HIGHER MATHEMATICS FOR GCSE

A complete course for the Higher tier

Brian Speed
Kevin Evans
Keith Gordon

Collins Educational
An imprint of HarperCollins*Publishers*

Acknowledgements

We are grateful to the following Examination Groups for permission to reproduce questions from their past examination papers and from specimen papers. Full details are given with each question. The Examination Groups accept no responsibility whatsoever for the accuracy or method of working in the answers given, which are solely the responsibility of the author and the publisher.

EDEXCEL Foundation (formerly University of London Examinations and Assessment Board: ULEAC)

Midland Examining Group (MEG)

Northern Examinations and Assessment Board (NEAB)

Northern Ireland Council for the Curriculum Examinations and Assessment (NICCEA)

Southern Examining Group (SEG)

Welsh Joint Education Committee (WJEC)

Every effort has been made to contact all copyright holders. If any have been inadvertently overlooked, the publisher would be pleased to make full acknowledgement at the first opportunity.

Published by Collins Educational
An imprint of HarperCollins*Publishers* Ltd
77–85 Fulham Palace Road
Hammersmith
London
W6 8JB

ISBN 0 00 322461 9

British Cataloguing in Publication Data
A catalogue record for this book is available from the British Library

Edited by John Day
Design and Illustration by Moondisks Ltd, Cambridge
Printed and bound by The Edinburgh Press, Edinburgh

Contents

1 Number 1 1
Percentage increase and decrease 1
Increase 1
Decrease 3
Compound interest 5
Using your calculator 5
Expressing one quantity as a percentage of another 7
Using your calculator 8
Finding the original quantity (reverse percentage) 9
Using your calculator 10
Rounding off 11
Decimal places 11
Significant figures 12
Approximation of calculations 13
Sensible rounding 15
Possible coursework tasks 17
Examination questions: coursework type 18
Examination questions 19

2 Shape 22
Sectors 25
Arc length and sector area 26
Area of a trapezium 28
Density 31
Cylinders 32
Volume 32
Surface area 32
Prisms, pyramids and cones 34
Volume of a prism 34
Volume of a pyramid 36
Volume and surface area of a cone 39
Volume and surface area of a sphere 41
Possible coursework tasks 42
Examination questions: coursework type 44
Examination questions 46

3 Algebra 1 51
Trial and improvement 56
Simultaneous equations 58
Elimination method 58
Problems solved by simultaneous equations 61
Transposition of formulae 63
Possible coursework tasks 64
Examination questions 65

4 Pythagoras and trigonometry 68
Pythagoras and real problems 70
Pythagoras in isosceles triangles 73
Pythagoras's theorem in three dimensions 75
Trigonometric ratios 78
Using your calculator 78
Working backwards: inverse functions 81
A closer look at the trigonometric ratios 83
Sine 83
Cosine 85
Tangent 88
Which ratio do I use? 90
In the real world 93
Special situations 95
Angle of elevation and angle of depression 96
Bearings and trigonometry 97
Isosceles triangle 99
Possible coursework tasks 101
Examination questions 102

5 Geometry 107
Angles in a polygon 108
Interior angles 109
Regular polygons 109
Special triangles 110
Equilateral triangle 110
Isosceles triangle 110
Special quadrilaterals 111
Trapezium 112
Parallelogram 112
Rhombus 112
Kite 112
Circles and angles 115
Angles in a circle 115
Cyclic quadrilaterals 118

Tangents to a circle 120
Alternate segment theorem 122
Possible coursework tasks 123
Examination questions 124

6 Transformation geometry **129**
Congruence 129
Conditions for congruent triangles 130
Notation 131
Transformations 132
Translation 132
Reflection 134
Rotation 137
Enlargement 139
Ray method 139
Co-ordinate method 140
Negative enlargement 140
Possible coursework tasks 144
Examination questions 145

Coursework example 1: Flight of stairs **150**

7 Constructions **153**
Bisectors 153
To construct a line bisector 153
To construct an angle bisector 154
Constructing 90° and 60° angles 155
The 90° angle 155
The 60° angle 155
Dropping a perpendicular from a point to a line 156
What is a locus? 158
Practical problems 159
Possible coursework tasks 163
Examination questions: coursework type 165
Examination questions 166

8 Number 2 **172**
Indices 172
Working out indices on your calculator 172
Two special powers 172
Negative indices 173
Rules for multiplying and dividing numbers in index form 174
Indices of the form $\frac{1}{n}$ 176
Indices of the form $\frac{a}{b}$ 177
Arithmetic of powers of 10 177
Multiplying 177
Dividing 178
Standard form 180
Standard form on a calculator 180
Rational and irrational numbers 182
The number line 182
Rational decimal numbers 184
Converting decimals into fractions 184
Terminating decimals 184
Recurring decimals 184
Surds 186
Possible coursework tasks 188
Examination questions: coursework type 189
Examination questions 189

9 Statistics 1 **192**
Frequency tables 192
Using your calculator 193
Grouped data 196
Discrete and continuous data 199
Discrete data 199
Continuous data 200
Charts 200
Frequency polygons 200
Bar charts and histograms 201
Using your calculator 202
Histograms with bars of unequal width 205
Surveys 210
Simple data collection sheet 210
Using your computer 210
Questionnaires 212
Sampling 214
Sampling methods 214
Sample size 215
Possible coursework tasks 218
Examination questions: coursework type 219
Examination questions 220

10 Algebra 2 225
Expansion 226
Simplification 227
Expand and simplify 227
Factorisation 228
Quadratic expansion and factorisation 229
Expanding squares 231
Quadratic factorisation 231
Difference of two squares 232
Solving the quadratic equation $x^2 + ax + b = 0$ 233
Factorising $ax^2 + bx + c$ 235
Solving the quadratic equation $ax^2 + bx + c = 0$ 235
By factorisation 235
By the quadratic formula 236
Quadratic equations with no solution 237
Problems solved by quadratic equations 238
Possible coursework tasks 241
Examination questions 242

11 Kinematics 245
Straight-line distance–time graphs 245
Gradient of distance–time graphs 248
Straight-line graphs 248
Curved graphs 251
Velocity 254
Straight-line velocity–time graphs 254
Area under a curve 257
Curved velocity–time graphs 259
Possible coursework tasks 262
Examination questions 263

12 Similarity 271
Similar triangles 271
Special cases of similar triangles 274
More complicated problems 277
Areas and volumes of similar shapes 279
Using area and volume ratios 283
Possible coursework tasks 285
Examination questions 286

13 Trigonometry 289
Some 2-D problems 289
Some 3-D problems 292
Trigonometric ratios of angles between 90° and 360° 296
Discovery activity 1: Sine 296
Discovery activity 2: Cosine 298
Discovery activity 3: Tangent 300
Solving any triangle 301
The sine rule 301
The ambiguous case 303
The cosine rule 305
Choosing the correct rule 309
Sine, cosine and tangent of 30°, 45° and 60° 311
Using sine to find the area of a triangle 312
Possible coursework tasks 314
Examination questions 315

14 Graphs 319
Finding the equation of a line from its graph 319
The equation $y = mx + c$ 319
Cover-up method for drawing graphs 322
Uses of graphs 323
Finding formulae or rules 324
Solving simultaneous equations 326
Quadratic graphs 327
Drawing accurate quadratic graphs 328
Roots of a quadratic equation 331
Square-root graphs 334
Reciprocal graphs 334
Cubic graphs 338
Solving equations by the method of intersection 341
Sketching graphs 345
Possible coursework tasks 347
Examination questions 348

15 Statistics 2 352
Scatter diagrams 352
Line of best fit 353
Correlation 353
Cumulative frequency diagrams 357
The median 359
The interquartile range 359
Measures of dispersion 364
Using your calculator 367
Use of standard deviation 367
Mean and standard deviation from a table of data 369
Using your calculator for a frequency table 371
Possible coursework tasks 373
Examination questions 375

16 Probability 381
- Terminology 381
- Finding probabilities 381
- Probability facts 386
- Mutually exclusive and exhaustive events 390
  - Complementary event 391
- Expectation 394
- Addition rule for events 395
- Combined events 397
  - Throwing two dice 397
  - Tossing coins 398
  - Other combined events and tree diagrams 400
- Using 'and' and 'or'. Independent events 407
  - 'At least' problems 408
  - More advanced use of 'and' and 'or' 410
- Conditional probability 413
- *Possible coursework tasks* 417
- *Examination questions* 418

17 Algebra 3 424
- Number sequences 424
  - Differences 424
  - Generalising to find the rule 425
  - Finding the nth term of a linear sequence 426
- General rules from given patterns 428
- Quadratic rules 431
  - The simpler rules 431
  - More complicated rules 432
- *Possible coursework tasks* 433
- *Examination questions: coursework type* 435
- *Examination questions* 435

Coursework example 2: Threes and ones problem 439

18 Dimensional analysis 443
- Length 443
- Area 444
- Volume 445
- Consistency 447
- *Examination questions* 449

19 Variation 452
- Direct variation 452
  - Proportions involving squares, cubes and square roots 454
- Inverse variation 456
- *Possible coursework tasks* 458
- *Examination questions* 459

20 Number and limits of accuracy 461
- Limits of accuracy 461
  - Upper and lower bounds 462
  - Percentage error 462
- Problems involving limits of accuracy 463
- *Examination questions* 465

21 Inequalities and regions 469
- Graphically representing inequalities 469
  - More than one inequality 471
- Problem solving 473
- Linear programming 477
- *Examination questions* 482

22 Vectors 486
- Definition of a vector 486
- Adding and subtracting vectors 487
- Vector geometry 491
- Vector force problems 497
- *Possible coursework tasks* 500
- *Examination questions* 501

23 Transformation of graphs 504
- Transformations of the graph of $y = f(x)$ 505
- *Possible coursework tasks* 512
- *Examination questions* 513

Appendix: Coursework guidance 518

Answers 520

1 Number 1

This chapter is going to ... introduce you to methods for calculating percentage increase and decrease, and compound interest. It then shows you how to express one quantity as a percentage of another, and how to reverse a percentage. Finally, it takes you through rounding off and approximating calculations.

What you should already know

- 'Per cent' means 'out of 100'. So that a statement such as 32% means 32 out of 100.
- To find P% of an amount T, you calculate

  $(P \times T) \div 100$

  For example, 4% of 30 kg is

  $(4 \times 30) \div 100 = 1.2$ kg
- Any percentage can be represented as a decimal by dividing by 100. For example,

  $65\% = 65 \div 100 = 0.65$
- The common fractions expressed as percentages:

  $\frac{1}{2} = 50\%$ $\frac{1}{4} = 25\%$ $\frac{3}{4} = 75\%$
  $\frac{1}{10} = 10\%$ $\frac{1}{5} = 20\%$ $\frac{1}{3} = 33\frac{1}{3}\%$

Percentage increase and decrease

Increase

There are three methods for increasing by a percentage.

Method 1
Find the increase and add it to the original amount. For example, to increase £6 by 5%

find 5% of £6: $(5 \times 6) \div 100 = £0.30$

add the £0.30 to the original amount: £6 + £0.30 = £6.30

Method 2

Change the percentage to a decimal, add 1, then multiply by the amount to be increased. For example, to increase £6 by 5%

change 5% to a decimal, add 1, then multiply by £6: $1.05 \times 6 = £6.30$

Method 3

Using the calculator **%** key.

Not all calculators operate in the same way, so you will have to find out how your calculator deals with percentage increase (if it does at all – since some don't).

For example, to increase £6 by 5%

you could try **6** **+** **5** **%** **=**

or **6** **×** **1** **0** **5** **%** **=**

You may not have to press the **=** key, depending on your type of calculator.

Check that you get the answer £6.30.

Exercise 1A

1 Increase each of the following by the given amount. (Use any method you like.)

a £60 by 4% **b** 12 kg by 8% **c** 450 g by 5% **d** 545 m by 10%
e £34 by 12% **f** £75 by 20% **g** 340 kg by 15% **h** 670 cm by 23%
i 130 g by 95% **j** £82 by 75%

2 Kevin, who was on a salary of £27 500, was given a pay rise of 7%. What was his new salary?

3 In 1990 the population of Melchester was 1 560 000. By 1995 that had increased by 8%. What was the population of Melchester in 1995?

4 A small firm made the same pay increase for all its employees: 5%.

a Calculate the new pay of each employee listed below. Each of their salaries before the increase is given.

Bob, caretaker, £16 500 Jean, superviser, £19 500
Anne, tea lady, £17 300 Brian, manager, £25 300

b Is the actual pay increase the same for each worker?

5 A bank pays 7% interest on the money that each saver keeps in the bank for a year. Allison keeps £385 in this bank for a year. How much will she have in the bank after the year?

6 In 1980 the number of cars on the roads of Sheffield was about 4200. Since then it has increased by 80%. Approximately how many cars are on the roads of Sheffield now?

7 An advertisement for a breakfast cereal states that a special offer packet contains 15% more cereal for the same price than a normal 500 g packet. How much breakfast cereal is in a special offer packet?

8 A headteacher was proud to point out that, since he had arrived at the school, its population then of 680 students had increased by 35%. How many students are now in the school?

9 At a school disco there are always about 20% more girls than boys. If at one disco there were 50 boys, how many girls were there?

10 VAT is a tax that the Government adds to the price of most goods and services. At the moment, it is 17.5% (except for fuel at 8%).

Calculate the price of the following goods in a shop after VAT of 17.5% has been added.

Goods	*Pre-VAT price*
TV set	£245
Microwave oven	£72
Desk	£115
Rug	£19.50

Decrease

There are three methods for decreasing by a percentage.

Method 1

Find the decrease and take it away from the original amount. For example, to decrease £8 by 4%

find 4% of £8: $(4 \times 8) \div 100 = £0.32$

take the £0.32 away from the original amount: $£8 - £0.32 = £7.68$

Method 2

Change the percentage to a decimal, take it away from 1, then multiply by the amount to be decreased. For example, to decrease by £8 by 4%

change 4% to a decimal and take from 1: $1 - 0.04 = 0.96$

multiply 0.96 by the original amount: $0.96 \times £8 = £7.68$

Method 3

Using the calculator % key.

You tried percentage increase with your calculator, now try percentage decrease by, perhaps, using subtraction instead of addition. For example, to decrease £8 by 5%

you could try 8 − 5 % =

or 9 5 % × 8 =

Here again, you may not have to press the **=** key.

Check that you get the answer £7.60.

Exercise 1B

1 Decrease each of the following by the given amount. (Use any method you like.)

a £10 by 6% **b** 25 kg by 8% **c** 236 g by 10% **d** 350 m by 3%
e £5 by 2% **f** 45 m by 12% **g** 860 m by 15% **h** 96 g by 13%
i 480 cm by 25% **j** 180 minutes by 35%

2 A car valued at £6500 last year is now worth 15% less. What is its value now?

3 A new P-plan diet guarantees that you will lose 12% of your weight in the first month. How much did the following people weigh after 1 month on the diet?

a Gillian, who started at 60 kg **b** Peter, who started at 75 kg
c Margaret, who started at 52 kg

4 A motor insurance firm offers no-claims discounts off the given premium, as follows:

1 year no claim	15% discount
2 years no claim	25% discount
3 years no claim	45% discount
4 years no claim	60% discount

Mr Speed and his family are all offered motor insurance from this firm:

Mr Speed, who has 4 years no-claim discount is quoted a premium of £140.
Mrs Speed, who has 1 year no-claim discount is quoted a premium of £350.
James, who has 3 years no-claim discount is quoted a premium of £230.
John, who has 2 years no-claim discount is quoted a premium of £450.

Calculate the actual amount each member of the family has to pay for the motor insurance.

5 A large factory employed 640 people. But it had to streamline its workforce and lose 30% of the workers. How big is the workforce now?

6 On the last day of the Christmas term, a school expects to have an absence rate of 6%. If the school population is 748 pupils, how many pupils will the school expect to see on the last day of the Christmas term?

7 Since the start of the National Lottery a particular charity called Young Ones said they now have a decrease of 45% in the money raised by scratch cards. If before the Lottery the charity had an annual income of £34 500 from their scratch cards, how much do they collect now?

8 Most speedometers in cars have an error of about 5% from the true reading. When my speedometer says I am driving at 70 mph,

a what is the slowest speed I could be doing
b what is the fastest speed I could be doing?

9 You are a member of a club which allows you to claim a 12% discount off any marked price in shops. What will you pay in total for the following goods?

Sweatshirt	£19
Track suit	£26

10 I read an advertisement in my local newspaper last week which stated: 'By lagging your roof and hot water system you will use 18% less fuel.' Since I was using an average of 640 units of gas a year, I thought I would lag my roof and my hot water system. How much gas would I expect to use now?

Compound interest

Compound interest is where the interest due at the end of a year on, for example, an amount of money in a savings account, is added to that amount and the new total amount then earns further interest at the same rate in the following year. This pattern is repeated year after year while the money is in the account. Therefore, the original amount grows bigger by the year, as does the actual amount of interest. In compound interest, the interest rate is always set at a fixed percentage for the whole period.

Example A bank pays 6% compound interest per year on all amounts in a savings account for that year. What is the final amount that Elizabeth will have in her account if she has kept £400 in her bank for 3 years?

The amount in the bank increases by 6% each year, so

after 1 year she will have £400 × 1.06 = £424
after 2 years she will have 424 × 1.06 = £449.44
after 3 years she will have £449.44 × 1.06 = £476.41 (rounded)

As you can see, the actual increase gets bigger and bigger.

From this example, you can see that you could have used £400 × $(1.06)^3$ to find the amount after 3 years. That is, you could have used the following formula for calculating the total amount due at any time:

$$\text{Total amount} = P \times (1 + x)^n$$

where P is the original amount invested, x is the rate of interest expressed as a decimal, and n is the number of years for which the money is invested.

So, in the above example, P = £400, $x = 0.06$, and $n = 3$.

Using your calculator

You may have noticed that you can do the above calculation on your calculator without having to write down all the intermediate steps.

To add on the 6% each time just means multiplying by 1.06 each time. That is, you can do the calculation as

4 0 0 × 1 • 0 6 × 1 • 0 6 × 1 • 0 6 =

or 4 0 0 × 1 0 6 % x^y 3 =

You need to find the method with which you are comfortable and which you understand.

The idea of compound interest does not only concern money. It can be about, for example, the growth in populations, increases in salaries and increases in body weight or height. Also the idea can involve regular reduction by a fixed percentage: for example, car depreciation, pollution losses, population losses and even water losses. Work through the next exercise and you will see the extent to which compound interest ideas are used.

Exercise 1C

1 A baby octopus increases its body weight by 5% each day for the first month of its life. In a safe ocean zoo, a baby octopus was born weighing 10 kg.

a What is its weight after

i 1 day **ii** 2 days **iii** 4 days **iv** 1 week?

b After how many days will the octopus first weigh over 15 kg?

2 A certain type of conifer hedging increases in height by 17% each year for the first 20 years. When I bought some of this hedging, it was all about 50 cm tall. How long will it take to grow 3 m tall?

3 The manager of a small family business offered his staff an annual pay increase of 4% every year they stayed with the firm.

a Gareth started work at the business on a salary of £8200. What salary will he be on after 4 years?

b Julie started work at the business on a salary of £9350. How many years will it be until she is earning a salary of over £20 000?

4 Scientists have been studying the shores of Scotland and estimate that due to pollution the seal population of those shores will decline at the rate of 15% each year. In 1995 they counted around 3000 seals on those shores.

a If nothing is done about pollution, how many seals will they expect to be there in

i 1996 **ii** 1997 **iii** 2000?

b How long will it take for the seal population to be less than 1000?

5 I am told that if I buy a new car its value will depreciate at the rate of 20% each year. I buy a car in 1996 priced at £8500. How much will the car be valued at in

a 1997 **b** 2000 **c** 2005?

6 At the peak of the drought during the summer of 1995, a reservoir in Derbyshire was losing water at the rate of 8% each day as the water-saving measures were being taken. On 1 August this reservoir held 2.1 million litres of water.

a At this rate of losing water, how much would have been in the reservoir on the following days?

i 2 August **ii** 4 August **iii** 8 August

b The danger point is when the water drops below 1 million litres. When would this have been if things had continued as they were?

7 Paul put a gift of £400 into a special savings account that offered him 9% compound interest if he promised to keep the money in for at least 2 years. How much was in this account after

a 2 years **b** 4 years **c** 6 years?

8 The population of a small country, Yebon, was only 46 000 in 1990, but it steadily increased by about 13% each year during the 1990s.

a Calculate the population in

i 1991 **ii** 1995 **iii** 1999

b If the country keeps increasing at this rate, when will its population be half a million?

9 How long will it take to accumulate one million pounds in the following situations?

a An investment of £100 000 at a rate of 12% compound interest.

b An investment of £50 000 at a rate of 16% compound interest.

10 A tree increases in height by 18% per year. When it is 1 year old, it is 8 cm tall. How long will it take the tree to grow to 10 m?

Expressing one quantity as a percentage of another

We express one quantity as a percentage of another by setting up the first quantity as a fraction of the second, and then converting that fraction to a percentage by simply multiplying it by 100.

For example, to express £5 as a percentage of £40

set up the fraction $\frac{5}{40}$ and multiply by 100

which becomes $(5 \times 100) \div 40 = 12.5\%$

We can use the method to calculate gain or loss in a financial transaction. For example, Bert buys a car for £1500 and sells it at £1800. What is his percentage gain?

The gain is £300, so the percentage gain is

$$\frac{300}{1500} \times 100 = 20\%$$

Notice how the percentage gain was found by

$$\frac{\text{Difference}}{\text{Original}} \times 100$$

Using your calculator

Here is another place you can use the **%** key on your calculator. For example, to express 5 as a percentage of 40

try **5** **÷** **4** **0** **%** **=**

You should get the answer 12.5%. You may not have to press the **=** key, depending on your type of calculator.

Exercise 1D

1 Express the following as percentages. (Give suitably rounded-off figures where necessary.)

a £5 of £20	**b** £4 of £6.60	**c** 241 kg of 520 kg
d 3 hours of 1 day	**e** 25 minutes of 1 hour	**f** 12 m of 20 m
g 125 g of 600 g	**h** 12 minutes of 2 hours	**i** 1 week of a year
j 1 month of 1 year	**k** 25 cm of 55 cm	**l** 105 g of 1 kg
m 5 oz of 16 oz	**n** 2.4 litres of 6 litres	**o** 8 days of 1 year
p 25p of £3	**q** 18p of £2.50	**r** 40 seconds of 1 day
s 8 hours of 1 year	**t** 5 mm of 4 cm	

2 Find, to 1 decimal place, the percentage profit on the following.

Item	*Retail price* (selling price)	*Wholesale price* (price the shop paid)
a CD player	£89	£60
b TV set	£345	£210
c Computer	£829	£750
d Video player	£199.99	£110
e Microwave oven	£98.50	£78

3 There were 3 pupils absent from a class of 27. What percentage were absent?

4 In 1995 the Melchester County Council raised £14 870 000 in rates. In 1996 it raised £15 597 000 in rates. What was the percentage increase?

5 John came home from school one day with his end-of-year test results. Change each of John's results to a percentage.

Maths	56 out of 75
English	46 out of 60
Science	78 out of 120
French	43 out of 80
Geography	76 out of 90
History	34 out of 40

6 In Greece in 1893, there were 5 563 100 acres of agricultural land. Of this

olives occupied	432 000 acres
currants occupied	168 000 acres
figs occupied	52 000 acres

a What percentage of the agricultural land was occupied by each commodity?

In Greece in 1993, there were 3 654 000 acres of agricultural land. Of this

olives occupied	237 000 acres
currants occupied	92 000 acres
figs occupied	51 000 acres

b What percentage of the agricultural land was occupied by each commodity in 1993?

c What changes are there in the percentage of the agricultural land occupied by each commodity?

7 Martin had an annual salary of £22 600 in 1995, which was increased to £23 100 in 1996. What percentage increase does this represent?

8 During the wet year of 1981, it rained in Manchester on 123 days of the year. What percentage of days were wet?

9 When Blackburn Rovers won the championship in 1995, they lost only 4 of their 42 league games. What percentage of games did they not lose?

10 In the year 1900 Britain's imports were as follows:

British Commonwealth	£109 530 635
USA	£138 789 261
France	£53 618 656
Other countries	£221 136 611

What percentage of the total imports came from each source?

Finding the original quantity (reverse percentage)

There are situations when we know a certain percentage and wish to get back to the original amount. For example, the 70 men who went on strike represented only 20% of the workforce. How large was the workforce?

Since 20% represents 70 people, then

1% will represent $70 \div 20$ people [Don't work it out.]
so 100% will represent $(70 \div 20) \times 100 = 350$

Hence the workforce is 350.

Using your calculator

You need to check this with your own calculator and see how it works. For example, if 42 represents 15% of an original amount, then

the original amount will be $(42 \div 15) \times 100 = 280$

or on the calculator try **4** **2** **÷** **1** **5** **%** **=**

(Again, the **=** key may not be needed.)

Exercise 1E

1 Find what 100% represents when

a 30% represents 63 kg **b** 20% represents £45 **c** 40% represents 320 g
d 25% represents 3 hours **e** 5% represents £23 **f** 14% represents 35 m
g 45% represents 27 cm **h** 4% represents £123 **i** 2.5% represents £5
j 12.5% represents 60 g **k** 8.5% represents £34 **l** 12.5% represents 115 m

2 On a gruelling army training session, only 28 youngsters survived the whole day. This represented 35% of the original group. How large was the original group?

3 VAT is a government tax added to goods and services. With VAT at 17.5%, what is the pre-VAT price of the following priced goods?

T shirt	£9.87	Tights	£1.41
Shorts	£6.11	Sweater	£12.62
Trainers	£29.14	Boots	£38.07

4 Ruth spends £8 each week on her social activities. This is 40% of her weekly income. How much is Ruth's weekly income ?

5 Howard spends £200 a month on food. This represents 24% of his monthly take-home pay. How much is his monthly take-home pay?

6 Tina's weekly pay is increased by 5% to £81.90. What was Tina's pay before the increase?

7 Dave sold his car for £2940, making a profit of 20% on the price he paid for it. How much did Dave pay for the car?

8 A particular rock is made up of: 18% sandstone, 52% shale and 30% limestone. A sample of this rock was found to contain 375 grams of limestone. How heavy was the sample?

9 If 38% of plastic bottles in a production line are blue and the remaining 7750 plastic bottles are brown, how many plastic bottles are blue?

10 I received £3.85 back from the tax office, which represented the 17.5% VAT on a piece of equipment. How much did I pay for this equipment in the first place?

11 A man's salary was increased by 5% in one year and reduced by 5% in the next year. Is his final salary greater or less than the original one and by how many per cent?

Rounding off

Decimal places

When a number is written in decimal form, the digits on the right-hand side of the decimal point are called the **decimal places**. For example,

6.83 is written to two decimal places
79.4 is written to one decimal place
0.526 is written to three decimal places

To round off a decimal number to a particular number of places, take these steps.

- Count down the decimal places from the point and look at the first digit you are going to remove.
- When this digit is less than 5, then just remove the unwanted places.
- When this digit is 5 or more, then add 1 to the last decimal place digit.

Here are some examples.

5.852 will round off to 5.85 to two decimal places
7.156 will round off to 7.16 to two decimal places
0.274 will round off to 0.3 to one decimal place
15.3518 will round off to 15.4 to one decimal place

Exercise 1F

1 Round off each of the following numbers to one decimal place.

a 4.83	**b** 3.79	**c** 2.16	**d** 8.25	**e** 3.673
f 46.935	**g** 23.883	**h** 9.549	**i** 11.08	**j** 33.509
k 7.054	**l** 46.800	**m** 0.057	**n** 0.109	**o** 0.599
p 64.99	**q** 213.86	**r** 76.07	**s** 455.177	**t** 50.999

2 Round off each of the following numbers to two decimal places.

a 5.783	**b** 2.358	**c** 0.977	**d** 33.085	**e** 6.007
f 23.5652	**g** 91.7895	**h** 7.995	**i** 2.3096	**j** 23.9158
k 5.9999	**l** 1.0075	**m** 3.5137	**n** 96.508	**o** 0.009
p 0.065	**q** 7.8091	**r** 569.899	**s** 300.004	**t** 0.0009

3 Round off each of the following to the number of decimal places (dp) indicated.

a 4.568 (1 dp)	**b** 0.0832 (2 dp)	**c** 45.715 93 (3 dp)	**d** 94.8531 (2 dp)
e 602.099 (1 dp)	**f** 671.7629 (2 dp)	**g** 7.1124 (1 dp)	**h** 6.903 54 (3 dp)
i 13.7809 (2 dp)	**j** 0.075 11 (1 dp)	**k** 4.001 84 (3 dp)	**l** 59.983 (1 dp)
m 11.9854 (2 dp)	**n** 899.995 85 (4 dp)	**o** 0.0499 (1 dp)	**p** 0.009 87 (2 dp)
q 0.000 78 (1 dp)	**r** 78.3925 (3 dp)	**s** 199.9999 (2 dp)	**t** 5.0907 (1 dp)

Significant figures

We often use significant figures when we want to approximate a number with quite a few digits in it.

Look at the following table which illustrates some numbers rounded off to one, two and three significant figures (sf).

One sf	8	50	200	90 000	0.000 07	0.003	0.4
Two sf	67	4.8	0.76	45 000	730	0.006 7	0.40
Three sf	312	65.9	40.3	0.0761	7.05	0.003 01	0.400

The steps taken to round off a number to a particular number of significant figures are very similar to those used for decimal places.

- From the left, count down the number of digits of the given significant figure. When the original number is less than 1, start counting from the first non-zero digit.
- Look at the next digit.
- When the next digit is less than 5, leave the digit on the left the same.
- When the next digit is equal to or greater than 5, add 1 to the digit on the left.
- Put in enough zeros to keep the number the right size.

For example, look at the following table which shows some numbers rounded off to one, two and three significant figures, respectively.

Number	Rounded to 1 sf	Rounded to 2 sf	Rounded to 3 sf
45 281	50 000	45 000	45 300
568.54	600	570	569
7.3782	7	7.5	7.38
8054	8000	8100	8050
99.8721	100	100	99.9
0.7002	0.7	0.70	0.700

Exercise 1G

1 Round off each of the following numbers to 1 significant figure.

a 46 313	**b** 57 123	**c** 30 569	**d** 94 558	**e** 85 299
f 54.26	**g** 85.18	**h** 27.09	**i** 96.432	**j** 167.77
k 0.5388	**l** 0.2823	**m** 0.005 84	**n** 0.047 85	**o** 0.000 876
p 9.9	**q** 89.5	**r** 90.78	**s** 199	**t** 999.99

2 What is the least and the greatest number of sweets that can be found in these jars?

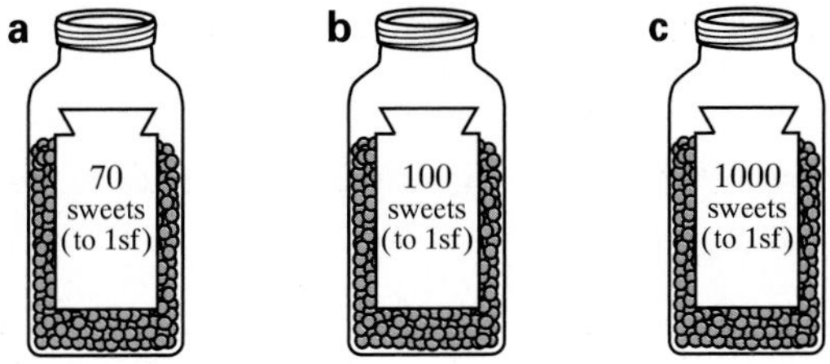

3 What is the least and the greatest number of people that can be found in these towns?

Elsecar population 800 (to 1 significant figure)

Hoyland population 1200 (to 2 significant figures)

Barnsley population 165 000 (to 3 significant figures)

4 What is the least and the greatest number of people that could have been at concerts at the following venues?

Huddersfield 11 000 (to 2 significant figures)

Leeds 27 500 (to 3 significant figures)

Middlesborough 20 000 (to 1 significant figure)

5 Round off each of the following numbers to 2 significant figures.

a 56 147	**b** 26 813	**c** 79 611	**d** 30 578	**e** 14 009
f 5876	**g** 1065	**h** 847	**i** 109	**j** 638.7
k 1.689	**l** 4.0854	**m** 2.658	**n** 8.0089	**o** 41.564
p 0.8006	**q** 0.458	**r** 0.0658	**s** 0.9996	**t** 0.009 82

6 Round off each of the following to the number of significant figures (sf) indicated.

a 57 402 (1 sf)	**b** 5288 (2 sf)	**c** 89.67 (3 sf)	**d** 105.6 (2 sf)
e 8.69 (1 sf)	**f** 1.087 (2 sf)	**g** 809.8 (3 sf)	**h** 4710 (1 sf)
i 66.51 (2 sf)	**j** 0.9785 (1 sf)	**k** 8.663 (1 sf)	**l** 9.7454 (3 sf)
m 12.65 (2 sf)	**n** 18.31 (1 sf)	**o** 869.89 (3 sf)	**p** 26.99 (1 sf)
q 0.073 61 (2 sf)	**r** 0.0099 (2 sf)	**s** 0.0905 (1 sf)	**t** 0.070 87 (3 sf)

Approximation of calculations

How do we approximate the value of a calculation? What do we actually do when we try to approximate an answer to a problem?

For example, what is the approximate answer to 35.1×6.58?

To approximate the answer in this and many other similar cases, we simply round off each number to 1 significant figure, then work out the sum. So in this case, the approximation is

$$35.1 \times 6.58 \approx 40 \times 7 = 280$$

Sometimes, especially when dividing, we round off a number to something more useful at 2 sf instead of at 1 sf. For example,

$$57.3 \div 6.87$$

Since 6.87 rounds off to 7, then round off 57.3 to 56 because 7 divides exactly into 56. Hence,

$$57.3 \div 6.87 \approx 56 \div 7 = 8$$

A quick approximation is always a great help on any calculation since it often stops your writing down a silly answer.

Exercise 1H

1 Find approximate answers to the following sums.

a 5435×7.31 **b** 5280×3.211 **c** $63.24 \times 3.514 \times 4.2$

d 3508×2.79 **e** $72.1 \times 3.225 \times 5.23$ **f** $470 \times 7.85 \times 0.99$

g $354 \div 79.8$ **h** $36.8 \div 1.876$ **i** $5974 \div 5.29$

j $208 \div 3.78$ **k** $1409 \div 64.28$ **l** $53.94 \div 8.502$

m $14.74 \div 2.65$ **n** $28.673 \div 7.24$ **o** $406.9 \div 23.78$

p $0.584 \div 0.0216$

(Check your answers on a calculator to see how close you were.)

2 By rounding off, find an approximate answer to these sums.

a $\dfrac{573 + 783}{107}$ **b** $\dfrac{783 - 572}{24}$ **c** $\dfrac{352 + 657}{999}$

d $\dfrac{1123 - 689}{354}$ **e** $\dfrac{589 + 773}{658 - 351}$ **f** $\dfrac{793 - 569}{998 - 667}$

g $\dfrac{354 + 656}{997 - 656}$ **h** $\dfrac{1124 - 661}{355 + 570}$ **i** $\dfrac{28.3 + 19.5}{87.4}$

j $\dfrac{78.3 - 22.6}{2.69}$ **k** $\dfrac{3.52 + 7.95}{9.9}$ **l** $\dfrac{11.78 + 67.8}{39.4}$

m $\dfrac{84.7 + 12.6}{65.7 - 11.2}$ **n** $\dfrac{32.8 + 71.4}{9.92 + 11.7}$ **o** $\dfrac{14.9 + 27.9}{62.3 - 15.3}$

p $\dfrac{12.7 + 34.9}{78.2 - 29.3}$

3 Find the approximate monthly pay of the following people whose annual salary is

a Paul £35 200 **b** Michael £25 600 **c** Jennifer £18 125 **d** Ross £8420

4 Find the approximate annual pay of the following people who earn:

a Kevin £270 a week **b** Malcolm £1528 a month **c** David £347 a week

5 A litre of paint will cover an area of about 8.7 m^2. Approximately how many litre cans will I need to buy to paint a room with a total surface area of 73 m^2?

6 A farmer bought 2713 kg of seed at a cost of £7.34 per kg. Find the approximate total cost of this seed.

7 A greengrocer sells a box of 450 oranges for £37. Approximately how much did each orange sell for?

8 Approximately how many 19p stamps can be bought for £5?

9 If a fuel is £3.15 per kilogram, about how much can I buy for £86?

10 It took me 6 hours and 40 minutes to drive from Sheffield to Bude, a distance of 295 miles. My car uses petrol at the rate of about 32 miles per gallon. The petrol cost £2.65 per gallon.

a Approximately how many miles did I do each hour?

b Approximately how many gallons of petrol did I use in going from Sheffield to Bude?

c What was the approximate cost of all the petrol I used in the journey to Bude and back again?

11 Mr Bradshaw wanted to find out how many bricks were in a chimney he was about to knock down. He counted 187 bricks in one row all the way round the chimney. He counted 53 rows of bricks up the chimney. Each brick weighed about 3.2 kg.

a Approximately how many bricks were in the chimney?

b Approximately how much did all the bricks weigh?

12 Kirsty arranges for magazines to be put into envelopes. She sorts out 178 magazines between 10.00 am and 1.00 pm. Approximately how many magazines will she be able to sort in a week in which she works for 17 hours?

13 An athlete trains often. Brian's daily training routine is to run 3.75 km every day. Approximately how much does he run in

a a week **b** a month **c** a year?

14 A box full of magazines weighs 8 kg. One magazine weighs about 15g. Approximately how many magazines are in the box?

15 An apple weighs about 280 grams.

a What is the approximate weight of a bag containing a dozen apples?

b Approximately how many apples will there be in a sack weighing 50 kg?

16 When typing John manages 85 words a minute. How long approximately will it take him to type a 2000 word essay?

Sensible rounding

You will be required to round off answers to problems to a suitable degree of accuracy without being told specifically what that is.

Generally, you can use common sense. For example, you would not give the length of a pencil as 14.574 cm, you would round off to something like 14.6 cm. If you were asked how many tins you need to buy to do a particular job, then you would give a whole-number answer and not something such as 5.91 tins.

It is hard to make rules about this, as there is much disagreement even among the 'experts' as to how you ought to do it. But, generally, when you are in any doubt as to how many significant figures to use for the final answer to a problem, round off to no more than one extra significant figure to the number used in the original data. (This particular type of rounding is used throughout the book.)

Exercise 1I

1 Round off each of the following figures to a suitable degree of accuracy.

a I am 1.7359 metres tall.

b It took me 5 minutes 44.83 seconds to mend the television.

c My hamster weighs 237.97 grams.

d The correct temperature at which to drink Earl Grey Tea is 82.739 °C.

e There were 34 827 people at the Test Match yesterday.

f In my collection I have 615 theatre programmes.

g The distance from Wath to Sheffield is 15.528 miles.

h My telephone number is 284519.

i The area of the floor is 13.673 m^2.

2 Rewrite the following article, rounding off all the numbers to a suitable degree of accuracy if they need to be.

> It was a hot day, the temperature was 81.699 °F and still rising. I had now walked 5.3289 km in just over 113.98 minutes. But I didn't care since I knew that the 43 275 people watching the race were cheering me on. I won by clipping 6.289 seconds off the record time. This was the 67th time it had happened since records first began in 1788. Well, next year I will only have 15 practice walks beforehand as I strive to beat the record by at least another 4.673 seconds.

3 How many test-tubes each holding 24 cm^3 of water can be filled from a 1 litre flask?

4 If I walk at an average speed of 70 metres per minute, how long will it take me to walk a distance of 3 km?

5 Keith earns £27 500 a year. How much does he earn in

a 1 month **b** 1 week **c** 1 day?

6 How many stamps 21p each can I buy for £12?

7 I travelled a distance of 450 miles in 6.4 hours. What was my average speed?

8 You need 1 teaspoon of cocoa to make a chocolate drink. Each teaspoon of cocoa is about 2.75 cm^3. How many chocolate drinks could you make from a tin that had 200 cm^3 of cocoa in it?

9 At Manchester United, it takes 160 minutes for 43 500 fans to get into the ground. On average, how many fans are let into the ground every minute?

10 A 5p coin weighs 4.2 grams. How much will one million pounds worth of 5p pieces weigh?

Possible coursework tasks

Elizabethan multiplication

Look at how the Elizabethans worked out 412×237.

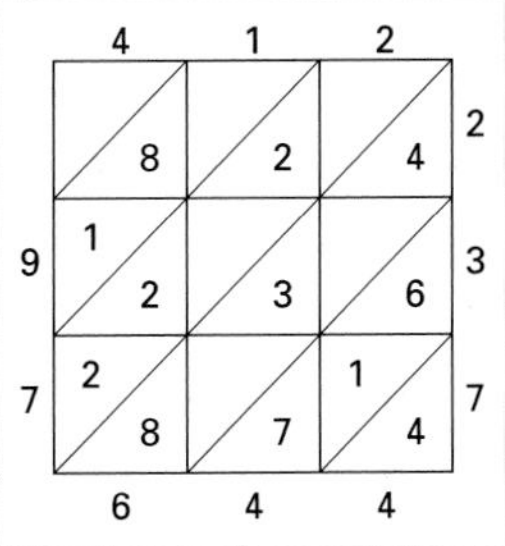

Investigate and see if you can find out

- how it works
- why it works
- how to work it yourself.

Russian multiplication

Look at this popular Russian way to do long multiplication.

36×17

~~36~~	~~17~~
~~18~~	~~34~~
9	68
~~4~~	~~136~~
~~2~~	~~272~~
1	544
	612

27×19

27	19
13	38
~~6~~	~~76~~
3	152
1	304
	513

Investigate and see if you can find out

- how it works
- why it works
- how to work it yourself.

Squares on a chessboard

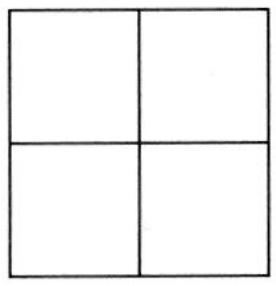

There are 5 squares in this diagram. How many squares are there on a chessboard?

Double your money

Suppose you put an amount in a building society deposit account that pays compound interest at 8% per annum and leave it there for a number of years.

How long will it take to double your money?

Egyptian fractions

The Ancient Egyptians expressed all fractions as the sum of unit fractions. That is, as the sum of fractions each of which has 1 as its numerator. For example,

$$\frac{3}{4} = \frac{1}{2} + \frac{1}{4} \quad \text{and} \quad \frac{7}{24} = \frac{1}{5} + \frac{1}{20} + \frac{1}{24}$$

Can you make up at least ten different sums that also use all ten digits?

Consecutive numbers

Take any three consecutive numbers, square the middle one and multiply the other two.

Investigate.

Products

The product of any two consecutive numbers is a multiple of 2.
The product of any three consecutive numbers is a multiple of 3.
The product of any four consecutive numbers is a multiple of ?

Investigate.

Examination questions: coursework type

Two brothers, Michael and Paul, usually save £1 each per week. Paul gets fed up with that and suggests changing to save

1p for the first week
2p the week after
4p the week after
8p the week after

so that each week he doubles what he saved the previous week. Michael continues to save £1 each week. Investigate

i the amounts saved by each over various times and comment
ii what might happen with different patterns of saving.

Examination questions

1 Tony bought a second-hand car for £7500. It decreased in value each year by 8% of its value at the beginning of that year. Calculate the value of the car 2 years after he bought it.
WJEC, Question 10, Paper 1, June 1994

2 In 1992 Nadir's total fuel bill was £480. In 1993 it was £552. What is the percentage increase in Nadir's fuel bill from 1992 to 1993?
WJEC, Question 11, Paper 1, June 1994

3 The size of the crowd at a football match is given as 34 700 to the nearest hundred.
a What is the lowest number that the crowd could be?
b What is the largest number that the crowd could be?
NEAB, Question 2, Specimen Paper 11, 1998

4 In 1990, a charity sold $2\frac{1}{4}$ million lottery tickets at 25p each. 80% of the money obtained was kept by the charity.
a Calculate the amount of money kept by the charity.
In 1991, the price of a lottery ticket fell by 20%. Sales of lottery tickets increased by 20%. 80% of the money obtained was kept by the charity.
b Calculate the percentage change in the amount of money kept by the charity.
ULEAC, Question 1, Paper 6, June 1995

5 a Use your calculator to work out the value of

$$\frac{6.08 \times (9.72)^2}{581 + 237}$$

Write down the full calculator display.
b i Write down a calculation that could be done mentally to check the answer to part **a** using numbers rounded to one significant figure.
ii Write down the answer to your calculation in part **b i**.
MEG, Question 4, Specimen Paper 6, 1998

6 a A particular CD costs a shopkeeper £9.20 from the wholesaler. The shopkeeper wants to make a profit of 35% on his costs. What price will the CD be in the shop?
b Another CD is offered in a sale at a discount of 15%. The sale price is £12.41. What was the price of the CD before the sale discount?
WJEC, Question 13, Specimen Paper 1,1998

7

Country	Population	Number of daily newspapers	Average number of people per daily newspaper
USA	248 760 000	1657	
UK	57 200 000	112	

In this question you should use the numbers given in the table rather than use estimates.

a Complete the table, giving your answers correct to 3 significant figures.

b Calculate, correct to 1 decimal place, the value of r in the statement:

'The average number of people per daily newspaper in the UK is r times the corresponding figure for the USA.'

WJEC, Question 3, Paper A1, June 1995

8 A new electronic typewriter costs £86.53. At the end of every year, its value falls by 15% of its value at the start of that year. Calculate the value of the typewriter at the end of 3 years. *ULEAC, Question 4, Paper 6, November 1994*

9 At the end of 1993 there were 5000 members of a certain rare breed of animal remaining in the world. It is predicted that their number will decrease by 12% each year.

a How many will be left at the end of 1996?

b By the end of which year will the number first be less than 2500?

MEG, Question 19, Specimen Paper 3, 1998

10 Nesta invests £508 in a bank account at an interest rate of 8.5% per annum.

a Calculate the interest on £508 after 1 year.

At the end of the first year the interest is added to her bank account. The interest rate remains at 8.5%.

b Calculate the total amount of money in Nesta's bank account at the end of the second year. *ULEAC, Specimen Paper 5, Question 6, 1998*

11 It takes 24 minutes to fill a swimming pool with 15 000 litres of water.

a The pool is increased in size so that it now holds 18 500 litres. How long will it now take to fill this pool with 18 500 litres of water?

b The pool had been filling with water for 15 minutes when the water was turned off. How much water was in the pool when the water was turned off?

NEAB, Question 1, Specimen Paper 2H, 1998

12 Esmi is organising a barbecue for 90 people. She wants to give each person a baked potato. Her local supermarket sells bags of baking potatoes. Each bag contains at least 8 and not more than 12 potatoes. How many bags should she buy to be sure to have enough potatoes? *NEAB, Question 7, Paper 2H, November 1995*

13 In 1994, the Humber Bridge lost money at a rate of £1.42 per second.

a How much money did the bridge lose in 1994 (365 days)?

One day, 15 274 vehicles crossed the Humber Bridge.

b What is the average number of vehicles per minute which crossed the bridge that day? *NEAB, Question 1, Paper 1H, November 1995*

14 Emma uses her calculator to work out

$$\frac{7.8 \times 5.2}{0.5 \times 16}$$

She gets the answer 5.07. Without using a calculator, she does a quick calculation to see whether her answer is about right. Explain how Emma can do this.

NEAB, Question 7, Paper 1H, November 1995

Summary

How well do you grade yourself?

To gain a grade **C**, you need to be able to round off your answers to a suitable degree of accuracy without being asked. You need also to be able to express one number as a percentage of another and to understand the equivalences between fractions, decimals and percentages.

To gain a grade **B**, you need to be able to use percentages to solve problems involving repeated changes and be able to calculate the original quantity given a particular percentage value.

To gain a grade **A**, you need to be able to sort out percentage problems, especially those requiring you to calculate reverse percentage.

What you should know after you have worked through Chapter 1

- What is meant by the terms ‘significant figures’ and ‘decimal places’.
- To find $P\%$ of an amount T, you calculate

  $$(P \times T) \div 100$$

- To calculate A as a percentage of B, you calculate

  $$\frac{A}{B} \times 100$$

- To calculate percentage gain, you calculate

  $$\frac{\text{Gain}}{\text{Original amount}} \times 100$$

- To calculate 100% when you know that $P\%$ represents an amount M, you calculate

  $$\frac{M}{P} \times 100$$

- How to calculate compound interest in several ways.

2 Shape

This chapter is going to ... show you how to calculate the areas of sectors and trapeziums, and introduce you to the types of problem that you will be able to solve with knowledge of area. It also introduces you to the methods for calculating the volumes and surface areas of several common shapes.

What you should already know

- The area of a rectangle is given by Area = Length × Breadth.
- The area of a triangle is given by Area = $\frac{1}{2}$ (Base length × Height).
- The circumference of a circle is given by $C = \pi D$, where D is the diameter of the circle.
- The area of a circle of radius r is given by Area = πr^2.
- The most accurate value of π that you can use is on your calculator. You should use it every time you have to work with π.
- The length of the diameter of a circle is twice the length of its radius. When you are given a radius in order to find a circumference, first double the radius to get the diameter.
- In problems using π, unless told otherwise, round off your answers to 3 sf.

If you feel you need to revise circle calculations, you should work through Exercises 2A and 2B.

Exercise 2A

1 Find the circumference of the following circles. Round off your answers to 1 dp.

a Diameter 5 cm **b** Diameter 8.2 cm **c** Radius 4 cm **d** Radius 5.8 cm
e Diameter 12 m **f** Radius 9 m **g** Diameter 1.3 cm **h** Radius 3.7 m
i Radius 1.9 cm **j** Diameter 4.6 mm **k** Diameter 5.8 m **l** Radius 0.8 cm

2 A bicycle wheel has a radius of 30 cm. The bicycle is cycled 50 km.

a What is the circumference of the bicycle wheel?
b How many complete revolutions will the wheel make over the 50 km?

3 A rope is wrapped 8 times round a capstan (cylindrical post), the diameter of which is 35 cm. How long is the rope?

4 On my watch the hour hand is 0.9 cm long, the minute hand 1.4 cm long.

a How far does the end of the minute hand travel in

i 1 minute **ii** 1 hour **iii** 1 day?

b How far does the end of the hour hand travel in

i 1 hour **ii** 1 week **iii** 1 minute?

5 A circular racing track has 5 lanes. Each lane is 1 m wide, and the radius of the inner lane is 32 m. In one race, the competitors have to run all the way round the track once, keeping in the same lanes in which they started.

a How far would each competitor run in each lane?

b Express the ratio of shortest run : longest run as a percentage.

6 The roller used on a cricket pitch has a radius of 70 cm.

a What is the circumference of the roller?

b How many revolutions does it make when rolling the pitch – a length of 20 m?

7 A semicircle is, as shown, exactly half a circle.

If a semicircle has a diameter of 6 cm, calculate

a its arc length **b** its total perimeter.

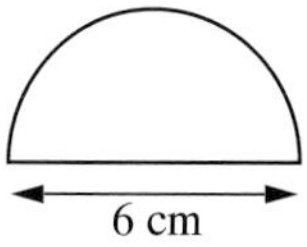

8 What is the total perimeter of a semicircle of diameter 15 cm?

9 What is the total perimeter of a circle of radius 7 cm?

10 How many complete revolutions will a car wheel, radius 25 cm, make in a journey of 285 km?

11 Assume that the human waist is circular.

a What are the distances around the waist of the following people?

Sue	waist radius of 10 cm	Dave	waist radius of 12 cm
Julie	waist radius of 11 cm	Brian	waist radius of 13 cm

b What interesting fact do the answers to the above tell you?

c What would be the difference in length between a rope stretched tightly round the earth and another rope always held 1 m above it?

12 A hamster has a treadmill of radius 6 cm.

a How far has he run when the wheel has made 100 complete revolutions?

b How many revolutions will be needed to cover 1 km?

Exercise 2B

1 Copy and complete the following table for each circle.

	Radius	Diameter	Circumference	Area
a	5 cm			
b	4.5 cm			
c		8 cm		
d			22 cm	
e	2.9 m			
f			110 m	
g		7.6 m		
h			121 m	
i	0.08 mm			

2 Calculate the area of each of these circles, giving your answers to 1 decimal place.

a Radius 5 cm **b** Diameter 9 m **c** Radius 13 cm

d Diameter 1 m **e** Radius 11 m **f** Diameter 67 cm

3 The diameter of each of these coins is

1p…2 cm 2p…2.6 cm 5p…1.7 cm 10p…2.4 cm

Calculate the area of one face of each coin.

4 Calculate the area of these shapes.

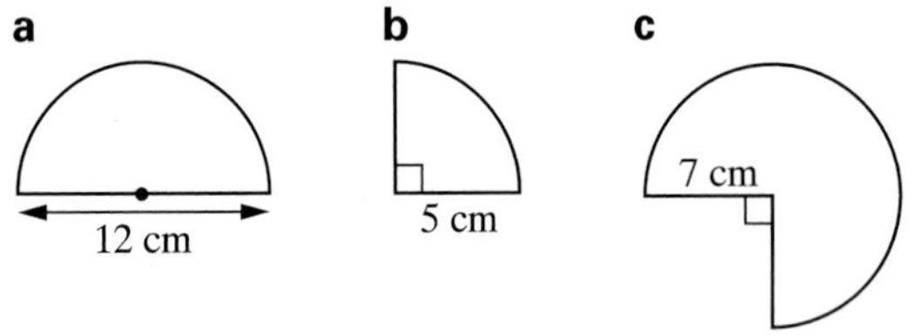

5 Calculate the area of these shapes.

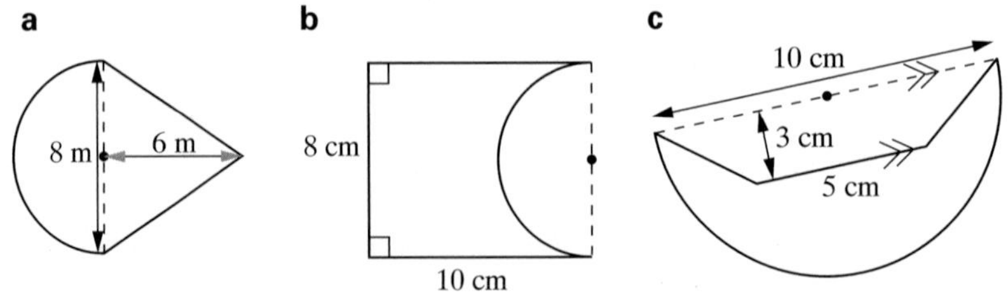

6 A garden has a circular lawn of diameter 30 m. There is a path 2 m wide all the way round the circumference. What is the area of this path?

7 Calculate the area of the shaded part of each of these diagrams.

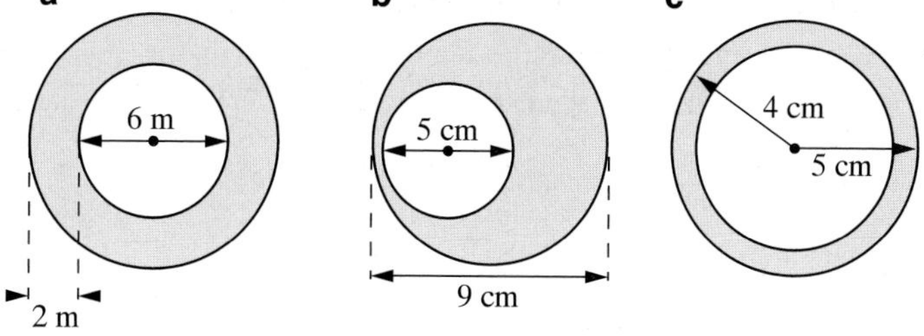

8 Metal discs are stamped from a rectangular sheet of metal, as shown in the diagram.

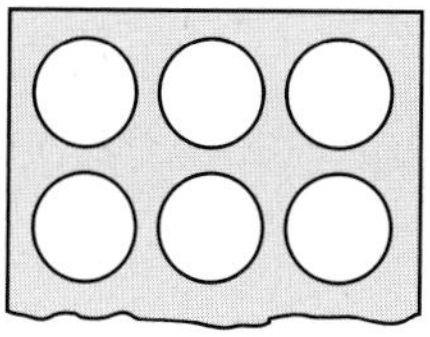

a What is the largest number of discs 3 cm in diameter that can be cut from a sheet which measures 10 cm by 16 cm?

b What would be the percentage waste from the original sheet of metal?

9 The whole area of a circular playground, radius 10 m, is to be covered in a rubber solution. This solution comes in cartons. Each carton contains enough solution to cover 2 m^2. How many cartons are needed?

10 The shaded shape consists of three semicircles. Calculate the perimeter and the area of the whole shape.

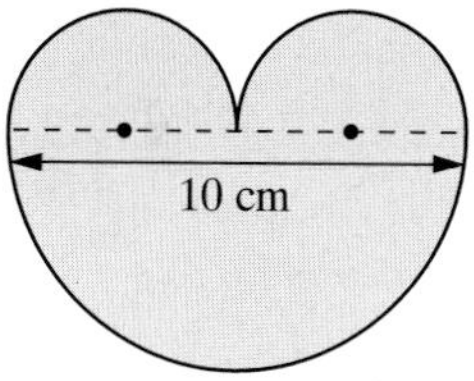

Sectors

A sector is part of a circle, bounded by two radii of the circle and one of the arcs formed by the intersection of these radii with the circumference.

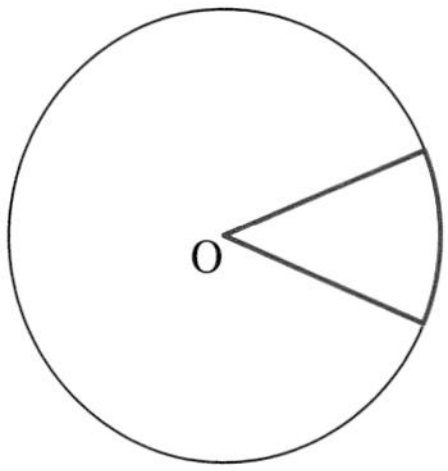

The angle subtended at the centre of the circle by the arc of a sector is known as the **angle of the sector**.

When a circle is divided into only two sectors, the larger one is called the **major sector** and the smaller one is called the **minor sector**.

Likewise, their arcs are called respectively the **major arc** and the **minor arc**.

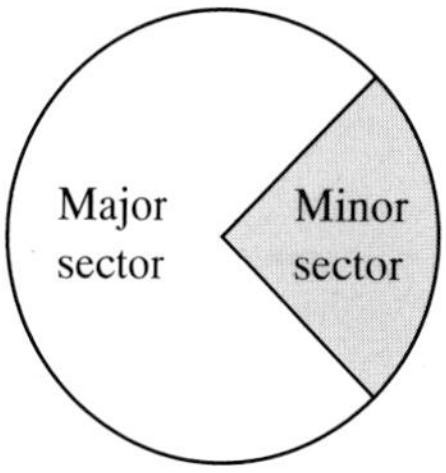

Arc length and sector area

A sector is a fraction of the whole circle, the size of the fraction being determined by the size of angle of the sector. For example, the sector shown in the diagram represents

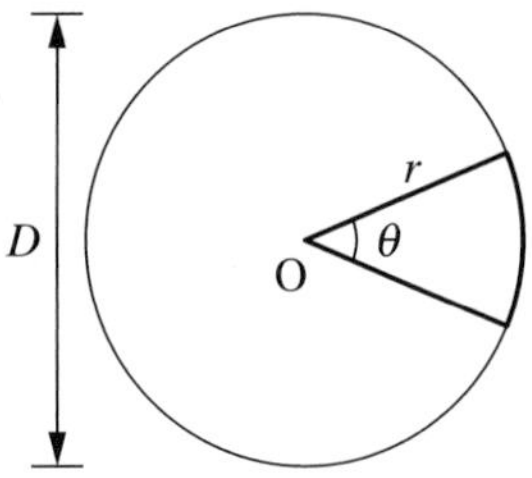

the fraction $\frac{\theta°}{360°}$. This applies to both its arc length and its area. Therefore,

$$\text{Arc length} = \frac{\theta°}{360°} \times \pi D$$

$$\text{Sector area} = \frac{\theta°}{360°} \times \pi r^2$$

Example Find the arc length and the area of the sector in the diagram.

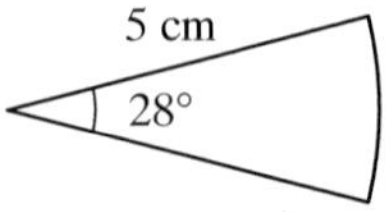

The sector angle is 28° and the radius is 5 cm. Therefore,

$$\text{Arc length} = \frac{28°}{360°} \times \pi \times 2 \times 5 = 2.4 \text{ cm} \quad (1 \text{ dp})$$

$$\text{Sector area} = \frac{28°}{360°} \times \pi \times 5^2 = 6.1 \text{ cm}^2 \quad (1 \text{ dp})$$

Exercise 2C

1 For each of these sectors, calculate

i arc length **ii** sector area

a

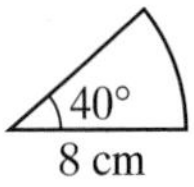

b

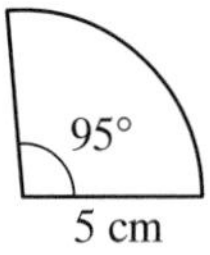

c

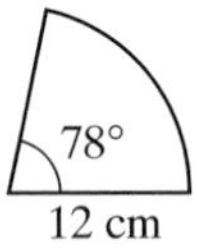

d

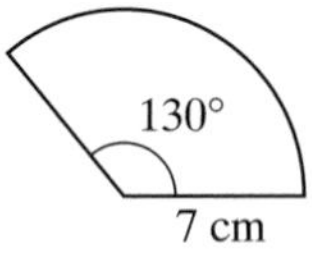

2 Calculate the arc length and the area of a sector whose arc subtends an angle of 154° at the centre of a circle of diameter 12 cm.

3 Calculate the total perimeter of each of these shapes.

a

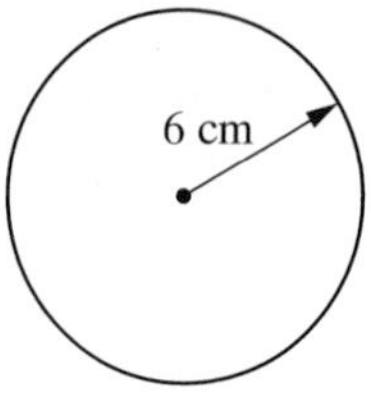

b

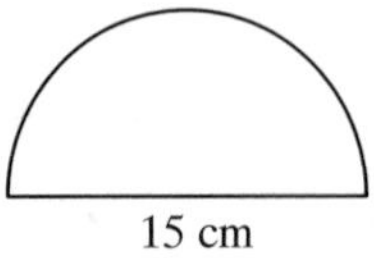

c

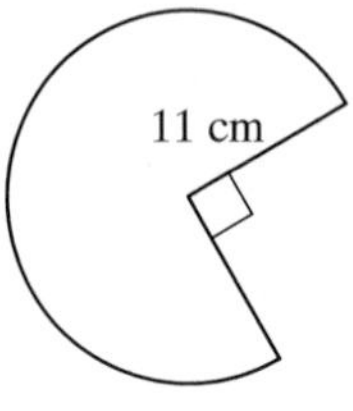

d

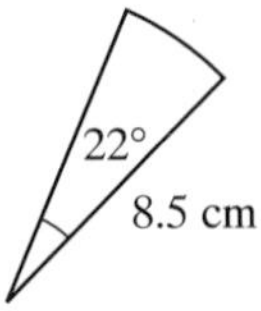

4 Calculate the area of each of these shapes.

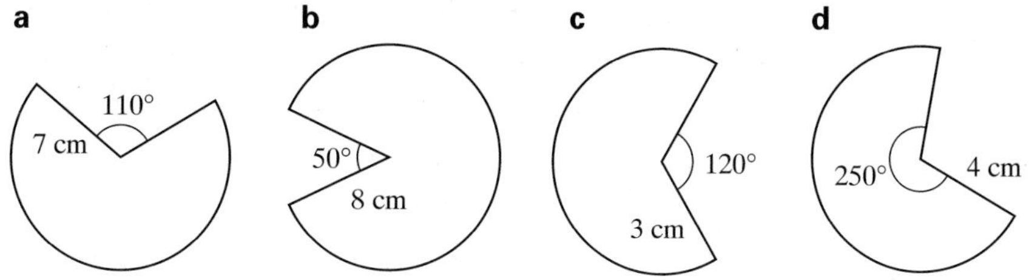

5 The planet Earth has a radius of 6400 km. Assume that it takes a day to make one complete revolution. Calculate the distance that a point on the Earth's equator moves round during

i 1 hour **ii** 1 minute **iii** 1 second

6 ABCD is a square of side length 8 cm. APC and AQC are arcs of the circles with centres D and B and radius 8 cm. Calculate the area of the shaded part.

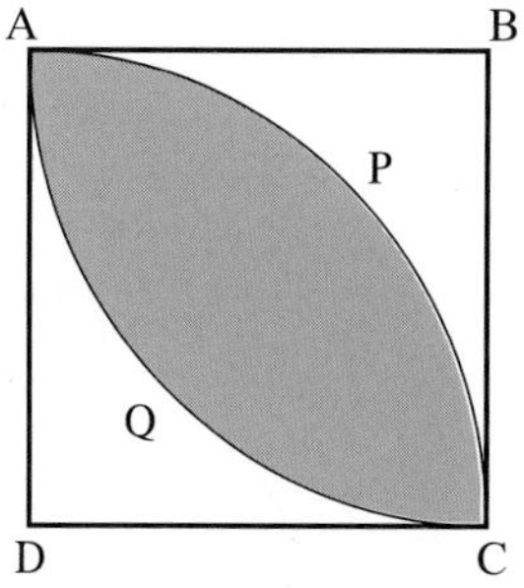

7 Find **i** the perimeter and **ii** the area of the shape below.

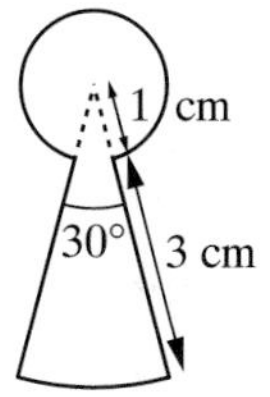

8 Calculate the area of the shaded shape on the right.

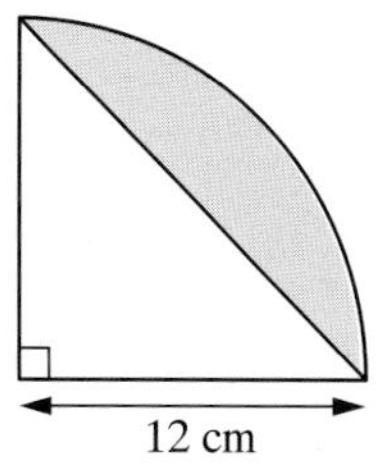

9 A pendulum of length 85 cm swings through an angle of 15°. Through what distance does the bob swing?

10 A sector of radius 8 cm has an area of 30 cm^2. Calculate the angle subtended by its arc at the centre of the circle.

11 A sector whose arc subtends an angle of 65° has an area of 50 cm^2. Calculate the radius of the sector.

12 Find some possible dimensions of a sector whose area is 1 m^2.

Area of a trapezium

The area of a trapezium is calculated by finding the average of the lengths of its parallel sides and multiplying this by the perpendicular distance between them.

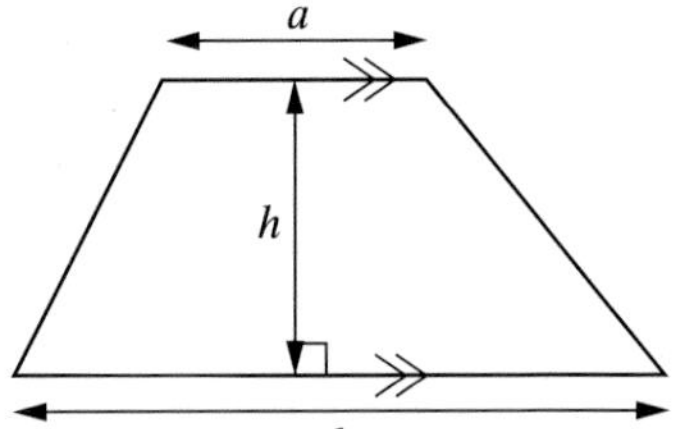

$$\text{Area} = h\left(\frac{a+b}{2}\right)$$

For example, the area of the trapezium ABCD is given by

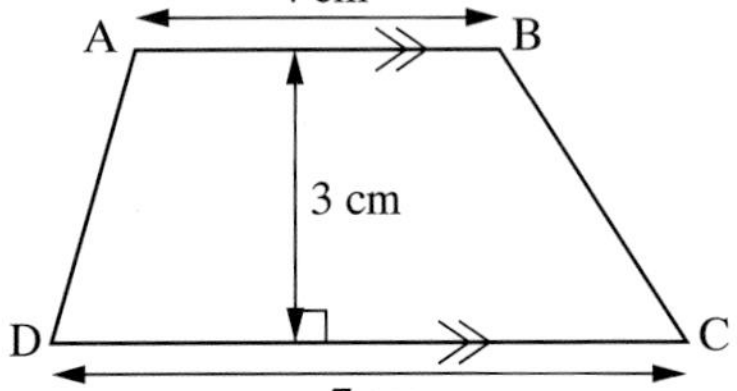

$$\text{Area} = 3 \times \left(\frac{4+7}{2}\right)$$

which equals 16.5 cm^2.

Exercise 2D

1 Copy and complete the following table for each trapezium.

	Parallel side 1	Parallel side 2	Vertical height	Area
a	8 cm	4 cm	5 cm	
b	10 cm	12 cm	7 cm	
c	7 cm	5 cm	4 cm	
d	5 cm	9 cm	6 cm	
e	3 m	13 m	5 m	
f	4 cm	10 cm		42 cm^2
g	7 cm	8 cm		22.5 cm^2
h	6 cm		5 cm	40 cm^2
i		7 cm	1.5 cm	7.5 cm^2
j		7.5 cm	6 cm	30 cm^2
k	4.8 cm	9.4 cm		85.2 cm^2

2 Calculate the perimeter and the area of each of these trapeziums.

a

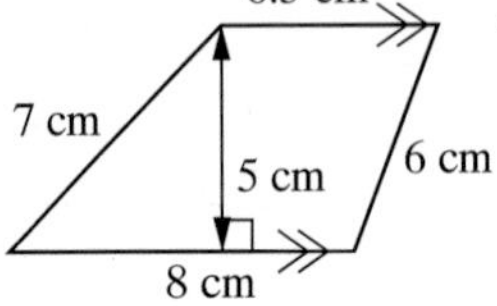

b

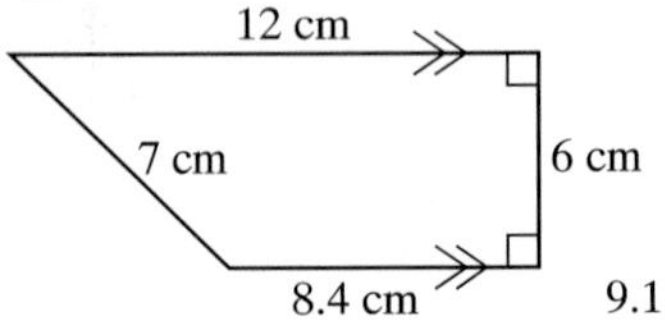

c

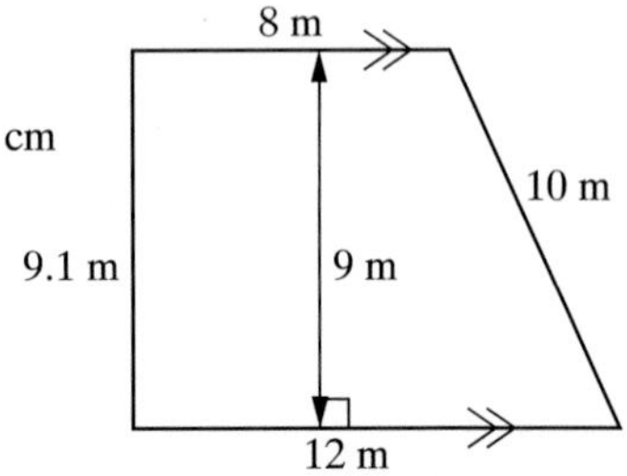

3 Calculate the area of each of these shapes.

a

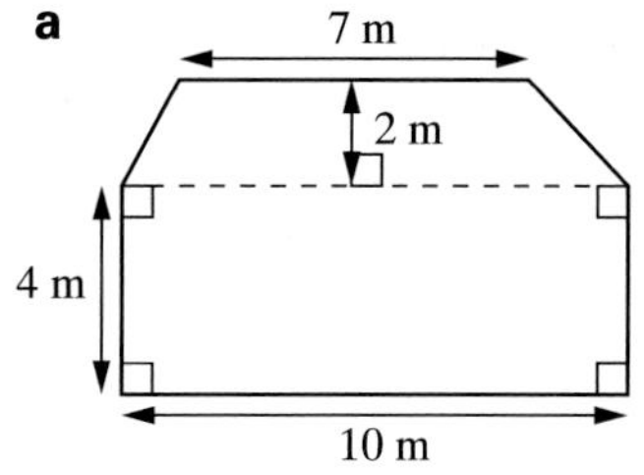

b

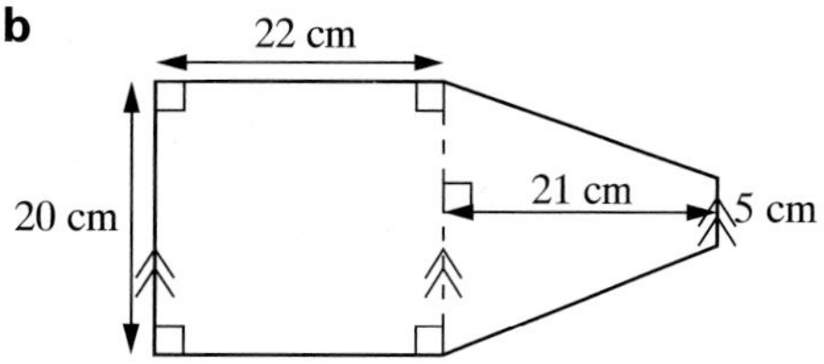

c

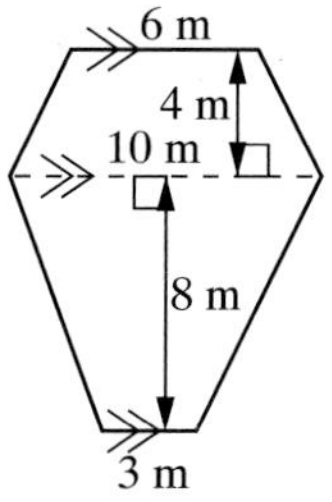

4 Calculate the area of the shaded part in each of these diagrams.

a

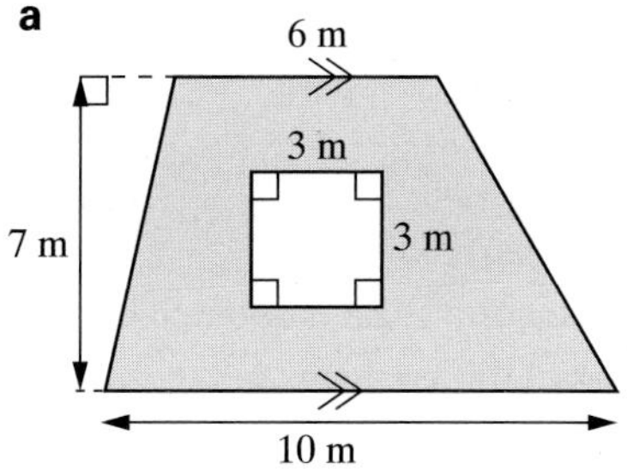

b

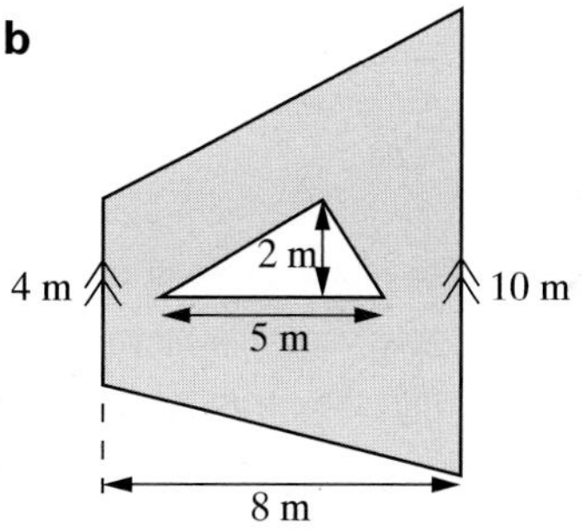

c

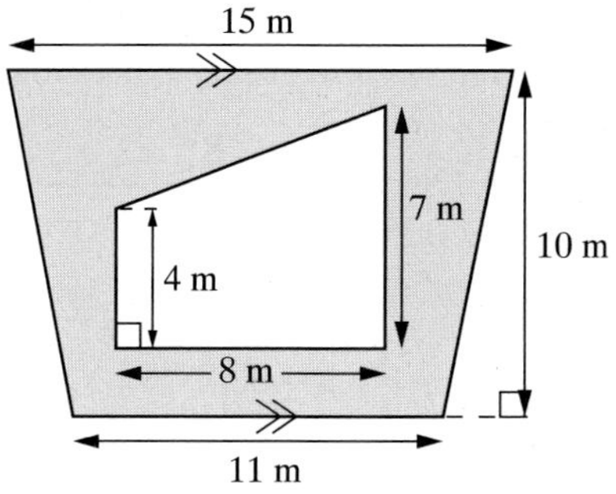

5 Which of the following shapes has the largest area?

a

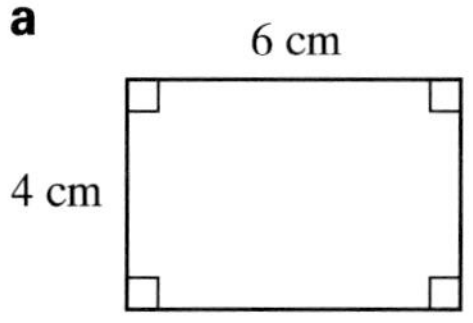

b

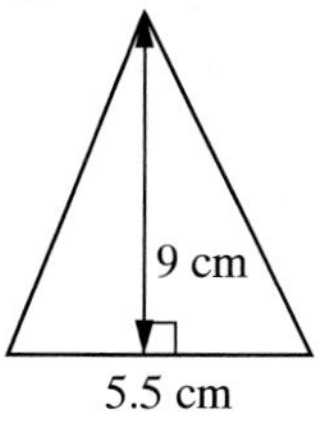

c

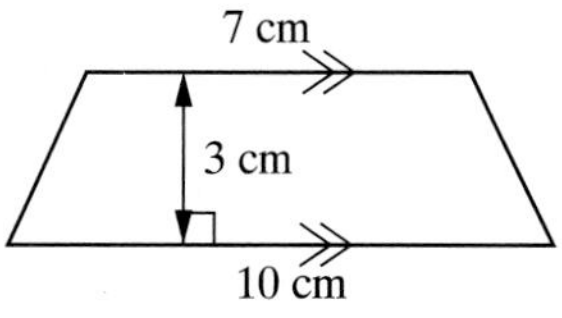

6 A trapezium has an area of 25 cm^2. Its vertical height is 5 cm. Write down 5 different possible pairs of lengths which the two parallel sides could be.

7 Which of the following shapes has the smallest area?

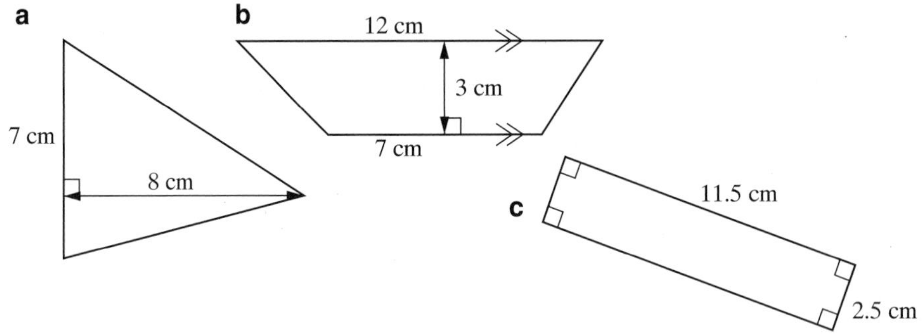

8 What percentage of this shape has been shaded?

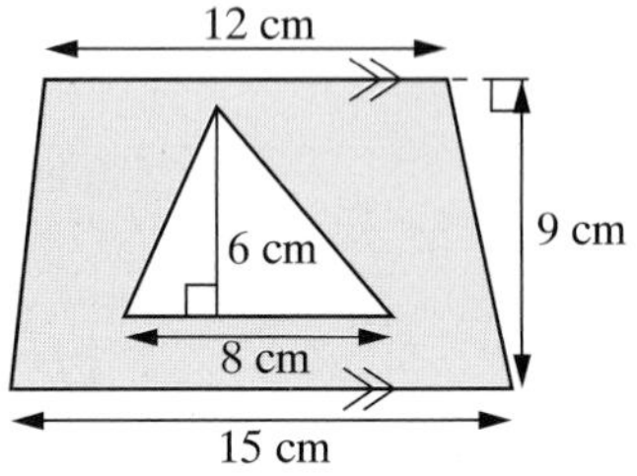

9 The shape of most of Egypt (see map) roughly approximates to a trapezium. The north coast is about 900 km long, the south boundary is about 1100 km long, and the vertical distance from north to south is about 1100 km.

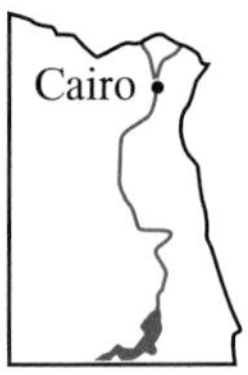

What is the approximate area of this part of Egypt?

10 Find the perimeter and the area of each parallelogram.

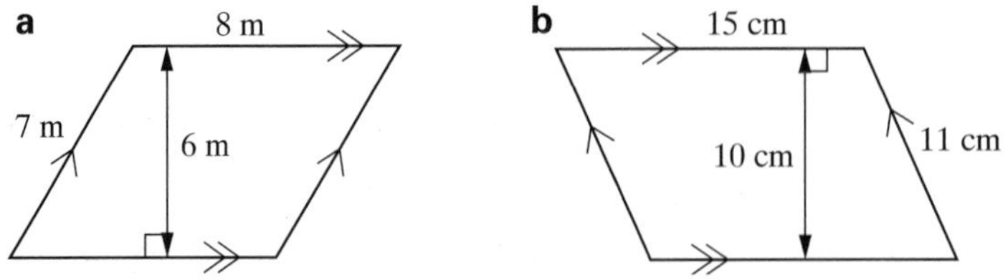

Density

Density is a rate of change. It is the mass of a substance per unit volume, usually expressed in grams per cm^3. The relationship between the three quantities is

$$\text{Density} = \frac{\text{Mass}}{\text{Volume}}$$

This is often remembered with the following triangle.

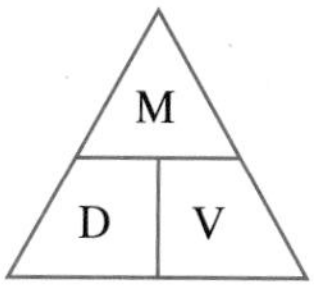

Mass = Density × Volume   Density = Mass ÷ Volume

Volume = Mass ÷ Density

Note Density is defined in terms of mass, which is commonly referred to as 'weight', although, strictly speaking, there is a difference between them (you may already have learnt about it in science). In this book, the two terms are assumed to have the same meaning.

Example 1 A piece of metal weighing 30 g has a volume of 4 cm^3. What is the density of the metal?

$$\text{Density} = \frac{30}{4} = 7.5 \text{ g/cm}^3$$

Example 2 What is the weight of a piece of rock which has a volume of 34 cm^3 and a density of 2.25 g/cm^3?

$$\text{Weight} = 34 \times 2.25 = 76.5 \text{ g}$$

Exercise 2E

1 Find the density of a piece of wood weighing 6 g and having a volume of 8 cm^3.

2 Calculate the density of a metal if 12 cm^3 of it weighs 100 g.

3 Calculate the weight of a piece of plastic, 20 cm^3 in volume, if its density is 1.6 g/cm^3.

4 Calculate the volume of a piece of wood which weighs 102 g and has a density of 0.85 g/cm^3.

5 Find the weight of a marble model, 56 cm^3 in volume, if the density of marble is 2.8 g/cm^3.

6 Calculate the volume of a liquid weighing 4 kg and having a density of 1.25 g/cm^3.

7 Find the density of the material of a pebble which weighs 34 g and has a volume of 12.5 cm^3.

8 It is estimated that the statue of Queen Victoria in Endcliffe Park, Sheffield, has a volume of about 4 m^3. The density of the material used to make the statue is 9.2 g/cm^3. What is the estimated weight of the statue?

9 I bought a 50 kg bag of coal, and estimated the total volume of coal to be about 28 000 cm^3. What is the density of coal in g/cm^3?

10 A 1 kg bag of sugar has a volume of about 625 cm^3. What is the density of sugar in g/cm^3?

Cylinders

Volume

The volume of a cylinder is found by multiplying the area of one of its circular ends by the length of the cylinder (or height if the cylinder is stood on end). That is,

$$\text{Volume} = \pi r^2 h$$

where r is the radius of the cylinder and h is its height or length.

Example What is the volume of a cylinder having radius 5 cm and height 12 cm?

$$\begin{aligned}\text{Volume} &= \text{End (or base) area} \times \text{Height}\\ &= \pi r^2 h\\ &= \pi \times 5^2 \times 12 = 942\ \text{cm}^3\end{aligned}$$

Surface area

The surface area of a cylinder is made up of the area of its curved surface plus the area of its two ends.

$$\begin{aligned}\text{Curved surface area} &= \text{Circumference of end} \times \text{Length of cylinder}\\ &= \pi D h\end{aligned}$$

$$\text{Area of one end} = \pi r^2$$

Therefore,

$$\text{Total surface area} = \pi D h + 2\pi r^2$$

Example What is the total surface area of a cylinder of radius 15 cm and height 2.5 m?

First, we must change the dimensions to a **common unit**: centimetres in this case.

$$\begin{aligned}\text{Total surface area} &= \pi \times 30 \times 250 + 2 \times \pi \times 15^2\\ &= 23\,562 + 1414\\ &= 24\,976\ \text{cm}^2\\ &= 25\,000\ \text{cm}^2 \quad \text{(3 sf)}\end{aligned}$$

Exercise 2F

1 Find **i** the volume and **ii** the curved surface area of each of these cylinders.

a Base radius 3 cm and height 8 cm.

b Base diameter 9 cm and height 7 cm.

c Base diameter 13.5 cm and height 15 cm.

d Base radius of 1.2 m and length 5.5 m.

2 Find **i** the volume and **ii** the total surface area of each of these cylinders.

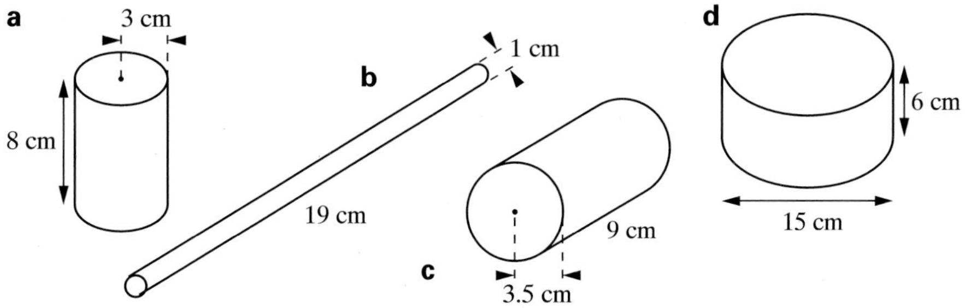

3 The diameter of a marble, cylindrical column is 60 cm and its height is 4.2 m. The cost of making this column is quoted as £67.50 a cubic metre. What is the estimated total cost of making the column?

4 Find the weight of a solid iron cylinder 55 cm high with a base diameter of 60 cm. The density of iron is 7.9 g/cm^3.

5 What is the radius of a cylinder, height 8 cm, with a volume of 200 cm^3?

6 What is the radius of a cylinder, height 12 cm, with a curved surface area of 226 cm^2.

7 What is the diameter of a cylinder, height 5 cm, with a volume of 150 cm^3?

8 A cylinder of height 14 cm has a curved surface area of 350 cm^2. Calculate the volume of this cylinder.

9 Calculate the curved surface area of a cylinder which has a height of 18 cm and a volume of 390 cm^3.

10 A cylindrical container is 65 cm in diameter. Water is poured into the container until it is 1 metre deep. How much water is in the container? (Remember 1000 cm^3 = 1 litre.)

11 A cylindrical can of soup has a diameter of 7 cm and a height of 9.5 cm. It is full of soup which weighs 625 g. What is the density of the soup?

12 An iron drainpipe has an outer diameter of 12 cm and an inner diameter of 11.5 cm.

a What volume of iron is in the 4 m long drainpipe?

b What is the mass of the drainpipe, given that iron has a density of 7.9 g/cm^3?

13 15 cm^3 of gold are rolled and made into wire 90 m long. Calculate the diameter of the wire.

14 A metal bar, 1 m long, and with a diameter of 6 cm, weighs 22 kg. What is the density of the metal from which the bar is made?

15 A solid iron cylinder of diameter 15 cm and height 12 cm is melted down to make wire 0.01 cm thick (diameter). What length of wire will be made?

16 What is the length of 0.015 cm thick wire made from a block of copper measuring 40 cm by 15 cm by 10 cm?

Prisms, pyramids and cones

Volume of a prism

A prism is a 3-D shape which has the same cross-section running all the way through it.

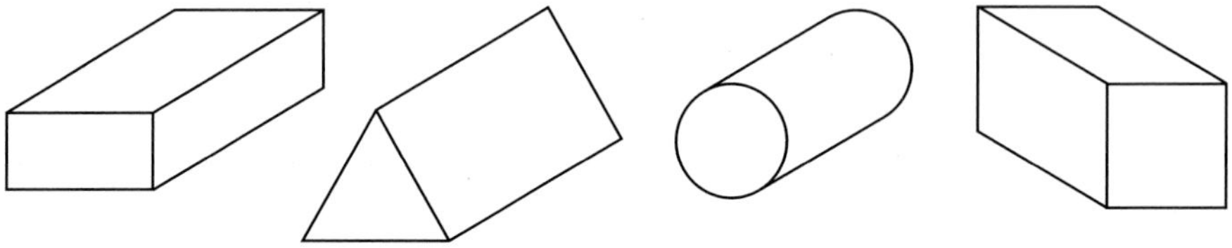

The volume of a prism is found by multiplying the area of its regular cross-section by the length of the prism (or height if the prism is stood on end). That is,

$$\text{Volume of prism} = \text{Area of cross-section} \times \text{Length}$$

$$V = A\ell$$

For example, the diagram shows a prism with a triangular cross-section, the area of which is

$$\frac{5 \times 7}{2} = 17.5 \text{ cm}^2$$

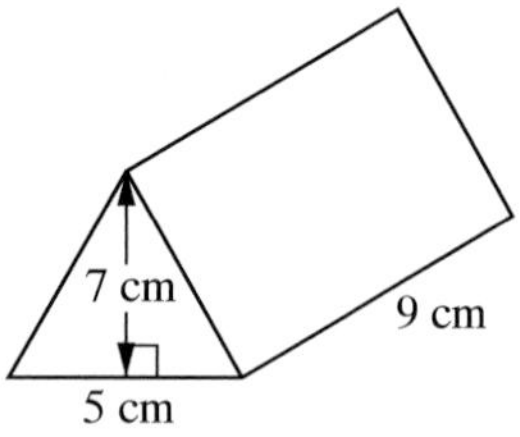

The volume is the area of its cross-section × length, which is

$$17.5 \text{ cm}^2 \times 9 \text{ cm} = 157.5 \text{ cm}^3$$

Exercise 2G

1 For each prism shown

i sketch the cross-section **ii** calculate the area of the cross-section

iii calculate the volume.

a

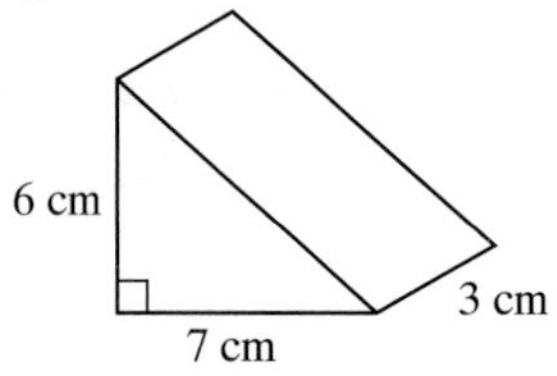

b

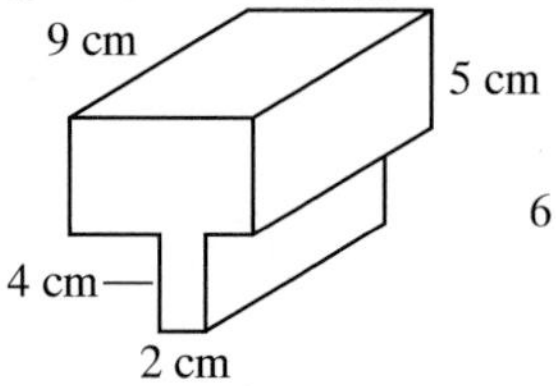

c

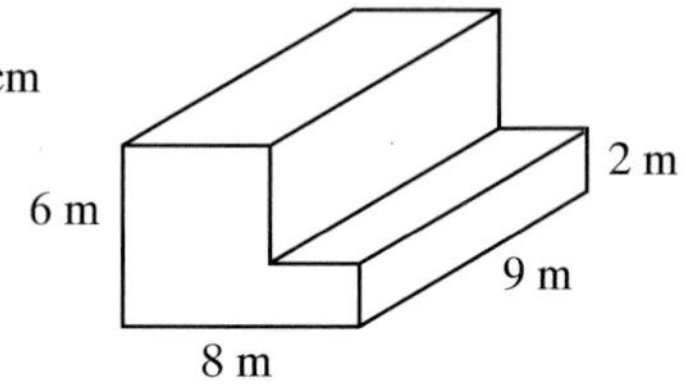

2 Calculate the volume of each of these prisms.

a

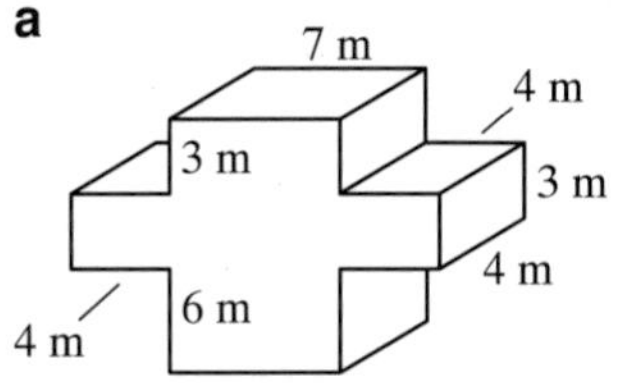

b

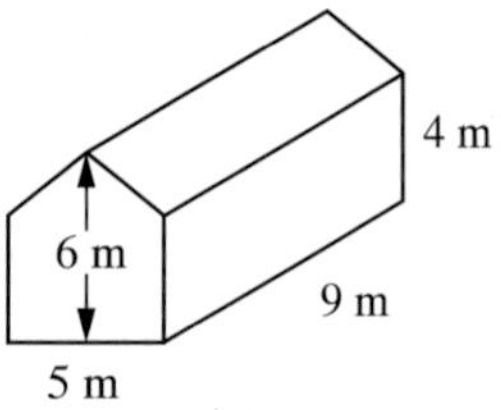

c

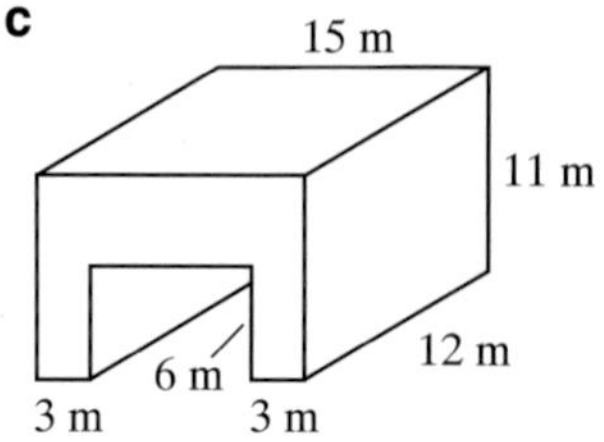

3 The uniform cross-section of a swimming pool is a trapezium with parallel sides, 1 m and 2.5 m, with a perpendicular distance of 30 m between them. The width of the pool is 10 m. How much water is in the pool when it is full?

4 A container is made in the shape shown. The top and bottom are the same size, both consisting of a rectangle, 4 cm by 9 cm, with a semicircle at each end. The depth is 3 cm. Find the volume of the container.

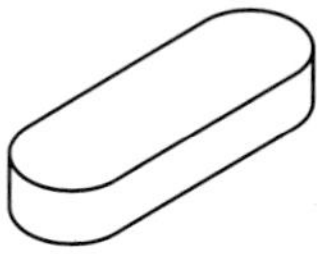

5 A lean-to is a prism as shown. Calculate the volume of air inside the lean-to.

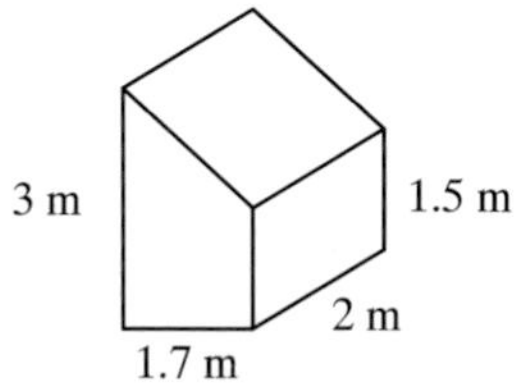

6 Each of these prisms has a regular cross-section in the shape of a right-angled triangle.

a Find the volume of each prism .

b Find the total surface area of each prism.

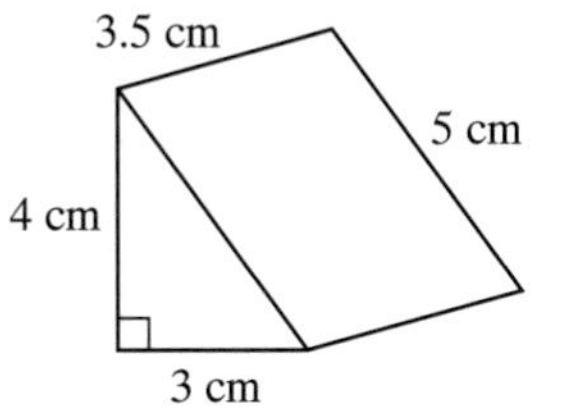

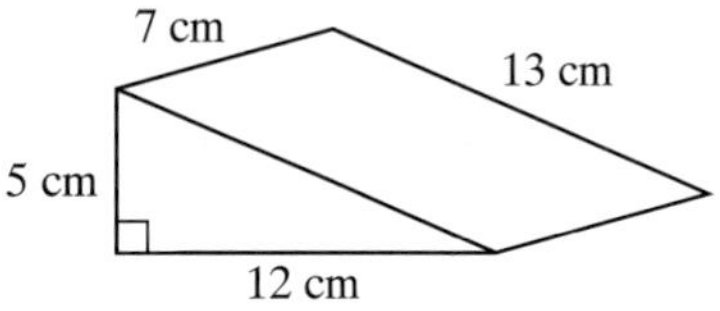

7 A tunnel is in the shape of a semicircle of radius 5 m, running for 500 m through a hill. Calculate the volume of soil removed when the tunnel was cut through the hill.

8 A horse trough is in the shape of a semicircular prism as shown. What volume of water will the trough hold when it is filled to the top?

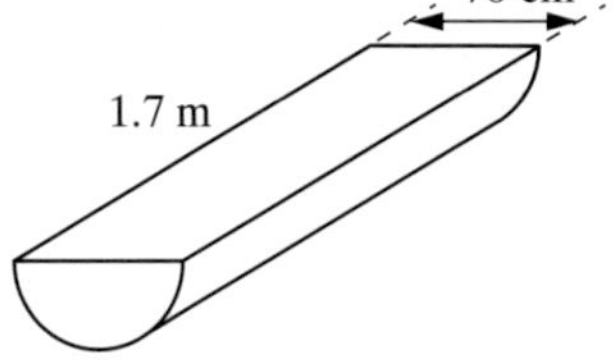

9 The dimensions of the cross-section of a girder, 2 m in length, are shown on the diagram. The girder is made of iron with a density of 7.9 g/cm³. What is the weight of the girder?

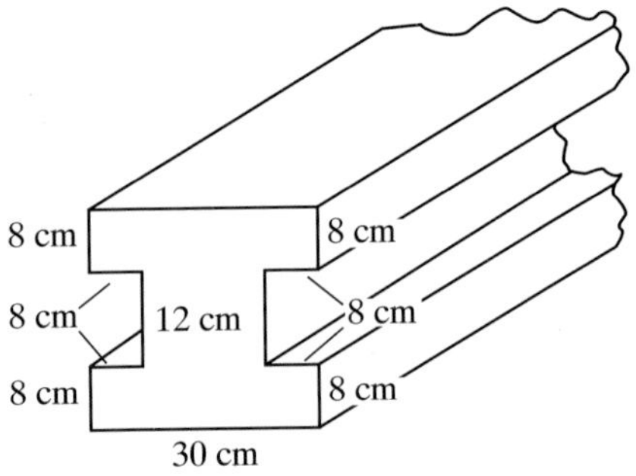

10 Which of these solids is

a the heaviest **b** the lightest?

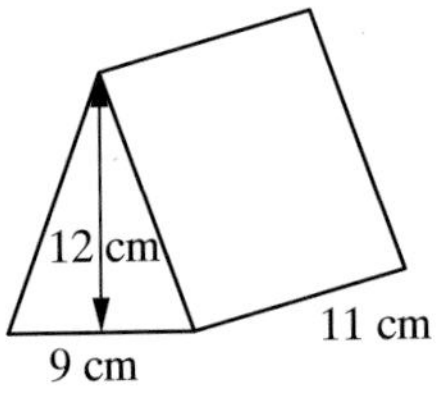

Density 4.8 g/cm³

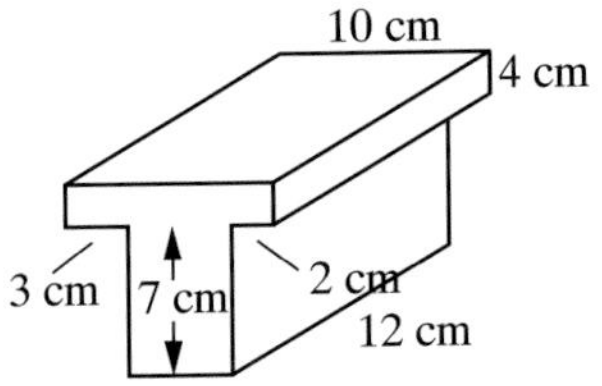

Density 3.2 g/cm³

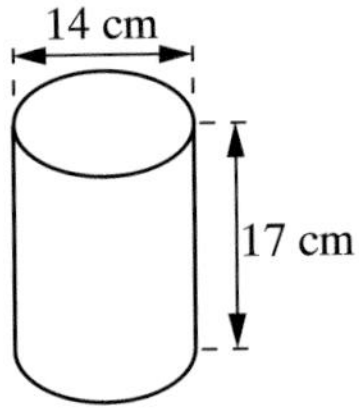

Density 1.1 g/cm³

11 A block of wood has a hole of radius 2.5 cm drilled out as shown on the diagram. Calculate the weight of the wood if its density is 0.95 g/cm³.

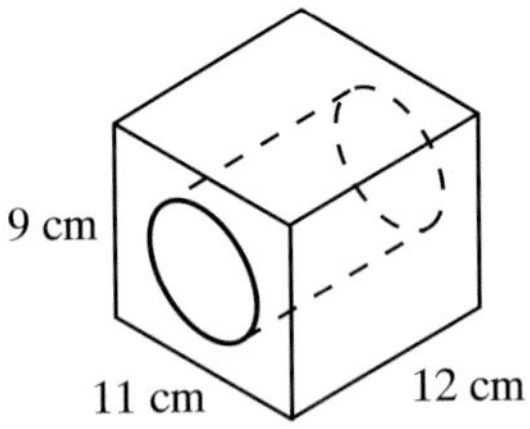

Volume of a pyramid

A pyramid is a 3-D shape with a base from which triangular faces rise to a common vertex, called the **apex**. The base can be any polygon, but is usually a triangle, a rectangle or a square.

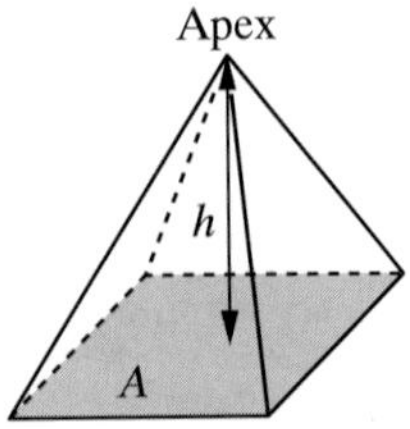

The volume of a pyramid is given by

$$\text{Volume} = \tfrac{1}{3} \times \text{Base area} \times \text{Vertical height}$$

$$V = \tfrac{1}{3}Ah$$

where A is the base area and h is the vertical height

Example 1 Calculate the volume of this pyramid.

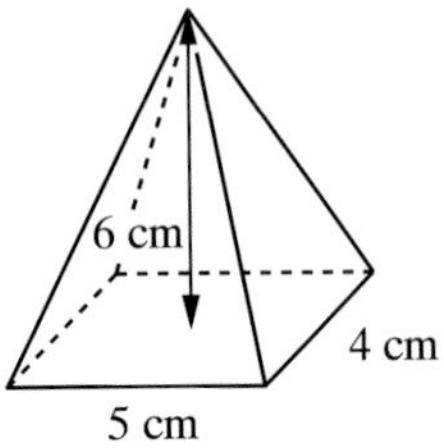

Base area = $5 \times 4 = 20\ \text{cm}^2$

Volume = $\tfrac{1}{3} \times 20 \times 6 = 40\ \text{cm}^3$

Example 2 A pyramid, with a square base of side 8 cm, has a volume of 320 cm^3. What is the vertical height of the pyramid?

Let h be the vertical height of the pyramid. Then,

$$\text{Volume} = \tfrac{1}{3} \times 64 \times h = 320$$

$$\frac{64\,h}{3} = 320$$

$$\Rightarrow \quad h = \frac{320 \times 3}{64}$$

$$\Rightarrow \quad h = 15 \text{ cm}$$

Exercise 2H

1 Calculate the volume of each of these pyramids, all with rectangular bases.

a

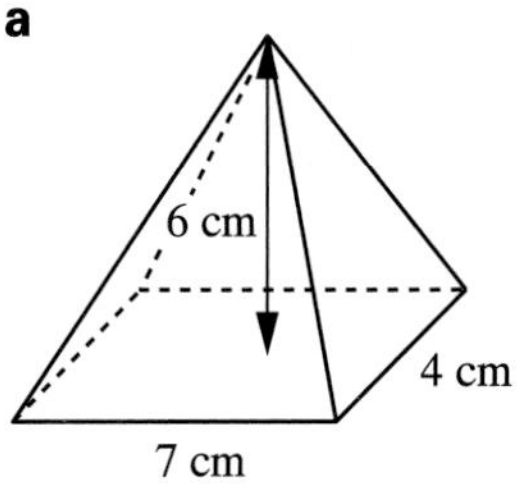

b

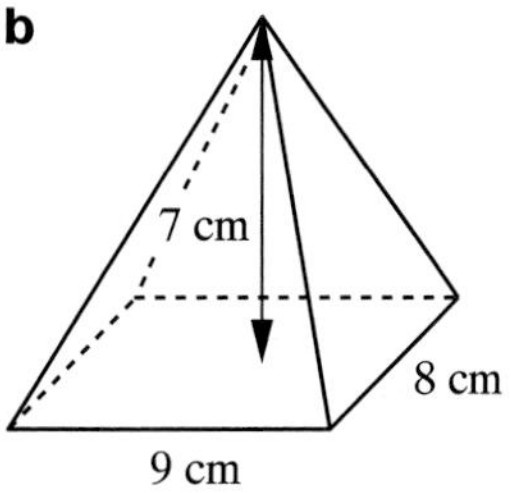

c

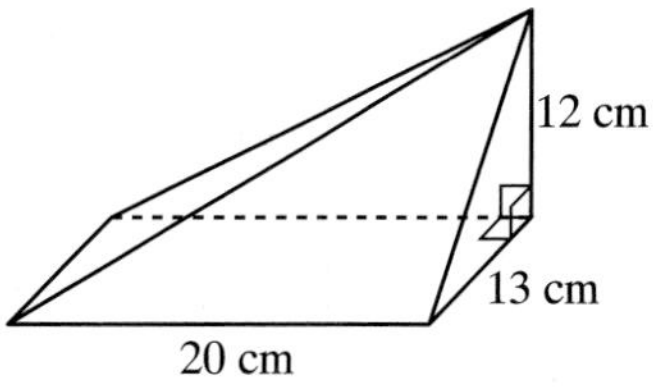

d

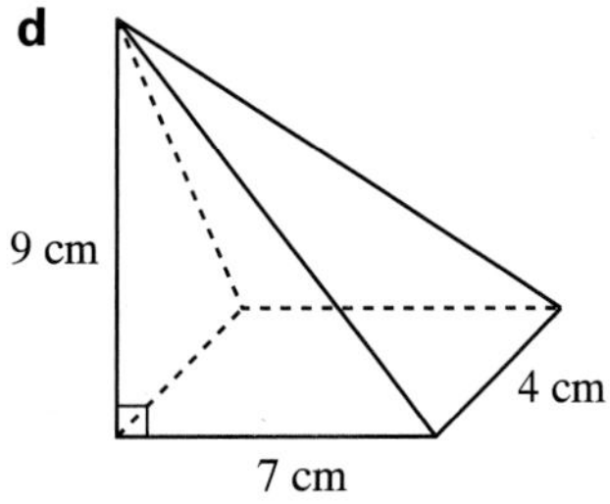

e

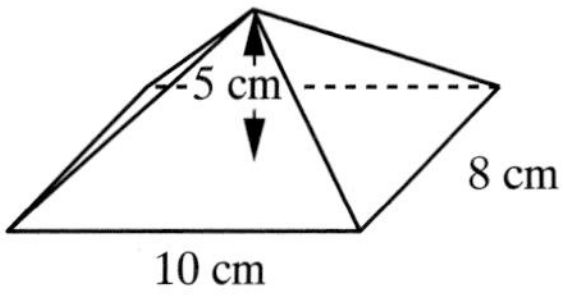

2 Calculate the volume of a pyramid having a square base of side 9 cm and a vertical height of 10 cm.

3 Calculate the volume of each of these shapes.

a

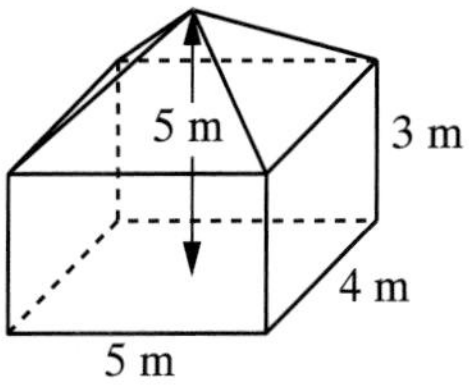

b

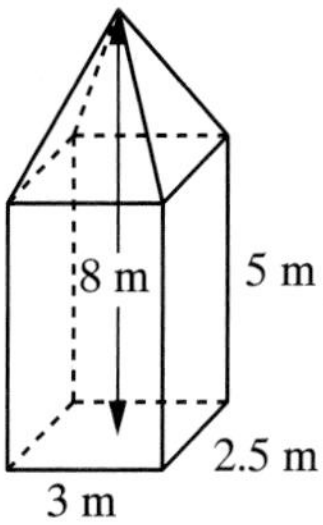

c

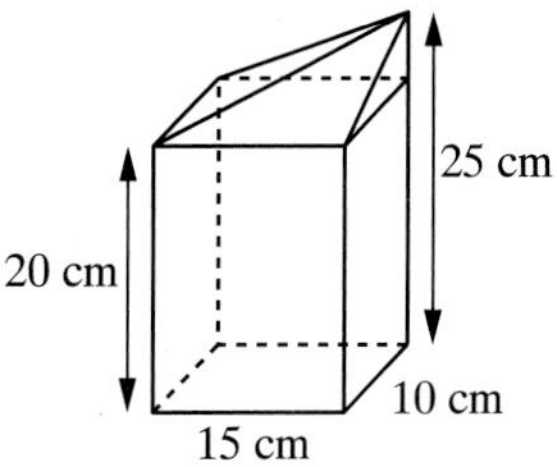

4 What is the weight of a solid pyramid having a square base of side 4 cm and a height of 3 cm, with a density of 13 g/cm^3?

5 A crystal is in the form of two square-based pyramids joined at their bases (see diagram). The crystal weighs 31.5 grams. What is its density?

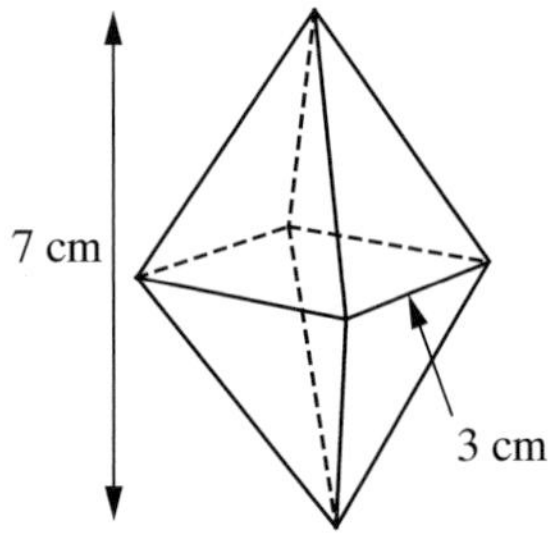

6 Find the weight of each of these pyramids

a

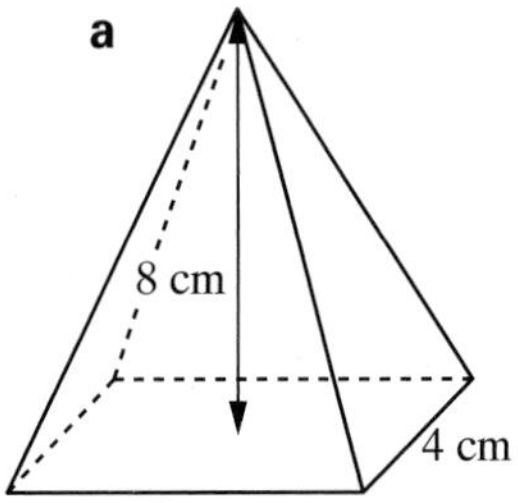

Density 2.7 g/cm^3

b

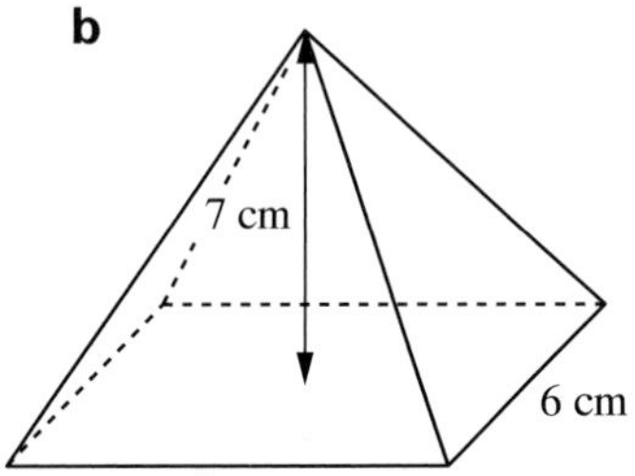

Density 3.5 g/cm^3

c

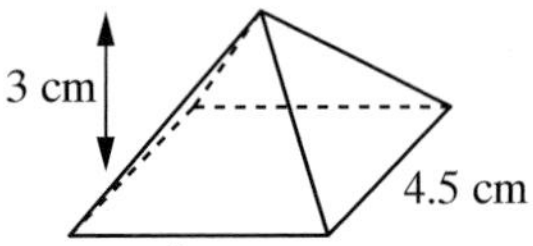

Density 2.1 g/cm^3

7 Calculate the length x in each of these rectangular-based pyramids.

a

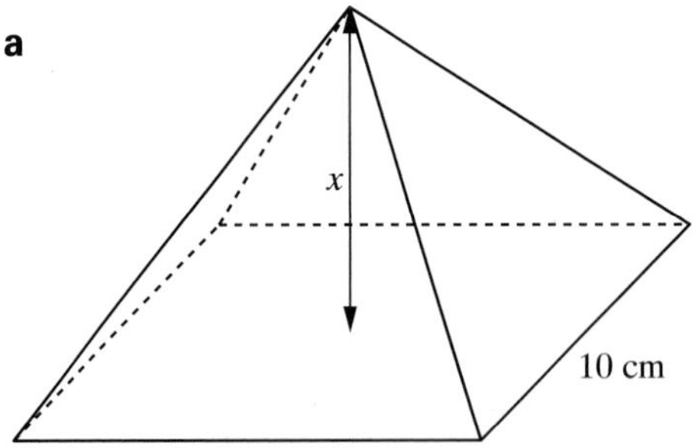

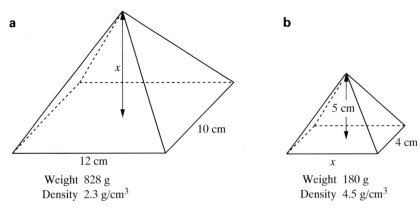

Weight 828 g
Density 2.3 g/cm^3

b

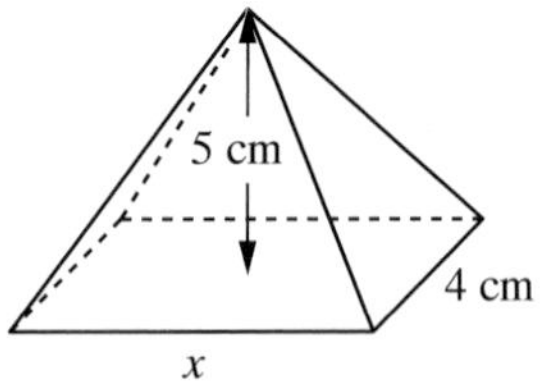

Weight 180 g
Density 4.5 g/cm^3

8 The pyramid in the diagram has its top 5 cm cut off as shown. The shape which is left is called a **frustum**. Calculate the volume of the frustum.

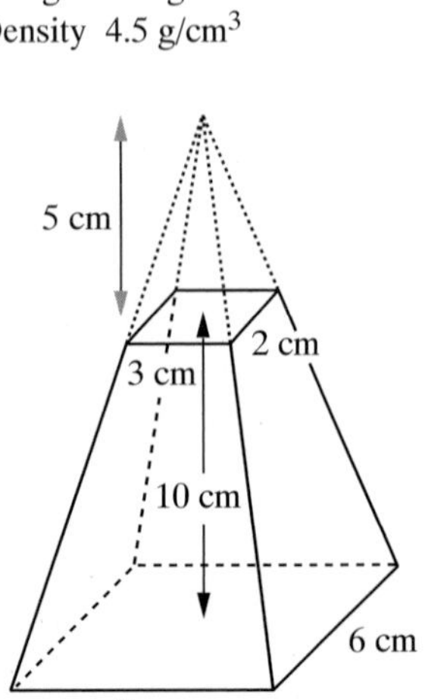

Volume and surface area of a cone

A cone can be treated as a pyramid with a circular base. Therefore, the formula for the volume of a cone is the same as that for a pyramid:

$$\text{Volume} = \tfrac{1}{3} \times \text{Base area} \times \text{Vertical height}$$

$$V = \tfrac{1}{3}\pi r^2 h$$

where r is the radius of the base and h is the vertical height of the cone.

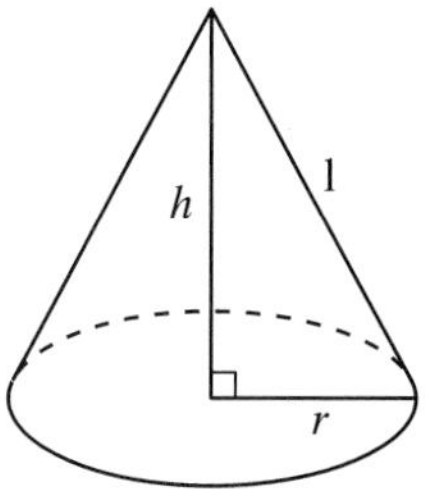

The curved surface area of a cone is given by

$$\text{Curved surface area} = \pi \times \text{Radius} \times \text{Slant height}$$

$$S = \pi r \ell$$

where ℓ is the slant height of the cone.

Note The base radius, the vertical height and the slant height of a cone form a right-angled triangle. So, from Pythagoras's theorem,

$$(\text{Slant height})^2 = (\text{Radius})^2 + (\text{Vertical height})^2$$

$$\ell^2 = r^2 + h^2$$

Example For the cone in the diagram, calculate **i** its volume and **ii** its total surface area.

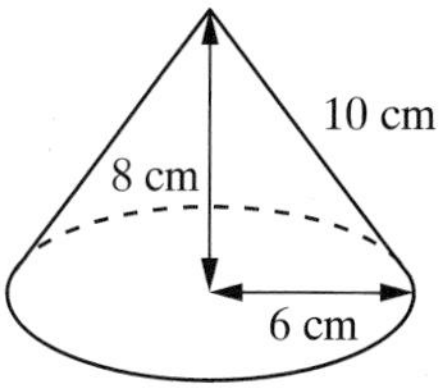

i The volume is given by

$$\tfrac{1}{3}\pi r^2 h = \tfrac{1}{3} \times \pi \times 36 \times 8 = 302 \text{ cm}^3 \quad (3 \text{ sf})$$

ii The total surface area is given by

$$\begin{aligned}\text{Curved surface area} + \text{Base area} &= \pi r \ell + \pi r^2 \\ &= \pi \times 6 \times 10 + \pi \times 36 \\ &= 188.495\,56 + 113.097\,34 \\ &= 302 \text{ cm}^2 \quad (3 \text{ sf})\end{aligned}$$

Exercise 2I

1 For each cone, calculate **i** its volume and **ii** its total surface area. (The units are cm.)

a

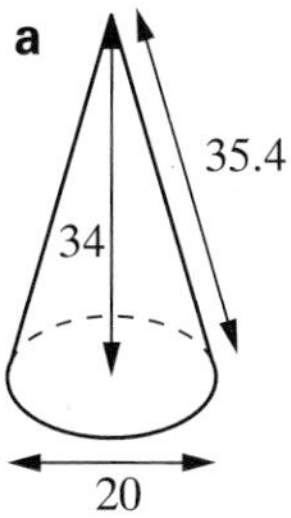

b

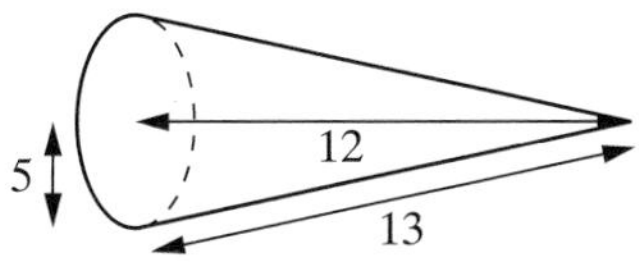

c

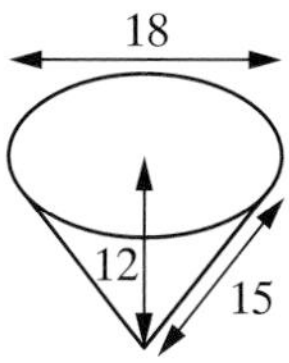

2 A solid cone, base radius 6 cm and vertical height 8 cm, is made of metal whose density is 3.1 g/cm^3. Find the weight of the cone.

3 Find the total surface area of a cone whose base radius is 3 cm and vertical height is 4 cm.

4 Find the total surface area of a cone whose base radius is 5 cm and vertical height is 12 cm.

5 In order to make a cone, a sector of angle 72° is cut from a circle whose radius is 6 cm.

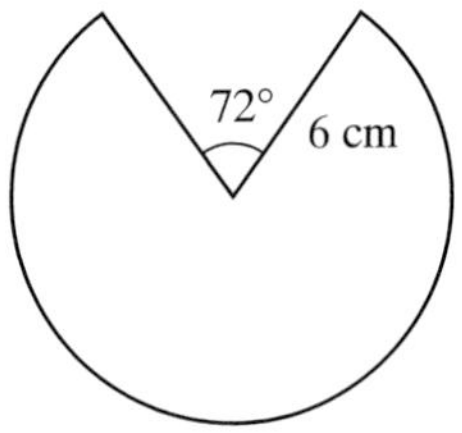

a Calculate the circumference of the base of the cone.
b Calculate the radius of the base of the cone.
c State the length of the slant height of the cone.
d Calculate the curved surface area of the cone.
e Calculate the vertical height of the cone.
f Calculate the volume of the cone.

6 Calculate the volume of each of these shapes.

a

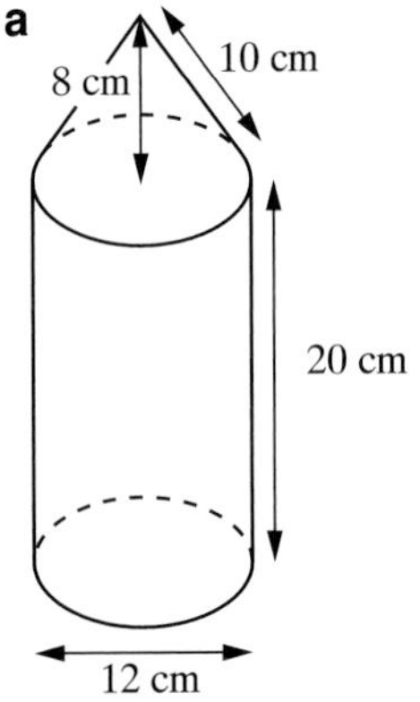

b

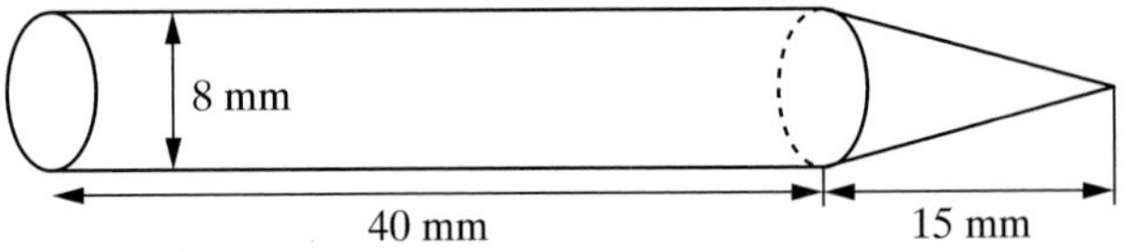

7 A container in the shape of a cone, base radius 10 cm and vertical height 19 cm, is full of water. The water is poured into an empty cylinder of radius 15 cm. How high is the water in the cylinder?

8 Calculate the volume of each of the cones which are to be made from the following cut-outs.

a

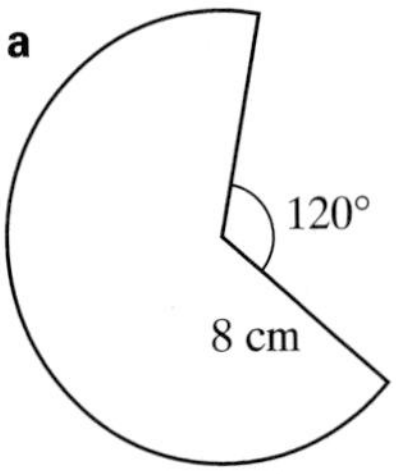

b

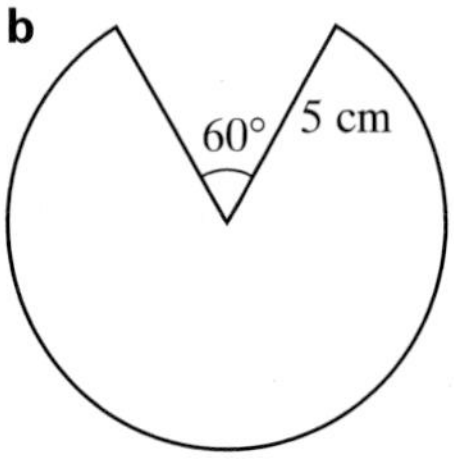

c

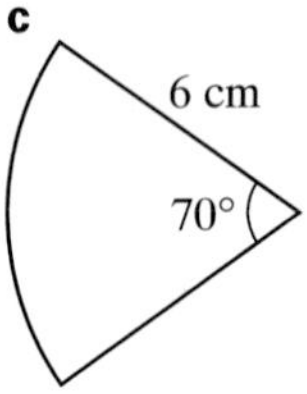

9 The model shown on the right is made from aluminium and is to be coated with gold.

a What is the weight of the model, given that the density of aluminium is 2.7 g/cm^3?

b The cost of coating with gold is £8 per cm^2. How much will it cost to have this model coated with gold?

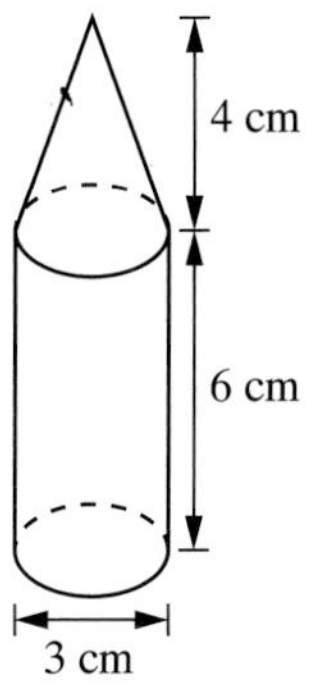

10 A solid cone, height 8 cm and base radius 4 cm, is placed in a cylindrical jar of radius 12 cm which contains just enough water to cover the cone completely. Find the rise in water level.

Volume and surface area of a sphere

The volume of a sphere, radius r, is given by

$$V = \tfrac{4}{3}\pi r^3$$

Its surface area is given by

$$A = 4\pi r^2$$

Example For a sphere of radius of 8 cm, calculate **i** its volume and **ii** its surface area.

i The volume of the sphere is given by

$$V = \tfrac{4}{3}\pi r^3$$
$$= \tfrac{4}{3} \times \pi \times 8^3 = 2150 \text{ cm}^3 \quad \text{(3 sf)}$$

ii The surface area of the sphere is given by

$$A = 4\pi r^2$$
$$= 4 \times \pi \times 8^2 = 804 \text{ cm}^2 \quad \text{(3 sf)}$$

Exercise 2J

1 Calculate the volume of each of these spheres.

i Radius 9.5 cm **ii** Radius 15 cm **iii** Diameter 25 cm

2 Calculate the surface area of each of these spheres.

i Radius 8.3 cm **ii** Radius 11.7 cm **iii** Diameter 35 cm

3 Calculate the volume and the surface area of a sphere with a diameter of 50 cm.

4 A sphere fits exactly into an open cubical box of side 25 cm. Calculate

i the surface area of the sphere

ii the volume of the sphere.

5 A metal sphere of radius 15 cm is melted down and recast into a solid cylinder of radius 6 cm. Calculate the height of the cylinder.

6 Lead has a density of 11.35 g/cm^3. Calculate the maximum number of shot (spherical lead pellets) of radius 1.5 mm which can be made from 1 kg of lead.

7 Calculate, correct to 1 decimal place, the radius of a sphere

a whose surface area is 150 cm^2

b whose volume is 150 cm^3.

8 The volume of a sphere is 25 m^3. Find its diameter.

9 What is the volume of a sphere whose surface area is 300 cm^2?

10 What is the surface area of a sphere whose volume is 200 cm^3?

11 Find the volume of rubber used in making a hollow ball which has an outer radius of 3 cm and is 2 mm thick.

12 In an experiment, a small spherical drop of oil was allowed to drop onto the surface of water so that it produced a thin film of oil covering a large area.

a The volume of one drop of oil was 11.5 mm^3. What was the radius of the drop?

b Calculate the number of drops of oil which could have been produced by 6 cm^3 of oil.

c A single drop of oil was found to produce a circular oil film whose area was 100 cm^2. Calculate the thickness of the film in millimetres.

Possible coursework tasks

Equable shapes

An 'equable shape' is defined as that shape for which the numerical value of its area is equal to the numerical value of its perimeter.

Investigate for different shapes.

Open box problem

A rectangular piece of card is made into an open box by cutting a square from each corner, as shown.

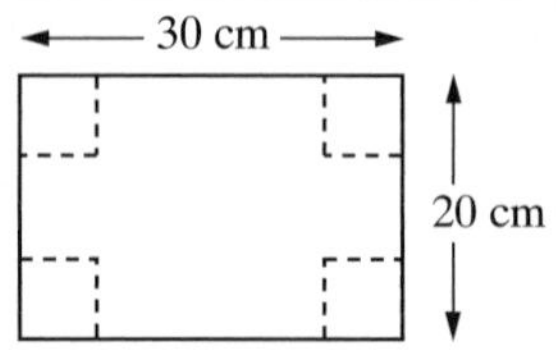

Investigate how to obtain a box which has the maximum volume. (You may find it easier to solve this problem using a spreadsheet.)

Canny problem

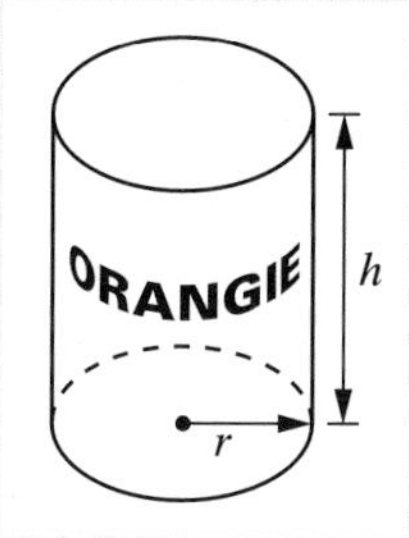

A manufacturer has to make a can to hold 1000 cm^3 of orange juice. Find the values of r and h which use the least amount of metal.

Magician's hat

A magician's hat is made from a circle of radius r by cutting out a sector, as shown in the diagram.

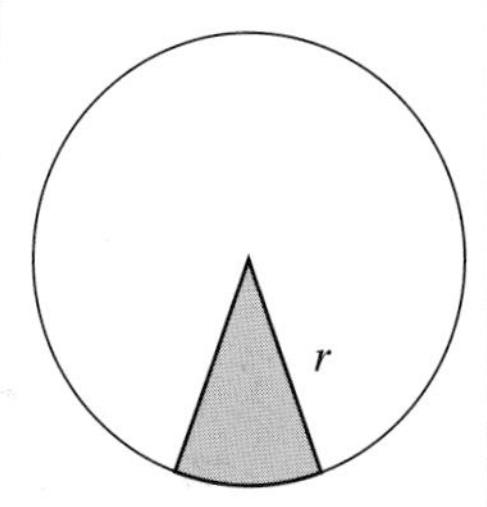

Find the greatest volume for the hat for different radii. (You may find it easier to solve this problem using a spreadsheet.)

Radian problem

Find the value of θ for which the arc length AB is the same length as the radius of the circle.

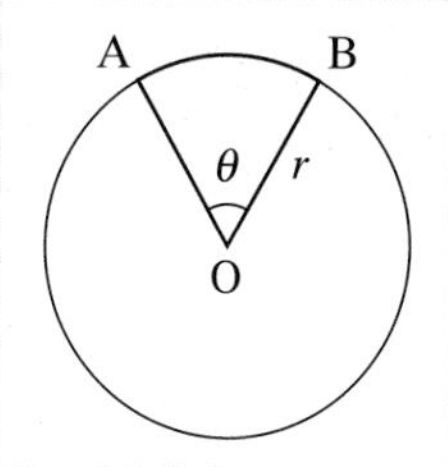

A problem with drink

Calculate the volume inside a wine bottle (or a similar container) by taking suitable measurements and shapes.

Compare your result with the amount stated on the bottle.

Equal areas and volumes

For each of a variety of 3-D shapes, find the measurements that give numerically the same value for the total surface area and the volume.

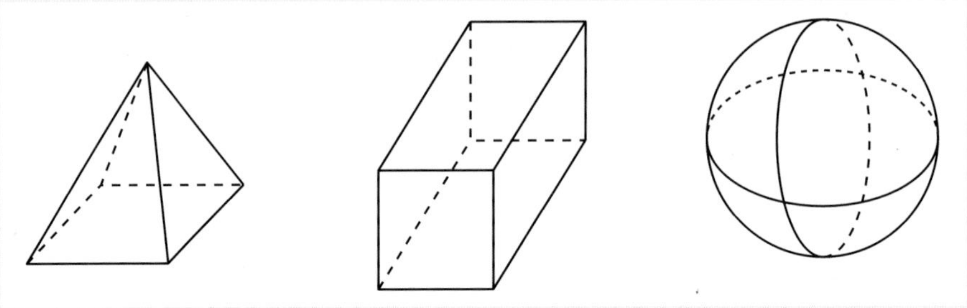

Examination questions: coursework type

1 The diagram shows a grid which has 6 dots along its length, 4 dots along its width. There are 8 dots inside the rectangle and 16 dots around its perimeter. Investigate the numbers of dots inside and on the perimeter of other rectangles which can be drawn on this grid.

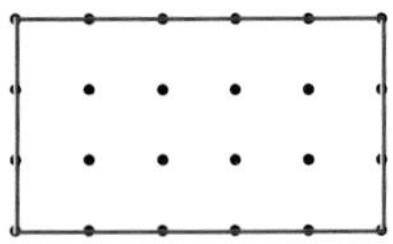

2 Suzie wants a new desk for her bedroom. She has seen one that she likes in a store. The kit costs £59.99.

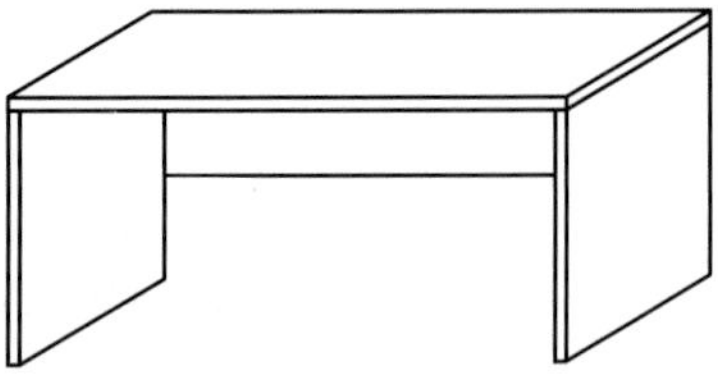

The desk top measures 120 cm × 60 cm and is 72 cm high. The back panel is 40 cm high.

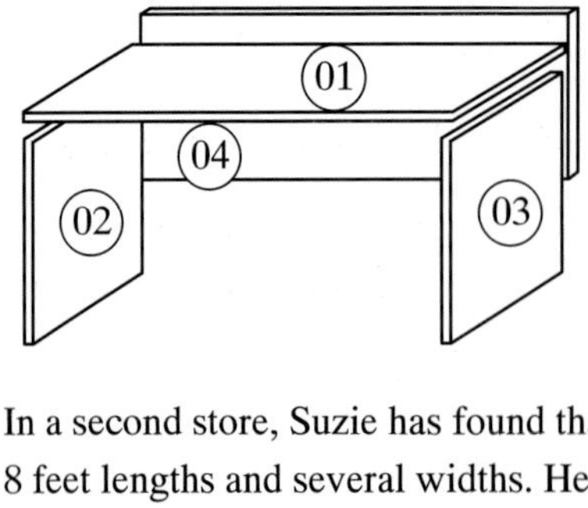

Parts list

01 Top
02 Left side
03 Right side
04 Back panel

In a second store, Suzie has found that a similar black-ash effect board is available in 8 feet lengths and several widths. Here are some prices.

Width in cm	30	40	50	60
Price	£8.29	£11.79	£15.49	£18.99

The store will cut boards to size free of charge. (Suzie also knows that 1 foot is just over 30 cm.)

Write your advice to Suzie.

- Should she buy the kit or make the desk herself?
- If she decides to make it herself, how should she ask for the boards to be cut?

NEAB, Question 1, Specimen Paper 3, 1998

3 Square panes of glass, 10 cm by 10 cm, are held together by thin strips of lead to form rectangular panels. Each panel also has a thin lead strip around its perimeter.

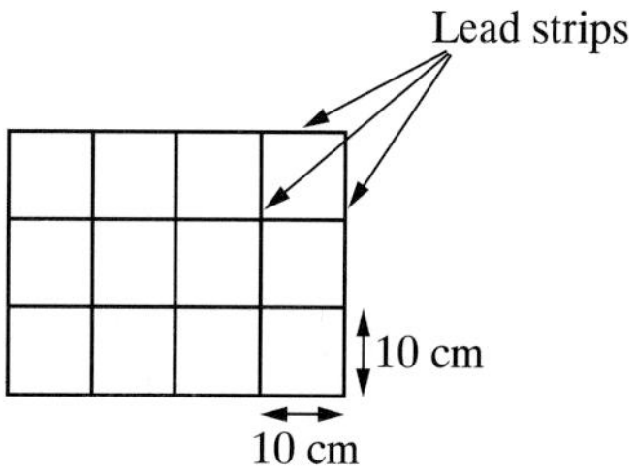

a Explain why arranging the panes of glass in a long thin rectangular panel uses more lead than arranging the same panes in other rectangular panels.

The rectangular panels made from the square panes of glass are also edged around the perimeter by a wooden strip.

Lead strip costs 28.3p per 10 cm
Wood strips costs 7.8p per 10 cm
10 cm by 10 cm panes of glass cost 12.5p each.

The rectangular panels have wooden and lead strips around the perimeter, with lead strips holding all the panes of glass together.

b Find the minimum cost of making a panel using 156 panes of glass. You must give your reasons for your choice of dimensions for the panel.

WJEC, Question 4, Paper A3, June 1995

4 Air passengers are allowed to take one item of hand luggage on the flight. Airlines have different rules about the size of the hand luggage.

Airline 1 Length + width + height of hand luggage must not be more than 150 cm.

Airline 2 The volume of hand luggage must not be more than 60 000 cm^3.

Investigate, for each airline, suitable designs of hand luggage which will satisfy the rule and be as large as possible, but made from the smallest amount of material.

SEG, Intermediate Coursework Task B, Specimen Paper, 1998

Examination questions

1 A factory produces plastic name tags by stamping discs from rectangular sheets of plastic. Each sheet of plastic is 40 cm long and 30 cm wide. The diameter of each disc is 5 cm. The diagram shows part of a sheet with discs cut from it.

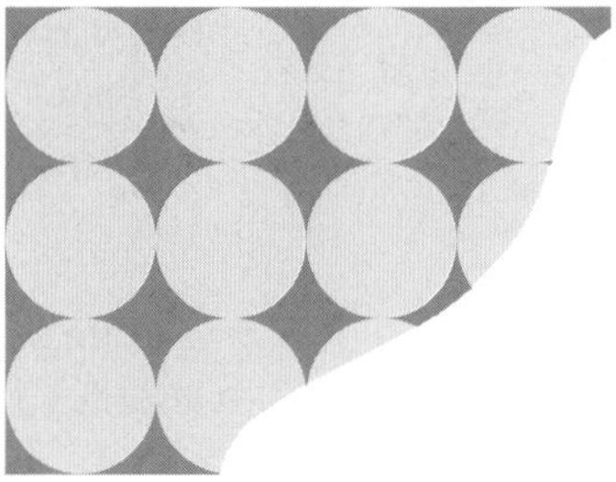

a How many discs can be cut from one sheet of plastic?

b What is the area of one sheet of plastic?

c What is the area of one disc?

d The plastic left after the discs are cut out is wasted. What percentage of each sheet of plastic is wasted? *WJEC, Question 7, Specimen Paper 2, 1998*

2 Louise does a sponsored bicycle ride. Each wheel of her bicycle is of radius 25 cm.

a Calculate the circumference of one of the wheels.

b She cycles 50 km. How many revolutions does a wheel make during the sponsored ride? *NEAB, Question 5, Paper 1, June 1995*

3 The diagram shows a running track. BA and DE are parallel and straight. They are each of length 90 metres. BCD and EFA are semicircular. They each have a diameter of length 70 metres.

a Calculate the perimeter of the track.

b Calculate the total area inside the track.

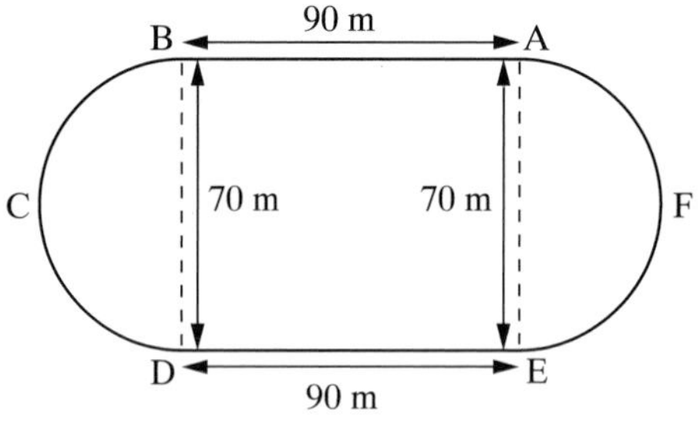

NEAB, Question 4, Paper 2, June 1995

4 A rubbish skip is a prism. The cross-section is an isosceles trapezium. This diagram shows the **inside** measurements of the cross-section.

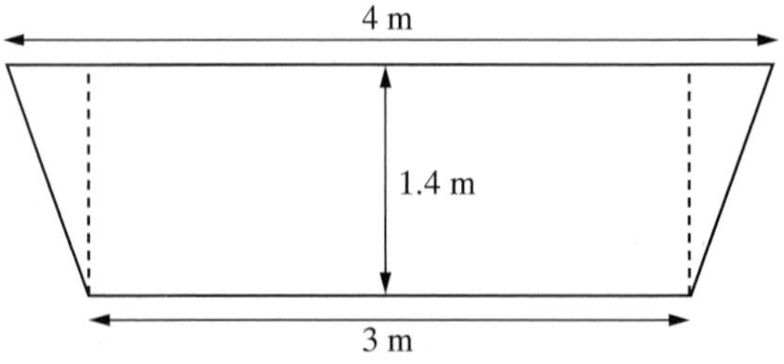

a The internal width of the skip is 2 m. It is filled with earth. The earth is level with the top of the skip. What is the volume of the earth in the skip?

b The density of the earth in the skip is 700 kg/m^3. What is the weight of the earth in the skip? *WJEC, Question 11ed, Specimen Paper 2, 1998*

5 A motorist fills the fuel tank of his car and a petrol can with petrol.

a The petrol can is cylindrical. It has a diameter of 16 cm and a height of 24 cm. Calculate, to the nearest litre, the amount of petrol in a full can.

b The motorist takes 20 seconds to fill the can. The motorist uses the same pump to fill the fuel tank in his car. It takes him 1 minute 48 seconds to fill the tank. How many litres of petrol did he put in the tank?

SEG, Question 7, Specimen Paper 10, 1998

6 A cylindrical tin of soup is 8.4 cm tall and has a base diameter of 7.0 cm.

a Calculate the area of the base of the tin.

b Calculate the capacity of the tin.

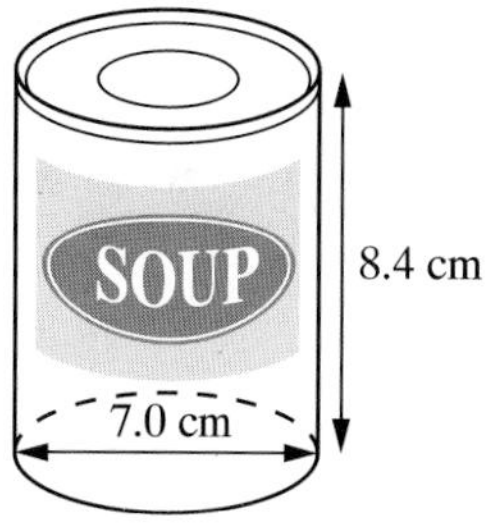

NEAB, Question 16, Specimen Paper 2, 1998

7 In Jane's classroom there is a bin. The bin is a cylinder with an open top. Jane uses the formula $A = \pi r(r + 2h)$ to calculate the surface area of the bin. The bin has a radius of 0.48 m and a height of 0.76 m. By using suitable approximations, show that the surface area of the bin is roughly 3 square metres.

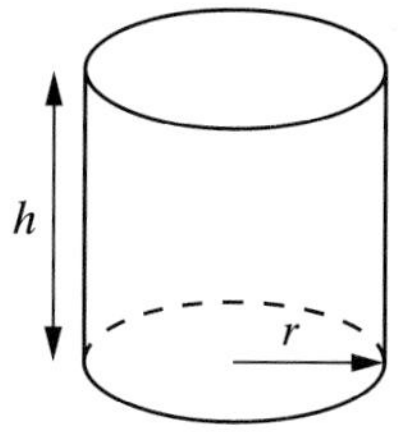

SEG, Question 11b, Specimen Paper 10, 1998

8 The diagram represents a tea packet in the shape of a cuboid.

a Calculate the volume of the packet.

There are 125 grams of tea in a full packet. Jason has to design a new packet that will contain 100 grams of tea when it is full.

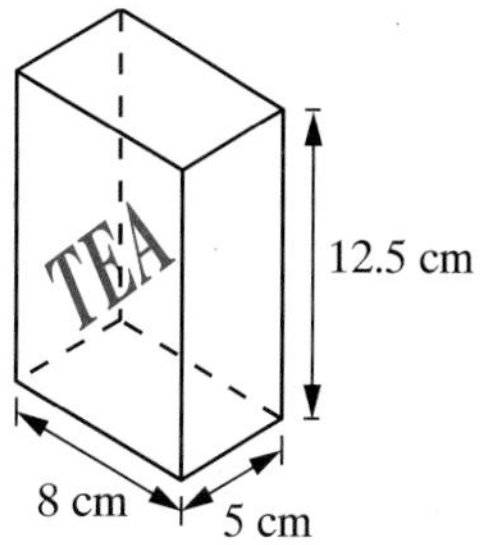

b **i** Work out the volume of the new packet.

ii Express the weight of the new packet as a percentage of the weight of the packet shown.

The new packet of tea is in the shape of a cuboid. The base of the new packet measures 7 cm by 6 cm.

c **i** Work out the area of the base of the new packet.

ii Calculate the height of the new packet.

ULEAC, Question 9, Paper 4, June 1994

9 Tomato soup is sold in cylindrical tins. Each tin has a base radius of 3.5 cm and a height of 12 cm.

a Calculate the volume of soup in a full tin.

b Mark has a full tin of tomato soup for dinner. He pours the soup into a cylindrical bowl of radius 7 cm. What is the depth of the soup in the bowl?

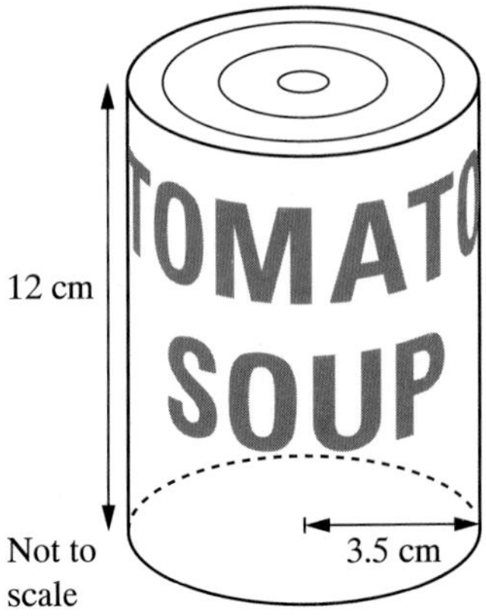

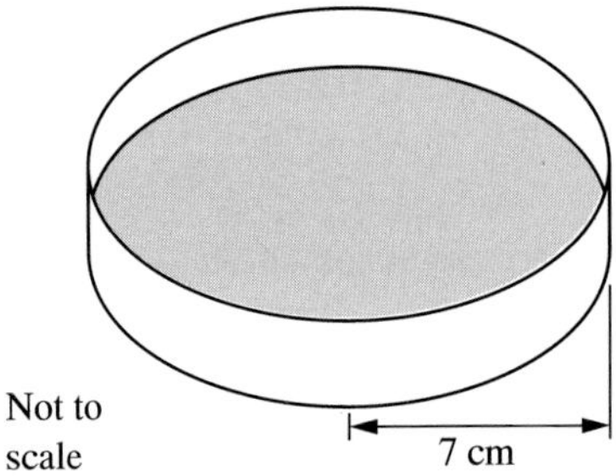

10 The diagram shows a paint trough in the shape of a prism. Each shaded end of the trough is a vertical trapezium. Calculate the volume of paint which the trough can hold when it is full

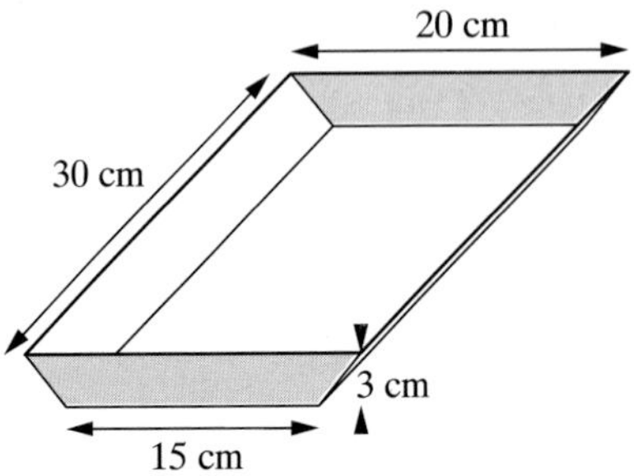

SEG, Question 14, Paper 5, June 1995

11 There is an infra-red sensor in a security system. The sensor can detect movement inside a sector of a circle. The radius of the circle is 15 m. The sector angle is 110°. Calculate the area of the sector.

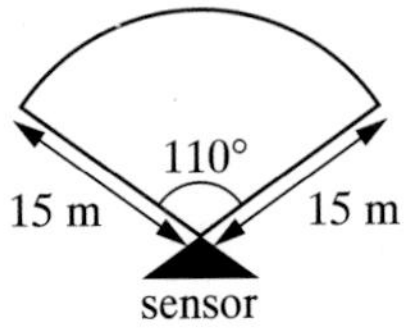

ULEAC, Question 11, Paper 5, November 1994

12 A spinning top, which consists of a cone of base radius 5 cm, height 9 cm and a hemisphere of radius 5 cm, is illustrated on the right.

a Calculate the volume of the spinning top.

b Calculate the total surface area of the spinning top.

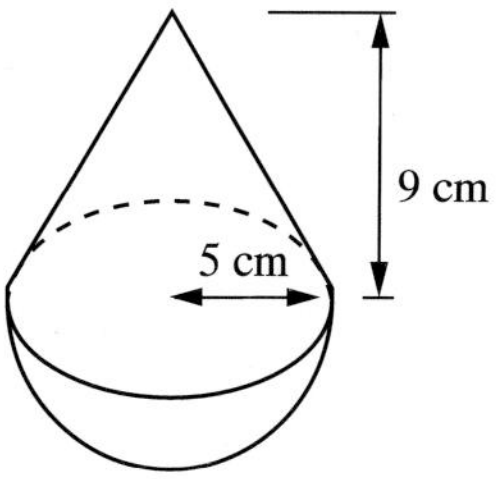

SEG, Question 11, Specimen Paper 15, 1998

13 a A symmetrically shaped timer is made from hollow hemispheres, cylinders and cones joined together as shown in the first diagram. It contains sand just sufficient to fill the top cone and cylinder sections. Calculate the volume of sand.

b When all the sand has run through, it collects as shown in the second diagram. Calculate the height, *h* cm, of sand in the cylindrical part of the timer.

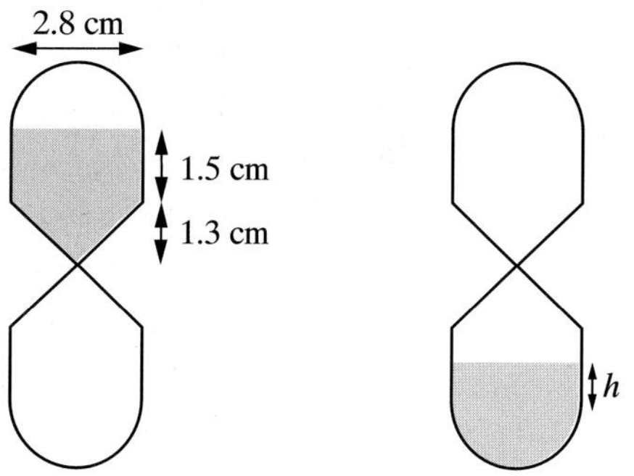

MEG, Question 18, Specimen Paper 5, 1998

14 A 'Corno' consists of ice cream in a biscuit cone. The diameter of the top of the cone is 6 cm and its vertical height is 12 cm. The shaded part of the diagram shows the ice cream in the cone. The ice cream goes down to a depth of 4 cm in the cone and forms a hemisphere on the top of the cone. Calculate the volume of ice cream in a 'Corno'.

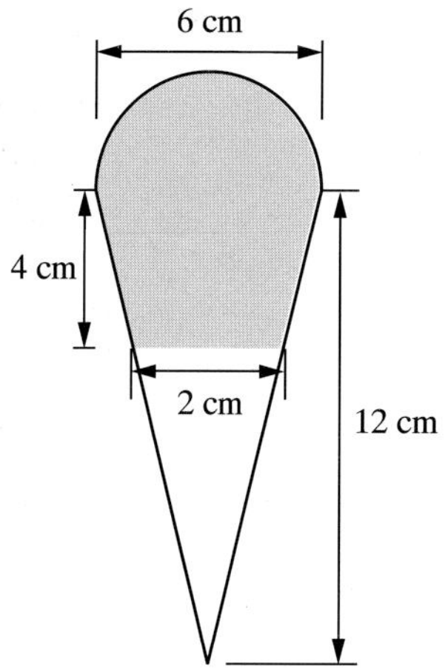

NEAB, Question 20, Specimen Paper 2, 1998

15 The sinker shown right is made up of a cone attached to a hemisphere. The overall height of the sinker is 9.9 cm. The diameter of the hemisphere is 5.2 cm. Calculate to the nearest unit

a the volume of the sinker

b the surface area of the sinker.

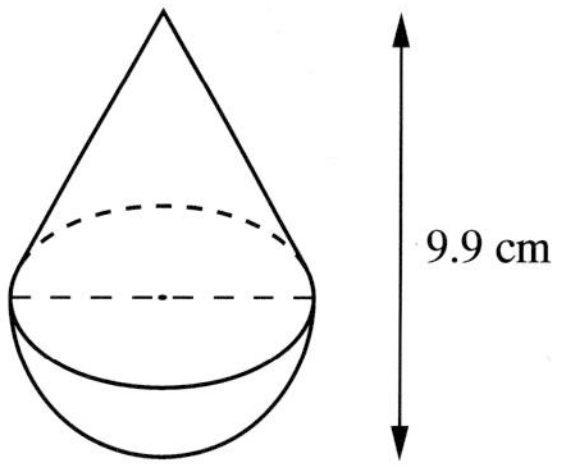

NICCEA, Question 1, Paper 4A, June 1995

Summary

How well do you grade yourself?

To gain a grade **C**, you need to be able to calculate the circumference and the area of a circle, and the area of a trapezium. You need also to be able to find the volumes of 3-D shapes such as cylinders and other regular prisms.

To gain a grade **B**, you need to be able to use the relationship between volume, density and weight to find any one from the other two.

To gain a grade **A**, you need to be able to calculate volumes and surface areas of 3-D shapes such as cylinders, pyramids, cones and spheres.

What you should know after you have worked through Chapter 2

- For a sector of radius r and angle θ

  $$\text{Arc length} = \frac{\theta°}{360°} \times 2 \times \pi \times r$$

  $$\text{Sector area} = \frac{\theta°}{360°} \times \pi \times r^2$$

- The area of a trapezium is given by

  $$A = h\left(\frac{a+b}{2}\right)$$

  where h is the vertical height, and a and b are the lengths of the two parallel sides.

- The volume of a prism is given by V = Regular cross-sectional area × Length.
- The volume of a cylinder is given by $V = \pi r^2 h$, where r is the radius and h is the height or length of the cylinder.
- The curved surface area of a cylinder is given by $S = \pi D h$, where D is the diameter and h is the height or length of the cylinder.
- The volume of a pyramid is given by $V = \frac{1}{3} \times$ Base area × Vertical height.
- The volume of a cone is given by $V = \frac{1}{3}\pi r^2 h$, where r is the base radius and h is the vertical height of the cone.
- The curved surface area of a cone is given by $S = \pi r \ell$, where r is the base radius and ℓ is the slant height of the cone.
- The volume of a sphere is given by $V = \frac{4}{3}\pi r^3$, where r is its radius.
- The surface area of a sphere is given by $A = 4\pi r^2$, where r is its radius.

3 Algebra 1

This chapter is going to ... remind you about the basic language of algebra and the algebraic processes that you will meet throughout this book. It leads you through simple linear equations to equations which are not so simple, including those that need to be solved by the method of trial and improvement. It also shows you ways of solving simultaneous equations.

What you should already know

- The basic language of algebra. For example,

$4 + x$	means add 4 to the number x
$x - 2$	means take 2 away from the number x
$a + b$	means add the number a to the number b
$7x$	means 7 multiplied by the number x
$\frac{x}{5}$	means the number x divided by 5
r^2	means the number r multiplied by itself

- Like terms only can be added or subtracted to simplify an expression. For example,

  $2x + 3x$ can be added to give $5x$
  but $2x + 3y$ cannot give anything simpler

- Expressions can be simplified by collecting like terms together. For example,

  $2x + 3y + 3x - y = 5x + 2y$

  (dealing with the x's first, then the y's).

- A number next to a bracket indicates a multiplication, and everything in the bracket can be multiplied by that number. For example,

$$3(2t - 5) = 3 \times 2t - 3 \times 5$$
$$= 6t - 15$$

Exercises 3A to 3G give you the opportunity to practise these basic skills.

Exercise 3A

1 Multiply out the following brackets, leaving the answer as simple as possible.

a $2(f + 3)$ **b** $3(k - 4)$ **c** $4(t + 1)$ **d** $3(2d + 3)$

e $4(3t - 2)$ **f** $2(5m + 3)$ **g** $4(5 + 2w)$ **h** $2(3 - 4x)$

i $3(4+ 5p)$ **j** $5(2t + 3w)$ **k** $4(3m - 2d)$ **l** $3(2x + 5y)$

m $2(4f + 3)$ **n** $5(8 - 2t)$ **o** $3(4g + 2t)$

2 Expand and simplify each of the following.

a $2(3x + y) + 3(x + 4y)$ **b** $5(2t + 3p) + 2(3t + 4p)$ **c** $4(x + 5y) + 3(2x + y)$

d $3(2p + t) + 5(3p + 2t)$ **e** $4(3x + 2y) + 2(x - 3y)$ **f** $5(2x - 3t) + 3(4x - 2t)$

g $3(2p + 4m) + 2(4p - m)$ **h** $2(5t - 4q) + 5(t - 3q)$ **i** $3(2x + 4y) - 2(x + 5y)$

j $4(3t - 2n) - 2(4t + n)$ **k** $2(3p + 2t) - 3(p - 4t)$ **l** $5(2x - 3y) - 2(3x - 2y)$

3 Give the total cost of

a 5 pens at 15p each **b** x pens at 15p each

c 4 pens at Ap each **d** y pens at Ap each

4 A boy went shopping with £A. He spent £B. How much has he got left?

5 Five ties cost £A. What is the cost of one tie?

6 My dad is 72 and I am T years old. How old will we both be in x years time?

7 I am twice as old as my son. I am T years old.

a How old is my son?

b How old will my son be in 4 years time?

c How old was I x years ago?

8 Joseph is given £t, John has £3 more than Joseph, Joy has £$2t$.

a How much more has Joy than Joseph?

b How much have they got altogether?

9 What is the total perimeter of these figures?

a A square of side $2x$. **b** An equilateral triangle of side $4m$.

c A regular hexagon of side $3t$.

10 A triathlon consists of swimming, cycling and running.

a The British championship consists of a 1.5 km swim, a 40 km cycle ride and a 10 km run. What is the total distance?

b A local club does a training session which consists of a 0.4 km swim, a 10 km cycle ride and a 5 km run. What is the total distance?

c Another club does a training session which consists of a 1 km swim, a 10 km cycle ride and an x km run. What is the total distance?

d How far in total is a triathlon that consists of an s km swim, a b km cycle ride and a r km run?

e The 'Ironman' triathlon is 140 miles in total distance. The swim is 2 miles and the run is a marathon of 26 miles. How long is the cycle ride?

f If a triathlon is T km long and the cycle ride is 20 km, what is the total distance of the run and the swim?

11 a At a concert 250 people paid £8 each for a seat in the gallery and 600 paid £5 each for a seat in the stalls. What was the total price paid to see the concert?

b At the same concert on another night, M people paid £8 each for a seat in the gallery and N people paid £5 each for a seat in the stalls. What was the total price paid to see this concert?

c At another concert, M people pay £G each for a seat in the gallery and N people pay £T each for a seat in the stalls. What is the total price paid to see this concert?

Exercise 3B

1 Find the value of $3x + 2$ when **i** $x = 2$ **ii** $x = 5$ **iii** $x = 10$

2 Find the value of $4k - 1$ when **i** $k = 1$ **ii** $k = 3$ **iii** $k = 11$

3 Find the value of $5 + 2t$ when **i** $t = 2$ **ii** $t = 5$ **iii** $t = 12$

4 Evaluate $15 - 2f$ when **i** $f = 3$ **ii** $f = 5$ **iii** $f = 8$

5 Evaluate $5m + 3$ when **i** $m = 2$ **ii** $m = 6$ **iii** $m = 15$

6 Evaluate $3d - 2$ when **i** $d = 4$ **ii** $d = 5$ **iii** $d = 20$

7 Find the value of $\frac{8 + 4h}{5}$ when **i** $h = 3$ **ii** $h = 7$ **iii** $h = 31$

8 Find the value of $\frac{25 - 3p}{2}$ when **i** $p = 4$ **ii** $p = 8$ **iii** $p = 10$

9 Find the value of $2x + 3$ when **i** $x = -1$ **ii** $x = -3$ **iii** $x = 1.5$

10 Evaluate $3w - 4$ when **i** $w = -1$ **ii** $w = -2$ **iii** $w = 3.5$

11 Evaluate $8 + 4g$ when **i** $g = -2$ **ii** $g = -5$ **iii** $g = 2.5$

12 Evaluate $10 - x$ when **i** $x = -2$ **ii** $x = -4$ **iii** $x = 5.6$

13 Find the value of $4b + 3$ when **i** $b = 2.5$ **ii** $b = -1.5$ **iii** $b = \frac{1}{2}$

14 Find the value of $6t - 5$ when **i** $t = 3.4$ **ii** $t = -2.5$ **iii** $t = \frac{3}{4}$

15 Find the value of $1 + 5y$ when **i** $y = 2.5$ **ii** $y = -3.4$ **iii** $y = \frac{1}{3}$

16 Evaluate $8 - 2t$ when **i** $t = 1.5$ **ii** $t = -2.3$ **iii** $t = \frac{3}{4}$

17 Evaluate $\frac{x}{3}$ when **i** $x = 6$ **ii** $x = 24$ **iii** $x = -30$

18 Evaluate $\frac{A}{4}$ when **i** $A = 12$ **ii** $A = 10$ **iii** $A = -20$

19 Find he value of $\frac{12}{y}$ when **i** $y = 2$ **ii** $y = 4$ **iii** $y = -6$

20 Find the value of $\frac{24}{x}$ when **i** $x = -5$ **ii** $x = \frac{1}{2}$ **iii** $x = \frac{3}{4}$

Exercise 3C

1 Where $A = \dfrac{4t + h}{t + h}$, find A when

a $t = 2$ and $h = 3$ **b** $t = 3$ and $h = 5$ **c** $t = 1$ and $h = 9$

2 Where $P = \dfrac{5w - 4y}{w + y}$, find P when

a $w = 3$ and $y = 2$ **b** $w = 6$ and $y = 4$ **c** $w = 2$ and $y = 3$

3 Where $T = \dfrac{2x + 3}{2 + x}$, find T when

a $x = 3$ **b** $x = -3$ **c** $x = 2.5$

4 Where $Y = x^2$, find Y when

a $x = 3$ **b** $x = -5$ **c** $x = 1.2$

5 Where $Z = \dfrac{y^2 + 3}{4 + y}$, find Z when

a $y = 4$ **b** $y = -6$ **c** $y = 8.5$

6 Where $A = b^2 + c^2$, find A when

a $b = 2$ and $c = 3$ **b** $b = 5$ and $c = 7$ **c** $b = -1$ and $c = -4$

7 Where $L = f^2 - g^2$, find L when

a $f = 6$ and $g = 3$ **b** $f = -3$ and $g = -2$ **c** $f = 5$ and $g = -5$

8 Where $C = \dfrac{N^2 + N}{N + 1}$, find C when

a $N = 4$ **b** $N = -3$ **c** $N = 1.5$

9 Where $T = P - n^2$, find T when

a $P = 100$ and $n = 5$ **b** $P = 17$ and $n = 3$ **c** $P = 10$ and $n = 4$

10 Where $A = \dfrac{180\,(n - 2)}{n + 5}$, find A when

a $n = 7$ **b** $n = 3$ **c** $n = 1$

In questions **11** to **15**, give your answers correct to a suitable degree of accuracy.

11 Where $A = \pi r^2$, find A when

a $r = 1.7$ **b** $r = 4.5$ **c** $r = 7.8$

12 Where $t = 10 - \sqrt{P}$, find t when

a $P = 10$ **b** $P = 25$ **c** $P = 8$

13 Where $W = \dfrac{v + 5}{m + 2}$, find W when

a $v = 3$ and $m = 7$ **b** $v = 2$ and $m = 3$ **c** $v = -3$ and $m = 8$

14 Where $K = \sqrt{(a + 3b)}$, find K when

a $a = 5$ and $b = 2$ **b** $a = 8$ and $b = -1$ **c** $a = 9$ and $b = 2.5$

15 Where $h = \sqrt{(a^2 + b^2)}$, find h when

a $a = 4$ and $b = 6$ **b** $a = 4.5$ and $b = 7.5$ **c** $a = -3$ and $b = -7$

Exercise 3D

Solve the following equations.

1 $3x + 5 = 11$ **2** $3x - 13 = 26$ **3** $3x - 7 = 32$ **4** $4y - 19 = 5$

5 $3a + 8 = 11$ **6** $2x + 8 = 14$ **7** $6 + y = 18$ **8** $8x + 4 = 12$

9 $2x - 10 = 8$ **10** $x + 4 = 60$ **11** $3y - 2 = 4$ **12** $3x - 4 = 11$

13 $5y + 3 = 18$ **14** $7 + 3t = 19$ **15** $5 + 4f = 15$ **16** $3 + 6k = 24$

17 $4x + 7 = 17$ **18** $5m - 3 = 17$ **19** $3t + 17 = 29$ **20** $6d + 3 = 30$

21 $5x + 2.5 = 10$ **22** $3y - 1.5 = 9$ **23** $5p + 4 = 10$ **24** $5t - 4 = 5$

Exercise 3E

Solve the following equations.

1 $\frac{x}{5} = 3$ **2** $\frac{t}{3} = 2$ **3** $\frac{y}{4} = 7$ **4** $\frac{k}{2} = 8$

5 $\frac{h}{8} = 5$ **6** $\frac{w}{6} = 4$ **7** $\frac{x}{4} + 5 = 7$ **8** $\frac{y}{2} - 3 = 5$

9 $\frac{f}{5} + 2 = 8$ **10** $\frac{w}{3} - 5 = 2$ **11** $\frac{x}{8} + 3 = 12$ **12** $\frac{m}{7} - 3 = 5$

13 $\frac{2x}{5} + 3 = 7$ **14** $\frac{4y}{3} - 2 = 6$ **15** $\frac{5t}{4} + 3 = 18$ **16** $\frac{3y}{2} - 1 = 8$

17 $\frac{2x}{3} + 5 = 12$ **18** $\frac{4x}{5} - 3 = 7$ **19** $\frac{5x}{2} + 3 = 2$ **20** $\frac{5x}{7} + 4 = 3$

Exercise 3F

Solve the following equations.

1 $2x + 8 = 6$ **2** $2t + 7 = 1$ **3** $10 + 3x = 4$ **4** $15 + 4y = 3$

5 $8 - 2x = 10$ **6** $9 - 4t = 17$ **7** $6 - 5x = 21$ **8** $\frac{x}{3} + 7 = 5$

9 $\frac{t}{5} + 3 = 1$ **10** $\frac{x+3}{2} = 5$ **11** $\frac{t-5}{4} = 3$ **12** $\frac{x+10}{2} = 3$

13 $\frac{2x+1}{3} = 5$ **14** $\frac{5y-2}{4} = 3$ **15** $\frac{4t+3}{2} = 5$ **16** $\frac{3x-1}{10} = 2$

17 $\frac{5x-2}{7} = 4$ **18** $\frac{6y+3}{9} = 1$ **19** $\frac{2x-3}{5} = 4$ **20** $\frac{5t+3}{4} = 1$

Exercise 3G

Solve the following equations.

1 $2(x + 5) = 16$ **2** $5(x - 3) = 20$ **3** $3(t + 1) = 18$ **4** $4(2x + 5) = 44$

5 $2(3y - 5) = 14$ **6** $5(4x + 3) = 135$ **7** $4(3t - 2) = 88$ **8** $6(2t + 5) = 42$

9 $2(3x + 1) = 11$ **10** $4(5y - 2) = 42$ **11** $6(3k + 5) = 39$ **12** $5(2x + 3) = 27$

13 $5(3y - 2) = 26$ **14** $2(7t - 3) = 57$ **15** $4(5x - 4) = 54$ **16** $9(3x - 5) = 9$

17 $2(x + 5) = 6$ **18** $5(x - 4) = -25$ **19** $3(t + 7) = 15$ **20** $2(3x + 11) = 10$

21 $4(5t + 8) = 12$ **22** $5(2x - 1) = -45$ **23** $7(3y + 5) = -7$ **24** $2(3x + 8) = 7$

Trial and improvement

Certain equations cannot be solved exactly. However, a close enough solution to such an equation can be found by the trial-and-improvement method. (Sometimes wrongly called the trial-and-error method.)

The idea is to keep trying different values in the equation which will take it closer and closer to its 'true' solution. This step-by-step process is continued until a value is found which gives a solution that is close enough to the accuracy required.

The trial-and-improvement method is the way in which computers are programmed to solve equations.

Example Solve the equation $x^2 + x = 100$, giving the solution to 2 decimal places.

Step 1 We must find the two consecutive whole numbers between which x lies. We do this by intelligent guessing.

Try $x = 10$: $100 + 10 = 110$ Too high – next trial needs to be much smaller.

Try $x = 9$: $81 + 9 = 90$ Much too low.

So we now know that the solution lies between $x = 9$ and $x = 10$.

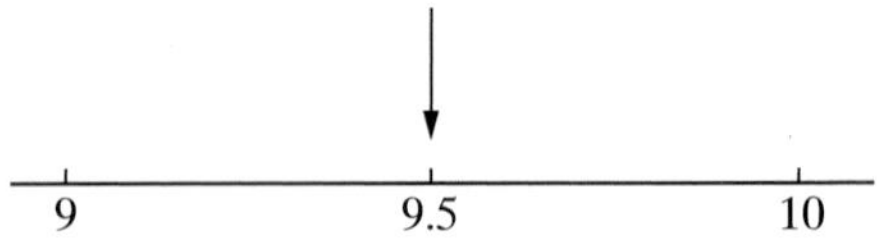

Step 2 We now must try 9.5, which is halfway between 9 and 10.

Try 9.5: $90.25 + 9.5 = 99.75$ Too small but very close.

So we attempt to improve this by trying 9.6.

Try 9.6: $92.16 + 9.6 = 101.76$ Much too high.

We now know the solution lies between 9.5 and 9.6.

Step 3 We now have to try 9.55, which is halfway between 9.5 and 9.6.

Try 9.55: $91.2025 + 9.55 = 100.7525$ Too high.

So we next try between 9.50 and 9.55 (close to halfway).

Try 9.53: $90.8209 + 9.53 = 100.3509$ Too high.

Try 9.52: $90.6304 + 9.52 = 100.1504$ Too high.

Try 9.51: $90.4401 + 9.51 = 99.9501$ Too low.

We now know the solution lies between 9.51 and 9.52, but which is closer?

Step 4 We cannot find which of these numbers is closer by just looking at them, because the differences between the values of the equation do not go up equally. So again we try the halfway value, which is 9.515.

Try 9.515: $90.535\,225 + 9.515 = 100.050\,23$ Too high.

So 9.51 is nearest to the true solution (to 2 decimal places).

If the question had asked for the solution to be given to 1 decimal place, we should have stopped at 9.55 because this value immediately shows us that 9.5 is the nearest solution to 1 decimal place.

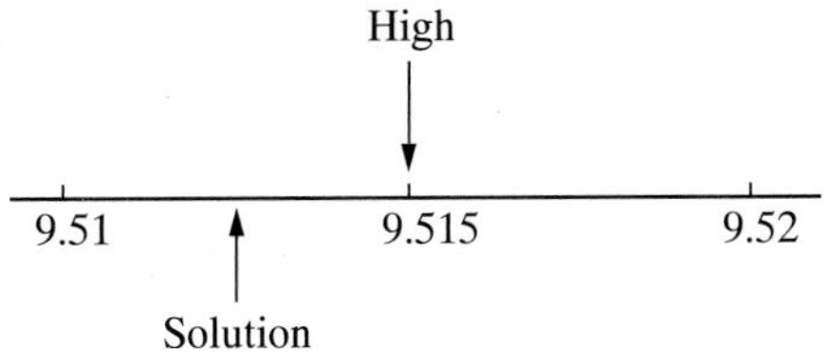

Exercise 3H

1 Find two consecutive **whole numbers** between which a solution to each of the following equations lies.

a $x^2 + x = 24$ **b** $x^2 + x = 61$ **c** $x^2 + x = 575$

2 Find a solution to each of the following equations to 1 decimal place.

a $x^2 + x = 33$ **b** $x^2 + x = 52$ **c** $x^2 + x = 79$

3 Find a solution to each of the following equations to 1 decimal place.

a $x^3 = 20$ **b** $x^3 - x = 28$ **c** $x^3 + x = 7$

4 Find a solution to each of the following equations to 1 decimal place.

a $x(x + 5) = 110$ **b** $x(x + 10) = 61$ **c** $x(x + 8) = 109$

Exercise 3I

1 A rectangle has an area of 100 cm². Its length is 5 cm longer than its width. Find, correct to 1 decimal place, the dimensions of the rectangle.

2 A gardener wants his rectangular lawn to be 10 m longer than the width, and the area of the lawn to be 550 m². What are the dimensions he should make his lawn? (Give your solution to 1 decimal place.)

3 A triangle has a vertical height 1 cm longer than its base length. Its area is 19 cm². What are the dimensions of the triangle? (Give your solution to 2 decimal places.)

4 A rectangular picture has a height 1 cm shorter than its length. Its area is 96 cm^2. What are the dimensions of the picture? (Give your solution to 1 decimal place.)

5 What are the dimensions, to 1 decimal place, of a cube that has a volume of 475 cm^3?

6 A square piece of card, whose area is 100 cm^2, has a square cut out from its middle so that the two pieces of card have the same area. What is the size of the cut-out square? (Give your answer to 1 decimal place.)

7 A square piece of card, whose area is 100 cm^2, is to have a square cut out at each corner, as in the diagram. What size must each cut-out square be if the area left is to be 50 cm^2? (Give your answers to 1 decimal place.)

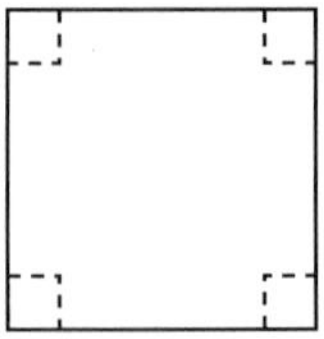

8 What is the length of a cube with volume 5.8 cm^3? (Give your answer to 2 decimal places.)

9 Find, correct to 1 decimal place, a solution to each of these equations.

a $x - \frac{1}{x} = 5$ **b** $x^2 - \frac{1}{x} = 10$ **c** $x^3 - \frac{1}{x} = 2$

10 Find, correct to 1 decimal place, the solution to $x^4 = 46$.

Simultaneous equations

A pair of simultaneous equations is exactly that – two equations (usually linear) for which we want the **same** solution, and which we therefore **solve together**. For example,

$x + y = 10$ has many solutions:

$x = 2, y = 8 \quad x = 4, y = 6 \quad x = 5, y = 5 \quad \ldots$

and $2x + y = 14$ has many solutions:

$x = 2, y = 10 \quad x = 3, y = 8 \quad x = 4, y = 6 \quad \ldots$

But only **one** solution, $x = 4$ and $y = 6$, satisfies both equations at the **same time**.

Elimination method

In this book, we solve simultaneous equations by the **elimination method** only. Follow through Examples 1 and 2 to see how this works.

Example 1 Solve $6x + y = 15$
$4x + y = 11$

Since the y-term in both equations is the same, we can subtract one equation from the other to give

$$2x = 4$$
$$\Rightarrow x = 2$$

We now substitute $x = 2$ into one of the original equations (usually the one with smallest numbers involved).

So substitute into $4x + y = 11$
which gives $8 + y = 11$
$\Rightarrow \quad y = 11 - 8$
$y = 3$

We should test our solution in the other original equation. So substitute $x = 2$ and $y = 3$ into $6x + y$, which gives $12 + 3 = 15$. This is correct, so we can confidently say the solution is $x = 2$ and $y = 3$.

Example 2 Solve $5x + y = 22$
$2x - y = 6$

Since both equations have the same y-term but **different** signs, we **add** the two equations, which gives

$7x = 28$
$\Rightarrow \quad x = 4$

We now substitute $x = 4$ into one of the original equations.

So substitute into $5x + y = 22$
which gives $20 + y = 22$
$\Rightarrow \quad y = 2$

We test our solution by putting $x = 4$ and $y = 2$ into the other equation $2x - y$, which gives $8 - 2 = 6$. This is correct, so our solution is $x = 4$ and $y = 2$.

Exercise 3J

Solve the following simultaneous equations by

- subtracting the equations when the identical terms have the same sign
- adding the equations when the identical terms have opposite signs.

1 $4x + y = 17$
$2x + y = 9$

2 $5x + 2y = 13$
$x + 2y = 9$

3 $2x + y = 7$
$5x - y = 14$

4 $3x + 2y = 19$
$2x - 2y = 6$

5 $3x - 4y = 17$
$x - 4y = 3$

6 $3x + 2y = 16$
$x - 2y = 4$

7 $x + 3y = 10$
$x + y = 6$

8 $2x + 5y = 24$
$2x + 3y = 16$

9 $3x - y = 4$
$2x + y = 11$

10 $2x + 5y = 37$
$2x + y = 11$

11 $4x - 3y = 7$
$x + 3y = 13$

12 $4x - y = 17$
$x - y = 2$

You were able to work out all the pairs of equations in Exercise 3J simply by adding or subtracting the equations in each pair. This does not always happen. So follow through the next worked example to see what to do when there are no identical terms to begin with.

Example 3 Solve $3x + 2y = 18$
$2x - y = 5$

Here we do not have any identical terms, so we have to make them because that is the only way we can solve such simultaneous equations by the elimination method. So multiply the second equation right through by 2 to match the y-terms:

$$(2x - y = 5) \times 2 \quad \Rightarrow \quad 4x - 2y = 10$$

Our pair of simultaneous equations is now

$$3x + 2y = 18$$
$$4x - 2y = 10$$

which can be solved by the method in Example 1.

Exercise 3K

Solve the following pairs of simultaneous equations by first changing one of the equations in each pair to obtain identical terms, and then adding or subtracting the equations to eliminate those terms.

1 $3x + 2y = 12$
$4x - y = 5$

2 $4x + 3y = 37$
$2x + y = 17$

3 $x + 3y = 7$
$2x - y = 7$

4 $2x + 3y = 19$
$6x + 2y = 22$

5 $5x - 2y = 14$
$3x - y = 9$

6 $10x - y = 3$
$3x + 2y = 17$

7 $2x + 5y = 9$
$x + 2y = 4$

8 $3x + 4y = 29$
$4x - 2y = 2$

9 $5x - 2y = 24$
$3x + y = 21$

10 $5x - 2y = 36$
$2x - 6y = 4$

11 $2x + 3y = 17$
$4x + 7y = 39$

12 $3x - 2y = 6$
$5x + 6y = 38$

There are also cases where **both** equations have to be changed to obtain identical terms. Follow through the next example to see how this is done.

Example 4 Solve $4x + 3y = 27$
$5x - 2y = 5$

Both equations have to be changed to obtain identical terms in either x or y. However, we can see that if we make the y-terms the same, we also eliminate the negative situation so this is obviously the better choice. We do this by multiplying the first equation by 2 and the second equation by 3, to give

$$(4x + 3y = 27) \times 2 \Rightarrow 8x + 6y = 54$$
$$\text{and } (5x - 2y = 5) \times 3 \Rightarrow 15x - 6y = 15$$

These are solved in the same way as in Example 1 to give the answer $x = 3$ and $y = 5$.

Exercise 3L

Solve the following simultaneous equations.

1 $5x + 2y = 20$
$4x + 3y = 23$

2 $3x + 4y = 25$
$2x + 3y = 18$

3 $10x - 2y = 2$
$4x + 3y = 16$

4 $3x + 2y = 22$
$4x - 3y = 18$

5 $3x + 2y = 27$
$4x + 5y = 43$

6 $5x - 3y = 11$
$2x + 4y = 20$

7 $2x + 5y = 15$
$3x - 2y = 13$

8 $2x + 3y = 30$
$5x + 7y = 71$

9 $2x - 3y = 15$
$5x + 7y = 52$

10 $3x - 2y = 15$
$2x - 3y = 5$

11 $5x - 3y = 14$
$4x - 5y = 6$

12 $3x + 2y = 28$
$2x + 7y = 47$

So far, all the simultaneous equations you have met in this chapter have had positive, whole numbers as their solutions. But you do need to be prepared to meet simultaneous equations that have negative and decimal solutions.

The next exercise is a selection of simultaneous equations whose solutions are negative or decimal or both.

Exercise 3M

Solve the following simultaneous equations.

1 $2x + y = 4$
$x - y = 5$

2 $5x + 2y = 11$
$3x + 4y = 8$

3 $5x + 4y = 11$
$2x + 3y = 9$

4 $4x + 2y = 14$
$2x + 3y = 15$

5 $3x - 4y = 4.5$
$2x + 2y = 10$

6 $x - 2y = 4$
$3x - y = -3$

7 $3x + 2y = 2$
$2x + 6y = 13$

8 $2x - 5y = 4$
$x - 4y = 5$

9 $6x + 2y = 14$
$3x - 5y = 10$

10 $2x + 4y = 15$
$x + 5y = 21$

11 $x - 5y = 15$
$3x - 7y = 17$

12 $3x - y = 5$
$x + 3y = -20$

Problems solved by simultaneous equations

We are now going to meet a type of problem which has to be expressed as a pair of simultaneous equations so that it can be solved. The next example shows you how to tackle such a problem.

Problem On holiday last year, I was talking over breakfast to two families about how much it cost them to go to the theatre. They couldn't remember how much was charged for each adult or each child, but they could both remember what they had paid altogether.

The Advani family, consisting of Mr and Mrs Advani with their daughter Rupa, paid £23.

The Shaw family, consisting of Mrs Shaw with her two children, Len and Sue, paid £17.50.

How much would I have to pay for my wife, my four children and me?

Solution We make a pair of simultaneous equations from the situation as follows.

Let x be the cost of an adult ticket, and y be the cost of a child's ticket. Then

$$2x + y = 23 \quad \text{for the Advani family}$$
$$\text{and } x + 2y = 17.5 \quad \text{for the Shaw family}$$

We solve these equations just as we have done in the previous examples, to obtain $x = £9.50$ and $y = £4$. I can now find my cost, which will be

$$(2 \times £9.50) + (4 \times £4) = £35$$

Exercise 3N

Read each situation carefully, then make a pair of simultaneous equations in order to solve the problem.

1 Amul and Kim have £10.70 between them. Amul has £3.70 more than Kim. How much does each have?

2 The two people in front of me were both buying stamps. One bought 10 second-class and five first-class stamps at a total cost of £3.05. The other bought 8 second-class and 10 first-class stamps at a total cost of £3.82. How much did I pay for 3 second-class and 4 first-class stamps?

3 At a local tea room I couldn't help noticing that at one table, where the customers had eaten 6 buns and had 3 teas, it had cost them £1.65. At another table, the customers had eaten 11 buns and had 7 teas at a total cost of £3.40. My family and I had 5 buns and 6 teas. What did it cost us?

4 Three chews and four bubblies cost 72p. Five chews and two bubblies cost 64p. What would three chews and five bubblies cost?

5 On a nut-and-bolt production line, all the nuts weighed the same and all the bolts weighed the same. An order of 50 nuts and 60 bolts weighed 10.6 kg. An order of 40 nuts and 30 bolts weighed 6.5 kg. What should an order of 60 nuts and 50 bolts weigh?

6 A taxi firm charges a fixed amount plus so much per mile. A journey of 6 miles costs £3.70. A journey of 10 miles costs £5.10. What would be the cost of a journey of 8 miles?

7 Two members of the same church went to the same shop to buy material to make Christingles. One bought 200 oranges and 220 candles at a cost of £65.60. The other bought 210 oranges and 200 candles at a cost of £63.30. They only needed 200 of each. How much should it have cost them?

8 When you book Bingham Hall for a conference, you pay a fixed booking fee plus a charge for each delegate at the conference. The total charge for a conference with 65 delegates was £192.50. The total charge for a conference with 40 delegates was £180. What will be the charge for a conference with 70 delegates?

9 My mother-in-law uses this formula to cook turkey:

$$T = a + bW$$

where T is the cooking time (minutes), W is the weight of the turkey (kg), and a and b are constants. She says it takes 4 hours 30 minutes to cook a 12 kg turkey, and 3 hours 10 minutes to cook an 8 kg turkey. How long will it take to cook a 5 kg turkey?

Transposition of formulae

The subject of a formula is the variable (letter) in the formula which stands on its own, usually on the left-hand side of the 'equals' sign. For example, x is the subject of each of the following

$$x = 5t + 4 \qquad x = 4(2y - 7) \qquad x = \frac{1}{t}$$

If we wish to change the existing subject to a different variable, we have to rearrange (transpose) the formula to get that variable on the left-hand side.

We do this by using the same rule as that for solving equations: move the terms concerned from one side of the 'equals' sign to the other.

Follow through Examples 1 and 2 below to see how the process works.

Example 1 Make m the subject of $T = 5m - 3$.

Move the 3 away from the $5m$: $T + 3 = 5m$

Move the 5 away from the m: $\frac{T + 3}{5} = m$

Change to opposite sides and the transposed formula becomes $m = \frac{T + 3}{5}$

Example 2 From the formula $C = m^2 - t$, **i** make m the subject, **ii** express t in terms of C and m.

i Make m the subject.
Move the t away from the m^2: $C + t = m^2$
Take the square root of both sides: $\sqrt{(C + t)} = m$
Change to opposite sides and the transformed formula becomes $m = \sqrt{(C + t)}$

ii Make t the subject.
Take over t to make it positive: $C + t = m^2$
Move the C away from the t: $t = m^2 - C$
The transformed formula is $t = m^2 - C$

Exercise 3P

1 $W = 3n + t$ **i** Make n the subject. **ii** Express t in terms of n and W.

2 $x = 5y - w$ **i** Make y the subject. **ii** Express w in terms of x and y.

3 $p = 7m + t$ **i** Make m the subject. **ii** Make t the subject.

4 $t = 2k - f$ **i** Express k in terms of f and t. **ii** Make f the subject.

5 $g = 6m + v$ **i** Express m in terms of v and g. **ii** Make v the subject.

6 $t = m^2$ Make m the subject.

7 $k = p^2$ Make p the subject.

8 $a = b^2 + 3$ Make b the subject.

9 $w = h^2 - 5$ Express h in terms of w.

10 $m = p^2 + 2$ Make p the subject.

11 $v = u^2 - t$ **i** Make t the subject. **ii** Make u the subject.

12 $k = m + n^2$ **i** Make m the subject. **ii** Make n the subject.

13 $T = 5r^2$ Make r the subject.

14 $P = 3t^2$ Make t the subject.

15 $K = 5n^2 + w$ **i** Make w the subject. **ii** Make n the subject.

Possible coursework tasks

Sheep pens

In a field a farmer has a number of sheep and a number of sheep pens.
If he puts 7 sheep into each pen, one sheep is left over.
If he puts 9 sheep into each pen, one pen is left over.
How many sheep and how many pens are there in the field?

Handshakes

At a meeting, there are n people who introduce themselves to everyone else in the room. How many handshakes will there be if every person shakes hands with every other person?

Prime example

Evaluate the expression $x^2 + x + 41$ for different values of x.

Investigate whether the expression generates prime numbers.

Examination questions

1 Given that $m = \frac{1}{2}$, $p = \frac{3}{4}$ and $t = -2$, calculate

a $mp + t$ **b** $\frac{(m + p)}{t}$

NEAB, Question 14, Paper 1, June 1995

2 a Short-sleeved shirts cost £x each. What is the cost of 6 of these shirts?

b Long-sleeved shirts cost £y each. What is the cost of 4 of these shirts?

c Write down the total cost of the 10 shirts.

d The short-sleeved shirts in part **a** are sold for £2 each less than the £x, if at least 20 are bought. What is the cost of 20 short-sleeved shirts at this new price?

WJEC, Question 8, Paper 1, June 1994

3 The diagram shows a square and a rectangle. The square has sides of length $2y$ metres. The rectangle has length $3y$ metres and breadth 3 metres.

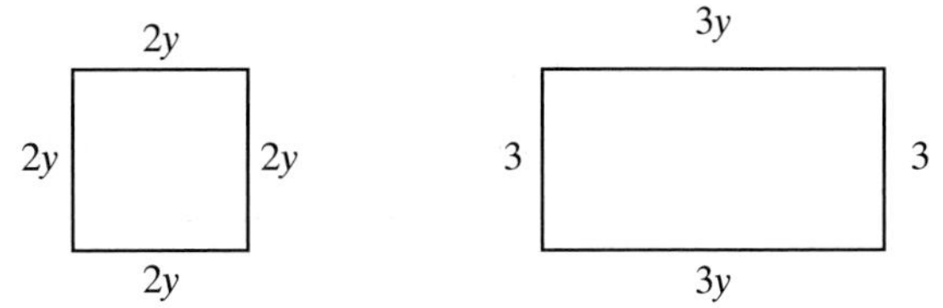

a i Find, in terms of y, the perimeter of the square.

ii Find, in terms of y, the perimeter of the rectangle.

b The perimeter of the square is equal to the perimeter of the rectangle. Work out the value of y.

c The areas of these two rectangles are the same. By solving the equation $2(x + 2) = 2(4x - 1)$, find the area of one of these rectangles.

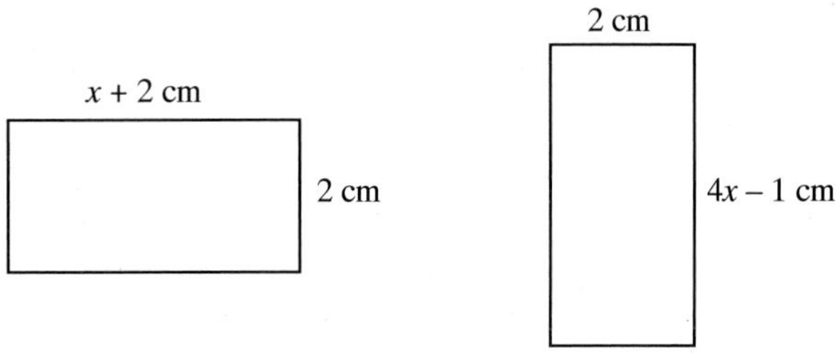

SEG, Question 9, Specimen Paper 11, 1998

4 In a certain rectangle the length of the longer sides are 3 cm more than the shorter sides Let x cm denote the length of each of the shorter sides.

a Write down, in terms of x, the length of each of the longer sides.

b Write down, in terms of x, the length of the perimeter of the rectangle. Simplify your answer as far as possible.

c Suppose the perimeter of the rectangle is 32 cm. Write down an equation that x satisfies and solve it to find the length of the sides of this rectangle.

WJEC, Question 9, Specimen Paper 1, 1998

5 a Write, in symbols, the rule

'To find y, double x and add 1.'

b Use your rule from part **a** to calculate the value of x when $y = 9$.

ULEAC, Question 5, Paper 4, June 1994

6 Paul is solving the equation

$$x^4 = 37$$

by a trial-and-improvement method. He sees that

$$2.1^4 = 19.4481$$
$$2.6^4 = 45.6976$$

Show how you would continue in this way to find the solution to the equation, correct to 1 decimal place. *WJEC, Question 14, Paper 1, June 1994*

7 The number x satisfies the equation $x^3 = 20$.

i Between which two consecutive whole numbers does x lie?

ii Use a trial-and-improvement method to find this value of x correct to one decimal place. Show all your working clearly. *NEAB, Question 11, Paper 2, June 1995*

8 A rocket is fired vertically upwards with velocity u metres per second. After t seconds the rocket's velocity, v metres per second, is given by the formula

$$v = u + gt$$

where g is a constant.

a Calculate v when $u = 100$, $g = -9.8$ and $t = 5$.

b Rearrange the formula to express t in terms of v, u and g.

c Calculate t when $u = 93.5$, $g = -9.8$ and $v = 20$.

NEAB, Question 4, Specimen Paper 1H, 1998

9 Greg sold 40 tickets for a concert. He sold x tickets at £2 each and y tickets at £3.50 each. He collected £92.

i Write down two equations connecting x and y.

ii Solve these simultaneous equations to find how many of each kind of ticket he sold.

NEAB, Question 13, Specimen Paper 1H, 1998

10 Solve the simultaneous equations

$4x - 3y = 18$
$5x + 2y = 11$ *WJEC, Question 17, Paper B1, June 1994*

11 Solve the simultaneous equations

$2a + 4c = 13$
$a + 3c = 8$ *NEAB, Question 18, Paper 1Q, June 1995*

12 The price, £P, of a cruise lasting t days is represented by the formula

$P = 40t + t^2$

a What is the price of a cruise lasting 3 days?

b The cost, £C, to run the cruise for t days is represented by the formula

$C = 500 + 80t$

i Rearrange this formula to make t the subject.

ii The cost of running a cruise was £900. For how many days did this cruise last?

NEAB, Question 2, Paper 1H, November 1995

Summary

How well do you grade yourself?

To gain a grade **C**, you need to be able to manipulate simple formulae, equations and expressions, and be able to solve simultaneous equations in which only one equation needs to be changed in order to eliminate a variable. You need also to be able to solve equations and problems by trial and improvement, and be able to make simple equations from situations and solve them.

To gain a grade **B**, you need to be able to substitute numerical fractions and negative values into expressions and formulae. You need also to be able to solve simultaneous equations where both equations need to be changed.

What you should know after you have worked through Chapter 3

- How to substitute values into expressions and evaluate them.
- How to solve simple linear equations.
- How to solve equations by trial and improvement.
- How to solve a variety of simultaneous linear equations.
- How to transpose a formula to change its subject.

4 Pythagoras and trigonometry

This chapter is going to … show you how to find the lengths and angles in right-angled triangles. It introduces you to the three basic trigonometric ratios, and helps you to recognise which of these ratios to use when solving right-angled triangles. It then shows you how to interpret practical problems and solve them using trigonometry.

What you should already know

- The sum of the three interior angles of a triangle is 180°.
- How to round off numbers to decimal places and significant figures.
- Pythagoras's theorem and how to use it to find the lengths of the sides of right-angled triangles.

You will need a scientific calculator with sin, cos and tan keys.

If you feel you need to revise the application of Pythagoras's theorem to solve right-angled triangles, you should work through Exercises 4A and 4B.

Exercise 4A

In each of the following triangles, find the hypotenuse, rounding off to a suitable degree of accuracy.

1

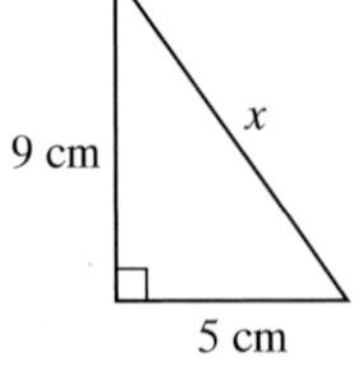

2

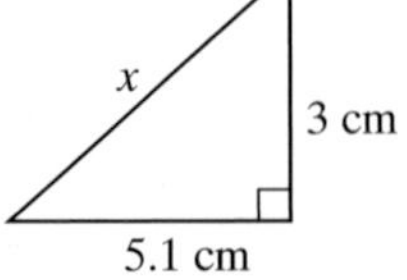

3

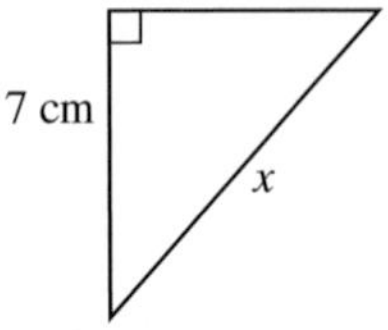

4

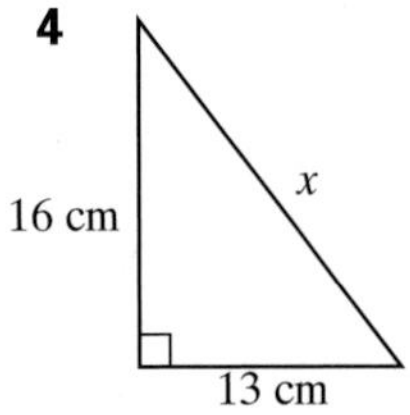

5

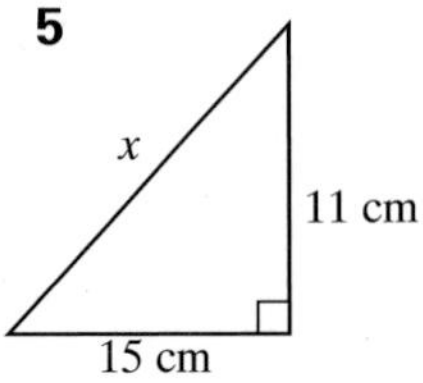

6

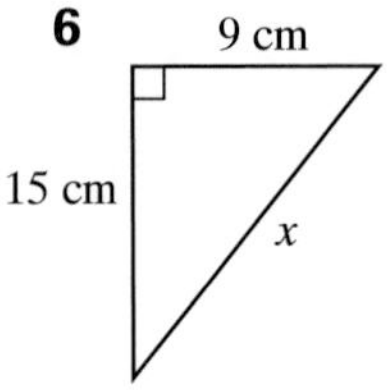

7

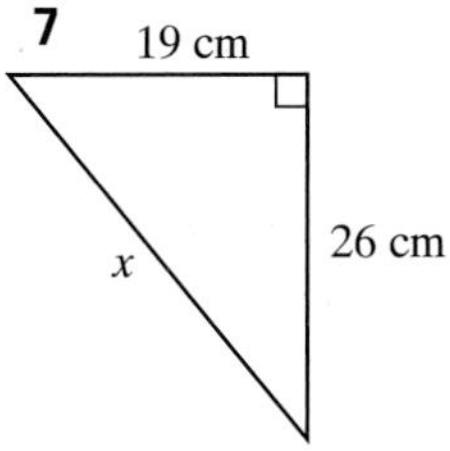

8

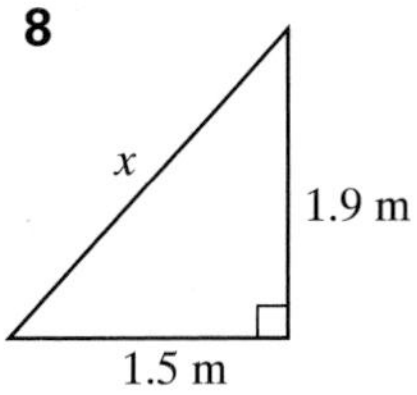

9

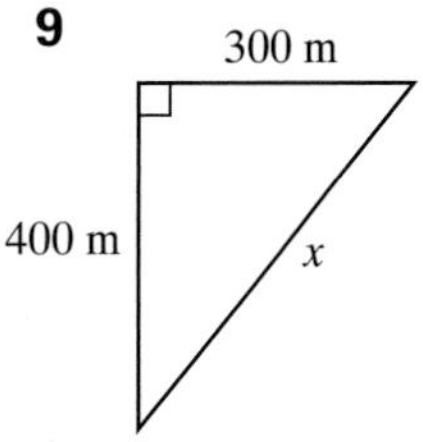

10

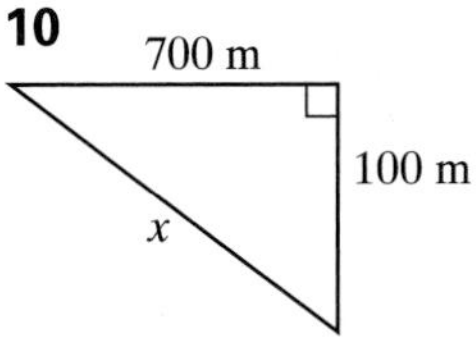

11

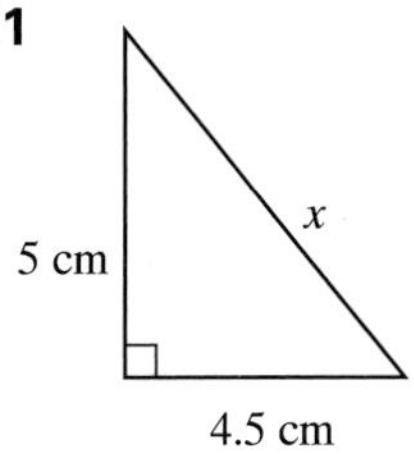

12

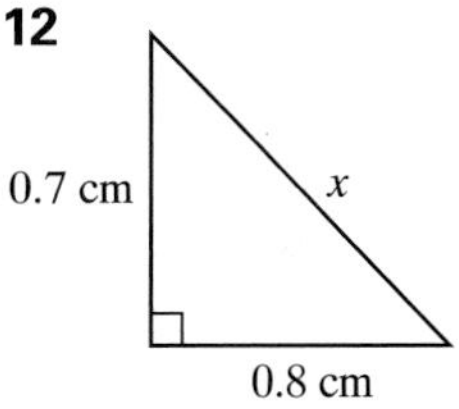

Exercise 4B

1 In each of the following triangles, find the length x to a suitable degree of accuracy.

a

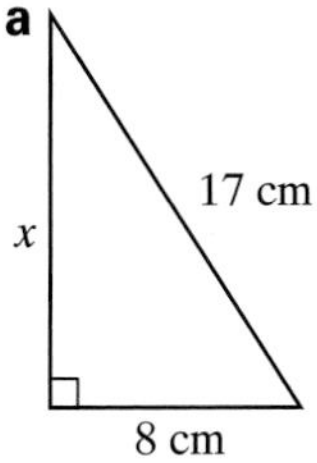

b

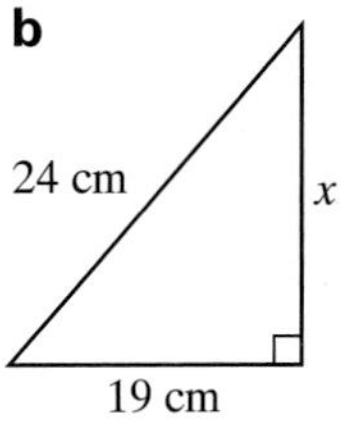

c

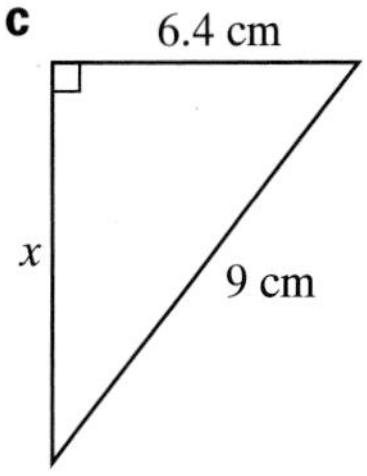

d

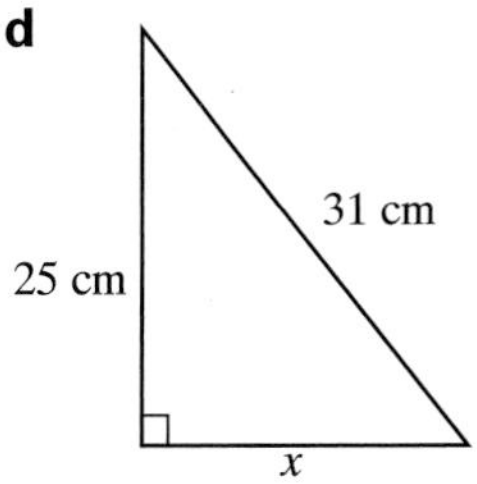

e

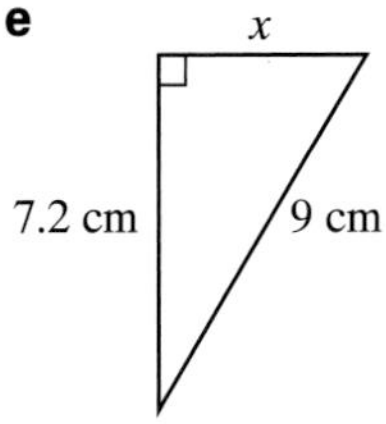

f

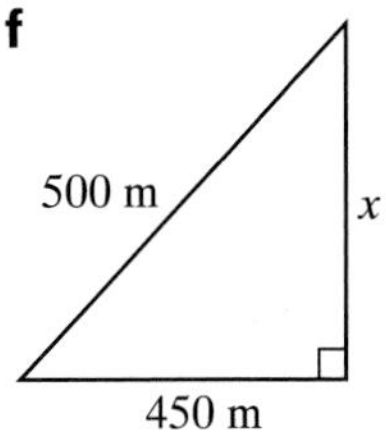

g

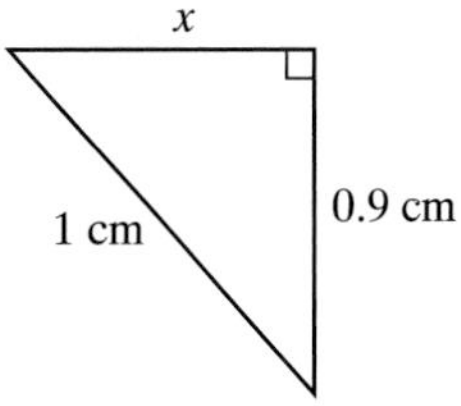

h

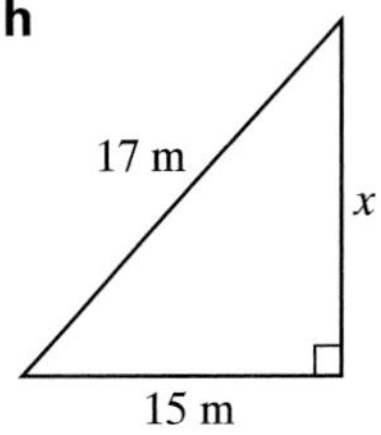

2 In each of the following triangles, find the length x to a suitable degree of accuracy.

a

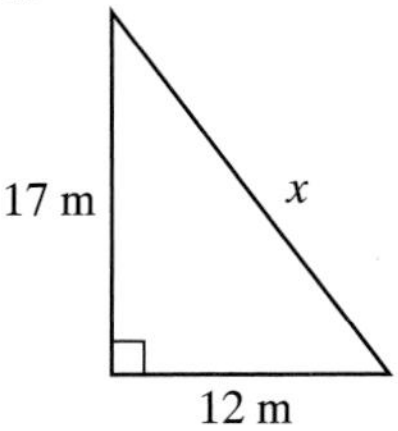

b

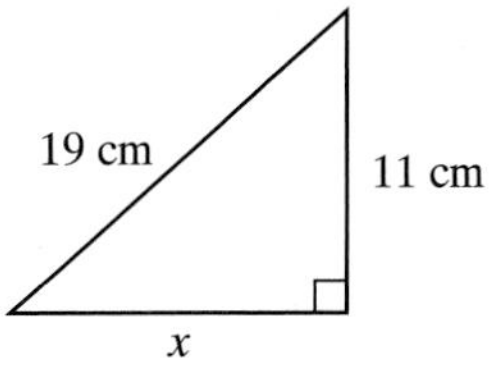

c

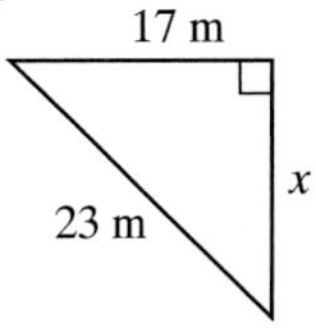

d

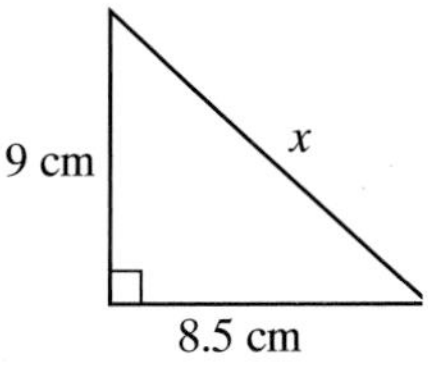

e

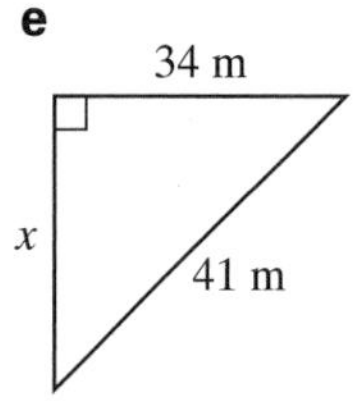

f

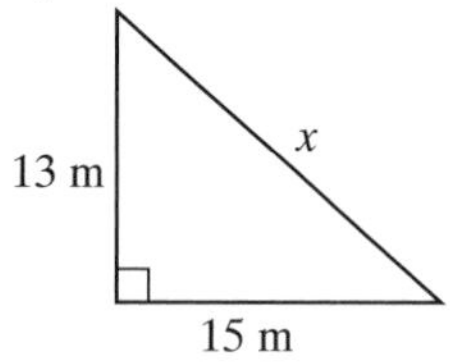

g

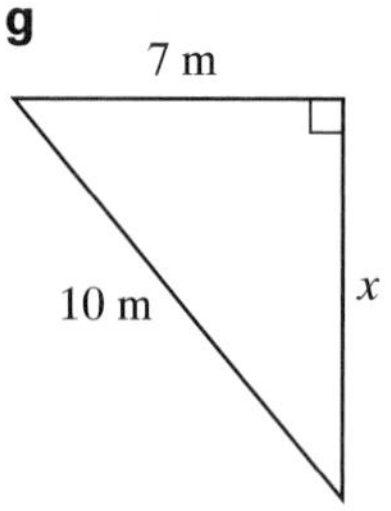

h

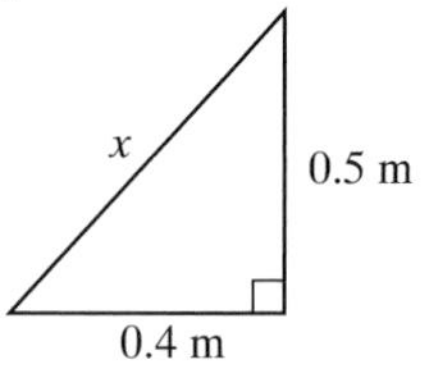

i

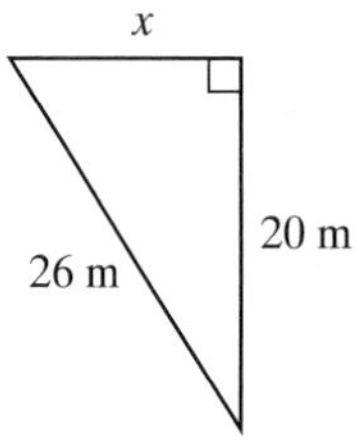

j

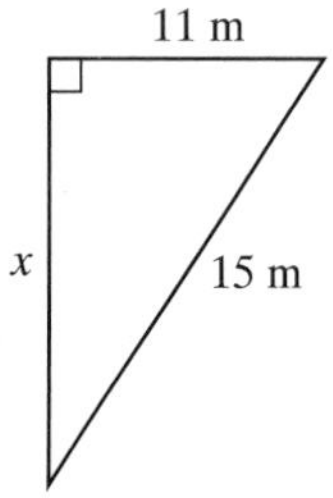

k

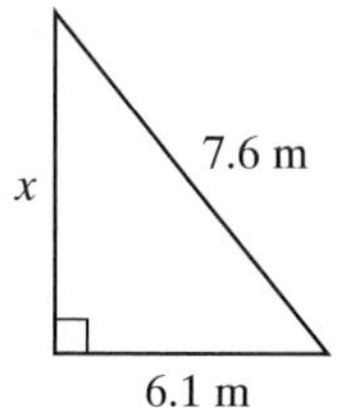

l

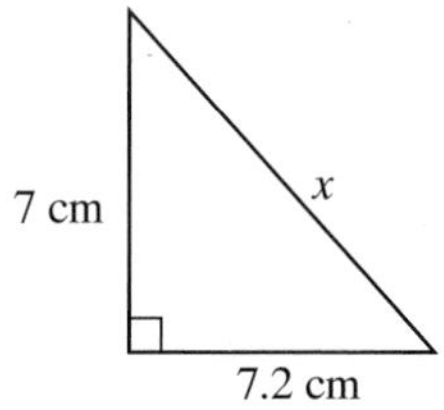

Pythagoras and real problems

Pythagoras's theorem can be used to solve certain practical problems. When a problem involves two lengths only:

- Draw a diagram from the problem that includes a right-angled triangle.
- Look at the diagram and decide which side has to be found: the hypotenuse or one of the other sides.
- If it's the hypotenuse, then square both numbers, add the squares and take the square root of the sum.
- If it's one of the other sides, then square both numbers, subtract the squares and take the square root of the difference.
- Finally, round off the answer.

Follow through the next example.

Example A plane leaves Manchester airport heading due east. It flies 160 km before turning due north. It then flies a further 280 km and lands.

What is the distance of the return flight if the plane flies straight back to Manchester airport?

First, sketch the situation.

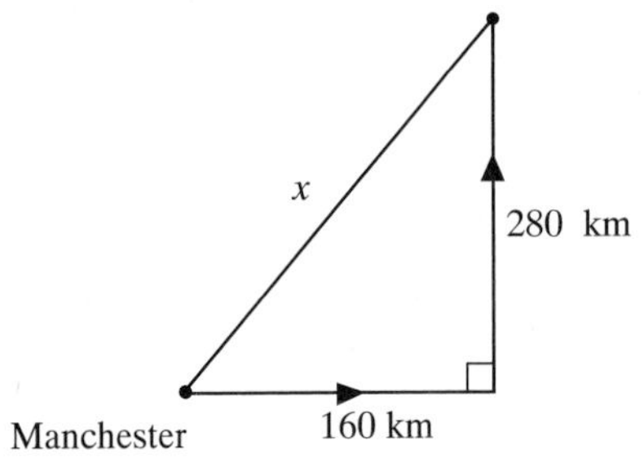

Using Pythagoras's theorem gives

$$x^2 = 160^2 + 280^2$$
$$= 25\,600 + 78\,400$$
$$= 104\,000$$
$$\Rightarrow \quad x = \sqrt{104\,000} = 322 \text{ km}$$

Remember the following tips when solving problems.

- Always sketch the right-angled triangle you need. Sometimes, the triangle is already drawn for you but some problems involve other lines and triangles that may confuse you. So identify which right-angled triangle you need and sketch it separately.
- Label the triangle with necessary information, such as the length of its sides, from the question. Label the side which is being found with an x.
- Set out your solution as we have above. Avoid short cuts, since they often cause errors. You gain marks in your examination for clearly showing how you are applying Pythagoras's theorem to the problem.
- Round off to a suitable degree of accuracy.

Exercise 4C

1 A ladder, 12 metres long, leans against a wall. The ladder reaches 10 metres up the wall. How far away from the foot of the wall is the foot of the ladder?

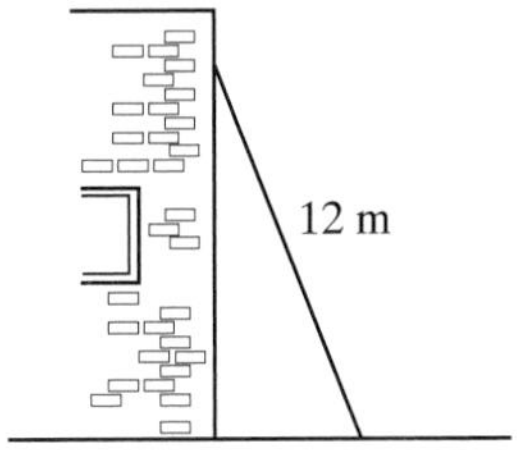

2 A model football pitch is 2 metres long and 0.5 metres wide. How long is the diagonal?

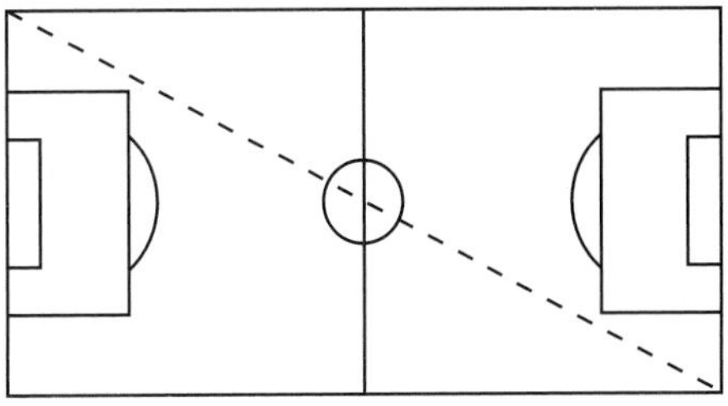

3 How long is the diagonal of a rectangle 6 metres long and 9 metres wide?

4 How long is the diagonal of a square with a side of 8 metres?

5 In a hockey game, a pass is made that goes 7 metres up the field and 6 metres across the field. How long was the actual pass?

6 A ship going from a port to a lighthouse steams 15 km east and 12 km north. How far is the lighthouse from the port?

7 A plane flies from London due north for 120 km before turning due west and flying for a further 85 km and landing at a secret location. How far from London is the secret location?

8 At the moment, three towns, A, B and C, are joined by two roads, as in the diagram. The council wants to make a road which runs directly from A to C. How much distance will the new road save?

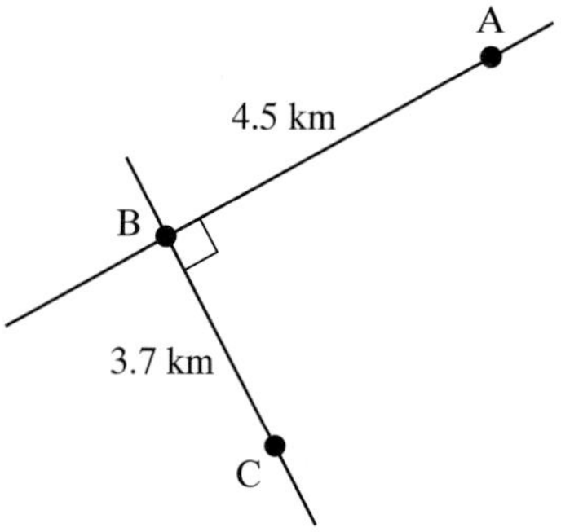

9 Some pedestrians wants to get from point X on one road to point Y on another. The two roads meet at right angles.

a If they follow the roads, how far will they walk?

b Instead of walking along the road, they take the shortcut, XY. Find the length of the shortcut.

c How much distance do they save?

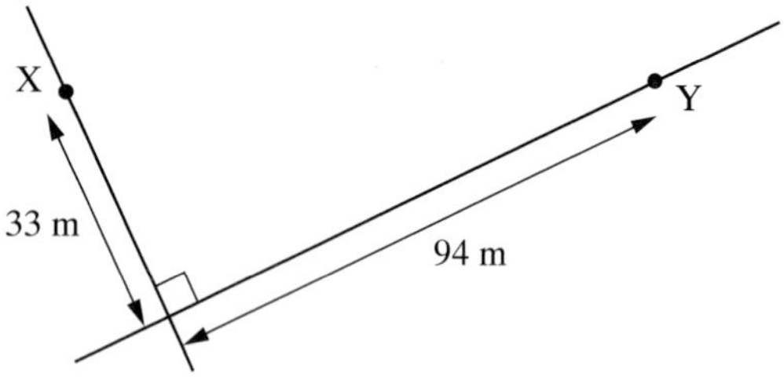

10 A mast on a sailboat is strengthened by a wire (called a stay), as shown on the diagram. The mast is 35 feet tall. The stay is 37 feet long. How far from the base of the mast does the stay reach?

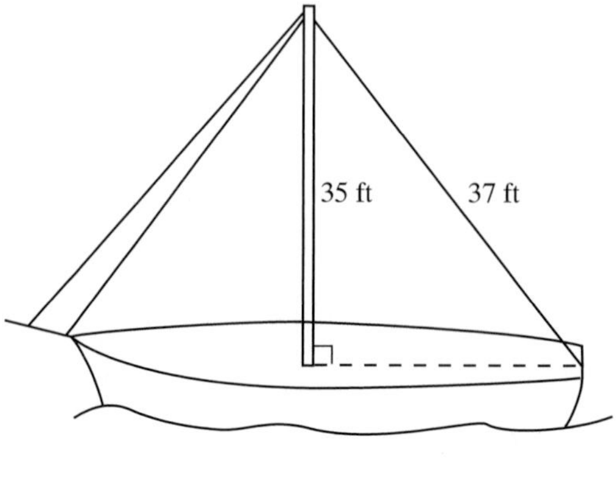

11 A 4-metre ladder is put up against a wall.

a How far up the wall will it reach when the foot of the ladder is 1 m away from the wall?

b When it reaches 3.6 m up the wall, how far is the foot of the ladder away from the wall?

12 A pole, 8 m high, is supported by metal wires, each 8.6 m long, attached to the top of the pole. How far from the foot of the pole are the wires fixed to the ground?

13 How long is the line that joins the two co-ordinates A(2, 6) and B(1, 1)?

14 The regulation for safe use of ladders states that for a 5 m ladder: The foot of the ladder must be placed between 1.6 m and 2.1 m from the foot of the wall.

a What is the maximum height the ladder can safely reach up the wall?

b What is the minimum height the ladder can safely reach up the wall?

15 A rectangle is 4.5 cm long. The length of its diagonal is 5.8 cm. What is the area of the rectangle?

16 A boat sails from port 31 km due north, then 27 km due east, then 21 km due north again. How far is it now from the port?

17 A plane leaves an airport and heads due west for 90 km before turning due south for 170 km and landing. How far is the plane now from the airport?

18 Two large trees, 5.5 m and 6.8 m tall, stand 120 m apart. A bird flies directly from the top of one tree to the top of the other. How far has the bird flown?

19 Is the triangle with sides 7 cm, 24 cm and 25 cm a right-angled triangle?

20 How long is the line that joins the two co-ordinates A(–2, 3) and B(4, –1).

Pythagoras in isosceles triangles

Every isosceles triangle has a line of symmetry that divides the triangle into two congruent right-angled triangles. So when you are faced with a problem involving an isosceles triangle, be aware that you are quite likely to have to split that triangle down the middle to create a right-angled triangle which will help you to solve the problem.

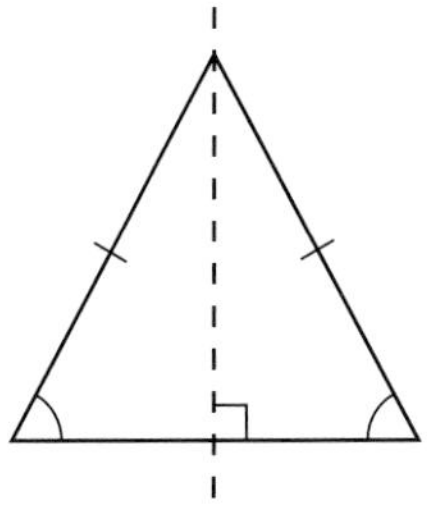

For example, suppose we have to find the area of this triangle.

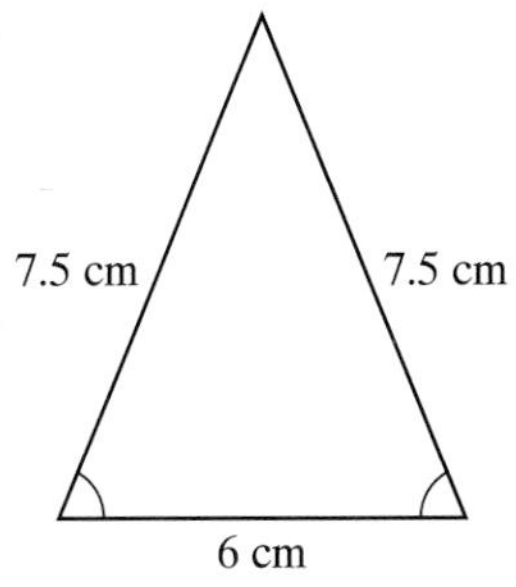

It is an isosceles triangle and we need to know its height to find its area. Splitting the triangle into two right-angled triangles will help us to find its height.

Call the height x. Then, using Pythagoras's theorem, we get

$$x^2 + 3^2 = 7.5^2$$

$$\Rightarrow \quad x^2 = 7.5^2 - 3^2$$

$= 56.25 - 9$

$= 47.25$

$\Rightarrow \quad x = \sqrt{47.25}$

$x = 6.87$

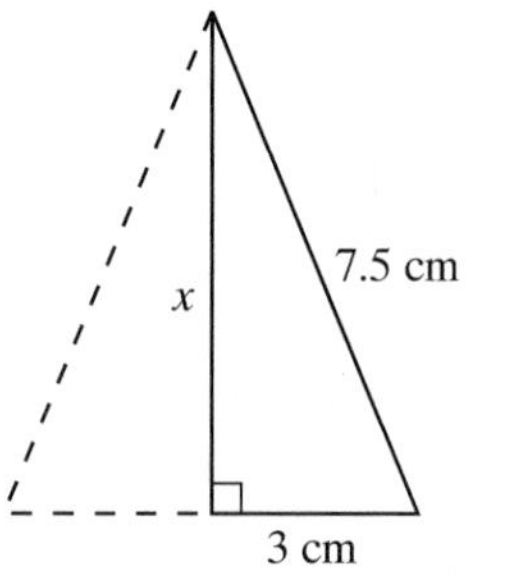

Keep the accurate figure in the calculator memory.

The area of the triangle is $\frac{1}{2} \times 6 \times 6.87$ (from the calculator memory), which is 20.6 cm^2.

Exercise 4D

1 Calculate the area of these isosceles triangles.

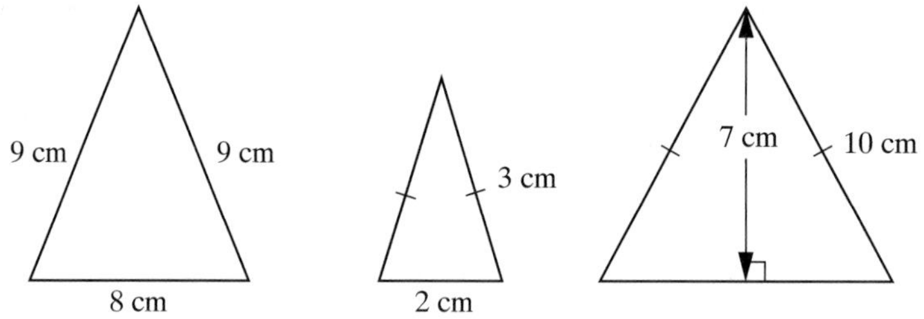

2 Calculate the area of an isosceles triangle whose sides are 8 cm, 8 cm and 6 cm.

3 Calculate the area of an equilateral triangle of side 6 cm.

4 Calculate the area of an equilateral triangle of side 8 cm.

5 An isosceles triangle has sides of 5 cm and 6 cm.

a Sketch the two different isosceles triangles that fit this data.

b Which of the two triangles has the greater area?

6 **a** Sketch a regular hexagon, showing all its lines of symmetry.

b Calculate the area of the hexagon if its side is 8 cm.

7 Calculate the area of a hexagon of side 10 cm.

8 Calculate the lengths marked x in these isosceles triangles.

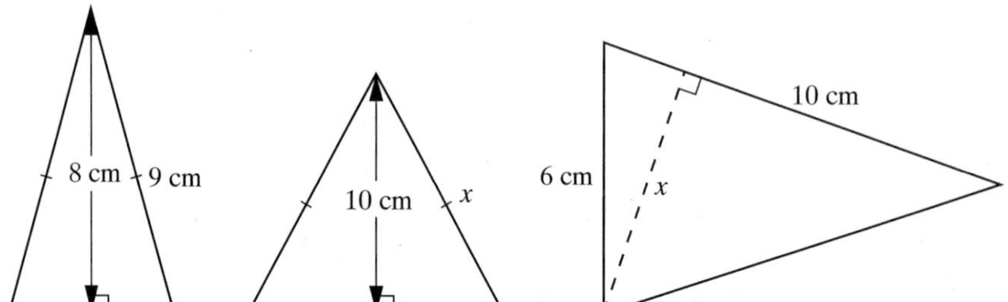

[**Hint:** Find the area first.]

Pythagoras's theorem in three dimensions

In the higher tier GCSE, there are questions which involve applying Pythagoras's theorem to 3-D situations. Such questions are usually accompanied by clearly labelled diagrams, which will help you quickly to identify the lengths and angles needed for your solutions.

You deal with these 3-D problems in exactly the same way as 2-D problems. That is:

- Identify the right-angled triangle you need, whose sides will be two given lengths and the length to be found.
- Redraw this triangle and label it with the given lengths and the length to be found (usually x or y).
- From your diagram, decide whether it is the hypotenuse or one of the other sides which has to be found.
- Solve the problem, rounding off to a suitable degree of accuracy.

Follow through the next example to see how this works.

Example What is the longest piece of straight wire that can be stored in a box 30 cm by 15 cm by 20 cm?

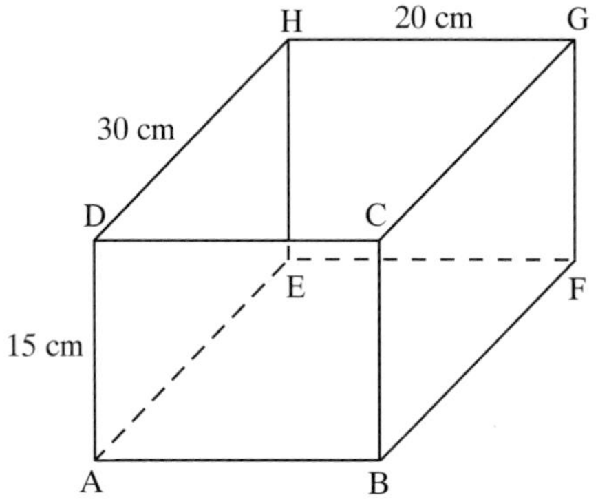

The longest distance across this box is any one of the diagonals AG, DF, CE, HB.

Let us take AG.

First, we identify a right-angled triangle containing AG and draw it. This gives us triangle AFG, which contains two lengths we do not know: AG, which we are trying to find, and AF, which is the diagonal of the base of the box.

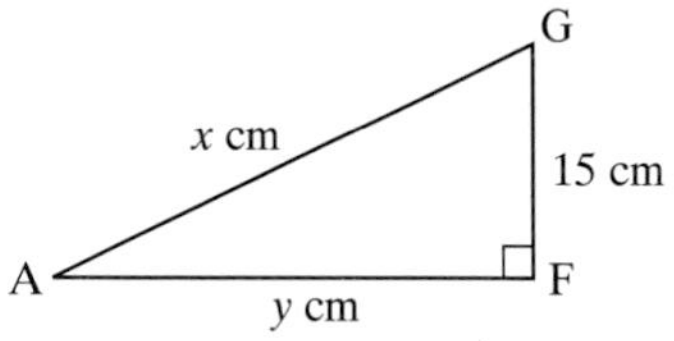

We next identify a right-angled triangle that contains the side AF and draw it.

This gives us triangle ABF. We can now find AF.

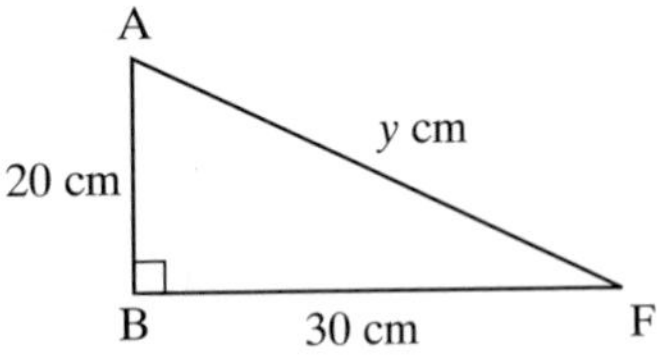

Let AF = y. Then by Pythagoras we obtain

$$y^2 = 30^2 + 20^2$$
$$y^2 = 1300$$
$$\Rightarrow \quad y = \sqrt{1300} = 36.0555 \text{ cm}$$

We can now find AG using triangle AFG.

Let AG = x. Then we obtain

$$x^2 = y^2 + 15^2$$
$$x^2 = 1300 + 225 = 1525$$
$$\Rightarrow \quad x = 39.1 \text{ cm} \quad (1 \text{ dp})$$

So, the longest straight wire that can be stored in the box is 39.1 cm.

Exercise 4E

1 A box measures 8 cm by 12 cm by 5 cm.

a Calculate the lengths of

i AC **ii** BG **iii** BE

b Calculate the diagonal distance BH.

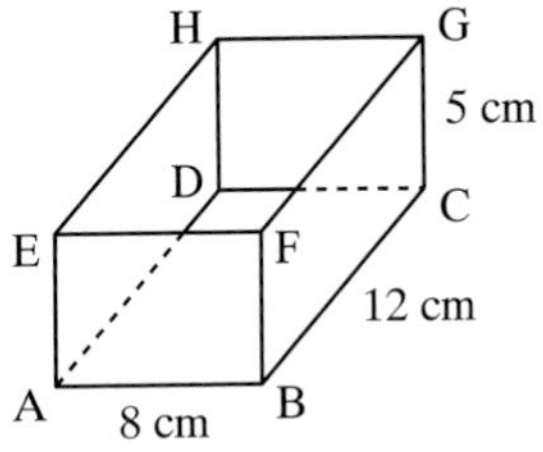

2 A garage is 5 m long, 3 m wide and 3 m high. Can a 7 m long pole be stored in it?

3 Spike, a spider, is at the corner S of the wedge shown in the diagram. Fred, a fly, is at the corner F of the same wedge.

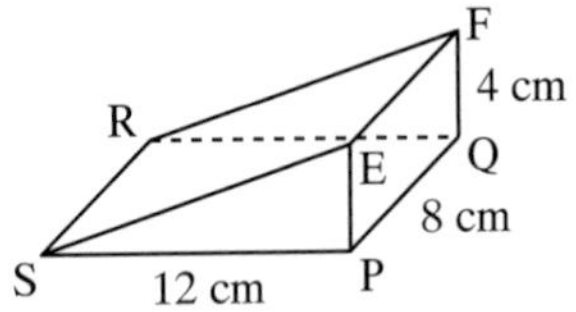

a Calculate the two distances Spike would have to travel to get to Fred if she used the edges of the wedge.

b Calculate the distance Spike would have to travel across the face of the wedge to get directly to Fred.

4 Fred is now at the top of a baked-beans can and Spike is directly below him on the base of the can. To catch Fred by surprise, Spike takes a diagonal route round the can. How far does Spike crawl? [**Hint:** Imagine the can opened out flat.]

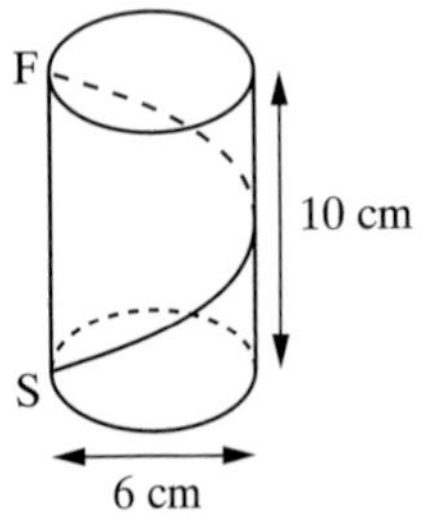

5 A corridor is 3 m wide and turns through a right angle, as in the diagram. What is the longest pole that can be carried along the corridor horizontally? If the corridor is 3 m high, what is the longest pole that can be carried along in any direction?

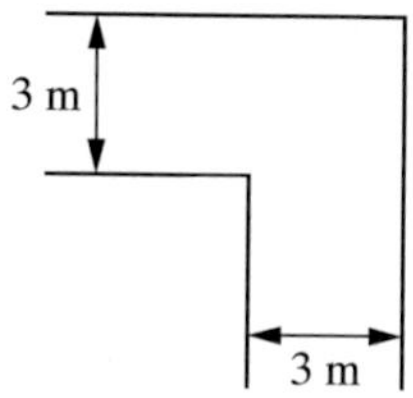

6 For the box shown on the right, find the lengths of

a DG

b HA

c DB

d AG

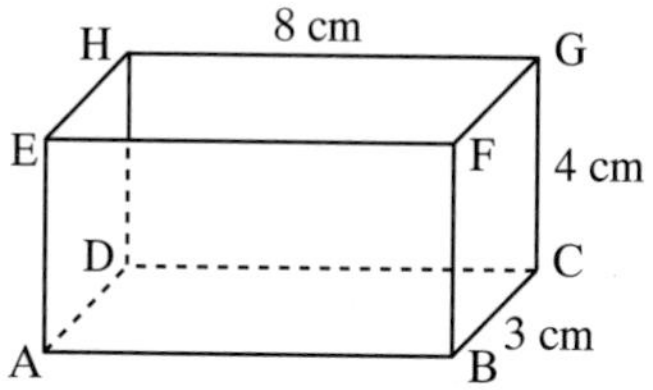

7 The diagram shows a square-based pyramid with base length 8 cm and sloping edges 9 cm. M is the mid-point of the side AB, X is the mid-point of the base, and E is directly above X.

a Calculate the length of the diagonal AC.

b Calculate EX, the height of the pyramid.

c Using triangle ABE, calculate the length EM.

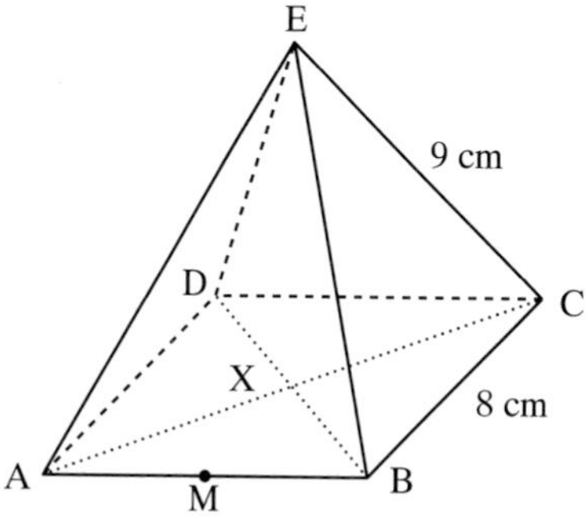

8 The diagram shows a cuboid framework with diagonal struts AG, AF and BG.

a Write down (or calculate) the length BG.

b Write down (or calculate) the length AF.

c Calculate the length AG.

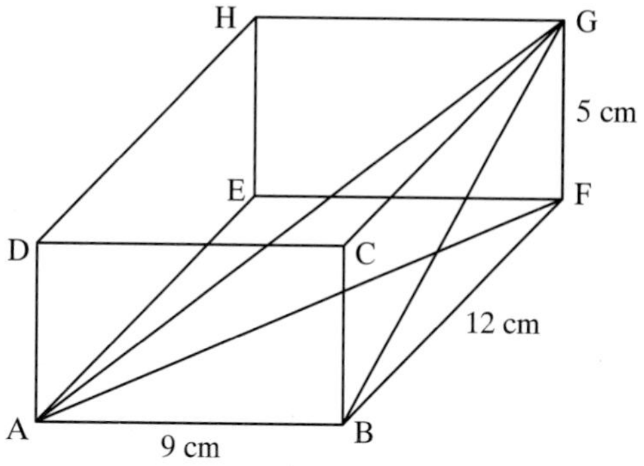

9 The diagram shows a cuboid with sides of 40 cm, 30 cm, and 22.5 cm. M is the mid-point of the side FG. Calculate (or write down) these lengths, giving your answer to 3 significant figures if necessary.

a AH **b** AG **c** AM **d** HM

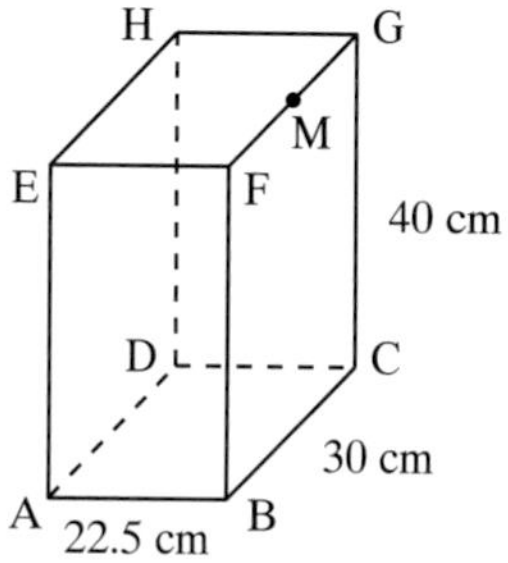

Trigonometric ratios

Trigonometry is concerned with the calculation of sides and angles in triangles, and involves the use of three important ratios: **sine**, **cosine** and **tangent**. These ratios are defined in terms of the sides of a right-angled triangle.

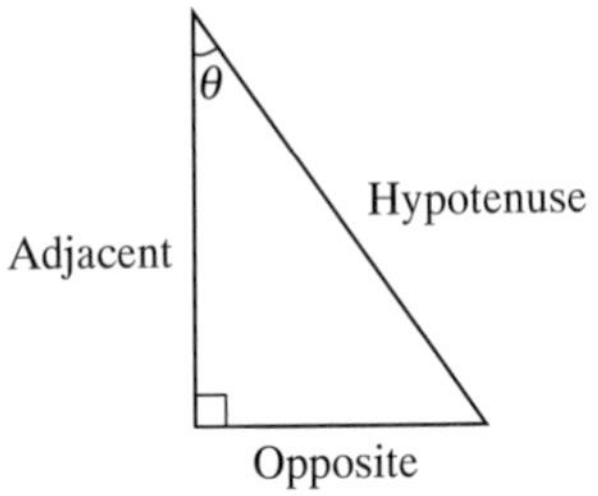

In a right-angled triangle:

- The side opposite the right angle is called the **hypotenuse**. It is the longest side.
- The side opposite the angle involved (θ) is called the **opposite**.
- The other side (next to both the right angle and the angle involved) is called the **adjacent**.

The sine, cosine and tangent ratios for θ are defined as

$$\text{sine } \theta = \frac{\text{Opposite}}{\text{Hypotenuse}} \qquad \text{cosine } \theta = \frac{\text{Adjacent}}{\text{Hypotenuse}} \qquad \text{tangent } \theta = \frac{\text{Opposite}}{\text{Adjacent}}$$

Memorising these may be helped by a mnenomic such as

Silly **O**ld **H**itler **C**ouldn't **A**dvance **H**is **T**roops **O**ver **A**frica

in which the first letter of each word is taken in order to give

$$S = \frac{O}{H} \qquad C = \frac{A}{H} \qquad T = \frac{O}{A}$$

Note The full names of these three ratios are never used in mathematical working, being shortened as follows:

sine **sin** cosine **cos** tangent **tan**

These abbreviated forms are also used on calculator keys.

Using your calculator

You can use your calculator to find the sine, cosine and tangent of **any** angle.

To find the sine, press the key label **sin**.
To find the cosine, press the key labelled **cos**.
To find the tangent, press the key labelled **tan**.

Make sure you can find sin, cos and tan on your calculator.

Important Make sure your calculator is working in **degrees**. When it is, D or DEG appears in the display.

Depending on your type of calculator, you need to be able to put it into 'degree mode' before you start working on sines, cosines and tangents. This can be done either

- by pressing the keys MODE 4
- or by pressing the key DEG until DEG is on display.

Try this **now** to make sure you can do it.

Example 1 Use your calculator to find the sine of 27° (written as sin 27°).

If you have an ordinary scientific calculator, the function is keyed in 'numbers first':

2 7 sin

The display should read 0.4539905. (You may have more or less digits depending on your calculator.) This is 0.454 to 3 sf.

If you have a graphics calculator or a certain type of 'algebraic logic' (DAL) calculator, you key in the function as it reads:

sin 2 7 EXE (EXE or ENTER may be = on your calculator.)

You should get the same value as above. If you don't then **consult** your calculator manual or your teacher.

Example 2 Use your calculator to find the cosine of 56° (written as cos 56°).

$\cos 56° = 0.5591929035 = 0.559$ to 3 sf

Check that you agree with this, using as many digits as your calculator allows.

Example 3 Use your calculator to work out $3 \times \cos 57°$ (written as $3 \cos 57°$).

Depending on your type of calculator, key in either

3 × 5 7 cos = or 3 × cos 5 7 =

Check that you get an answer of 1.634 to 3 decimal places (actual 1.633917105).

Exercise 4F

1 Find these values, rounding off your answers to 3 sf.

a sin 43°	**b** sin 56°	**c** sin 67.2°	**d** sin 90°
e sin 45°	**f** sin 20°	**g** sin 22°	**h** sin 0°
i sin 35°	**j** sin 75°	**k** sin 89°	**l** sin 71°

2 Find these values, rounding off your answers to 3 sf.

a cos 43°	**b** cos 56°	**c** cos 67.2°	**d** cos 90°
e cos 45°	**f** cos 20°	**g** cos 22°	**h** cos 0°
i cos 35°	**j** cos 75°	**k** cos 89°	**l** cos 71°

3 From your answers to questions **1** and **2**, what angle has the same value for sine and cosine?

4 a i What is sin 35°? **ii** What is cos 55°?
b i What is sin 12°? **ii** What is cos 78°?
c i What is cos 67°? **ii** What is sin 23°?
d What connects the values in parts **a**, **b** and **c**?
e Copy and complete these sentences.
i sin 15° is the same as cos …
ii cos 82° is the same as sin …
iii sin x is the same as cos …

5 Use your calculator to work out the value of

a tan 43° **b** tan 56° **c** tan 67.2° **d** tan 90°
e tan 45° **f** tan 20° **g** tan 22° **h** tan 0°
i tan 35° **j** tan 75° **k** tan 89° **l** tan 71°

6 Use your calculator to work out the value of

a sin 73° **b** cos 26° **c** tan 65.2° **d** sin 88°
e cos 35° **f** tan 30° **g** sin 28° **h** cos 5°
i tan 37° **j** sin 73° **k** cos 79° **l** tan 79°

7 What is so different about tan compared with both sin and cos?

8 Use your calculator to work out the value of

a 5 sin 65° **b** 6 cos 42° **c** 12 sin 17° **d** 3 cos 78°
e 6 sin 90° **f** 5 sin 0° **g** 12 cos 73° **h** 9 sin 12°

9 Use your calculator to work out the value of

a 5 tan 65° **b** 6 tan 42° **c** 12 tan 17° **d** 3 tan 78°
e 6 tan 90° **f** 5 tan 0° **g** 12 tan 73° **h** 9 tan 12°

10 Use your calculator to work out the value of

a 4 sin 63° **b** 7 tan 52° **c** 18 cos 37° **d** 4 tan 68°
e 5 tan 80° **f** 9 cos 8° **g** 19 tan 74° **h** 7 sin 22°

11 Use your calculator to work out the value of

a $\frac{5}{\sin 63°}$ **b** $\frac{6}{\cos 32°}$ **c** $\frac{12}{\sin 37°}$ **d** $\frac{3}{\cos 48°}$

e $\frac{6}{\sin 90°}$ **f** $\frac{5}{\sin 30°}$ **g** $\frac{12}{\sin 73°}$ **h** $\frac{9}{\sin 12°}$

12 Use your calculator to work out the value of

a $\frac{3}{\tan 64°}$ **b** $\frac{7}{\tan 42°}$ **c** $\frac{13}{\tan 36°}$ **d** $\frac{23}{\tan 58°}$

e $\frac{5}{\tan 89°}$ **f** $\frac{6}{\tan 40°}$ **g** $\frac{16}{\tan 63°}$ **h** $\frac{8}{\tan 22°}$

13 Use your calculator to work out the value of

a $8 \sin 75°$ **b** $\dfrac{19}{\sin 23°}$ **c** $7 \cos 71°$ **d** $\dfrac{15}{\sin 81°}$

e $\dfrac{23}{\sin 54°}$ **f** $23 \sin 17°$ **g** $\dfrac{12}{\sin 34°}$ **h** $17 \sin 85°$

14 Use your calculator to work out the value of

a $8 \tan 75°$ **b** $\dfrac{19}{\tan 23°}$ **c** $7 \tan 71°$ **d** $\dfrac{15}{\tan 81°}$

e $\dfrac{23}{\tan 54°}$ **f** $23 \tan 17°$ **g** $\dfrac{12}{\tan 34°}$ **h** $17 \tan 85°$

15 Use your calculator to work out the value of

a $\dfrac{6}{\sin 66°}$ **b** $\dfrac{8}{\tan 32°}$ **c** $\dfrac{14}{\cos 76°}$ **d** $\dfrac{24}{\tan 68°}$

e $\dfrac{8}{\tan 79°}$ **f** $\dfrac{5}{\cos 50°}$ **g** $\dfrac{17}{\tan 65°}$ **h** $\dfrac{9}{\sin 32°}$

16 Use your calculator to work out the value of

a $7 \sin 85°$ **b** $\dfrac{12}{\cos 53°}$ **c** $8 \tan 61°$ **d** $\dfrac{35}{\tan 71°}$

e $\dfrac{13}{\cos 34°}$ **f** $27 \tan 47°$ **g** $\dfrac{19}{\sin 64°}$ **h** $18 \cos 75°$

Working backwards: inverse functions

The sine of 54° is 0.809 016 9944 (to 10 dp).
The sine of 55° is 0.819 152 0443 (to 10 dp).

What angle has a sine of 0.815?

Obviously, it is between 54° and 55°, so we could probably use a trial-and-improvement method to find it. But there is an easier way which uses the **inverse functions** of your calculator.

An inverse function can be accessed in several different ways. For example, that for sine may be any of these:

2ndF sin   SHIFT sin   INV sin

The inverse function printed above the sine key is usually given in either of the following ways:

$\sin^{-1}$ / sin   or   arcsin / sin

You will need to find out how your calculator deals with inverse functions.

When you do the inverse sine of 0.815, you should get 54.58736189°.

It is usually acceptable in trigonometry to round off angles to 1 decimal place, so the angle with a sine of 0.815 is 54.6° (to 1 dp).

Try these three examples.

1 Find the angle with a cosine of 0.654. Then check that your calculator gives an answer of 49.15613192 = 49.2° (1 dp).

2 Find the angle with a sine of (3 ÷ 4). How you solve this will depend on your type of calculator. So key in either

3 ÷ 4 = INV sin   or   INV sin (3 ÷ 4) EXE

Check that you get an answer of 48.6° to 1 dp (actual 48.59037789).

3 Find the angle with a tangent of 0.75. Check that your calculator gives an answer of 36.869898 = 36.9° (1 dp).

Exercise 4G

Use your calculator to find the answers to the following. Give your answers to 1 dp.

1 What angles have sines of

a 0.5 **b** 0.785 **c** 0.64 **d** 0.877
e 0.999 **f** 0.707 **g** 0.102 **h** 0.722
i 0.888 **j** 0.2 **k** 0.7 **l** 0.75

2 What angles have cosines of

a 0.5 **b** 0.785 **c** 0.64 **d** 0.877
e 0.999 **f** 0.707 **g** 0.102 **h** 0.722
i 0.888 **j** 0.2 **k** 0.7 **l** 0.75

3 What angles have tangents of

a 0.6 **b** 0.38 **c** 0.974 **d** 0.247
e 0.3058 **f** 0.895 **g** 1.05 **h** 1.287
i 1.78 **j** 1.975 **k** 2.67 **l** 4.38

4 What angles have sines of

a 4 ÷ 5 **b** 2 ÷ 3 **c** 7 ÷ 10 **d** 5 ÷ 6
e 1 ÷ 24 **f** 5 ÷ 13 **g** 24 ÷ 25 **h** 1 ÷ 4

5 What angles have cosines of

a 4 ÷ 5 **b** 2 ÷ 3 **c** 7 ÷ 10 **d** 5 ÷ 6
e 1 ÷ 24 **f** 5 ÷ 13 **g** 24 ÷ 25 **h** 1 ÷ 4

6 What angles have tangents of

a 3 ÷ 5 **b** 7 ÷ 9 **c** 2 ÷ 7 **d** 9 ÷ 5
e 11 ÷ 7 **f** 6 ÷ 5 **g** 3 ÷ 4 **h** 1 ÷ 11

7 What happens when you try to find the angle with a sine of 1.2? What is the largest value of sine you can put into your calculator without getting an error when you ask for the inverse sine? What is the smallest?

8 **a** **i** What angle has a sine of 0.3? (Keep the answer in your calculator memory.)
ii What angle has a cosine of 0.3?
iii Add the two accurate answers of parts **i** and **ii** together.
b Will you always get the same answer to the above no matter what number you start with?

A closer look at the trigonometric ratios

Sine

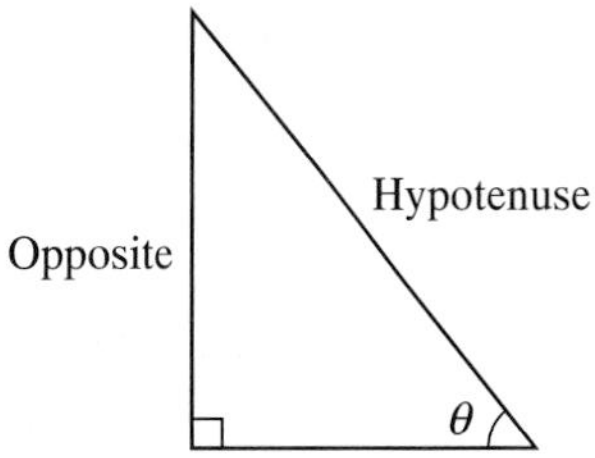

Remember

$$\text{sine } \theta = \frac{\text{Opposite}}{\text{Hypotenuse}}$$

Example 1 Find the angle θ, given that the opposite side is 7 cm and the hypotenuse is 10 cm.

Draw a diagram. [This is an **essential step.**]

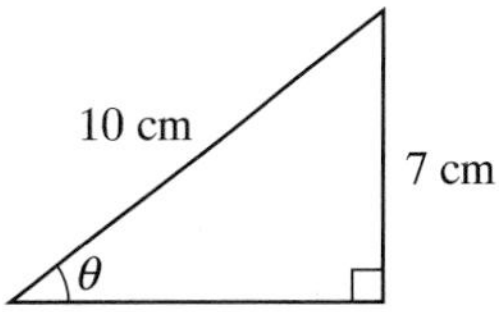

From the information given, we cannot directly find the angle and so we use the sine of the angle.

$$\sin \theta = \frac{\text{Opposite}}{\text{Hypotenuse}} = \frac{7}{10} = 0.7$$

What angle has a sine of 0.7? To find out, use the inverse sine function on your calculator.

Check that you get 44.4° to 1 dp.

Example 2 Find the length of the side marked a in this triangle.

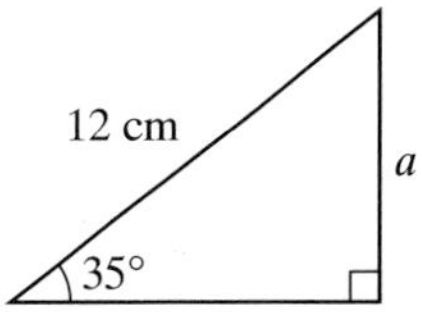

Side a is the opposite, so we use sin 35°.

$$\sin 35° = \frac{\text{Opposite}}{\text{Hypotenuse}} = \frac{\text{Opposite}}{12}$$

$$\Rightarrow \quad \text{Opposite} = \text{Hypotenuse} \times \sin 35°$$

$$\Rightarrow \quad a = 12 \times \sin 35° = 6.9 \text{ cm}$$

Example 3 Find the hypotenuse of this triangle.

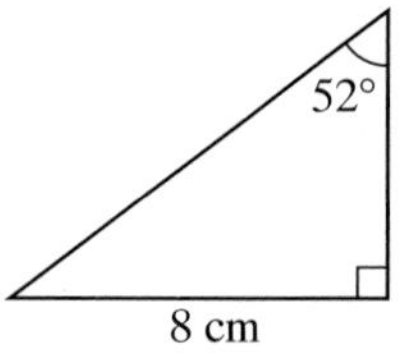

Note that although the angle is in the other 'corner', the opposite (8 cm) is again given. So we use

$$\sin 52° = \frac{8}{\text{Hypotenuse}}$$

$$\Rightarrow \quad \text{Hypotenuse} \times \sin 52° = 8$$

$$\Rightarrow \quad \text{Hypotenuse} = \frac{8}{\sin 52°} = 10.2 \text{ cm}$$

Exercise 4H

1 Find the angle marked x in each of these triangles.

a

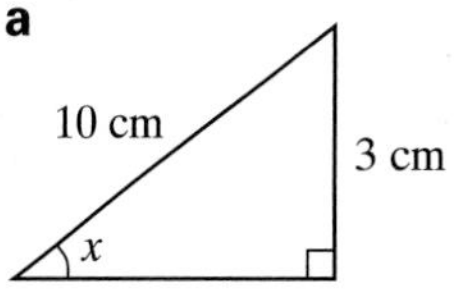

b

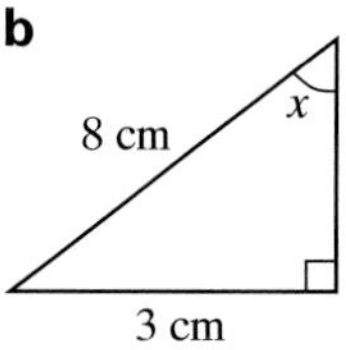

c

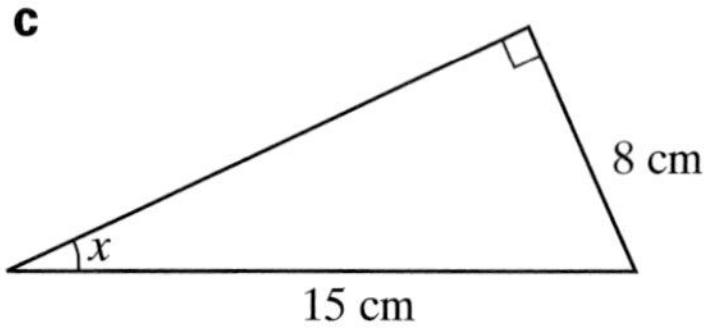

2 Find the side marked x in each of these triangles.

a

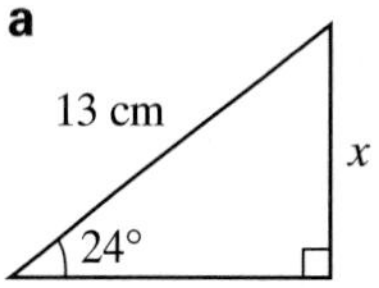

b

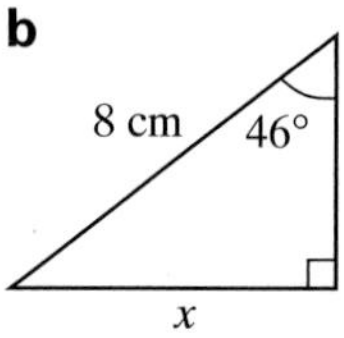

c

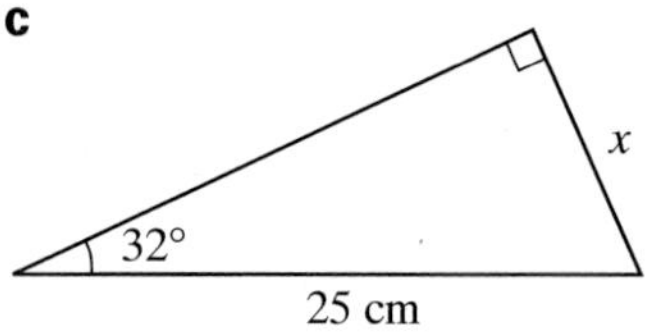

3 Find the side marked x in each of these triangles.

a

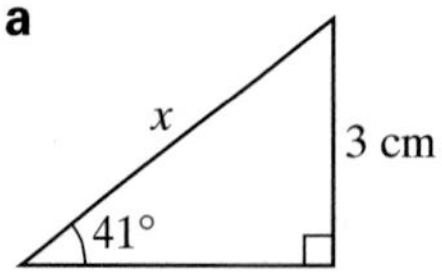

b

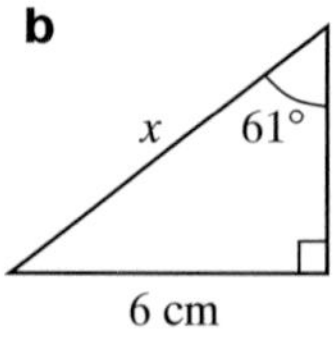

c

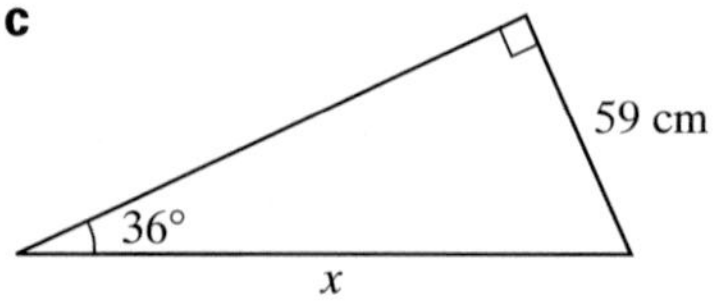

4 Find the side marked x in each of these triangles.

a

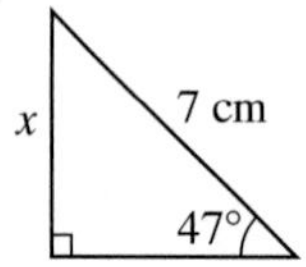

b

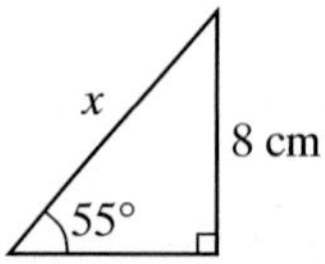

c

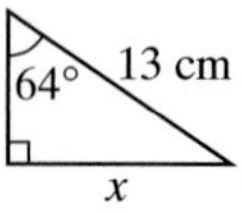

d

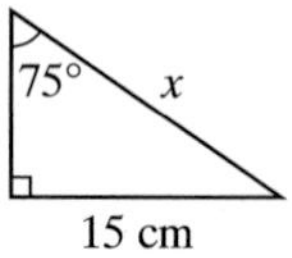

e

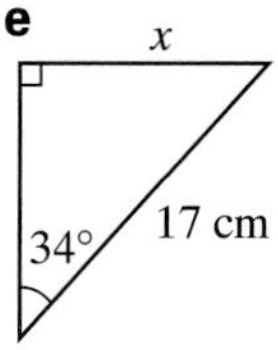

f

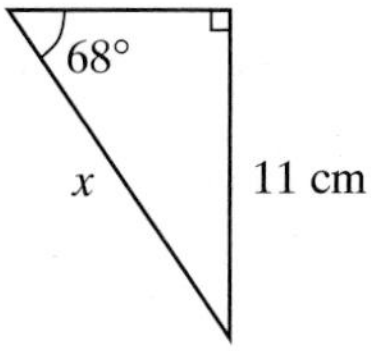

g

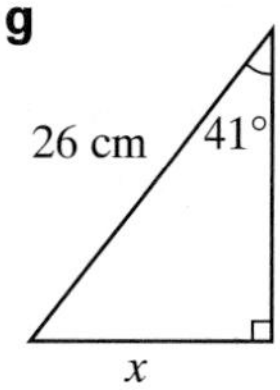

h

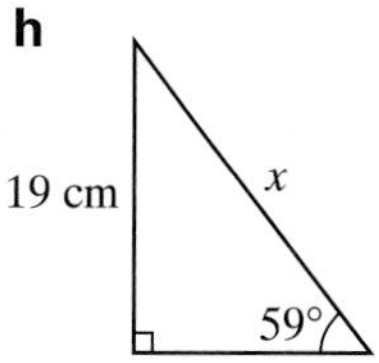

5 Find the value of *x* in each of these triangles.

a

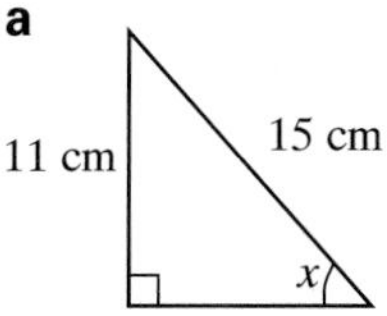

b

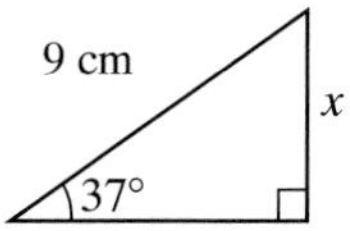

c

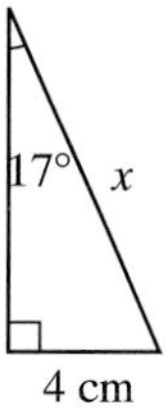

d

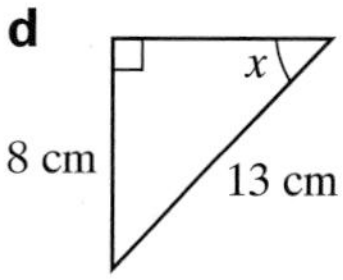

e

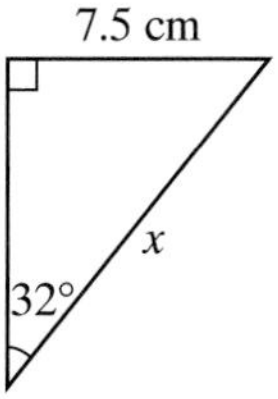

f

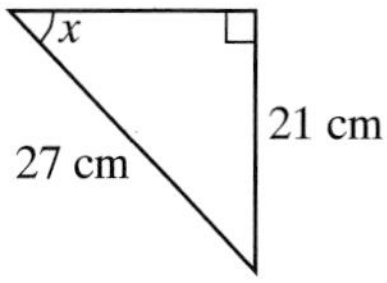

g

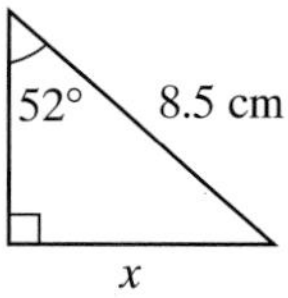

h

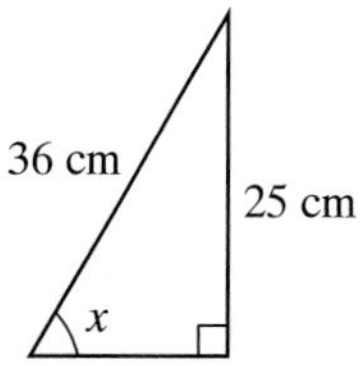

Cosine

Remember

$$\text{cosine } \theta = \frac{\text{Adjacent}}{\text{Hypotenuse}}$$

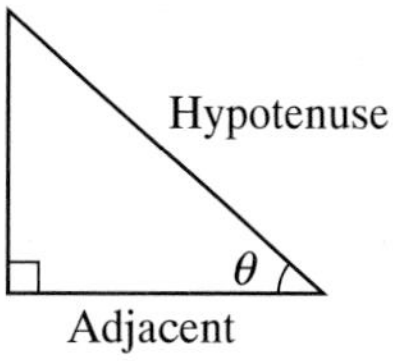

Example 1 Find the angle θ, given that the adjacent side is 5 cm and the hypotenuse is 12 cm.

Draw a diagram. [This is an **essential step**.]

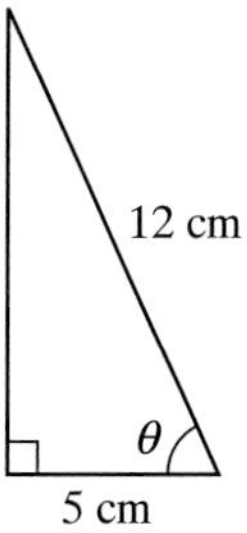

From the information given, we cannot directly find the angle and so we use the cosine of the angle.

$$\cos \theta = \frac{\text{Adjacent}}{\text{Hypotenuse}} = \frac{5}{12} = 0.416\,6667$$

What angle has a cosine of 0.416 6667? To find out, use the inverse cosine function on your calculator.

Check that you get 65.4° to 1 dp.

Example 2 Find the side marked a in this triangle.

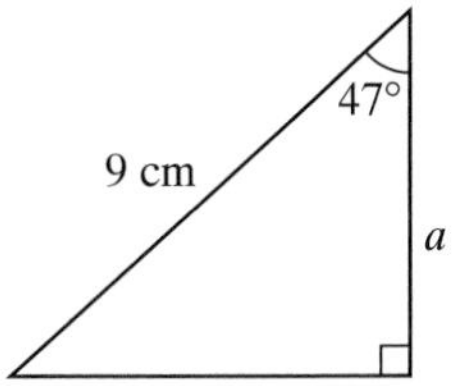

Side a is the adjacent, so we use cos 47°.

$$\cos 47° = \frac{\text{Adjacent}}{\text{Hypotenuse}} = \frac{a}{9}$$

$$\Rightarrow \quad a = 9 \times \cos 47° = 6.14 \text{ cm}$$

Example 3 Find the hypotenuse of this triangle.

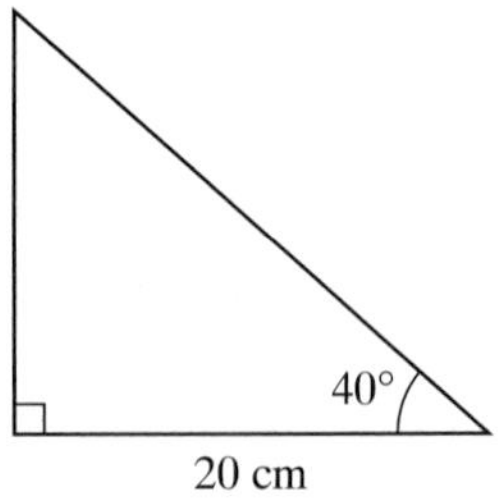

Side 20 cm is the adjacent, so we use cos 40°.

$$\cos 40° = \frac{20}{\text{Hypotenuse}}$$

$$\Rightarrow \quad \text{Hypotenuse} = \frac{20}{\cos 40°} = 26.1 \text{ cm}$$

Exercise 4I

1 Find the angle marked x in each of these triangles.

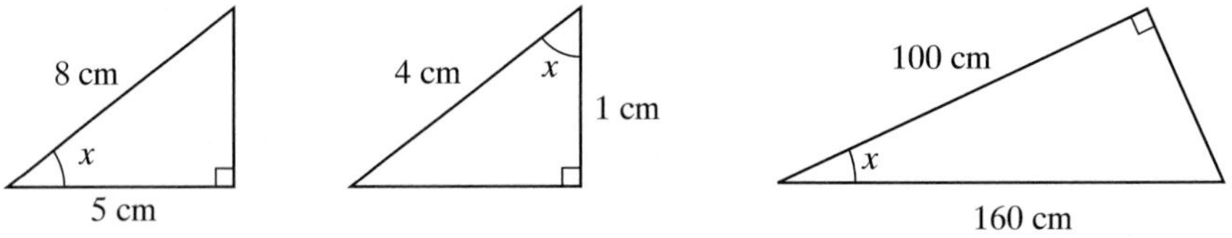

2 Find the side marked x in each of these triangles.

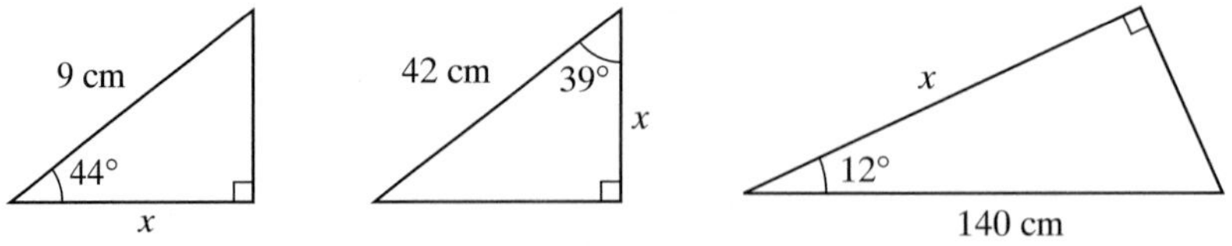

3 Find the side marked x in each of these triangles.

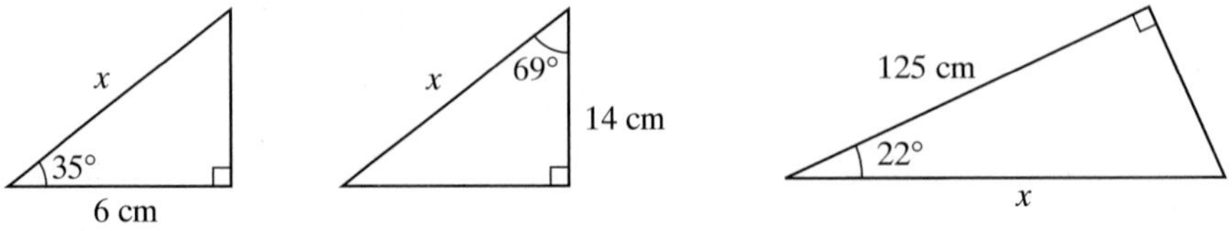

4 Find the side marked x in each of these triangles.

a

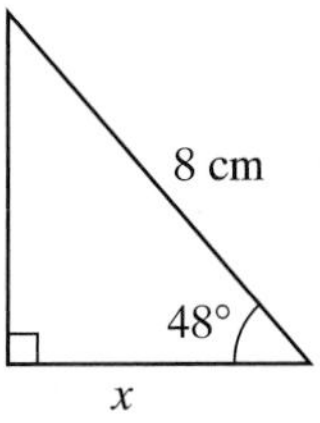

b

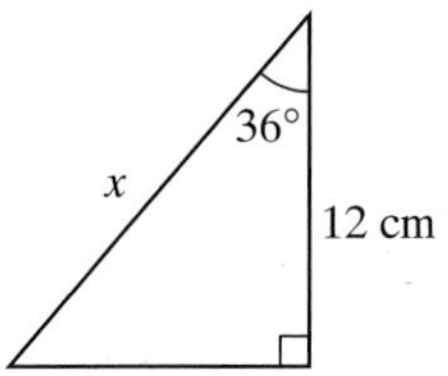

c

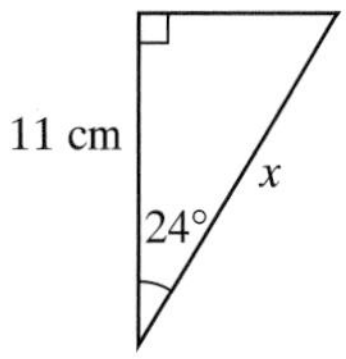

d

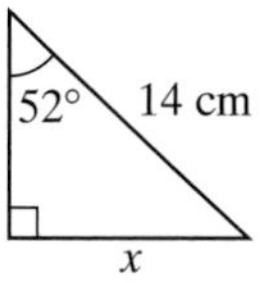

e

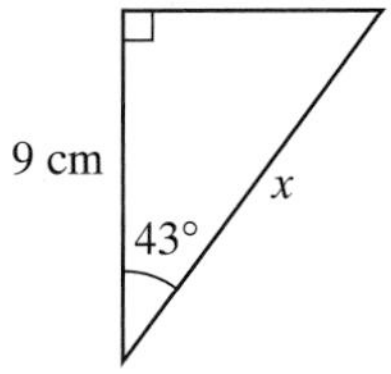

f

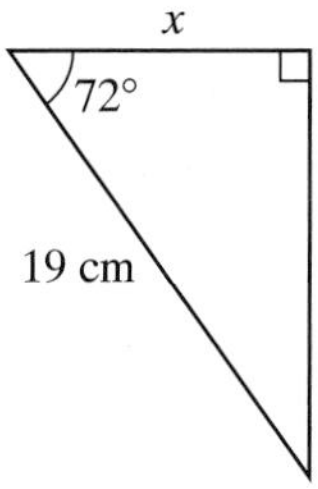

g

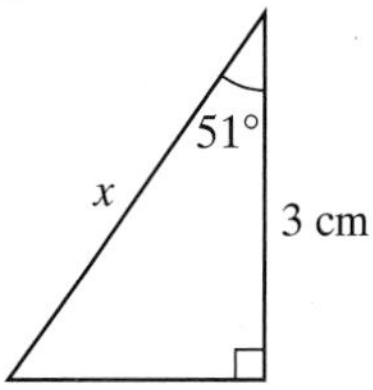

h

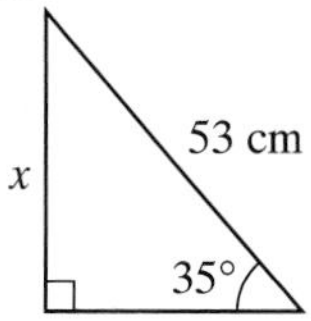

5 Find the value of x in each of these triangles.

a

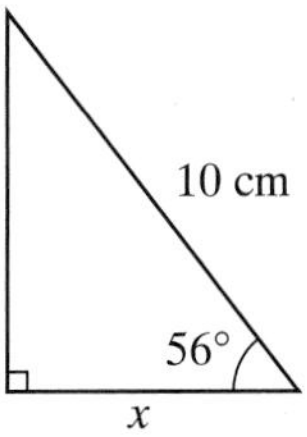

b

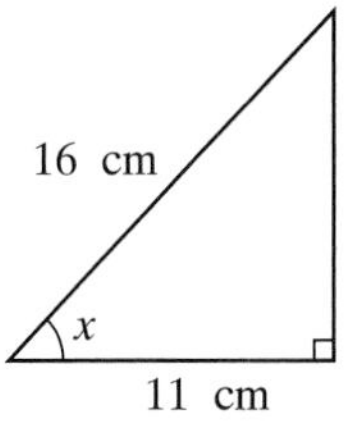

c

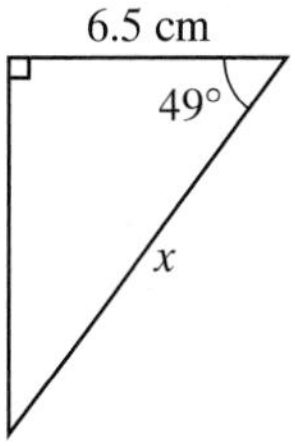

d

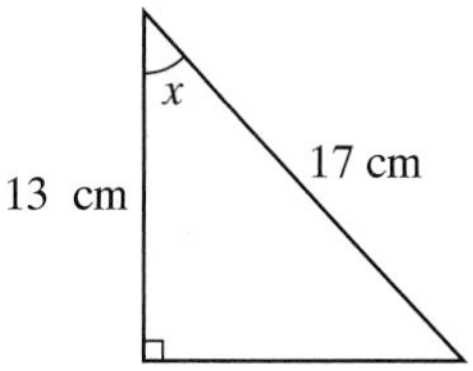

e

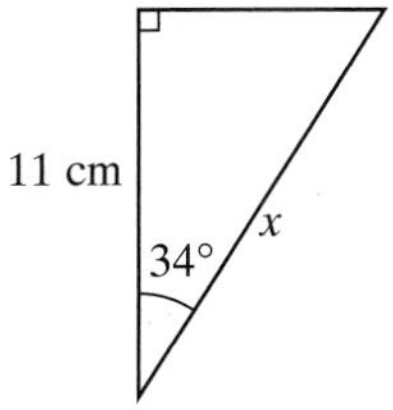

f

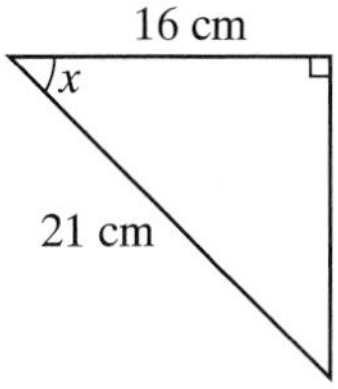

g

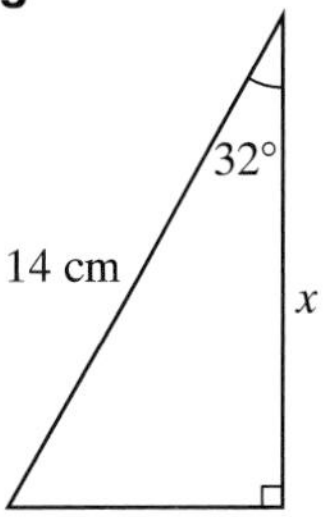

h

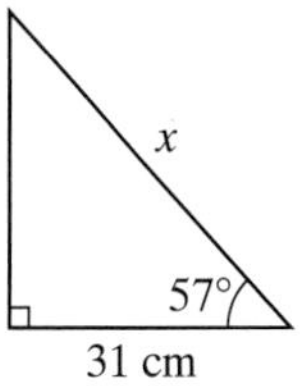

Tangent

Remember

$$\text{tangent } \theta = \frac{\text{Opposite}}{\text{Adjacent}}$$

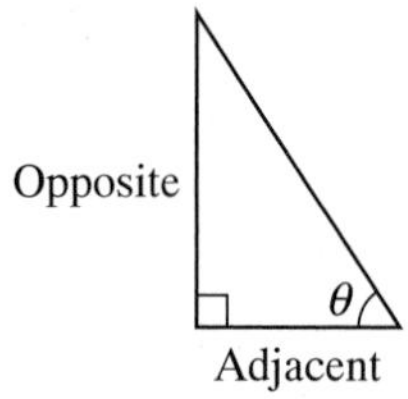

Example 1 Find the angle θ, given that the opposite side is 3 cm and the adjacent side is 4 cm.

Draw a diagram. [This is an **essential step**.]

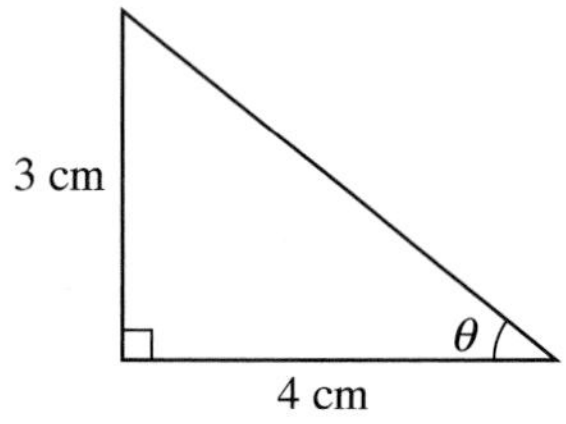

From the information given, we cannot directly find the angle and so we use the tangent of the angle.

$$\tan \theta = \frac{\text{Opposite}}{\text{Adjacent}} = \frac{3}{4} = 0.75$$

What angle has a tangent of 0.75? To find out, use the inverse tangent function on your calculator.

Check that you get 36.9° to 1 dp.

Example 2 Find the side marked x in this triangle.

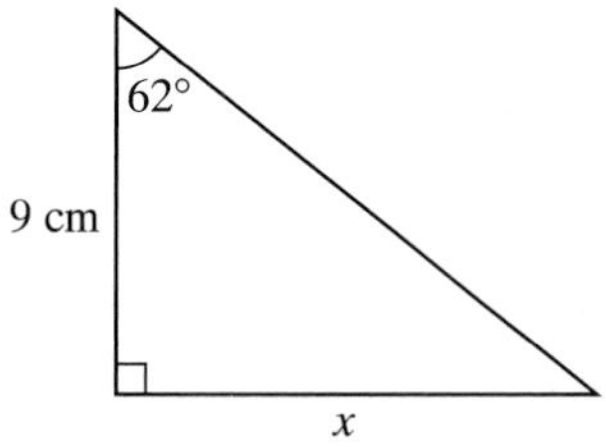

Note that the angle is in the other 'corner', so side x is the opposite and tan 62° is given by

$$\tan 62° = \frac{\text{Opposite}}{9} = \frac{x}{9}$$

$$\Rightarrow \quad = 9 \times \tan 62° = 16.9 \text{ cm}$$

Example 3 Find the side marked a in this triangle.

Side a is the adjacent, so tan 35° is given by

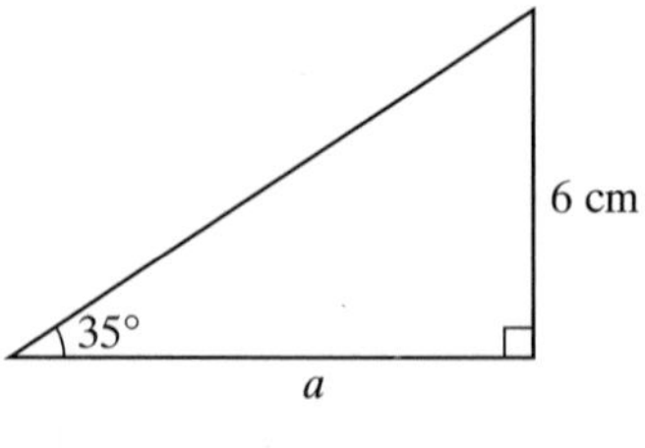

$$\tan 35° = \frac{6}{a}$$

$$\Rightarrow \quad a = \frac{6}{\tan 35°} = 8.6 \text{ cm}$$

Exercise 4J

1 Find the angle marked x in each of these triangles.

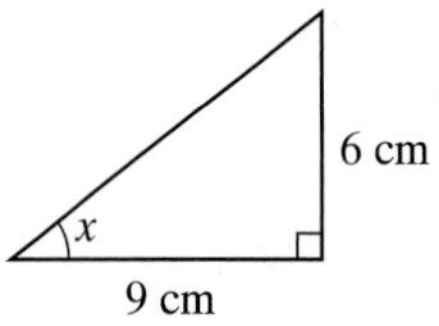

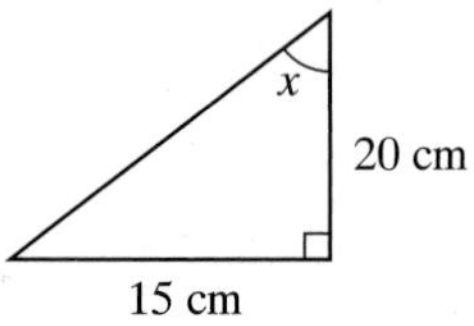

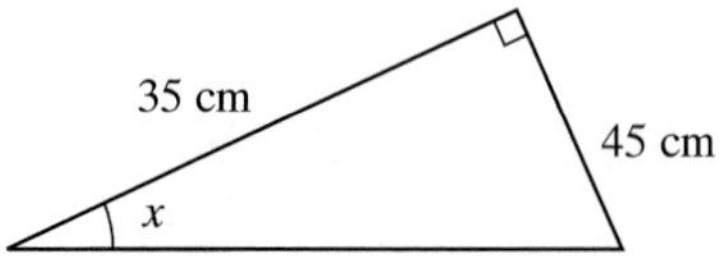

2 Find the side marked x in each of these triangles.

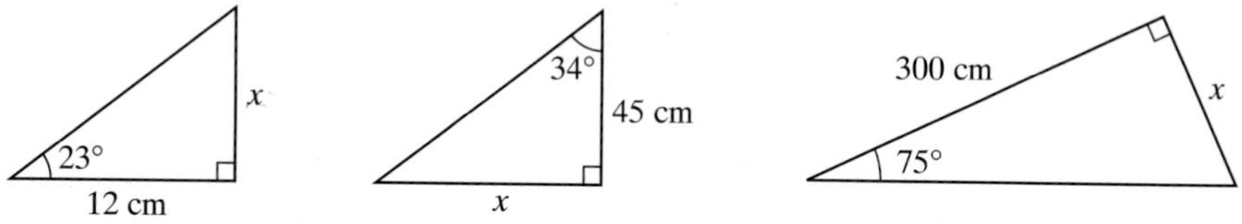

3 Find the side marked x in each of these triangles.

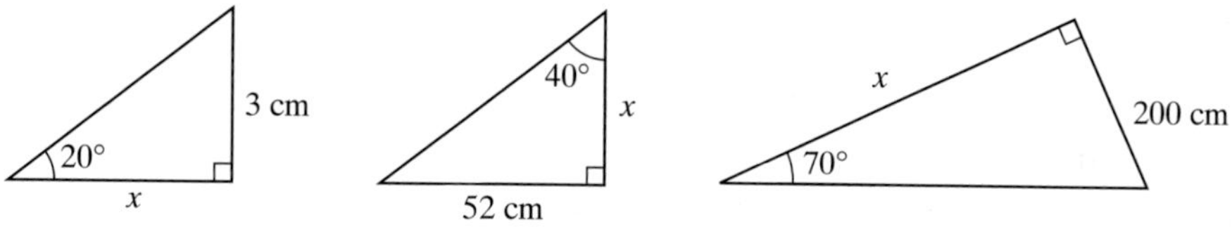

4 Find the side marked x in each of these triangles.

a

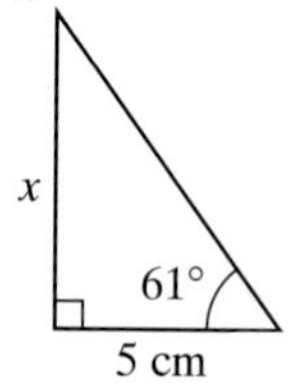

b

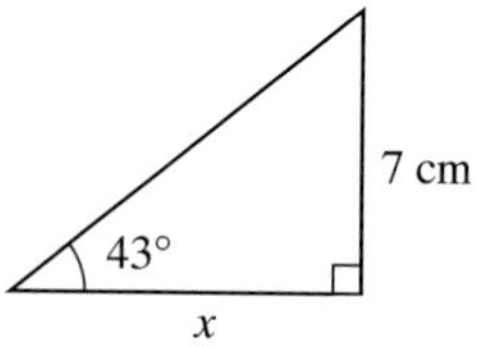

c

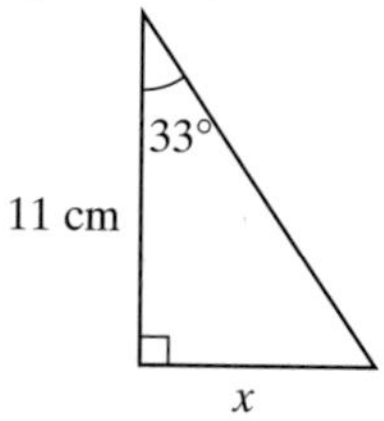

d

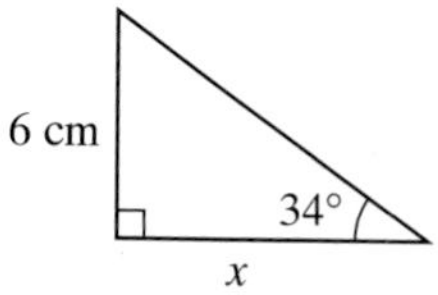

e

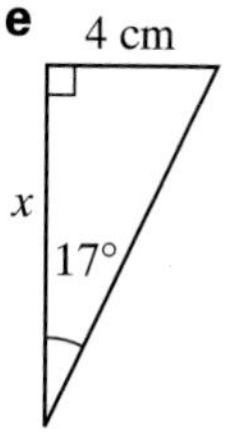

f

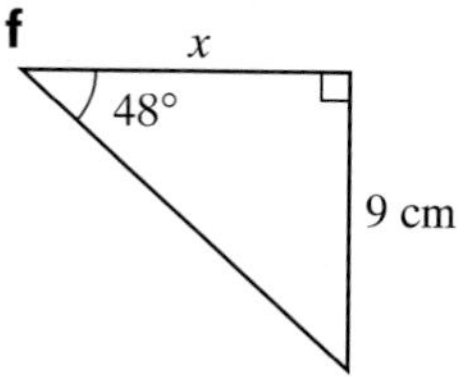

g

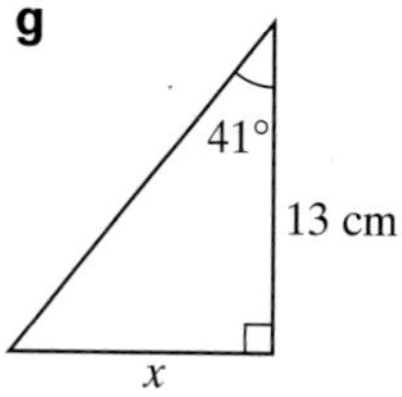

h

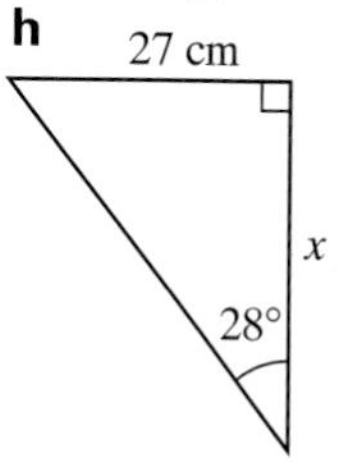

5 Find the value x in each of these triangles.

a

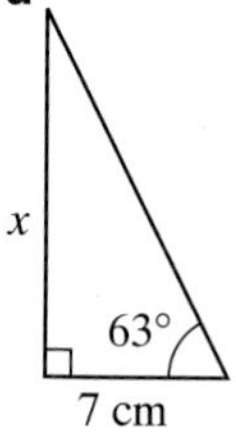

b

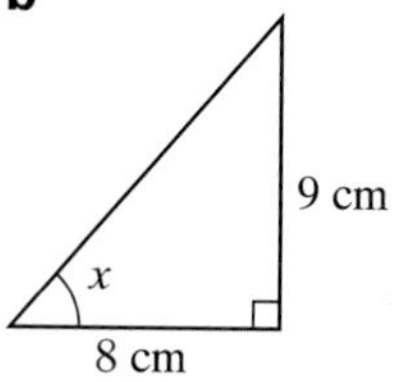

c

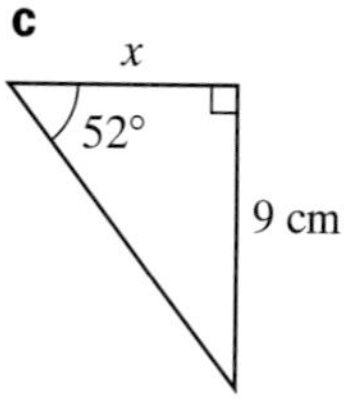

d

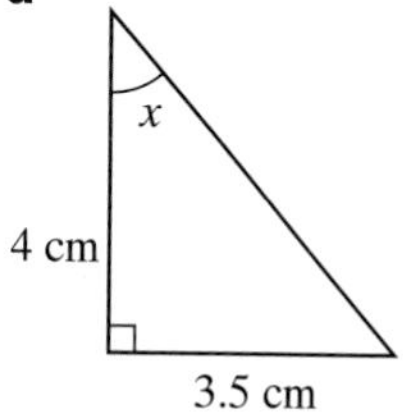

e

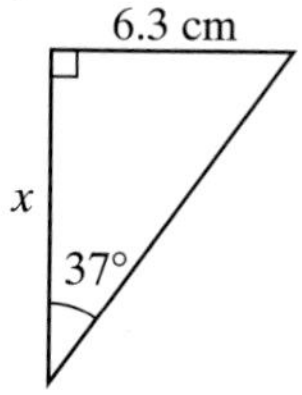

f

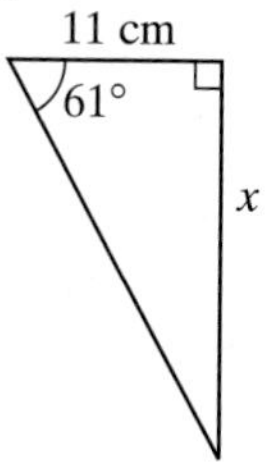

g

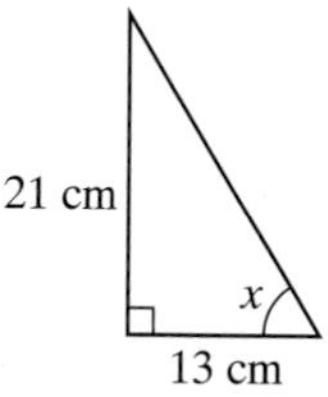

h

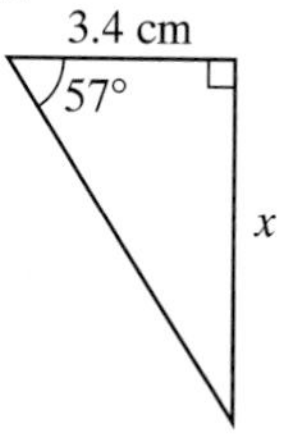

Which ratio do I use?

The difficulty with any trigonometric problem is knowing which ratio to use to solve it.

Examples 1 to 4 on this page and the next show you how to determine which ratio you need in any given situation.

Example 1 Find the side marked x in this triangle.

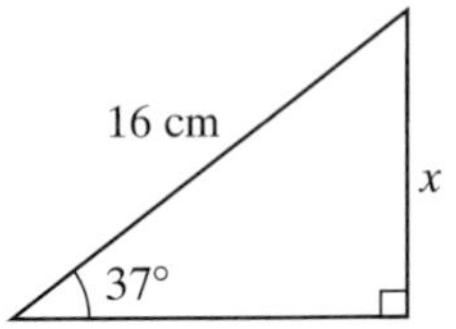

Step 1 Identify what information is given and what needs to be found. Namely, x is **opposite** the angle and 16 cm is the **hypotenuse**

Step 2 Decide which ratio to use. Only one ratio uses opposite and hypotenuse: **sine**.

Step 3 Remember: $\sin \theta = \dfrac{\text{Opposite}}{\text{Hypotenuse}}$

Step 4 Put in the numbers and letters: $\sin 37° = \dfrac{x}{16}$

Step 5 Rearrange the expression and work out the answer: $x = 16 \sin 37° = 9.629\,0404$

Step 6 Give the answer to an appropriate degree of accuracy: $x = 9.63$ (3 sf)

The answer has been given to 3 sf because the 16 cm was to 2 sf. We have gone to one more figure, as discussed on page 16.

In reality, you do not write down every step as above. Step 1 can be done by marking the triangle. Step 2 is done in your head. Steps 3–6 are what you write down.

Remember that examiners will want to see evidence of working. Any reasonable attempt at identifying the sides and using a ratio will probably get you some method marks – but only if the fraction is the right way round.

The following example is set out in a way that requires the **minimum** amount of working but gets **maximum** marks.

Example 2 Find the side marked x in this triangle.

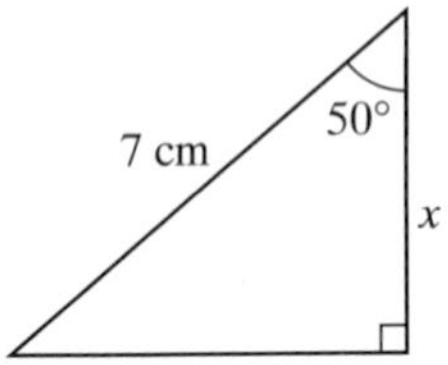

Mark on the triangle the sides we know and want to know (O, A or H).

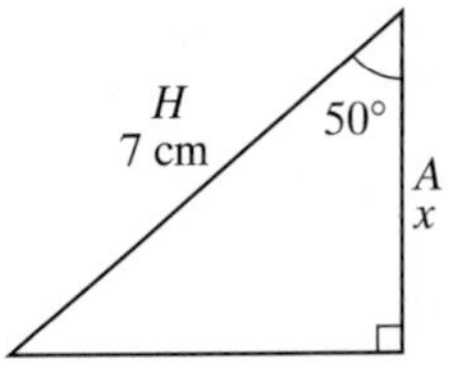

Recognise it is a cosine problem because we have A and H. So

$$\cos 50° = \frac{x}{7}$$

$$\Rightarrow \quad x = 7 \cos 50° = 4.5 \text{ cm}$$

Example 3 Find the angle marked x in this triangle.

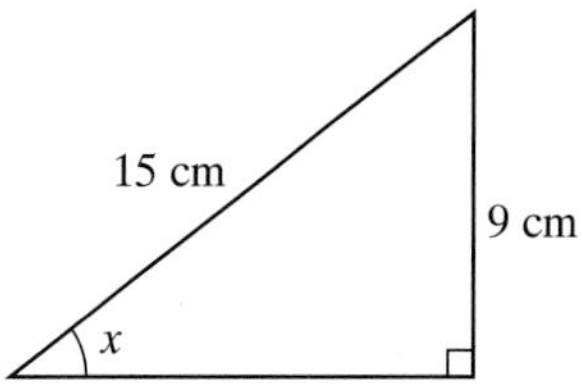

Mark on the triangle what we know and want to know.

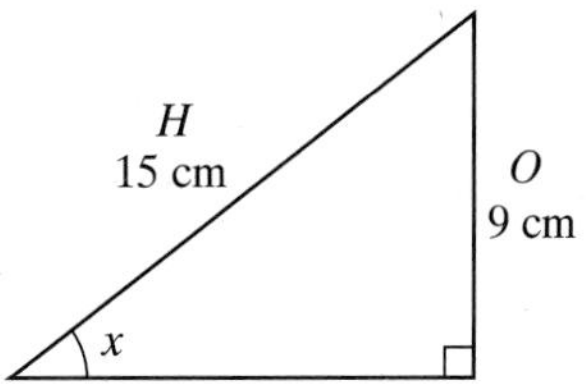

Recognise it is a sine problem because we have O and H. So

$$\sin x = \frac{9}{15} = 0.6$$

$$\Rightarrow \quad x = 36.9°$$

Example 4 Find the angle marked x in this triangle.

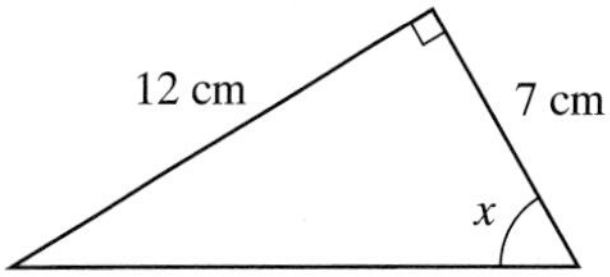

This triangle is not oriented in the usual way. So be careful when deciding which sides are which. If you are unsure, redraw the triangle so that it is oriented in a way that makes more sense. (This is the same as turning the page round to look at the triangle a different way.)

Mark on the triangle what we know and want to know.

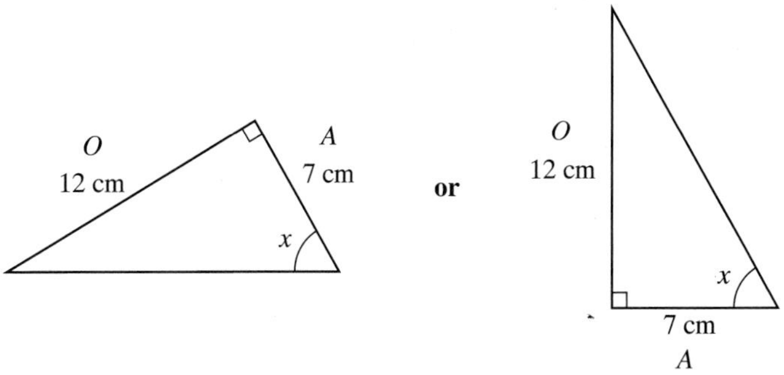

Recognise it is a tangent problem because we have O and A. So

$$\tan x = \frac{12}{7} = 1.714$$

$$\Rightarrow \quad x = 59.7°$$

Exercise 4K

1 Find the length marked x in each of these triangles.

a

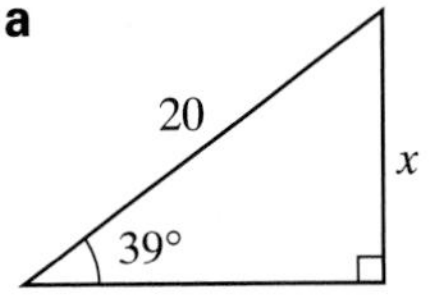

b

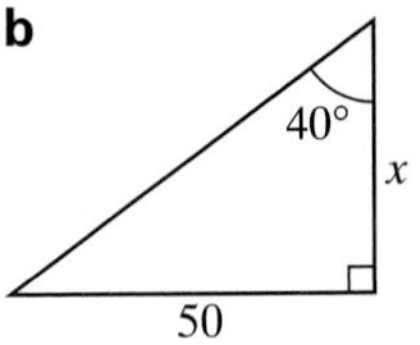

c

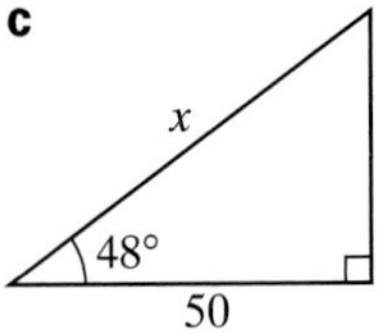

d

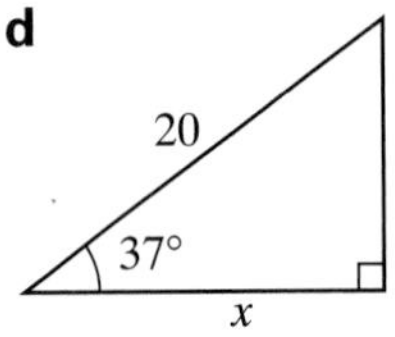

e

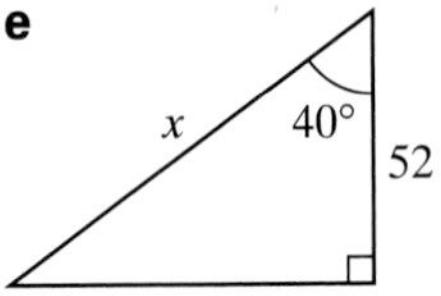

f

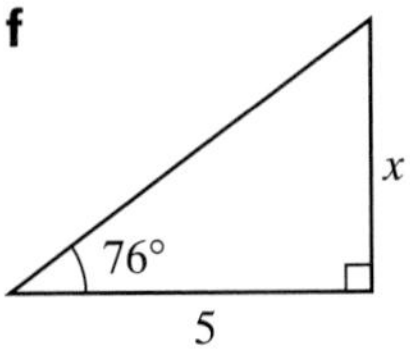

g

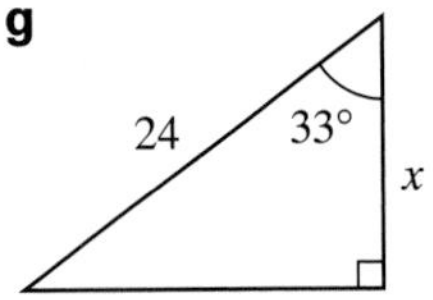

h

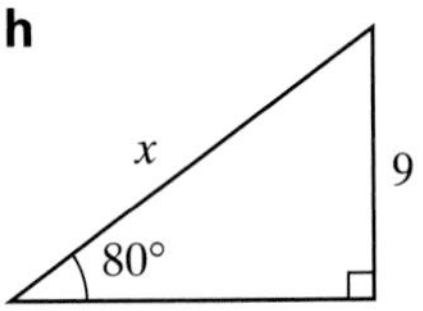

i

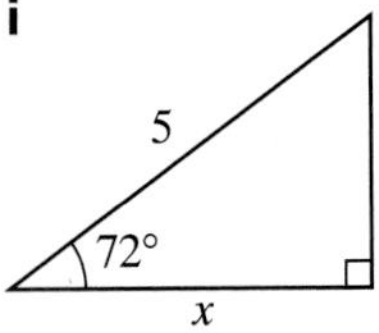

2 Find the angle marked x in each of these triangles.

a

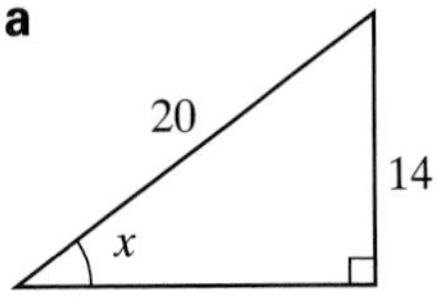

b

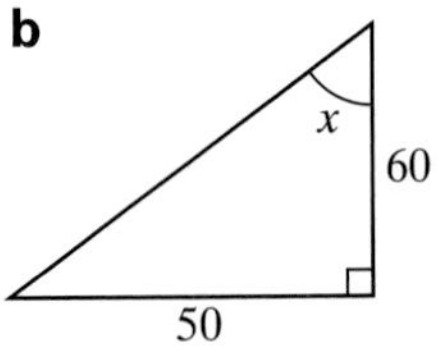

c

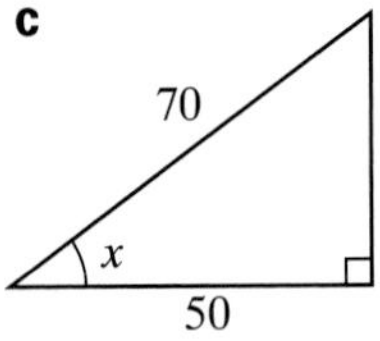

d

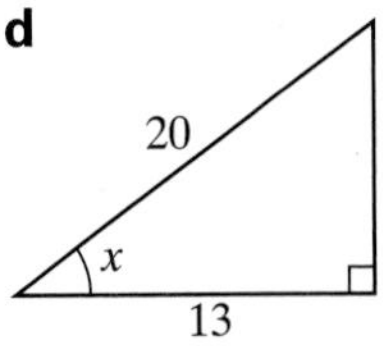

e

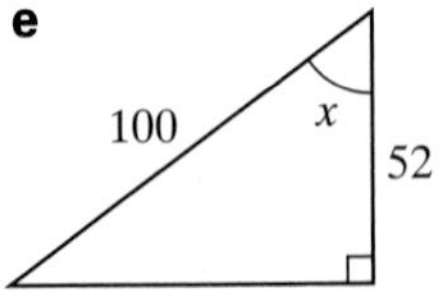

f

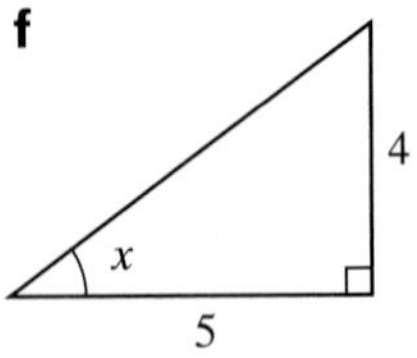

g

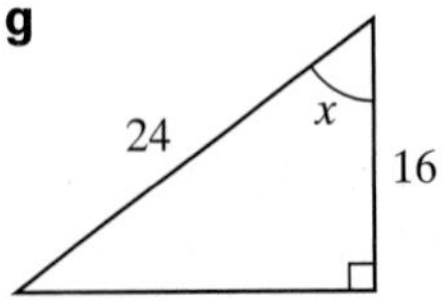

h

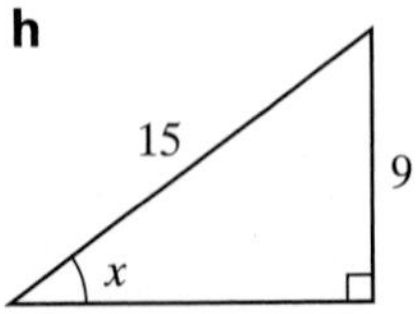

i

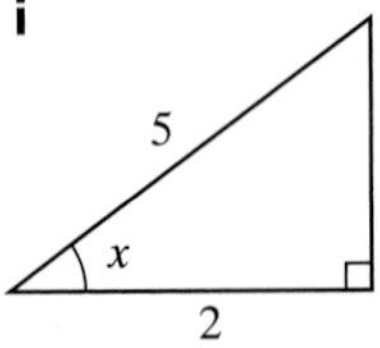

3 Find the angle or length marked x in each of these triangles.

a

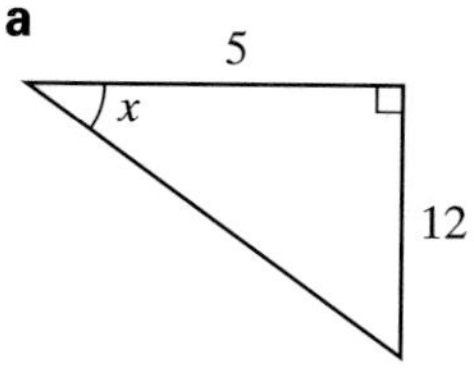

b

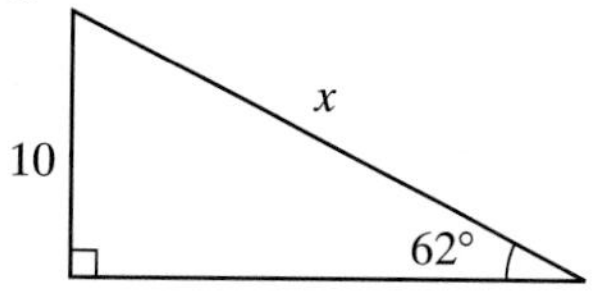

c

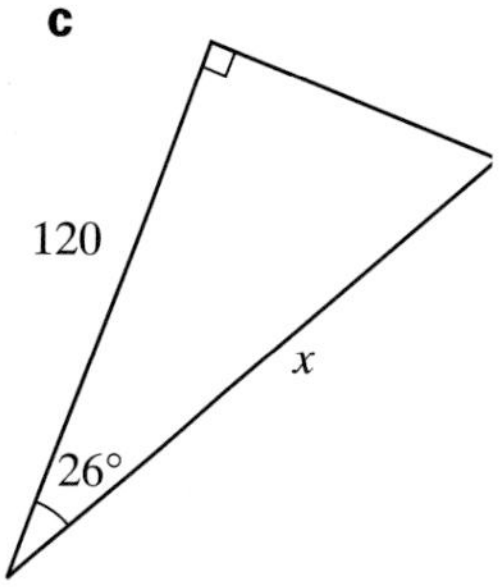

d

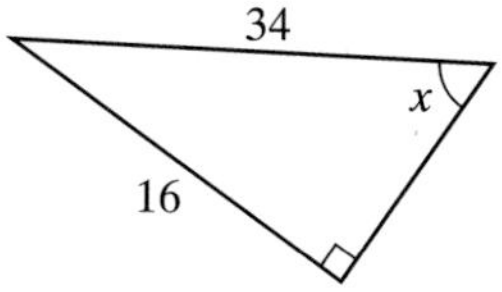

e

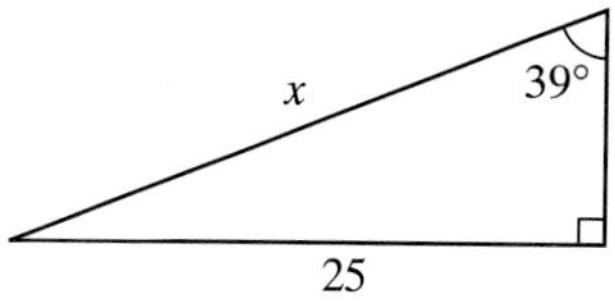

f

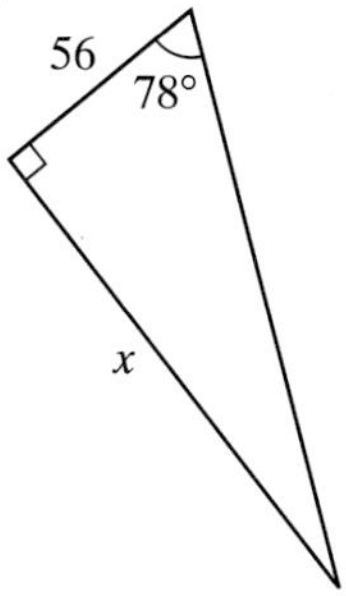

g

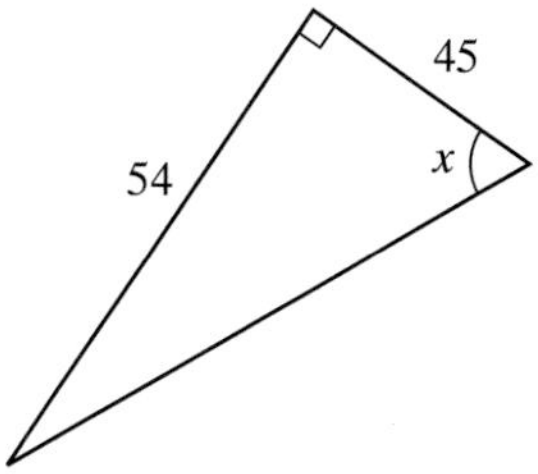

h

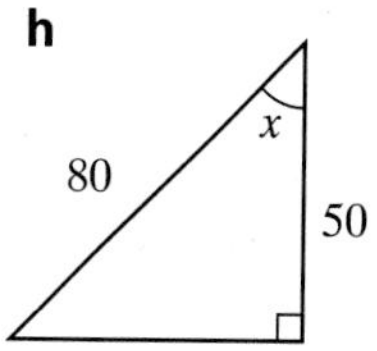

i

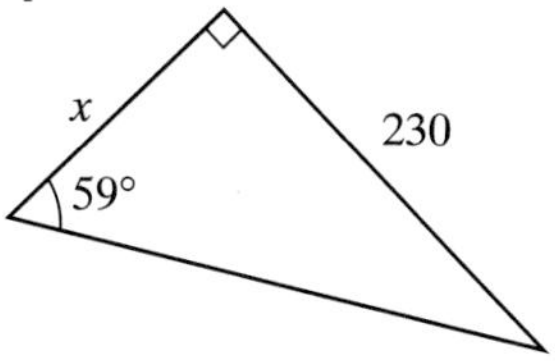

j

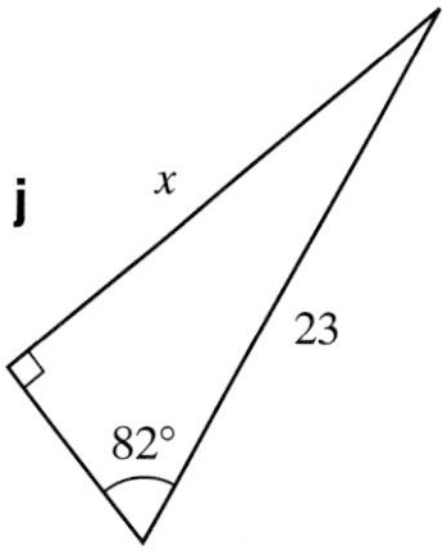

In the real world

Most trigonometry problems in GCSE examinations do not come as a straightforward triangle. Usually, solving a triangle is part of solving a practical problem. In this case, you **must draw** the triangle. Sometimes, the triangle to be used is a section of the diagram that accompanies the problem. Even in this case, **redraw** the triangle as a **separate** diagram. This will avoid any confusion and help you not only correctly to identify the sides but also to choose the correct ratio.

Example A window cleaner has a ladder which is 7 m long. He leans it against a wall so that the foot of the ladder is 3 m from the wall. What angle does the ladder make with the wall?

Draw the situation as a right-angled triangle.

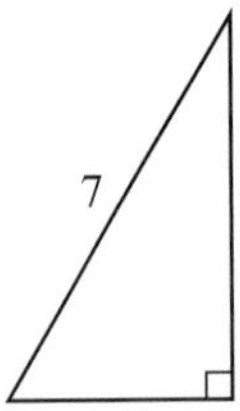

Then mark the sides and angle.

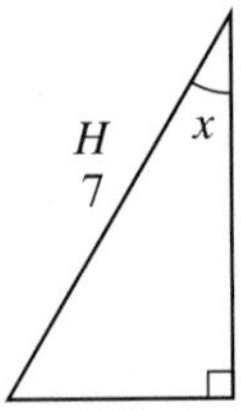

Recognise it is a sine problem because we have O and H. So

$$\sin x = \frac{3}{7} = 0.428$$

$$\Rightarrow \quad x = 25.4°$$

Exercise 4L

In questions **1** to **7**:

- Draw the triangle required.
- Put on the information given (angles and/or sides).
- Put on x for the unknown angle or side.
- Mark on two of O, A or H as appropriate.
- Choose the ratio to use.
- Write out the ratio with the numbers in.
- Rearrange if necessary, then work out the answer.

1 A ladder 6 m long rests against a wall. The foot of the ladder is 2.5 m from the base of the wall. What angle does the ladder make with the ground?

2 The ladder in question **1** has a 'safe angle' with the ground of between 60° and 70°. What are the safe limits for the distance of the foot of the ladder from the wall?

3 Another ladder of length 10 m is placed so that it reaches 7 m up the wall. What angle does it make with the ground?

4 Yet another ladder is placed so that it makes an angle of 76° with the ground. When the foot of the ladder is 1.7 m from the foot of the wall, how high up the wall does the ladder reach?

5 Use trigonometry to calculate the length of the ladder in question **4**.

6 Use trigonometry to calculate the angle that the diagonal makes with the long side of a rectangle 10 cm by 6 cm.

7 Use trigonometry to calculate the length of the diagonal of a square with side 4 cm.

8 The diagram on the right shows a frame for a bookcase. What angle does the diagonal strut make with the long side? Use trigonometry to calculate the length of the strut.

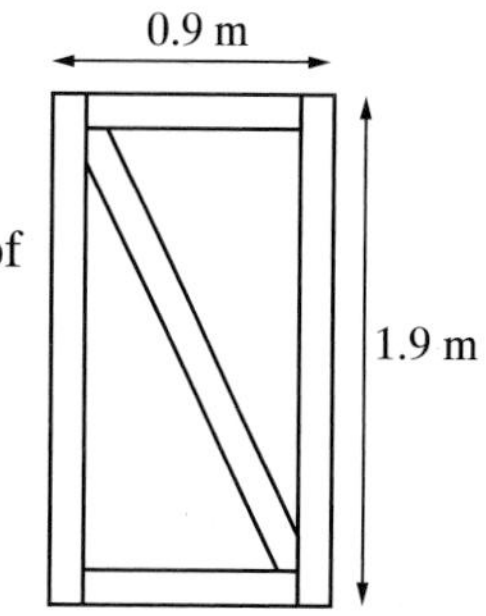

9 The diagram below shows a roof truss. What angle will the roof make with the horizontal? Use trigonometry to calculate the length of the sloping strut.

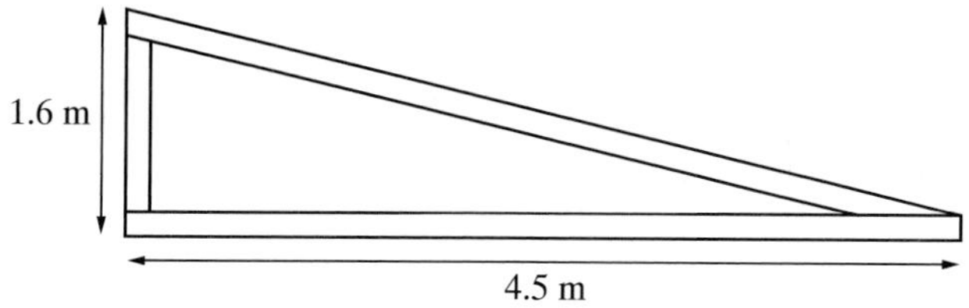

10 Building regulations state that the angle of a roof must be at least 25° to the horizontal. If the width of the roof truss in question **9** cannot be decreased, by how much does the vertical strut need to be increased so that the truss meets the regulations?

11 Alicia paces out 100 m from the base of a church. She then measures the angle to the top of the spire as 23°. How high is the church spire?

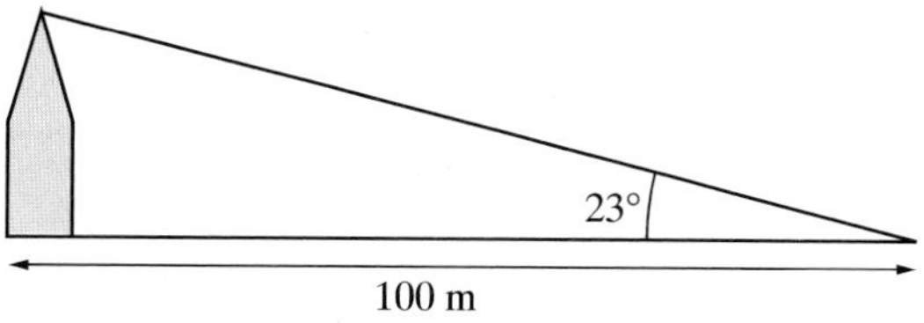

12 A girl is flying a kite on a string 32 m long. The string which is being held at 1 m above the ground, makes an angle of 39° with the horizontal. How high is the kite?

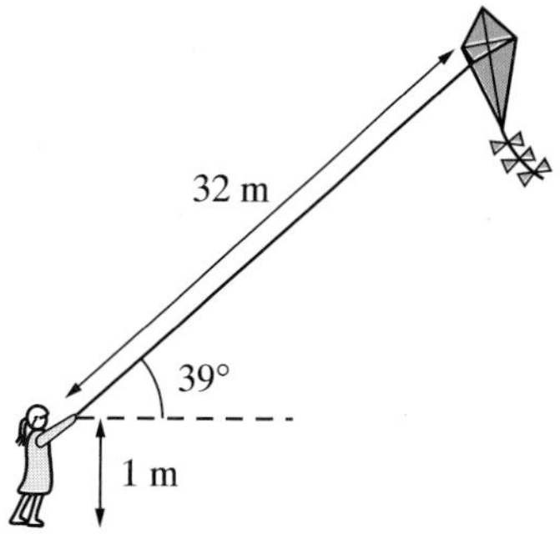

Special situations

A variety of special situations occur in trigonometry problems. These are commonly used in GCSE examinations because they give examiners opportunities to ask questions related to everyday experiences.

Angle of elevation and angle of depression

When you look **up** at an aircraft in the sky, the angle through which your line of sight turns from looking straight ahead (the horizontal) is called the **angle of elevation.**

When you are standing on a high point and look **down** at an object, the angle through which your line of sight turns from looking straight ahead (the horizontal) is called the **angle of depression.**

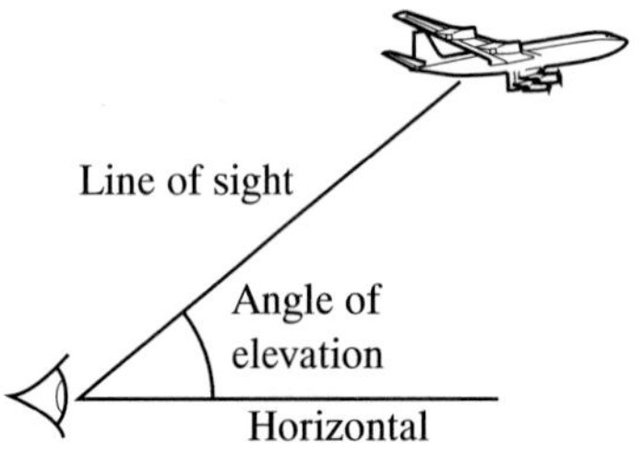

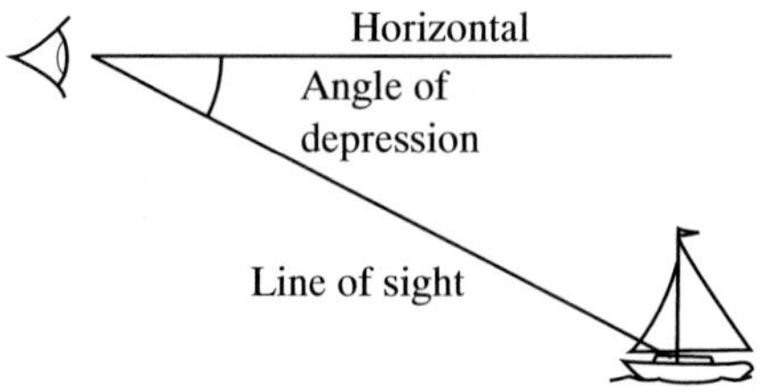

Example From the top of a vertical cliff, 100 m high, Andrew sees a boat out at sea. The angle of depression from Andrew to the boat is 42°. How far from the base of the cliff is the boat?

The diagram of the situation is shown in figure **i**.

From this, we get the triangle shown in figure **ii**.

i

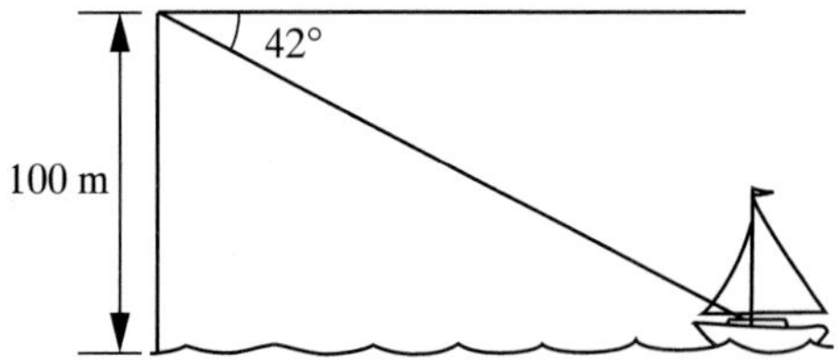

ii

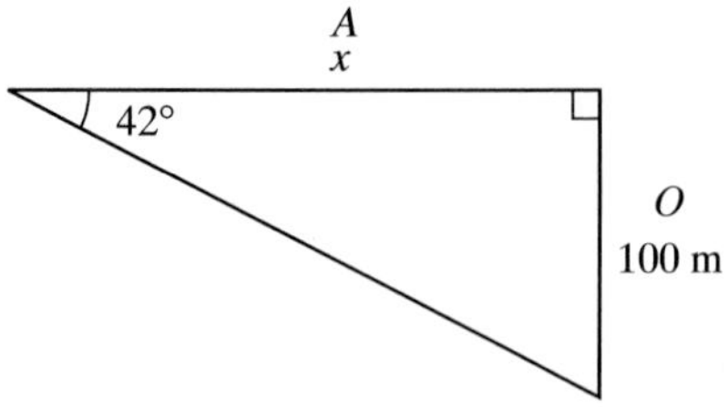

From figure **ii**, we see that this is a tangent problem. So

$$\tan 42° = \frac{100}{x}$$

$$\Rightarrow \quad x = \frac{100}{\tan 42°} = 111 \text{ m} \quad (3 \text{ sf})$$

Exercise 4M

1 Eric sees an aircraft in the sky. The aircraft is at a horizontal distance of 25 km from Eric. The angle of elevation is 22°. How high is the aircraft?

2 A passenger in the same aircraft hears the pilot say that they are flying at an altitude of 4000 m and are 10 km from the airport. If the passenger can see the airport, what is the angle of depression?

3 A man standing 200 m from the base of a television transmitter looks at the top of it and notices that the angle of elevation of the top is 65°. How high is the tower?

4 From the top of a vertical cliff, 200 m high, a boat has an angle of depression of 52°. How far from the base of the cliff is the boat?

5 From a boat, the angle of elevation of the foot of a lighthouse on the edge of a cliff is 34°. If the cliff is 150 m high, how far from the base of the cliff is the boat? If the lighthouse is 50 m high, what would the angle of elevation of the top of the lighthouse from the boat be?

6 A bird flies from the top of a 12 m tall tree, at an angle of depression of 34°, to catch a worm on the ground.

a How far does the bird actually fly?

b How far was the worm from the base of the tree?

7 I stand about 50 m away from a building. The angle of elevation from me to the top of the building is about 15°. How tall is the building?

8 The top of a ski run is 100 m above the finishing line. The run is 300 m long. What is the angle of depression of the ski run?

Bearings and trigonometry

A bearing is the direction of one place from another. The usual way of giving a bearing is as an angle measured from north in a clockwise direction. This is how a navigational compass and a surveyor's compass measure bearings.

A bearing is always written as a three-digit number. The diagram shows how this works, using the main compass points as examples.

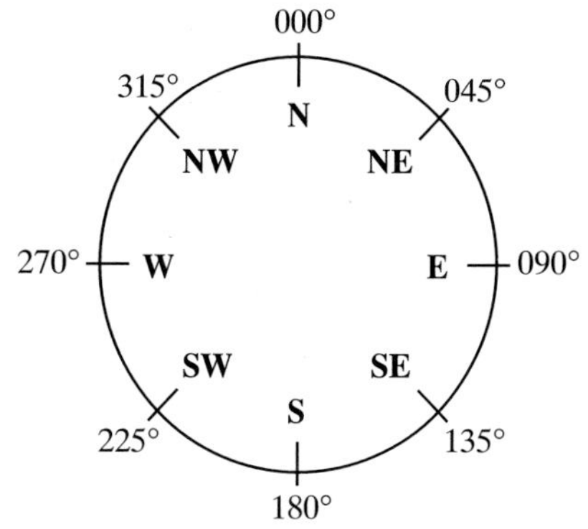

When working with bearings, these three rules must be followed:

- Always start from **north**.
- Always measure **clockwise**.
- Always give a bearing (in degrees) as a **three-digit number**.

The difficulty with trigonometric problems involving bearings is dealing with those angles greater than 90° whose trigonometric ratios have negative values. To avoid this, we have to find a right-angled triangle that we can readily use.

The example on the next page shows you how to deal with such a situation.

Example A ship sails on a bearing of 120° for 50 km. How far east has it travelled?

The diagram of the situation is shown in figure **i**. From this, we get the acute-angled triangle shown in figure **ii**.

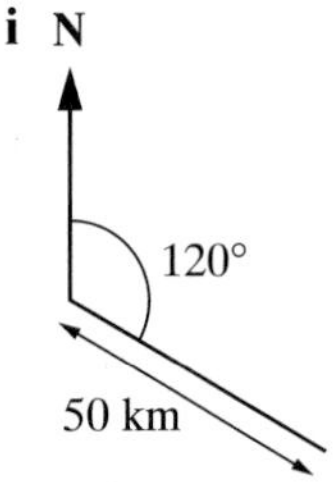

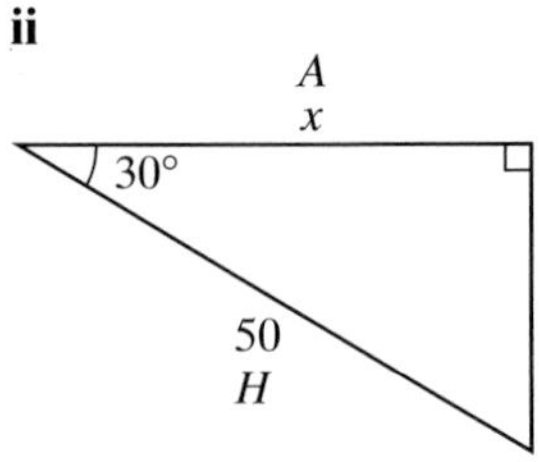

From figure **ii**, we see that this is a cosine problem. So

$$\cos 30° = \frac{x}{50}$$

$$\Rightarrow \quad x = 50 \cos 30° = 43.301 = 43.3 \quad \text{(3 sf)}$$

Exercise 4N

1 **a** A ship sails for 75 km on a bearing of 078°. How far east has it travelled?
b How far north has the ship sailed?

2 Lopham is 17 miles from Wath on a bearing of 210°.
a How far south of Wath is Lopham?
b How far east of Lopham is Wath?

3 A plane sets off from an airport and flies due east for 120 km, then turns to fly due south for 70 km before landing at Seddeth. What is the bearing of Seddeth from the airport?

4 A helicopter leaves an army base and flies 60 km on a bearing of 278°.
a How far west has the helicopter flown?
b How far north has the helicopter flown?

5 A ship sails from a port on a bearing of 117° for 35 km before heading due north for 40 km and docking at Angle Bay.
a How far south had the ship sailed before turning?
b How far north had the ship sailed from the port to Angle Bay?
c How far east is Angle Bay from the port?
d What is the bearing from the port to Angle Bay?

6 Mountain A is due west of a walker. Mountain B is due north of the walker. The guidebook says that mountain B is 4.3 km from mountain A, on a bearing of 58°. How far is the walker from mountain B?

7 The diagram shows the relative distances and bearings of three ships A, B and C.

a How far north of A is B? (Distance x on diagram.)

b How far north of B is C? (Distance y on diagram.)

c How far west of A is C? (Distance z on diagram.)

d What is the bearing of A from C? (Angle $w°$ on diagram.)

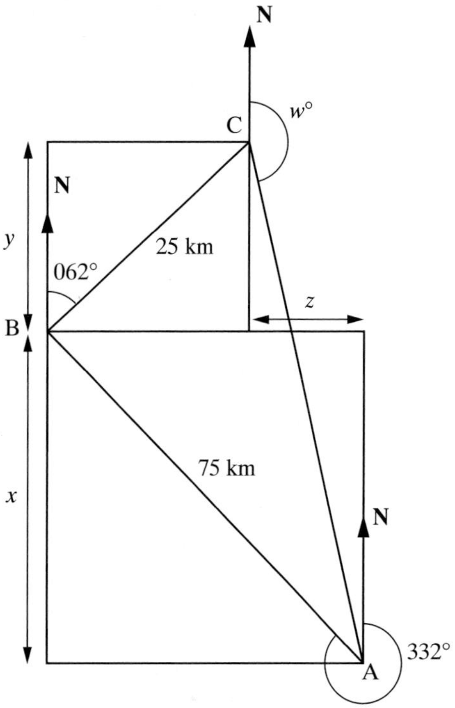

8 A ship sails from port A for 42 km on a bearing of 130° to point B. It then changes course and sails for 24 km on a bearing of 040° to point C, where it breaks down and anchors. What distance and on what bearing will a helicopter have to fly from port A to go directly to the ship at C?

Isosceles triangle

Isosceles triangles often feature in trigonometry problems because such a triangle can be split into two right-angled triangles that are congruent.

Example **a** Find the length x in this triangle. **b** Calculate the area of the triangle.

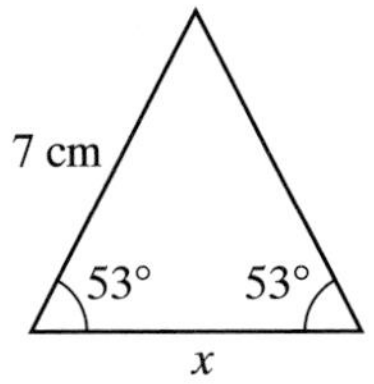

We look for a right-angled triangle. So draw a perpendicular from the apex of the triangle to its base, splitting the triangle into two congruent, right-angled triangles.

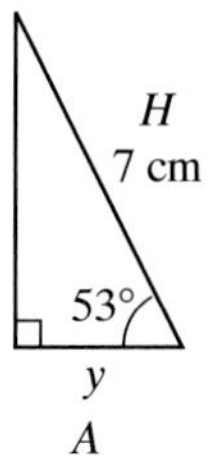

a To find the length y $(= \frac{1}{2}x)$, use the cosine of 53°, which gives

$$\cos 53° = \frac{y}{7}$$

$$\Rightarrow \quad y = 7 \cos 53° = 4.2 \text{ cm}$$

So the length $x = 2y = 8.4$ cm.

b To find the area of the original triangle, we need to find its vertical height, h. We have two choices, both of which involve the right-angled triangle of part **a**. We can use either Pythagoras's theorem ($h^2 + y^2 = 7^2$) or trigonometry. It is safer to use trigonometry again, since we are then still using known information.

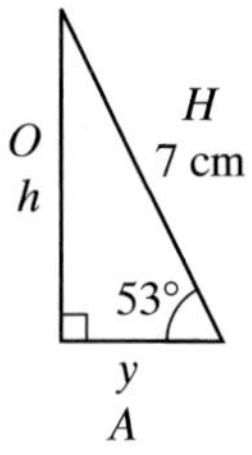

This is a sine problem, so

$$\sin 53° = \frac{h}{7}$$

$$\Rightarrow \quad h = 7 \sin 53° = 5.6 \text{ cm} \quad \text{(Keep the accurate figure in the calculator.)}$$

The area of the triangle = $\frac{1}{2}$ × base × height. (We should use the most accurate figures we have for this calculation.)

$$\text{Area} = \frac{1}{2} \times 8.425\,4103 \times 5.590\,4486$$

$$= 23.55 \text{ cm}^2$$

You are not expected to write down these 8-figure numbers, just to use them.

Note: If we use the rounded-off values to calculate the area, the answer would be 23.52, which is significantly different from the one calculated using the most accurate data. So **never** use rounded-off data when you can use accurate data – unless you are just estimating.

Exercise 4P

In questions **1** to **4** find the side or angle marked x.

1

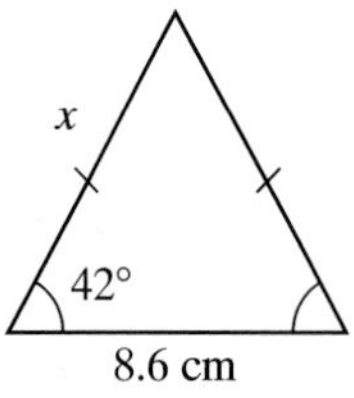

2

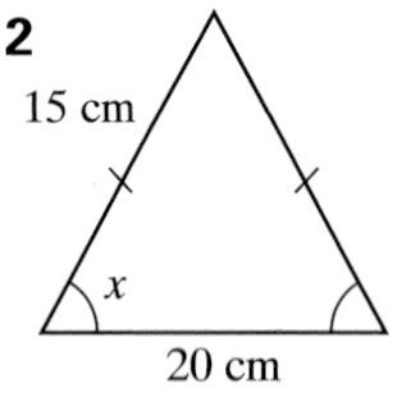

3

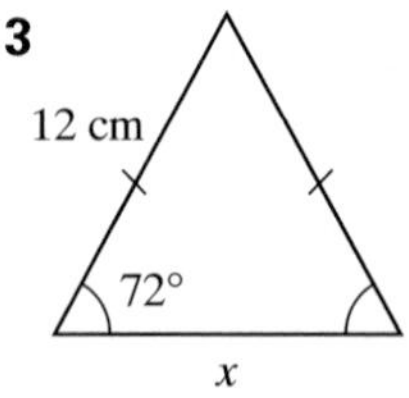

4

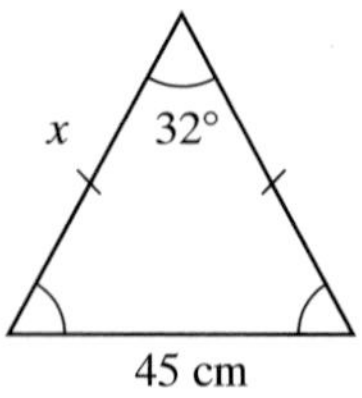

5 This diagram below shows a roof truss. How wide is the roof?

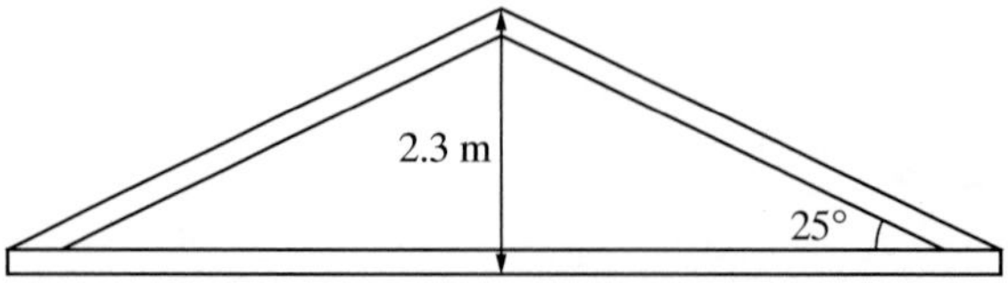

6 Calculate the area of each of these triangles.

a

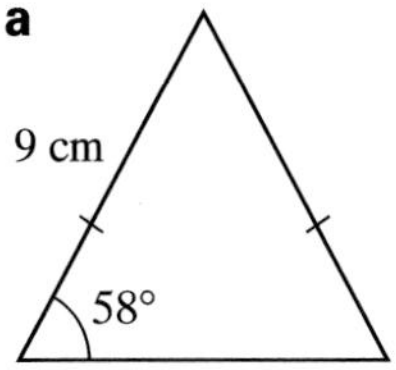

b

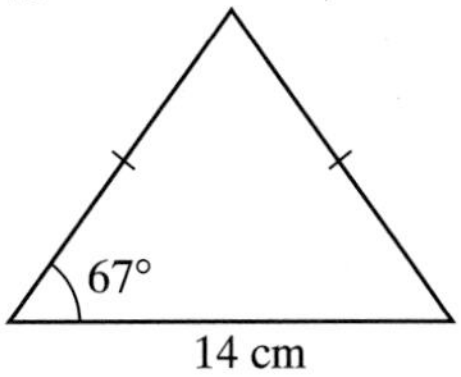

c

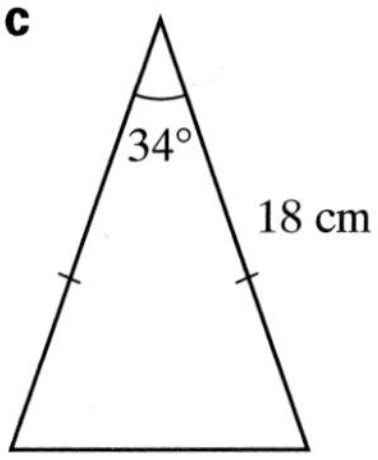

d

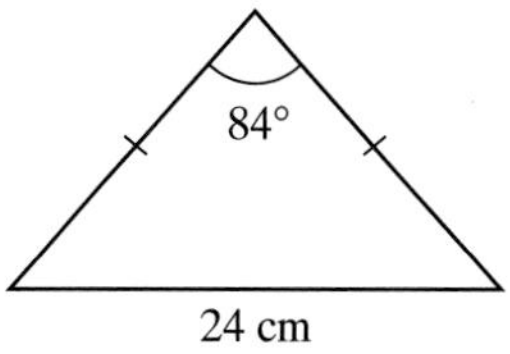

Possible coursework tasks

Trig squared

a Calculate **i** sin 73° **ii** cos 73°

b Calculate **i** $(\sin 73°)^2$ **ii** $(\cos 73°)^2$

c Calculate $(\sin 73°)^2 + (\cos 73°)^2$

d What do you notice?

e Investigate for other angles.

Sine waves

Draw the graph of $y = \sin x$, using multiples of 5° up to 90° as the values of x. You should find that the points you have plotted join up to make a curve. What happens if you go over 90°? (You may be able to do this investigation with a computer graph plotter.)

Special trig ratios

Use the diagram to find cos 60° without using a calculator.
What about sin 60° and tan 60°?
What about sin 30°, cos 30° and tan 30°?
Draw another triangle to find cos 45° without using a calculator.

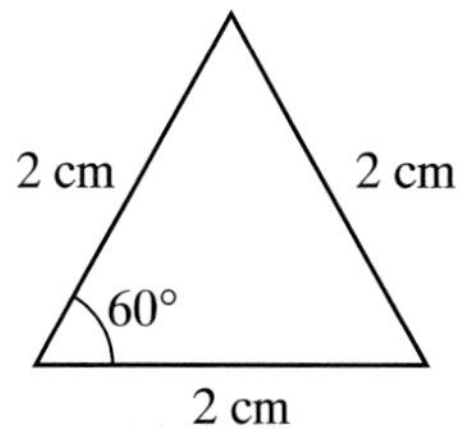

Rectangle in a semicircle

A rectangle can be drawn inside a semicircle as shown in the diagram. Investigate the area for different rectangles that can be drawn inside the semicircle.

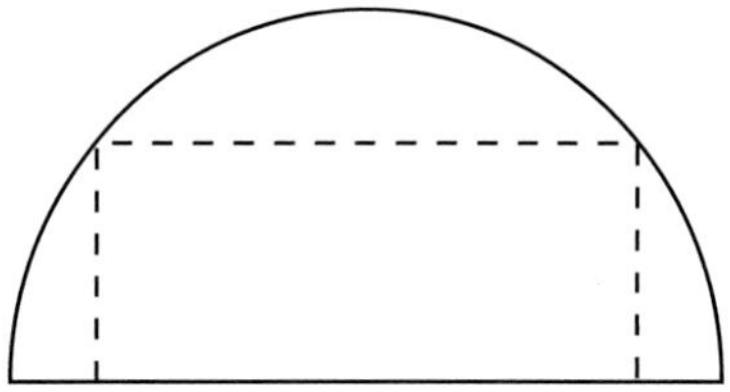

Practical trigonometry

You are standing on one side of a very wide river. There is no way of crossing it or bridging it. You have a 100-metre tape measure and a clinometer (for measuring angles).
Show how, using the equipment, you can calculate the width of the river.

Examination questions

1 The diagram shows the end view of the framework for a sports arena stand. Calculate the length AB.

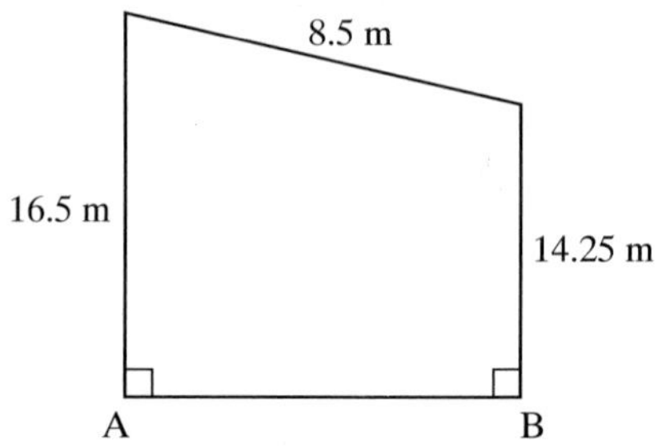

NEAB, Question 22, Specimen Paper 1, 1998

2 The diagram represents Nelson's voyage from Great Yarmouth to position B. Nelson's boat sails due east from Great Yarmouth for 14 km to position A. The boat then changes course and sails for 20 km to position B. On a map, the distance between G and A is 56 cm.

a Work out the scale of the map.

b Calculate the distance, in km, of B from Great Yarmouth.

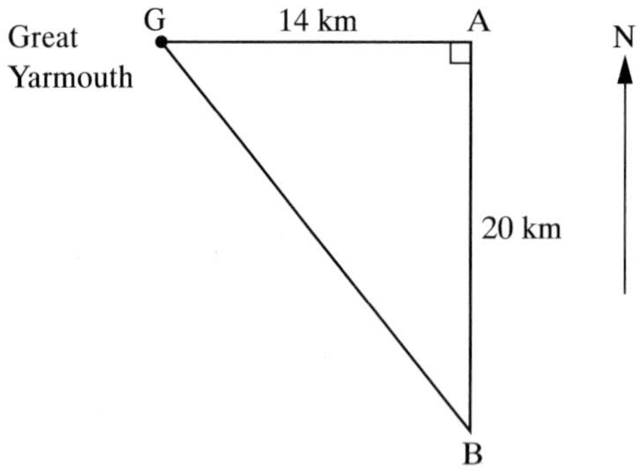

ULEAC, Question 14, Specimen Paper 3, 1998

3 This diagram is not drawn to scale. It shows the cross-section of a swimming pool 50 m long. It is 3 m deep at the deep end. The deepest part of the pool is 12 m long.

a Calculate the length of the sloping bottom of the pool AB.

b The pool is 7.5 m wide. What is its volume?

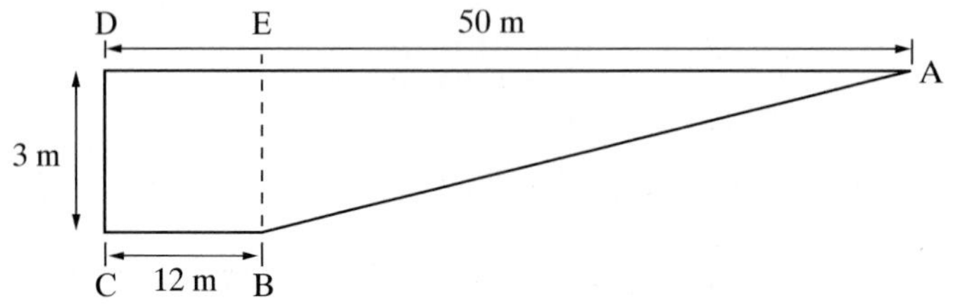

4 Beryl said that if the sides of a triangle were 14 cm, 11 cm and 9 cm, then it would be a right-angled triangle. Kevin said that it would not be a right-angled triangle. Who is correct, and why?

NEAB, Question 5, Paper 11, June 1995

5 An isosceles triangle has two sides of 12 cm and one of 7 cm. What is the area of the triangle?

NEAB, Question 8, Specimen Paper 2H, 1998

6 When an aeroplane takes off, its ascent is in two stages. These two stages are shown in the diagram as AB and BC.

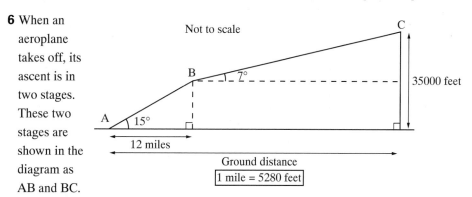

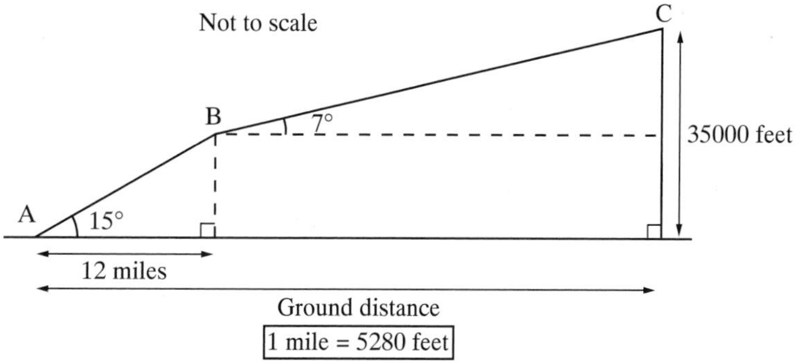

a In the first stage, the aeroplane climbs at an angle of 15° to the horizontal. Calculate the height it has reached when it has covered a ground distance of 12 miles. Give your answer correct to the nearest thousand feet.

b In the second stage, the aeroplane climbs at an angle of 7° to the horizontal. At the end of its ascent it has reached a height of 35 000 feet above the ground. Calculate the total ground distance it has covered. Give your answer in miles to a reasonable degree of accuracy.

NEAB, Question 15, Paper Q2, June 1995

7 a The diagram shows an isosceles triangle of base 10 mm and height 12 mm.

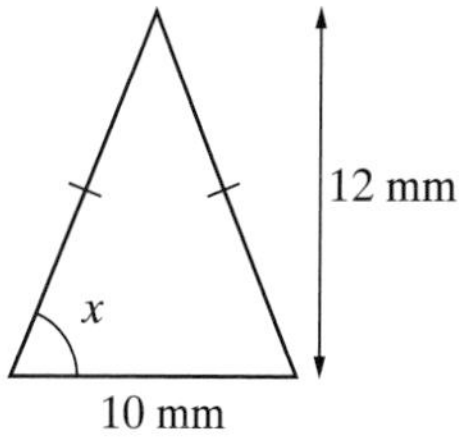

i Calculate the area of the triangle.

ii Write down the value of tan x, giving your answer as a decimal.

iii Calculate the size of angle x.

b In the right-angled triangle ABC, the hypotenuse AC is 35 cm, and the angle ACB is 48°. Calculate the length of the shortest side of the triangle.

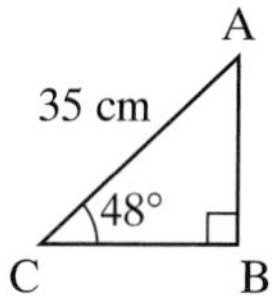

NEAB, Question 21, Paper 1, November 1995

8 The diagram shows a roofing frame frame ABCD.

AB = 7 m, BC = 5 m, DB = 3 m, angle ABD = angle DBC = 90°

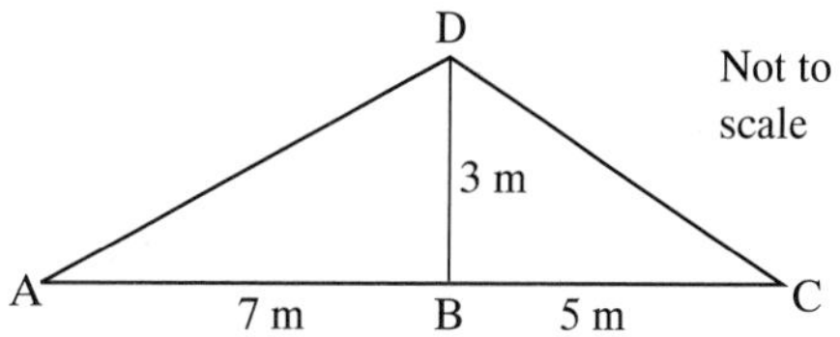

a Calculate the length of AD.

b Calculate the size of angle DCB.

MEG, Question 14, Paper 2, June 1994

9 A crane is used to lift a load by means of a hook on the end of a steel rope.

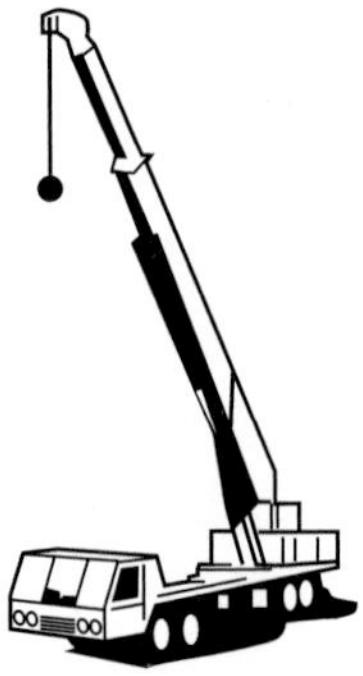

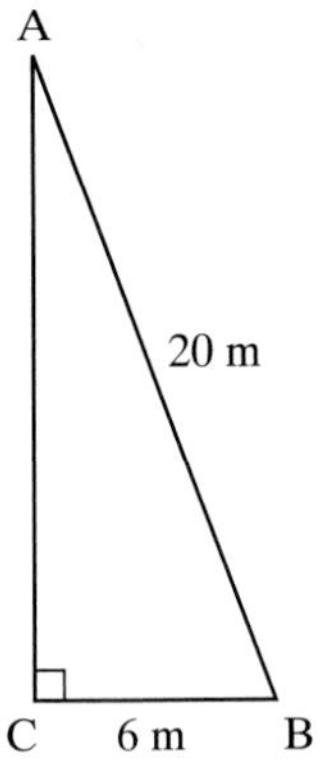

a **i** The jib of the crane is 20 metres long. A load is placed at a point C which is 6 metres horizontally from the base B of the jib. Calculate the length of the rope AC required to reach the load.

ii Calculate the angle the jib makes with the horizontal in this position.

b The jib is extended to 30 metres and moved to an angle of 65° with the horizontal. Calculate the vertical height of the tip of the jib above the base.

NICCEA, Question 19, Paper 3, June 1995

10 The diagram shows an 8 m ladder leaning against a wall. Instructions for finding the safest position for the foot of the ladder are also given.

The safest position for your ladder

Instructions
The safest distance for the foot of the ladder from the wall is one quarter of the length of the ladder

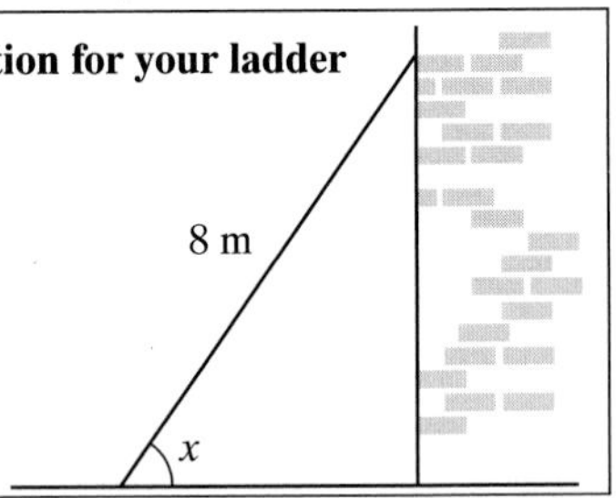

a An 8 m ladder is placed against a wall using the safety instructions above. Calculate the size of the angle marked x.

b Use trigonometry to calculate how far up the wall this ladder will reach when it is in the safest position.

NEAB, Question 17, Paper 1Q, November 1994

11 A top of a vertical cliff is 60 m above sea level. At 23.45 on Thursday, a life raft is 1800 m from the base of the cliff.

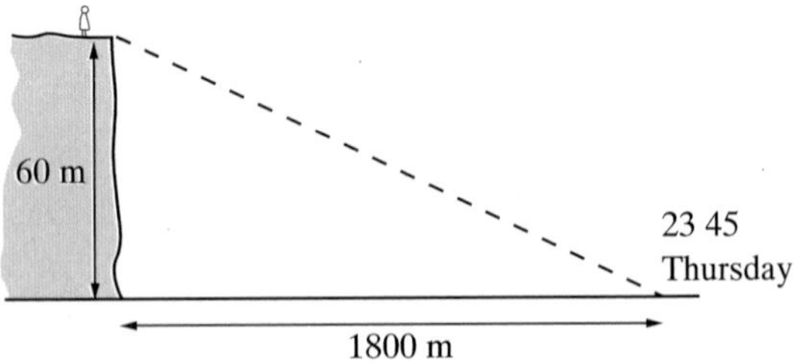

a Calculate the angle of elevation of the top of the cliff from the life raft.

b At 01.15 on Friday, the angle of elevation of the top of the cliff from the life raft is 7.6°. How far from the foot of the cliff is the life raft?

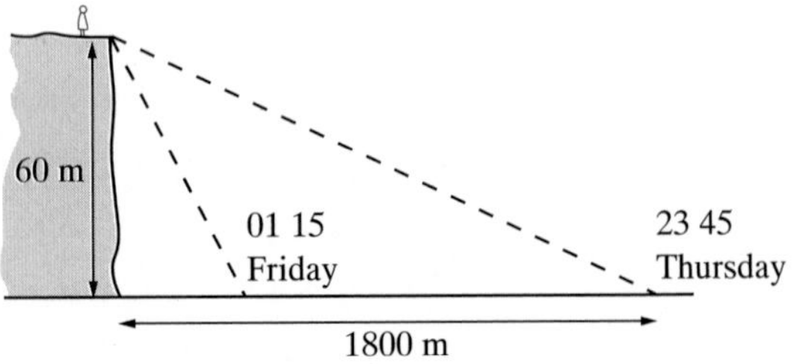

c At what speed is the life raft drifting towards the cliff?

WJEC, Question 14, Specimen Paper 2, 1998

12 In the diagram, ABCD is a parallelogram.

a Calculate the height, DN, of the parallelogram.

b Calculate the area of the parallelogram.

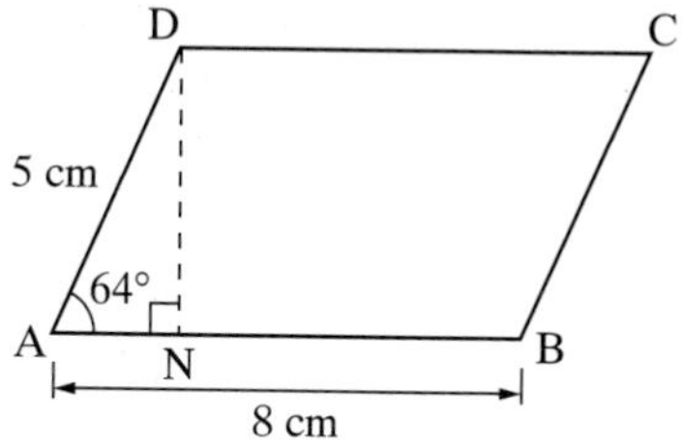

MEG, Question 14, Specimen Paper 3

13 An aeroplane is flying from Leeds (L) to London Heathrow (H). It flies 150 miles on a bearing 136° to a point A. It then turns through 90° and flies the final 80 miles to H.

a i Show clearly why the angle marked x is equal to 46°.

ii Give the bearing of H from A.

b Use Pythagoras' theorem to calculate the distance LH.

c i Calculate the size of the angle marked y.

ii Work out the bearing of L from H.

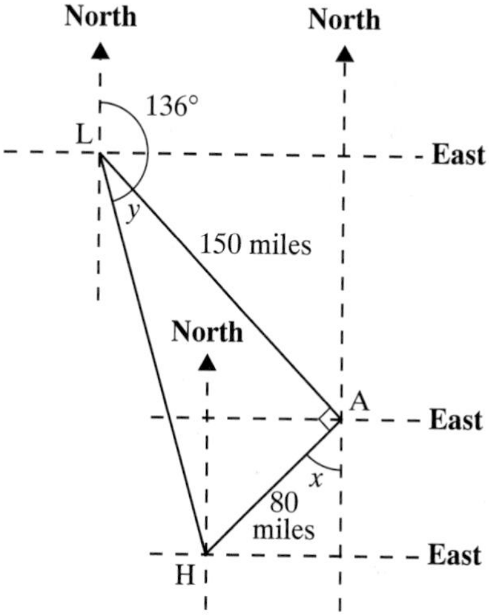

NEAB, Question 12, Paper Q2, November 1994

Summary

How well do you grade yourself?

To gain a grade **C**, you need to be able to show you understand and can use Pythagoras's theorem. You need also to be able to use sine, cosine and tangent in right-angled triangles when solving problems in two dimensions. These problems will usually be restricted to finding angles and short sides.

To gain a grade **B**, you need to be able to draw out of a complicated situation the application of Pythagoras's theorem. You need also to be able to use sine, cosine and tangent in right-angled triangles when solving problems in two dimensions. These problems may include finding the hypotenuse, for example. They may also involve angles of depression and elevation, and bearings. Generally, questions for grade **B** will require you to interpret a practical situation before solving the trigonometry problem.

To gain a grade **A**, you need to be able to apply Pythagoras's theorem and trigonometry when solving problems in three dimensions.

What you should know after you have worked through Chapter 4

- How to use Pythagoras's theorem to find the hypotenuse or a short side of a right-angled triangle, given the two other sides.
- How to draw out a right-angled triangle from a 2-D or 3-D problem and label it with necessary information.
- The three basic trigonometric ratios:

$$\text{sine } \theta = \frac{\text{Opposite}}{\text{Hypotenuse}} \qquad \text{cosine } \theta = \frac{\text{Adjacent}}{\text{Hypotenuse}} \qquad \text{tangent} = \frac{\text{Opposite}}{\text{Adjacent}}$$

- In a right-angled triangle:
  - Given one side and one angle (other than the right angle), calculate the lengths of the other two sides.
  - Given two sides, calculate the two angles (other than the right angle).
- Interpret a practical situation to obtain a right-angled triangle which can be used to solve the problem.

5 Geometry

This chapter is going to ... revise the properties of polygons (including all the special quadrilaterals) and the ways of finding the size of their angles. It then introduces you to the properties of angles in a circle and to tangents.

What you should already know

- **Vertically opposite angles**

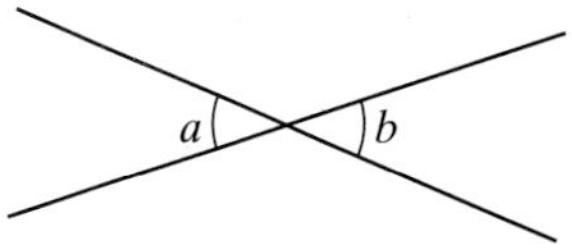

Vertically opposite angles are equal.

The angles labelled *a* and *b* are vertically opposite angles.

- **Angles on a line**

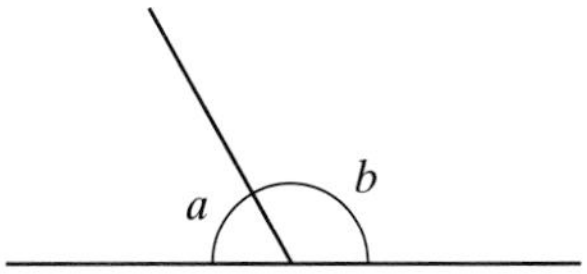

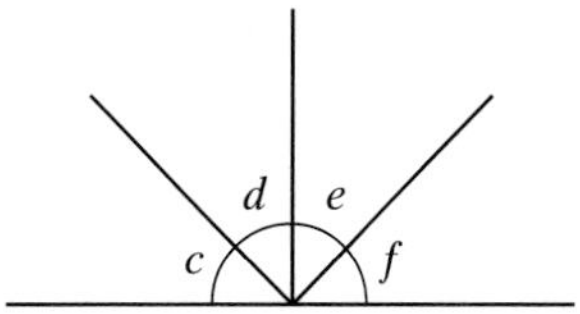

The angles on a straight line add up to 180°, that is $a + b = 180°$. This is true for any number of angles on a line. For example,

$$c + d + e + f = 180°$$

- **Angles around a point**

The sum of the angles around a point is 360°. For example,

$$a + b + c + d + e = 360°$$

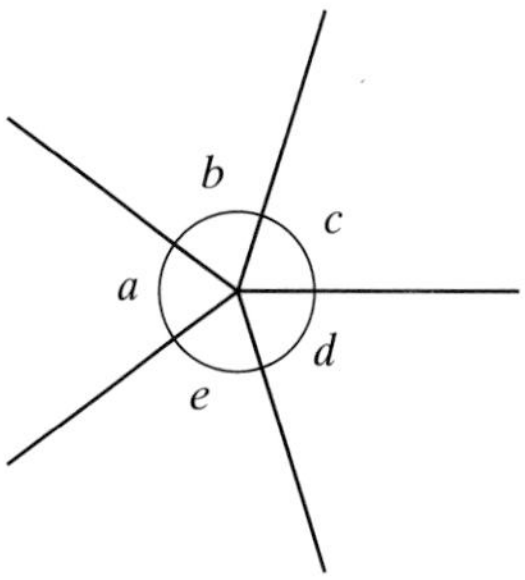

- **Angles in a triangle**

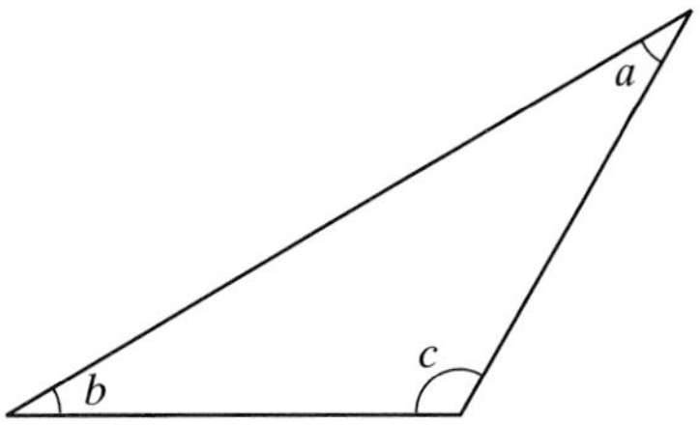

The three interior angles of a triangle add up to 180°. That is

$$a + b + c = 180°$$

- **Parallel lines**

A line which cuts parallel lines is called a **transversal**. The equal angles so formed are called **alternate angles**.

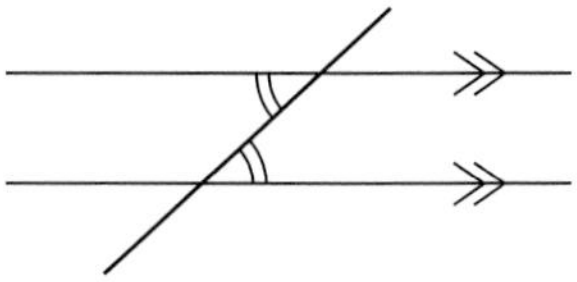

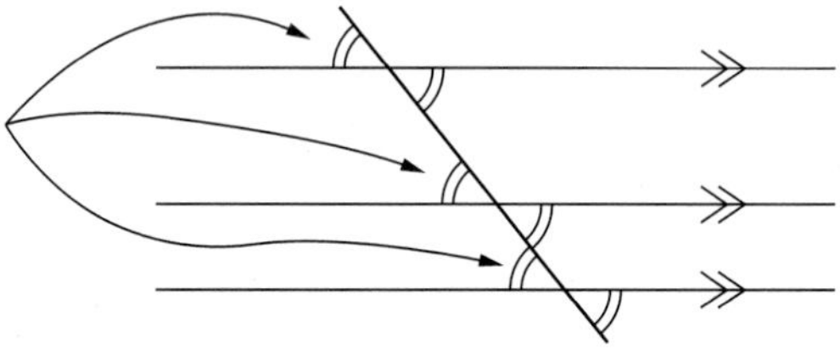

Because of their positions, the angles shown above are called **corresponding angles**.

Two angles positioned like *a* and *b*, which add up to 180°, are called **allied angles**.

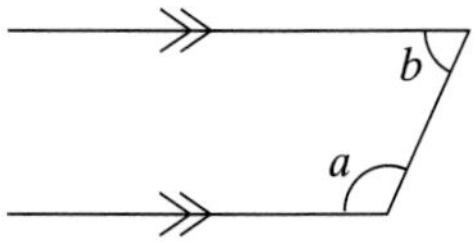

Angles in a polygon

A polygon has two kinds of angle:

- interior angles (angles made by adjacent sides of the polygon and lying inside the polygon)
- exterior angles (angles lying on the outside of the polygon)

The exterior angles of **any** polygon add up to 360°.

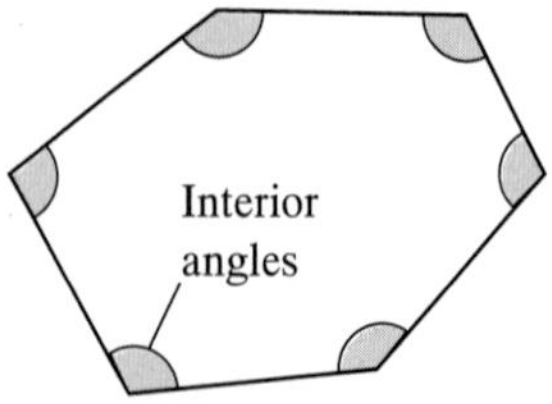

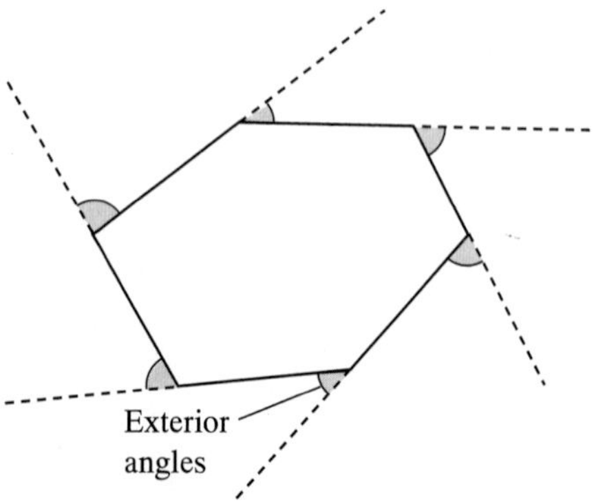

Interior angles

You can find the sum of the interior angles of any polygon by splitting it into triangles.

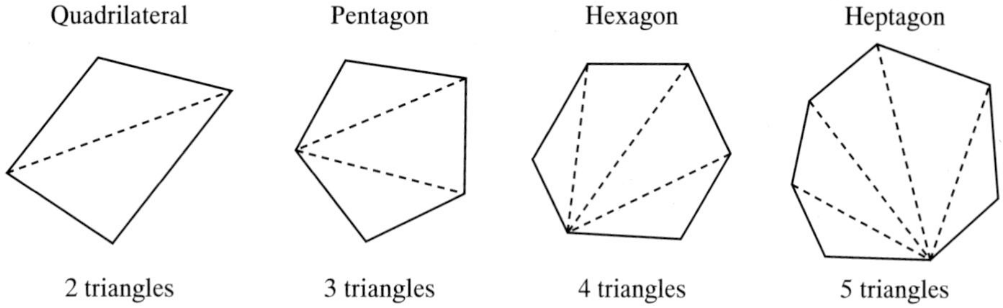

Since we already know that the angles in a triangle add up to 180°, the sum of the interior angles in a polygon is found by multiplying the number of triangles in the polygon by 180°, as shown in this table.

Shape	Name	Sum of interior angles
4-sided	Quadrilateral	$2 \times 180° = 360°$
5-sided	Pentagon	$3 \times 180° = 540°$
6-sided	Hexagon	$4 \times 180° = 720°$
7-sided	Heptagon	$5 \times 180° = 900°$
8-sided	Octagon	$6 \times 180° = 1080°$

As you can see from the table, for an N-sided polygon, the sum of the interior angles is $(N - 2) \times 180°$.

As you see from the diagram, the sum of an exterior angle and its adjacent interior angle is 180°.

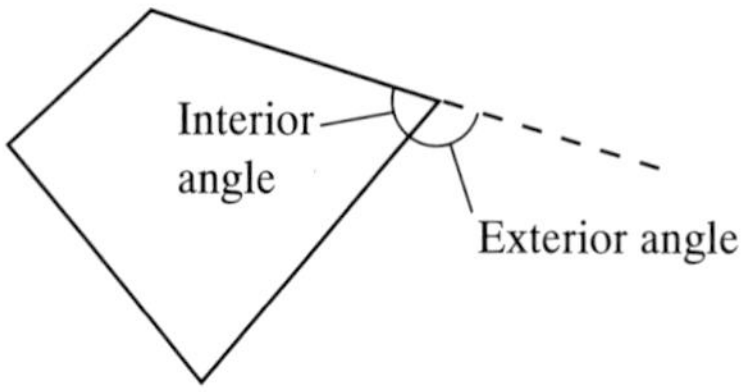

Regular polygons

A polygon is regular if all its interior angles are equal and all its sides have the same length.

Here are two simple rules for calculating the interior and the exterior angles of regular polygons.

- The exterior angle of a regular N-sided polygon = $360° \div N$
- The interior angle of a regular N-sided polygon = 180° – exterior angle
  $= 180° - (360° \div N)$

Special triangles

Equilateral triangle

An equilateral triangle is a triangle with all its sides equal. Therefore, all three interior angles are 60°.

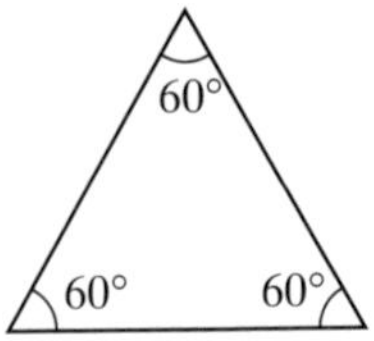

Isosceles triangle

An isosceles triangle is a triangle with two equal sides, and therefore with two equal angles (at the foot of the equal sides). Notice how we mark the equal sides and equal angles.

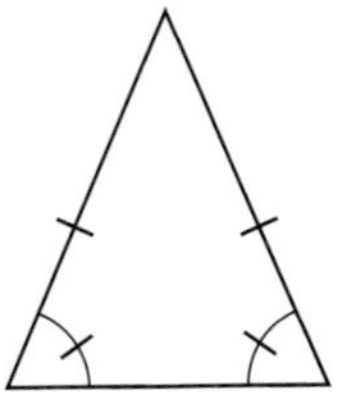

Exercise 5A

1 Calculate the sum of the interior angles of polygons with

a 10 sides **b** 15 sides **c** 100 sides **d** 45 sides

2 Calculate the size of the interior angle of regular polygons with

a 12 sides **b** 20 sides **c** 9 sides **d** 60 sides

3 Find the number of sides of the polygon with the interior angle sum of

a 1260° **b** 2340° **c** 18 000° **d** 8640°

4 Find the number of sides of the regular polygon with an exterior angle of

a 24° **b** 10° **c** 15° **d** 5°

5 Find the number of sides of the regular polygon with an interior angle of

a 150° **b** 140° **c** 162° **d** 171°

6 Calculate the size of the unknown angle in each of these polygons.

a

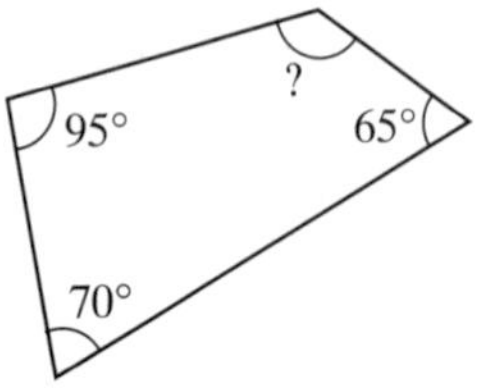

b

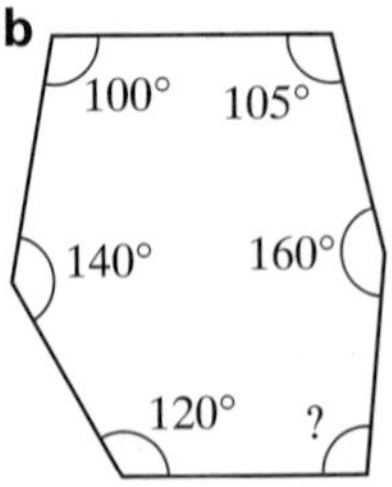

c

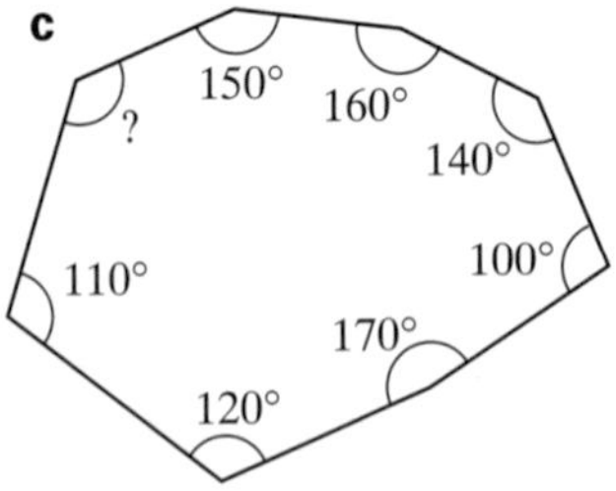

7 Find the value of x in each of these polygons.

a

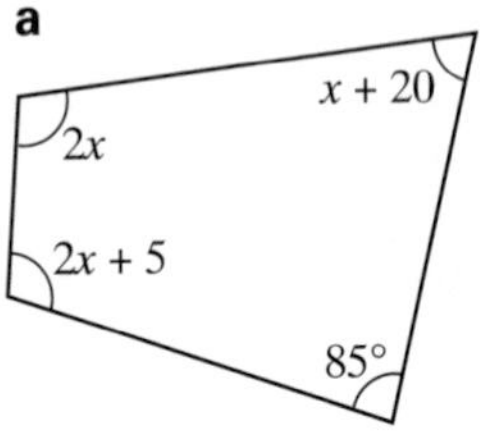

b

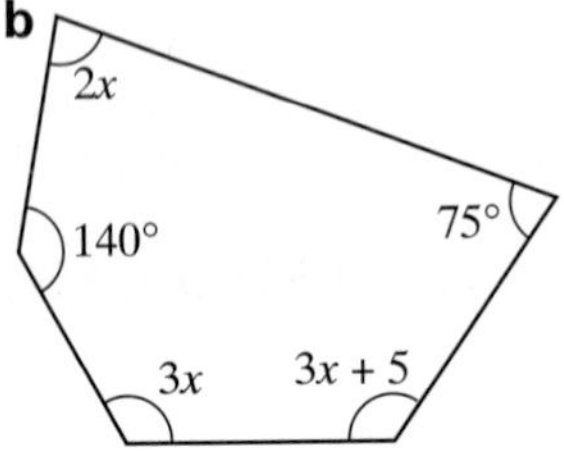

c

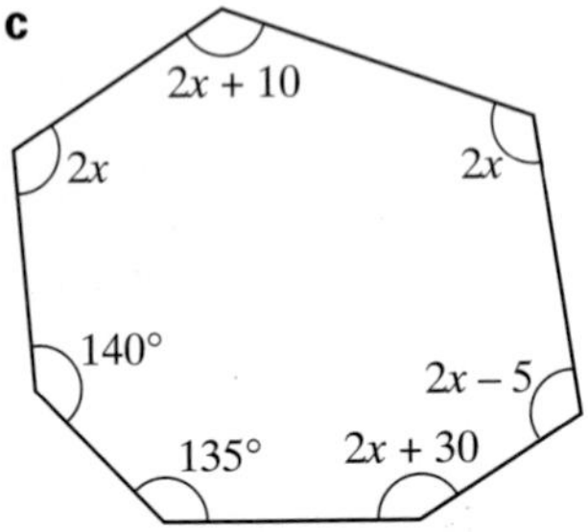

8 What is the name of the regular polygon whose interior angles are twice its exterior angles?

9 Wesley measured all the interior angles in a polygon. He added them up to make 991°, but he had missed out one angle.

a What type of polygon did Wesley measure?

b What is the size of the missing angle?

10 Calculate the lettered angles in each triangle.

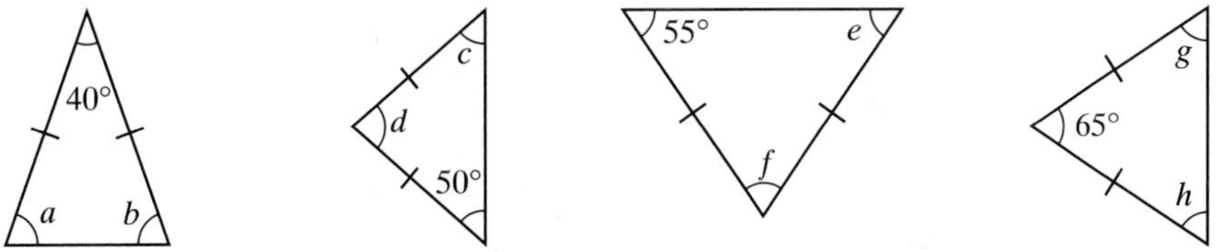

11 Calculate the two identical angles in an isosceles triangle when the other angle is

a 30° **b** 80° **c** 56° **d** 100°

12 An isosceles triangle has an angle of 50°. Sketch the two different possible triangles that match this description, showing what each angle is.

13 The three angles of an isosceles triangle are $2x$, $x - 10$ and $x - 10$. What is the actual size of each angle?

14 Calculate the lettered angles in these diagrams.

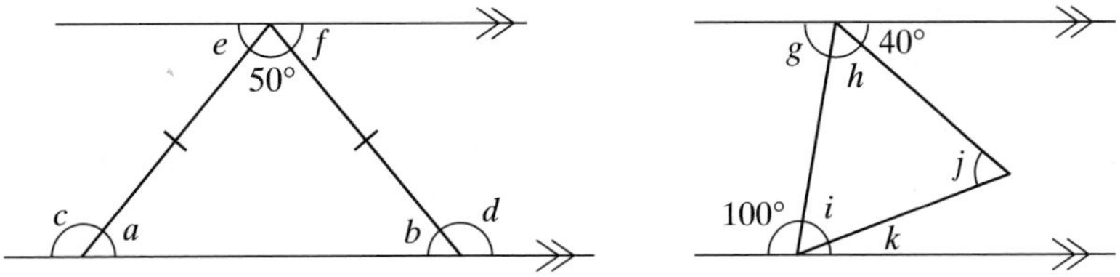

15 Given that ABCDE is a regular pentagon, calculate

a angle BCD **b** angle BCA **c** angle ACD

16 Given that ABCDEF is a regular hexagon, calculate

a angle ABC **b** angle ACD **c** angle ADE

17 Given that ABCDEFGH is a regular octagon, calculate

a angle DEF **b** angle AEF **c** angle EAF

Special quadrilaterals

You should be able to recognise and name the four quadrilaterals featured on the next page.

You should also know their angle properties.

Trapezium

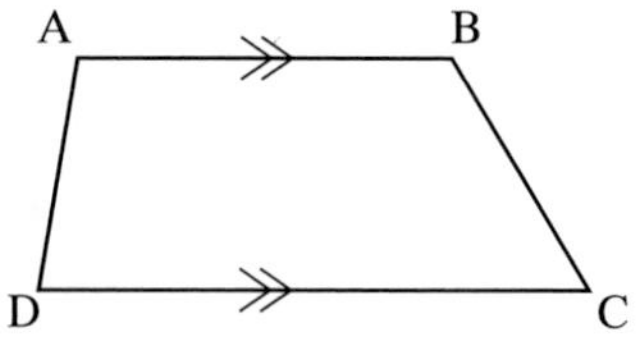

- A trapezium has two parallel sides.
- The sum of the interior angles at the ends of each non-parallel side is 180°, that is

  $\angle A + \angle D = 180°$ and $\angle B + \angle C = 180°$

Parallelogram

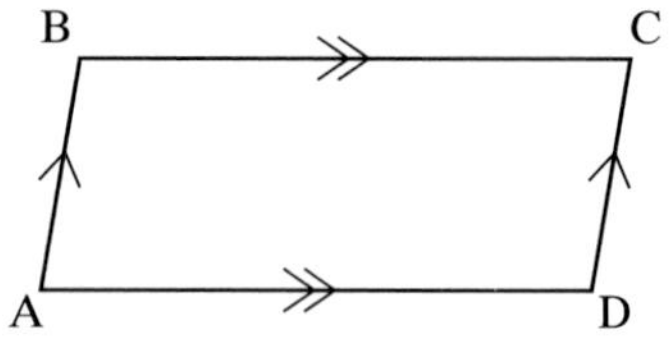

- A parallelogram has opposite sides parallel.
- Its opposite sides are equal.
- Its diagonals bisect each other.
- Its opposite angles are equal, that is

  $\angle A = \angle C$ and $\angle B = \angle D$

Rhombus

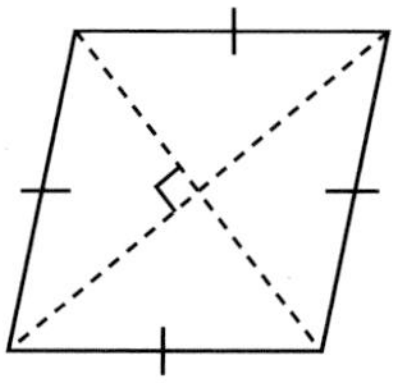

- A rhombus is a parallelogram with all its sides equal.
- Its diagonals bisect each other at right angles.
- Its diagonals also bisect the angles.

Kite

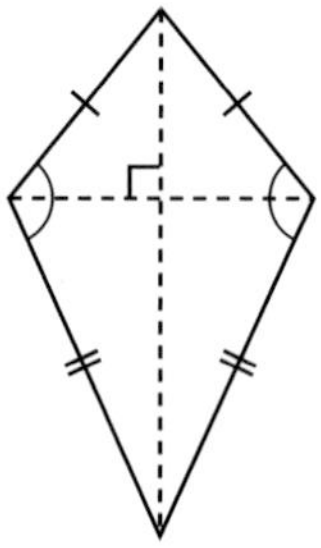

- A kite is a quadrilateral with two pairs of equal adjacent sides.
- Its longer diagonal bisects its shorter diagonal at right angles.
- The opposite angles between the sides of different lengths are equal.

Exercise 5B

1 For each of these trapeziums, calculate the value of the lettered angles.

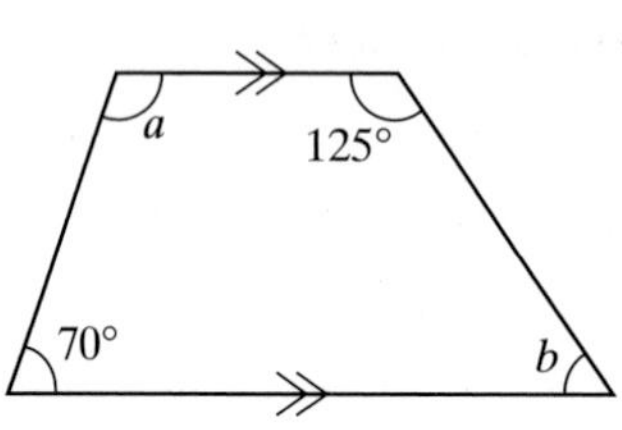

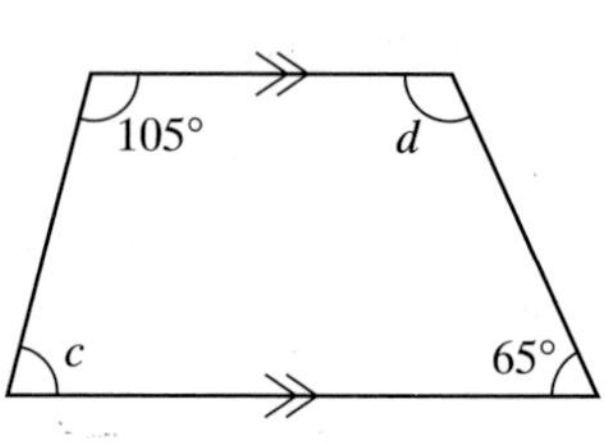

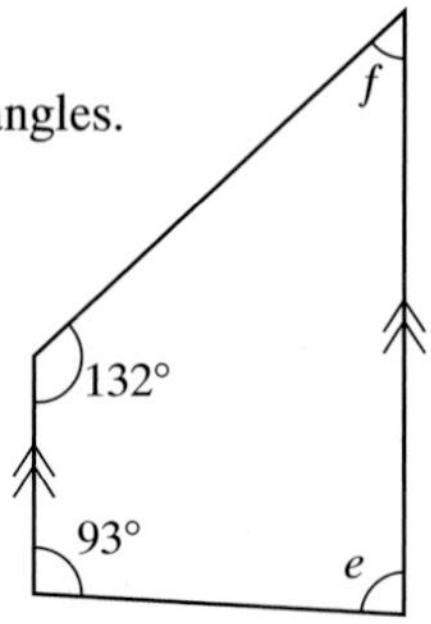

2 For each of these parallelograms, calculate the value of the lettered angles.

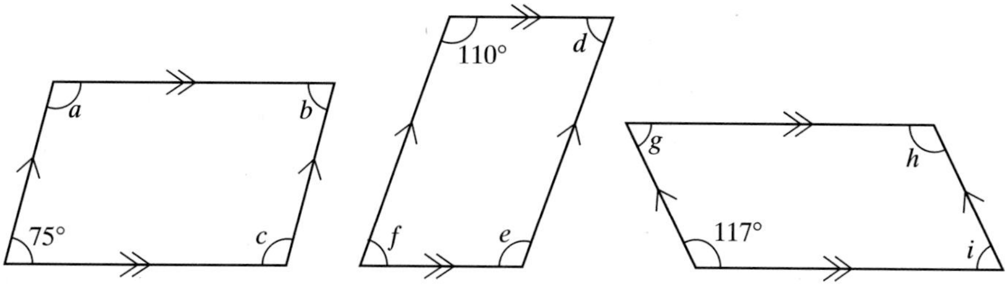

3 For each of these kites, calculate the value of the lettered angles.

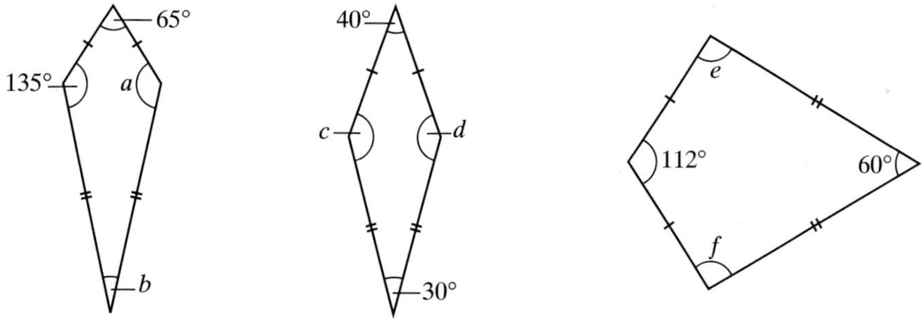

4 For each of these rhombuses, calculate the value of the lettered angles.

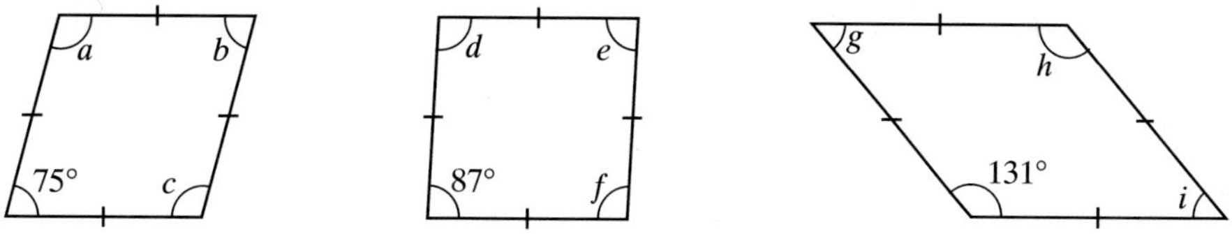

5 For each of these shapes, calculate the value of the lettered angles.

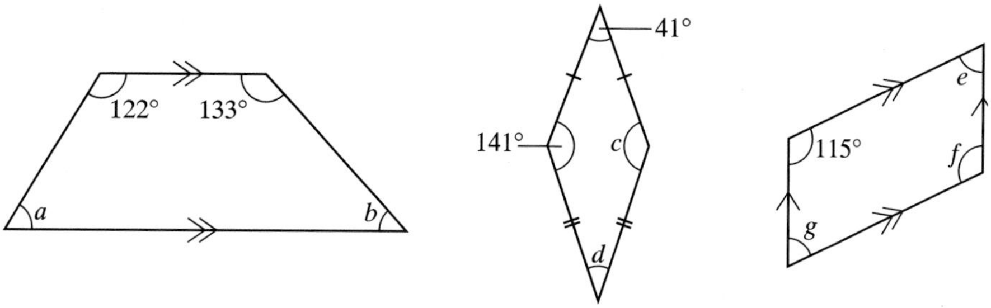

6 Calculate the values of x and y in each of these parallelograms.

a

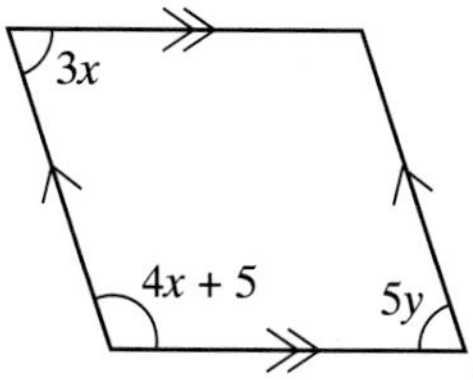

b

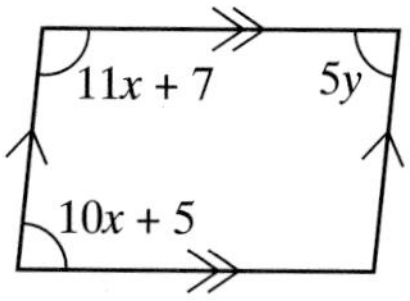

c

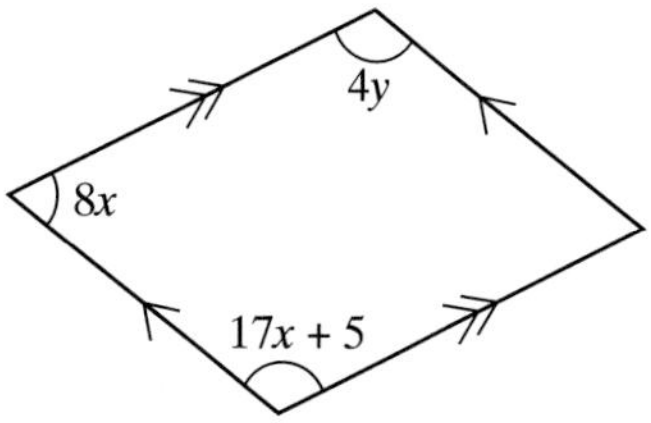

7 For each of these shapes, calculate the value of the lettered angles.

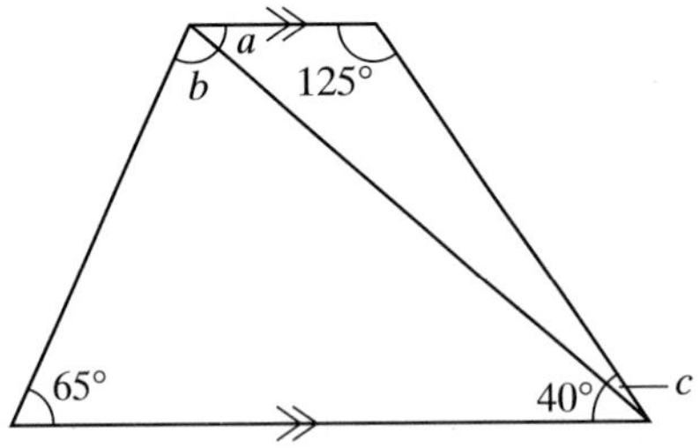

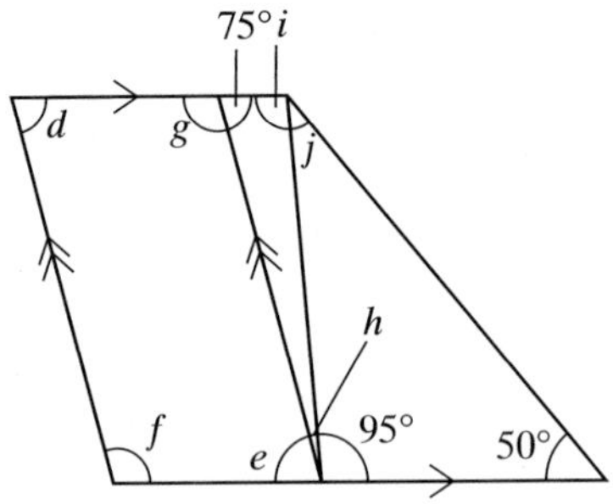

8 Calculate the values of x and y in each of these trapeziums.

a

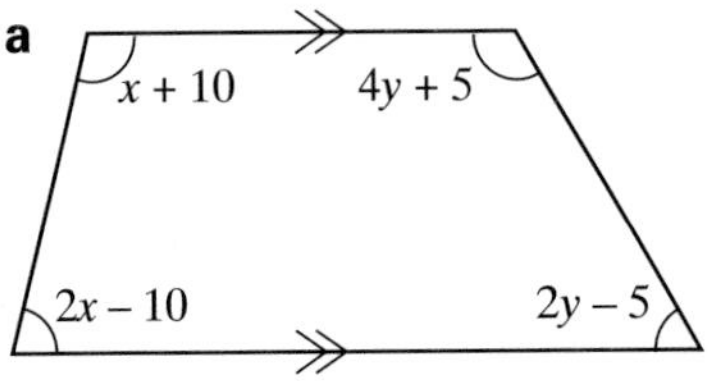

b

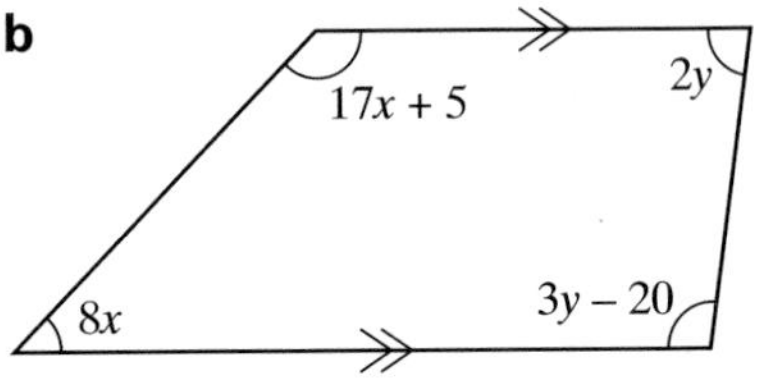

9 Calculate the value of x in each of these rhombuses.

a

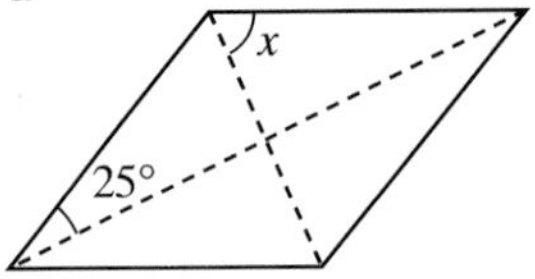

b

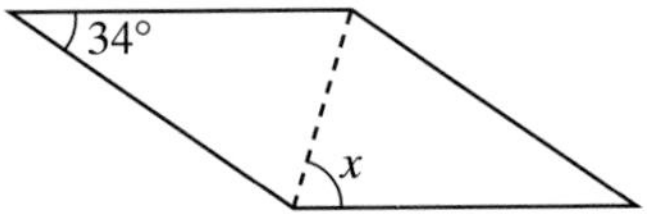

c

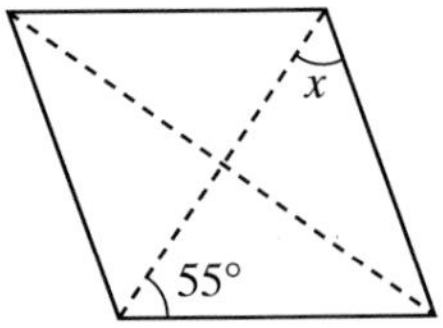

10 Calculate the values of the letters in each of these shapes.

a

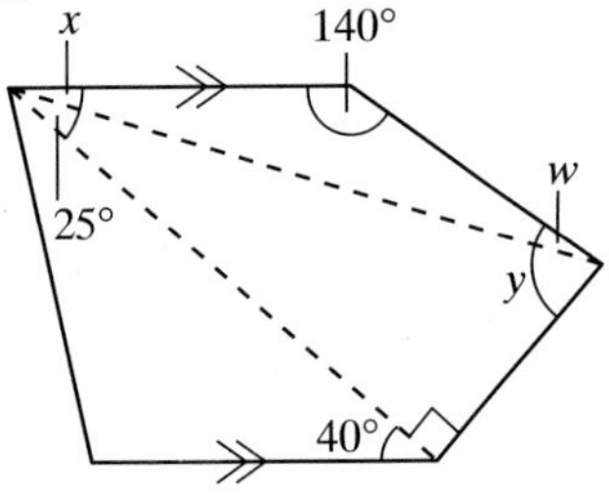

b

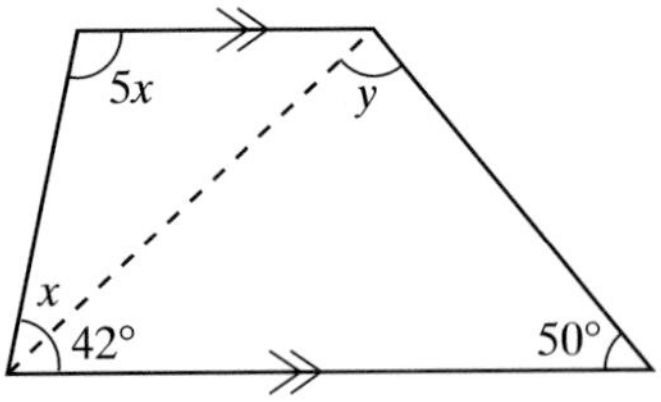

c

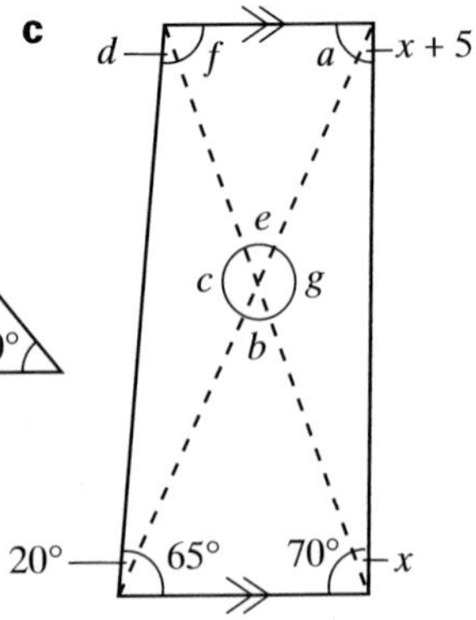

11 Find the value of x in each of these quadrilaterals and hence state the type of quadrilateral it is.

a One with angles $x + 10$, $x + 20$, $2x + 20$, $2x + 10$

b One with angles $x - 10$, $2x + 10$, $x - 10$, $2x + 10$

c One with angles $x - 10$, $2x$, $5x - 10$, $5x - 10$

d One with angles $4x + 10$, $5x - 10$, $3x + 30$, $2x + 50$

Circles and angles

Angles in a circle

Here are three theorems you need to know. Try proving them for yourself.

- An angle at the centre of a circle is twice any angle at the circumference subtended by the same arc.

  $\angle AOB = 2 \times \angle ACB$

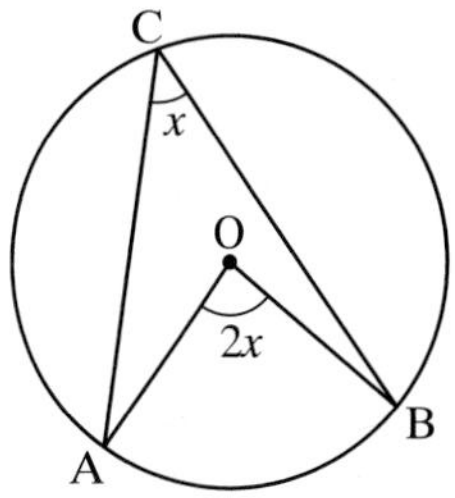

- Every angle at the circumference of a semicircle that is subtended by the diameter of the semicircle is a right angle.

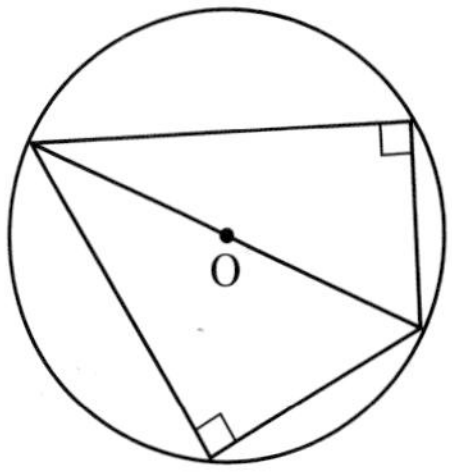

- Angles at the circumference in the same segment of a circle are equal. (That is, they are subtended by the same arc.)

  $\angle AC_1B = \angle AC_2B = \angle AC_3B = \angle AC_4B$

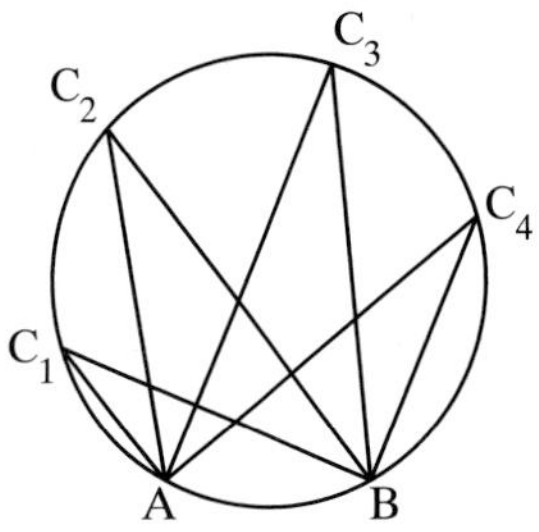

Follow through Examples 1 to 3 to see how these theorems are applied.

Example 1 O is the centre of each circle. Find the angles marked *a* and *b* in each circle.

i

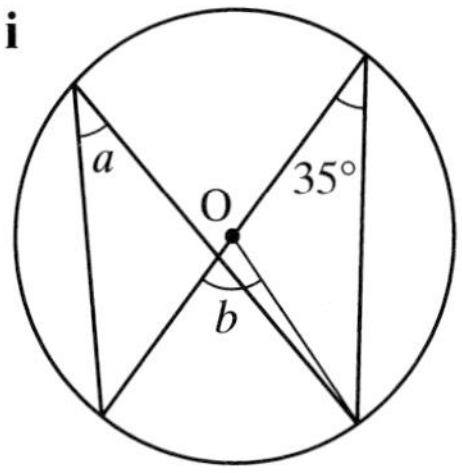

ii

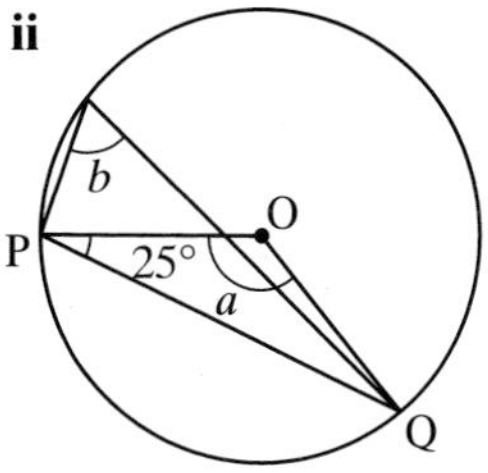

i $a = 35°$ (Angles in same segment)

$b = 2 \times 35°$ (Angle at centre = Twice angle at circumference)

$= 70°$

ii With OP = QP, triangle OPQ is isosceles. So the sum of the angles in this triangle is given by

$$a + (2 \times 25°) = 180°$$
$$\Rightarrow \quad a = 180° - (2 \times 25°)$$
$$= 130°$$

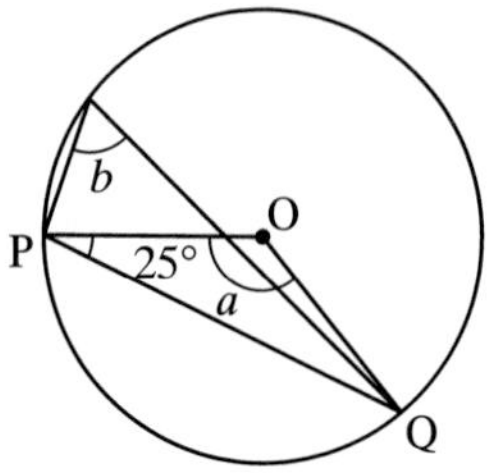

$b = \frac{1}{2} \times 130°$ (Angle at circumference)
$= 65°$

Example 2 O is the centre of the circle. PQR is a straight line. Find the angle labelled a.

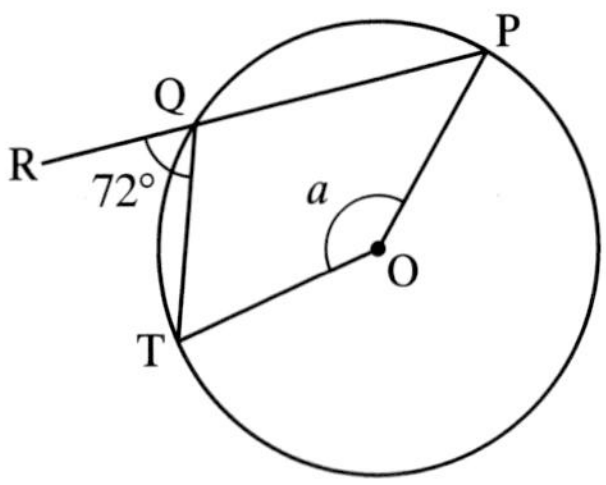

$\angle PQT = 180° - 72°$
$\angle PQT = 108°$
(Reflex) $\angle POT = 2 \times 108°$ (Angle at centre)
$= 216°$

$a + 216° = 360°$ (Sum of angles around a point)
$\Rightarrow \quad a = 360° - 216°$
$= 144°$

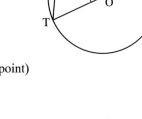

Example 3 O is the centre of the circle. POQ is parallel to TR. Find the angles labelled a and b.

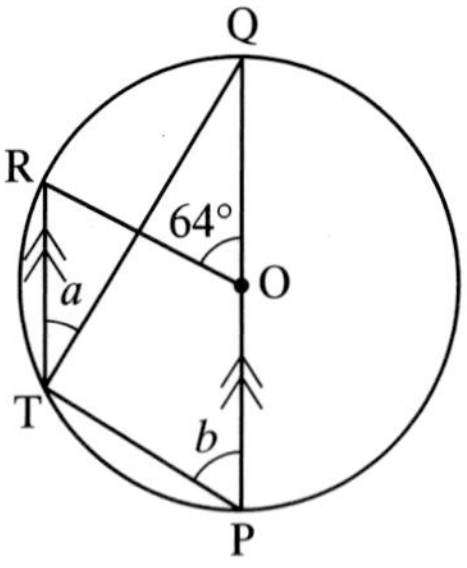

$a = \frac{1}{2} \times 64°$ (Angle at circumference)
$= 32°$

$\angle TQP = a$ (Alternate angles)
$= 32°$
$\angle PTQ = 90°$ (Angle in a semicircle)
$b + 90° + 32° = 180°$ (Sum of angles in $\triangle PQT$)
$\Rightarrow \quad b = 180° - 122° = 58°$

Exercise 5C

1 Find the value of x in each of these circles with centre O.

a

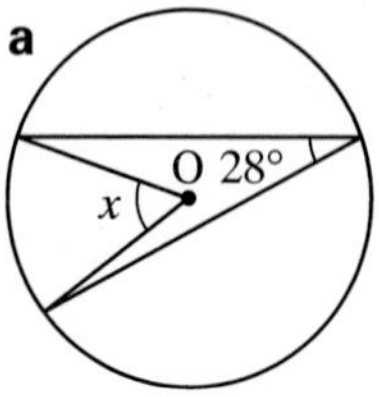

b

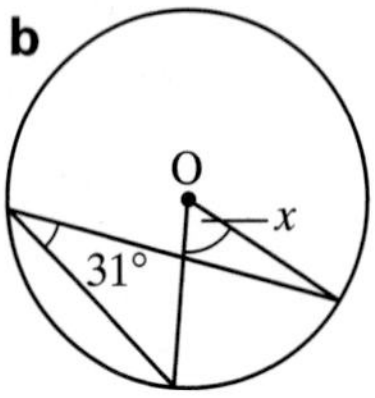

c

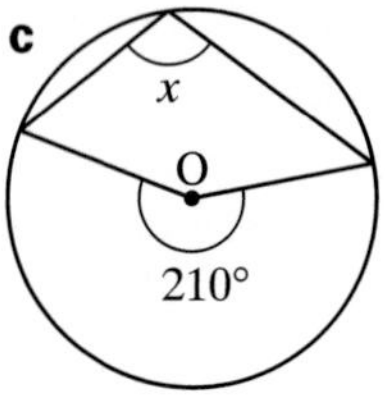

d

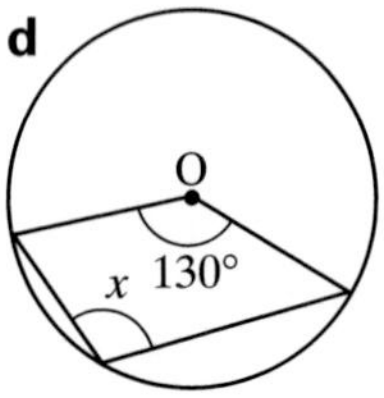

e

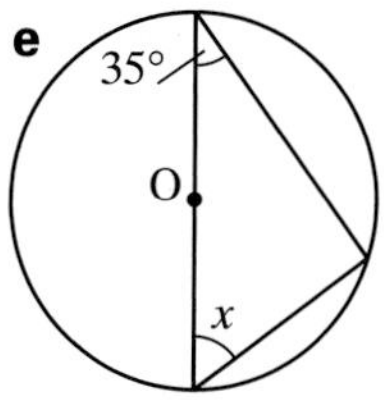

f

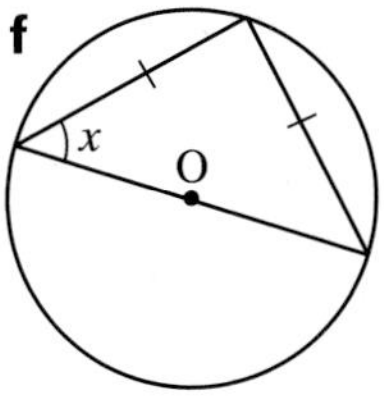

g

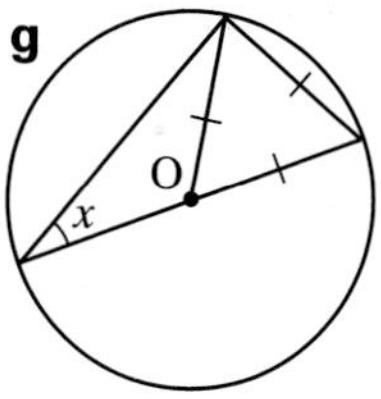

h

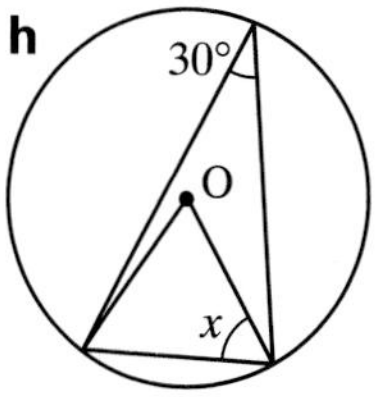

i

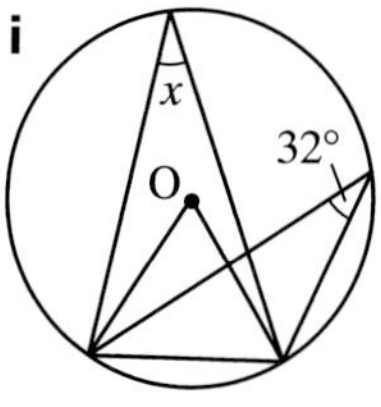

j

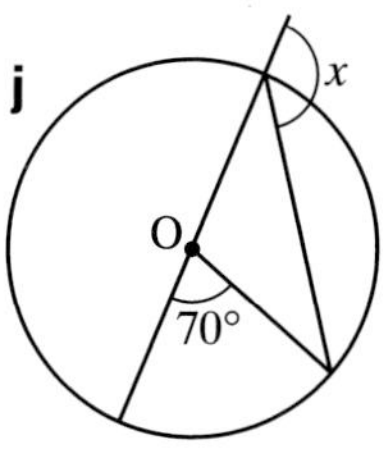

k

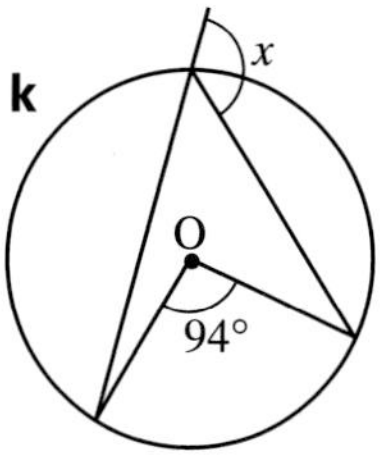

l

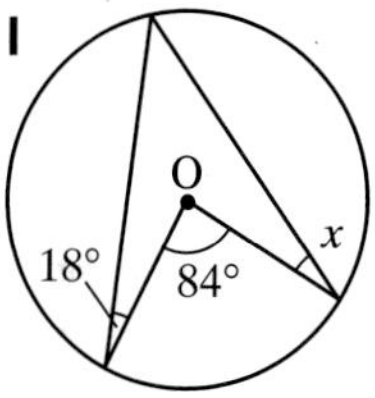

2 Find the value of x in each of these circles with centre O.

a

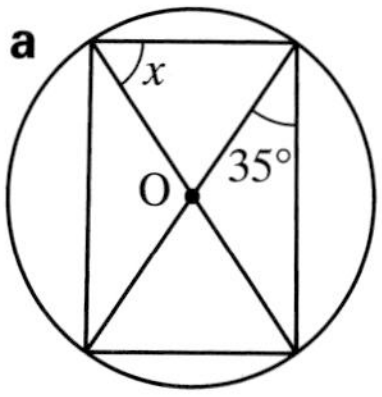

b

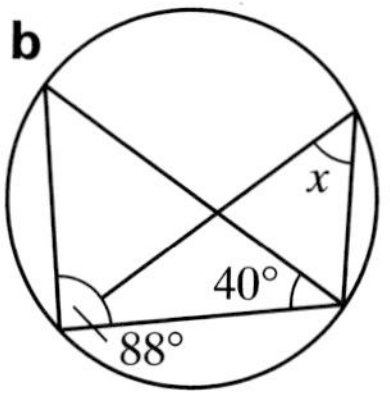

c

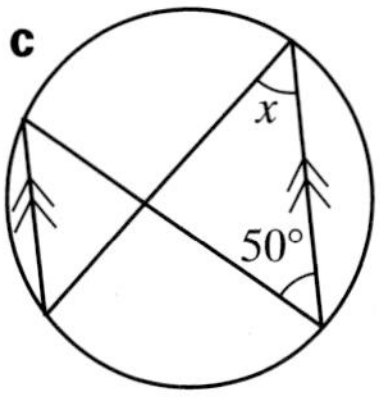

d

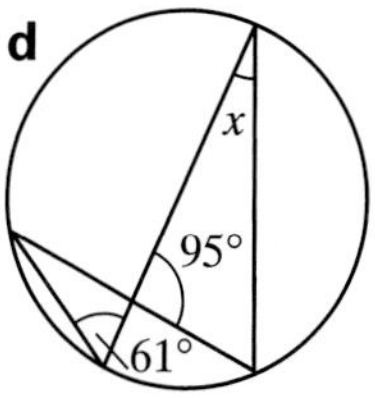

e

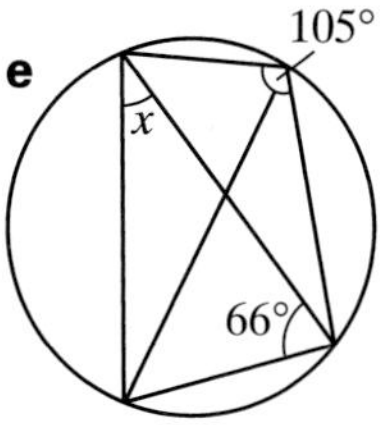

f

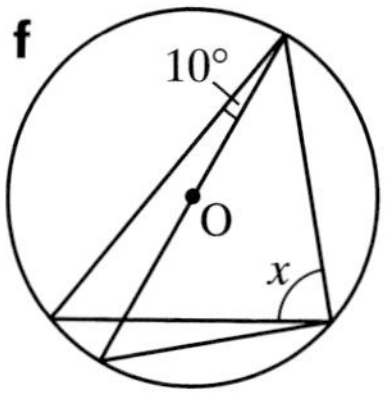

g

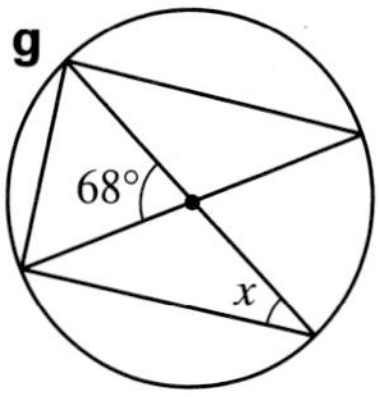

h

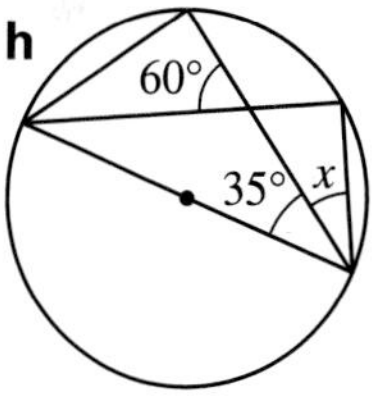

3 In the diagram, O is the centre of the circle. Find

a ∠ADB

b ∠DBA

c ∠CAD

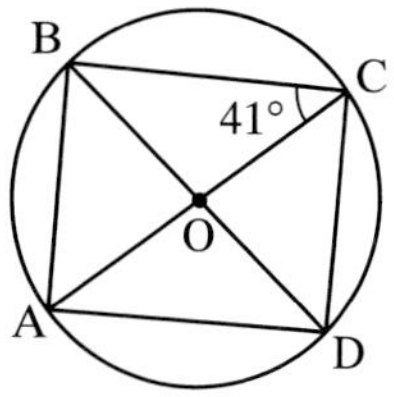

4 In the diagram, O is the centre of the circle. Find x.

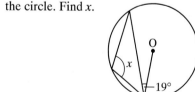

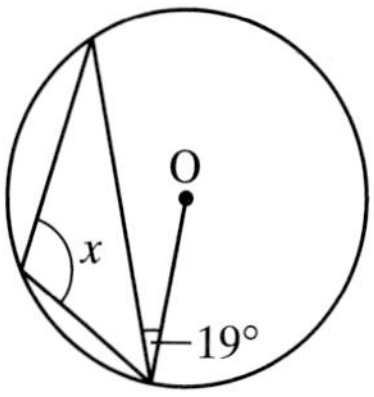

5 In the diagram, O is the centre of the circle. Find

a ∠EDF

b ∠DEG

c ∠EGF

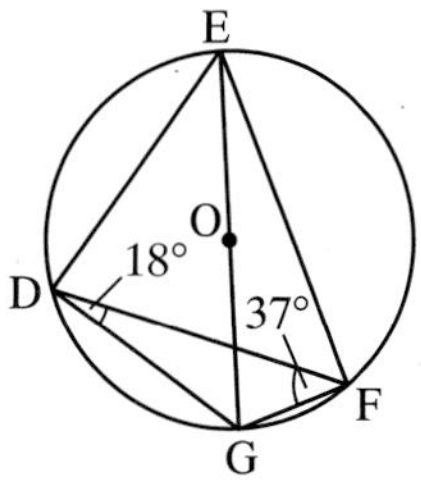

6 In the diagram, O is the centre, AD a diameter of the circle. Find x.

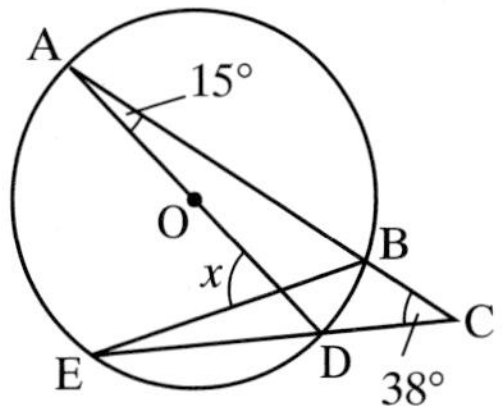

7 Find the values of x and y in each of these circles with centre O.

a

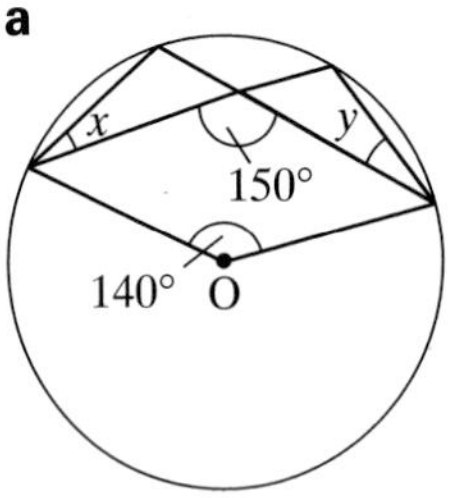

b

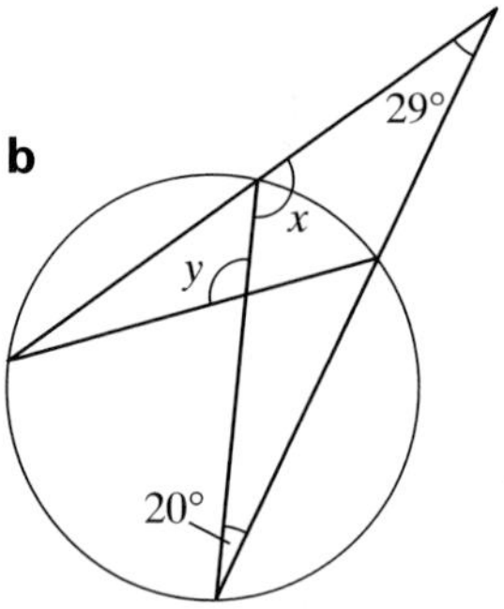

c

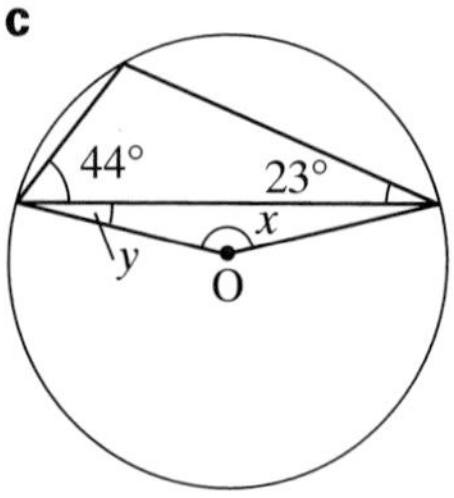

d

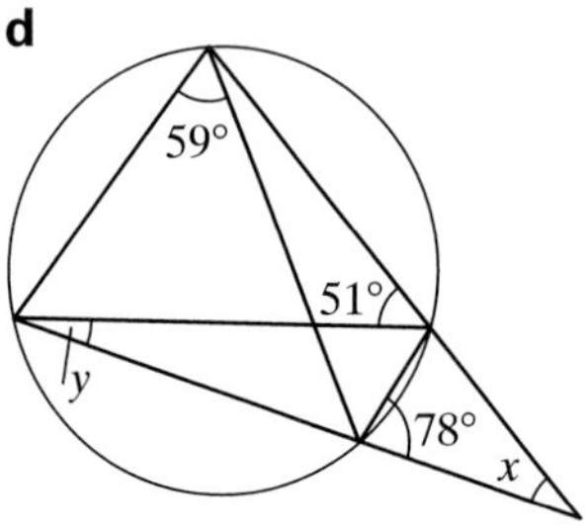

e

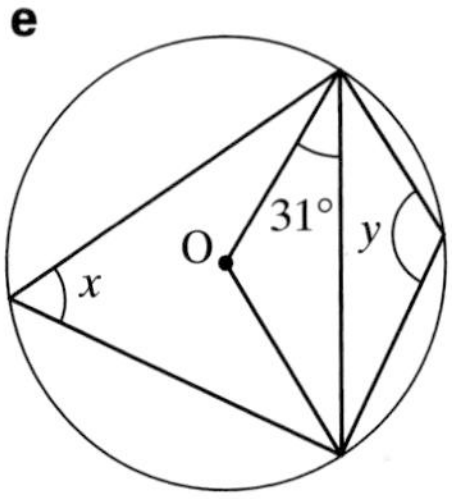

f

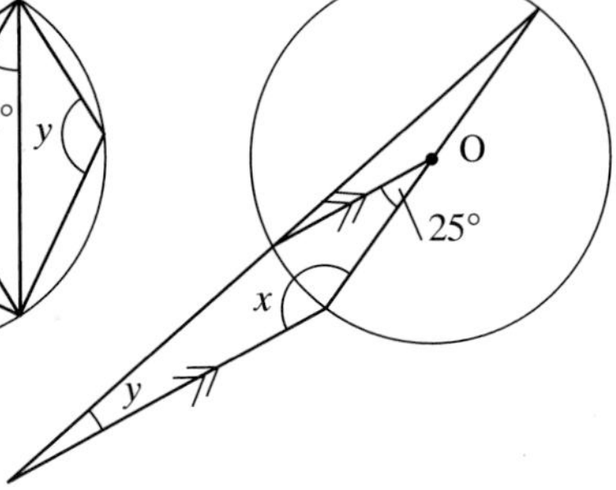

Cyclic quadrilaterals

A quadrilateral whose four vertices lie on the circumference of a circle is called a **cyclic quadrilateral**.

The sum of the opposite angles of a cyclic quadrilateral is 180°. (See the example on the right.)

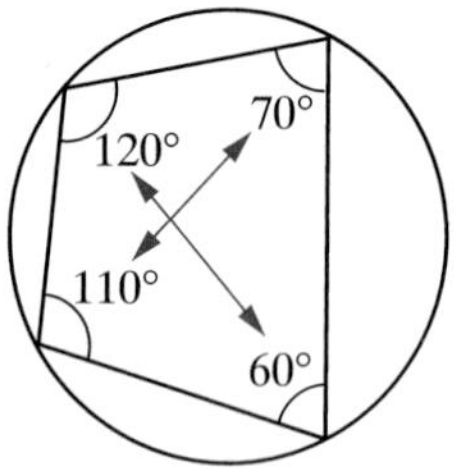

Exercise 5D

1 Find the size of the lettered angles in each of these circles.

a

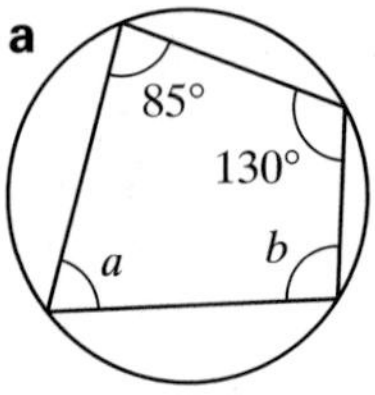

b

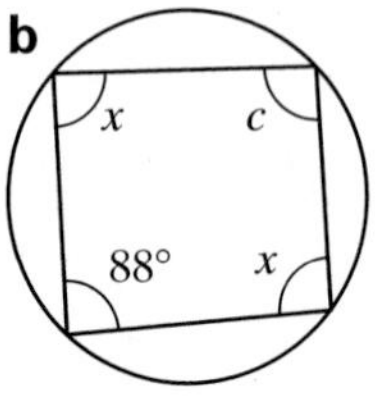

c

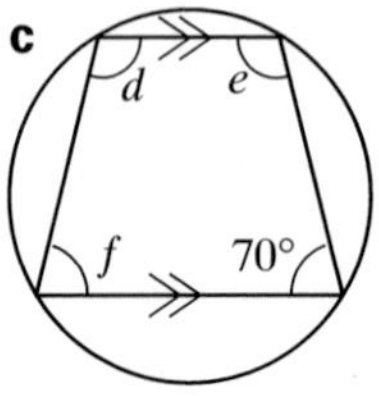

d

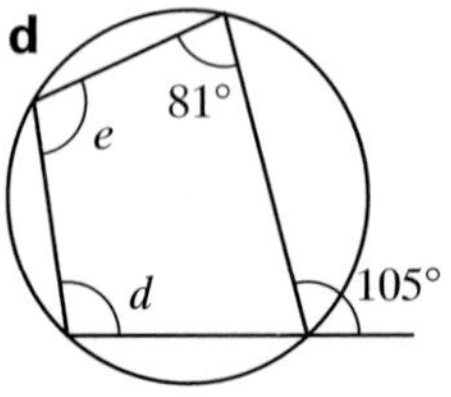

e

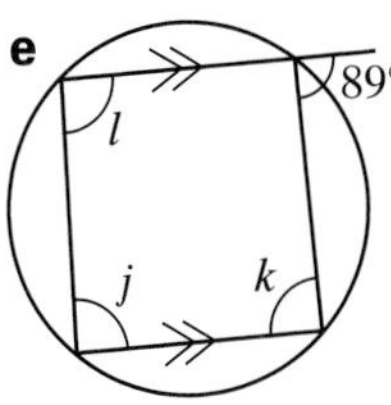

f

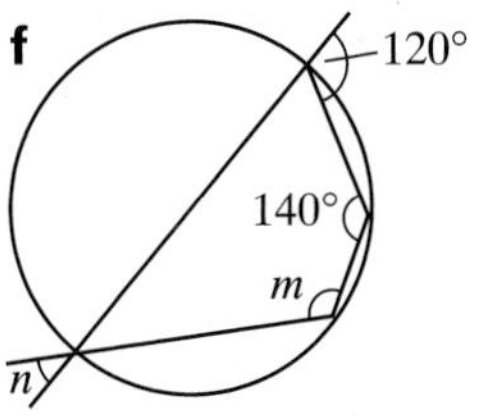

g

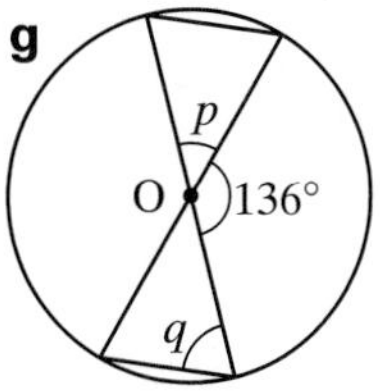

h

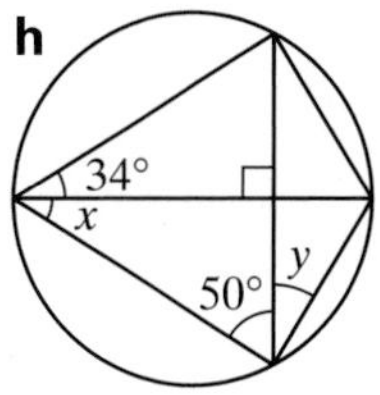

2 Find the values of x and y in each of these circles, centre O.

a

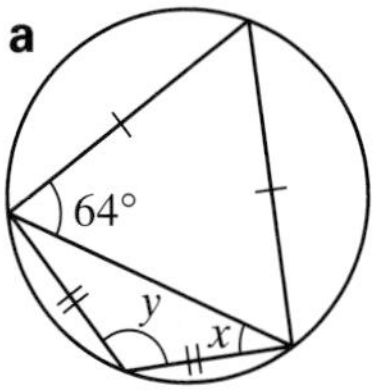

b

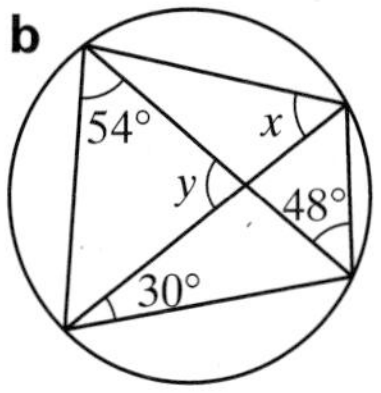

c

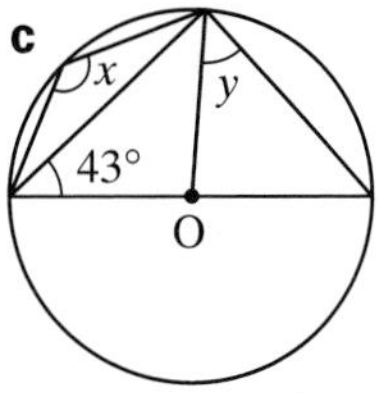

d

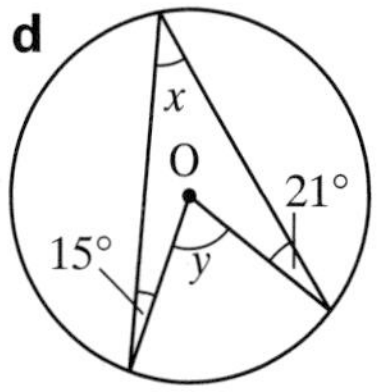

e

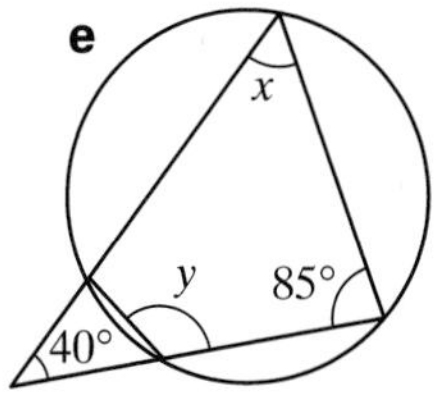

f

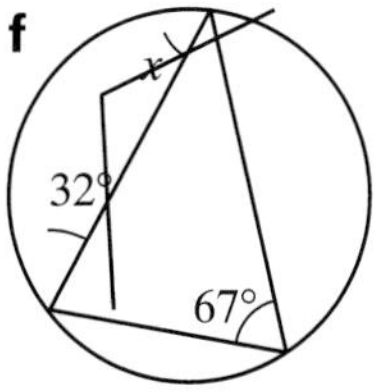

g

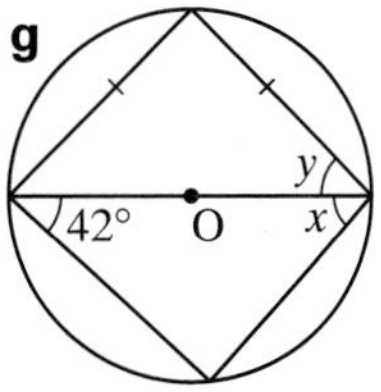

h

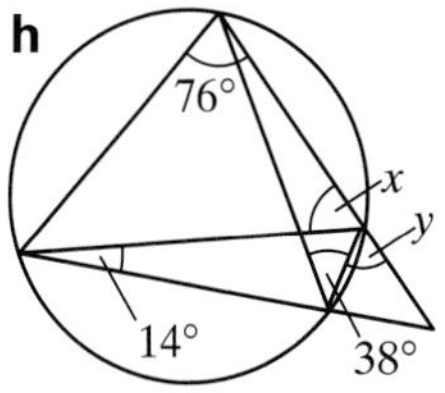

3 Find the values of x and y in each of these circles, centre O.

a

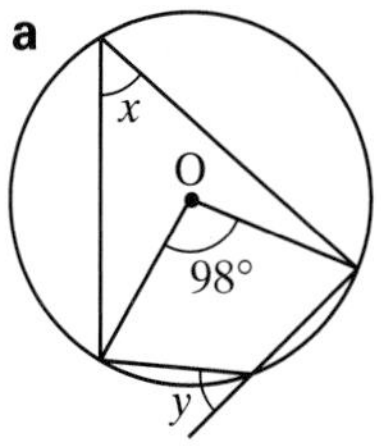

b

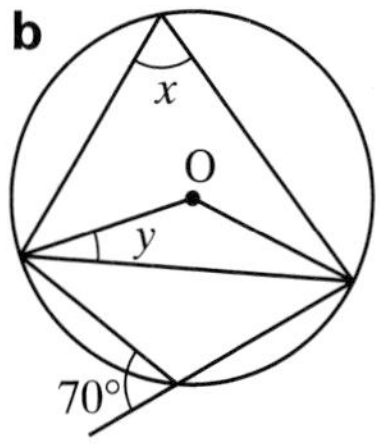

c

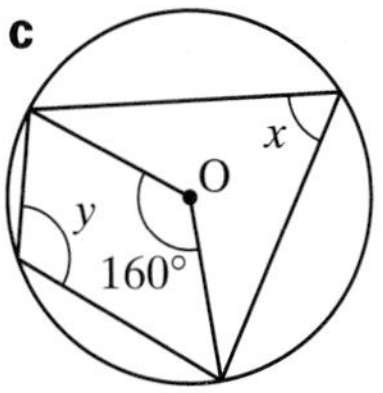

d

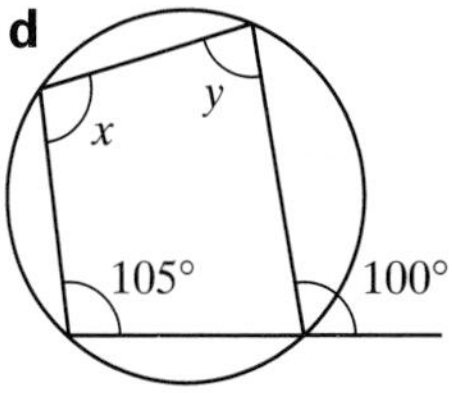

4 Find the values of x and y in each of these circles.

a

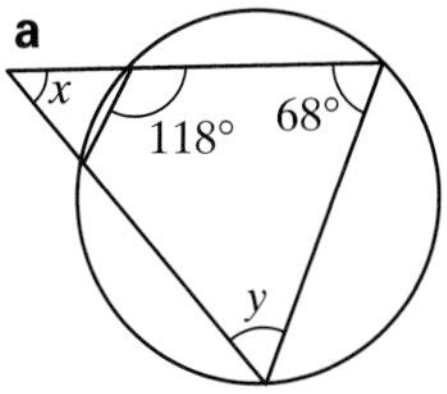

b

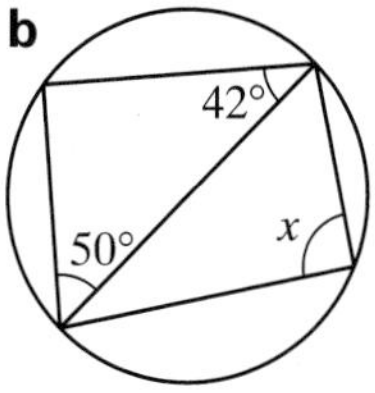

c

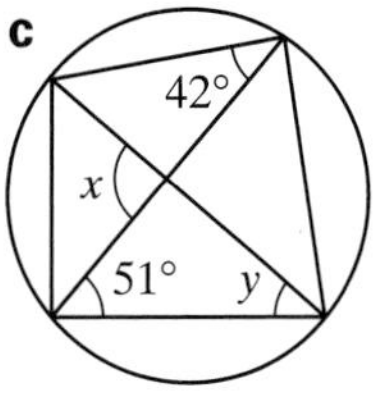

d

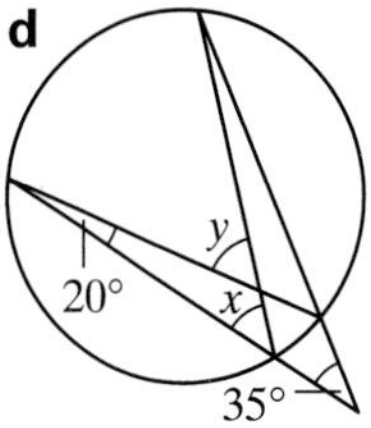

5 Find the values of x and y in each of these circles, centre O.

a

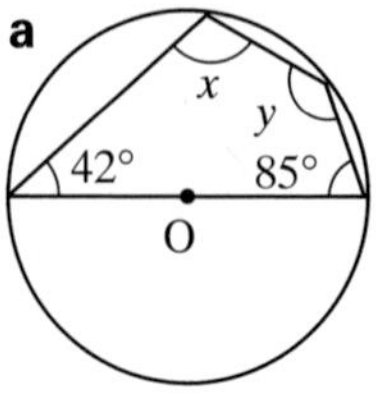

b

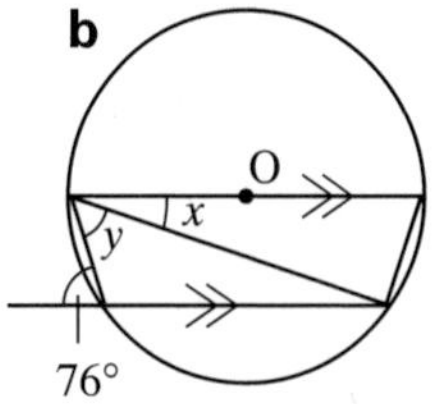

c

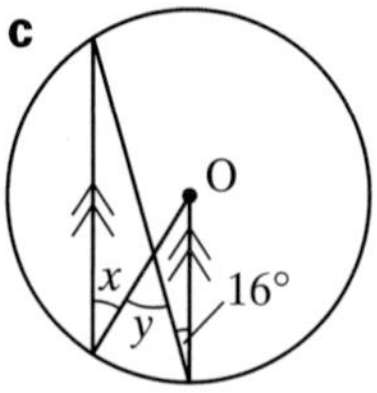

d

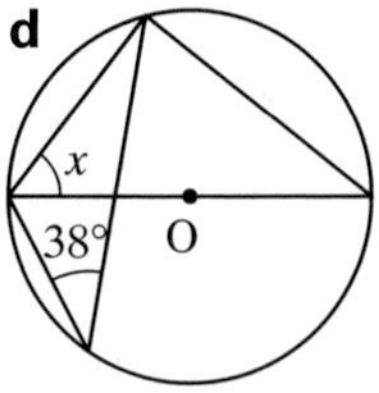

6 The cyclic quadrilateral PQRT has ∠ROQ equal to 38°. POT is a diameter of a circle, centre O and parallel to QR. Calculate

a ∠ROT **b** ∠QRT

Tangents to a circle

A tangent is a straight line that **touches** a circle **at one point only**. This point is called the **point of contact**.

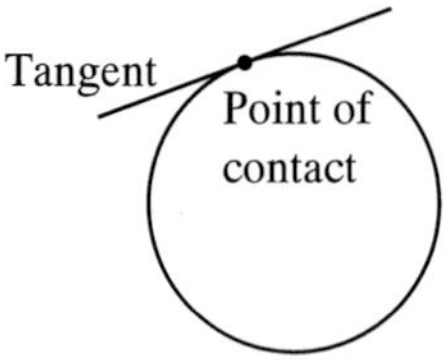

There are three other important properties of tangents which you need to know.

- A tangent to a circle is perpendicular to the radius drawn to the point of contact.
- Tangents to a circle from an external point are equal in length to the point of contact.
- The line joining the external point to the centre of the circle bisects the angle between the tangents.

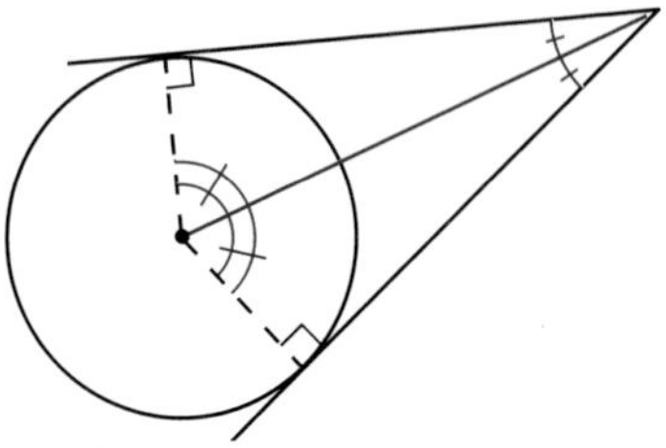

Exercise 5E

1 In each diagram, TP and TQ are tangents to a circle, centre O. Find each value of x.

a

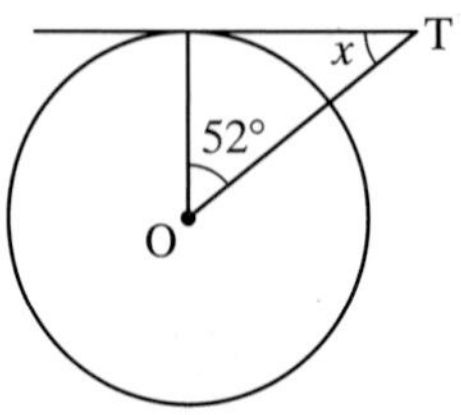

b

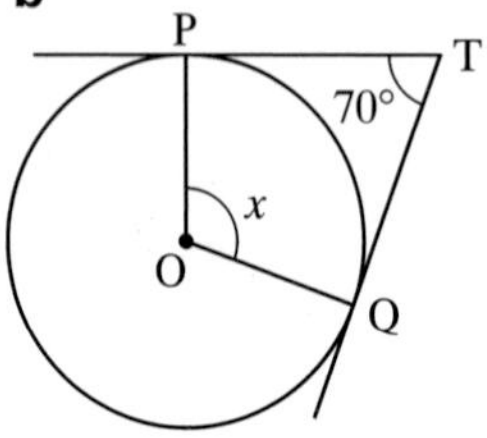

c

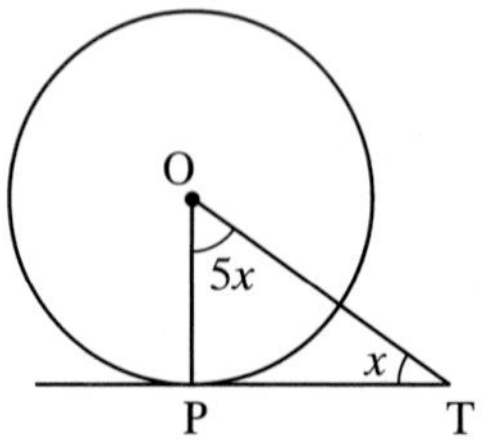

d

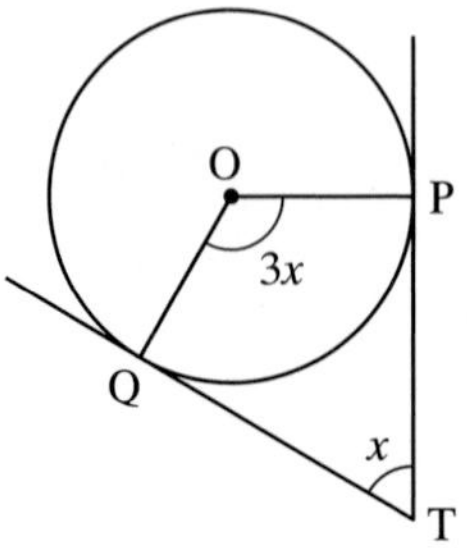

2 Each diagram shows a tangent to a circle, centre O. Find each value of y.

a

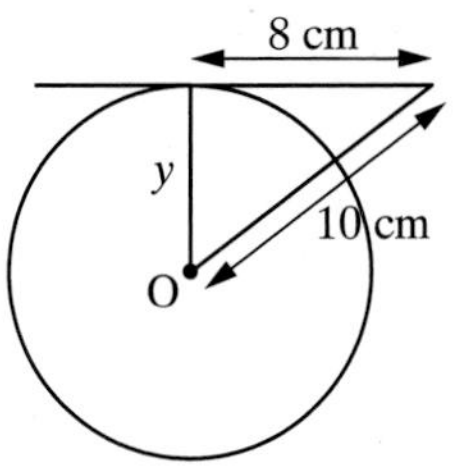

b

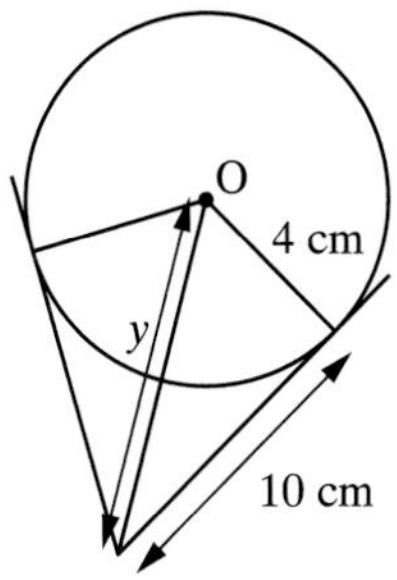

c

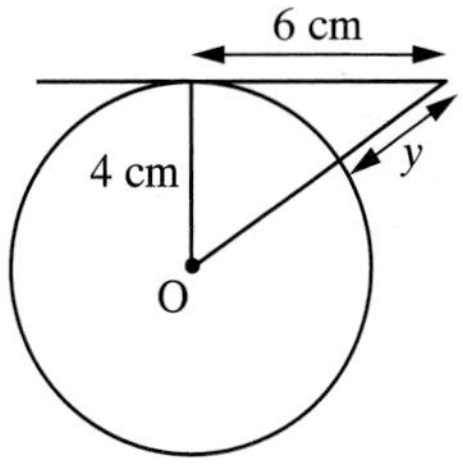

d

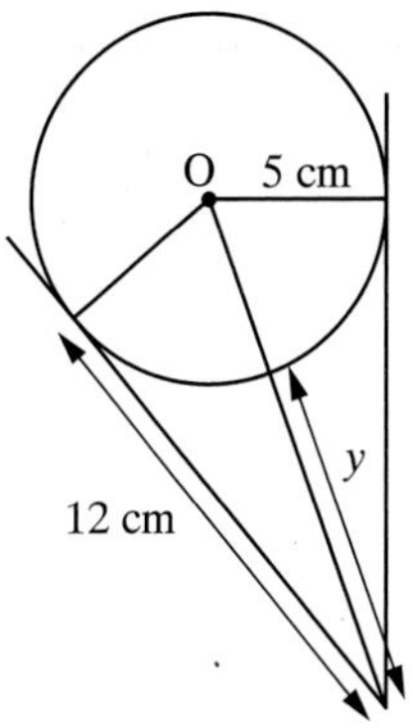

3 Each diagram shows a tangent to a circle, centre O. Find x and y in each case.

a

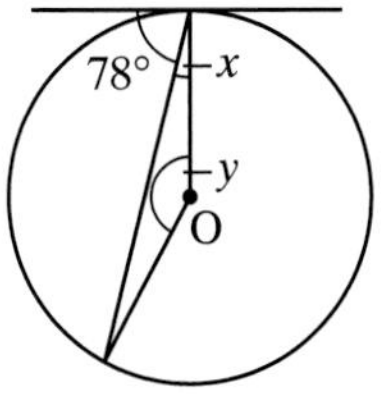

b

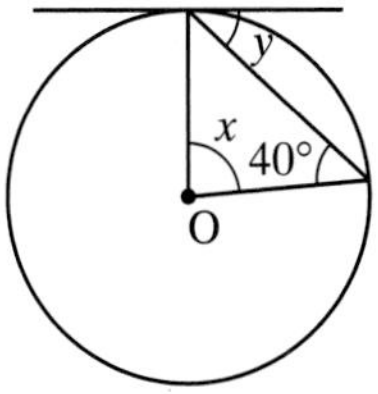

c

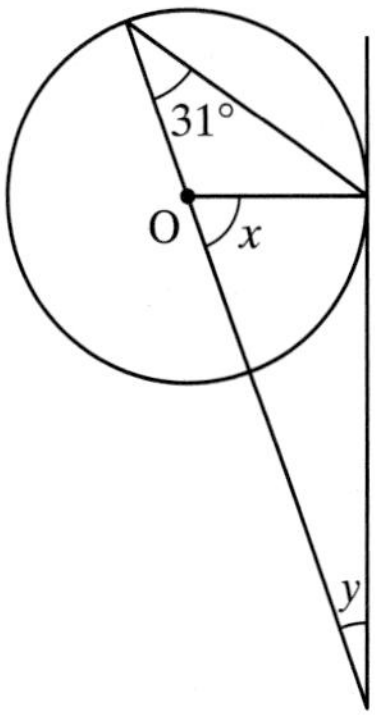

d

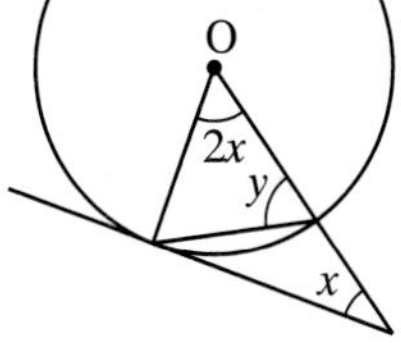

4 In each of the diagrams, TP and TQ are tangents to the circle, centre O. Find each value of x.

a

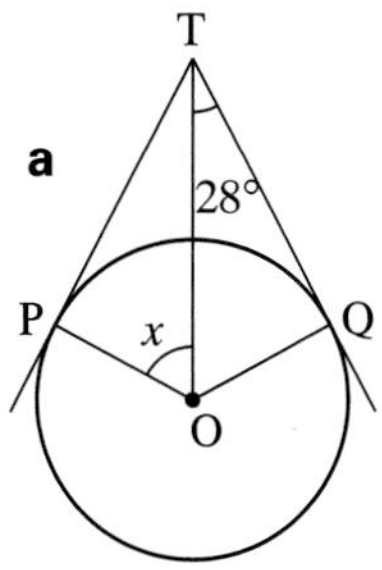

b

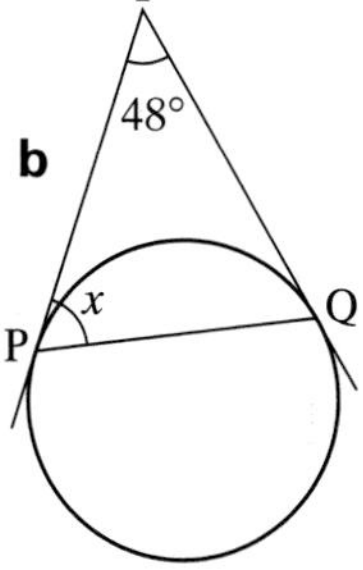

c

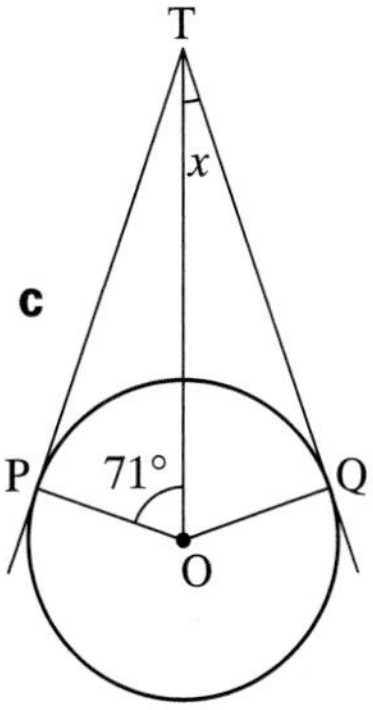

d

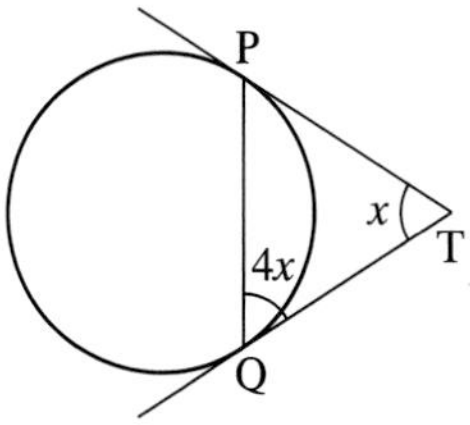

5 Three circles are drawn so that they just touch each other on the outside. Their centres form a triangle with sides 10 cm, 9 cm and 7 cm. What is the total area of the three circles?

6 A point P is 8.5 cm from the centre of a circle. A tangent from P to the circle is 7.2 cm long. What is the area of the circle?

7 Two circles with the same centre have radii of 7 cm and 12 cm respectively. A tangent to the inner circle cuts the outer circle at A and B. Find the length of AB.

Alternate segment theorem

PTQ is the tangent to a circle at T. The segment containing ∠TBA is known as the **alternate segment** of ∠PTA, because it is on the other side of the chord AT from ∠PTA.

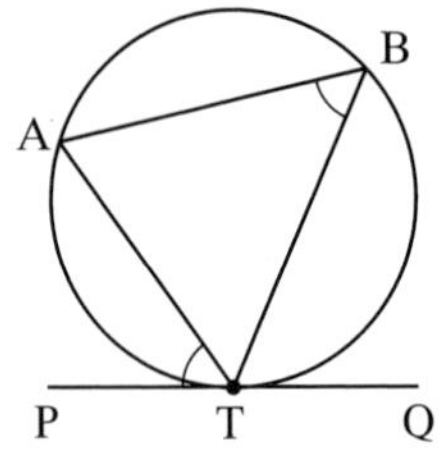

Theorem The angle between a tangent and a chord through the point of contact is equal to the angle in the alternate segment.

Example In the diagram, find **a** ∠ATS and **b** ∠TSR.

a ∠ATS = 80° (Angle in alternate segment)

b ∠TSR = 70° (Angle in alternate segment)

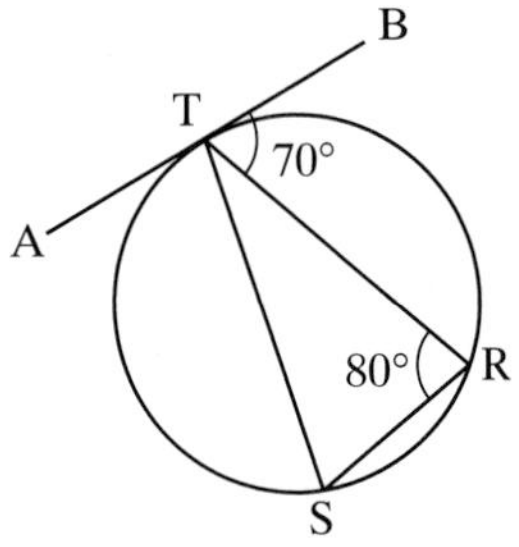

Exercise 5F

1 Find the size of each lettered angle.

a

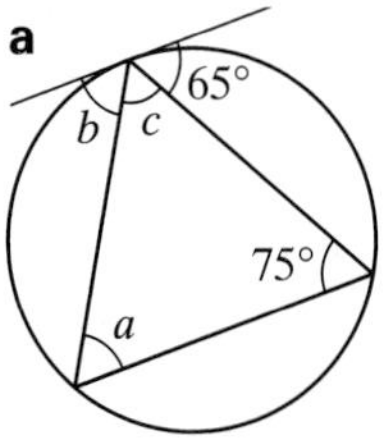

b

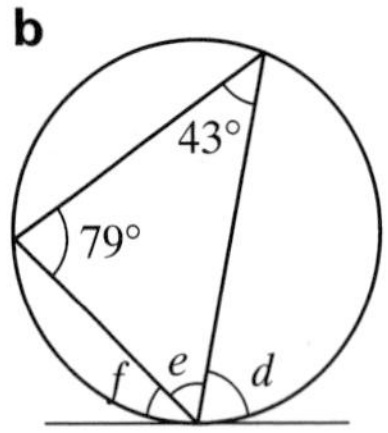

c

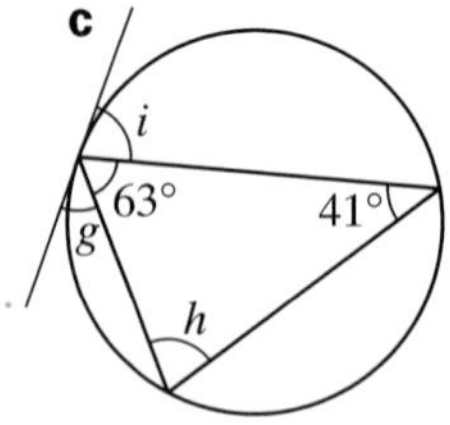

d

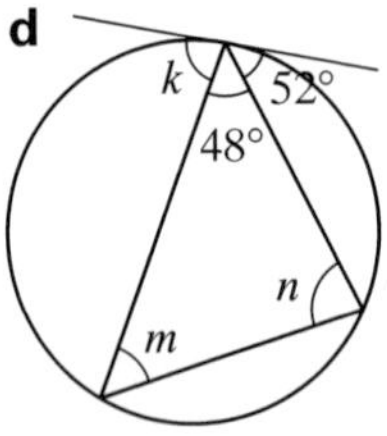

2 In each diagram, find the size of a, b, c and d.

a

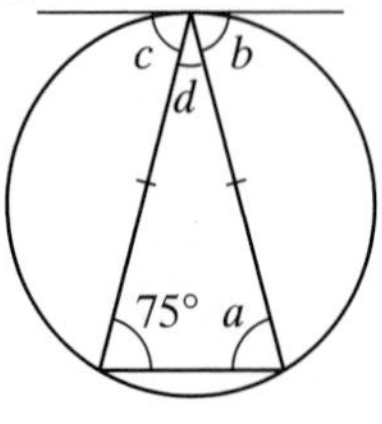

b

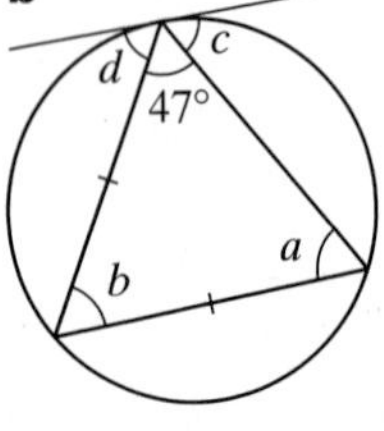

c

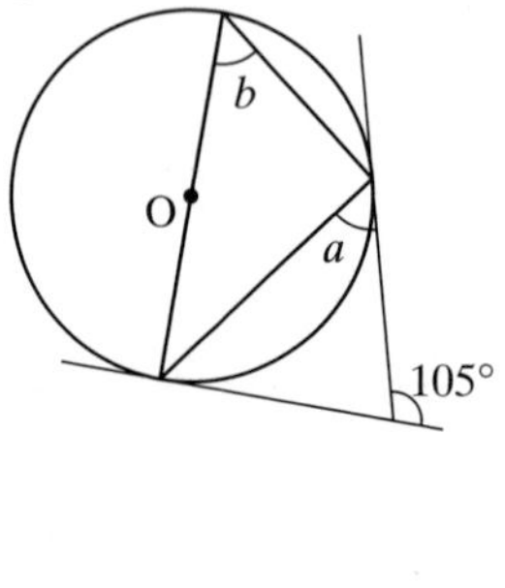

d

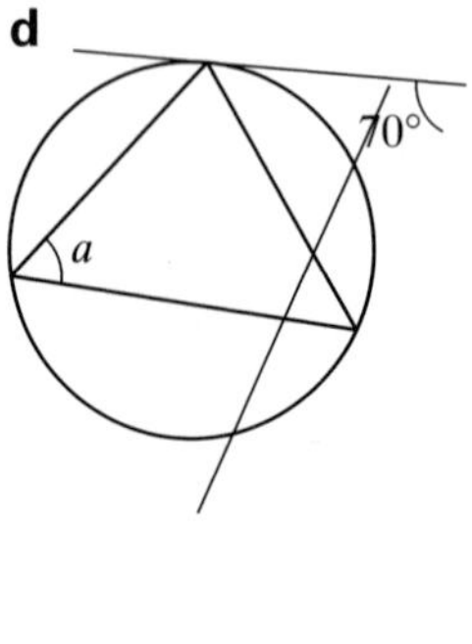

3 In each diagram, find the value of x.

a

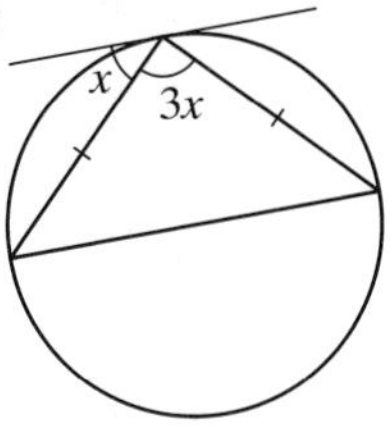

b

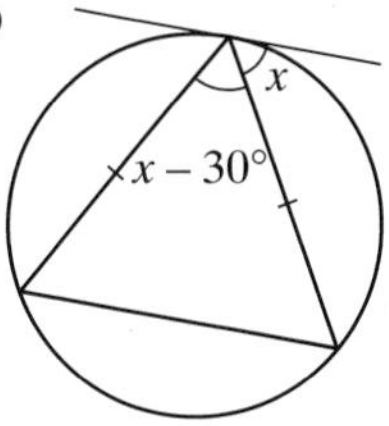

4 ATB is a tangent to the circle, centre O. Find the values of x, y and z in each case.

a

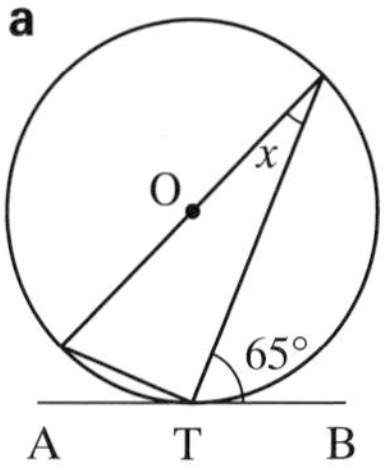

b

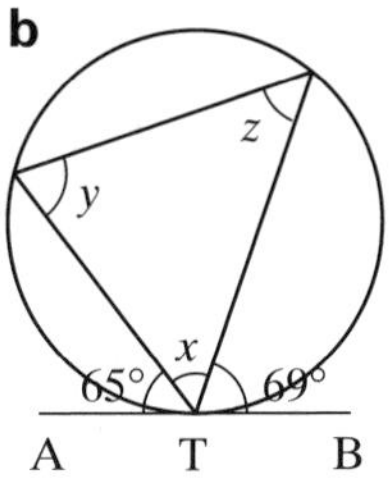

c

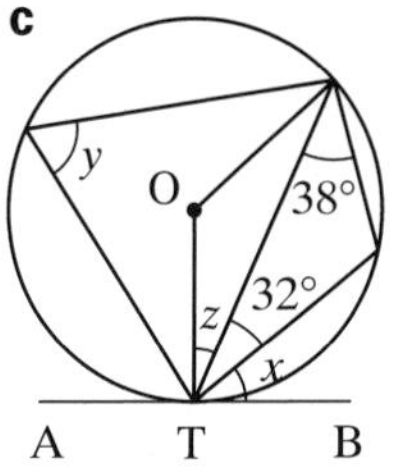

d

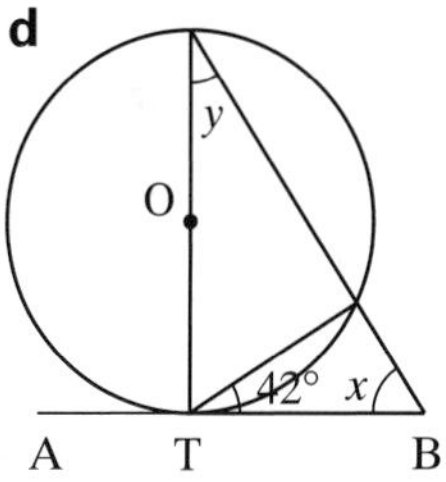

Possible coursework tasks

Fertile triangles

Start with any equilateral triangle and continue the given pattern using equilateral triangles at each stage.

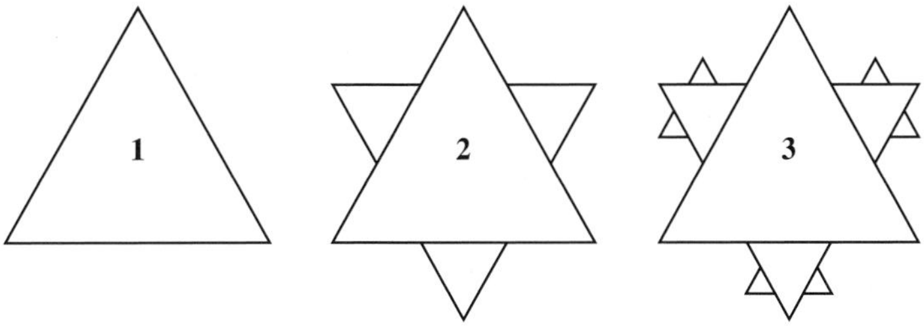

Investigate the perimeter and area of the shape at each stage.

Dotty parallel lines

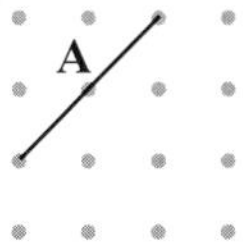

How many lines can be drawn on the grid which are parallel to line A and have the same length as line A?

Investigate for different lines and grids.

Interior and exterior right angles

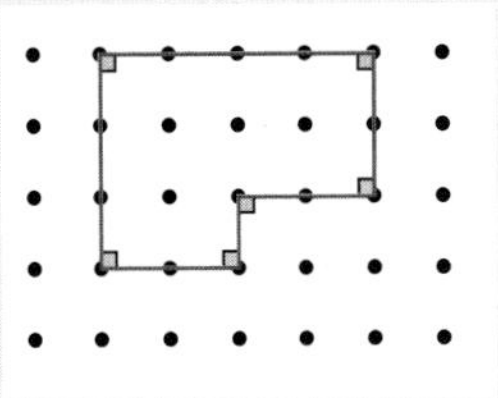

The shape is made by drawing only horizontal and vertical lines.

There are five right angles inside the shape and one outside the shape.

Investigate for other shapes.

Star patterns

Draw a pentagon and put in all its diagonals.
How many diagonals have you drawn?

Investigate for other polygons.

Examination questions

1

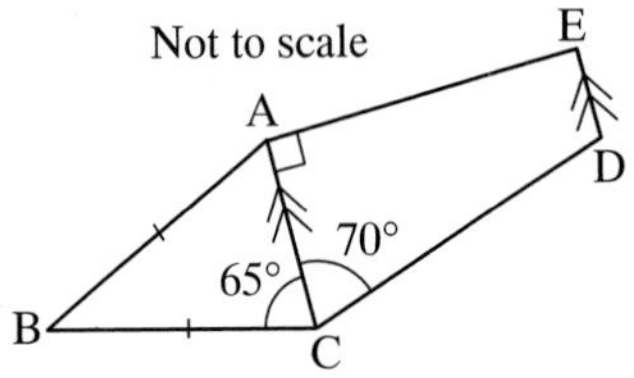

The pentagon ABCDE is the frame for Ibrahim's mountain bike. ABC is an isosceles triangle in which AB = BC and angle BCA = 65°. In the quadrilateral ACDE, angle ACD = 70°, angle CAE = 90° and AC is parallel to ED.

a **i** Calculate the size of angle ABC.

ii What facts about the angles of a triangle did you use in your calculation?

b Calculate the size of angle CDE.

c The radius of the wheel is 34 cm. Calculate the circumference of the wheel.

MEG, Question 2, Specimen Paper 4, 1998

2 A workbench is standing on a horizontal floor.
The side view of the bench is shown.
The legs AB and CD are equal in length and joined at E.

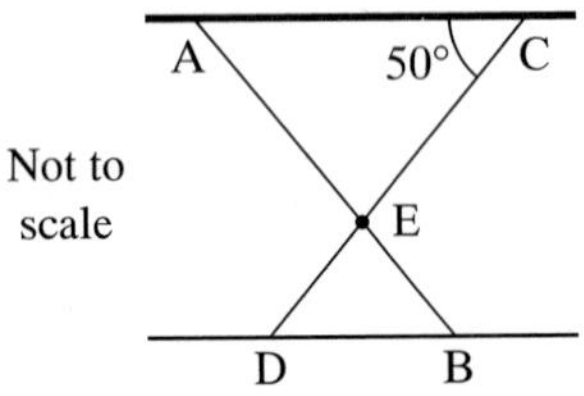

AE = EC
Angle ACD = 50°

a Work out the size of angle BAC giving a reason for your answer.

b Work out the size of angle AEC giving a reason for your answer.

SEG, Question 13, Paper 3, June 1994

3 A regular octagon, drawn opposite, has eight sides. One side of the octagon has been extended to form angle p.

a Work out the size of angle p.

b Work out the size of angle q.

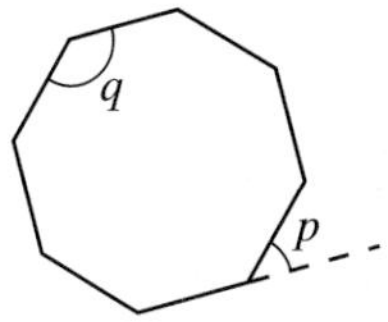

SEG, Question 14, Paper 3, June 1994

4 The diagram represents a regular pentagon with 2 of its lines of symmetry shown.

a Write down the value of angle p.

b Find the size of angle

i q **ii** r

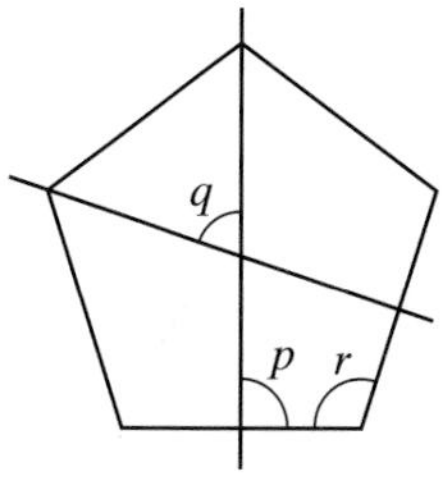

NEAB, Question 13, Specimen Paper 2, 1998

5 PQR is an equilateral triangle. PRS is an isosceles triangle with PR = RS.

a When SPR = 20°, what is the size of angle QRS?

b **i** When PQ is parallel to RS, what name is given to quadrilateral PQSR?

ii Give a reason for your answer.

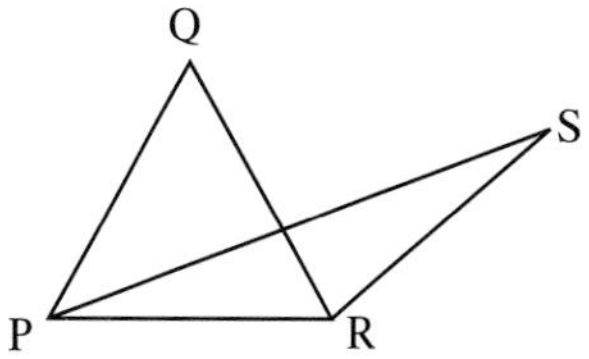

SEG, Question 5, Specimen Paper 10, 1998

6 The framework for some staging consists of three equilateral triangles ABE, EDB and DBC as shown in the diagram.

You must give a reason for each of your answers in this question.

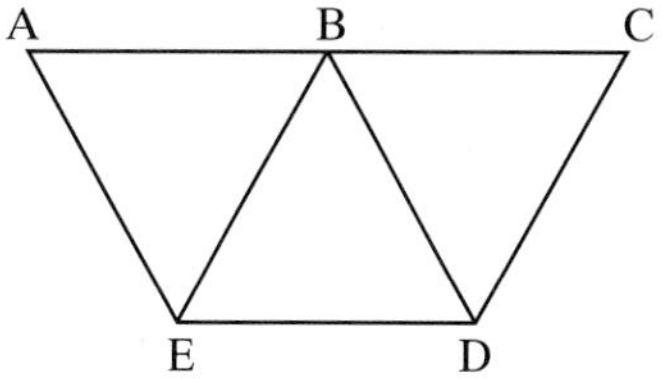

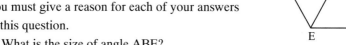

a What is the size of angle ABE?

b What is the size of angle EBC?

c What do your answers to parts **a** and **b** tell you about the points A, B and C?

d What is the size of angle BED?

e What do your answers to parts **a** and **d** tell you about the lines AB and ED?

WJEC, Question 4, Specimen Paper 2, 1998

7 The diagram shows the positions of three places A, B and C. AB is the same length as AC.

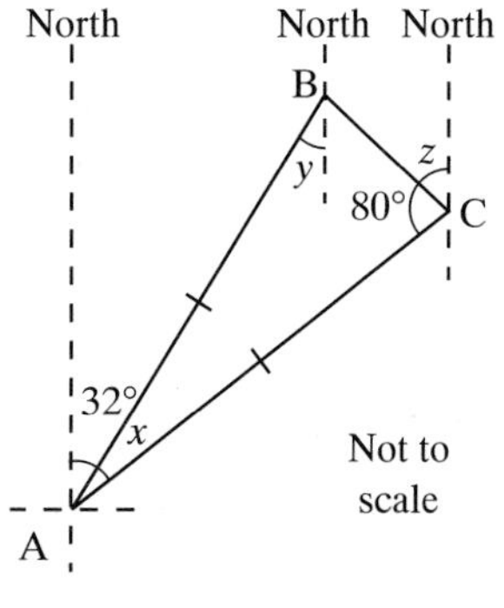

i Calculate the size of the angle marked x.

ii Explain why the angle marked y is equal to 32°.

iii Calculate the size of the angle marked z.

NEAB, Question 7, Paper 2H, June 1995

8 The diagram shows a circle, centre O. The chord BA is parallel to the tangent QC. QBP and QCR are tangents. Calculate the value of an angle x and and angle y.

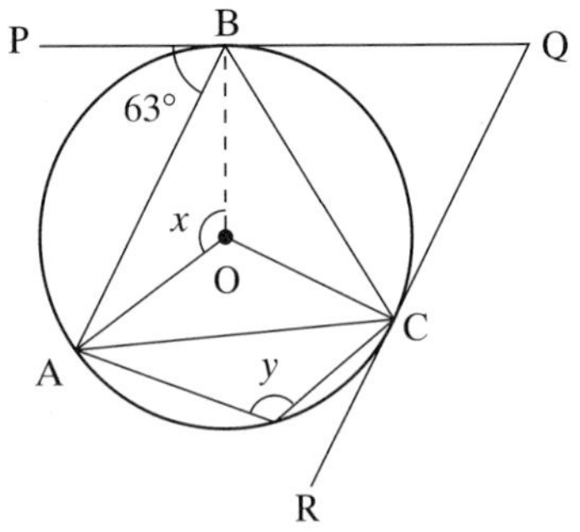

SEG, Question 13, Specimen Paper 15, 1998

9 TPK is a tangent to the circle. TSQ is a straight line. PQ = QR. Calculate the size of

a angle PQR

b angle QRS

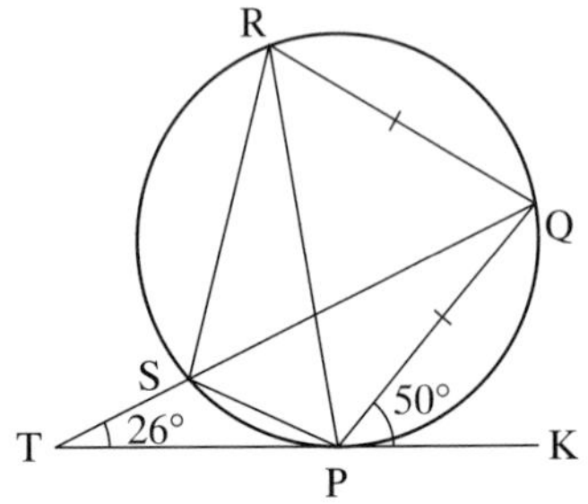

NEAB, Question 16, Specimen Paper 2H, 1998

10 ABCD is a circle, centre O. XAB is a straight line.
Angle BCD = 96°

a Find the values of p and q.

YBZ is the tangent to the circle at B.
Angle AOB = 144°

b Find the value of r.

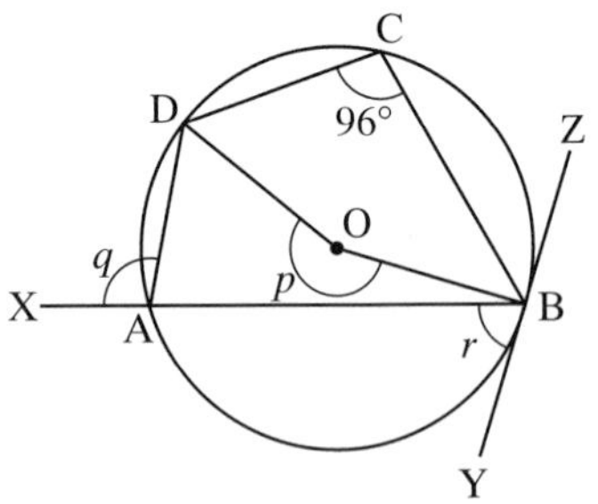

MEG, Question 3, Specimen SMP Paper 6, 1998

11 a O is the centre of the circle. P, K, Q and N are points on the circumference. QT is the tangent to the circle at Q. Calculate the values of m and n.

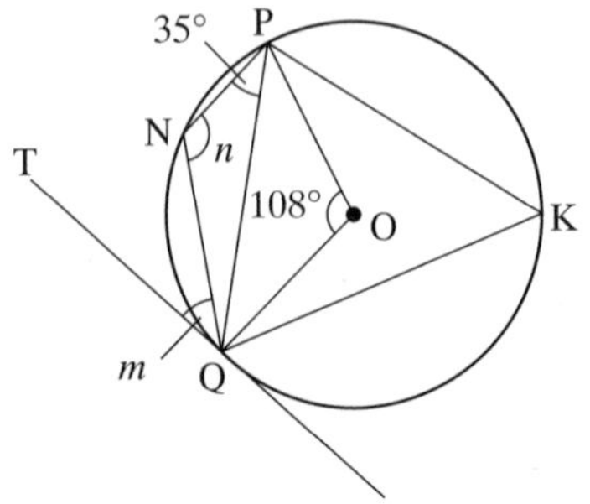

b ABC and ADE are straight lines. CE is a diameter. Angle DCE = $x°$ and angle BCD = $2x°$. Find, in terms of x, the sizes of the angles

i ABD **ii** DBE **iii** BAD

c Explain why BE × AC = AE × CD.

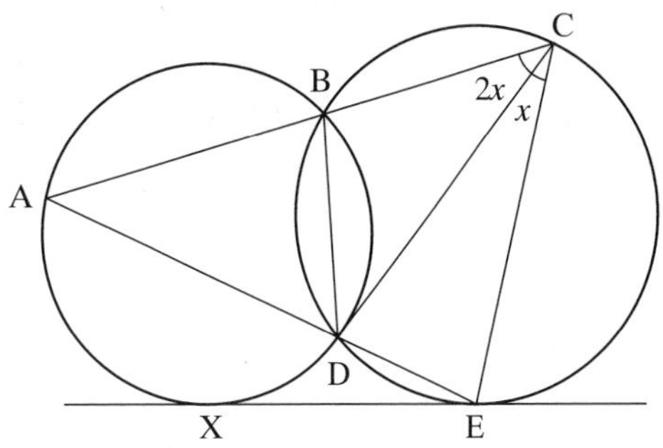

ULEAC, Question 12, Specimen Paper 6, 1998

12 AT and BT are tangents to the circle, centre C. P is a point on the circumference as shown. Angle BAT = 65°. Calculate the size of

a x **b** y **c** z

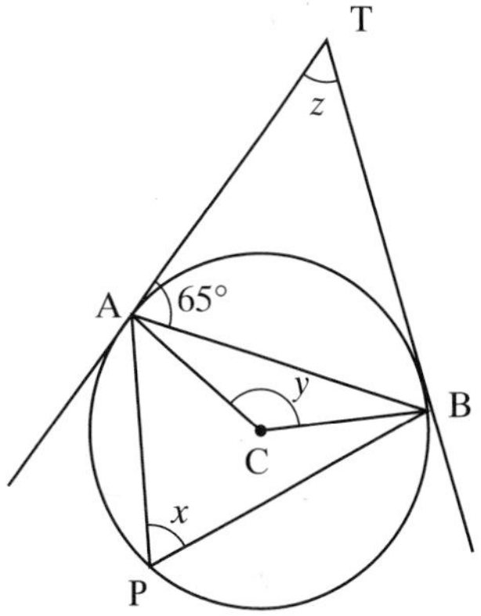

NEAB, Question 13, Paper 1H, June 1995

Summary

How well do you grade yourself?

To gain a grade **C**, you need to be able to solve problems using the angle properties of polygons and the properties of intersecting and parallel lines.

To gain a grade **B**, you need to be familiar with the properties of each different type of quadrilateral and be able clearly to give reasons to support answers to problems involving angles.

To gain a grade **A**, you need to know and be able to use circle theorems: angles at the centre, angles in the same segment, angles in a semicircle. You need also to know the properties of a cyclic quadrilateral and the alternate segment theorem.

What you should know after you have worked through Chapter 5

- Corresponding angles are equal. The sum of **allied** angles is 180°.
- For an N-sided polygon, the sum of the interior angles = $(N - 2) \times 180°$.
  The exterior angle of a regular N-sided polygon = $360° \div N$.
  Its interior angle = $180° - (360° \div N)$.
- An angle at the centre of a circle is twice any angle at the circumference subtended by the same arc.
- Every angle at the circumference of a semicircle that is subtended by a diameter of the semicircle is a right angle.
- Angles at the circumference in the same segment of a circle are equal.
- The sum of the opposite angles of a cyclic quadrilateral is 180°.
- A tangent is a straight line that touches a circle at one point only. This point is called the point of contact.
- A tangent is perpendicular to the radius at the point of contact.
- Tangents to a circle from an external point are equal in length to the point of contact. The line joining the external point to the centre of the circle bisects the angle between the tangents.
- The alternate segment theorem: the angle between a tangent and a chord through the point of contact is equal to the angle in the alternate segment.

6 Transformation geometry

This chapter is going to ... show you what is meant by congruence and then introduce you to geometric transformation, which involves the movement and enlargement of shapes.

What you should already know

- Be able to identify simple line graphs and their equations, such as these two, which occur often.

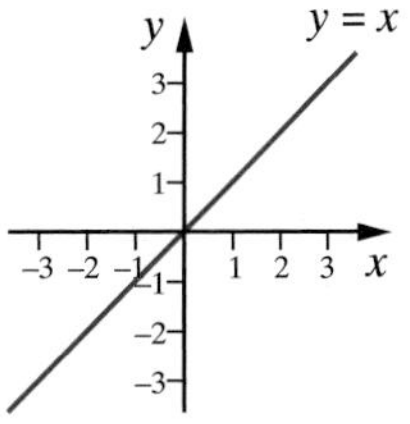

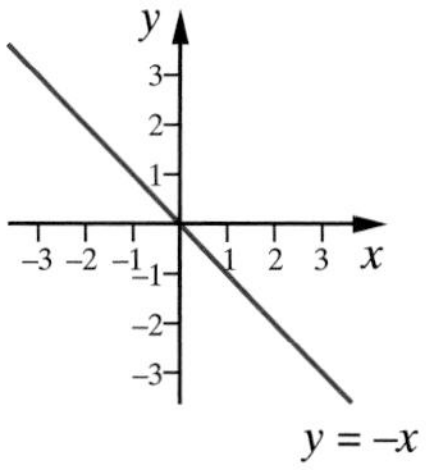

- Be able to recognise the equations of lines such as those below.

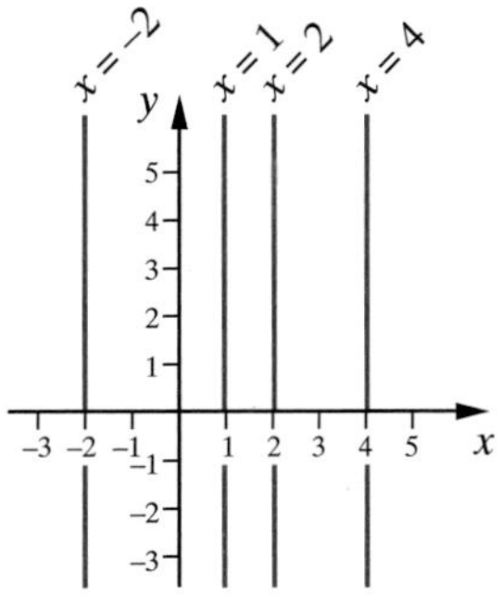

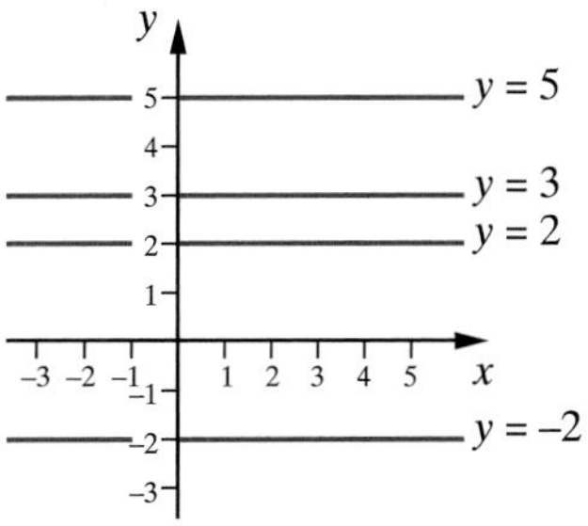

Congruence

Two shapes are congruent if they fit exactly on each other. For example, these triangles are all congruent.

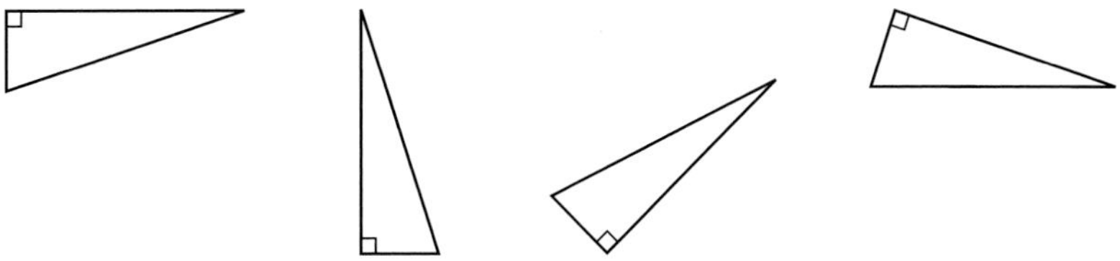

Notice that the triangles can be differently orientated (turned in different directions).

Conditions for congruent triangles

One of the following conditions is sufficient for two triangles to be congruent.

- All three sides of one triangle are equal to the corresponding sides of the other triangle.

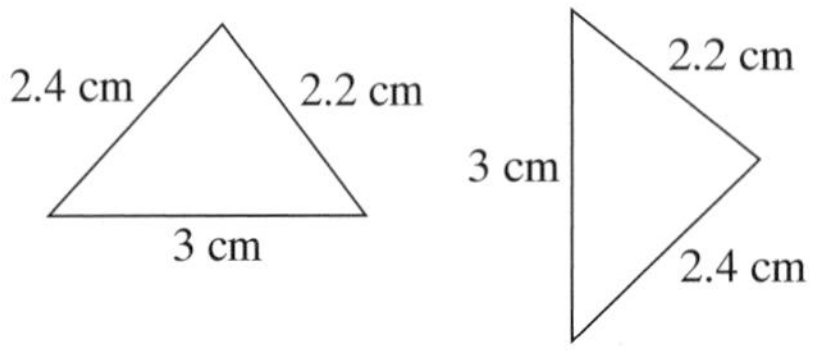

This is known as SSS (side, side, side).

- Two sides and the angle between them of one triangle are equal to the corresponding sides and angle of the other triangle.

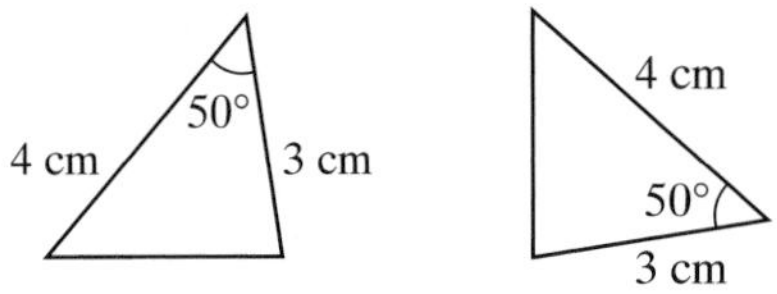

This is known as SAS (side, angle, side).

- Two angles and the side between them of one triangle are equal to the corresponding angles and side of the other triangle.

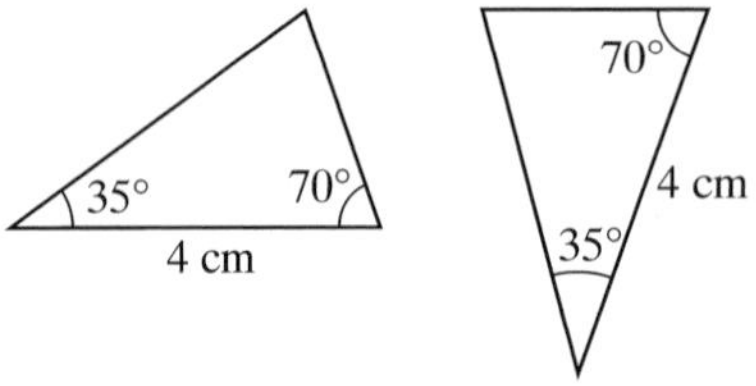

This is known as ASA (angle, side, angle).

- Both triangles have a right angle, equal hypotenuse and another side which is equal.

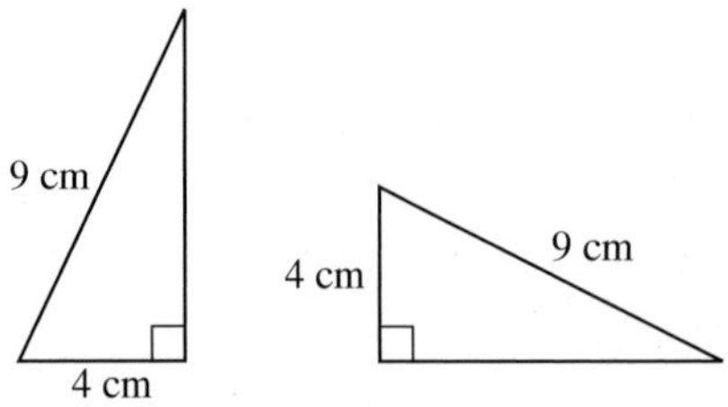

This is known as RHS (right angle, hypotenuse, side).

Notation

When we say that triangle ABC is congruent to triangle PQR, it should imply that

$\angle A = \angle P$	AB = PQ
$\angle B = \angle Q$	BC = QR
$\angle C = \angle R$	AC = PR

In other words, the points ABC correspond exactly to the points PQR in that order.

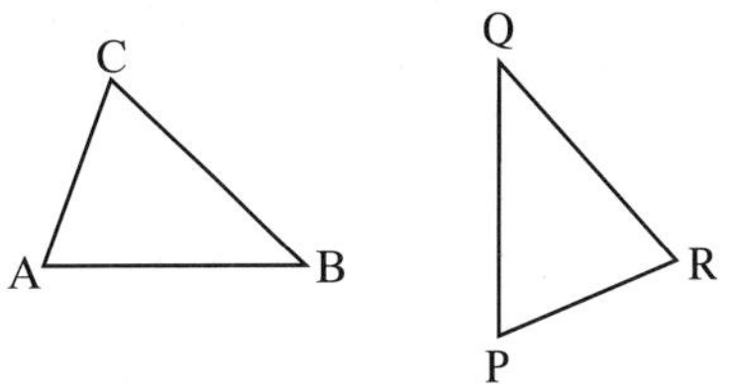

Exercise 6A

1 State whether each pair of triangles **a** to **h** is congruent, giving the reasons if they are.

a

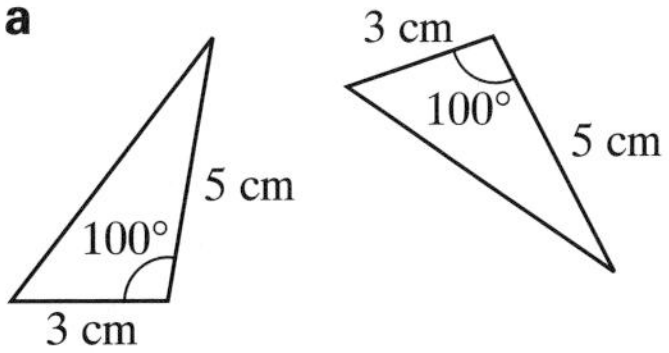

b

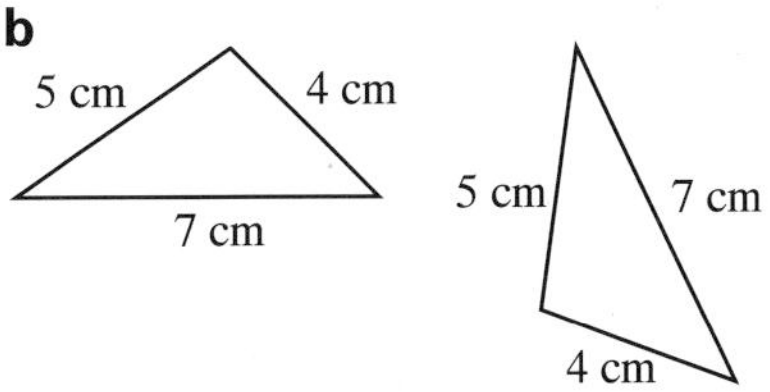

c

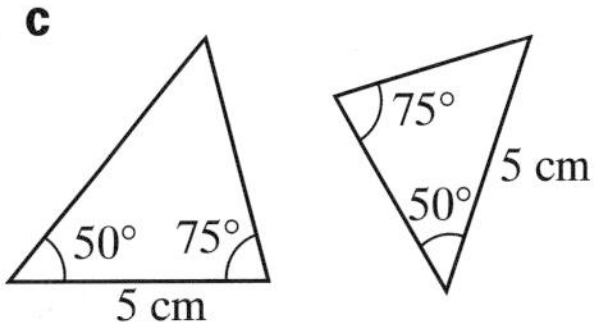

d

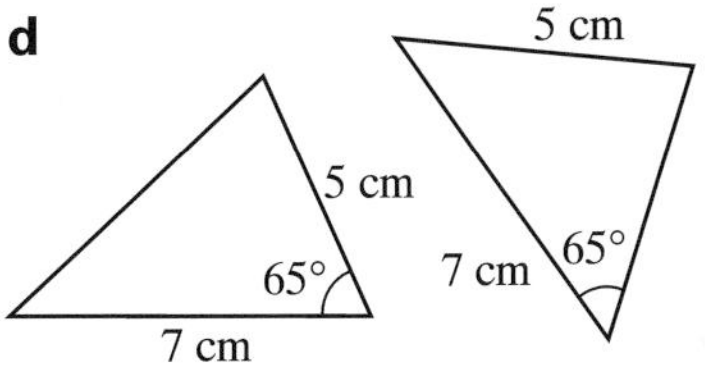

e

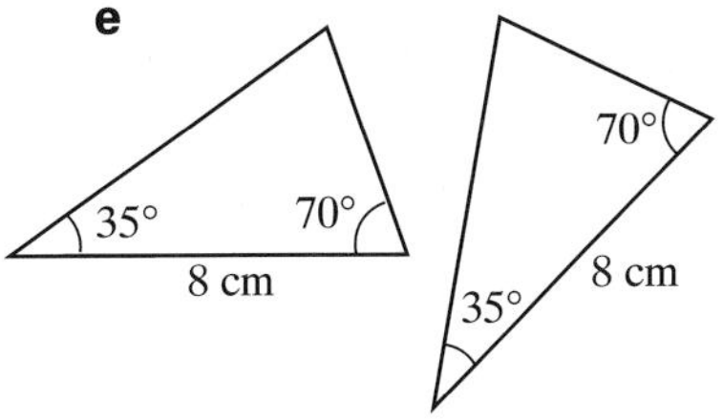

f

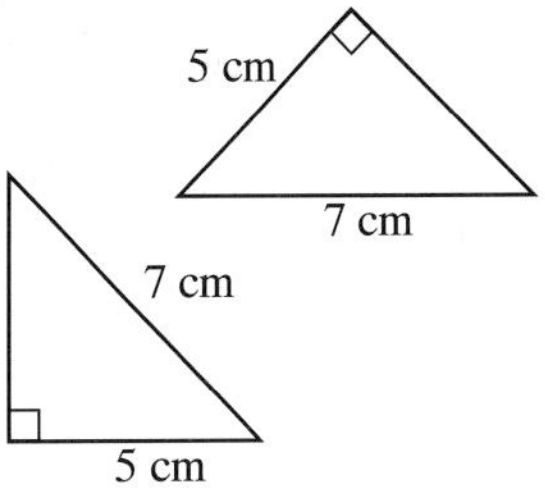

g

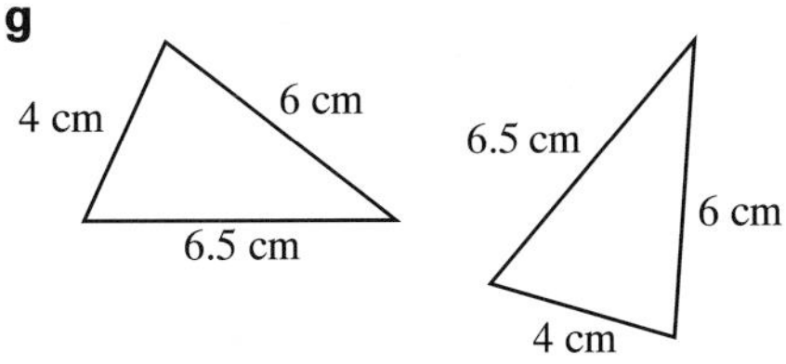

h

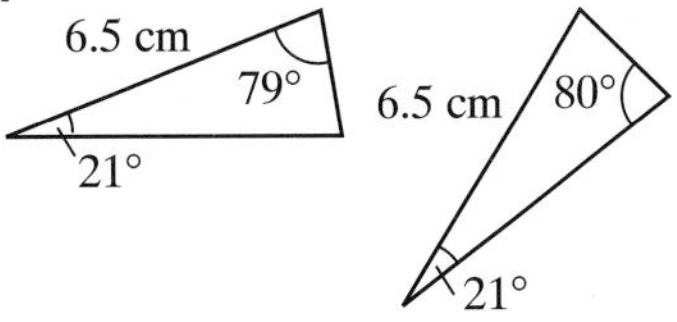

2 Draw a square PQRS. Draw in the diagonals PR and QS. Which triangles are congruent to each other?

3 Draw a rectangle EFGH. Draw in the diagonals EG and FH. Which triangles are congruent to each other?

4 Draw a parallelogram ABCD. Draw in the diagonals AC and BD. Which triangles are congruent to each other?

5 Draw an isosceles triangle ABC where AB = AC. Draw the line from A to the mid-point of BC. Which triangles are congruent to each other?

6 State whether each pair of triangles given below is congruent or not. If they are congruent, give the reason and state which points correspond to which.

a ABC where AB = 8 cm, BC = 9 cm, AC = 7.4 cm.
PQR where PQ = 9 cm, QR = 7.4 cm, PR = 8 cm.

b ABC where AB = 7.5 cm, AC = 8 cm, angle A = 50°.
PQR where PQ = 8 cm, QR = 75 mm, angle R = 50°.

c ABC where AB = 5 cm, BC = 6 cm, angle B = 35°.
PQR where PQ = 6 cm, QR = 50 mm, angle Q = 35°

d ABC where AB = 6 cm, angle B = 35°, angle C = 115°.
PQR where PQ = 6 cm, angle Q = 115°, angle R = 35°.

7 Given that triangle ABC is congruent to triangle PQR, $\angle A = 60°$, $\angle B = 80°$ and AB = 5 cm, find

i $\angle P$ **ii** $\angle Q$ **iii** $\angle R$ **iv** PQ

8 Given that ABCD is congruent to PQRS, $\angle A = 110°$, $\angle B = 55°$, $\angle C = 85°$ and RS = 4 cm, find

i $\angle P$ **ii** $\angle Q$ **iii** $\angle R$ **iv** $\angle S$ **v** CD

Transformations

Geometrical transformation changes the positions, or sizes, of shapes on a plane in particular ways. We shall deal with the four basic ways of changing the position and size of shapes: **translation**, **reflection**, **rotation** and **enlargement**.

All of these transformations, except enlargement, keep a shape congruent with itself.

Translation

Translation is the movement of a shape from one place to another without reflecting it or rotating it. It is sometimes called a 'glide', since the shape appears to glide from one place to another. Every point in the shape moves in the same direction and through the same distance.

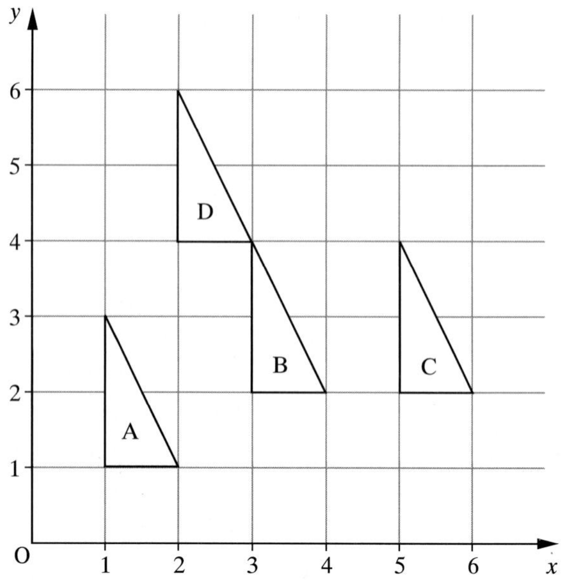

We describe such changes of position using vectors. In such a vector, the move from one point to another is represented

by the combination of a horizontal shift and a vertical shift. For example, take the case, shown in this diagram, of a triangle being moved from A to D, via B and C, and then back to A.

The vector describing the translation from A to B is $\begin{pmatrix} 2 \\ 1 \end{pmatrix}$.

The vector describing the translation from B to C is $\begin{pmatrix} 2 \\ 0 \end{pmatrix}$.

The vector describing the translation from C to D is $\begin{pmatrix} -3 \\ 2 \end{pmatrix}$.

The vector describing the translation from D to A is $\begin{pmatrix} -1 \\ -3 \end{pmatrix}$.

Notice

- The top number describes the horizontal movement. To the right +, to the left –.
- The bottom number describes the vertical movement. Upwards +, downwards –.

Exercise 6B

1 Describe with vectors these translations.

a **i** A to B	**ii** A to C	**iii** A to D	**iv** A to E	**v** A to F	**vi** A to G
b **i** B to A	**ii** B to C	**iii** B to D	**iv** B to E	**v** B to F	**vi** B to G
c **i** C to A	**ii** C to B	**iii** C to D	**iv** C to E	**v** C to F	**vi** C to G
d **i** D to E	**ii** E to B	**iii** F to C	**iv** G to D	**v** F to G	**vi** G to E

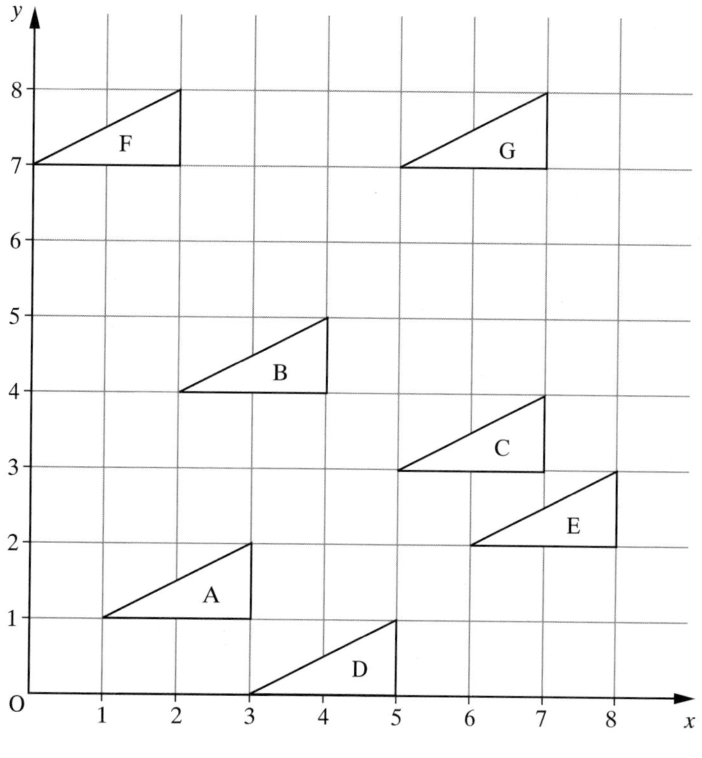

2 **a** Draw the triangle with co-ordinates A(1, 1), B(2, 1) and C(1, 3).

b Draw the image of ABC after a translation with vector $\begin{pmatrix} 2 \\ 3 \end{pmatrix}$. Label this P.

c Draw the image of ABC after a translation with vector $\begin{pmatrix} -1 \\ 2 \end{pmatrix}$. Label this Q.

d Draw the image of ABC after a translation with vector $\begin{pmatrix} 3 \\ -2 \end{pmatrix}$. Label this R.

e Draw the image of ABC after a translation with vector $\begin{pmatrix} -2 \\ -4 \end{pmatrix}$. Label this S.

3 Using your diagram from question **2**, describe the translation that will move

a P to Q **b** Q to R **c** R to S **d** S to P

e R to P **f** S to Q **g** R to Q **e** P to S

4 Take a 10×10 grid and the triangle A(0, 0), B(1, 0) and C(0, 1). How many different translations are there that use integer values only and will move the triangle ABC to somewhere in the grid? (Do not draw them all.)

Reflection

Reflection is the movement of a shape so that it becomes a mirror image of itself. For example,

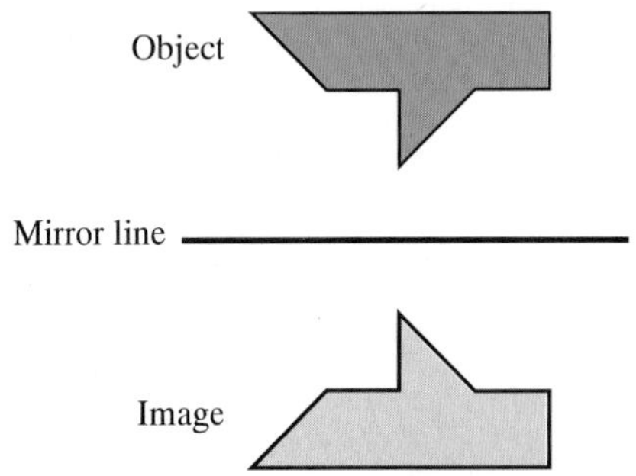

Notice the reflection of each point in the original shape (called the object) is perpendicular to the mirror line. So if you 'fold' the whole diagram along the mirror line, any object point will coincide with its reflection (also called its image point).

Exercise 6C

1 Draw these figures on squared paper and then draw the reflection of each in the given mirror line.

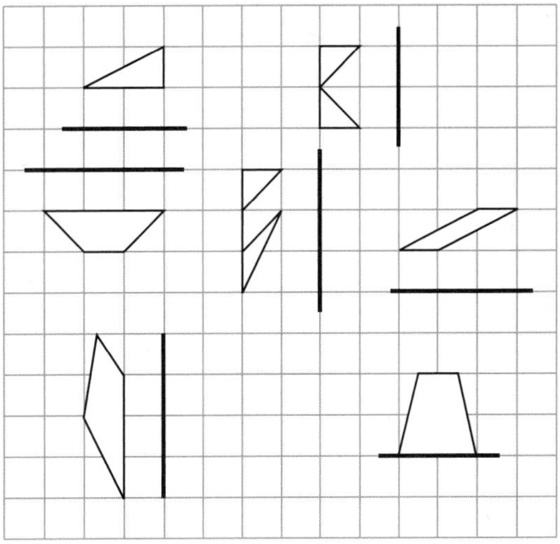

2 Draw these figures on squared paper and then draw the reflection of each in the given mirror line.

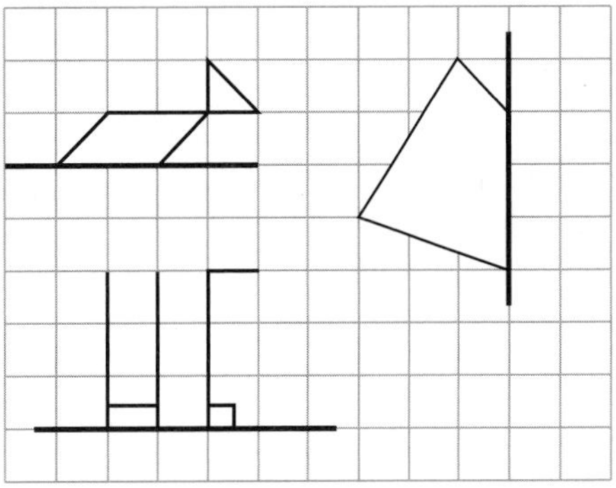

3 a Draw a pair of axes, *x*-axis from –5 to 5, *y*-axis from –5 to 5.

b Draw the triangle with co-ordinates A(1, 1), B(3, 1), C(4, 5).

c Reflect the triangle ABC in the *x*-axis. Label the image P.

d Reflect triangle P in the *y*-axis. Label the image Q.

e Reflect triangle Q in the *x*-axis, label it R.

f Describe the reflection that will move triangle ABC to triangle R.

4 a Repeat the steps of question **3** but start with any shape you like.

b Is your answer to part **f** the same as before?

c Would the final answer in part **d** always be the same no matter what shape you started with?

5 Draw these figures on squared paper and then draw the reflection of each in the given mirror line.

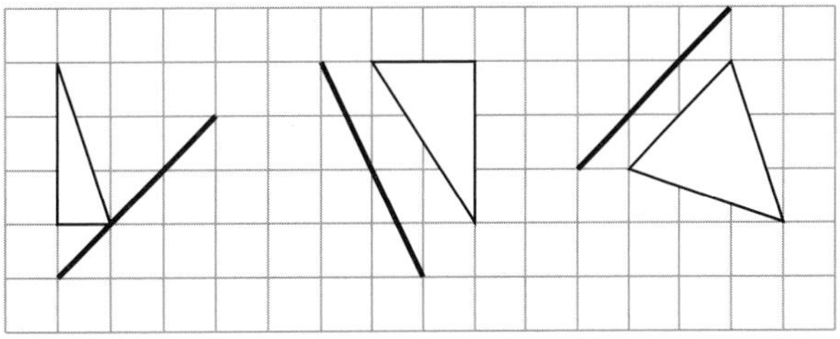

6 Draw these figures on squared paper and then draw the reflection of each in the given mirror line.

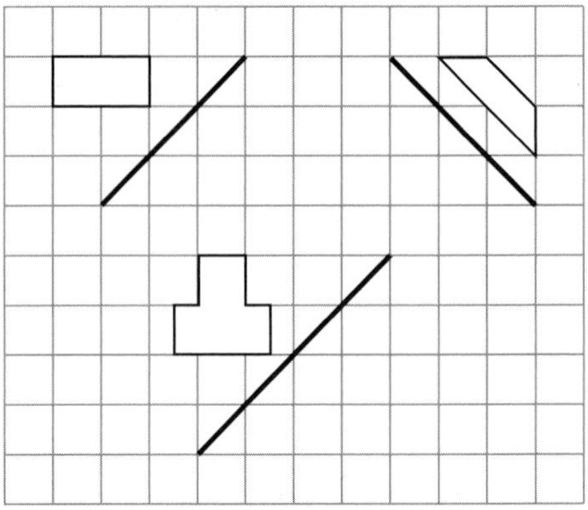

7 a Draw a pair of axes and the lines $y = x$ and $y = -x$, as shown.

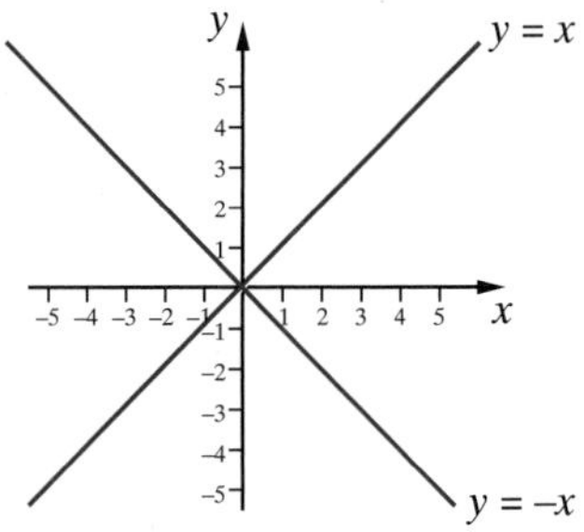

b Draw the triangle with co-ordinates A(2, 1), B(5, 1), C(5, 3).

c Draw the reflection of triangle ABC in the x-axis and label the image P.

d Draw the reflection of triangle P in the line $y = -x$ and label the image Q.

e Draw the reflection of triangle Q in the y-axis and label the image R.

f Draw the reflection of triangle R in the line $y = x$ and label the image S.

g Draw the reflection of triangle S in the x-axis and label the image T.

h Draw the reflection of triangle T in the line $y = -x$ and label the image U.

i Draw the reflection of triangle U in the y-axis and label the image W.

j What single reflection will move triangle W to triangle ABC?

8 a Repeat the steps of question **7** but start with any shape you like.

b Is your answer to part **j** the same as before?

c Would your answer to part **j** always be the same no matter what shape you started with?

9 a Draw a pair of axes where both the x and y values are from –5 to 5.

b Draw, in the first quadrant, any triangle ABC and write down the co-ordinates of each vertex.

c i Reflect triangle ABC in the x-axis and label the image A′B′C′, where A′ is the image of A etc.

ii Write down the co-ordinates of A′, B′ and C′.

iii What connection is there between A, B, C and A′, B′, C′?

iv Will this connection always be so?

10 Repeat question **9**, but reflect triangle ABC in the y-axis.

11 Repeat question **9**, but reflect triangle ABC in the line $y = x$.

12 Repeat question **9**, but reflect triangle ABC in the line $y = -x$.

Rotation

Rotation moves a shape to a new position by turning it about a fixed point called the **centre of rotation**.

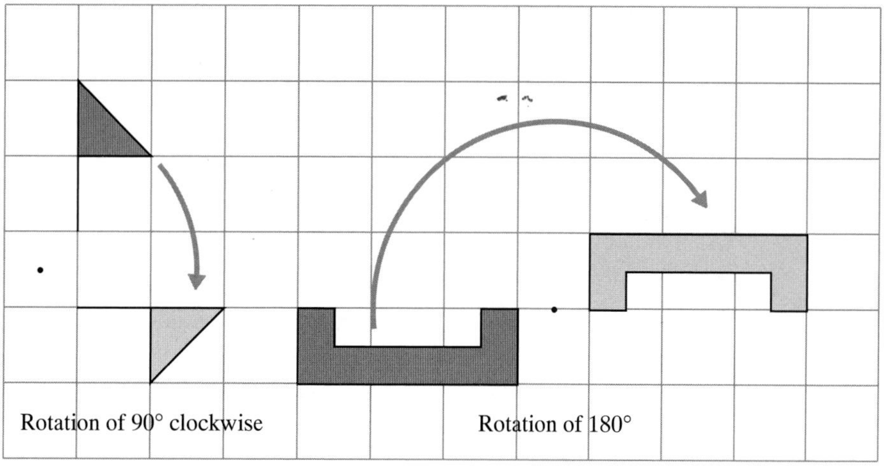

Notice

- The angle of rotation has direction, usually expressed as clockwise or anticlockwise.
- The position of the centre of rotation is always specified.

The rotations which most often appear in examination questions are 90° and 180° about the origin.

Exercise 6D

1 On squared paper, draw these shapes and centres of rotation.

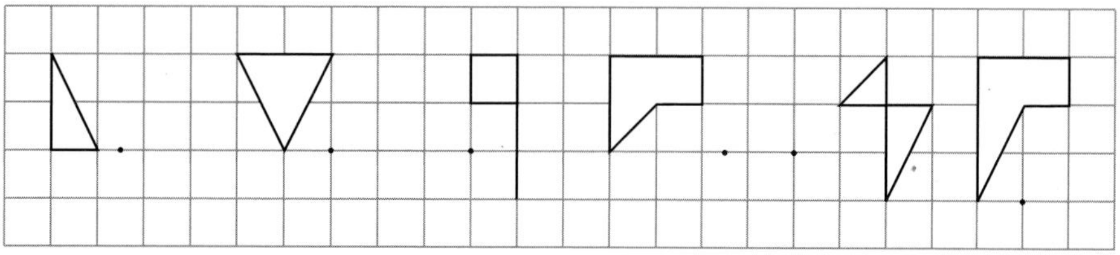

a Rotate each shape about its centre of rotation

i first by 90° clockwise **ii** then by a further 180°

b Describe, in each case, the transformation that would take the original shape to the final image.

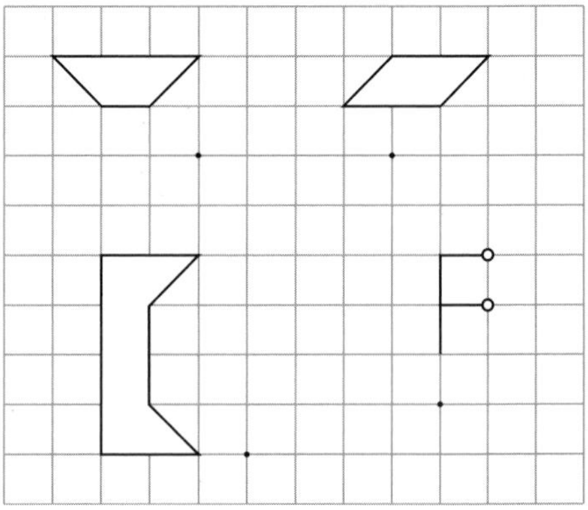

2 On squared paper draw these shapes and centres of rotation.

a Rotate each shape about its centre of rotation

i first by 90° anticlockwise

ii then by a further 180°

b Describe, in each case, the transformation that would take the original shape to the final image.

3 Draw some rotations to show that by rotating 180° clockwise you get the same result as you do by rotating 180° anticlockwise.

4 What other rotations are equivalent to these rotations?

a 270° clockwise   **b** 90° clockwise

c 60° anticlockwise   **d** 100° anticlockwise

5 a Draw a pair of axes where both the x and y values are from –5 to 5.

b Draw, in the first quadrant, any triangle ABC and write down the co-ordinates of each point.

c i Rotate triangle ABC 90° clockwise about the origin (0, 0) and label the image A′, B′, C′, where A′ is the image of A etc.

ii Write down the co-ordinate of A′, B′, C′.

iii What connection is there between A, B, C and A′, B′, C′?

iv Will this connection always be so?

6 Repeat question **5**, but rotate triangle ABC 180° clockwise.

7 Repeat question **5**, but rotate triangle ABC 90° anticlockwise.

8 a Draw a pair of axes where both the x and y values are from –5 to 5.

b Draw the triangle with vertices A(2, 1), B(3, 1), C(3, 5).

c Reflect ABC in the x-axis, then reflect the image in the y-axis. Label the final position A′B′C′.

d Describe the transformation that will take ABC directly to A′B′C′.

e Will this always happen no matter what shape you start with?

f Will this still happen if you reflect in the y-axis first, then reflect in the x-axis?

9 a Draw a regular hexagon ABCDEF with centre O.

b Using O as the centre of rotation, describe a transformation that will move

i triangle AOB to triangle BOC   **ii** triangle AOB to triangle COD

iii triangle AOB to triangle DOE   **iv** triangle AOB to triangle EOF

c Describe the transformations that will move the rhombus ABCO to

i rhombus BCDO   **ii** rhombus DEFO

10 ABCDE is a regular pentagon with centre O.

a What transformation will move

i triangle DOE to triangle EOA

ii quadrilateral ABCO to quadrilateral BCDO?

b Name all the triangles congruent to

i AOB **ii** ADC

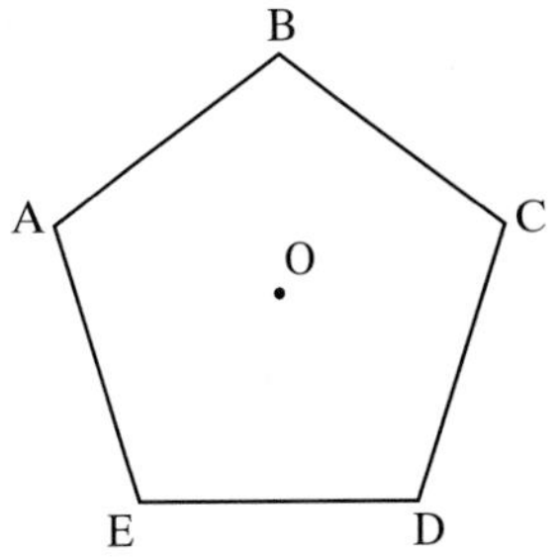

Enlargement

Enlargement changes the size of a shape to give a similar image. It always has a **centre of enlargement** and a **scale factor**. Every length of the enlargement will be

Original length × Scale factor

The distance of each image point on the enlargement from the centre of enlargement will be

Distance of original point from centre of enlargement × Scale factor

For example, this diagram shows an enlargement by scale factor 3 of a triangle ABC.

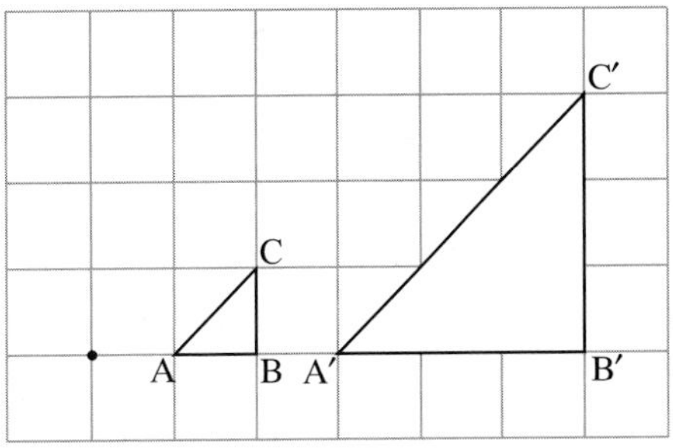

Notice

- Each length on the enlargement A′B′C′ is three times the corresponding length on the original shape.
- The distance of any point on the enlargement from the centre of enlargement is three times longer than the corresponding distance on the original shape.

There are two distinct ways to enlarge a shape: the ray method and the co-ordinate method.

Ray method

This is the **only** way to construct an enlargement when the diagram is not on a grid. The example on the right shows an enlargement by scale factor 3 made by the ray method.

Notice that the rays have been drawn from the centre of enlargement to each vertex and beyond.

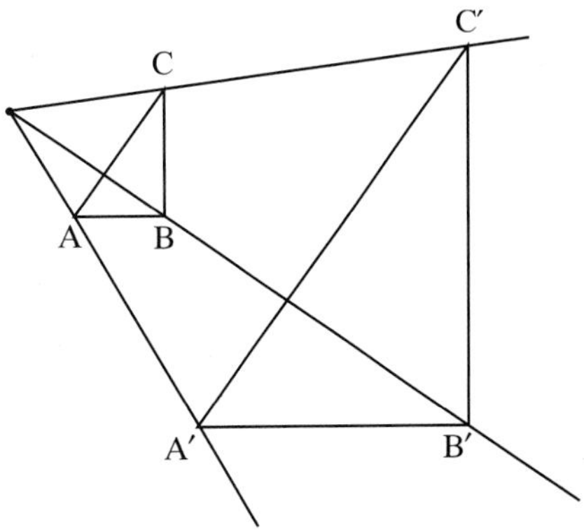

The distance from each vertex on triangle ABC to the centre of enlargement was measured and multiplied by 3 to give the distance of each image vertex from the centre of enlargement. Once each image vertex has been found, the whole image shape can then be drawn.

Check the measurements and see for yourself how the calculations have been done. Notice again that each line is three times longer in the enlargement.

Co-ordinate method

In the diagram below, an enlargement has been made by scale factor 3 from the centre of enlargement $(1, 2)$.

The co-ordinates of each image vertex were found as follows.

First, we worked out the horizontal and vertical distances from each original vertex to the centre of enlargement.

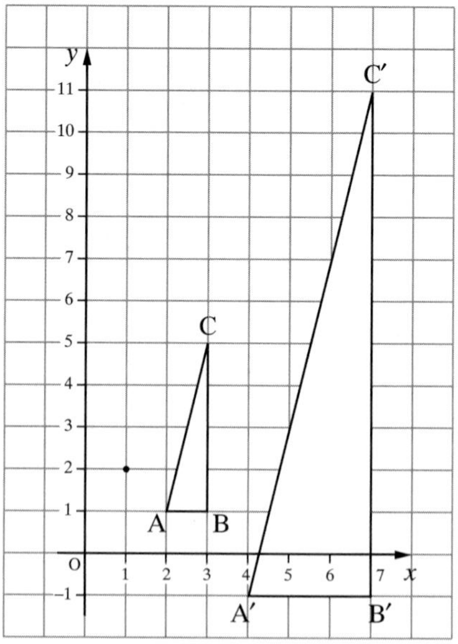

Then we multiplied each of these distances by 3 to find the position of each image vertex.

For example, take the calculations to find the co-ordinates of C′.

From the centre of enlargement $(1, 2)$ to point $C(3, 5)$

horizontal distance $= 3 - 1 = 2$

vertical distance $= 5 - 2 = 3$

Make these 3 times longer to give

new horizontal distance $= 6$

new vertical distance $= 9$

So the co-ordinates of C′ are

$(1 + 6, 2 + 9) = (7, 11)$

Notice again that each line is three times longer in the enlargement.

Negative enlargement

Negative enlargement produces an image shape on the opposite side of the centre of enlargement to the original shape.

In the example shown at the top of the next page, ABC has been enlarged by scale factor -2, with the centre of enlargement at $(1, 0)$.

You can transform from ABC to A′B′C′ by either the ray method or the co-ordinate method, but calculating the new lengths on the opposite side of the centre of enlargement to the original shape.

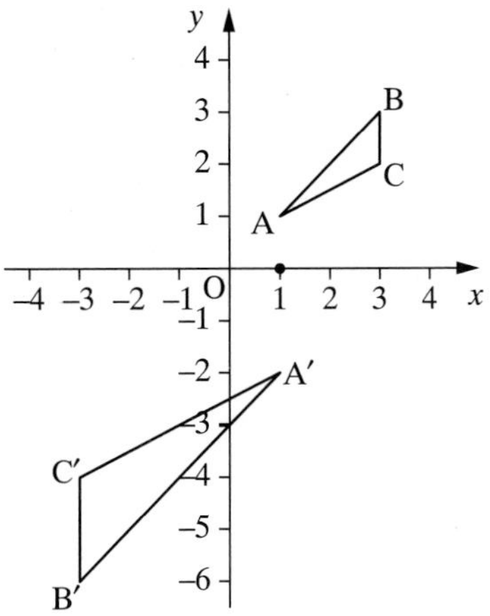

Exercise 6E

1 Copy each of these figures with its centre of enlargement. Then enlarge it by the given scale factor, using the ray method.

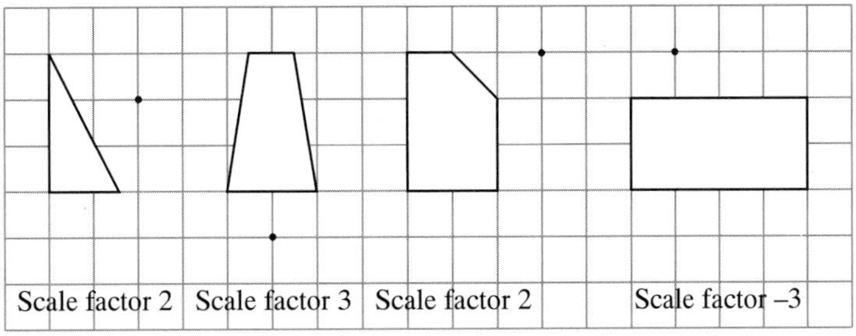

2 Copy each of these shapes on squared paper and enlarge it from the given centre of enlargement by the given scale factor. Use the co-ordinate method.

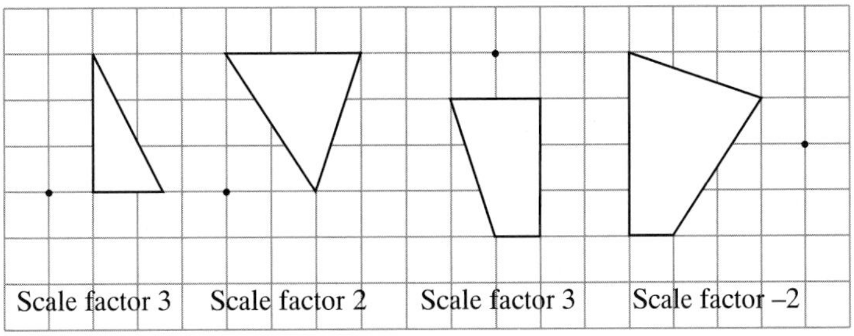

3 **a** Draw on squared paper a triangle ABC.

b Mark four different centres of enlargement on your diagram:

one above your triangle	one to the left of your triangle
one below your triangle	one to the right of your triangle.

d What do you notice about each enlarged shape?

4 'Strange but True'… you can have an enlargement in mathematics that is actually smaller than the original shape! This happens when you 'enlarge' a shape by a fractional scale factor. For example, try 'enlarging' these shapes by scale factor $\frac{1}{2}$.

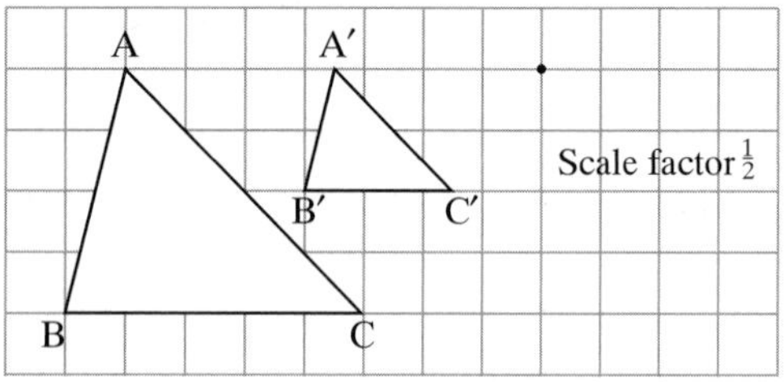

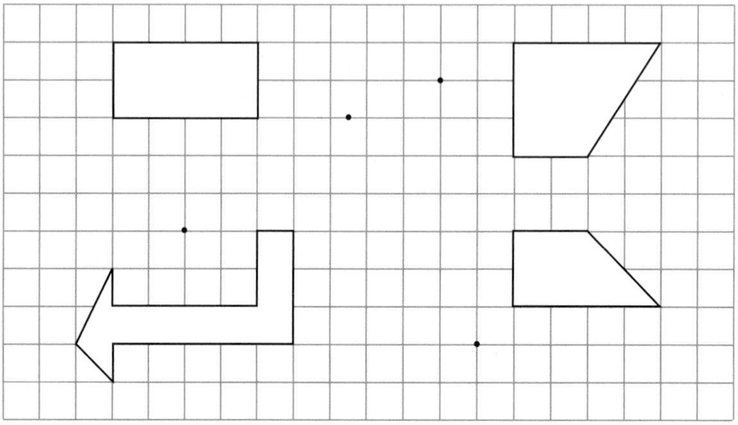

5 Draw the enlargement of each shape at the given scale factor.

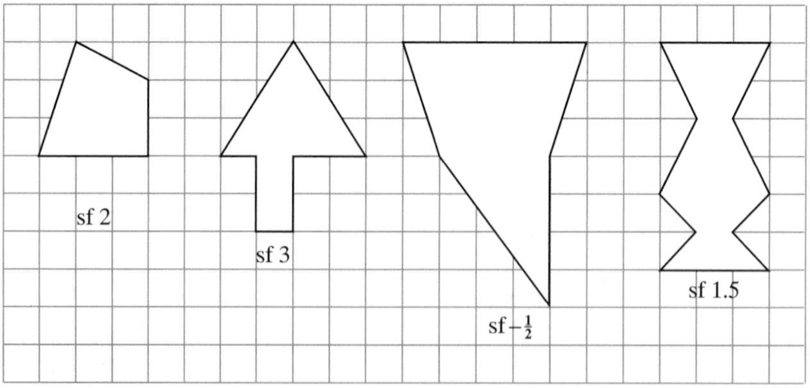

6 When you draw an enlargement:

a What effect does moving the centre of enlargement have on the enlarged shape?

b What is not affected by moving the centre of enlargement?

Exercise 6F

1 Describe fully the transformation that will move the shaded triangle to each of the positions A–F.

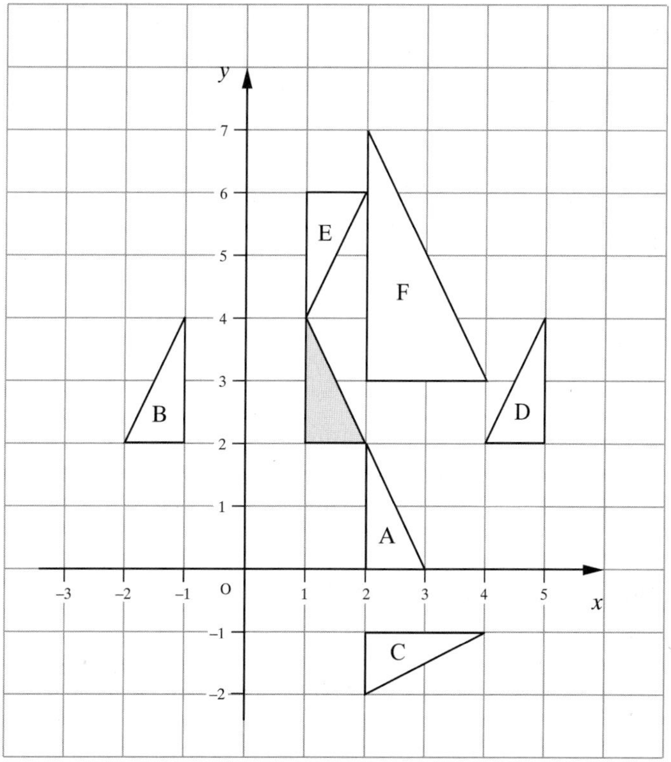

2 Describe fully the transformation that will move

a T_1 to T_2

b T_1 to T_6

c T_2 to T_3

d T_6 to T_2

e T_6 to T_5

f T_5 to T_4

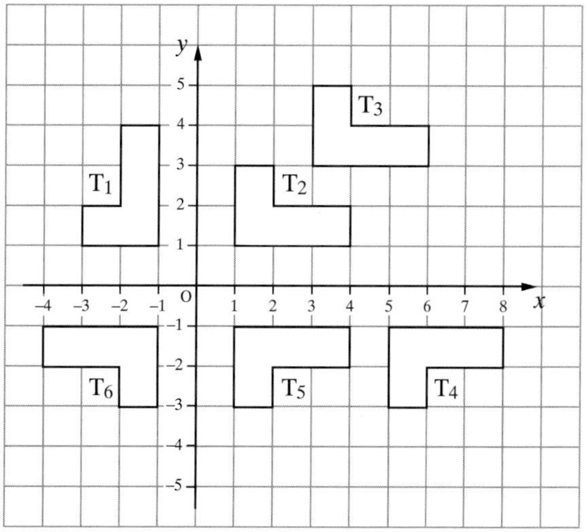

3 **a** Plot a triangle T with vertices (1, 1), (2, 1), (1, 3).
b Reflect triangle T in the y-axis and label the image T_b.
c Rotate triangle T_b 90° anticlockwise about the origin and label the image T_c.
d Reflect triangle T_c in the y-axis and label the image T_d.
e Describe fully the transformation that will move triangle T_d back to triangle T.

4 The point P(3, 4) is reflected in the x-axis, then rotated by 90° clockwise about the origin. What are the co-ordinates of the image of P?

5 A point Q(5, 2) is rotated by 180°, then reflected in the x-axis.
a What are the co-ordinates of the image point of Q?
b What single transformation would have taken point Q directly to the image point?

6 Find the co-ordinates of the image of the point (3, 5) after a clockwise rotation of 90° about the point (1, 3).

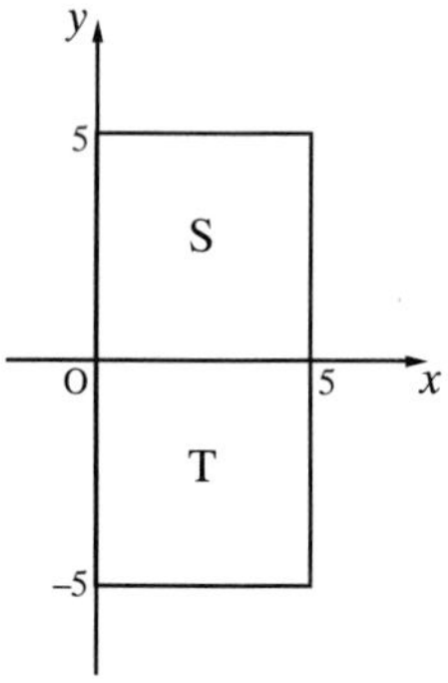

7 Describe fully at least three different transformations that could move the square labelled S to the square labelled T.

8 The point A(4, 4) has been transformed to the point A′ (4, –4). Describe as many different transformations as you can that could transform point A to point A′.

9 Describe the single transformation equivalent to: reflection in the y-axis followed by reflection in the x-axis.

Possible coursework tasks

Keep turning left

The shape is made by following the instructions.

** • Draw a line 1 cm long.
- Rotate left 90° and draw a line 3 cm long.
- Rotate left 90° and draw a line 2 cm long.
- Rotate left 90° and draw a line 1 cm long.
- Go back to **.

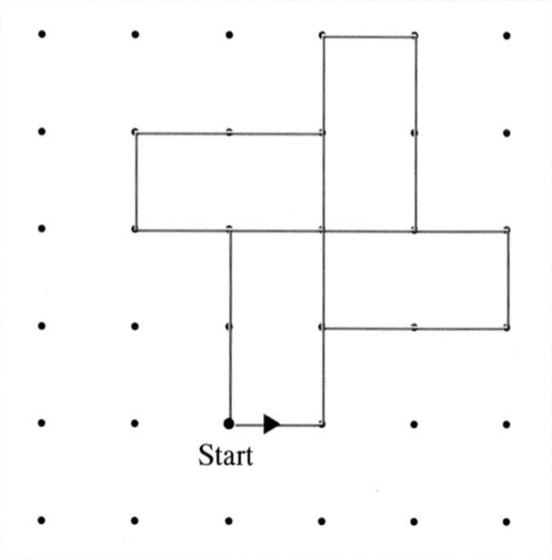

Call this pattern (1, 3, 2). What other patterns can you make using different numbers?

Vectorial areas

The vector describing the translation from O to A is $\begin{pmatrix}3\\4\end{pmatrix}$.

The vector describing the translation from O to B is $\begin{pmatrix}6\\4\end{pmatrix}$.

The area of the triangle is 6 square units.

Can you find a connection between the two vectors and the area of the triangle?

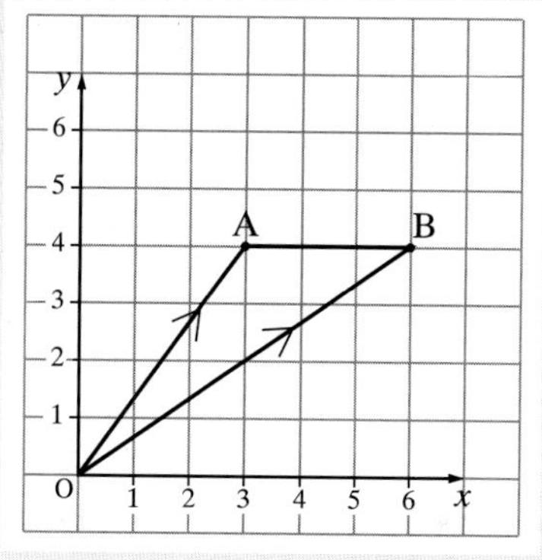

What's the change?

There are 4 different transformations which leave a rectangle in the same position although its vertices may have changed.

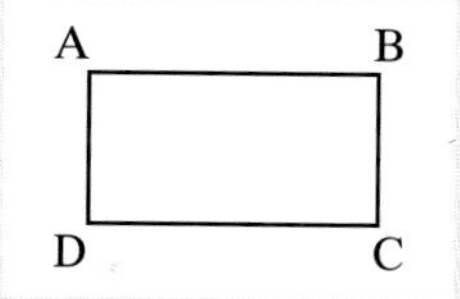

a Can you find all four?
Let this be called the 'symmetry group of order 4' for the rectangle.

b Investigate the order of the symmetry group for other shapes.

Reams of paper

Paper sizes are coded with a letter and a number: For example, A4 and A3 as used in school.

Investigate paper sizes and scale factors.

Examination questions

1 Which triangle is congruent to ABC? State why.

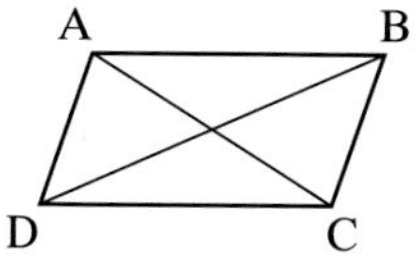

NEAB, Question 5, Specimen Paper 2H, 1998

2 The diagram shows three identical rhombuses P, Q and T.

a Explain why angle x is 120°.

b Rhombus Q can be rotated onto rhombus T.

i Mark a centre of rotation on the diagram.

ii State the angle of rotation.

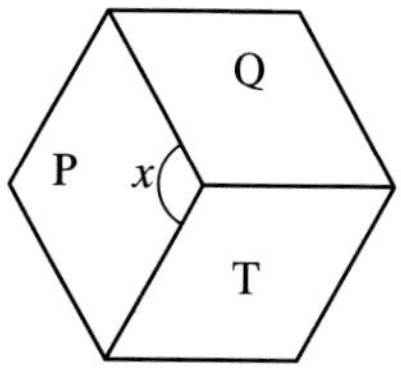

NEAB, Question 2 Paper 1, June 1995

3 **a** Describe fully the single transformation that will transform the shape labelled A to the shaded shape.

b On the grid draw the shape labelled A after it has been rotated 90° clockwise about the origin. Label it B.

c On the grid enlarge the shape labelled A by a scale factor of 2 from the centre of enlargement P(6, 1).

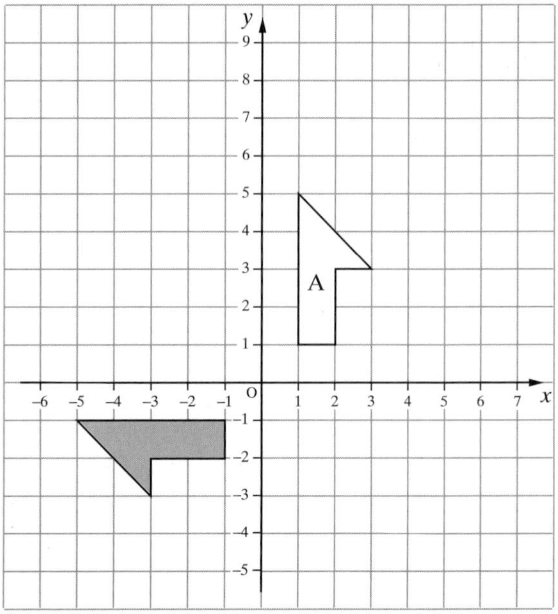

NEAB, Question 13, Paper 1, November 1995

4 The parallelogram ABCD has vertices at (6, 3), (9, 3), (12, 9) and (9, 9) respectively.

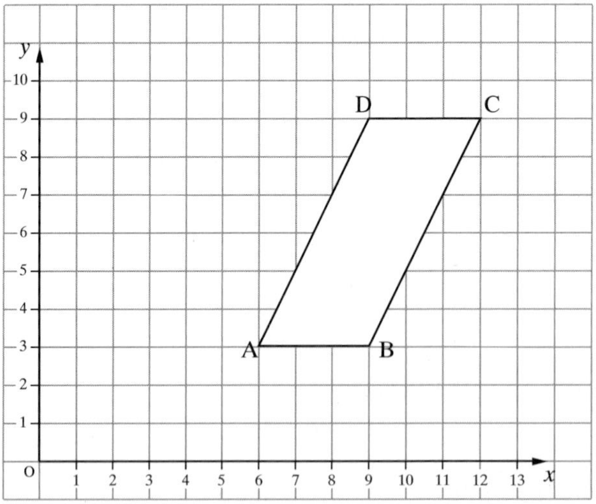

a An enlargement, scale factor $\frac{2}{3}$ and centre (0, 0), transforms parallelogram ABCD onto parallelogram $A_1B_1C_1D_1$. Draw the parallelogram $A_1B_1C_1D_1$.

b The parallelogram $A_1B_1C_1D_1$ can be transformed back onto the parallelogram ABCD by a single transformation. Describe fully this transformation

SEG, Question 5, Specimen Paper 16, 1998

5 The sketch shows the position of a rectangle ABCD.

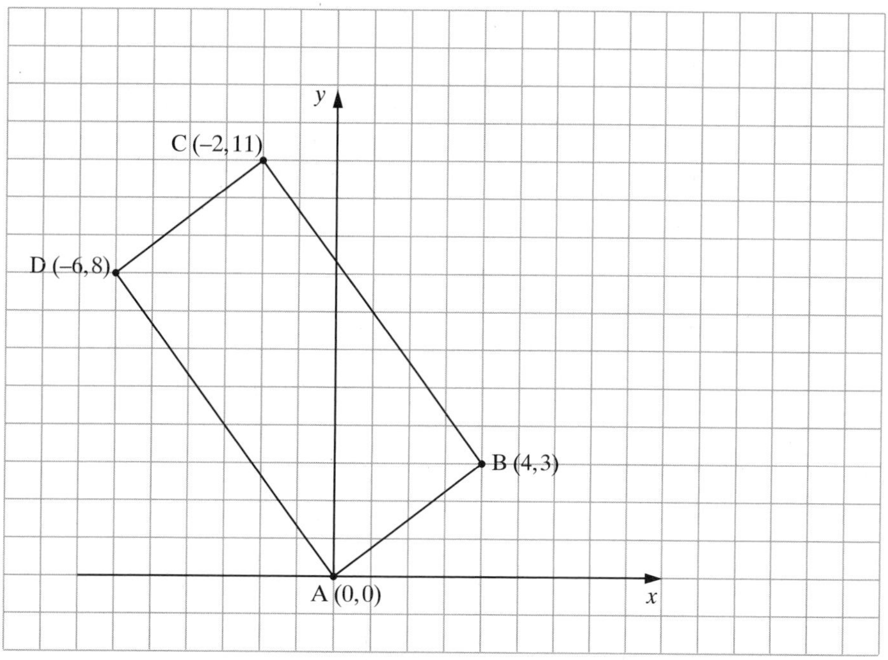

a The rectangle ABCD is reflected in the line $x = 4$ to give rectangle $A_1B_1C_1D_1$. What are the co-ordinates of C_1?

b The rectangle ABCD is rotated about A anticlockwise through 90° to give $A_2B_2C_2D_2$. What are the co-ordinates of B_2?

c The rectangle is enlarged by scale factor 2, centre of enlargement A. What are the co-ordinates of the new position of B? *SEG, Question 2, Specimen Paper 10, 1998*

6 The diagram shows a regular pentagon ABCDE.
List all the triangles in the pentagon congruent to ADC.

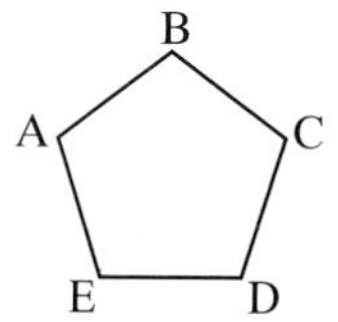

NEAB, Question 6, Specimen Paper 2H, 1998

7 Describe fully the single transformation which maps the triangle A onto the triangle C.

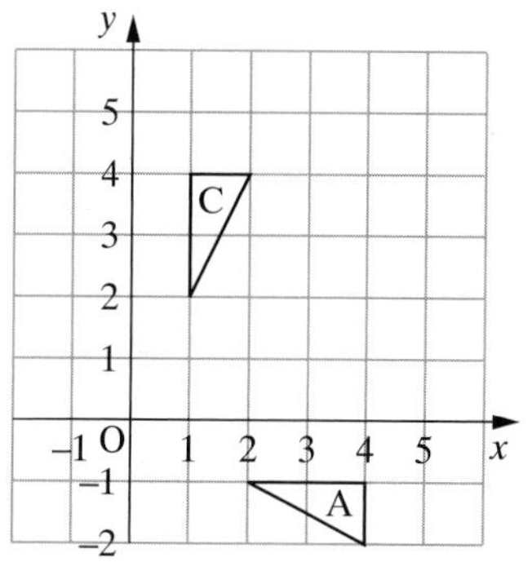

ULEAC, Question 8, Specimen Paper 6, 1998

8 A computer game involves moving a car round a circuit by writing column vectors.

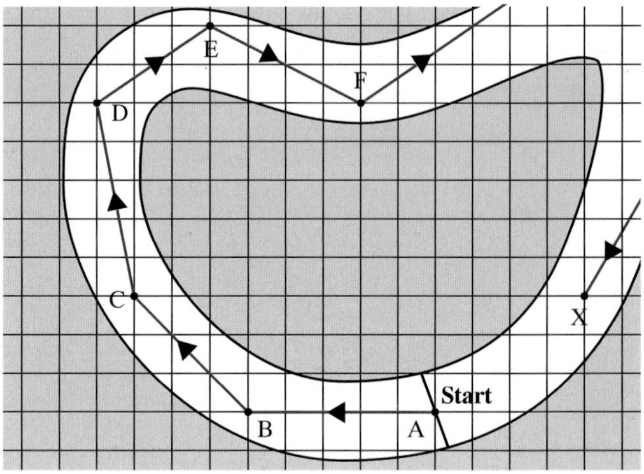

a Write the column vector to get from A to B.

b Write the column vector to get from E to F.

c What is the sum of the column vectors that take the car round the circuit from A to X?

MEG, Question 1, Specimen SMP Paper 5, 1998

9 What single transformation will be equivalent to: a reflection in the x-axis, followed by a reflection in the y-axis? *NEAB, Question 4, Specimen Paper 1H, 1998*

Summary

How well do you grade yourself?

To gain a grade **C**, you need to be able to enlarge a shape by a positive whole-number scale factor and a fraction scale factor, and be able to change the position of a shape using reflection, rotation and translation.

To gain a grade **B**, you need to be able to state clearly why two triangles are congruent.

To gain a grade **A**, you need to be able to use negative scale factors and rotations about any point.

What you should know after you have worked through Chapter 6

- Congruence: Two or more shapes are congruent if they fit exactly on one another.
- Translation: This is the movement of a shape from one place to another without reflecting it or rotating it. Every point in the shape moves in the same direction and through the same distance. Such changes of position are described using vectors which express the move from one point to another in terms of a horizontal shift and a vertical shift.
- Reflection: This is the movement of a shape so that it becomes a mirror image of itself. The reflection of each point in the original shape (the object) is perpendicular to the mirror line.

- Rotation: This moves a shape to a new position by turning it about a fixed point, called the centre of rotation.
  - The angle of rotation has direction – clockwise or anticlockwise.
  - The position of the centre of rotation is always specified.
- Enlargement: This changes the size of a shape (object) to give a similar image. The original lengths are multiplied by a scale factor to obtain the image lengths.

  The enlargement is always made from a centre of enlargement. The distance of each image point from the centre of enlargement is the distance of each object point from the centre of enlargement multiplied by the scale factor.

Coursework examples

Here and at one other place in the book examples are given of completed coursework that show what typical higher tier students should achieve. They provide you with guidance for your own coursework, showing in detail:

- The type of things you have to do and how to score the different levels of marks.
- What the marks have been awarded for, at each stage.

The examples will thus help you to decide whether your own coursework needs to be improved in certain respects.

You will find further help in the Appendix (page 518). This contains the definitions of columns A, B and C, together with descriptions of what each mark will be awarded for, which will give you a better understanding of the things you ought to show in your own coursework.

Coursework example 1

Flight of stairs

Refer to the Appendix for a summary of coursework marks.

Problem statement

Find the total volume of a flight of stairs.

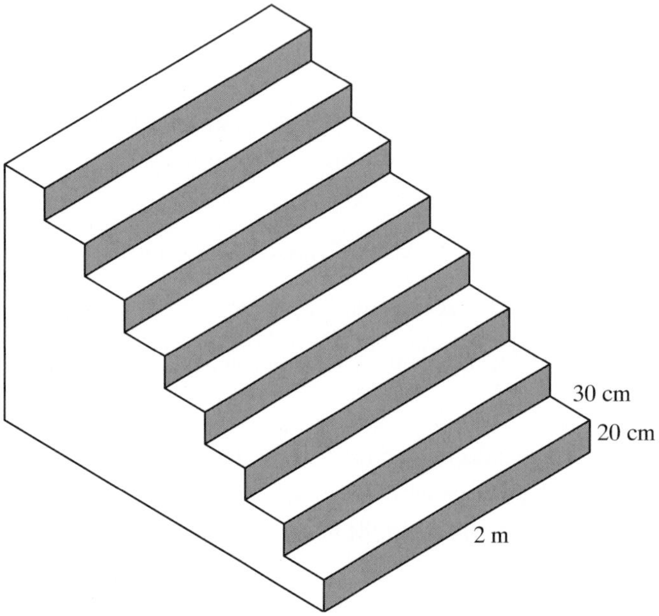

Possible solution

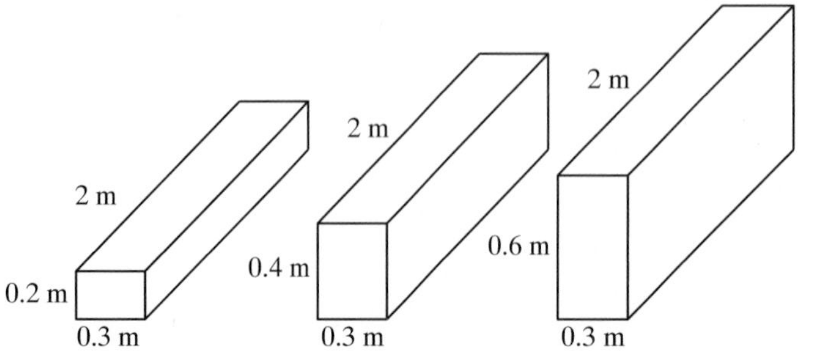

Volume of 1st step $= 0.2 \times 0.3 \times 2 = 0.12\ m^3$

Volume of 2nd step $= 0.4 \times 0.3 \times 2 = 0.24\ m^3$

Volume of 3rd step $= 0.6 \times 0.3 \times 2 = 0.36\ m^3$

Notes

A	B	C	
4			Task broken down into smaller stages.

Therefore, the volume of each step is $0.12 \times$ step number.
So, following the pattern, the volume of the 4th step is $0.48\ \text{m}^3$.

In the diagram, there are 8 steps. Therefore,

$$V = 0.12 + 0.24 + 0.36 + 0.48 + 0.6 + 0.72 + 0.84 + 0.96 = 4.32\ \text{m}^3$$

where V is the total volume of the flight of stairs.

I am now going to look at a flight of stairs with n steps.

From the above pattern, the volume of the nth step is $0.12n$.
Therefore, the total volume of the flight with n steps is

$$\begin{aligned} V &= 0.12 + 0.24 + 0.36 + \dots + 0.12n \\ &= 0.12\,(1 + 2 + 3 + \dots + n) \end{aligned}$$

This formula involves summing the first n natural numbers. The pattern will be:

1
$1 + 2 = 3$
$1 + 2 + 3 = 6$
$1 + 2 + 3 + 4 = 10$
$1 + 2 + 3 + 4 + 5 = 15$

The totals are just the sequence of triangle numbers with the next total being the 6th triangle number. That is,

$$\frac{6 \times 7}{2} = 21$$

Therefore, the sum of the first n natural numbers $= \dfrac{n(n+1)}{2}$

Therefore, for a flight of n steps

$$V = \frac{0.12n(n+1)}{2} = 0.06n(n+1)$$

I can now find the volume of a flight of n steps with the dimensions of each one as in the diagram below.

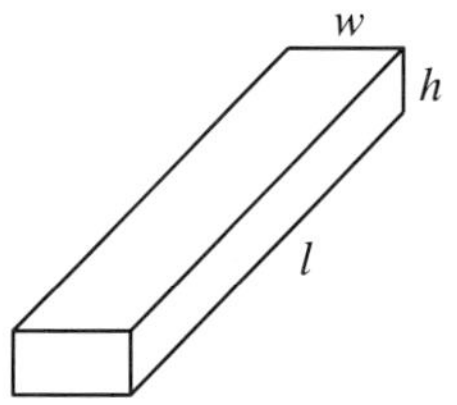

$$\begin{aligned} V &= hlw + 2hlw + 3hlw + \dots + nhlw \\ &= hlw\,(1 + 2 + 3 + \dots + n) \end{aligned}$$

$$\Rightarrow \quad V = \frac{hlwn(n+1)}{2}$$

A	B	C	
		4	Generalisation given.
5			Introduces own question to give a fuller solution.
	4		Information given in a variety of forms.
	5		An alternative approach by using triangle numbers.
		5	Generalisation justified by use of algebra.
	6		Follows a new line of enquiry.
	6		Consistent use of algebraic notation.
		6	General solution found.

This has given me the idea to look at summing different sequences that have the same form. For example,

$$3 + 5 + 7 + 9 \quad \text{and} \quad 5 + 8 + 11 + 14 + 17$$

The nth term for the first is $2n + 1$, and for the second is $3n + 2$.

Here I have taken two linear sequences whose first terms are different, but for which the difference between consecutive terms is the same.

I think I can now write down an algebraic expression for sequences of this type.

For such a sequence, let the first term be a and the difference between the terms be d. Then the sum S of n terms of the sequence is

$$S = a + (a + d) + (a + 2d) + (a + 3d) + \ldots + (a + [n - 2]d) + a + [n - 1]d)$$

I am now going to show how to find a formula for S.

I first write the terms of the sequence in order, and then again in reverse order, as shown below.

$$S = a + (a + d) + (a + 2d) + (a + 3d) + \ldots + (a + [n - 2]d) + (a + [n - 1]d)$$

$$S = (a + [n - 1]d) + (a + [n - 2]d) + \ldots + (a + 3d) + (a + 2d) + (a + d) + a$$

I add together both sequences to obtain

$$2S = (2a + [n - 1]d) + (2a + [(n - 1]d) + (2a + [n - 1]d) + \ldots + (2a + [n - 1]d)$$

Since there are n terms, this gives

$$2S = n(2a + [n - 1]d)$$

$$\Rightarrow \quad S = \frac{n(2a + [n - 1]d)}{2}$$

I can now use this formula to sum any sequence which has a linear nth term.

Example Find the sum of

$$4 + 9 + 14 + 19 + 24 + 29 + 34 + 39 + 44 + 49 + 54 + 59$$

Here, $a = 4$, $d = 5$ and $n = 12$. Therefore,

$$S = \frac{12\,(8 + [11 \times 5])}{2} = \frac{12 \times 63}{2} = 378$$

A	B	C	
7	7	7	Develops the idea further, using three variables with accurate use of algebra and justifications.
8			Explores an unfamiliar area of mathematics.
	8		An efficient and concise solution.
	8		A full proof provided.
			Final marks: (i) 8 (ii) 8 (iii) 8

7 Constructions

This chapter is going to ... show you how to construct a line bisector, an angle bisector, a right angle and an angle of 60°, using only a pair of compasses, a pencil and a ruler. It then introduces you to the idea of a locus, and to some of the more common loci. It also shows you how to use these loci in practical situations.

What you should already know

- How to use a protractor.
- How to use a pair of compasses.
- How to construct triangles.
- How to work out simple problems involving bearings.
- Understand the idea of a scale when it applies to maps.
- A plan view of a situation is what you would see when looking down from above.

Bisectors

To bisect means to divide in half. So a bisector divides something into two equal parts.

- A line bisector divides a straight line into two equal lengths.
- An angle bisector is the straight line which divides an angle into two equal angles.

To construct a line bisector

It is usually more accurate to construct a line bisector than to measure its position (the midpoint of the line).

- Here is a line to bisect.

- Open your compasses to a radius of about three quarters of the length of the line. Using each end of the line as a centre, draw two intersecting arcs without changing the radius of your compasses.

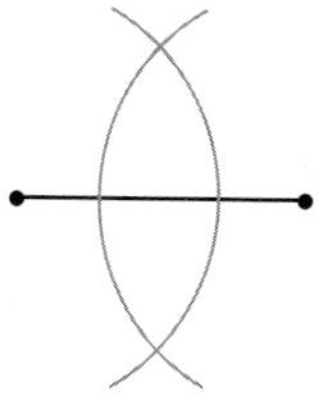

- Join the two points at which the arcs intersect. This line is the **perpendicular bisector** of the original line.

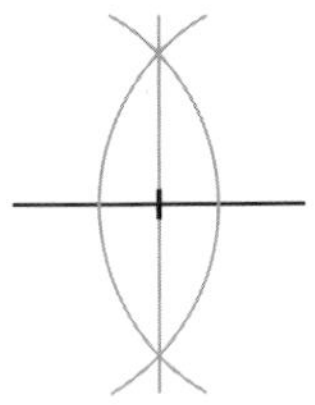

To construct an angle bisector

It is much more accurate to construct an angle bisector than to measure its position.

- Here is an angle to bisect.

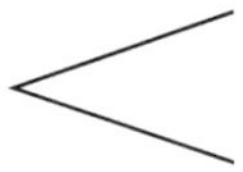

- Open your compasses to any reasonable radius that is less than the length of the shorter line. If in doubt, go for about 3 cm. With the vertex of the angle as centre, draw an arc through both lines.

- With centres at the two points at which this arc intersects the lines, draw two more arcs so that they intersect. (The radius of the compasses may have to be increased to do this.)

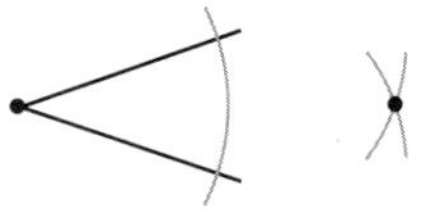

- Join the point at which these two arcs intersect to the vertex of the angle.

This line is the **angle bisector**.

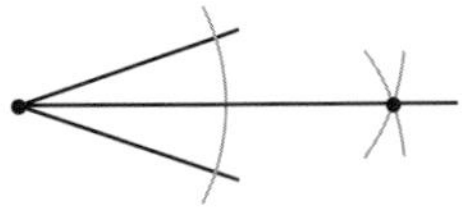

Exercise 7A

1 Draw a line 7 cm long. Bisect it with a pair of compasses. Check your accuracy by seeing if each half is 3.5 cm.

2 **a** Draw any triangle whose sides are between 5 cm and 10 cm.
b On each side construct the line bisector.
All your line bisectors should intersect at the same point.
c Use this point as the centre of a circle that only touches each vertex of the triangle. Draw this circle.

3 Repeat question **2** with a different triangle and check that you get a similar result.

4 **a** Draw a quadrilateral whose opposite angles add up to 180°.
b On each side construct the line bisector.
They all should intersect at the same point.
c Use this point as the centre of a circle that only touches the quadrilateral at each vertex. Draw this circle.

5 **a** Draw an angle of 50°.
b Construct the angle bisector.
c Check how accurate you have been by measuring each half. Both should be 25°.

6 **a** Draw any triangle whose sides are between 5 cm and 10 cm.
b At each angle construct the angle bisector.
All three bisectors should intersect at the same point.
c Use this point as the centre of a circle that only touches the sides of the triangle without cutting through them.

Constructing 90° and 60° angles

The 90° angle

The following method will produce an angle of 90° at a particular point on a line.

- Open your compasses to about 2 or 3 cm. With the given point as centre, draw two short arcs to intersect the line each side of the point.

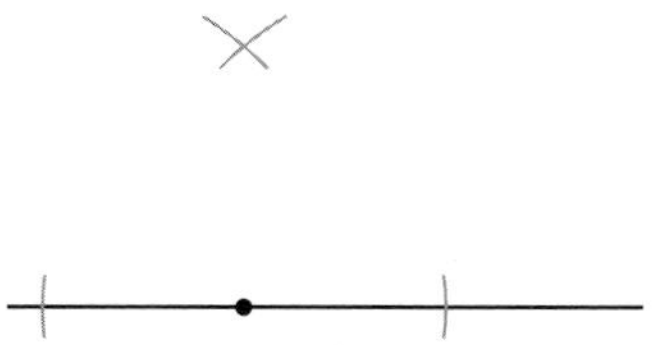

- Now extend the radius of your compasses to about 3 or 4 cm. With centres at the two points at which the arcs intersect the line, draw two arcs to intersect each other above the line.

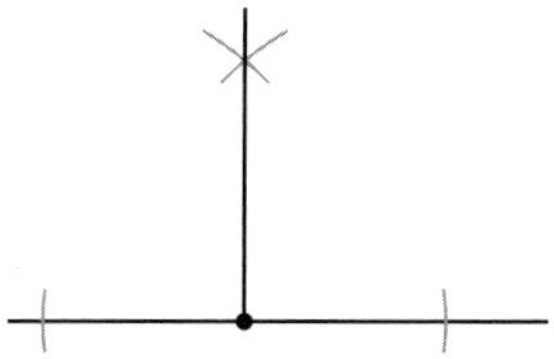

- Join the point at which these two arcs intersect to the given point on the line.

The two lines form the required angle of 90°.

Note that if you needed to construct a 90° angle at the end of a line, you would first have to extend the line.

You could be even more accurate by also drawing two arcs *underneath* the line, which would give three points in line.

The 60° angle

An angle of 60° is usually wanted at an end of a line, so on the next page we give a method for constructing it in that position.

- Open your compasses to about 3 cm. With the end of the line as centre, draw an arc from above to intersect the line.

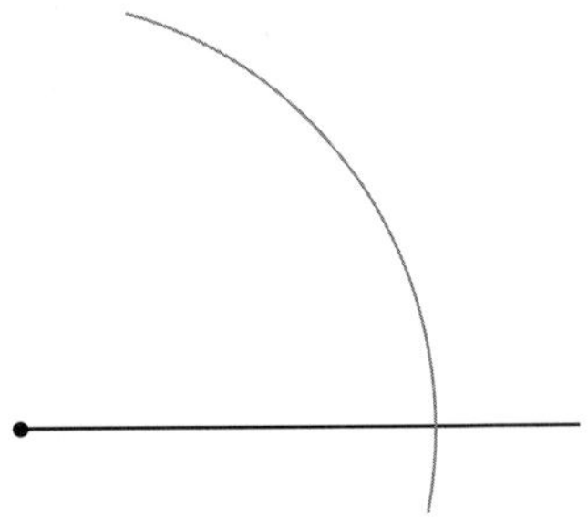

- With this point of intersection as centre, draw a second arc which passes through the end of the line to intersect the first arc.

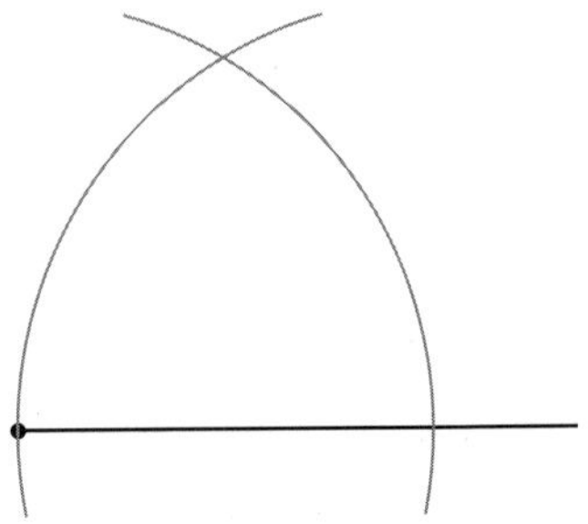

- Join the point of intersection of the arcs to the end of the line. The two lines make an angle of 60°.

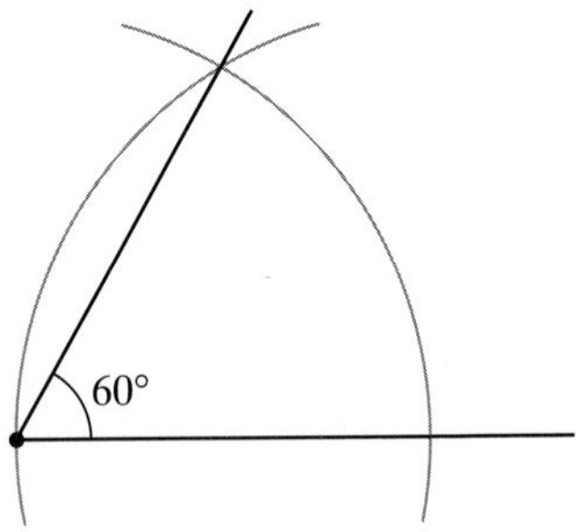

Dropping a perpendicular from a point to a line

You will meet situations for which you will need to be able to construct a perpendicular to a line that passes through a given point above the line. Here is the method.

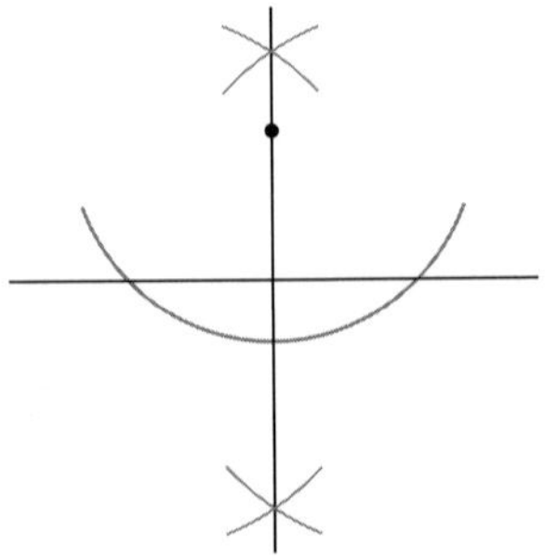

- With the point above the line as centre, draw an arc which twice intersects the line.
- With centres at these two points of intersection, draw two arcs to intersect each other both above and below the line.
- Join the two points at which the arcs intersect . The resulting line passes through the given point and intersects the given line at 90°.

Examination note When a question says '*construct*', you must use **only** compasses – no protractor. When it says '*draw*', you may use whatever you can to produce an accurate diagram.

But also note, when constructing you may use your protractor to check your accuracy.

Exercise 7B

1 Construct these triangles accurately without using a protractor.

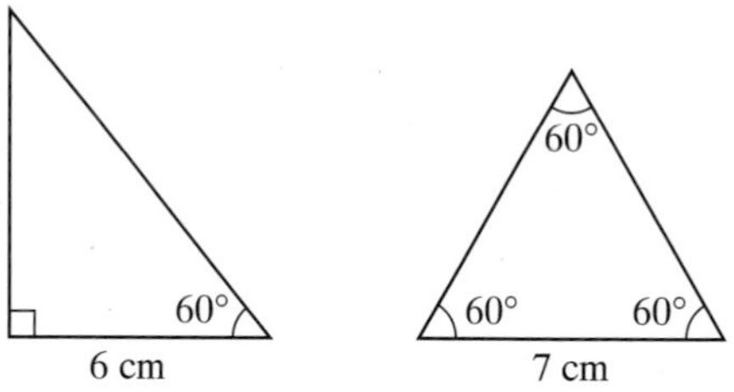

2 a Without using a protractor, construct a square of side 6 cm.

b See how accurate you have been by constructing an angle bisector on any of the right angles and seeing whether this also cuts through the opposite right angle.

3 With ruler and compasses only, construct these triangles.

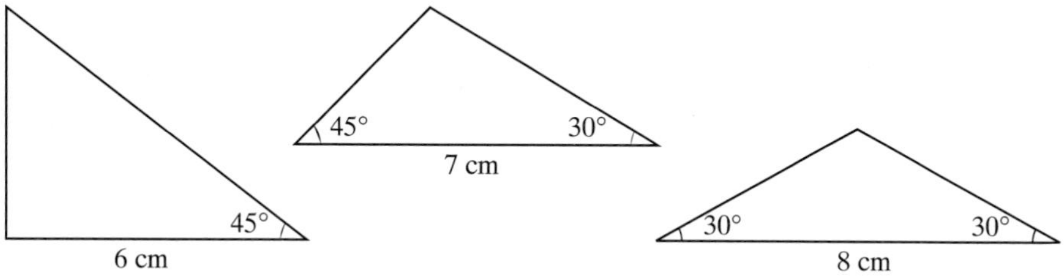

4 a Construct an angle of 90°.

b Bisect this angle to construct an angle of 45°.

5 a Construct these angles.

i 30° **ii** 15° **iii** 22.5° **iv** 75° [30° + 45°]

b Calculate your percentage error of each angle constructed.

6 Construct an isosceles triangle ABC, where AB = AC = 7 cm and ∠CAB = 120°.

7 Construct a trapezium whose parallel sides are 8 cm and 6 cm, and having an angle of 60° at each end of the longer side.

8 a Construct the triangle ABC, where AB = 7 cm, ∠BAC = 60° and ∠ABC = 45°.

b Measure the lengths of AC and BC.

9 a Construct the triangle PQR, where PQ = 8 cm, ∠RPQ = 30° and ∠PQR = 45°.

b Measure the lengths of PR and RQ.

10 Construct the parallelogram which has sides of 6 cm and 8 cm with an angle of 105°.

11 Draw a straight line and mark a point above the line. Construct the perpendicular which passes through that point to the line.

What is a locus?

A locus (plural loci) is the movement of a point according to a rule.

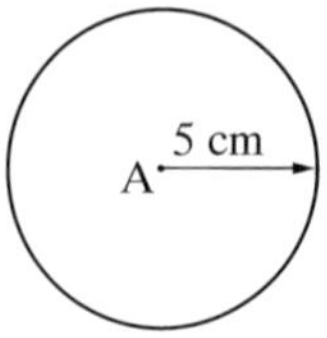

For example, a point P that moves so that it is always at a distance of 5 cm from a fixed point A will have a locus that is a circle of radius 5 cm.

To express this mathematically, we say:

The locus of the point P is such that AP = 5 cm

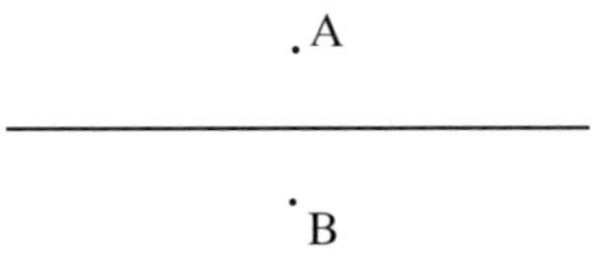

Another point P moves so that it is always the same distance from two fixed points A and B.

To express this mathematically, we say:

The locus of the point P is such that AP = BP

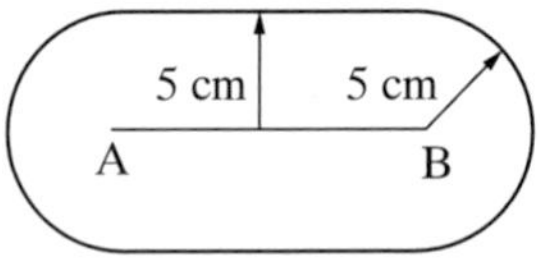

A point that moves so that it is always 5 cm from a line B will trace a 'sausage' or 'racetrack' shape around the line.

This is difficult to express mathematically. In your GCSE examination, you will usually get practical situations rather than abstract mathematical ones. For example, a point that is always 5 m from a long, straight wall will have a locus that is in a line parallel to the wall and 5 m from it.

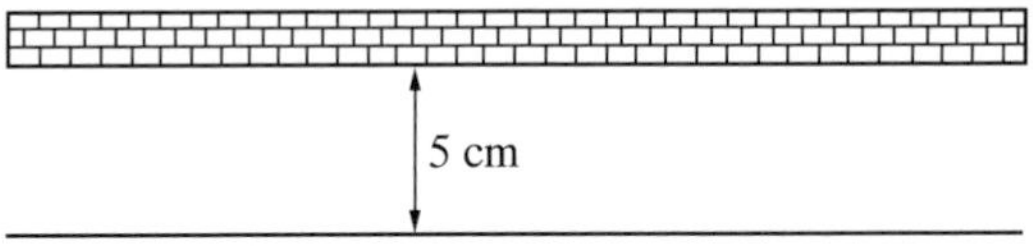

The four examples of loci just given occur frequently.

Imagine a grassy, flat field in which a horse is tethered to a stake by a rope that is 10 m long. What is the shape of the area that the horse can graze?

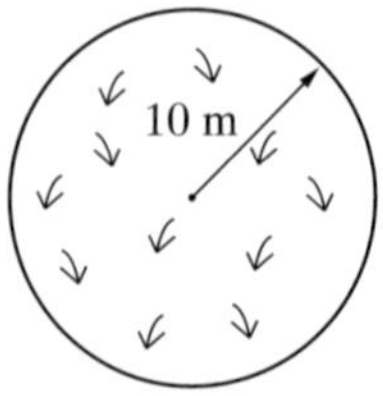

In reality, the horse may not be able to reach the full 10 m if the rope is tied round its neck but we ignore fine details like that. We 'model' the situation by saying that the horse can move around in a 10 m circle and graze all the grass within that circle.

In this example, the locus is the whole of the area inside the circle. We express this mathematically as

The locus of the point P is such that $AP \leq 10$ m

Exercise 7C

1 A is a fixed point. Sketch the locus of the point P when

a AP = 2 cm **b** AP = 4 cm **c** AP = 5 cm

2 A and B are two fixed points 5 cm apart. Sketch the locus of the point P for the following situations:

a AP = BP **b** AP = 4 cm and BP = 4 cm

c P is always within 2 cm of the line AB.

3 A horse is tethered in a field on a rope 4 m long. Describe or sketch the area that the horse can graze.

4 The same horse is still tethered by the same rope but there is now a long, straight fence running 2 m from the stake. Sketch the area that the horse can now graze.

5 ABCD is a square of side 4 cm. In each of the following loci, the point P moves only inside the square. Sketch the locus in each case.

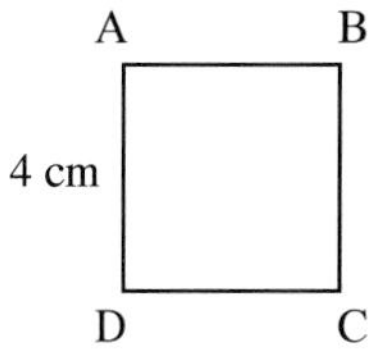

a AP = BP **b** AP < BP **c** AP = CP

d CP < 4 cm **e** CP > 2 cm **f** CP > 5 cm

6 One of the following diagrams is the locus of a point on the rim of a bicycle wheel as it moves along a flat road. Which is it?

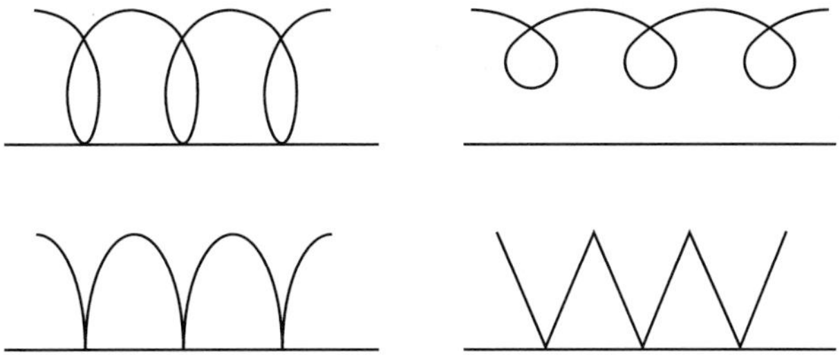

7 Draw the locus of the centre of the wheel for the bicycle in question **6**.

Practical problems

Most of the loci problems in your GCSE examination will be of a practical nature, as in the next example.

Example Imagine that a radio company wants to find a site for a transmitter. The transmitter must be the same distance from Doncaster and Leeds and within 20 miles of Sheffield.

In mathematical terms, this means we are concerned with the perpendicular bisector between Leeds and Doncaster and the area within a circle of radius 20 miles from Sheffield.

The map, drawn to a scale of 1 cm = 10 miles, illustrates the situation and shows that the transmitter can be built anywhere along the thick black line.

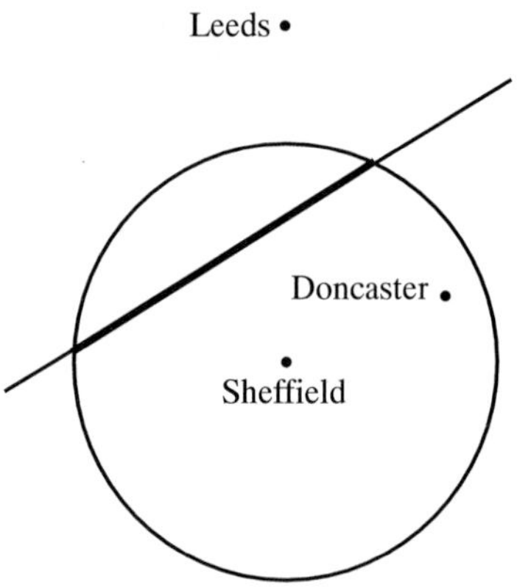

Exercise 7D

For questions **1** to **7**, you should start by sketching the picture given in each question on a 6×6 grid, each square of which is 1 cm by 1 cm. The scale for each question is given.

1 A goat is tethered by a rope, 7 m long, in a corner of a field with a fence at each side. What is the locus of the area that the goat can graze? Use a scale of 1 cm ≡ 2 m.

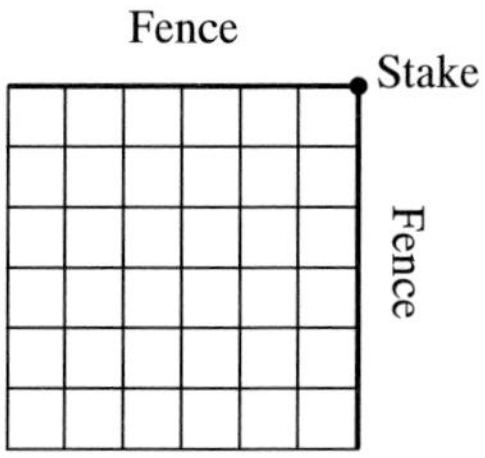

2 A horse in a field is tethered to a stake by a rope 6 m long. What is the locus of the area that the horse can graze? Use a scale of 1 cm ≡ 2 m.

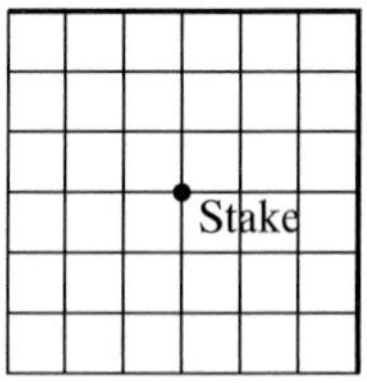

3 A cow is tethered to a rail at the top of a fence 6 m long. The rope is 3 m long. Sketch the area that the cow can graze. Use a scale of 1 cm ≡ 2 m.

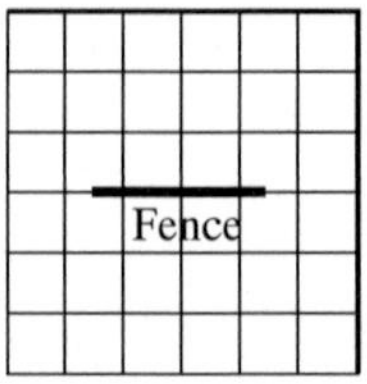

4 A horse is tethered to a stake near a corner of a fenced field, at a point 4 m from each fence. The rope is 6 m long. Sketch the area that the horse can graze. Use a scale of 1 cm ≡ 2 m.

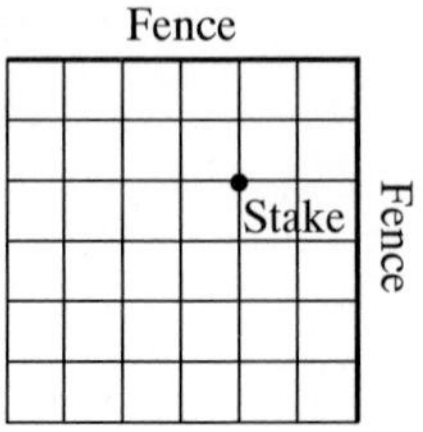

5 A horse is tethered to a corner of a shed, 2 m by 1 m. The rope is 2 m long. Sketch the area that the horse can graze. Use a scale of 1 cm ≡ 1 m.

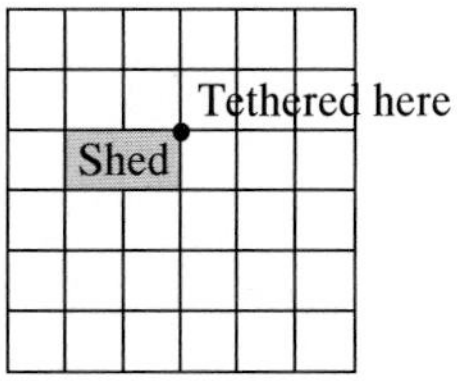

6 A goat is tethered by a 4 m rope to a stake at one corner of a pen, 4 m by 3 m. Sketch the area of the pen on which the goat cannot graze. Use a scale of 1 cm ≡1 m.

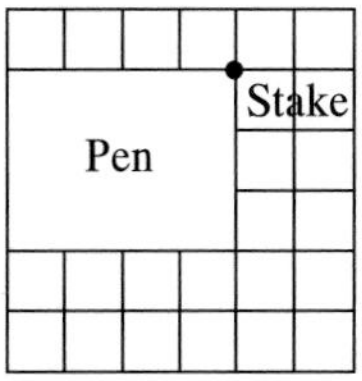

7 A puppy is tethered to a stake by a rope, 3 m long, on a flat lawn on which are two raised brick flower beds. The stake is situated at one corner of a bed, as shown. Sketch the area that the puppy is free to roam in. Use a scale of 1 cm ≡ 1 m.

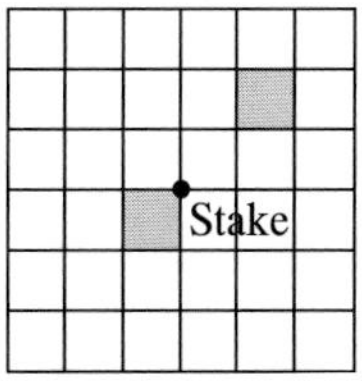

For questions **8** to **15**, you should use a copy of the map on page 162. For each question, trace the map and mark on those points that are relevant to that question.

8 A radio station broadcasts from London on a frequency of 1000 kHz with a range of 300 km. Another radio station broadcasts from Glasgow on the same frequency with a range of 200 km.

a Sketch the area to which each station can broadcast.

b Will they interfere with each other?

c If the Glasgow station increases its range to 400 km, will they then interfere with each other?

9 The radar at Leeds airport has a range of 200 km. The radar at Exeter airport has a range of 200 km.

a Will a plane flying over Glasgow be detected by the Leeds radar?

b Sketch the area where a plane can be picked up by both radars at the same time.

10 A radio transmitter is to be built according to the following rules.

i It has to be the same distance from York and Birmingham.

ii It must be within 350 km of Glasgow.

iii It must be within 250 km of London.

a Sketch the line that is the same distance from York and Birmingham.

b Sketch the area that is within 350 km of Glasgow and 250 km of London.

c Show clearly the possible places at which the transmitter could be built.

11 A radio transmitter centred at Birmingham is designed to give good reception in an area greater than 150 km and less than 250 km from the transmitter. Sketch the area of good reception.

Glasgow
Newcastle upon Tyne
North Sea
York
Leeds
Irish Sea
Manchester
Sheffield
Norwich
Birmingham
London
Bristol
Exeter
0
50
100
150
200
250 miles
0
50
100
150
200
250
300
350 km

12 Three radio stations pick up a distress call from a boat in the Irish Sea. The station at Glasgow can tell from the strength of the signal that the boat is within 300 km of the station. The station at York can tell that the boat is between 200 km and 300 km from York. The station at London can tell that it is less than 400 km from London. Sketch the area where the boat could be.

13 Sketch the area that is between 200 km and 300 km from Newcastle upon Tyne, and between 150 km and 250 km from Bristol.

14 An oil rig is situated in the North Sea in such a position that it is the same distance from Newcastle upon Tyne and Manchester. It is also the same distance from Sheffield and Norwich. Draw the line that shows all the points that are the same distance from Newcastle upon Tyne and Manchester. Repeat for the points that are the same distance from Sheffield and Norwich and find out where the oil rig is located.

15 Whilst looking at a map, Fred notices that his house is the same distance from Glasgow, Norwich and Exeter. Where is it?

16 Wathsea Harbour is as shown in the diagram. A boat sets off from point A and steers so that it keeps the same distance from the sea-wall and the West Pier. Another boat sets off from B and steers so that it keeps the same distance from the East Pier and the sea-wall. Copy the diagram below, and on your diagram show accurately the path of each boat.

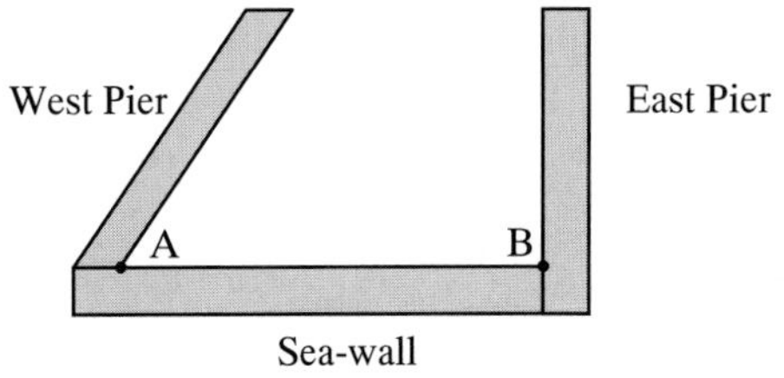

Possible coursework tasks

Find the centre

P is a point on the circumference of a circle whose centre is unknown. Show how you can construct a diameter passing through P. Show how to locate the centre of the circle. You should use ruler and compasses only.

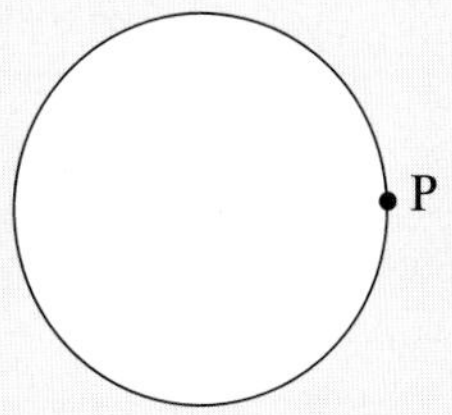

Dangerous ladders

A window cleaner is climbing a ladder when, unfortunately, the ladder slips down the wall. If he is halfway up the ladder when this happens, draw diagrams to show the locus of his path as he clings to the ladder.

Investigate the locus of his path for different positions on the ladder.

Toppling boxes

A square box is rolled along the ground. The box will rotate about D to end up in the position shown on the diagram. The locus of A as it moves is also shown.

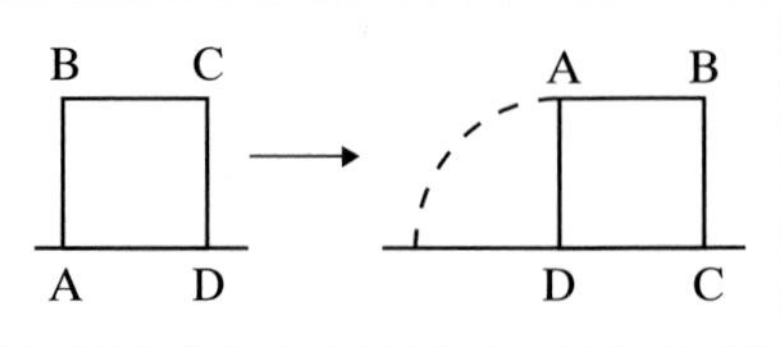

Complete the locus of A until A is on the ground again. What is the locus of A if the box is a cuboid?

Investigate for different-shaped boxes.

Changing loci

X and Y are fixed points. The point P can change its position under the condition

$$PX = kPY \quad \text{for } k = 1, 2, 3, 4, \ldots$$

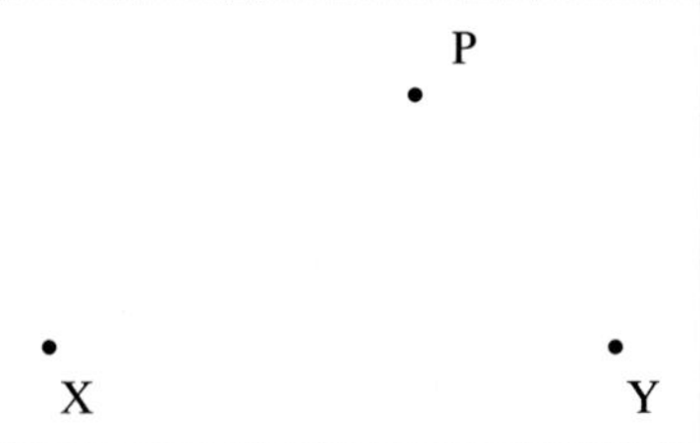

Investigate the locus of P for different values of k.

The conchoid

XY is a fixed line and O is a fixed point. Lines OP are drawn such that PQ is a fixed distance. Three positions for P are shown on the diagram.

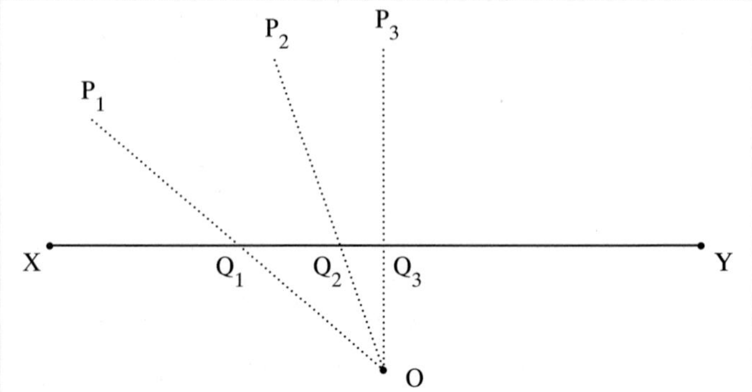

By plotting other points, show the locus of P. Investigate other possible loci in this situation.

Billy the goat

Billy the goat is tethered by a rope to a corner of a square field. How long should the rope be if Billy is to have access to just half of the field?

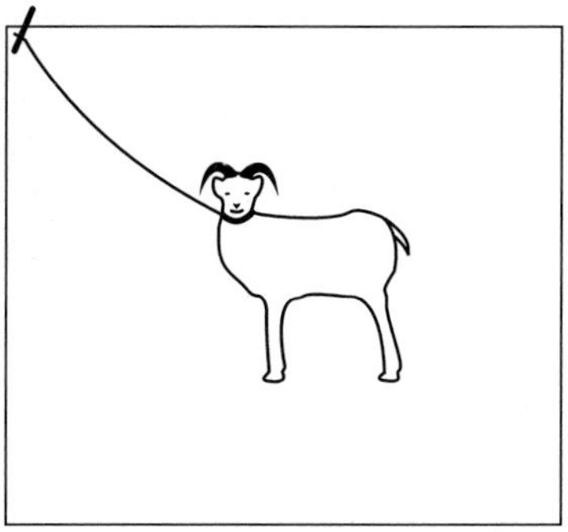

Spiralling outwards

The point P is at a distance r from O.
The angle between OP and the x-axis is θ (measured in an anticlockwise direction).

If $r = \theta$, find the locus of P for different values of θ.

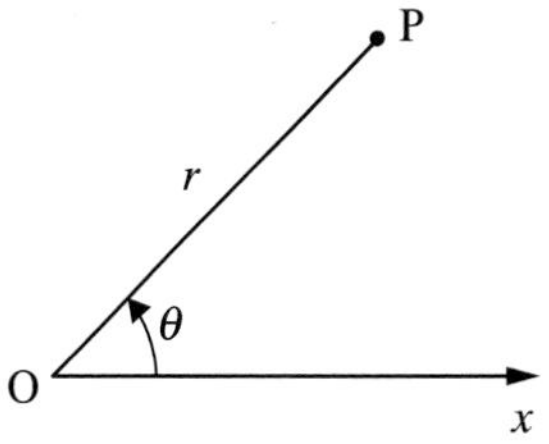

Examination questions: coursework type

1 **a** 'The perpendicular bisector of any chord in a circle is a diameter of that circle.'
b 'The angle bisector of any two chords in a circle is a diameter of that circle.'
Test each statement out and state whether you can say for each one:
i It may be true. **ii** It is always true.
iii It is sometimes not true. **iv** It is never true.

2 Fred has a goat called Billy. Billy grazes in a square field, 60 ft by 60 ft which has a footpath running diagonally across it from B to D. Fred has lots of rope and he wants Billy to have the maximum amount of grass to eat, but Billy must not be able to cross over the footpath. Fred has worked out that the best place to tether Billy is to a post in one of the corners, A or C, as shown in the diagram.

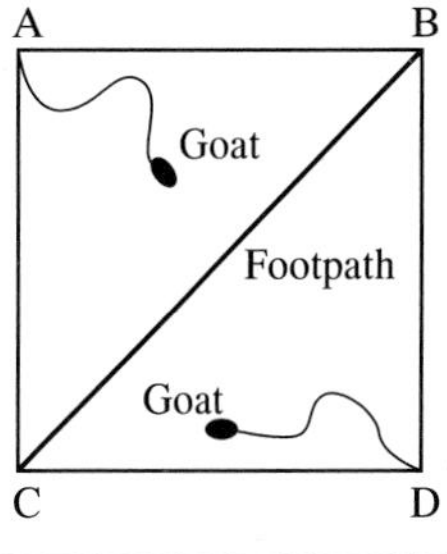

Fred also has a rectangular field which measures 60 ft by 180 ft. This field also has a footpath running diagonally across it. Sometimes he wants Billy to graze in this

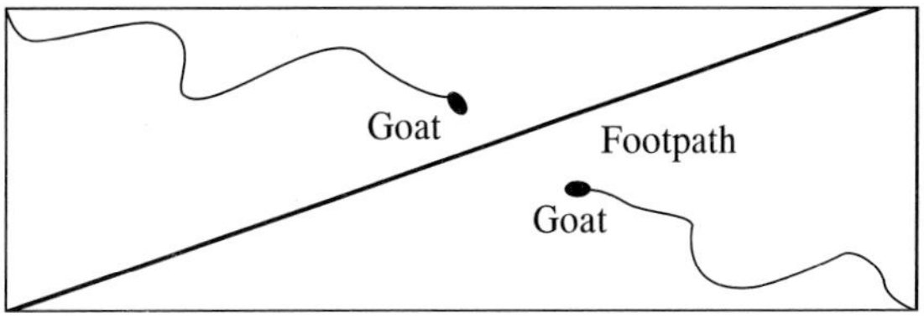

rectangular field without being able to cross over the footpath. He thinks the best places to tether Billy are the corners, as shown in the diagram.
Is Fred correct? Can you find any better places?

You may use any combination of accurate drawing, measurement and calculation. Explain your method and reasons fully. (You will need to draw scale diagrams.)

NEAB, Question 4, Paper 3, June 1995

Examination questions

1 The front of the main building of Andrew's school is parallel to the edge of the playing field and 100 metres from it. Andrew stands at a point A on the edge of the playing fields. He measures the bearing of one corner of the front of the building as 015° and the bearing of the other corner as 330°.

a Using the scale of 1 cm to 10 metres, construct a scale drawing to show the positions of the two corners relative to the edge of the playing fields.

b From the scale drawing find the length of the building.

NICCEA Question 7, Paper 3, June 1995

2 The diagram shows a map of part of the North Devon coast. The bearing of a ship from Hartland Point is 070°. Its bearing from Appledore is 320°. Showing your construction lines, mark the position of the ship on the map. Label the position with the letter S.

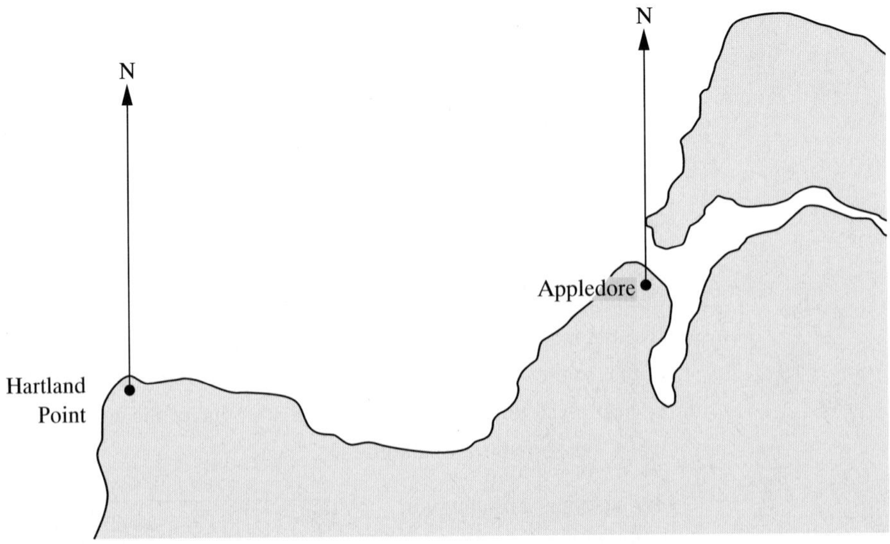

MEG, Question 7, Paper 2, 1994

3 The diagram shows a park with two ice-cream sellers A and B. People always go to the ice-cream seller nearest to them. Shade the region of the park from which people go to ice-cream seller B.

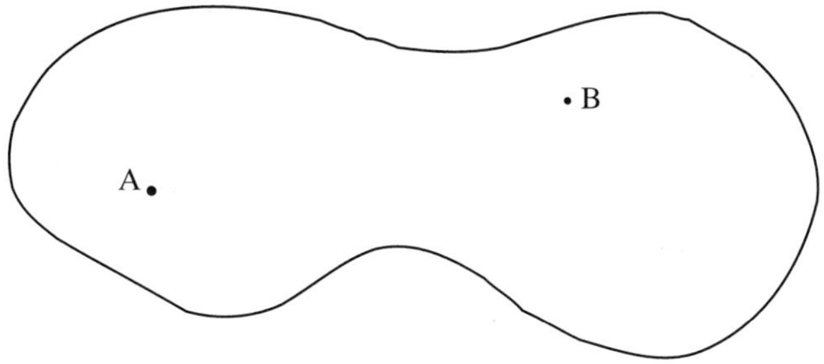

WJEC, Question 14, Paper 2, June 1994

4 The diagram shows a wheel, centre P, inside a rectangular frame. The wheel rolls around the inside of the frame so that it is always touching the frame. Draw the locus of the point P.

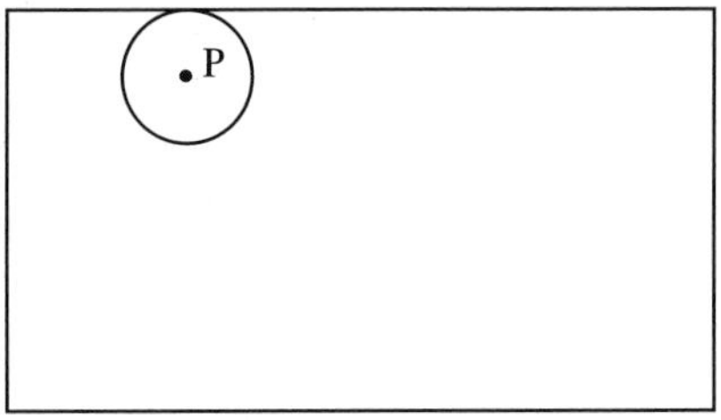

WJEC, Question 18, Paper 2, June 1994

5 The diagram shows a field ABCD. The line AB is 80 m long. The line BC is 50 m long. The diagram is drawn to a scale of 1 cm to 10 m. Treasure is hidden in the field.

a The treasure is at an equal distance from the sides AB and AD. Construct the locus of points for which this is true.

b The treasure is also 60 m from the corner C. Construct the locus of points for which this is true.

c Mark with an X the position of the treasure. *SEG, Question 16, Paper 4, June 1994*

6 The map shows part of a coastline and a coastguard station. 1 cm on the map represents 2 km.

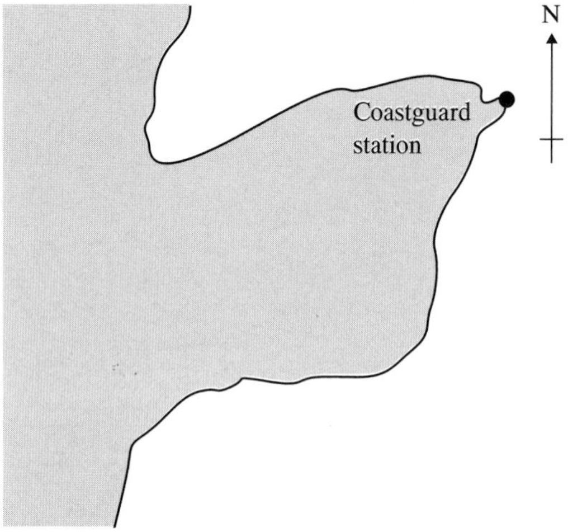

A ship is 12 km from the coastguard station on a bearing of 160°.

a Plot the position of the ship from the coastguard station, using a scale of 1 cm to represent 2 km.

It is not safe for ships to come within 6 km of the coastguard station.

b Shade the area on the map which is less than 6 km from the coastguard station.

ULEAC, Question 12, Paper 4, June 1994

7 Two ships A and B both hear a distress signal from a fishing boat. The positions of A and B are shown on the map, which is drawn using a scale of 1 cm to represent 1 km. The fishing boat is less than 4 km from ship A and is less than 4.5 km from ship B.

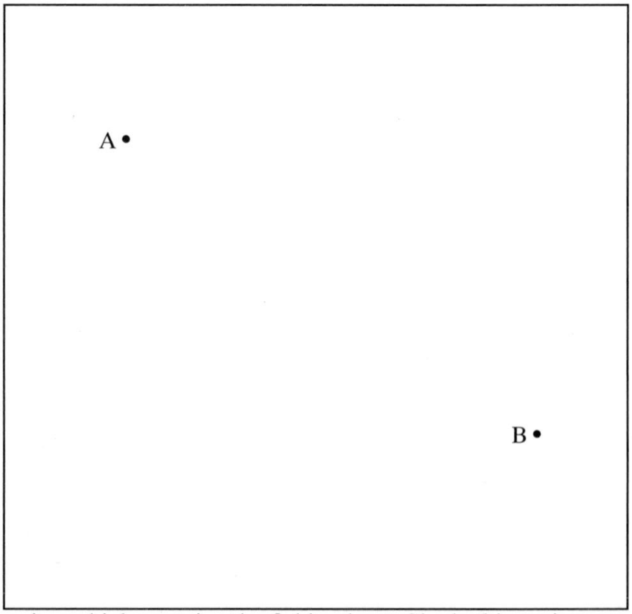

A helicopter pilot sees that the fishing boat is nearer to ship A than to ship B. Use accurate construction to show the region which contains the fishing boat. Shade this region.

NEAB, Question 2, Paper 2H, June 1995

8 A new radio telephone transmission mast is to provide services for the three towns Axon, Beaver and Caxton. The position of the three towns is shown. The diagram is drawn to a scale of 1 cm to 10 km.

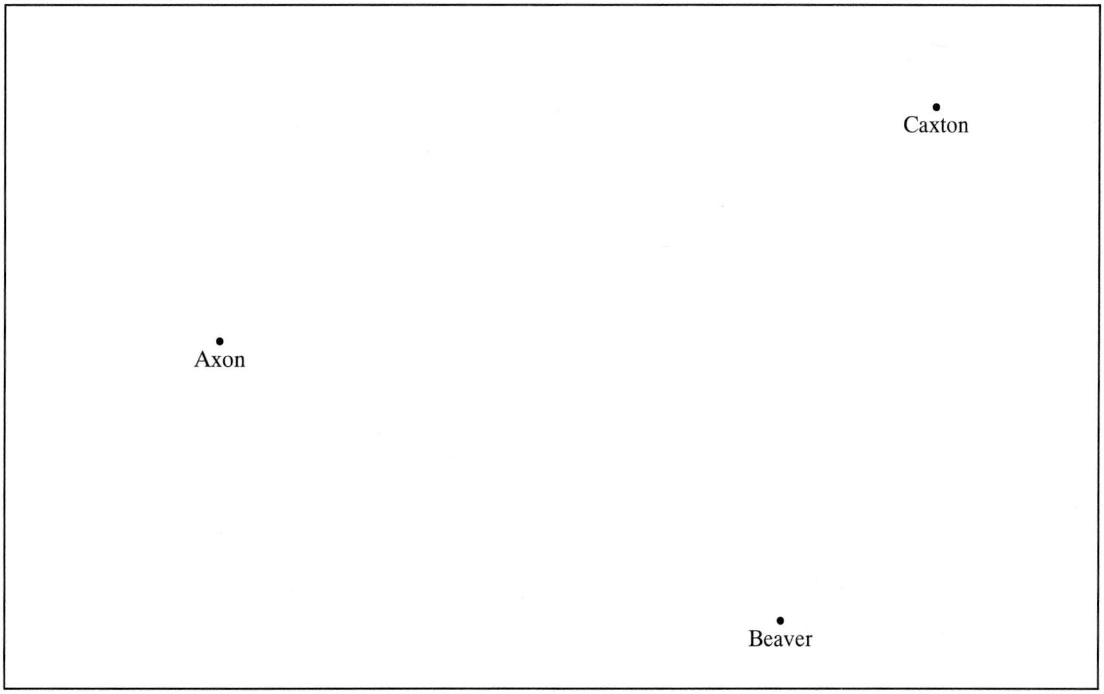

a The mast is located within the triangle formed by Axon, Beaver and Caxton so that it is

i equidistant from Axon and Beaver, and

ii 70 km from Caxton.

Construct the position of the mast on the diagram. Mark with an X the position of the mast.

b A helicopter flies directly from Beaver to Caxton at an average speed of 250 km/h. How long does the flight take? (Give your answer in minutes to the nearest minute.)

SEG, Question 12, Specimen Paper 14, 1998

9 The base AB of the triangle ABC is fixed. The point C can move, but the area of the triangle ABC stays the same. Describe or draw the locus of the point C.

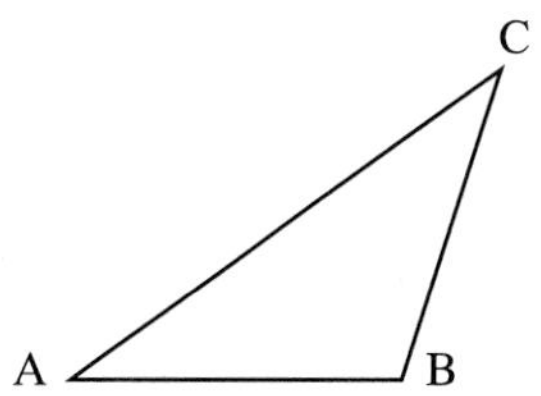

NEAB, Question 3, Paper 2H, November 1994

10 The diagram shows a theatre stage. It is drawn using a scale 1:200. The line AB is 10 cm long.

a What is the distance from A to B on the stage?

b A microphone is placed so that is is equidistant from C and D, and 12 m from BD. Show the position of the microphone accurately on the diagram.

c The area of the stage is 276 m^2. A smaller theatre has a similar stage, with AB 10 m long. What is the area of the smaller stage. *WJEC, Question 4, Specimen Paper 2, 1998*

Summary

How well do you grade yourself?

To gain a grade **C**, you need to be able to construct accurately to the nearest degree and to draw good scale diagrams. You need also to be able to express a problem in terms of a locus and to know which locus is wanted.

To gain a grade **B**, you need to be able to sketch and interpret complicated loci which involve more than one condition.

What you should know after you have worked through Chapter 7

- How to construct both line and angle bisectors.
- How to construct angles of 90° and 60°.
- How to drop a perpendicular from a point to a line.
- Understand what is meant by a locus.
- How to draw a locus about a point, a line or a plane shape.
- How to draw a locus that depends on the bisecting of lines or angles or both.
- Be able to recognise when a locus is being asked for.

8 Number 2

This chapter is going to ... show you how to express and manipulate numbers in index form (including fractional and negative indices) and how to express very large and very small numbers in standard form. It then introduces you to the idea of rational and irrational numbers, leading on to the conversion into fractions of both terminating and recurring decimals, and to the manipulation of surds.

What you should already know

- How to convert a fraction into a decimal.
- How to find the lowest common denominator of two or more fractions.
- The rules for manipulating indices.

Indices

You will recall how we use indices (also called 'powers'). For example,

$$3 \times 3 \times 3 \times 3 \times 3 \times 3 \times 3 \times 3 = 3^8$$
$$13 \times 13 \times 13 \times 13 \times 13 = 13^5$$

Working out indices on your calculator

For example, how do we work out the value of 5^7 on a calculator?

We could do the sum as $5 \times 5 \times 5 \times 5 \times 5 \times 5 \times 5 =$. But if we tried to key this sum, we would probably end up missing a number or pressing a wrong key. Instead, we use the power key x^y or, on some calculators, y^x . So

$5^7 =$ 5 x^y 7 = 78 125

Make sure you know where to find the power key on your calculator. It may be an INV or SHIFT function.

Two special powers

Choose any number, say 5, and use your calculator to raise it to the power 1. You will find that $5^1 = 5$. That is, a number raised to the power 1 stays the same number. This is true for **any** number, so we do not normally write down the power 1.

Choose any number, say 9, and use your calculator to raise it to the power 0. You will find that $9^0 = 1$. This is true for **any** number raised to the power 0. The answer is **always** 1.

Exercise 8A

1 Write these expressions using power notation. Do not work them out yet.

a $2 \times 2 \times 2 \times 2$ **b** $3 \times 3 \times 3 \times 3 \times 3$
c 7×7 **d** $5 \times 5 \times 5$
e $10 \times 10 \times 10 \times 10 \times 10 \times 10 \times 10$ **f** $6 \times 6 \times 6 \times 6$
g 4 **h** $1 \times 1 \times 1 \times 1 \times 1 \times 1 \times 1$
i $0.5 \times 0.5 \times 0.5 \times 0.5$ **j** $100 \times 100 \times 100$

2 Write these power terms out in full. Do not work them out yet.

a 3^4 **b** 9^3 **c** 6^2 **d** 10^5 **e** 2^{10}
f 8^1 **g** 0.1^3 **h** 2.5^2 **i** 0.7^3 **j** 1000^2

3 Using the power key on your calculator (or another method), work out the values of the power terms in question **1**.

4 Using the power key on your calculator (or another method), work out the values of the power terms in question **2**.

5 Without using a calculator, work out the values of these power terms.

a 2^0 **b** 4^1 **c** 5^0 **d** 1^9 **e** 1^{235}

6 The answers to question **5**, parts **d** and **e**, should tell you something special about powers of 1. What is it?

7 Write the answer to question **1**, part **j** as a power of 10.

8 Write the answer to question **2**, part **j** as a power of 10.

9 Using your calculator, or otherwise, work out the values of these power terms.

a $(-1)^0$ **b** $(-1)^1$ **c** $(-1)^2$ **d** $(-1)^4$ **e** $(-1)^5$

10 Using your answers to question **9**, write down the answers to these.

a $(-1)^8$ **b** $(-1)^{11}$ **c** $(-1)^{99}$ **d** $(-1)^{80}$ **e** $(-1)^{126}$

Negative indices

A negative index is a convenient way of writing the reciprocal of a number or term. (That is, one divided by that number or term.) For example,

$$x^{-a} = \frac{1}{x^a}$$

Here are some other examples:

$$5^{-2} = \frac{1}{5^2} \qquad 3^{-1} = \frac{1}{3} \qquad 5x^{-2} = \frac{5}{x^2}$$

Exercise 8B

1 Write down each of these in fraction form.

a 5^{-3} **b** 6^{-1} **c** 10^{-5} **d** 3^{-2} **e** 8^{-4}

f 9^{-1} **g** w^{-2} **h** t^{-1} **i** x^{-m} **j** $4m^{-3}$

2 Write down each of these in negative index form.

a $\frac{1}{3^2}$ **b** $\frac{1}{5}$ **c** $\frac{1}{10^3}$ **d** $\frac{1}{m}$ **e** $\frac{1}{t^n}$

3 Change each of the following expressions into an index form of the type shown.

a All of the form 2^n

i 16 **ii** $\frac{1}{2}$ **iii** $\frac{1}{16}$ **iv** -8

b All of the form 10^n

i 1000 **ii** $\frac{1}{10}$ **iii** $\frac{1}{100}$ **iv** 1 million

c All of the form 5^n

i 125 **ii** $\frac{1}{5}$ **iii** $\frac{1}{25}$ **iv** $\frac{1}{3125}$

d All of the form 3^n

i 9 **ii** $\frac{1}{27}$ **iii** $\frac{1}{81}$ **iv** -6561

4 Rewrite each of the following in fraction form.

a $5x^{-3}$ **b** $6t^{-1}$ **c** $7m^{-2}$ **d** $4q^{-4}$ **e** $10y^{-5}$

f $\frac{1}{2}x^{-3}$ **g** $\frac{1}{4}m^{-1}$ **h** $\frac{3}{4}t^{-4}$ **i** $\frac{4}{5}y^{-3}$ **j** $\frac{7}{8}x^{-5}$

5 Change each fraction to index form.

a $\frac{7}{x^3}$ **b** $\frac{10}{p}$ **c** $\frac{5}{t^2}$ **d** $\frac{8}{m^5}$ **e** $\frac{3}{y}$

6 Find the value of each of the following, where the letters have the given values.

a Where $x = 5$

i x^2 **ii** x^{-3} **iii** $4x^{-1}$

b Where $t = 4$

i t^3 **ii** t^{-2} **iii** $5t^{-4}$

c Where $m = 2$

i m^3 **ii** m^{-5} **iii** $9m^{-1}$

d Where $w = 10$

i w^6 **ii** w^{-3} **iii** $25w^{-2}$

Rules for multiplying and dividing numbers in index form

When we **multiply** together powers of the same number or variable, we **add** the indices. For example,

$$3^4 \times 3^5 = 3^{(4+5)} = 3^9$$
$$2^3 \times 2^4 \times 2^5 = 2^{12}$$
$$10^4 \times 10^{-2} = 10^2$$
$$10^{-3} \times 10^{-1} = 10^{-4}$$
$$a^x \times a^y = a^{(x+y)}$$

When we **divide** powers of the same number or variable, we **subtract** the indices. For example,

$a^4 \div a^3 = a^{(4-3)} = a^1 = a$
$b^4 \div b^7 = b^{-3}$
$10^4 \div 10^{-2} = 10^6$
$10^{-2} \div 10^{-4} = 10^2$
$a^x \div a^y = a^{(x-y)}$

When we **raise** a power term to a further power, we **multiply** the indices. For example,

$(a^2)^3 = a^{2 \times 3} = a^6$
$(a^{-2})^4 = a^{-8}$
$(a^2)^6 = a^{12}$
$(a^x)^y = a^{xy}$

Here are some examples of different kinds of power sums.

$2a^2 \times 3a^4 = (2 \times 3) \times (a^2 \times a^4) = 6 \times a^6 = 6a^6$
$4a^2b^3 \times 2ab^2 = (4 \times 2) \times (a^2 \times a) \times (b^3 \times b^2) = 8a^3b^5$
$12a^5 \div 3a^2 = (12 \div 3) \times (a^5 \div a^2) = 4a^3$
$(2a^2)^3 = (2)^3 \times (a^2)^3 = 8 \times a^6 = 8a^6$

Exercise 8C

1 Write these as single powers of 5.

a $5^2 \times 5^2$ **b** $5^4 \times 5^6$ **c** $5^2 \times 5^3$ **d** 5×5^2 **e** $5^6 \times 5^9$ **f** 5×5^8
g $5^{-2} \times 5^4$ **h** $5^6 \times 5^{-3}$ **i** $5^{-2} \times 5^{-3}$

2 Write these as single powers of 6.

a $6^5 \div 6^2$ **b** $6^7 \div 6^2$ **c** $6^3 \div 6^2$ **d** $6^4 \div 6^4$ **e** $6^5 \div 6^4$ **f** $6^2 \div 6^4$
g $6^4 \div 6^{-2}$ **h** $6^{-3} \div 6^4$ **i** $6^{-3} \div 6^{-5}$

3 Write these as single powers of 4.

a $(4^2)^3$ **b** $(4^3)^5$ **c** $(4^1)^6$ **d** $(4^3)^{-2}$ **e** $(4^{-2})^{-3}$ **f** $(4^7)^0$

4 Simplify these and write them as single powers of a.

a $a^2 \times a$ **b** $a^3 \times a^2$ **c** $a^4 \times a^3$ **d** $a^6 \div a^2$ **e** $a^3 \div a$ **f** $a^5 \div a^4$

5 Simplify these expressions.

a $2a^2 \times 3a^3$ **b** $4a^3 \times 5a$ **c** $2a^{-2} \times 4a^5$ **d** $3a^4 \times 3a^{-2}$ **e** $3a^2 \times 5a^{-2}$
f $(2a^2)^3$ **g** $-2a^2 \times 3a^2$ **h** $-4a^3 \times -2a^5$ **i** $-2a^4 \times 5a^{-7}$

6 Simplify these expressions.

a $6a^3 \div 2a^2$ **b** $12a^5 \div 3a^2$ **c** $15a^5 \div 5a$ **d** $18a^{-2} \div 3a^{-1}$
e $24a^5 \div 6a^{-2}$ **f** $30a \div 6a^5$

7 Simplify these expressions.

a $2a^2b^3 \times 4a^3b$ **b** $5a^2b^4 \times 2ab^{-3}$ **c** $6a^2b^3 \times 5a^{-4}b^{-5}$ **d** $12a^2b^4 \div 6ab$
e $24a^{-3}b^4 \div 3a^2b^{-3}$

8 Simplify these expressions.

a $\dfrac{6a^4b^3}{2ab}$ **b** $\dfrac{2a^2bc^2 \times 6abc^3}{4ab^2c}$ **c** $\dfrac{3abc \times 4a^3b^2c \times 6c^2}{9a^2bc}$

Indices of the form $\frac{1}{n}$

Consider the problem $7^x \times 7^x = 7$. This can be written as

$$7^{(x+x)} = 7$$
$$7^{2x} = 7^1$$
$$\Rightarrow \quad 2x = 1$$
$$x = \tfrac{1}{2}$$

If we now substitute $x = \frac{1}{2}$ back into the original equation, we see that

$$7^{\frac{1}{2}} \times 7^{\frac{1}{2}} = 7$$

This makes $7^{\frac{1}{2}}$ the same as $\sqrt{7}$.

You can similarly show that $7^{\frac{1}{3}}$ is the same as $\sqrt[3]{7}$. And that, generally,

$$x^{\frac{1}{n}} = \sqrt[n]{x} \quad (n\text{th root of } x)$$

For example,

$$49^{\frac{1}{2}} = \sqrt{49} = 7 \qquad 8^{\frac{1}{3}} = \sqrt[3]{8} = 2$$

$$10\,000^{\frac{1}{4}} = \sqrt[4]{10\,000} = 10 \qquad 36^{-\frac{1}{2}} = \frac{1}{\sqrt{36}} = \frac{1}{6}$$

Exercise 8D

Evaluate the following.

1 $25^{\frac{1}{2}}$ **2** $100^{\frac{1}{2}}$ **3** $64^{\frac{1}{2}}$ **4** $81^{\frac{1}{2}}$

5 $625^{\frac{1}{2}}$ **6** $27^{\frac{1}{3}}$ **7** $64^{\frac{1}{3}}$ **8** $1000^{\frac{1}{3}}$

9 $125^{\frac{1}{3}}$ **10** $512^{\frac{1}{3}}$ **11** $144^{\frac{1}{2}}$ **12** $400^{\frac{1}{2}}$

13 $625^{\frac{1}{4}}$ **14** $81^{\frac{1}{4}}$ **15** $100\,000^{\frac{1}{5}}$ **16** $729^{\frac{1}{6}}$

17 $32^{\frac{1}{5}}$ **18** $1024^{\frac{1}{10}}$ **19** $1296^{\frac{1}{4}}$ **20** $216^{\frac{1}{3}}$

21 $16^{-\frac{1}{4}}$ **22** $8^{-\frac{1}{3}}$ **23** $81^{-\frac{1}{4}}$ **24** $3125^{-\frac{1}{5}}$

25 $1\,000\,000^{-\frac{1}{6}}$ **26** $\left(\frac{25}{36}\right)^{\frac{1}{2}}$ **27** $\left(\frac{100}{36}\right)^{\frac{1}{2}}$ **28** $\left(\frac{64}{81}\right)^{\frac{1}{2}}$

29 $\left(\frac{81}{25}\right)^{\frac{1}{2}}$ **30** $\left(\frac{25}{64}\right)^{\frac{1}{2}}$ **31** $\left(\frac{27}{125}\right)^{\frac{1}{3}}$ **32** $\left(\frac{8}{512}\right)^{\frac{1}{3}}$

33 $\left(\frac{1000}{64}\right)^{\frac{1}{3}}$ **34** $\left(\frac{64}{125}\right)^{\frac{1}{3}}$ **35** $\left(\frac{512}{343}\right)^{\frac{1}{3}}$ **36** $\left(\frac{64}{729}\right)^{\frac{1}{6}}$

37 $\left(\frac{243}{1024}\right)^{\frac{1}{5}}$ **38** $\left(\frac{1024}{59\,049}\right)^{\frac{1}{10}}$ **39** $\left(\frac{625}{2401}\right)^{\frac{1}{4}}$ **40** $\left(\frac{343}{512}\right)^{\frac{1}{3}}$

Indices of the form $\frac{a}{b}$

Here are two examples of this form.

$$t^{\frac{2}{3}} = t^{\frac{1}{3}} \times t^{\frac{1}{3}} = (\sqrt[3]{t})^2 \qquad 81^{\frac{3}{4}} = (\sqrt[4]{81})^3 = 3^3 = 27$$

Exercise 8E

1 Evaluate the following.

a $32^{\frac{4}{5}}$ **b** $125^{\frac{2}{3}}$ **c** $1296^{\frac{3}{4}}$ **d** $243^{\frac{4}{5}}$

2 Rewrite the following in index form.

a $\sqrt[3]{t^2}$ **b** $\sqrt[4]{m^3}$ **c** $\sqrt[5]{k^2}$ **d** $\sqrt{x^3}$

3 Evaluate the following.

a $8^{\frac{2}{3}}$ **b** $27^{\frac{7}{3}}$ **c** $16^{\frac{3}{2}}$ **d** $625^{1.25}$

e $25^{1.5}$ **f** $36^{3.5}$ **g** $16^{-1.25}$ **h** $81^{2.75}$

4 **a** Draw the graph of $y = 2^x$ for $x = -2$ to 5.

b Use your graph to estimate the square root of 2.

5 **a** Draw the graph of $y = 3^x$ for $x = -2$ to 4.

b Use your graph to estimate the cube root of 3.

6 Using a trial-and-improvement method, or otherwise, solve these equations.

a $5^x = 50$ **b** $7^x = 77$ **c** $9^x = 999$

You could try to use the x^y key on your calculator.

Arithmetic of powers of 10

Multiplying

The easiest number to multiply by is probably zero, because any number multiplied by zero is zero. The next easiest number to multiply by is 1, because any number multiplied by 1 stays the same. After that it is a matter of opinion, but it is generally accepted that multiplying by 10 is simple.

To multiply by any power of 10, we simply move the decimal point according to these two rules:

- When the index is **positive**, move the decimal point to the **right** by the same number of places as the value of the index.
- When the index is **negative**, move the decimal place to the **left** by the same number of places as the value of the index.

For example,

$12.356 \times 10^2 = 1235.6$ $\quad$ $3.45 \times 10^1 = 34.5$

$753.4 \times 10^{-2} = 7.534$ $\quad$ $6789 \times 10^{-1} = 678.9$

In certain cases, we have to insert the 'hidden' zeros. For example,

$75 \times 10^4 = 750\,000$ $\quad$ $2.04 \times 10^5 = 204\,000$

$6.78 \times 10^{-3} = 0.006\,78$ $\quad$ $0.897 \times 10^{-4} = 0.000\,0897$

Dividing

To divide by any power of 10, we simply move the decimal point according to these two rules:

- When the index is **positive**, move the decimal point to the **left** by the same number of places as the value of the index.
- When the index is **negative**, move the decimal place to the **right** by the same number of places as the value of the index.

For example,

$712.35 \div 10^2 = 7.1235$ $\quad$ $38.45 \div 10^1 = 3.845$

$3.463 \div 10^{-2} = 346.3$ $\quad$ $6.789 \div 10^{-1} = 67.89$

In certain cases, we have to insert the 'hidden' zeros. For example,

$75 \div 10^4 = 0.0075$ $\quad$ $2.04 \div 10^5 = 0.000\,0204$

$6.78 \div 10^{-3} = 6780$ $\quad$ $0.08 \div 10^{-4} = 800$

When doing the next exercise, remember

$$
\begin{aligned}
10\,000 &= 10 \times 10 \times 10 \times 10 = 10^4 \\
1\,000 &= 10 \times 10 \times 10 = 10^3 \\
100 &= 10 \times 10 = 10^2 \\
10 &= 10 = 10^1 \\
1 &= 10^0 \\
0.1 &= 1 \div 10 = 10^{-1} \\
0.01 &= 1 \div 100 = 10^{-2} \\
0.001 &= 1 \div 1000 = 10^{-3}
\end{aligned}
$$

Exercise 8F

1 Write down the value of

a 3.1×10 **b** 3.1×100 **c** 3.1×1000 **d** $3.1 \times 10\,000$

2 Write down the value of

a 6.5×10 **b** 6.5×10^2 **c** 6.5×10^3 **d** 6.5×10^4

3 Write down the value of

a $3.1 \div 10$ **b** $3.1 \div 100$ **c** $3.1 \div 1000$ **d** $3.1 \div 10\,000$

4 Write down the value of

a $6.5 \div 10$ **b** $6.5 \div 10^2$ **c** $6.5 \div 10^3$ **d** $6.5 \div 10^4$

5 Without using a calculator, evaluate the following.

a 2.5×100 **b** 3.45×10 **c** 4.67×1000 **d** 34.6×10
e 20.789×10 **f** 56.78×1000 **g** 2.46×10^2 **h** 0.076×10
i 0.076×10^3 **j** 0.897×10^5 **k** 0.865×1000 **l** 100.5×10^2
m 0.999×10^6 **n** 234.56×10^2 **o** 98.7654×10^3 **p** 43.23×10^6
q 78.679×10^2 **r** 203.67×10^1 **s** 76.43×10 **t** 34.578×10^5
u $0.003\,4578 \times 10^5$ **v** 0.0006×10^7 **w** $0.005\,67 \times 10^4$ **x** 56.0045×10^4
y $0.909\,07 \times 10^4$ **z** 70.086×10^3

6 Without using a calculator, evaluate the following.

a $2.5 \div 100$ **b** $3.45 \div 10$ **c** $4.67 \div 1000$ **d** $34.6 \div 10$
e $20.789 \div 100$ **f** $56.78 \div 1000$ **g** $2.46 \div 10^2$ **h** $0.076 \div 10$
i $0.076 \div 10^3$ **j** $0.897 \div 10^5$ **k** $0.865 \div 1000$ **l** $100.5 \div 10^2$
m $0.999 \div 10^6$ **n** $234.56 \div 10^2$ **o** $98.7654 \div 10^3$ **p** $43.23 \div 10^6$
q $78.679 \div 10^2$ **r** $203.67 \div 10^1$ **s** $76.43 \div 10$ **t** $34.578 \div 10^5$
u $0.003\,4578 \div 10^5$ **v** $0.0006 \div 10^7$ **w** $0.005\,67 \div 10^4$ **x** $56.0045 \div 10^4$
y $0.909\,07 \div 10^4$ **z** $70.086 \div 10^3$

7 Without using a calculator, evaluate the following.

a 200×300 **b** 30×4000 **c** 50×200 **d** 60×700
e 70×300 **f** 10×30 **g** 3×50 **h** 200×7
i 200×500 **j** 100×2000 **k** 20×1400 **l** 30×30
m $(20)^2$ **n** $(20)^3$ **o** $(400)^2$ **p** 30×150
q 40×200 **r** 50×5000 **s** 40×250 **t** 300×2
u 6×500 **v** 30×2000 **w** $20 \times 40 \times 5000$ **x** $20 \times 20 \times 900$
y $200 \times 4000 \times 60\,000$ **z** $20 \times 50 \times 400 \times 3000$

8 Without using a calculator, evaluate the following.

a $2000 \div 400$ **b** $3000 \div 60$ **c** $5000 \div 200$ **d** $6000 \div 200$
e $2100 \div 300$ **f** $9000 \div 30$ **g** $300 \div 50$ **h** $2100 \div 70$
i $2000 \div 500$ **j** $10\,000 \div 2000$ **k** $2800 \div 1400$ **l** $3000 \div 30$
m $2000 \div 50$ **n** $80\,000 \div 400$ **o** $400 \div 20$ **p** $3000 \div 150$
q $400 \div 200$ **r** $5000 \div 5000$ **s** $4000 \div 250$ **t** $300 \div 2$
u $6000 \div 500$ **v** $30\,000 \div 2000$ **w** $2000 \times 40 \div 2000$ **x** $200 \times 20 \div 800$
y $200 \times 6000 \div 30\,000$ **z** $20 \times 80 \times 600 \div 3000$

9 Without using a calculator, evaluate the following.

a 2.3×10^2 **b** 5.789×10^5 **c** 4.79×10^3 **d** 5.7×10^7
e 2.16×10^2 **f** 1.05×10^4 **g** 3.2×10^{-4} **h** 9.87×10^3

Standard form

This is also known as standard index or SI form. On calculators, it is usually called Scientific Notation.

Standard form is a way of writing large and small numbers using powers of 10. In this form, a number is given a value between 1 and 10 multiplied by a power of 10. That is,

$a \times 10^n$ where $1 \leq a < 10$, and n is a whole number

This is the way you will find standard form defined in your examination formula sheet.

Follow through these examples to see how numbers are written in this way.

$52 = 5.2 \times 10 = 5.2 \times 10^1$
$73 = 7.3 \times 10 = 7.3 \times 10^1$
$625 = 6.25 \times 100 = 6.25 \times 10^2$
$389 = 3.89 \times 100 = 3.89 \times 10^2$
$3147 = 3.147 \times 1000 = 3.147 \times 10^3$

The numbers at the right are in standard form.

When writing a number in this way, two rules must always be followed:

- The first part must be a number between 1 and 10 (1 is allowed but 10 isn't).
- The second part must be a whole number (negative or positive) power of 10. Note that we would **not normally** write the power 1.

Standard form on a calculator

A number such as 123 000 000 000 is obviously difficult to key into a calculator. Instead, you enter it in standard form (assuming you are using a scientific calculator):

$123\,000\,000\,000 = 1.23 \times 10^{11}$

The key strokes to enter this into your calculator will be

[1] [•] [2] [3] [EXP] [1] [1] (On some calculators EXP is EE.)

Your calculator display should now show

1.23 [11] or 1.23 [11]

Be careful when you get an answer like this on your calculator. It needs to be written properly in standard form with × 10, not copied exactly as shown on the calculator display.

Standard form of numbers less than 1

These numbers are written in standard form. Make sure that you understand how they are formed.

a $0.4 = 4 \times 10^{-1}$ | **b** $0.05 = 5 \times 10^{-2}$
c $0.007 = 7 \times 10^{-3}$ | **d** $0.123 = 1.23 \times 10^{-1}$
e $0.0085 = 8.5 \times 10^{-3}$ | **f** $0.0032 = 3.2 \times 10^{-3}$
g $0.007\,65 = 7.65 \times 10^{-3}$ | **h** $0.9804 = 9.804 \times 10^{-1}$
i $0.0098 = 9.8 \times 10^{-3}$ | **j** $0.000\,0078 = 7.8 \times 10^{-6}$

On a calculator you will enter 1.23×10^{-6}, for example, as

1 • 2 3 EXP +/– 6

or 1 • 2 3 EXP 6 +/–

How you enter such numbers will depend on your type of calculator. Try some of the numbers **a** to **j** (above) to see what happens.

Exercise 8G

1 Write down the value of

a 3.1×0.1 **b** 3.1×0.01 **c** 3.1×0.001 **d** 3.1×0.0001

2 Write down the value of

a 6.5×10^{-1} **b** 6.5×10^{-2} **c** 6.5×10^{-3} **d** 6.5×10^{-4}

3 a What is the largest number you can enter into your calculator?

b What is the smallest number you can enter into your calculator?

4 Work out the value of

a $3.1 \div 0.1$ **b** $3.1 \div 0.01$ **c** $3.1 \div 0.001$ **d** $3.1 \div 0.0001$

You will probably need a calculator for this question.

5 Work out the value of

a $6.5 \div 10^{-1}$ **b** $6.5 \div 10^{-2}$ **c** $6.5 \div 10^{-3}$ **d** $6.5 \div 10^{-4}$

You will probably need a calculator for this question.

6 Write these numbers out in full.

a 2.5×10^2 **b** 3.45×10 **c** 4.67×10^{-3} **d** 3.46×10
e 2.0789×10^{-2} **f** 5.678×10^3 **g** 2.46×10^2 **h** 7.6×10
i 7.6×10^3 **j** 8.97×10^5 **k** 8.65×10^{-3} **l** 1.005×10^2
m 9.99×10^{-6} **n** 2.3456×10^2 **o** $9.876\,54 \times 10^3$ **p** 4.323×10^6
q $7.8679 \quad 10^{-2}$ **r** 2.0367×10^{-1} **s** 7.643×10 **t** 3.4578×10^{-5}
u 3.4578×10^5 **v** 6×10^7 **w** 5.67×10^{-4} **x** $5.600\,45 \times 10^4$
y 9.0907×10^4 **z** 7.0086×10^{-3}

7 Write these numbers in standard form.

a 250	**b** 0.345	**c** 46700	**d** 3 400 000 000
e 20 780 000 000	**f** 0.000 5678	**g** 2460	**h** 0.076
i 0.000 76	**j** 0.897	**k** 8650	**l** 100.5
m 0.999	**n** 234.56	**o** 98.7654	**p** 43.23
q 7867.9	**r** 203.67	**s** 76.43	**t** 34.578
u 0.003 4578	**v** 0.0006	**w** 0.005 67	**x** 56.0045
y 0.909 07	**z** 70.086		

In questions **8** to **11**, write the numbers given in each question in standard form.

8 One of the busiest bridges in the world is the Howrah Bridge in Calcutta. It is 72 feet wide and 1500 feet long. It carries 57 000 vehicles a day.

9 One year, 27 797 runners completed the New York Marathon.

10 The largest number of dominoes ever toppled by one person is 281 581, although 30 people set up and toppled 1 382 101.

11 The asteroid Phaethon comes within 12 980 000 miles of the sun, whilst the asteroid Pholus reaches at its furthest point a distance of 2 997 million miles from the earth. The closest asteroid ever to earth came within 93 000 miles.

12 These numbers are not in standard form. Write them in standard form.

a 56.7×10^2	**b** 234.6×10^3	**c** 0.06×10^4
d 34.6×10^{-2}	**e** 0.07×10^{-2}	**f** 56×10
g $2 \times 3 \times 10^5$	**h** $2 \times 10^2 \times 35$	**i** 35×10^{-7}
j 160×10^{-2}	**k** 100×10^{-2}	**l** 10×10^2
m 23 million	**n** 0.0003×10^{-2}	**o** 25.6×10^5
p $2 \times 10^4 \times 54 \times 10^3$	**q** $16 \times 10^2 \times 3 \times 10^{-1}$	**r** $2 \times 10^4 \times 56 \times 10^{-4}$
s $54 \times 10^3 \div 2 \times 10^2$	**t** $18 \times 10^2 \div 3 \times 10^3$	**u** $56 \times 10^3 \div 2 \times 10^{-2}$

Rational and irrational numbers

The number line

The number line is a straight line on which every number, including zero, is represented by a point.

Points to the right of 0 at a distance of 1 unit, 2 units, 3 units, … represent the positive integers 1, 2, 3, … . Points to the left of 0 at a distance of 1 unit, 2 units, 3 units, … represent the negative integers –1, –2, –3, … . The intermediate points represent the fractions or decimals. For example, $\frac{1}{3}$ is placed between 0 and 1, 3.4 between 3 and 4, and $-1\frac{2}{3}$ between –1 and –2.

In theory, the number line spans minus infinity to plus infinity, but in practice we only ever use that, usually short, section of the line which includes only those numbers with which we are dealing at the time. Such a section might be, for example,

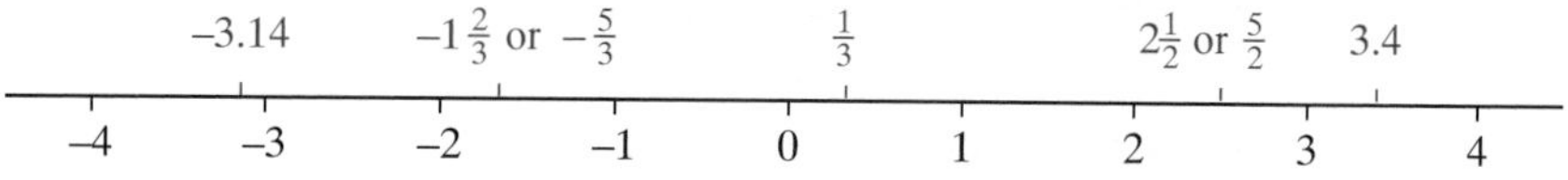

Sometimes we need to enlarge a very small section of the number line so that we can more precisely locate a number. Here is an example of such a situation:

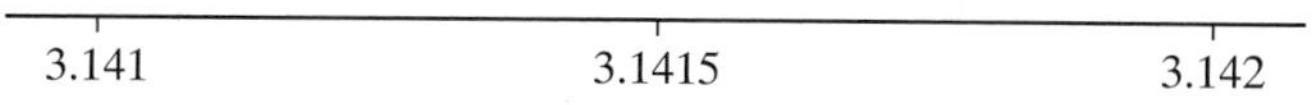

Numbers such as $\frac{1}{3}$, $2\frac{1}{2}$, 3.4, $-1\frac{2}{3}$ and 3.14, which can be precisely located on the number line, are known as **rational numbers**. A rational number is formally defined as a number that can be expressed as the quotient of two integers which do not have a common factor. That is, a rational number can be written in the form

$$\frac{a}{b}$$

where both a and b are integers. It follows that **all integers** are rational numbers.

Some numbers, such as π, $\sqrt{2}$, $\sqrt[3]{10}$ and $\sqrt[7]{100}$, exist on the number line but cannot be precisely located on it because their values are decimals with an unending string of digits to the right of the decimal point which do not even repeat (recur). Such a number is called an **irrational number**.

A close approximation to the position of an irrational number can be obtained by enlarging a small section of the number line in the region of the number, such as shown above and in the solution by trial and improvement given on pages 56–57.

Exercise 8H

1 State which of the following are irrational.

a π **b** $\sqrt{5}$ **c** $\sqrt{16}$ **d** 0.97 **e** 4π

f $1\frac{3}{4}$ **g** $6 + \pi$ **h** $1 - \sqrt{2}$ **i** $\frac{1}{\pi}$ **j** $\sqrt{\pi}$

2 Write down an irrational number between

a 2 and 3 **b** 8 and 10 **c** 21 and 30 **d** 55 and 56

3 What can be added to each of the following to make a rational number?

a $\sqrt{3}$ **b** $\pi - 2$ **c** 5π **d** $\sqrt{2} - \sqrt{3}$ **e** $\pi + 7$

4 What can be multiplied to each of the following to make a rational number?

a π **b** $\sqrt{7}$ **c** $\sqrt{\frac{2}{3}}$ **d** $\frac{1}{\pi}$ **e** $\frac{\pi}{5}^{2}$

5 Investigate the validity of the following statements.

a The square of an irrational number is rational.

b The product of two irrational numbers is rational

c The square root of a prime number is irrational.

Rational decimal numbers

A rational number can be expressed as a decimal which is either a **terminating decimal** or a **recurring decimal**.

A terminating decimal contains a finite number of digits (decimal places). For example, changing $\frac{3}{16}$ into a decimal gives 0.1875 exactly.

A recurring decimal contains a digit or a block of digits that repeats. For example, changing $\frac{5}{9}$ into a decimal gives 0.5555 …, while changing $\frac{14}{27}$ into a decimal gives 0.518 518 5 … with the recurring block 518.

Recurring decimals are indicated by a dot placed over the first and last digits in the recurring block: for example, 0.5555… becomes $0.\dot{5}$, and 0.518 518 5… becomes $0.\dot{5}1\dot{8}$, and 0.583 33 becomes $0.58\dot{3}$

Converting decimals into fractions

Terminating decimals

When converting a terminating decimal, the numerator of the fraction is formed from the decimal, and its denominator is given by 10^n, where n is the number of decimal places.

Because the terminating decimal ends at a specific decimal place, we know the place value at which the numerator ends. For example,

$$0.7 = \frac{7}{10} \qquad 0.045 = \frac{45}{1000} = \frac{9}{200}$$

$$2.34 = \frac{234}{100} = \frac{117}{50} = 2\tfrac{17}{50}$$

$$0.625 = \frac{625}{1000} = \frac{5}{8}$$

Recurring decimals

Follow through Examples 1 and 2, which show the method for converting a recurring decimal to a fraction.

Example 1 Convert $0.\dot{7}$ to a fraction.

Let x be the fraction. Then

$$x = 0.777\,777\,777\ldots \quad (1)$$

Multiply (1) by 10 $\quad 10x = 7.777\,777\,777\ldots \quad (2)$

Subtract (2) – (1) $\quad 9x = 7$

$$\Rightarrow \quad x = \frac{7}{9}$$

Example 2 Convert $0.\dot{5}6\dot{4}$ to a fraction.

Let x be the fraction. Then

$$x = 0.564564564\ldots \quad (1)$$

Multiply (1) by 1000 $\quad 1000x = 564.564\,564\,564\ldots \quad (2)$

Subtract (2) – (1) $\quad 999x = 564$

$$\Rightarrow \quad x = \frac{564}{999} = \frac{188}{333}$$

Exercise 8I

1 Work out each of these fractions as a decimal. Give them as terminating decimals or recurring decimals as appropriate.

a $\frac{1}{2}$ **b** $\frac{1}{3}$ **c** $\frac{1}{4}$ **d** $\frac{1}{5}$ **e** $\frac{1}{6}$

f $\frac{1}{7}$ **g** $\frac{1}{8}$ **h** $\frac{1}{9}$ **i** $\frac{1}{10}$ **j** $\frac{1}{13}$

2 There are several patterns to be found in recurring decimals. For example,

$\frac{1}{7} = 0.142\,857\,142\,857\,142\,857\,142\,857\ldots$

$\frac{2}{7} = 0.285\,714\,285\,714\,285\,714\,285\,714\ldots$

$\frac{3}{7} = 0.428\,571\,428\,571\,428\,571\,428\,571\ldots$

and so on

a Write down the decimals for $\frac{4}{7}$, $\frac{5}{7}$, $\frac{6}{7}$ to 24 decimal places.

b What do you notice?

3 Write each of these fractions as a decimal. Use this to write the list in order of size, smallest first.

$\frac{4}{9}$ $\quad \frac{5}{11}$ $\quad \frac{3}{7}$ $\quad \frac{9}{22}$ $\quad \frac{16}{37}$ $\quad \frac{6}{13}$

4 Write each of the following as a fraction with a denominator of 120. Use this to put them in order of size, smallest first.

$\frac{19}{60}$ $\quad \frac{7}{24}$ $\quad \frac{3}{10}$ $\quad \frac{2}{5}$ $\quad \frac{5}{12}$

5 Convert each of these terminating decimals to a fraction.

a 0.125 **b** 0.34 **c** 0.725 **d** 0.3125

e 0.89 **f** 0.05 **g** 2.35 **h** 0.218 75

6 $x = 0.242\,424\ldots$

a What is $100x$?

b By subtracting the original value from your answer to part **a**, work out the value of $99x$.

c What is x as a fraction?

7 Convert each of these recurring decimals to a fraction.

a $0.\dot{8}$	**b** $0.\dot{3}\dot{4}$	**c** $0.\dot{4}\dot{5}$	**d** $0.\dot{5}6\dot{7}$
e $0.\dot{4}$	**f** $0.0\dot{4}$	**g** $0.1\dot{4}$	**h** $0.0\dot{4}\dot{5}$
i $2.\dot{7}$	**j** $7.\dot{6}\dot{3}$	**k** $3.\dot{3}$	**l** $2.\dot{0}\dot{6}$

8 **a** $\frac{1}{7}$ is a recurring decimal. $(\frac{1}{7})^2 = \frac{1}{49}$ is also a recurring decimal.
Is it true that when you square any fraction that is a recurring decimal, you get another fraction that is also a recurring decimal? Try this with at least four numerical examples before you make a decision.

b $\frac{1}{4}$ is a terminating decimal. $(\frac{1}{4})^2 = \frac{1}{16}$ is also a terminating decimal.
Is it true that when you square any fraction that is a terminating decimal, you get another fraction that is also a terminating decimal? Try this with at least four numerical examples before you make a decision.

c What type of fraction do you get when you multiply a fraction that gives a recurring decimal by another fraction that gives a terminating decimal? Try this with at least four numerical examples before you make a decision.

Surds

It is useful at higher levels of mathematics to be able to work with surds, which are roots of numbers written as, for example,

$$\sqrt{2} \qquad \sqrt{5} \qquad \sqrt{15} \qquad \sqrt{9} \qquad \sqrt{3} \qquad \sqrt{10}$$

Four general rules governing surds (which you can prove yourself by taking numerical examples) are

$$\sqrt{a} \times \sqrt{b} = \sqrt{ab} \qquad C\sqrt{a} \times D\sqrt{b} = CD\sqrt{ab}$$

$$\sqrt{a} \div \sqrt{b} = \sqrt{\frac{a}{b}} \qquad C\sqrt{a} \div D\sqrt{b} = \frac{C}{D}\sqrt{\frac{a}{b}}$$

For example,

$$\sqrt{2} \times \sqrt{2} = \sqrt{4} = 2 \qquad \sqrt{2} \times \sqrt{10} = \sqrt{20} = \sqrt{(4 \times 5)} = \sqrt{4} \times \sqrt{5} = 2\sqrt{5}$$

$$\sqrt{2} \times \sqrt{3} = \sqrt{6} \qquad \sqrt{6} \times \sqrt{15} = \sqrt{90} = \sqrt{9} \times \sqrt{10} = 3\sqrt{10}$$

$$\sqrt{2} \times \sqrt{8} = \sqrt{16} = 4 \qquad 3\sqrt{5} \times 4\sqrt{3} = 12\sqrt{15}$$

Exercise 8J

1 Work out each of the following in simplified form.

a $\sqrt{2} \times \sqrt{3}$ **b** $\sqrt{5} \times \sqrt{3}$ **c** $\sqrt{2} \times \sqrt{2}$ **d** $\sqrt{2} \times \sqrt{8}$
e $\sqrt{5} \times \sqrt{8}$ **f** $\sqrt{3} \times \sqrt{3}$ **g** $\sqrt{6} \times \sqrt{2}$ **h** $\sqrt{7} \times \sqrt{3}$
i $\sqrt{2} \times \sqrt{7}$ **j** $\sqrt{2} \times \sqrt{18}$ **k** $\sqrt{6} \times \sqrt{6}$ **l** $\sqrt{5} \times \sqrt{6}$

2 Work out each of the following in surd form.

a $\sqrt{12} \div \sqrt{3}$ **b** $\sqrt{15} \div \sqrt{3}$ **c** $\sqrt{12} \div \sqrt{2}$ **d** $\sqrt{24} \div \sqrt{8}$
e $\sqrt{40} \div \sqrt{8}$ **f** $\sqrt{3} \div \sqrt{3}$ **g** $\sqrt{6} \div \sqrt{2}$ **h** $\sqrt{21} \div \sqrt{3}$
i $\sqrt{28} \div \sqrt{7}$ **j** $\sqrt{48} \div \sqrt{8}$ **k** $\sqrt{6} \div \sqrt{6}$ **l** $\sqrt{54} \div \sqrt{6}$

3 Work out each of the following in surd form.

a $\sqrt{2} \times \sqrt{3} \times \sqrt{2}$ **b** $\sqrt{5} \times \sqrt{3} \times \sqrt{15}$ **c** $\sqrt{2} \times \sqrt{2} \times \sqrt{8}$ **d** $\sqrt{2} \times \sqrt{8} \times \sqrt{3}$
e $\sqrt{5} \times \sqrt{8} \times \sqrt{8}$ **f** $\sqrt{3} \times \sqrt{3} \times \sqrt{3}$ **g** $\sqrt{6} \times \sqrt{2} \times \sqrt{48}$ **h** $\sqrt{7} \times \sqrt{3} \times \sqrt{3}$
i $\sqrt{2} \times \sqrt{7} \times \sqrt{2}$ **j** $\sqrt{2} \times \sqrt{18} \times \sqrt{5}$ **k** $\sqrt{6} \times \sqrt{6} \times \sqrt{3}$ **l** $\sqrt{5} \times \sqrt{6} \times \sqrt{30}$

4 Work out each of the following in surd form.

a $\sqrt{2} \times \sqrt{3} \div \sqrt{2}$ **b** $\sqrt{5} \times \sqrt{3} \div \sqrt{15}$ **c** $\sqrt{32} \times \sqrt{2} \div \sqrt{8}$ **d** $\sqrt{2} \times \sqrt{8} \div \sqrt{8}$
e $\sqrt{5} \times \sqrt{8} \div \sqrt{8}$ **f** $\sqrt{3} \times \sqrt{3} \div \sqrt{3}$ **g** $\sqrt{8} \times \sqrt{12} \div \sqrt{48}$ **h** $\sqrt{7} \times \sqrt{3} \div \sqrt{3}$
i $\sqrt{2} \times \sqrt{7} \div \sqrt{2}$ **j** $\sqrt{2} \times \sqrt{18} \div \sqrt{3}$ **k** $\sqrt{6} \times \sqrt{6} \div \sqrt{3}$ **l** $\sqrt{5} \times \sqrt{6} \div \sqrt{30}$

5 Simplify each of these expressions.

a $\sqrt{a} \times \sqrt{a}$ **b** $\sqrt{a} \div \sqrt{a}$ **c** $\sqrt{a} \times \sqrt{a} \div \sqrt{a}$

6 Simplify each of the following surds into the form $a\sqrt{b}$.

a $\sqrt{18}$ **b** $\sqrt{24}$ **c** $\sqrt{12}$ **d** $\sqrt{50}$
e $\sqrt{8}$ **f** $\sqrt{27}$ **g** $\sqrt{48}$ **h** $\sqrt{75}$
i $\sqrt{45}$ **j** $\sqrt{63}$ **k** $\sqrt{32}$ **l** $\sqrt{200}$
m $\sqrt{1000}$ **n** $\sqrt{250}$ **o** $\sqrt{98}$ **p** $\sqrt{243}$

7 Simplify each of these.

a $2\sqrt{18} \times 3\sqrt{2}$ **b** $4\sqrt{24} \times 2\sqrt{5}$ **c** $3\sqrt{12} \times 3\sqrt{3}$ **d** $2\sqrt{8} \times 2\sqrt{8}$
e $2\sqrt{27} \times 4\sqrt{8}$ **f** $2\sqrt{48} \times 3\sqrt{8}$ **g** $2\sqrt{45} \times 3\sqrt{3}$ **h** $2\sqrt{63} \times 2\sqrt{7}$
i $2\sqrt{32} \times 4\sqrt{2}$ **j** $\sqrt{1000} \times \sqrt{10}$ **k** $\sqrt{250} \times \sqrt{10}$ **l** $2\sqrt{98} \times 2\sqrt{2}$

8 Simplify each of these.

a $4\sqrt{2} \times 5\sqrt{3}$ **b** $2\sqrt{5} \times 3\sqrt{3}$ **c** $4\sqrt{2} \times 3\sqrt{2}$ **d** $2\sqrt{2} \times 2\sqrt{8}$
e $2\sqrt{5} \times 3\sqrt{8}$ **f** $3\sqrt{3} \times 2\sqrt{3}$ **g** $2\sqrt{6} \times 5\sqrt{2}$ **h** $5\sqrt{7} \times 2\sqrt{3}$
i $2\sqrt{2} \times 3\sqrt{7}$ **j** $2\sqrt{2} \times 3\sqrt{18}$ **k** $2\sqrt{6} \times 2\sqrt{6}$ **l** $4\sqrt{5} \times 3\sqrt{6}$

9 Simplify each of these.

a $6\sqrt{12} \div 2\sqrt{3}$ **b** $3\sqrt{15} \div \sqrt{3}$ **c** $6\sqrt{12} \div \sqrt{2}$ **d** $4\sqrt{24} \div 2\sqrt{8}$
e $12\sqrt{40} \div 3\sqrt{8}$ **f** $5\sqrt{3} \div \sqrt{3}$ **g** $14\sqrt{6} \div 2\sqrt{2}$ **h** $4\sqrt{21} \div 2\sqrt{3}$
i $9\sqrt{28} \div 3\sqrt{7}$ **j** $12\sqrt{56} \div 6\sqrt{8}$ **k** $25\sqrt{6} \div 5\sqrt{6}$ **l** $32\sqrt{54} \div 4\sqrt{6}$

10 Simplify each of these.

a $4\sqrt{2} \times \sqrt{3} \div 2\sqrt{2}$ **b** $4\sqrt{5} \times \sqrt{3} \div \sqrt{15}$ **c** $2\sqrt{32} \times 3\sqrt{2} \div 2\sqrt{8}$
d $6\sqrt{2} \times 2\sqrt{8} \div 3\sqrt{8}$ **e** $3\sqrt{5} \times 4\sqrt{8} \div 2\sqrt{8}$ **f** $12\sqrt{3} \times 4\sqrt{3} \div 2\sqrt{3}$
g $3\sqrt{8} \times 3\sqrt{12} \div 3\sqrt{48}$ **h** $4\sqrt{7} \times 2\sqrt{3} \div 8\sqrt{3}$ **i** $15\sqrt{2} \times 2\sqrt{7} \div 3\sqrt{2}$
j $8\sqrt{2} \times 2\sqrt{18} \div 4\sqrt{3}$ **k** $5\sqrt{6} \times 5\sqrt{6} \div 5\sqrt{3}$ **l** $2\sqrt{5} \times 3\sqrt{6} \div \sqrt{30}$

11 Simplify each of these expressions.

a $a\sqrt{b} \times c\sqrt{b}$ **b** $a\sqrt{b} \div c\sqrt{b}$ **c** $a\sqrt{b} \times c\sqrt{b} \div a\sqrt{b}$

12 Find the value of a that makes each of these surds true.

a $\sqrt{5} \times \sqrt{a} = 100$ **b** $\sqrt{6} \times \sqrt{a} = 12$ **c** $\sqrt{10} \times 2\sqrt{a} = 20$

d $2\sqrt{6} \times 3\sqrt{a} = 72$ **e** $2\sqrt{a} \times \sqrt{a} = 6$ **f** $3\sqrt{a} \times 3\sqrt{a} = 54$

13 The following rules are not true. Try some numerical examples to show this.

a $\sqrt{(a + b)} = \sqrt{a} + \sqrt{b}$

b $\sqrt{(a - b)} = \sqrt{a} - \sqrt{b}$

14 Simplify the following.

a $\left(\frac{\sqrt{3}}{2}\right)^2$ **b** $\left(\frac{5}{\sqrt{3}}\right)^2$ **c** $\left(\frac{\sqrt{5}}{4}\right)^2$ **d** $\left(\frac{6}{\sqrt{3}}\right)^2$ **e** $\left(\frac{\sqrt{8}}{2}\right)^2$

Possible coursework tasks

Fermat's primes

The mathematician Fermat (1601–65) discovered that some prime numbers are the sum of two square numbers. For example,

$$29 = 2^2 + 5^2$$

Investigate this for other prime numbers.

p powers

Investigate whether $n^p - n$ is a multiple of p.

Irrational number

Prove that $\sqrt{2}$ is an irrational number.

'Log' problem

Investigate powers of 10 which use decimal indices: for example, $10^{2.5}$.

Five fives

Which is largest: 5^{5555} or 55^{555} or 555^{55}?

Examination questions: coursework type

The number 169 is a square number. It has factors 1, 13 and 169. Investigate the truth of the statement:

'All square numbers have only three factors.'

Investigate the truth of this statement:

'There are no numbers x and y such that $x^2 - 2y^2 = 1$.'

WJEC, Question 3, Paper 3, June 1995

Examination questions

1 Find the value of **i** 9^4 **ii** 5^{-2} *NEAB, Question 22, Specimen Paper 2, 1998*

2 a At certain times Jupiter is approximately 775 000 000 kilometres from the sun. Express this distance in standard form.

b The mass of a proton is 1.67×10^{-24} grams and the mass of an electron is 9.109×10^{-28} grams. Evaluate

$$\frac{\text{Mass of proton}}{\text{Mass of electron}}$$

correct to the nearest whole number. *WJEC, Question 14, Specimen Paper 1, 1998*

3 The mass of one atom of oxygen is given as 2.66×10^{-23} grams. The mass of one atom of hydrogen is given as 1.67×10^{-24} grams.

a Find the difference in mass between one atom of oxygen and one atom of hydrogen.

b A molecule of water contains two atoms of hydrogen and one atom of oxygen.

i Calculate the mass of one molecule of water.

ii Calculate the number of molecules of water in 1 gram of water.

NEAB, Question 15, Paper 2, November 1994

4 The number 10^{100} is called a googol.

a Write the number 50 googols in standard index form.

A nanometre is 10^{-9} metres.

b Write 50 nanometres in metres. Give your answer in standard form.

ULEAC, Question 23, Paper 4, June 1994

5 A light year is the distance travelled by light in 365 days. The speed of light is 3.0×10^5 kilometres per second. The distance to the nearest star is 4.0×10^{13} kilometres. How many light years is it to the nearest star? Give your answer to an appropriate degree of accuracy. *SEG, Question 17, Specimen Paper 13, 1998*

6 a The approximate population of the United Kingdom is given in standard form as 5.2×10^7. Write this as an ordinary number.

b The thickness of grade A paper is 6.0×10^{-2} cm. Grade B paper is twice as thick as grade A. Calculate, in centimetres, the thickness of grade B paper. Write your answer in standard form. *SEG, Question 7, Paper 4, June 1994*

7 a Evaluate $8^{\frac{1}{3}}$.

b Write $16^{-\frac{1}{2}} \times 2^{-3}$ as a power of 2.

c Given that $32^y = 2$, find the value of y. *NEAB, Question 17, Specimen Paper 2H, 1998*

8 a Which of the following numbers are rational?

i $1 + \sqrt{2}$ **ii** $\frac{\pi}{2}$ **iii** $3^0 + 3^{-1} + 3^{-2}$

b When p and q are two different irrational numbers, $p \times q$ can be rational. Write down one example to show this.

c Write down a fraction which is equal to the recurring decimal $0.0\dot{3}\dot{6}$.

SEG, Question 1, Specimen Paper 16, 1998

9 $m = 5$ $n = -7$

a Write down the exact value of the following, leaving your answers as integers or fractions if you can, otherwise as an irrational number.

i $m^2 - n^2$ **ii** $m^{\frac{1}{2}}$ **iii** n^{-3}

b Simplify $(4 - \sqrt{5})^2$ as far as possible, without using a calculator.

NEAB, Question 15, Specimen Paper 2H, 1998

10 a Write 1.61 as a rational number in the form $\frac{a}{b}$, where a and b are whole numbers.

Given that $n = 1.777\ldots$

b i Write down the value of $10n$.

ii Hence write down the value of $9n$.

iii Express n as a rational number, in the form $\frac{a}{b}$, where a and b are whole numbers.

c Write down an irrational number which has a value between $\sqrt{10}$ and $\sqrt{11}$.

NEAB, Question 13, Paper 1R, November 1995

Summary

How well do you grade yourself?

To gain a grade **C**, you need to be able to multiply and divide numbers written in index form.

To gain a grade **B**, you need to be able to write numbers in standard form and use these in various problems.

To gain a grade **A**, you need to understand rational and irrational numbers and be able to manipulate them. You need also to know how to use the rules of indices for negative and fractional values.

What you should know after you have worked through Chapter 8

- How to write numbers in standard form and compare their sizes.
- How to solve problems using numbers in standard form.
- How to manipulate indices, both integer (positive and negative) and fractional.
- What rational and irrational numbers are.
- What surds are and how to manipulate them.

9 Statistics 1

This chapter is going to ... introduce you to frequency tables, from which you can create frequency polygons, bar charts and histograms, and find averages. It then shows you how best to conduct surveys, construct questionnaires and use sampling techniques.

What you should already know

- The **mode** is the item of data that occurs the most.
- The **median** is the item of data in the middle once all the items have been put in order of size, from lowest to highest.
- The **mean** is the sum total of all the items of data divided by the number of items. The mean is usually written as $\bar{x}$.
- The **range** is the difference between the highest item of data and the lowest.

Frequency tables

When a lot of information has been gathered, it is often convenient to put it together in a frequency table. From this table you can then find the values of the four averages. For example, a survey was done on the number of people in each car leaving the Meadowhall Shopping Centre, in Sheffield. The results are summarised in the table below.

Number of people in each car	1	2	3	4	5	6
Frequency	45	198	121	76	52	13

- The modal number of people in a car is easy to spot. It is the number with the largest frequency of 198. Hence, the modal number is 2.
- The median number of people in a car is found by working out where the middle of the set of numbers is located. First, we add up frequencies to get the total number of cars surveyed, which comes to 505. Next, we calculate the middle position:

  $(505 + 1) \div 2 = 253$

  We now need to count the frequencies across the table to find which group contains the 253rd item. The 243rd item is the end of the group with 2 in a car. Therefore, the 253rd item must be in the group with 3 in a car. Hence, the median number in a car is 3.

- The mean number of people in a car is found by adding together all the people and then dividing this total by the number of cars surveyed.

Number in a car	Frequency	Number in these cars
1	45	$1 \times 45 = 45$
2	198	$2 \times 198 = 396$
3	121	$3 \times 121 = 363$
4	76	$4 \times 76 = 304$
5	52	$5 \times 52 = 260$
6	13	$6 \times 13 = 78$
Totals	505	1446

Hence, the mean number of people in a car is $1446 \div 505 = 2.9$.

Notice that, although we cannot have 2.9 people, the mean often does work out to be a decimal number, and hence needs rounding off. One decimal place is appropriate here.

Using your calculator

The previous example can also be done by using the statistical mode which is available on some calculators. However, not all calculators are the same, so you will have to either read your instruction manual or experiment with the statistical keys on your calculator. You may find one labelled

DATA or M+ or Σ+ or $\bar{x}$ where $\bar{x}$ is printed in blue.

Try the following key strokes.

1 × 4 5 DATA 2 × 1 9 8 DATA …

6 × 1 3 DATA $\bar{x}$

Now find $\bar{x}$ on your calculator. You may first have to use INV or 2ndF

You can use n to check the number of items in your survey.

Exercise 9A

1 Find **i** the mode, **ii** the median and **iii** the mean from each frequency table below.

a A survey of the shoe sizes of all the Y10 boys in a school gave these results.

Shoe size	4	5	6	7	8	9	10
Number of pupils	12	30	34	35	23	8	3

b A survey of the number of eggs laid by hens over a period of one week gave these results.

Number of eggs	0	1	2	3	4	5	6
Frequency	6	8	15	35	48	37	12

c This is a record of the number of babies born each day over 1 week in a small maternity unit.

Number of babies	0	1	2	3	4	5	6	7	8	9	10	11	12	13	14
Frequency	1	1	1	2	2	2	3	5	9	8	6	4	5	2	1

d A school did a survey on how many times in a week pupils arrived late at school. These are the findings.

Number of times late	0	1	2	3	4	5
Frequency	481	34	23	15	3	4

2 A survey of the number of children in each family of a school's intake gave these results.

Number of children	1	2	3	4	5
Frequency	214	328	97	26	3

a Assuming each child at the school is shown in the data, how many children are at the school?

b Calculate the mean number of children in a family.

c How many families have this mean number of children?

d How many families would consider themselves average from this survey?

3 A dentist kept records of how many teeth he extracted from his patients.

In 1970 he extracted 598 teeth from 271 patients.
In 1980 he extracted 332 teeth from 196 patients.
In 1990 he extracted 374 teeth from 288 patients.

a Calculate the average number of teeth taken from each patient in each year.

b Explain why you think the average number of teeth extracted falls each year.

4 The number of league goals scored by a Premier team over a season is given in the table below.

Number of goals scored	0	1	2	3	4	5	6	7
Number of matches	4	9	10	11	4	2	1	1

a How many games were played that season?

b What is the range of goals scored?

c What is the modal number of goals scored?

d What is the median number of goals scored?

e What is the mean number of goals scored?

f Which average do you think the team's supporters would say is the average number of goals scored by the team that season?

g If the team also scored 25 goals in six cup matches that season, what was mean number of goals the team scored throughout the whole season?

5 The teachers in a school were asked to indicate the average number of hours they spent each day marking. The table summarises their replies.

Number of hours spent marking	1	2	3	4	5	6
Number of teachers	9	12	10	8	6	1

a How many teachers were at the school?

b What is the modal number of hours spent marking?

c What is the mean number of hours spent marking?

6 100 cases of apples delivered to a supermarket were inspected and the number of bad apples counted.

Bad apples	0	1	2	3	4	5	6	7	8	9
Frequency	52	29	9	3	2	1	3	0	0	1

What is

a the modal number of bad apples per case

b the mean number of bad apples per case?

7 Two dice are thrown together 60 times. The sum of the scores is shown below.

Score	2	3	4	5	6	7	8	9	10	11	12
Frequency	1	2	6	9	12	15	6	5	2	1	1

Find **a** the modal score, **b** the median score and **c** the mean score.

8 During a 1 month period, the number of days off by 100 workers in a factory were noted as follows.

Number of days off	0	1	2	3	4
Number of workers	35	42	16	4	3

Calculate

a the modal number of days off

b the median number of days off

c the mean number of days off.

9 Two friends often played golf together. They recorded their scores for each hole over the last five games to compare who was more consistent and who was the better player. Their results were summarised in the following table.

No. of shots to hole ball	1	2	3	4	5	6	7	8	9
Roger	0	0	0	14	37	27	12	0	0
Brian	5	12	15	18	14	8	8	8	2

a What is the modal score for each player?
b What is the range of scores for each player?
c What is the median score for each player?
d What is the mean score for each player?
e Which player is the more consistent and explain why?
f Who would you say is the better player and state why?

10 The table below shows the number of passengers in each of 100 taxis leaving London Airport one day.

No. of passengers in a taxi	1	2	3	4
No. of taxis	x	40	y	26

a Find the value of $x + y$.
b If the mean number of passengers per taxi is 2.66, show that $x + 3y = 82$.
c Find the values of x and y by solving appropriate equations.
d State the median of the number of passengers per taxi.

Grouped data

Sometimes the information we are given is grouped in some way, as in the table below, which shows the range of pocket money given to Y10 students in a particular class.

Pocket money (£)	0.00–1.00	1.01–2.00	2.01–3.00	3.01–4.00	4.01–5.00
No. of students	2	5	5	9	15

The modal group is still easy to pick out, since it is simply the one with the largest frequency. Here the modal group is £4.01–£5.00.

The median will be in the middle of a group, and the way to find it is to draw a particular type of graph called a **cumulative frequency curve**, which you will meet on pages 357–63.

The mean can only be estimated, since we do not have all the information. To estimate the mean, we simply assume that each person in each group has the 'mid-way' amount, then we proceed to build up the following table.

Note how we find the mid-way value. The two end values are added together and then divided by two. The result could be rounded off to the nearest penny if we wished, since it is only an estimate, but it is usual not to round off until the final calculation is complete.

Pocket money (£)	Frequency (f)	Mid-way (m)	$f \times m$
0.00–1.00	2	0.50	$2 \times 0.50 = 1.00$
1.01–2.00	5	1.505	$5 \times 1.505 = 7.525$
2.01–3.00	5	2.505	$5 \times 2.505 = 12.525$
3.01–4.00	9	3.505	$9 \times 3.505 = 31.545$
4.01–5.00	15	4.505	$15 \times 4.505 = 67.575$
Totals	36		120.170

The estimated mean will be £120.17 ÷ 36 = £3.34 (rounded off).

There are several different ways of giving the groups in a grouped-frequency table. For example, the group headings in the first table could have been given as:

Pocket money £p $\quad 0 \le p \le 1 \quad 1 < p \le 2 \quad 2 < p \le 3 \quad 3 < p \le 4 \quad 4 < p \le 5$

where, for instance, $2 < p \le 3$ means 'the pocket money is more than £2 but less than or equal to £3'.

You will meet different ways of using inequalities in this type of table. Usually, it will make little difference to the middle value but could make it simpler to find the middle.

Exercise 9B

1 Find for each table of values given below

i the modal group

ii an estimate for the mean.

a

Score	0–10	11–20	21–30	31–40	41–50
Frequency	4	6	11	17	9

b

Records	0–100	101–200	201–300	301–400	401–500	501–600
Frequency	95	56	32	21	9	3

c

Cost (£)	0.00–5.00	5.01–10.00	10.01–15.00	15.01–20.00
Frequency	16	27	19	13

d

Weeks	0–3	4–6	7–9	10–12	13–15
Frequency	5	8	14	10	7

2 Jason brought 100 pebbles back from the beach and weighed them all to the nearest gram. His results are summarised in the table below.

Weight (grams)	40–60	61–70	71–80	81–90	91–100	101–140
Frequency	5	9	22	27	26	11

Find

a the modal weight of the pebbles

b an estimate of the total weight of all the pebbles

c an estimate of the mean weight of the pebbles.

3 A gardener measured the heights of all his daffodils to the nearest centimetre and summarised his results as follows.

Height (cm)	10–14	15–18	19–22	23–26	27–40
Frequency	21	57	65	52	12

a How many daffodils did the gardener have?

b What is the modal height of the daffodils?

c What is the estimated mean height of the daffodils?

4 In the Y10 end-of-year exams the results were grouped for easy comparison.

Marks	0–10	11–20	21–30	31–40	41–50	51–60	61–70	71–80	81–90	91–100
Frequency	3	5	11	19	34	26	18	10	6	2

Find

a the modal mark

b the estimated mean mark.

c What percentage of marks were over 70?

5 A survey was made to see how quickly the AA attended calls which were not on a motorway. The following table summarises the results.

Time (min)	0–15	16–30	31–45	46–60	61–75	76–90	91–105
Frequency	2	23	48	31	27	18	11

a How many calls were used in the survey?

b Estimate the mean time taken per call.

c Which average would the AA use for the average call-out time?

d What percentage of calls do the AA get to within the hour?

6 A certain London train was notorious for arriving late. So a survey was carried out over a month to see just how bad the problem was. The table summarises the results.

Minutes late	0–2	3–4	5–6	7–8	9–10	11–12
Frequency	9	6	5	4	4	2

a Estimate the mean number of minutes late.

b Which average would the rail company use?

c Do you think the criticism of the rail company is justified by these results? Fully explain your reasons.

7 One hundred light bulbs were tested by their manufacturer to see whether the average life span of the manufacturer's bulbs was over 200 hours. The following table summarises the results.

Life span (h)	150–175	176–200	201–225	226–250	251–275
Frequency	24	45	18	10	3

a What is the modal length of time a bulb lasts?
b What percentage of bulbs last longer than 200 hours?
c Estimate the mean life span of the light bulbs.
d Do you think the test shows that the average life span is over 200 hours? Fully explain your answers.

8 I grew tomatoes last year and weighed each one to see what I had grown. I put the results into the following table.

Weight (grams)	41–80	81–100	101–120	121–140	141–160	161–200	201–250
Frequency	5	15	24	39	26	17	6

a How many tomatoes did I grow last year?
b Estimate the mean weight of my tomatoes last year.

9 The owners of a boutique did a survey to find the average age of people using the boutique. The table summarises the results.

Age (years)	14–18	19–20	21–26	27–35	36–50
Frequency	26	24	19	16	11

What do you think is the average age of the people using the boutique?

10 Three supermarkets each claimed to have the lowest average price increase over the year. The following table summarises their average price increases.

Price increase (p)	0–5	6–10	11–15	16–20	21–25	26–30	31–35
Soundbuy	4	10	14	23	19	8	2
Springfields	5	11	12	19	25	9	6
Setco	3	8	15	31	21	7	3

Using their average price increases, make a comparison of the supermarkets and write a report on which supermarket, in your opinion, has the lowest price increases over the year. Don't forget to justify your answers.

Discrete and continuous data

You will need to be able to recognise the important difference between discrete data and continuous data.

Discrete data

This is data which consists of a set of separate numbers. For example, goals scored, marks in a test, number of children, shoe sizes.

Continuous data

This is data which can have an infinite number of different values. It is always rounded-off information. For example, height, weight, time, area, capacity. When representing continuous data on an axis in a chart you need to be careful how you represent it, and be clear about what rounding off has taken place in obtaining the data.

Charts

To help people understand it, statistical information is often presented in pictorial or diagrammatic form, which includes the pie chart, the frequency polygon, the bar chart and the histogram.

Frequency polygons

Frequency polygons can be used to represent both ungrouped data and grouped data, as shown in Example 1 and Example 2 respectively.

Example 1

No. of children	0	1	2	3	4	5
Frequency, f	12	23	36	28	16	11

This is the frequency polygon for the **ungrouped data** in the table.

Notice the following:

- We simply plot the co-ordinates from each ordered pair in the table.
- We complete the polygon by joining up the plotted points with straight lines.

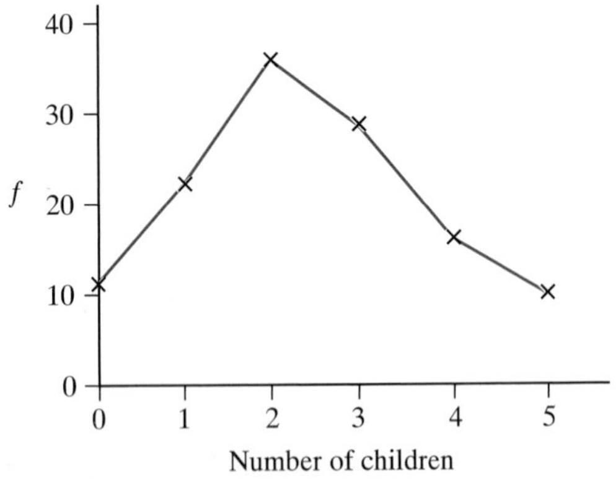

Example 2

Score	1–5	6–10	11–15	16–20	21–25	26–30
Frequency, f	4	13	25	32	17	9

The frequency polygon for the **grouped data** in the table is shown at the top of the next page.

Notice the following:

- We use the mid-point of each group, just as we did in estimating the mean.

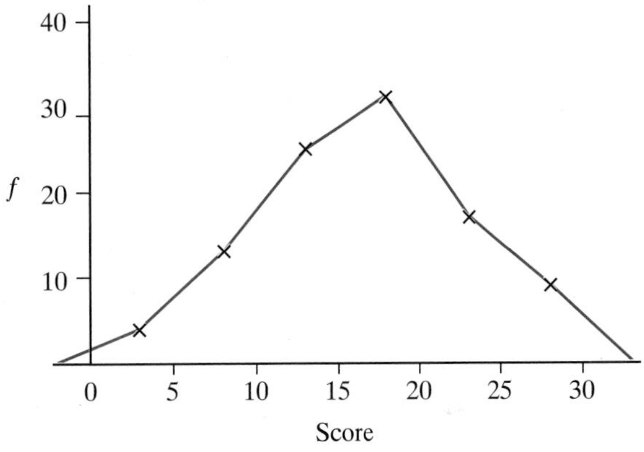

- We plot the ordered pairs of mid-points with frequency, namely,

  $(3, 4), (8, 13), (13, 25),$
  $(18, 32), (23, 17), (28, 9)$

- We complete the polygon by joining up the plotted points with straight lines and bringing it down to 0 on the frequency axis to intercept the score axis 5 units back from the first plotted point $(3, 4)$ and 5 units on from the last plotted point $(28, 9)$.

Bar charts and histograms

You should already be familiar with the bar chart in which the vertical axis represents frequency, and the horizontal axis represents the type of data. (Sometimes it is more convenient to have the axes the other way.)

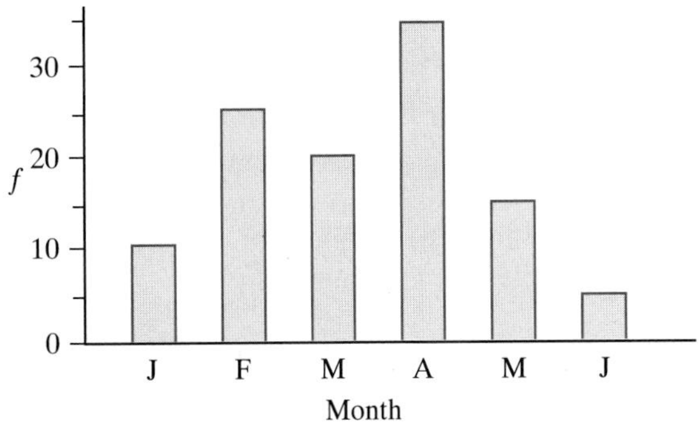

A histogram looks similar to a bar chart but there are four fundamental differences.

- There are no gaps between the bars.
- The horizontal axis has a continuous scale since it represents continuous data, such as time, weight or length.
- The area of each bar represents the class or group frequency of the bar.
- The vertical axis is labelled 'Frequency density', where

$$\text{Frequency density} = \frac{\text{Frequency of class interval}}{\text{Width of class interval}}$$

When the data is not continuous, a simple bar chart is used. For example, the runs scored in a test match or the goals scored by a hockey team.

Look at the histogram below, which has been drawn from this table of times taken by people to walk to work, measured to the nearest minute.

Time (min)	1–4	5–8	9–12	13–16
Frequency	8	12	10	7
Frequency density	2	3	2.5	1.75

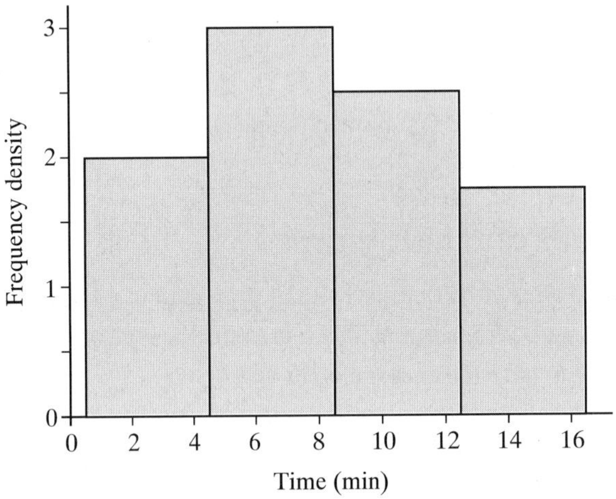

Notice that each histogram bar starts at the **least possible** time and finishes at the **greatest possible** time for its group. For example, in the time interval 5–8 minutes,

the least possible time is $4\frac{1}{2}$ minutes
the greatest possible time is $8\frac{1}{2}$ minutes

In the same way, the bar for 9–12 minutes starts at $8\frac{1}{2}$ minutes and finishes at $12\frac{1}{2}$ minutes.

The $8\frac{1}{2}$ and $12\frac{1}{2}$ minutes are called respectively the **lower** and **upper bounds** for the interval.

Using your calculator

Histograms can also be drawn on graphics calculators or by using computer software packages. If you have access to either of these, try to use them.

Exercise 9C

1 The table shows the range of heights of the girls in Y11 at a London school.

Height (cm)	121–130	131–140	141–150	151–160	161–170
Frequency	15	37	25	13	5

i Draw a frequency polygon from this data.
ii Draw a histogram from this data.
iii Estimate the mean height of the girls.

2 After a spelling test, all the results were collated for girls and boys as below.

Number correct	1–4	5–8	9–12	13–16	17–20
Boys	3	7	21	26	15
Girls	4	8	17	23	20

i Draw frequency polygons to illustrate the differences between the boys' scores and the girls' scores.
ii Estimate the mean score for boys and girls separately, and comment on the results.

3 The following table shows how many students were absent from one particular class throughout the year.

Students absent	0–1	2–3	4–5	6–7	8–9
Frequency	48	32	12	3	1

i Draw a frequency polygon to illustrate the data.
ii Estimate the mean number of absences each lesson.
iii Why is a histogram not a particularly useful chart to draw for this information?

4 The table below shows the number of goals scored by a hockey team in one season.

Goals	0–1	2–4	5–8	9–13	14–19
Frequency	3	9	7	5	2

i Draw the frequency polygon for this data.
ii Estimate the mean number of goals scored per game this season.

5 A doctor was concerned at the length of time her patients had to wait to see her when they came to the morning surgery. The survey she did gave her the following results.

Time (min)	1–10	11–20	21–30	31–40	41–50	51–60
Monday	5	8	17	9	7	4
Wednesday	9	8	16	3	2	1
Friday	7	6	18	2	1	1

i Draw a frequency polygon for each day on the same pair of axes.
ii What is the average amount of time spent waiting each day?
iii Why might the average time for each day be different?

6 At a maternity clinic, the following data was collected one month on the weights at birth of the babies born in that month. The weights were recorded to the nearest kg.

Weight (kg)	3	4	5	6	7	8
Boys	4	26	11	8	4	3
Girls	5	28	14	5	2	1

i Were more girls or boys born that month?

ii How many babies were born at the unit that month?

iii Draw a frequency polygon for each sex on the same pair of axes.

iv Draw a histogram for the combined weights of the babies.

v What was the average weight of each sex? Comment on your results.

7 In a survey of over 200 families about the number of children in a family, the following results were obtained.

Number of children	1	2	3	4
Frequency	69	134	19	7

i What is the mean number of children per family?

ii Why is the data not particularly suitable for a frequency polygon or a histogram to be drawn?

8 The wages paid to Saturday workers in a market were found to be:

Wages (£)	6–10	11–15	16–20	21–25	26–30
Age 16–17	12	9	8	3	0
Age 18–20	6	15	11	8	2

i What are the average Saturday wages paid to each age group?

ii Illustrate the difference between each age group on a frequency polygon.

9 The speeds achieved by computer secretaries are given in this table.

Speed (words/min)	21–30	31–40	41–50	51–60	61–70
Frequency	3	7	12	8	3

i Draw a histogram to illustrate the data.

ii Estimate the mean speed of the secretaries.

iii What percentage have a speed over 50 words per minute?

10 The number of passengers in each taxi leaving a night-club one night were:

Passengers	1	2	3	4	5	6
Frequency	8	15	23	9	6	2

i How many taxis were in the survey?

ii What is the mean number of passengers in each taxi?

iii Draw a frequency polygon from the given data.

Histograms with bars of unequal width

Sometimes the data in a frequency distribution are grouped into classes whose intervals are different. That is, the resulting histogram has bars of unequal width.

Now, it is the area of a bar in a histogram that represents the class frequency of the bar. So, in the case of an unequal-width histogram, the height of each bar is found by dividing its class frequency by its class interval width (bar width), which is the difference between the lower and upper bounds for each interval.

Conversely, given a histogram, any of its class frequencies can be found by multiplying the height of the corresponding bar by its width.

It is for this reason that the scale on the vertical axes of histograms is nearly always 'Frequency density' (see page 202).

Example The heights of a group of girls were measured to the nearest centimetre. The results were classified as shown in the table.

Height (*h*, nearest cm)	152–153	154	155	156–159	160
Frequency	64	43	47	96	12

First we need to appreciate that the classes have lower and upper bounds. These are:

Class (cm)	Lower bound	Upper bound	Interval width
152–153	151.5	153.5	2
154	153.5	154.5	1
155	154.5	155.5	1
156–159	155.5	159.5	4
160	159.5	160.5	1

So the heights of the bars on the frequency density scale are:

Class (cm)	Frequency	Interval width	Frequency density
152–153	64	2	$64 \div 2 = 32$
154	43	1	43
155	47	1	47
1656–159	96	4	$96 \div 4 = 24$
160	12	1	12

The histogram for the above data is shown on the next page.

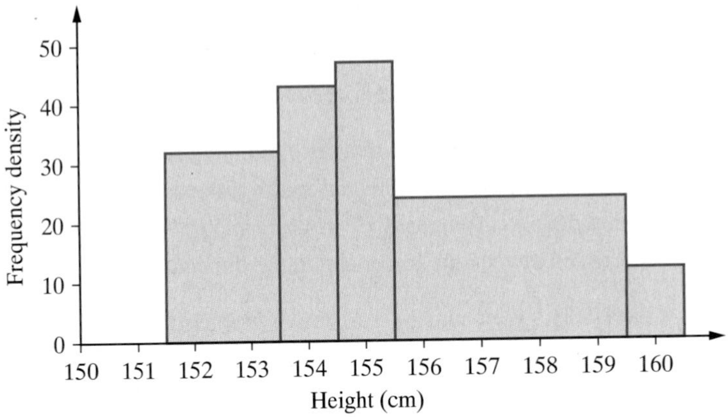

Exercise 9D

1 Draw histograms for the following grouped frequency distributions.

a

Temperature (nearest °C)	10	11–12	13–15	16	17	18–20
Frequency	5	13	18	4	3	6

b

Wage (nearest £1000)	7000	8000–10 000	11 000–15 000	16 000–20 000
Frequency	16	54	62	25

c

Age (nearest year)	11–13	14–15	16	17–20
Frequency	51	36	12	20

d

Pressure (mm)	745–754	755–759	760–764	765–774
Frequency	4	6	14	10

e

Time (nearest minute)	1–8	9–12	13–15	16–20
Frequency	72	84	54	35

2 For each of the frequency distributions illustrated in the histograms on the next page:

i Write down the grouped frequency table.

ii State the modal group.

iii Estimate the median by finding where the whole area is divided into two equal parts.

iv Estimate the mean of the distribution.

a

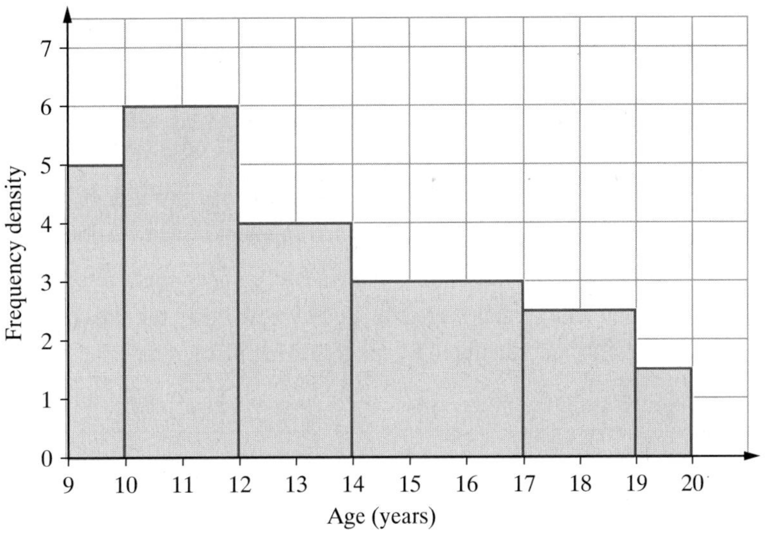
Frequency density
0
1
2
3
4
5
6
7
9 10 11 12 13 14 15 16 17 18 19 20
Age (years)

b

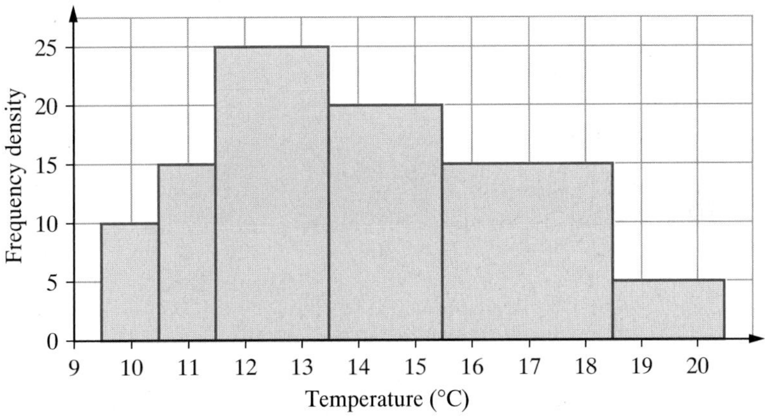
Frequency density
0
5
10
15
20
25
9 10 11 12 13 14 15 16 17 18 19 20
Temperature (°C)

c

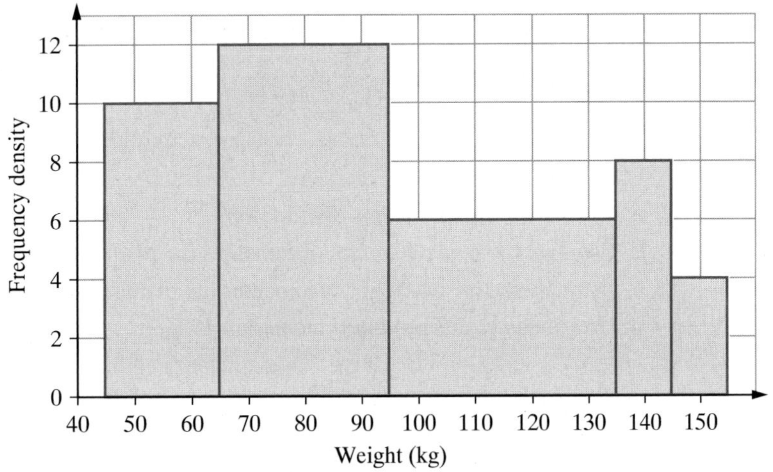
Frequency density
0
2
4
6
8
10
12
40 50 60 70 80 90 100 110 120 130 140 150
Weight (kg)

3 All the patients in a hospital were asked how long it was since they last saw a doctor. The results, given to the nearest hour, were:

Hours	1	2–3	4–6	7–10	11–16	17–24
Frequency	8	15	21	35	44	8

a Find the median time since a patient last saw a doctor.

b Estimate the mean time since a patient last saw a doctor.

4 The London trains were always late, so one month a survey was undertaken to find how many trains were late, and by how many minutes (to the nearest minute). The results are illustrated by the following histogram.

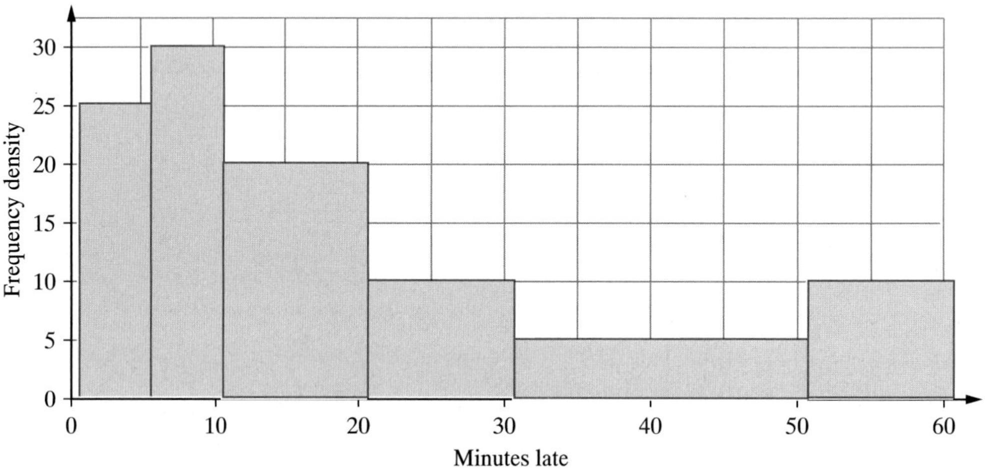

a How many trains were in the survey?

b What is the median time of delay?

c How many trains were delayed for longer than 15 minutes?

5 One summer, Albert monitored the weight of tomatoes grown on each of his plants. His results are summarised in the following table.

Weight (nearest kg)	8–9	10–12	13–16	17–20	21–25
Frequency	8	15	28	16	10

a Draw a histogram for this distribution.

b Estimate the median weight of tomatoes the plants produced.

c Estimate the mean weight of tomatoes the plants produced.

d How many plants produced more than 15 kg?

6 A survey was carried out to find the speeds of cars passing a particular point on the M1. The histogram illustrates the results of the survey.

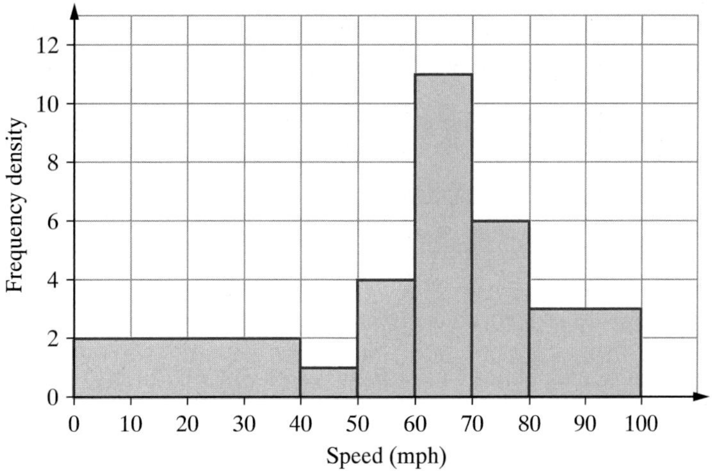

a Copy and complete the table below.

Speed, v (mph)	$0 < v \leq 40$	$40 < v \leq 50$	$50 < v \leq 60$	$60 < v \leq 70$	$70 < v \leq 80$	$80 < v \leq 100$
Frequency		10	40	110		

b Find the number of cars included in the survey.

c Work out an estimate of the median speed of the cars on this part of the M1.

d Work out an estimate of the mean speed of the cars on this part of the M1.

7 The following information was gathered about the range of pocket money given to 14 year olds.

Pocket money (£)	0.01–2.00	2.01–4.00	4.01–5.00	5.01–8.00	8.01–10.00
Girls	8	15	22	12	4
Boys	6	11	25	15	6

a Represent the information about the boys on a histogram.

b Represent both sets of data with a frequency polygon, using the same pair of axes.

c What is the mean amount of pocket money given to each sex? Comment on your answer.

8 The sales of the *Star Newspaper* over 65 years was recorded as:

Years	1930–50	1951–70	1971–80	1981–90	1991–95
Copies	62 000	68 000	71 000	75 000	63 000

a Illustrate this information on a histogram.

b Illustrate this information with a frequency polygon.

c Which diagram best illustrates the data?

Surveys

A survey is an organised way of asking a lot of people a few, well constructed questions, or of making a lot of observations in an experiment, in order to reach a conclusion about something.

We use surveys to test out people's opinions or to test a hypothesis.

Simple data collection sheet

If you need just to collect some data to analyse, you will have to design a simple data capture sheet. For example: 'Where do you want to go to for the Y10 trip at the end of term – Blackpool, Alton Towers, The Great Western Show or London?'

You would put this question one day to a lot of Y10, and enter their answers straight onto a data capture sheet, as below.

Place	**Tally**	f
Blackpool	𝍸 𝍸 𝍸 𝍸 |||	
Alton Towers	𝍸 𝍸 𝍸 𝍸 𝍸 𝍸	
	𝍸 𝍸 𝍸 |	
The Great Western Show	𝍸 𝍸 ||||	
London	𝍸 𝍸 𝍸 𝍸 ||	

Notice how plenty of space is made for the tally marks, and how the tallies are 'gated' in groups of five to make counting easier when the survey is complete.

This is a good, simple data collection sheet because

- only one question ('Where do you want to go?') has to be asked
- all the possible venues are listed
- the answer from each interviewee can be easily and quickly tallied, then on to the next interviewee.

Notice, too, that since the question listed specific places, they must appear on the data collection sheet. You would lose many marks in an examination if you just asked the open question: 'Where do you want to go?'

Using your computer

Once the data has been collected for your survey, it can be put into a computer database. This allows the data to be stored and amended or updated at a later date if necessary.

From the database, suitable diagrams can easily be drawn within the software and averages calculated for you. Your results can then be published in, for example, the school magazine.

Exercise 9E

1 'People like the supermarket to open on Sundays.'

a To see whether this statement is true, design a data collection sheet which will allow you to capture data while standing outside a supermarket.

b Does it matter on which day you collect data outside the supermarket?

2 The school tuck shop wanted to know which types of chocolate it should get in to sell – plain, milk, fruit and nut, wholenut or white chocolate.

a Design a data collection sheet which you could use to ask the pupils in your school which of these chocolate types are their favourite.

b Invent the first 30 entries on the chart.

3 When you throw two dice together, what numbers are you most likely to get?

a Design a data collection sheet on which you can record the data from an experiment in which two dice are thrown together and note the sum of the two numbers shown on the dice.

b Carry out this experiment for at least 100 throws.

c Which numbers are most likely to occur?

d Illustrate your results on a frequency polygon.

4 Which letters of the alphabet do printers use the most?

a Design a data collection sheet to record the frequency of each letter used on any page in this book.

b Carry out the experiment on any page you choose.

c Which letters are used the most?

5 What kind of vehicles pass your school each day? Design a data collection sheet to record the data necessary for a survey which will answer this question.

6 What types of television programme do your age group watch the most? Is it crime, romance, comedy, documentary, sport or something else? Design a data collection sheet to be used in a survey of your age group.

7 What do people of your age tend to spend their money on? Is it sport, magazines, clubs, cinema, sweets, clothes or something else? Design a data collection sheet to be used in a survey of your age group.

8 Who uses the buses the most in the mornings? Is it pensioners, mums, school children, the unemployed or some other group? Design a data collection sheet to be used in a survey of who uses the buses.

9 Who in your house gets up first most mornings? Is it mum, dad, a big brother, a little sister, you or who? Design a data collection sheet to be used in a survey of who gets up first.

10 Design a data collection sheet to be used in a survey of the usual time Y10s get up in the morning to go to school.

Questionnaires

When you are putting together a questionnaire, you must think very carefully about the sorts of question you are going to ask. Here are four rules that you should always follow.

- Never ask a leading question designed to get a particular response.
- Never ask a personal, irrelevant question.
- Keep each question as simple as possible.
- Include a question that will get a response from whomever is asked.

The following types of question are **badly constructed** and should never appear in any questionnaire.

What is your age? This is personal. Many people will not want to answer.

Slaughtering animals for food is cruel to the poor defenceless animals. Don't you agree? This is a leading question, designed to get a 'yes'.

Do you go to discos when abroad? This can be answered only by those who have been abroad.

When you first get up in a morning and decide to have some sort of breakfast that might be made by somebody else, do you feel obliged to eat it all or not? This is a too complicated question.

The following types of question are **well constructed**.

Which age group are you in? 0–20 21–30 31–50 over 50

Do you think it is cruel to kill animals for meat to feed humans?

If you went abroad would you consider going to a disco?

Do you eat all your breakfast?

A questionnaire is usually put together to test a hypothesis or a statement. For example: 'People buy cheaper milk from the supermarket and they don't mind not getting it on their doorstep. They'd rather go out and buy it.'

A questionnaire designed to test whether this statement is true or not should include these questions:

'Do you have milk delivered to your doorstep?'
'Do you buy cheaper milk from the supermarket?'
'Would you buy your milk only from the supermarket?'

Once these questions have been answered, they can be looked at to see whether or not the majority of people hold views that agree with the statement.

Exercise 9F

1 Design a questionnaire to see whether or not the following statement is true in your area.

> 'Tall men marry tall women, and short men marry short women.'

2 Design a questionnaire to test the following statement.

> 'People under 16 do not know what is meant by all the jargon used in the business news on TV, but the over twenties do.'

3 'Women think that men are bad drivers, while men think that women are slow drivers and that nobody drives as well as they do.'

Design a questionnaire to test this statement.

4 'Wood lice will only live in cold, damp places.'

Design an experiment to test whether this hypothesis is true or not.

5 'The under twenties feel quite at ease with computers, while the over forties would rather not bother with them. The 20–40s always try to look good with computers.'

Design a questionnaire to test this statement.

6 'Most school children arrive at school having had a good breakfast of either bread or cereal and a warm drink.'

I don't think this statement is true, do you? Design a questionnaire to be used to test the statement to see whether it is false or not.

7 Design a questionnaire to test the following hypothesis.

> 'The older you get, the less sleep you need.'

8 'People leave football matches early because their team is either losing or playing badly. They never come out early to avoid traffic queues or to get home quickly for tea.'

Design a questionnaire to test this statement for any truth.

9 Design a questionnaire to test this statement.

> 'Everybody has played with a piano, but unless you learn to play before you are 12, you will not play the piano well.'

10 A head teacher wanted to find out if his pupils thought they had too much, too little or just the right amount of homework. She also wanted to know the parents' views about homework.

Design a questionnaire that could be used to find the data the head teacher needs to look at.

Sampling

Statisticians often have to carry out surveys to collect information and test hypotheses about the **population** of a wide variety of things. (In statistics, the term 'population' does not only mean a group of people. It also means a group of objects or events.)

It is seldom possible to survey a whole population, mainly because such a survey would cost too much and take a long time. Also there are populations for which it would be physically impossible to survey every member: for example, finding the average length of eels in the North Sea. So a statistician chooses a small part of the population to survey and assumes that the results for this **sample** are representative of the whole population.

Therefore, to ensure the accuracy of a survey, two questions have to be considered:

- Will the sample be representative of the whole population and thereby eliminate bias?
- How large should the sample be to give results which are valid for the whole population?

Sampling methods

There are two main types of sample: **random** and **stratified**.

In a random sample, every member of the population has an equal chance of being chosen. For example, it may be the first 100 people met in a survey, or 100 names picked from a hat, or 100 names taken at random from the electoral register or a telephone directory.

In a stratified sample, the population is first divided into categories and the number of members in each category determined. The sample is then made up of these categories in the same proportions as they are in the population. The required numbers in each category are chosen by random sampling.

Example A school has numbers as in the table.

School year	Boys	Girls	Total
7	52	68	120
8	46	51	97
9	62	59	121
10	47	61	108
11	39	55	94
Total number in school			540

To obtain a random sample, we could, for example, simply ask the first 100 students as they came into school. But to obtain a sample of 100 students stratified according to the school years and the gender of the students, we would have to calculate the number of girls and boys from each year which must be represented in the sample. We would therefore proceed as follows.

Year 7 students in sample = $\frac{120}{540} \times 100 = 22$

of which $\frac{52}{120} \times 22 = 10$ must be boys and so 12 must be girls

Year 8 students in sample = $\frac{97}{540} \times 100 = 18$

of which $\frac{46}{97} \times 18 = 9$ must be boys and so 9 must be girls

We would continue like this for Years 9 to 11 until we had obtained the number of boys and the number of girls from each and every year needed in the survey.

Sample size

Before the sampling of a population can begin, it is necessary to determine how much data needs to be collected to ensure that the sample is representative of the population. This is called the **sample size**.

Two factors determine sample size:

- The desired precision with which the sample represents the population.
- The amount of money available to meet the cost of collecting the sample data.

The greater the precision desired, the larger the sample size needs to be. But the larger the sample size, the higher the cost will be. Therefore, the benefit of achieving high accuracy in a sample will always have to be set against the cost of achieving it.

There are statistical procedures for determining the most suitable sample size, but these are beyond the scope of the GCSE syllabus.

The next example addresses some of the problems associated with obtaining an unbiased sample.

Example You are going to conduct a survey among an audience of 30 000 people at a rock concert. How would you choose the sample?

1 You would not want to question all of them, so you might settle for a sample size of 2%, which is 600 people.

2 Assuming that there will be as many men at the concert as women, you would need the sample to contain the same proportion of each, namely,

300 men and 300 women

3 Assuming that about 20% of the audience will be aged under 20, you would also need the sample to contain

120 people aged under 20 (20% of 600)
and 480 people aged 20 and over (600 – 120 or 80% of 600)

4 You would also need to select people from different parts of the auditorium in equal proportions so as to get a balanced view. Say this breaks down into three equal groups of people, taken respectively from the front, the back and the middle of the auditorium. So, you would further need the sample to consist of

200 people at the front 200 at the back 200 in the middle

5 If you now assume that one researcher can survey 40 concert-goers, you would arrive at the following sampling strategy:

$600 \div 40 = 15$ researchers to conduct the survey

$15 \div 3 = 5$ researchers in each part of the auditorium

Each researcher would need to question: 4 men aged under 20, 16 men aged 20 and over and 4 women aged under 20, 16 women aged 20 and over.

Exercise 9G

1 For a school project you have been asked to do a presentation of the lunchtime arrangements of the pupils in your school. You decide to interview a sample of pupils. How will you choose those you wish to interview if you want your results to be reliable? Give three reasons for your decisions.

2 Comment on the reliability of the following ways of finding a sample.

- **a** Find out about smoking by asking 50 people in a non-smoking part of a restaurant.
- **b** Find out how many homes have video recorders by asking 100 people outside a video hire shop.
- **c** Find the most popular make of car by counting 100 cars in a city car park.
- **d** Find a year representative on a school's council by picking a name out of a hat.
- **e** Decide whether the potatoes have cooked properly by testing one with a fork.

3 Comment on the way the following samples have been taken. For those that are not satisfactory, suggest a better way to find a more reliable sample.

- **a** Joseph had a discussion with his dad about pocket money. To get some information, he asked 15 of his friends how much pocket money they each received.
- **b** Douglas wanted to find out what proportion of his school went abroad for holidays, so he asked the first 20 people he came across in the school yard.
- **c** A teacher wanted to know which lesson his pupils enjoyed most. So he asked them all.

d It has been suggested that more females go to church than males. So Ruth did a survey in her church that Sunday and counted the number of females there.

e A group of local people asked for a crossing on a busy road. The council conducted a survey by asking a randomly selected 100 people in the neighbourhood.

4 For a school project you have been asked to do a presentation of the social activities of the pupils in your school. You decide to interview a sample of pupils. How will you choose the pupils you wish to interview if you want your results to be reliable? Give three reasons for your decisions.

5 A fast-food pizza chain attempted to estimate the number of people who would eat pizzas in a certain town. They telephoned 50 people in the town one evening and asked: 'Have you eaten a pizza in the last month?' Eleven people said 'Yes'. The pizza chain stated that 22% of the town's population eat pizzas. Give three criticisms of this method of estimation.

6 **a** Adam is writing a questionnaire for a survey about the Meadowhall shopping centre in Sheffield. He is told that fewer local people visit Meadowhall than people from further away. He is also told that the local people spend less money per visit. Write two questions which would help him to test these ideas. Each question should include at least three options for a response. People are asked to choose one of these options.

b For another survey, Adam investigates how much is spent at the chocolate machines by students at his school. The number of students in each year group is shown.

Year group	7	2	3	10	11
Number of students	143	132	156	131	108

Explain, with calculations, how Adam obtains a stratified random sample of 100 students for his survey.

7 Claire made a survey of pupils in her school. She wanted to find out their opinions on eating facilities in the school. The size of each year group in the school is shown below.

Year group	Boys	Girls	Total
8	96	78	174
9	84	86	170
10	84	91	175
11	82	85	167
6th form	83	117	200
			886

Claire took a sample of 90 pupils.

a Explain why she should not have sampled equal numbers of boys and girls in the sixth form.

b Calculate the number of pupils she should have sampled in the sixth form.

Possible coursework tasks

If available, you could use a computer software package for these tasks.

School dinners

'School dinners are good value.'

Investigate the opinions of different people.

Advertisements

'There is too much time devoted to adverts on TV.'

Investigate who thinks this is true.

Win the pools

'There are more draws in the Premier Division than there are in Division Three.'

Investigate whether this is true or not.

Win the National Lottery

One week, the six main balls drawn out in the National Lottery were

21, 29, 31, 32, 34, 48

Is the average of these numbers higher than usual? What is the usual average of the Lottery numbers.

Geometric mean

For a set of n data points $x_1, x_2, x_4, x_5, \ldots, x_n$, the geometric mean is given by

$$G = \sqrt[n]{(x_1 \cdot x_2 \cdot x_4 \cdot x_5, \cdot \ldots, x_n)}$$

Investigate G.

Examination questions: coursework type

1 This diagram has been drawn to exaggerate the difference between the contributions two youth clubs made to charity.

a Explain how the diagram is misleading.

b Draw a diagram which displays the information in a way which is not misleading.

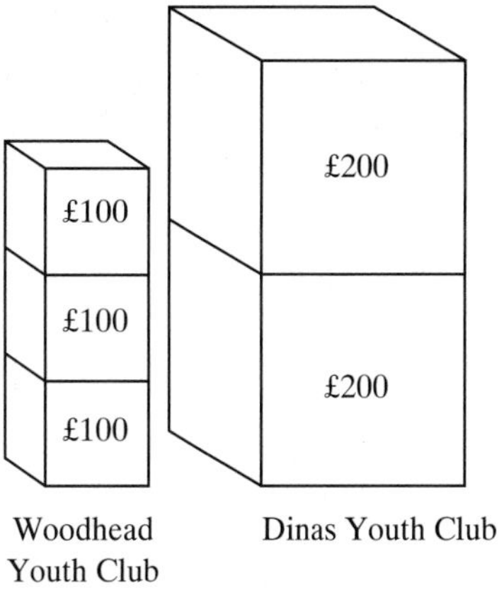

WJEC, Question 3, Specimen Paper 3, 1998

2 Class 11B is doing a survey about pocket money. Each pupil says how much he or she has each week. These are the results.

£5	£4	£5	0	£5	£5	£7.50	£3	0	£6
£3	£2.50	0	£4	£4	£2	£5	0	£1	£7
£6	£5	£5	£4	£5	£5	0	£10	0	£2

a Ceri is a pupil in class 11B. She has £2 pocket money a week. She thinks she should get more. Use the survey data to help her argue for more pocket money.

b Tom is in class 11C. Class 11C is also doing a survey about pocket money. Tom compares the data for the two classes. This is what he writes.

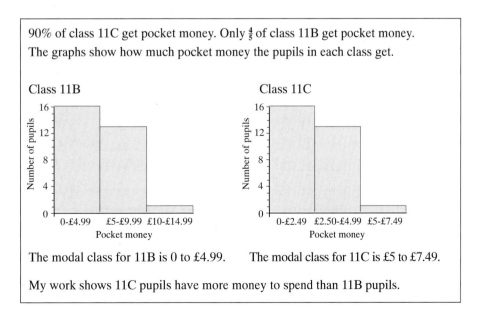

> 90% of class 11C get pocket money. Only $\frac{4}{5}$ of class 11B get pocket money.
> The graphs show how much pocket money the pupils in each class get.
>
> Class 11B
>
> 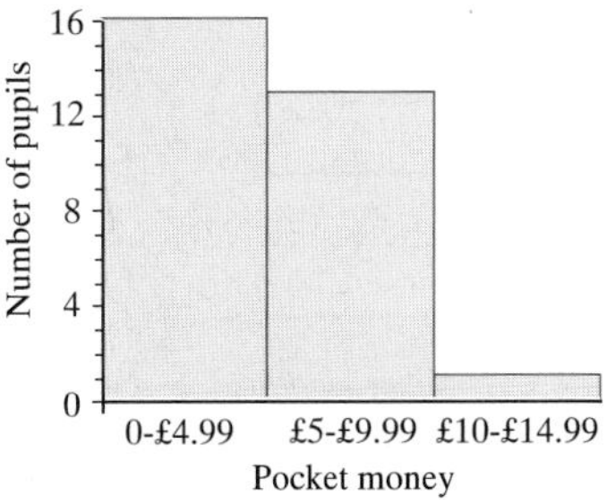
>
>
> Class 11C
>
> 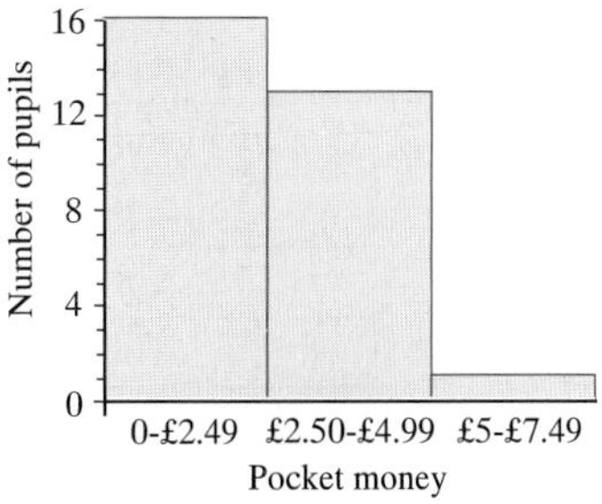
>
>
> The modal class for 11B is 0 to £4.99. The modal class for 11C is £5 to £7.49.
>
> My work shows 11C pupils have more money to spend than 11B pupils.

Criticise Tom's work.

NEAB, Question 4, Paper 3Q, June 1995

Examination questions

1 Coles sells furniture and will deliver up to a distance of 20 miles. The diagram shows the delivery charges made by Coles. The table shows the information in the diagram and also the number of deliveries made in the first week of May 1994.

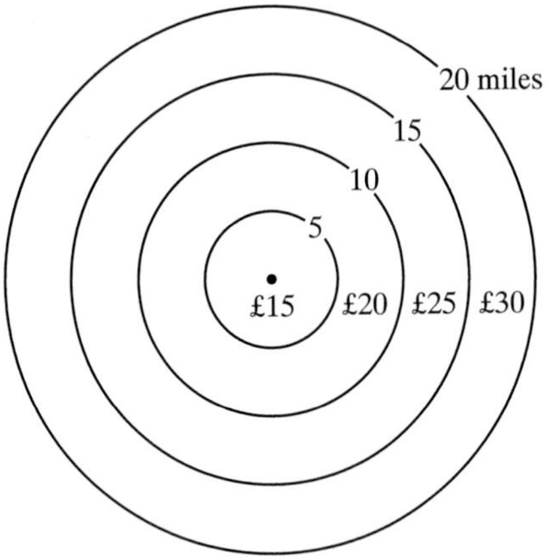

Distance (d) from Coles in miles	Delivery charge in pounds	Number of deliveries
$0 \le d < 5$	15	27
$5 \le d < 10$	20	11
$10 \le d < 15$	25	8
$15 \le d < 20$	30	4

a Calculate the mean charge per delivery for these deliveries.

b Calculate an estimate for the mean distance of the customers' homes from Coles.

ULEAC, Question 19, Paper 7, June 1994

2 Mrs Wilson wants to sell her herd of dairy cows. A buyer will need to know the herd's average daily yield of milk. The daily milk yield, p litres, is monitored over 5 weeks. The table below shows the results of this survey.

Milk yield, p litres	Frequency
$140 \le p < 145$	3
$145 \le p < 150$	5
$150 \le p < 155$	9
$155 \le p < 160$	6
$160 \le p < 165$	8
$165 \le p < 170$	4
Total	35

a Mrs Wilson finds the modal class for the daily average. What is this value?

b Calculate an estimated mean daily milk yield.

c Which is the more suitable average for the buyer to use? Give a reason for your answer.

NEAB, Question 16, Specimen Paper 1, 1998

3 Twenty-nine children are asked how much pocket money they were given last week. Their replies are shown in this frequency table.

Pocket money (£)	Frequency (f)
0–£1.00	12
£1.00–£2.00	9
£2.00–£3.00	6
£3.00–£4.00	2

a Which is the modal class?

b Calculate an estimate of the mean amount of pocket money received per child.

NEAB, Question 15, Paper 1, June 1995

4 A forester measures the heights of 100 trees, correct to the nearest metre. This table shows her results.

Height to nearest metre	1 to 5	6 to 10	11 to 15	16 to 20	21 to 25
Frequency	12	23	33	26	6

a Calculate an estimate of the mean height of the trees in the sample.

b Draw a frequency polygon to show the forester's results.

c The forester also measures the heights of 100 trees in a different wood. This frequency polygon shows these results. The mean of this set of data is 13.2 m. How does this second set of 100 trees compare with the first set?

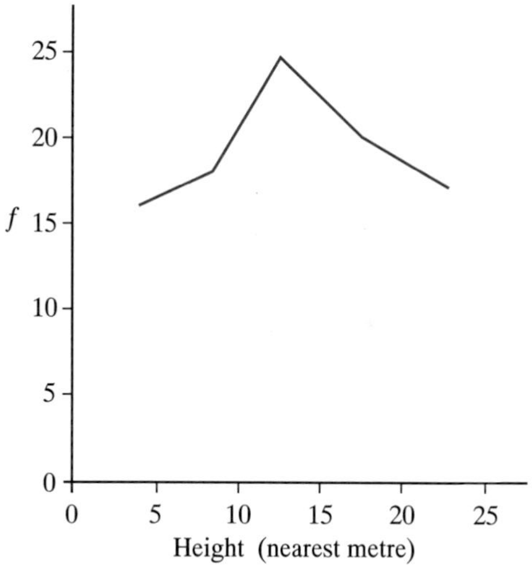

WJEC, Question 10, Specimen Paper 2, 1998

5 Kay is doing a survey to find out what people think about the amount of sport on television. She designs two questions.

A

Most people think there is far too much sport on television. Do you agree?

Yes ☐ No ☐

B

What do you think about the amount of sport on television?

Too little ☐ About right ☐ Too much ☐

a Which is the better one for her to use? Give a reason for your answer.

b Write down, with a reason, **one** other question that she could ask in her survey.

c She asks people shopping on a Saturday afternoon. Why is this likely to result in a biased survey?

WJEC, Question 7, Paper 2, June 1994

6 A newspaper boy keeps a record of the amount of tips he receives for his morning round at Christmas.

Amount	Frequency	Mid-point	Mid-point × frequency
1p to £1.00	6		
£1.01 to £2.00	9		
£2.01 to £3.00	12		
£3.01 to £4.00	3		
£4.01 to £5.00	3		

He puts them into a grouped frequency table.

a Which is the modal group?

b Calculate an estimate of the mean amount he receives in tips.

c The frequency polygon below shows the distribution of tips received for an evening round in the same area. Draw a frequency polygon to show the distribution of tips for the morning round on the same diagram.

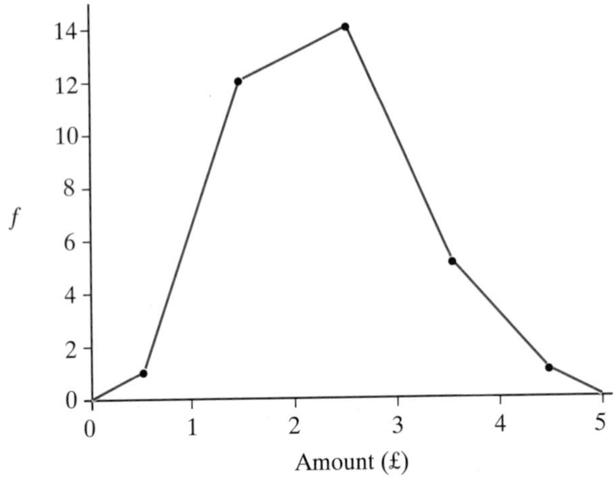

d Describe **one** difference between the two distributions.

WJEC, Question 13, Paper 2, June 1994

7 A gardener tests a fertiliser. He grows some tomatoes with the fertiliser and some without. He records the weights of all the tomatoes grown.

Weight, W (grams)	Frequency	
	With fertiliser	Without fertiliser
$50 \leq W < 100$	10	2
$100 \leq W < 150$	15	42
$150 \leq W < 200$	55	46
$200 \leq W < 250$	53	41
$250 \leq W < 300$	17	34
$300 \leq W < 350$	8	1

a Draw a frequency polygon for each distribution, clearly indicating which is with fertiliser, and which is without fertiliser.

b Use the frequency polygons to compare the effects of the fertiliser.

NEAB, Question 5, Paper 1R, June 1996

8 A bus company attempted to estimate the number of people who travel on local buses in a certain town. They telephone 100 people in the town one evening and asked: 'Have you travelled by bus in the last week?' Nineteen people said 'Yes'. The bus company concluded that 19% of the town's population travel on local buses. Give three criticisms of this method of estimation. *MEG, Question 14, Specimen Paper 6A, 1998*

9 Sam was making a survey of pupils in his school. He wanted to find out their opinions on noise pollution by motor bikes. The size of each year group is shown below.

Year group	Boys	Girls	Total
8	85	65	150
9	72	75	147
10	74	78	152
11	77	72	149
6th form	93	107	200
			798

Sam took a sample of 80 pupils.

a Explain whether or not he should have sampled equal numbers of boys and girls in Year 8.

b Calculate the number of pupils he should have sampled in Year 8.

ULEAC, Question 17, Specimen Paper 5, 1998

10 The waiting times for customers at a Post Office counter are as follows.

Waiting time (minutes)	Frequency
$0 \le x < 1$	12
$1 \le x < 2$	8
$2 \le x < 3$	8
$3 \le x < 4$	12
$4 \le x < 7$	12

a Draw a histogram of these waiting times.

b Show an estimate of the median on your histogram. Show your working.

Summary

How well do you grade yourself?

To gain a grade **C**, you need to be able to construct and interpret frequency diagrams, and test a hypothesis. You need also to be able to find the modal group and estimate the mean of a set of grouped data, choosing the most appropriate type of average, and be able to use measures of average and range with frequency polygons to compare distributions.

To gain a grade **B**, you need to be able to read and construct a histogram. You also must be able to criticise and create questionnaires to a test a hypothesis.

To gain a grade **A**, you need to be able to understand the methods of sampling, and must know how these methods, as well as sample size, may affect the reliability of conclusions drawn. You need also to be able to select and justify a sample and a method to investigate a population. And you must be able to construct histograms which have unequal intervals and use frequency density.

What you should know after you have worked through Chapter 9

- How to interpret frequency tables and find averages from both simple and grouped frequency tables.
- How to read and create frequency polygons and histograms.
- How to create a questionnaire to test a hypothesis.
- How to use random and stratified samples.

10 Algebra 2

This chapter is going to ... show you how to expand algebraic expressions involving brackets, and how to factorise an expression back into brackets. It will also show you how to create a quadratic expression, and how to factorise and solve quadratic equations.

What you should already know

- How to combine algebraic expressions. For example,

  $2 \times t = 2t$

  $m \times t = mt$

  $2t \times 5 = 10t$

  $3y \times 2m = 6my$

- The convention that states: always put the letters in alphabetical order. In other words, do not write $2ba$, but $2ab$.

- How to multiply together similar terms. Remember: the indices are added together. For example,

  $t \times t = t^2$ (Also remember: $t = t^1$)

  $3t \times 2t = 6t^2$

  $3t^2 \times 4t = 12t^3$

  $2t^3 \times 4t^2 = 8t^5$

Exercise 10A

Evaluate these expressions, writing them as simply as possible.

1 $2 \times 3t$ **2** $3 \times 4y$ **3** $5y \times 3$ **4** $2w \times 4$

5 $3t \times t$ **6** $5b \times b$ **7** $2w \times w$ **8** $5y \times 3y$

9 $4p \times 2p$ **10** $3t \times 2t$ **11** $4m \times 3m$ **12** $5t \times 3\mathrm{t}$

13 $m \times 2t$ **14** $3y \times w$ **15** $5t \times q$ **16** $n \times 6m$

17 $3t \times 2q$ **18** $4f \times 3g$ **19** $5h \times 2k$ **20** $3p \times 7\mathrm{r}$

21 $y^2 \times y$ **22** $t \times t^2$ **23** $3m \times m^2$ **24** $4t^2 \times t$

25 $3n \times 2n^2$ **26** $4r^2 \times 5r$ **27** $t^2 \times t^2$ **28** $h^3 \times h^2$

29 $3n^2 \times 4n^3$ **30** $5t^3 \times 2t^4$ **31** $3a^4 \times 2a^3$ **32** $k^5 \times 4k^2$

33 $-t^2 \times -t$ **34** $-2y \times -3y$ **35** $-4d^2 \times -3d$ **36** $-3p^4 \times -5p^2$

37 $3mp \times p$ **38** $2ty \times 3t$ **39** $3mn \times 2m$ **40** $4mp \times 2mp$

Expansion

In mathematics, the term 'expand' usually means 'multiply out'. For example, expressions such as $3(y + 2)$ and $4y^2(2y + 3)$ can be expanded by multiplying out.

You need to remember that there is an invisible multiplication sign between the outside number and the bracket. So that $3(y + 2)$ is really $3 \times (y + 2)$, and $4y^2(2y + 3)$ is really $4y^2 \times (2y + 3)$.

We expand by multiplying **everything inside** the bracket by what is outside the bracket. So in the case of the above two examples,

$$3(y + 2) = 3 \times (y + 2) = 3y + 6$$
$$4y^2(2y + 3) = 4y^2 \times (2y + 3) = 8y^3 + 12y^2$$

Look at these next examples of expansion, which show clearly how the term outside the bracket has been multiplied to the terms inside it.

$2(m + 3) = 2m + 6$	$y(y^2 - 4x) = y^3 - 4xy$
$3(2t + 5) = 6t + 15$	$3x^2(4x + 5) = 12x^3 + 15x^2$
$m(p + 7) = mp + 7m$	$-3(2 + 3x) = -6 - 9x$
$x(x - 6) = x^2 - 6x$	$-2x(3 - 4x) = -6x + 8x^2$
$4t(t + 2) = 4t^2 + 8t$	$3t(2 + 5t - p) = 6t + 15t^2 - 3pt$

Note The signs change when a negative quantity is outside the bracket. For example,

$a(b + c) = ab + ac$	$a(b - c) = ab - ac$
$-a(b + c) = -ab - ac$	$-a(b - c) = -ab + ac$

Exercise 10B

Expand these expressions.

1 $2(3 + m)$ **2** $5(2 + l)$ **3** $3(4 - y)$ **4** $4(5 + 2k)$

5 $3(2 - 4f)$ **6** $2(5 - 3w)$ **7** $3(g + h)$ **8** $5(2k + 3m)$

9 $4(3d - 2n)$ **10** $t(t + 3)$ **11** $m(m + 5)$ **12** $k(k - 3)$

13 $g(3g + 2)$ **14** $y(5y - 1)$ **15** $p(5 - 3p)$ **16** $3m(m + 4)$

17 $4t(t - 1)$ **18** $2k(4 - k)$ **19** $4g(2g + 5)$ **20** $5h(3h - 2)$

21 $3t(5 - 4t)$ **22** $3d(2d + 4e)$ **23** $2y(3y + 4k)$ **24** $5m(3m - 2p)$

25 $y(y^2 + 5)$ **26** $h(h^3 + 7)$ **27** $k(k^2 - 5)$ **28** $3t(t^2 + 4)$

29 $4h(h^3 - 1)$ **30** $5g(g^3 - 2)$ **31** $4m(3m^2 + m)$ **32** $5k(2k^3 + k^2)$

33 $3d(5d^2 - d^3)$ **34** $3w(2w^2 + t)$ **35** $5a(3a^2 - 2b)$ **36** $3p(4p^3 - 5m)$

37 $m^2(5 + 4m)$ **38** $t^3(t + 2t)$ **39** $g^2(5t - 4g^2)$ **40** $3t^2(5t + m)$

41 $4h^2(3h + 2g)$ **42** $2m^2(4m + m^2)$

Simplification

Simplification is the process whereby an expression is written down as simply as possible, any like terms being combined. Like terms are terms which have the same letter(s) raised to the same power and can differ only in their numerical coefficients (numbers in front). For example,

m, $3m$, $4m$, $-m$ and $76m$ are all like terms in m
t^2, $4t^2$, $7t^2$, $-t^2$, $-3t^2$ and $98t^2$ are all like terms in t^2
pt, $5pt$, $-2pt$, $7pt$, $-3pt$ and $103pt$ are all like terms in pt

Note also that all the terms in tp are also like terms to all the terms in pt.

In simplifying an expression, only like terms can be added or subtracted. For example,

$4m + 3m = 7m$ $\quad 3y + 4y + 3 = 7y + 3$ $\quad 4h - h = 3h$
$2t^2 + 5t^2 = 7t^2$ $\quad 2m + 6 + 3m = 5m + 6$ $\quad 7t + 8 - 2t = 5t + 8$
$3ab + 2ab = 5ab$ $\quad 5k - 2k = 3k$ $\quad 10g - 4 - 3g = 7g - 4$

Expand and simplify

This process often occurs in mathematics and is illustrated by Examples 1 and 2.

1 $3(4 + m) + 2(5 + 2m)$
$= 12 + 3m + 10 + 4m = 22 + 7m$

2 $3t(5t + 4) - 2t(3t - 5)$
$= 15t^2 + 12t - 6t^2 + 10t = 9t^2 + 22t$

Exercise 10C

1 Simplify these expressions.

a $4t + 3t$ **b** $5m + 4m$ **c** $2y + y$ **d** $3d + 2d + 4d$
e $5e - 2e$ **f** $7g - 5g$ **g** $4p - p$ **h** $3t - t$
i $2t^2 + 3t^2$ **j** $6y^2 - 2y^2$ **k** $3ab + 2ab$ **l** $7a^2d - 4a^2d$

2 Expand and simplify.

a $3(4 + t) + 2(5 + t)$ **b** $5(3 + 2k) + 3(2 + 3k)$ **c** $4(1 + 3m) + 2(3 + 2m)$
d $2(5 + 4y) + 3(2 + 3y)$ **e** $4(3 + 2f) + 2(5 - 3f)$ **f** $5(1 + 3g) + 3(3 - 4g)$
g $3(2 + 5t) + 4(1 - t)$ **h** $4(3 + 3w) + 2(5 - 4w)$

3 Expand and simplify.

a $4(3 + 2h) - 2(5 + 3h)$ **b** $5(3g + 4) - 3(2g + 5)$ **c** $3(4y + 5) - 2(3y + 2)$
d $3(5t + 2) - 2(4t + 5)$ **e** $5(5k + 2) - 2(4k - 3)$ **f** $4(4e + 3) - 2(5e - 4)$
g $3(5m - 2) - 2(4m - 5)$ **h** $2(6t - 1) - 3(3t - 4)$

4 Expand and simplify.

a $m(4 + p) + p(3 + m)$ **b** $k(3 + 2h) + h(4 + 3k)$ **c** $t(2 + 3n) + n(3 + 4t)$

d $p(2q + 3) + q(4p + 7)$ **e** $3h(2 + 3j) + 2j(2h + 3)$ **f** $2y(3t + 4) + 3t(2 + 5y)$
g $4r(3 + 4p) + 3p(8 - r)$ **h** $5k(3m + 4) - 2m(3 - 2k)$

5 Expand and simplify.
a $t(3t+ 4) + 3t(3 + 2t)$ **b** $2y(3 + 4y) + y(5y - 1)$ **c** $4w(2w + 3) + 3w(2 - w)$
d $5p(3p + 4) - 2p(3 - 4p)$ **e** $3m(2m - 1) + 2m(5 - m)$ **f** $6d(4 - 2d) + d(3d - 2)$
g $4e(3e - 5) - 2e(e - 7)$ **h** $3k(2k + p) - 2k(3p - 4k)$

6 Expand and simplify.
a $4a(2b + 3c) + 3b(3a + 2c)$ **b** $3y(4w + 2t) + 2w(3y - 4t)$
c $2g(3h - k) + 5h(2g - 2k)$ **d** $3h(2t - p) + 4t(h - 3p)$
e $a(3b - 2c) - 2b(a - 3c)$ **f** $4p(3q - 2w) - 2w(p - q)$
g $5m(2n - 3p) - 2n(3p - 2m)$ **h** $2r(3r + r^2) - 3r^2(4 - 2r)$

Factorisation

Factorisation is the opposite of expansion. It puts an expression back into the brackets it may have come from.

In factorisation, we have to look for the common factors in **every** term of the expression. Follow through the examples below to see how this works.

$6t + 9m = 3(2t + 3m)$
$6my + 4py = 2y(3m + 2p)$
$5k^2 - 25k = 5k(k - 5)$

Notice that if you multiply out each answer you will get the expressions you started with.

Exercise 10D

Factorise the following expressions.

1 $6m + 12t$ **2** $9t + 3p$ **3** $8m + 12k$ **4** $4r + 8t$
5 $mn + 3m$ **6** $5g^2 + 3g$ **7** $4w - 6t$ **8** $8p - 6k$
9 $16h - 10k$ **10** $2mp + 2mk$ **11** $4bc + 2bk$ **12** $6ab + 4ac$
13 $3y^2 + 2y$ **14** $4t^2 - 3t$ **15** $4d^2 - 2d$ **16** $3m^2 - 3mp$
17 $6p^2 + 9pt$ **18** $8pt + 6mp$ **19** $8ab - 4bc$ **20** $12a^2 - 8ab$
21 $9mt - 6pt$ **22** $16at^2 + 12at$ **23** $5b^2c - 10bc$ **24** $8abc + 6bed$
25 $4a^2 + 6a + 8$ **26** $6ab + 9bc + 3bd$ **27** $5t^2 + 4t + at$ **28** $6mt^2 - 3mt + 9m^2t$
29 $8ab^2 + 2ab - 4a^2b$ **30** $10pt^2 + 15pt + 5p^2t$

Factorise the following expressions where possible. List those which cannot factorise.

31 $7m - 6t$ **32** $5m + 2mp$ **33** $t^2 - 7t$ **34** $8pt + 5ab$
35 $4m^2 - 6mp$ **36** $a^2 + b$ **37** $4a^2 - 5ab$ **38** $3ab + 4cd$
39 $5ab - 3b^2c$

Quadratic expansion and factorisation

A quadratic expression is one in which the highest power of its terms is 2. For example,

$y^2 \qquad 3t^2 + 5t \qquad 5m^2 + 3m + 8$

An expression such as $(3y + 2)(4y - 5)$ can be expanded to give a quadratic expression. This multiplying out of such pairs of brackets is usually called **quadratic expansion**.

The rule for expanding such expressions as $(t + 5)(3t - 4)$ is similar to that for expanding single brackets: multiply everything in one bracket by everything in the other bracket.

Follow through Examples 1 to 3 below to see how a pair of brackets can be expanded. Notice how we split up the first bracket and make each of its terms multiply the second bracket. We then simplify the outcome.

Example 1 Expand $(x + 3)(x + 4)$.

$$\begin{aligned}(x + 3)(x + 4) &= x(x + 4) + 3(x + 4)\\ &= x^2 + 4x + 3x + 12\\ &= x^2 + 7x + 12\end{aligned}$$

Example 2 Expand $(t + 5)(t - 2)$.

$$\begin{aligned}(t + 5)(t - 2) &= t(t - 2) + 5(t - 2)\\ &= t^2 - 2t + 5t - 10\\ &= t^2 + 3t - 10\end{aligned}$$

Example 3 Expand $(k - 3)(k - 2)$.

$$\begin{aligned}(k - 3)(k - 2) &= k(k - 2) - 3(k - 2)\\ &= k^2 - 2k - 3k + 6\\ &= k^2 - 5k + 6\end{aligned}$$

Warning Be careful with the signs, since this is the main place where marks are lost in examination questions involving the expansion of brackets.

Exercise 10E

Expand the following expressions.

1 $(x + 3)(x + 2)$ **2** $(t + 4)(t + 3)$ **3** $(w + 1)(w + 3)$ **4** $(m + 5)(m + 1)$

5 $(k + 3)(k + 5)$ **6** $(a + 4)(a + 1)$ **7** $(x + 4)(x - 2)$ **8** $(t + 5)(t - 3)$

9 $(w + 3)(w - 1)$ **10** $(f + 2)(f - 3)$ **11** $(g + 1)(g - 4)$ **12** $(y + 4)(y - 3)$

13 $(x - 3)(x + 4)$ **14** $(p - 2)(p + 1)$ **15** $(k - 4)(k + 2)$ **16** $(y - 2)(y + 5)$

17 $(a - 1)(a + 3)$ **18** $(t - 3)(t + 4)$ **19** $(x - 4)(x - 1)$ **20** $(r - 3)(r - 2)$

21 $(m - 3)(m - 1)$ **22** $(g - 4)(g - 2)$ **23** $(h - 5)(h - 3)$ **24** $(n - 1)(n - 4)$

25 $(5 + x)(4 + x)$ **26** $(6 + t)(3 - t)$ **27** $(3 - b)(5 + b)$ **28** $(5 - y)(1 - y)$

29 $(2 + p)(p - 3)$ **30** $(5 - k)(k - 2)$

The expansions of the expressions below follow a pattern. Work out the first few and try to spot the pattern that will allow you immediately to write down the answers to the rest.

31 $(x + 3)(x - 3)$ **32** $(t + 5)(t - 5)$ **33** $(m + 4)(m - 4)$ **34** $(t + 2)(t - 2)$

35 $(y + 8)(y - 8)$ **36** $(p + 1)(p - 1)$ **37** $(5 + x)(5 - x)$ **38** $(7 + g)(7 - g)$

39 $(x - 6)(x + 6)$

All the algebraic terms in x^2 in Exercise 10E have a coefficient of 1 or –1. The next two examples show you what to do if you have to expand brackets containing terms in x^2 whose coefficients are not 1 or –1.

Example 1 Expand $(2t + 3)(3t + 1)$.

$$\begin{aligned}(2t + 3)(3t + 1) &= 2t(3t + 1) + 3(3t + 1)\\ &= 6t^2 + 2t + 9t + 3\\ &= 6t^2 + 11t + 3\end{aligned}$$

Example 2 Expand $(4x - 1)(3x - 5)$.

$$\begin{aligned}(4x - 1)(3x - 5) &= 4x(3x - 5) - (3x - 5)\\ &= 12x^2 - 20x - 3x + 5\\ &= 12x^2 - 23x + 5\end{aligned}$$

[Note: $-(3x - 5)$ is the same as $-1(3x - 5)$.]

Exercise 10F

Expand the following expressions.

1 $(2x + 3)(3x + 1)$ **2** $(3y + 2)(4y + 3)$ **3** $(3t + 1)(2t + 5)$ **4** $(4t + 3)(2t - 1)$

5 $(5m + 2)(2m - 3)$ **6** $(4k + 3)(3k - 5)$ **7** $(3p - 2)(2p + 5)$ **8** $(5w + 2)(2w + 3)$

9 $(2a - 3)(3a + 1)$ **10** $(4r - 3)(2r - 1)$ **11** $(3g - 2)(5g - 2)$ **12** $(4d - 1)(3d + 2)$

13 $(5 + 2p)(3 + 4p)$ **14** $(2 + 3t)(1 + 2t)$ **15** $(4 + 3p)(2p + 1)$ **16** $(6 + 5t)(1 - 2t)$

17 $(4 + 3n)(3 - 2n)$ **18** $(2 + 3f)(2f - 3)$ **19** $(3 - 2q)(4 + 5q)$ **20** $(1 - 3p)(3 + 2p)$

21 $(4 - 2t)(3t + 1)$ **22** $(3 - 4r)(1 - 2r)$ **23** $(5 - 2x)(1 - 4x)$ **24** $(3 - 4m)(3m - 2)$

25 $(x + y)(2x + 3y)$ **26** $(3y + t)(2y - 4t)$ **27** $(4x - 5y)(2x + y)$ **28** $(2x - 3y)(x - 2y)$

29 $(5m - 2p)(m + 3p)$ **30** $(t - 3k)(4t - k)$

Exercise 10G

Try to spot the pattern in the following expressions so that you can immediately write down their expansions.

1 $(2x + 1)(2x - 1)$ **2** $(3t + 2)(3t - 2)$ **3** $(5y + 3)(5y - 3)$ **4** $(4m + 3)(4m - 3)$
5 $(2k - 3)(2k + 3)$ **6** $(4h - 1)(4h + 1)$ **7** $(2 + 3x)(2 - 3x)$ **8** $(5 + 2t)(5 - 2t)$
9 $(6 - 5y)(6 + 5y)$ **10** $(a + b)(a - b)$ **11** $(3t + k)(3t - k)$ **12** $(2m - 3p)(2m + 3p)$
13 $(5k + g)(5k - g)$ **14** $(ab + cd)(ab - cd)$ **15** $(a^2 + b^2)(a^2 - b^2)$

Expanding squares

Example 1 Expand $(x + 3)^2$.

$$\begin{aligned}(x + 3)^2 &= (x + 3)(x + 3)\\ &= x(x + 3) + 3(x + 3)\\ &= x^2 + 3x + 3x + 9\\ &= x^2 + 6x + 9\end{aligned}$$

Example 2 Expand $(3x - 2)^2$.

$$\begin{aligned}(3x - 2)^2 &= (3x - 2)(3x - 2)\\ &= 3x(3x - 2) - 2(3x - 2)\\ &= 9x^2 - 6x - 6x + 4\\ &= 9x^2 - 12x + 4\end{aligned}$$

Exercise 10H

Expand the following squares.

1 $(x + 5)^2$ **2** $(m + 4)^2$ **3** $(6 + t)^2$ **4** $(3 + p)^2$
5 $(m - 3)^2$ **6** $(t - 5)^2$ **7** $(4 - m)^2$ **8** $(7 - k)^2$
9 $(3x + 1)^2$ **10** $(4t + 3)^2$ **11** $(2 + 5y)^2$ **12** $(3 + 2m)^2$
13 $(4t - 3)^2$ **14** $(3x - 2)^2$ **15** $(2 - 5t)^2$ **16** $(6 - 5r)^2$
17 $(x + y)^2$ **18** $(m - n)^2$ **19** $(2t + y)^2$ **20** $(m - 3n)^2$

Quadratic factorisation

This is putting a quadratic expression back into its brackets (if possible). We start with the factorisation of quadratic expressions of the type

$$x^2 + ax + b$$

where a and b are integers.

Sometimes it is easy to put a quadratic expression back into its brackets, other times it seems hard. However, there are three simple rules that will help you to factorise.

- The signs start off the brackets.

$x^2 + ax + b = (x + ?)(x + ?)$ Since everything is positive.
$x^2 - ax + b = (x - ?)(x - ?)$ Since $-ve \times -ve = +ve$.

- When the **second** sign in the expression is a ***plus***, both bracket signs are the **same** as the **first** sign.
- When the **second** sign is a ***minus***, the bracket signs are **different**.

$x^2 + ax - b = (x + ?)(x - ?)$ Since $+ve \times -ve = -ve$.
$x^2 - ax - b = (x + ?)(x - ?)$

- Next, look at the **last** number, b, in the expression. When multiplied together, the two numbers in the brackets must give b.
- Finally, look at the **middle** number, a.
  - When the bracket signs are the **same**, the **sum** of the numbers in the brackets must be a.
  - When the bracket signs are **different**, the **difference** between the numbers in the brackets must be a.

Exercise 10I

Factorise the following.

1 $x^2 + 5x + 6$	**2** $t^2 + 5t + 4$	**3** $m^2 + 7m + 10$	**4** $k^2 + 10k + 24$
5 $p^2 + 14p + 24$	**6** $r^2 + 9r + 18$	**7** $w^2 + 11w + 18$	**8** $x^2 + 7x + 12$
9 $a^2 + 8a + 12$	**10** $k^2 + 10k + 21$	**11** $f^2 + 22f + 21$	**12** $b^2 + 20b + 96$
13 $t^2 - 5t + 6$	**14** $d^2 - 5g + 4$	**15** $g^2 - 7g + 10$	**16** $x^2 - 15x + 36$
17 $c^2 - 18c + 32$	**18** $t^2 - 13t + 36$	**19** $y^2 - 16y + 48$	**20** $j^2 - 14j + 48$
21 $p^2 - 8p + 15$	**22** $y^2 + 5y - 6$	**23** $t^2 + 2t - 8$	**24** $x^2 + 3x - 10$
25 $m^2 - 4m - 12$	**26** $r^2 - 6r - 7$	**27** $n^2 - 3n - 18$	**28** $m^2 - 7m - 44$
29 $w^2 - 2w - 24$	**30** $t^2 - t - 90$	**31** $h^2 - h - 72$	**32** $t^2 - 2t - 63$
33 $d^2 + 2d + 1$	**34** $y^2 + 20y + 100$	**35** $t^2 - 8t + 16$	**36** $m^2 - 18m + 81$
37 $x^2 - 24x + 144$	**38** $d^2 - d - 12$	**39** $t^2 - t - 20$	**40** $q^2 - q - 56$
41 $p^2 + p - 2$	**42** $v^2 + 2v - 35$	**43** $t^2 + 4t + 3$	**44** $m^2 - 3m - 4$
45 $x^2 - x - 6$			

Difference of two squares

In Exercise 10G, you multiplied out, for example, $(a + b)(a - b)$ and obtained $a^2 - b^2$.

This type of quadratic expression with only two terms, both of which are perfect squares separated by a minus sign, is called the **difference of two squares**. You should have found that all the expansions in Exercise 10G are the differences of two squares.

The exercise illustrates a system of factorisation that will **always** work for the difference of two squares such as

$x^2 - 9$ $x^2 - 25$ $x^2 - 4$ $x^2 - 100$

- Recognise the pattern of the expression as x^2 minus a square number n^2.
- Its factors are $(x + n)(x - n)$.

Example Factorise $x^2 - 36$.

- Recognise the difference of two squares x^2 and 6^2.
- So it factorises to $(x + 6)(x - 6)$.

Expanding the brackets shows that they do come from the original expression.

Similarly $x^2 - 169 = (x + 13)(x - 13)$

Exercise 10J

Each of these is the difference of two squares. Factorise them.

1 $x^2 - 9$	**2** $t^2 - 25$	**3** $m^2 - 16$	**4** $9 - x^2$
5 $49 - t^2$	**6** $k^2 - 100$	**7** $4 - y^2$	**8** $x^2 - 64$
9 $t^2 - 81$	**10** $x^2 - y^2$	**11** $x^2 - 4y^2$	**12** $x^2 - 9y^2$
13 $9x^2 - 1$	**14** $16x^2 - 9$	**15** $25x^2 - 64$	**16** $4x^2 - 9y^2$
17 $9t^2 - 4w^2$	**18** $16y^2 - 25x^2$		

Solving the quadratic equation $x^2 + ax + b = 0$

To solve a quadratic equation such as $x^2 - 2x - 3 = 0$, you first have to be able to factorise it. Follow through Examples 1 to 3 below to see how this is done.

Example 1 Solve $x^2 + 6x + 5 = 0$.

This factorises into $(x + 5)(x + 1) = 0$

The only way this expression can ever equal 0 is if the value of one of the brackets is 0. Hence

either $(x + 5) = 0$ or $(x + 1) = 0$

$\Rightarrow x + 5 = 0$ or $x + 1 = 0$

$\Rightarrow x = -5$ or $x = -1$

So the solution is $x = -5$ and $x = -1$.

Example 2 Solve $x^2 + 3x - 10 = 0$.

This factorises into $(x + 5)(x - 2) = 0$

Hence $x + 5 = 0$ or $x - 2 = 0$

$\Rightarrow x = -5$ or $x = 2$

So the solution is $x = -5$ and $x = 2$.

Example 3 Solve $x^2 - 6x + 9 = 0$.

This factorises into $(x - 3)(x - 3) = 0$

The equation has **repeated roots**. That is $(x - 3)^2 = 0$

Hence, there is only one solution, $x = 3$.

Exercise 10K

Solve these equations.

1 $(x + 2)(x + 5) = 0$
2 $(t + 3)(t + 1) = 0$
3 $(a + 6)(a + 4) = 0$
4 $(x + 3)(x - 2) = 0$
5 $(x + 1)(x - 3) = 0$
6 $(t + 4)(t - 5) = 0$
7 $(x - 1)(x + 2) = 0$
8 $(x - 2)(x + 5) = 0$
9 $(a - 7)(a + 4) = 0$
10 $(x - 3)(x - 2) = 0$
11 $(x - 1)(x - 5) = 0$
12 $(a - 4)(a - 3) = 0$

First factorise, then solve these equations.

13 $x^2 + 5x + 4 = 0$
14 $x^2 + 11x + 18 = 0$
15 $x^2 - 6x + 8 = 0$
16 $x^2 - 8x + 15 = 0$
17 $x^2 - 3x - 10 = 0$
18 $x^2 - 2x - 15 = 0$
19 $t^2 + 4t - 12 = 0$
20 $t^2 + 3t - 18 = 0$
21 $x^2 - x - 2 = 0$
22 $x^2 + 4x + 4 = 0$
23 $m^2 + 10m + 25 = 0$
24 $t^2 - 8t + 16 = 0$
25 $t^2 + 8t + 12 = 0$
26 $k^2 - 2k - 15 = 0$
27 $a^2 - 14a + 49 = 0$

First rearrange these equations, then solve them.

28 $x^2 + 10x = -24$
29 $x^2 - 18x = -32$
30 $x^2 + 2x = 24$
31 $x^2 + 3x = 54$
32 $t^2 + 7t = 30$
33 $x^2 - 7x = 44$
34 $t^2 - t = 72$
35 $x^2 = 17x - 72$
36 $x^2 + 1 = 2x$

Factorising $ax^2 + bx + c$

We can adapt the method for factorising $x^2 + ax + b$ to take into account the factors of the coefficient of x^2. Follow through the next example to see how this is done.

Example Factorise $3x^2 + 8x + 4$.

- First we note that both signs are positive. So both bracket signs must be positive.
- As 3 has only 3×1 as factors, the brackets must start

  $(3x + \quad)(x + \quad)$

- Next, we note that the factors of 4 are 4×1 and 2×2.
- We now have to find which pair of factors of 4 combine with 3×1 to give 8.

$$\begin{array}{c|c} 3 & 4\ 2 \\ 1 & 1\ 2 \end{array}$$

We see that the combination 3×2
1×2 adds up to 8.

- So, the complete factorisation becomes

  $(3x + 2)(x + 2)$

Exercise 10L

Factorise the following expressions.

1 $2x^2 + 5x + 2$ **2** $7x^2 + 8x + 1$ **3** $4x^2 + 3x - 7$ **4** $24t^2 + 19t + 2$

5 $15t^2 + 2t - 1$ **6** $16x^2 - 8x + 1$ **7** $6y^2 + 33y - 63$ **8** $4y^2 + 8y - 96$

9 $8x^2 + 10x - 3$ **10** $6t^2 + 13t + 5$ **11** $3x^2 - 16x - 12$ **12** $7x^2 - 37x + 10$

Solving the quadratic equation $ax^2 + bx + c = 0$

By factorisation

The method is similar to that used to solve equations of the form $x^2 + ax + b = 0$. That is, we have to find two factors of $ax^2 + bx + c$ whose product is 0. Follow through the example to see how this is done.

Example Solve $12x^2 - 28x = -15$.

First, rearrange the equation to equal 0.

$12x^2 - 28x + 15 = 0$

This factorises into $(2x - 3)(6x - 5) = 0$

The only way this product can equal 0 is if the value of one of the brackets is 0. Hence,

$$\begin{aligned} &\text{either } 2x - 3 = 0 &&\text{or}\quad 6x - 5 = 0 \\ &\Rightarrow\quad 2x = 3 &&\text{or}\quad 6x = 5 \\ &\Rightarrow\quad x = \frac{3}{2} &&\text{or}\quad x = \frac{5}{6} \end{aligned}$$

So the solution is $x = 1\frac{1}{2}$ and $x = \frac{5}{6}$.

Note It is almost always the case that if a solution is a fraction which is then changed into a rounded-off decimal number, the original equation cannot be evaluated exactly using that decimal number. So it is preferable to leave the solution in its fraction form. This is called the **rational form.**

Exercise 10M

Give your answers either in rational form or as mixed numbers.

1 Solve the following equations.

a $3x^2 + 8x - 3 = 0$ **b** $6x^2 - 5x - 4 = 0$ **c** $5x^2 - 9x - 2 = 0$
d $4t^2 - 4t - 35 = 0$ **e** $18t^2 + 9t + 1 = 0$ **f** $3t^2 - 14t + 8 = 0$
g $2x^2 + 5x - 3 = 0$ **h** $12x^2 - 16x - 35 = 0$ **i** $15t^2 + 4t - 35 = 0$
j $28x^2 - 85x + 63 = 0$ **k** $24x^2 - 19x + 2 = 0$ **l** $16t^2 + 8t + 1 = 0$
m $4x^2 + 12x + 9 = 0$ **n** $25t^2 - 20t + 4 = 0$ **p** $9m^2 - 24m + 16 = 0$

2 Solve the following equations.

a $x^2 - x = 42$ **b** $8x(x + 1) = 30$ **c** $(x + 1)(x - 2) = 40$
d $13x^2 = 11 - 2x$ **e** $(x + 1)(x - 2) = 4$ **f** $10x^2 - x = 2$
g $39x^2 = 44 - 131x$ **h** $76x - 15 = 96x^2$ **i** $8x - 16 - x^2 = 0$
j $(2x - 1)(x - 2) = 5$ **k** $5 + 2x^2 = -7x$ **l** $2m^2 = 27 + 3m$
m $9x^2 + 25 = 30x$ **n** $4x^2 + 49 = 28x$ **p** $2t^2 - t = 15$

By the quadratic formula

Many quadratic equations cannot be solved by factorisation because they do not have simple factors. Try to factorise, for example, $x^2 - 4x - 3 = 0$ or $3x^2 - 6x + 2 = 0$. You will find it is impossible.

The only way to solve this type of equation is to use the **quadratic formula.** This formula can be used to solve **any** quadratic equation that is **soluble.** (Some are not, which the quadratic formula would immediately show. See the next section.)

The solution of the equation $ax^2 + bx + c = 0$ is given by

$$x = \frac{-b \pm \sqrt{b^2 - 4ac}}{2a}$$

This is the quadratic formula.

The symbol ± states that the square root has a positive and a negative value, **both** of which must be used in solving for x.

Follow through the next example, which shows how to apply the quadratic equation.

Example Solve $5x^2 - 11x - 4 = 0$, correct to 2 decimal places.

Take the quadratic formula

$$x = \frac{-b \pm \sqrt{b^2 - 4ac}}{2a}$$

and put $a = 5$, $b = -11$ and $c = -4$, which gives

$$x = \frac{11 \pm \sqrt{121 - 4(5)(-4)}}{10}$$

$$= \frac{11 \pm \sqrt{201}}{10}$$

$$\Rightarrow \quad x = 2.52 \quad \text{or} \quad -0.32$$

On your calculator, first work out $\sqrt{(b^2 - 4ac)}$ and then put its value into the calculator memory to use twice in the solution.

Examination tip If you are asked to solve a quadratic equation to one or two decimal places, you can be sure that it can be solved **only** by the quadratic formula.

Exercise 10N

Solve the following equations using the quadratic formula. Give your answers to 2 dp.

1 $2x^2 + x - 8 = 0$ **2** $3x^2 + 5x + 1 = 0$ **3** $x^2 - x - 10 = 0$

4 $5x^2 + 2x - 1 = 0$ **5** $7x^2 + 12x + 2 = 0$ **6** $3x^2 + 11x + 9 = 0$

7 $4x^2 + 9x + 3 = 0$ **8** $6x^2 + 22x + 19 = 0$ **9** $x^2 + 3x - 6 = 0$

10 $3x^2 - 7x + 1 = 0$ **11** $2x^2 + 11x + 4 = 0$ **12** $4x^2 + 5x - 3 = 0$

13 $4x^2 - 9x + 4 = 0$ **14** $7x^2 + 3x - 2 = 0$ **15** $5x^2 - 10x + 1 = 0$

Quadratic equations with no solution

Consider the quantity $(b^2 - 4ac)$ in the quadratic formula

$$x = \frac{-b \pm \sqrt{b^2 - 4ac}}{2a}$$

When $b^2 < 4ac$, $(b^2 - 4ac)$ is negative. So its square root is that of a negative number. Such a square root cannot be found and therefore there are no solutions.

Example Solve $x^2 + 3x + 5 = 0$ using the formula $x = \dfrac{-b \pm \sqrt{b^2 - 4ac}}{2a}$.

We notice that $(b^2 - 4ac)$ becomes $(9 - 20) = -11$, which gives $\sqrt{-11}$. Therefore, there are no solutions for x.

Hence $x^2 + 3x + 5 = 0$ has no solutions.

Note The way in which the quantity $(b^2 - 4ac)$ affects the solution of a quadratic equation can be stated as follows:

- When $b^2 - 4ac > 0$, its square root can be found and two distinct solutions are thus obtained for the equation.
- When $b^2 - 4ac = 0$, its square root is zero, giving a repeated root, $-\dfrac{b}{2a}$, and therefore just one solution.
- When $b^2 - 4ac < 0$, its square root is that of a negative number. Such a square root cannot be found and therefore there is no solution.

Exercise 10P

Solve the following equations. Where there is a solution, give your answer correct to 2 decimal places.

1 $3x^2 + 2x = 4$ **2** $2x^2 - 2 = 7x$ **3** $5x^2 = 8x - 2$ **4** $3x^2 = 7 - x$

5 $(3 - x) = (4x - 3)^2$ **6** $(x - 1)^2 = 17$ **7** $5x^2 + 5x + 3 = 0$ **8** $4x^2 + 3x = -2$

9 $x(5x - 1) = 2$ **10** $x(6 + x) = 1$ **11** $17x^2 = x - 2$ **12** $x^2 + 5x = 3$

13 On a graphics calculator, try to write a program to solve a quadratic equation for any values of a, b or c.

Problems solved by quadratic equations

You are likely to have to solve a problem which involves generating a quadratic equation and finding its solution.

Follow through Examples 1 to 3, which show you how to tackle such problems.

Example 1 Find the sides of the right-angled triangle shown in the diagram.

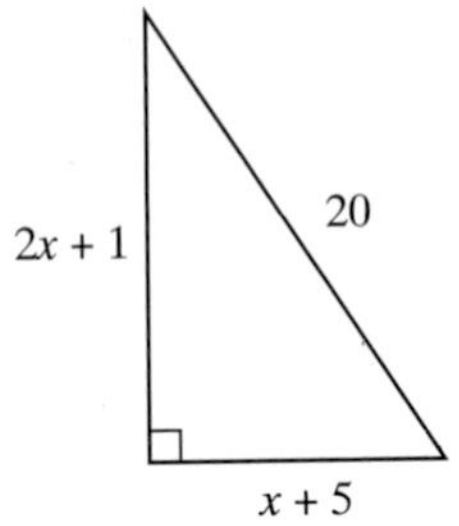

Applying the theorem of Pythagoras gives

$$(x + 5)^2 + (2x + 1)^2 = 20^2$$
$$(x^2 + 10x + 25) + (4x^2 + 4x + 1) = 400$$
$$5x^2 + 14x + 26 = 400$$
$$5x^2 + 14x - 374 = 0$$

Take the quadratic formula

$$x = \frac{-b \pm \sqrt{b^2 - 4ac}}{2a}$$

and put $a = 5$, $b = 14$ and $c = -374$, which gives

$$x = \frac{-14 \pm \sqrt{196 + 7480}}{10}$$

$$\Rightarrow \quad x = -10.16 \quad \text{or} \quad 7.36$$

We reject the negative value for x because this would give negative lengths. So we take $x = 7.36$, which gives the following lengths: 12.36, 15.72 and 20.

Example 2 Solve the equation $x - \frac{2}{x} = 5$. Give your answer to 2 decimal places.

Multiply through by x to give

$$x^2 - \frac{2x}{x} = 5x$$

which simplifies to

$$x^2 - 2 = 5x$$

$$\Rightarrow \quad x^2 - 5x - 2 = 0$$

Putting $a = 1$, $b = -5$ and $c = -2$ into the quadratic formula gives

$$x = \frac{5 \pm \sqrt{25 + 8}}{2}$$

$$\Rightarrow \quad x = 5.37 \quad \text{or} \quad -0.37$$

Example 3 A coach driver undertook a journey of 300 km. Her actual average speed turned out to be 10 km/h slower than expected. Therefore, she took 1 hour longer over the journey than expected. Find her actual average speed.

Let the driver's actual average speed be x km/h. So the estimated speed would have been $(x + 10)$ km/h.

$$\text{Time taken} = \frac{\text{Distance travelled}}{\text{Speed}}$$

At x km/h, she did the journey in $\frac{300}{x}$ hours.

At $(x + 10)$ km/h, she would have done the journey in $\frac{300}{x + 10}$ hours.

Since the journey took 1 hour longer than expected, then

$$\frac{300}{x} = \frac{300}{x+10} + 1$$

$$= \frac{300 + x + 10}{x+10} = \frac{310 + x}{x+10}$$

$$\Rightarrow \quad 300(x + 10) = x(310 + x)$$

$$\Rightarrow \quad 300x + 3000 = 310x + x^2$$

Rearranging gives

$$x^2 + 10x - 3000 = 0$$

This factorises into

$$(x + 60)(x - 50) = 0$$

$$\Rightarrow \quad x = -60 \quad \text{or} \quad 50$$

The coach driver's average speed could not be –60 km/h, so it has to be 50 km/h.

Exercise 10Q

1 The sides of a right-angled triangle are x, $(x + 2)$ and $(2x - 2)$. Find the actual dimensions of the triangle.

2 The length of a rectangle is 5 m more than its width. Its area is 300 m^2. Find the actual dimensions of the rectangle.

3 The average weight of a group of people is 45.2 kg. A newcomer to the group weighs 51 kg, which increases the average weight by 0.2 kg. How many people are now in the group?

4 Solve the equation $x + \frac{3}{x} = 7$. Give your answers correct to 2 decimal places.

5 Solve, to 2 decimal places, the equation $2x + \frac{5}{x} = 8$.

6 A tennis court has an area of 224 m^2. If the length were decreased by 1 m and the width increased by 1 m, the area would be increased by 1 m^2. Find the dimensions of the court.

7 On a journey of 400 km, the driver of a train calculates that if he were to increase his average speed by 2 km/h, he would take 20 minutes less. Find his average speed.

8 The difference of the squares of two positive numbers whose difference is 2, is 184. Find these two numbers.

9 The length of a carpet is 1 m more than its width. Its area is 9 m^2. Find the dimensions of the carpet to 2 decimal places.

10 The two shorter sides of a right-angled triangle differ by 2 cm. The area is 24 cm^2. Find the shortest side of the triangle.

11 Helen worked out that she could save 30 minutes on a 45 km journey if she travelled at an average speed which was 15 km/h faster than that at which she had planned to travel. Find the speed at which Helen had originally planned to travel.

12 Claire intended to spend £3.20 on balloons for her party. But each balloon cost her 2p more than she expected, so she had to buy 8 fewer balloons. Find the cost of each balloon.

13 The sum of a number and its reciprocal is 2.05. What are the two numbers?

14 A woman buys goods for £$60x$ and sells them for £$(600 - 6x)$ at a loss of x%. Find x.

15 A train has a scheduled time for its journey. If the train averages 50 km/h, it arrives 12 minutes early. If the train averages 45 km/h, it arrives 20 minutes late. Find how long the train should take for the journey.

16 A rectangular garden measures 15 m by 11 m and is surrounded by a path of uniform width whose area is 41.25 m^2. Find the width of the path.

Possible coursework tasks

Expanding brackets

$$(x + 1)^2 = x^2 + 2x + 1$$

a Can you expand $(x + 1)^3$?

b Investigate $(x + 1)^n$.

Sums and products

Solve $x^2 - 5x + 6 = 0$.

a What is the sum of the solutions?

b What is the product of the solutions?

c Investigate these for other quadratic equations.

Imaginary numbers

Imagine that you could find $\sqrt{-1}$.

Let $\sqrt{-1} = i$.

This would mean that $\sqrt{-4} = 2i$.

Investigate 'imaginary numbers' when using the quadratic formula.

Examination questions

1 Factorise fully $3t + 6t^2$. *NEAB, Question 2, Specimen Paper 1H, 1998*

2 a Factorise completely $12p^2q - 15pq^2$.

b Expand and simplify $(2x - 3)(x + 5)$.

c The cost, C pence, of printing n party invitations is given by

$$C = 120 + 40n$$

Find a formula for n in terms of C. *MEG, Question 18, Paper 2, June 1994*

3 a Factorise $2ab - a$.

b Solve the equations:

i $3(x - 1) = 15$ **ii** $x^2 - 5x + 6 = 0$ *SEG, Question 18, Specimen Paper 13, 1998*

4 a i Factorise fully the expression $2\pi r^2 + 2\pi rh$.

ii Multiply out $(2x + 3)(x + 4)$. Simplify your answer.

b A possible points system for the high jump event in athletics is given by

$$P = a(M - b)^2$$

M is the height jumped in cm, P is the number of points awarded, and a and b are non-zero positive constants.

i Zero points are scored for a height jumped of 75 cm. What is the value of the constant b?

ii Express M in terms of P, a and b. *SEG, Question 18, Specimen Paper 14, 1998*

5 a Expand the following expression, simplifying your answer as far as possible.

$$(2x - 5)(x - 3)$$

b Make b the subject of the formula

$$c = fc + fb$$

WJEC, Question 26, Paper 1, June 1994

6 A rectangle has a length of $(x + 5)$ cm and a width of $(x - 2)$ cm.

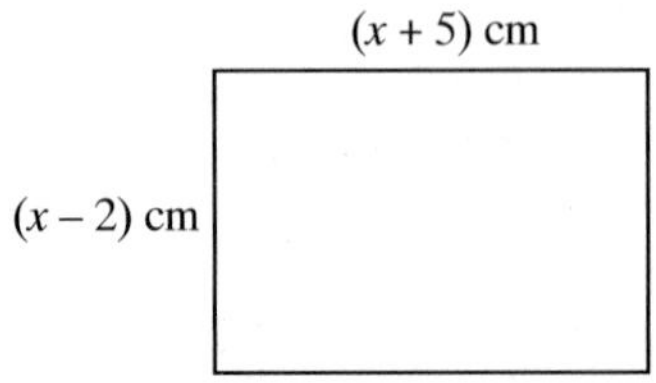

a If the perimeter of the rectangle is 24 cm, what is the value of x?

b i If the area of the rectangle is 60 cm^2, show that $x^2 + 3x - 70 = 0$.

ii Find the value of x when the area of the rectangle is 60 cm^2.

NEAB, Question 23, Specimen Paper 2I, 1998

7 a i Multiply out $4x(x + 3)$.

ii Multiply out and simplify $(2x + 3)(2x + 3)$.

b Four identical rectangular tiles are placed around a square tile as shown in the diagram. Using your answers to part **a**, or otherwise, find the area of the square tile.

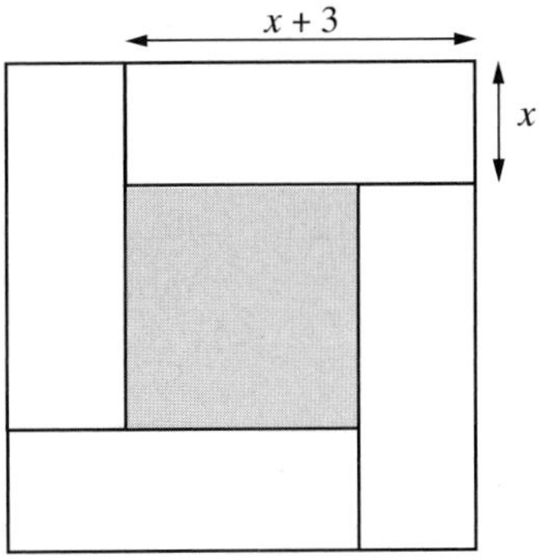

NEAB, Question 14, Paper 2, June 1995

8 a Simplify $\frac{x^2 - 9}{3x - 9}$.

b Solve the equation $12x^2 - 25x + 12 = 0$. *NEAB, Question 16, Paper 1R, November 1995*

9 Solve the equation $x^2 = 5x + 7$, giving your answers correct to 3 siginificant figures..

NEAB, Question 16, Specimen Paper 1R, November 1995

10 $x + \frac{1}{x} = 3$

a Show that this equation can be rearranged as $x^2 - 3x + 1 = 0$.

b Solve this equation to find the values of x correct to 2 decimal places.

NEAB, Question 12, Paper 2R, November 1995

11 Gareth took part in a 26-mile road race.

a He ran the first 15 miles at an average speed of x mph. He ran the last 11 miles at an average speed of $(x - 2)$ mph. Write down an expression, in terms of x, for the time he took to complete the 26-mile race.

b Gareth took 4 hours to complete the race. Using your answer to part **a**, form an equation in terms of x.

c i Simplify your equation and show that it can be written as

$$2x^2 - 17x + 15 = 0$$

ii Solve this equation and obtain Gareth's average speed over the first 15 miles of the race. *NEAB, Question 14, Specimen Paper 2H, 1998*

12 The perimeter of a rectangle is 20 cm. The length of the rectangle is x cm, and the area is 11 cm^2.

a Form an equation in x and show that the equation can be simplified to the form

$$x^2 - 10x + 11 = 0$$

b Solve this equation to find the length and width of the rectangle. Give your answers to an appropriate degree of accuracy. *SEG, Question 20, Paper 15, June 1995*

Summary

How well do you grade yourself?

To gain a grade **C**, you need to be able to manipulate simple formulae, equations and expressions. You need also to be able to expand a two-bracket expression.

To gain a grade **B**, you need to be able to factorise quadratic expressions and solve quadratic equations by factorising.

To gain a grade **A**, you need to be able to factorise $ax^2 + bx + c$, and solve any quadratic equation by factorisation or formula.

To gain a grade **A***, you need to be able to solve problems which involve quadratic equations.

What you should know after you have worked through Chapter 10

- How to expand expressions such as $5m(2m - t)$.
- How to expand expressions such as $(3x - 2)(4x + 5)$.
- How to factorise into either one or two brackets.
- How to solve the quadratic equation $ax^2 + bx + c = 0$.
- How to use the quadratic formula.

11 Kinematics

This chapter is going to … show you how to use graphs to find speed, velocity, acceleration and distance travelled. It will introduce you to the idea of the gradient of linear and curved graphs, with special reference to its application to distance–time and velocity–time graphs. It will then show you how to find the area under linear and curved velocity–time graphs.

What you should already know

- How to extract information from a travel graph.

Straight-line distance–time graphs

Sometimes when using distance–time graphs, you will need to change the given units of speed. So work through Examples 1 and 2 to remind yourself of the process.

1 Change 15 metres per second to kilometres per hour.

15 m/s = 15 × 60 × 60 metres per hour = 54 000 m/h
54 000 m/h = 54 000 ÷ 1000 km/h = 54 km/h

2 Change 24 kilometres per hour to metres per minute.

24 km/h = 24 × 1000 m/h = 24 000 m/h
24 000 m/h = 24 000 ÷ 60 m/min = 400 m/min

Exercise 11A

1 Paul was travelling in his car to a meeting. He set off from home at 7.00 am, and stopped on the way for a break. This distance–time graph illustrates his journey.

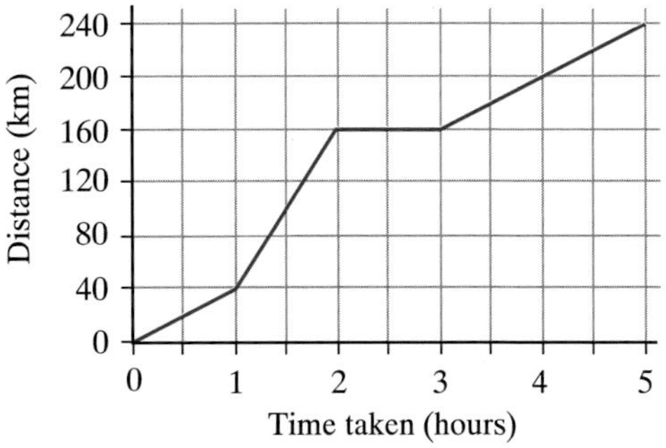

a At what time did he
  i stop for his break
  ii set off after his break
  iii get to his meeting place?

b At what average speed was he travelling
  i over the first hour
  ii over the second hour
  iii for the last part of his journey?

2 James was travelling to Cornwall on his holidays. This distance–time graph illustrates his journey.

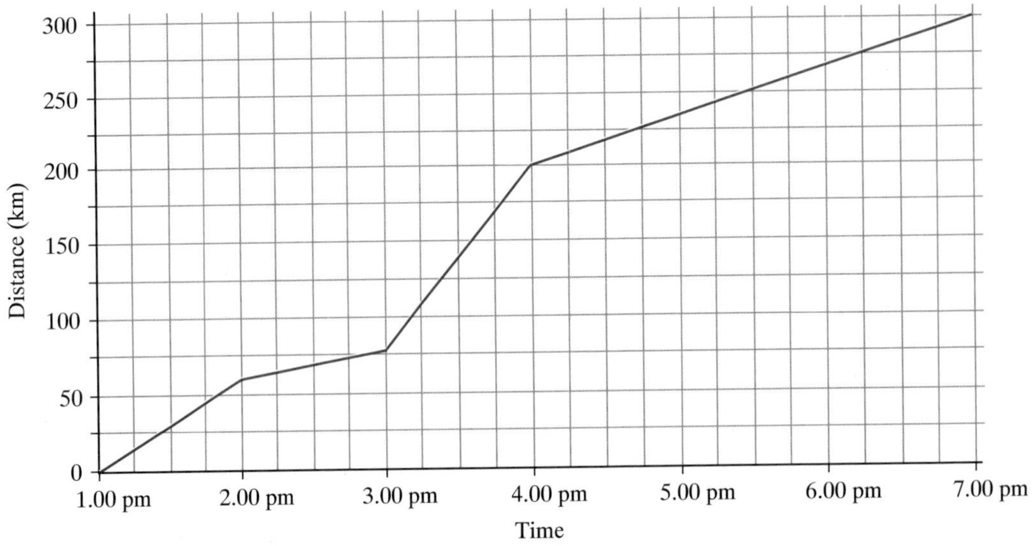

a His fastest speed was on the motorway.

i How much motorway did he use?

ii What was his average speed on the motorway.

b **i** When did he travel the slowest?

ii What was his slowest average speed?

3 Richard and Paul had a race. The distance covered is illustrated below.

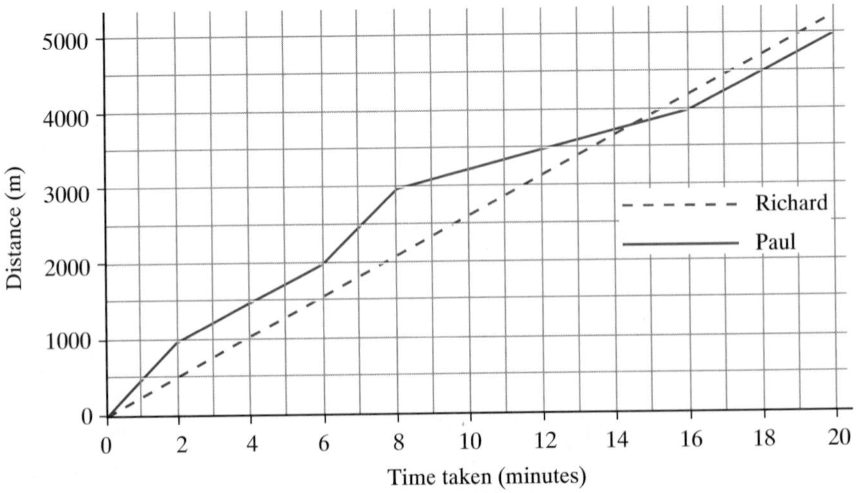

a Paul ran a steady race. What is his average speed in

i metres per minute **ii** km/h?

b Richard ran in spurts. What was his quickest average speed?

c Who won the race and by how much?

4 Azam and Jafar were having a race. The distance–time graph below illustrates the distances covered.

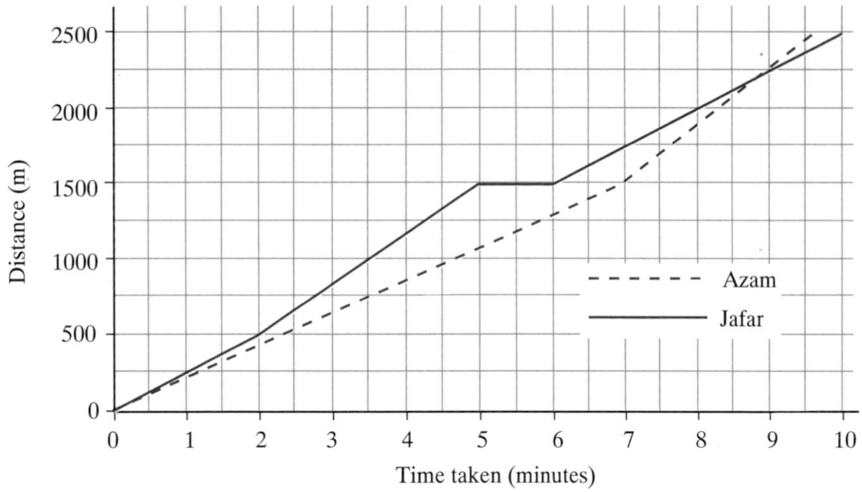

a Jafar stopped in the middle of the race. Why might this have happened?

b Write a description of this race, but do not include actual speeds.

c What was the fastest average speed that was run by

i Azam in metres per minute

ii Jafar in kilometres per hour?

5 Three school friends all set off from school at the same time, 3.45 pm. They all lived 12 km away from the school. The distance–time graph below illustrates their journeys.

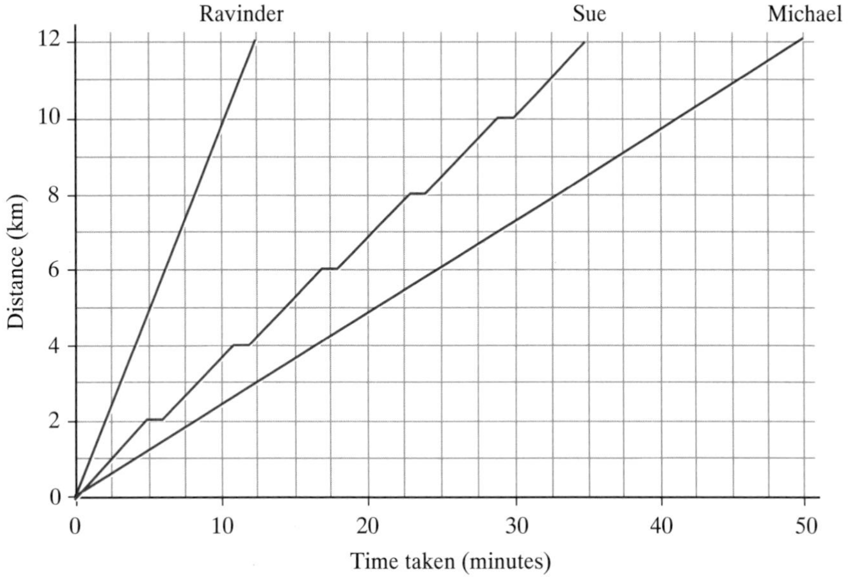

One of the friends went by bus, one cycled and one was taken by car.

a Who used which transport?

b At what time did each friend get home?

c When the bus was moving, what was its average speed in km/min?

d What was Michael's average speed on the journey home? Give your answer in km/h.

6 Three friends, Patrick, Araf and Sean, ran a 1000 metres race. The race is illustrated on the distance–time graph below.

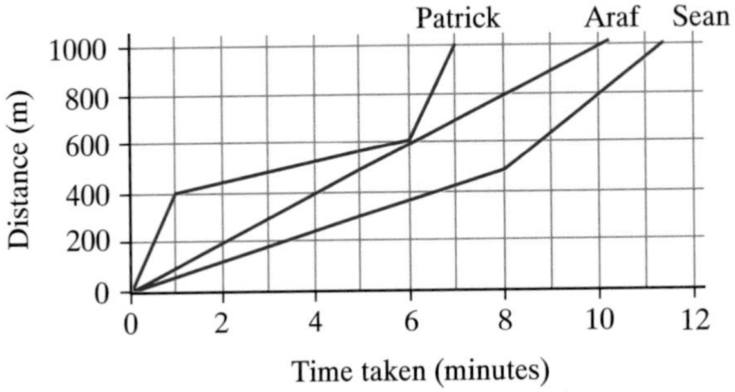

a Describe the race of each friend.

b i What is the average speed of Araf in m/s?

ii What is this speed in km/h?

Gradient of distance–time graphs

Straight-line graphs

The gradient of a straight line is a measure of its slope.

The gradient of the line shown below can be found by constructing a right-angled triangle whose hypotenuse (sloping side) is on the line. The gradient is then given by

$$\text{Gradient} = \frac{\text{Distance measured vertically}}{\text{Distance measured horizontally}} = \frac{6}{4} = 1.5$$

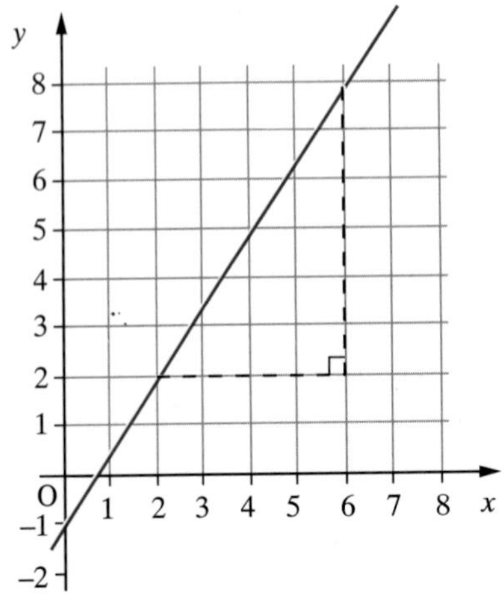

Look at the following examples of straight lines and their gradients.

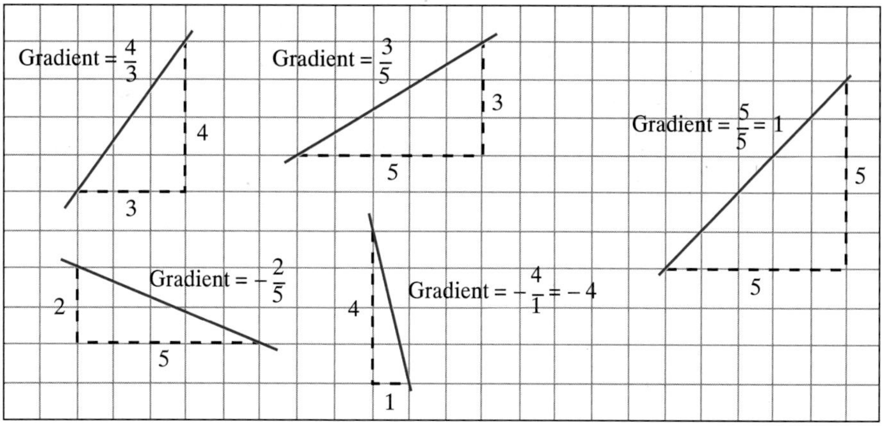

Notice Lines which slope downwards from left to right have **negative gradient**s.

In the case of a straight-line graph between two quantities, its gradient is found using the **scales** on its axes, **not** the actual number of grid squares. It usually represents a third quantity whose value we want to know. For example, look at the next graph.

The gradient on this distance–time graph represents average speed.

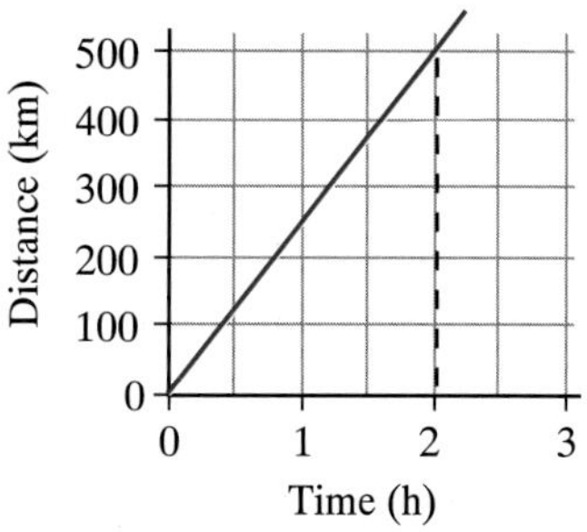

Gradient = $\frac{500}{2}$ = 250 km/h

Exercise 11B

1 Calculate the gradient of each line.

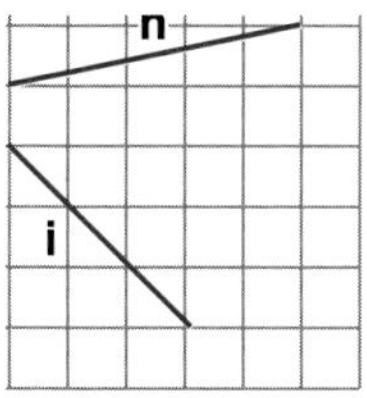

2 Calculate the gradient of each line, using the scales on the axes.

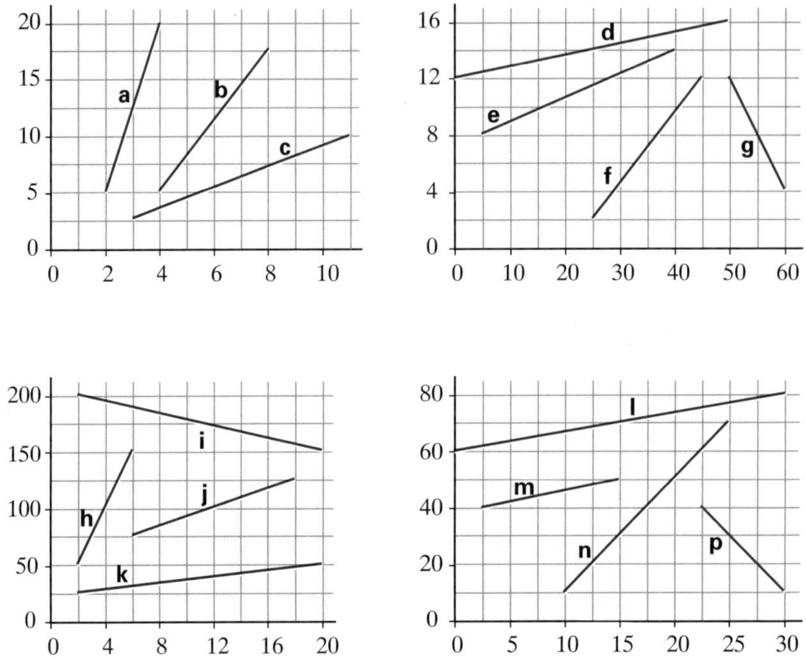

3 Calculate the average speed of the journey represented by each line in the following diagrams.

a

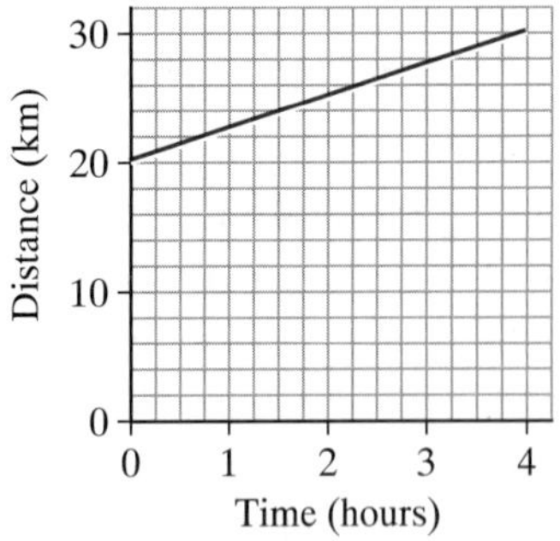

b

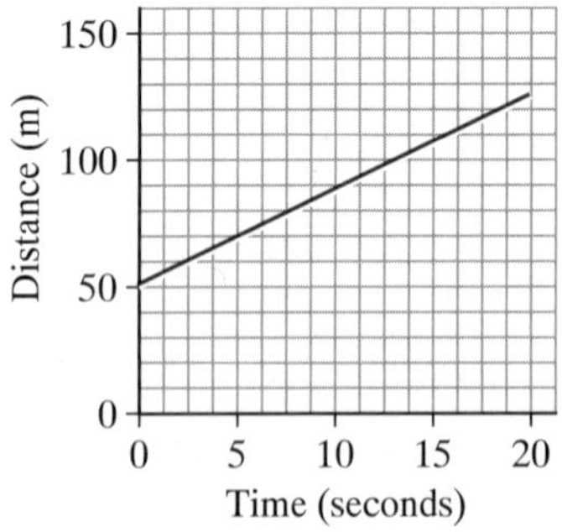

c

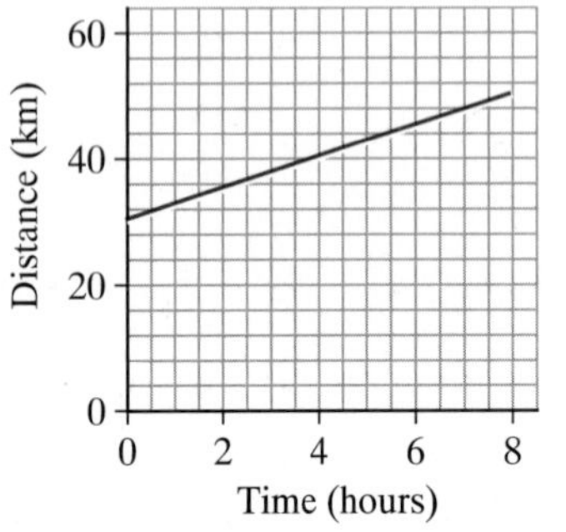

4 From each diagram below, calculate the speed between each stage of the journey.

a

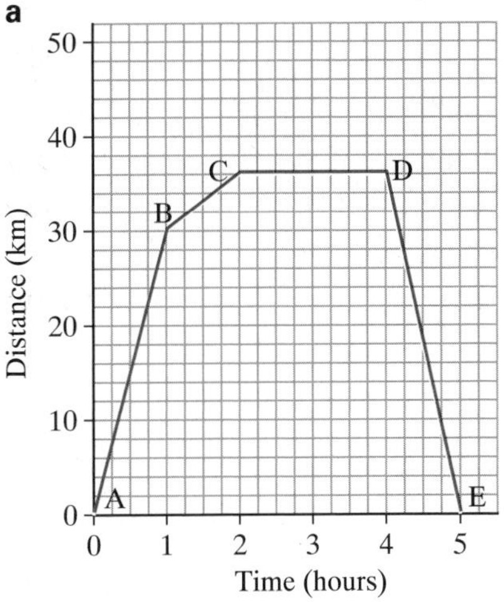

b

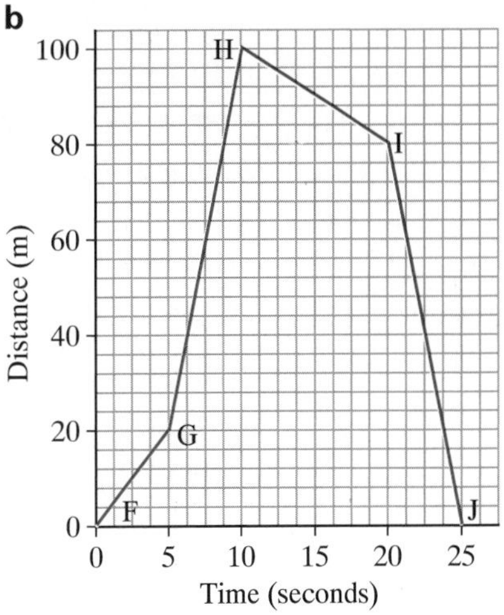

Curved graphs

When the speed of an object is continually changing, the distance–time graph is a curved line whose gradient is continually changing. But we can still use the idea of a gradient to find the average speed over a given time interval, and the speed at a particular instant.

For example, the diagram on the right shows a car journey over a 2-hour period.

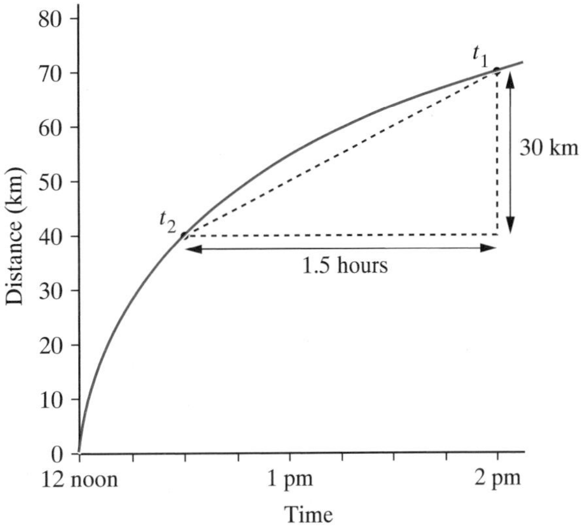

Average speed The average speed between times t_1 and t_2 is found by calculating the gradient of the chord joining the points on the curve that correspond to those times. So, to find the average speed between, say, 12.30 and 14.00, we draw the chord t_1t_2. Then

$$\text{Average speed} = \text{Gradient of } t_1t_2 = \frac{30}{1.5} = 20 \text{ km/h}$$

Instantaneous speed Instantaneous speed changes along a distance–time curve. However, at any given time, t, the instantaneous speed is given by the gradient of the tangent to the curve at t.

So, to find the instantaneous speed at a point on a distance–time curve, you first have to draw the tangent to the curve at that point. Then you calculate its gradient.

To draw a tangent at a given point, you position a ruler on the curve so that only that point can be seen in that region. When you are satisfied that the ruler is correctly positioned, draw the tangent.

For example, to find the instantaneous speed at 12 noon, draw the tangent to the curve at t = 12 noon. This is shown as CD on the graph. The gradient of CD is

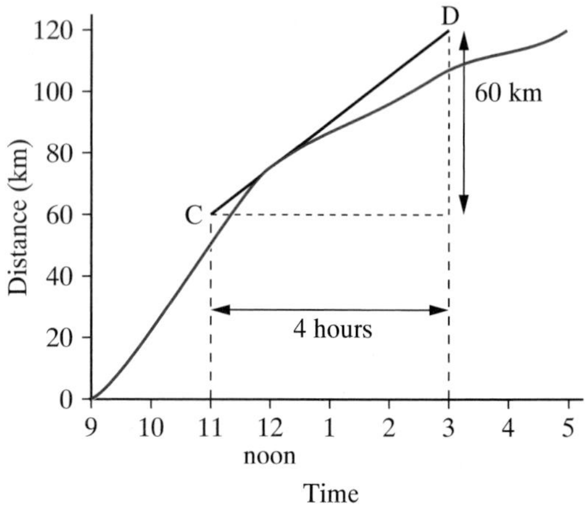

$$\frac{60}{4} = 15$$

So, the instantaneous speed at 12 noon is 15 km/h.

Note A negative gradient on a distance–time graph indicates the return journey.

Exercise 11C

1 The table shows the height, d metres, of a ball from the ground t seconds after being kicked.

t (seconds)	0	1	2	3	4	5	6	7	8
d (metres)	0	4	7	9	10	10.5	9	5	0

a Draw the graph of d against t.

b Find the average speed of the ball from

i $t = 1$ to 2 **ii** $t = 5$ to 7

c Find the speed of the ball at

i $t = 2.5$ **ii** $t = 6$

2 A pebble was thrown out to sea from the top of a cliff. After t seconds, its height was h metres above sea level, as shown in the table below.

t (seconds)	0	0.5	1	1.5	2	2.5	3	3.5	4	4.5	5
h (metres)	15	20.5	24	26.5	27	26.5	24	20.5	15	8.5	0

a Draw the graph of h against t.

b Find the average speed of the pebble from

i $t = 1$ to 2 **ii** $t = 4$ to 5

c Find the speed of the pebble at

i $t = 0.5$ **ii** $t = 3.5$

3 A boat journey was timed as shown in the following table, which gives the distances covered after each hour.

***t* (hours)**	0	1	2	3	4
***d* (km)**	0	10	50	100	130

a Draw the graph of d against t.

b Find the average speed of the boat during the second hour of the journey.

c Find the speed of the boat at

i $t = 1$ **ii** $t = 3.5$

4 The total distance, d km, travelled by a bus on a tour around York, was recorded every half-hour, as shown in the table.

Time	10.00	10.30	11.00	11.30	12.00	12.30
***d* (km)**	0	5	12	23	42	48

a Draw the graph of d against time.

b Find the average speed of the tour

i over the first 15 minutes **ii** between 11.15 and 11.45

5 An athlete ran from Sheffield to Wath. Her distance, d km, from Sheffield at various times is given in the table.

Time	07.30	08.00	08.30	09.00	09.30
***d* (km)**	0	5	13	18	24

a Draw the graph of d against time.

b Find the average speed of the athlete

i from 07.45 to 08.15 **ii** from 08.30 to 09.10

c Find the speed of the athlete at

i 7.45 **ii** 9.15

6 A mother drives to Manchester Airport to pick up her son, and then drives straight back home. The table shows her distance, d km, from home at various times.

Time	13.00	13.10	13.20	13.30	13.40	13.50	14.00	14.10
***d* (km)**	0	9	19	38	46	33	15	0

a Draw the graph of d against time.

b Find the mother's average speed over the first 15 minutes.

c Estimate the speed the mother was travelling at

i 14.00 **ii** 13.25

Velocity

In our calculations of speed, we have ignored the sign of the gradient. The sign of the gradient of a distance–time graph gives the **direction of travel**. Once we introduce the direction of travel into our calculations, then we must use the term **velocity** instead of speed. Velocity at time t is the gradient of the distance–time graph at t, **including its sign**.

Straight-line velocity–time graphs

When the velocity of a moving object is plotted against time, two quantities can be found from the graph: acceleration and distance travelled.

- The **gradient** of the velocity–time graph at any time t is equal to the **acceleration** of the object at that time.

  Acceleration is rate of change of velocity, so when the gradient becomes negative, the object is slowing down. Negative acceleration is called **deceleration**.

- The **area** under the velocity–time graph is equal to the **distance travelled**.

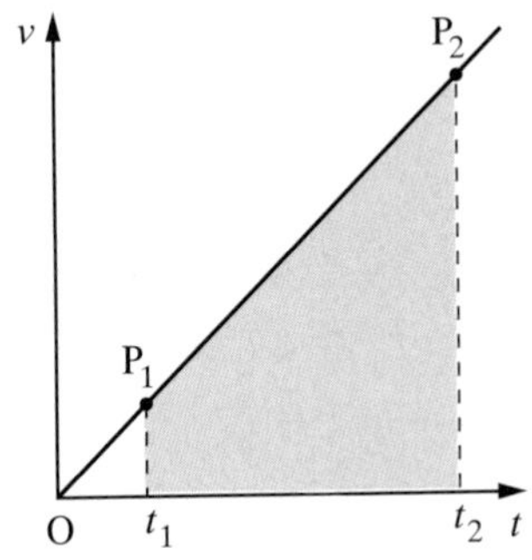

For example, in the diagram on the right, the area under the graph between P_1 and P_2 (that is the area enclosed by the graph, the horizontal time axis, and the ordinates at t_1 and t_2) is equal to the distance travelled between t_1 and t_2. (Remember: the area is calculated using the **scales** on the axes, **not** the number of grid squares.)

We can easily verify this fact. Take, for example, the velocity–time graph (also shown on the right) of a vehicle travelling at a constant velocity of 30 km/h, for 2 hours.

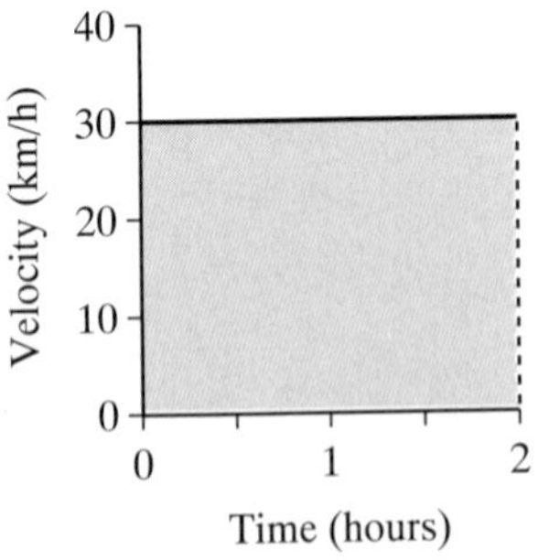

Distance travelled = Velocity × Time
$= 30 \times 2 = 60$

Area under graph up to 2-hour ordinate $= 30 \times 2 = 60$

Therefore, the distance travelled is equal to the area under the graph.

Follow through the next example, which shows in detail both applications of a velocity–time graph.

Example At the top of the next page is the velocity–time graph of a particle over a 6 seconds period, drawn from measurements made during a scientific experiment.

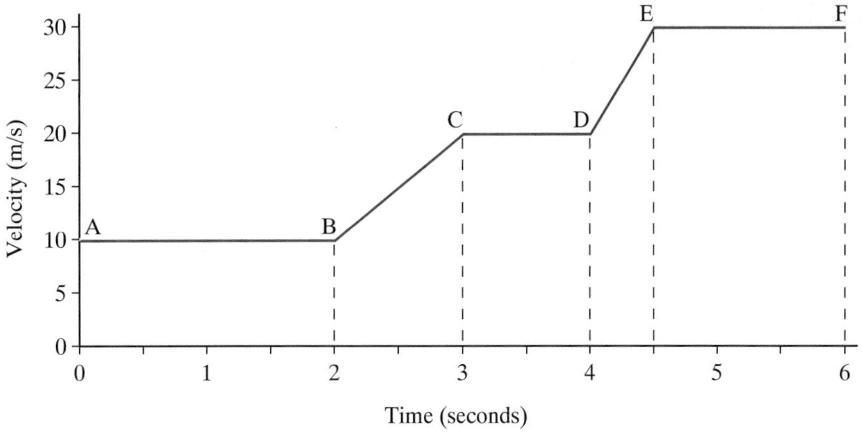

The graph shows a constant particle velocity of 10 m/s for the first 2 seconds (AB). Then the velocity increases uniformly from 10 m/s to 20 m/s over 1 second (BC). Then follows another period of constant velocity (20 m/s) over 1 second (CD), after which the velocity increases uniformly from 20 m/s to 30 m/s in 0.5 seconds (DE). During the final 1.5 seconds the velocity is constant at 30 m/s.

Acceleration There are two periods of acceleration: BC and DE.

$$\text{Acceleration over BC} = \text{Gradient of BC} = \frac{10 \text{ m/s}}{1 \text{ s}} = 10 \text{ m/s}^2$$

$$\text{Acceleration over DE} = \text{Gradient of DE} = \frac{10 \text{ m/s}}{0.5 \text{ s}} = 20 \text{ m/s}^2$$

Distance travelled The distance travelled over the five periods of time are found as follows.

The area under the graph from A to B represents the distance travelled at 10 m/s for 2 seconds, which is 20 metres. (Notice that the area under AB is $2 \times 10 = 20$.)

The area under BC, which is a trapezium, is $\frac{1}{2}(10 + 20) = 15$. So the distance travelled during the second period is 15 metres.

The area under CD is $1 \times 20 = 20$. So the distance travelled during the third period is 20 metres.

The area under DE, which is a trapezium, is $0.5 \times \frac{1}{2}(20 + 30) = 12.5$. So the distance travelled during the fourth period is 12.5 metres.

The area under EF is $1.5 \times 30 = 45$. So the distance travelled during the final period is 45 metres.

Therefore, the total distance travelled by the particle in 6 seconds is $20 + 15 + 20 + 12.5 + 45 = 112.5$ metres.

Exercise 11D

1 The diagram shows the velocity of a model car over 6 seconds.

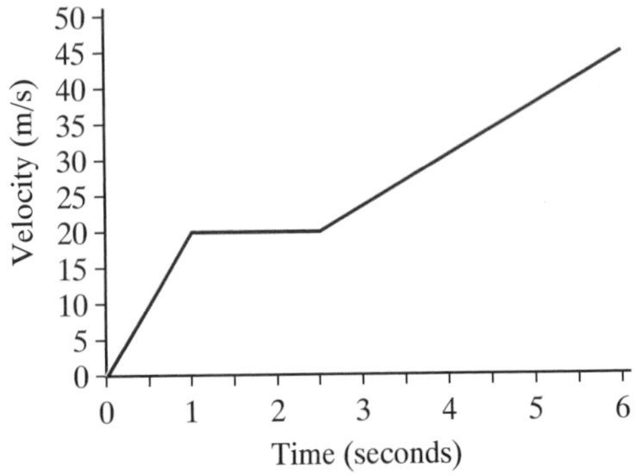

a Calculate the acceleration

i over the first second **ii** after 5 seconds

b Calculate the total distance the model car has travelled in these 6 seconds.

2 The diagram shows the velocity–time graph for a short tram journey between stops. Find

a how far the tram travelled in the first 30 seconds

b the total distance travelled.

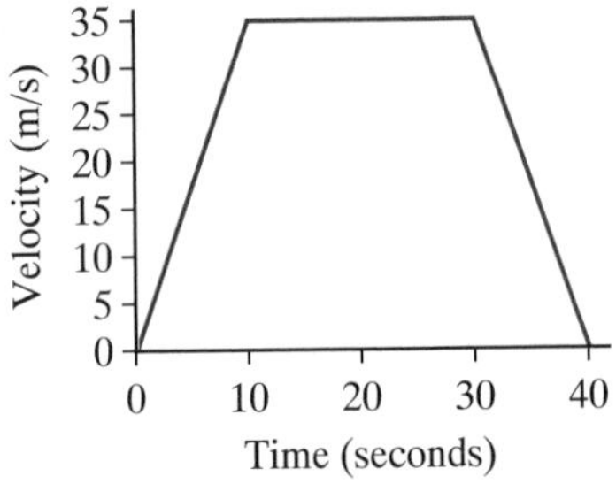

3 The diagram shows the velocity of a boat over an 18-hour period. Calculate

a the times at which the boat was travelling at a constant velocity

b the total distance travelled

c the average speed of the whole journey.

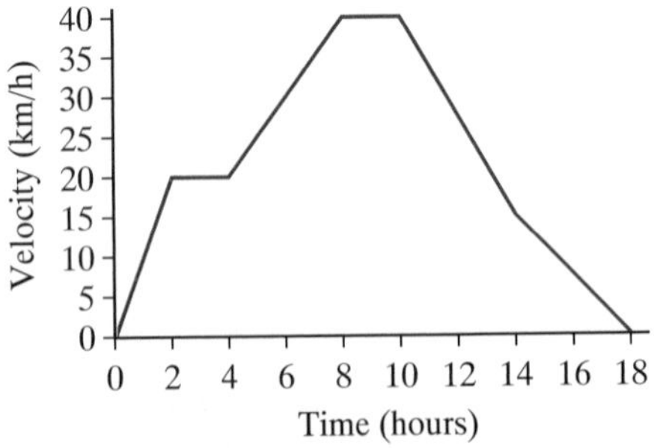

4 An aircraft flying at a constant height of 300 m dropped a load fitted to a parachute. During the times stated, the velocity of the parachute was as follows:

0–2 seconds	The load accelerated uniformly up to 20 m/s
2–6 seconds	The parachute opened, which brought the velocity down uniformly to 2 m/s
After 6 seconds	The load fell with a constant speed of 2 m/s

a Draw a velocity–time graph for the first 8 seconds.

b Find the distance fallen in the first 6 seconds.

c Find the total time taken for the load to reach the ground.

5 Starting from rest (zero velocity), a particle travels as indicated below.

- Accelerates at a constant rate over 5 seconds to reach 15 m/s.
- Keeps this velocity for 10 seconds.
- Accelerates over the next 5 seconds to reach 25 m/s.
- Steadily slows down to reach rest (zero velocity) over the next 10 seconds.

a Draw the velocity–time graph.

b Calculate the acceleration over the first 5 seconds.

c Calculate the total distance travelled by the particle.

d Calculate the average speed of the particle.

6 A particle starts from rest and travels for 10 seconds with constant acceleration. At the end of the 10 seconds, it has travelled 450 m and reached a speed of v m/s.

a Find v and construct a velocity–time graph.

b Find

i the velocity of the particle after 5 seconds **ii** its acceleration

Area under a curve

Without using more advanced mathematics, it is not possible to find the exact value of the area under a curve. Therefore, we have to estimate it. The best way to do this is to divide the area into several vertical strips (trapeziums), find the area of each one, and then sum the lot.

Example Find the area under the curve shown in the diagram.

First, we divide the area under the curve into vertical strips of equal width. (Eight will be enough in this case.) Then we approximate the arcs AB, BC, …, HI by straight lines, to form six trapeziums and two triangles.

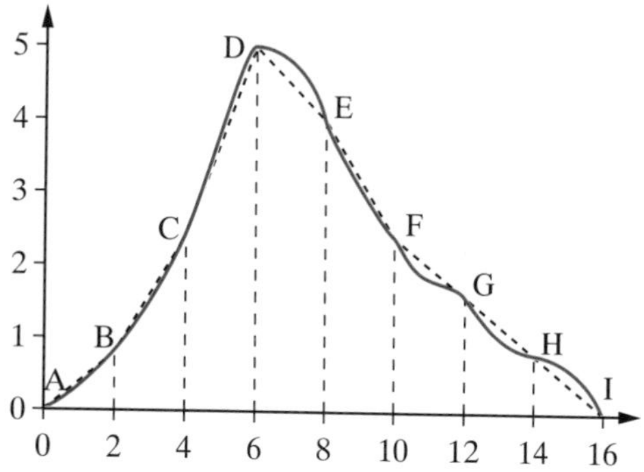

(There are two triangles, instead of two trapeziums, because both ends of the graph come down to the horizontal axis.)

Therefore, the approximate value, T_a, of the total area under the curve is given by the sum of the areas of these six trapeziums and two triangles. Denoting each area by the line under which it is situated, we therefore have

$$\begin{aligned}T_a &= AB + BC + CD + DE + EF + FG + GH + HI\\ &= \tfrac{1}{2}(2 \times 0.8) + 2 \times \tfrac{1}{2}(0.8 + 2.4) + 2 \times \tfrac{1}{2}(2.4 + 5) + 2 \times \tfrac{1}{2}(5 + 4) + 2 \times \tfrac{1}{2}(4 + 2.4)\\ &\quad + 2 \times \tfrac{1}{2}(2.4 + 1.6) + 2 \times \tfrac{1}{2}(1.6 + 0.8) + \tfrac{1}{2}(2 \times 0.8)\\ &= 0.8 + 3.2 + 7.4 + 9 + 6.4 + 4.0 + 2.4 + 0.8\\ &= 34\end{aligned}$$

Note Some trapeziums fall outside the curve, while the others fall inside. This method of estimation depends on the assumption that the 'oversized' trapeziums will compensate for the 'undersized' trapeziums.

Exercise 11E

1 Estimate the area under each of the following curves using the strips given.

a

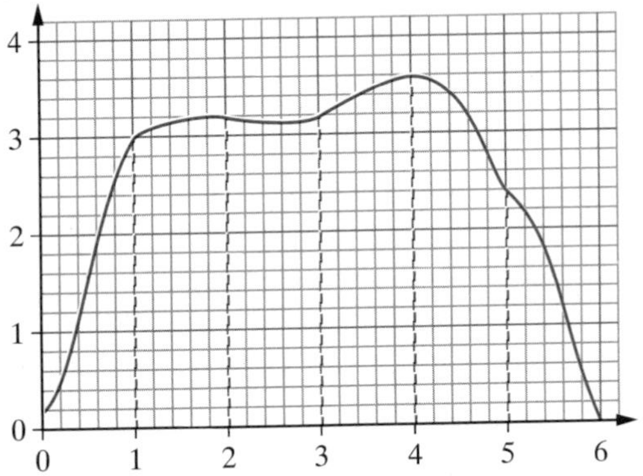

b

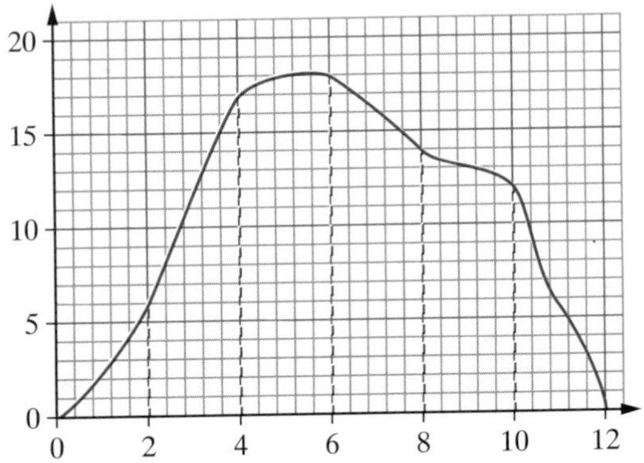

c

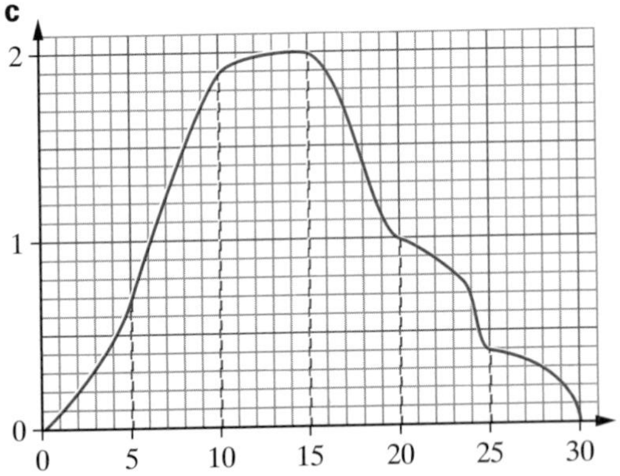

d

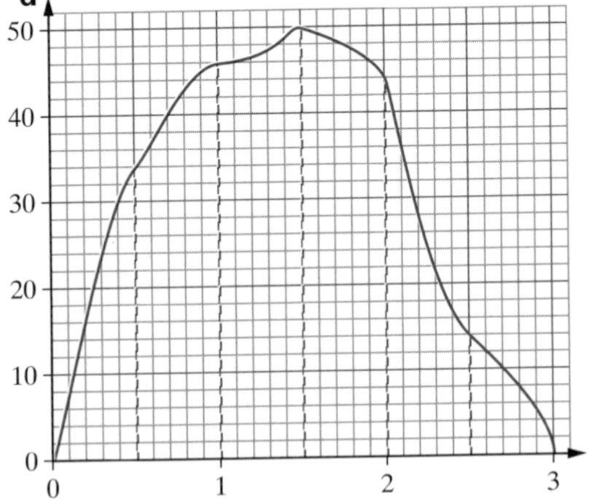

2 By drawing suitable strips, estimate the area under each curve.

a

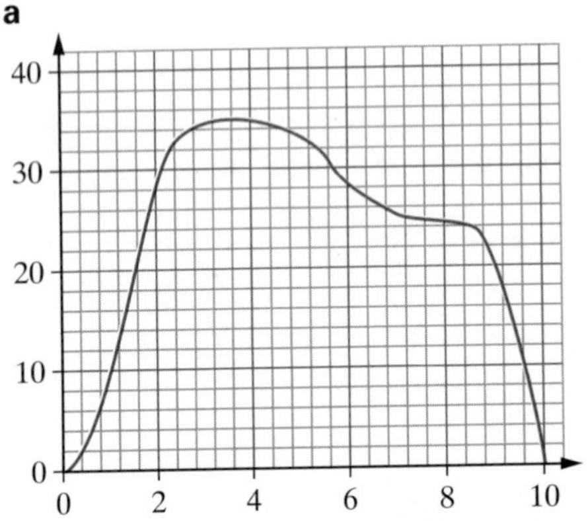

b

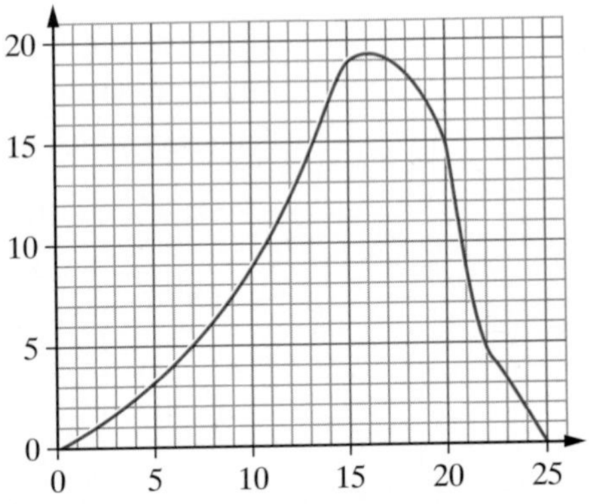

c

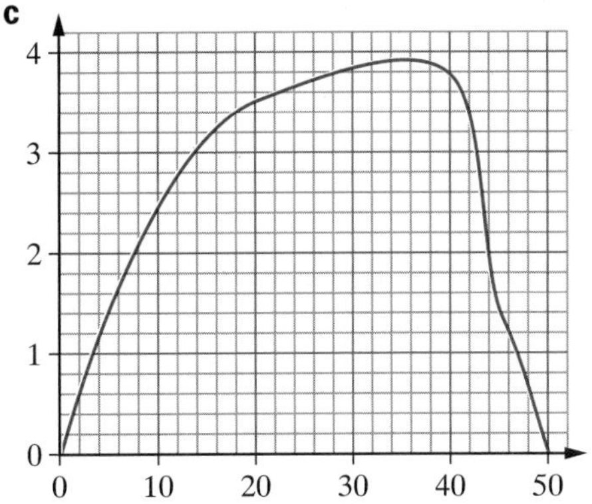

d

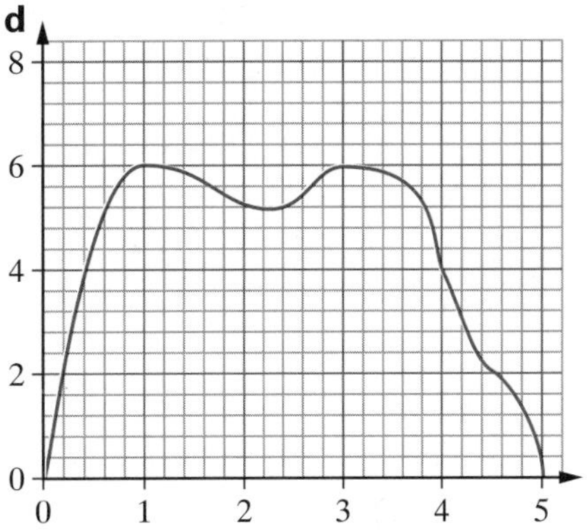

Curved velocity–time graphs

In reality, most situations give curved velocity–time graphs. The data that we can derive from them are the same as for the straight-line graphs:

- The **acceleration** at any point is given by the **gradient** of the tangent to the curve at that point.
- The **distance travelled** is the estimated **area** under the curve.

Example The velocity of a particle is shown on the velocity–time graph below. Calculate

a the acceleration after 15 seconds

b the total distance travelled over the 80 seconds.

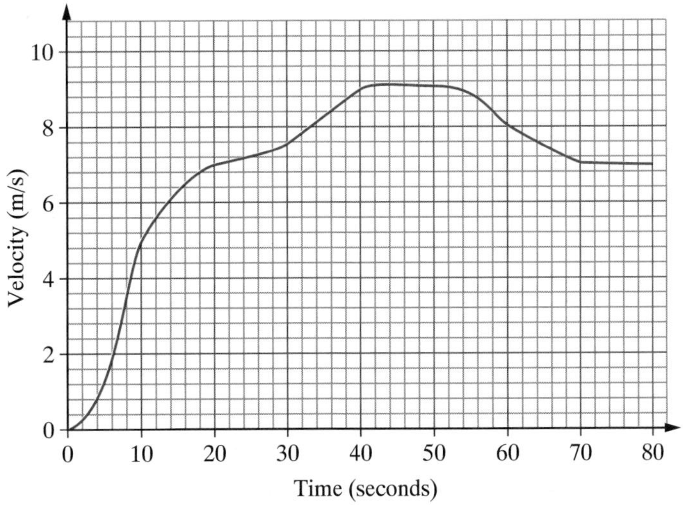

a To obtain the required acceleration, draw the tangent AC at $t = 15$ and find its gradient.

From triangle ABC,

$$\text{Gradient} = \frac{5.6}{40} = 0.14$$

Therefore, the acceleration after 15 seconds is 0.14 m/s^2.

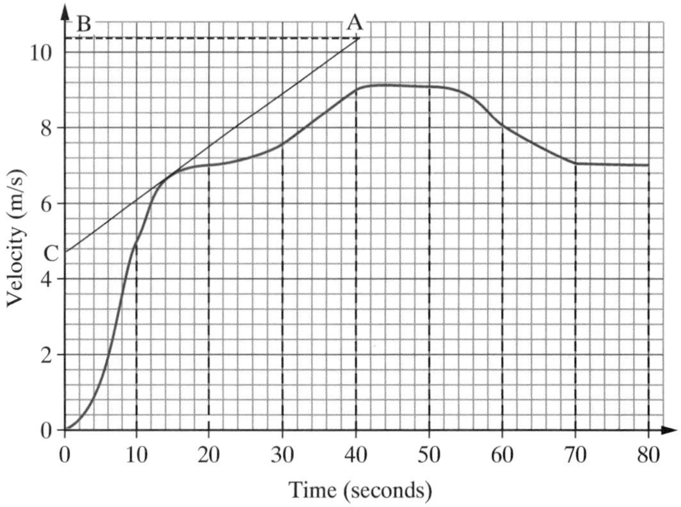

b The total distance is given by the area under the curve, the approximate value of which is found by dividing this area into eight strips, as follows:

$$\frac{1}{2}(10 \times 5) + \frac{10}{2}(5 + 7) + \frac{10}{2}(7 + 7.6) + \frac{10}{2}(7.6 + 9) + \frac{10}{2}(9 + 9)$$

$$+ \frac{10}{2}(9 + 8) + \frac{10}{2}(8 + 7) + \frac{10}{2}(7 + 7)$$

$$= 25 + 60 + 73 + 83 + 90 + 85 + 75 + 70 = 561$$

Since this is an approximation, it would be sensible to round off to 560 m.

Exercise 11F

1 The table shows the velocity, v metres per second, of a particle after t seconds.

t (s)	0	1.6	3.2	4.8	6.4	8
v (m/s)	12	11.7	10.7	9.1	6.9	4

a Plot the points on a velocity–time graph and join them with a smooth curve.

b Describe the motion of the particle.

c Calculate the acceleration after

i 2 seconds **ii** 6 seconds

d Calculate the distance travelled over the 8 seconds.

2 The diagram shows the speed of a cyclist during a road race. Find

a the acceleration after

i 5 minutes **ii** 35 minutes

b the total distance travelled in the race

c the average speed over the whole race.

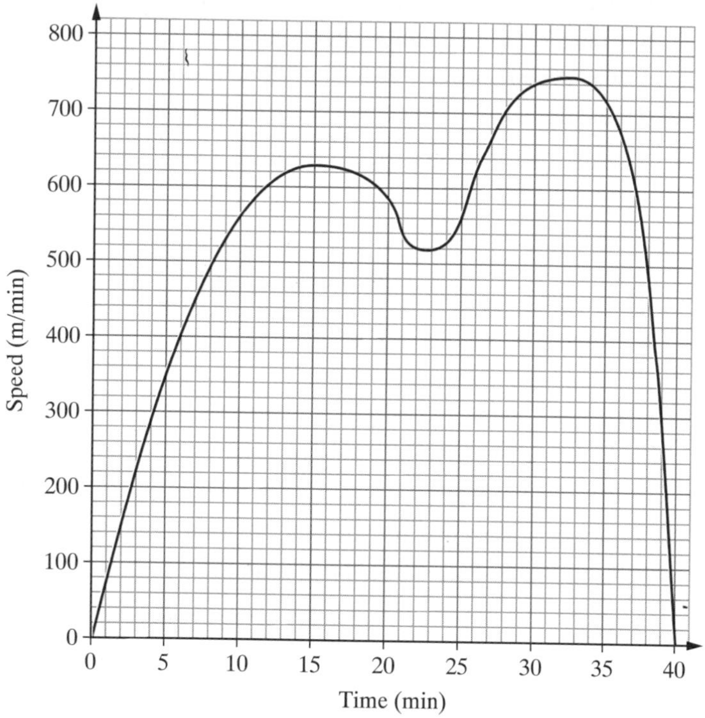

3 The speed of a boat is observed at 10-second intervals over 1 minute. The observations are recorded in the table.

Time (s)	0	10	20	30	40	50	60
Speed (m/s)	0	6	16	29	38	39	40

a Plot the points on a velocity–time graph and join them with a smooth curve.

b Estimate the acceleration

i after 30 seconds **ii** when the speed is 34 m/s

c Estimate the total distance covered by the boat over the minute.

4 The recorded speeds of a train at intervals of 1 minute during a journey of 8 minutes are as follows.

0 13 34 45 48 48 42 24 0 km/h

a Draw the velocity–time graph.

b Estimate the total length of the journey over the full 8 minutes.

5 A rocket was fired and its velocity, v km/min, was estimated every half minute after firing. The following table was constructed.

t (min)	0	0.5	1	1.5	2	2.5	3	3.5
v (km/min)	0	0.2	0.5	2.25	6	12.5	22.5	40

a Draw the velocity–time graph.

b Estimate the acceleration after 3 minutes.

c Find the distance covered in the third minute.

d Find the distance covered in the first 3 minutes.

6 A particle moved with a speed of v m/s at each recorded time of t seconds. The results are given in the table.

t (s)	0	2	4	6	8	10	12
v (m/s)	0	20	30	20	30	40	45

a Estimate the acceleration after 2.5 seconds.

b Estimate the distance travelled

i in the first 4 seconds **ii** during the 9th second

iii over the whole 12 seconds

c Estimate the average speed of the particle over the 12 seconds.

7 A car accelerates uniformly from rest to a speed of 120 km/h after 30 seconds. Estimate the distance covered in this time.

8 A car slows down, at first gradually and then very quickly, from a speed of 120 km/h to 40 km/h in 10 seconds. Estimate the distance covered in this time.

Possible coursework tasks

The trapezium rule

To estimate the area under a curve, we divide the area into strips of equal width.

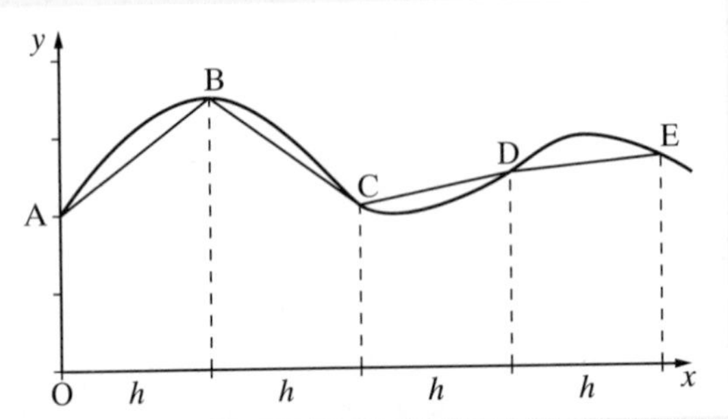

If the co-ordinates of A, B, C, D, E, … are respectively (x_0, y_0), (x_1, y_1), (x_2, y_2), (x_3, y_3), (x_4, y_4), …, and the width of each strip is h, can you develop a rule for estimating the area under the curve?

Find a formula for using any number of strips.

Swimming pools

A swimming pool is being filled at the local sports centre.

The hosepipe delivers water at a constant rate and it takes 30 minutes to fill a pool.

a Draw a graph to show how the depth of water (d) varies with time (t) as the pool fills with water.

b Draw graphs as in part **a** for the two pools whose regular cross-sections are shown below. Each pool takes 30 minutes to fill.

c Draw your own pools and comment on anything you notice for each one.

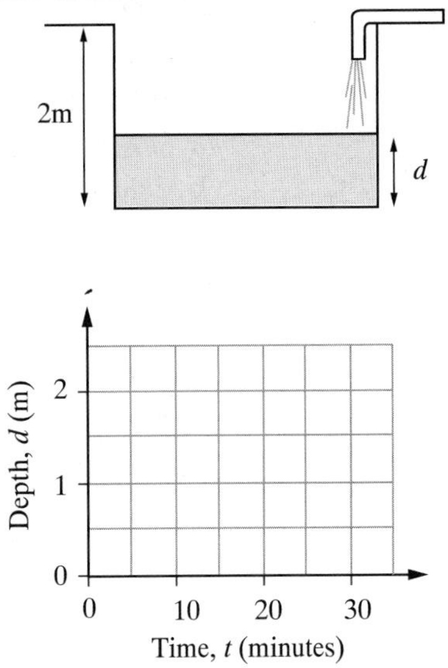

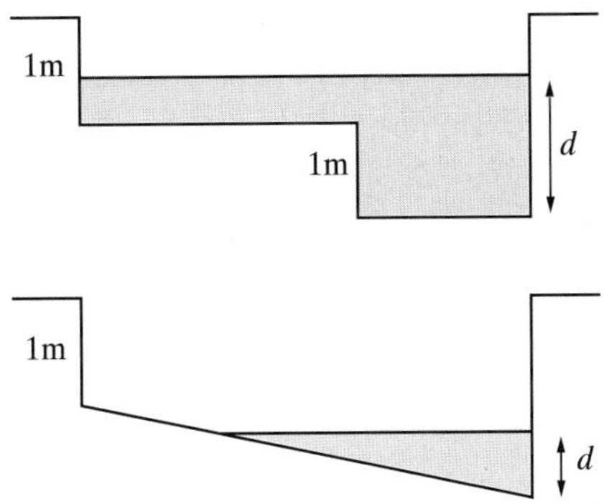

Examination questions

1 The distance–time graph shows the journeys made by a van and a car starting from Oxford, travelling to Luton, and returning to Oxford.

a How far had the car travelled when it met the van for the second time?

b Calculate, in miles per hour, the average speed of the car between 0959 and 1000.

c During which period of time was the van travelling at its greatest average speed?

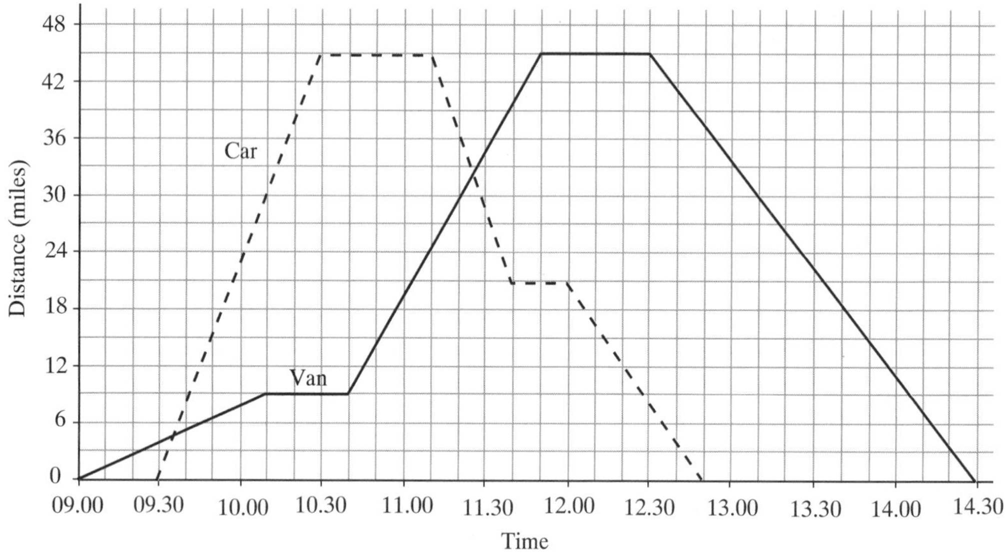

SEG, Question 9, Specimen Paper 14, 1998

2 Jennifer walks from Corfe Castle to Wareham Forest and then returns to Corfe Castle. The travel graph of her journey is shown.

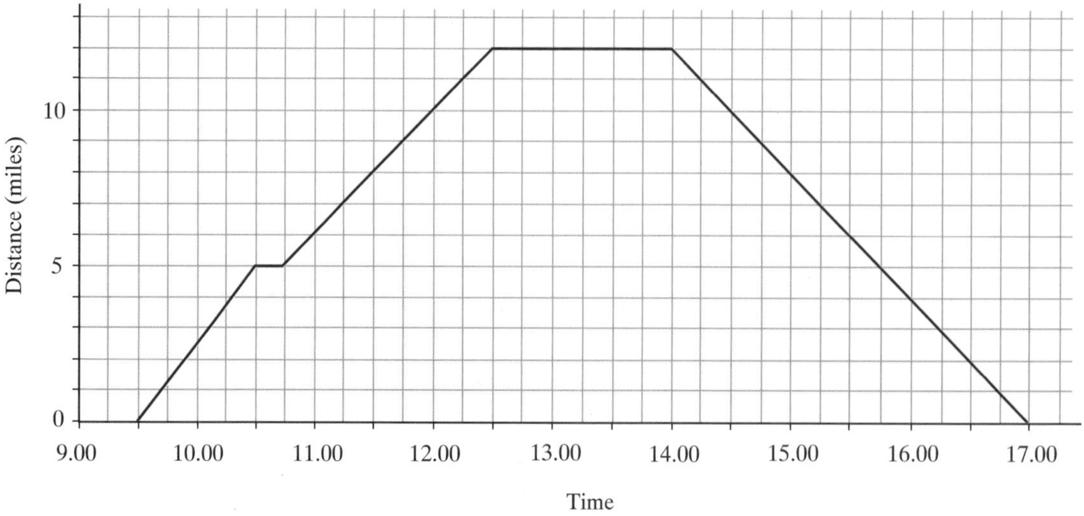

a At what time did Jennifer leave Corfe Castle?

b How far from Wareham Forest did Jennifer make her first stop?

c Jennifer had lunch at Wareham Forest. How many minutes did she stop for lunch?

d At what average speed did Jennifer walk back from Wareham Forest to Corfe Castle?

SEG, Question 10, Paper 3, June 1994

3 The graph below represents the journey of a train that travels from Shrewsbury to Hereford and then on to Newport.

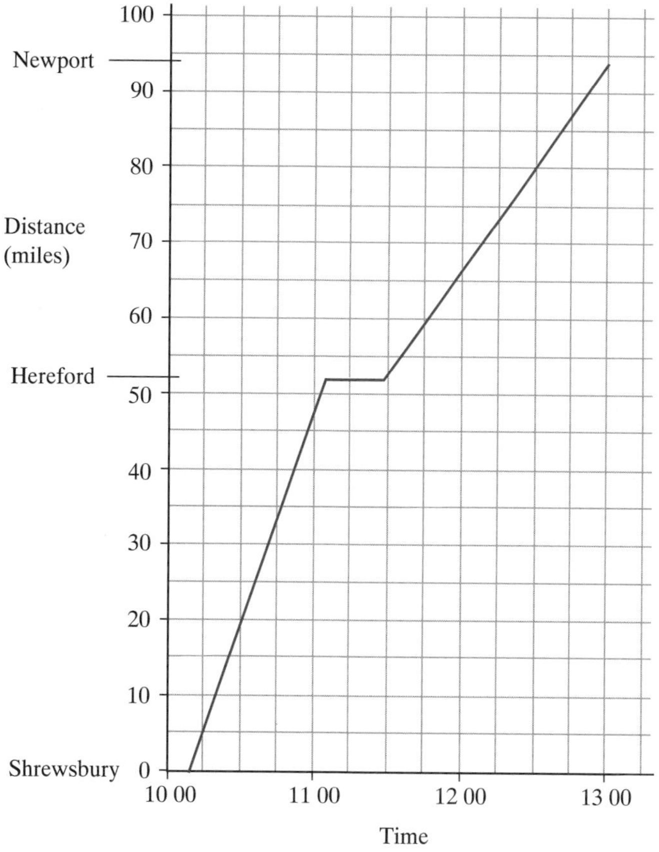

a Draw a copy of the graph.

b What was the average speed of the train from Shrewsbury to Hereford?

c How long did the train wait at Hereford?

d Without calculating another average speed, show how the graph can tell whether or not the average speed of the train from Hereford to Newport was more than its average speed from Shrewsbury to Hereford.

e Another train starts from Newport at 11.15 and travels non-stop to Shrewsbury at an average speed of 60 mph. Draw the graph of its journey on your graph.

f Write down how far from Hereford the trains were when they passed each other.

WJEC, Question 11, Specimen Paper 1, 1998

4 Here is a velocity–time graph of a car travelling between two sets of traffic lights.

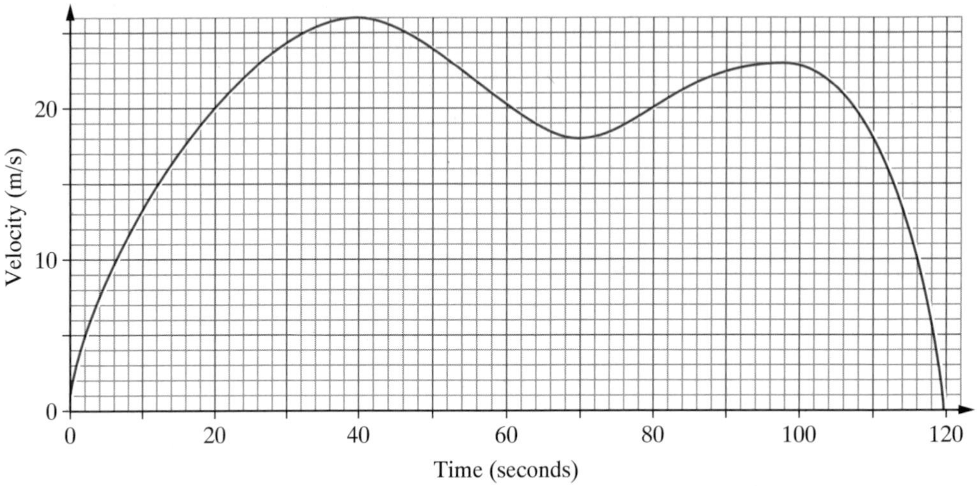

a Calculate an estimate for the acceleration of the car when the time is equal to 20 seconds.

b Calculate an estimate for the total distance travelled by the car.

ULEAC, Question 10, Specimen Paper 6, 1998

5

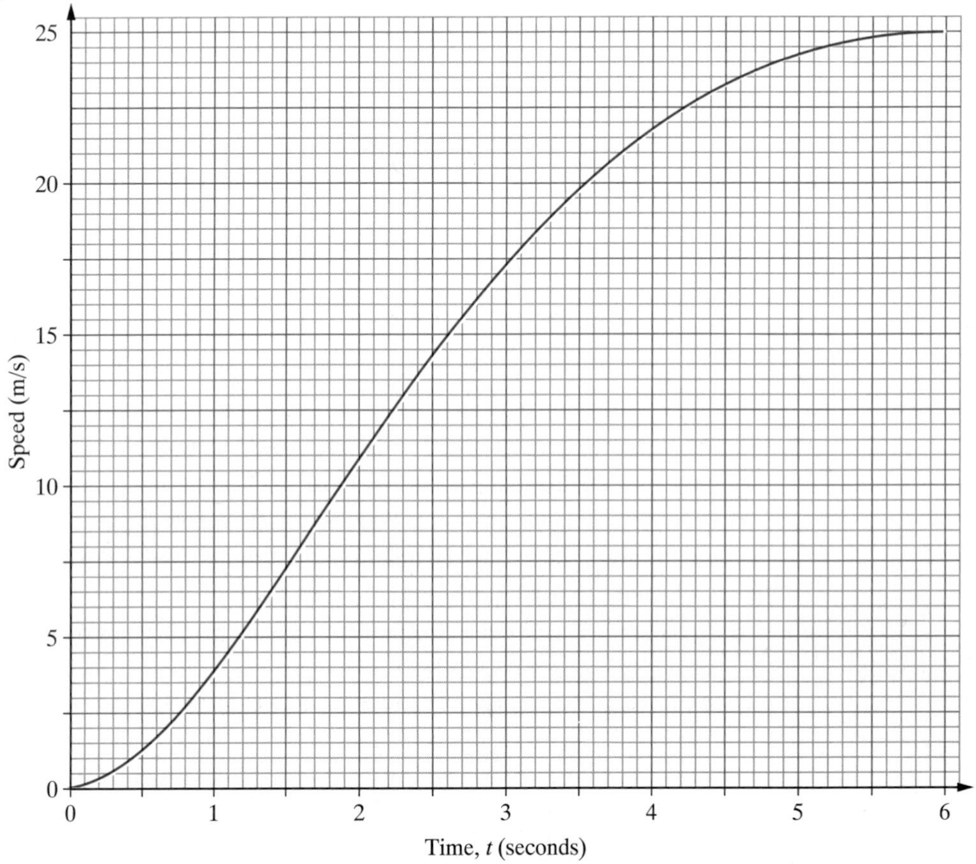

The graph on page 266 shows how a car's speed, measured in metres per second, varies in the first 6 seconds after the car moves away from some traffic lights.

a **i** Draw the tangent at the point on the curve where $t = 5$ seconds.

ii Find the gradient of this tangent.

b Making your method clear, estimate the area beneath the graph between $t = 0$ and $t = 6$. Hence estimate the distance travelled by the car in the first 6 seconds.

MEG, Question 13, Specimen Paper 6, 1998

6 The graph shows the velocity of a car over the time interval $0 < t < 20$, where t is time in seconds and v is velocity in metres per second.

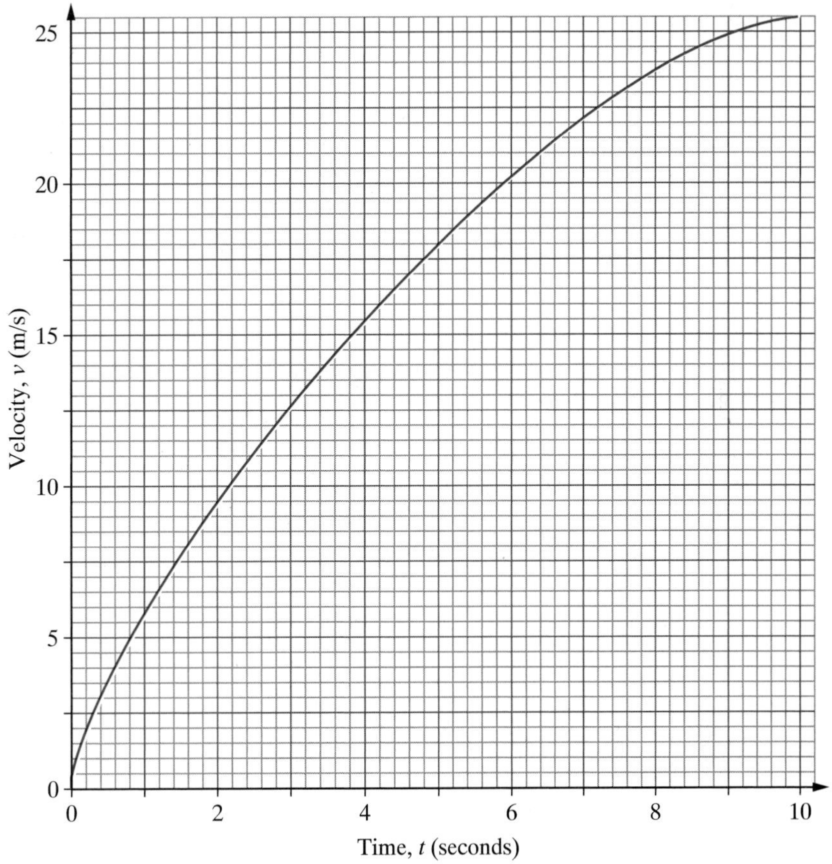

a Use the graph to estimate the acceleration of the car at $t = 7.5$.

b **i** Estimate the area under the graph for the interval $0 \le t \le 10$

ii What does this area represent?

SEG, Question 18, Specimen Paper 15, 1998

7 The graph at the top of the next page shows the distance, in metres, travelled by a cyclist during the first 30 seconds of a race.

a Use the graph to estimate the greatest speed, in metres per second, reached by the cyclist during the first 30 seconds.

b Calculate the average speed, in metres per second, of the cyclist during the first 30 seconds.

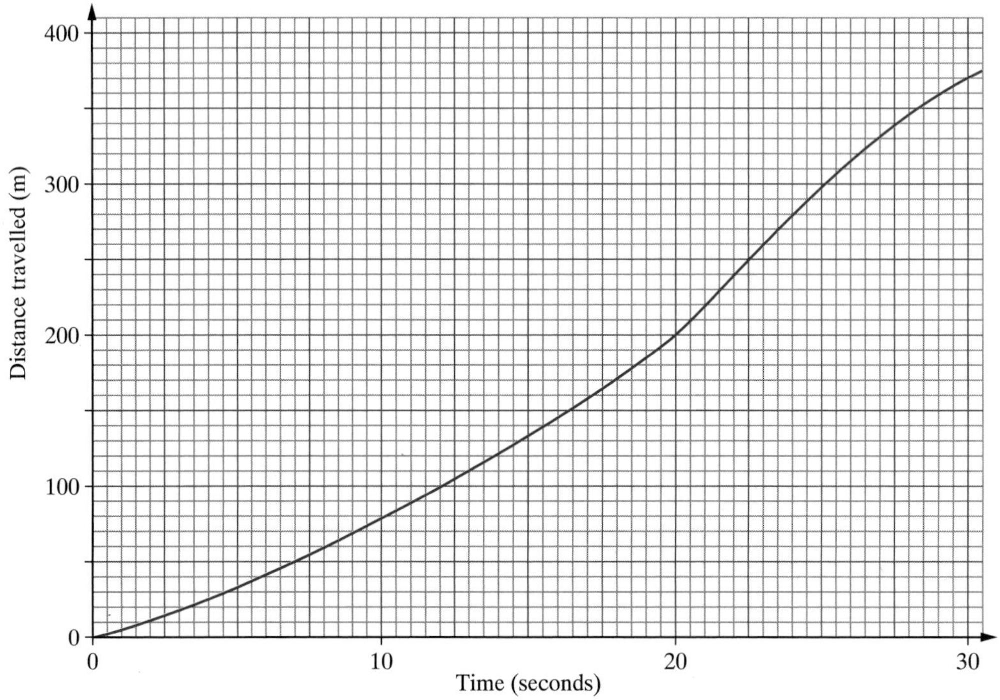

c The graph below shows the speed, in metres per second, of the cyclist during the last 40 seconds of the race. Use the graph to estimate the distance travelled, in metres, by the cyclist during the last 40 seconds of the race.

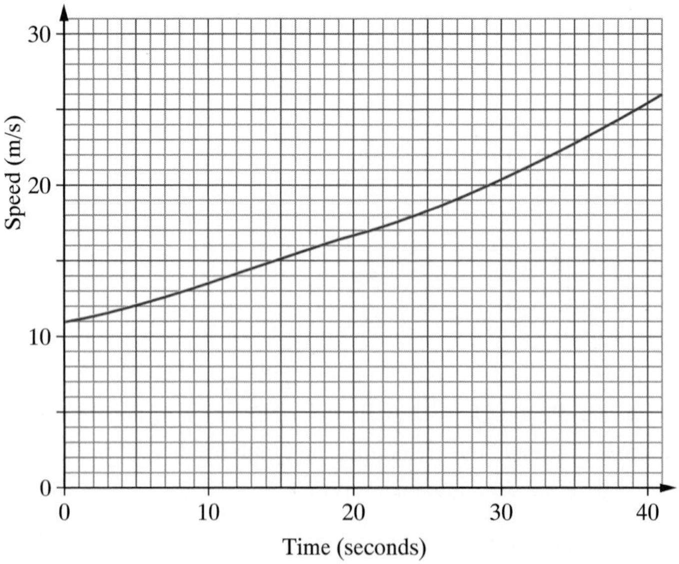

NEAB, Question 16, Paper 2R, November 1995

8 A train normally travels between two stations A and B at a steady speed of 90 kilometres per hour. On a particular day the driver had to stop at a red signal between the stations. The speed–time graph is shown below.

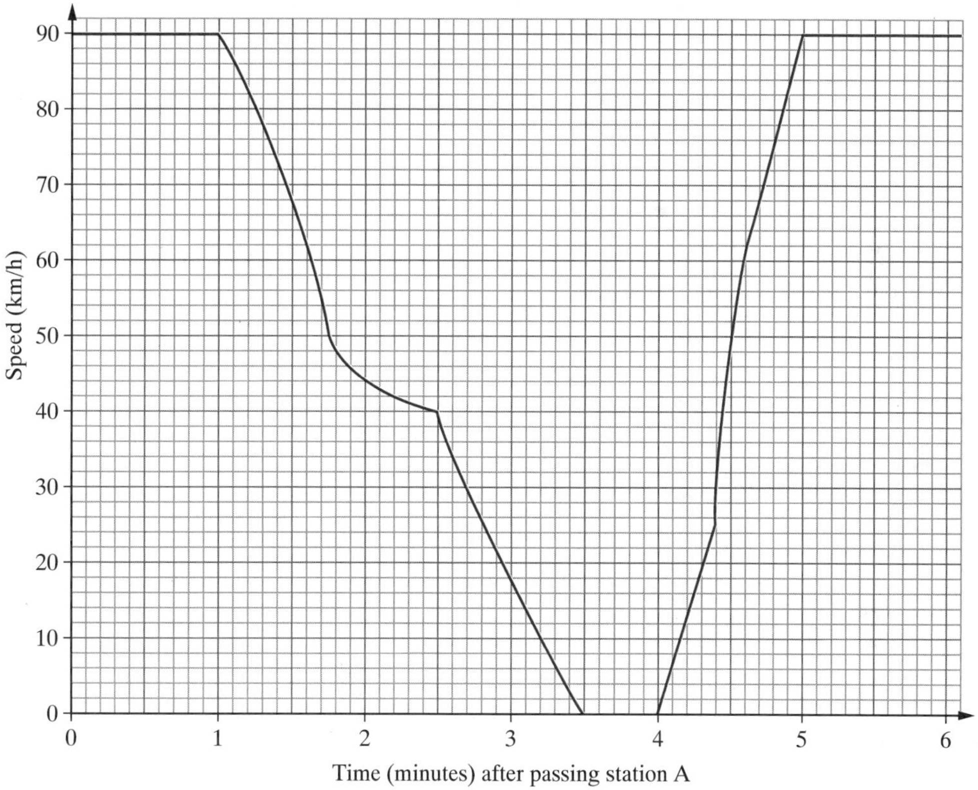

a **i** From the graph, estimate the deceleration of the train, in kilometres per hour per minute, two minutes after passing station A.

ii Express this deceleration in metres per second^2.

b Estimate the distance of the signal from station A.

NEAB, Question 15, Paper 1R, June 1996

9 **a** Each of the four graphs on the next page represents **one** of the following **five** situations.

Situation A A ball rolling from rest down a smooth slope for 4 seconds.

Situation B A ball thrown vertically upwards and caught by the thrower 4 seconds later.

Situation C A train travelling at a constant speed of 15 m/s taking 4 seconds to pass through a tunnel.

Situation D The first 4 seconds of a sprinter's 100 metre race.

Situation E A lift setting off from one floor and stopping 4 seconds later at the next floor.

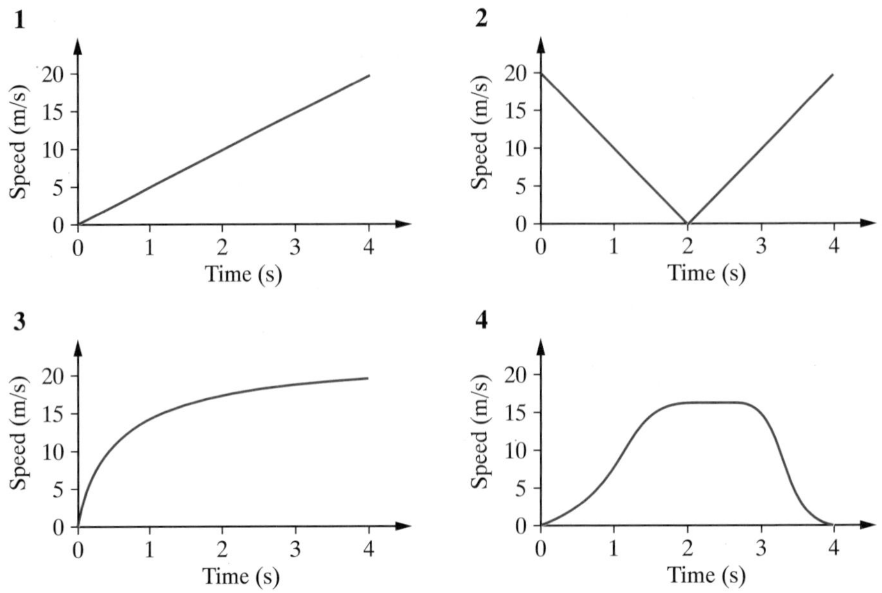

Match each graph with one of the five situations.

b One of the situations A, B, C, D or E does not match any of the four graphs drawn in part **a**. Sketch the speed–time graph for this situation.

NEAB, Question 16, Paper 2, November 1994

Summary

To gain a grade **C**, you need to be able to calculate the gradient of a straight-line graph as well as find speed from a distance–time graph.

To gain a grade **B**, you need to be able to interpret the gradient on a straight-line graph.

To gain a grade **A**, you need to be able to use any distance–time graph to estimate velocities, and any velocity–time graph to estimate acceleration and the total distance travelled.

What you should know after you have worked through Chapter 11

- How to find the gradient of a straight line.
- How to draw and interpret distance–time graphs.
- The relevance of the gradient of a straight-line graph.
- How to find velocities from a distance–time graph.
- How to find acceleration and total distance travelled from a velocity–time graph.

12 Similarity

This chapter is going to ... introduce you to similar triangles. It will show you how to work out the scale factor between similar figures, and how to use this to calculate unknown sides in such figures. It will also show you how to use the scale factor between similar shapes to calculate areas and volumes.

What you should already know

- What congruent triangles are.
- How to calculate a ratio.
- How to work out the square and cube of numbers.
- How to solve equations of the form $\frac{x}{9} = \frac{2}{3}$.

Similar triangles

Triangles are similar if their corresponding angles are equal. Their corresponding sides are then in the same ratio.

Example The triangles ABC and PQR are similar. Find the length of the side PR.

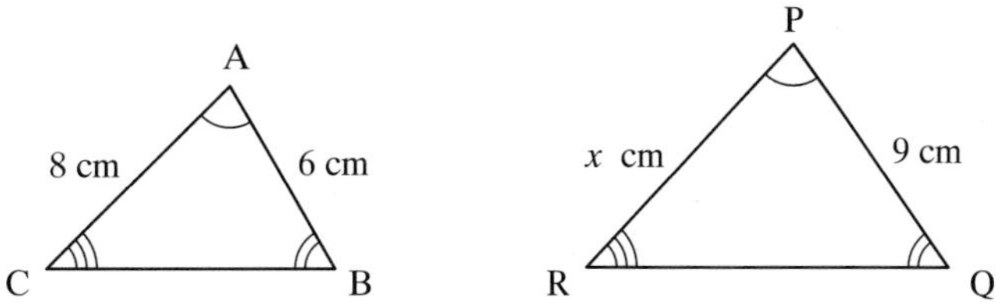

Take two pairs of corresponding sides, one pair of which must contain the unknown x. Form each pair into a fraction, so that x is on top. Since these fractions must be equal,

$$\frac{PR}{A} = \frac{PQ}{AB}$$

$$\frac{x}{8} = \frac{9}{6}$$

To find x:

$$x = \frac{9 \times 8}{6} \quad \Rightarrow \quad x = \frac{72}{6} = 12 \text{ cm}$$

Exercise 12A

1 These diagrams are drawn to scale. What is the scale factor of the enlargement in each case?

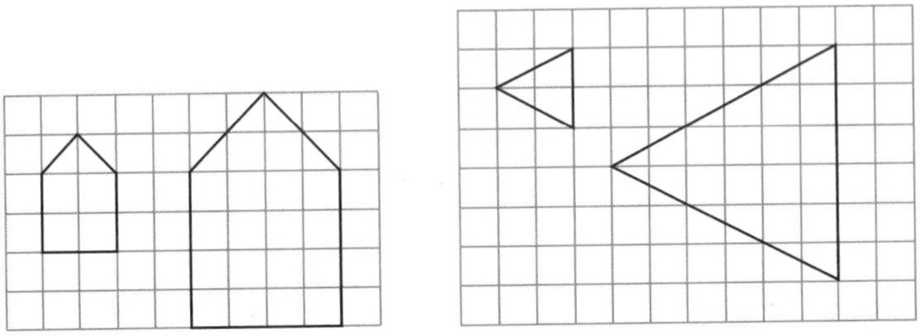

2 Are the following pairs of shapes similar? If so, give the scale factor. If not, give a reason.

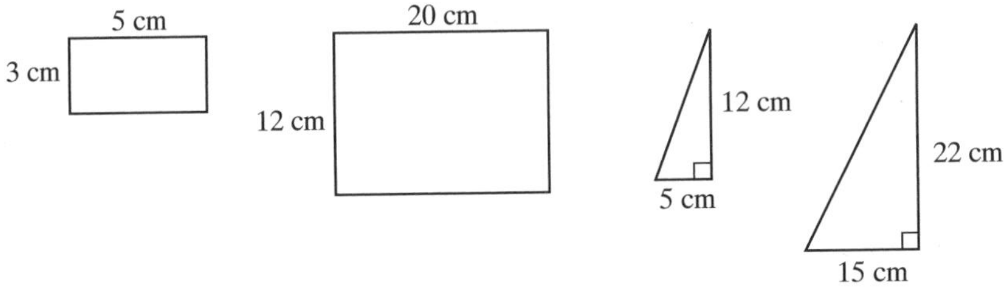

3 **a** Explain why these shapes are similar.
b Give the ratio of the sides.
c Which angle corresponds to angle C?
d Which side corresponds to side QP?

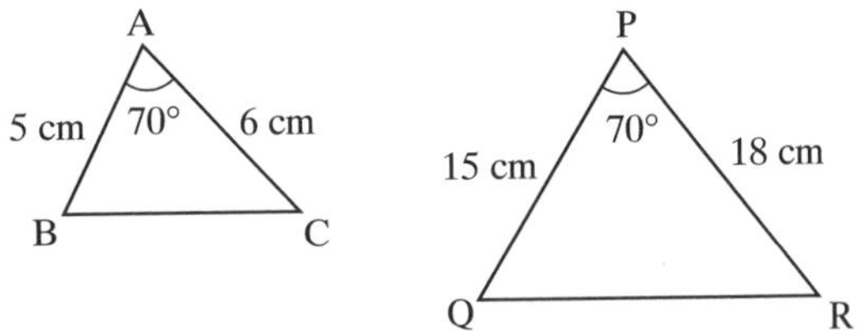

4 **a** Explain why these shapes are similar.
b What is the ratio of the corresponding sides?
c Which angle corresponds to angle B?

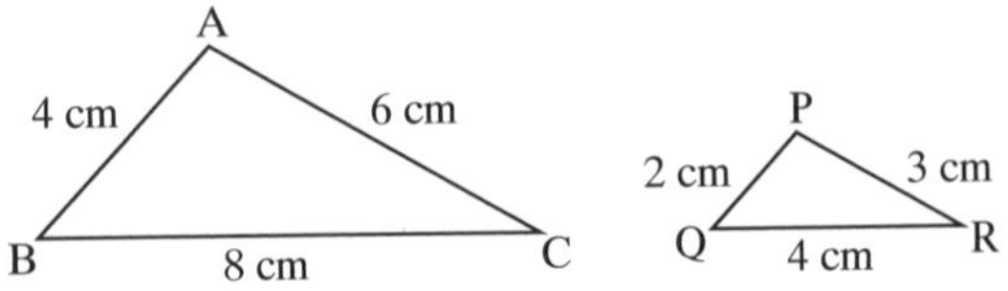

5 **a** Explain why these shapes are similar.
b Which angle corresponds to angle A?
c Which side corresponds to side AC?

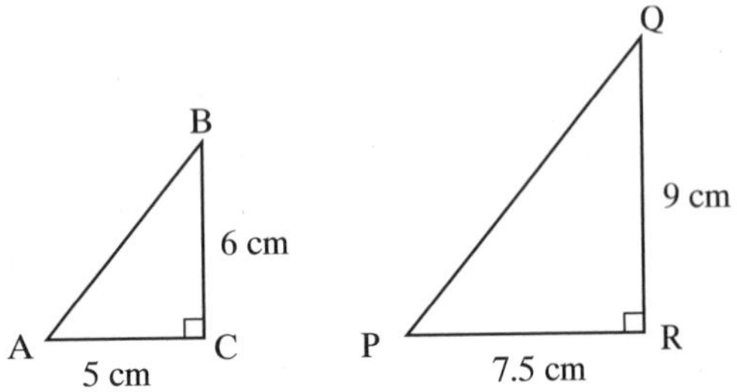

6 **a** Explain why triangle ABC is similar to triangle AQR.

b Which angle corresponds to the angle at B?

c Which side of triangle AQR corresponds to side AC of triangle ABC? Your answers to question **5** may help you.

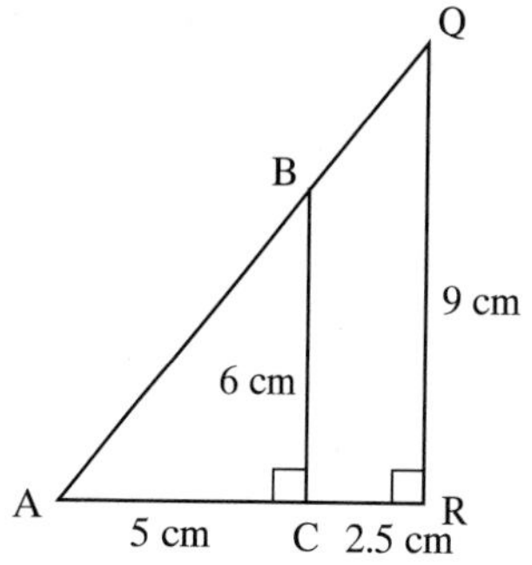

7 In the diagrams **a** to **h** below, find the lengths of the sides as requested. Each pair of shapes are similar but not drawn to scale.

a Find x.

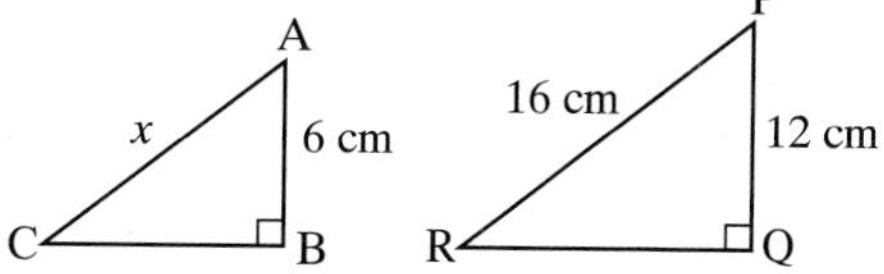

b Find PQ.

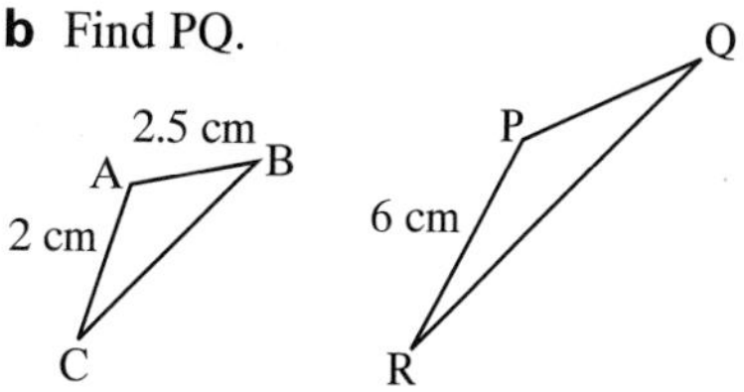

c Find x.

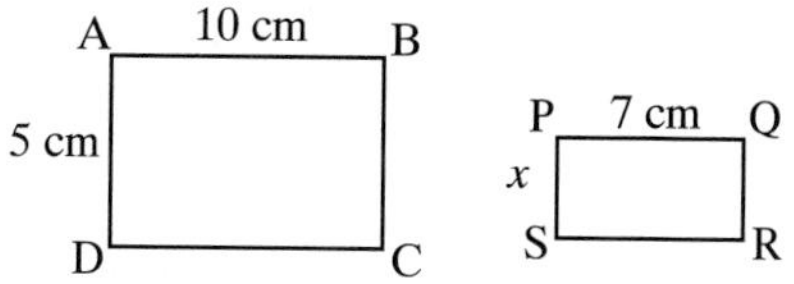

d Find x and y.

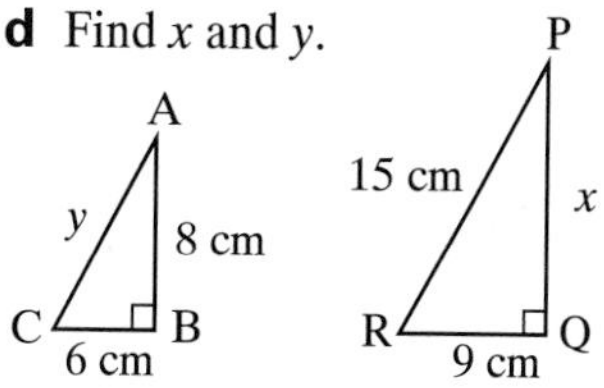

e Find x and y.

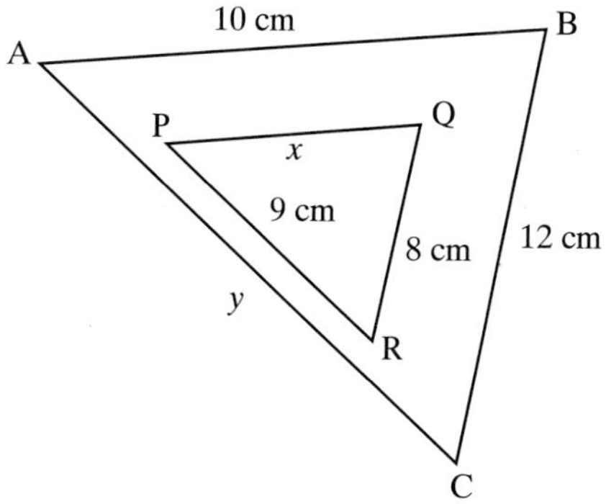

f Find x and y.

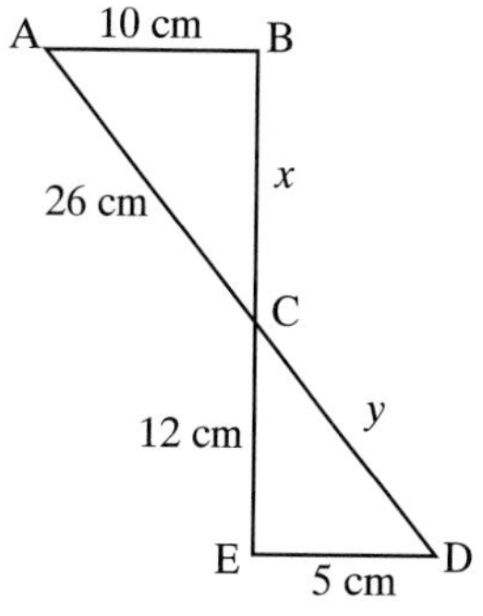

g Find AB and PQ.

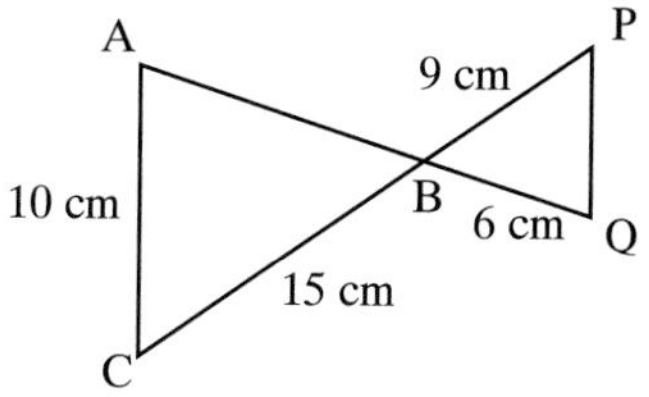

h Find QR.

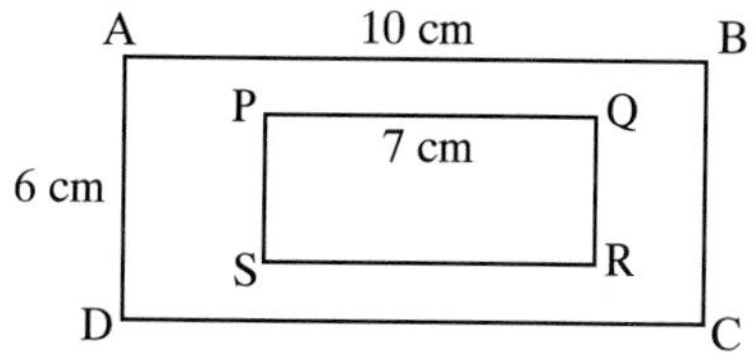

8 **a** Explain why these two triangles are similar.
b What is the ratio of their sides?
c Use Pythagoras's theorem to calculate the side of AC of triangle ABC.
d Write down the length of the side PR of triangle PQR.

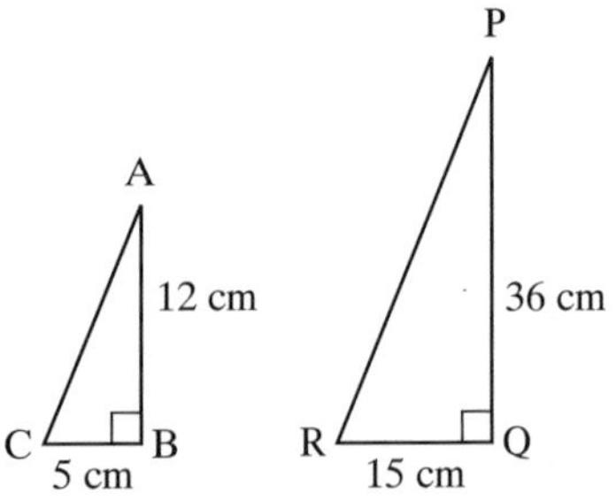

9 A model railway is made to a scale of 1:40. If the model bridge is 12 cm high, how high would a real railway bridge be? Give your answer in metres.

Special cases of similar triangles

Example 1 Find the sides marked x and y in these triangles (not drawn to scale).

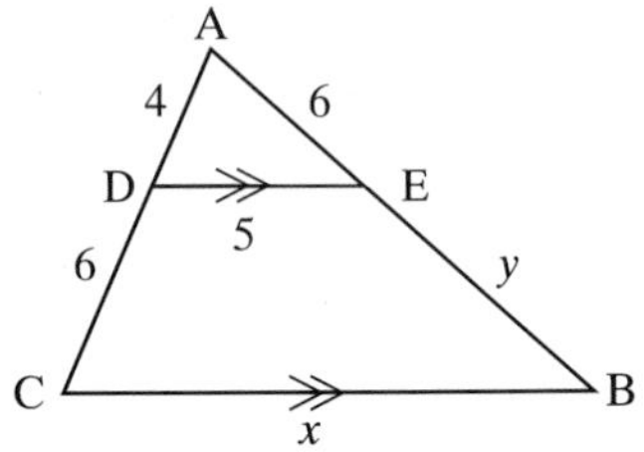

Triangles AED and ABC are similar. So using the corresponding sides CB, DE with AC, AD gives

$$\frac{x}{5} = \frac{10}{4}$$

$$\Rightarrow \quad x = \frac{10 \times 5}{4} = 12.5$$

Using the corresponding sides AE, AB with AD, AC gives

$$\frac{y+6}{6} = \frac{10}{4}$$

$$\Rightarrow y = \frac{6 \times 10}{4} - 6 = 9$$

Example 2 Ahmed wants to work out the height of a tall building. He walks 100 paces from the building and sticks a pole, 6 feet long, vertically into the ground. He then walks another 10 paces on the same line and notices that when he looks from ground level, the top of the pole and the top of the building are in line. How tall is the building?

First, draw a diagram of the situation and label it.

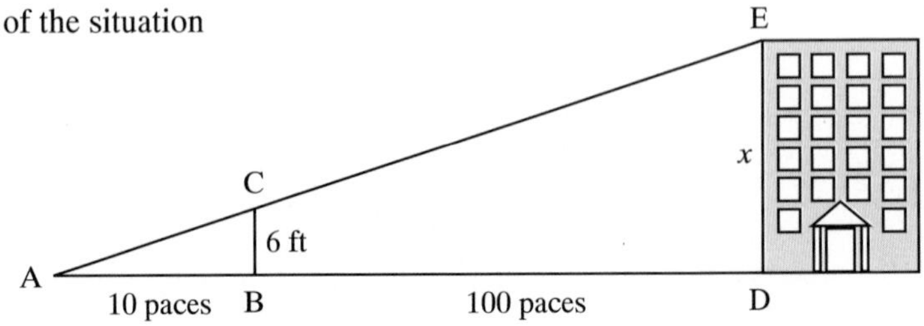

Using corresponding sides ED, CB with AD, AB gives

$$\frac{x}{6} = \frac{110}{10}$$

$$\Rightarrow \quad x = \frac{110 \times 6}{10} = 66$$

Hence the building is 66 feet high.

Exercise 12B

1 In each of the cases below, state a pair of similar triangles and find the length marked x. Separate the similar triangles if it makes it easier for you.

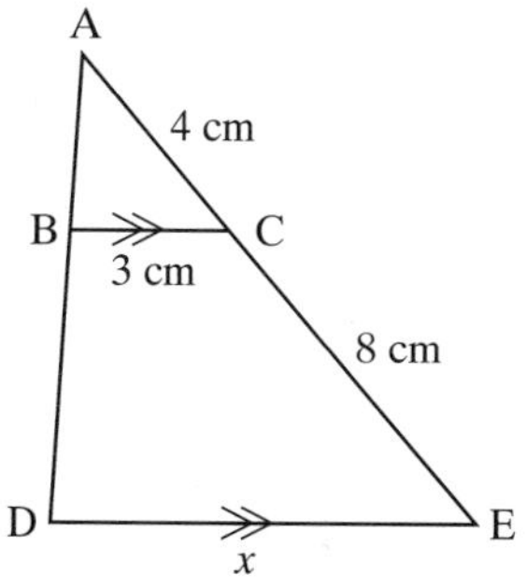

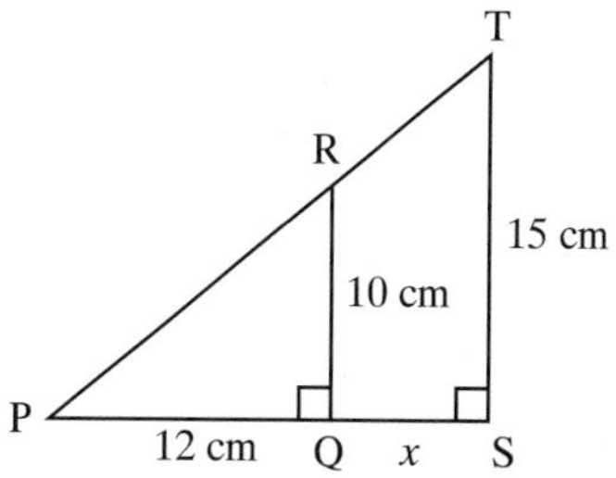

2 In the diagrams **a** to **h** below, find the lengths of the sides as requested.

a Find x.

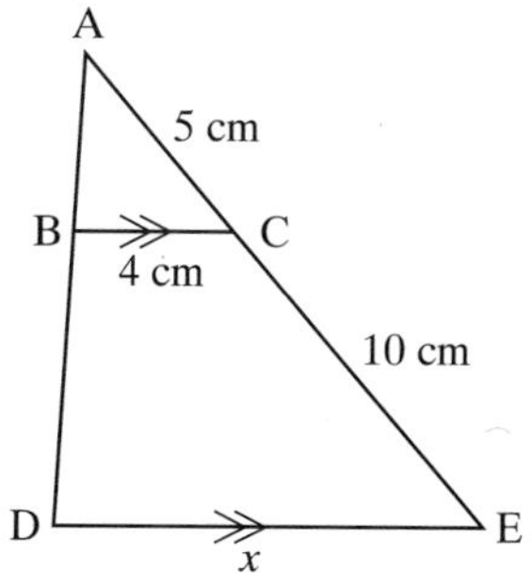

b Find x.

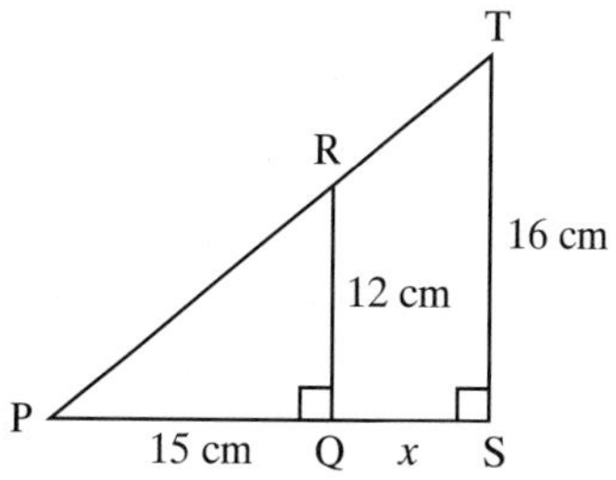

c Find x.

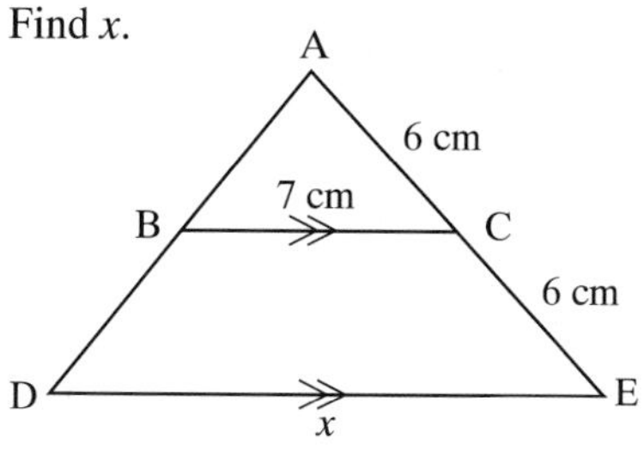

d Find CE.

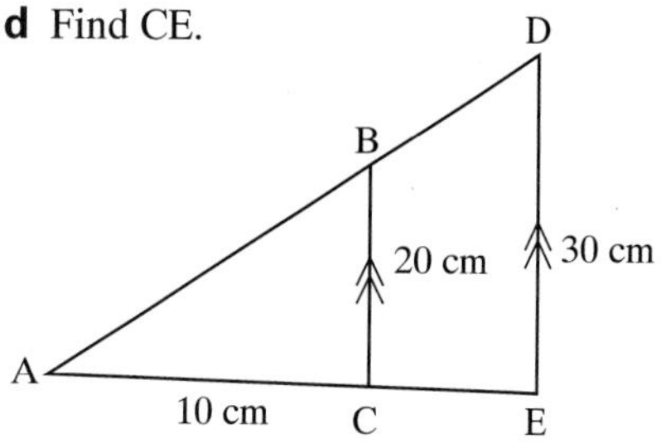

e Find x and y.

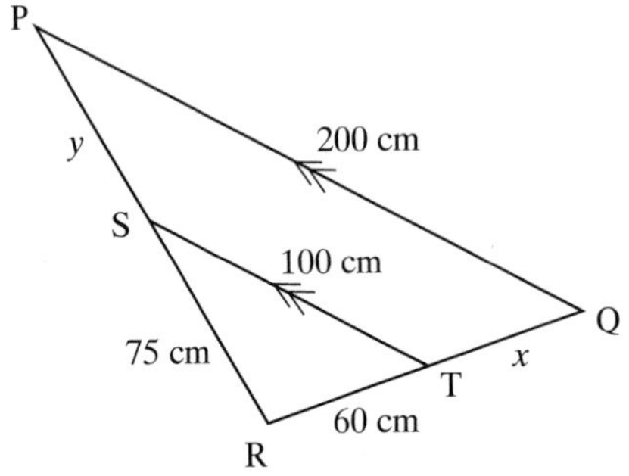

f Find PQ and PS.

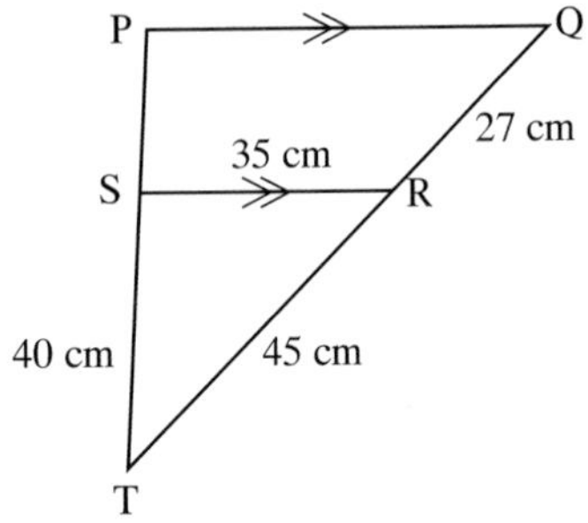

g Find x and y.

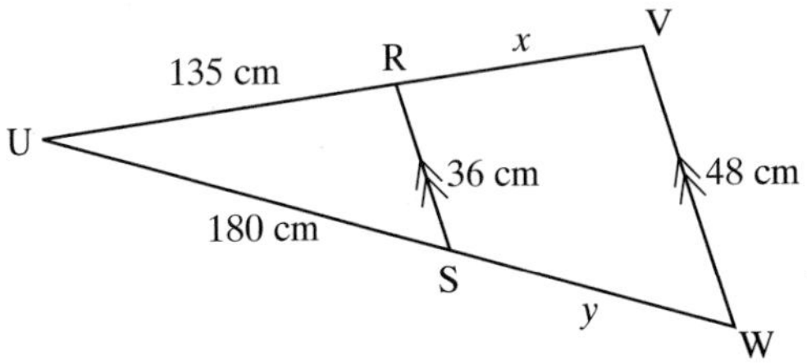

h Find DC and EB.

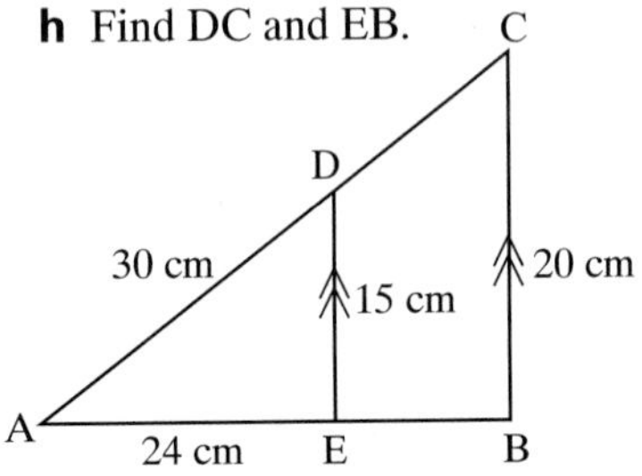

3 This diagram shows a method of working out the height of a tower.

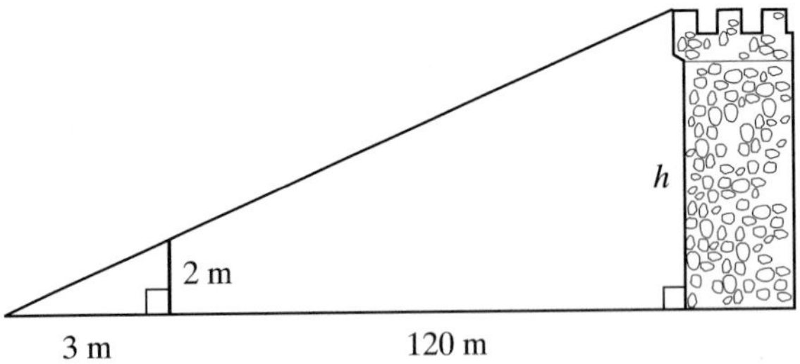

A stick, 2 metres long, is placed vertically 120 metres from the base of a tower so that the top of the tower and the top of the stick is in line with a point on the ground 3 metres from the base of the stick. How high is the tower?

4 It is known that a factory chimney is 330 feet high. Patrick paces out distances as shown in the diagram, so that the top of the chimney and the top of the flag pole are in line with each other. How high is the flag pole?

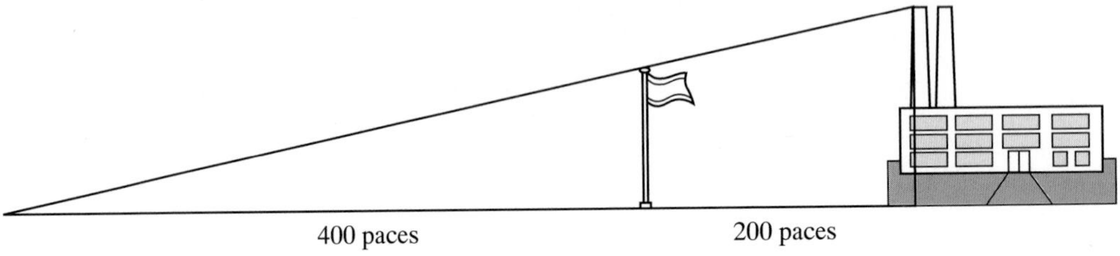

5 The shadow of a tree and the shadow of a golf flag coincide, as shown in the diagram. How high is the tree?

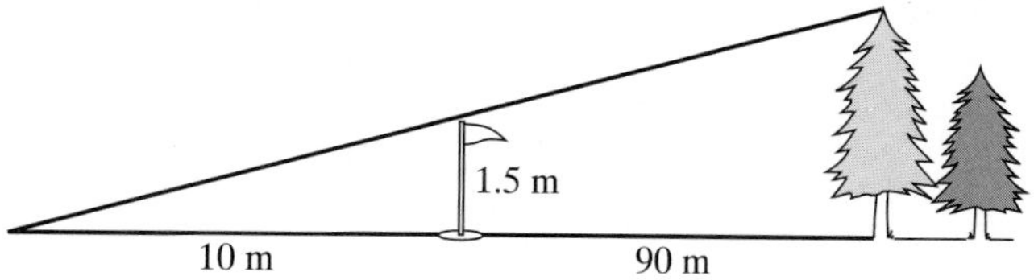

6 Find the lengths DE, FG and HJ.

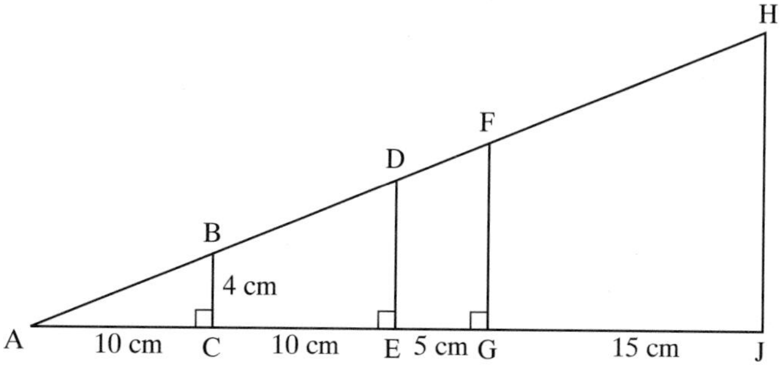

7 Find the height of a pole which casts a shadow of 1.5 metres when at the same time a man of height 165 cm casts a shadow of 80 cm.

8 Andrew, who is about 120 cm tall, notices that when he stands at the bottom of his garden, which is 20 metres away from his house, his dad, who is about 180 cm tall, looks as big as the house when he is about 2.5 metres away. How high is the house?

More complicated problems

The information given in a similar triangle situation can be more complicated than anything you have so far met, and you will need to have good algebraic skills to deal with it. The example on the next page is typical of the more complicated problem you may be asked to solve, so follow it through carefully.

Example Find the value of x in this triangle.

We know that triangle ABC is similar to triangle ADE.

Splitting the triangles up may help us to see what will be awkward (and often missed).

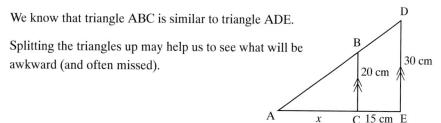

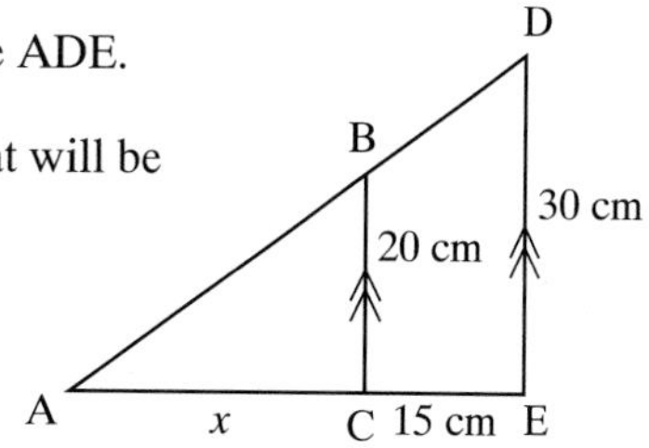

So our equation will be

$$\frac{x + 15}{x} = \frac{30}{20}$$

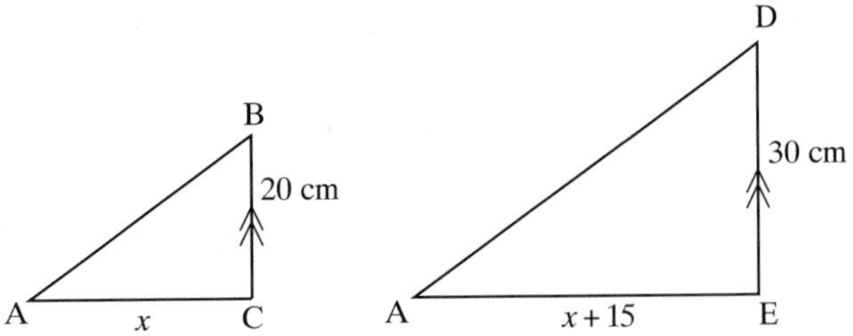

Cross multiplying (moving each of the two bottom terms to the opposite side and multiplying) gives

$$20x + 300 = 30x$$

$$\Rightarrow \quad 300 = 10x \quad \Rightarrow \quad x = 30 \text{ cm}$$

Exercise 12C

Find the lengths x and y in the diagrams **1** to **8**.

1

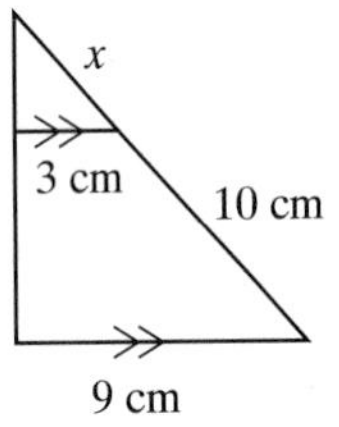

2

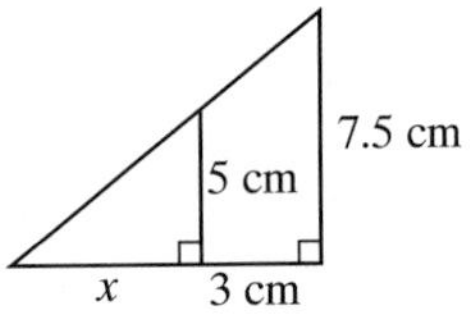

3

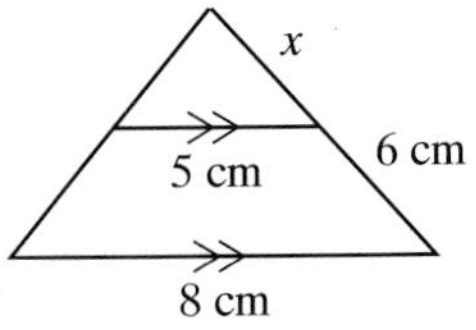

4

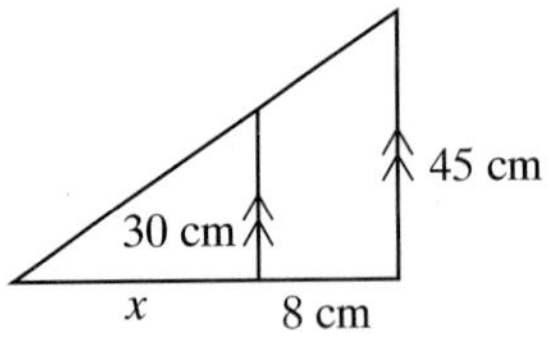

5

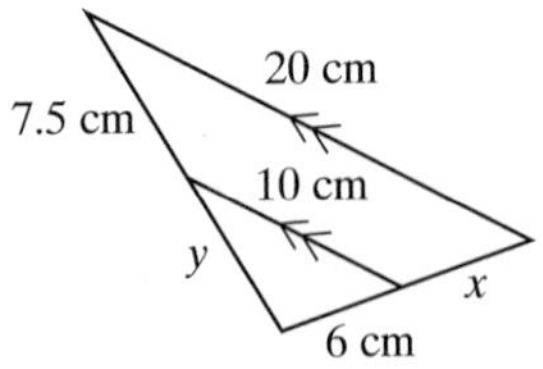

6

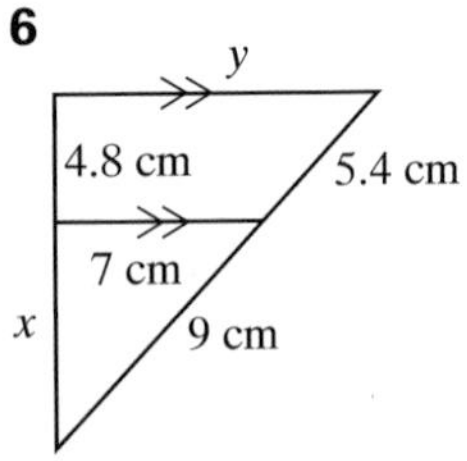

7

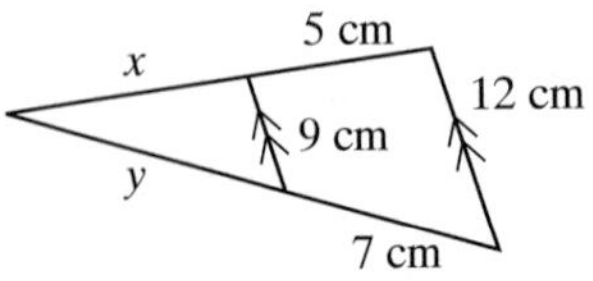

8

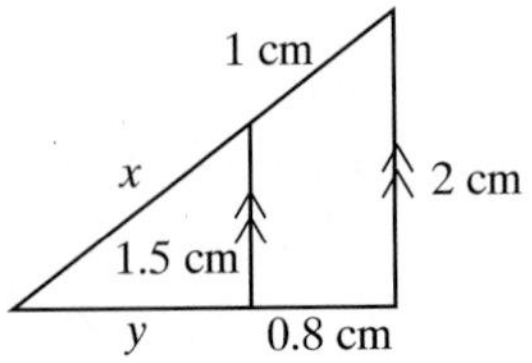

Areas and volumes of similar shapes

There are relationships between the lengths, areas and volumes of similar shapes.

You saw on pages 139–41 that when a plane shape is enlarged by a given scale factor to form a new, similar shape, the corresponding lengths of the original shape and the new shape are all in the same ratio, which is equal to the scale factor. This scale factor of the lengths is called the **length ratio**.

Two similar shapes also have an **area ratio**, which is equal to the ratio of the squares of their corresponding lengths. That is, the **square of the length ratio**.

Likewise, two 3-D shapes are similar if their corresponding lengths are in the same ratio. Their **volume ratio** is equal to the ratio of the cubes of their corresponding lengths. That is, the **cube of the length ratio**.

Generally, the relationship between similar shapes can be expressed as

Length ratio $x : y$
Area ratio $x^2 : y^2$
Volume ratio $x^3 : y^3$

Examples 1 to 3 show you how to use these three ratios.

Example 1 A model yacht is made to a scale of $\frac{1}{20}$ of the size of the real yacht. The area of the sail of the model is 150 cm^2. What is the area of the sail of the real yacht?

At first sight, it may appear that we do not have enough information to solve this problem, but it can be done as follows.

Length ratio = 1 : 20
Area ratio = 1 : 400 (Square of the length ratio)

Area of real sail = 400 × area of model sail
= 400 × 150
= 60 000 cm^2 = 6 m^2

Example 2 A bottle has a base radius of 4 cm, a height of 15 cm and a capacity of 650 cm^3. A similar bottle has a base radius of 3 cm.

a What is the length ratio?

b What is the volume ratio?

c What is the volume of the smaller bottle?

a The length ratio is given by the ratio of the two radii. That is, 4 : 3.

b The volume ratio is therefore $4^3 : 3^3 = 64:27$.

c Let v be the volume of the smaller bottle. Then the volume ratio is

$$\frac{\text{Volume of smaller bottle}}{\text{Volume of larger bottle}} = \frac{v}{650} = \frac{27}{64}$$

$$\Rightarrow \quad v = \frac{27 \times 650}{64} = 274 \text{ cm}^3 \quad (3 \text{ sf})$$

Example 3 The cost of a paint can, height 20 cm, is £2.00 and its label has an area of 24 cm^2.

a What is the cost of a similar can, 30 cm high?

b Assuming the labels are similar, what will be the area of the label on the larger can?

a The cost of the paint is proportional to the volume of the can.

Length ratio $= 20 : 30 = 2 : 3$

Volume ratio $= 2^3 : 3^3 = 8 : 27$

Let P be the cost of the larger can. Then the cost ratio is

$$\frac{\text{Cost of larger can}}{\text{Cost of smaller can}} = \frac{P}{2}$$

Therefore,

$$\frac{P}{2} = \frac{27}{8}$$

$$\Rightarrow \quad P = \frac{27 \times 2}{8} = £6.75$$

b Area ratio $= 2^2 : 3^2 = 4 : 9$

Let A be the area of the larger label. Then the area ratio is

$$\frac{\text{Larger label area}}{\text{Smaller label area}} = \frac{A}{24}$$

Therefore,

$$\frac{A}{24} = \frac{9}{4}$$

$$\Rightarrow \quad A = \frac{9 \times 24}{4} = 54 \text{ cm}^2$$

Exercise 12D

1 The length ratio between two similar solids is 2:5.

a What is the area ratio between the solids?

b What is the volume ratio between the solids?

2 The length ratio between two similar solids is 4:7.

a What is the area ratio between the solids?

b What is the volume ratio between the solids?

3 Copy and complete this table.

Linear scale factor	Linear ratio	Linear fraction	Area scale factor	Volume scale factor
2	1 : 2	$\frac{2}{1}$		
3				
$\frac{1}{4}$	4 : 1	$\frac{1}{4}$		$\frac{1}{64}$
			25	
				$\frac{1}{1000}$
	1 : 7			
	5 : 1			
			$\frac{1}{4}$	

4 Some years ago, a famous beer advertisement showed a bar attendant taking an ordinary pint glass and filling it with beer underneath the counter. When the glass reappeared, it was full of beer and its width and height were twice those of the original glass. The slogan on the advertisement was 'The pint that thinks it's a quart'. (A quart is 2 pints.)

a What was the length ratio of the two glasses used in the advertisement?

b What was the volume ratio of the two glasses?

c The smaller glass held a pint. How much would the larger glass have held?

d Is the advertisement fair?

5 A shape has an area of 15 cm^2. What is the area of a similar shape whose lengths are three times the corresponding lengths of the first shape.

6 A toy brick has a surface area of 14 cm^2. What would be the surface area of a similar toy brick whose lengths are

a twice the corresponding lengths of the first brick

b three times the corresponding lengths of the first brick?

7 A sheepskin rug covers 12 ft^2 of floor. What area would be covered by a rug whose lengths are

a twice the corresponding lengths of the first rug

b half the corresponding lengths of the first rug?

8 A brick has a volume of 300 cm^3. What would be the volume of a similar brick whose lengths are

a twice the corresponding lengths of the first brick

b three times the corresponding lengths of the first brick?

9 Thirty cubic centimetres of clay were used to make a model sheep. What volume of clay would be needed to make a similar model sheep whose lengths are

a five times the corresponding lengths of the first model

b one half of the corresponding lengths of the first model?

10 A can of paint, 6 cm high, holds a half a litre of paint. How much paint would go into a similar can which is 12 cm high?

11 It takes 1 litre of paint to fill a can of height 10 cm. How much paint does it take to fill a similar can of height 45 cm?

12 It takes 1.5 litres of paint to fill a can of height 12 cm.

a How much paint does it take to fill a similar can whose dimensions are $1\frac{1}{2}$ times the corresponding dimensions of the first can?

b Which of the information given is not needed to be able to answer part **a**?

13 To make a certain dress, it took 2.4 m^2 of material. How much material would a similar dress need if its lengths were

a 1.5 times the corresponding lengths of the first dress

b three quarters of the corresponding lengths of the first dress?

14 A model statue is 10 cm high and has a volume of 100 cm^3. The real statue is 2.4 m high. What is the volume of the real statue? Give your answer in m^3.

15 A small can of paint costs 75p. What is the cost of a larger similar can whose circumference is twice that of the smaller can? Assume that the cost is based only on the volume of paint in the can.

16 A triangle has sides of 3, 4 and 5 cm. Its area is 6 cm^2. How long are the sides of a similar triangle that has an area of 24 cm^2?

17 A ball with a radius of r cm has a volume of 10 cm^3. What is the radius of a ball with a volume of 270 cm^3?

18 Calculate the area of each of the shaded faces and hence calculate the volume of each of these solids. (They are not drawn to scale.)

a

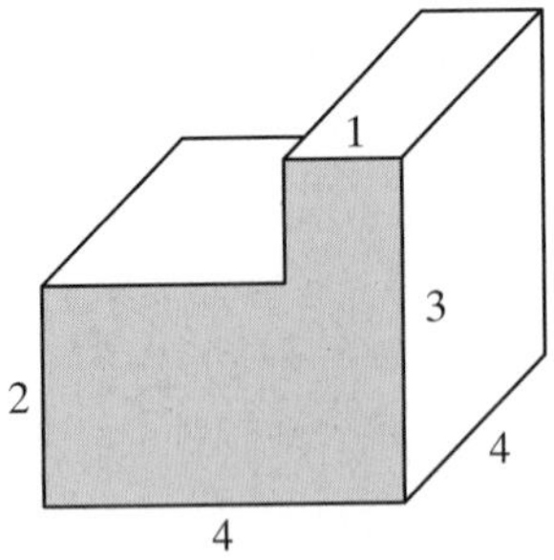

b

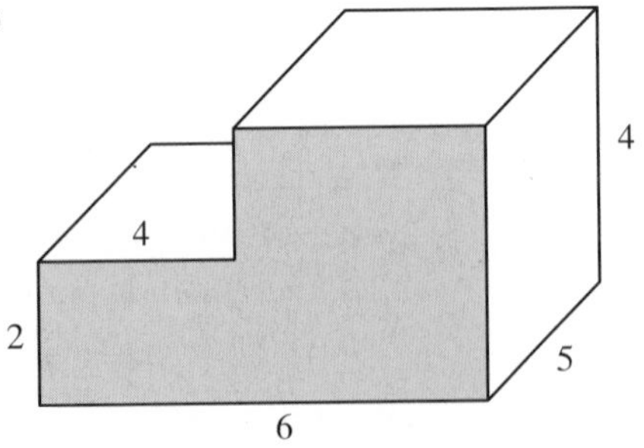

c

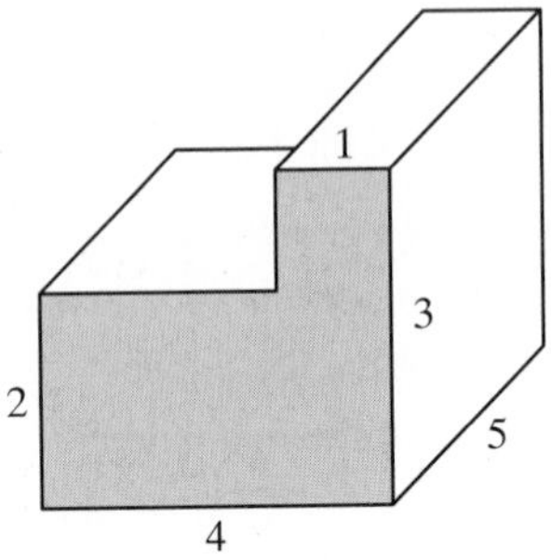

d

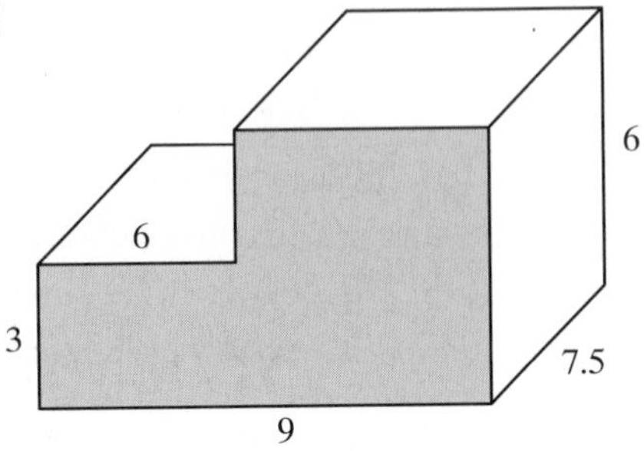

e Which two solids are similar?

Using area and volume ratios

In some problems involving similar shapes, the length ratio is not given, so we have to start with the area ratio or the volume ratio. We usually then need first to find the length ratio in order to proceed with the solution. Follow through Examples 1 to 3 to see how this is done.

Example 1 A manufacturer makes a range of clown hats that are all similar in shape. The smallest hat is 8 cm tall and uses 180 cm^2 of card. What will be the height of a hat made from 300 cm^2 of card?

The area ratio is 180 : 300.
Therefore, the length ratio is $\sqrt{180} : \sqrt{300}$. (Do not calculate these yet.)

Let the height of the larger hat be H, then

$$\frac{H}{8} = \frac{\sqrt{300}}{\sqrt{180}} = \sqrt{\frac{300}{180}}$$

$$\Rightarrow \quad H = 8 \times \sqrt{\frac{300}{180}} = 10.3 \text{ cm} \quad (1 \text{ dp})$$

Example 2 A supermarket stocks similar small and large cans of soup. The areas of their labels are 110 cm^2 and 190 cm^2 respectively. The weight of a small can is 450 g. What will be the weight of a large can?

The area ratio is 110 : 190.
Therefore, the length ratio is $\sqrt{110} : \sqrt{190}$. (Do not calculate these yet.)
So the weight ratio is $(\sqrt{110})^3 : (\sqrt{190})^3$.

Let the weight of a large can be W, then

$$\frac{W}{450} = \frac{(\sqrt{190})^3}{(\sqrt{110})^3} = \left(\sqrt{\frac{900}{110}}\right)^3$$

$$\Rightarrow \quad W = 450 \times \left(\sqrt{\frac{900}{110}}\right)^3 = 1020 \text{ g} \quad (3 \text{ sf})$$

Example 3 Two similar cans hold respectively 1.5 litres and 2.5 litres of paint. The area of the label on the smaller can is 85 cm^2. What is the area of the label on the larger can?

The volume ratio is 1.5 : 2.5.
Therefore, the length ratio is $\sqrt[3]{1.5} : \sqrt[3]{2.5}$. (Do not calculate these yet.)
So the area ratio is $(\sqrt[3]{1.5})^2 : (\sqrt[3]{2.5})^2$.

Let the area of the label on the larger can be A, then

$$\frac{A}{85} = \frac{(\sqrt[3]{2.5})^2}{(\sqrt[3]{1.5})^2} = \left(\sqrt[3]{\frac{2.5}{1.5}}\right)^2$$

$$\Rightarrow \quad A = 85 \times \left(\sqrt[3]{\frac{2.5}{1.5}}\right)^2 = 119 \text{ cm}^2 \quad (3 \text{ sf})$$

Exercise 12E

1 A firm produces three sizes of similarly shaped labels for its products. Their areas are 150 cm^2, 250 cm^2 and 400 cm^2. The 250 cm^2 label just fits around a can of height 8 cm. Find the heights of similar cans around which the other two labels would just fit.

2 A firm makes similar gift boxes in three different sizes: small, medium and large. The areas of their lids are

small 30 cm^2 medium 50 cm^2 large 75 cm^2

The medium box is 5.5 cm high. Find the heights of the other two sizes.

3 A cone, height 8 cm, can be made from a piece of card with an area of 140 cm^2. What is the height of a similar cone made from a similar piece of card with an area of 200 cm^2?

4 It takes 5.6 litres of paint to paint a chimney which is 3 m high. What is the tallest similar chimney that can be painted with 8 litres of paint?

5 A man takes 45 minutes to mow a lawn 25 m long. How long would it take him to mow a similar lawn only 15 m long?

6 A piece of card, 1200 cm^2 in area, will make a tube 13 cm long. What is the length of a similar tube made from a similar piece of card with an area of 500 cm^2?

7 All television screens are similar. If a screen of area 220 cm^2 has a diagonal length of 21 cm, what will be the diagonal length of a screen of area 350 cm^2?

8 Two similar statues, made from the same bronze, are placed in a school. One weighs 300 g, the other weighs 2 kg. The height of the smaller statue is 9 cm. What is the height of the larger statue?

9 A supermarket sells similar cans of pasta rings in three different sizes: small, medium and large. The sizes of the labels around the cans are

small can 24 cm^2 medium can 46 cm^2 large can 78 cm^2

The medium size can is 6 cm tall with a weight of 380 g. Calculate

a the heights of the other two sizes

b the weights of the other two sizes.

10 Two similar bottles are 20 cm and 14 cm high. The smaller bottle holds 850 ml. Find the capacity of the larger one.

11 A statue weighs 840 kg. A similar statue was made out of the same material but two fifths the height of the first one. What was the weight of the smaller statue?

12 A model stands on a base of area 12 cm^2. A smaller but similar model, made of the same material, stands on a base of area 7.5 cm^2. Calculate the weight of the smaller model if the larger one is 3.5 kg.

13 The areas of the bases of two similar jugs are in the ratio 5 : 8.

a Find the ratio of the heights of the jugs.

b What is the capacity of the smaller jug if the capacity of the larger one is 2 litres?

14 A solid silver statue was melted down to make 100 000 similar miniatures, each 2 cm high. How tall was the original statue?

15 Two similar models have volumes 12 m^3 and 30 m^3. If the surface area of one of them is 2.4 m^2, what are the possible surface areas of the other model?

Possible coursework tasks

Similar co-ordinates

Triangle ABC is similar to triangle A′B′C′.

Investigate the relationship between the co-ordinates of any two similar triangles.

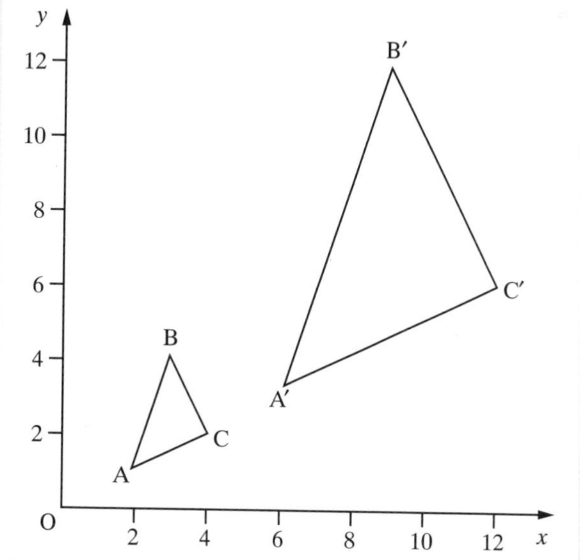

Growing cubes

Find a relationship between the total surface area of a cube and its volume.

Investigate for other shapes.

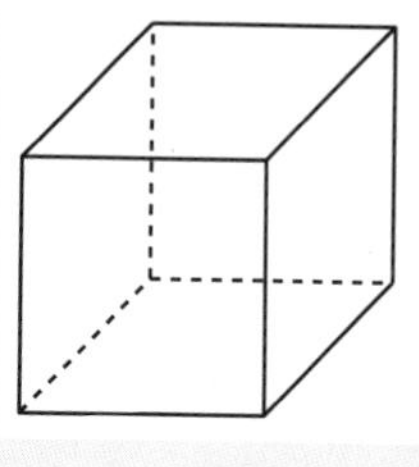

Golden rectangles

The square ABEF is removed from the rectangle ACDF.
If the remaining rectangle BCDE is similar to the original rectangle ACDF, then the rectangles are called Golden Rectangles.

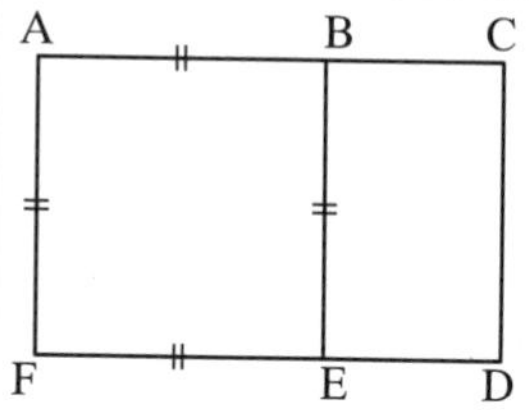

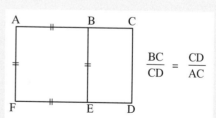

$$\frac{BC}{CD} = \frac{CD}{AC}$$

Investigate Golden Rectangles.

Examination questions

1 A school badge is made in two sizes.
The width of the small size is 3 cm. The large size is an enlargement of the small size in the ratio 2:3. Calculate the width of the large size badge.

SEG, Question 3, Paper 4, June 1994

2 Calculate the length OY.

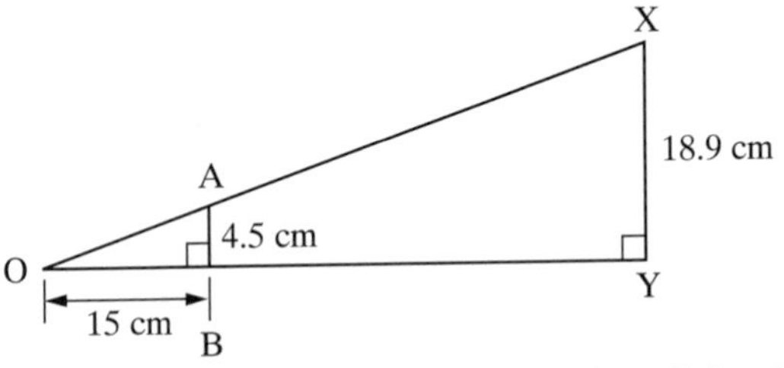

ULEAC, Question 27, Paper 7, June 1994

3 I stood 420 m away from the OUB Centre, the tallest building in Singapore. I held a piece of wood 40 cm long at arm's length, 60 cm away from my eye. The piece of wood, held vertically, just blocked the building from my view. Use similar triangles to calculate the height, h metres, of the building

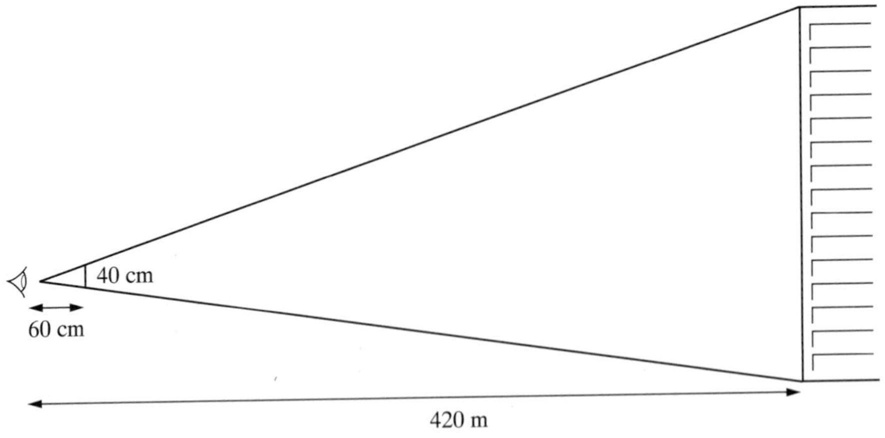

NEAB, Question 20, Paper 1, June 1995

4 The model of a cross-section of a roof is illustrated below.
BC = 6 cm, CE = 3 cm and CD = 9 cm.
Triangles ABE and DCE are similar triangles with angle
BAE = angle CDE. Calculate the length of AB.

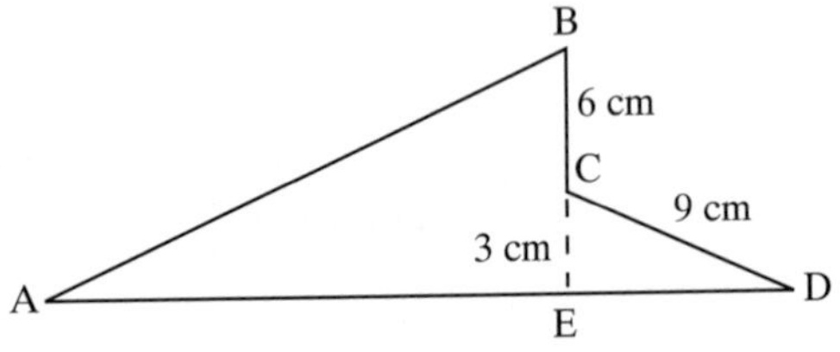

SEG, Question 10, Specimen Paper 14, 1998

5 The diagram shows two vertical lines, AB and CD, of lengths 4 cm and 12 cm. BFD is a horizontal line. E is the intersection of AD and BC.

a **i** Write down a triangle that is similar to triangle BEF.

ii Use these similar triangles to calculate the height marked *h*.

b CD is gradually moved closer to AB. Describe what happens to the height *h*.

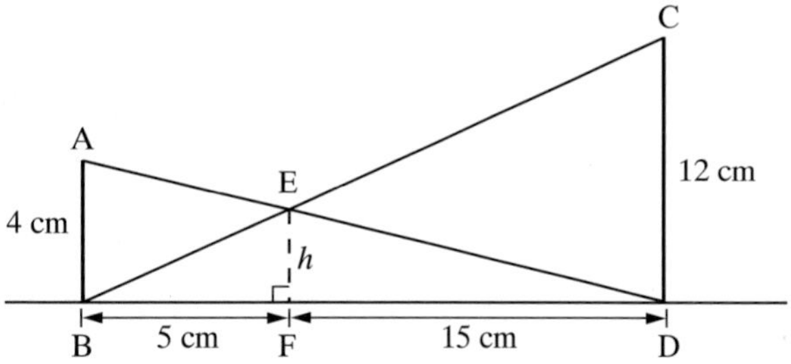

NEAB, Question 16, Paper 1, June 1994

6 In the diagram CD = 4 metres, CE = 3 metres and BC = 5 metres. AB is parallel to DE. ACE and BCD are straight lines.

a Explain why triangle ABC is similar to triangle EDC.

b Calculate the length of AC.

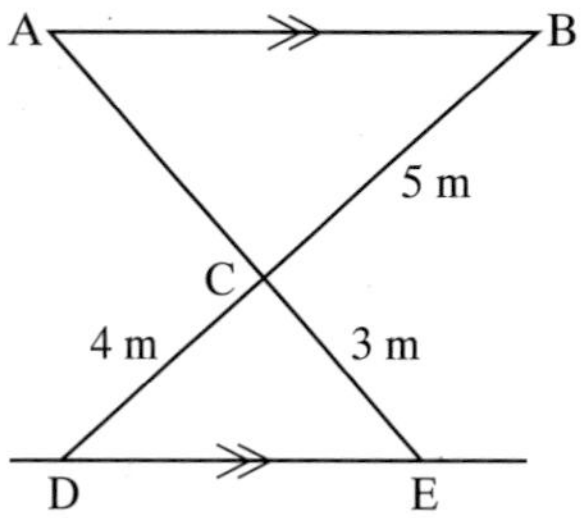

ULEAC, Question 23, Paper 4, June 1995

7 Find the height of a tree which casts a shadow of 1.2 metres, when at the same moment in the same place a woman of height 140 cm casts a shadow of 60 cm.

8 **a** State which two triangles are similar.

b Calculate the lengths of

i x **ii** y

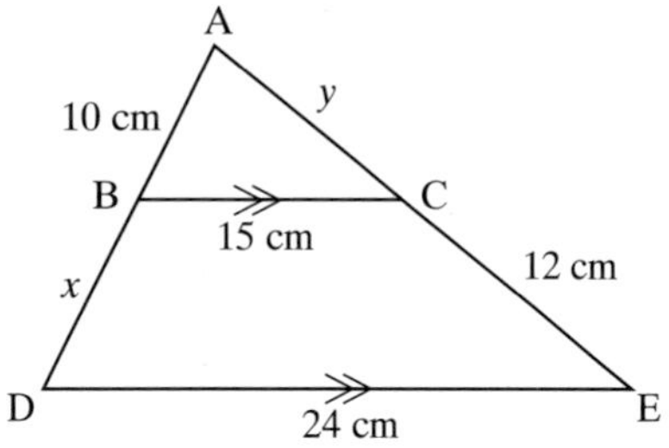

NEAB, Question 8, Specimen Paper 2H, 1998

9 The shape of a plastic medicine dispenser is a section of a cone, as shown on the right. The upper and lower radii of the section, CD and BE, are 2.7 cm and 1.2 cm respectively. The centre of the base of the section, C, is 3.6 cm above the vertex of the cone, A. Calculate the capacity of the medicine dispenser.

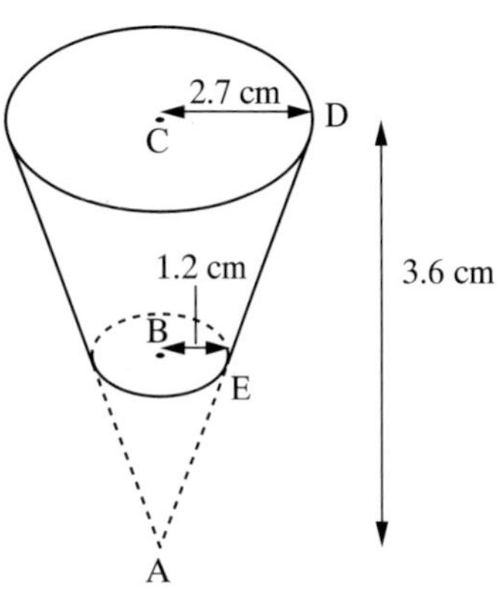

WJEC, Question 10, Specimen Paper 2, 1998

10 The ratio of the height of P to the height of Q is 3 : 2. The volume of P is 5.4 cm^3. Calculate the volume of Q.

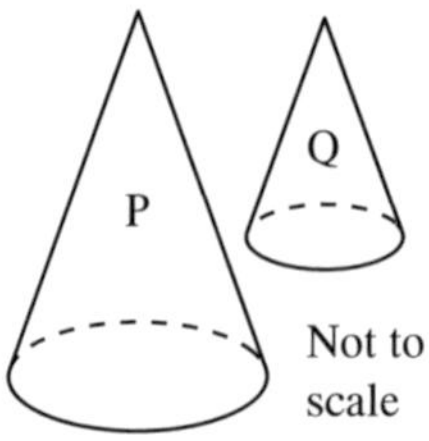

SEG, Question 7b, Specimen Paper 15, 1998

Summary

How well do you grade yourself?

To gain a grade **C**, you need to know why two shapes are similar. You need also to be able to work out unknown sides using ratios, and be able to solve simple problems using length scale factors between two similar shapes.

To gain a grade **B**, you need to be able to work out the unknown side in one of two similar shapes, using an equation.

To gain a grade **A**, you need to be able to evaluate problems using area and volume ratios in similar shapes.

What you should know after you have worked through Chapter 12

- How to find the ratios between two similar shapes.
- How to work out unknown lengths, areas and volumes of similar 3-D shapes.
- How to solve practical problems using similar shapes.
- How to solve problems involving area and volume ratios.

13 Trigonometry

This chapter is going to ... show you how to use trigonometry in more complicated 2-D situations, and also in simple 3-D situations. You will see the connection between Pythagoras's theorem and trigonometry in triangles with special angles, and its application to problems. You will then be introduced to the sine and cosine rules which are used to solve triangles that do not have a right angle.

What you should already know

- How to think in three dimensions.
- How to calculate the angles and sides of a right-angled triangle.
- How to make an isosceles triangle into two right-angled triangles in solving problems trigonometrically.
- When using trigonometric functions, your calculator should be in degree mode.

Some 2-D problems

Example 1 In triangle ABC, AB = 6 cm, BC = 9 cm and angle ABC = 52°. Calculate

a the length of the perpendicular from A to BC

b the area of the triangle.

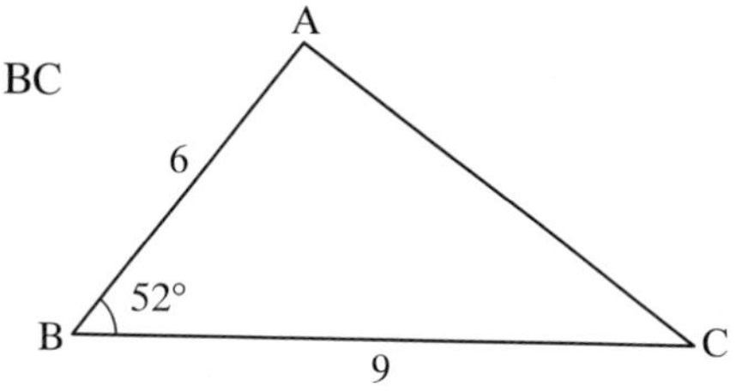

a Drop the perpendicular from A to BC to form the right-angled triangle ADB.

Let h be the length of the perpendicular AD. Then

$$h = 6 \sin 52° = 4.73 \quad \text{(3 sf)}$$

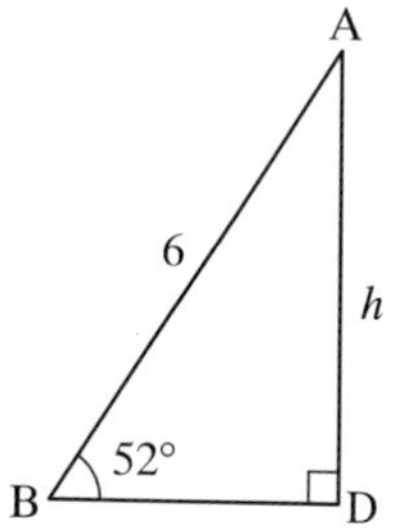

b The area of triangle ADB is given by

$$\text{Area} = \tfrac{1}{2} \times \text{Base} \times \text{Height}$$
$$= \tfrac{1}{2} \times 9 \times h = 21.3 \text{ cm}^2 \quad \text{(3 sf)}$$

Example 2 SR is a diameter of a circle whose radius is 25 cm. PQ is a chord at right angles to SR. X is the mid-point of PQ. The length of XR is 1 cm. Calculate the length of the arc PQ.

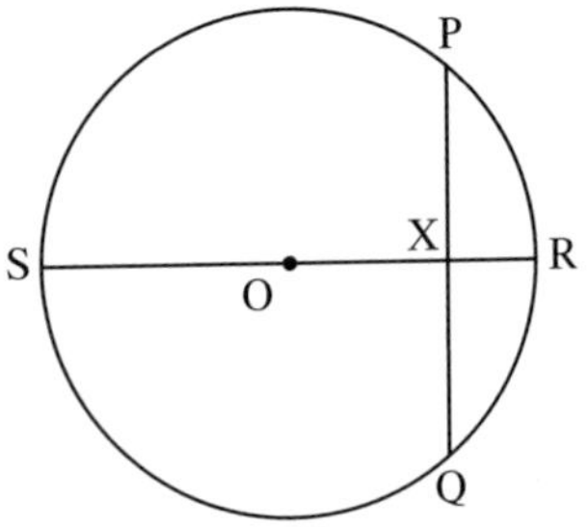

To find the length of the arc PQ, we need first to find the angle it subtends at the centre of the circle. (See page 26.)

So we join P to the centre of the circle O to obtain the angle POX, which is equal to half the angle subtended by PQ at O.

In right-angled triangle POX,

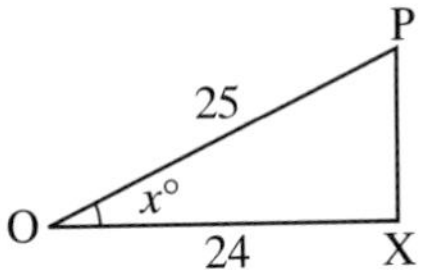

$$OX = OR - XR$$
$$= 25 - 1 = 24$$

Therefore,

$$\cos x = \frac{24}{25}$$

$$\Rightarrow \quad x = \cos^{-1} 0.96 = 16.26°$$

So, the angle subtended at the centre by the arc PQ is $2 \times 16.26° = 32.52°$, giving the length of the arc PQ as

$$\frac{32.52}{360} \times 2 \times \pi \times 25 = 14.2 \text{ cm} \quad (3 \text{ sf})$$

Exercise 13A

1 AC and BC are tangents to a circle of radius 7 cm. Calculate the length of AB.

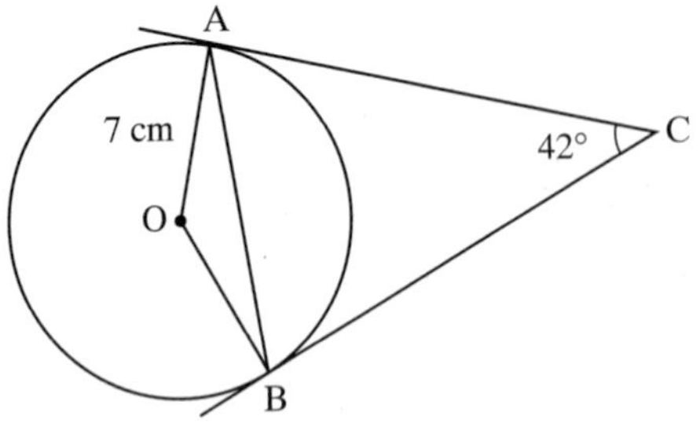

2 CD, length 20 cm, is a diameter of a circle. AB, length 12 cm, is a chord at right angles to DC. Calculate the angle AOB.

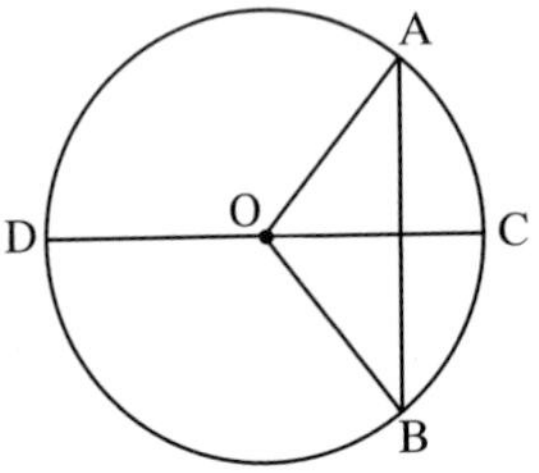

3 Calculate the length of AB.

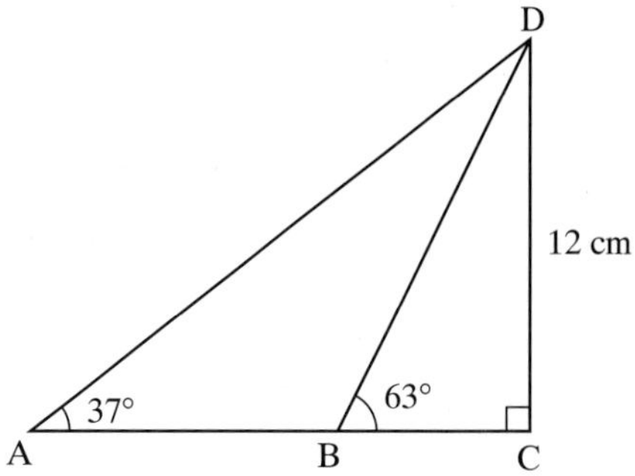

4 A building has a ledge halfway up, as shown in the diagram. Alf measures the length AB as 100 m, the angle CAB as 31° and the angle EAB as 42°. Use this information to calculate the width of the ledge CD.

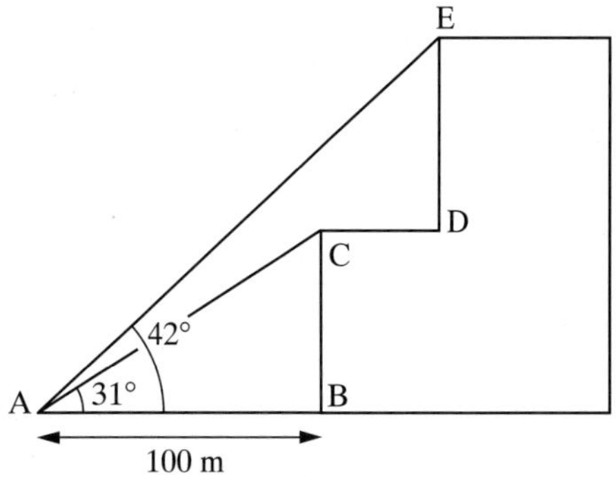

5 AB and CD are two equal, perpendicular chords of a circle that intersect at X. The circle is of radius 6 cm and the angle COA is 113°. Calculate

a the length AC

b the length XB [**Hint:** AX = XC]

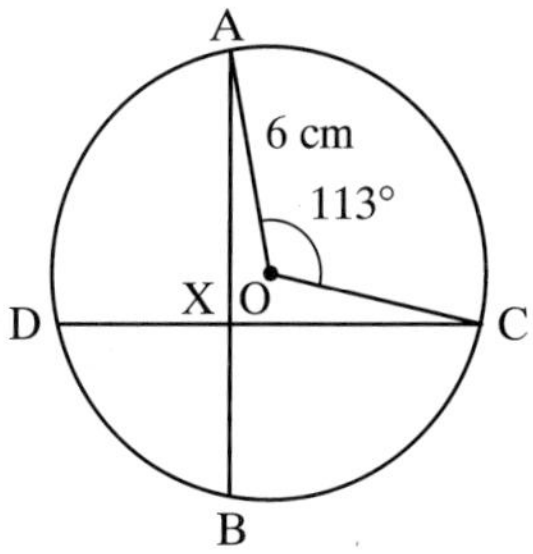

6 A vertical flagpole PQ is held by a wooden framework framework, as shown in the diagram. The framework is in the same vertical plane. Angle SRP = 25°, SQ = 6 m and PR = 4 m. Calculate the size of the angle QRP.

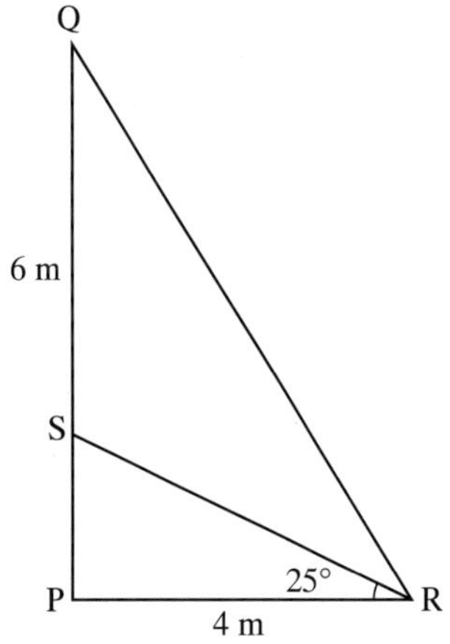

Some 3-D problems

Solving a problem set in three dimensions nearly always involves identifying a right-angled triangle that contains the length or angle required. This triangle will have to contain (apart from the right angle) two known measures from which the required calculation can be made.

It is essential to extract from its 3-D situation the triangle you are going to use and redraw it as a separate, plane, right-angled triangle. (It is rarely the case that the required triangle appears as a true right-angled triangle in its 3-D representation. Even if it does, it should still be redrawn as a separate figure.)

The redrawn triangle should be annotated with the known quantities and the unknown quantity to be found.

Follow through Examples 1 and 2 to see how the procedure works.

Example 1 The diagram shows a cuboid 22.5 cm by 40 cm by 30 cm. M is the mid-point of FG. Calculate

a angle ABE
b angle ECA
c angle EMH

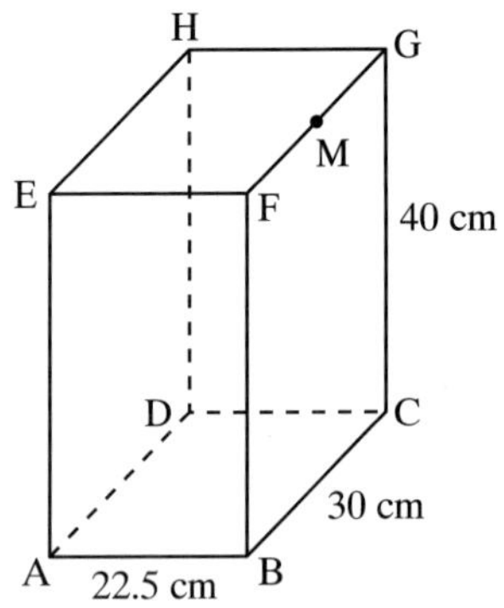

a The right-angled triangle containing the angle required is ABE.

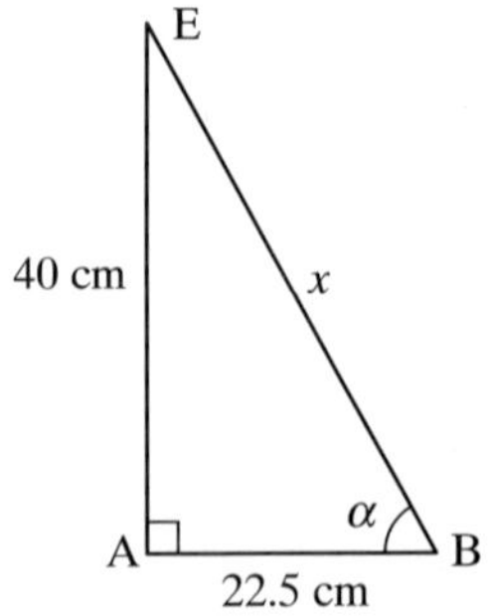

Solving for α gives

$$\tan \alpha = \frac{40}{22.5} = 1.7777$$

$$\Rightarrow \quad \alpha = \tan^{-1} 1.7777 = 60.6° \quad (3 \text{ sf})$$

b The right-angled triangle containing the angle required is ACE, but for which only AE is known. Therefore, we need to find AC by applying Pythagoras to the right-angled triangle ABC.

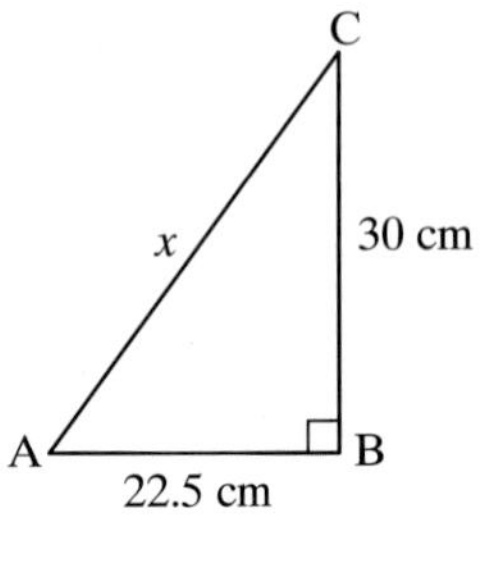

$$x^2 = (22.5)^2 + (30)^2$$

$$\Rightarrow \quad x = 37.5$$

Returning to triangle ACE, we obtain

$$\tan \beta = \frac{40}{37.5} = 1.0666$$

$$\Rightarrow \quad \beta = 46.8° \quad \text{(3 sf)}$$

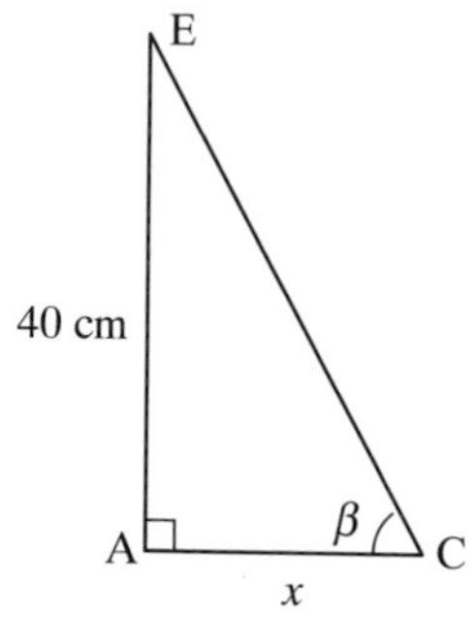

c EMH is an isosceles triangle.

Drop the perpendicular from M to N, the mid-point of HE, to form two right-angled triangles. Angle HMN equals angle EMN, and HN = NE = 15 cm.

Taking triangle MEN, we obtain

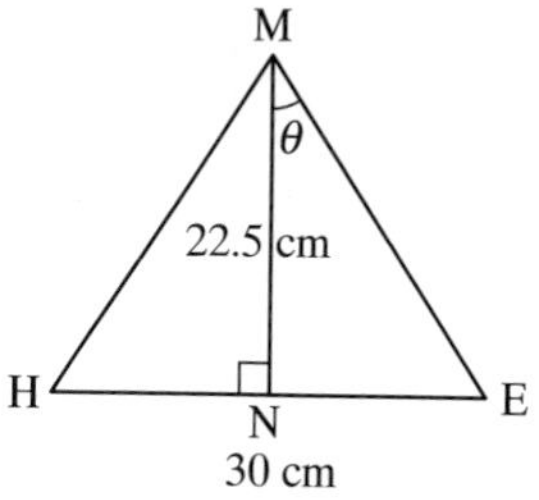

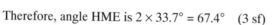

$$\tan \theta = \frac{15}{22.5} = 0.666\,66$$

$$\Rightarrow \quad \theta = \tan^{-1} 0.666\,66 = 33.7°$$

Therefore, angle HME is $2 \times 33.7° = 67.4°$ (3 sf)

Example 2 A, B and C are three points at ground level. They are in the same horizontal plane. C is 50 km east of B. B is north of A. C is on a bearing of 050° from A.

An aircraft, flying in an easterly direction, passes over B and over C at the same height. When it passes over B, the angle of elevation from A is 12°. Find the angle of elevation of the aircraft from A when it is over C.

First, draw a diagram containing all the known information.

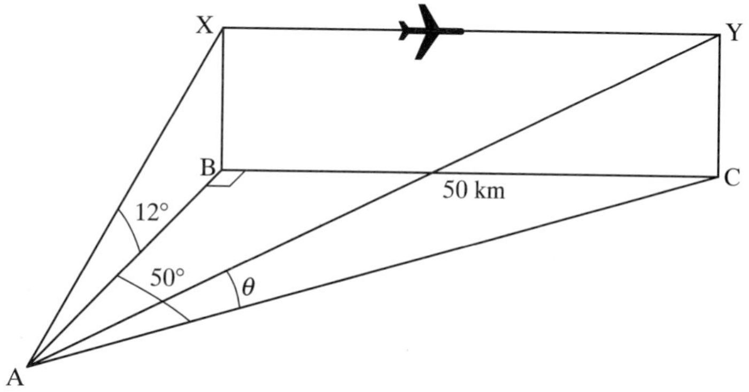

Next, use the right-angled triangle ABC to calculate AB and AC.

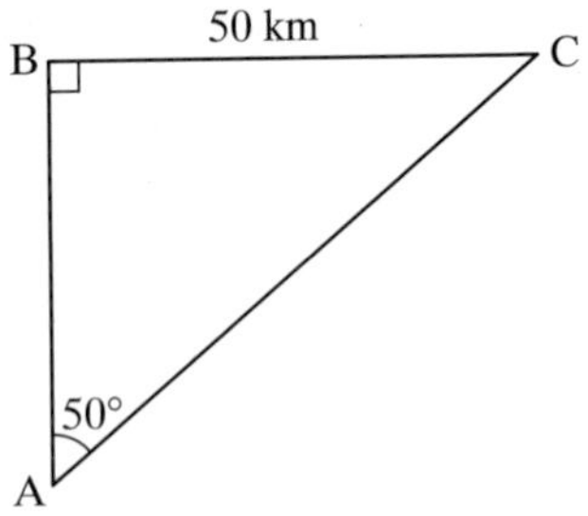

$$AB = \frac{50}{\tan 50°} = 41.95 \text{ km} \quad (2 \text{ dp})$$

$$AC = \frac{50}{\sin 50°} = 65.27 \text{ km} \quad (2 \text{ dp})$$

Then use the right-angled triangle ABX to calculate BX.

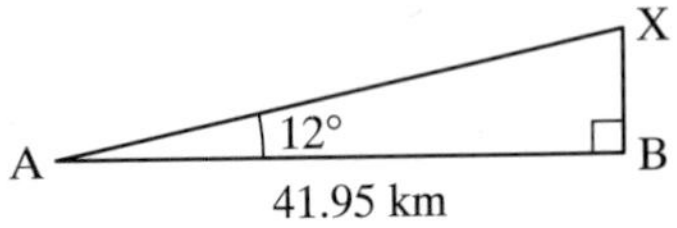

$$BX = 41.95 \tan 12° = 8.92 \text{ km} \quad (2 \text{ dp})$$

Finally, use the right-angled triangle ACY to calculate the required angle of elevation, θ.

$$\tan \theta = \frac{8.92}{65.27} = 0.1367$$

$$\Rightarrow \quad \theta = \tan^{-1} 0.1367 = 7.8° \quad (2 \text{ sf})$$

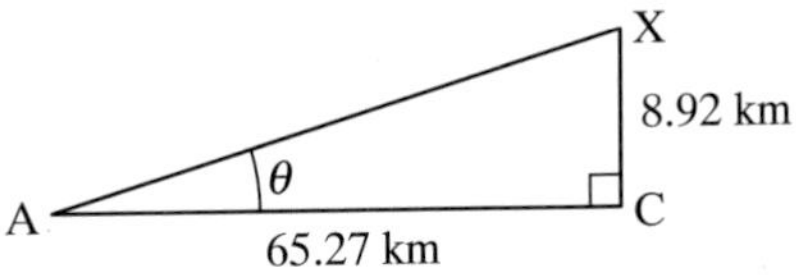

Exercise 13B

1 The diagram shows a pyramid. The base is a horizontal rectangle ABCD, 20 cm by 15 cm. The length of each sloping edge is 24 cm. The apex, V, is over the centre of the rectangular base. Calculate

a the size of the angle VAC

b the height of the pyramid

c the volume of the pyramid

d the size of the angle between the face VAD and the base ABCD.

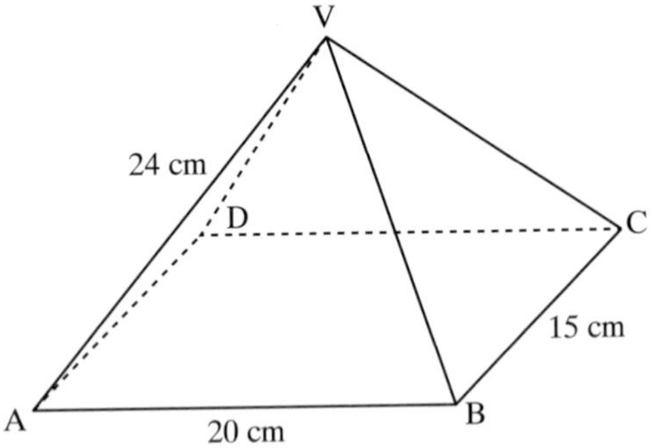

2 The diagram shows the roof of a building. The base ABCD is a horizontal rectangle 7 m by 4 m. The triangular ends are equilateral triangles. Each side of the roof is an isosceles trapezium. The length of the top of the roof, EF, is 5 m. Calculate

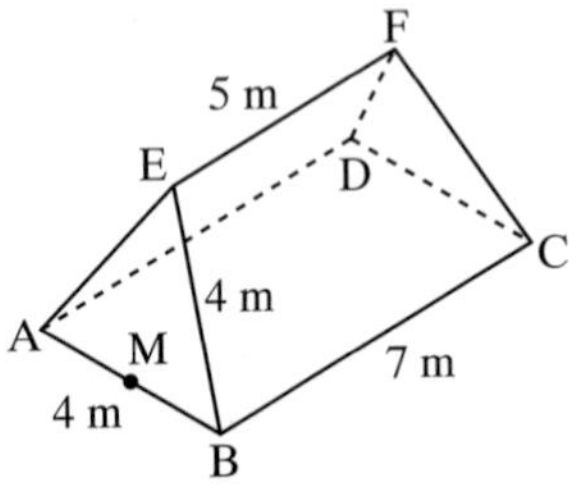

a the length EM, where M is the mid-point of AB

b the size of angle EBC

c the size of the angle between the face EAB and the base ABCD

d the surface area of the roof (excluding the base).

3 ABCD is a vertical rectangular plane. EDC is a horizontal triangular plane. Angle CDE = 90°, AB = 10 cm, BC = 4 cm and ED = 9 cm. Calculate the size of

a angle AED **b** angle DEC

c EC **d** angle BEC

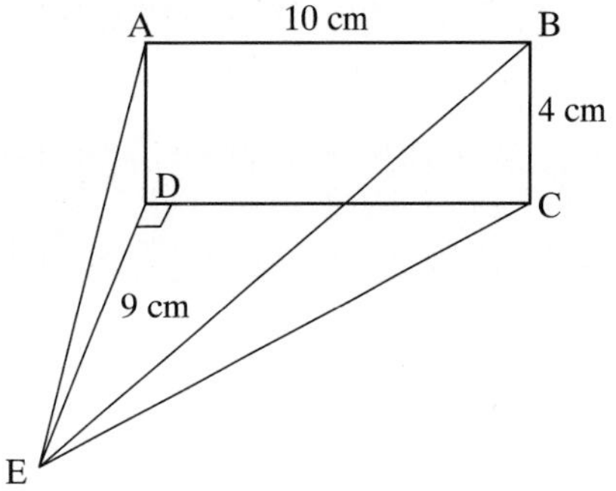

4 The diagram shows a tetrahedron. The base ABC is a horizontal equilateral triangle of side 8 cm. The vertex D is 5 cm directly above the point B. Calculate

a the size of angle DCB

b the size of the angle between the face ADC and the face ABC.

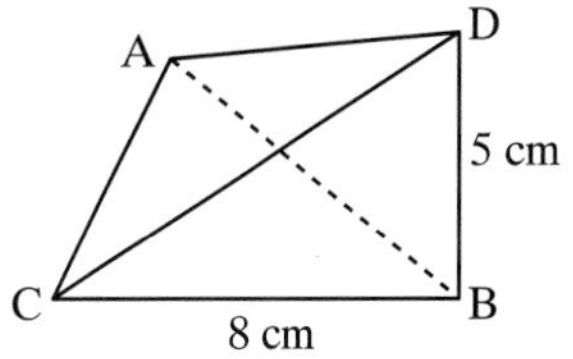

5 The diagram shows a tetrahedron, each face of which is an equilateral triangle of side 6 m. The lines AN and BM meet the sides CB and AC at a right angle. The lines AN and BM intersect at X, which is directly below the vertex, D. Calculate

a the distance AX

b the angle between the side DBC and the base ABC.

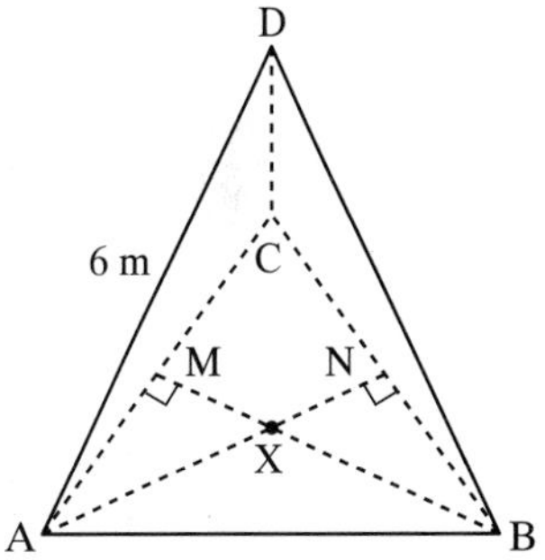

Trigonometric ratios of angles between 90° and 360°

Discovery activity 1

a Copy and complete this table using your calculator and rounding off to 3 dp.

x	**sin x**	x	**sin x**	x	**sin x**	x	**sin x**
0°		180°		180°		360°	
15°		165°		195°		335°	
30°		150°		210°		320°	
45°		135°		225°		315°	
60°		120°		240°		300°	
75°		105°		255°		285°	
90°		90°		270°		270°	

b Comment on what you notice about the sine of each acute angle, and the sines of its corresponding non-acute angles.

c Draw a graph sin x against x.

d Comment on any symmetries your graph has.

You should have discovered these three facts:

- When $90° < x < 180°$ $\sin x = \sin(180° - x)$

  For example $\sin 153° = \sin(180° - 153°) = \sin 27° = 0.454$

- When $180° < x < 270°$ $\sin x = -\sin(x - 180°)$

  For example $\sin 214° = -\sin(214° - 180°) = -\sin 34° = -0.559$

- When $270° < x < 360°$ $\sin x = -\sin(360° - x)$

  For example $\sin 287° = -\sin(360° - 287°) = -\sin 73° = -0.956$

Note

- Each and every value of sine between –1 and 1 gives **two** angles between 0° and 360°.
- When the value of sine is positive, both angles are between 0° and 180°.
- When the value of sine is negative, both angles are between 180° and 360°.

Example 1 Find the angles whose sine is 0.56.

We know that both angles are between 0° and 180°.

Using our calculator to find $\sin^{-1} 0.56$, we obtain 34.1°.

The other angle is, therefore,

$$180 - 34.1 = 145.9°$$

So, the angles are 34.1° and 145.9°.

Example 2 Find the angles whose sine is −0.197.

We know that both angles are between 180° and 360°.

Using our calculator to find $\sin^{-1} 0.197$, we obtain 11.4°.

So the angles are

$$180° + 11.4° \quad \text{and} \quad 360° - 11.4°$$

which give 191.4° and 348.6°.

You can always use your calculator to check your answer to this type of problem by first keying in the angle and then keying in the appropriate trigonometric function (which would be sine in the above examples).

Exercise 13C

State the two angles between 0° and 360° for each of these sine values.

1 0.6	**2** 0.8	**3** 0.75	**4** 0.37
5 0.654	**6** −0.7	**7** −0.25	**8** −0.32
9 −0.175	**10** −0.814	**11** 0.471	**12** 0.947
13 −0.342	**14** −0.097	**15** 0.553	**16** −0.5
17 0.145	**18** −0.318	**19** 0.745	**20** −0.893

Discovery activity 2

a Copy and complete this table using your calculator and rounding off to 3 dp.

x	$\cos x$	x	$\cos x$	x	$\cos x$	x	$\cos x$
0°		180°		180°		360°	
15°		165°		195°		335°	
30°		150°		210°		320°	
45°		135°		225°		315°	
60°		120°		240°		300°	
75°		105°		255°		285°	
90°		90°		270°		270°	

b Comment on what you notice about the cosines of the angles.

c Draw a graph of $\cos x$ against x.

d Comment on the symmetry of the graph.

You should have discovered these three facts:

- When $90° < x < 180°$ $\quad \cos x = -\cos(180 - x)°$

  For example $\quad \cos 161° = -\cos(180° - 161°) = -\cos 19° = -0.946$ (3 sf)

- When $180° < x < 270°$ $\quad \cos x = -\cos(x - 180°)$

  For example $\quad \cos 245° = -\cos(245° - 180°) = -\cos 65° = -0.423$ (3 sf)

- When $270° < x < 360°$ $\quad \cos x = \cos(360° - x)$

  For example $\quad \cos 310° = -\cos(360° - 310°) = \cos 50° = 0.643$ (3 sf)

Notice

- Each and every value of cosine between –1 and 1 gives **two** angles between 0° and 360°.
- When the value of cosine is positive, one angle is between 0° and 90°, and the other is between 270° and 360°.
- When the value of cosine is negative, both angles are between 90° and 270°.

Example 1 Find the angles whose cosine is 0.75.

We know that one angle is between 0° and 90°, and that the other is between 270° and 360°.

Using our calculator to find $\cos^{-1}$ 0.75, we obtain 41.4°.

The other angle is, therefore,

$$360° - 41.4° = 318.6°$$

So, the angles are 41.4° and 318.6°.

Example 2 Find the angles whose cosine is –0.285.

We know that both angles are between 90° and 270°.

Using our calculator to find $\cos^{-1}$ 0.285, we obtain 73.4°.

The two angles are, therefore,

$$180° - 73.4° \quad \text{and} \quad 180° + 73.4°$$

which give 106.6° and 253.4°.

Here again, you can use your calculator to check your answer, as already described but keying in cosine.

Exercise 13D

State the two angles between 0° and 360° for each of these cosine values.

1 0.6	**2** 0.58	**3** 0.458	**4** 0.575
5 0.185	**6** –0.8	**7** –0.25	**8** –0.175
9 –0.361	**10** –0.974	**11** 0.196	**12** 0.714
13 –0.418	**14** –0.308	**15** 0.558	**16** –0.055
17 –0.664	**18** 0.505	**19** 0.795	**20** –0.334

Exercise 13E

1 Write down the sine of each of these angles.

a 135° **b** 269° **c** 305° **d** 133°

2 Write down the cosine of each of these angles.

a 129° **b** 209° **c** 95° **d** 357°

3 Write down the two possible values of x (0° < x < 360°) for each equation. Give your answer to 1 dp.

a $\sin x = 0.361$ **b** $\sin x = -0.486$ **c** $\cos x = 0.641$

d $\cos x = -0.866$ **e** $\sin x = 0.874$ **f** $\cos x = 0.874$

4 Find two angles such that the sine of each is 0.5.

5 cos 41° = 0.755. What is cos 139°? (Do not use a calculator.)

6 Write down the value of each of the following, correct to 3 sf.

a sin 50° + cos 50° **b** cos 120° – sin 120° **c** sin 136° + cos 223°

d sin 175° + cos 257° **e** sin 114° – sin 210° **f** cos 123° + sin 177°

7 It is suggested that $(\sin x)^2 + (\cos x)^2 = 1$ is true for all values of x. Test out this suggestion to see if you agree.

8 Suppose the sine key on your calculator is broken, but not the cosine key. Show how you could calculate

a sin 25° **b** sin 130°

9 Find a solution to these equations.

a $\sin(x + 20°) = 0.5$ **b** $\cos(5x) = 0.45$

10 By any suitable method, find the solution to the equation $\sin x = (\cos x)^2$

Discovery activity 3

a Try to find tan 90°. What do you notice?

Which is the closest angle to 90° for which you can find the tangent on your calculator?

What is the largest value that you can get on your calculator?

b Find values of tan x where $0° < x < 360°$. Draw a graph of your results.

State some rules for finding both angles between 0° and 360° that have any given tangent.

Example 1 Find the angles between 0° and 360° whose tangent is 0.875.

We know that one angle is between 0° and 90°, and that the other is between 180° and 270°.

Using our calculator to find $\tan^{-1} 0.875$, we obtain 41.2°.

The other angle is, therefore,

$$180° + 41.2° = 221.2°$$

So, the angles are 41.2° and 221.2°.

Example 2 Find the angles between 0° and 360° whose tangent is –1.5.

We know that one angle is between 90° and 180°, and that the other is between 270° and 360°.

Using our calculator to find $\tan^{-1} 1.5$, we obtain 56.3°.

The angles are, therefore,

$$180° - 56.3° \quad \text{and} \quad 360° - 56.3°$$

which give 123.7° and 303.7°.

Exercise 13F

State the angles between 0° and 360° for each of these tangent values.

1 0.258	**2** 0.785	**3** 1.19	**4** 1.875
5 2.55	**6** –0.358	**7** –0.634	**8** –0.987
9 –1.67	**10** –3.68	**11** 1.397	**12** 0.907
13 –0.355	**14** –1.153	**15** 4.15	**16** –2.05
17 –0.098	**18** 0.998	**19** 1.208	**20** –2.5

Solving any triangle

We have already established that any triangle has six elements: three sides and three angles. To solve a triangle (that is, to find any unknown angles or sides), we need to know at least three of the elements. Any combination of three elements – **except that of all three angles** – is enough to work out the rest. In a right-angled triangle, one of the known elements is, of course, the right angle.

When we need to solve a triangle which contains no right angle, we can use one or the other of two rules, depending on what is known about the triangle. These are the **sine rule** and the **cosine rule**.

The sine rule

Take a triangle ABC and draw the perpendicular from A to the opposite side BC.

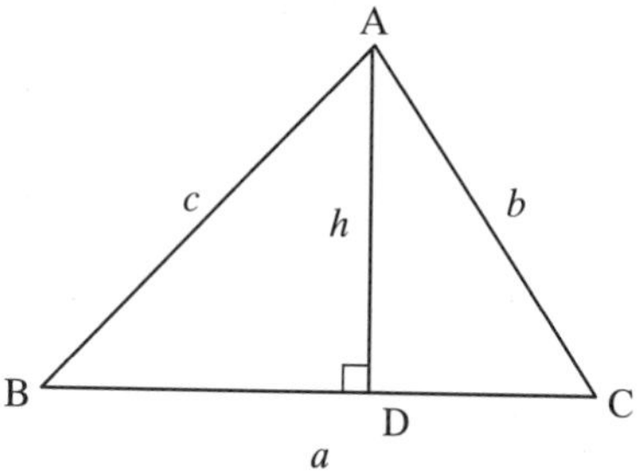

From right-angled triangle ADB

$$h = c \sin B$$

From right-angled triangle ADC

$$h = b \sin C$$

Therefore,

$$c \sin B = b \sin C$$

which can be rearranged to give

$$\frac{c}{\sin C} = \frac{b}{\sin B}$$

By drawing a perpendicular from each of the other two vertices to the opposite side (or by algebraic symmetry), we see that

$$\frac{a}{\sin A} = \frac{c}{\sin C} \quad \text{and that} \quad \frac{a}{\sin A} = \frac{b}{\sin B}$$

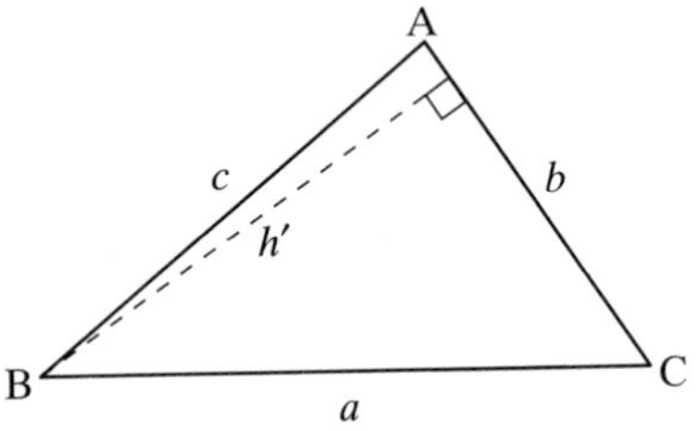

These are usually combined in the form

$$\frac{a}{\sin A} = \frac{b}{\sin B} = \frac{c}{\sin C}$$

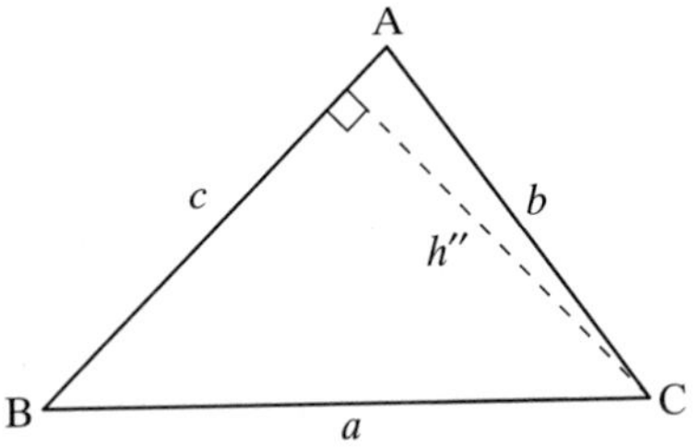

which can be inverted to give

$$\frac{\sin A}{a} = \frac{\sin B}{b} = \frac{\sin C}{c}$$

Usually, a triangle is not conveniently labelled as in the diagram above. So, when using the sine rule, it is easier to remember to proceed as follows: take each side in turn, divide it by the sine of the angle opposite, and then equate the resulting quotients.

Note

- When you are calculating a **side**, use the rule with the **sides on top**.
- When you are calculating an **angle**, use the rule with the **sines on top**.

Example 1 In triangle ABC, find the value of x.

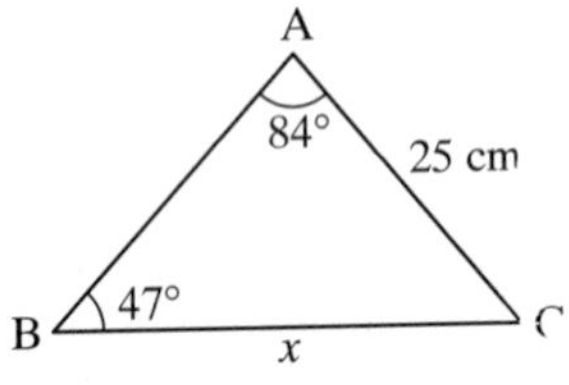

Use the sine rule with sides on top, which gives

$$\frac{x}{\sin 84°} = \frac{25}{\sin 47°}$$

$$\Rightarrow \quad x = \frac{25 \sin 84°}{\sin 47°} = 34.0 \text{ cm} \quad (3 \text{ sf})$$

Example 2 In the triangle ABC, find the value of x.

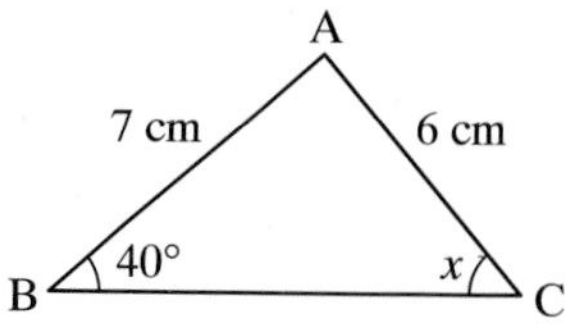

Use the sine rule with sines on top, which gives

$$\frac{\sin x}{7} = \frac{\sin 40°}{6}$$

$$\Rightarrow \quad \sin x = \frac{7 \sin 40°}{6} = 0.7499$$

$$\Rightarrow \quad x = \sin^{-1} 0.7499 = 48.6° \quad \text{(3 sf)}$$

The ambiguous case

Example In triangle ABC, AB = 9 cm, AC = 7 cm and angle ABC = 40°. Find the angle ACB.

As we sketch triangle ABC, we realise that C can have two positions, giving two different configurations.

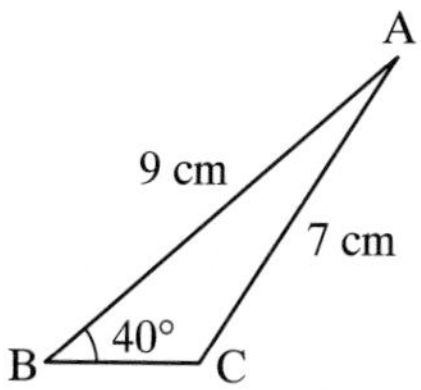

or

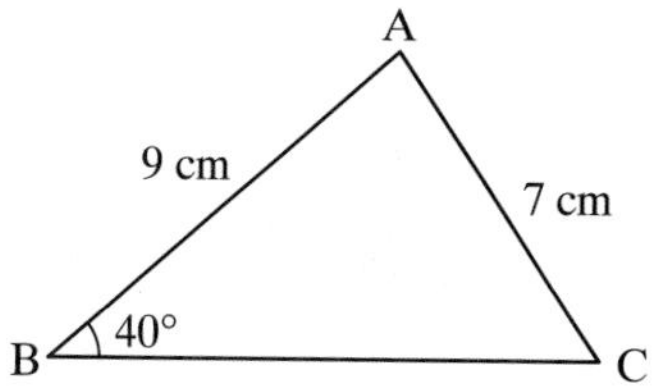

But we still proceed as in the normal sine-rule situation, obtaining

$$\frac{\sin C}{9} = \frac{\sin 40°}{7}$$

$$\Rightarrow \quad \sin C = \frac{9 \sin 40°}{7} = 34.0 \text{ cm} \quad \text{(3 sf)}$$

$$= 0.8264$$

Keying inverse sine on our calculator gives $C = 55.7°$. But there is another angle with a sine of 0.8264, given by (180° – 55.7°) = 124.3°.

These two values for C give the two different situations shown above.

When an illustration of the triangle is given, it will be clear whether the required angle is acute or obtuse. When an illustration is not given, the more likely answer is an acute angle.

Examiners will not try to catch you out with the ambiguous case. They will indicate clearly what is required, either with the aid of a diagram or by stating it.

Exercise 13G

1 Find the length x in each of these triangles

a

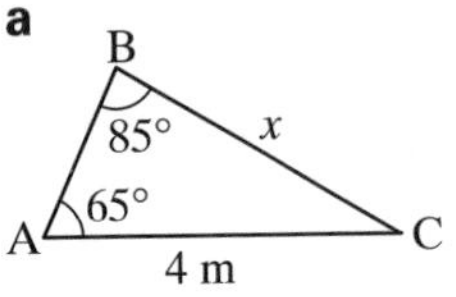

b

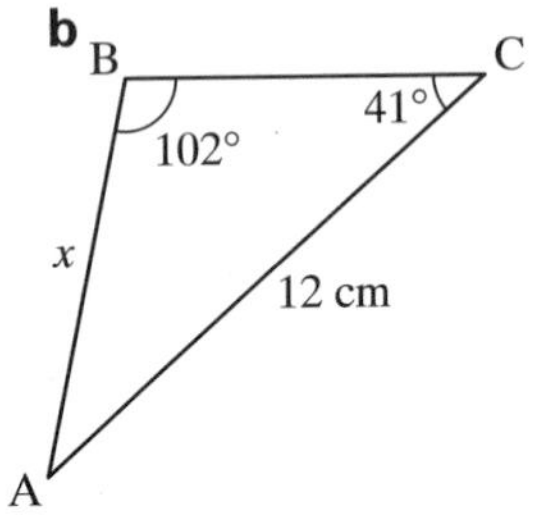

c

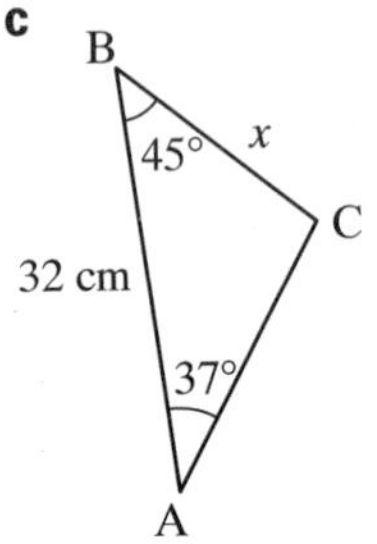

2 Find the angle x in each of these triangles

a

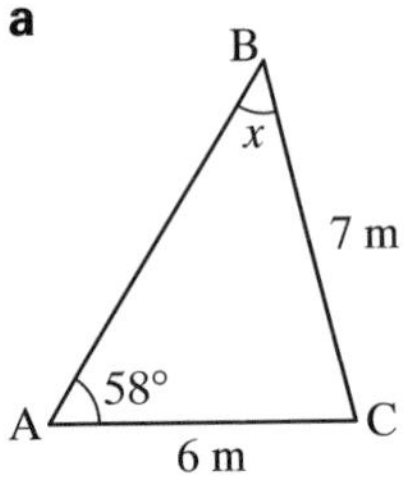

b

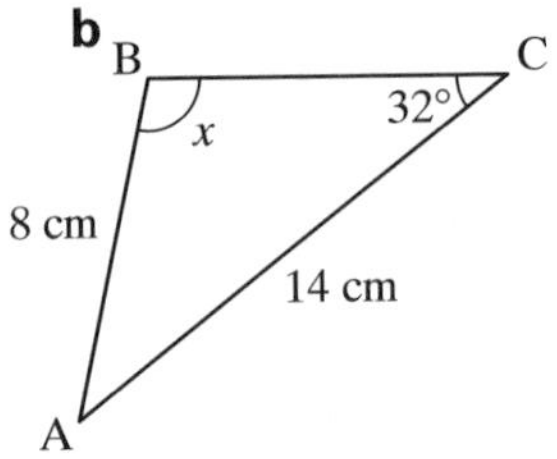

c

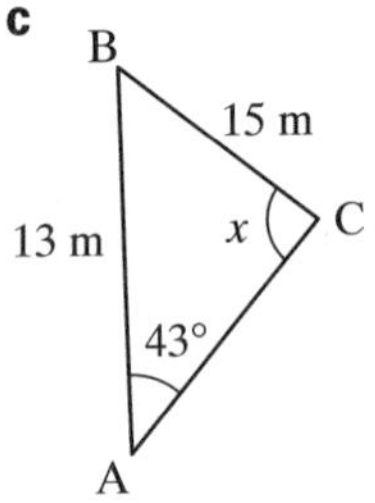

3 In triangle ABC, the angle at A is 38°, the side AB is 10 cm and the side BC is 8 cm. Find the two possible values of the angle at C.

4 In triangle ABC, the angle at A is 42°, the side AB is 16 cm and the side BC is 10 cm. Find the two possible values of the side AC.

5 To find the height of a tower standing on a small hill, Mary made the following measurements (see diagram).

From a point B, the angle of elevation of C is 20°, the angle of elevation of A is 50°, and the distance BC is 25 m.

Calculate

a angle ABC **b** angle BAC

c Using the sine rule and triangle ABC, calculate the height h of the tower.

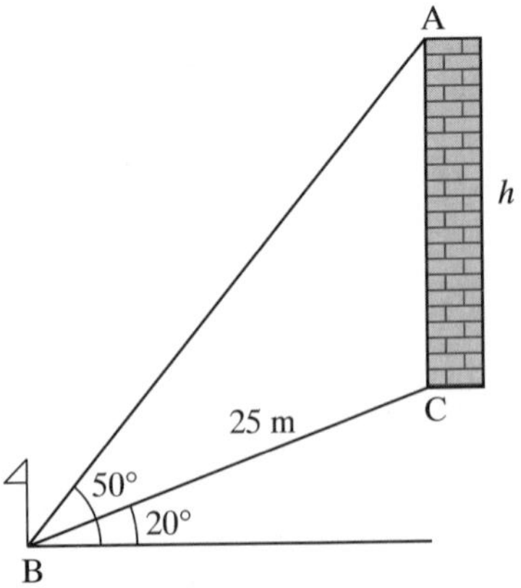

6 Use the information on this sketch to calculate the width, w, of the river.

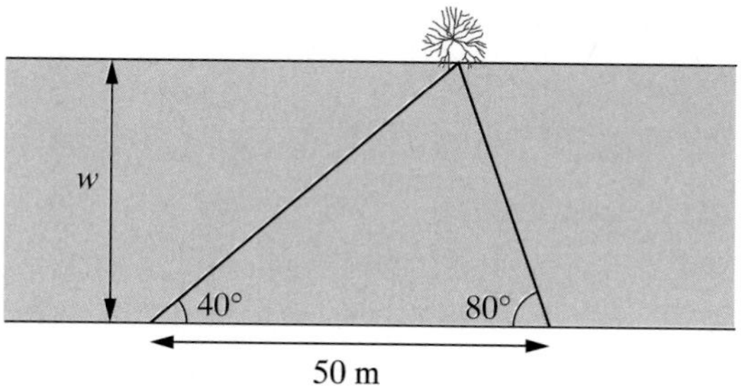

7 An old building is unsafe, so it is protected by a fence. To work out the height of the building, Annie made the measurements shown on the diagram.

a Use the sine rule to work out the distance AB.

b Calculate the height of the building.

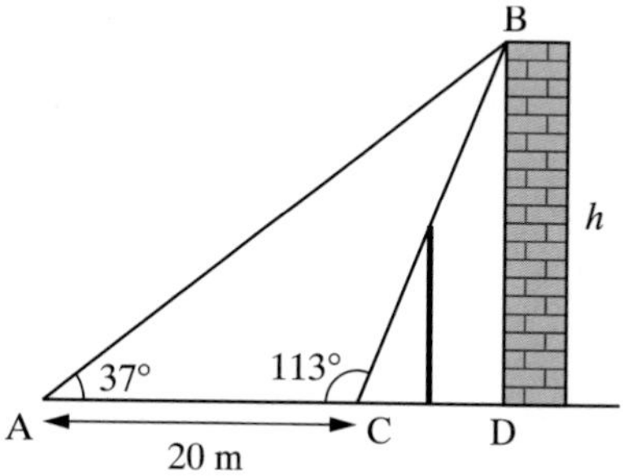

8 A weight is hung from a horizontal beam using two strings. The shorter string is 2.5 m long and makes an angle of 71° with the horizontal. The longer string makes an angle of 43° with the horizontal. What is the length of the longer string?

9 An aircraft is flying over an army base. Suddenly, two searchlights, 3 km apart, are switched on. The two beams of light meet on the aircraft at an angle of 125° vertically above the line joining the searchlights. One of the beams of light makes an angle of 31° with the horizontal. Calculate the height of the aircraft.

10 Two ships leave a port in directions that are 41° from each other. After half an hour, the ships are 11 km apart. If the speed of the slower ship is 7 km/h, what is the speed of the faster ship?

The cosine rule

Take the triangle, shown on the right, where D is the foot of the perpendicular to BC from A.

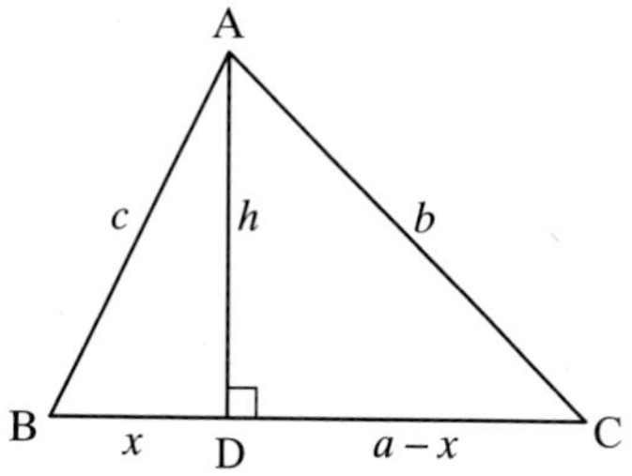

Using Pythagoras on triangle BDA

$$h^2 = c^2 - x^2$$

Using Pythagoras on triangle ADC

$$h^2 = b^2 - (a - x)^2$$

Therefore,

$$c^2 - x^2 = b^2 - (a - x)^2$$
$$c^2 - x^2 = b^2 - a^2 + 2ax - x^2$$
$$\Rightarrow \quad c^2 = b^2 - a^2 + 2ax$$

From triangle BDA $\quad x = c \cos B$

Hence

$$c^2 = b^2 - a^2 + 2ac \cos B$$

Rearranging gives

$$b^2 = a^2 + c^2 - 2ac \cos B$$

By algebraic symmetry

$$a^2 = b^2 + c^2 - 2bc \cos A \quad \text{and} \quad c^2 = a^2 + b^2 - 2ab \cos C$$

This is the **cosine rule**, which can be best remembered by the diagram on the right, where

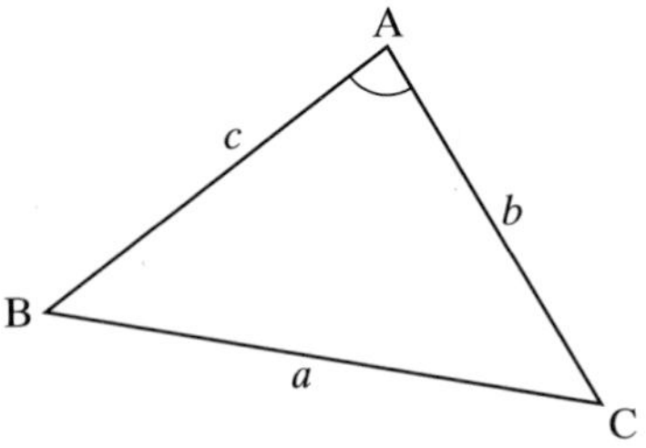

$$a^2 = b^2 + c^2 - 2bc \cos A$$

Note the symmetry of the rule and how the rule works using two adjacent sides and the angle between them.

The formula can be rearranged to find any of the three angles:

$$\cos A = \frac{b^2 + c^2 - a^2}{2bc}$$

$$\cos B = \frac{a^2 + c^2 - b^2}{2ac}$$

$$\cos C = \frac{a^2 + b^2 - c^2}{2ab}$$

The next three examples show you how to use the cosine rule.

Example 1 Find x in this triangle.

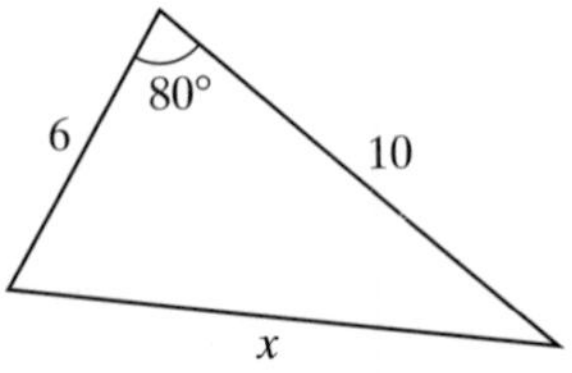

By the cosine rule

$$x^2 = 6^2 + 10^2 - 2 \times 6 \times 10 \times \cos 80°$$
$$x^2 = 115.16$$
$$\Rightarrow \quad x = 10.7 \quad \text{(3 sf)}$$

Example 2 Find x in this triangle.

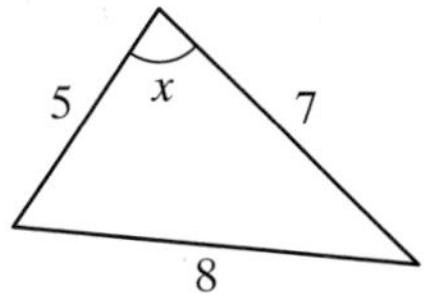

By the cosine rule

$$\cos x = \frac{5^2 + 7^2 - 8^2}{2 \times 5 \times 7} = 0.1428$$

$$\Rightarrow \quad x = 81.8° \quad (3 \text{ sf})$$

Example 3 A ship sails from a port on a bearing of 055° for 40 km. It then changes course to 123° for another 50 km. On what course should the ship be steered to get it straight back to the port?

The diagram for this question is

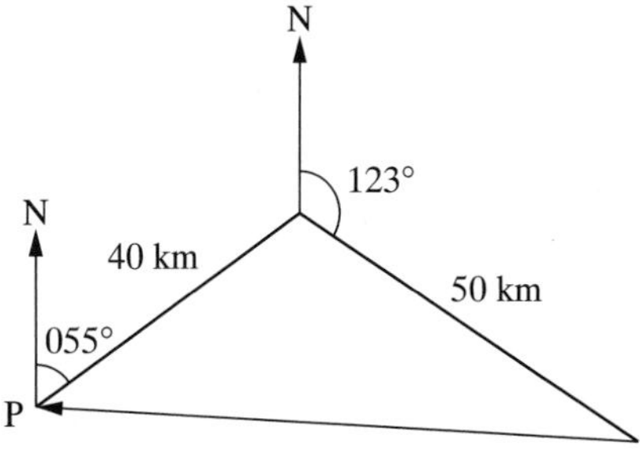

Previously, we have solved this type of problem using right-angled triangles. This method could be applied here but it would involve at least six separate calculations.

With the aid of the cosine and sine rules, however, we can reduce the solution to two separate calculations, as follows.

The course diagram gives the triangle PAB (on the right), where angle PAB is found by using alternate angles and angles on a line (55° + 180° – 123° = 112°).

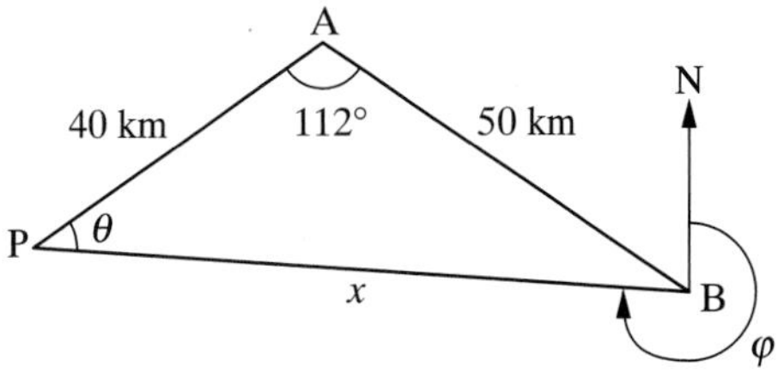

Let φ be the bearing to be steered, then

$$\varphi = \theta + 55° + 180°$$

To find θ, we first have to obtain PB = x, using the cosine rule:

$$x^2 = 40^2 + 50^2 - 2 \times 40 \times 50 \times \cos 112°$$

(Remember: the cosine of 112° is negative.)

$$\Rightarrow \quad x^2 = 5598.43$$
$$\Rightarrow \quad x = 74.82 \text{ km}$$

We can now find θ from the sine rule:

$$\frac{\sin \theta}{50} = \frac{\sin 112°}{74.82}$$

$$\Rightarrow \quad \sin \theta = \frac{50 \times \sin 112°}{74.82} = 0.6196$$

$$\Rightarrow \quad \theta = 38.3°$$

So the ship should be steered on a bearing of

$$(55° + 38.3°) + 180° = 273.3°$$

Exercise 13H

1 Find the length x in each of these triangles.

a

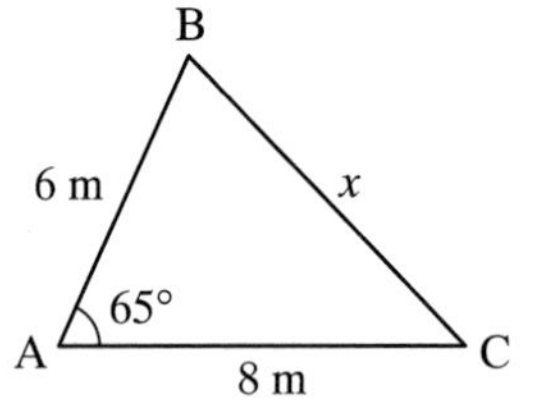

b

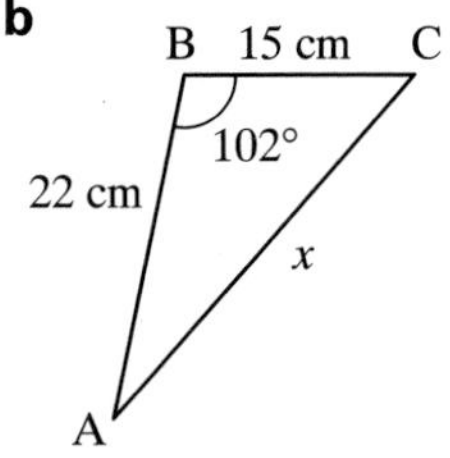

c

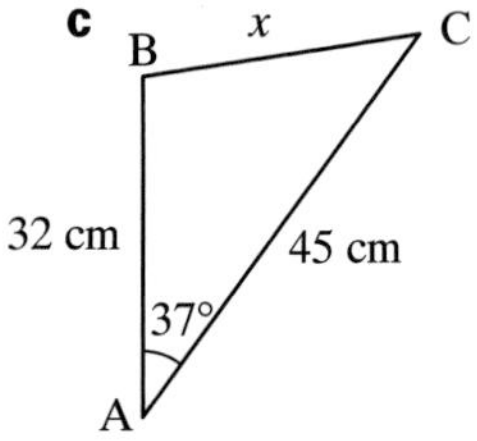

2 Find the angle x in each of these triangles.

a

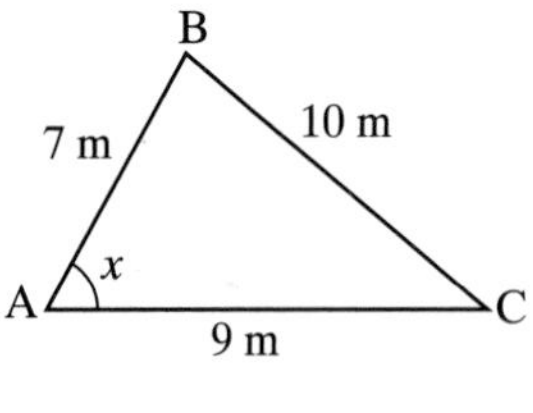

b

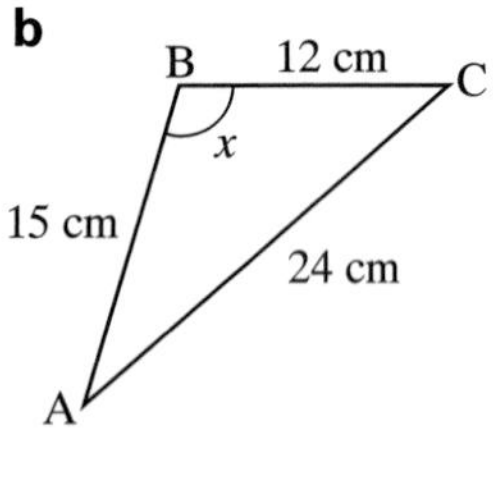

c

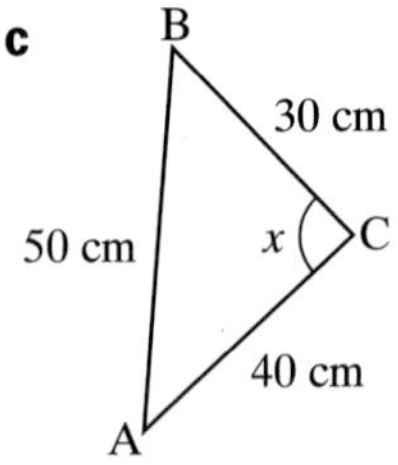

3 In triangle ABC, AB = 5 cm, BC = 6 cm and angle ABC = 55°. Find AC.

4 A quadrilateral ABCD has AD = 6 cm, DC = 9 cm, AB = 10 cm and BC = 12 cm. Angle ADC = 120°. Calculate angle ABC.

5 A triangle has two sides of length 30 cm and an angle of 50°. Unfortunately, the position of the angle is not known. Sketch the two possible triangles and use them to work out the two possible lengths of the third side of the triangle.

6 A triangle has two sides of length 40 cm and an angle of 110°. Work out the length of the third side of the triangle.

7 A ship sails from a port on a bearing of 050° for 50 km then turns on a bearing of 140° for 40 km. A crewman is taken ill, so the ship drops anchor. What course and distance should a rescue helicopter from the port fly to reach the ship in the shortest possible time?

8 The three sides of a triangle are given as $3a$, $5a$ and $7a$. Calculate the smallest angle in the triangle.

9 The diagram shows a trapezium ABCD. AB = 6.7 cm, AD = 7.2 cm, CB = 9.3 cm and angle DAB = 100°. Calculate

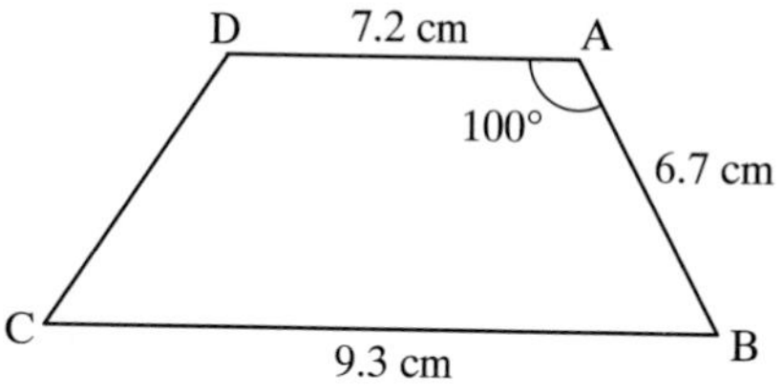

a length DB
b angle DBA
c angle DBC
d length DC
e area of the trapezium

10 ABCD is a trapezium where AB is parallel to CD. AB = 4 cm, BC = 5 cm, CD = 8 cm, DA = 6 cm. A line BX is parallel to AD and cuts DC at X. Calculate
a angle BCD **b** length BD

Choosing the correct rule

When solving triangles, there are only four situations that can occur, each of which can be solved completely in three stages.

- **Two sides and the included angle**
  1. Use the cosine rule to find the third side.
  2. Use the sine rule to find either of the other angles.
  3. Use the sum of the angles in a triangle to find the third angle.

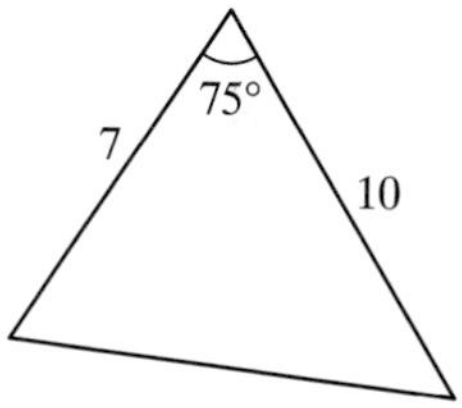

- **Two angles and a side**
  1. Use the sum of the angles in a triangle to find the third angle.
  2, 3. Use the sine rule to find the other two sides.

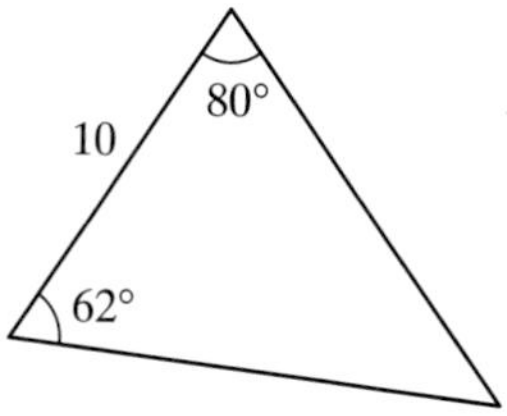

- **Three sides**
  1. Use the cosine rule to find one angle.
  2. Use the sine rule to find another angle.
  3. Use the sum of the angles in a triangle to find the third angle.

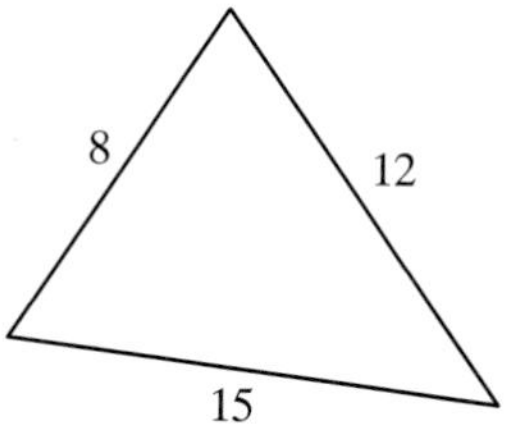

- **Two sides and a non-included angle**
  This is the ambiguous case already covered (page 303).
  1 Use the sine rule to find the two possible values of the appropriate angle.
  2 Use the sum of the angles in a triangle to find the two possible values of the third angle.
  3 Use the sine rule to find the two possible values for the length of the third side.

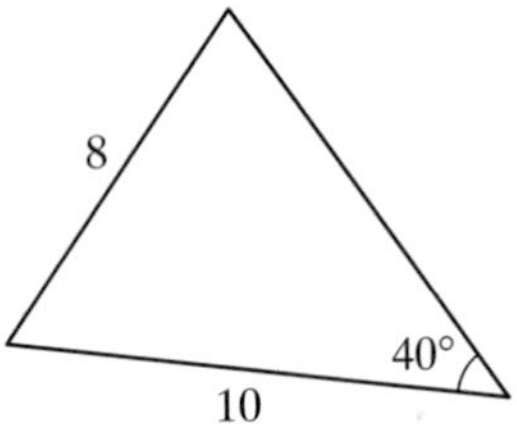

Note Apply the sine rule wherever you can – it is always easier to use than the cosine rule. The cosine rule should never need to be used more than once.

Exercise 13I

1 Find the length or angle x in each of these triangles.

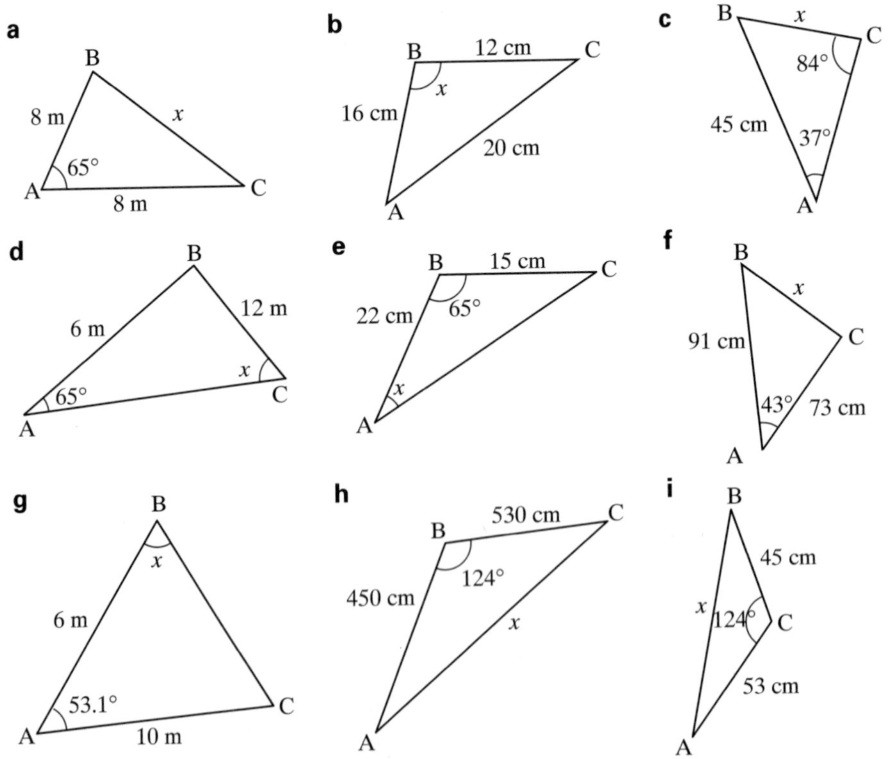

2 The hands of a clock have lengths 3 cm and 5 cm. Find the distance between the tips of the hands at 4 o'clock.

3 A spacecraft is seen hovering at a point which is in the same vertical plane as two towns, X and F. Its distances from X and F are 8.5 km and 12 km respectively. The angle of elevation of the spacecraft when observed from F is 43°. Calculate the distance between the two towns.

4 Two boats, Mary Jo and Suzie, leave port at the same time. Mary Jo sails at 10 knots on a bearing of 065°. Suzie sails on a bearing of 120° and after 1 hour Mary Jo is on a bearing of 330° from Suzie. What is Suzie's speed? (A knot is a nautical mile per hour.)

5 Two ships leave port at the same time, Darling Dave sailing at 12 knots on a bearing of 055°, and Merry Mary at 18 knots on a bearing of 280°.

a How far apart are the two ships after 1 hour?

b What is the bearing of Merry Mary from Darling Dave?

Sine, cosine and tangent of 30°, 45° and 60°

Example 1 Using an equilateral triangle whose sides are 2 units, write down expressions for the sine, cosine and tangent of 60° and 30°.

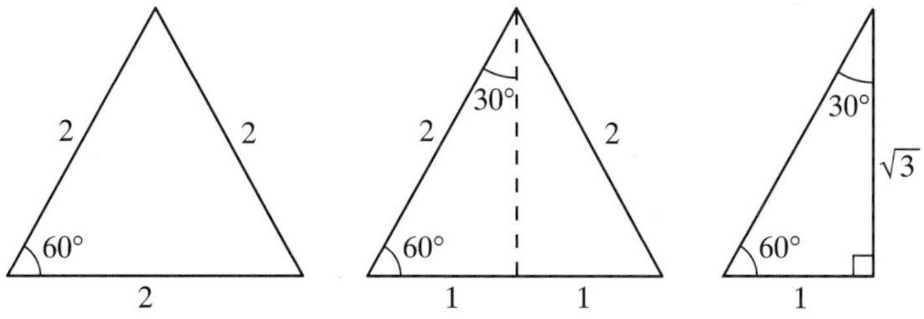

Divide the equilateral triangle into two equal right-angled triangles and take one of them as shown above.

From the definition of sine, cosine and tangent, we obtain

$$\sin 60° = \frac{\sqrt{3}}{2} \qquad \cos 60° = \frac{1}{2} \qquad \tan 60° = \sqrt{3}$$

and

$$\sin 30° = \frac{1}{2} \qquad \cos 30° = \frac{\sqrt{3}}{2} \qquad \tan 30° = \frac{1}{\sqrt{3}} = \frac{\sqrt{3}}{3}$$

Example 2 Using a right-angled isosceles triangle whose equal sides are 1 unit, find the sine, cosine and tangent of 45°.

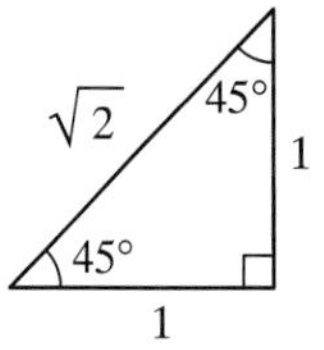

The hypotenuse of the triangle is √2 units.

From the definition of sine, cosine and tangent, we obtain

$$\sin 45° = \frac{1}{\sqrt{2}} = \frac{\sqrt{2}}{2} \qquad \cos 45° = \frac{1}{\sqrt{2}} = \frac{\sqrt{2}}{2} \qquad \tan 45° = 1$$

Exercise 13J

1 The sine of angle x is $\frac{4}{5}$. Without using a calculator, work out the cosine of angle x.

2 The cosine of angle x is $\frac{3}{\sqrt{15}}$. Without using a calculator, work out the sine of angle x.

3 The two short sides of a right-angled triangle are $\sqrt{6}$ and $\sqrt{13}$. Without using a calculator, write down the exact value of the hypotenuse of this triangle, and the exact value of the sine, cosine and tangent of the smallest angle in the triangle.

4 The tangent of angle A is $\frac{6}{11}$. Use this fact to label two sides of the triangle.

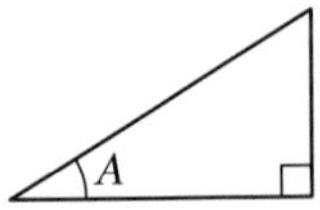

a Calculate the third side of the triangle

b Write down the exact values of $\sin A$ and $\cos A$.

5 Calculate the exact value of the area of an equilateral triangle of side 24 cm.

6 Work out the exact value of the area of a right-angled isosceles triangle whose hypotenuse is 40 cm.

Using sine to find the area of a triangle

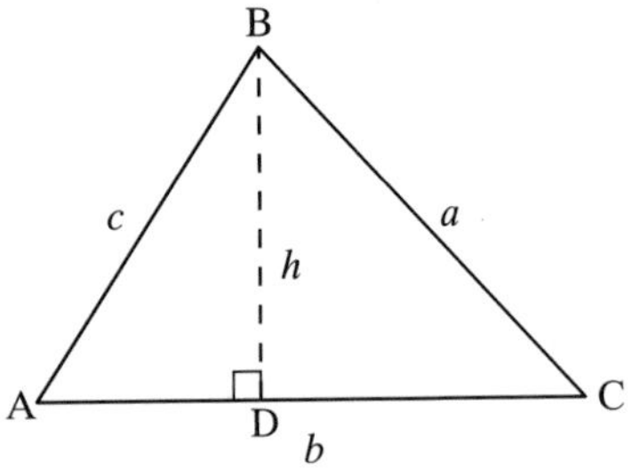

Take triangle ABC, whose vertical height is BD and whose base is AC.

Let BD = h and AC = b, then the area of the triangle is given by

$$\tfrac{1}{2} \times \text{AC} \times \text{BD} = \tfrac{1}{2}bh$$

However, in triangle BCD

$$h = \text{BC} \sin C = a \sin C$$

where BC = a.

Substituting into $\frac{1}{2}bh$ gives

$$\tfrac{1}{2}b \times (a \sin C) = \tfrac{1}{2}ab \sin C$$

as the area of the triangle.

By taking the perpendicular from A to its opposite side BC, and the perpendicular from C to its opposite side AB, we can show that the area of the triangle is also given by

$$\tfrac{1}{2}ac \sin B \quad \text{and} \quad \tfrac{1}{2}bc \sin A$$

Note the pattern: the area is given by the product of two sides multiplied by the sine of the included angle.

Two different situations are illustrated in Examples 1 and 2. Follow them through.

Example 1 Find the area of triangle ABC.

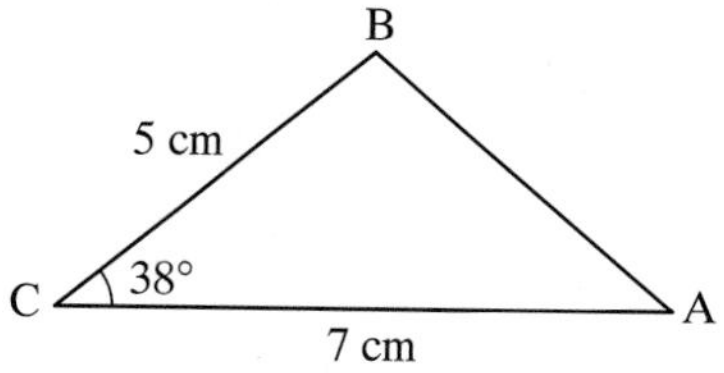

Area = $\frac{1}{2}ab \sin C$

$= \frac{1}{2} \times 5 \times 7 \times \sin 38° = 10.8 \text{ cm}^2$ (3 sf)

Example 2 Find the area of triangle ABC.

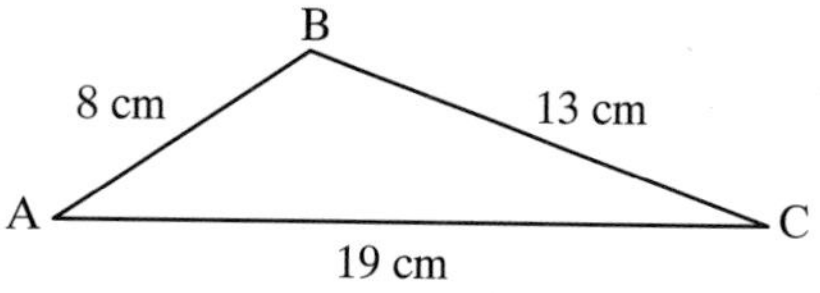

We have all three sides but no angle. So first we must find an angle in order to apply the area sine rule.

Find angle C, using the cosine rule:

$$\cos C = \frac{a^2 + b^2 - c^2}{2ab}$$

$$= \frac{13^2 + 19^2 - 8^2}{2 \times 13 \times 19} = 0.9433$$

$$\Rightarrow \quad C = \cos^{-1} 0.9433 = 19.4°$$

(Keep the exact value in your calculator memory.)

Now we apply the area sine rule:

$$\frac{1}{2}ab \sin C = \frac{1}{2} \times 13 \times 19 \times \sin 19.4°$$

$$= 41.0 \text{ cm}^2 \quad \text{(3 sf)}$$

Exercise 13K

1 Find the area of each of the following triangles.

a Triangle ABC where BC = 7 cm, AC = 8 cm and angle ACB = 59°.

b Triangle ABC where angle BAC = 86°, AC = 6.7 cm and AB = 8 cm.

c Triangle PQR where QR = 27 cm, PR = 19 cm and angle QRP = 109°.

d Triangle XYZ where XY = 231 m, XZ = 191 cm and angle YXZ = 73°.

e Triangle LMN where LN = 63 cm, LM = 39 cm and angle NLM = 85°.

2 The area of triangle ABC is 27 cm^2. If BC = 14 cm and angle BCA = 115°, find AC.

3 In a quadrilateral ABCD, DC = 4 cm, BD = 11 cm, angle BAD = 32°, angle ABD = 48° and angle BDC = 61°. Calculate the area of the quadrilateral.

4 The area of triangle LMN is 113 cm^2, LM = 16 cm and MN = 21 cm. Calculate

a angle LMN **b** angle MNL

5 A board is in the shape of a triangle with sides 60 cm, 70 cm and 80 cm. Find the area of the board.

6 Two circles, centres P and Q, have radii of 6 cm and 7 cm respectively. The circles intersect at X and Y. Given that PQ = 9 cm, find the area of triangle PXQ.

7 The points A, B and C are on the circumference of a circle, centre O and radius 7 cm. AB = 4 cm and BC = 3.5 cm. Calculate

a angle AOB **b** area of quadrilateral OABC.

Possible coursework tasks

Rectangles in a semicircle

A rectangle can be drawn inside a semicircle, as shown in the diagram.

Investigate the area of different rectangles that can be drawn inside the semicircle.

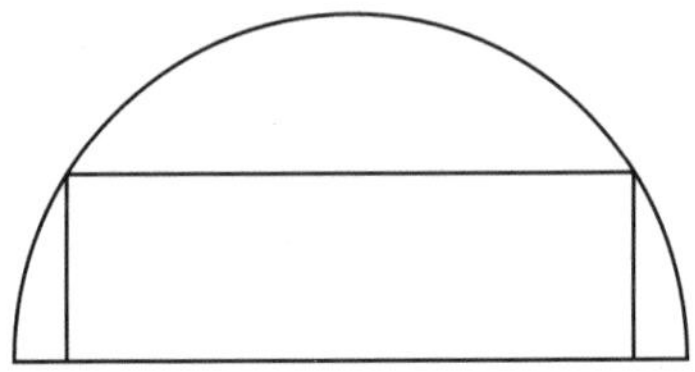

Snooker table

For this 'snooker table' the ball starts at A and ends up in pocket B.

Investigate for different sized 'snooker tables'.

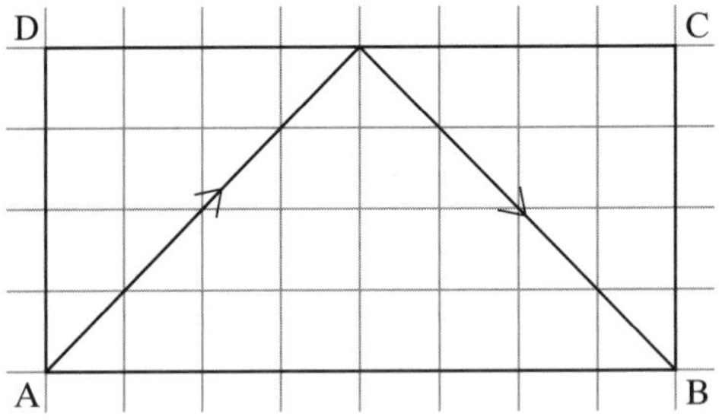

Wrappers

A chocolate bar is to be wrapped in a rectangular piece of silver foil.

Investigate the most economical way of doing this.

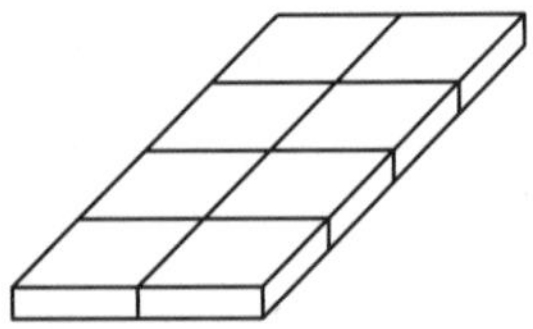

The circumcircle

R is the radius of the circumcircle of triangle ABC.

Can you find a relationship between R and the sine rule?

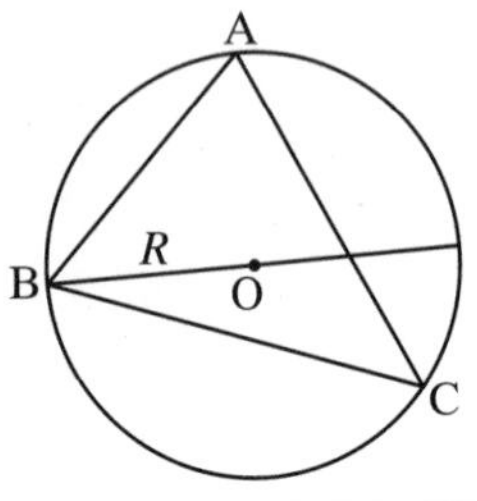

Hero's formula

The area of triangle ABC can be calculated by using Hero's formula:

$$A = \sqrt{s(s-a)(s-b)(s-c)}$$

where s is the semi-perimeter, that is

$$s = \frac{a+b+c}{2}$$

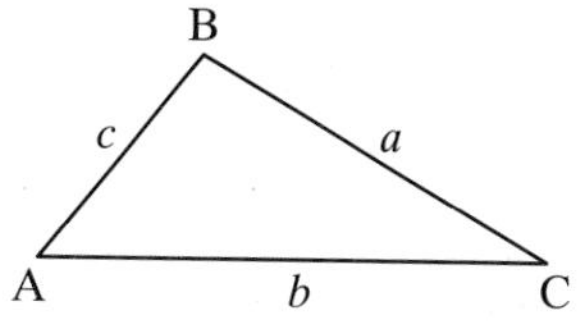

Investigate how you could prove Hero's formula.

Combining trigonometric ratios

Investigate graphs of the form

$$y = a \cos x + b \sin x$$

You may find a computer graphical package useful for this.

DEG/RAD/GRA

When solving trigonometry problems, you must remember to put your calculator in DEGREE mode.

You may have noticed that your calculator has two other modes for use in trigonometry: RAD and GRA

Investigate the RAD and GRA modes on a calculator.

Examination questions

1 In triangle ABC, the length of side AB is 42 cm to the nearest cm. The length of side AC is 35 cm to the nearest cm, and angle C is 61° to the nearest degree. What is the largest possible size that angle B could be? *NEAB, Question 13, Specimen Paper 2H, 1998*

2 A helicopter leaves a heliport H and flies 3.2 km on a bearing of 128° to a checkpoint C. It then flies 4.7 km on a bearing of 066° to its base B.

a Show that angle HCB is 118°.

b Calculate the direct distance from the heliport H to the base B.

NEAB, Question 20, Specimen Paper 1H, 1998

3 A port, B, is 20 km north east of another port, A. A lighthouse, L, is 5 km from B on a bearing of 260° from B.

a Calculate the distance AL.

b Calculate, to the nearest degree, the bearing of L from A.

NEAB, Question 18, Paper 1H, November 1995

4 In triangle ABC, AC = 7.6 cm, angle BAC = 35°, angle ACB = 65°. The length of AB is x cm. The size of angle ABC is θ.

a **i** Write down the value of θ.

ii Hence calculate the value of x.

Alison constructs this triangle by first drawing the side AC. She then uses a protractor to draw the angles at A and C. In constructing the triangle, the length of AC is measured correct to the nearest mm. The angles at A and C are measured correct to the nearest degree.

b **i** Write down the minimum value θ can take.

ii Calculate the maximum and minimum values x can take.

NEAB, Question 15, Paper 2H, June 1995

5 A vertical telegraph pole, PQ, is 9.4 m tall and stands on sloping ground, QS.
A metal cable, RS, is attached to the ground at the point S and to the pole at the point R, where R is 0.5 m below P. The distance QS is 3.7 m and angle PQS is 125°.

a Calculate the length of the cable, RS.

b Calculate the angle that the cable makes with the vertical.

WJEC, Question 15, Paper 2, June 1996

6 The 'folly tower' in the grounds of Poldark Castle is in the shape of a tetrahedron VPQR standing on a prism FGHPQR. The cross-section PQR is an equilateral triangle of side 9.0 m. VP = VQ = VR = 20.5 m. PF = QG = RH = 28.0 m. M is the mid-point of QR.

a **i** Use triangle PQR to find the length of PM.

ii Use triangle VQR to find the length of VM.

b Find the size of angle VPM.

c Find the height of V above the base FGH. Give your answer to an appropriate degree of accuracy.

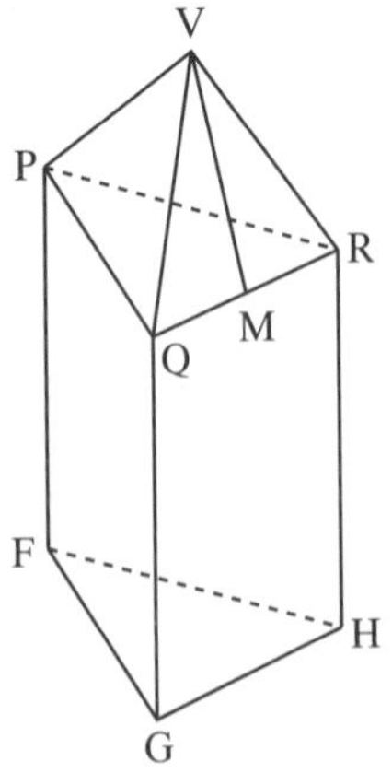

MEG, Question 13, Specimen Paper 6, 1998

7 In triangle OAB, OA = 3 m, OB = 8 m and angle AOB = 15°.

a Calculate, correct to 2 decimal places, the area of triangle OAB.

b Calculate the length of the side AB.

MEG, Question 9, Specimen Paper 6, 1998

8 The positions of the 6th, 7th and 8th holes on a putting green are shown in the diagram. The distances between the holes are given in yards.

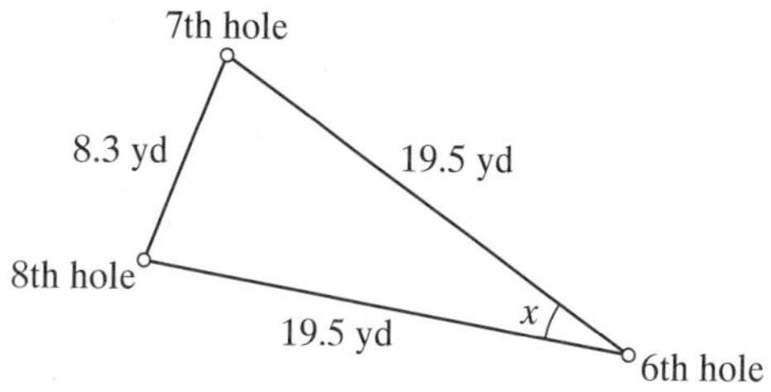

a Calculate the size of the angle marked x on the diagram.

b When playing, Joyce walks from the 7th to the 8th hole in an arc of a circle, with the centre of the circle at the 6th hole. How far does she walk?

SEG, Question 4, Specimen Paper 16, 1998

9 A surveyor wishes to measure the height of a church. Measuring the angle of elevation, she finds that the angle increases from 30° to 35° after walking 20 metres towards the church. What is the height of the church?

SEG, Question 17, Specimen Paper 15, 1998

10 The banks of a river are straight and parallel. To find the width of the river, two points, A and B, are chosen 50 m apart. The angles made with a tree at C on the opposite bank are measured as angle CAB = 56°, angle CBA = 40°. Calculate the width of the river.

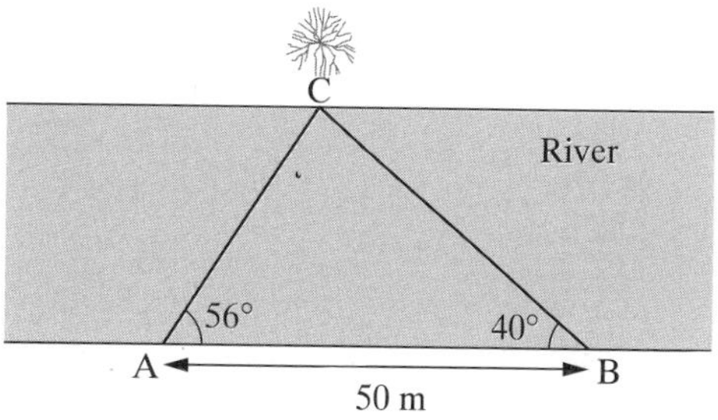

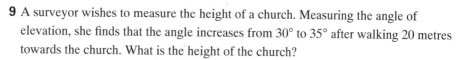

SEG, Question 14, Paper 6, June 1995

Summary

How well do you grade yourself?

To gain a grade **C**, you need to be able to solve simple 2-D trigonometry problems.

To gain a grade **B**, you need to be able to solve isosceles-triangle problems and 2-D trigonometry problems where the hypotenuse may need to be found.

To gain a grade **A**, you need to be able to solve simple 3-D trigonometry problems. You need also to be able to solve triangles using the sine and cosine rules, including the area sine rule.

What you should know after you have worked through Chapter 13

- How to solve problems in two and three dimensions using trigonometry.
- How to draw the graphs of the trigonometric functions.
- How to find the trigonometric ratios for angles between 0° and 360°.
- How to find both angles between 0° and 360° that have the same trigonometric ratio.
- How to use the sine and cosine rules.
- How to find the area of a triangle, knowing two sides and the included angle.
- How to find the exact trigonometric ratios of 30°, 45° and 60°.

14 Graphs

This chapter is going to ... show you how to find the equation of a given graph, how to use graphs to solve simultaneous equations, and how to draw a variety of non-linear graphs from their equations. It will also help you to recognise quadratic, cubic and reciprocal graphs, and show you how to use these graphs to solve equations.

What you should already know

- How to read and plot co-ordinates.
- How to substitute into simple algebraic formulae.
- How to draw graphs from linear equations.

Finding the equation of a line from its graph

The equation $y = mx + c$

When a graph can be expressed in the form $y = mx + c$, the coefficient of x, m, is the gradient, and the constant term, c, is the intercept on the y-axis.

This means that if we know the gradient, m, of a line and its intercept, c, on the y-axis, we can write down the equation of the line immediately. For example, if $m = 3$ and $c = -5$, the equation of the line is $y = 3x - 5$.

All linear graphs are of the form $y = mx + c$.

This gives us a method of finding the equation of any line drawn on a pair of co-ordinate axes.

Example Find the equation of the line shown in the diagram.

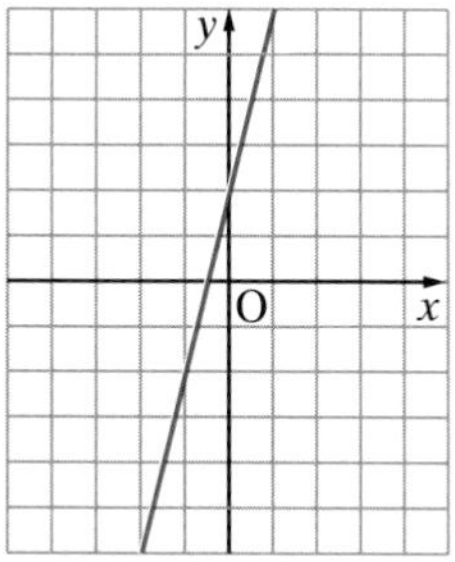

First, we find where the graph crosses the y-axis (diagram **A**). So $c = 2$.

Next, we measure the gradient of the line (diagram **B**). So $m = 4$.

Finally, we write down the equation of the line: $y = 4x + 2$.

A

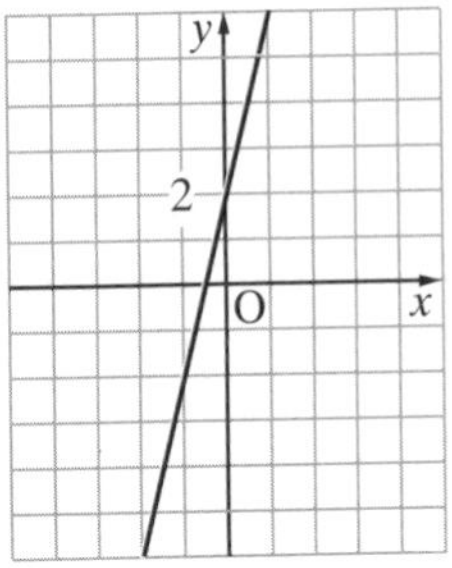

B

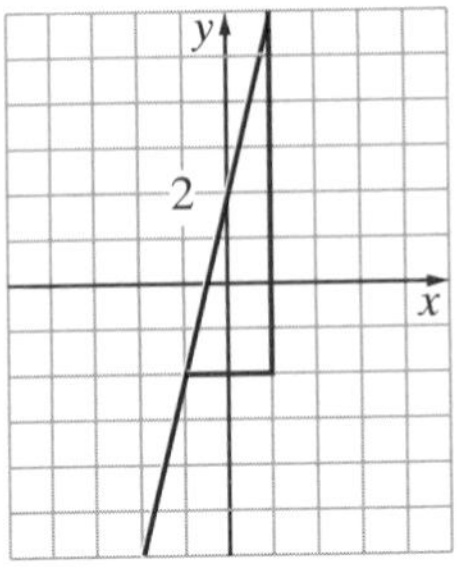

y-step = 8
x-step = 2
Gradient = $8 \div 2 = 4$

Exercise 14A

1 Give the equation of each of these lines, all of which have positive gradients.

a

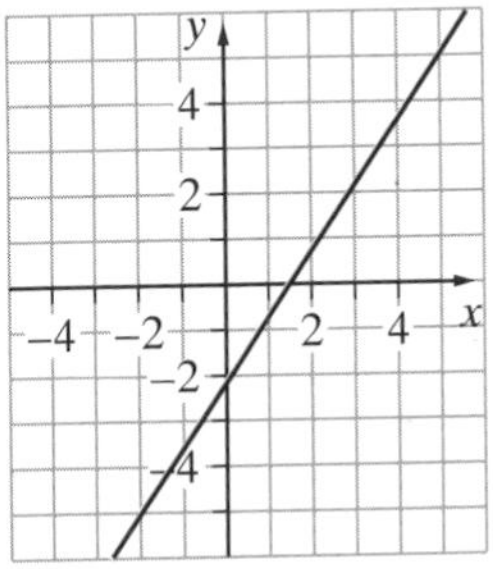

b

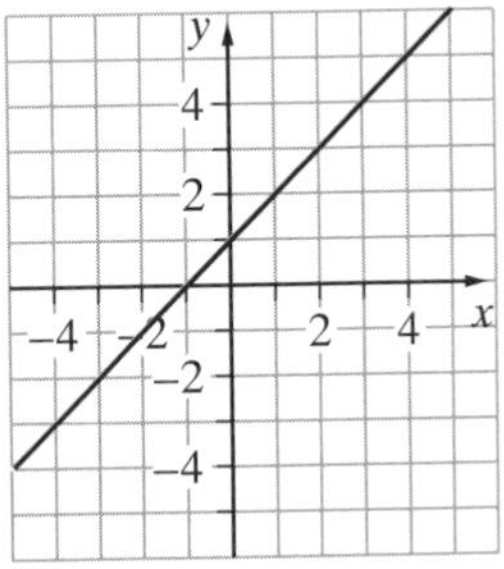

c

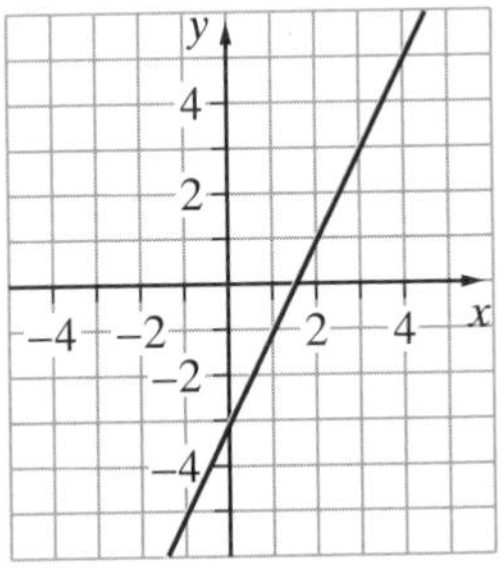

d

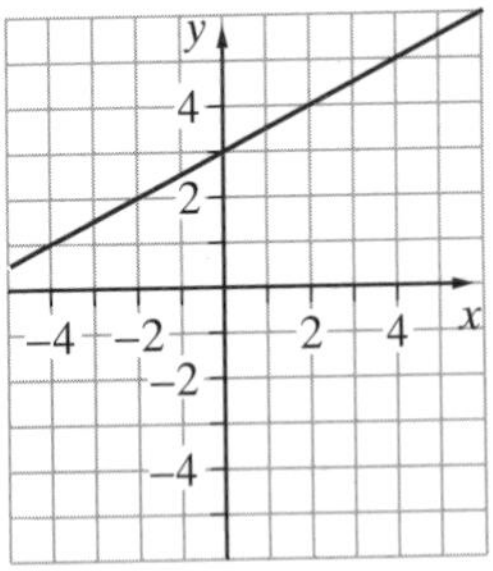

e

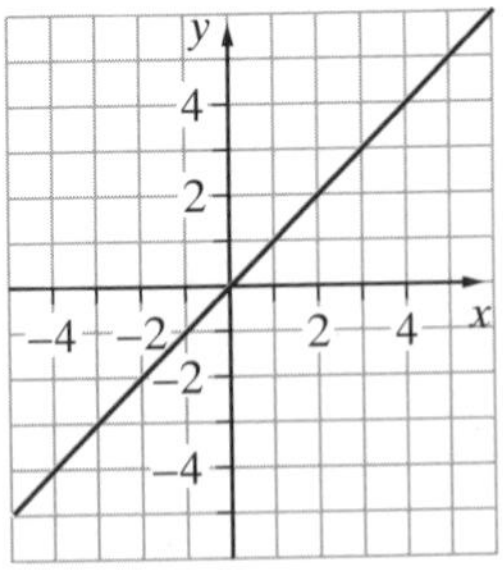

f

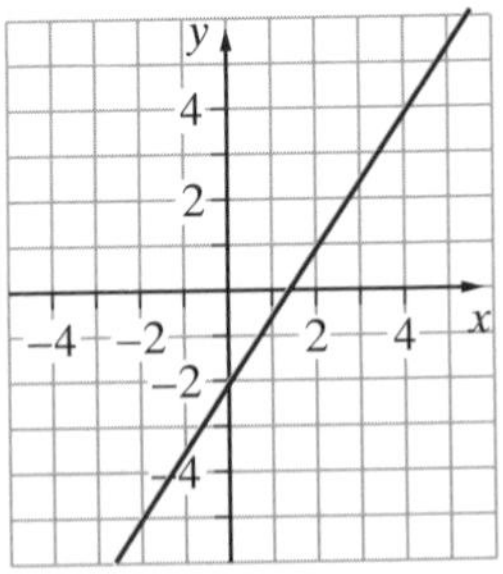

g

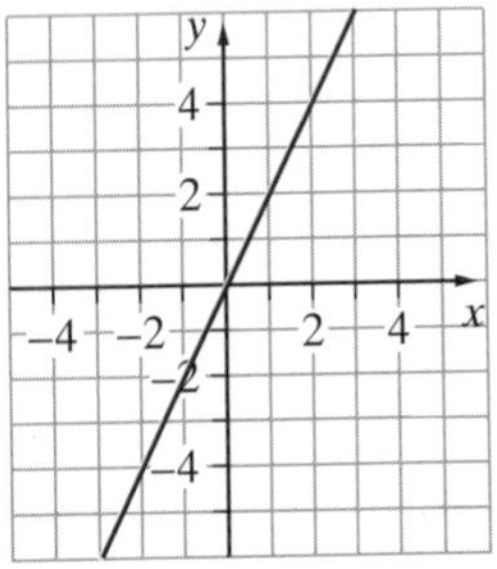

h

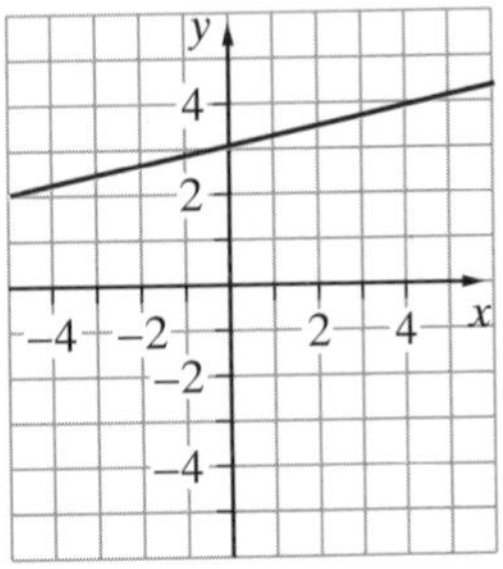

i

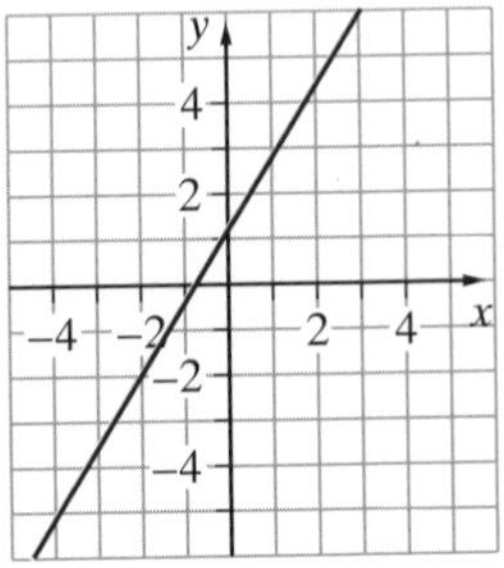

2 In each of these grids, there are two lines.

a

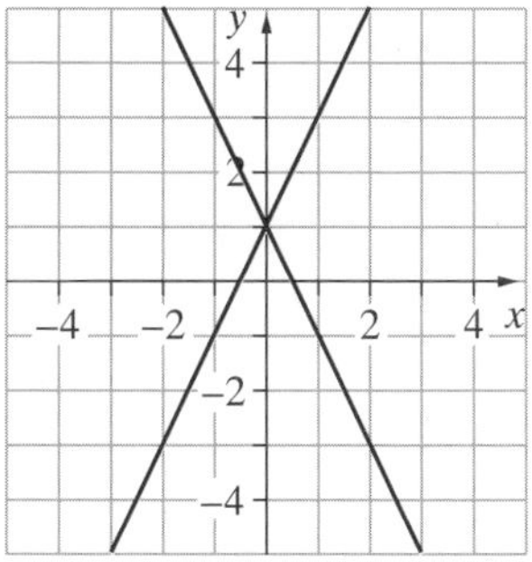

b

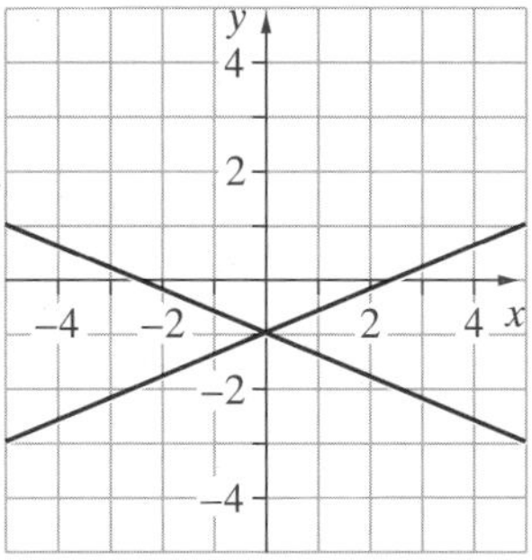

c

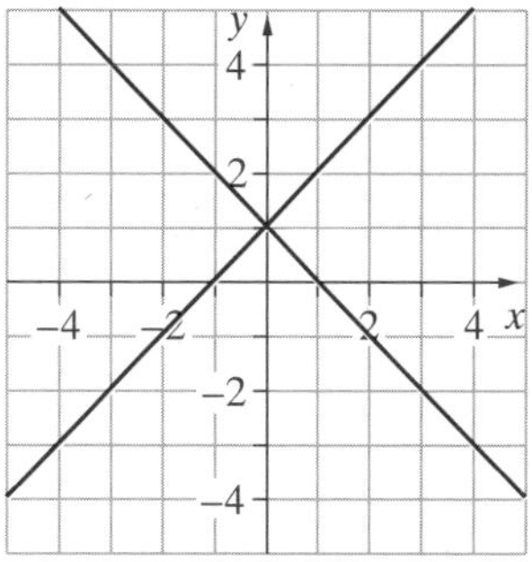

For each grid:

i Find the equation of each of the lines.

ii Describe any symmetries that you can see.

iii What connection is there between the gradients of each pair of lines?

3 Give the equation of each of these lines, all of which have negative gradients.

a

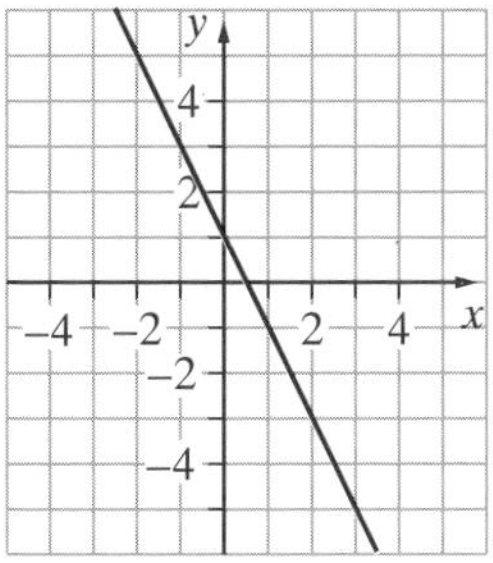

b

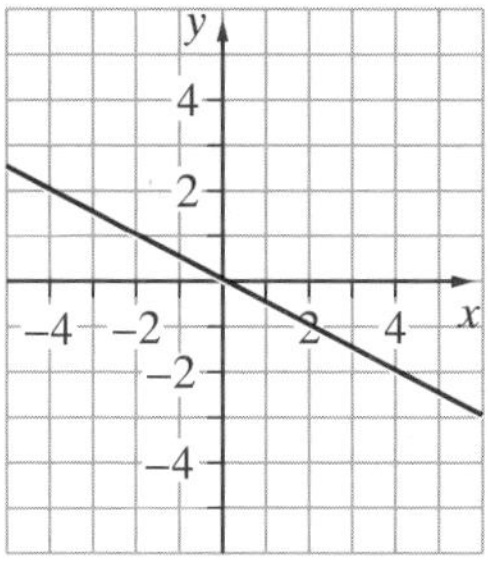

c

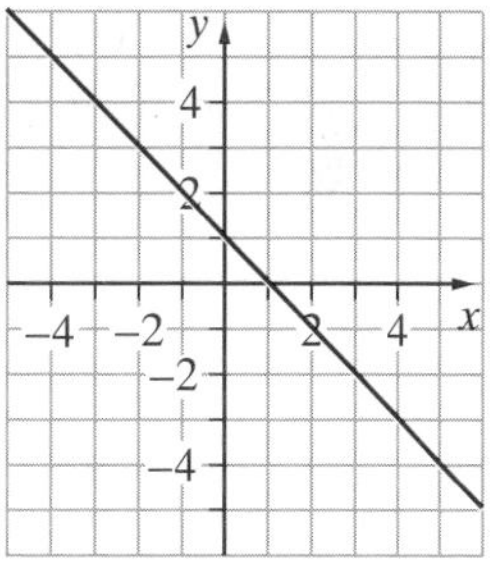

d

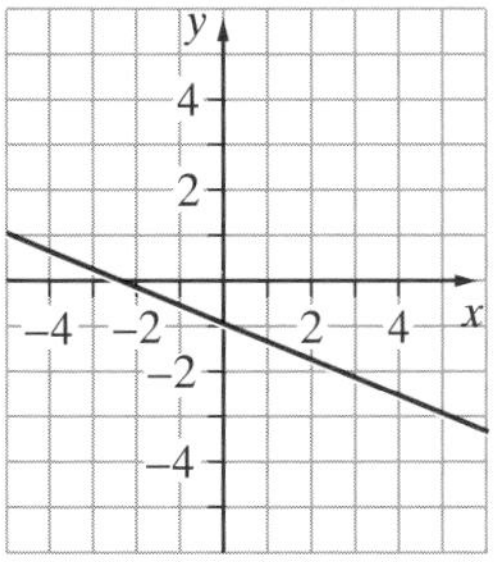

e

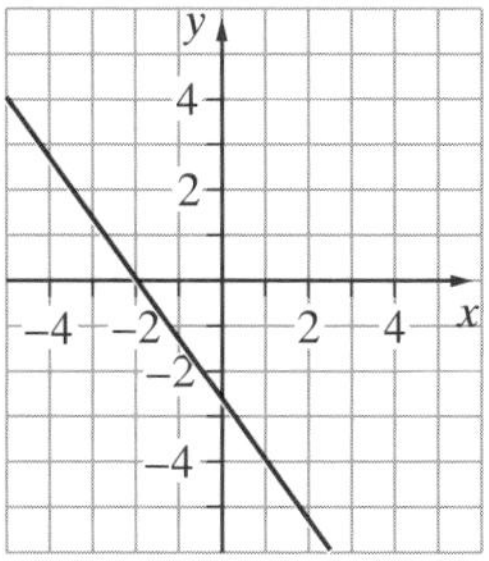

4 In each of these grids, there are three lines. One of them is $y = x$.

a

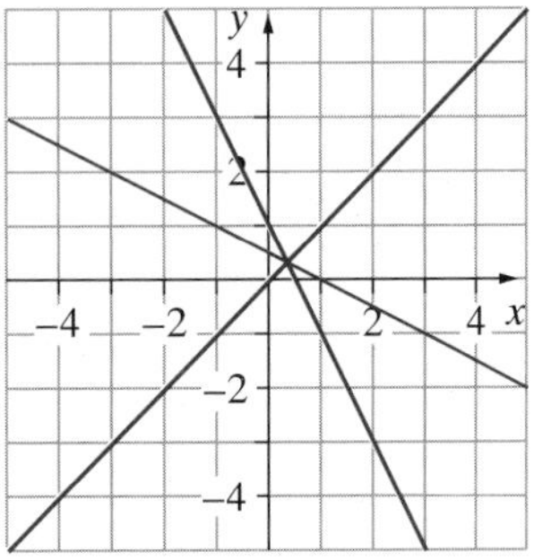

b

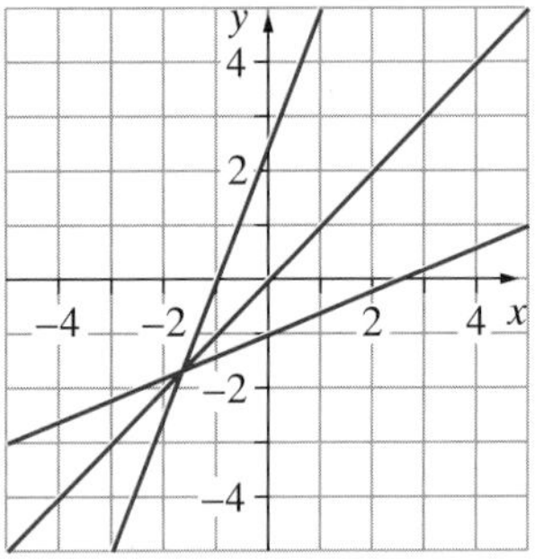

c

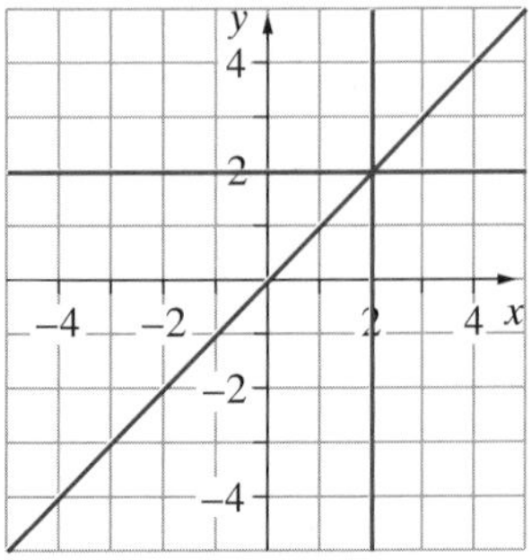

For each grid:

i Find the equation of each of the other two lines.

ii Describe any symmetries that you can see.

iii What connection is there between the gradients of each pair of lines?

Cover-up method for drawing graphs

The x-axis has the equation $\mathbf{y = 0}$. This means that all points on that axis have a y-value of 0.

The y-axis has the equation $\mathbf{x = 0}$. This means that all points on the y-axis have an x-value of 0. We can use this fact to draw any line that has an equation of the form $ax + by = c$.

Example Draw the graph of $4x + 5y = 20$.

Because the value of x is 0 on the y-axis, we can solve the equation for y:

$$4(0) + 5y = 20$$
$$5y = 20$$
$$\Rightarrow \quad y = 4$$

Hence, the line passes through the point (0, 4) on the y-axis (diagram **A**).

Because the value of y is 0 on the x-axis, we can also solve the equation for x:

$$4x + 5(0) = 20$$
$$4x = 20$$
$$\Rightarrow \quad x = 5$$

Hence, the line passes through the point (5, 0) on the x axis (diagram **B**). We need only two points to draw a line. (Normally, we would like a third point but in this case we can accept two.) The graph is drawn by joining the points (0, 4) and (5, 0) (diagram **C**).

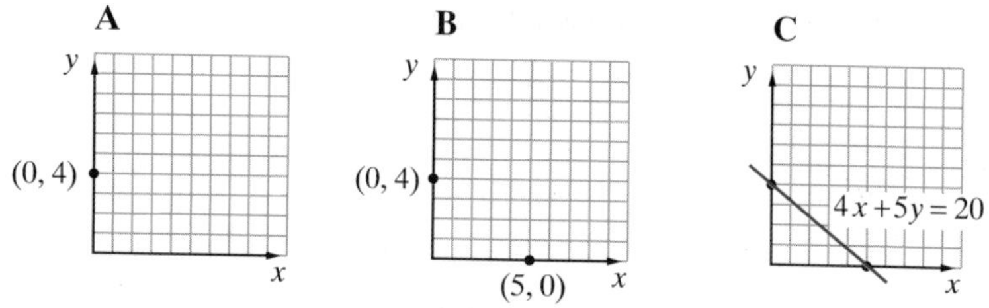

This type of equation can be drawn very easily, without much working at all, using the **cover-up** method.

Start with the equation	$4x + 5y = 20$
Cover up the x-term	[cover] $+ 5y = 20$
Solve the equation	$y = 4$
Now cover up the y-term	$4x +$ [cover] $= 20$
Solve the equation	$x = 5$

Giving the points 5 on the x-axis and 4 on the y-axis.

Exercise 14B

1 Draw these lines using the cover-up method. Use the same grid, taking x from –10 to 10 and y from –10 to 10. If the grid gets too 'crowded', draw another.

a $3x + 2y = 6$ **b** $4x + 3y = 12$ **c** $4x - 5y = 20$ **d** $x + y = 10$
e $3x - 2y = 18$ **f** $x - y = 4$ **g** $5x - 2y = 15$ **h** $2x - 3y = 15$
i $6x + 5y = 30$ **j** $x + y = -5$ **k** $x + y = 3$ **l** $x - y = -4$

2 **a** Using the cover-up method, draw the following lines on the same grid.
i $2x + y = 4$ **ii** $x - 2y = 2$
b Where do the lines cross?

3 **a** Using the cover-up method, draw the following lines on the same grid.
i $x + 2y = 6$ **ii** $2x - y = 2$
b Where do the lines cross?

4 **a** Using the cover-up method, draw the following lines on the same grid.
i $x + y = 6$ **ii** $x - y = 2$
b Where do the lines cross?

Uses of graphs

On pages 245–70, you met two uses of graphs in kinematics. Two other uses of graphs which we will now consider are finding formulae and solving simultaneous equations. Solving quadratic and other equations by graphical methods is covered on pages 331, 338–9 and 341–2.

Finding formulae or rules

Example A taxi fare will cost you more the further you go. The graph on the right illustrates the fares in one part of England.

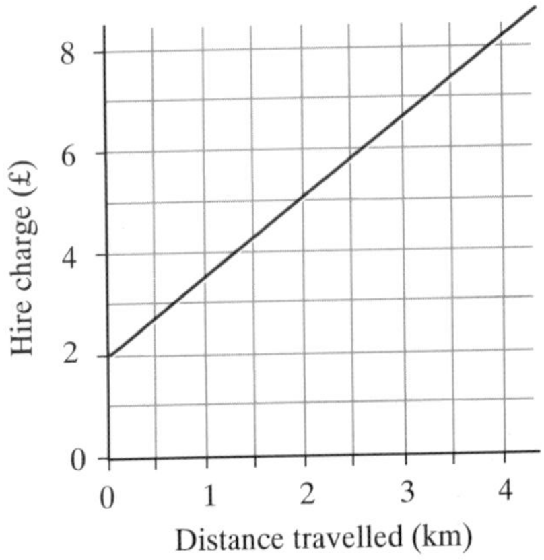

The taxi company charges a basic hire fee to start with of £2.00. This is shown on the graph as the point where the line cuts through the hire-charge axis (when distance travelled is 0).

The gradient of the line is

$$\frac{8-2}{4} = \frac{6}{4} = 1.5$$

This represents the hire charge per kilometre travelled.

So the total hire charge is made up of two parts: a basic hire charge of £2.00 and an additional charge of £1.50 per kilometre travelled. This can be put in a formula as

Hire charge = £2.00 + £1.50 per kilometre.

In this example, £2.00 is the constant term in the formula (the equation of the graph).

Exercise 14C

1 This graph is a conversion graph between °C and °F.

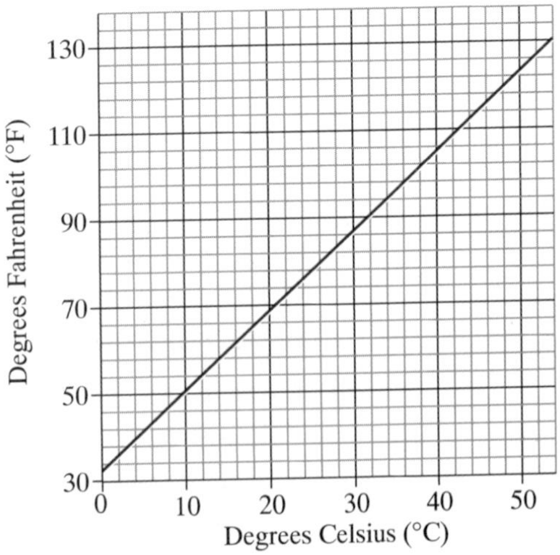

a How many °F are equivalent to 0 °C?

b What is the gradient of the line?

c From your answers to parts **a** and **b**, write down a rule which can be used to convert °C to °F.

2 The following graph illustrates the charges for fuel.

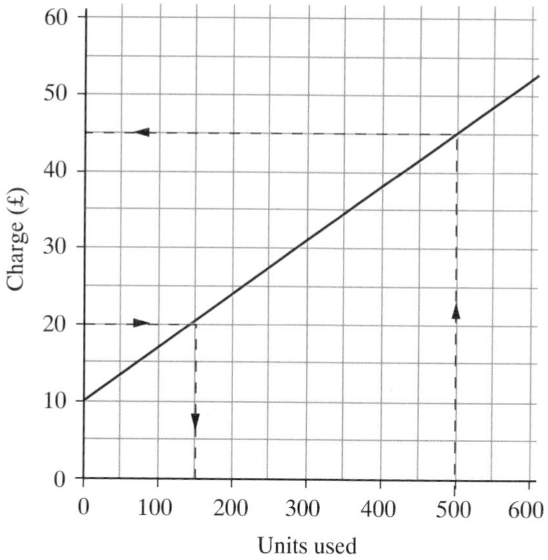

a What is the gradient of the line?

b The standing charge is the basic charge before the cost per unit is added. What is the standing charge?

c Write down the rule used to work out the total charge for different amounts of units used.

3 This graph shows the hire charge for heaters over so many days.

a Calculate the gradient of the line.

b What is the basic charge before the daily hire charge is added on?

c Write down the rule used to work out the total hire charge.

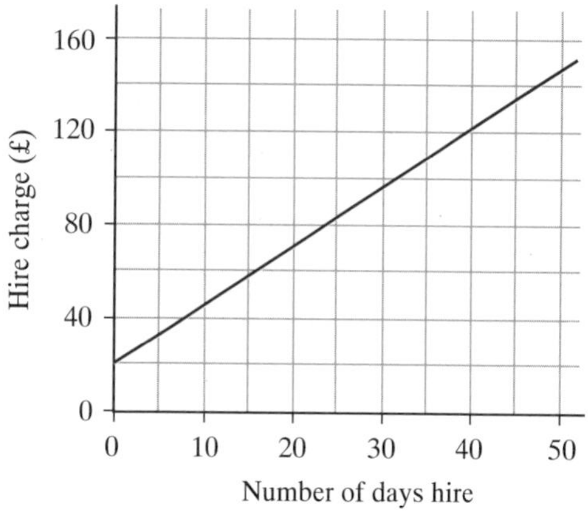

4 This graph shows the hire charge for a conference centre depending on the number of people at the conference.

a Calculate the gradient of the line.

b What is the basic fee for hiring the conference centre?

c Write down the rule used to work out the total hire charge for the centre.

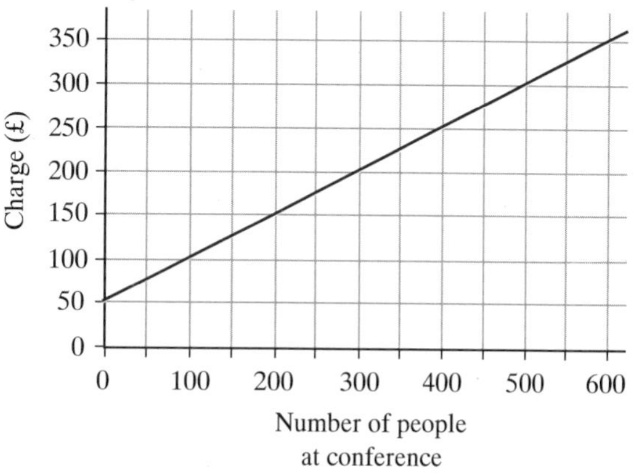

5 This graph shows the length of a spring for different weights attached to it.

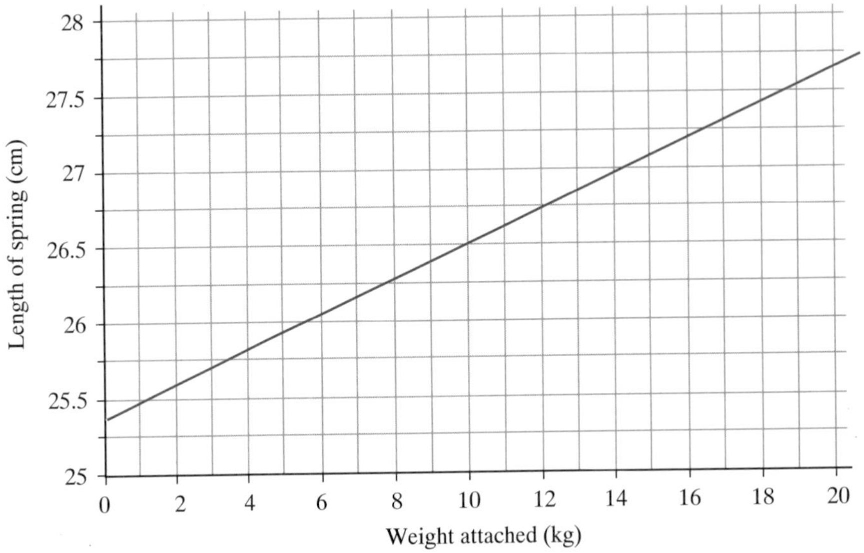

a Calculate the gradient of the line.

b How long is the spring when no weight is attached to it?

c By how much does the spring extend per kilogram?

d Write down the rule for finding the length of the spring for different weights.

Solving simultaneous equations

Example By drawing their graphs on the same grid, find the solution of the simultaneous equations

a $3x + y = 6$ **b** $y = 4x - 1$

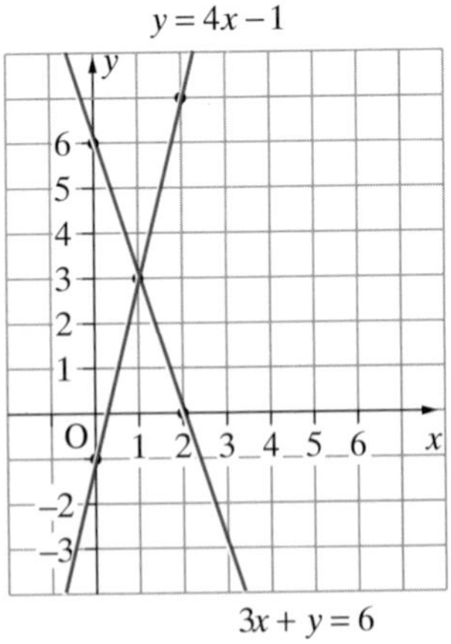

a The first graph is drawn using the cover-up method. It crosses the x-axis at (2, 0) and the y-axis at (0, 6).

b This graph can be drawn by finding some points or by the gradient–intercept method. If we use the gradient–intercept method, the graph crosses the y-axis at –1 and has a gradient of 4.

The point where the graphs intersect is (1, 3). So the solution to the simultaneous equations is $x = 1, y = 3$.

Exercise 14D

By drawing their graphs, find the solution of each of these pairs of simultaneous equations.

1 $x + 4y = 8$
$x - y = 3$

2 $y = 2x - 1$
$3x + 2y = 12$

3 $y = 2x + 4$
$y = x + 7$

4 $y = x$
$x + y = 10$

5 $y = 2x + 3$
$5x + y = 10$

6 $y = 5x + 1$
$y = 2x + 10$

7 $y = x + 8$
$x + y = 4$

8 $y - 3x = 9$
$y = x - 3$

9 $y = -x$
$y = 4x - 5$

10 $3x + 2y = 18$
$y = 3x$

11 $y = 3x + 2$
$y + x = 10$

12 $y = \frac{x}{3} + 1$
$x + y = 11$

Quadratic graphs

A quadratic graph has a term in x^2 in its equation. All of the following are quadratic equations and each would produce a quadratic graph.

$y = x^2$ $\quad y = x^2 + 5$ $\quad y = x^2 - 3x$

$y = x^2 + 5x + 6$ $\quad y = 3x^2 - 5x + 4$

Example Draw the graph of $y = x^2 + 5x + 6$ for $-5 \le x \le 3$.

Make a table, as shown below. Work out each row (x^2, $5x$, 6) separately, adding them together to obtain the values of y. Then plot the points from the table.

x	–5	–4	–3	–2	–1	0	1	2	3
x^2	25	16	9	4	1	0	1	4	9
$5x$	–25	–20	–15	–10	–5	0	5	10	15
6	6	6	6	6	6	6	6	6	6
y	6	2	0	0	2	6	12	20	30

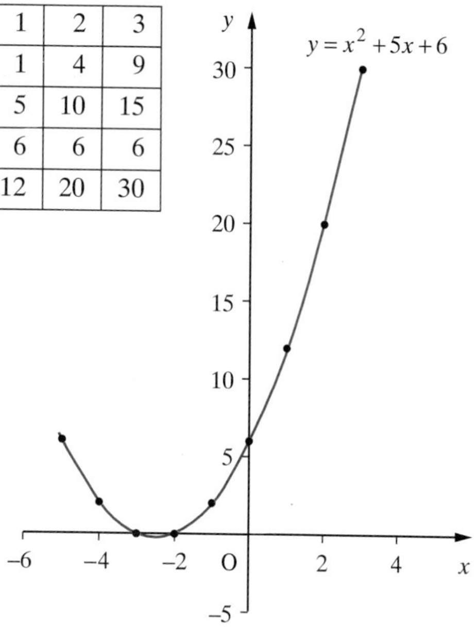

Note that in an examination paper you may be given only the first and last rows, with some values filled in. For example,

x	–5	–4	–3	–2	–1	0	1	2	3
y	6		0		2				30

In this case, you would either construct your own table, or work out the remaining y-values with a calculator.

Drawing accurate quadratic graphs

Note that, although it is difficult to draw accurate curves, examiners work to a **tolerance of only 1 mm**.

Here are some of the more common ways in which marks are lost in an examination (see also diagrams).

- When the points are too far apart, a curve tends to 'wobble'.
- Drawing curves in small sections leads to 'feathering'.
- The place where a curve should turn sharply is drawn 'flat'.
- A line is drawn through a point which, clearly, has been incorrectly plotted.

Wobbly curve

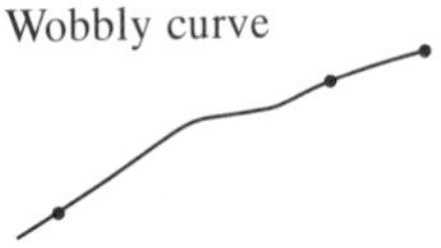

Feathering

Flat bottom

Miscalculated point

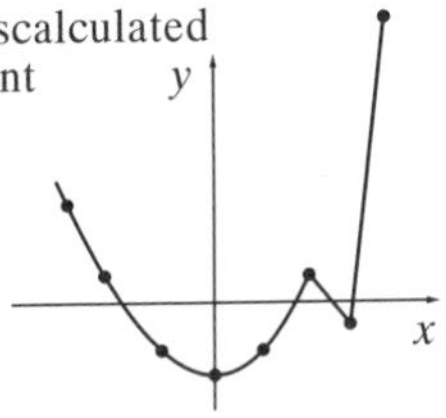

A quadratic graph drawn correctly will always give a smooth curve.

Exercise 14E

1 a Copy and complete the table for the graph of $y = 3x^2$ for $-3 \leq x \leq 3$.

x	–3	–2	–1	0	1	2	3
y	27		3			12	

b Use your graph to find the value of y when $x = -1.5$.

c Use your graph to find the values of x that give a y-value of 10.

2 a Copy and complete the table for the graph of $y = x^2 + 2$ for $-5 \leq x \leq 5$.

x	−5	−4	−3	−2	−1	0	1	2	3	4	5
$y = x^2 + 2$	27		11					6			

b Use your graph to find the value of y when $x = -2.5$.

c Use your graph to find the values of x that give a y-value of 14.

3 a Copy and complete the table for the graph of $y = x^2 - 3x$ for $-5 \leq x \leq 5$.

x	−5	−4	−3	−2	−1	0	1	2	3	4	5
x^2	25		9					4			
$-3x$	15							−6			
y	40							−2			

b Use your graph to find the value of y when $x = 3.5$.

c Use your graph to find the values of x that give a y-value of 5.

4 a Copy and complete the table for the graph of $y = x^2 - 2x - 8$ for $-5 \leq x \leq 5$.

x	−5	−4	−3	−2	−1	0	1	2	3	4	5
x^2	25		9					4			
$-2x$	10							−4			
-8	−8							−8			
y	27							−8			

b Use your graph to find the value of y when $x = 0.5$.

c Use your graph to find the values of x that give a y-value of −3.

5 a Copy and complete the table for the graph of $y = x^2 - 5x + 4$ for $-2 \leq x \leq 5$.

x	−2	−1	0	1	2	3	4	5
y	18		4			−2		

b Use your graph to find the value of y when $x = -0.5$.

c Use your graph to find the values of x that give a y-value of 3.

6 a Copy and complete the table for the graph of $y = x^2 + 2x - 1$ for $-3 \leq x \leq 3$.

x	−3	−2	−1	0	1	2	3
x^2	9				1	4	
$+2x$	−6		−2			4	
-1	−1	−1				−1	
y	2					7	

b Use your graph to find the y-value when $x = -2.5$.

c Use your graph to find the values of x that give a y-value of 1.

d On the same axes, draw the graph of $y = \frac{x}{2} + 2$.

e Where do the graphs $y = x^2 + 2x - 1$ and $y = \frac{x}{2} + 2$ cross?

7 a Copy and complete the table for the graph of $y = x^2 + 2x + 3$ for $-3 \le x \le 3$.

x	−3	−2	−1	0	1	2	3
x^2	9				1	4	
$-2x$	6					−4	
+3	+3					+3	
y	18					3	

b Use your graph to find the y-value when $x = 1.5$.

c Use your graph to find the values of x that give a y-value of 4.

d On the same axes, draw the graph of $y = 2x + 8$.

e Where do the graphs $y = x^2 - 2x + 3$ and $y = 2x + 8$ cross?

8 a Copy and complete the table for the graph of $y = x^2 - x + 6$ for $-3 \le x \le 3$.

x	−3	−2	−1	0	1	2	3
x^2	9				1	4	
$-x$	3					−2	
+6	+6					+6	
y	18					8	

b Use your graph to find the y-value when $x = 2.5$.

c Use your graph to find the values of x that give a y-value of 8.

d Copy and complete the table to draw the graph of $y = x^2 + 5$ on the same axes.

x	−3	−2	−1	0	1	2	3
y	14		6				14

e Where do the graphs $y = x^2 - x + 6$ and $y = x^2 + 5$ cross?

9 a Copy and complete the table for the graph of $y = x^2 + 2x + 1$ for $-3 \le x \le 3$.

x	−3	−2	−1	0	1	2	3
x^2	9				1	4	
$+2x$	−6					4	
+1	+1					+1	
y	4						

b Use your graph to find the y-value when $x = 1.7$.

c Use your graph to find the values of x that give a y-value of 2.

d On the same axes, draw the graph of $y = 2x + 2$.

e Where do the graphs $y = x^2 + 2x + 1$ and $y = 2x + 2$ cross?

10 a Copy and complete the table for the graph of $y = 2x^2 - 5x - 3$ for $-2 \le x \le 4$.

x	−2	−1.5	−1	−0.5	0	0.5	1	1.5	2	2.5	3	3.5	4
y	15	9			−3	−5				−3			9

b Where does the graph cross the x-axis?

Roots of a quadratic equation

If you look at your answer to question **10** in Exercise 14E, you will see that the graph crosses the x-axis at $x = -0.5$ and $x = 3$. Since the x-axis is the line $y = 0$, the y-value at any point on the axis is zero (see page 322). So, you have found the answer to the equation

$$0 = 2x^2 - 5x - 3 \quad \text{that is} \quad 2x^2 - 5x - 3 = 0$$

You met equations of this type on pages 233–40. They are known as quadratic equations. You solved them either by factorisation or by using the quadratic formula. That is, you found the values of x that made them true. Such values are called the **roots** of an equation. So in the case of the quadratic equation $2x^2 - 5x - 3 = 0$, its roots are -0.5 and 3.

Let's check these values:

For $x = 3$ $\quad 2(3)^2 - 5(3) - 3 = 18 - 15 - 3 = 0$

For $x = 0.5$ $\quad 2(-0.5)^2 - 5(-0.5) - 3 = 0.5 + 2.5 - 3 = 0$

We can find the roots of a quadratic equation by drawing its graph and finding where the graph crosses the x-axis.

Example

a Draw the graph of $y = x^2 - 3x - 4$ for $-2 \le x \le 5$.

b Use your graph to find the roots of the equation $x^2 - 3x - 4 = 0$.

a Set up a table.

x	-2	-1	0	1	2	3	4	5
x^2	4	1	0	1	4	9	16	25
$-3x$	6	3	0	-3	-6	-9	-12	-15
-4	-4	-4	-4	-4	-4	-4	-4	-4
y	6	0	-4	-6	-6	-4	0	6

Draw the graph.

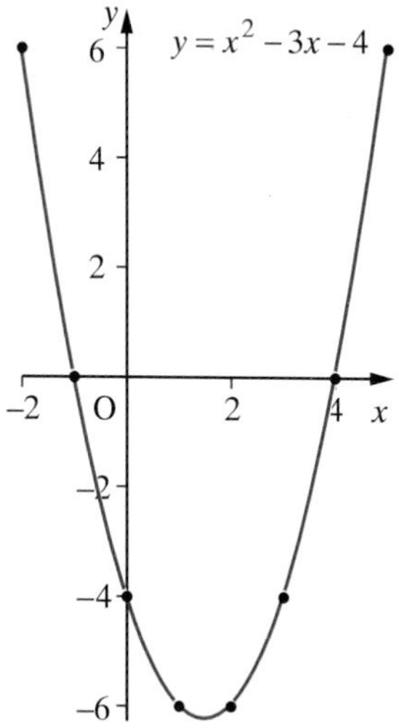

b The points where the graph crosses the x-axis are -1 and 4.

So, the roots of $x^2 - 3x - 4 = 0$ are $x = -1$ and $x = 4$.

Exercise 14F

1 a Copy and complete the table to draw the graph of $y = x^2 - 4$ for $-4 \leq x \leq 4$.

x	−4	−3	−2	−1	0	1	2	3	4
y	12			−3				5	

b Use your graph to find the roots of $x^2 - 4 = 0$.

2 a Copy and complete the table to draw the graph of $y = x^2 - 9$ for $-4 \leq x \leq 4$.

x	−4	−3	−2	−1	0	1	2	3	4
y	7				−9			0	

b Use your graph to find the roots of $x^2 - 9 = 0$.

3 a Look at the equations of the graphs you drew in questions **1** and **2**. Is there a connection between the numbers in each equation and its roots?

b Before you draw the graphs in parts **c** and **d**, try to predict what their roots will be.

c Copy and complete the table to draw the graph of $y = x^2 - 1$ for $-4 \leq x \leq 4$.

x	−4	−3	−2	−1	0	1	2	3	4
y	15				−1			8	

d Copy and complete the table to draw the graph of $y = x^2 - 5$ for $-4 \leq x \leq 4$.

x	−4	−3	−2	−1	0	1	2	3	4
y	11		−1					4	

e Were your predictions correct?

4 a Copy and complete the table to draw the graph of $y = x^2 + 4x$ for $-5 \leq x \leq 2$.

x	−5	−4	−3	−2	−1	0	1	2
x^2	25			4			1	
$+4x$	−20			−8			4	
y	5			−4			5	

b Use your graph to find the roots of the equation $x^2 + 4x = 0$.

5 a Copy and complete the table to draw the graph of $y = x^2 - 6x$ for $-2 \leq x \leq 8$.

x	−2	−1	0	1	2	3	4	5	6	7	8
x^2	4			1			16				
$-6x$	12			−6			−24				
y	16			−5			−8				

b Use your graph to find the roots of the equation $x^2 - 6x = 0$.

6 a Copy and complete the table to draw the graph of $y = x^2 + 3x$ for $-5 \leq x \leq 3$.

x	−5	−4	−3	−2	−1	0	1	2	3
y	10			−2				10	

b Use your graph to find the roots of the equation $x^2 + 3x = 0$.

7 a Look at the equations of the graphs you drew in questions **4**, **5** and **6**. Is there a connection between the numbers in each equation and the roots?

b Before you draw the graphs in parts **c** and **d**, try to predict what their roots will be.

c Copy and complete the table to draw the graph of $y = x^2 - 3x$ for $-2 \leq x \leq 5$.

x	−2	−1	0	1	2	3	4	5
y	10			−2				10

d Copy and complete the table to draw the graph of $y = x^2 + 5x$ for $-6 \leq x \leq 2$.

x	−6	−5	−4	−3	−2	−1	0	1	2
y	6			−6				6	

e Were your predictions correct?

8 a Copy and complete the table to draw the graph of $y = x^2 - 4x + 4$ for $-1 \leq x \leq 3$.

x	−1	0	1	2	3
y	9				1

b Use your graph to find the roots of the equation $x^2 - 4x + 4 = 0$.

c What happens with the roots?

9 a Copy and complete the table to draw the graph of $y = x^2 - 6x + 3$ for $-1 \leq x \leq 7$.

x	−1	0	1	2	3	4	5	6	7
y	10			−5			−2		

b Use your graph to find the roots of the equation $x^2 - 6x + 3 = 0$.

10 a Copy and complete the table to draw the graph of $y = 2x^2 + 5x - 6$ for $-5 \leq x \leq 2$.

x	−5	−4	−3	−2	−1	0	1	2
y								

b Use your graph to find the roots of the equation $2x^2 + 5x - 6 = 0$.

Square-root graphs

The graph of $y = \sqrt{x}$ is one you should be able to recognise and draw.

When you are working out co-ordinates in order to plot $y = \sqrt{x}$, remember that for every value of x (except $x = 0$) there are two square roots, one positive and the other negative, which give two pairs of co-ordinates. For example,

when $x = 1$, $y = \pm 1$ giving co-ordinates $(1, -1)$ and $(1, 1)$

when $x = 4$, $y = \pm 2$ giving co-ordinates $(4, -2)$ and $(4, 2)$

In the case of $x = 0$, $y = 0$ and so there is only one pair of co-ordinates: $(0, 0)$.

Using these five points, you can draw the graph.

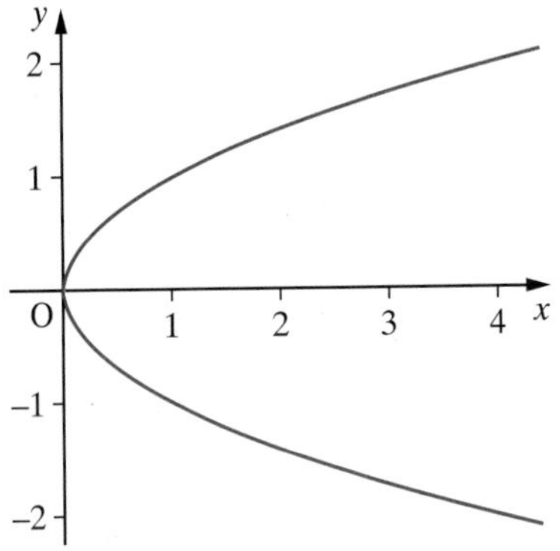

Reciprocal graphs

A reciprocal equation has the form $y = \frac{a}{x}$.

Examples of reciprocal equations or graphs are

$$y = \frac{1}{x} \qquad y = \frac{4}{x} \qquad y = -\frac{3}{x}$$

All reciprocal graphs have a similar shape and some symmetry properties.

Example Complete the table to draw the graph of $y = \frac{1}{x}$ for $-4 \le x \le 4$.

x	–4	–3	–2	–1	1	2	3	4
y								

Values are rounded off to two decimal places, as it is unlikely that you could plot a value more accurately than this. The completed table is

x	–4	–3	–2	–1	1	2	3	4
y	–0.25	–0.33	–0.5	–1	1	0.5	0.33	0.25

The graph plotted from these values is shown in **A**. This is not much of a graph and does not show the properties of the reciprocal function. If we take x-values from -0.8 to 0.8 in steps of 0.2, we get the next table.

Note that we cannot use $x = 0$ since $\frac{1}{0}$ is infinity.

x	-0.8	-0.6	-0.4	-0.2	0.2	0.4	0.6	0.8
y	-1.25	-1.67	-2.5	-5	5	2.5	1.67	1.25

Plotting these points as well gives the graph in **B**.

A

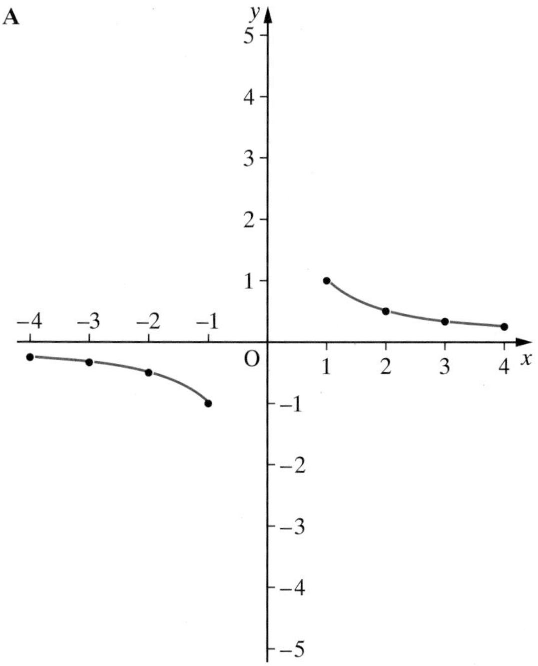

B

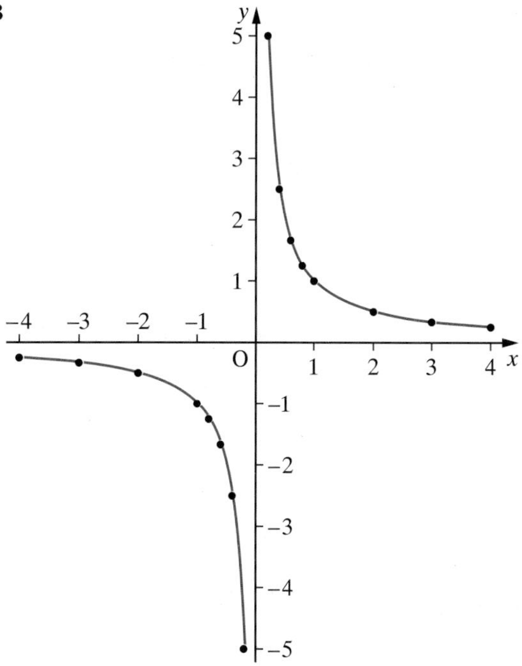

From the graph in **B**, the following properties can be seen.

- The lines $y = x$ and $y = -x$ are lines of symmetry.
- The closer x gets to zero, the nearer the graph gets to the y-axis.
- As x increases, the graph gets closer to the x-axis.

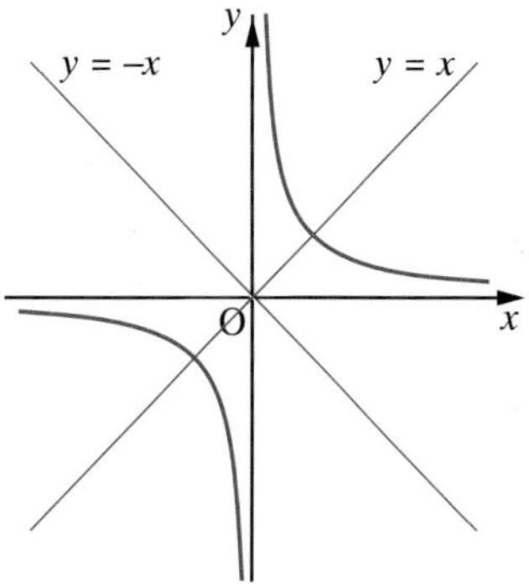

The graph never actually touches the axes, it just gets closer and closer to them. A line to which a graph gets closer but never touches or crosses is called an **asymptote**.

These properties are true for **all reciprocal graphs**.

Exercise 14G

1 a Complete the table to draw the graph of $y = \frac{2}{x}$ for $-4 \leq x \leq 4$.

x	0.2	0.4	0.5	0.8	1	1.5	2	3	4
y	10.00		4.00	2.50			1.00		0.50

b Use your graph to find

i the y-value when $x = 2.5$ **ii** the x-value when $y = -1.25$

2 a Complete the table to draw the graph of $y = \frac{4}{x}$ for $-10 \leq x \leq 10$.

x	0.4	0.5	0.8	1	2	4	5	8	10
y	10.00		5.00				0.80		0.40

b Use your graph to find

i the y-value when $x = 6$ **ii** the x-value when $y = -6$

3 a Complete the table to draw the graph of $y = \frac{1}{x}$ for $-15 \leq x \leq 15$.

x	0.1	0.2	0.3	0.5	0.8	1	3	5	10	15
y	10.00		3.33			1.00			0.10	

b Use your graph to find

i the y-value when $x = 8$ **ii** the x-value when $y = -4$

4 a Complete the table to draw the graph of $y = 5\sqrt{x}$ for $0 \leq x \leq 5$.

x	0	1	2	3	4	5
$\sqrt{x}$					2 and –2	
$y = 5\sqrt{x}$					10 and –10	

b Use your graph to find

i the values of y when $x = 3.5$ **ii** the value of x when $y = 8$

5 a Complete the table to draw the graph of $y = \frac{1}{2}\sqrt{x}$ for $0 \leq x \leq 5$.

x	0	1	2	3	4	5
$\sqrt{x}$					2 and –2	
$y = \frac{1}{2}\sqrt{x}$					1 and –1	

b Use your graph to find

i the values of y when $x = 2.5$ **ii** the value of x when $y = 0.75$

6 a Complete the table to draw the graph of $y = \sqrt{x-3}$ for $0 \le x \le 8$.

x	3	4	5	6	7	8
$x - 3$					4	
$y = \sqrt{x-3}$					2 and –2	

b Use your graph to find

i the values of y when $x = 6.5$ **ii** the value of x when $y = 1.5$

7 a Complete the table to draw the graph of $y = \dfrac{100}{x}$ for $-400 \le x \le 400$.

x	10	20	40	50	80	100	200	300	400
y	10.00		2.5			1.00			0.25

b Use your graph to find

i the y-value when $x = -150$ **ii** the x-value when $y = 4$

8 a Complete the table to draw the graph of $y = \dfrac{1}{x}$ for $-5 \le x \le 5$.

x	0.1	0.2	0.4	0.5	1	2	2.5	4	5
y	10.00		2.5		1.00				0.2

b On the same axes, draw the line $x + y = 5$.

c Use your graph to find the x-values of the points where the graphs cross.

9 a Complete the table to draw the graph of $y = \dfrac{5}{x}$ for $-20 \le x \le 20$.

x	0.2	0.4	0.5	1	2	5	10	15	20
y	25.00		10						0.25

b On the same axes, draw the line $y = x + 10$.

c Use your graph to find the x-value of the points where the graphs cross.

10 a Complete the table to draw the graph of $y = \dfrac{2}{x} + 1$ for $-4 \le x \le 4$.

x	–4	–2	–1.5	–1	–0.8	–0.5	–0.4	–0.2	0.2	0.4	0.5	0.8	1	1.5	2	4
y	0.5	0.0				–3.0			11		5.00	3.50			2.00	1.5

b Complete the table to draw the graph of $y = \dfrac{2}{x} - 3$ for $-4 \le x \le 4$. Use the same axes as graph **a**.

x	–4	–2	–1.5	–1	–0.8	–0.5	–0.4	–0.2	0.2	0.4	0.5	0.8	1	1.5	2	4
y	–3.5	–4.0				–7.0			7.0		1.00	–0.5			–2.0	–2.5

c Compare your graphs with the one you drew in question **1**. Describe the differences.

Cubic graphs

A cubic function or graph is one which contains a term in x^3. The following are examples of cubic graphs

$$y = x^3 \qquad y = x^3 - 2x^2 - 3x - 4 \qquad y = x^3 - x^2 - 4x + 4$$

The techniques used to draw them are exactly the same as those for quadratic and reciprocal graphs.

Example

a Complete the table to draw the graph of $y = x^3 - x^2 - 4x + 4$ for $-3 \le x \le 3$.

x	−3	−2.5	−2	−1.5	−1	−0.5	0	0.5	1	1.5	2	2.5	3
y	−20.00		0.00		6.00		4.00	1.88				3.38	10.00

b Use the graph to find the solution of the equation $x^3 - x^2 - 4x - 1 = 0$.

a The completed table (to two decimal places) is given below and the graph is shown below right.

x	−3	−2.5	−2	−1.5	−1	−0.5	0	0.5	1	1.5	2	2.5	3
y	−20.00	−7.88	0.00	4.38	6.00	5.63	4.00	1.88	0.00	−0.88	0.00	3.38	10.00

b We need to see the similarity between the equation of the graph, $y = x^3 - x^2 - 4x + 4$, and the equation to be solved, $x^3 - x^2 - 4x - 1 = 0$. So we rearrange the equation to be solved as

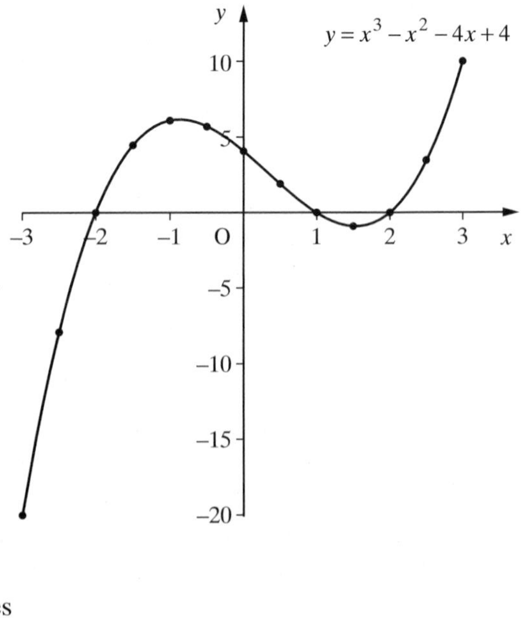

$$x^3 - x^2 - 4x + 4 = something$$

That is, we want to make the left-hand side of the equation to be solved the same as the right-hand side of the equation of the graph. We can do this by adding 5 to the −1 to make +4. So we add 5 to **both** sides of the equation to be solved, which gives

$$x^3 - x^2 - 4x - 1 + 5 = 0 + 5$$
$$x^3 - x^2 - 4x + 4 = 5$$

Hence, we simply need to draw the straight line $y = 5$ and find the x co-ordinates of the points where it crosses $y = x^3 - x^2 - 4x + 4$.

The solutions can now be read from the graph as $x = -1.4, -0.3$ and 2.7.

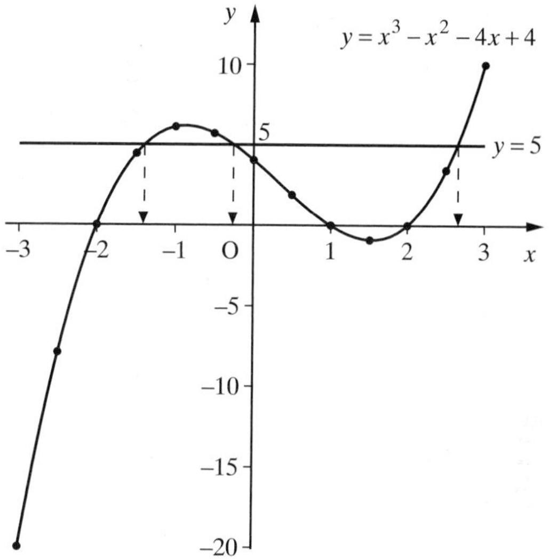

Exercise 14H

1 a Complete the table to draw the graph of $y = x^3 + 3$ for $-3 \leq x \leq 3$.

x	−3	−2.5	−2	−1.5	−1	−0.5	0	0.5	1	1.5	2	2.5	3
y	−24.00	−12.63			2.00		3.00	3.13			11.00		30.00

b Use your graph to find the y-value for an x-value of 1.2.

2 a Complete the table to draw the graph of $y = 2x^3$ for $-3 \leq x \leq 3$.

x	−3	−2.5	−2	−1.5	−1	−0.5	0	0.5	1	1.5	2	2.5	3
y		−31.25		−6.75			0.00	0.25			16.00		

b Use your graph to find the y-value for an x-value of 2.7.

3 a Complete the table to draw the graph of $y = -x^3$ for $-3 \leq x \leq 3$.

x	−3	−2.5	−2	−1.5	−1	−0.5	0	0.5	1	1.5	2	2.5	3
y	27.00		8.00	3.38			0.00	−0.13			−8.00	−15.63	

b Use your graph to find the y-value for an x-value of −0.6.

4 a Complete the table to draw the graph of $y = x^3 + 3x$ for $-3 \leq x \leq 3$.

x	−3	−2.5	−2	−1.5	−1	−0.5	0	0.5	1	1.5	2	2.5	3
y	−36.00		−14.00	−7.88			0.00	1.63				23.13	

b Use your graph to find the x-value for a y-value of 2.

5 a Complete the table to draw the graph of $y = x^3 - 3x^2 - 3x$ for $-3 \leq x \leq 3$.

x	−3	−2.5	−2	−1.5	−1	−0.5	0	0.5	1	1.5	2	2.5	3
y	−45.00		−14.00	−5.63			0.00	−0.63				−10.63	

b Use your graph to find the y-value for an x-value of 1.8.

6 a Complete the table to draw the graph of $y = x^3 - 3x + 1$ for $-3 \leq x \leq 3$.

x	−3	−2.5	−2	−1.5	−1	−0.5	0	0.5	1	1.5	2	2.5	3
y	−17.00		−1.00	2.13			1.00	−0.38				9.13	

b Use your graph to find the roots of the equation $x^3 - 3x + 1 = 0$.

7 a Complete the table to draw the graph of $y = x^3 - 3x^2 + 1$ for $-2 \leq x \leq 4$.

x	−2	−1.5	−1	−0.5	0	0.5	1	1.5	2	2.5	3	3.5	4
y	−19.00		−3.00	0.13			−1.00	−2.38				7.13	

b Use your graph to solve the equation $x^3 - 3x^2 - 2 = 0$.

8 a Complete the table to draw the graph of $y = x^3 - 6x + 2$ for $-3 \leq x \leq 3$.

x	−3	−2.5	−2	−1.5	−1	−0.5	0	0.5	1	1.5	2	2.5	3
y	−7.00		6.00	7.63			2.00	−0.88				2.63	

b Use your graph to solve the equation $x^3 - 6x + 3 = 0$.

9 a Complete the table to draw the graph of $y = x^3 - 2x + 5$ for $-3 \leq x \leq 3$.

x	−3	−2.5	−2	−1.5	−1	−0.5	0	0.5	1	1.5	2	2.5	3
y	−16.00		1.00	4.63			5.00	4.13				15.63	

b On the same axes, draw the graph of $y = x + 6$.

c Use your graph to find the x-values of the points where the graphs cross.

10 a Complete the table to draw the graph of $y = x^3 - 2x + 1$ for $-3 \leq x \leq 3$.

x	−3	−2.5	−2	−1.5	−1	−0.5	0	0.5	1	1.5	2	2.5	3
y	−20.00		−3.00	0.63			1.00	0.13				11.63	

b On the same axes, draw the graph of $y = x$.

c Use your graph to find the x-values of the points where the graphs cross.

11 Sketch a copy of each of these graphs and label it as linear, quadratic, reciprocal, cubic or none of these.

a

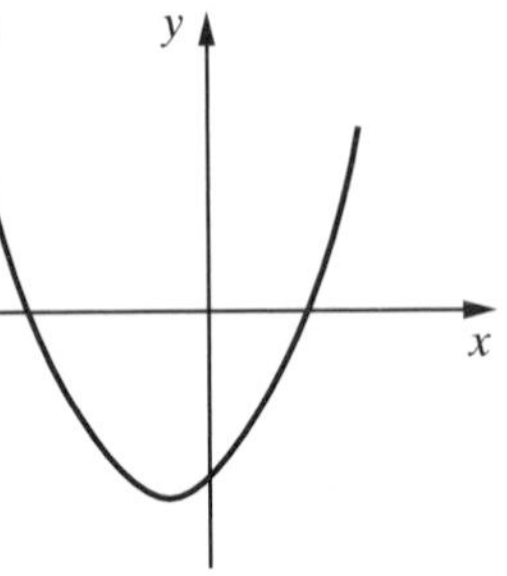

b

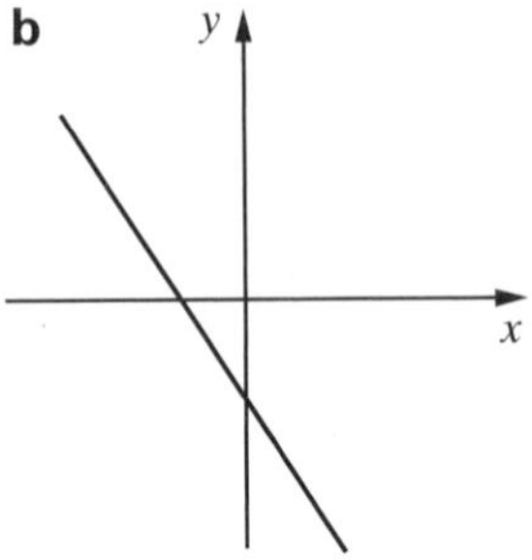

c

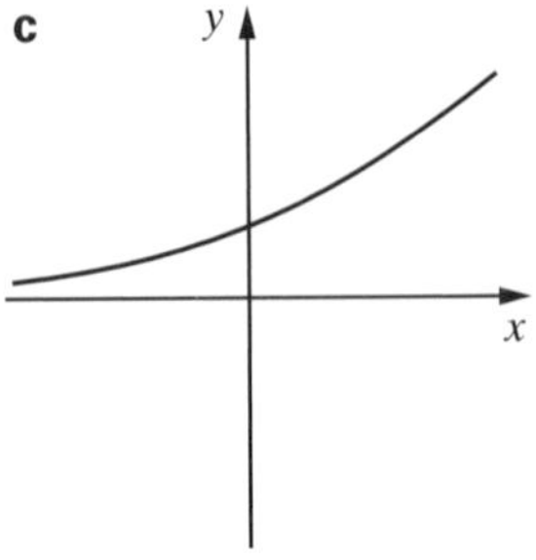

d

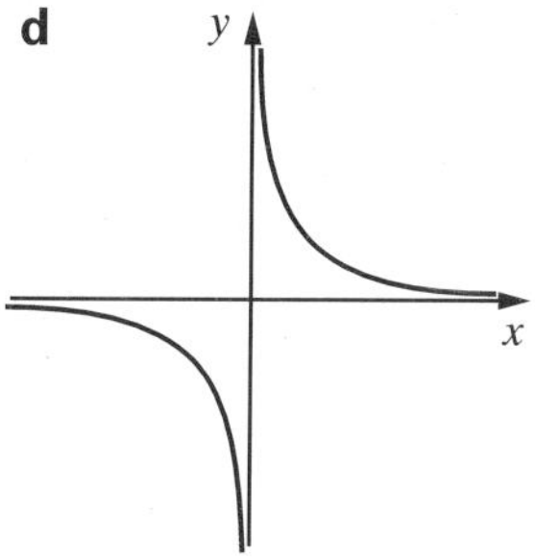

e

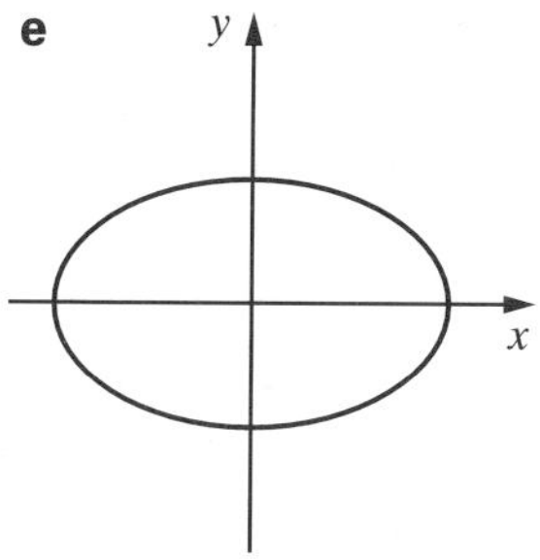

f

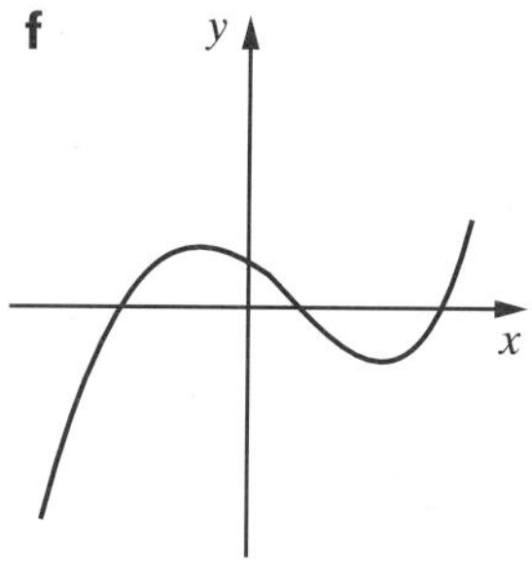

g

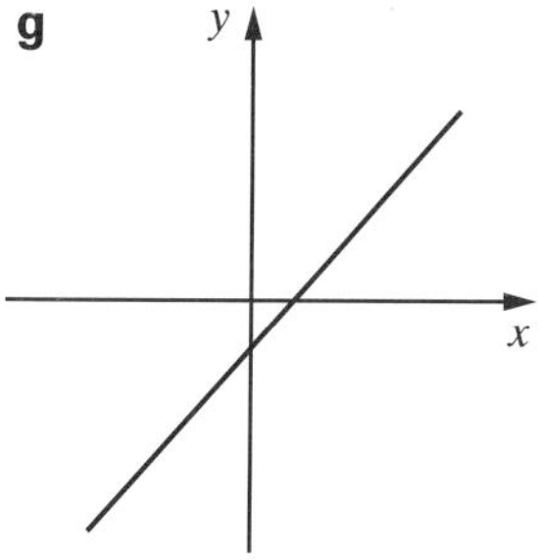

h

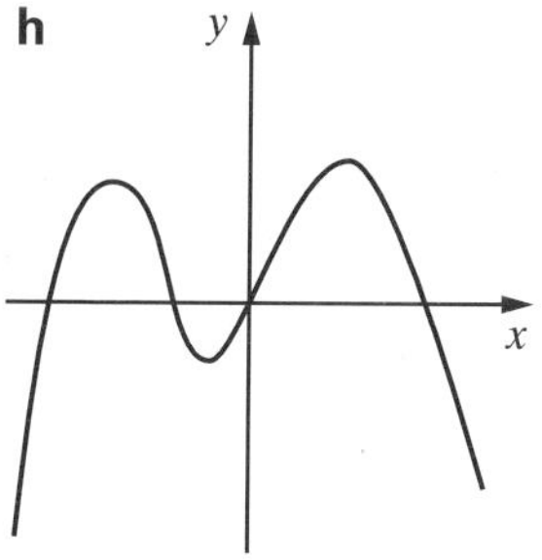

i

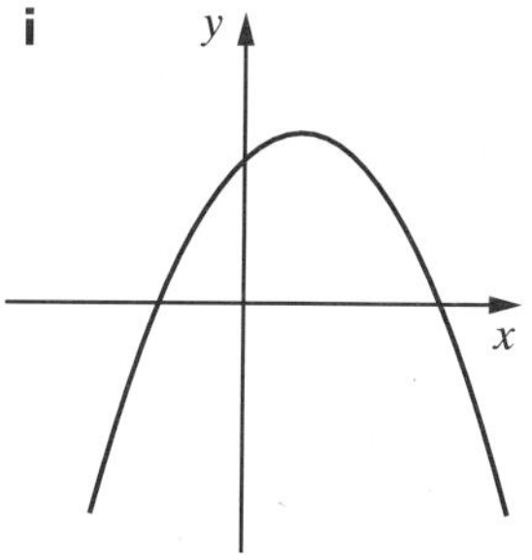

Solving equations by the method of intersection

Many equations can be solved by drawing two intersecting graphs on the same axes and using the x-value(s) of their point(s) of intersection. (In the GCSE examination, you are very likely to be presented with two drawn graphs and asked to use them to solve a given equation.)

Follow through the next example, which shows how this method works.

Example Show how each equation given below can be solved using the graph of $y = x^3 - 2x - 2$ and its intersection with another graph. In each case, give the equation of the other graph and the solution(s).

a $x^3 - 2x - 4 = 0$ **b** $x^3 - 3x - 3 = 0$

The equation to be solved is rearranged in the form of the given equation, in this case $y = x^3 - 2x - 2$. That is, the left-hand side of the equation to be solved is made the same as the right-hand side of the given equation.

a So, $x^3 - 2x - 4 = 0$ is rearranged as

$$x^3 - 2x - 4 + (2) = 0 + (2)$$

That is $x^3 - 2x - 2 = 2$

The graphs of $y = x^3 - 2x - 2$ and $y = 2$ are then drawn on the same axes.

The intersection of these two graphs is the solution of $x^3 - 2x - 4 = 0$.

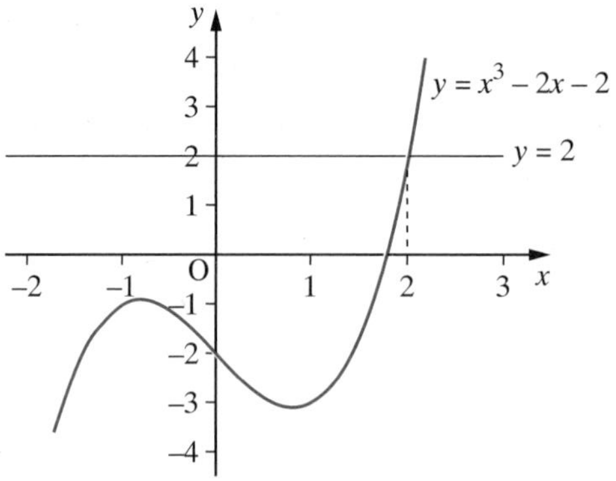

The other graph is $y = 2$ and the solution is $x = 2$.

b Here, $x^3 - 3x - 3 = 0$ is rearranged as

$$x^3 - 3x + (x) - 3 + (1) = x + 1$$

That is $$x^3 - 2x - 2 = x + 1$$

The graph of $y = x^3 - 2x - 2$ and $y = x + 1$ are then drawn on the same axes.

The intersection of the two graphs is the solution of $x^3 - 3x - 3 = 0$.

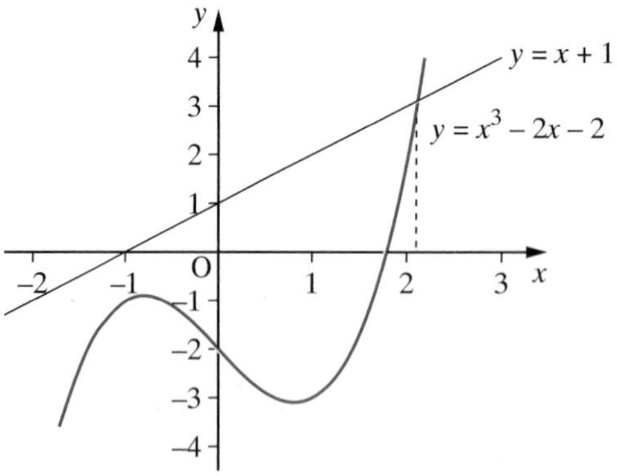

The other graph is $y = x + 1$ and the solution is $x = 2.1$

Exercise 14I

In questions **1** to **5**, use the graphs given here. In questions **6** to **10**, either draw the graphs yourself or use a graphics calculator to draw them.

1 Below is the graph of $y = x^2 - 3x - 6$. Use this graph to solve

a $x^2 - 3x - 6 = 0$ **b** $x^2 - 3x - 6 = 4$ **c** $x^2 - 3x - 2 = 0$ **d** $2x^2 - 6x + 2 = 0$

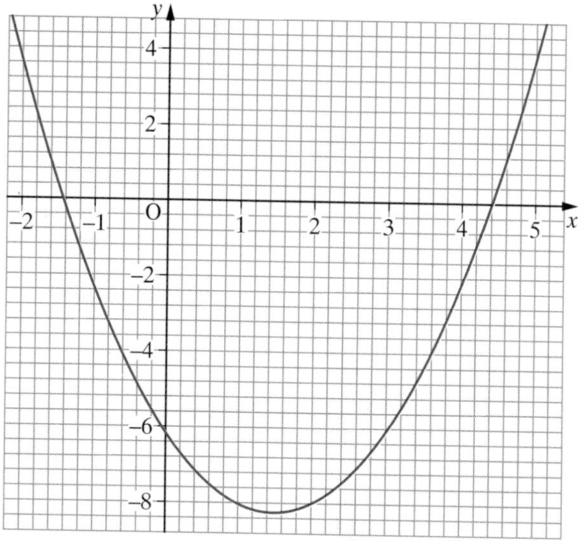

2 Below is the graph of $y = x^2 + 4x - 5$. Use this graph to solve

a $x^2 + 4x - 5 = 0$ **b** $x^2 + 4x - 5 = 2$ **c** $x^2 + 4x - 4 = 0$ **d** $3x^2 + 12x + 6 = 0$

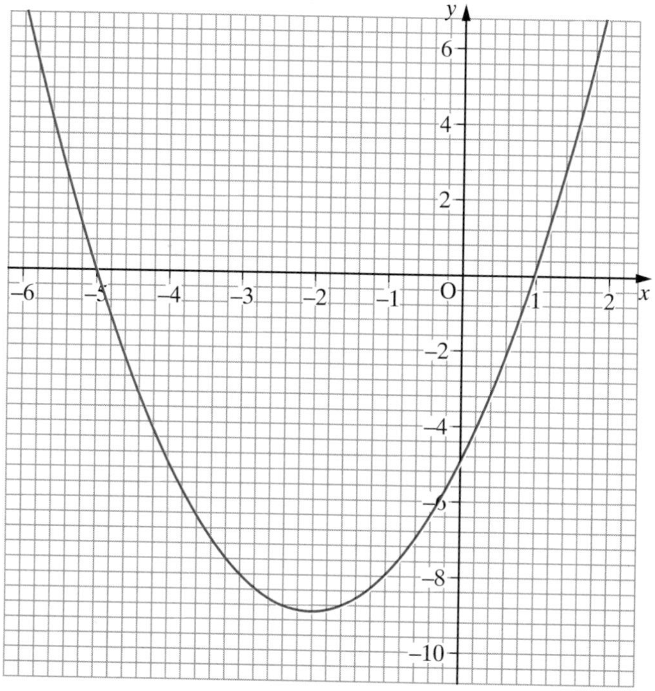

3 Below are the graphs of $y = x^2 - 5x + 3$ and $y = x + 3$. Use these graphs to solve

a $x^2 - 5x + 3 = 0$ **b** $x^2 - 5x + 3 = 2$ **c** $x^2 - 5x - 2 = 0$ **d** $x^2 - 6x = 0$

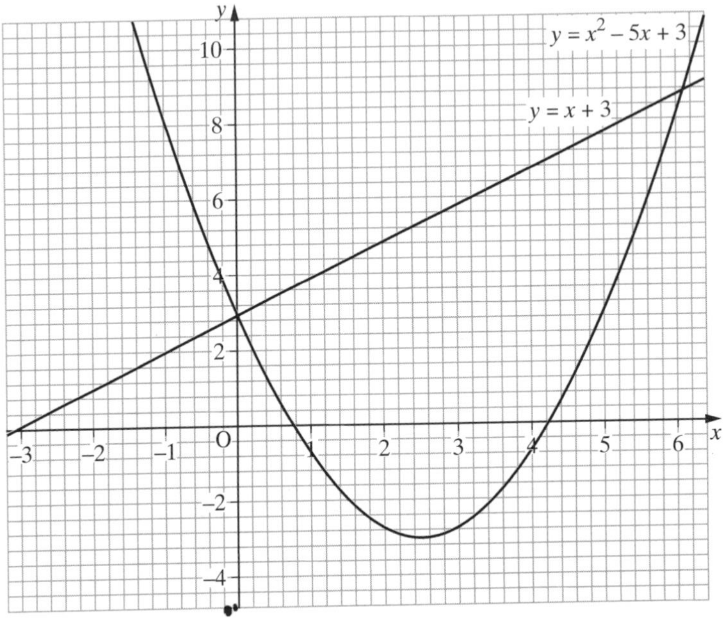

4 Alongside are the graphs of $y = x^2 - 2$ and $y = x + 2$. Use these graphs to solve

a $x^2 - 2 = 0$

b $x^2 - 2 = 3$

c $x^2 - 4 = 0$

d $x^2 - x - 4 = 0$

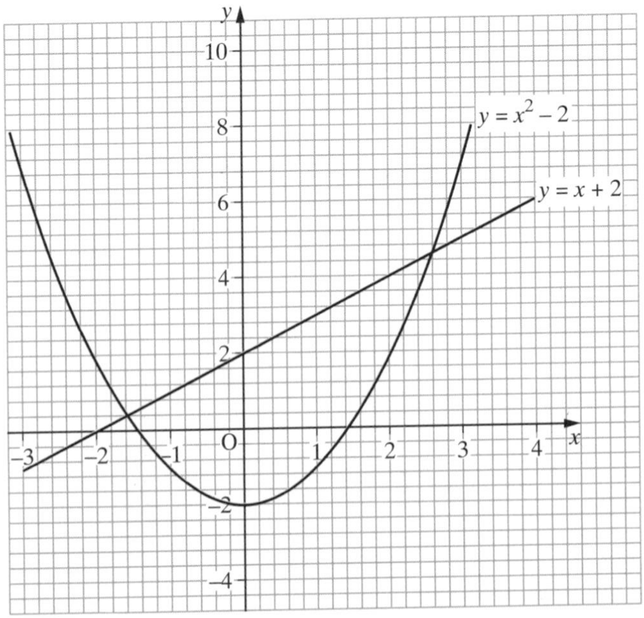

5 Alongside are the graphs of $y = x^3 - 2x^2$, $y = 2x + 1$ and $y = x - 1$. Use these graphs to solve

a $x^3 - 2x^2 = 0$

b $x^3 - 2x^2 = 3$

c $x^3 - 2x^2 + 1 = 0$

d $x^3 - 2x^2 - 2x - 1 = 0$

e $x^3 - 2x^2 - x + 1 = 0$

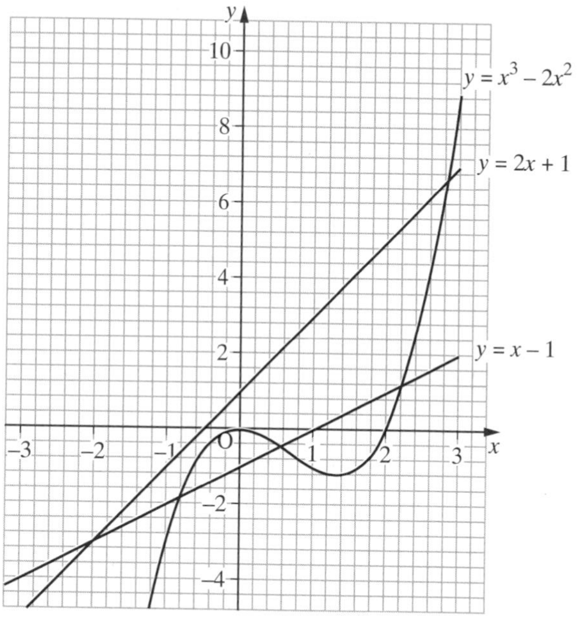

6 Draw the graph of $y = x^2 - 4x - 2$. Use your graph to solve

a $x^2 - 4x - 2 = 0$ **b** $x^2 - 4x - 5 = 0$

7 Draw the graph of $y = 2x^2 - 5$. Use your graph to solve

a $2x^2 - 5 = 0$ **b** $2x^2 - 3 = 0$

8 Draw the graphs of $y = x^2 - 3$ and $y = x + 2$ on the same axes. Use your graphs to solve

a $x^2 - 5 = 0$ **b** $x^2 - x - 5 = 0$

9 Draw the graphs of $y = x^2 - 3x - 2$ and $y = 2x - 3$ on the same axes. Use your graphs to solve

a $x^2 - 3x - 1 = 0$ **b** $x^2 - 5x + 1 = 0$

10 Draw the graphs of $y = x^3 - 2x^2 + 3x - 4$ and $y = 3x - 1$ on the same axes. Use your graphs to solve

a $x^3 - 2x^2 + 3x - 6 = 0$ **b** $x^3 - 2x^2 - 3 = 0$

Sketching graphs

When you are asked to sketch a graph, you do not plot a series of points but simply show the shape and position of the curve, and indicate a few key points, such as the intersection of the curve with either or both axes, or a maximum or minimum point.

Example 1 Sketch the graph of $y = x^2 + 3$.

This is a quadratic graph, so you know the shape of the curve, and you can see that when $x = 0$, $y = 3$. So the graph will look as in the diagram on the right.

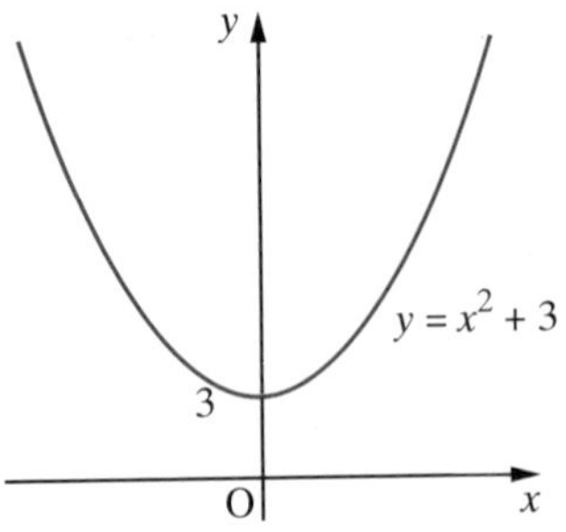

Example 2 Sketch the graph of $y = \dfrac{1}{x + 2}$.

This is a reciprocal graph, so you know the shape of the curve in both quadrants. You can see that there is an asymptote at $x = -2$, and another at $y = 0$. Also you can see that when $x = 0$, $y = \frac{1}{2}$, so the graph will look as in the diagram on the right.

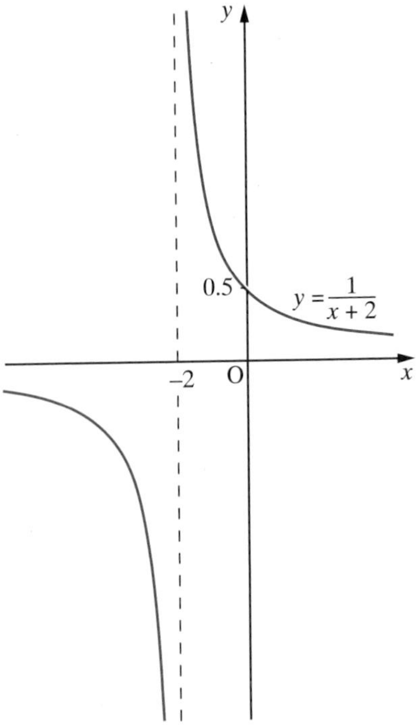

Exercise 14J

Sketch the graph of each of the following functions, pointing out any co-ordinates on the graph which are known.

1 $y = 2x - 5$ **2** $y = x^2 - 1$ **3** $y = x(x + 4)$ **4** $y = (x + 1)(x - 2)$

5 $y = 3x + 1$ **6** $y = \sqrt{x}$ **7** $y = \sqrt{x + 4}$ **8** $y = \dfrac{1}{(x + 4)}$

9 $y = x^3 - 5$ **10** $y = \dfrac{1}{(x + 4)^2}$ **11** $y = 10 - x^2$ **12** $y = \dfrac{1}{x^2}$

Possible coursework tasks

Quadratic graphs

The general form of a quadratic graph is

$$y = ax^2 + bx + c$$

Investigate what happens to the graph if the values of a, b and c change.

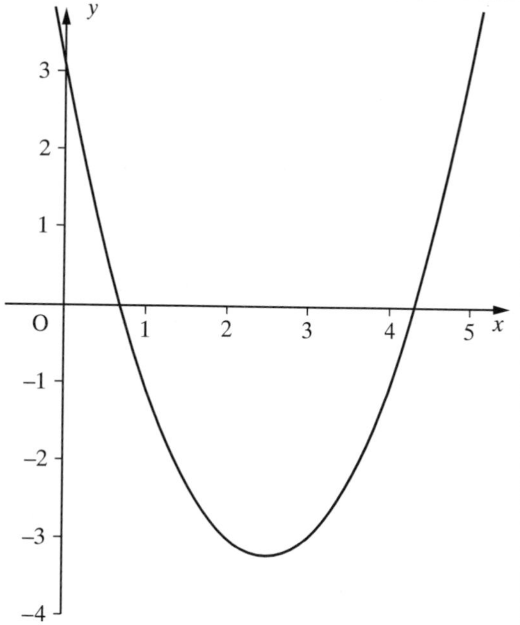

Stationary points

All quadratic graphs are of the form $y = ax^2 + bx + c$.
They all have either a maximum point or a minimum point. These are also known as stationary points.

Investigate stationary points.

Gradient functions

By drawing tangents work out the gradients at various points on the curves $y = x^2$, $y = x^3$, … .

Find a relationship between the gradient at any point and the x co-ordinate at that point.

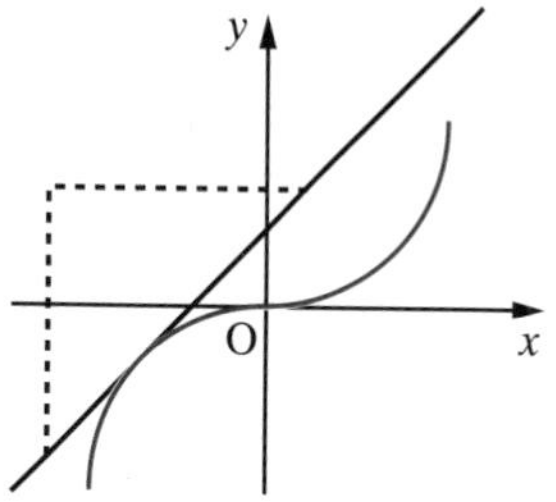

Rational graphs

Investigate graphs of the form $y = \dfrac{ax + b}{cx + d}$

Note *In all these investigations, you would find it helpful to use either a graphics calculator or a graphical computer package.*

Examination questions

1 The line $y = x$ has been drawn.

a On a copy of the diagram,

i draw the graph of $y = 2x - 1$ for values of x from -1 to 3

ii draw the image of $y = 2x - 1$ when it is reflected in the line $y = x$. Label this image L.

b i Calculate the gradient of line L.

ii For the line L write down the value of y when $x = 0$.

iii Write down the equation of the line L.

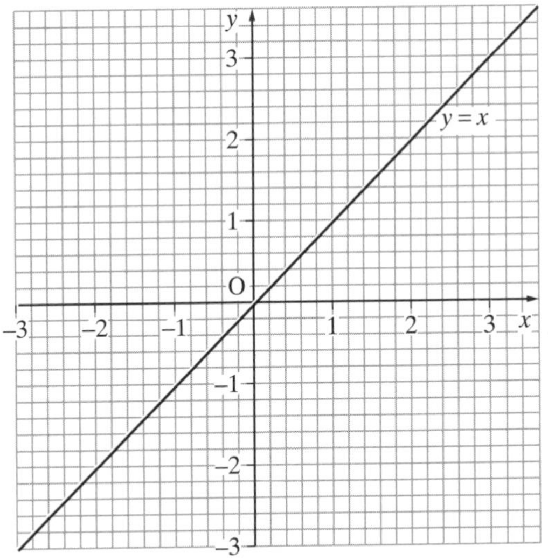

NEAB, Question 11, Paper 2, November 1994

2 a On a pair of axes $0 \le x \le 5$ and $-5 \le y \le 15$, draw the graphs of

i $y = 4x - 3$ **ii** $y = 6 - 2x$

b Use the graphs to solve the simultaneous equations

$$y = 4x - 3$$
$$y = 6 - 2x$$

NICCEA, Question 6, Paper 3. June 1995

3 The table shows the largest quantity of salt, w grams, which can be dissolved in a beaker of water at temperature t °C.

t °C	10	20	25	30	40	50	60
w grams	54	58	60	62	66	70	74

a On a grid $0 \le t \le 60$ and $0 \le w \le 80$, plot the points and draw a graph to illustrate this information.

b Use your graph to find

i the lowest temperature at which 63 g of salt will dissolve in the water

ii the largest amount of salt that will dissolve in the water at 44 °C.

c i The equation of the graph is of the form $w = at + b$. Use your graph to estimate the constants a and b.

ii Use the equation to calculate the largest amount of salt which will dissolve in the water at 95 °C.

NEAB, Question 19, Paper 1, June 1995

4 Jane buys 3 litres of oil and 40 litres of petrol for £30. Richard buys 2 litres of oil and 10 litres of petrol for £10. The cost of 1 litre of oil is £x. The cost of 1 litre of petrol is £y.

Therefore $3x + 40y = 30$

and $2x + 10y = 10$

a Draw on a suitable pair of axes the two graphs of these equations.

b What is the cost of 1 litre of petrol?

SEG, Question 9, Specimen Paper 13, 1998

5 The radius, r, and value, v, of gold coins were measured and recorded.

r (cm)	0.5	1	1.5	2	2.5
v (£)	250	1000	2250	4000	6250

a Which of the following graphs represents the information shown in the table.

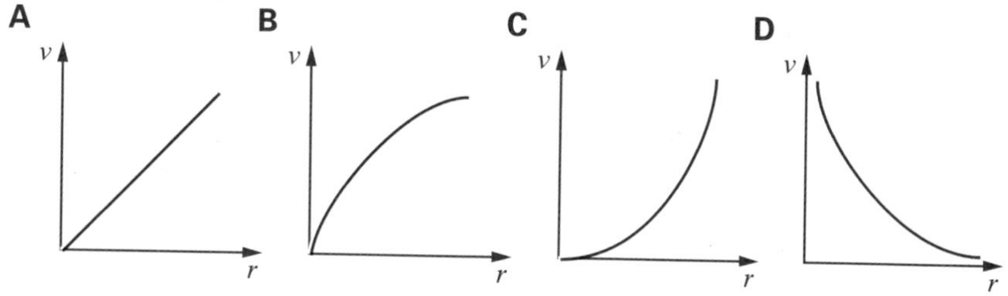

b Which of these equations describes the information shown in the table?

$v = k\sqrt{r}$ $\quad v = kr$ $\quad v = kr^2$ $\quad v = \dfrac{k}{r}$

SEG, Question 13, Specimen Paper 13, 1998

6 The graph of $y = x^3 - 6x$ for $-2.8 \leq x \leq +2.8$ is drawn on the right.

a Use the graph to find the two positive solutions of the equation $x^3 - 6x = -3$.

b On a copy of the diagram, draw the graph of the straight line $y = 2 - x$.

c i Find the x co-ordinates of the points of intersection of the curve $y = x^3 - 6x$ and the straight line $y = 2 - x$.

ii Hence, write down an equation whose solutions are the three values of x.

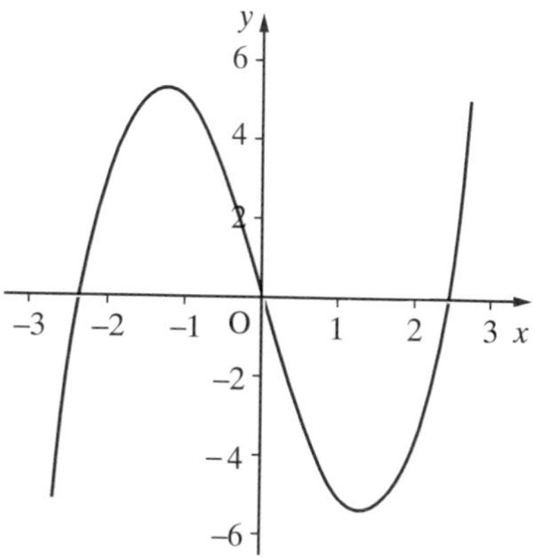

NICCEA, Question 8, Paper 4a, June 1995

7 The distance, d metres, a car travels in time t seconds is given by the formula $d = 2.5\,t^2$.

a Complete the following table of d for some values of t.

Time, t	0	1	2	3	4	5	6	7	8
Distance, d	0	2.5	10	22.5		62.5	90		160

b On graph paper, plot the points represented in the table and draw a smooth curve passing through your points.

c Use your graph to estimate the distance travelled by the car in the first 6.5 seconds.

d Use your graph to estimate how long it takes the car to travel the first 50 metres.

WJEC, Question 15, Paper 1, June 1994

8 a Complete the following table for $y = x^2 - 3x$.

x	−2	−1	0	1	2	3	4	5
y		4	0		−2		4	

b On a pair of axes draw the graph of $y = x^2 - 3x$.

c Use your graph to find the two solutions of the equation $x^2 - 3x = -1$.

MEG, Question 12, Specimen Paper 4, 1998

9 a Draw the graph of $y = x^2$ for $-1 \leq x \leq 4$.

b By drawing a suitable straight line on the same diagram, estimate, correct to one decimal place, the solutions to the equation $x^2 - 2x - 1 = 0$.

SEG, Question 9, Specimen Paper 26, 1998

10 a The equation of the straight line shown in the diagram is

$$x = \frac{y-3}{2}$$

This equation can be written in the form $y = mx + c$. Find the values of m and c.

b Find, by drawing tangents to the curve $y = x^2 + 1$,

i the gradient when $x = 1$

ii the gradient when $x = 0$

c Use the graph to find approximate solutions of $x^2 - 2x - 2 = 0$.

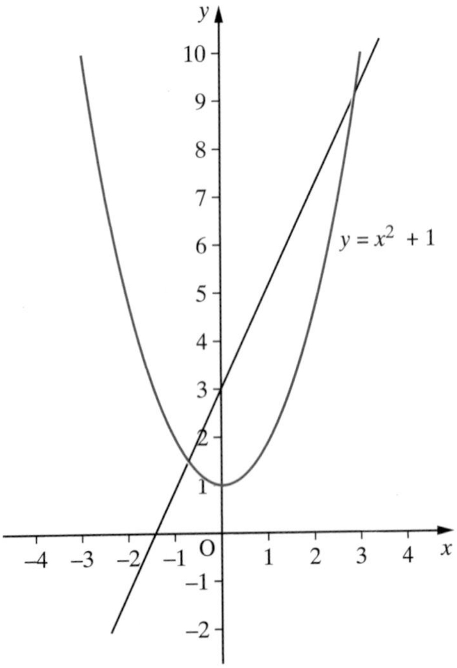

SEG, Question 9, Paper 6, November 1994

Summary

How well do you grade yourself?

To gain a grade **C**, you need to be able to draw any straight-line graph, measure its gradient and give its equation. You need also to be able to recognise and plot any quadratic, cubic or reciporocal graph using a table or any other method, and to use such graphs to solve quadratic and cubic equations.

To gain a grade **B**, you need to be able to solve simultaneous equations using graphical methods. You need also to be able to sketch any quadratic, cubic or reciprocal graph using its properties, and to know how the shape of a graph changes with different coefficients.

To gain a grade **A**, you need to be able to solve problems using intersections and gradients of graphs.

What you should know after you have worked through Chapter 14

- How to draw graphs of a variety of functions such as $y = a$, $x = a$, $y = mx + c$, $ax + by = c$, $y = ax^2 + bx + c$, $y = ax^3$ and $y = \frac{a}{x}$.
- How to solve two linear simultaneous equations using graphs.
- How to solve quadratic and cubic equations using graphs.
- How to recognise quadratic, cubic and reciprocal graphs, and how to sketch graphs of these functions according to their coefficients.

15 Statistics 2

This chapter is going to ... show you how to plot a scatter diagram, draw a line of best fit and use it to predict values. It will also show you how to plot a cumulative frequency diagram and use it to find the median, the quartiles and the interquartile range of a set of data.

What you should already know

- How to calculate the mean of discrete data from a frequency table.
- How to plot co-ordinates.
- How to recognise a positive or a negative gradient.
- Statistics is the study of information. We use statistics to analyse data, compare data and make predictions from our results.

Scatter diagrams

A scatter diagram (also called a scattergraph, or scattergram) is a method of comparing two variables by plotting on a graph their corresponding values (usually taken from a table). In other words, treating them just like a set of (x, y) co-ordinates, as shown in this scatter diagram, in which the marks scored in an English test are plotted against the marks scored in a mathematics test.

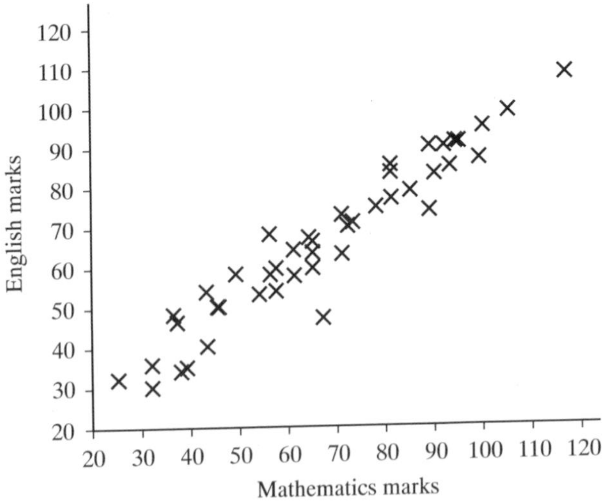

This graph shows **positive correlation**. This means that pupils who get high marks in mathematics tests also tend to get high marks in English tests.

Line of best fit

This is a straight line that goes through the middle of the data, passing as close to as many points as possible. There are ways of working out the position of the line exactly but they are beyond the scope of the GCSE syllabus, so it is acceptable to draw a line of best fit by eye.

A true line of best fit would go through a point that is the mean point of the data. For the scatter diagram on page 352, this would be the point (66,65) because its co-ordinates are the means of the mathematics and English scores respectively. Unless you are asked specifically to do so, this is not required in an examination answer. It takes too much time to work out the mean values and, anyway, in most cases you will be putting the line of best fit onto a scatter diagram that has already been drawn for you.

Correlation

Here are three statements that may or may not be true.

The taller people are, the wider their arm span is likely to be.
The older a car is, the lower its value will be.
The distance you live from your place of work will affect how much you earn.

These relationships could be tested by collecting data and plotting the data on a scatter diagram. For example, the first statement may give a scatter diagram like that on the right. This has a **positive correlation** because the data has a clear 'trend' and we can draw a line of best fit with a positive gradient that passes quite close to most of the points. From such a scatter diagram we could say that the taller someone is, the wider the arm span.

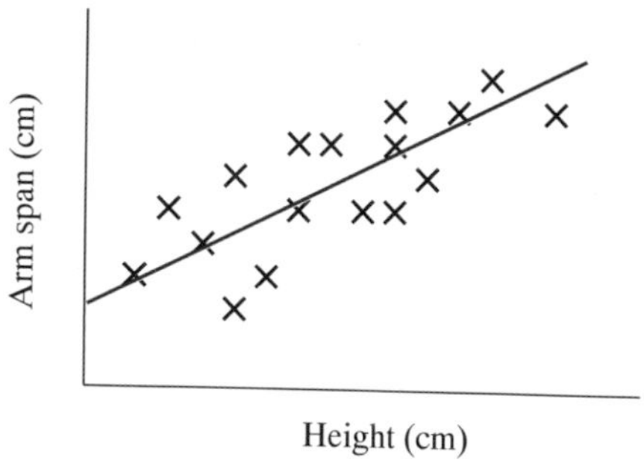

Testing the second statement may give a scatter diagram like that on the right. This has a **negative correlation** because the data has a clear 'trend' and we can draw a line of best fit with a negative gradient that passes quite close to most of the points. From such a scatter diagram we could say that as a car gets older, its value decreases.

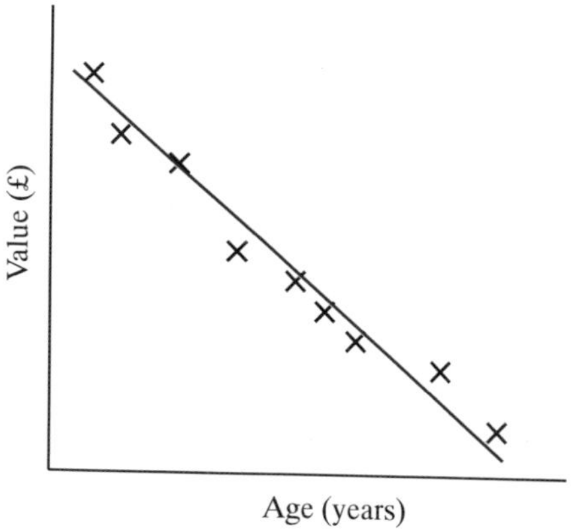

Testing the third statement may give a scatter diagram like that on the right. This scatter diagram has no correlation. It is not possible to draw a line of best fit. We could therefore say there is no relationship between the distance a person lives from his or her work and how much the person earns.

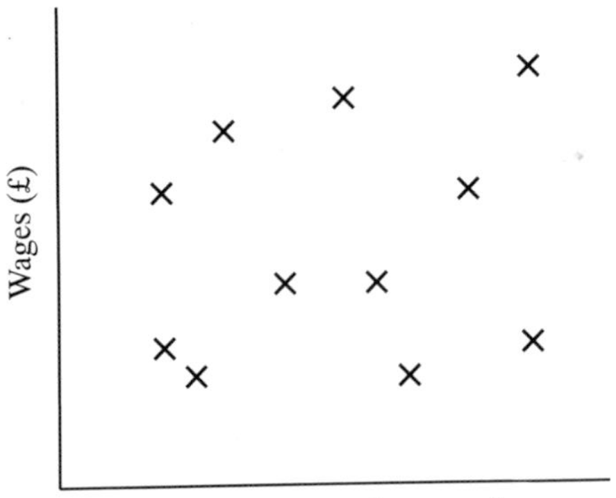

Example This table shows the ages of 10 army PE instructors, and the time, in seconds, each took to run 100 m during a test.

Age	24	32	23	50	45	25	35	45	22	39	**Mean = 34**
Time	10.8	11.2	11.1	13.6	12.7	12	12.1	13	10.9	12.6	**Mean = 12**

a Plot the data on a scatter diagram and draw the line of best fit.

b One of the instructors had a sprained leg at the time of the test. He was 26 years old. How long would you expect him to have taken to run 100 m?

a The diagram shows all 10 points plotted. The mean point has also been plotted. [Remember: this will not be necessary in an examination unless asked for.]

The line of best fit has been drawn and the lines of interpolation giving the expected time for an instructor aged 26 have been inserted.

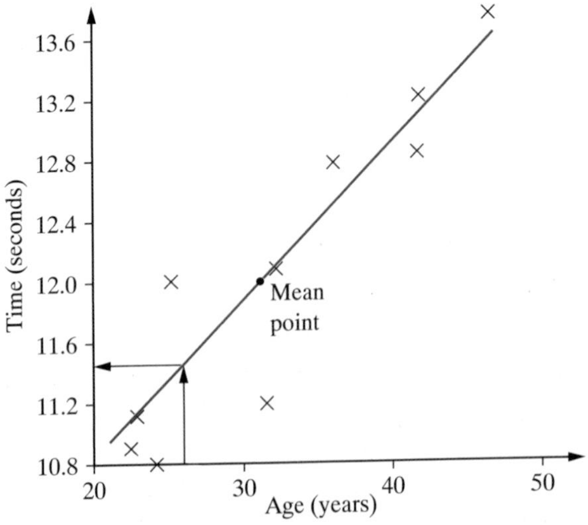

b The expected time for the 26-year-old PE instructor is 11.4 seconds.

Exercise 15A

1 Describe the correlation of each of these graphs

a

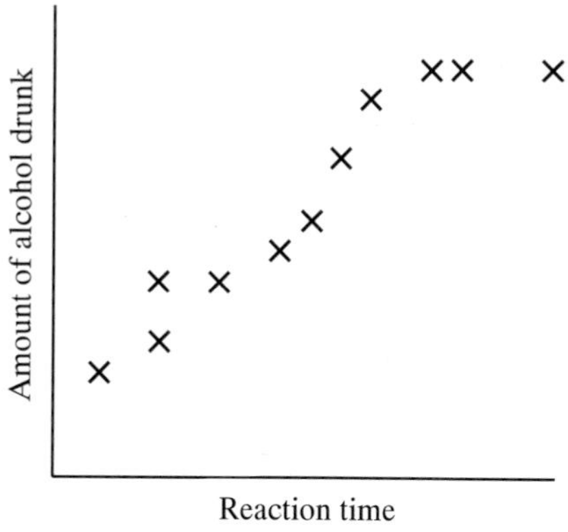

b

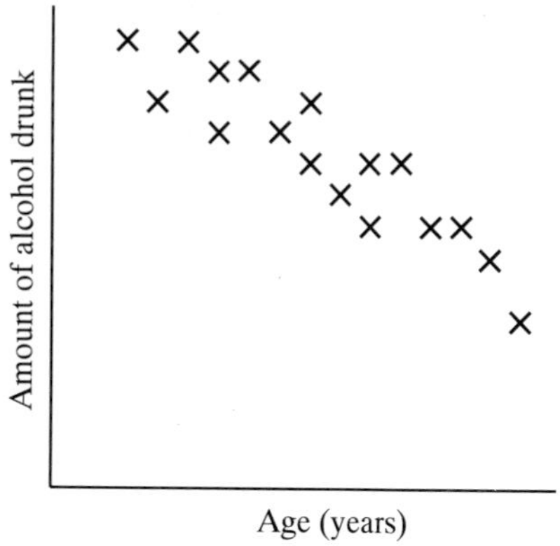

c

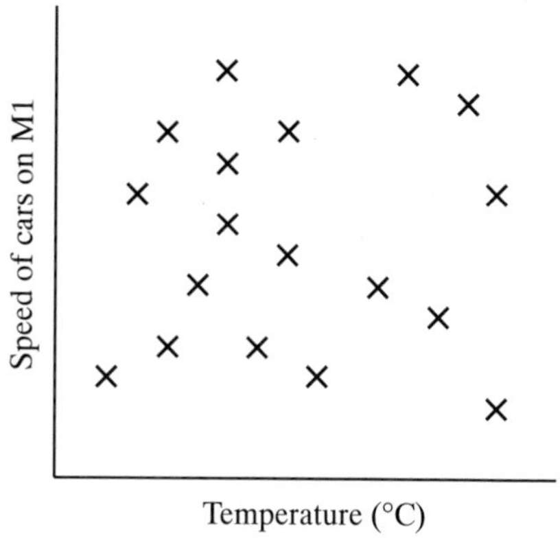

d

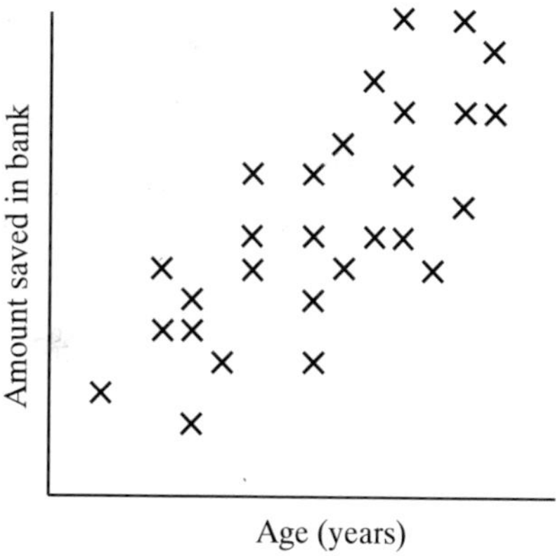

2 Write in words what graph **1a** tells you.

3 Write in words what graph **1b** tells you.

4 Write in words what graph **1c** tells you.

5 Write in words what graph **1d** tells you.

6 The table below shows the results of a science experiment in which a ball is rolled along a desk top. The speed of the ball is measured at various points.

Distance from start (cm)	10	20	30	40	50	60	70	80
Speed (cm/s)	18	16	13	10	7	5	3	0

a Plot the data on a scatter diagram. **b** Draw the line of best fit.

c If the ball's speed had been measured at 5 cm from the start, what is it likely to have been?

d How far from the start was the ball when its speed was 12 cm/s?

7 The table below shows the marks for 10 pupils in their mathematics and geography examinations.

Pupil	Anna	Beryl	Cath	Dema	Ethyl	Fatima	Greta	Hannah	Imogen	Joan
Maths	57	65	34	87	42	35	59	61	25	35
Geog	45	61	30	78	41	36	35	57	23	34

a Plot the data on a scatter diagram and draw a line of best fit. Take the x-axis for the mathematics scores and mark it from 20 to 100. Take the y-axis for the geography scores and mark it from 20 to 100.

b One of the pupils was ill when she took the geography examination. Which pupil was it most likely to be?

c If another pupil, Kate, was absent for the geography examination but scored 75 in mathematics, what mark would you expect her to get in geography?

d If another pupil, Lynne, was absent for the mathematics examination but scored 65 in geography, what mark would you expect her to get in mathematics?

8 The heights, in centimetres, of 20 mothers and their 15 year-old daughters were measured. These are the results.

Mother	153	162	147	183	174	169	152	164	186	178
Daughter	145	155	142	167	167	151	145	152	163	168
Mother	175	173	158	168	181	173	166	162	180	156
Daughter	172	167	160	154	170	164	156	150	160	152

a Plot these results on a scatter diagram.
Take the x-axis for the mothers' heights from 140 to 200.
Take the y-axis for the daughters' heights from 140 to 200.

b Draw a line of best fit.

c Is it true that the tall mothers have tall daughters?

9 The government wanted to see how much the prices of houses had risen over the last ten years in different areas of Britain. They surveyed 10 houses that had been sold 10 years ago and had them valued at today's prices.

This table shows the value of the houses (in thousands of pounds) ten years ago and today.

House	A	B	C	D	E	F	G	H	I	J
Value 10 years ago	32	54	89	25	43	58	38	47	95	39
Value today	43	61	94	34	56	67	46	56	105	48

a Plot the data on a scatter diagram.
Take the x-axis as the price 10 years ago and mark it from 20 to 100.
Take the y-axis as the price today and mark it from 20 to 110.

b Draw the line of best fit through the data.

c What would you expect a house worth £65 000 ten years ago to be worth today?

d Apart from inflation, what other factors could have affected the rise or fall in the value of a house?

e Would you say that there was a correlation between the value of a house 10 years ago and the value of the same house today?

10 A form teacher surveyed his class and asked them to say how many hours per week they spent playing sport and how many hours a week they spent watching TV. This table shows the results of the survey.

Pupil	1	2	3	4	5	6	7	8	9	10
Hours playing sport	12	3	5	15	11	0	9	7	6	12
Hours watching TV	18	26	24	16	19	27	12	13	17	14

Pupil	11	12	13	14	15	16	17	18	19	20
Hours playing sport	12	10	7	6	7	3	1	2	0	12
Hours watching TV	22	16	18	22	12	28	18	20	25	13

a Plot these results on a scatter diagram.
Take the x-axis as the number of hours playing sport and mark it from 0 to 20.
Take the y-axis as the number of hours watching TV and mark it from 0 to 30.

b Why can you not draw a line of best fit through the data?

c If you knew that another pupil from the form watched 8 hours of TV a week, would you be able to predict how long she or he spent playing sport?

Cumulative frequency diagrams

This section will show you how to find a measure of dispersion – the **interquartile range** – using a graph. This method also enables you to find the median. The advantage of the interquartile range is that it eliminates extreme values and bases the measure of spread on the middle 50% of the data.

For example, the marks for the 50 pupils in the mathematics test (see page 352) could be put into a grouped table, as shown at the top of the next page. Note that it includes a column for the **cumulative frequency**, which is found by adding each frequency to the sum of all preceding frequencies.

This data can then be used to plot a graph of the top point of each group against its cumulative frequency. That is, the points to be plotted are (30, 1), (40, 7), (50, 13), (60, 21) etc, which will give the graph shown on the next page.

Mark	Number of pupils	Cumulative frequency
21 to 30	1	1
31 to 40	6	7
41 to 50	6	13
51 to 60	8	21
61 to 70	8	29
71 to 80	6	35
81 to 90	7	42
91 to 100	6	48
101 to 110	1	49
111 to 120	1	50

Note The cumulative frequency is **always** the vertical (y) axis.

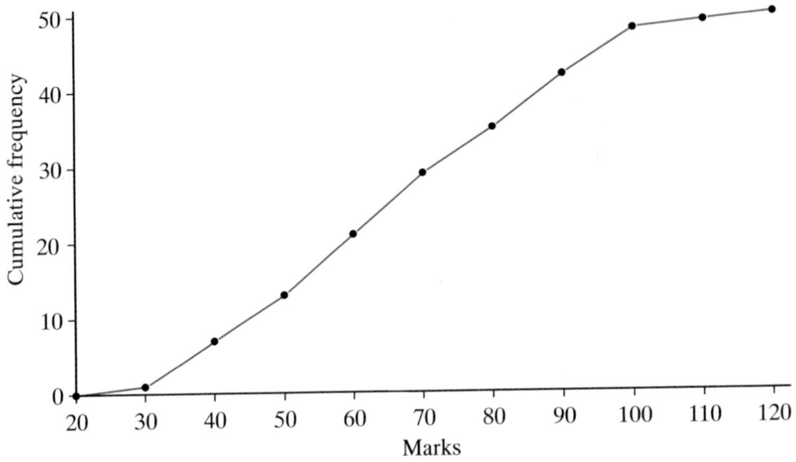

Also note that the scales on both axes are labelled at each graduation mark, in the usual way. **Do not** label the scales as shown below – it is **wrong**.

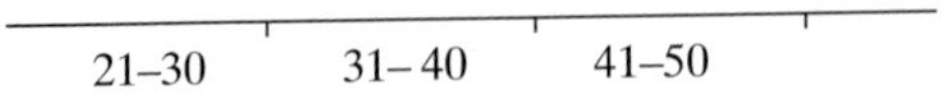

The plotted points can be joined in two different ways:

- by straight lines, to give a **cumulative frequency polygon**
- by a freehand curve, to give a **cumulative frequency curve** or **ogive**.

They are both called cumulative frequency diagrams.

In an examination you are most likely to be asked to draw a cumulative frequency diagram, and the type (polygon or curve) is up to you. Both will give similar results.

The cumulative frequency diagram can be used in several ways, as you will now see.

The median

The median is the middle item of data once all the items have been put in order of size, from lowest to highest. So, if we have n items of data plotted as a cumulative frequency diagram, the median can be found from the middle value of the cumulative frequency, that is the $\frac{n}{2}$th value.

But remember, if we want to find the median from a simple list of discrete data, we **must** use the $\left(\frac{n+1}{2}\right)$th value. The reason for the difference is that the cumulative frequency diagram treats the data as continuous.

There are 50 values in the table on page 358. The middle value will be the 25th value. Draw a horizontal line from the 25th value to meet the graph then go down to the horizontal axis. This will give an estimate of the median. In this example, the median is about 65.

The interquartile range

By dividing the cumulative frequency into four parts, we obtain **quartiles** and the **interquartile range**.

The **lower quartile** is the item one quarter of the way up the cumulative frequency axis and is found by looking at the $\frac{n}{4}$th value.

The **upper quartile** is the item three-quarters of the way up the cumulative frequency axis and is found by looking at the $\frac{3n}{4}$th value.

The **interquartile range** is the difference between the lower and upper quartiles.

These are illustrated on the graph below.

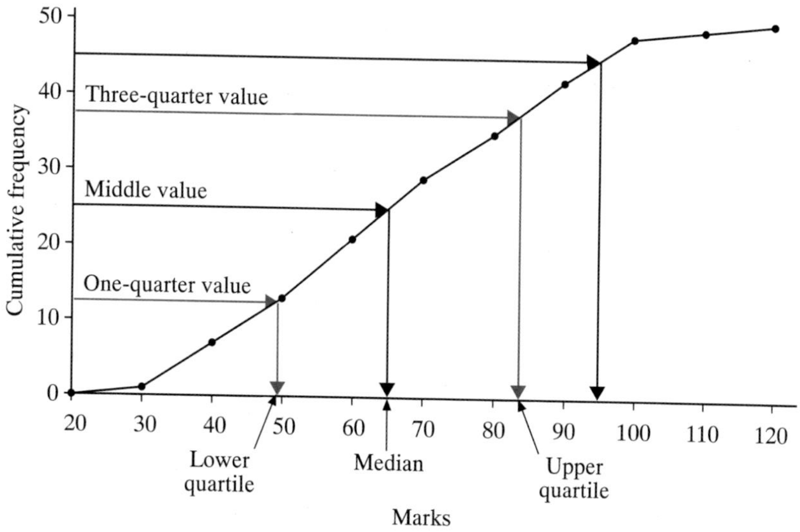

The quarter and three-quarter values out of 50 values are the 12.5th value and the 37.5th value. Draw lines across to the cumulative frequency curve from these values and down to the horizontal axis. These give the lower and upper quartiles. In this example, the lower quartile is 48, the upper quartile is 83, and the interquartile range is 83 – 48 = 35.

Note that questions like these are often followed up with an extra question such as: 'The Head of Mathematics decides to give a special award to the top 10% of pupils. What would the cut-off mark be?'

The top 10% would be the top 5 pupils (10% of 50 is 5). Draw a line across from 45 pupils to the graph and down to the horizontal axis. This gives a cut-off mark of 96.

Example The table below shows the marks of 100 pupils in a mathematics SAT.

a Draw a cumulative frequency curve.
b Use your graph to find the median and the interquartile range.
c Pupils who score less than 44 do not get a SAT level awarded. How many pupils will not get a SAT level?

Mark	Number of pupils	Cumulative frequency
$21 \le x \le 30$	3	3
$31 \le x \le 40$	9	12
$41 \le x \le 50$	12	24
$51 \le x \le 60$	15	39
$61 \le x \le 70$	22	61
$71 \le x \le 80$	16	77
$81 \le x \le 90$	10	87
$91 \le x \le 100$	8	95
$101 \le x \le 110$	3	98
$111 \le x \le 120$	2	100

Note The groups are given in a different way to those in the table on page 358. You will meet several ways of giving groups (for example, 21–30, $20 < x \le 30$, $21 < x < 30$) but the important thing to remember is to plot the **top point** of each group against the corresponding **cumulative frequency**.

a Draw the graph and put on the lines for the median (50th value), lower and upper quartiles (25th and 75th values). Then at 44 on the mark axis draw a perpendicular line to intersect the graph, and at the point of intersection draw a horizontal line across to the cumulative frequency axis, as shown.

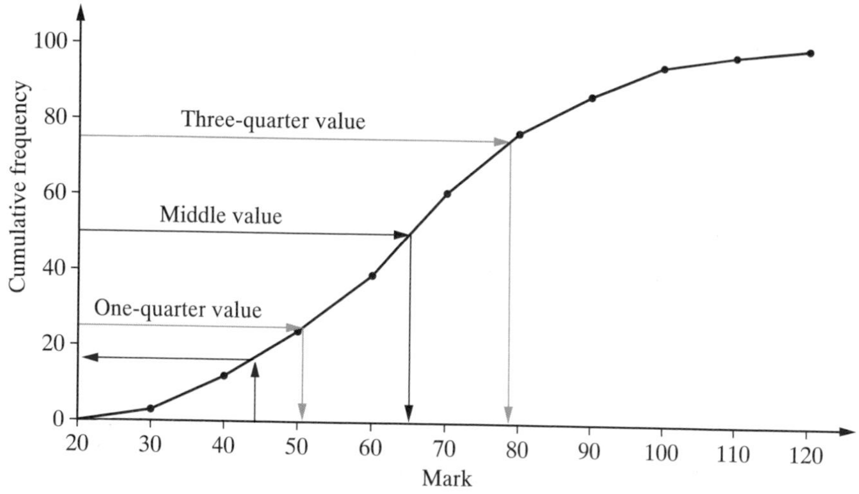

b The required answers are read from the graph as

Median = 65

Lower quartile = 51

Upper quartile = 79

Interquartile range = 79 – 51 = 28

c Number of pupils without a SAT level = 17

Note An alternative way in which the table could have been set out is shown below. This arrangement has the advantage that the points to be plotted are taken straight from the last two columns. You have to decide which method you prefer. In examination papers, the columns of tables are sometimes given without headings, so you will need to be familiar with all the different ways in which the data can be set out.

Mark	Number of pupils	Less than	Cumulative frequency
$21 \le x \le 30$	3	30	3
$31 \le x \le 40$	9	40	12
$41 \le x \le 50$	12	50	24
$51 \le x \le 60$	15	60	39
$61 \le x \le 70$	22	70	61
$71 \le x \le 80$	16	80	77
$81 \le x \le 90$	10	90	87
$91 \le x \le 100$	8	100	95
$101 \le x \le 110$	3	110	98
$111 \le x \le 120$	2	120	100

Exercise 15B

1 A class of 30 children were asked to estimate a minute. Their teacher recorded the times they actually said. This table shows the results.

a Copy the table and complete a cumulative frequency column.

b Draw a cumulative frequency diagram.

c Use your diagram to estimate the median time and the interquartile range.

Time (seconds)	Number of pupils
$20 < x \leq 30$	1
$30 < x \leq 40$	3
$40 < x \leq 50$	6
$50 < x \leq 60$	12
$60 < x \leq 70$	3
$70 < x \leq 80$	3
$80 < x \leq 90$	2

2 A group of 50 pensioners were given the same task as the children in question **1**. Their results are shown in the table.

a Copy the table and complete a cumulative frequency column.

b Draw a cumulative frequency diagram.

c Use your diagram to estimate the median time and the interquartile range.

d Which group, the children or the pensioners, would you say was better at estimating time? Give a reason for your answer.

Time (seconds)	Number of pensioners
$10 < x \leq 20$	1
$20 < x \leq 30$	2
$30 < x \leq 40$	2
$40 < x \leq 50$	9
$50 < x \leq 60$	17
$60 < x \leq 70$	13
$70 < x \leq 80$	3
$80 < x \leq 90$	2
$90 < x \leq 100$	1

3 The sizes of 360 secondary schools in South Yorkshire are recorded in the table.

a Copy the table and complete a cumulative frequency column.

b Draw a cumulative frequency diagram.

c Use your diagram to estimate the median size of the schools and the interquartile range.

d Schools with less than 350 pupils are threatened with closure. About how many schools are these?

Number of pupils	Number of schools
100–199	12
200–299	18
300–399	33
400–499	50
500–599	63
600–699	74
700–799	64
800–899	35
900–999	11

4 The temperature at a seaside resort was recorded over a period of 50 days. The table shows the results.

a Copy the table and complete a cumulative frequency column.

b Draw a cumulative frequency diagram.

c Use your diagram to estimate the median temperature and the interquartile range.

Temperature (°F)	Number of days
41–45	2
46–50	3
51–55	5
56–60	6
61–65	6
66–70	9
71–75	8
76–80	6
81–85	5

5 At the school charity fête, a game consists of throwing three darts and recording the total score. The results of the first 80 people to throw are recorded in the table.

a Copy the table and complete a cumulative frequency column.

b Draw a cumulative frequency diagram.

c Use your diagram to estimate the median score and the interquartile range.

d People who score over 90 get a prize. About what percentage of the people get a prize?

Total score	Number of players
$1 \le x \le 20$	9
$21 \le x \le 40$	13
$41 \le x \le 60$	23
$61 \le x \le 80$	15
$81 \le x \le 100$	11
$101 \le x \le 120$	7
$121 \le x \le 140$	2

6 One hundred pupils in a school were asked to say how much pocket money they each get in a week. The results are in the table.

a Copy the table and complete a cumulative frequency column.

b Draw a cumulative frequency diagram.

c Use your diagram to estimate the median amount of pocket money and the interquartile range.

Amount of pocket money (p)	Number of pupils
51–100	6
101–150	10
151–200	20
201–250	28
251–300	18
301–350	11
351–400	5
401–450	2

7 The parents of the same 100 pupils were asked to state their monthly salaries.

a Copy the table and complete a cumulative frequency column.

b Draw a cumulative frequency diagram.

c Estimate the median monthly salary and the interquartile range.

d What percentage of the parents had an annual salary greater than £10 000?

Monthly salary (£)	Number of parents
651–700	8
701–750	14
751–800	25
801–850	35
851–900	14
901–950	4

Measures of dispersion

Another method commonly used to compare data is the **measure of dispersion**, also called the **measure of spread**.

You have already met two measures of dispersion:

- **Range**, which is calculated by subtracting the smallest value in the set of data from the largest.
- **Interquartile range**, which is the difference between the upper and lower quartiles (page 359).

The range is not a good measure of dispersion, as it does not eliminate extreme values. The interquartile range is a better measure, as it takes the central half of the data. The only drawback is that it is centred about the median which may not be the best measure of location.

A much better measure of dispersion centred about the mean is the **standard deviation**.

There are two methods for calculating standard deviation, illustrated by the following examples.

Method 1

Calculate the mean and the standard deviation of the heights of the people in group A.

Group A

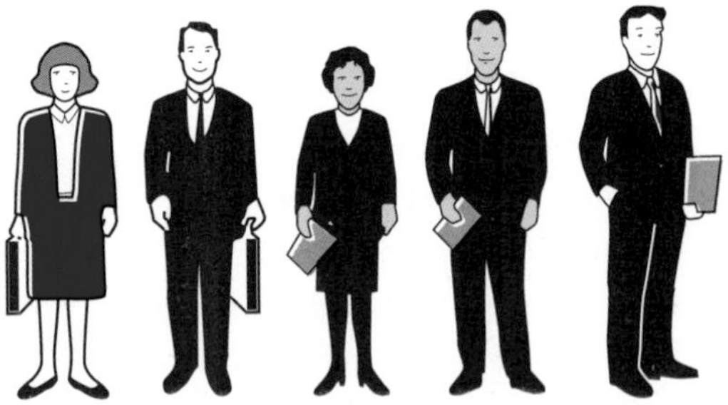

1.62 m   1.73 m   1.60 m   1.75 m   1.75 m

First, calculate the mean height, $\overline{x}$, given by

$$\overline{x} = \frac{\Sigma x}{n}$$

where Σ, the capital Greek letter sigma, means 'sum of', and n is the number of items of data. So in this case

$$\overline{x} = \frac{1.62 + 1.73 + 1.60 + 1.75 + 1.75}{5}$$

$$\Rightarrow \quad \overline{x} = 1.69$$

Next, find the difference between each height and the mean height, $(x - \bar{x})$, which gives

$1.62 - 1.69 = -0.07$
$1.73 - 1.69 = 0.04$
$1.60 - 1.69 = -0.09$
$1.75 - 1.69 = 0.06$
$1.75 - 1.69 = 0.06$

Then, square each of these differences (to eliminate the negative values) and sum them:

$$\Sigma (x - \bar{x})^2 = (-0.07)^2 + (0.04)^2 + (-0.09)^2 + (0.06)^2 + (0.06)^2 = 0.0218$$

where $(x - \bar{x})^2$ is the square of each difference.

Divide this total by the number of items of data, which gives

$$\frac{\Sigma(x - \bar{x})^2}{n} = \frac{0.0218}{5} = 0.004\,36$$

Take the square root of this result:

$$\sqrt{\frac{\Sigma(x - \bar{x})^2}{n}} = \sqrt{0.00\,436}$$

$$= 0.0660 = 0.07 \quad (2 \text{ dp})$$

This is the **standard deviation** and is given by the formula

$$\sigma = \sqrt{\frac{\Sigma(x - \bar{x})^2}{n}}$$

where σ, the lower-case Greek letter sigma, represents standard deviation.

The main part of the calculation can also be set out in a table like this:

x	$x - \bar{x}$	$(x - \bar{x})^2$
1.62	−0.07	0.0049
1.73	0.04	0.0016
1.60	−0.09	0.0081
1.75	0.06	0.0036
1.75	0.06	0.0036
	Total	0.0218

Method 2

Calculate the mean and the standard deviation of the heights of the people in group B.

Group B

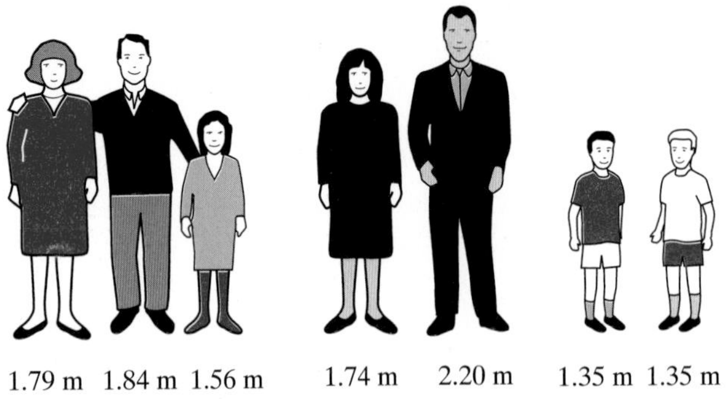

The method is best done using a table of x and x^2, as shown below. First calculate each value of x^2, then sum the values of x and those of x^2.

	x	x^2
	1.79	3.2041
	1.84	3.3856
	1.56	2.4336
	1.74	3.0276
	2.20	4.8400
	1.35	1.8225
	1.35	1.8225
Totals	11.83	20.5359

From this, calculate the mean of x,

$$\bar{x} = 11.83 \div 7 = 1.69$$

and the standard deviation, which in this case is given by

$$\sigma = \sqrt{\frac{\sum x^2}{n} - \bar{x}^2}$$

$$\Rightarrow \quad \sigma = \sqrt{\frac{20.5359}{7} - (1.69)^2} \quad = 0.28 \quad (2 \text{ dp})$$

Note The formula for Method 2 is given in the GCSE formulae sheet as

$$\sigma = \sqrt{\frac{\sum x^2}{n} - \left(\frac{\sum x}{n}\right)^2}$$

where $\left(\frac{\sum x}{n}\right)^2 = \bar{x}^2$

The second method is easier if the mean is not known.

Calculators use the second method. If needed, information such as $\sum x$ and $\sum x^2$ can also be extracted from the calculator.

As you are expected to be familiar with the mean and the standard deviation, you need to be able to use your calculator to find them.

Using your calculator

First put your calculator into statistics mode by pressing one of the following keys:

SD or SAT or $\Sigma+$ or M+

SD or SAT will usually appear on the display. (On a graphics calculator, the operation mode key is different but the method is similar.)

Enter each number followed by

x or DATA or $\Sigma+$ or M+

The mean and the standard deviation are found by pressing $\bar{x}$ and σn or σx. But you may have to use INV or 2ndF first.

Some calculators have a $\sigma n{-}1$ key. Be careful **not** to use it.

Your calculator will also have Σx, Σx^2 and n keys.

After each calculation remember to clear your data. On most calculators this is done by pressing SAC or CA.

Example Find the mean and the standard deviation for 3, 8, 5 and 7.

First key

3 DATA 8 DATA 5 DATA 7 DATA

Then press $\bar{x}$. (You may first have to use INV or 2ndF.) You should get 5.75.

Finally, press σn. You should get 1.92 (2 dp).

Use of standard deviation

Using standard deviation, we can compare, for example, the two age groups A and B. Although both groups have the same mean height, we can see that group B has a much greater variance in the heights of its members than group A. Hence, the heights of the members of group B deviate much more from the mean, while the members of group A are all very similar in height.

Exercise 15C

Use a calculator to check your answers.

1 Find the mean and the standard deviation of the following sets of data. Use Method 1.

a 2, 5, 6, 8, 9
b 7, 9, 11, 13, 18
c 102, 105, 108, 110, 115
d 201, 202, 203, 204, 205
e 68.6, 72.3, 75.6, 78.1
f −2, −1, −1, 0, 2, 4, 5
g 71, 72, 78, 80, 85
h 29.3, 31.8, 33.9, 34.9, 40.0, 40.1

2 Find the mean and the standard deviation of the following sets of data. Use Method 2.

a 4, 7, 8, 8, 11
b 17, 19, 21, 23, 28
c 82, 85, 88, 89, 92
d 201, 202, 203, 204, 205
e 65, 71, 76, 76
f −4, −2, −1, 0, 2, 5, 7
g 91, 92, 98, 100, 105
h 29, 32, 35, 36, 42, 43

3 Five numbers, 4, 5, 7, 8 and x, have a mean of 6.

a What is the value of x?
b What is the standard deviation of the numbers?

4 a Calculate the mean and the standard deviation of 4, 7, 8, 9, 12.
b Calculate the mean and standard deviation of 14, 17, 18, 19, 22.
c Using your answers to parts **a** and **b**, write down the mean and the standard deviation of 24, 27, 28, 29, 32.

5 For a set of ten numbers, $\sum x = 40$, $\sum x^2 = 1160$. Find the standard deviation of the set.

6 For a set of five numbers, $\sum x = 45$, $\sum x^2 = 202$. Find the standard deviation of the set.

7 For a set of six numbers, $\sum(x - \overline{x})^2 = 150$. Find the standard deviation of the set.

8 The captain of the netball team needs to pick a player for an important match. She has to choose between Paula and Rose. She has the number of points they have scored from their last few matches. These are

Paula 7, 8, 6, 8, 7, 12, 6, 10 Rose 2, 4, 4, 4, 6, 8, 10, 10, 16, 16

a Calculate the mean and the standard deviation for Paula.
b Calculate the mean and standard deviation for Rose.
c Who would you pick and why?

9 Five numbers, 4, 8, 10, x and y, have a mean of 10 and a standard deviation of 4. Find the values of x and y.

10 In the 1996 Northern Counties Road Relays, teams of six runners each ran a 4-mile leg. The three winning teams had these times for each of their six runners.

First team: Salford Harriers 19.50, 19.47, 19.43, 19.30, 20.01, 19.40

Second team: Bingley Harriers 19.42, 20.32, 20.09, 19.50, 19.34, 19.36

Third team: Sunderland 20.40, 20.40, 20.36, 19.23, 20.29, 19.45

a Calculate the mean and the standard deviation of each team. (Remember that the times above are in minutes and seconds.)
b One of the top three teams has to be chosen to represent Northern Counties at the National Road Relays. Which team should be chosen and why?

Mean and standard deviation from a table of data

Large sets of data often contain repeated values. For example, these are the marks of 20 pupils in a mathematics test.

4, 5, 6, 5, 5, 4, 4, 7, 8, 10, 7, 4, 7, 8, 5, 6, 6, 5, 9, 6

Normally, they would be put in a frequency table or, as is more likely in an examination paper, presented like the first two columns of the table shown below.

There are two ways to calculate the standard deviation in this case. Both are very similar to the two methods for individual data.

Method 1

First, calculate the mean. To do this, generate the first three columns of the table shown below. The mean is given by

$$\bar{x} = \frac{\Sigma fx}{n}$$

where $n = \Sigma f$ is the number of items of data.

$$\Rightarrow \quad \bar{x} = \frac{121}{20} = 6.05$$

Having found $\bar{x}$, complete the rest of the table, as shown.

x	f	fx	$(x-\bar{x})$	$(x-\bar{x})^2$	$f \times (x-\bar{x})^2$
4	4	16	−2.05	4.2025	16.81
5	5	25	−1.05	1.1025	5.5125
6	4	24	−0.05	0.0025	0.01
7	3	21	0.95	0.9025	2.7075
8	2	16	1.95	3.8025	7.605
9	1	9	2.95	8.7025	8.7025
10	1	10	3.95	15.6025	15.6025
Totals	20	121		**Total $\Sigma f(x-\bar{x})^2$**	56.95

The standard deviation is given by

$$\sigma = \sqrt{\frac{\Sigma f(x-\bar{x})^2}{n}}$$

$$\Rightarrow \quad \sigma = \sqrt{\frac{56.95}{20}} \quad \text{(Substituting the total of column 6)}$$

$$= 1.69 \quad \text{(3 sf)}$$

Method 2

In this method, the complete table is generated first. (Note where it is different from the table of Method 1.)

x	f	x^2	fx	fx^2
4	4	16	16	64
5	5	25	25	125
6	4	36	24	144
7	3	49	21	147
8	2	64	16	128
9	1	81	9	81
10	1	100	10	100
Totals	20		121	789

The mean is given by

$$\bar{x} = \frac{\Sigma fx}{n}$$

$$\Rightarrow \quad \bar{x} = \frac{121}{20} = 6.05$$

The standard deviation is given by

$$\sigma = \sqrt{\frac{\Sigma fx^2}{n} - \bar{x}^2} \quad \text{(Substituting the total of column 5)}$$

$$\Rightarrow \quad \sigma = \sqrt{\frac{789}{20} - (6.05)^2}$$

$$= 1.69 \quad \text{(3 sf)}$$

Note Another formula for the standard deviation is

$$\sigma = \sqrt{\frac{\Sigma fx^2}{\Sigma f} - \left(\frac{\Sigma fx}{\Sigma f}\right)^2}$$

This formula is not given in the GCSE formulae sheet.

Example The table shows the number of heads obtained when four coins are tossed 160 times. Work out the mean and the standard deviation of the number of heads.

Heads, x	**Frequency, f**
0	8
1	42
2	55
3	44
4	11

Use Method 1.

x	f	fx	$(x-\bar{x})$	$(x-\bar{x})^2$	$f\times(x-\bar{x})^2$
0	8	0	−2.05	4.2025	33.62
1	42	42	−1.05	1.1025	46.305
2	55	110	−0.05	0.0025	0.1375
3	44	132	0.95	0.9025	39.71
4	11	44	1.95	3.8025	41.8275
Totals	160	328		**Total** $\sum f(x-\bar{x})^2$	161.6

The mean is given by

$$\bar{x} = \frac{\sum fx}{n} = \frac{328}{160} = 2.05$$

The standard deviation is given by

$$\sigma = \sqrt{\frac{\sum f(x-\bar{x})^2}{n}} = \sqrt{\frac{161.6}{160}} = 1.00 \quad \text{(3sf)}$$

Using your calculator for a frequency table

Follow through the next example, noting especially the **strict order** in which the input must be keyed. For example, each item of the data **always precedes** its frequency.

Example Find the mean and the standard deviation for this frequency table.

x	f
4	2
5	3
6	4
7	1

Enter as

4 × 2 DATA 5 × 3 DATA 6 × 4 DATA 7 × 1 DATA

Then $\bar{x}$ = 5.4 and σn = 0.92 (2 dp)

Note Always clear your calculator of old data before starting a new calculation, by pressing SAC or CA.

Exercise 15D

Use a calculator to check your answers

1 The times (to the nearest minute) of the first 20 phone calls made from an office in a morning are

2, 5, 5, 7, 3, 4, 5, 6, 7, 8, 2, 12, 2, 5, 2, 5, 7, 9, 10, 2

Put these times into a frequency table and, using Method 1, calculate the mean and the standard deviation of the call times.

2 Calculate the mean and the standard deviation of the data in these tables.

a

x	f
0	2
1	4
2	6
3	5
4	3

b

x	f
22	4
23	6
24	7
25	6
26	4
27	3

c

x	f
100	2
101	4
102	6
103	5
104	3

d

x	f
6.7	12
7.3	41
7.8	66
8.1	43
8.5	27

e

x	f
2.2	8
3.2	13
4.2	16
5.2	3

f

x	f
0.07	12
0.09	17
0.14	25
0.17	36
0.26	17
0.27	13

3 a A dice is thrown 180 times. The results are shown in the table.

Score	1	2	3	4	5	6
Frequency	21	20	19	20	19	21

i Calculate the mean and the standard deviation of the scores from the dice.

ii Square the standard deviation.

b Two dice are thrown 120 times. The results are shown in the table.

Score	2	3	4	5	6	7	8	9	10	11	12
Frequency	5	11	15	20	25	31	24	19	16	9	5

i Calculate the mean and the standard deviation of the scores from the two dice.

ii Square the standard deviation.

c What is the approximate relationship between the answers to parts **a** and **b**?

d If three dice are thrown, estimate the mean and the standard deviation of the total scores from all three dice.

4 a Copy and complete this table to calculate the mean and the standard deviation.

Mark, x	121	126	131	136	141	146
Frequency, f	2	3	5	6	5	4

b 121 is subtracted from each of the values in the table above and the result is divided by 5. This gives the table below.

Mark, x	0	1	2	3	4	5
Frequency, f	2	3	5	6	5	4

Calculate the mean and the standard deviation for this table.

i Multiply the mean by 5 and add 121.

ii Multiply the standard deviation by 5.

c What connects your answers to parts **bi** and **bii** and your answers to part **a**?

d What advantage does the second table have over the first?

5 The tables below show the results of two classes in a mathematics test.

Class 1

Mark, x	0	1	2	3	4	5	6	7	8	9	10
Frequency, f	0	1	4	6	5	4	5	6	1	2	1

Class 2

Mark, x	0	1	2	3	4	5	6	7	8	9	10
Frequency, f	0	0	2	2	10	11	5	4	1	1	0

a Calculate the mean and the standard deviation for each class.

b Which class did better in the test? Why?

6 During the first six weeks in a new job Mrs Best recorded how long it took her from getting out of bed to walking through the office door. The results are shown in the table.

Time, x (min)	80	85	90	95	100	105
Frequency, f	6	4	10	5	3	2

a Calculate the mean and the standard deviation of the data.

b Mrs Best has to arrive at work by 9.00 am. If she is late more than five times in a 30-day period, she will be sacked. She decides to set her alarm for 7.30 am. Is this a good idea? Justify your answer.

Possible coursework tasks

Who's a big head, then?

Investigate the circumference of a person's head and his/her height.

Watching TV is bad for your maths

'Young people today watch too much television. This is bound to affect their test results in mathematics.'

Draw up a suitable questionnaire to test the validity of this statement.

Get up!

Do a survey of your class to find out at what time your classmates get up in the morning on school days.

Is there a relationship between the getting-up time and the time it takes to get to school?

Gulliver's journey into mathematics

'… they measured my right thumb, and desired no more; for a mathematical computation that twice round my thumb is once round the wrist and so on to the neck and the waist …'

Investigate this extract taken from Swift's *Gulliver's Travels*.

Pulse rate

A person's pulse rate is affected by various things. Try to set up some experiments to investigate these effects. You may use diagrams to show your results.

Can you suggest any hypohtesis from your results?

Reaction time

Use a reaction ruler to design experiments to test people's reaction times.

Green for Go!

Design experiments to show the effect that traffic lights have on traffic flow.

For some of these coursework tasks, you may find it helpful first to design a questionnaire. The data can then be put onto a computer database. Statistical diagrams can also be drawn using the computer database. Their use will improve the presentation of your work.

Examination questions

1 Ten people entered a craft competition. Their displays of work were awarded marks by two different judges.

Competitor	A	B	C	D	E	F	G	H	I	J
First judge	90	35	60	15	95	25	5	100	70	45
Second judge	75	30	55	20	75	30	10	85	65	40

The table shows the marks that the two judges gave to each of the competitors.

a Draw a scatter diagram to show this information, and on your diagram draw a line of best fit.

b A late entry was given 75 marks by the first judge. Use your scatter diagram to estimate the mark that might have been given by the second judge. (Show how you found your answer.)

NEAB, Question 7, Paper 1, June 1995

2 This table gives you the marks scored by pupils in a French test and in a German test.

French	15	35	34	23	35	27	36	34	23	24	30	40	25	35	20
German	20	37	35	25	33	30	39	36	27	20	33	35	27	32	28

a Work out the range of the pupils' marks in French.

b Draw a scattergraph of the marks scored in the French and German tests.

c Draw the line of best fit on the diagram.

d Use your line of best fit to estimate the mark of a pupil's test in French when their mark in German was 23.

e Describe the relationship between the marks scored in the two tests.

ULEAC, Question 8, Specimen Paper 4, 1998

3 A researcher asks people how many visits they have made to a city during the last three months and how far they live from the city. This table shows her results.

Visits to city	10	5	13	2	6	16	15	11		Mean	9.75
Distance (km)	5	8	3	9	7	1	3	4		Mean	5

a Draw a scatter diagram to show these results.

b Draw a line of best fit on your scatter diagram.

c Approximately how many visits would you expect from a person who lives 2 km from the city to have made during the last three months?

WJEC, Question 8, Specimen Paper 2, 1998

4 A marathon is held in London every year.

a One year, 100 people were running for a charity. The scatter diagram shows the ages of these 100 runners and the times they took.

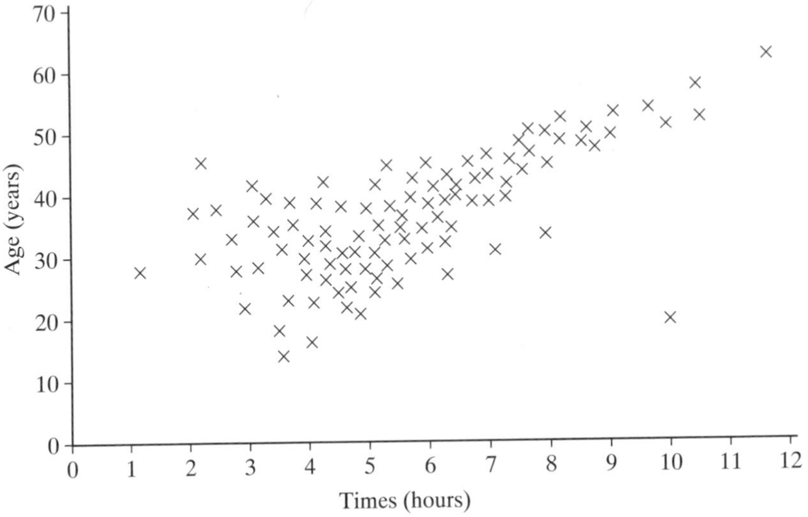

What does the scatter diagram tell you?

b The table shows the times taken by the 50 men and the 50 women in the marathon. Draw a frequency polygon to show the distribution of times taken by the 50 men.

Time taken, t (hours)	Men	Women
$2 < t \leq 3$	9	3
$3 < t \leq 4$	18	7
$4 < t \leq 5$	12	16
$5 < t \leq 6$	6	18
$6 < t \leq 7$	4	4
$7 < t \leq 8$	1	2

c The frequency polygon for the women's times is different from that for the men's times. Describe how they differ. (You do not need to draw the frequency polygon for the women.)

d The median time and the modal time for the men are both in the range of 3 to 4 hours. Write down the range that contains

i the median women's time

ii the modal women's time.

NEAB, Question 13, Paper 1, November 1994

5 Laura and Joy played 40 games of golf together. The table shows Laura's scores.

Scores, x	$70 < x \leq 80$	$80 < x \leq 90$	$90 < x \leq 100$	$100 < x \leq 110$	$110 < x \leq 120$
Frequency	1	4	15	17	3

a Draw a cumulative frequency diagram to show Laura's scores.

b Making your method clear, use your graph to find

i Laura's median score **ii** the interquartile range of her scores.

c Joy's median score was 103. The interquartile range of her score was 6.

i Who was the more consistent player? Give a reason for your choice.

ii The winner of a game of golf is the one with the lowest score. Who won most of these 40 games? Give a reason for your choice. *NEAB, Question 16, Paper 2, June 1995*

6 A school entered 80 pupils for an examination. The results are shown in the table.

Mark, x	$0 < x \leq 20$	$20 < x \leq 40$	$40 < x \leq 60$	$60 < x \leq 80$	$80 < x \leq 100$
Number of pupils	2	14	28	26	10

a Calculate an estimate of the mean.

b Complete a cumulative frequency table and draw a cumulative frequency diagram.

c i Use your graph to estimate the median mark.

ii 12 of these pupils were given a grade A. Use your graph to estimate the lowest mark for which grade A was given. *NEAB, Question 13, Paper 2, November 1994*

7 The speeds, in miles per hour (mph), of 200 cars travelling on the A320 road were measured. The results are shown in the table.

a Draw a cumulative frequency graph to show these figures.

b Use your graph to find an estimate for

i the median speed (in mph)

ii the interquartile range (in mph)

iii the percentage of cars travelling at less than 48 miles per hour.

Speed (mph)	**Cumulative frequency**
Not exceeding 20	1
Not exceeding 25	5
Not exceeding 30	14
Not exceeding 35	28
Not exceeding 40	66
Not exceeding 45	113
Not exceeding 50	164
Not exceeding 55	196
Not exceeding 60	200
Total	200

ULEAC, Question 14, Specimen Paper 4, 1998

8 The table below illustrates the age distribution in a village of 360 people.

Age	0–	10–	20–	30–	40–	50–	60–	70–	80–100
Frequency	44	51	59	68	50	35	31	18	4

a Draw a cumulative frequency diagram to illustrate this data.

b Use your graph to estimate

i the number of villagers who are more than 25 years old

ii the median

iii the interquartile range. *SEG, Question 17, Specimen Paper 14, 1998*

9 This table shows the results for 160 pupils in a test.

Mark	0 to 19	20 to 39	40 to 49	50 to 59	60 to 69	70 to 99
Frequency	5	18	29	65	32	11

a Complete a cumulative frequency table and draw a cumulative frequency diagram to show these results.

b Copy and complete the table at the top of the next page to show the median and interquartile range for this distribution.

Median	**Lower quartile**	**Upper quartile**	**Interquartile range**

c The top 60% of pupils passed the test. What was the pass mark?

WJEC, Question 12, Specimen Paper 2, 1998

10 A survey was made of the time spent by each of 500 customers at the check-outs of a supermarket. The results were recorded in the frequency table.

Time, t (minutes)	**Frequency**
$0 < t \leq 1$	83
$1 < t \leq 2$	138
$2 < t \leq 3$	141
$3 < t \leq 4$	68
$4 < t \leq 5$	45
$5 < t \leq 6$	25

a Calculate the mean time spent by each customer at a check-out.

b Complete a cumulative frequency table and then draw the cumulative frequency curve.

c Use your graph to estimate

i the median time **ii** the interquartile range.

d The supermarket is open for $8\frac{1}{2}$ hours on a Saturday and approximately 1000 customers are expected. Use any appropriate average to estimate the number of check-outs which should be used.

NICCEA, Question 14, Paper 3, June 1995

11 In an experiment. Cathy has to take readings of radioactive emissions from six pieces of rock. Her readings are 490, 497, 511, 500, 479 and 484.

a Calculate the mean and the standard deviation of her readings.

b Cathy's teacher then told her that the electronic counter she was using was faulty and each reading was 10 emissions too high. Cathy used her original answers for the mean and the standard deviation to write down their true values. Explain how she did this.

NEAB, Question 17, Specimen Paper 2H, 1998

12 A small building company employs ten people. The weekly pay of each is as follows:

£150 £150 £200 £220 £220 £240 £260 £290 £290 £350

The mean weekly pay for these employees is £237.

a Calculate the standard deviation of the weekly pay.

A building project is completed early and each person in the company receives a bonus on their weekly pay.

b The manager suggests that everyone should receive a bonus of £24.50 added to their usual weekly pay. What effect would this have on the mean and the standard deviation of the weekly pay?

c The foreman suggests that everyone should receive a bonus of 10% added to their usual weekly pay. What effect would this have on the mean and standard deviation of the weekly pay?

d Which of these proposals should be implemented to give the greater benefit to the greater number of employees? Explain your answer.

SEG, Question 17, Specimen Paper 16, 1998

Summary

How well do you grade yourself?

To gain a grade **C**, you need to be able to draw a line of best fit on a scatter diagram by inspection. You need also to be able to draw a cumulative frequency diagram.

To gain a grade **B**, you need to be able to interpret a scatter diagram and have a knowledge of positive and negative correlation. You need also to be able to solve problems using a cumulative frequency diagram.

To gain a grade **A**, you need to be able to calculate standard deviation from different frequency distributions.

What you should know after you have worked through Chapter 15

- How to plot points on a scatter diagram.
- How to recognise positive and negative correlation from a scatter diagram, and also the condition of no correlation.
- How to draw an accurate line of best fit on a scatter diagram, and use it to make predictions.
- How to construct a cumulative frequency diagram.
- The difference between a cumulative frequency polygon and a cumulative frequency curve.

- How to find from a cumulative frequency diagram
  - the median using the $\frac{n}{2}$th value
  - the lower quartile using the $\frac{n}{4}$th value
  - the upper quartile using the $\frac{3n}{4}$th value
  - the interquartile range.
- How to calculate standard deviation from different frequency distributions.

16 Probability

This chapter is going to ... remind you of the basic definition of probability. It will show you the difference between experimental probability and theoretical probability and how these quantities are related to each other. It will also show you how to deal with combined events by using a probability space diagram, such as a tree diagram, or by considering all the outcomes of an experiment.

What you should already know

- Basic ideas of probability.
- The probability scale goes from 0 to 1.
- How to cancel, add, subtract and multiply fractions (using a calculator if necessary).
- Probability can be expressed as a fraction, a decimal, or a percentage.

You have already met probability. Exercise 16A is essentially revision and could be missed out if you are sure that you know what probability means.

Terminology

The topic of probability has its own special terminology which will be explained as it arises. For example, a **trial** is one go at performing something, such as throwing a dice or tossing a coin. So, if we throw a dice 10 times, we perform 10 trials.

Two other probability terms are **event** and **outcome**. An event is anything whose probability we want to measure. An outcome is any way in which an event can happen.

Note 'Dice' is used in this book in preference to 'die' for the singular form of the noun, as well as for the plural. This is in keeping with growing common usage, including in examination papers.

Finding probabilities

There are three ways in which the probability of an event can be found.

- **First method** If we can work out the theoretical probability of an event – for example, drawing a King from a pack of cards – this is called **using equally likely outcomes**.
- **Second method** Some events, such as buying a certain brand of dog food, cannot be calculated using equally likely outcomes. To find the probability of such an event, we can perform an experiment such as we already have or conduct a survey. This is called **collecting experimental data**. The more data we collect, the better the estimate is.
- **Third method** The probability of some events, such as an earthquake occurring in Japan, cannot be found by either of the above methods. One of the things we can do is to look at data collected over a long period of time and make an estimate (sometimes called a 'best guess') at the chance of the event happening. This is called **looking at historical data**.

Example Which method (A, B or C) would you use to estimate the probabilities of the events **a** to **e**?

A: Use equally likely outcomes
B: Conduct a survey/collect data
C: Look at historical data.

a Someone in your class will go abroad for a holiday this year.
b You will win the National Lottery.
c Your bus home will be late.
d It will snow on Christmas Day.
e You will pick a red seven from a pack of cards.

a You would have to ask all the members of your class what they intended to do for their holidays this year. You would therefore conduct a survey, Method B.
b The odds on winning are about 14 million to 1, so this is an equally likely outcome, Method A.
c If you catch the bus every day, you can collect data over several weeks. This would be Method C.
d If you check whether it snowed on Christmas Day for the last few years you would be able to make a good estimate of the probability. This would be Method C.
e There are 2 red sevens out of 52 cards, so the probability of picking one can be calculated:

$$\text{P(red seven)} = \frac{2}{52} = \frac{1}{26}$$

This is Method A.

Exercise 16A

1 Naseer throws a dice and records the number of sixes that he gets after various numbers of throws. The table shows his results.

Number of throws	10	50	100	200	500	1000	2000
Number of sixes	2	4	10	21	74	163	329

a Calculate the experimental probability of a six at each stage that Naseer recorded his results.

b How many ways can a dice land?

c How many of these ways give a six?

d What is the theoretical probability of throwing a six with a dice?

e If Naseer threw the dice a total of 6000 times, how many sixes would you expect him to get?

2 Marie made a five-sided spinner, like the one shown in the diagram She used it to play a board game with her friend Sarah. The girls thought that the spinner wasn't very fair as it seemed to land on some numbers more than others. They threw the spinner 200 times and recorded the results. The results are shown in the table.

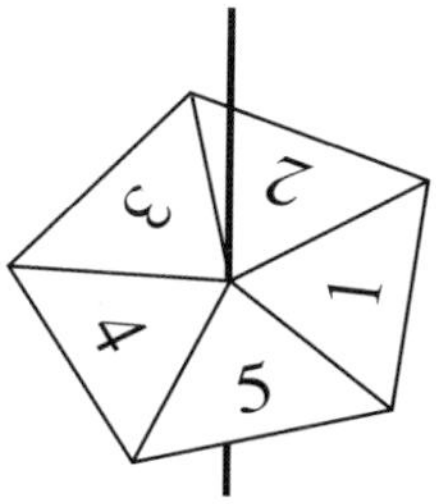

Side spinner lands on	1	2	3	4	5
Number of times	19	27	32	53	69

a Work out the experimental probability of each number.

b How many times would you expect each number to occur if the spinner is fair?

c Do you think that the spinner is fair? Give a reason for your answer.

3 Sarah thought she could make a much more accurate spinner. After she had made it she tested it and recorded how many times she threw a 5. Her results were:

Number of throws	10	50	100	500
Number of fives	3	12	32	107

a Sarah made a mistake in recording the number of fives. Which number in the second row above is wrong? Give a reason for your answer.

b These are the full results for 500 throws.

Side spinner lands on	1	2	3	4	5
Number of times	96	112	87	98	107

Do you think the spinner is fair? Give a reason for your answer.

4 A sampling bottle contains 20 balls. The balls are either black or white. (A sampling bottle is a sealed bottle with a clear plastic tube at one end into which one of the balls can be tipped.) Kenny conducts an experiment to see how many black balls are in the bottle. He takes various numbers of samples and records how many of them showed a black ball. The results are shown in the table on the next page.

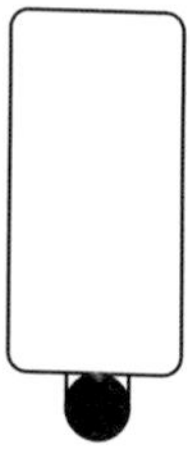

Number of samples	Number of black balls	Experimental probability
10	2	
100	25	
200	76	
500	210	
1000	385	
5000	1987	

a Copy the table and calculate the experimental probability of getting a black ball at each stage.

b Using this information, how many black balls do you think are in the bottle?

5 Another sampling bottle contains red, white and blue balls. It is known that there are 20 balls in the bottle altogether. Carrie performs an experiment to see how many of each colour are in the bottle. She starts off putting down a tally each time a colour shows in the clear plastic tube.

Red	White	Blue
卌 卌 卌 卌 ||	卌 卌 卌 |||	卌 卌 ||

Unfortunately, she forgets to count how many times she performs the experiment, so every now and again she counts up the tallies and records them in a table (see below).

Red	White	Blue	Total
22	18	12	42
48	31	16	95
65	37	24	126
107	61	32	211
152	93	62	307
206	128	84	418

The experimental probability of the red balls is calculated by dividing the frequency of red by the total number of trials, so at each stage these are

0.524 0.505 0.516 0.507 0.495 0.493

These answers are rounded off to 3 significant figures.

a Calculate the experimental probabilities of the white balls at each stage to 3 sf.

b Calculate the experimental probabilities of the blue balls at each stage to 3 sf.

c Round off the final experimental probabilities for Carrie's 418 trials to 1 decimal place.

d What is the total of the answers in part **c**?

e How many of each colour do you think are in the bottle? Explain your answer.

6 Using card and a cocktail stick, make a six-sided spinner, as shown below.

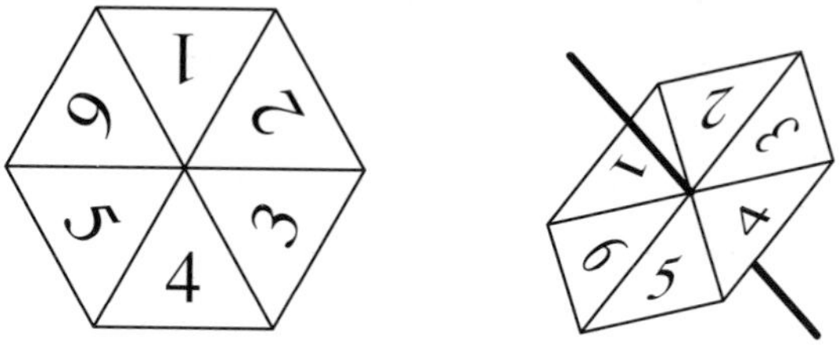

When you have made the spinner, spin it 120 times and record your results in a table like the one below.

Number	Tally	Total
1	𝍸 ||	
2	||||	

a Which number occurred the most?

b How many times would you expect to get each number?

c Is your spinner fair?

d Explain your answer to part **c**.

7 Use a set of number cards from 1 to 10 (or make your own set) and work with a partner. Take it in turns to choose a card and keep a record each time of what card you get. Shuffle the cards each time and repeat the experiment 60 times. Put your results in a copy of this table.

Score	1	2	3	4	5	6	7	8	9	10
Total										

a How many times would you expect to get each number?

b Do you think you and your partner conducted this experiment fairly?

c Explain your answer to part **b**.

8 Which of these methods would you use to estimate or state the probability of each of the events **a** to **h**?

Method A: Equally likely outcomes
Method B: Survey or experiment
Method C: Look at historical data

a How people will vote in the next election.

b A drawing pin dropped on a desk will land point up.

c A Premier League team will win the FA Cup.

d You will win a school raffle.

e The next car to drive down the road will be red.

f You will throw a 'double six' with two dice.

g Someone in your class likes classical music.

h A person picked at random from your school will be a vegetarian.

9 A four-sided dice has faces numbered 1, 2, 3 and 4. The 'score' is the face on which it lands. Five pupils throw the dice to see if it is biased. They each throw it a different number of times. Their results are shown in the table.

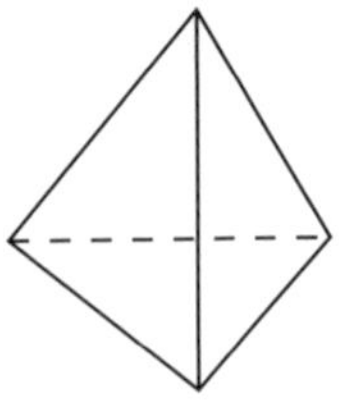

Pupil	Total number of throws	Score			
		1	2	3	4
Alfred	20	7	6	3	4
Brian	50	19	16	8	7
Caryl	250	102	76	42	30
Deema	80	25	25	12	18
Emma	150	61	46	26	17

a Which pupil will have the most reliable set of results? Why?

b Add up all the score columns and work out the relative frequency of each score.

c Is the dice biased? Explain your answer.

10 If you were about to choose a card from a pack of yellow cards numbered from 1 to 10, what would be the chance of each of the events **a** to **i** occurring? Copy and complete each of these statements with a word or phrase chosen from 'impossible', 'not likely', '50–50 chance', 'quite likely', or 'certain'.

a The likelihood that the next card chosen will be a four is ......

b The likelihood that the next card chosen will be pink is ......

c The likelihood that the next card chosen will be a seven is ......

d The likelihood that the next card chosen will be a number less than 11 is ......

e The likelihood that the next card chosen will be a number bigger than 11 is ......

f The likelihood that the next card chosen will be an even number is ......

g The likelihood that the next card chosen will be a number more than 5 is ......

h The likelihood that the next card chosen will be a multiple of 1 is ......

i The likelihood that the next card chosen will be a prime number is ......

Probability facts

The probability of a **certain** event is **1** and the probability of an **impossible** event is **0**. Probability is **never greater than 1 or less than 0**.

Many probability examples involve coins, dice and packs of cards. Here is a reminder of their outcomes.

- A coin has two outcomes: head or tail.
- An ordinary six-sided dice has six outcomes: 1, 2, 3, 4, 5, 6.

- A pack of cards consists of 52 cards divided into four suits: Hearts (red), Spades (black), Diamonds (red), and Clubs (black). Each suit consists of 13 cards bearing the following values: 2, 3, 4, 5, 6, 7, 8, 9, 10, Jack, Queen, King and Ace. The Jack, Queen and King are called 'picture cards'. (The Ace is sometimes also called a picture card.) So the total number of outcomes is 52.

Probability is defined as

$$\text{P(event)} = \frac{\text{Number of ways the event can happen}}{\text{Total number of all possible outcomes}}$$

This definition always leads to a fraction which should be cancelled down to its simplest form. This can be done with most scientific calculators. Make sure that you know how to cancel down fractions with or without a calculator. It is acceptable to give a probability as a decimal but fractions are better.

This definition can be used to work out the probability of events, as the following example shows.

Example A card is drawn from a pack of cards. What is the probability that it is one of the following?

a a red card **b** a Spade **c** a seven
d a picture card **e** a number less than 5 **f** a red King

a There are 26 red cards, so P(red card) = $\frac{26}{52} = \frac{1}{2}$

b There are 13 Spades, so P(Spade) = $\frac{13}{52} = \frac{1}{4}$

c There are 4 sevens, so P(seven) = $\frac{4}{52} = \frac{1}{13}$

d There are 12 picture cards, so P(picture card) = $\frac{12}{52} = \frac{3}{13}$

e If we count the value of an Ace as 1, there are 16 cards each of whose value is less than 5. So, P(number less than 5) = $\frac{16}{52} = \frac{4}{13}$

f There are 2 red Kings, so P(red King) = $\frac{2}{52} = \frac{1}{26}$

Another probability term is: **at random**. This means 'without looking' or 'not knowing what the outcome is in advance'.

Exercise 16B

1 What is the probability of each of the following?

a Throwing a 2 with a dice.

b Throwing a 6 with a dice.

c Tossing a coin and getting a tail.

d Drawing a Queen from a pack of cards.

e Drawing a Heart from a pack of cards.

f Drawing a black card from a pack of cards.

g Throwing a 2 or a 6 with a dice.

h Drawing a black Queen from a pack of cards.

i Drawing an Ace from a pack of cards.

j Throwing a 7 with a dice.

2 What is the probability of each of the following?

a Throwing an even number with a dice.

b Throwing a prime number with a dice.

c Getting a Heart or a Club from a pack of cards.

d Drawing the King of Hearts from a pack of cards.

e Drawing a picture card or an Ace from a pack of cards.

f Drawing the Seven of Diamonds from a pack of cards.

3 A bag contains only blue balls. If I take one out at random, what is the probability that

a I get a black ball **b** I get a blue ball?

4 The numbers 1 to 10 inclusive are placed in a hat. Bob takes a number out of the bag without looking. What is the probability that he draws

a the number 7 **b** an even number **c** a number greater than 6

d a number less than 3 **e** a number between 3 and 8?

5 A bag contains 1 blue ball, 1 pink ball and 1 black ball. Joan takes a ball from the bag without looking. What is the probability that she takes out

a the blue ball **b** the pink ball **c** a ball that is not black?

6 A pencil case contains 6 red pens and 5 blue pens. Geoff takes a pen out without looking at what it is. What is the probability that he takes out

a a red pen **b** a blue pen **c** a pen that is not blue?

7 A bag contains 50 balls. Ten are green, 15 are red and the rest are white. Gemma takes a ball from the bag at random. What is the probability that she takes

a a green ball **b** a white ball **c** a ball that is not white

d a ball that is green or white?

8 A box contains 7 bags of cheese and onion crisps, 2 bags of beef crisps and 6 bags of plain crisps. Iklil takes a bag of crisps out at random. What is the probability that he gets

a a bag of cheese and onion crisps **b** a bag of beef crisps

c a bag of crisps that are not cheese and onion **d** a bag of prawn cracker crisps

e a bag of crisps that is either plain or beef?

9 In a Christmas raffle, 2500 tickets are sold. One family has 50 tickets. What is the probability that that family wins the first prize?

10 Arthur, Brenda, Charles, Doris and Eliza are in the same class. Their teacher wants two pupils to do a special job.

a Write down all the possible combinations of two people. For example, Arthur and Brenda, Arthur and Charles (there are 10 combinations altogether).

b How many pairs give two boys?

c What is the probability of choosing two boys?

d How many pairs give a boy and a girl?

e What is the probability of choosing a boy and a girl?

f What is the probability of choosing two girls?

11 A bag contains 10 chocolates. Six are soft centred and the rest are hard centred. I take out one chocolate and eat it.

a What is the probability that I get a hard-centred chocolate?

b If the first chocolate I get is hard centred

i how many hard centres are left **ii** how many chocolates are left?

c After I have eaten the first chocolate, a hard centre, I pick another one. What is the probability that I pick

i a hard centre **ii** a soft centre?

12 An ordinary six-sided dice has 2 red faces, 1 blue face and 3 green faces. If this dice is thrown, what is the probability that the top face will be

a red **b** green **c** not blue

d black **e** red, green or blue?

13 Eight-sided dice are used in adventure games. They are marked with the numbers 1 to 8. The score is the uppermost face. If an eight-sided dice is thrown, what is the probability that the score will be

a a number in the 3 times table **b** a factor of 10

c a square number **d** a triangle number

e a number that is not prime **f** not a square number?

14 Indicate on a copy of the number line the approximate position of each of the events **a** to **g**.

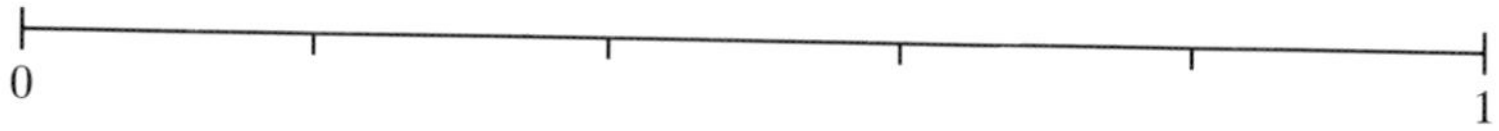

a A baby born to a family will be a girl.

b Sitting next to someone born in February.

c It will rain on the moon.

d It will rain somewhere in Britain next year.

e A computer crashing while in normal use.

f Drawing a Spade from a pack of cards.

g Throwing a number bigger than 2 with a dice.

15 Packets of jelly babies contain 20 sweets. It is known that there are five each of red, green, orange and black jelly babies.

a John takes out a sweet and eats it. Explain why the probability of getting any colour is $\frac{1}{4}$.

b Mary now takes out a sweet. Explain why the probability of getting any colour is **not** $\frac{1}{4}$.

Mutually exclusive and exhaustive events

If a bag contains 3 black, 2 yellow and 5 white balls and only one ball is allowed to be taken at random from the bag, then by the basic definition of probability

$$P(\text{black ball}) = \frac{3}{10}$$

$$P(\text{yellow ball}) = \frac{2}{10} = \frac{1}{5}$$

$$P(\text{white ball}) = \frac{5}{10} = \frac{1}{2}$$

We can also say that the probability of choosing a black ball or a yellow ball is $\frac{5}{10} = \frac{1}{2}$.

The events 'picking a yellow ball' and 'picking a black ball' can never happen at the same time when only one ball is taken out. That is, a ball can be either black or yellow. Such events are called **mutually exclusive**. Other examples of mutually exclusive events are tossing a head or a tail with a coin, drawing a King or an Ace from a pack of cards and throwing an even or an odd number with a dice.

An example of events that are not mutually exclusive would be drawing a red card or a King from a pack of cards. There are two red Kings, so these events could be true at the same time.

Example 1 If an ordinary dice is thrown, what is the probability of throwing

a an even number **b** an odd number?

c What is the total of the answers to parts **a** and **b**?

d Is it possible to get a score on a dice that is both odd and even?

a $P(\text{even}) = \frac{1}{2}$ **b** $P(\text{odd}) = \frac{1}{2}$ **c** $\frac{1}{2} + \frac{1}{2} = 1$ **d** No

Events such as those in Example 1 are mutually exclusive because they can never happen at the same time. Because there are no other possibilities, they are also called **exhaustive** events. The probabilities of exhaustive events **add up to 1**.

Example 2 A bag contains only black and white balls. The probability of picking at random a black ball from the bag is $\frac{7}{10}$.

a What is the probability of picking a white ball from the bag?
b Can you say how many black and white balls are in the bag?

a As the event 'picking a white ball' and the event 'picking a black ball' are mutually exclusive and exhaustive then

$$P(\text{white}) = 1 - P(\text{black}) = 1 - \frac{7}{10} = \frac{3}{10}$$

b We cannot say precisely what the number of balls is although we can say that there could be 7 black and 3 white, 14 black and 6 white, or any combination of black and white balls in the ratio 7:3.

Complementary event

If we have an event A, the complementary event of A is

Event A **not** happening

Any event is mutually exclusive and exhaustive to its complementary event. That is,

P(event A not happening) = 1 – P(event A happening)

which can be stated as

P(event) + P(complementary event) = 1

For example, the probability of getting a 4 from a pack of cards is $\frac{4}{52} = \frac{1}{13}$, so the probability of **not** getting a 4 is

$$1 - \frac{1}{13} = \frac{12}{13}$$

Exercise 16C

1 Say whether these pairs of events are mutually exclusive or not.
  a Tossing a head with a coin/tossing a tail with a coin.
  b Throwing a number less than 3 with a dice/throwing a number greater than 3 with a dice.
  c Drawing a Spade from a pack of cards/drawing an Ace from a pack of cards.
  d Drawing a Spade from a pack of cards/drawing a red card from a pack of cards.
  e If two people are to be chosen from three girls and two boys: choosing two girls/choosing two boys.
  f Drawing a red card from a pack of cards/drawing a black card from a pack of cards.

2 Which of the pairs of mutually exclusive events in question **1** are also exhaustive?

3 Each morning I run to work or get a lift. The probability that I run to work is $\frac{2}{5}$. What is the probability that I get a lift?

4 A letter is to be chosen at random from this set of letter-cards.

S T A T I S T I C S

a What is the probability the letter is

i an S **ii** a T **iii** a vowel?

b Which of these pairs of events are mutually exclusive?

i Picking an S / picking a T. **ii** Picking an S / picking a vowel.

iii Picking an S / picking a consonant. **iv** Picking a vowel / picking a consonant.

c Which pair of mutually exclusive events in part **b** is also exhaustive?

5 Two people are to be chosen for a job from this set of five people.

Jane Dave Anne Jack John

a List all of the possible pairs (there are 10 altogether).

b What is the probability that the pair of people chosen will be

i both female

ii both male

iii both have the same initial

iv have different initials?

c Which of these pairs of events are mutually exclusive?

i Picking two women / picking two men.

ii Picking two people of the same sex / picking two people of opposite sex.

iii Picking two people with the same initial / picking two men.

iv Picking two people with the same initial / picking two women.

d Which pair of mutually exclusive events in part **c** is also exhaustive?

6 A spinner consists of an outer ring of coloured sectors and an inner circle of numbered sectors, as shown.

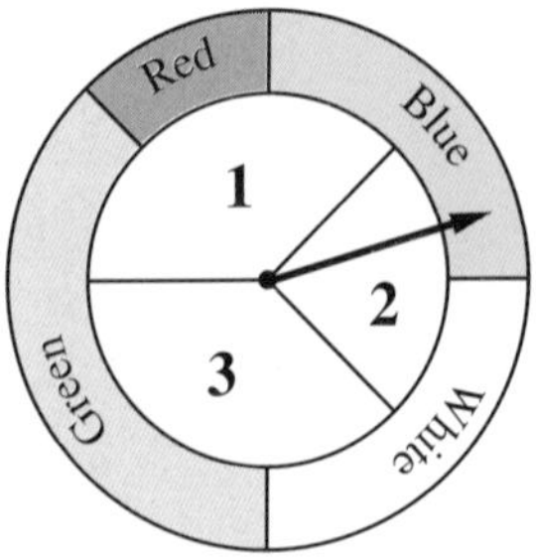

a The probability of getting 2 is $\frac{1}{4}$. The probabilities of getting 1 or 3 are equal. What is the probability of getting 3?

b The probability of getting blue is $\frac{1}{4}$. The probability of getting white $\frac{1}{4}$. The probability of getting green is $\frac{3}{8}$. What is the probability of getting red?

c Which of these pairs of events are mutually exclusive?

i Getting 3/getting 2. **ii** Getting 3/getting green.

iii Getting 3/getting blue. **iv** Getting blue/getting red.

d Explain why it is not possible to get a colour that is mutually exclusive to the event 'getting an odd number'.

7 At the morning break, I have the choice of coffee, tea or hot chocolate. If the probability I choose coffee is $\frac{3}{5}$, the probability I choose tea is $\frac{1}{4}$, what is the probability I choose hot chocolate?

8 Assemblies at school are always taken by the head, the deputy head or the senior teacher. If the head takes the assembly, the probability that he goes over time is $\frac{1}{2}$. If the deputy takes the assembly, the probability that he goes over time is $\frac{1}{4}$. Explain why it is not necessarily true to say that the probability that the senior teacher goes over time is $\frac{1}{4}$.

9 An electronic device chooses random numbers from 1 to 49. Here is a list of events.

Event A: the number chosen is odd
Event B: the number chosen is even
Event C: the number chosen is a square number
Event D: the number chosen is a multiple of 3
Event E: the number chosen is a triangle number
Event F: the number chosen is a multiple of 6
Event G: the number chosen is a factor of 30

For each of the pairs of events **i** to **x**, say whether they are

a mutually exclusive **b** exhaustive

c If they are not mutually exclusive, give an example of a number that fits both events.

i Event A and Event B **ii** Event A and Event C
iii Event B and Event D **iv** Event C and Event D
v Event D and Event F **vi** Event C and Event G
vii Event E and Event G **viii** Event A and Event E
ix Event A and Event F **x** Event B and Event F

10 A hotelier conducted a survey of guests staying at her hotel. The table shows some of the results of her survey.

Type of guest	Probability
Man	0.7
Woman	0.3
American man	0.2
American woman	0.05
Vegetarian	0.3
Married	0.6

a A guest was chosen at random. From the table, work out the probability that
i the guest was American
ii the guest was single
iii the guest was not a vegetarian.

b Explain why it is not possible to work out from the table the probability of a guest being a married vegetarian.

c From the table, give two pairs of types of guest that would form a pair of mutually exclusive events.

d From the table, give one pair of types of guest that would form a pair of exhaustive events.

Expectation

When we know the probability of an event, we can predict how many times we would expect that event to happen in a certain number of trials.

Note that this is what we **expect**. It is not what is going to happen. If what we expected always happened, life would be very dull and boring and the National Lottery would be a waste of time.

Example Four in 10 of every car sold in Britain are made by Japanese companies.

a What is the probability that the next car to drive down your road will be Japanese?
b If there are 2000 cars in a multistorey car park, how many of them would you expect to be Japanese?

a P(Japanese car) = $\frac{4}{10} = \frac{2}{5} = 0.4$

b Expected number of Japanese cars in 2000 cars = $2000 \times 0.4 = 800$ cars

Exercise 16D

1 I throw an ordinary dice 150 times. How many times can I expect to get a score of 6?

2 I toss a coin 2000 times. How many times can I expect to get a head?

3 I draw a card from a pack of cards and replace it. I do this 520 times. How many times would I expect to get
a a black card **b** a King **c** a Heart **d** the King of Hearts?

4 The ball in a roulette wheel can land on any number between 0 and 36. I always bet on the same number, 13. If I play all evening and there is a total of 185 spins of the wheel in that time, how many times could I expect to win?

5 I have 20 tickets for a raffle and I know that the probability of my winning the prize is 0.05. How many tickets were sold altogether in the raffle?

6 In a bag there are 30 balls, 15 of which are red, 5 yellow, 5 green, and 5 blue. A ball is taken out at random and then replaced. This is repeated 300 times. How many times would I expect to get
a a red ball **b** a yellow or blue ball
c a ball that is not blue **d** a pink ball?

7 The same experiment described in question **6** is carried out 1000 times. Approximately how many times would you expect to get
a a green ball **b** a ball that is not blue?

8 A sampling bottle (as described in question **4** of Exercise 23A contains red and white balls. It is known that the probability of getting a red ball is 0.3 when 1500 samples are taken. How many of them would you expect to give a white ball?

9 Josie said: 'When I throw a dice, I expect to get a score of 3.5.'
'Impossible,' said Paul, 'You can't score 3.5 with a dice.'
'Do this and I'll prove it', said Josie.

a An ordinary dice is thrown 60 times. Fill in the table for the expected number of times each score will occur.

Score	1	2	3	4	5	6
Expected occurrences						

b Now work out the average score that is expected over 60 throws.

c There is an easy way to get an answer of 3.5 for the expected average score. Can you see what it is?

Addition rule for events

We have used this rule already but it has not yet been formally defined.

When two events are mutually exclusive, we can work out the probability of either of them occurring by **adding together the separate probabilities**.

Example A bag contains 12 red balls, 8 green balls, 5 blue balls and 15 black balls. A ball is drawn at random. What is the probability that it is

a red **b** black **c** red or black
d not green **e** neither green nor blue?

a $P(\text{red}) = \frac{12}{40} = \frac{3}{10}$

b $P(\text{black}) = \frac{15}{40} = \frac{3}{8}$

c $P(\text{red or black}) = P(\text{red}) + P(\text{black}) = \frac{3}{10} + \frac{3}{8} = \frac{27}{40}$

d $P(\text{not green}) = \frac{32}{40} = \frac{4}{5}$

e $P(\text{neither green nor blue}) = P(\text{red or black}) = \frac{27}{40}$

The last part is another example of how confusing probability can be. You might say

$$P(\text{neither green nor blue}) = P(\text{not green}) + P(\text{not blue}) = \frac{32}{40} + \frac{35}{40} = \frac{67}{40}$$

This cannot be correct, as $\frac{67}{40}$ is greater than 1. In fact, the events 'not green' and 'not blue' are not mutually exclusive, as there are lots of balls that are true for both events.

Tossing coins

Tossing one coin

There are two equally likely outcomes, head or tail:

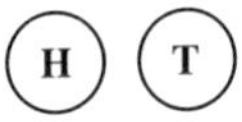

Tossing two coins together

There are four equally likely outcomes:

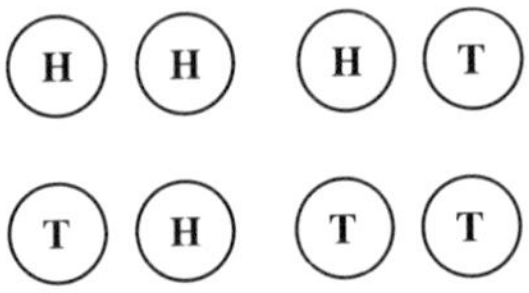

$$P(2\text{ heads}) = \frac{1}{4}$$

$$P(\text{head or tail}) = 2\text{ ways out of }4 = \frac{2}{4} = \frac{1}{2}$$

Tossing three coins together

There are eight equally likely outcomes:

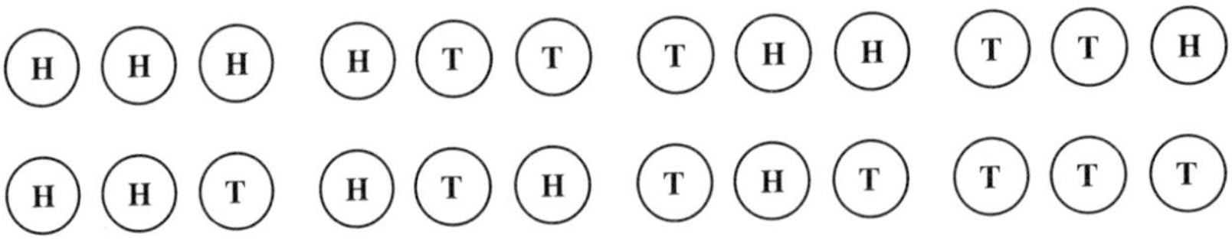

$$P(\text{same on all 3 coins}) = P(3\text{ heads})\text{ or }P(3\text{ tails}) = \frac{1}{8} + \frac{1}{8} = \frac{1}{4}$$

$$P(2\text{ heads and 1 tail}) = 3\text{ ways out of }8 = \frac{3}{8}$$

Tossing a coin and throwing a dice

There are 12 equally likely outcomes:

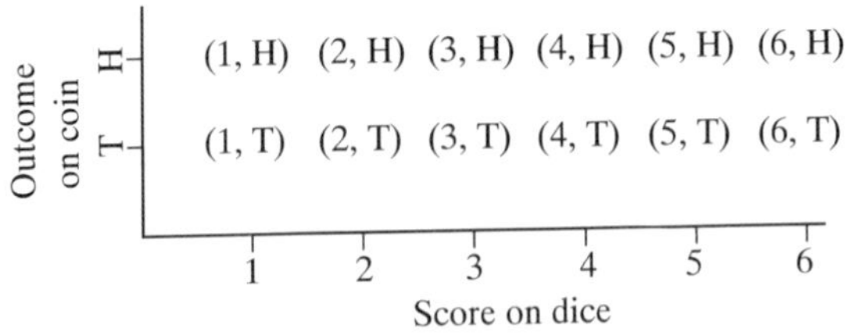

$$P(\text{head and an even number}) = 3\text{ ways out of }12 = \frac{3}{12} = \frac{1}{4}$$

Exercise 16F

1 To answer these questions, use the diagram on page 397 for the total scores when two dice are thrown together.

a What is the most likely score? **b** Which two scores are least likely?

c Write down the probabilities of all scores from 2 to 12.

d What is the probability of a score that is

i bigger than 10 **ii** between 3 and 7 **iii** even

iv a square number **v** a prime number **vi** a triangle number?

2 Using the diagram on page 397 that shows, as co-ordinates, the outcomes when two dice are thrown together, what is the probability that

a the score is an even 'double' **b** at least one of the dice shows 2

c the score on one dice is twice the score on the other dice

d at least one of the dice shows a multiple of 3?

3 Using the diagram on page 397 that shows, as co-ordinates, the outcomes when two dice are thrown together, what is the probability that

a both dice show a 6

b at least one of the dice will show a six

c exactly one dice shows a six?

4 The diagram shows the score for the event 'the difference between the scores when two dice are thrown'. Copy and complete the diagram.

Score on second dice						
6	5	4			1	0
5	4	3				1
4	3					
3	2					
2	1					
1	0					
	1	2	3	4	5	6

Score on first dice

For the event described above, what is the probability of a difference of

a 1 **b** 0 **c** 4

d 6 **e** an odd number?

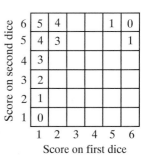

5 When two coins are tossed together, what is the probability of

a 2 heads **b** a head and a tail **c** at least 1 tail **d** no tails?

Use the diagram of the outcomes when two coins are tossed together, on page 398.

6 When three coins are tossed together, what is the probability of

a 3 heads **b** 2 heads and 1 tail **c** at least 1 tail **d** no tails?

7 When one coin is tossed there are two outcomes. When two coins are tossed, there are four outcomes. When three coins are tossed, there are eight outcomes.

a How many outcomes will there be when four coins are tossed?

b How many outcomes will there be when five coins are tossed?

c How many outcomes will there be when ten coins are tossed?

d How many outcomes will there be when n coins are tossed?

8 When a dice and a coin are thrown together, what is the probability of each of the following outcomes?

a You get a head on the coin and a 6 on the dice.

b You get a tail on the coin and an even number on the dice.

c You get a head on the coin and a square number on the dice.

Use the diagram on page 398 that shows the outcomes when a dice and a coin are thrown together.

9 Two five-sided spinners are spun together and the total core of the faces that they land on is worked out. Copy and complete the probability space diagram on the right.

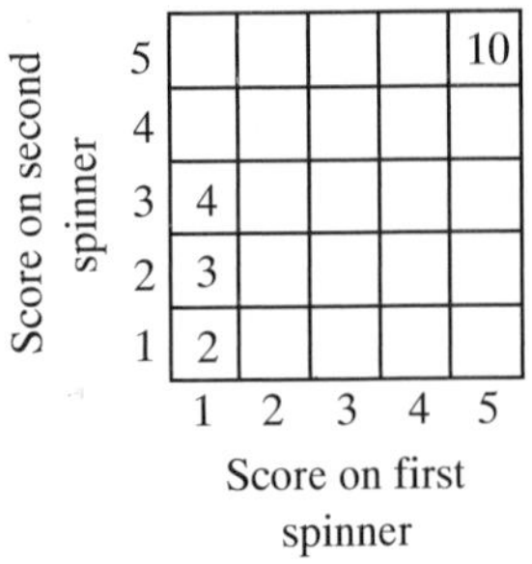

a What is the most likely score?

b When two five-sided spinners are spun together, what is the probability that

i the total score is 5

ii the total score is an even number

iii the score is a 'double'

iv the score is less than 7?

Other combined events and tree diagrams

Imagine we have to draw two cards from this pack of cards, but we must replace the first card before we select the second card.

One way we could show all the outcomes of this experiment is to construct a **probability space diagram**. For example, it could be an array set in a pair of axes, like those used for the two dice (see page 397), or a pictogram, like those used for the coins, or simply a list of all the outcomes. By showing all the outcomes of our experiment as array, we obtain the diagram above right.

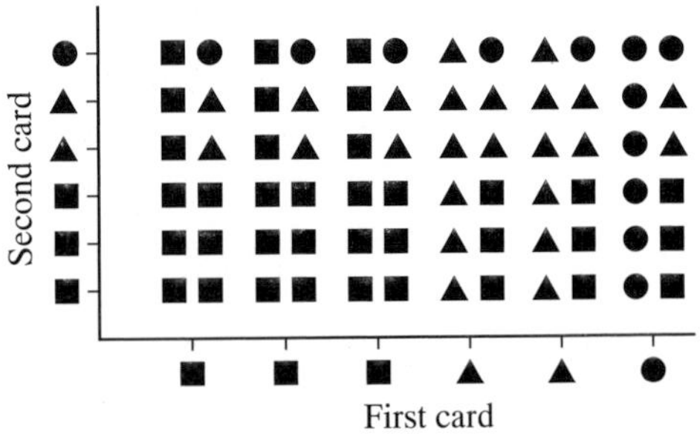

From the diagram, we can see immediately that the probability of picking, say, two squares is 9 out of 36. So,

$$\text{P(2 squares)} = \frac{9}{36} = \frac{1}{4}$$

Example Using the above diagram, what is the probability of getting the following?

a a square and a triangle (in any order) **b** two circles **c** two shapes the same

a There are 12 combinations which give a square and a triangle together. These become 6 when a square is chosen first or when a triangle is chosen first. So,

$$\text{P(square and triangle, in any order)} = \frac{12}{36} = \frac{1}{3}$$

b There is only one combination which gives two circles. So,

$$\text{P(2 circles)} = \frac{1}{36}$$

c There are 9 combinations of two squares together, 4 combinations of two triangles together, and one combination of two circles together. These give a total of 14 combinations with two shapes the same. So,

$$\text{P(2 shapes the same)} = \frac{14}{36} = \frac{7}{18}$$

An alternative method is to use a **tree diagram** (also a probability space diagram).

When we pick the first card, there are three possible outcomes: a square, a triangle or a circle. For a single event,

$$\text{P(square)} = \frac{1}{2} \qquad \text{P(triangle)} = \frac{1}{3} \qquad \text{P(circle)} = \frac{1}{6}$$

We can show this by depicting each event as a **branch** and writing its probability on the branch.

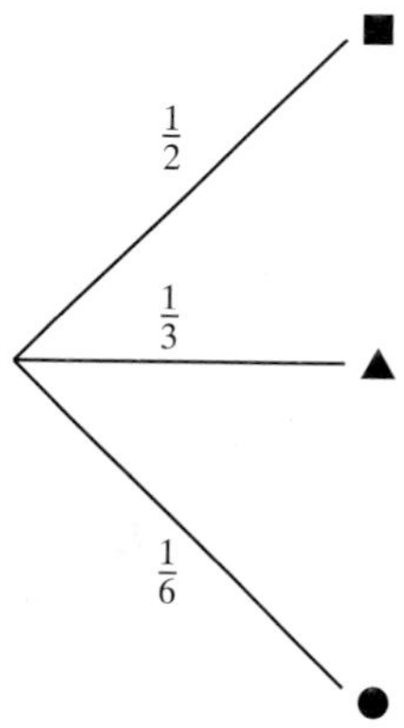

The diagram can then be extended to take into account a second choice. Because the first card has been replaced, we can still pick a square, a triangle or a circle. This is true no matter what is chosen the first time. We can demonstrate this by adding three more branches to the squares branch in the diagram.

Here is the complete tree diagram. The probabilities are worked out as explained below.

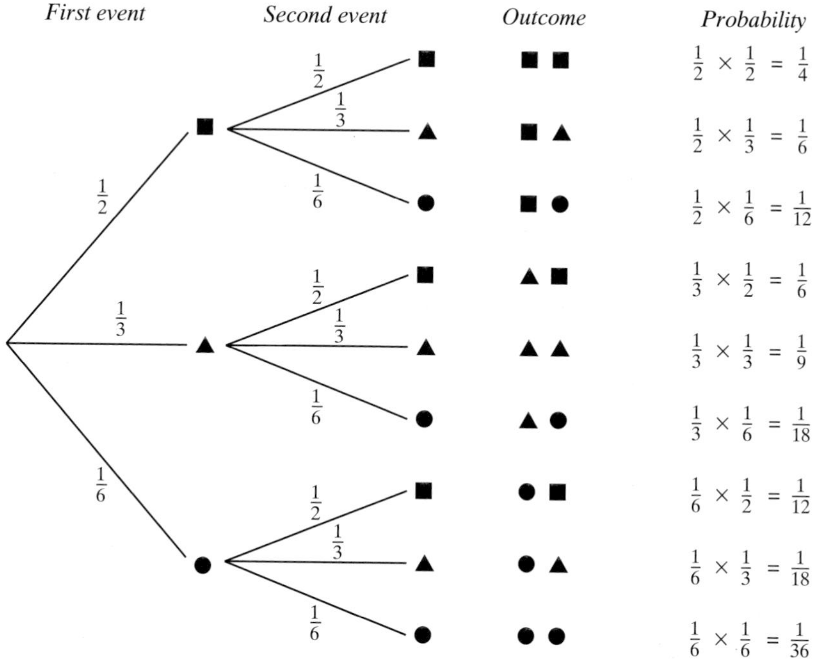

The probability of any outcome is calculated by multiplying together the probabilities on its branches. For instance,

$$P(2\text{ squares}) = \frac{1}{2} \times \frac{1}{2} = \frac{1}{4}$$

$$P(\text{triangle followed by circle}) = \frac{1}{3} \times \frac{1}{6} = \frac{1}{18}$$

Example Using the tree diagram on page 401, what is the probability of obtaining

a two triangles
b a circle followed by a triangle
c a square and a triangle, in any order
d two circles
e two shapes the same?

a $P(2\text{ triangles}) = \frac{1}{9}$

b $P(\text{circle followed by triangle}) = \frac{1}{18}$

c There are two places in the outcome column which have a square and a triangle. These are the second and fourth rows. The probability of each is $\frac{1}{6}$, so their combined probability is given by the addition rule:

$$P(\text{square and triangle, in any order}) = \frac{1}{6} + \frac{1}{6} = \frac{1}{3}$$

d $P(2\text{ circles}) = \frac{1}{36}$

e There are three places in the outcome column which have two shapes the same. These are the first, fifth and last rows. The probabilities are respectively $\frac{1}{4}$, $\frac{1}{9}$ and $\frac{1}{36}$, so their combined probability is given by the addition rule:

$$P(\text{two shapes the same}) = \frac{1}{4} + \frac{1}{9} + \frac{1}{36} = \frac{7}{18}$$

Note that the answers to parts **c**, **d** and **e** are the same as the answers in the previous example.

Exercise 16G

1 A coin is tossed twice. Copy and complete the tree diagram below to show all the outcomes.

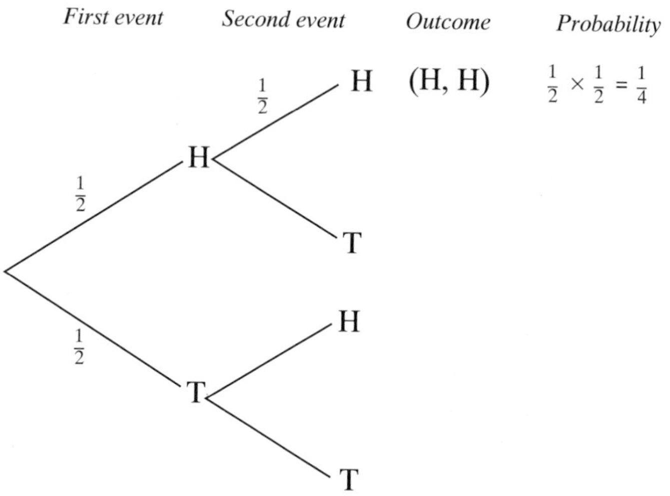

Use your tree diagram to work out the probability of

a getting two heads **b** getting a head and a tail **c** getting at least one tail

2 On my way to work, I drive through two sets of road works with traffic lights which only show green or red. I know that the probability of the first set being green is $\frac{1}{3}$ and the probability of the second set being green is $\frac{1}{2}$.

a What is the probability that the first set of lights will be red?

b What is the probability that the second set of lights will be red?

c Copy and complete the tree diagram below, showing the possible outcomes of passing through both sets of lights.

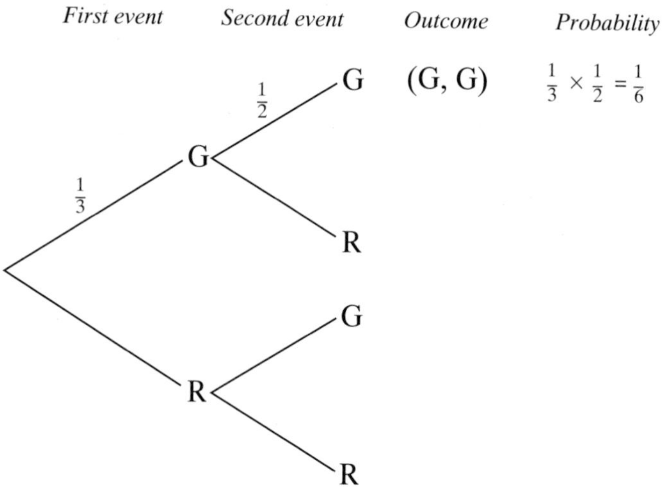

d Using the tree diagram, what is the probability of the following outcomes?

i I do not get held up at either set of lights.

ii I get held up at exactly one set of lights.

iii I get held up at least once.

e Over a term I make 90 journeys to work. On how many days can I expect to get two green lights?

3 Six out of every 10 cars in Britain are foreign made.

a What is the probability that any car will be British made?

b Two cars can be seen approaching in the distance. Draw a tree diagram to work out the probability that

i both cars will be British made

ii one car will be British and the other car will be foreign made.

4 A card is drawn from a pack of cards. It is replaced, the pack is shuffled and another card is drawn.

a What is the probability that either card was an Ace?

b What is the probability that either card was not an Ace?

c Draw a tree diagram to show the outcomes of two cards being drawn as described. Use the tree diagram to work out the probability that

i both cards will be Aces **ii** at least one of the cards will be an Ace.

5 A prison work party consists of five criminals. Two of them are robbers and the other three are fraudsters. Two of them are to be picked for a special job.

a The first member of the special job detail is picked at random. What is the probability that he is

i a robber **ii** a fraudster?

b If the first person chosen is a robber,

i how many criminals are left to choose from

ii how many of them are robbers?

c If the first person chosen is a fraudster,

i how many criminals are left to choose from

ii how many of them are robbers?

d Copy and complete the tree diagram below.

e Use the tree diagram to work out the probability that

i both criminals chosen are of the same type

ii there is at least one robber chosen.

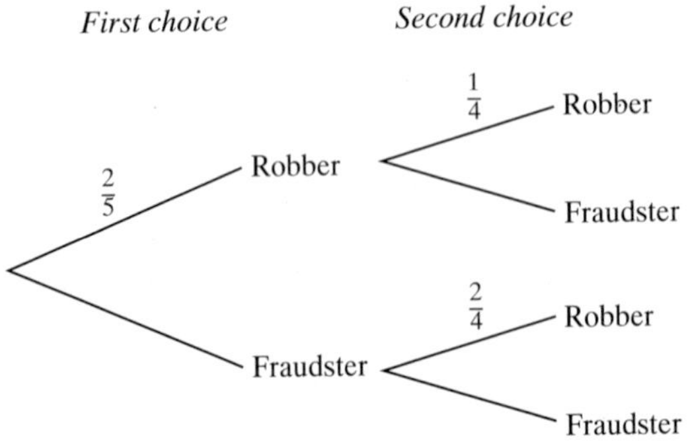

6 Three coins are tossed. Complete the tree diagram below and use it to answer the questions.

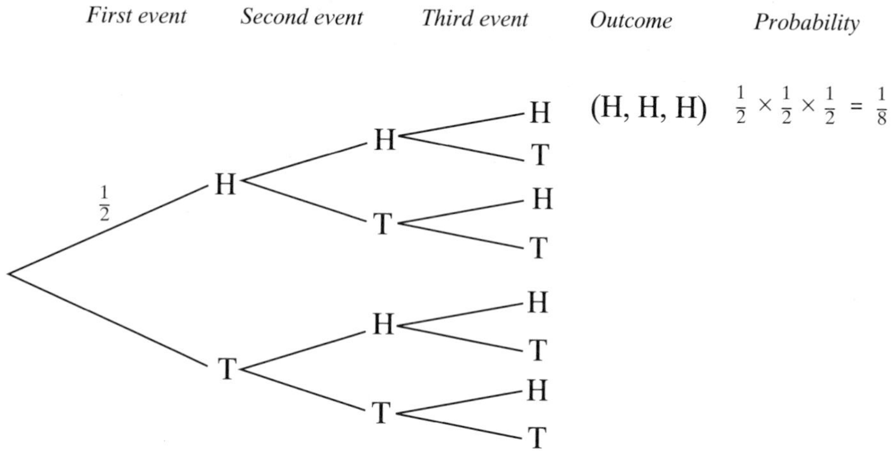

If a coin is tossed three times, what is the probability that you get

a three heads **b** two heads and a tail **c** at least one tail?

7 Thomas has to take a three-part language examination paper. The first part is speaking. He has a 0.4 chance of passing this. The second is listening. He has a 0.5 chance of passing this. The third part is writing. He has a 0.7 chance of passing this. Draw a tree diagram covering three events where the first event is passing or failing the speaking part of the examination, the second event is passing or failing the listening part, and the third event is passing or failing the writing part.

a If he passes all three parts, his father will give him £20. What is the probability that he gets the money?

b If he passes two parts only, he can resit the third part. What is the chance he will have to resit?

c If he fails all three parts, he will be thrown off the course. What is the chance he is thrown off the course?

8 In a group of ten girls, six like the pop group Smudge and four like the pop group Mirage. Two girls are to be chosen for a pop quiz.

a What is the probability that the first girl chosen will be a Smudge fan?

b Draw a tree diagram to show the outcomes of choosing two girls and which pop groups they like (Remember: once a girl has been chosen the first time she cannot be chosen again.)

c Use your tree diagram to work out the probability that

i both girls chosen will like Smudge

ii both girls chosen will like the same group

iii both girls chosen will like different groups.

9 There are three white and one brown eggs in an egg box. Sanjay decides to make a two-egg omelette. He takes each egg from the box without looking at its colour.

a What is the probability that the first egg taken is brown?

b If the first egg taken is brown, what is the probability that the second egg taken will also be brown?

c Copy and complete this tree diagram.

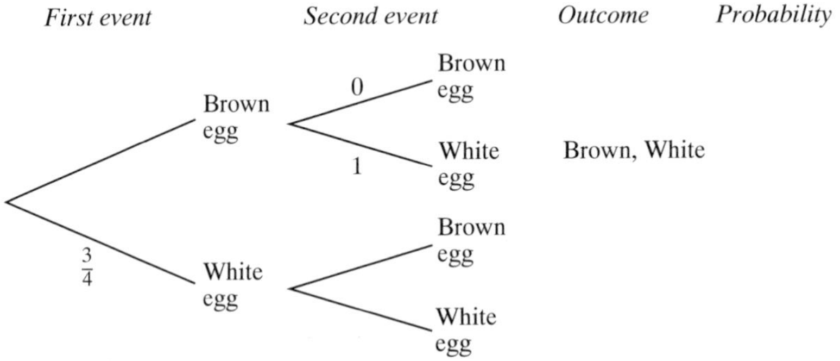

d What is the probability that Sanjay gets an omelette made from

i two white eggs **ii** one white and one brown egg **iii** two brown eggs?

10 Look at all the tree diagrams that have been drawn so far.

a What do the probabilities across any set of branches (outlined in the diagram below) always add up to?

b What do the final probabilities (outlined in the diagram below) always add up to?

c You should now be able to fill in all of the missing values in the diagram.

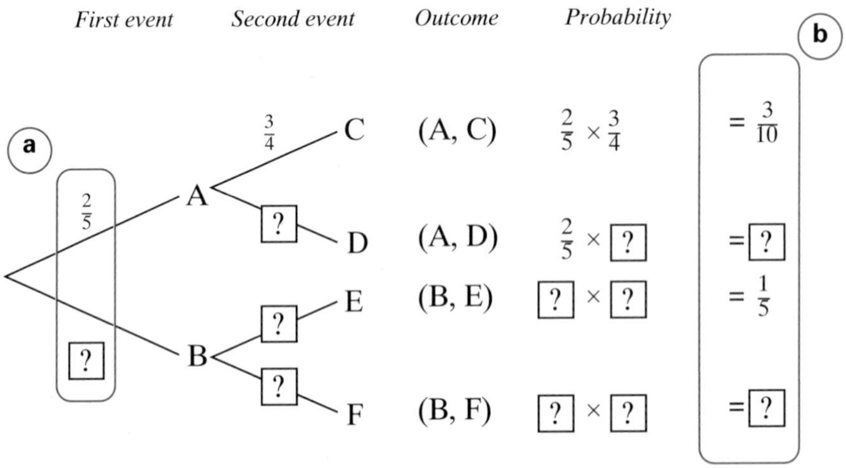

Using 'and' and 'or'. Independent events

If the outcome of event A does not effect the outcome of event B, then events A and B are called **independent events**. Most of the combined events we have looked at so far have been independent events.

It is possible to work out problems on combined events without using tree diagrams. The method explained in the next example is basically the same as that of a tree diagram but uses the words **and** and **or**.

Example The chance that Ashley hits a target with an arrow is $\frac{1}{4}$. He has two shots at the target. What is the probability that he

a hits the target both times

b hits the target once only

c hits the target at least once?

a P(hits **both** times) = P(first shot hits **and** second shot hits) = $\frac{1}{4} \times \frac{1}{4} = \frac{1}{16}$

b P(hits the target once only) = P(first hits **and** second misses **or** first misses **and** second hits) = $\left(\frac{1}{4} \times \frac{3}{4}\right) + \left(\frac{3}{4} \times \frac{1}{4}\right) = \frac{3}{8}$

c P(hits at least once) = P(both hit **or** one hits) = $\frac{1}{16} + \frac{3}{8} = \frac{7}{16}$

Exercise 16H

1 Alf tosses a coin twice. The coin is biased so it has a probability of landing a head of $\frac{2}{3}$. What is the probability that he gets

a two heads **b** a head and a tail (in any order)?

2 Bernice draws a card from a pack of cards, replaces it, shuffles the pack and then draws another card. What is the probability that the cards are

a both Aces **b** an Ace and a King (in any order)?

3 Charles draws a card from a pack of cards, does not replace it and then draws another card. What is the probability that the cards are

a both Aces **b** an Ace and a King (in any order)?

4 A dice is thrown twice. What is the probability that both scores are

a even **b** one even and one odd (in any order)?

5 I throw a dice three times. What is the probability of getting three sixes?

6 A bag contains 15 white beads and 10 black beads. I take out a bead at random, replace it and take out another bead. What is the probability that

a both beads are black **b** one bead is black and the other white (in any order)?

7 A bag contains 15 white beads and 10 black beads. I take out a bead at random, do not replace it and take out another bead. What is the probability that

a both beads are black **b** one bead is black and the other white (in any order)?

8 The probability that I am late for work on Monday is 0.4. The probability that I am late on Tuesday is 0.2. What is the probability of each of the following outcomes?

a I am late for work on Monday and Tuesday.

b I am late for work on Monday and on time on Tuesday.

c I am on time on both Monday and Tuesday.

9 Thomas has to take a three-part language examination paper. The first part is speaking. He has a 0.7 chance of passing this. The second part is listening. He has a 0.6 chance of passing this. The third part is writing. He has a 0.8 chance of passing this.

a If he passes all three parts, his father will give him £20. What is the probability that he gets the money?

b If he passes two parts only, he can resit the third part. What is the chance he will have to resit?

c If he fails all three parts, he will be thrown off the course. What is the chance he is thrown off the course?

10 There are five white and one brown eggs in an egg box. Kate decides to make a two-egg omelette. She takes each egg from the box without looking at its colour.

a What is the probability that the first egg taken is brown?

b If the first egg taken is brown, what is the probability that the second egg taken will be brown?

c What is the probability that Kate gets an omelette made from

i two white eggs **ii** one white and one brown egg **iii** two brown eggs?

'At least' problems

In examination questions concerning combined events, it is common to ask for the probability of at least one of the events occurring. There are two ways to solve such problems:

- All possibilities can be written out, which takes a long time.
- Use

$$P(\text{at least one}) = 1 - P(\text{none})$$

This is much easier to work out and there is less chance of making a mistake.

Example A bag contains 7 red and 3 black balls. A ball is taken out and replaced. This is repeated three times. What is the probability of getting

a no red balls **b** at least one red ball?

a P(no reds) = P(black, black, black) = $\frac{7}{10} \times \frac{7}{10} \times \frac{7}{10} = 0.343$

b P(at least one red) = 1 – P(no reds) = 1 – 0.343 = 0.657

Note The answer to part **b** is 1 minus the answer to part **a**. Examination questions often build up answers in this manner.

Exercise 16I

1 A dice is thrown three times.

a What is the probability of not getting a 2?

b What is the probability of at least one 2?

2 Four coins are thrown. What is the probability of

a 4 tails **b** at least 1 head?

3 Adam, Bashir and Clem take a mathematics test. The probability that Adam passes is 0.6, the probability that Bashir passes is 0.9, and the probability that Clem passes is 0.7. What is the probability that

a all three pass **b** Bashir and Adam pass but Clem does not

c all three fail **d** at least one passes?

4 A bag contains 4 red and 6 blue balls. A ball is taken out and replaced. Another ball is taken out. What is the probability that

a both balls are red **b** both balls are blue **c** at least one is red?

5 A bag contains 4 red and 6 blue balls. A ball is taken out and **not** replaced. Another ball is taken out. What is the probability that

a both balls are red **b** both balls are blue **c** at least one is red?

6 a A dice is thrown three times. What is the probability of

i 3 sixes **ii** no sixes **iii** at least one six?

b A dice is thrown four times. What is the probability of

i 4 sixes **ii** no sixes **iii** at least one six?

c A dice is thrown five times. What is the probability of

i 5 sixes **ii** no sixes **iii** at least one six?

d A dice is thrown n times. What is the probability of

i n sixes **ii** no sixes **iii** at least one six?

7 The probability that the school canteen serves chips on any day is $\frac{2}{3}$. In a week of 5 days, what is the probability that

a chips are served every day **b** chips are not served on any day

c chips are served on at least one day?

8 The probability that Steve is late for work is $\frac{5}{6}$. The probability that Nigel is late for work is $\frac{9}{10}$. The probability that Gary is late for work is $\frac{1}{2}$. What is the probability that on a particular day

a all three are late **b** none of them is late **c** at least one is late?

9 A class has 13 boys and 12 girls. Two of the class are to be chosen at random to do a task for their teacher. What is the probability that

a both are girls **b** at least one is a boy?

10 Alice has 10 CDs. Six are rock CDs and four are dance CDs. She loads three at random into her multi-player CD system. What is the probability that

a all three are dance **b** at least one is rock?

More advanced use of 'and' and 'or'

We have already seen how certain probability problems can be solved either by tree diagrams or by the use of the *and/or* method. Both methods are basically the same but the *and/or* method works better in the case of three events following one another or in situations where the number of outcomes of one event is greater than two. This is simply because the tree diagram would get too large and involved.

Example Three cards are to be drawn from a pack of cards. Each card is to be replaced before the next one is drawn. What is the probability that the cards will be

a 3 Kings **b** exactly 2 Kings and 1 other card
c no Kings **d** at least 1 King?

Let K be the event 'Drawing a King'. Let N be the event 'Not drawing a King'. Then we obtain

a $\mathrm{P}(KKK) = \frac{1}{13} \times \frac{1}{13} \times \frac{1}{13} = \frac{1}{2197}$

b $\mathrm{P}(\text{exactly 2 Kings}) = \mathrm{P}(KKN) \text{ or } \mathrm{P}(KNK) \text{ or } \mathrm{P}(NKK)$

$$= \left(\frac{1}{13} \times \frac{1}{13} \times \frac{12}{13}\right) + \left(\frac{1}{13} \times \frac{12}{13} \times \frac{1}{13}\right) + \left(\frac{12}{13} \times \frac{1}{13} \times \frac{1}{13}\right)$$

$$= \frac{36}{2197}$$

c $\mathrm{P}(\text{no Kings}) = \mathrm{P}(NNN) = \frac{12}{13} \times \frac{12}{13} \times \frac{12}{13} = \frac{1728}{2197}$

d $\mathrm{P}(\text{at least 1 King}) = 1 - \mathrm{P}(\text{no Kings}) = 1 - \frac{1728}{2197} = \frac{469}{2197}$

Note that in part **b** the notation stands for the probability that the first card is a King, the second is a King and the third is not a King; or the first is a King, the second is not a King and the third is a King; or the first is not a King, the second is a King and the third is a King.

Note also that the probability of each component of part **b** is exactly the same. So we could have done the calculation as

$$3 \times \frac{1}{13} \times \frac{1}{13} \times \frac{12}{13} = \frac{36}{2197}$$

Patterns of this kind often occur in probability.

Exercise 16J

1 A bag contains 3 black balls and 7 red balls. A ball is taken out and replaced. This is repeated twice. What is the probability that

a all 3 are black **b** exactly 2 are black

c exactly 1 is black **d** none is black?

2 A bag contains 4 blue balls and 6 white balls. A ball is taken out but not replaced. This is repeated twice. What is the probability that

a all 3 are blue **b** exactly 2 are blue

c exactly 1 is blue **d** none is blue?

3 A dice is thrown 4 times . What is the probability that

a 4 sixes are thrown **b** no sixes are thrown

c exactly one six is thrown?

4 On my way to work I pass three sets of traffic lights. The probability that the first is green is $\frac{1}{2}$. The probability that the second is green is $\frac{1}{3}$. The probability that the third is green is $\frac{2}{3}$. What is the probability that

a all three are green **b** exactly two are green

c exactly one is green **d** none is green

e at least one is green?

5 Alf is late for school with a probability of 0.9. Bert is late with a probability of 0.7. Chas is late with a probability of 0.6. On any particular day what is the probability of

a exactly one of them being late **b** exactly two of them being late?

6 Daisy takes four A-levels. The probability that she will pass English is 0.7. The probability that she will pass history is 0.6. The probability she will pass geography is 0.8. The probability that she will pass general studies is 0.9. What is the probability that she will pass

a all four subjects **b** exactly three subjects

c at least three subjects?

7 The driving test is now in two parts. A written test and a practical test. It is known that 90% of people who take the written test pass and 60% of people who take the practical test pass. A person who passes the written test does not have to take it again. A person who fails the practical test does have to take it again.

a What is the probability that someone passes the written test?

b What is the probability that someone passes the practical test?

c What is the probability that someone passes both tests?

d What is the probability that someone passes the written test but takes two attempts to pass the practical test?

8 Six out of ten cars in Britain are made by foreign manufacturers. Three cars can be seen approaching in the distance.

a What is the probability that the first one is foreign?

b The first car is going so fast that its make could not be made out. What is the probability that the second car is foreign?

c What is the probability that exactly two of them are foreign?

d Explain why, if the first car is foreign, the probability of the second car being foreign is still 6 out of 10.

9 Each day Mr Smith runs home. He has a choice of three routes: the road, the fields or the canal path. The road route is 4 miles, the fields route is 6 miles and the canal route is 5 miles. In a three-day period, what is the probability that Mr Smith runs a total distance of

a exactly 17 miles

b exactly 13 miles

c exactly 15 miles

d over 17 miles?

10 A rock climber attempts a difficult route. There are three hard moves at points A, B and C in the climb. The climber has a probability of 0.6, 0.3 and 0.7 respectively of completing each of these moves. What is the probability that the climber

a completes the climb

b fails at move A

c fails at move B

d fails at move C

Conditional probability

The term **conditional probability** is used to describe the situation when the probability of an event is dependent on the outcome of another event. For instance, if a card is taken from a pack and not returned, then the probabilities for the next card drawn will be altered. The following example illustrates this situation.

Example A bag contains 9 balls, of which 5 are white and 4 are black.

A ball is taken out and not replaced. Another is then taken out. If the first ball removed is black, what is the probability that

a the second ball will be black **b** both balls will be black?

When a black ball is removed, there are 5 white balls and 3 black balls left, reducing the total to 8.

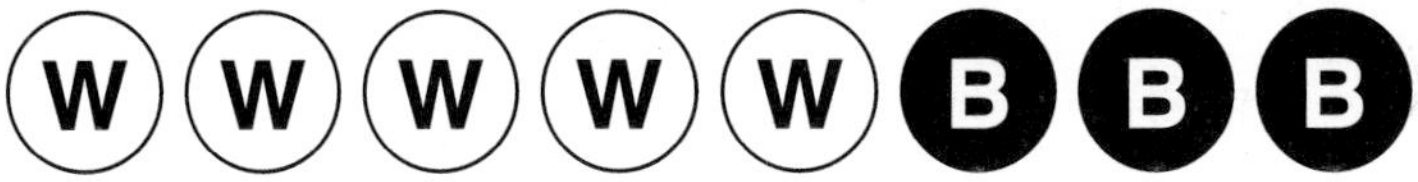

Hence, when the second ball is taken out,

a P(second ball black) = $\frac{3}{8}$

b P(both balls black) = $\frac{4}{9} \times \frac{3}{8} = \frac{1}{6}$

Exercise 16K

1 A box contains 10 red and 15 yellow balls. One is taken out and not replaced. Another is taken out.

a If the first ball taken out is red, what is the probability that the second ball is

i red **ii** yellow?

b If the first ball taken out is yellow, what is the probability that the second ball is

i red **ii** yellow?

2 A fruit bowl contains 6 Granny Smith apples and 8 Golden Delicious apples. Kevin takes two apples at random.

a If the first apple is a Granny Smith, what is the probability that the second is

i a Granny Smith **ii** a Golden Delicious?

b What is the probability that

i both are Granny Smiths **ii** both are Golden Delicious?

3 Ann has a bargain box of tins. They are unlabelled but she knows that 6 tins contain soup and 4 contain peaches.

a She opens 2 tins. What is the probability that

i they are both soup **ii** they are both peaches?

b What is the probability that she has to open 2 tins before she gets a tin of peaches?

c What is the probability that she has to open 3 tins before she gets a tin of peaches?

d What is the probability that she will get a tin of soup if she opens 5 tins?

4 I put six CDs in my multi-player and put it on random play. Each CD has 10 tracks. Once a track is played, it is not played again.

a What is the chance that track 5 on CD 6 is the first one played?

b What is the maximum number of tracks that could be played before a track from CD 6 is played?

5 One in three cars on British roads is made in Britain. A car comes down the road. It is a British-made car. John says that the probability of the next car being British made is one in two because a British-made car has just gone past. Explain why he is wrong.

6 A bag contains 3 black balls and 7 red balls. A ball is taken out and not replaced. This is repeated twice. What is the probability that

a all 3 are black **b** exactly 2 are black

c exactly 1 is black **d** none is black?

7 One my way to work, I pass two sets of traffic lights. The probability that the first is green is $\frac{1}{3}$. If the first is green, the probability that the second is green is $\frac{1}{3}$. If the first is red, the probability that the second is green is $\frac{2}{3}$. What is the probability that

a both are green **b** none is green

c exactly one is green **d** at least one is green?

8 A hand of five cards is dealt. What is the probability that

a all five are Spades

b all five are the same suit

c they are four Aces and any other card

d they are four of a kind and any other card?

9 An engineering test is in two parts. A written test and a practical test. It is known that 90% who take the written test pass. When a person passes the written test the probability that he/she will also pass the practical test is 60%. When a person fails the written test the probability that he/she will pass the practical test is 20%.

a What is the probability that someone passes both tests?

b What is the probability that someone passes one test?

c What is the probability that someone fails both tests?

d What is the combined probability of the answers to parts **a**, **b** and **c**?

10 Each day Mr Smith runs home from work. He has a choice of three routes. The road, the fields or the canal path. On Monday, each route has an equal probability of being chosen. The route chosen on any day will not be picked the next day and so each of the other two routes has an equal probability of being chosen.

a Write down all the possible combinations so that Mr Smith runs home via the canal path on Wednesday (there are four of them).

b Calculate the probability that Mr Smith runs home via the canal path on Wednesday.

c Calculate the probability that Mr Smth runs home via the canal path on Tuesday.

d Using your results from parts **b** and **c**, write down the probability that Mr Smith runs home via the canal path on Thursday.

e Explain the answers to parts **b**, **c** and **d**.

Exercise 16L

This exercise contains a variety of questions which together cover all the aspects of probability dealt with in this chapter.

1 Draw a tree diagram to show the outcome of tossing 2 coins. Use it, or some other method, to find the probability of

a 2 heads **b** at least 1 tail

2 What is the chance of tossing a coin four times and getting

a 4 heads in a row **b** no heads at all **c** at least 1 head?

3 A bag contains 4 black and 3 white balls. Three balls are taken out one at a time.

a If the balls are put back each time, what is the probability of getting

i 3 black balls **ii** at least 1 black ball?

b If the balls are not put back each time, what is the probability of getting

i 3 black balls **ii** at least 1 black ball?

4 Two cards are drawn one at a time from a pack of cards. The cards are replaced each time. What is the probability that at least one of them is a Spade?

5 Two cards are drawn from a pack of cards. The cards are not replaced each time. What is the probability that at least one of them is a Spade?

6 A box contains 100 batteries. It is known that 30 of them are dead. John needs two batteries for his calculator. He takes two out. What is the probability that

a both of them are dead **b** at least one of them works?

7 From the same box of 100 batteries (question **6**), Janet takes out four batteries for her radio. The radio will work if three or four of the batteries are good. What is the probability that the radio will work?

8 a A fair dice is thrown twice. What is the probability of getting at least one six?

b A fair dice is thrown three times. What is the probability of getting at least one six?

c A fair dice is thrown four times. What is the probability of getting at least one six?

d A fair dice is thrown n times. What is the probability of getting at least one six?

9 An ordinary dice and a tetrahedral (four-sided) dice, whose faces are numbered 1, 2, 3 and 4, are thrown together. The score on the ordinary dice is the uppermost face. The score on the tetrahedral dice is the face it lands on. Show by means of a sample space diagram, or a list of all outcomes, that there are 24 outcomes with total scores from 2 to 10. What is the probability of

a a total score of 8 **b** at least one 3 on either dice?

10 In a blind-tasting test between Popsi Cola and Hoca Cola, the probability that Alf will pick Popsi is $\frac{1}{3}$, the probability that Bo will pick Popsi is $\frac{2}{5}$, and the probability that Cy will pick Popsi is $\frac{3}{4}$. What is the probability that

a all 3 pick Popsi
b exactly 2 pick Popsi
c exactly 1 picks Popsi
d none of them picks Popsi
e at least 1 picks Popsi?

11 In a Skuta car from Estovolakia, the probability that the engine fails in the first year is $\frac{1}{4}$. The probability that the steering fails in the first year is $\frac{1}{5}$. And the probability that the gearbox fails in the first year is $\frac{1}{6}$. Calculate the probability that, in the first year,

a nothing fails
b exactly one of the components fails
c at least one component fails.
d If 2000 cars are sold, how many will not be returned in their first year for some sort of repair?

12 On average, Steve is late for school one day each week (of 5 days).

a What is the probability that he is late on any one day?
b In a week of 5 days, what is the probability that
  i he is late every day
  ii he is late exactly once
  iii he is never late
  iv he is late at least once?

13 Five T-shirts are hung out at random on a washing line. Three are red and two are blue. Using R and B, write down all 10 possible combinations: for example, RRRBB, RRBBR, … . What is the probability of

a 2 red shirts being next to each other
b 2 blue shirts being next to each other

14 Dan has 5 socks in a drawer, of which 3 are blue and 2 are black. He takes out 2 socks. What is the probability that

a both socks are blue
b both socks are black
c he gets a pair of socks
d at least one of the socks is blue?

15 Jane loads up her six-changer multi CD player at random with a choice from 10 CDs. Six of them are pop and 4 are dance. What is the probability that

a all 6 CDs are pop
b all 6 CDs are dance
c at least one of them is a dance CD?

16 Ten balls, numbered 1 to 10, are in a bag. Two are taken out and not put back. What is the probability that

a both balls are even
b both balls are odd
c at least one ball is odd
d both balls are prime numbers?

17 Steve has a probability of 0.8 of scoring a penalty. Nigel has a probability of 0.7 of scoring a penalty. They both need to take a penalty at the end of penalty shoot-out. What is the probability that

a both of them score **b** both of them miss

c at least one of them scores?

18 One in ten people are left handed. Ten people are in a room. What is the probability that

a all 10 are left-handed **b** all 10 are right-handed

c at least one of them is left-handed?

19 A ball is dropped into a maze at A. It can go either side of A, B, C, etc with equal chance.

a Show that the probability that the ball lands in slot 1 is $\frac{1}{8}$.

b Show that the probability that the ball lands in slot 2 is $\frac{3}{8}$.

c Sixteen balls are dropped into the maze at A. How many would you expect to land in slot 3?

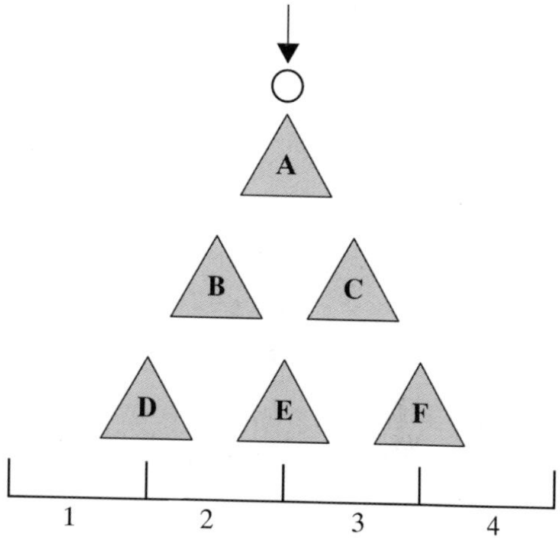

Possible coursework tasks

First to get a six

Investigate how many times a dice has to be thrown before a six is first obtained.

The National Lottery

Find ways of drawing tree diagrams which will help you to obtain the probability of winning the jackpot on the National Lottery.

Colour matching

A bag contains r red balls and b blue ones. Find the probability of choosing various combinations of the two colours.

Pascal's maze

The diagram shows a board with nails spaced out to form a triangular maze.

A marble is rolled into the maze at the top. It makes its way through the maze by bouncing, either to the left or to the right, off each nail.

Investigate the number of ways in which a marble can hit each nail from the start.

Buffon's experiment

Take a large sheet of paper and a matchstick. Draw a series of parallel lines on the paper that are exactly a matchstick-length apart.

Drop the matchstick onto the paper from a convenient height and count the number of times the matchstick falls across any line.

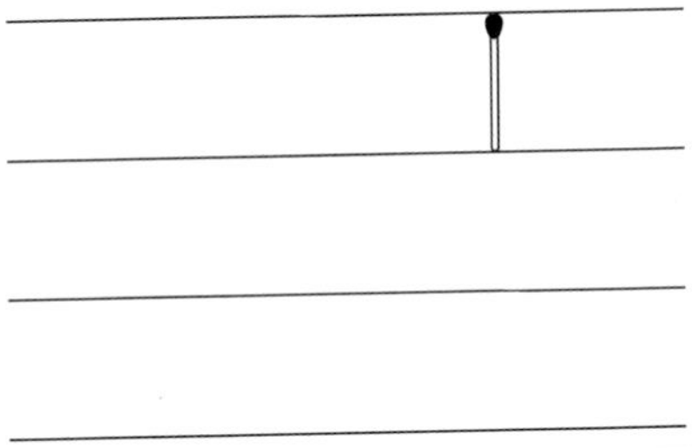

Buffon discovered that there is a relationship between π and the number of times the matchstick crosses the line. Can you find Buffon's relationship?

Examination questions

1 When you drop a match box on to a table, there are three ways it can land.

Jane has found that the probability of the match box landing 'on its end' is approximately 0.1 and the probability of it landing 'on its side' is approximately 0.6.

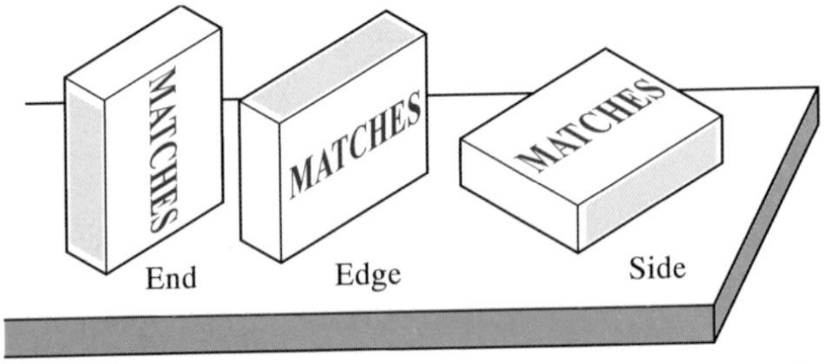

a Jane drops two identical match boxes. What is the probability that both boxes will land 'on their edges'?

b Jane and Sarah are playing a game.

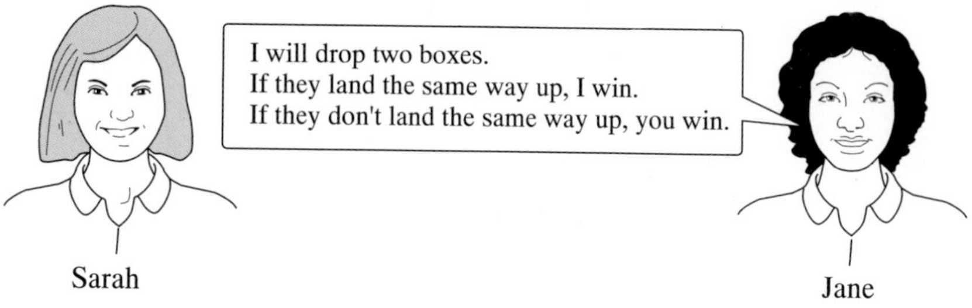
I will drop two boxes.
If they land the same way up, I win.
If they don't land the same way up, you win.
Sarah
Jane

Who is more likely to win the game? Show all your working.

NEAB, Question 21, Specimen Paper 11, 1998

2 The diagram shows two sets of cards, **A** and **B**.

One card is chosen at random from set **A**. One card is chosen at random from set **B**.

a i List all the possible outcomes. The two numbers are added together.

ii What is the probability of getting a total of 5?

iii What is the probability of getting a total that is **not** 5?

A new card is added to the set **B**.

One card is chosen at random from **A**. One card is chosen at random from **B**.

b i How many possible outcomes are there now?

ii Explain why adding the new card does not change the number of outcomes that have a total of 5.

iii Adding the new card does change the probability of getting a total of 5. What is now the probability of getting a total of 5?

SEG, Question 10, Specimen Paper 13, 1998

3 Sharna has bought 10 tickets for the Instant National Lottery. She has won a prize on one of them. She says:

This shows that the chance of winning a prize in the Instant National Lottery is $\frac{1}{10}$.

Is she correct? You must give a reason for your answer.

WJEC, Question 5, Specimen Paper 2, 1998

4a There are four socks in a drawer.

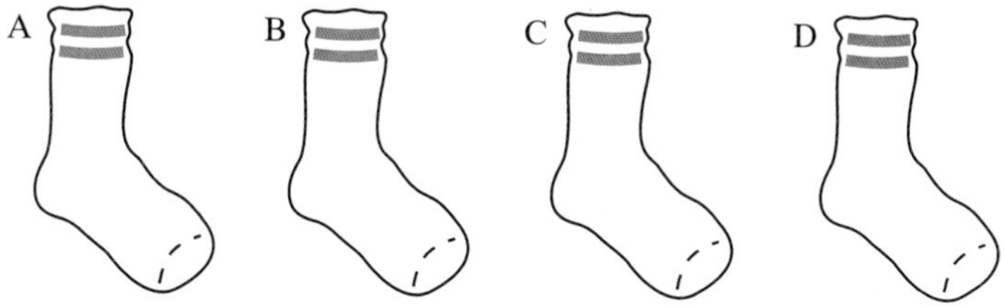
A
B
C
D

i Two socks are chosen at random. One possible choice is A and B. Write down the other five possible choices.

ii Two of the socks in the drawer are white and two are black.
If two of the socks are chosen at random, what is the probability that a black pair will be chosen?

b Another drawer contains red socks and green socks. The probability of choosing a red pair is 0.33. What is the probability that a red pair will **not** be chosen?

NEAB, Question 4, Paper 2Q, November 1994

5 When I answer the telephone the call is never for me. Half the calls are for my daughter Janette. One-third of them are for my son Glen. The rest are for my wife Barbara.

a I answer the telephone twice this evening. Calculate the probability that

i the first call will be for Barbara

ii both calls will be for Barbara.

b The probability that both these calls are for Janette is $\frac{1}{4}$. The probability that they are both for Glen is $\frac{1}{9}$. Calculate the probability that either they are both for Janette or both for Glen.

NEAB, Question 13, Paper 2Q, June 1995

6 A bag contains a number of counters. Each counter is coloured red, blue, yellow or green. Each counter is numbered 1, 2, or 3. The table shows the probability of colour and number for these counters.

	Colour of counter			
Number on counter	Red	Blue	Yellow	Green
1	0.2	0	0.1	0
2	0.2	0.1	0.1	0
3	0.1	0.1	0	0.1

a A counter is taken from the bag at random.

i What is the probability that it is red **and** numbered 2?

ii What is the probability that it is green **or** numbered 2?

iii What is the probability that it is red **or** numbered 2?

b There are two green counters in the bag. How many counters are in the bag altogether?

SEG, Question 15, Specimen Paper 14, 1998

7 Zaheda conducted a probability experiment using a packet of 20 sweets. She counted the number of sweets of each colour. Her results are shown in the table.

Red	Green	Orange
12	3	5

Zaheda is going to take one sweet at random from the packet. Write down the probability

i that Zaheda will take a green sweet from the packet

ii that the sweet Zaheda takes will **not** be red.

ULEAC, Question 4, Specimen Paper 3, 1998

8 Rob has a bag containing 3 blue balls, 4 red balls and 1 green ball. Sarah has a bag containing 2 blue balls and 3 red balls. The balls are identical except for the colour. Rob chooses a ball at random from his bag and Sarah chooses a ball at random from her bag.

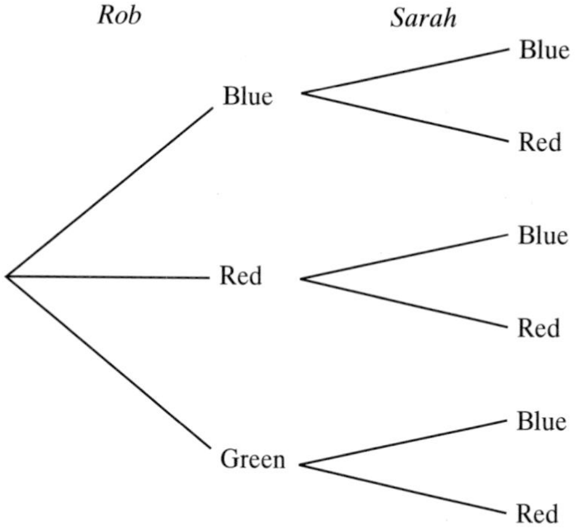

a On a copy of the tree diagram, write the probability of each of the events on the appropriate branch.

b Calculate the probability that both Rob and Sarah will choose a blue ball.

c Calculate the probability that the ball chosen by Rob will be a different colour from the ball chosen by Sarah.

MEG, Question 19, Specimen Paper 3, 1998

9 The probability of different numbers of births per week in a village are as follows.

Number of births	0	1	2	3
Probability	0.4	0.3	0.2	0.1

The probability of different numbers of deaths per week in the village are as follows.

Number of deaths	0	1	2	3
Probability	0.1	0.3	0.4	0.2

Assume that the number of births per week and the number of deaths per week are independent.

a Find the probability that during any particular week, there are exactly two births and two deaths.

b Find the probability that during any particular week, the number of births and deaths are the same.

SEG, Question 19, Specimen Paper 13, 1998

10 A bag contains 7 toffees and 5 mints.

a What is the probability that a sweet taken from the bag at random will be a toffee?

b Another bag contains 4 fruit drops and 6 mints. James takes one sweet from each bag without looking. Complete this tree diagram to show the possible outcomes and their probabilities.

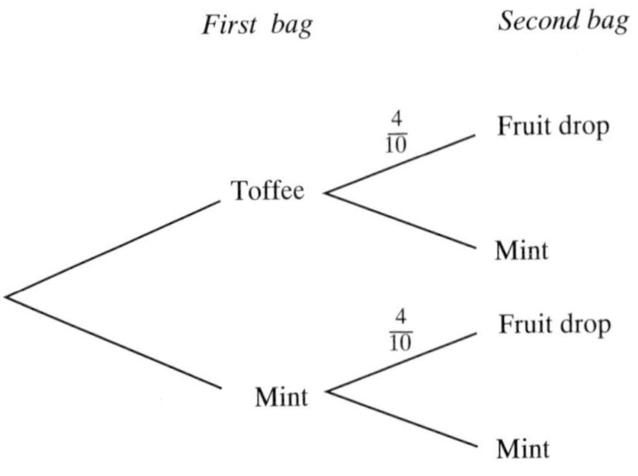

c What is the probability that James takes

i two mints **ii** exactly one mint?

WJEC, Question 13, Specimen Paper 2, 1998

Summary

How well do you grade yourself?

To gain a grade **C**, you need to be able to understand relative frequency as an estimate of probability and be able to use this to compare outcomes of experiments. You need also to be able to calculate the probability of a combined event using either a tree diagram or some other type of probability space diagram. And you need to be able to work out the probability of an event not happening and the probability of the event happening, and to know what mutually exclusive events are.

To gain a grade **B**, you need to be able to work out the probabilities of combined events using theoretical considerations of all the likely outcomes, and to solve problems using the words *and* and *or*.

To gain a grade **A**, you need to be able to recognise when and how to use conditional probability.

What you should know after you have worked through Chapter 16

- How to calculate the experimental probability of an event from data supplied.
- How to calculate the theoretical probability of an event from consideration of all outcomes of the event.
- That as the number of trials of an event increases, the experimental probability of the event gets closer to its theoretical probability.

- How to use either a tree diagram or some other type of probability space diagram to calculate the probability of combined events.
- How to work out the probability of mutually exclusive events.
- How to use the words *and* and *or* to solve combined events problems.
- How to use conditional probability

17 Algebra 3

This chapter is going to ... show you how to recognise rules for sequences and how to express these rules in formulae. It will then explain what is meant by the *n*th term, and show you how to find it for simple sequences.

What you should already know

- How to use the methods of algebra and indices.

Number sequences

A number sequence is a set of numbers with a rule to find every number (term) in the sequence. This rule could be a simple addition or multiplication which takes you from one term to the next, but often it is more tricky than that. So you need to look most carefully at the pattern of a sequence.

Look at these sequences and their rules.

3, 6, 12, 24 … doubling the last term each time … 48, 96, …

2, 5, 8, 11, … adding 3 to the last term each time … 14, 17, …

1, 10, 100, 1000, … multiplying the last term by 10 each time … 10 000, 100 000

1, 8, 15, 22, … adding 7 to the last term each time … 29, 36, …

These are all quite straightforward once you have looked for the link from one term to the next (consecutive terms).

Differences

For some sequences we need to look at the differences between consecutive terms to determine the pattern.

Example Find the next two terms of the sequence 1, 3, 6, 10, 15, …

Looking at the differences between each pair of consecutive terms, we notice

```
1   3   6   10   15
  ↑   ↑   ↑    ↑
  2   3   4    5
```

So we can continue the sequence as follows:

1 3 6 10 15 21 28

↑ ↑ ↑ ↑ └ +6 ┘└ +7 ┘

2 3 4 5

The differences usually form a number sequence of their own, so you need to find out the sequence of the differences before you can expand the original sequence.

Generalising to find the rule

When using a number sequence, we sometimes need to know, say, its 50th term, or even a bigger number in the sequence. To do so, we need to find the generalised form of the rule which produces the sequence.

Let's first look at the problem backwards. That is, we'll take a rule and see how it produces a sequence.

Example 1 A sequence is formed by the rule $3n + 1$, where $n = 1, 2, 3, 4, 5, 6, \ldots$. Write down the sequence.

Substituting $n = 1, 2, 3, 4, \ldots$ in turn, we get

$(3 \times 1 + 1)$,	$(3 \times 2 + 1)$,	$(3 \times 3 + 1)$,	$(3 \times 4 + 1)$,	$(3 \times 5 + 1)$,	…
4	7	10	13	16	

So the sequence is 4, 7, 10, 13, 16, … .

Notice that the difference between each term and the next is always 3, which is the coefficient of n.

Example 2 The nth term of a sequence is $4n - 3$. Write down the sequence.

Taking n to be 1, 2, 3, 4, … in turn, we get

$(4 \times 1 - 3)$,	$(4 \times 2 - 3)$,	$(4 \times 3 - 3)$,	$(4 \times 4 - 3)$,	…
1	5	9	13	

So the sequence is 1, 5, 9, 13, … .

Notice again how the difference between each term and the next is the same as the coefficient of n.

Exercise 17A

1 Use each of the following rules to write down the first five terms of a sequence.

a $2n + 1$ for $n = 1, 2, 3, 4, \ldots$

b $3n - 2$ for $n = 1, 2, 3, 4, \ldots$

c $5n + 2$ for $n = 1, 2, 3, 4, \ldots$

d n^2 for $n = 1, 2, 3, 4, \ldots$

e $n^2 + 3$ for $n = 1, 2, 3, 4, \ldots$

2 Write down the first five terms of the sequence which has its nth term as

a $n + 3$ **b** $3n - 1$ **c** $5n - 2$ **d** $n^2 - 1$ **e** $4n + 5$

3 Write down the first six terms of the sequence of fractions $\frac{n-1}{n+1}$ for $n = 1, 2, 3, 4, \ldots$

4 A sequence is formed by the rule $\frac{1}{2} \times n \times (n + 1)$ for $n = 1, 2, 3, 4, \ldots$

a Write down the first six terms of this sequence.

b This is a well-known sequence with a name you have met before. What is it?

5 $n!$ is a mathematical shorthand for $n \times (n - 1) \times (n - 2) \times (n - 3) \times \ldots \times 2 \times 1$.

a Calculate $n!$ for $n = 4, 5$ and 6.

b Find the ! key on your calculator. What is the largest value of n that gives you an answer on the calculator?

Finding the *n*th term of a linear sequence

A linear sequence has the **same difference** between each term and the next.
For example,

2, 5, 8, 11, 14, … difference of 3
5, 7, 9, 11, 13, … difference of 2

The nth term of a linear sequence is **always** of the form $An + b$, where

- A, the coefficient of n, is the difference between each term and the next term (consecutive terms).
- b is the difference between the first term and A.

Example 1 Find the nth term of the sequence 5, 7, 9, 11, 13, …

The difference between consecutive terms is 2. So the first part of the nth term is $2n$.
Subtract the difference 2 from the first term 5, which gives $5 - 2 = 3$.
So the nth term is given by $2n + 3$.
(You can test it by substituting $n = 1, 2, 3, 4, \ldots$.)

Example 2 From the sequence 5, 12, 19, 26, 33, … find

a the nth term **b** the 50th term **c** the first term that is greater than 1000

a The difference between consecutive terms is 7. So the first part of the nth term is $7n$.
Subtract the difference 7 from the first term 5, which gives $5 - 7 = -2$.
So the nth term is given by $7n - 2$.

b The 50th term is found by substituting $n = 50$ into the rule, $7n - 2$. So

$$\begin{aligned}\text{50th term} &= 7 \times 50 - 2 = 350 - 2 \\ &= 348\end{aligned}$$

c The first term that is greater than 1000 is given by

$$7n - 2 > 1000$$
$$\Rightarrow 7n > 1000 + 2$$
$$\Rightarrow n > \frac{1002}{7}$$
$$n > 143.14$$

So the first term (which has to be a whole number) over 1000 is the 144th.

Exercise 17B

1 Find the *n*th term in each of these linear sequences.

a 3, 5, 7, 9, 11, … **b** 5, 9, 13, 17, 21, … **c** 8, 13, 18, 23, 28, …
d 2, 8, 14, 20, 26, … **e** 5, 8, 11, 14, 17, … **f** 2, 9, 16, 23, 30, …
g 1, 5, 9, 13, 17, … **h** 3, 7, 11, 15, 19, … **i** 2, 5, 8, 11, 14, …
j 2, 12, 22, 32, … **k** 8, 12, 16, 20, … **l** 4, 9, 14, 19, 24, …

2 Find the 50th term in each of these linear sequences.

a 4, 7, 10, 13, 16, … **b** 7, 9, 11, 13, 15, … **c** 3, 8, 13, 18, 23, …
d 1, 5, 9, 13, 17, … **e** 2, 10, 18, 26, … **f** 5, 6, 7, 8, 9, …
g 6, 11, 16, 21, 26, … **h** 3, 11, 19, 27, 35, … **i** 1, 4, 7, 10, 13, …
j 21, 24, 27, 30, 33, … **k** 12, 19, 26, 33, 40, … **l** 1, 9, 17, 25, 33, …

3 **a** Which term of the sequence 5, 8, 11, 14, 17, … is the first one to be greater than 100?
b Which term of the sequence 1, 8, 15, 22, 29, … is the first one to be greater than 200?
c Which term of the sequence 4, 9, 14, 19, 24, … is the closest to 500?

4 For each sequence **a** to **j**, find

i the *n*th term **ii** the 100th term **iii** the term closest to 100

a 5, 9, 13, 17, 21, … **b** 3, 5, 7, 9, 11, 13, … **c** 4, 7, 10, 13, 16, …
d 8, 10, 12, 14, 16, … **e** 9, 13, 17, 21, … **f** 6, 11, 16, 21, …
g 0, 3, 6, 9, 12, … **h** 2, 8, 14, 20, 26, … **i** 7, 15, 23, 31, …
j 25, 27, 29, 31, …

5 A sequence of fractions is $\frac{3}{4}, \frac{5}{7}, \frac{7}{10}, \frac{9}{13}, \frac{11}{16}, \ldots$

a Find the *n*th term in the sequence.
b By changing each fraction to a decimal, can you see any pattern at all?
c What, as a decimal, will be the value of the
 i 100th term **ii** 1000th term?
d Use your answers to part **c** to predict what the 10 000th term and the millionth term are. (Check these out on your calculator.)

6 Repeat the above set of questions for $\frac{3}{6}, \frac{7}{11}, \frac{11}{16}, \frac{15}{21}, \frac{19}{26}, \ldots$

General rules from given patterns

Many problem-solving situations that you are likely to meet involve number sequences. So you do need to be able to formulate general rules from given number patterns.

Exercise 17C

1 A pattern of squares is built up from matchsticks as shown.

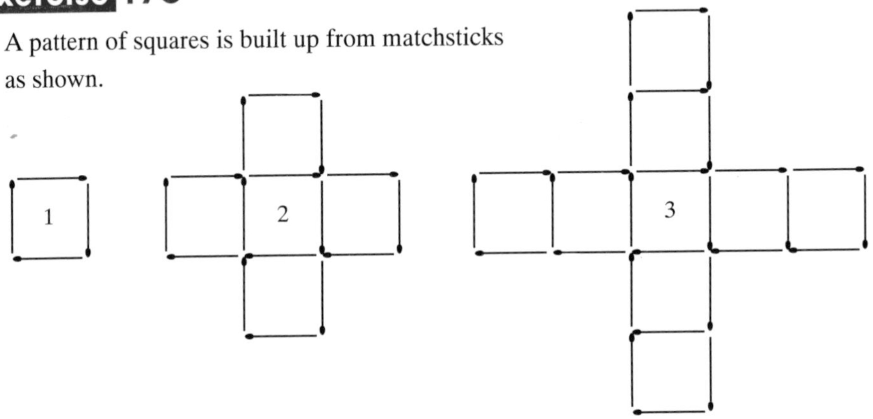

a Draw the 4th diagram.

b How many squares are in the nth diagram?

c How many squares are in the 25th diagram?

d With 200 squares, which is the biggest diagram that could be made?

2 A pattern of triangles is built up from matchsticks.

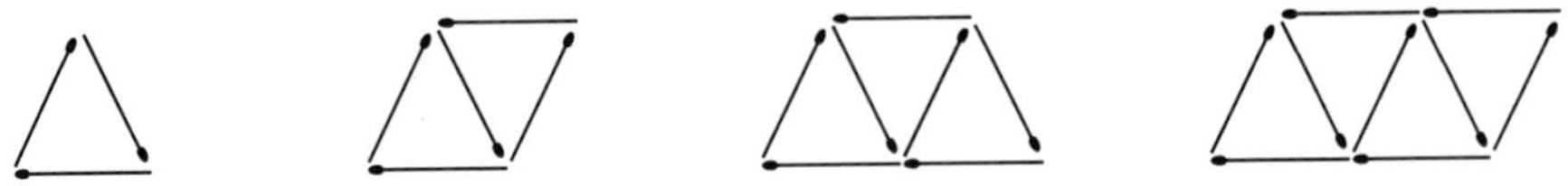

1 2 3 4

a Draw the 5th set of triangles in this pattern.

b How many matchsticks are needed for the nth set of triangles?

c How many matchsticks are needed to make the 60th set of triangles?

d If there are only 100 matchsticks, which is the largest set of triangles that could be made?

3 A conference centre had tables each of which could sit 6 people. When put together, the tables could seat people as shown.

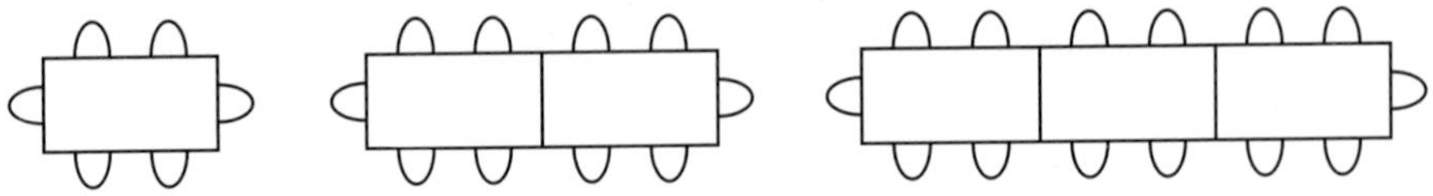

1 2 3

a How many people could be seated at 4 tables?

b How many people could be seated at n tables put together in this way?

c A conference had 50 people who wished to use the tables in this way. How many tables would they need?

4 A pattern of squares is put together as shown.

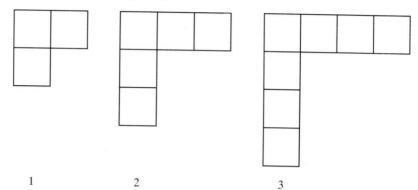

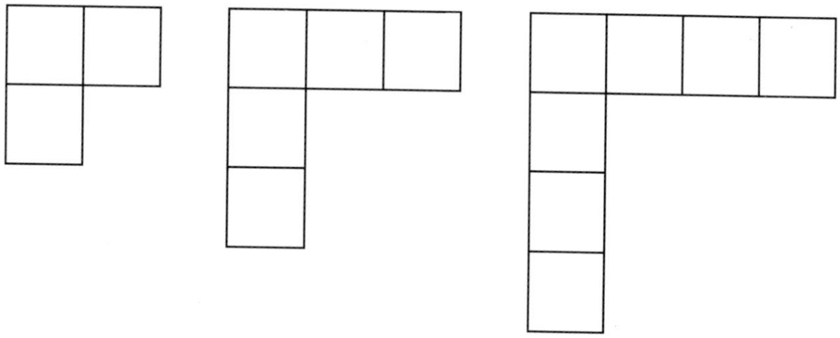

1 2 3

a Draw the 4th diagram.

b How many squares are in the nth diagram?

c How many squares are in the 50th diagram?

d With 300 squares, what is the biggest diagram that could be made?

5 Prepacked fencing units come in the shape shown on the right, made of 4 pieces of wood. When you put them together in stages to make a fence, you also need joining pieces, so the fence will start to build up as shown below.

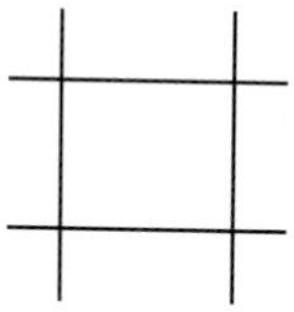

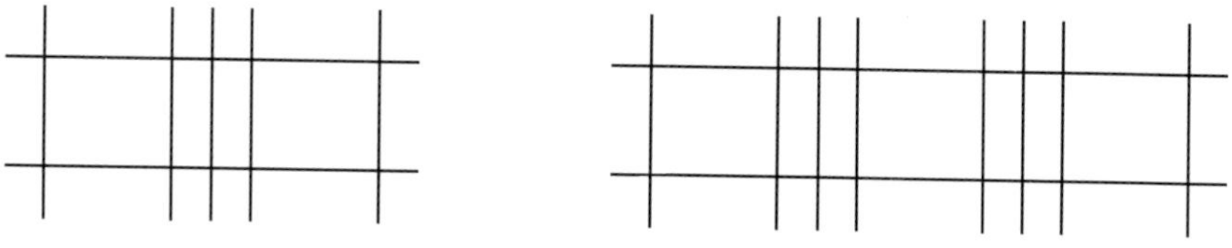

2 3

a How many pieces of wood would you have in a fence made up in

i 5 stages **ii** n stages **iii** 45 stages?

b I made a fence out of 124 pieces of wood. How many stages did I use?

6 Lamp-posts are put at the end of every 100 m stretch of a motorway, as shown,

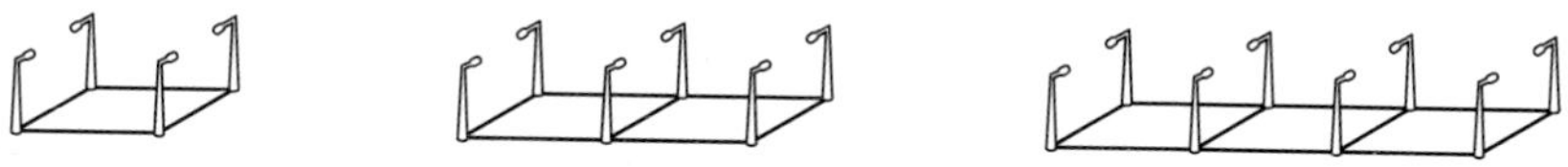

1 2 3

a How many lamp-posts are needed for

i 900 m of this motorway **ii** 8 km of this motorway?

b The M99 is a motorway being built. The contractor has ordered 1598 lamp-posts. How long is this motorway?

7 Regular pentagons of side length 1 cm are joined together to make a pattern as shown.

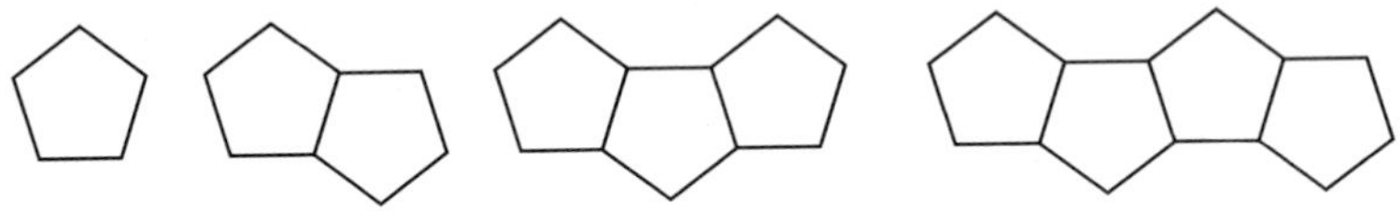

1 2 3 4

Copy this pattern and write down the perimeter of each shape.

a What is the perimeter of patterns like this made from

i 6 pentagons **ii** *n* pentagons **iii** 50 pentagons?

b What is the largest number of pentagons that can be put together like this to have a perimeter less than 1000 cm?

8 A school dining hall had tables in the shape of a trapezium. Each table could seat 5 people, as shown on the right. When the tables were joined together as shown below, each table couldn't seat as many people.

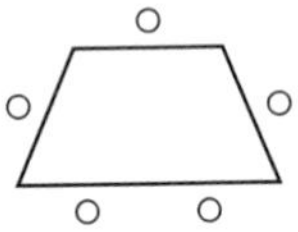

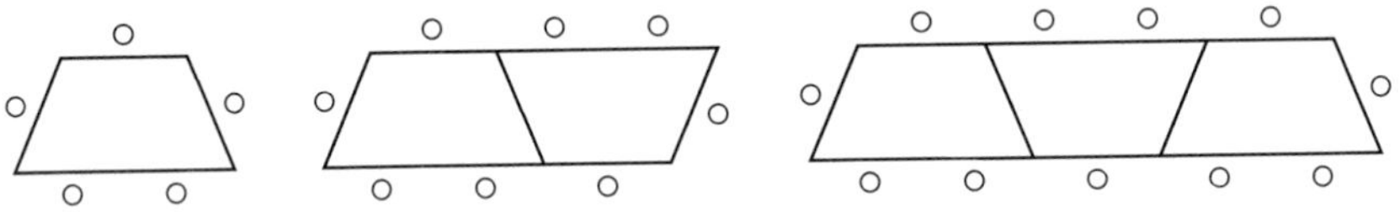

1 2 3

a In this arrangement, how many could be seated if they used

i 4 tables **ii** *n* tables **iii** 13 tables?

b For an outside charity event, up to 200 people had to be seated. How many tables like this did they need?

9 A window can be split into small panes, as shown.

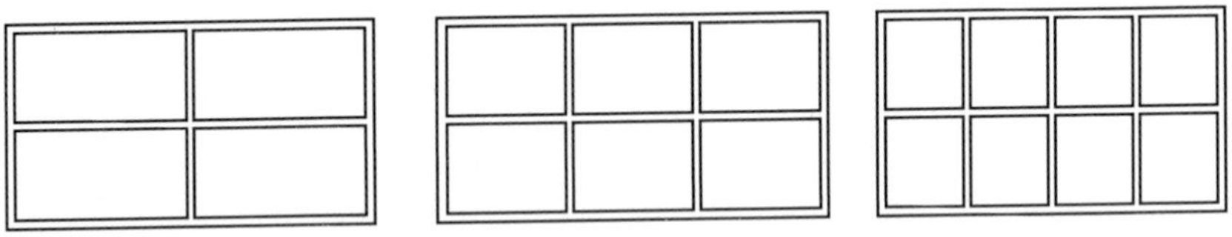

1 strut 2 struts 3 struts

a How many panes are there in a window with the following number of struts?

i 4 struts **ii** *n* struts **iii** 9 struts

b A window like this was made with 30 panes. How many struts did it have?

10 When setting out tins to make a display of a certain height, you need to know how many tins to start with at the bottom.

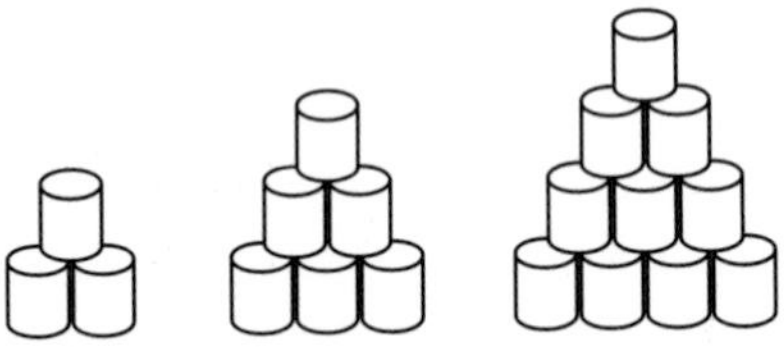

a How many tins are needed on the bottom if you wish the display to be

i 5 tins high **ii** *n* tins high **iii** 18 tins high?

b I saw a shop assistant starting to build a display, and noticed he was starting with 20 tins on the bottom. How high was the display when it was finished?

Quadratic rules

Some problem-solving situations involve number sequences which are governed by a quadratic rule. You met some of these patterns in Exercise 17A, where we have, for example, n^2, $n^2 + 3$ and $n^2 - 1$.

You can always identify a pattern as being quadratic from its **second differences**, which are **constant**. (A second difference is the result of subtracting one difference between consecutive terms from the next difference.)

The simpler rules

These sequences will nearly always be based on n^2 alone. So you do need to recognise the pattern 1, 4, 9, 16, 25, … .

The differences between consecutive terms of this pattern are the odd numbers 3, 5, 7, 9, … . So if you find that the differences form an odd-number sequence, you know the pattern is based on n^2.

Follow through the next two examples to see how sequences can be spotted when they are based on n^2.

Example 1 Find the nth term in the sequence 2, 5, 10, 17, 26, … .

The differences are the odd numbers 3, 5, 7, 9, … so we know the rule is based on n^2.

Next, we look for a link with the square numbers. We do this by subtracting from each term the corresponding square number:

2	5	10	17	26
−1	−4	−9	−16	−25
1	1	1	1	1

Clearly, the link is +1, so the nth term is $n^2 + 1$.

(You should always quickly check the generalisation by substituting $n = 1, 2, 3, 4$ to see whether it does work.)

Example 2 Find the nth term in the sequence 1, 6, 13, 22, 33, ….

The differences are 5, 7, 9, 11, … so we know the pattern is based on n^2.

Next, we have to find the link. We notice that the first difference is 5 not 3, which means that the series of square numbers we use starts at 4, not at 1.

It follows that to obtain 4, 9, 16, 25, … from the original sequence simply add 3 to each term of that sequence.

So to get from the square numbers to the sequence 1, 6, 13, 22, 33, … we have to use $(n + 1)^2$, since the sequence is based on 4, 9, 16, ….

The final step in finding the rule is to take away the 3, which gives the nth term as $(n + 1)^2 - 3$.

More complicated rules

Example Find the nth term in the sequence 2, 6, 12, 20, 30, …

An examination of the differences tells us that the sequence is not linear, and is not based on n^2 alone. So we look at the second differences and find that they all are the same. The sequence is therefore quadratic, its nth term being given by an expression of the form

$$an^2 + bn + c$$

where a, b and c are constants.

Next, we take the first three terms of the sequence to obtain three equations in a, b and c which we can solve simultaneously:

First term	$n = 1$	$a + b + c = 2$	(1)
Second term	$n = 2$	$4a + 2b + c = 6$	(2)
Third term	$n = 3$	$9a + 3b + c = 12$	(3)

Subtract (1) from (2) to obtain $3a + b = 4$ (4)

Subtract (2) from (3) to obtain $5a + b = 6$ (5)

Solve for a by subtracting (4) from (5), which gives

$$2a = 2 \quad \Rightarrow \quad a = 1$$

Substitute $a = 1$ into (4) to obtain $b = 1$. Then substitute $a = 1$ and $b = 1$ into (1) to obtain $c = 0$.

Putting these values into $an^2 + bn + c$ gives the nth term as $n^2 + n$, which factorises into $n(n + 1)$.

This method will enable you to generalise **any** quadratic sequence. But always do look first for simple relationships before plunging into this method. Many of the sequences you will meet can easily be generalised by other procedures.

Exercise 17D

1 For each of the sequences **a** to **e**

i write down the next two terms **ii** find the nth term.

a 0, 3, 8, 15, 24, … **b** 3, 6, 11, 18, 27, … **c** 4, 7, 12, 19, 28, …

d –1, 2, 7, 14, 23, … **e** 11, 14, 19, 26, …

2 For each of the sequences **a** to **e**

i write down the next two terms **ii** find the nth term.

a 5, 10, 17, 26, … **b** 3, 8, 15, 24, … **c** 9, 14, 21, 30, …

d 10, 17, 26, 37, … **e** 8, 15, 24, 35, …

3 Look at each of the following sequences to see whether the rule is linear, quadratic on n^2 alone or fully quadratic Then

i write down the nth term **ii** write down the 50th term.

a 5, 8, 13, 20, 29, … **b** 5, 8, 11, 14, 17, … **c** 3, 8, 15, 24, 35, …

d 5, 12, 21, 32, 45, … **e** 3, 6, 11, 18, 27, … **f** 1, 6, 11, 16, 21, …

Possible coursework tasks

Fibonacci sequences

The Fibonacci sequence is 1, 1, 2, 3, 5, 8, … . Can you see the pattern?

Make up some other Fibonacci sequences starting with a different pair of numbers each time.

For Fibonacci sequences investigate the following:

a The ratio of successive terms.

b Take any three consecutive Fibonacci numbers, multiply the outside numbers and square the middle number.

c Take any four consecutive Fibonacci numbers, compare the product of the outside numbers with the product of the inside numbers.

d Invent different Fibonacci sequences of your own: for example, start with 1, 1, 1 and the next term is the sum of the previous three.

The above problems can be done on a computer spreadsheet. You may be able to find other patterns which perhaps haven't yet been discovered!

Squared numbers summed

$$1^2 + 2^2 = 5$$

$$1^2 + 2^2 + 3^2 = 14$$

Investigate $1^2 + 2^2 + 3^2 + \ldots + n^2 = ?$

A journey to infinity

Use your calculator or a computer spreadsheet to investigate these 'infinite' sequences.

a $1 + \frac{1}{2} + \frac{1}{4} + \frac{1}{8} + \ldots$

b $\frac{1}{3} + \frac{1}{9} + \frac{1}{27} + \frac{1}{81} + \ldots$

c $\frac{1}{2} - \frac{1}{4} + \frac{1}{8} - \frac{1}{16} + \ldots$

d $\frac{1}{3} - \frac{1}{9} + \frac{1}{27} - \frac{1}{81} + \ldots$

Wallis sequence

Evaluate each line and investigate what happens when you continue the sequence.

$2 \times \frac{2}{1} \times \frac{2}{3} =$

$2 \times \frac{2}{1} \times \frac{2}{3} \times \frac{4}{3} =$

$2 \times \frac{2}{1} \times \frac{2}{3} \times \frac{4}{3} \times \frac{4}{5} =$

$2 \times \frac{2}{1} \times \frac{2}{3} \times \frac{4}{3} \times \frac{4}{5} \times \frac{6}{5} =$

Round and round

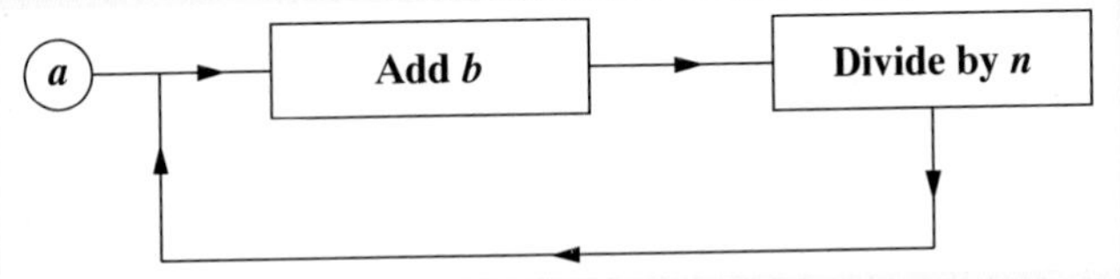

Investigate.

Bouncing ball

A rubber ball is dropped from a height of 4 m. After each bounce, it rises to three quarters of the height it reached on its previous bounce.

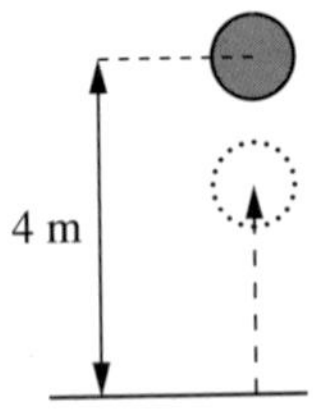

Investigate the total distance the ball travels before it comes to rest.

Induction

Can you prove the following?

a $5^n + 3$ is always a multiple of 4.

b $2^n + 2^{n+1}$ is always a multiple of 6.

c $6^n + 4$ is always a multiple of 10.

d $3^n + 3^{n+1} + 3^{n+2}$ is always a multiple of 13.

Some relativity

Einstein's theory of relativity states that the mass, m, of an object as measured by an observer depends on the speed of the object, and is given by

$$m = \frac{m_0}{\sqrt{1 - \frac{v^2}{c^2}}}$$

where m_0 is the mass of the object at rest
v is its speed relative to the observer
c is the speed of light (300 000 km/s)

Investigate the mass of the object as its speed increases relative to the observer.

Examination questions: coursework type

Rene has made designs with matchsticks.

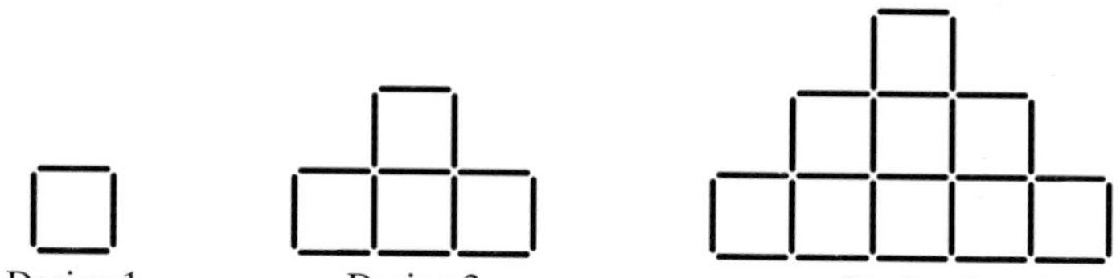

Rene has made a table of results.

Design number	1	2	3
Number of squares	1	4	9

a Without drawing, write down **two** ways of calculating the number of squares in design 10.

b Describe **two** ways of calculating the number of squares in any such design.

c Look again at the designs Rene has made with matchsticks. Suggest a different investigation that could be carried out using Rene's designs.

d Carry out the investigation you have suggested in part **c**.

WJEC, Question 2, Specimen Paper HP3, 1998

Examination questions

1 **a** A number pattern begins 1, 1, 2, 3, 5, 8, …

i What is the next number in this pattern?

ii The number pattern is continued. Explain how you would find the eighth number in the pattern.

b Another number pattern begins 1, 4, 7, 10, 13, … . Write down, in terms of n, the nth term in this pattern. *SEG, Question 1, Specimen Paper 13, 1998*

2 **a** A sequence is given by $\frac{1}{2}, \frac{2}{3}, \frac{3}{4}, \frac{4}{5}, \ldots$. Write down
i the 11th term of this sequence **ii** the nth term of this sequence.
b Each term of a second sequence is the reciprocal of the corresponding term of the sequence given in part **a**. Write down the first four terms of the second sequence.
NEAB, Question 3, Paper 1R, November 1995

3 **a** Write down the next two numbers in the number pattern 3, 7, 11, 15, 19, … .
b Write down in words what you think the rule is for finding the next number in the pattern from the one before it.
c Write down what you think the rule is for finding the nth number in the pattern.
WJEC, Question 6, Specimen Paper 1, 1998

4 Sheep enclosures are built using fences and posts.

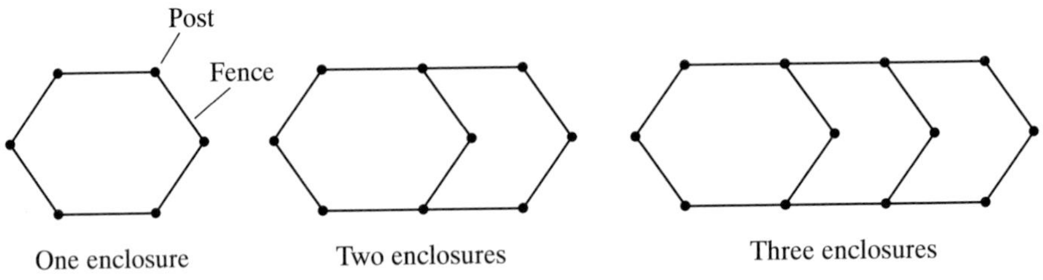

a **i** Sketch four enclosures in a row.
ii Sketch five enclosures in a row.
b Copy and complete the table below.

Number of enclosures	1	2	3	4	5	6	7	8
Number of posts	6	9	12					

c Work out the number of posts needed for 20 enclosures in a row.
d Write down an expression to find the number of posts needed for n enclosures in a row. *ULEAC, Question 10, Paper 4, June 1994*

5 There is a relationship between the terms in rows A, B and C.

Row A	1	2	3	4	5
Row B	1	4	9	16	25
Row C	2	6	12	20	30

a What is the formula for the nth term in row B?
b What is the formula for the nth term in row C?
NEAB, Question 20, Specimen Paper 2, 1998

6 Look at the three sequences below.

Sequence p 4, 6, 8, 10, …
Sequence q 3, 8, 15, 24, 35, …
Sequence r 5, 10, 17, …

a The sequence r is obtained from sequences p and q as follows.

$\sqrt{(4^2 + 3^2)} = 5$ $\sqrt{(6^2 + 8^2)} = 10$ $\sqrt{(8^2 + 15^2)} = 17$ etc

i Use the numbers 10 and 24 to calculate the fourth term of sequence r.
ii Calculate the fifth term of sequence r.
b i Find the tenth term of sequence p.
ii Find the sixth term of sequence q.
c i Write down the nth term of sequence p.
ii The nth term of sequence q is $n^2 + kn$, where k represents a number. Find the value of k.

NEAB, Question 11, Paper 2I, June 1996

7 The picture shows a pattern of cards.

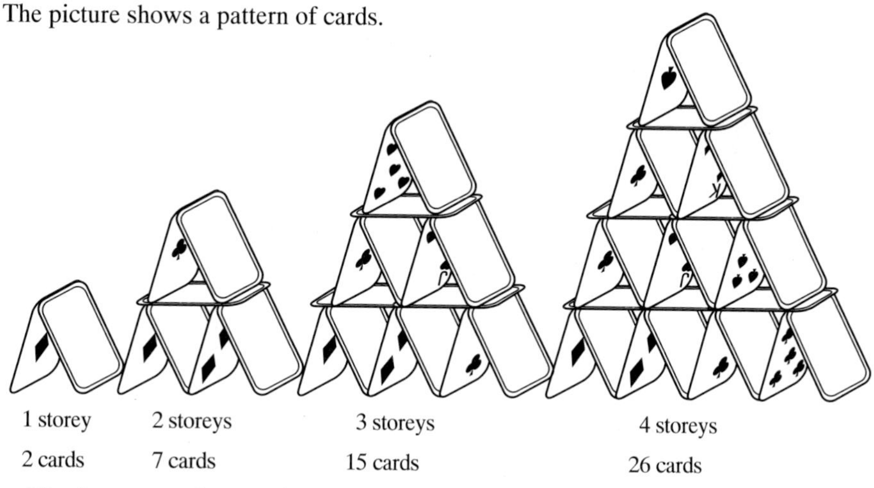

a The four-storey house of cards is to be made into a five-storey house of cards. How many more cards are needed?
b Look at the sequence 2, 7, 15, 26 …
i Calculate the sixth term in this sequence.
ii Explain how you found your answer.
c The number of cards, C, needed to make a house of cards with S storeys, is given by the formula

$$C = aS^2 + bS$$

where a and b represent numbers.
i Use some of the information given at the beginning of the question to show that

$$2 = a + b \quad \text{and} \quad 7 = 4a + 2b$$

ii Solve these two equations simultaneously to find the numbers a and b.

NEAB, Question 12, Paper 2, June 1995

Summary

How well do you grade yourself?

To gain a grade **C**, you need to be able to find the rules of a quadratic pattern and the nth term in a quadratic sequence. You need also to be able to explain how you found the rule of a sequence.

To gain a grade **B**, you need to be able to find the nth term of any given sequence. You need also to be able easily to recognise which sequences are based on n^2 alone and which are more complicated to find, but be able to do so.

What you should know after you have worked through Chapter 17

- Be able to recognise a number pattern and explain how the pattern is made.
- Be able to recognise a linear sequence and find its nth term.
- Be able to recognise when a sequence is not linear and therefore look for a quadratic rule.
- Be able to recognise when a sequence is based on n^2 alone.
- Start to look for the more complicated quadratic rules and be able to find them.

Coursework example 2

Refer to the Appendix for a summary of coursework marks.

Threes and ones problem

Problem statement

The integer 5 can be formed by summing 3 and 1 in **four different ways**:

$$\begin{aligned}5 &= 1 + 1 + 1 + 1 + 1\\ &= 3 + 1 + 1\\ &= 1 + 3 + 1\\ &= 1 + 1 + 3\end{aligned}$$

Investigate how many different ways positive integers can be formed by summing 3 and 1.

Possible solution

To start the investigation, I am going to find how many different ways there are for the first seven integers and then put my results into a table to see whether there is a pattern.

1 $1 = 1$

2 $2 = 1 + 1$

3 $3 = 1 + 1 + 1$
$= 3$

4 $4 = 1 + 1 + 1 + 1$
$= 3 + 1$
$= 1 + 3$

5 $5 = 1 + 1 + 1 + 1 + 1$
$= 3 + 1 + 1$
$= 1 + 3 + 1$
$= 1 + 1 + 3$

6 $6 = 1 + 1 + 1 + 1 + 1 + 1$
$= 3 + 1 + 1 + 1$
$= 1 + 3 + 1 + 1$
$= 1 + 1 + 3 + 1$
$= 1 + 1 + 1 + 3$
$= 3 + 3$

7 $7 = 1 + 1 + 1 + 1 + 1 + 1 + 1$
$= 3 + 1 + 1 + 1 + 1$
$= 1 + 3 + 1 + 1 + 1$
$= 1 + 1 + 3 + 1 + 1$
$= 1 + 1 + 1 + 3 + 1$
$= 1 + 1 + 1 + 1 + 3$
$= 3 + 3 + 1$
$= 3 + 1 + 3$
$= 1 + 3 + 3$

Notes

A	B	C	
4			Task broken down into small stages.

Integer (n)	1	2	3	4	5	6	7
No. of ways (x)	1	1	2	3	4	6	9

A | B | C

At first the pattern looks quite complicated, but I do spot that, for example, 9 = 6 + 3 and 6 = 4 + 2.

So the rule might be:

> To find the number of ways for any integer n, add the number of ways for the previous integer to the number of ways for the third previous integer.

My prediction for 8 is, therefore, 9 + 4 = 13.

Before I test my prediction, I've also noticed that I may not have to list all the ways (which would soon become very tedious), because some of them are just rearrangements of 3s and 1s in the same group.

The table below shows the different groups with their number of rearrangements for the integer 8.

B: 4 — Information given in a variety of forms.

Number of rearrangements for 8					
Group	Example	No. of 3s	No. of 1s	No. in group	No. of ways
1	1+1+1+1+1+1+1 + 1	0	8	8	1
2	3+1+1+1+1+1	1	5	6	6
3	3+3+1+1	2	2	4	6
				Total	13

So, the total is 13 and my rule has worked.

C: 4 — Generalisation tested.

I am now going to find a formula for this rule.

If I let x_n be the total number of rearrangements of 3s and 1s for any integer n, then I have found that for the integer 8

A: 5 — Poses own question.

$$x_8 = x_7 + x_5$$
$$= 9 + 4 = 13$$

B: 5 — Introduces own notation to improve presentation.

So my formula is

$$x_n = x_{n-1} + x_{n-3}$$

for any integer n.

But the formula cannot work for $n \leq 3$, because I can see no meaning for x_0 or x_{-1}. Therefore, I need to know x_1, x_2 and x_3.

C: 5 — Generalisation justified by formula.

I first need to see if there is a quicker way to find the number of rearrangements for each group, because it will soon become very cumbersome to work them out in full.

A	B	C	

I found from an A-level textbook that the number of rearrangements of the members of a group is called the 'permutations' of the group. I also found that I could obtain the permutations of a group by using the ${}_nC_r$ key on my calculator. For example, the number of permutations (or 'perms') of the group AAAABBB is

A 6 — Starts to develop a new line of enquiry.

$${}_7C_3 = 35$$

C 6 — Makes further progress.

where $n = 7$ is the total number of letters in the group and $r = 3$ is the number of Bs in the group.

I note that using the number of As instead of the number of Bs gives ${}_7C_4$, which also equals 35.

B 6 — Consistent use of notation.

What about the number of perms for the group AAAAAAA?

I know there is only one perm for this group. This should mean that ${}_7C_0$ or ${}_7C_7 = 1$. I check them on my calculator and both give the answer 1.

I can use ${}_nC_r$ for my 3s and 1s examples, where n is the total number of 3s and 1s in the group and r is the number of 1s in the group. For example, the number of perms of 3 + 3 + 3 + 1 + 1 is given by

A 7 — Introduces other features into the problem.

$${}_5C_2 = 10$$

and the number of perms of 3 + 3 + 1 + 1 + 1 + 1 + 1 + 1 is given by

B 7 — Accurate use of notation.

$${}_8C_6 = 28$$

I am going to use this method to obtain the number of perms of 3s and 1s for the integer 9.

From my formula

C 7 — Justifies solution.

$$x_9 = x_8 + x_6 = 13 + 6 = 19$$

Using perms gives

Number of rearrangements for 9					
Group	Example	No. of 3s	No. of 1s	No. in group	No. of perms
1	1+1+1+1+1+1+1+1+1	0	9	9	${}_9C_9 = 1$
2	3+1+1+1+1+1+1	1	6	7	${}_7C_6 = 7$
3	3+3+1+1+1	2	3	5	${}_5C_3 = 10$
4	3+3+3	3	0	3	${}_3C_0 = 1$
				Total	19

I will now work out x_{10} using permutations:

A 8 — Explores a new area of mathematics.

$$x_{10} = {}_{10}C_{10} + {}_8C_7 + {}_6C_4 + {}_4C_1$$

$$= 1 + 8 + 15 + 4 = 28$$

For each consecutive value of ${}_nC_r$, the value of n decreases by 2 and the value of r decreases by 3 for $r \geq 0$.

From my formula

$$x_{10} = x_9 + x_7 = 19 + 9 = 28$$

so it works. This means I can now work out x_n without having to know any previous values.

Example Find the number of ways 15 can be summed using 3s and 1s.

$$x_{15} = {}_{15}C_{15} + {}_{13}C_{12} + {}_{11}C_9 + {}_9C_6 + {}_7C_3 + {}_5C_0$$
$$= 1 + 13 + 55 + 84 + 35 + 1 = 189$$

Final formula

The number of ways n can be summed using 3s and 1s is given by

$$x_n = {}_nC_n + {}_{n-2}C_{n-3} + {}_{n-4}C_{n-6} + {}_{n-6}C_{n-9} + \ldots$$

which is continued while $r \geq 0$ in the value of ${}_nC_r$.

A	B	C	
	8		Efficient and concise use of symbols.
		8	A rigorous justification.

Final marks
(i) 8 (ii) 8 (iii) 8

18 Dimensional analysis

This chapter is going to … tell you how to decide whether a formula represents length, area or volume.

What you should already know

- The formulae for the areas and volumes of common shapes.

Length

When we have an unknown length or distance in a problem, we represent it by a single letter, followed by the unit in which it is measured. For example,

t centimetres x miles y kilometres

Example Find the perimeters of these shapes.

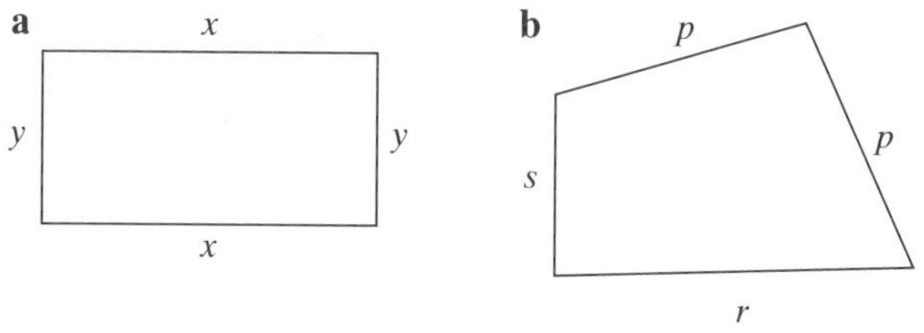

Shape **a** is a rectangle. Its perimeter is

$$P = x + y + x + y = 2x + 2y$$

Shape **b** is irregular. Its perimeter is

$$P = p + p + r + s = 2p + r + s$$

In the example, each letter is a length and has the **dimension** or measure of length, i.e. centimetre, metre, kilometre, etc. The numbers (coefficients) written before the letters are **not** lengths and therefore have **no** dimensions. So, for example, $2x$, $2y$ or $2p$ has the **same** dimension as x, y or p respectively.

When just one length is involved in a calculation or formula, the calculation or formula is said to have **one dimension** or **1D**, which is represented by the symbol **[L]**.

Exercise 18A

Find an expression for the perimeter of each of these shapes.

1

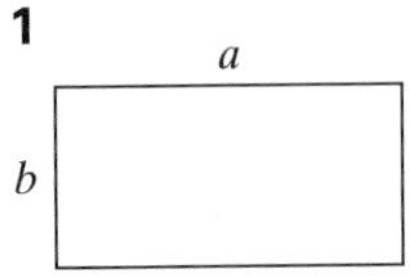

2

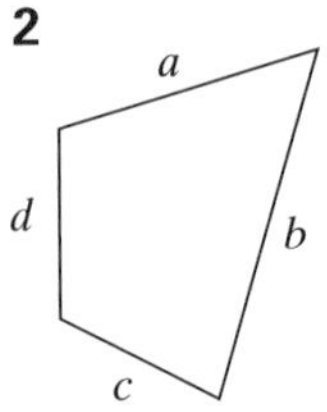

3

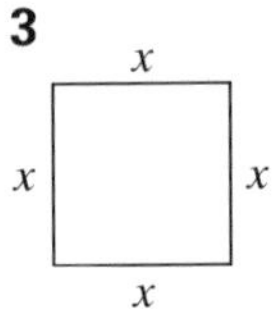

4

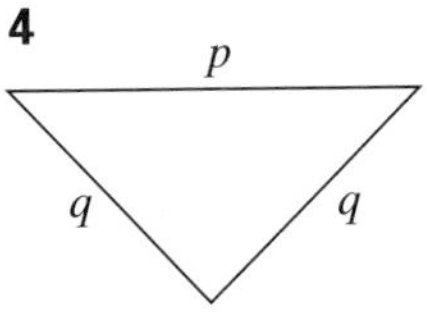

5

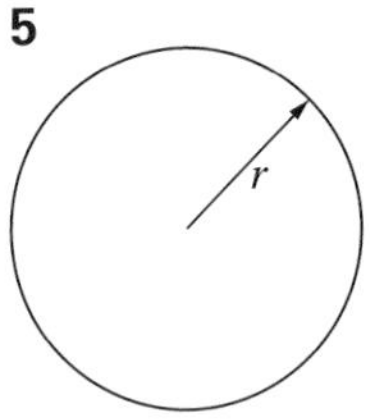

6

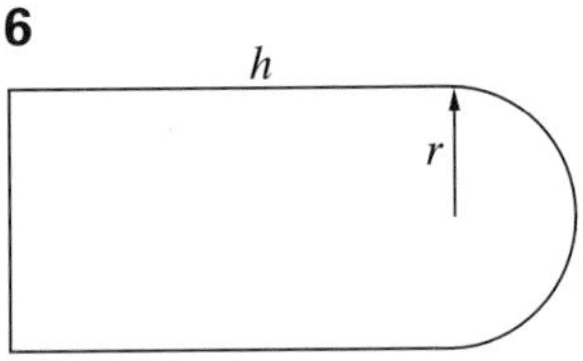

Area

Look at these four examples of formulae for calculating area.

$A = lb$ gives the area of a rectangle
$A = x^2$ gives the area of a square
$A = 2ab + 2ac + 2bc$ gives the surface area of a cuboid
$A = \pi r^2$ gives the area of a circle

These formulae have one thing in common. They all consist of terms that are the product of two lengths. We recognise this by counting the number of letters in each term of the formula. The first formula has two (l and b). The second has two (x and x). The third has three terms, each of two letters (a and b, a and c, b and c). The fourth also has only two letters (r and r) because π is a number (3.14159…) which has no dimension.

Hence, we can recognise formulae for area because they only have terms that consist of two letters. That is, two lengths multiplied together. They therefore have **two dimensions** or **2D**, represented by the symbol **[L × L]** or **[L^2]**. Here, again, numbers not defined as lengths have no dimensions.

This confirms the units in which area is usually measured. For example,

square metres (m × m or m^2) square inches (in × in or in^2)
square centimetres (cm × cm or cm^2)

Exercise 18B

1 Find a formula for each of these areas.

a

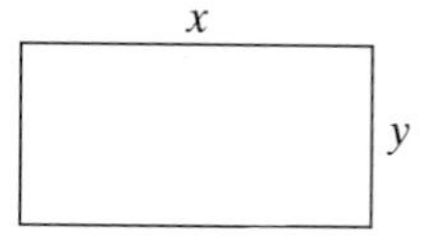

b

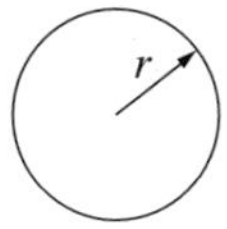

c

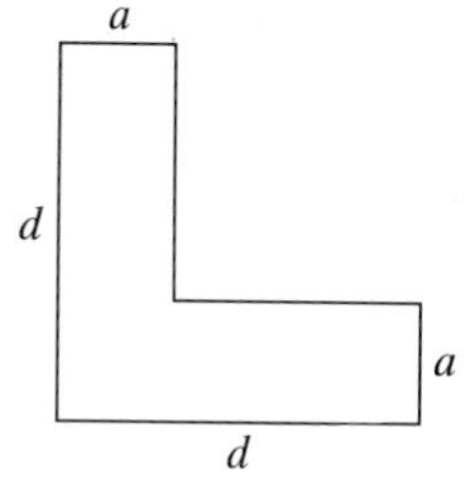

d

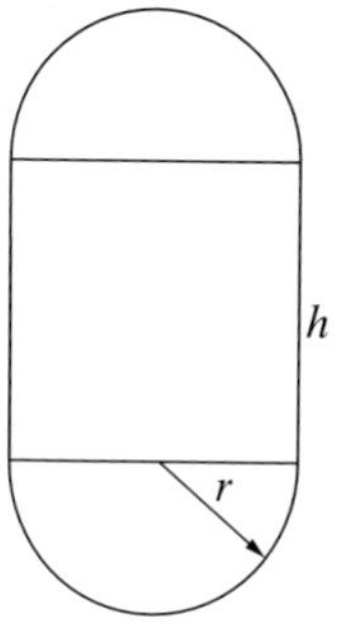

2 Find an expression for the area of each of these shapes.

a

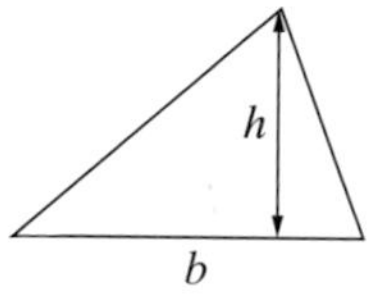

b

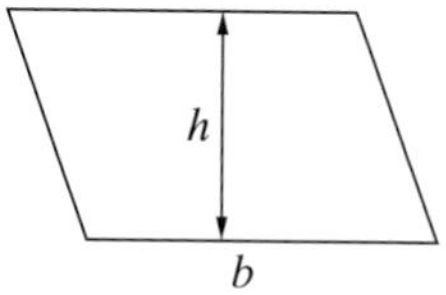

c

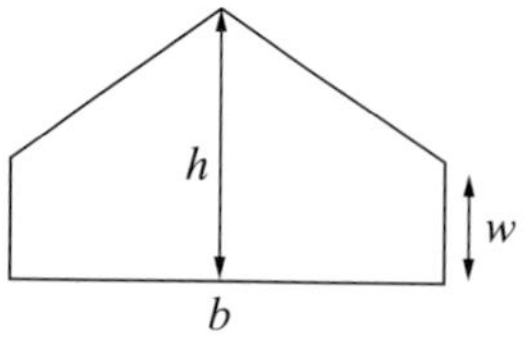

d

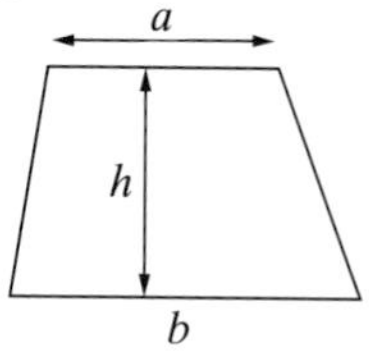

e

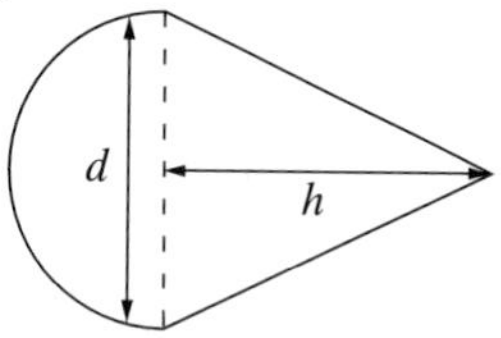

f

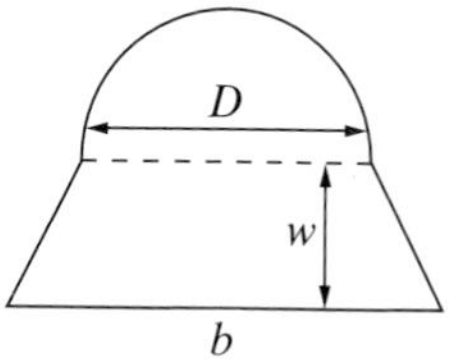

Volume

Look at these three examples of formulae for calculating volume.

$V = lbh$ gives the volume of a cuboid

$V = x^3$ gives the volume of a cube

$V = \pi r^2 h + \frac{4}{3}\pi r^3$ gives the volume of a cylinder with hemispherical ends

Again, these formulae have one thing in common. They all consist of terms that are the product of three lengths. We recognise this by counting the number of letters in each term of the formula. The first formula has three (l, b and h). The second has three (x, x and x). The third has two terms, each of three letters (r, r and h; r, r and r). Remember, π has no dimension.

Hence, we can recognise formulae for volume because they only have terms that consist of three letters. That is, three lengths multiplied together. They therefore have

three dimensions or **3D**, represented by the symbol **[L × L × L]** or **[L^3]**. Once more, numbers not defined as lengths have no dimensions.

This confirms the units in which volume is usually measured. For example,

cubic metres (m × m × m or m^3)   cubic inches (in × in × in or in^3)
cubic centimetres (cm × cm × cm or cm^3)

Exercise 18C

Find a formula for each of these volumes.

1

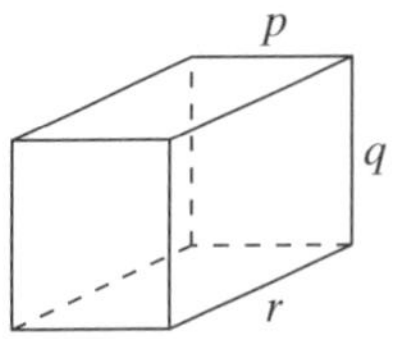

2

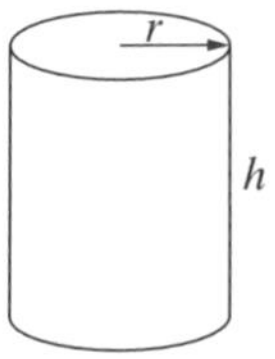

3

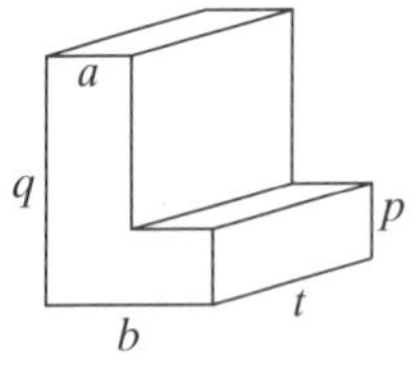

4

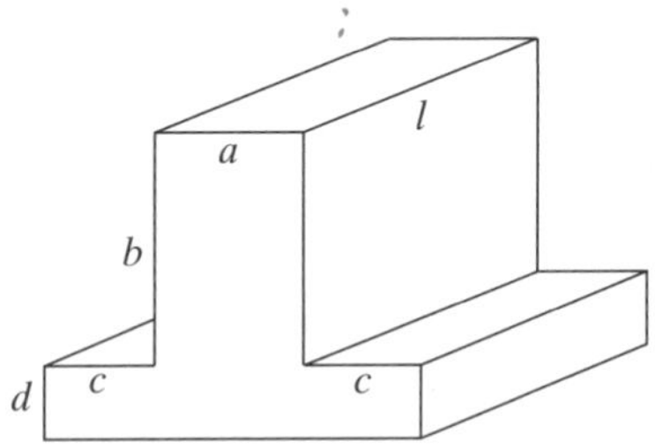

5

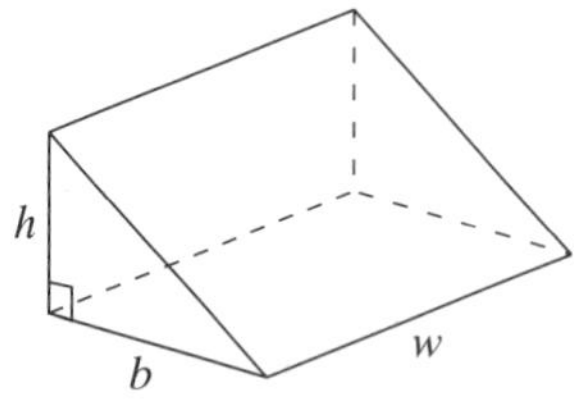

6

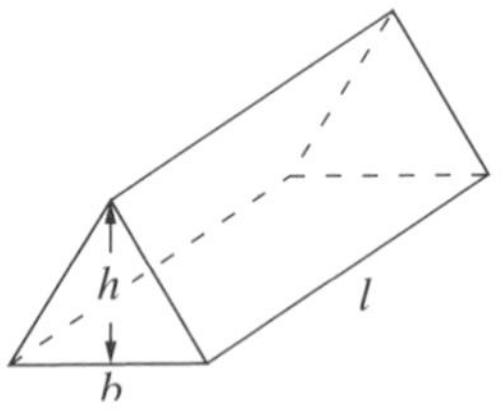

Exercise 18D

1 Indicate by L, A, V or [L], [L^2], [L^3] whether the following quantities are lengths, areas or volumes, or none of these (N).

a 1 mile
b 5 cm^3
c $3x$ centimetres
d 65 cm^2
e 4π cm
f 10 km
g 4π cm^3
h 3 m^3
i 6 mph
j Diameter of a circle
k Mass of the moon
l Region inside a square
m Space inside a football
n Surface of a cone

o Amount of air in a room
p Amount of pop in a can
q Value of an antique painting
r 18 inches
s 3 acres
t 7 litres
u Rise and fall of the tide
v Wattage of a light bulb
w Noise made by a radio
x Bearing of a ship from a harbour
y Altitude of an aircraft
z 8 tonnes

2 Each of these represents a length, an area or a volume. Indicate by writing L, A or V which it is.

a x^2
b $2y$
c πa
d πab
e xyz
f $3x^3$
g x^2y
h $2xy$
i $4y$
j $3ab^2$
k $4xz$
l $5z$
m abc
n $ab + bc$
o $abc + d^3$
p $2ab + 3bc$
q $a^2b + ab^2$
r $a^2 + b^2$
s πa^2
t $\frac{abc}{d}$
u $\frac{(ab + bc)}{d}$
v $\frac{ab}{2}$
w $(a + b)^2$
x $4a^2 + 2ab$
y $3abc + 2abd + 4bcd + 2acd$
z $4\pi r^3 + \pi r^2h$

Consistency

One way in which scientists and mathematicians check complicated formulae to see whether they are correct is to test for **consistency**. That is, to check that every term is of the same **order** (dimension) and represents the same **unit**. We are only concerned with lengths, areas and volumes, so it is easy for us to test for consistency.

Each term in a formula must have the correct number of dimensions. It is not possible to have a formula with a mixture of terms, some of which have, for example, one dimension and some two dimensions. When terms are found to be mixed, the formula is said to be **inconsistent** and is rejected.

Example

i Which of these formulae are consistent?

ii If any are consistent, do they represent a length, an area or a volume?

a $a + bc$
b $\pi r^2 + ab$
c $r^3 + 2\pi r^2$
d $\frac{(ab^2 + a^2b)}{2}$
e $\frac{\pi(R^2 + r^2)}{x}$

Formula **a** is inconsistent because the first term has one letter (order 1), and the second has two letters (order 2). Hence, it is a mixture of length and area. So it has no meaning, i.e. $[L] + [L^2]$ is not possible.

Formula **b** is consistent because the first term has two letters (r and r) multiplied by a dimensionless number (π), and the second term also has two letters (a and b). Hence the formula could represent an area, i.e. $[L^2] + [L^2] = [L^2]$ is true.

Formula **c** is inconsistent because the first term is of order 3 and the second term is of order 2. It is a mixture of area and volume, so it has no meaning, i.e. $[L^3] + [L^2]$ is not possible.

Formula **d** is consistent. Each term is of order 3 and the whole expression could represent a volume, i.e. $[L^3] + [L^3] = [L^3]$ is true.

Formula **e** is also consistent. There are two terms of order 2 on the top line and one term of order 1 on the bottom. One dimension can be cancelled to give two terms of order 1. Hence the formula could represent a length, i.e. $[L^2]/[L] = [L]$ is true.

Exercise 18E

1 Indicate whether each of these formulae is consistent (C) or inconsistent (I).

a $a + b$ **b** $a^2 + b$ **c** $a^2 + b^2$ **d** $ab + c$

e $ab + c^2$ **f** $a^3 + bc$ **g** $a^3 + abc$ **h** $a^2 + abc$

i $3a^2 + bc$ **j** $4a^3b + 2ab^2$ **k** $3abc + 2x^2y$ **l** $3a(ab + bc)$

m $4a^2 + 3ab$ **n** $\pi a^2(a + b)$ **o** $\pi a^2 + 2r^2$ **p** $\pi r^2h + \pi rh$

q $\pi r^2(R + r)$ **r** $\dfrac{(ab + bc)}{d}$ **s** $a(b^2 + c)$ **t** $\pi ab + \pi bc$

u $(a + b)(c + d)$ **v** $\pi(a + b)(a^2 + b^2)$ **w** $\pi(a^2 + b^2)$ **x** $\pi^2(a + b)$

y $\pi r^2h + \pi r^3$

2 **i** Write down whether each formula is consistent (C) or inconsistent (I).

ii When it is consistent, say whether it represents a length (L), an area (A) or a volume (V).

a $\pi a + \pi b$ **b** $2\pi r^2 + h$ **c** $\pi r^2h + 2\pi r^3$ **d** $2\pi r + h$

e $2\pi rh + 4\pi r^3$ **f** $\dfrac{\pi r}{6} + \pi a^2$ **g** $r^2h + \pi rh^2$ **h** $\pi r^2(r + h)$

i $\pi r^2h + 2r^3 + \dfrac{h^2r}{6}$ **j** $2\pi r^3 + 3\pi r^2h$ **k** $4\pi a + 3x$ **l** $3\pi r^2a + 2\pi r$

m $\dfrac{\pi r^2h}{3} + \dfrac{\pi r^3}{3} + x^3$

3 What power * would make each formula consistent?

a $\pi abc + a^*b$ **b** $\dfrac{\pi r^*h}{2} + \pi h^* + \dfrac{rh^2}{2}$

c $\pi a(b^* + ac)$ **d** $a^*b + ab^* + c^3$

4 Kerry has worked out a volume formula as

$$V = \frac{(2hD^2 + hd)}{4}$$

It is wrong. Why?

Examination questions

1 Taking l, b h and r to be lengths, complete the table to show which of the formulae 1, 2, 3, 4, or 5 denotes length, area or volume.

	Formula
Length	
Area	
Volume	

Formulae: 1 $h^2(l + b)$
2 $\pi r(l + r)$
3 $4(l + b)^2$
4 $\pi\sqrt{(h^2 - b^2)}$
5 $b^2(\frac{h}{3} + l)$

NICCEA, Question 11, Paper 3, June 1995

2 One of the formulae in the list below can be used to calculate the area of material needed to make the curved surface of the lampshade in the diagram.

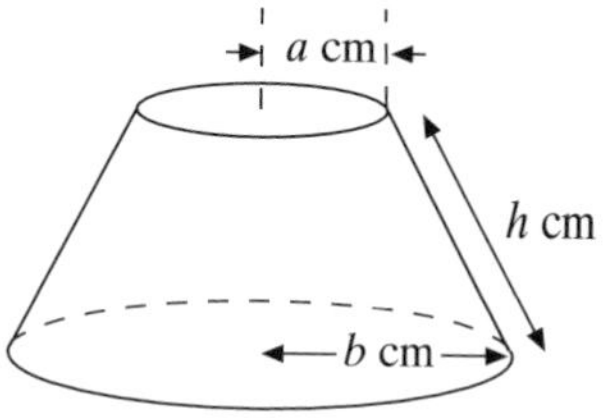

i $\pi h(a + b)^2$ **ii** $\pi h^2(a + b)$ **iii** $\pi h(a + b)$ **iv** $\pi h^2(a + b)^2$

State which formula is correct. Give a reason for your answer.

MEG, Question 20, Paper 2, June 1994

3 The expressions shown in the table below can be used to calculate lengths, areas or volumes of various shapes. π, 2, 4 and 1 are numbers which have no dimensions. The letters r, l, b and h represent lengths. Put a tick in the box underneath those expressions that can be used to calculate a volume.

$2\pi r$	$4\pi r^2$	$\pi r^2 h$	πr^2	lbh	$\frac{1}{2}bh$

ULEAC, Question 25, Paper 7, June 1994

4 In the following formulae, r and h each represent a length.

a For each formula, state whether it represents a length, an area, a volume or none of these.

i $2\pi r^2$ **ii** $r^2(r + h)$ **iii** $\sqrt{(r^2 + h^2 + rh)}$ **iv** $\frac{r^3}{h}$ **v** $3r + rh$

b Explain your answer to part **v**.

MEG, Question 18, Paper 2, November 1994

5 The dimensions of four cuboids are shown.

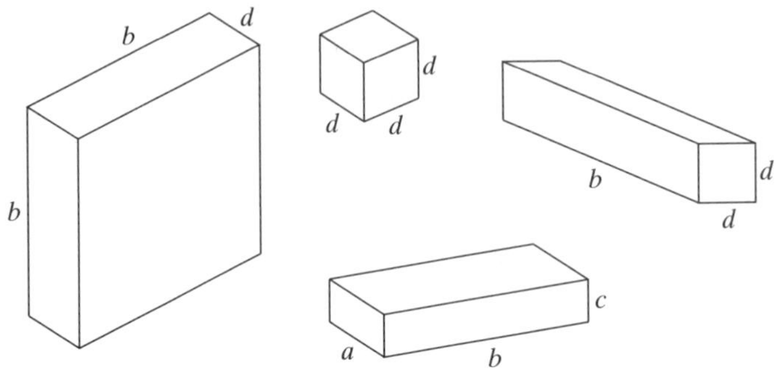

These expressions

abc $\quad 4d$ $\quad d^2$ $\quad 2(a + b)$ $\quad bd$ $\quad d^3$

give the perimeter of a face of one of the cuboids, or the area of a face of one of the cuboids, or the volume of one of the cuboids. Complete the statements below with Perimeter, Area or Volume.

abc gives a ……

$2(a + b)$ gives a ……

bd gives a …….

ULEAC, Question 21, Paper 3, November 1994

6 This diagram shows the cross-section of a warehouse.

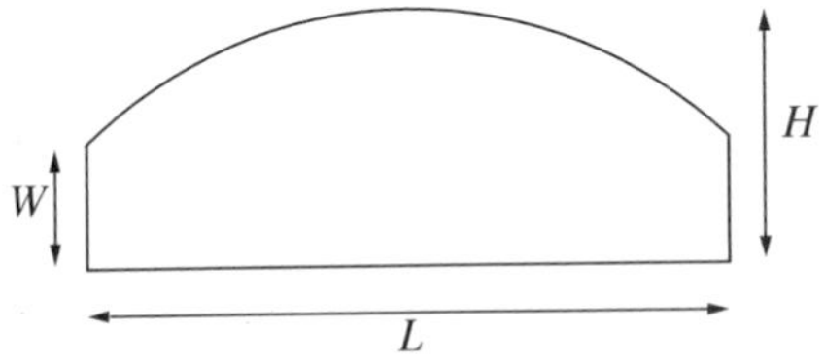

The top of the roof is H metres above the floor. The side walls are W metres high. The width of the warehouse is L metres.

An estate agent wants to estimate the area of cross-section of the warehouse.

a Explain why the formula

$$A = \frac{(8H + 2W + L)}{10}$$

cannot be a suitable formula for him to use.

b Look at these formulae.

i $A = \dfrac{8WHL}{10}$ **ii** $A = \dfrac{L(8H + 2W)}{10}$ **iii** $A = \dfrac{LW + 8H}{10}$

One of these formulae can be used to estimate the area of cross-section.

Which is it? Give a reason for your answer.

WJEC, Question 18, Paper 2, June 1995

7 The diagram shows a child's play brick in the shape of a prism.
The following formulae represent certain quantities connected with this prism.

$\pi ab \quad \pi(a + b) \quad \pi abl \quad \pi(a + b)l$

Which of the formulae represent areas?

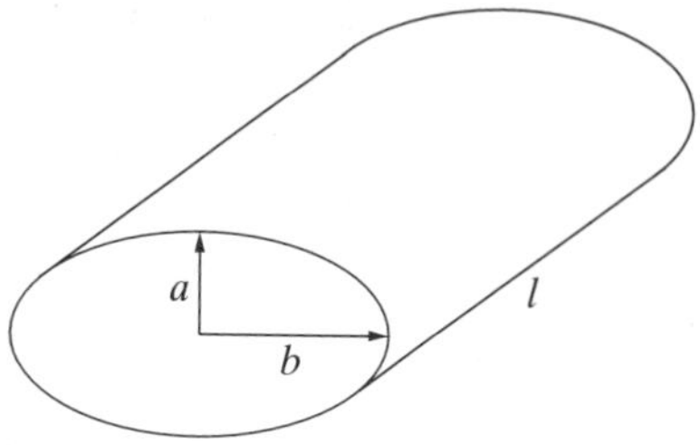

SEG, Question 18, Paper 4, 1995

Summary

How well do you grade yourself?

To gain a grade **C**, you need to be able to calculate lengths, areas, and volumes of plane shapes and right prisms.

To gain a grade **B**, you need to be able to recognise whether a formula is dimensionally consistent and whether it represents a length, an area or a volume.

What you should know after you have worked through Chapter 18

- Be able to recognise whether a formula is 1D, 2D or 3D.
- Be able to recognise when a formula is not consistent and state the reasons why.

19 Variation

This chapter is going to … introduce you to the two different types of variation: direct and inverse. It will show you how different types of problem can be solved using variation.

What you should already know

- The routines of algebraic substitution and solving equations.
- How to deal with squares and square roots in formulae.

Direct variation

The term 'direct variation' has the same meaning as 'direct proportion'.

There is direct variation (or direct proportion) between two variables when one variable is a simple multiple of the other. That is, their ratio is a constant.

Look at Examples 1 and 2.

1 1 kilogram = 2.2 pounds — There is a multiplying factor of 2.2 between kilograms and pounds.

2 Area of a circle = πr^2 — There is a multiplying factor of π between the area of a circle and the square of its radius.

An examination question involving direct variation usually requires you first to find this multiplying factor (called the **constant of proportionality**), then to use it to solve a problem.

The symbol for variation or proportion is $\propto$.

So the statement 'Pay is directly proportional to time' can be mathematically written as

$$\text{Pay} \propto \text{Time}$$

which implies that

$$\text{Pay} = k \times \text{Time}$$

where k is the constant of proportionality.

Follow through the next example to see how the constant of proportionality can be used to solve a problem.

Example The cost of an article is directly proportional to the time spent making it. An article taking 6 hours to make costs £30. Find

a the cost of an article that takes 5 hours to make

b the length of time it takes to make an article costing £40.

Let C be the cost of making an article and t the time it takes. We then have

$$C \propto t$$

$$\Rightarrow \quad C = kt$$

where k is the constant of proportionality.

Since C = £30 when t = 6 hours, then

$$30 = 6k$$

$$\Rightarrow \quad \frac{30}{6} = k$$

$$\Rightarrow \quad k = 5$$

So the formula is $C = 5t$

a When $t = 5$ hours $C = 5 \times 5 = 25$

So the cost is £25.

b When C = £40 $40 = 5 \times t$

$$\Rightarrow \quad \frac{40}{5} = t \quad \Rightarrow \quad t = 8$$

So the making time is 8 hours.

Exercise 19A

In each case, first find k, the constant of proportionality, and then the formula connecting the variables.

1 T is directly proportional to M. If $T = 20$ when $m = 4$, find

a T when $M = 3$ **b** M when $T = 10$

2 W is directly proportional to F. If $W = 45$ when $F = 3$, find

a W when $F = 5$ **b** F when $W = 90$

3 P is directly proportional to A. If $P = 150$ when $A = 2$, find

a P when $A = 3$ **b** A when $P = 450$

4 A is directly proportional to t. If $A = 15$ when $t = 5$, find

a A when $t = 8$ **b** t when $A = 18$

5 Q varies directly with P. If $Q = 100$ when $P = 2$, find

a Q when $P = 3$ **b** P when $Q = 300$

6 X varies directly with Y. If $X = 17.5$ when $Y = 7$, find

a X when $Y = 9$ **b** Y when $X = 30$

7 T varies directly with M. If $T = 10.8$ when $M = 6$, find

a T when $M = 11$ **b** M when $T = 25.2$

8 The distance covered by a train is directly proportional to the time taken. The train travels 105 miles in 3 hours.

a What distance will the train cover in 5 hours?

b What time will it take for the train to cover 280 miles?

9 The cost of fuel delivered to your door is directly proportional to the weight received. When 250 kg is delivered, it costs £47.50.

a How much will it cost to have 350 kg delivered?

b How much would be delivered if the cost were £33.25?

10 The number of children who can play safely in a playground is directly proportional to the area of the playground. A playground with an area of 210 m^2 is safe for 60 children.

a How many children can safely play in a playground of area 154 m^2?

b A play-group has 24 children. What is the smallest playground area in which they could safely play?

Proportions involving squares, cubes and square roots

The process is the same as for a linear direct variation, as the next example shows.

Example The cost of a circular badge is directly proportional to the square of its radius. The cost of a badge with a radius of 2 cm is 68p.

a Find the cost of a badge of radius 2.4 cm.

b Find the radius of a badge costing £1.53.

Let C be the cost and r the radius of a badge. Then

$$C \propto r^2$$

$$\Rightarrow \quad C = kr^2$$

where k is the constant of proportionality.

$C = 68\text{p}$ when $r = 2$ cm. So

$$68 = 4k$$

$$\Rightarrow \quad \frac{68}{4} = k \quad \Rightarrow \quad k = 17$$

Hence the formula is $C = 17r^2$

a When $r = 2.4$ cm $\quad C = 17 \times 2.4^2 = 97.92$

Rounding off gives the cost as 98p.

b When $C = 153$p $\quad 153 = 17r^2$

$$\Rightarrow \frac{153}{17} = 9 = r^2$$

$$\Rightarrow r = \sqrt{9} = 3$$

Hence, the radius is 3 cm.

Exercise 19B

In each case, first find k, the constant of proportionality, and then the formula connecting the variables.

1 T is directly proportional to x^2. If $T = 36$ when $x = 3$, find
a T when $x = 5$ **b** x when $T = 400$

2 W is directly proportional to M^2. If $W = 12$ when $M = 2$, find
a W when $M = 3$ **b** M when $W = 75$

3 A is directly proportional to r^2. If $A = 48$ when $r = 4$, find
a A when $r = 5$ **b** r when $A = 12$

4 T is directly proportional to p^2. If $T = 45$ when $p = 3$, find
a T when $p = 2$ **b** p when $T = 125$

5 D varies directly with F^2. If $D = 96$ when $F = 8$, find
a D when $F = 4$ **b** F when $D = 54$

6 E varies directly with $\sqrt{C}$. If $E = 40$ when $C = 25$, find
a E when $C = 49$ **b** C when $E = 10.4$

7 X is directly proportional to $\sqrt{Y}$. If $X = 128$ when $Y = 16$, find
a X when $Y = 36$ **b** Y when $X = 48$

8 H is directly proportional to $\sqrt{t}$. If $H = 20.8$ when $t = 4$, find
a H when $t = 1.21$ **b** t when $H = 93.6$

9 P is directly proportional to f^3. If $P = 400$ when $f = 10$, find
a P when $f = 4$ **b** f when $P = 50$

10 V varies directly with t^3. If $V = 50$ when $t = 10$, find
a V when $t = 8$ **b** t when $V = 6.25$

11 The cost of serving tea and biscuits varies directly with the square root of the number of people at the buffet. It costs £25 to serve tea and biscuits to 100 people.
a How much will it cost to serve tea and biscuits to 400 people?
b For a cost of £37.50, how many could be served tea and biscuits?

12 The temperature, in °C, in an experiment varied directly with the square of the pressure, in atmospheres. The temperature was 20 °C when the pressure was 5 atm.

a What will the temperature be at 2 atm?

b What will the pressure be at 80 °C?

13 The weight, in grams, of ball bearings varies directly with the cube of the radius measured in millimetres. A ball bearing of radius 4 mm has a weight of 115.2 g.

a What will a ball bearing of radius 6 mm weigh?

b A ball bearing has a weight of 45 g. What is its radius?

14 The energy, in J, of a particle varies directly with the square of its speed in m/s. A particle moving at 20 m/s has 50 J of energy.

a How much energy has a particle moving at 4 m/s?

b At what speed is a particle moving if it has 200 J of energy?

15 The cost, in £, of a trip varies directly with the square root of the number of miles travelled. The cost of a 100-mile trip is £35.

a What is the cost of a 500-mile trip? (To the nearest £.)

b What is the distance of a trip costing £70?

Inverse variation

There is inverse variation between two variables when one variable is directly proportional to the reciprocal of the other. That is, the product of the two variables is constant. So, as one variable increases, the other decreases.

For example, the faster you travel over a given distance, the less time it takes. So there is an inverse variation between speed and time. We say speed is inversely proportional to time.

$$S \propto \frac{1}{T} \quad \text{and so} \quad S = \frac{k}{T}$$

which can be written as $ST = k$.

Follow through the next example to see how this works.

Example M is inversely proportional to R. If $M = 9$ when $R = 4$, find

a M when $R = 2$ **b** R when $M = 3$

From the first statement, we have

$$M \propto \frac{1}{R} \Rightarrow M = \frac{k}{R}$$

where k is the constant of proportionality.

When $M = 9$ and $R = 4$, we get $9 = \frac{k}{4}$

$$\Rightarrow 9 \times 4 = k \Rightarrow k = 36$$

So the formula is $M = \frac{36}{R}$

a When $R = 2$, then $M = \frac{36}{2} = 18$

b When $M = 3$, then $3 = \frac{36}{R}$

$$\Rightarrow \quad 3R = 36 \quad \Rightarrow \quad R = 12$$

Exercise 19C

In each case, first find the formula connecting the variables.

1 T is inversely proportional to m. If $T = 6$ when $m = 2$, find
a T when $m = 4$ **b** m when $T = 4.8$

2 W is inversely proportional to x. If $W = 5$ when $x = 12$, find
a W when $x = 3$ **b** x when $W = 10$

3 H is inversely proportional to $(p + 2)$. If $H = 4$ when $p = 5$, find
a H when $p = 8$ **b** p when $H = 10$

4 Q varies inversely with $(5 - t)$. If $Q = 8$ when $t = 3$, find
a Q when $t = 10$ **b** t when $Q = 16$

5 M varies inversely with t^2. If $M = 9$ when $t = 2$, find
a M when $t = 3$ **b** t when $M = 1.44$

6 C is inversely proportional to f^2. If $C = 16$ when $f = 3$, find
a C when $f = 5$ **b** f when $C = 9$

7 W is inversely proportional to $\sqrt{T}$. If $W = 6$ when $T = 16$, find
a W when $T = 25$ **b** T when $W = 2.4$

8 H varies inversely with $\sqrt{g}$. If $H = 12$ when $g = 9$, find
a H when $g = 64$ **b** g when $H = 30$

9 The grant available to a section of society was inversely proportional to the number of people needing the grant. When 30 people needed a grant, they received £60 each.
a What would the grant have been if 120 people had needed one?
b If the grant had been £50 each, how many people would have received it?

10 While doing underwater tests in one part of an ocean, a team of scientists noticed that the temperature in °C was inversely proportional to the depth in kilometres. When the temperature was 6 °C, the scientists were at a depth of 4 km.
a What would have been the temperature at a depth of 8 km?
b To what depth would they have had to go to find the temperature at 2 °C?

11 The top prize in a raffle was inversely proportional to square of the number of winners. When there were two winners, the top prize was £30.

a What would be the top prize if there were 6 winners?

b If the top prize were £2.40, how many winners would there be?

12 A new engine was being tested, but it had serious problems. The distance, in km, it went without breaking down was inversely proportional to the square of its speed in m/s. When the speed was 12 m/s, the engine lasted 3 km.

a Find the distance covered before a breakdown when the speed is 15 m/s.

b On one test, the engine broke down after 6.75 km. What was the speed?

13 In a balloon it was noticed that the pressure, in atmospheres, was inversely proportional to the square root of the height, in metres. When the balloon was at a height of 25 m, the pressure was 1.44 atm.

a What was the pressure at a height of 9 m?

b What would have been the height if the pressure was 0.72 atm?

14 The amount of waste which a firm produces, measured in tonnes per hour, is inversely proportional to the square root of the size of the filter beds, measured in m^2. At the moment, the firm produces 1.25 tonnes per hour of waste, with filter beds of size 0.16 m^2.

a The filter beds used to be only 0.01 m^2. How much waste did they produce then?

b How much waste would be produced if the filter beds were 0.75 m^2?

Possible coursework tasks

These investigations provide an opportunity for practical work. You will require several pieces of equipment, and a lot of time and patience.

Remember that data can be easily shown on a computer spreadsheet or in a computer database.

First to the floor

When both systems are released at the same time, which weight hits the floor first?

Investigate for different weights.

Equipment required: string, different weights, pulleys.

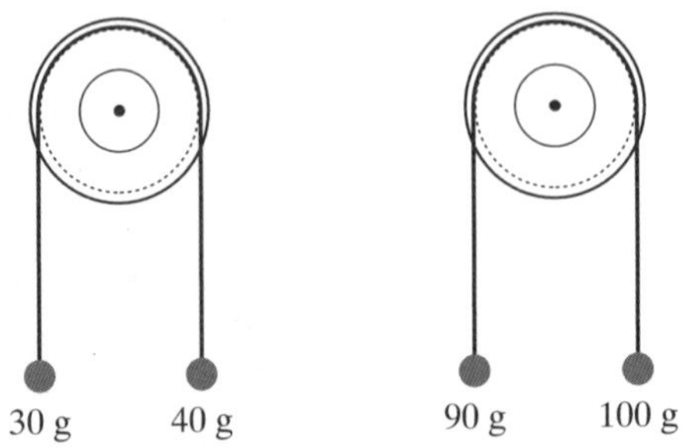

Pendulum problem

A pendulum can be easily made from a piece of string of length L and a bob of weight W.

When the bob is pulled to one side of the vertical line through the point of suspension and then released, it will swing back and forth. The time taken by the pendulum to swing from its starting position across to the other side and back is known as the **period** of the pendulum. It is usually denoted by T.

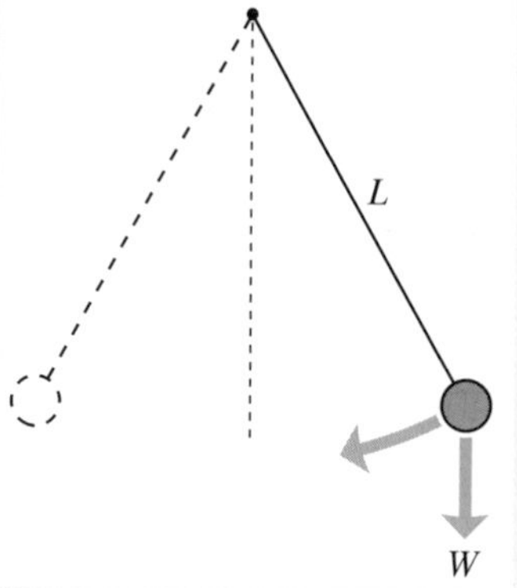

Investigate the relationship between T, L and W.

Equipment required: string, one-metre rule, weights (actual or made from Plasticine), stopwatch.

Examination questions

1 Given that y is directly proportional to x^2 and that $y = 2$ when $x = 3$, find the value of y when $x = 6$.

2 Y is inversely proportional to X^2. Given that $Y = 2$ when $X = 3$,
i express Y in terms of X **ii** find the value of Y when $X = 5$.

3 Given that y is inversely proportional to $(x + 3)$ and that $y = 4$ when $x = 2$,
i express y in term of x **ii** find the value of y when $x = 7$.

4 When a stone is thrown upwards with an initial speed of s metres per second, it reaches a maximum height, h metres. Given that h varies directly as the square of s and that $h = 5$ when $s = 10$,
a work out a formula connecting h and s
b calculate the value of s when $h = 20$. *ULEAC, Question 9, Specimen Paper 5, 1998*

5 Two variables, x and y, vary in such a way that y is inversely proportional to the square of x.
a When $x = 4$, $y = 5$. Find the formula giving y in terms of x.
b Find the value of y when $x = 5$. *WJEC, Question 25, Paper 1, June 1994*

6 The weight of a metal sphere varies directly as the cube of its radius. The weight of a metal sphere of radius 3 cm is 1.02 kg. Calculate the weight of a metal sphere of radius 5 cm. *NEAB, Question 21, Paper 1, June 1995*

7 The perceived brightness of a bulb varies inversely with the square of the distance away from the bulb. If the brightness of a bulb is 4 candle power at a distance of 4 metres, what is the brightness at a distance of 8 metres?

8 The distance that can be seen out to sea on a clear day varies directly as the square root of the height above sea level. At a height of 6 metres above sea level, you can see 10 km on a clear day. What distance will you be able to see on a clear day from a height of 60 metres above sea level? *NEAB, Question 5, Specimen Paper 1, 1998*

9 T is directly proportional to the positive square root of M. $T = 32$ when $M = 16$.

a Find an expression for T in terms of M.

b Calculate T when M is 100.

c Calculate M when T is 9.6 *NEAB, Question 16, Specimen Paper 1H, 1998*

10 Given that y is inversely proportional to the square of x, and that y is 12 when $x = 3$,

a find an expression for y in terms of x

b calculate **i** y when $x = 6$ **ii** x when $y = 27$

WJEC, Question 12, Specimen Paper 1H, 1998

Summary

How well do you grade yourself?

To gain a grade **A**, you need to be able to find formulae describing direct or inverse variation and to use them to solve problems involving direct or inverse variation.

What you should know after you have worked through Chapter 19

- How to recognise direct and inverse variations.
- What a constant of proportionality is and how to calculate it.
- How to find formulae describing direct or inverse variation.
- How to solve problems involving direct or inverse variation.

20 Number and limits of accuracy

This chapter is going to ... show you how to use limits of accuracy in calculations, and how to recognise when the answer to a calculation will be affected by the accuracy of the values used in the calculation. It will also introduce you to the calculation of percentage error.

What you should already know

- The limits between which the actual value of a number may lie when the number is expressed to a given accuracy.

Limits of accuracy

Any recorded measurement will have been rounded off to some degree of accuracy. This defines the possible true value before rounding off took place and hence the limits of accuracy. The range of values between the limits of accuracy is called the **rounding error**.

For example, a length of 53.7 cm is given to 1 decimal place, which means

- its smallest possible value is 53.65 cm
- its largest possible value is 53.749 999 999…

so, the limits of accuracy are

$$53.65 \leq 53.7 < 53.75$$

Exercise 20A

Write down the limits of accuracy for each of the following values which are to the given degree of accuracy.

a 6 cm (1 sf)	**b** 17 kg (2 sf)	**c** 32 min (2 sf)	**d** 238 km (3 sf)
e 7.3 m (1 dp)	**f** 25.8 kg (1 dp)	**g** 3.4 h (1 dp)	**h** 87 g (2 sf)
i 4.23 mm (2 dp)	**j** 2.19 kg (2 dp)	**k** 12.67 min (2 dp)	**l** 25 m (2 sf)
m 40 cm (1 sf)	**n** 600 g (2 sf)	**o** 30 min (1 sf)	**p** 1000 m (2 sf)
q 4.0 m (1 dp)	**r** 7.04 kg (2 dp)	**s** 12.0 s (1 dp)	**t** 7.00 m (2 dp)

Upper and lower bounds

A journey of 26 miles measured to the nearest mile could actually be as long as 26.499 9999... miles or as short as 25.5 miles. It could **not** be 26.5 miles, as this would round off to 27 miles. However, 26.499 999 99... is **virtually the same** as 26.5.

We overcome this difficulty by saying that 26.5 is the **upper bound** of the measured value and 25.5 is its **lower bound**. We therefore write the answer as

$$25.5 \leq \text{Actual distance} < 26.5$$

which states that the actual distance is **greater than or equal to** 25.5 but **less than** 26.5.

Although it is not wrong to give the upper bound as 26.499 99... it is mathematically neater to give 26.5. It is wrong, however, to give the upper bound as 26.4 or 26.49. So, when stating an upper bound, always follow the accepted practice, as demonstrated here, which eliminates the difficulties that arise with recurring decimals.

Percentage error

The error made by rounding off can be expressed as a percentage:

$$\text{Percentage error} = \frac{\text{Error}}{\text{Actual value}} \times 100$$

$$\text{Greatest percentage error} = \frac{\text{Largest error}}{\text{Least possible value}} \times 100$$

The greatest percentage errors are at the upper and lower bounds.

Example Calculate the greatest percentage error in a height of 156 cm given to 3 sf.

The limits of accuracy are $155.5 \leq 156 < 156.5$

We have, therefore,

the largest error that could be made = 0.5 cm (either + or −)
the least possible value = 155.5 cm

which give

$$\text{Greatest percentage error} = \frac{0.5}{155.5} \times 100 = 0.322\% \quad (3\text{ dp})$$

Exercise 20B

1 Find the greatest percentage error of each of the following measures.

a 8 m (1 sf)	**b** 26 kg (2 sf)	**c** 25 min (2 sf)	**d** 85 g (2 sf)
e 2.40 m (2 dp)	**f** 0.2 kg (1 dp)	**g** 0.06 s (2 dp)	**h** 300 g (1 sf)
i 0.7 m (1 dp)	**j** 366 d (3 sf)	**k** 170 weeks (2 sf)	**l** 210 g (2 sf)

7 A carton of apple juice has the shape of a cuboid with a square base of side 6.8 cm and a height of 18.4 cm. Each of these measurements is correct to one decimal place.

a Given that 5000 such cartons must be filled, calculate the volume of juice necessary to be certain of filling all the cartons.

b Calculate the maximum number of cartons that could be filled with this volume of juice. *MEG, Question 17, Specimen Paper 5, 1998*

8 Cars are timed over a stretch of road using a digital timer, which counts in tenths of a second. The digits change at the end of each complete tenth of a second. The time for one car is shown as 41.8 seconds.

a Complete the inequality below to show the possible times taken by the car.

$$\ldots\ldots \leq \text{Time of car in seconds} < \ldots\ldots$$

b The stretch of road is 800 m long, correct to the nearest 10 metres. Calculate the minimum speed the car could have been travelling. Give your result in metres per second, correct to 2 decimal places.

c Another car's speed is calculated as 31.73 metres per second (correct to 2 decimal places). Convert this speed to miles per hour. [1 metre per second = 2.237 miles per hour (correct to 3 decimal places).] Give your answer to an appropriate degree of accuracy. Show clearly why it is not possible to give a more exact answer.

NEAB, Question 8, Specimen Paper 2H, 1998

9 Ohm's law states that the voltage, V volts, the current, I amps, and the resistance, R ohms, of an electrical circuit are connected by the formula

$$V = IR$$

Anwar is carrying out an experiment to find the resistance, R ohms. He measures V to be 6 volts and I to be 0.2 amps.

a Without using a calculator, work out the value of R. Show all your working.

b Anwar is told that his value of V has a maximum possible error ±2%. He is also told that his value of I has a maximum possible error of ±5%. Within what limits must the value of R lie? *NEAB, Question 13, Paper 2R, November 1995*

10 A stop-watch records the time for the winner of a 100-metre race as 10.4 seconds, measured to the nearest one tenth of a second.

a What are the greatest and least possible times for the winner?

b The length of the 100-metre track is correct to the nearest 10 cm. What are the greatest and least possible lengths of the track?

c What is the fastest possible average speed of the winner, with a time of 10.4 seconds in the 100-metre race? *NEAB, Question 4, Paper 1R, November 1995*

Summary

How well do you grade yourself?

To gain a grade **B**, you need to be able to find upper and lower bounds from measures of given accuracy.

To gain a grade **A**, you need to be able to evaluate limits of accuracy for compound measures and determine the percentage errors while working with limits of accuracy in length and associated measures.

What you should know after you have worked through Chapter 20

- How to use limits of accuracy in calculations.
- How the answer to a calculation may be affected by the accuracy of the values used in the calculation.
- How to find the greatest percentage error in a calculation involving continuous data.

21 Inequalities and regions

This chapter is going to … show you how to find a region that obeys an algebraic inequality, and introduce you to the method of problem solving by considering different regions on a graph.

What you should already know

- What an inequality is.
- How to draw a graph from any linear equation.

Graphically representing inequalities

A linear inequality can be plotted on a graph. The result is a **region** that lies on one side of a straight line or the other. You will recognise an inequality by the fact that it looks like an equation but instead of the equals sign it has an inequality sign: <, >, ≤, or ≥.

The following are examples of linear inequalities which can be represented on a graph.

$y < 3 \qquad x > 7 \qquad -3 \leq y < 5 \qquad y \geq 2x + 3 \qquad 2x + 3y < 6 \qquad y \leq x$

The method for graphing an inequality is to draw the boundary line that defines the inequality. This is found by replacing the inequality sign with an equals sign.

When a strict inequality is stated, i.e. < or > are used, the boundary line should be drawn as a **dashed** line to show that it is **not included** in the range of values. But when ≤ or ≥ are used to state the inequality, the boundary line should be drawn as a **solid** line to show that the boundary is **included**.

After the boundary line has been drawn, the **required region is shaded**.

To confirm on which side of the line the region lies, choose any point that is not on the boundary line and test it in the inequality. If it satisfies the inequality, that is the side required. If it doesn't, the other side is required.

Work through the six examples on the next two pages to see how the procedure is applied.

Example Show each of the following inequalities on a graph.

$y \leq 3$ $\quad x > 7$ $\quad -3 \leq y < 5$ $\quad y \leq 2x + 3$ $\quad 2x + 3y < 6$ $\quad y \leq x$

a Draw the line $y = 3$. Since the inequality is stated as $\leq$, the line is **solid**. Test a point that is not on the line The **origin** is always a good choice if possible, as 0 is easy to test. Putting 0 into the inequality gives $0 \leq 3$. The inequality is satisfied and so the region containing the origin is the side we want. Shade it in.

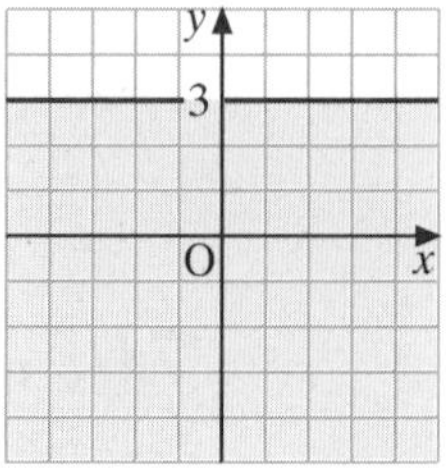

$y \leq 3$

b Since the inequality is stated as >, the line is **dashed**. Draw the line $x = 7$. Test the origin (0, 0), which gives $0 > 7$. This is not true, so we want the other side of the line to the origin. Shade it in.

$x > 7$

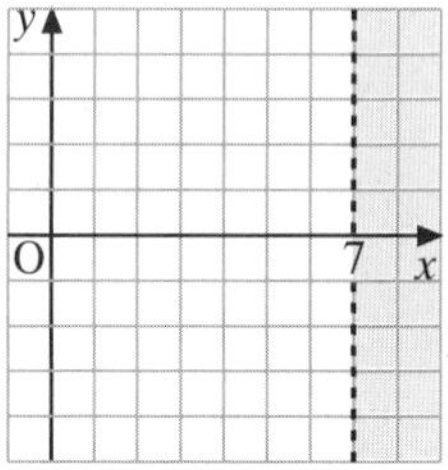

c Draw the lines $y = -3$ (solid for $\leq$) and $y = 5$ (dashed for <). Test a point that is not on either line, say (0, 0). Zero is between –3 and 5, so the required region lies between the lines. Shade it in.

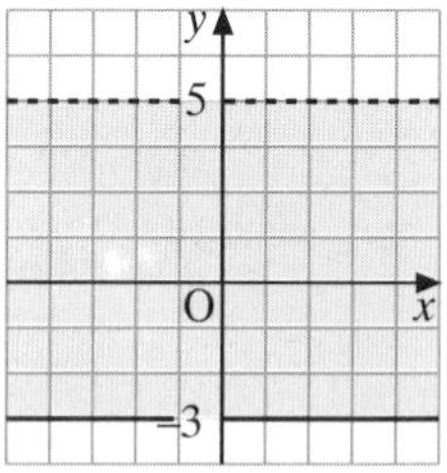

$-3 \leq y < 5$

d Draw the line $y = 2x + 3$. Since the inequality is stated as $\leq$, the line is solid. Test a point that is not on the line, (0, 0). Putting these x and y-values in the inequality gives $0 \leq 2(0) + 3$, which is true. So the region that includes the origin is what we want. Shade it in.

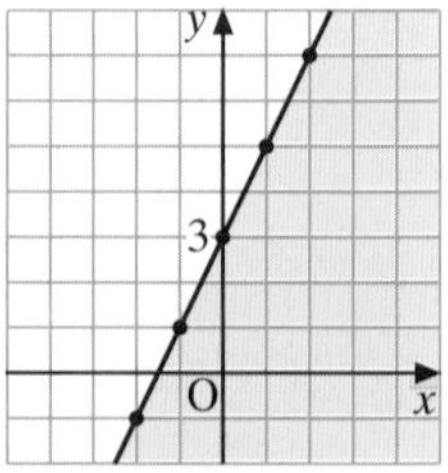

$y \leq 2x + 3$

e Draw the line $2x + 3y = 6$. Since the inequality is stated as <, the line is dashed. Test a point that is not on the line, say (0, 0). Is it true that $2(0) + 3(0) < 6$? The answer is yes, so the origin is in the region that we want. Shade it in.

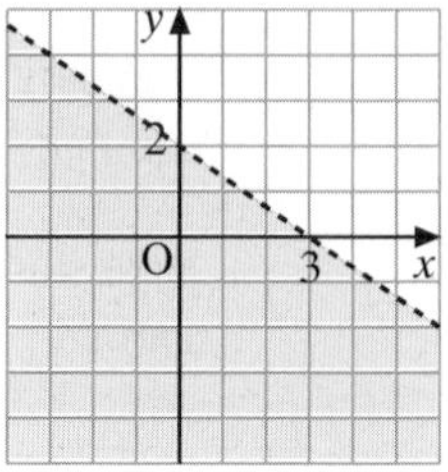

$2x + 3y < 6$

f Draw the line $y = x$. Since the inequality is stated as $\leq$, the line is solid. This time the origin is on the line, so pick any other point, say (1, 3). Putting $x = 1$ and $y = 3$ in the inequality gives $3 \leq 1$. The answer is not true, so the point (1, 3) is not in the region we want. Shade in the other side to (1, 3).

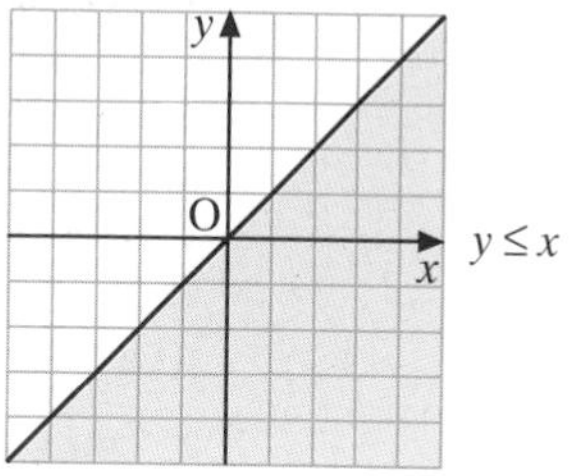

More than one inequality

When we have to show a region that satisfies more than one inequality, it is clearer to **shade out** the regions **not required**, so that the **required region** is left **blank**.

Example

a On the same grid, shade out the regions that represent the inequalities
  i $x > 2$ **ii** $y \geq x$ **iii** $x + y < 8$

b Are the points (3, 4), (2, 6) and (3, 3) in the region that satisfies all three inequalities?

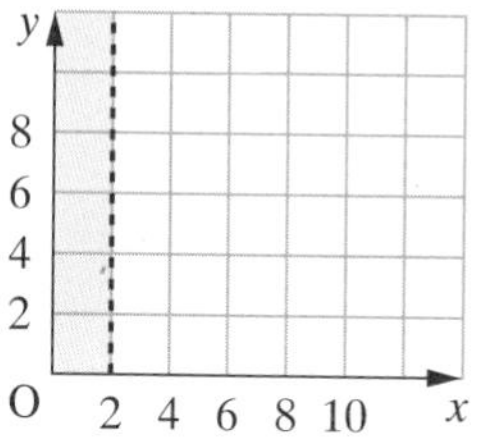

i

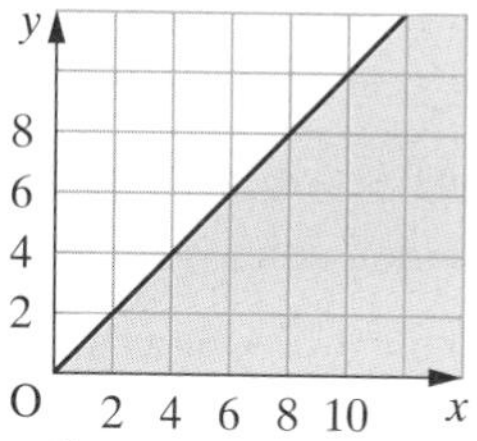

ii

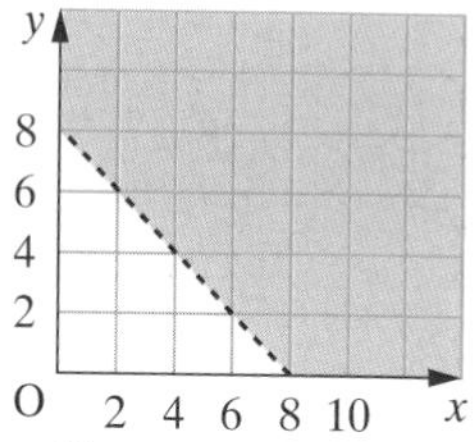

iii

a i This region is shown unshaded in diagram **i**. The boundary line is $x = 2$ (dashed).

ii This region is shown unshaded in diagram **ii**. The boundary line is $y = x$ (solid).

iii This region is shown unshaded in diagram **iii**. The boundary line is $x + y = 8$ (dashed).

The regions have first been drawn separately so that each may be clearly seen. The diagram on the right shows all three regions on the same grid. The white triangular area defines the region that satisfies all three inequalities.

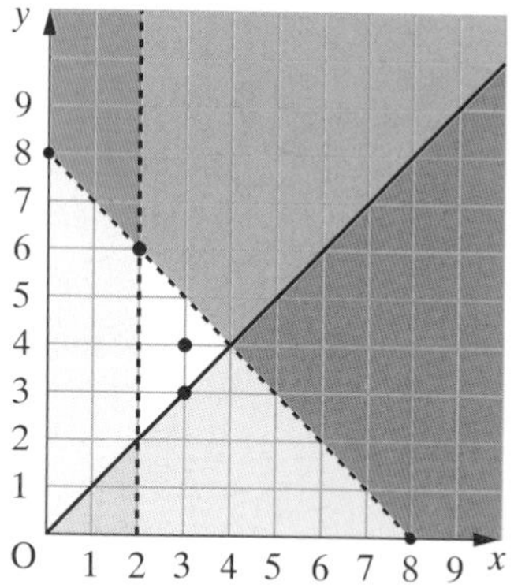

b i The point (3, 4) is clearly within the region that satisfies all three inequalities.

ii The point (2, 6) is on the boundary line $x = 2$ and $x + y = 8$. As these are dashed lines, they are not included in the region defined by all three inequalities. So, the point (2, 6) is also not in this region.

iii The point (3, 3) is on the boundary line $y = x$. As this is a solid line, it is included in the region defined by all three inequalities. So, the point (3, 3) is also included in this region.

Exercise 21A

1 a Draw the line $x = 2$ (as a solid line).
b Shade the region defined by $x \leq 2$.

2 a Draw the line $y = -3$ (as a dashed line).
b Shade the region defined by $y < -3$.

3 a Draw the line $x = -2$ (as a solid line).
b Draw the line $x = 1$ (as a solid line) on the same grid.
c Shade the region defined by $-2 \leq x \leq 1$.

4 a Draw the line $y = -1$ (as a dashed line).
b Draw the line $y = 4$ (as a solid line) on the same grid.
c Shade the region defined by $-1 < y \leq 4$.

5 a On the same grid, draw the regions defined by the inequalities
i $-3 \leq x \leq 6$ **ii** $-4 < y \leq 5$
b Are the following points in the region defined by both inequalities?
i (2, 2) **ii** (1, 5) **iii** (–2, –4)

6 a Draw the line $y = 2x - 1$ (as a dashed line).
b Shade the region defined by $y < 2x - 1$.

7 a Draw the line $3x - 4y = 12$ (as a solid line).
b Shade the region defined by $3x - 4y \leq 12$.

8 a Draw the line $y = \frac{1}{2}x + 3$ (as a solid line).
b Shade the region defined by $y \geq \frac{1}{2}x + 3$.

9 a Draw the line $y = -3$ (as a dashed line).
b Shade the region defined by $y < -3$.

10 a Draw the line $y = 3x - 4$ (as a solid line).
b Draw the line $x + y = 10$ (as a solid line) on the same diagram.
c Shade out the region defined by $y \geq 3x - 4$.
d Shade out the region defined by $x + y \leq 10$.
e Are the following points in the region defined by both inequalities?
i (2, 1) **ii** (2, 2) **iii** (2, 3)

11 a Draw the line $y = x$ (as a solid line).
b Draw the line $2x + 5y = 10$ (as a solid line) on the same diagram.
c Draw the line $2x + y = 6$ (as a dashed line) on the same diagram.
d Shade out the region defined by $y \geq x$.
e Shade out the region defined by $2x + 5y \geq 10$.
f Shade out the region defined by $2x + y < 6$.
g Are the following points in the region defined by these inequalities?
i (1, 1) **ii** (2, 2) **iii** (3, 3)

12 a On the same grid, draw the regions defined by the following inequalities.
i $y > x - 3$ **ii** $3y + 4x \leq 24$ **iii** $x \geq 2$

b Are the following points in the region defined by all three inequalities?
i (1, 1) **ii** (2, 2) **iii** (3, 3) **iv** (4, 4)

Problem solving

Inequalities can arise in the solution of certain kinds of problem. The next example illustrates such a situation.

Example James has to buy drinks for himself and four friends. He has £2.50 to spend. A can of Cola cost 60 pence and a can of Orange cost 40 pence. He buys x cans of Cola and y cans of Orange.

a Explain why **i** $x + y \geq 5$ **ii** $6x + 4y \leq 25$

b Write down all the possible numbers of each type of drink he can buy.

a i James needs to buy at least five cans as there are five people. So the total number of cans of Cola and Orange must be at least five. This is expressed as

$$x + y \geq 5$$

ii x cans of Cola cost $60x$ pence, and y cans of Orange cost $40y$ pence. So

$$\text{Total cost} = 60x + 40y$$

But he has only 250 pence to spend, so total cost cannot exceed 250 pence. Hence,

$$60x + 40y \leq 250$$

This cancels through by 10 to give

$$6x + 4y \leq 25$$

b By trying different values of x and y, the following four combinations are found to satisfy the condition:

1 can of Cola and 4 cans of Orange
2 cans of Cola and 3 cans of Orange
5 or 6 cans of Orange

Exercise 21B

1 A company sells two types of bicycle, the Chapper and the Graffiti. A Chapper costs £148 and a Graffiti cost £125.

a How much do x Chappers cost?
b How much do y Graffitis cost?
c How much do x Chappers and y Graffiti cost altogether?

2 A school tuck shop sells Pluto bars at 19p each, Pogo mints at 15p per packet and Chews at 3p each. How much do each of the following orders cost?

a 2 Pluto bars and a packet of Pogo mints.

b x Pluto bars and y packets of Pogo mints.

c x Pluto bars, y packets of Pogo mints and z Chews.

d d Pluto bars, f packets of Pogo mints and 7 Chews.

3 A computer firm makes two types of machine. The Z210 and the Z310. The price of the Z210 is £A and that of the Z310 is £B. How much are

a x Z210s and y Z310s

b x Z210s and twice as many Z310s

c 9 Z210s and $(9 + y)$ Z310s?

4 If $x + y > 40$, which of the following may be true?

a $x > 40$ **b** $x + y \leq 20$ **c** $x - y = 10$ **d** $x \leq 5$

5 A bookshelf holds P paperback and H hardback books. The bookshelf can hold a total of 400 books. Which of the following may be true?

a $P + H < 300$ **b** $P \geq H$ **c** $P + H > 500$

6 A school uses two coach firms, Excel and Storms, to take pupils home from school. An Excel coach holds 40 pupils and a Storm coach holds 50 pupils. 1500 pupils need to be taken home by coach. If E Excel coaches and S Storm coaches are used, explain why

$$4E + 5S \geq 150$$

7 A boy goes to the fair with £6.00 in his pocket. He likes only rides on the big wheel and eating hot dogs. A big-wheel ride costs £1.50 and a hot dog costs £2.00. He has W big wheel rides and D hot dogs. Explain why

a $W \leq 4$ **b** $D \leq 3$ **c** $3W + 4D \leq 12$

d If he cannot eat more than 2 hot dogs without being ill, write down an inequality that must be true.

e Which of these combinations of big-wheel rides and hot dogs are possible if they obey all of the above conditions?

i 2 big wheel rides and 1 hot dog

ii 3 big wheel rides and 2 hot dogs

iii 2 big wheel rides and 2 hot dogs

iv 1 big wheel ride and 1 hot dog.

8 Pens cost 45p each and pencils cost 25p each. Jane has £2.00 with which to buy pens and pencils. She buys x pens and y pencils.

a Write down an inequality that must be true.

b She must have at least two more pencils than pens. Write down an inequality that must be true.

Exercise 21C

1 Mushtaq has to buy some apples and some pears. He has £3.00 to spend. Apples cost 30p each and pears cost 40p each. He must buy at least 2 apples and at least 3 pears, and at least 7 fruits altogether. He buys x apples and y pears.

a Explain each of these inequalities.

i $3x + 4y \leq 30$ **ii** $x \geq 2$ **iii** $y \geq 3$ **iv** $x + y \geq 7$

b Which of these combinations satisfy all of the above inequalities?

i 3 apples and 3 pears **ii** 4 apples and 5 pears

iii 0 apples and 7 pears **iv** 3 apples and 5 pears

2 A shop decides to stock only sofas and beds. A sofa takes up 4 m^2 of floor area and is worth £300. A bed takes up 3 m^2 of floor area and is worth £500. The shop has 48 m^2 of floor space for stock. The insurance policy will allow a total of only £6000 of stock to be in the shop at any one time. The shop stocks x sofas and y beds.

a Explain each of these inequalities.

i $4x + 3y \leq 48$ **ii** $3x + 5y \leq 60$

b Which of these combinations satisfy both of the above inequalities?

i 10 sofas and no beds **ii** 8 sofas and 6 beds

iii 10 sofas and 5 beds **iv** 6 sofas and 8 beds

3 The 300 pupils in Year 7 are to go on a trip to Adern Towers theme park. The local bus company has 6 forty-seat coaches and 5 fifty-seat coaches. The school hires x forty-seat coaches and y fifty-seat coaches.

a Explain each of these inequalities

i $4x + 5y \geq 30$ **ii** $x \leq 6$ **iii** $y \leq 5$

b Check that each of these combinations obeys each of the inequalities above.

i 6 forty-seaters and 2 fifty-seaters

ii 2 forty-seaters and 5 fifty-seaters

iii 4 forty-seaters and 3 fifty-seaters

iv 3 forty-seaters and 4 fifty-seaters

c The cost of hiring each coach is £100 for a forty-seater and £120 for a fifty-seater. Which of the combinations in part **b** would be the cheapest option?

d There is one combination that is even cheaper than the answer to part **c**. What is it?

4 To entertain the children at a birthday party, Amy decides to hire some videos. She can hire two types of video: cartoons which last 30 minutes and cost 75p each to hire, and animations which last 45 minutes and cost £1.00 each to hire. She needs to entertain the children for 3 hours and she has £6.00 to spend. So that the children do not get bored, she wants at least two of each type of video. She hires x cartoons and y animations.

a Explain each of these inequalities

i $2x + 3y \leq 12$ **ii** $3x + 4y \leq 24$

b Write down two other inequalities that must be true.

c Which of these combinations obeys all of the inequalities above?

i 2 cartoons and 4 animations **ii** 2 cartoons and 5 animations

iii 1 cartoon and 5 animations **iv** 3 cartoons and 2 animations

d Of the combinations in part **c** that work, which one would be cheapest to hire?

5 Dave has a fish tank that holds 30 gallons of water. He wants to put two types of fish into it. One is the fantail, which need at least a gallon of water per fish and cost £2.50 each. The other is the rainbow, which need at least 2 gallons of water per fish and cost £1.50 each. Dave wants more rainbows than fantails. He has £37.50 to spend, and buys x fantails and y rainbows.

a Explain each of these inequalities

i $x + 2y \leq 30$ **ii** $5x + 3y \leq 75.$ **iii** $x < y$

b Write down one other inequality that must be true.

c Which of these combinations obey all of the inequalities above?

i 10 fantails and 12 rainbows

ii 7 fantails and 8 rainbows

iii 10 fantails and 9 rainbows

iv 10 fantails and 10 rainbows

v 8 fantails and 11 rainbows

d Which of the combinations in part **c** that work is the cheapest?

6 A lorry can carry two types of pre-packed pallet. Pallet A takes up 2 m^3 of space and weighs 1.25 tonnes. Pallet B takes up 3 m^3 of space and weighs 2.5 tonnes. The lorry has a capacity of 48 m^3 and a maximum load of 37.5 tonnes. The lorry is carrying x of pallet A and y of pallet B. Write down two inequalities that must be true for this situation.

7 A farmer decides to start keeping ostriches and emus instead of cows. He has 300 acres of fields. Each ostrich needs 2 acres and each emu needs 1.5 acres. An ostrich gives 50 kg of meat and an emu 40 kg. The farmer can get a contract with a local meat-pie company if he can supply at least 6000 kg of meat. The ratio of the number of ostriches to the number of emus must never be more than 2:1, otherwise the ostriches attack the emus. The farmer gets x ostriches and y emus. Write down three inequalities that satisfy the given conditions.

8 A school party stays for a week at a hotel which can offer two types of room for pupils. The 'basic', which holds two people, and the 'large', which holds four. There are 40 pupils in the school party. A 'basic' room costs £100 per week, and a 'large' room costs £150 per week. The hotel has only 10 'basic' and 7 'large' rooms available. The school has charged the pupils £45 each to cover accommodation costs. The party takes x 'basic' and y 'large' rooms. Write down four inequalities that satisfy the given conditions.

9 An examiner has a stock of questions. 'Short' questions, which carry 8 marks and take 15 minutes to do, and 'long' questions, which take 30 minutes to do and carry 20 marks. There must be at least the same number of short questions as long questions.

The examination lasts 3 hours, so the total time needed to do the questions must be less than this. Also, the examinations must offer at least 100 marks, so the total marks available from the questions must be greater than this. The examiner sets x 'short' questions and y 'long' questions. Write down three inequalities that satisfy the given conditions.

10 Alf is on a diet. He eats only PowerBics, which have 4 g of fat and 300 calories, or SlimBars, which have 6 g of fat and 500 calories. He needs to keep his daily fat intake below 24 g and his daily calorie intake above 1500 calories. Because they taste so awful, Alf cannot take more than 4 PowerBics a day or more than 3 SlimBars a day. In one day he eats x PowerBics and y SlimBars. Write down four inequalities that satisfy the given conditions.

Linear programming

Linear programming is a graphical method for solving problems which have several conditions that must be satisfied simultaneously. Such a problem forms the next example.

Example An agency wants to take at least 600 tonnes of emergency supplies on to a ferry. It has eighteen 30-tonne trucks and twelve 40-tonne trucks, and 24 drivers are available. The ferry company charges £200 for each 30-tonne truck and £300 for each 40-tonne truck. The agency uses x 30-tonne trucks and y 40-tonne trucks. Find the following:

a The cheapest option that satisfies the conditions.
b The least number of trucks that could be used.

First, write down the inequalities that describe the given conditions.

Number of trucks	30 tonnes	$x \le 18$	(1)
	40 tonnes	$y \le 12$	(2)
Weight of supplies		$30x + 40y \ge 600$	
		$\Rightarrow \quad 3x + 4y \ge 60$	(3)
Number of drivers		$x + y \le 24$	(4)

Next, plot these inequalities on a graph, leaving **unshaded** the region that satisfies all of them. This region is called the **feasible region**.

(The size of the grid is usually given in an examination. In this case, an x-axis from 0 to 24 and a y-axis from 0 to 24 are needed.)

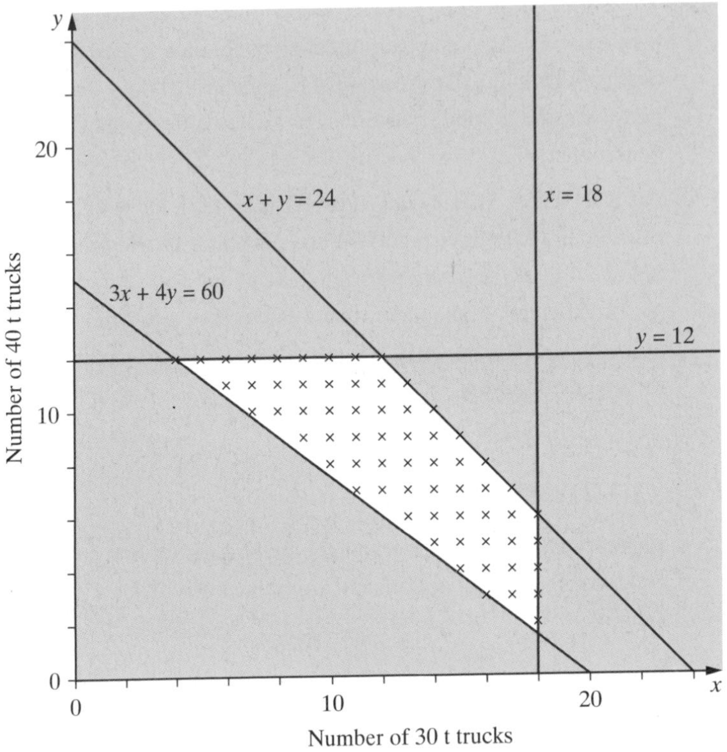

Within the feasible region, there are several possible pairs of values of x and y that satisfy the conditions. These are marked with crosses. To obtain the solutions to the problem we could test every one of these points, but this would take too long. Instead, we test the points **nearest to the corners** of the region. These are (4, 12), (12, 12), (18, 6), (18, 2).

a The ferry costs given by this set of test points are

(4, 12)	$4 \times 200 + 12 \times 300 = £4400$
(12, 12)	$12 \times 200 + 12 \times 300 = £6000$
(18, 6)	$18 \times 200 + 6 \times 300 = £5400$
(18, 2)	$18 \times 200 + 2 \times 300 = £4200$

So the cheapest option is eighteen 30-tonne trucks and two 40-tonne trucks.

b The least number of trucks is sixteen, comprising four 30-tonne and twelve 40-tonne trucks.

Exercise 21D

The situations in questions **1** to **10** below are identical to those in questions **1** to **10** in Exercise 21C. Shade out the regions not required, leaving the feasible region blank. Label the feasible region as R.

1 Mushtaq has to buy some apples and some pears. He has £3.00 to spend. Apples cost 30p each and pears cost 40p each. He must buy at least 2 apples and at least 3 pears. He must buy at least 7 fruits altogether. He buys x apples and y pears.

a Find four inequalities from this situation and represent them on the same grid.

b Which combination of apples and pears gives the largest number of fruits?

c Which combination gives the cheapest option?

2 A shop decides to stock only sofas and beds. A sofa takes up 4 m^2 of floor area and is worth £300. A bed takes up 3 m^2 of floor area and is worth £500. The shop has 48 m^2 of floor space for stock. The insurance policy will allow a total of only £6000 of stock to be in the shop at any one time. The shop stocks x sofas and y beds.

a Show, on the same grid, the two inequalities which express this situation.

b The shopkeeper wants to display as many items as possible. Which combination of beds and sofas does this?

c The accountant wants to keep the greatest amount of money tied up in stock. Which combination would do this?

3 The 300 pupils in Year 7 are to go on a trip to Adern Towers theme park. The local bus company has 6 forty-seat coaches and 5 fifty-seat coaches. The cost of hiring each coach is £100 for a forty seater and £120 for a fifty seater. The school hires x forty seaters and y fifty seaters.

a Write down three inequalities from this situation and represent them on the same grid.

b The theme park would like the fewest number of coaches. Which combination would do this?

c The school bursar would like the cheapest option possible. Show that this is the same combination that you found in part **d** of question **3**, Exercise 21C.

4 To entertain the children at a birthday party, Amy decides to hire some videos. She can hire two types of video: cartoons which last 30 minutes and cost 75p each to hire, and animations which last 45 minutes and cost £1.00 each to hire. She needs to entertain the children for 3 hours and she has £6.00 to spend. So that the children do not get bored, she wants at least two of each type of video. She hires x cartoons and y animations.

a Draw all four inequalities from this situation on the same grid.

b The children would like the maximum amount of time on the videos. Which combination would do this?

c Amy would like the cheapest option possible. Which combination would do this?

5 Dave has a fish tank that holds 30 gallons of water. He wants to put two types of fish into it. One is the fantail, which need at least a gallon of water per fish and cost £2.50 each. The other fish is the rainbow, which need at least 2 gallons of water per fish and cost £1.50 each. Dave wants more rainbows then fantails. He has £37.50 to spend on fish, and buys x fantails and y rainbows.

a Write down five inequalities from this situation and represent them all on the same grid.

b Dave wants the greatest number of fish possible. Which combination would do this?

c Dave's wife wants the cheapest option. Which combination would do this?

6 A lorry can carry two types of pre-packed pallet. Pallet A takes up 2 m^3 of space and weighs 1.25 tonnes. Pallet B takes up 3 m^3 of space and weighs 2.5 tonnes. The lorry has a capacity of 48 m^3 and a maximum load of 37.5 tonnes. The lorry is carrying x of pallet A and y of pallet B.

a Write down two inequalities from the description above and draw them both on the same grid.

Each of pallet A gives a profit to the lorry company of £15.50. Each of pallet B gives a profit of £25.

b Which combination of pallets would give the maximum profit?

7 A farmer decides to start keeping ostriches and emus instead of cows. He has 300 acres of fields. Each ostrich needs 2 acres and each emu needs 1.5 acres. An ostrich gives 50 kg of meat and an emu 40 kg. The farmer can get a contract with a local meat-pie company if he can supply at least 5500 kg of meat. The ratio of the number of ostriches to the number of emus must never be more than 2:1, otherwise the ostriches attack the emus. The farmer gets x ostriches and y emus.

a Write down three inequalities that satisfy the conditions above and show them on the same grid.

b What is the smallest total number of birds that the farmer could keep to satisfy all of the inequalities?

c Each ostrich costs £5 a week to feed and each emu costs £3 a week to feed. Which combination of birds is the cheapest to keep?

8 A school party stays for a week at a hotel which can offer two types of room for pupils. The 'basic', which holds two people, and the 'large', which holds four. There are 40 pupils in the school party. A 'basic' room costs £100 per week, and a 'large' room costs £150 per week. The hotel has only 10 'basic' and 7 'large' rooms available. The school has charged the pupils £45 each to cover accommodation costs. The party takes x 'basic' and y 'large' rooms.

a Draw the four inequalities described above on the same diagram.

b What is the cheapest combination of rooms?

c The teacher in charge books the cheapest combination of rooms. When he arrives at the hotel with the 23 girls and 17 boys, he realises that he has made a serious mistake. What could it be?

9 An examiner has a stock of questions. 'Short' questions, which carry 8 marks and take 15 minutes to do, and 'long' questions, which take 30 minutes to do and carry 20 marks. There must be at least the same number of short questions as long questions. The examination lasts 3 hours, so the total time needed to do the questions must be less than this. Also, the examination must offer at least 100 marks, so the total marks available from the questions must be greater than this. The examiner sets x 'short' questions and y 'long' questions.

a Write down three inequalities from the above situation and represent them all on the same grid.

b What is the smallest total number of questions?

c How many marks would this combination of questions give?

d How much time would this combination of questions take?

10 Alf is on a diet. He eats only PowerBics, which have 4 g of fat and 300 calories, or SlimBars, which have 6 g of fat and 500 calories. He needs to keep his daily fat intake below 24 g and his daily calorie intake above 1500 calories. Because they taste so awful, Alf cannot take more than 4 PowerBics a day or more than 3 SlimBars a day. In one day he eats x PowerBics and y SlimBars.

a Draw the four inequalities defined above on the same diagram.

b What is the smallest total number of PowerBics and SlimBars Alf could eat in a day?

c A PowerBic costs £2.50. A SlimBar costs £3.50. Which combination would cost Alf the least?

11 A builder has a plot of land with an area of 12 000 ft^2. He builds two types of house, the Balmoral and the Sandringham. The Balmoral takes an area of 1500 ft^2 and the Sandringham 2000 ft^2. Building a Balmoral requires 5 workers each day and building a Sandringham requires 3 workers each day. The builder has 30 workers available each day. He builds x Balmorals and y Sandringhams.

a Explain why $3x + 4y \leq 24$ and $5x + 3y \leq 30$.

b Draw these two inequalities on the same diagram.

c The profit on any house is £4000. What combination of houses should be built to give the most profit.

12 Julie is organising her wedding cars. She needs to take 20 people to the church. The local car-hire company has two limousines. The Canardley holds 4 people and costs £50 to hire. The Rapture holds 5 people and costs £60 to hire. Her budget for car hire is £300. The car-hire company has only four Canardleys and three Raptures. Julie hires x Canardleys and y Raptures.

a Write down four inequalities that are true for the above information.

b Draw these four inequalities on the same diagram.

c Julie wants to spend as little as possible. What combination does this?

Examination questions

1 The school hall seats a maximum audience of 200 people for performances. Tickets for the school concert cost £2 or £3 each. The school needs to raise at least £450 from this concert. It is decided that the number of £3 tickets must not be greater than twice the number of £2 tickets. There are x tickets at £2 each and y tickets at £3 each.

a Explain why

i $x + y \leq 200$ **ii** $2x + 3y \geq 450$ **iii** $y \leq 2x$

The graphs of $x + y = 200$, $2x + 3y = 450$ and $y = 2x$ are drawn on the grid.

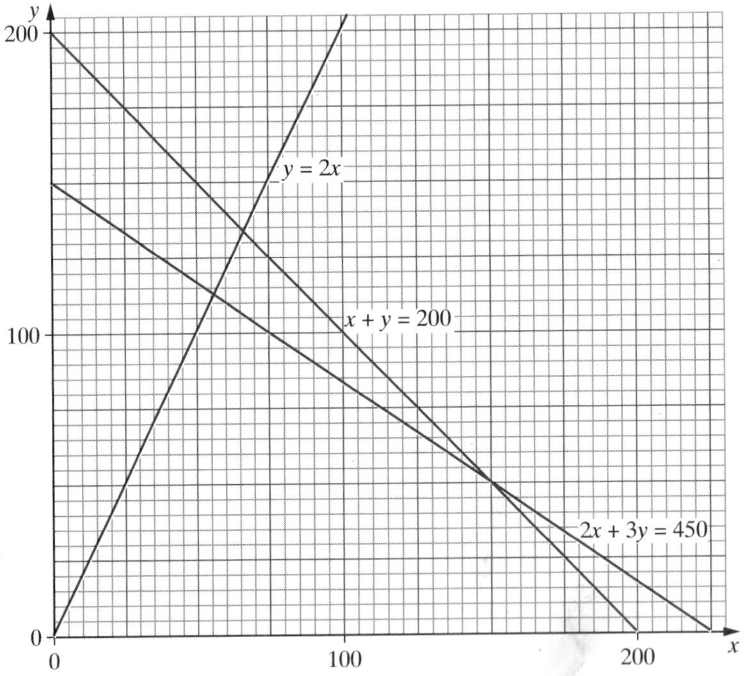

b Leave unshaded the region of the grid which satisfies all three inequalities.

c **i** Hence find the number of £2 and £3 tickets which should be sold to obtain the maximum profit.

ii State this profit.

NEAB, Question 14, Paper 2R, June 1995

2 **a** Draw a pair of graphs to solve the simultaneous equations

$$y = x + 1$$
$$3x + 2y = 12$$

b $s = y - 1$ and $t = 3x + 2y$

Find the values of s and t at the points (2, 1) and (4, 6).

c On your diagram for part **a**, show the region for which

$x \geq 0$ $y \leq 0$ $y - x \leq 1$ $3x + 2y \leq 12$

MEG, Question 1, Specimen Paper 6, 1998

3 Write down the three inequalities which define the triangular region ABC.

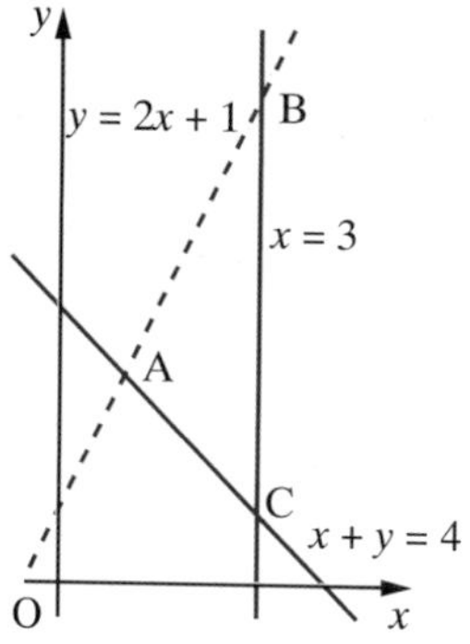

MEG, Question 7, Specimen Paper 5, 1998

4 **a** On a pair of axes, leave unshaded the region represented by the following inequalities.

i $x \leq 3$ **ii** $y > 1$ **iii** $2y - 2x \leq 1$

b Write down the co-ordinates of all the points whose co-ordinates are integers and lie in the region which satisfy all the inequalities in part **a**.

WJEC, Question 17, Specimen Paper H1, 1998

5 **a** Write down the equations of the three lines marked (i), (ii) and (iii) on the grid.

b Write down three inequalities necessary to describe the region ABC.

(p, q) are the co-ordinates of any point of the region ABC.

c Find the values of p and q which give the maximum value of $2p + 5q$.

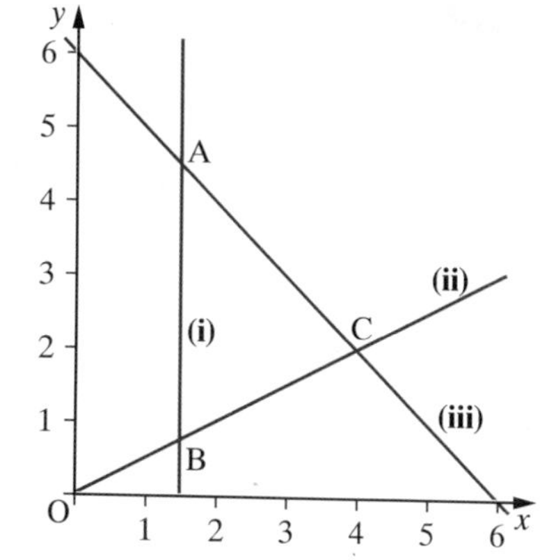

NEAB, Question 17, Paper 1R, November 1995

6 The firm Leisure Breaks is opening a new site for caravans and tents. Each caravan plot requires 100 m^2 of land and each tent plot 50 m^2. There is a total of 1000 m^2 of land available. For each caravan rented, the firm makes £3 profit per night and for each tent £7 per night. To cover costs, the firm needs to make at least £42 profit per night. The local council say that there can be no more than twice as many tents as caravans. Let c represent the number of caravan plots occupied and t the number of tent plots occupied.

a Write down three inequalities which must be true, and represent these on a diagram. By shading the regions not required, find the region that satisfies all of these conditions.

b Find the maximum value of $c + t$, subject to all three conditions, where c and t are integers.

SEG, Question 16, Specimen Paper 16, 1998

7 You are organising a school trip for 560 people, both staff and pupils. You need a coach firm to provide the transport. The local coach firm has two types of coach.

Double decker	*Capacity* 60 people	*Cost* £50 per hour	*Coaches available* 6
Single decker	*Capacity* 40 people	*Cost* £40 per hour	*Coaches available* 15

a It is decided to hire x double-deck coaches and y single-deck coaches. Explain why x and y must satisfy

$$60x + 40y \geq 560$$

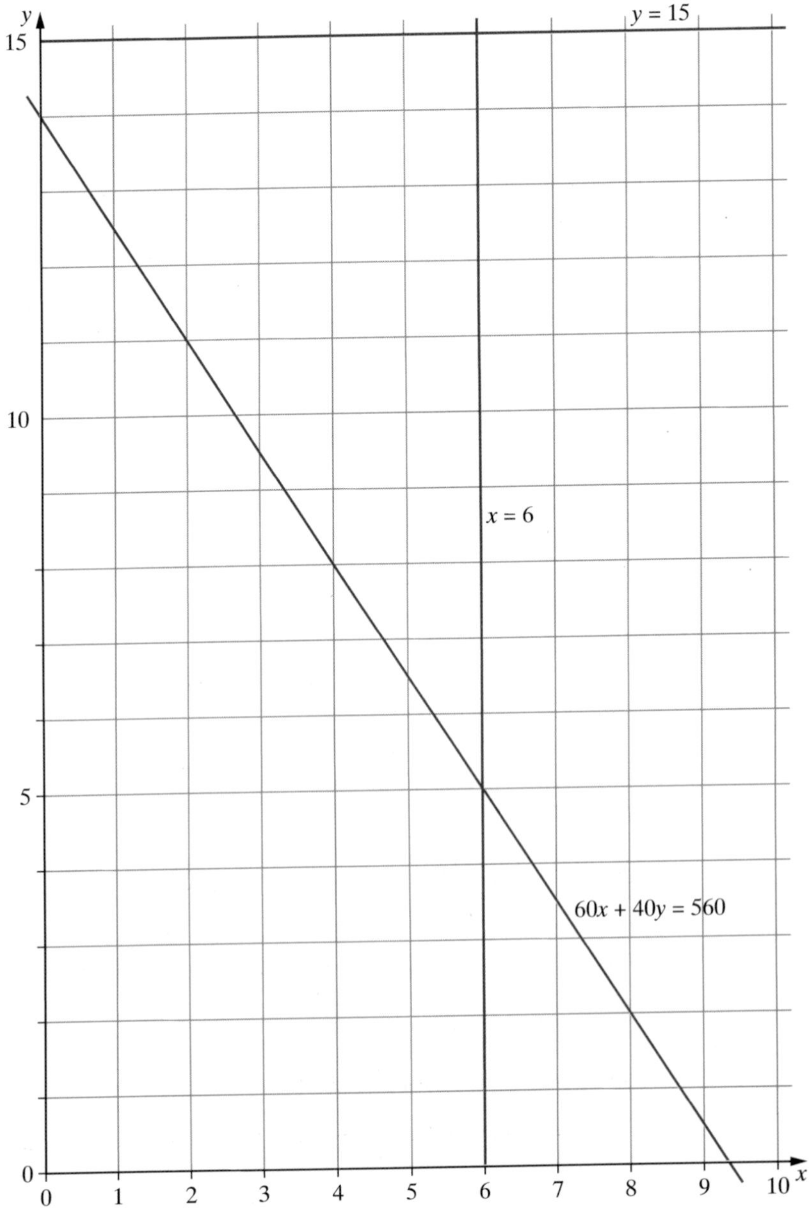

b The lines $x = 6$, $y = 15$ and $60x + 40y = 560$ are drawn on the axes. Identify the feasible region if

$$0 \leq x \leq 6 \qquad 0 \leq y \leq 15 \quad \text{and} \quad 60x + 40y \geq 560$$

c The total cost is given by

$$C = 50x + 40y$$

Use the graph to find the values of x and y which satisfy all the inequalities and give a minimum value to C. *SEG, Question 20, Paper 6, November 1994*

8 A council decides to buy some boats for use on their boating lake. They decide to buy at least 4, but not more than 8 canoes and at least 3 dinghies. The maximum number of boats allowed on the lake is 14.

a Using c as the number of canoes and d as the number of dinghies, write down four inequalities which represent the conditions given above.

b Illustrate these four regions on the same grid in order to show, by not shading, the region which gives the possible combinations of canoes and dinghies.

c The council are prepared to spend a maximum of £1000 on these boats. Each canoe will cost £100 and each dinghy £80. Use the graphs to find the largest total number of boats they can buy.

Summary

How well do you grade yourself?

To gain a grade **B**, you need to be able graphically to represent a region that satisfies an inequality.

To gain a grade **A**, you need to be able graphically to represent a region that simultaneously satisfies more than one inequality.

To gain a grade **A***, you need to be able to translate a problem into inequalities and give the feasible region.

What you should know after you have worked through Chapter 21

- How to create algebraic inequalities from verbal statements.
- How to graph inequalities.
- How to depict a region satisfying more than one inequality.
- How to solve practical problems through linear programming techniques.

22 Vectors

This chapter is going to ... extend your ideas about vectors. It will show you how vectors can be used in geometry and how they can be applied in the solution of practical problems.

What you should already know

- How column vectors are used to describe translations.
- Pythagoras and trigonometry.
- Sine and cosine rules.

Definition of a vector

A **vector** is a quantity which has both **magnitude** (size) and **direction**. It can be represented by a straight line which is drawn in the direction of the vector and whose length represents the magnitude of the vector. Usually, the line includes an arrowhead.

Four examples of vectors are

- Velocity: such as 550 mph on a bearing of 032°.
- Acceleration: such as 300 m/s^2 along x-axis.
- Displacement: such as 7 km due west.
- Force: such as 270 N acting vertically downwards.

A quantity which is completely described by its magnitude, and has no direction associated with it, is called a **scalar**. The mass of a bus (10 tonnes) is an example of a scalar. Another example is a linear measure, such as 25.4 mm.

Multiplying a vector by a number (scalar) **alters** its **magnitude** (length) but **not** its **direction**. For example, the vector 2**a** is twice as long as the vector **a**, but in the same direction.

The negative of a vector has the **same magnitude** as the vector but **opposite direction**.

Notation In printed works, a vector is usually represented by a bold single letter (for example, **a**) or as a line between two points with an arrow above (for example, $\overrightarrow{XY}$).

Adding and subtracting vectors

We can take any two vectors **a** and **b** which are non-parallel (so-called **independent vectors**) and obtain the following diagrams.

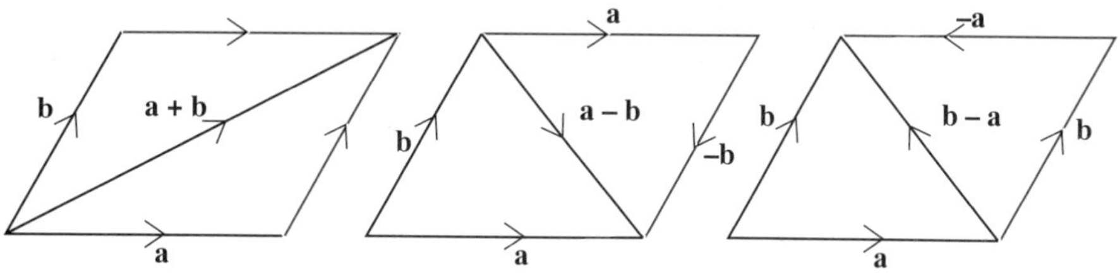

Look at the parallelogram grid below.

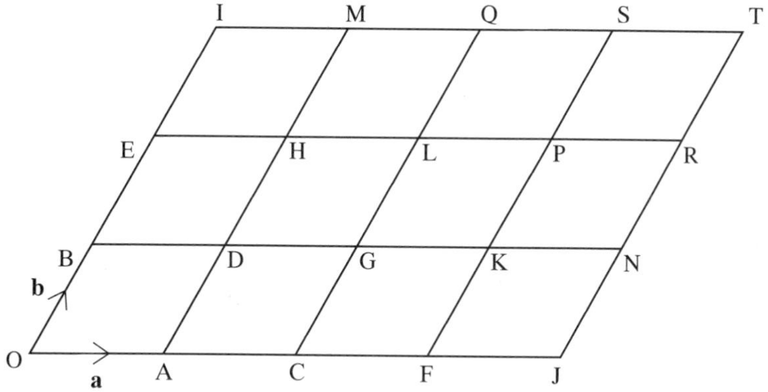

a and **b** are two independent vectors that form the **basis** of this grid. It is possible to define the position, with reference to O, of any point on this grid by a vector expressed in terms of **a** and **b**. Such a vector is called a **position vector**.

For example, the position vector of K is $\overrightarrow{OK}$ or **k** = 3**a** + **b**, the position vector of E is $\overrightarrow{OE}$ or **e** = 2**b**. The vector $\overrightarrow{HT}$ = 3**a** + **b**, the vector $\overrightarrow{MK}$ = 2**a** – 2**b**, and the vector $\overrightarrow{TP}$ = –**a** – **b**.

Note $\overrightarrow{OK}$ and $\overrightarrow{HT}$ are called **equal vectors** because they have exactly the **same length** and are in the **same direction**. $\overrightarrow{MK}$ and $\overrightarrow{PN}$ are **parallel vectors** but $\overrightarrow{MK}$ is twice the magnitude of $\overrightarrow{PN}$.

Example

a Using the grid above, state the following vectors.

i $\overrightarrow{BH}$	**ii** $\overrightarrow{HP}$	**iii** $\overrightarrow{GT}$
iv $\overrightarrow{TI}$	**v** $\overrightarrow{FH}$	**vi** $\overrightarrow{BQ}$

b What is the relationship between the following vectors?

i $\overrightarrow{BH}$ and $\overrightarrow{GT}$	**ii** $\overrightarrow{BQ}$ and $\overrightarrow{GT}$	**iii** $\overrightarrow{HP}$ and $\overrightarrow{TI}$

c Explain why the vectors $\overrightarrow{BH}$ and $\overrightarrow{BQ}$ show that B, H and Q lie on the same straight line.

a **i** $\mathbf{a} + \mathbf{b}$ **ii** $2\mathbf{a}$ **iii** $2\mathbf{a} + 2\mathbf{b}$

iv $-4\mathbf{a}$ **v** $-2\mathbf{a} + 2\mathbf{b}$ **vi** $2\mathbf{a} + 2\mathbf{b}$

b **i** $\overrightarrow{BH}$ and $\overrightarrow{GT}$ are parallel and $\overrightarrow{GT}$ is twice the length of $\overrightarrow{BH}$.

ii $\overrightarrow{BQ}$ and $\overrightarrow{GT}$ are equal.

iii $\overrightarrow{HP}$ and $\overrightarrow{TI}$ are in opposite direction and $\overrightarrow{TI}$ is twice the length of $\overrightarrow{HP}$.

c $\overrightarrow{BH}$ and $\overrightarrow{BQ}$ are parallel and start at the same point B. Therefore, they must lie on the same straight line.

Exercise 22A

1 On the grid below, $\overrightarrow{OA}$ is **a** and $\overrightarrow{OB}$ is **b**.

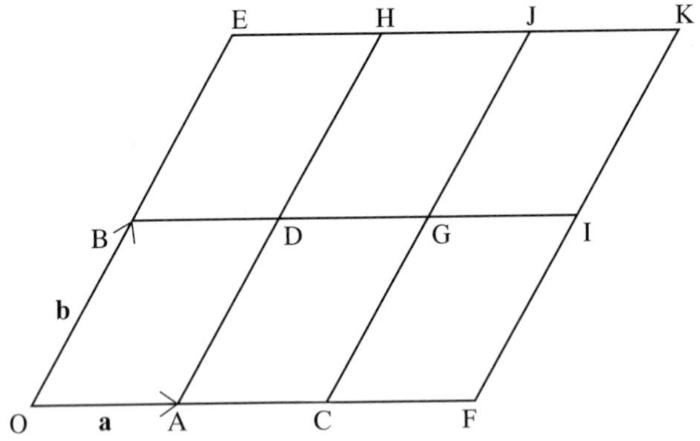

a Name three other vectors equivalent to **a**.

b Name three other vectors equivalent to **b**.

c Name three other vectors equivalent to –**a**.

d Name three other vectors equivalent to –**b**.

2 Using the same grid as in question **1**, give the following vectors in terms of **a** and **b**.

a $\overrightarrow{OC}$ **b** $\overrightarrow{OE}$ **c** $\overrightarrow{OD}$ **d** $\overrightarrow{OG}$

e $\overrightarrow{OJ}$ **f** $\overrightarrow{OH}$ **g** $\overrightarrow{AG}$ **h** $\overrightarrow{AK}$

i $\overrightarrow{BK}$ **j** $\overrightarrow{DI}$ **k** $\overrightarrow{GJ}$ **l** $\overrightarrow{DK}$

3 a What do the answers to parts **2c** and **2g** tell you about the vectors $\overrightarrow{OD}$ and $\overrightarrow{AG}$?

b On the grid in question **1**, there are three vectors equivalent to $\overrightarrow{OG}$. Name all three.

4 a What do the answers to parts **2c** and **2e** tell you about vectors $\overrightarrow{OD}$ and $\overrightarrow{OJ}$?

b On the grid in question **1**, there is one other vector that is twice the size of $\overrightarrow{OD}$. Which is it?

c On the grid in question **1**, there are three vectors that are three times the size of $\overrightarrow{OA}$. Name all three.

5

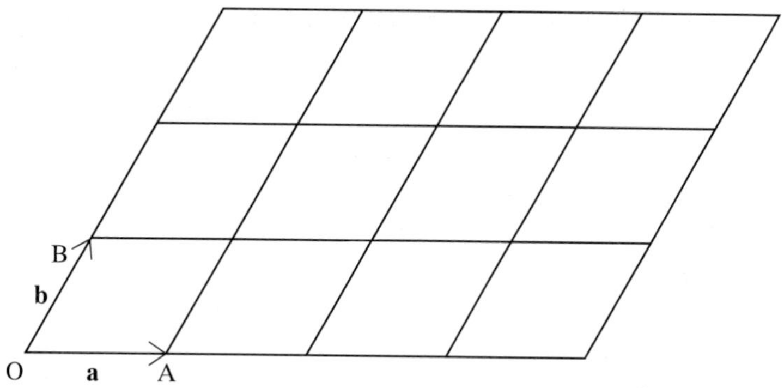

On a copy of the grid above, mark on the points C to P such that

a $\overrightarrow{OC} = 2\mathbf{a} + 3\mathbf{b}$ **b** $\overrightarrow{OD} = 2\mathbf{a} + \mathbf{b}$ **c** $\overrightarrow{OE} = \mathbf{a} + 2\mathbf{b}$

d $\overrightarrow{OF} = 3\mathbf{b}$ **e** $\overrightarrow{OG} = 4\mathbf{a}$ **f** $\overrightarrow{OH} = 4\mathbf{a} + 2\mathbf{b}$

g $\overrightarrow{OI} = 3\mathbf{a} + 3\mathbf{b}$ **h** $\overrightarrow{OJ} = \mathbf{a} + \mathbf{b}$ **i** $\overrightarrow{OK} = 2\mathbf{a} + 2\mathbf{b}$

j $\overrightarrow{OM} = 2\mathbf{a} + \frac{3}{2}\mathbf{b}$ **k** $\overrightarrow{ON} = \frac{1}{2}\mathbf{a} + 2\mathbf{b}$ **l** $\overrightarrow{OP} = \frac{5}{2}\mathbf{a} + \frac{3}{2}\mathbf{b}$

6 a Look at the diagram in question **5**. What can you say about the points O, J, K and I?

b How could you tell this by looking at the vectors for parts **5g**, **5h** and **5i**?

c There is another point on the same straight line as O and D. Which is it?

d Complete these statements and then mark the appropriate points on the diagram you drew for question **5**.

i The point Q is on the straight line ODH. The vector $\overrightarrow{OQ}$ is given by

$\overrightarrow{OQ} = \mathbf{a} + \ldots\ldots\ \mathbf{b}$

ii The point R is on the straight line ODH. The vector $\overrightarrow{OR}$ is given by

$\overrightarrow{OR} = 3\mathbf{a} + \ldots\ldots\ \mathbf{b}$

e Complete the following statement.

Any point on the line ODH has a vector $n\mathbf{a}$ + …… **b**, where n is any number.

7 On the grid below, $\overrightarrow{OA}$ is **a** and $\overrightarrow{OB}$ is **b**.

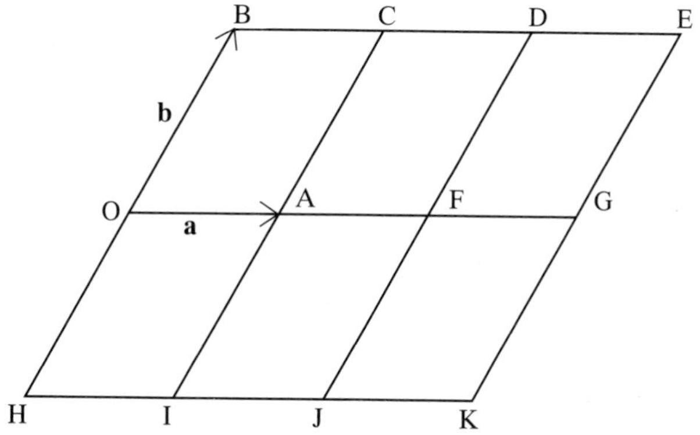

Give the following vectors in terms of **a** and **b**.

a $\overrightarrow{OH}$ **b** $\overrightarrow{OK}$ **c** $\overrightarrow{OJ}$ **d** $\overrightarrow{OI}$

e $\overrightarrow{OC}$ **f** $\overrightarrow{CO}$ **g** $\overrightarrow{AK}$ **h** $\overrightarrow{DI}$

i $\overrightarrow{JE}$ **j** $\overrightarrow{AB}$ **k** $\overrightarrow{CK}$ **l** $\overrightarrow{DK}$

8 a What do the answers to parts **7e** and **7f** tell you about the vectors $\overrightarrow{OC}$ and $\overrightarrow{CO}$?

b On the grid in question **7**, there are five other vectors 'opposite' to $\overrightarrow{OC}$. Name at least three.

9 a What do the answers to parts **7j** and **7k** tell you about vectors $\overrightarrow{AB}$ and $\overrightarrow{CK}$?

b On the grid in question **7**, there are two vectors that are twice the size of $\overrightarrow{AB}$ and in the opposite direction. Name both.

c On the grid in question **7**, there are three vectors that are three times the size of $\overrightarrow{OA}$ and in the opposite direction. Name all three.

10 On a copy of the grid below, mark on the points C to P such that

a $\overrightarrow{OC} = 2\mathbf{a} - \mathbf{b}$ **b** $\overrightarrow{OD} = 2\mathbf{a} + \mathbf{b}$ **c** $\overrightarrow{OE} = \mathbf{a} - 2\mathbf{b}$

d $\overrightarrow{OF} = \mathbf{b} - 2\mathbf{a}$ **e** $\overrightarrow{OG} = -\mathbf{a}$ **f** $\overrightarrow{OH} = -\mathbf{a} - 2\mathbf{b}$

g $\overrightarrow{OI} = 2\mathbf{a} - 2\mathbf{b}$ **h** $\overrightarrow{OJ} = -\mathbf{a} + \mathbf{b}$ **i** $\overrightarrow{OK} = -\mathbf{a} - \mathbf{b}$

j $\overrightarrow{OM} = -\mathbf{a} - \frac{3}{2}\mathbf{b}$ **k** $\overrightarrow{ON} = -\frac{1}{2}\mathbf{a} - 2\mathbf{b}$ **l** $\overrightarrow{OP} = \frac{3}{2}\mathbf{a} - \frac{3}{2}\mathbf{b}$

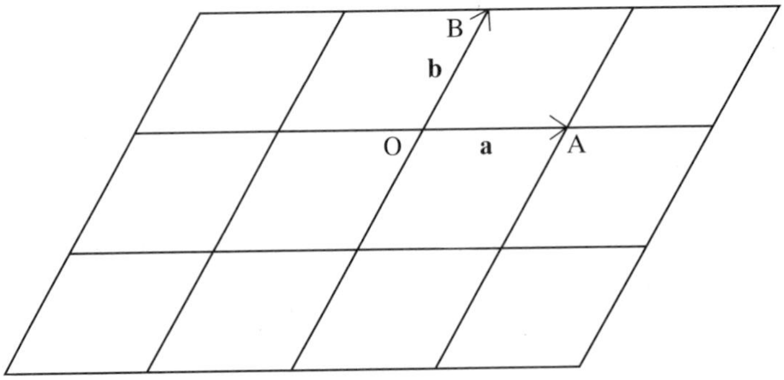

11 The grid below shows the vectors $\overrightarrow{OA} = \mathbf{a}$ and $\overrightarrow{OB} = \mathbf{b}$.

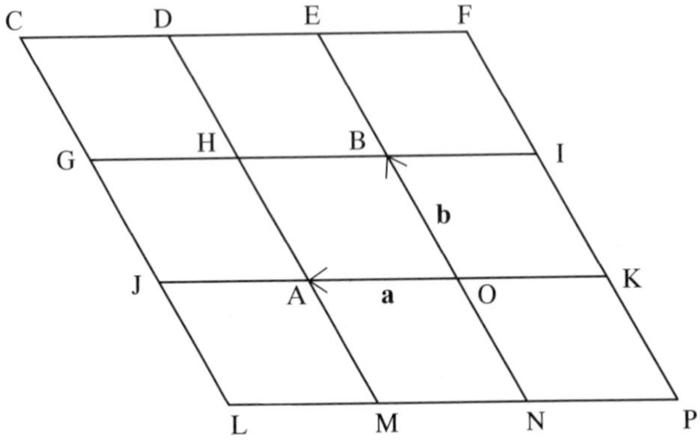

a Name three vectors equivalent to **a** + **b**.

b Name three vectors equivalent to **a** – **b**.

c Name three vectors equivalent to **b** – **a**.

d Name three vectors equivalent to –**a** – **b**.

e Name three vectors equivalent to 2**a** – **b**.

f Name three vectors equivalent to 2**b** – **a**.

g Name any one vector equivalent to

i 3**a** – **b**	**ii** 2(**a** + **b**)	**iii** 3**a** – 2**b**
iv 3(**a** – **b**)	**v** 3(**b** – **a**)	**vi** 3(**a** + **b**)
vii –3(**a** + **b**)	**viii** 2**a** + **b** – 3**a** – 2**b**	**ix** 2(2**a** + **b**) – 3(**a** – **b**)

12 The points P, Q and R lie on a straight line. The vector $\overrightarrow{PQ}$ is 2**a** + **b**, where **a** and **b** are vectors. Which of the following vectors could be the vector $\overrightarrow{PR}$ and which could not be the vector $\overrightarrow{PR}$ (two of each).

a 2**a** + 2**b** **b** 4**a** + 2**b** **c** 2**a** – **b** **d** –6**a** – 3**b**

13 The points P, Q and R lie on a straight line. The vector $\overrightarrow{PQ}$ is 3**a** – **b**, where **a** and **b** are vectors.

a Write down any other vector that could represent $\overrightarrow{PR}$.

b How can you tell from the vector $\overrightarrow{PS}$ that S lies on the same straight line as P, Q and R?

Vector geometry

Vectors can be used to prove many results in geometry, as the following examples show.

Example 1 In the diagram, $\overrightarrow{OA}$ = **a** , $\overrightarrow{OB}$ = **b**, and $\overrightarrow{BC}$ = 1.5**a**. M is the mid-point of $\overrightarrow{BC}$, N is the mid-point of $\overrightarrow{AC}$ and P is the mid-point of $\overrightarrow{OB}$.

a Find in terms of **a** and **b** the vectors

i $\overrightarrow{AC}$ **ii** $\overrightarrow{OM}$ **iii** $\overrightarrow{BN}$

b Prove that $\overrightarrow{PN}$ is parallel to $\overrightarrow{OA}$.

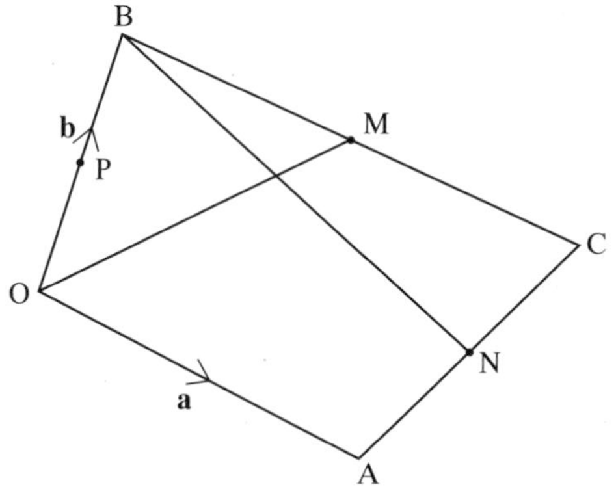

a i We have to get from A to C in terms of vectors that we know: for example,

$$\overrightarrow{AC} = \overrightarrow{AO} + \overrightarrow{OB} + \overrightarrow{BC}$$

Now $\overrightarrow{AO} = -\overrightarrow{OA}$, so we can write

$$\overrightarrow{AC} = -\mathbf{a} + \mathbf{b} + \tfrac{3}{2}\mathbf{a}$$

$$= \tfrac{1}{2}\mathbf{a} + \mathbf{b}$$

Note that the letters 'match up' as we go from A to C, and that the negative of a vector represented by any pair of letters is formed by reversing the letters.

ii In the same way

$$\overrightarrow{OM} = \overrightarrow{OB} + \overrightarrow{BM} = \overrightarrow{OB} + \tfrac{1}{2}\overrightarrow{BC}$$
$$= \mathbf{b} + \tfrac{1}{2}(\tfrac{3}{2}\mathbf{a})$$

$$= \tfrac{3}{4}\mathbf{a} + \mathbf{b}$$

iii $\overrightarrow{BN} = \overrightarrow{BC} + \overrightarrow{CN} = \overrightarrow{BC} - \tfrac{1}{2}\overrightarrow{AC}$

$$= \tfrac{3}{2}\mathbf{a} - \tfrac{1}{2}(\tfrac{3}{2}\mathbf{a} + \mathbf{b})$$
$$= \tfrac{3}{2}\mathbf{a} - \tfrac{3}{4}\mathbf{a} - \tfrac{1}{2}\mathbf{b}$$
$$= \tfrac{3}{4}\mathbf{a} - \tfrac{1}{2}\mathbf{b}$$

Note that if we did this as $\overrightarrow{BN} = \overrightarrow{BO} + \overrightarrow{OA} + \overrightarrow{AN}$, we would get the same result.

b $\overrightarrow{PN} = \overrightarrow{PO} + \overrightarrow{OA} + \overrightarrow{AN}$

$$= \tfrac{1}{2}(-\mathbf{b}) + \mathbf{a} + \tfrac{1}{2}(\tfrac{1}{2}\mathbf{a} + \mathbf{b})$$
$$= -\tfrac{1}{2}\mathbf{b} + \mathbf{a} + \tfrac{1}{4}\mathbf{a} + \tfrac{1}{2}\mathbf{b}$$
$$= \tfrac{5}{4}\mathbf{a}$$

$\overrightarrow{PN}$ is a multiple of **a** only, so must be parallel to $\overrightarrow{OA}$.

Example 2 OACB is a parallelogram. $\overrightarrow{OA}$ is represented by the vector **a**. $\overrightarrow{OB}$ is represented by the vector **b**. P is a point $\tfrac{2}{3}$ the distance from O to C, and M is the mid-point of $\overrightarrow{AC}$. Show that B, P and M lie on the same straight line.

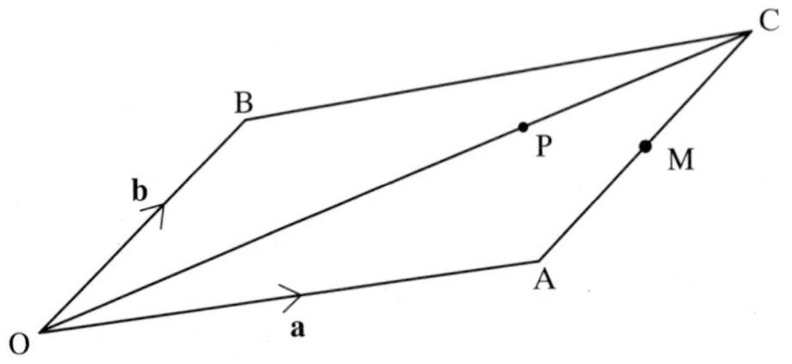

$\overrightarrow{OC} = \overrightarrow{OA} + \overrightarrow{AC} = \mathbf{a} + \mathbf{b}$

$\overrightarrow{OP} = \frac{2}{3}\overrightarrow{OC} = \frac{2}{3}\mathbf{a} + \frac{2}{3}\mathbf{b}$

$\overrightarrow{OM} = \overrightarrow{OA} + \overrightarrow{AM} = \overrightarrow{OA} + \frac{1}{2}\overrightarrow{AC} = \mathbf{a} + \frac{1}{2}\mathbf{b}$

$\overrightarrow{BP} = \overrightarrow{BO} + \overrightarrow{OP} = -\mathbf{b} + \frac{2}{3}\mathbf{a} + \frac{2}{3}\mathbf{b} = \frac{2}{3}\mathbf{a} - \frac{1}{3}\mathbf{b}$

$\overrightarrow{BM} = \overrightarrow{BO} + \overrightarrow{OM} = -\mathbf{b} + \mathbf{a} + \frac{1}{2}\mathbf{b} = \mathbf{a} - \frac{1}{2}\mathbf{b}$

Therefore, $\overrightarrow{BM}$ is a multiple of $\overrightarrow{BP}$ ($\overrightarrow{BM} = \frac{3}{2}\overrightarrow{BP}$).

Therefore, $\overrightarrow{BP}$ and $\overrightarrow{BM}$ are parallel and as they have a common point, B, they must lie on the same straight line.

Exercise 22B

1 The diagram shows the vectors $\overrightarrow{OA} = \mathbf{a}$ and $\overrightarrow{OB} = \mathbf{b}$. M is the mid-point of AB.

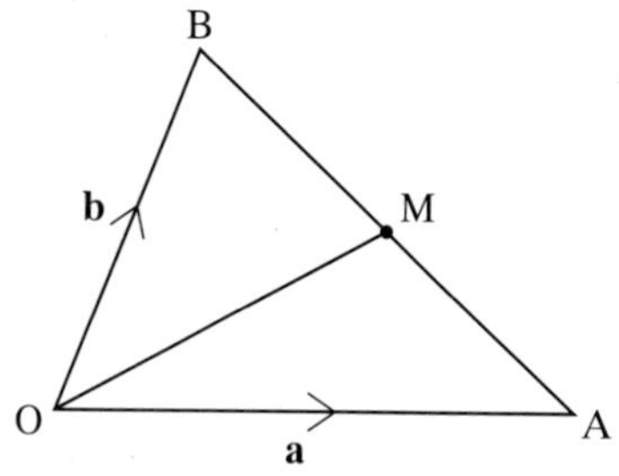

a **i** Work out the vector $\overrightarrow{AB}$.
  ii Work out the vector $\overrightarrow{AM}$.
  iii Explain why $\overrightarrow{OM} = \overrightarrow{OA} + \overrightarrow{AM}$.
  iv Using your answers to parts **ii** and **iii**, work out $\overrightarrow{OM}$ in terms of **a** and **b**.

b **i** Work out the vector $\overrightarrow{BA}$.
  ii Work out the vector $\overrightarrow{BM}$.
  iii Explain why $\overrightarrow{OM} = \overrightarrow{OB} + \overrightarrow{BM}$.
  iv Using your answers to parts **ii** and **iii**, work out $\overrightarrow{OM}$ in terms of **a** and **b**.

c Copy the diagram above and show on it the vector **a** + **b**.

d Describe in geometrical terms the position of M in relation to $\overrightarrow{OA}$ and $\overrightarrow{OB}$.

2 The diagram shows the vectors $\overrightarrow{OA} = \mathbf{a}$ and $\overrightarrow{OC} = -\mathbf{b}$. N is the mid-point of $\overrightarrow{AC}$.

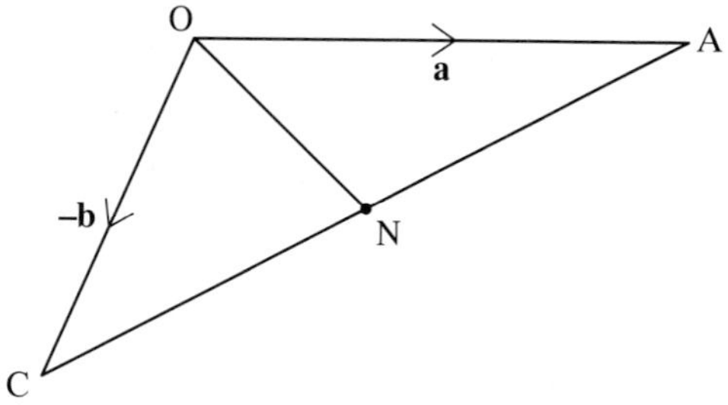

a **i** Work out the vector $\overrightarrow{AC}$.
  ii Work out the vector $\overrightarrow{AN}$.
  iii Explain why $\overrightarrow{ON} = \overrightarrow{OA} + \overrightarrow{AN}$.
  iv Using your answers to parts **ii** and **iii**, work out $\overrightarrow{ON}$ in terms of **a** and **b**.

b **i** Work out the vector $\overrightarrow{CA}$.
  ii Work out the vector $\overrightarrow{CN}$.
  iii Explain why $\overrightarrow{ON} = \overrightarrow{OC} + \overrightarrow{CN}$.
  iv Using your answers to parts **ii** and **iii**, work out $\overrightarrow{ON}$ in terms of **a** and **b**.

c Copy the diagram above and show on it the vector **a** – **b**.

d Describe in geometrical terms the position of N in relation to $\overrightarrow{OA}$ and $\overrightarrow{OC}$.

3 Copy this diagram and on it draw vectors that represent

a $\mathbf{a} + \mathbf{b}$ **b** $\mathbf{a} - \mathbf{b}$

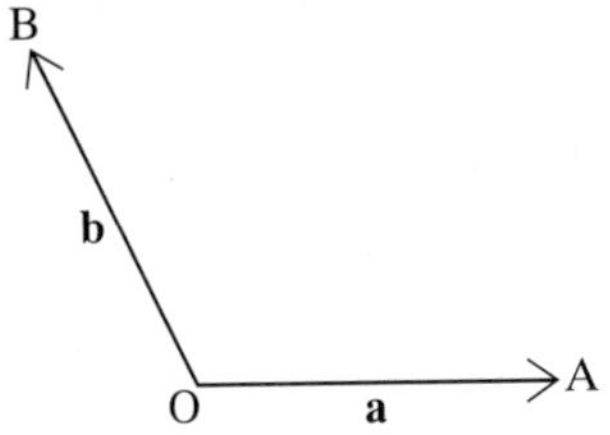

4 The diagram shows the vectors $\overrightarrow{OA} = \mathbf{a}$ and $\overrightarrow{OB} = \mathbf{b}$. The point C divides the line $\overrightarrow{AB}$ in the ratio 1:2 (i.e. $\overrightarrow{AC}$ is $\frac{1}{3}$ the distance from A to B).

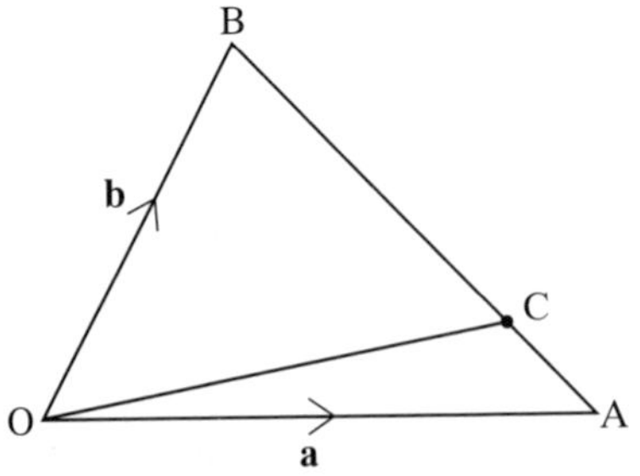

a i Work out the vector $\overrightarrow{AB}$.

ii Work out the vector $\overrightarrow{AC}$.

iii Work out the vector $\overrightarrow{OC}$ in terms of **a** and **b**.

b If C now divides the line $\overrightarrow{AB}$ in the ratio 1:3 (i.e. AC is $\frac{1}{4}$ the distance from A to B), write down the vector that represents $\overrightarrow{OC}$.

5 The diagram shows the vectors $\overrightarrow{OA} = \mathbf{a}$ and $\overrightarrow{OB} = \mathbf{b}$.

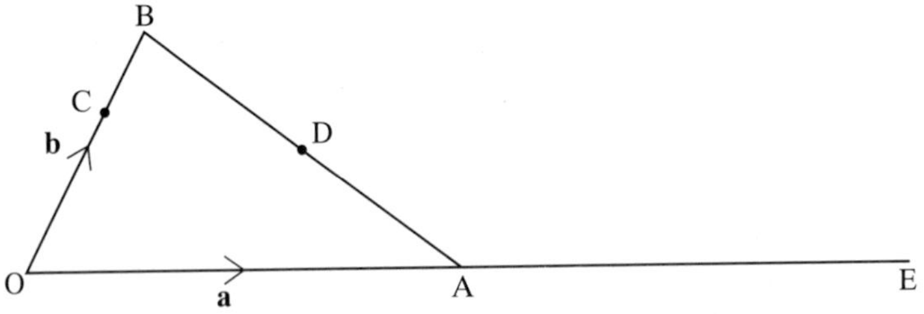

The point C divides $\overrightarrow{AB}$ in the ratio 2:1 (i.e. AC is $\frac{2}{3}$ the distance from O to B, and the point E is such that $\overrightarrow{OE} = 2\,\overrightarrow{OA}$. D is the mid-point of AB.)

a Write down (or work out) these vectors in terms of **a** and **b**.

i $\overrightarrow{OC}$ **ii** $\overrightarrow{OD}$ **iii** $\overrightarrow{CO}$

b The vector $\overrightarrow{CD}$ can be written as $\overrightarrow{CD} = \overrightarrow{CO} + \overrightarrow{OD}$. Use this fact to work out $\overrightarrow{CD}$ in terms of **a** and **b**.

c Write down a similar rule to that in part **b** for the vector $\overrightarrow{DE}$. Use this rule to work out $\overrightarrow{DE}$ in terms of **a** and **b**.

d Explain why C, D and E lie on the same straight line.

6 ABCDEF is a regular hexagon. $\overrightarrow{AB}$ is represented by the vector **a**, and $\overrightarrow{BC}$ by the vector **b**.

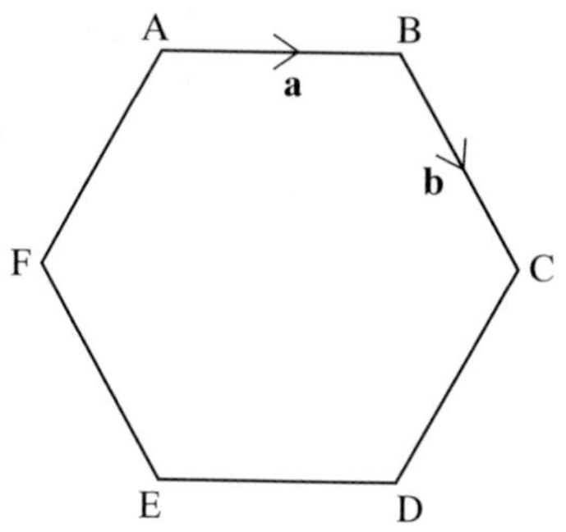

a By means of a diagram, or otherwise, explain why $\overrightarrow{CD} = \mathbf{b} - \mathbf{a}$.

b Express these vectors in terms of **a** and **b**.

i $\overrightarrow{DE}$ **ii** $\overrightarrow{EF}$ **iii** $\overrightarrow{FA}$

c Work out the answer to

$$\overrightarrow{AB} + \overrightarrow{BC} + \overrightarrow{CD} + \overrightarrow{DE} + \overrightarrow{EF} + \overrightarrow{FA}$$

Explain your answer.

d Express these vectors in terms of **a** and **b**.

i $\overrightarrow{AD}$ **ii** $\overrightarrow{BE}$ **iii** $\overrightarrow{CF}$

iv $\overrightarrow{AE}$ **v** $\overrightarrow{DF}$

7 ABCDEFGH is a regular octagon. $\overrightarrow{AB}$ is represented by the vector **a**, and $\overrightarrow{BC}$ by the vector **b**.

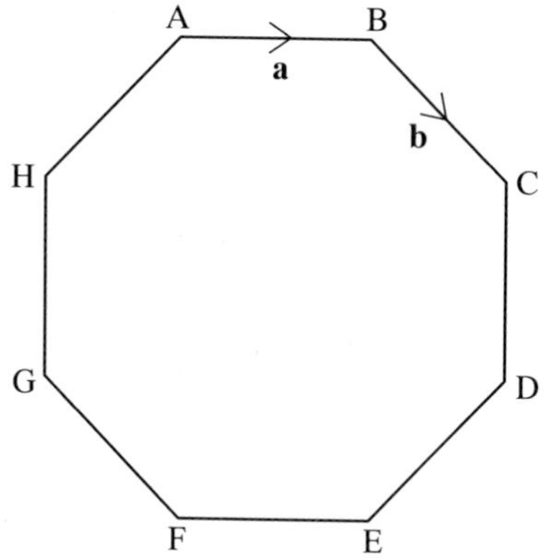

a By means of a diagram, or otherwise, explain why $\overrightarrow{CD} = \sqrt{2}\mathbf{b} - \mathbf{a}$.

b By means of a diagram, or otherwise, explain why $\overrightarrow{DE} = \mathbf{b} - \sqrt{2}\mathbf{a}$.

c Express the following vectors in terms of **a** and **b**.

i $\overrightarrow{EF}$ **ii** $\overrightarrow{FG}$

iii $\overrightarrow{GH}$ **iv** $\overrightarrow{HA}$

v $\overrightarrow{HC}$ **vi** $\overrightarrow{AD}$

vii $\overrightarrow{BE}$ **viii** $\overrightarrow{BF}$

8 In the quadrilateral OABC, M, N, P and Q are the mid-points of the sides as shown. $\overrightarrow{OA}$ is represented by the vector **a**, and $\overrightarrow{OC}$ by the vector **c**. The diagonal $\overrightarrow{OB}$ is represented by the vector **b**.

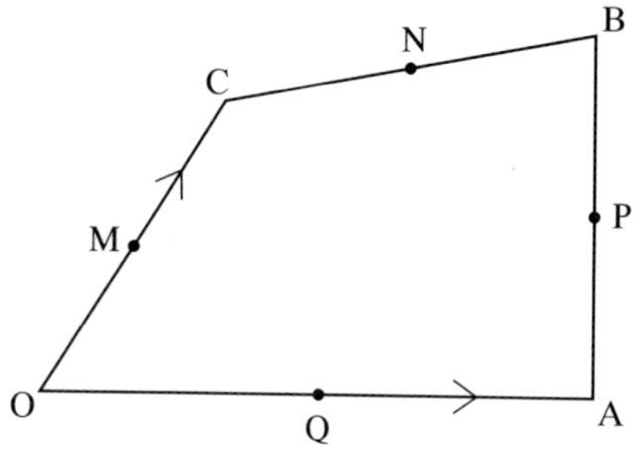

a Express these vectors in terms of **a**, **b** and **c**.

i $\overrightarrow{AB}$ **ii** $\overrightarrow{AP}$ **iii** $\overrightarrow{OP}$

Give your answers as simply as possible.

b i Express the vector $\overrightarrow{ON}$ in terms of **b** and **c**.

ii Hence express the vector $\overrightarrow{PN}$ in terms of **a** and **c**.

c i Express the vector $\overrightarrow{QM}$ in terms of **a** and **c**.

ii What relationship is there between $\overrightarrow{PN}$ and $\overrightarrow{QM}$?

iii What sort of quadrilateral is PNMQ?

d Prove that $\overrightarrow{AC} = 2\,\overrightarrow{QM}$.

9 In the triangle OAB, P is the mid-point of AB, X is the mid-point of OD, $\overrightarrow{OA} = \mathbf{a}$ and $\overrightarrow{OB} = \mathbf{b}$. Q is the point that divides OP in the ratio 2:1.

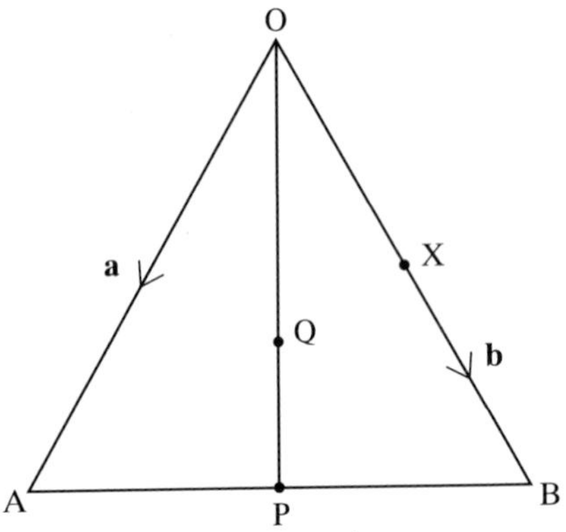

a Express in terms of **a** and **b** the vectors

i $\overrightarrow{AB}$ **ii** $\overrightarrow{AP}$

iii $\overrightarrow{OP}$ **iv** $\overrightarrow{OQ}$

v $\overrightarrow{AQ}$ **vi** $\overrightarrow{AX}$

b Deduce that $\overrightarrow{AX} = k\overrightarrow{AQ}$, where k is a scalar, and find the value of k.

10 L, M, N, P, Q, R are the mid-points of the line segments, as shown. $\overrightarrow{OA} = \mathbf{a}$, $\overrightarrow{OB} = \mathbf{b}$, $\overrightarrow{OC} = \mathbf{c}$.

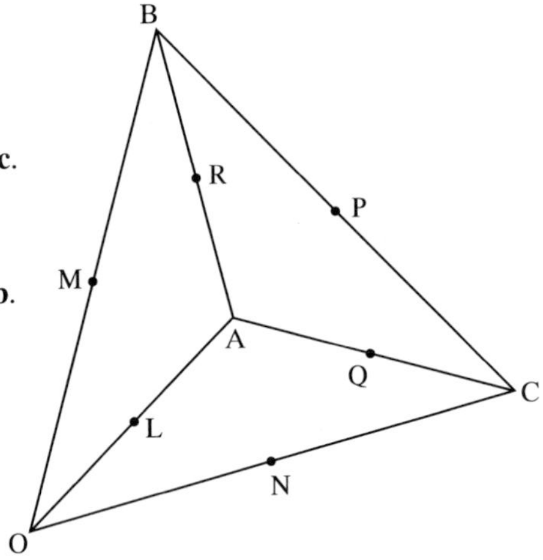

a Express these vectors in terms of **a** and **c**.

i $\overrightarrow{OL}$ **ii** $\overrightarrow{AC}$

iii $\overrightarrow{OQ}$ **iv** $\overrightarrow{LQ}$

b Express these vectors in terms of **a** and **b**.

i $\overrightarrow{LM}$ **ii** $\overrightarrow{QP}$

c Explain why the quadrilateral LMPQ is a parallelogram.

d Find two other sets of four points that form parallelograms.

11 In the diagram, $\overrightarrow{OA} = 2\mathbf{a} + 3\mathbf{b}$, $\overrightarrow{OB} = 3\mathbf{a} + 2\mathbf{b}$ and $\overrightarrow{OC} = 5\mathbf{a}$.

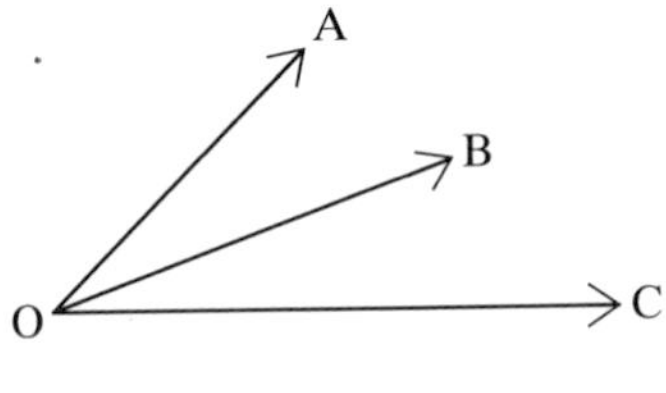

a Find the vectors $\overrightarrow{AB}$, $\overrightarrow{AC}$ and $\overrightarrow{BC}$.

b What do your results in part **a** show?

c Explain how you could have obtained the result in part **b** by working out only two of the vectors in part **a**.

12 OXYZ is a parallelogram. $\overrightarrow{OX} = \mathbf{x}$ and $\overrightarrow{OY} = \mathbf{y}$. $\overrightarrow{OP} = \frac{1}{3}\mathbf{x}$, $\overrightarrow{OQ} = \frac{1}{6}\mathbf{y}$ and $\overrightarrow{OR} = \frac{1}{4}\mathbf{y}$.

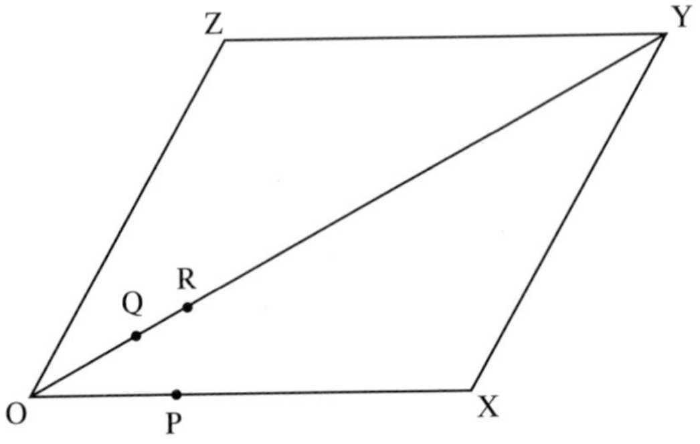

a Express these vectors in terms of **x** and **y**.

i $\overrightarrow{QP}$ **ii** $\overrightarrow{OZ}$

iii $\overrightarrow{ZR}$

b Show that $\overrightarrow{QP} = \frac{1}{6}\overrightarrow{ZX}$

c Show that $\overrightarrow{ZR}$ and $\overrightarrow{RP}$ are in the same direction and find the ratio of their lengths.

Vector force problems

Many physical quantities are vectors, so vector methods can be used to solve problems in which such quantities are involved, as the next two examples show.

Example 1 John sets off to swim across a river. He starts directly opposite a tree and he swims at 2 m/s at right angles to the bank. The current in the river is 4 m/s. If the river is 40 metres wide, how far down the bank from the tree will John be when he reaches the other side?

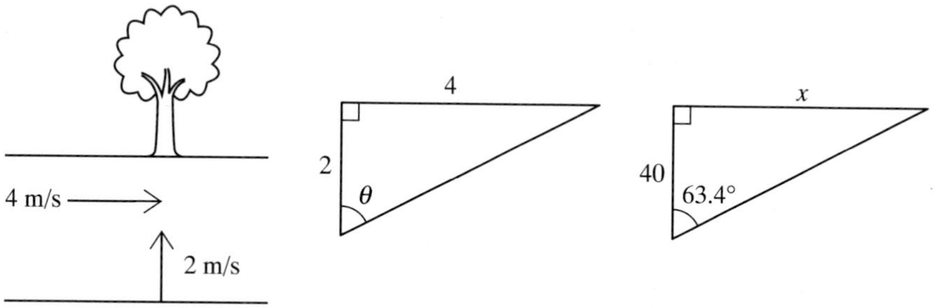

As John swims 2 m across the river, he is moved 4 m down the river by the current. This gives a triangle (above centre), in which

$$\tan \theta = \frac{4}{2} = 2$$

$$\Rightarrow \quad \theta = 63.4°$$

Let x be the distance downstream from the tree. Then

$$x = 40 \tan 63.4° = 80 \text{ m}$$

Example 2 Two boys are trying to drag a sledge along a straight path. They pull with forces of 50 N and 40 N at angles to the path of 20° and 30° respectively. Show on a sketch the resultant force and calculate the direction, relative to the path, in which the sledge moves. [N is the abbreviation for a unit of force called the newton.]

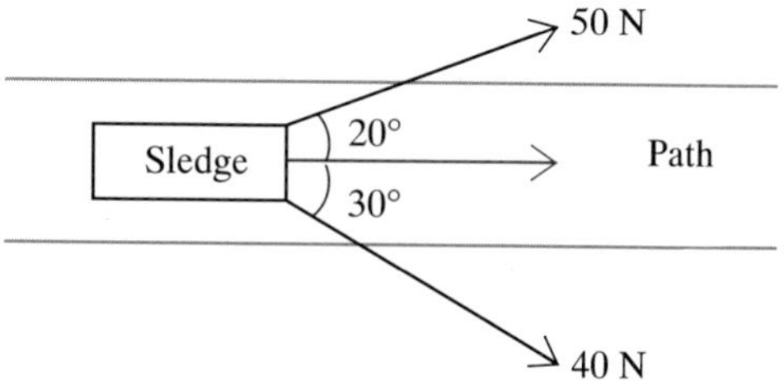

Putting the two forces together gives

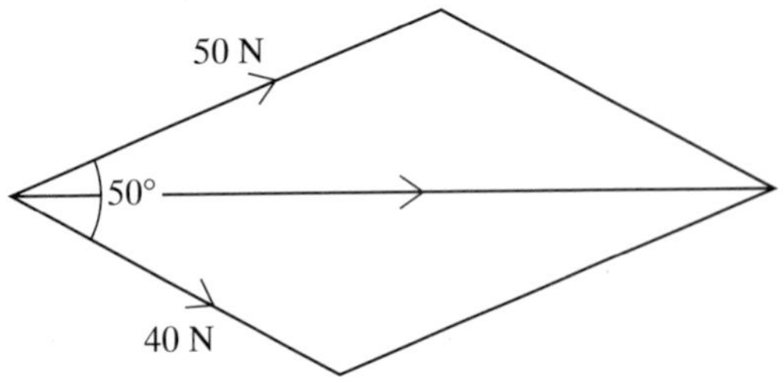

The resultant force is the diagonal of this parallelogram, which can be solved by the sine and cosine rules.

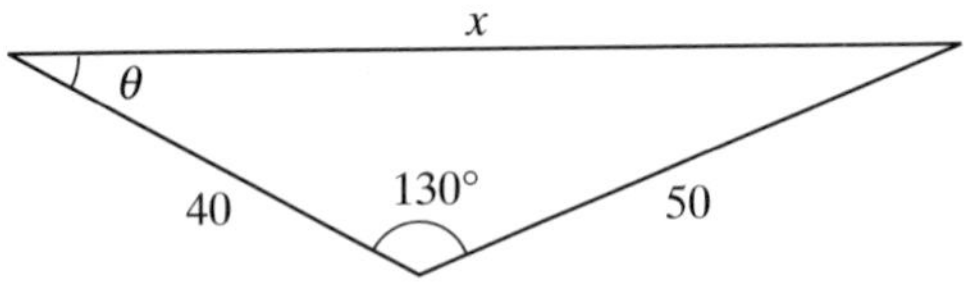

First, find the length, x, of the diagonal:

$$x^2 = 40^2 + 50^2 - 2 \times 40 \times 50 \times \cos 130°$$

$$\Rightarrow \quad x = 81.7 \text{ N}$$

Then, solve for θ:

$$\frac{\sin \theta}{50} = \frac{\sin 130°}{81.7}$$

$$\Rightarrow \quad \theta = \sin^{-1}\left(\frac{50 \sin 130°}{81.7}\right) = 28°$$

So, the direction, relative to path, in which the sledge moves is

$$30° - \theta = 30° - 28° = 2°$$

Exercise 22C

1 In the following diagrams, two forces are acting on a body. For each case, sketch the resultant force and find its direction in relation to force **A**.

a

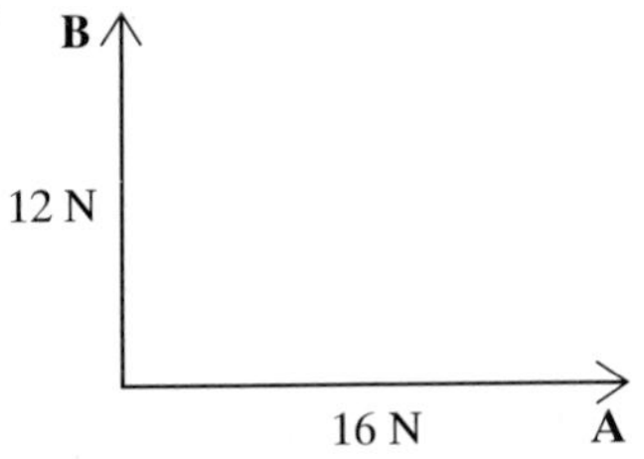

b

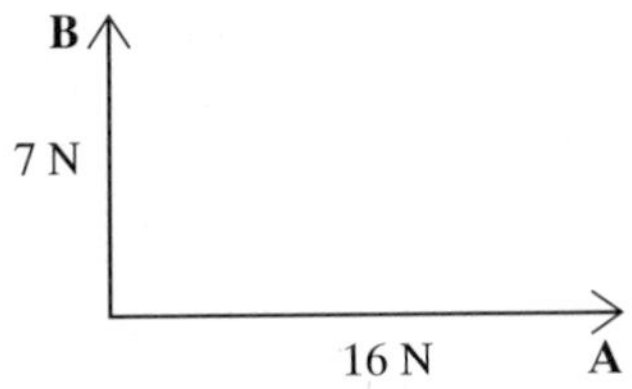

c

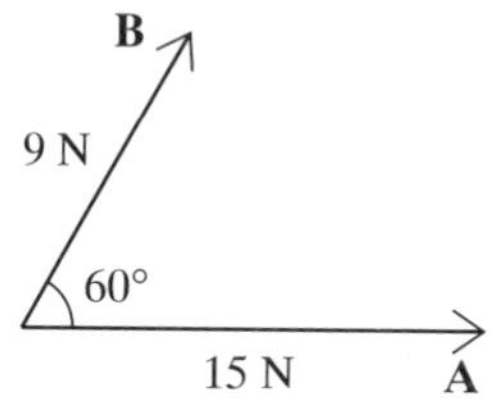

d

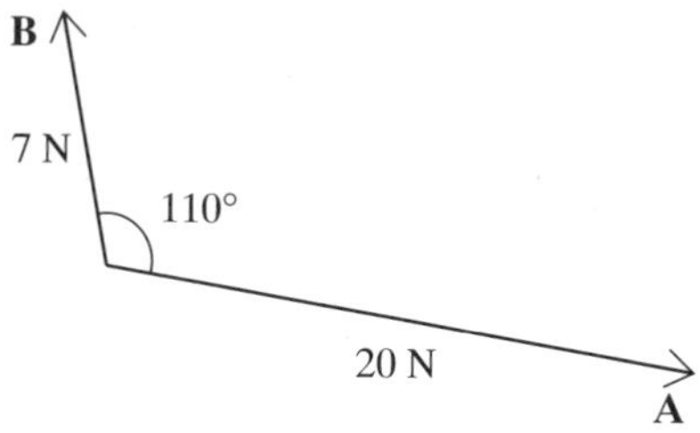

2 An aircraft is flying at 500 mph through a wind of 80 mph blowing from the west. It is being steered due north. What is the actual bearing of the aircraft?

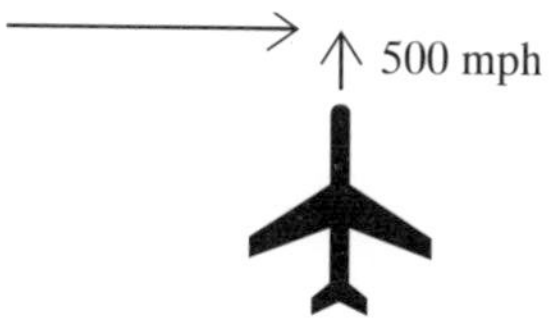

3 A boy swims across a river. He can swim at 4 m/s. The current is flowing at 2 m/s. In what direction should he swim to make sure that he goes straight across the river?

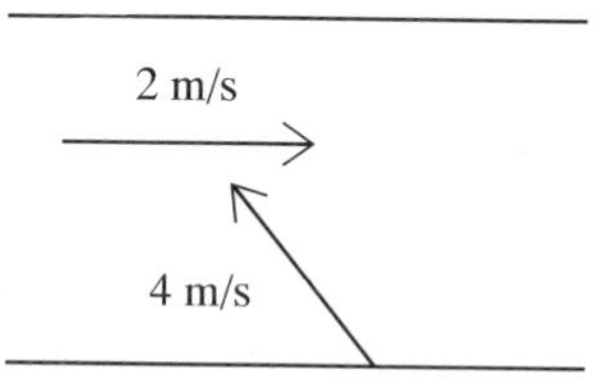

4 Two cranes are trying to lift a derailed locomotive that weighs 150 t. If they exert the forces shown in the diagram, will the locomotive be lifted?

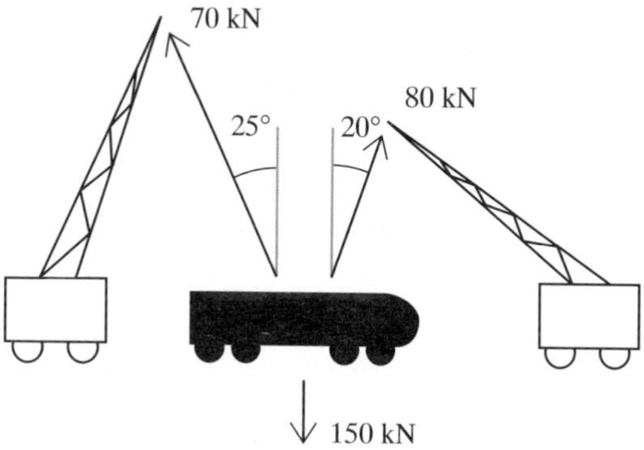

5 Ann and Beryl are arguing over a doll. They each grap a pigtail and a leg and pull as in the diagram. Assuming that the doll stays in one piece, which girl gets the doll?

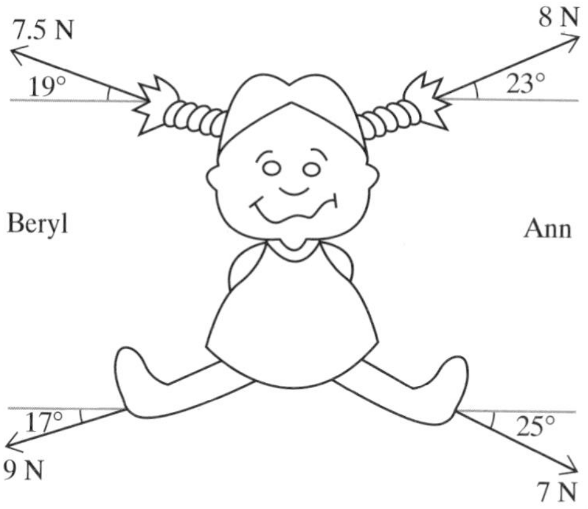

6 An aircraft is flying on a course of 335° with an air speed of 450 km/h. The wind is blowing from 048° at 55 km/h. Find the actual bearing of the aircraft, and its actual speed (as recorded from the ground).

7 An aircraft is flying on a course of 245° with an air speed of 200 km/h. The wind is blowing and the aircraft actually flies on a bearing of 265°. Its actual speed is 235 km/h (as recorded on the ground). What is the speed and direction of the wind?

8 A boat sets sail and attempts to sail due east at 15 km/h, but it is taken off course by a current of 5 km/h flowing in the south-west direction. Find the resultant speed of the boat and the bearing on which it sails.

9 A swimmer wants to swim across a river to a point exactly opposite from where he is standing. He can swim in still water at a speed of 5 km/h. The river is flowing at 1.9 km/h.

a Find the angle to the river bank at which the swimmer has to head.

b If the river is 30 m wide, how long will he take to cross it?

10 A boat is heading in a direction of 192° at a speed of 23 km/h, but the boatman has actually set his course on a bearing of 205° and a speed of 25 km/h. Find the speed and the direction of the current taking him off this course.

Possible coursework tasks

What is an argument?

The position vector of **A** can be written as

$$\mathbf{a} = \begin{pmatrix} x \\ y \end{pmatrix}$$

We can define the argument of **a** to be the angle the vector makes in an anticlockwise direction with the positive x-axis. This is shown as θ in the diagram.

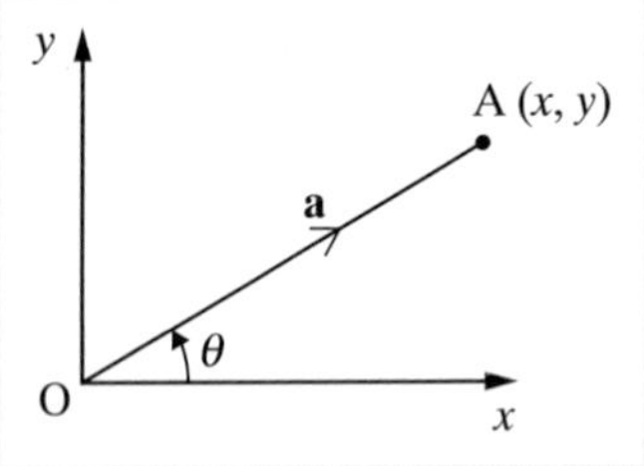

Investigate the argument for any position vector.

Perpendicular vectors

Draw any two vectors that are perpendicular to each other.

Can you find a rule which determines whether any two vectors are perpendicular to each other?

3-D vectors

In 3-D space, we can find the co-ordinates of a point by using the Cartesian axes x, y and z, as in the diagram. So, the point P will have the co-ordinates (2, 3, 4). P will also have a position vector

$$\mathbf{p} = \begin{pmatrix} 2 \\ 3 \\ 4 \end{pmatrix}$$

Investigate 3-D vectors.

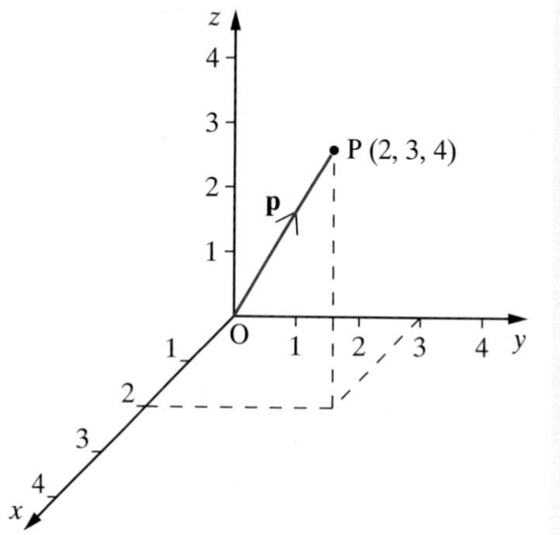

Examination questions

1 In the rhombus ABCD, E and F are the mid-points of BC and DC respectively. Given that $\overrightarrow{AB} = \mathbf{p}$ and $\overrightarrow{AD} = \mathbf{q}$, find the following vectors in terms of **p** and **q**.

i $\overrightarrow{AE}$ **ii** $\overrightarrow{BD}$ **iii** $\overrightarrow{AF}$

iv Show that EF is parallel to BD and is half its length.

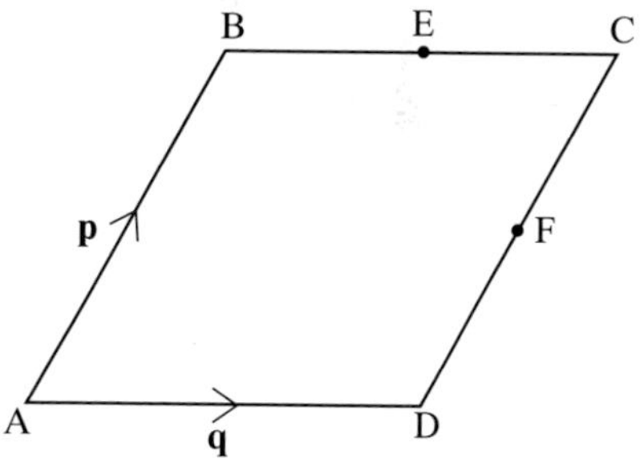

WJEC, Question 12, Specimen Paper 2H, 1998

2

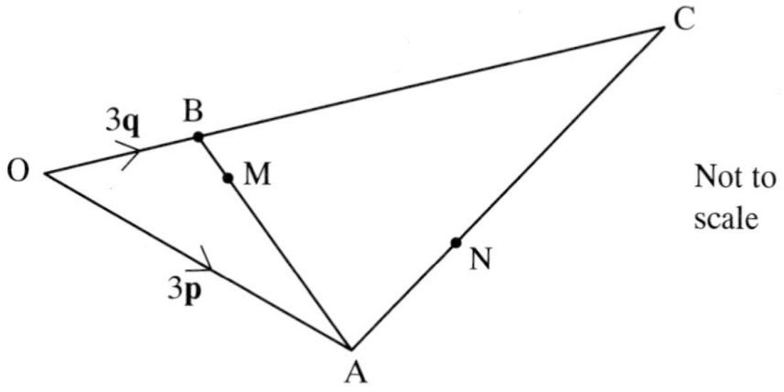

a Express $\overrightarrow{AC}$ in terms of $\overrightarrow{AB}$ and $\overrightarrow{BC}$.

b Given that $\overrightarrow{OA} = 3\mathbf{p}$, $\overrightarrow{OB} = 3\mathbf{q}$ and $\overrightarrow{OC} = 4\overrightarrow{OB}$, show that $\overrightarrow{AC} = 12\mathbf{q} - 3\mathbf{p}$.

c Given that $\overrightarrow{AM} = \frac{2}{3}\overrightarrow{AB}$ and $\overrightarrow{AN} = \frac{1}{3}\overrightarrow{AC}$,

i show that $\overrightarrow{OM} = \mathbf{p} + 2\mathbf{q}$

ii express $\overrightarrow{ON}$ in terms of **p** and **q**.

d What can you say about the points O, M and N?

NEAB, Question 20, Specimen Paper 1H, 1998

3

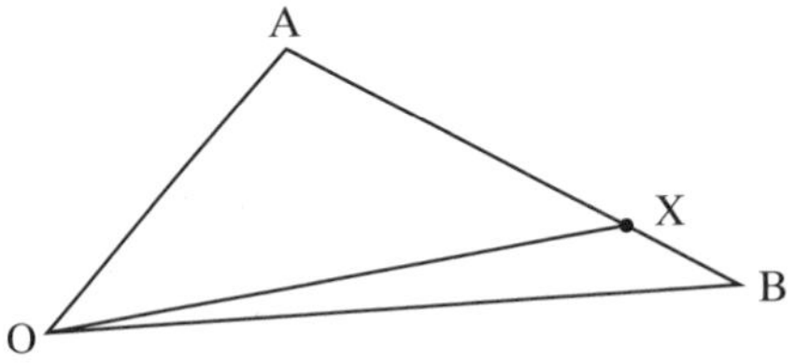

In the diagram, X is the point on AB such that AX = 3XB. Given that OA = 8**a** and OB = 4**b**, express in terms of **a** and/or **b**.

i AB **ii** AX **iii** OX

MEG, Question 11, Specimen Paper 5, 1998

4 A model power boat can travel at 0.75 m/s in still water. It is released from a point P on the bank of a river which flows at 0.4 m/s. The river is 15 m wide. The boat is aimed continually in a direction perpendicular to the flow of the river, as shown in the diagram.

a Find

i the resultant speed of the boat

ii the direction in which the boat actually travels across the river.

b i How far downstream from P does the boat land on the opposite bank?

ii How long does the boat take to cross the river?

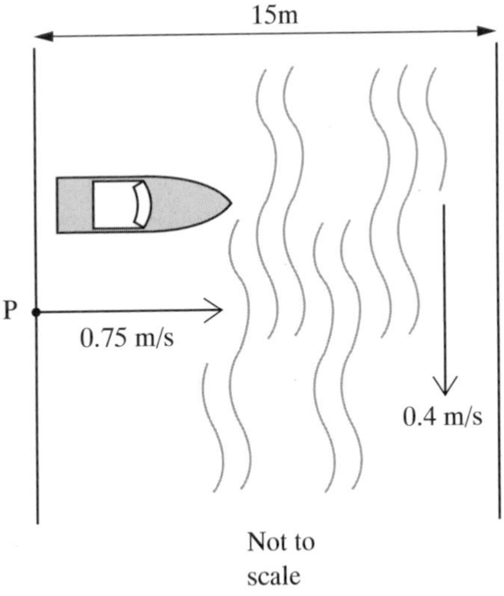

NEAB, Question 10, Paper 2R, June 1995

5

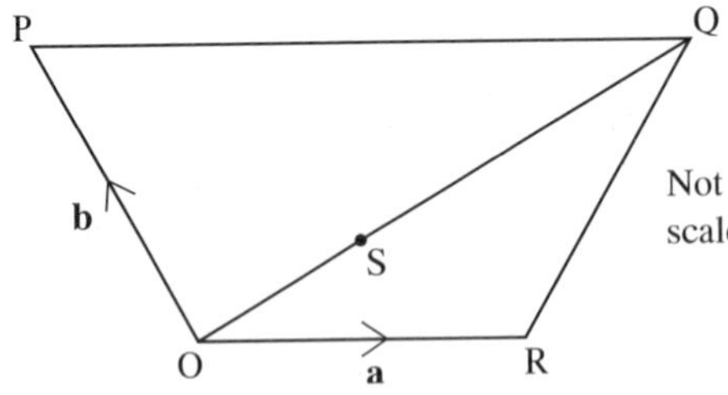

The diagram shows the position of points O, P, Q and R with vectors **a** and **b** acting along OR and OP respectively.

$\overrightarrow{OR} = \mathbf{a}$ $\quad \overrightarrow{OP} = \mathbf{b}$ $\quad \overrightarrow{OS} = \frac{1}{3}\overrightarrow{OQ}$ $\quad \overrightarrow{PQ} = 2\overrightarrow{OR}$

By expressing $\overrightarrow{PS}$ and $\overrightarrow{RS}$ in terms of the vectors **a** and **b**, find the ratio PS : SR and explain the relationship between the points P, S and R.

SEG, Question 10, Specimen Paper 16, 1998

6 PQRS and PSTU are parallelograms.
$\overrightarrow{PQ}$ is **a**, $\overrightarrow{PS}$ is **b**, and $\overrightarrow{ST}$ is **c**. Find in terms of **a**, **b** and **c** expressions in their simplest forms for

i $\overrightarrow{PT}$ **ii** $\overrightarrow{US}$

iii $\overrightarrow{PX}$, where X is the mid-point of QT

iv $\frac{1}{2}(\overrightarrow{PQ} + \overrightarrow{PT})$

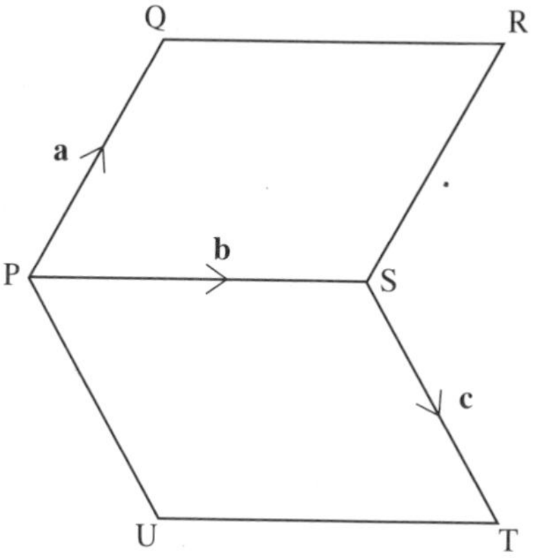

ULEAC, Question 14, Specimen Paper 5, 1998

7 A boat is heading in a direction 071° at a speed which in still water would be 15 km/h. It is carried off course by a current of 6 km/h in a direction 145°. Find the boat's actual speed and direction.

8 A ferry crosses a river to a spot exactly opposite its start. The speed of the boat in still water is 6 m/s, and the current flows at 2 m/s. Find the angle to the bank at which the boat must head.

Summary

How well do you grade yourself?

To gain a grade **A**, you need to be able to apply vector methods to geometry in two dimensions.

To gain a grade **A***, you need to be able to find resultant vectors. You need also to be able to apply vector methods to solve problems.

What you should know after you have worked through Chapter 22

- How to find the sum and difference of two vectors.
- How to apply vector methods to 2-D geometrical situations.
- How to solve problems involving forces by the use of vectors.

23 Transformation of graphs

This chapter is going to … show you how to transform graphs and how to recognise the relationships between graphs from their equations.

What you should already know

- Geometric transformation by translation, reflection and stretching.
- A translation is described by a column vector.
- A reflection is described by a mirror line.
- A stretch is an enlargement that takes place in one direction only. It is described by the scale factor and the direction of the stretch.

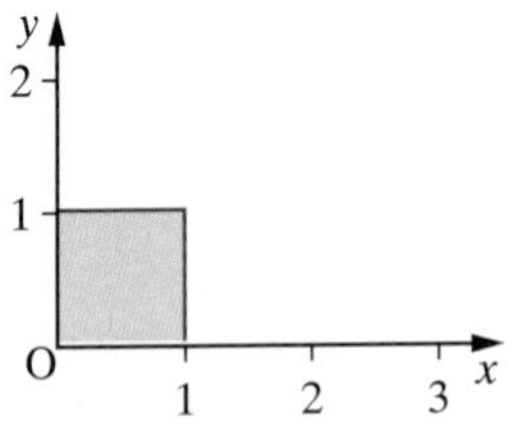

Original

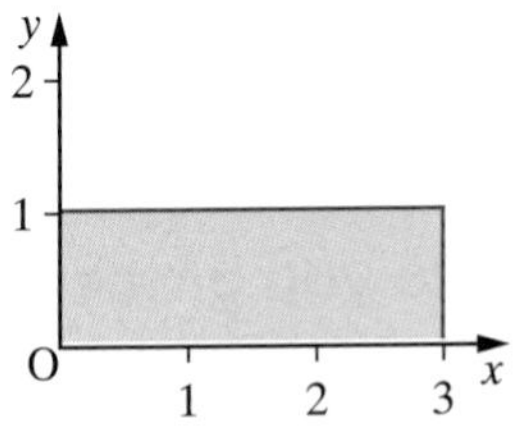

Stretch scale factor 3 in x-direction

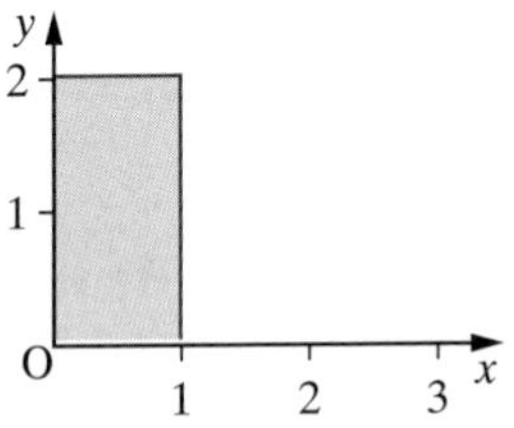

Stretch scale factor 2 in y-direction

- The graphs of $y = x^2$, $y = x^3$, $y = \sin x$, $y = \cos x$, $y = \tan x$ and $y = \frac{1}{x}$.

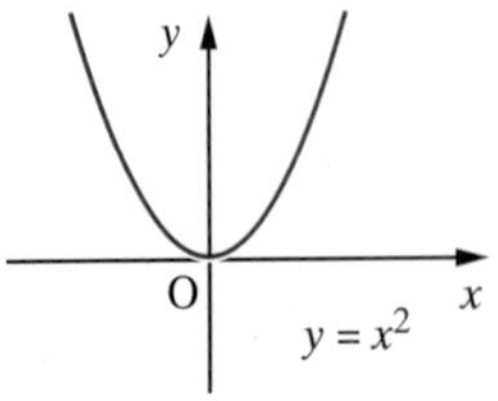

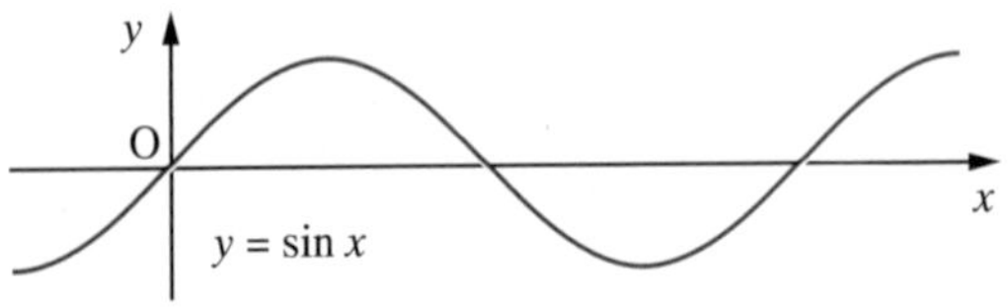

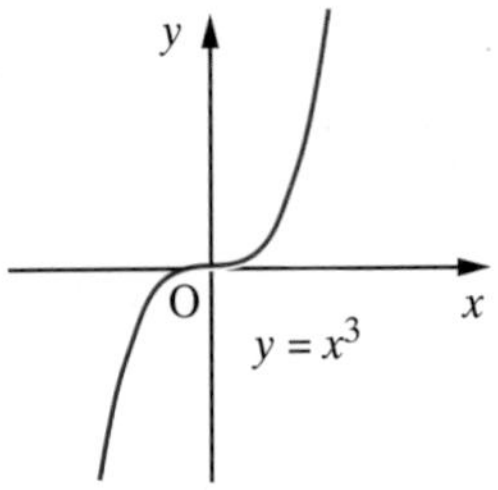

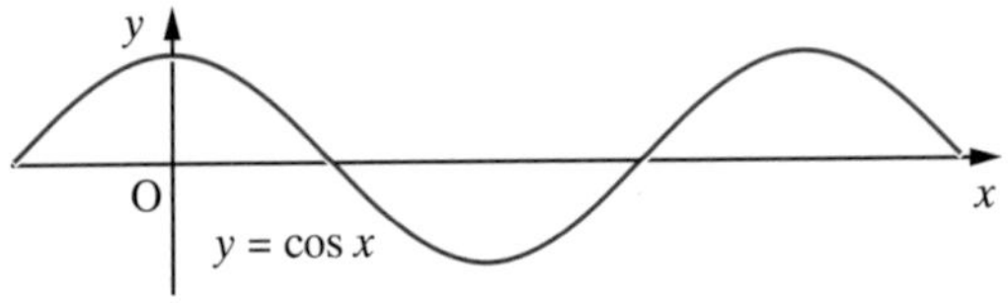

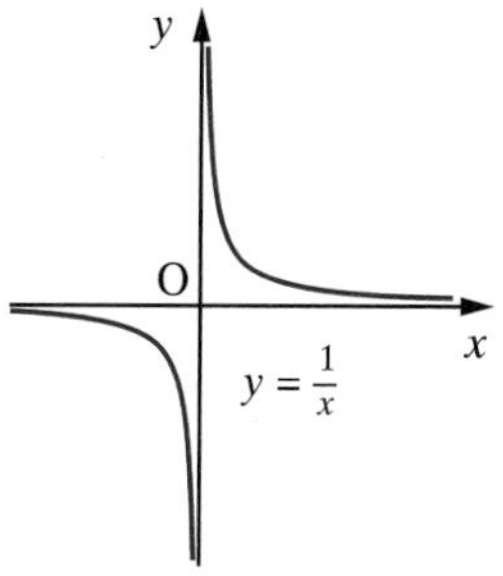

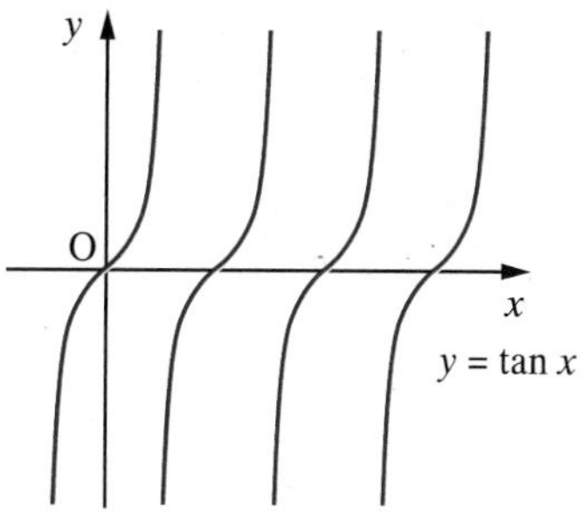

On this page and the next, we present six general statements or rules about transforming graphs.

We use the notation f(x) to represent a function of x. A function of x is any algebraic expression in which x is the only variable: for example,

$$x + 3 \quad 5x \quad 2x - 7 \quad x^2 \quad x^3 + 2x - 1 \quad \sin x \quad \frac{1}{x}$$

(This work is much easier to understand if you have access to a graphics calculator or a graph-drawing computer program.)

Transformations of the graph of $y = f(x)$

The graph on the right represents any function $y = f(x)$.

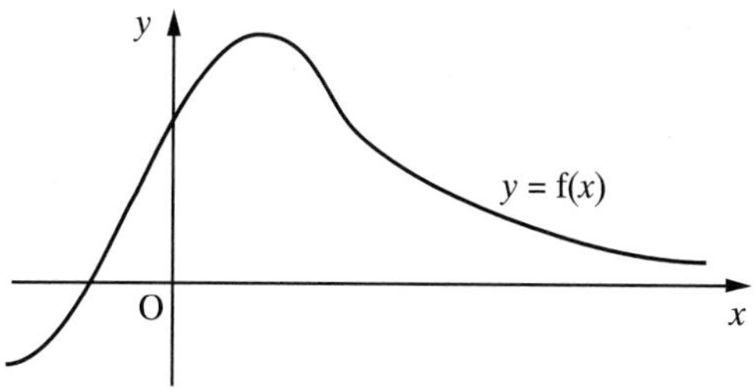

Rule 1 The graph of $y = f(x) + a$ is a translation of the graph of $y = f(x)$ by a vector $\begin{pmatrix} 0 \\ a \end{pmatrix}$.

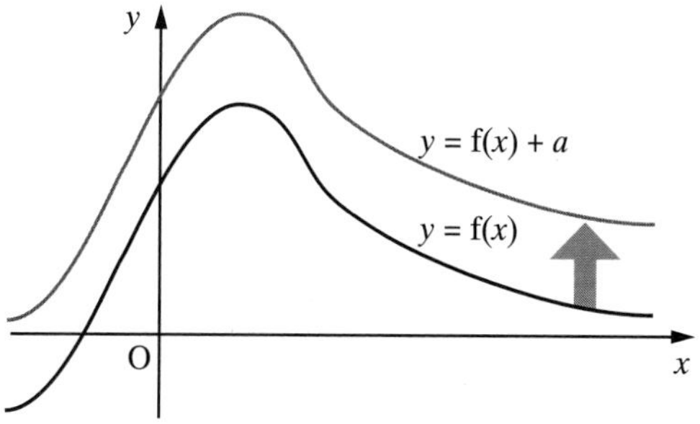

Rule 2 The graph of $y = f(x - a)$ is a translation of the graph of $y = f(x)$ by a vector $\begin{pmatrix} a \\ 0 \end{pmatrix}$.

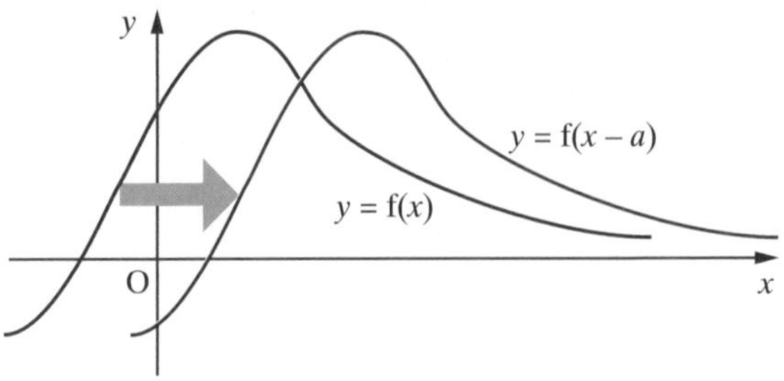

Rule 3 The graph of $y = kf(x)$ is a stretch of the graph $y = f(x)$ by a scale factor of k in the y-direction.

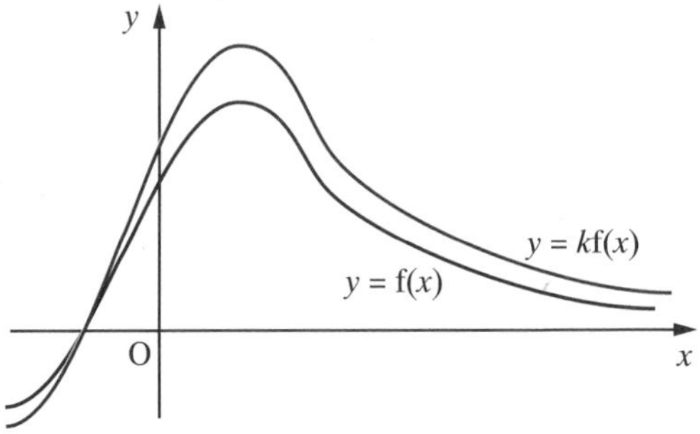

Rule 4 The graph of $y = f(tx)$ is a stretch of the graph $y = f(x)$ by a scale factor of $\frac{1}{t}$ in the x-direction.

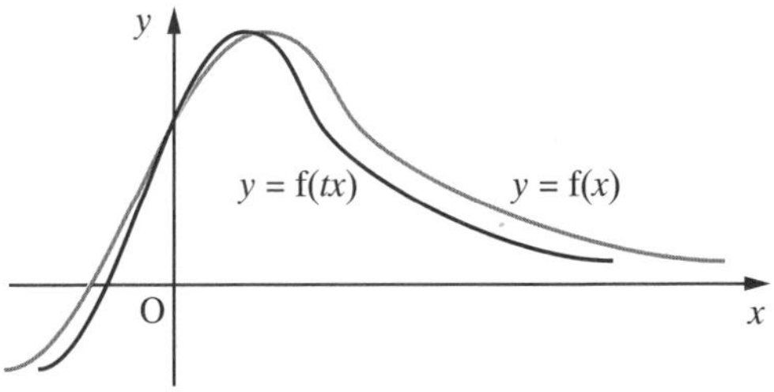

Rule 5 The graph of $y = -f(x)$ is the reflection of the graph $y = f(x)$ in the x-axis

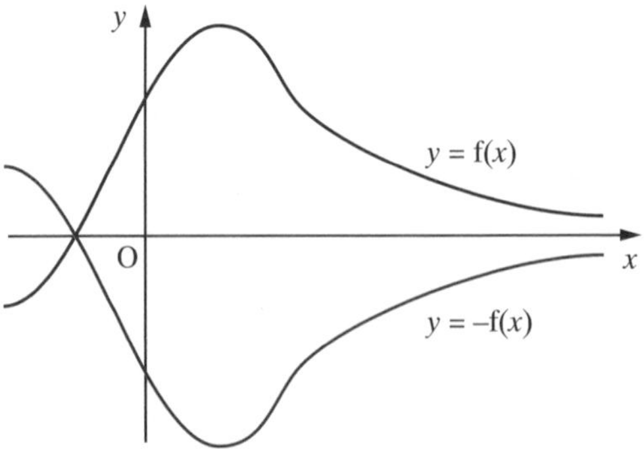

Rule 6 The graph of $y = f(-x)$ is the reflection of the graph $y = f(x)$ in the y-axis

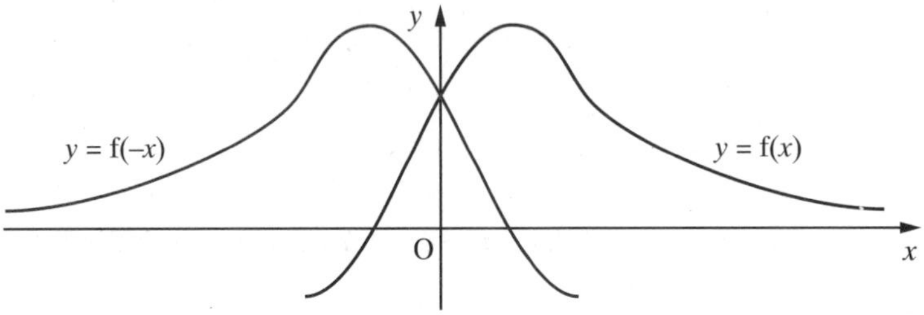

Example Sketch the graphs of

a $y = x^2$ **b** $y = 5x^2$ **c** $y = x^2 - 5$

d $y = -x^2$ **e** $y = (x - 5)^2$ **f** $y = 2x^2 + 3$

and describe the transformation(s) that change graph **a** to each of the other graphs.

Graph **a** is the basic graph to which we apply the rules to make the necessary transformations: graph **b** uses Rule 3, graph **c** uses Rule 1, graph **d** uses Rule 5, graph **e** uses Rule 2, and graph **f** uses Rules 3 and 1.

The graphs are

a

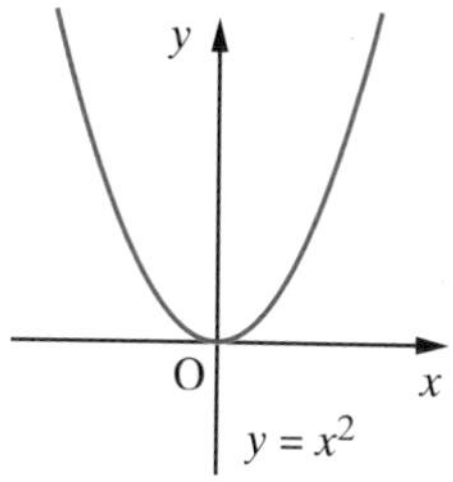

b

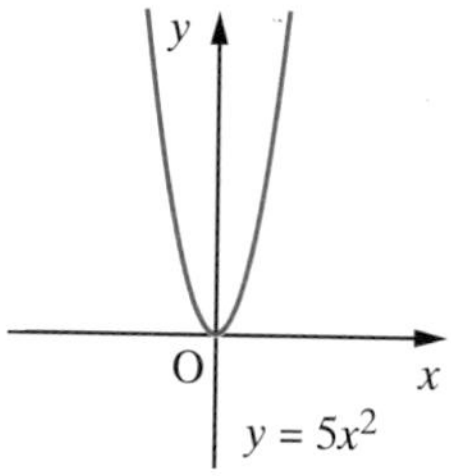

c

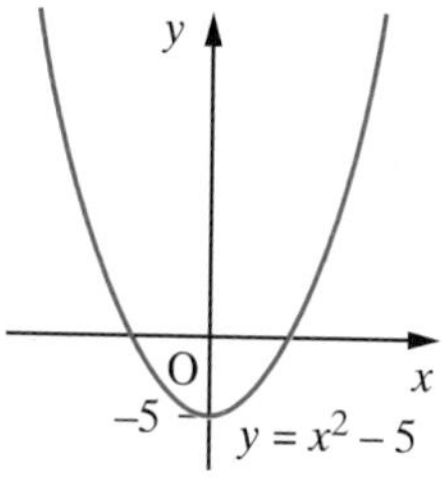

d

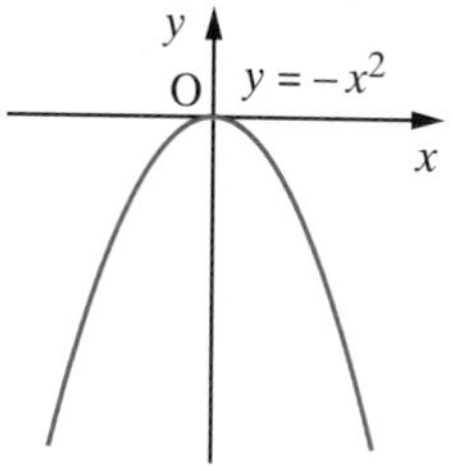

e

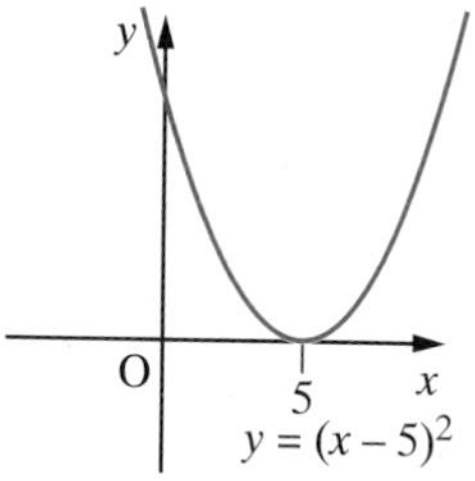

f

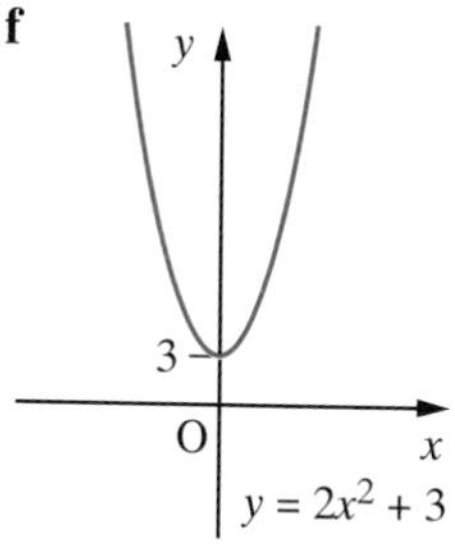

The transformations are

Graph **b** is a stretch of scale factor 5 in the y-direction.

Graph **c** is a translation of $\begin{pmatrix} 0 \\ -5 \end{pmatrix}$.

Graph **d** is a reflection in the x-axis.

Graph **e** is a translation of $\begin{pmatrix} 5 \\ 0 \end{pmatrix}$.

Graph **f** is a stretch of scale factor 2 in the y-direction, followed by a translation of $\begin{pmatrix} 0 \\ 3 \end{pmatrix}$

Exercise 23A

1 On the same axes sketch the graphs of

a $y = x^2$ **b** $y = 3x^2$ **c** $y = \frac{1}{2}x^2$ **d** $10x^2$

e Describe the transformation(s) that take(s) the graph in part **a** to each of the graphs in parts **b** to **d**.

2 On the same axes sketch the graphs of

a $y = x^2$ **b** $y = x^2 + 3$ **c** $y = x^2 - 1$ **d** $y = 2x^2 + 1$

e Describe the transformation(s) that take(s) the graph in part **a** to each of the graphs in parts **b** to **d**.

3 On the same axes sketch the graphs of

a $y = x^2$ **b** $y = (x + 3)^2$ **c** $y = (x - 1)^2$ **d** $y = 2(x - 2)^2$

e Describe the transformation(s) that take the graph in part **a** to each of the graphs in parts **b** to **d**.

4 On the same axes sketch the graphs of

a $y = x^2$ **b** $y = (x +3)^2 - 1$ **c** $y = 4(x - 1)^2 + 3$

d Describe the transformation(s) that take(s) the graph in part **a** to each of the graphs in parts **b** and **c**.

5 On the same axes sketch the graphs of

a $y = x^2$ **b** $y = -x^2 + 3$ **c** $y = -3x^2$ **d** $y = -2x^2 + 1$

e Describe the transformation(s) that take(s) the graph in part **a** to each of the graphs in parts **b** to **d**.

6 On the same axes sketch the graphs of

a $y = \sin x$ **b** $y = 2 \sin x$ **c** $y = \frac{1}{2} \sin x$ **d** $y = 10 \sin x$

e Describe the transformation(s) that take(s) the graph in part **a** to each of the graphs in parts **b** to **d**.

7 On the same axes sketch the graphs of

a $y = \sin x$ **b** $y = \sin 3x$ **c** $y = \sin \frac{x}{2}$ **d** $y = 5 \sin 2x$

e Describe the transformation(s) that take(s) the graph in part **a** to each of the graphs in parts **b** to **d**.

8 On the same axes sketch the graphs of

a $y = \sin x$ **b** $y = \sin (x + 90°)$

c $y = \sin (x - 45°)$ **d** $y = 2 \sin (x - 90°)$

e Describe the transformation(s) that take(s) the graph in part **a** to the graphs in parts **b** to **d**.

9 On the same axes sketch the graphs of

a $y = \sin x$ **b** $y = \sin x + 2$ **c** $y = \sin x - 3$ **d** $y = 2 \sin x + 1$

e Describe the transformation(s) that take(s) the graph in part **a** to each of the graphs in parts **b** to **d**.

10 On the same axes sketch the graphs of

a $y = \sin x$ **b** $y = -\sin x$ **c** $y = \sin (-x)$ **d** $y = -\sin (-x)$

e Describe the transformation(s) that take(s) the graph in part **a** to each of the graphs in parts **b** to **d**.

11 On the same axes sketch the graphs of

a $y = \cos x$ **b** $y = 2\cos x$ **c** $y = \cos(x - 60°)$ **d** $y = \cos x + 2$

e Describe the transformation(s) that take(s) the graph in part **a** to each of the graphs in parts **b** to **d**.

12 Explain why the graphs of $y = \tan x$ and $y = \tan(x - 180°)$ are the same.

13 a Describe the transformations of the graph of $y = x^2$ needed to obtain the graphs of

i $4x^2$ **ii** $9x^2$ **iii** $16x^2$

b Describe the transformations of the graph of $y = x^2$ needed to obtain the graphs of

i $(2x)^2$ **ii** $(3x)^2$ **iii** $(4x)^2$

c Describe two different transformations that take the graph of $y = x^2$ to the graph of $y = (ax)^2$, where a is a positive number.

14 On the right is a sketch of the function $y = f(x)$.

Use this to sketch

a $y = f(x) + 2$ **b** $y = 2f(x)$

c $y = f(x - 3)$ **d** $y = -f(x)$

e $y = 2f(x) + 3$ **f** $y = -f(x) - 2$

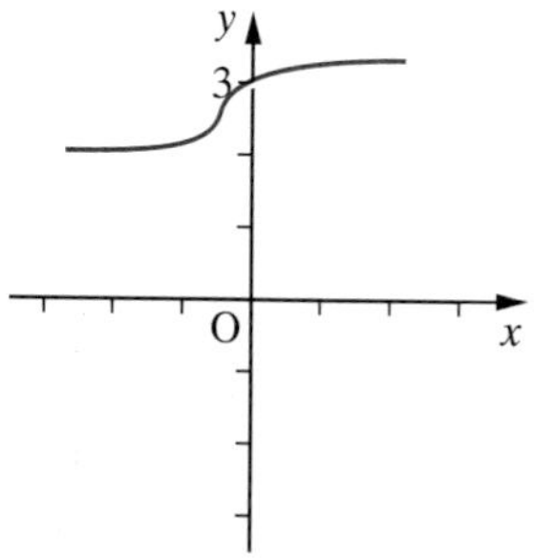

15 What is the equation of the graph obtained when the following transformations are performed on the graph of $y = x^2$?

a Stretch by a factor of 5 in the y-direction.

b Translation of $\begin{pmatrix} 0 \\ 7 \end{pmatrix}$.

c Translation of $\begin{pmatrix} -3 \\ 0 \end{pmatrix}$.

d Stretch by a factor of 3 in the y-direction followed by a translation of $\begin{pmatrix} 0 \\ 4 \end{pmatrix}$.

e Translation of $\begin{pmatrix} -2 \\ -3 \end{pmatrix}$.

f Reflection in the x-axis, followed by a stretch, scale factor 3, in the y-direction.

16 What is the equation of the graph obtained when the following transformations are performed on the graph of $y = \cos x$?

a Stretch by a factor of 6 in the y-direction.

b Translation of $\begin{pmatrix} 0 \\ 3 \end{pmatrix}$.

c Translation of $\begin{pmatrix} -30 \\ 0 \end{pmatrix}$.

d Stretch by a factor of 3 in the y-direction followed by a translation of $\begin{pmatrix} 0 \\ -2 \end{pmatrix}$.

e Translation of $\begin{pmatrix} 45 \\ -2 \end{pmatrix}$.

17 a Sketch the graph $y = x^3$.

b Use your sketch in part **a** to draw the graphs obtained after $y = x^3$ is transformed as follows.

i Reflection in the x-axis.

ii Translation of $\begin{pmatrix} 0 \\ -2 \end{pmatrix}$.

iii Stretch by a scale factor of 3 in the y-direction.

iv Translation of $\begin{pmatrix} -2 \\ 0 \end{pmatrix}$.

c Give the equation of each of the graphs obtained in part **b**.

18 a Sketch the graph of $y = \dfrac{1}{x}$.

b Use your sketch in part **a** to draw the graphs obtained after $y = \dfrac{1}{x}$ is transformed as follows.

i Translation of $\begin{pmatrix} 0 \\ 4 \end{pmatrix}$.

ii Translation of $\begin{pmatrix} 4 \\ 0 \end{pmatrix}$.

iii Stretch, scale factor 3 in the y-direction.

iv Stretch, scale factor $\frac{1}{2}$ in the x-direction.

c Give the equation of each of the graphs obtained in part **b**.

19 The graphs below are all transformations of $y = x^2$. Two points through which each graph passes are indicated. Use this information to work out the equation of each graph.

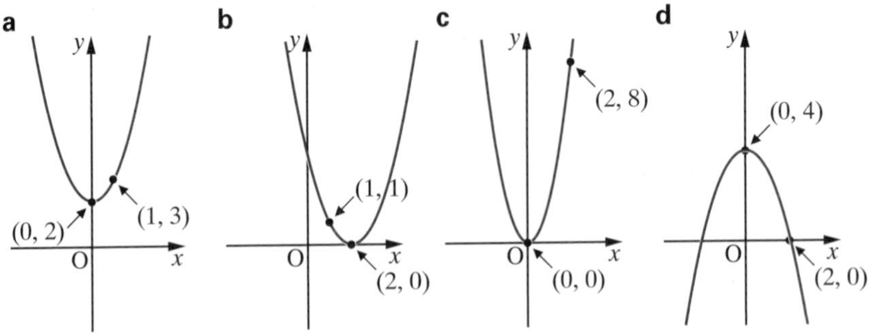

20 The graphs below are all transformations of $y = \sin x$. Two points through which each graph passes are indicated. Use this information to work out the equation of each graph.

a

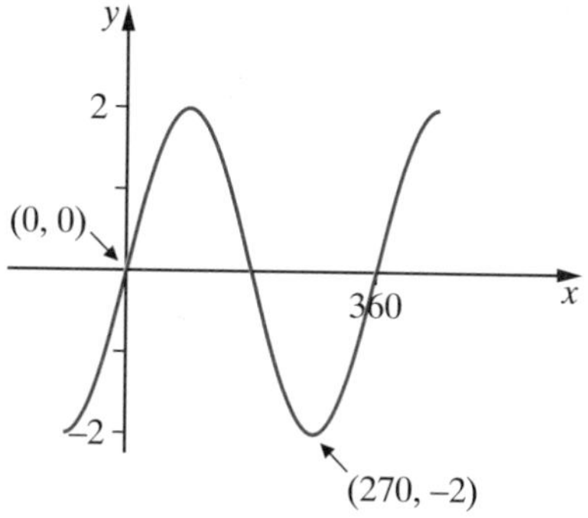

b

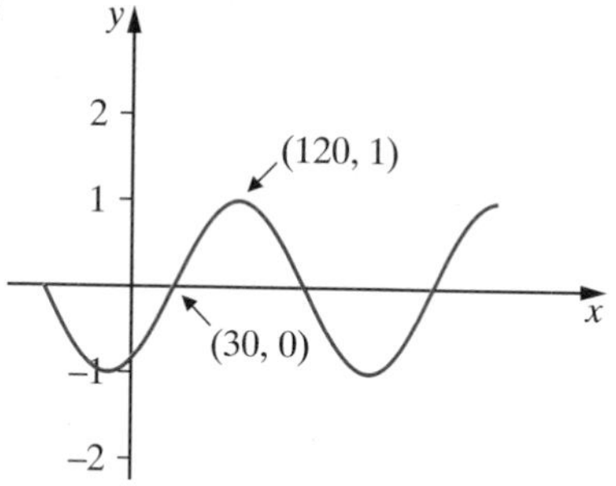

c

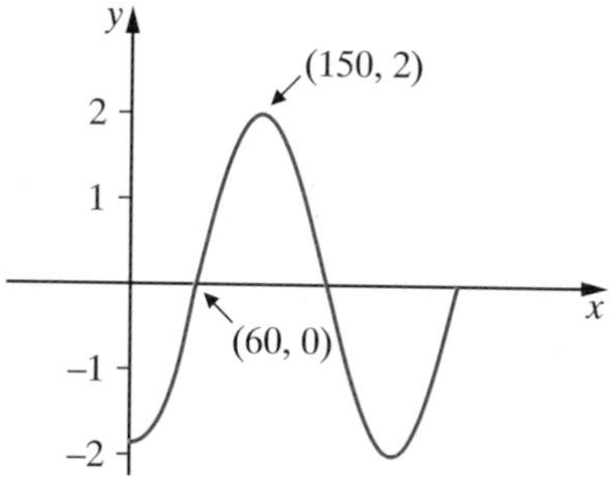

d

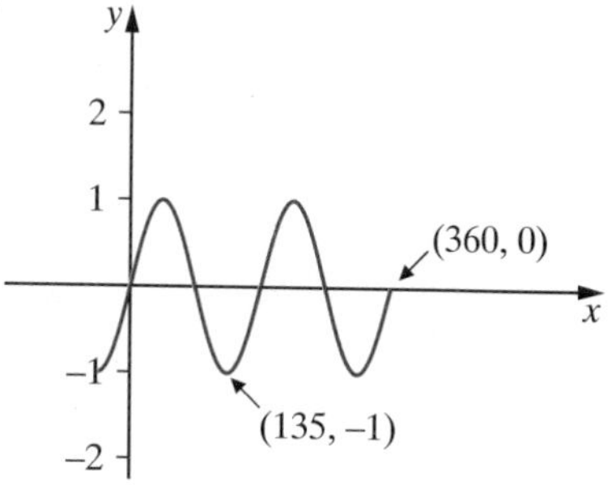

21 Below are the graphs of $y = \sin x$ and $y = \cos x$.

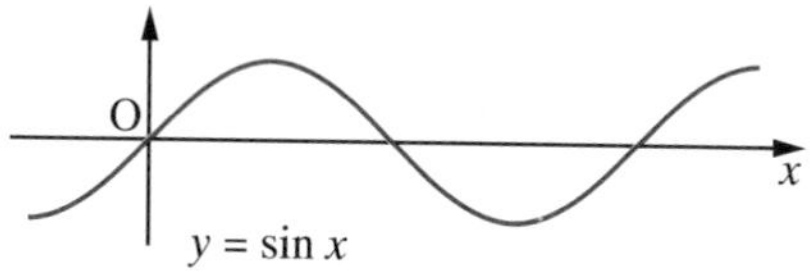

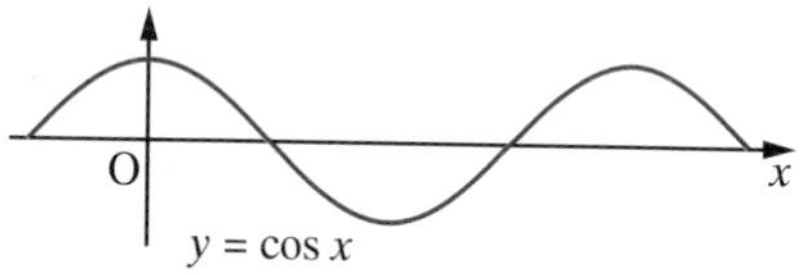

a Describe a series of transformations that would take the first graph to the second.

b Which of these is equivalent to $y = \cos x$?

i $y = \sin(x + 90°)$ **ii** $y = -\sin(x - 90°)$ **iii** $y = 2\cos\frac{x}{2}$

22 A

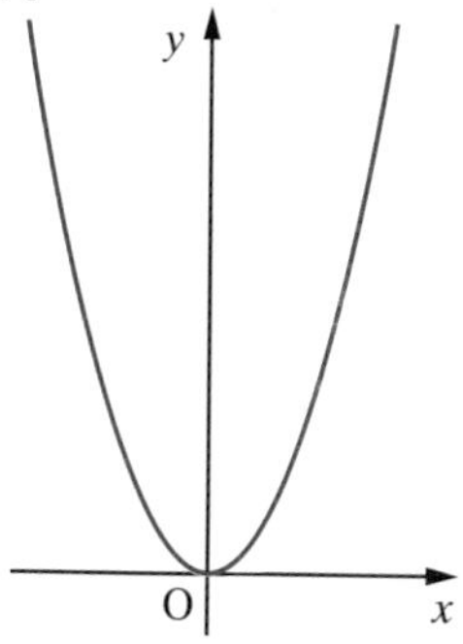

B

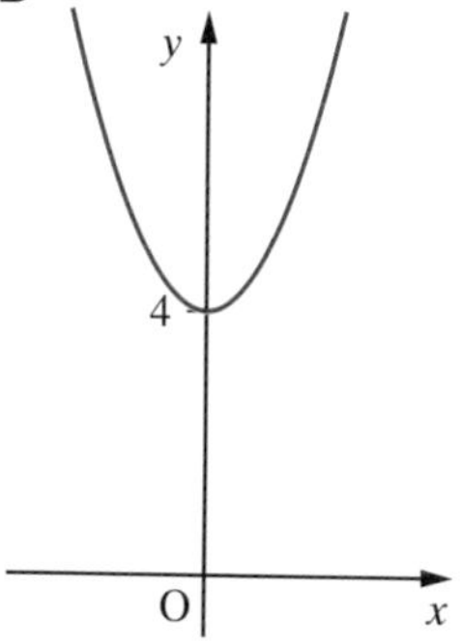

C

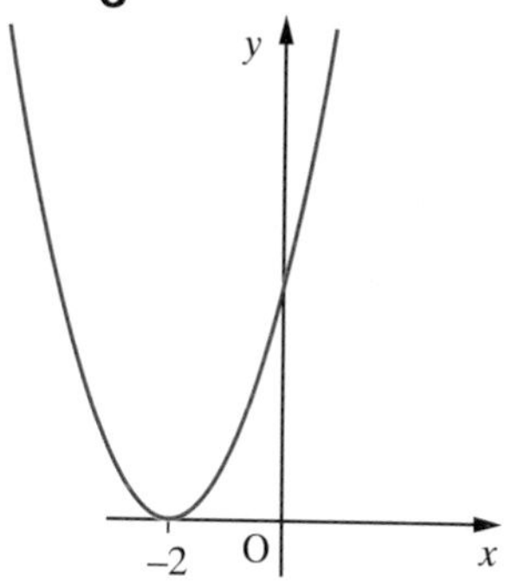

D

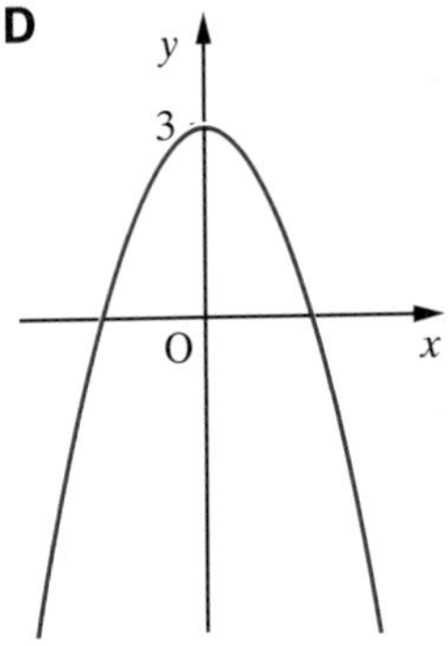

E

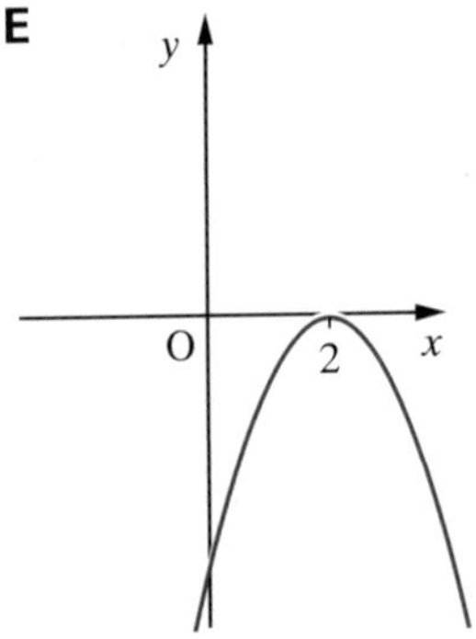

Match each of the graphs **A**, **B** ,**C**, **D** and **E** to one of these equations.

i $y = x^2$ **ii** $y = -x^2 + 3$ **iii** $y = -(x - 2)^2$

iv $y = (x + 2)^2$ **v** $y = x^2 + 4$

Possible coursework tasks

Parabolic transformations

The quadratic function $f(x) = ax^2 + bx + c$ is always a translation of $y = x^2$.

Can you define the transformation in terms of a, b and c?

Trigonometric transformations

The trigonometric function $f(x) = a \sin x + b \cos x$ is always a transformation of $y = \sin x$.

Can you define the transformation in terms of a and b?

For these two investigations it would be an advantage to have access to a graphics calculator or a graph-drawing computer program.

Examination questions

1 On the right is a sketch of the graph of $y = f(x)$ where $f(x) = (x + 3)(x - 2)(x - 4)$

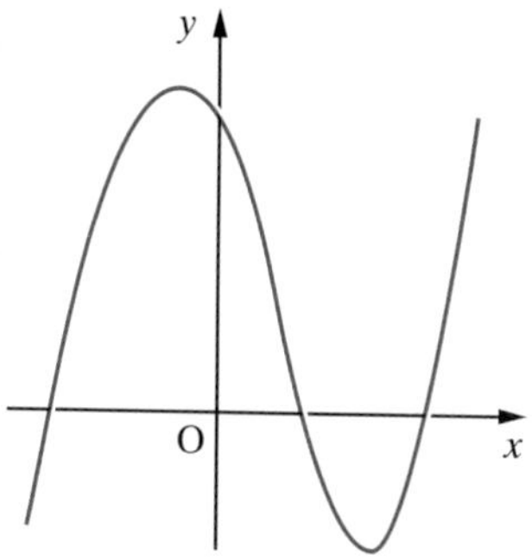

a Calculate the value of f(0).

b Sketch the graph of $y = f(-x)$.

c Describe the single geometric transformation which maps the graph of $y = f(x)$ onto the graph of $y = f(-x)$.

d The equation $f(x) = f(-x)$ has a solution $x = 0$. It also has a positive solution x such that

$$n < x < n + 1$$

where n is a positive integer. Write down the value of n.

ULEAC, Question 15, Specimen Paper 5, 1998

2 The function $y = f(x)$ is defined for $0 < x < 2$. The function is sketched on the right.

a Sketch $y = f(x + 1)$.

b Sketch $y = f(\frac{1}{2}x)$.

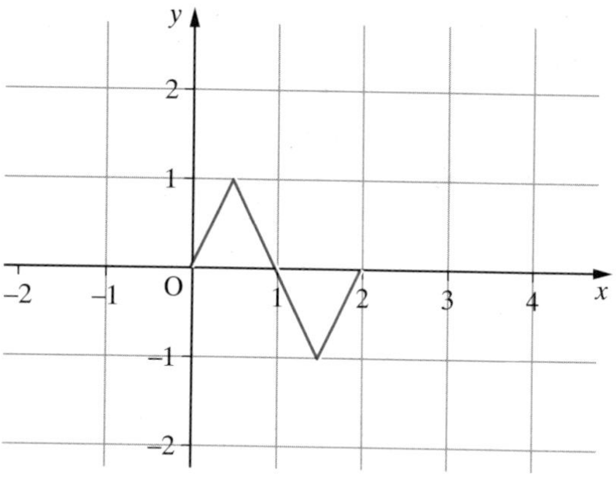

SEG, Question 15, Specimen Paper 16, 1998

3 The table shows some values of the function $f(x) = (x - 2)^2 + 4$, where $-3 < x < 4$.

x	–3	–2	–1	0	1	2	3	4
$f(x)$	29	20	13	8	5	4	5	8

a Draw the graph of $y = f(x)$.

b On the same axes, draw the graph of $y = x^2$.

c Describe how the graph of $y = (x - 2)^2 + 4$ can be obtained from the graph of $y = x^2$ by a transformation. State clearly what this transformation is.

NEAB, Question 19, Specimen Paper 1H, 1998

4 The diagram shows a sketch of $y = x^4$. Sketch the following curves, marking clearly the co-ordinates of the points where the curve meets each axis.

i $y = -x^4$

ii $y = 2 + x^4$

iii $y = (x + 3)^4$

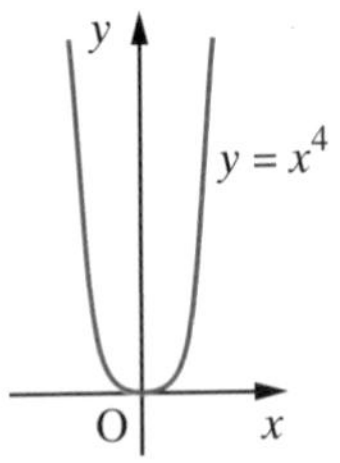

WJEC, Question 15, Specimen Paper H1, 1998

5 The graph of $y = f(x)$ has been drawn. Sketch the graph of $y = f(x + 2)$.

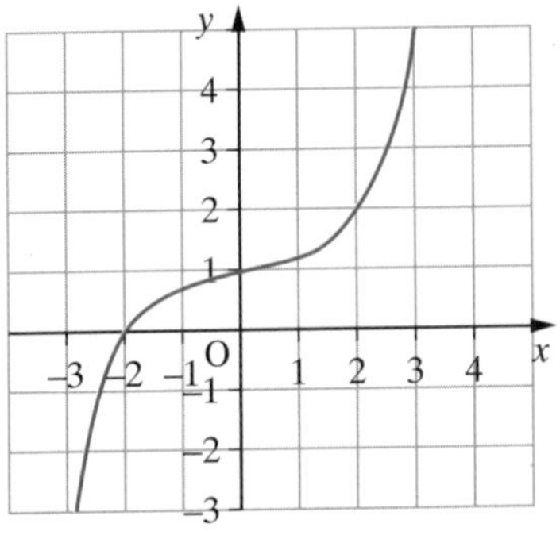

6 On the right is the graph of a function $y = f(x)$.

i Draw the graph of $y = f(\frac{1}{2}x)$

ii Write down, in terms of f, the equation of the graph below.

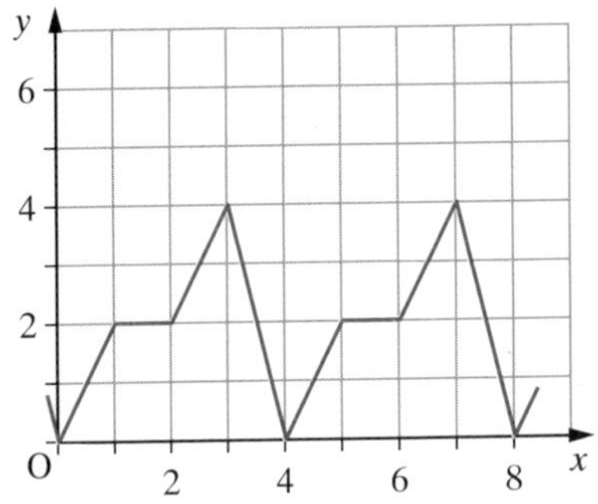

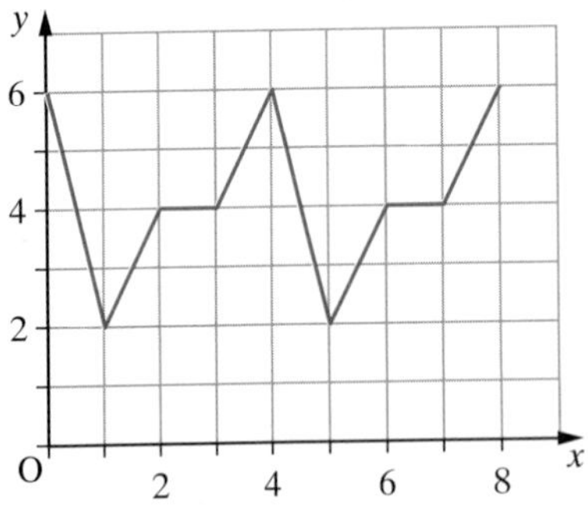

MEG, SMP 1–16, Question 7, Specimen Paper 6, June 1998

7 Sketch and label the functions $y = x^3$ and $y = x^3 + 2$ on the same pair of axes.

SEG, Question 8, Paper 6, November 1994

8 The graph of $y = f(x)$, where $f(x) = \dfrac{x}{x+1}$, is sketched on the right. Sketch the graphs of

i $y = f(x - 1)$

ii $y = f(2x)$

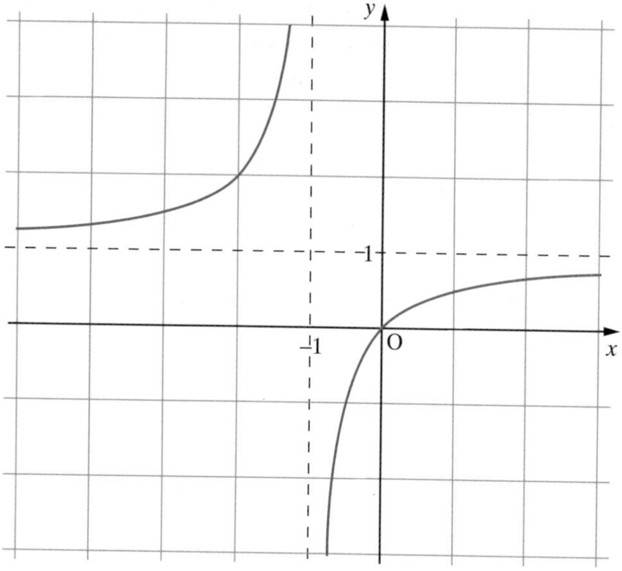

SEG, Question 10, Paper 6, June 1995

9 A graph of $y = f(x)$ has been drawn. Sketch the graph of

i $y = f(x) - 2$

ii $y = f(x - 2)$

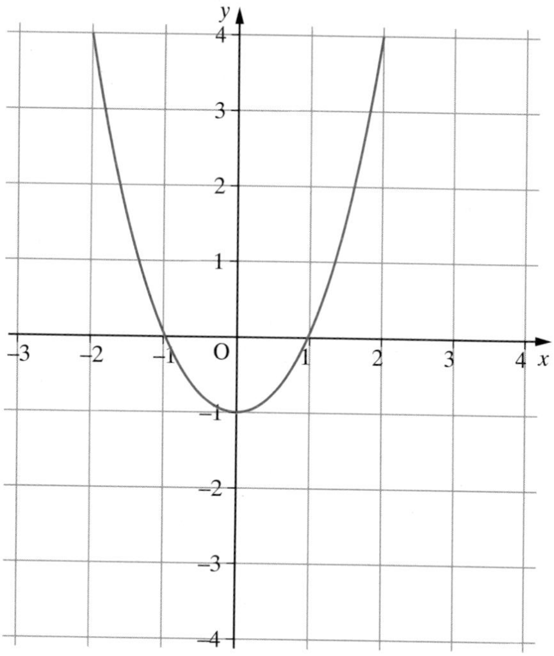

10 The diagram shows the graph of $y = 3x^2 - x^3$ for values of x from -2 to 4.

i On the diagram, draw the reflection of the graph in the x-axis.

ii Write down the equation of this reflection.

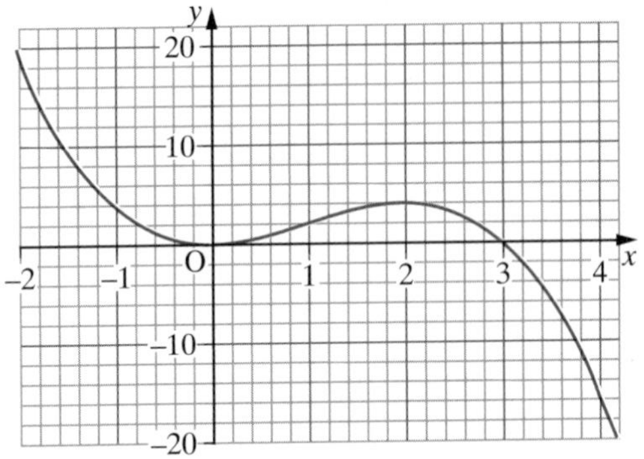

MEG, Question 10, Specimen Paper 6, 1998

Summary

How well do you grade yourself?

To gain a grade **A**, you need to be able to transform the graph of a function.

To gain a grade **A***, you need to be able to identify the equation of a function from its graph which has been formed by a transformation on a known function.

What you should know after you have worked through Chapter 23

- How to sketch the graphs of functions such as $y = f(ax)$ and $y = f(x + a)$ from the known graph of $y = f(x)$.
- How to describe from their graphs the transformation of one function into another.
- How to identify equations from the graphs of transformations of known graphs.

Appendix: Coursework guidance

When you have completed a coursework task, you will usually be given three scores or marks. The table opposite gives you some idea what these marks mean.

Strand i: Decisions This is about how you decide to solve a particular problem and then to ask your own questions to extend the problem. This corresponds to column **A** in each coursework example.

Strand ii: Presentation This is about how you present your work. It involves making tables of results, drawing graphs, using algebraic notation or using computer software. This corresponds to column **B** in each coursework example.

Strand iii: Reasons This is about finding solutions to problems and drawing conclusions. You need to find patterns, rules or formulae, and explain how you obtained them. This corresponds to column **C** in each coursework example.

In the two examples in the book, you can see how the marks are given at each stage of the solution. For example, 7 in column **B** means that a mark of 7 has been awarded in Strand ii. By carefully studying these examples, you should be able to improve your coursework marks.

At the end of your GCSE coursework you will be given a total mark found by taking your **best** mark in each column and adding them together. If you sit an examination paper instead of doing coursework, your answers will be marked in a similar way.

Mark	Strand i: Making and monitoring decisions to solve problems	Strand ii: Communicating mathematically	Strand iii: Developing skills of mathematical reasoning
	COLUMN A	COLUMN B	COLUMN C
1	Show that you understand the problem by giving an example	Explain how you intend to start solving the problem	Find easy examples that fit the problem
2	Choose a suitable method to help you solve the problem	Write out your results clearly and carefully	Look for any pattern in your results
3	Identify the necessary information and check that your results are sensible	Show your results in a table, or use diagrams, or use simple algebra	Explain the pattern of, or find a rule for, your results
4	Break the problem down into easy and more manageable stages	Link your tables, graphs and diagrams with a clear explanation	Give another example to show that your pattern or rule works
5	Introduce some questions of your own to find out more about the problem	Explain how you have improved the presentation of your work to make it clearer	Explain why your rule works, using algebra if possible
6	Develop the problem further by introducing some questions that use more complicated mathematics	Develop the problem further using algebra or other forms of notation	Comment constructively on your solutions to show that you fully understand the problem
7	Analyse the problem carefully by considering a number of different approaches	Show that you can present an accurate and convincing mathematical solution	Give reasons why you are considering using different approaches to solve the problem
8	Explore a context or area of mathematics that is unfamiliar	Use mathematical techniques efficiently to give a complete and concise solution	Give a proof in your solution to a more complex problem

Answers

Exercise 1A

1 **a** £62.40 **b** 12.96 kg **c** 472.5 g **d** 599.5 m **e** £38.08 **f** £90 **g** 391 kg **h** 824.1 cm **i** 253.5 g **j** £143.50 **2** £29 425 **3** 1 690 200 **4** **a** Bob £17 325, Jean £20 475, Anne £18 165, Brian £26 565 **b** No **5** £411.95 **6** 7600 **7** 575 g **8** 918 **9** 60 **10** TV £287.88, microwave £84.60, desk £135.13, rug £22.91

Exercise 1B

1 **a** £9.40 **b** 23 kg **c** 212.4 g **d** 339.5 m **e** £4.90 **f** 39.6 m **g** 731 m **h** 83.52 g **i** 360 cm **j** 117 min **2** £5525 **3** **a** 52.8 kg **b** 66 kg **c** 45.76 kg **4** Mr Speed £56, Mrs Speed £297.50, James £126.50, John £337.50 **5** 448 **6** 703 **7** £18 975 **8** **a** 66.5 mph **b** 73.5 mph **9** Sweatshirt £16.72, tracksuit £22.88 **10** 524.8 units

Exercise 1C

1 **a** **i** 10.5 kg **ii** 11.03 kg **iii** 12.16 kg **iv** 14.07 kg **b** 9 **2** 12 years **3** **a** £9592.84 **b** 20 years **4** **a** **i** 2550 **ii** 2168 **iii** 1331 **b** 7 years **5** **a** £6800 **b** £3481.60 **c** £1140.85 **6** **a** **i** 1.9 million litres **ii** 1.6 million litres **iii** 1.2 million litres **b** 10 August **7** **a** £475.24 **b** £564.63 **c** £670.84 **8** **a** **i** 51 980 **ii** 84 752 **iii** 138 185 **b** 2010 **9** **a** 21 yrs **b** 21 yr **10** 30 yr

Exercise 1D

1 **a** 25% **b** 60.61% **c** 46.35% **d** 12.5% **e** 41.67% **f** 60% **g** 20.83% **h** 10% **i** 1.92% **j** 8.33% **k** 45.5% **l** 10.5% **m** 31.25% **n** 40% **o** 2.19% **p** 8.33% **q** 7.2% **r** 0.05% **s** 0.09% **t** 12.5% **2** **a** 48.3% **b** 64.3% **c** 10.5% **d** 81.8% **e** 26.3% **3** 11.1% **4** 4.9% **5** Maths 74.7%, English 76.7%, science 65%, French 53.8%, geography 84.4%, history 85% **6** **a** Olives 7.8%, currants 3.0%, figs 0.9% **b** Olives 6.5%, currants 2.5%, figs 1.4% **c** Olives –1.3%, currants –0.5%, figs +0.5% **7** 2.2% **8** 33.7% **9** 90.5% **10** Commonwealth 20.9%, USA 26.5%, France 10.3%, other 42.3%

Exercise 1E

1 **a** 210 kg **b** £225 **c** 800 g **d** 12 h **e** £460 **f** 250 m **g** 60 cm **h** £3075 **i** £200 **j** 480 g **k** £400 **l** 920 m **2** 80 **3** T-shirt £8.40, tights £1.20, shorts £5.20, sweater £10.74, trainers £24.80, boots £32.40 **4** £20 **5** £833.33 **6** £78 **7** £2450 **8** 2.083 kg **9** 4750 **10** £25.85 **11** 1.25% less

Exercise 1F

1 **a** 4.8 **b** 3.8 **c** 2.2 **d** 8.3 **e** 3.7 **f** 46.9 **g** 23.9 **h** 9.5 **i** 11.1 **j** 33.5 **k** 7.1 **l** 46.8 **m** 0.1 **n** 0.1 **o** 0.6 **p** 65.0 **q** 213.9 **r** 76.1 **s** 455.2 **t** 51.0 **2** **a** 5.78 **b** 2.36 **c** 0.98 **d** 33.09 **e** 6.01 **f** 23.57 **g** 91.79 **h** 8.00 **i** 2.31 **j** 23.92 **k** 6.00 **l** 1.01 **m** 3.51 **n** 96.51 **o** 0.01 **p** 0.07 **q** 7.81 **r** 569.90 **s** 300.00 **t** 0.00 **3** **a** 4.6 **b** 0.08 **c** 45.716 **d** 94.85 **e** 602.1 **f** 671.76 **g** 7.1 **h** 6.904 **i** 13.78 **j** 0.1 **k** 4.002 **l** 60.0 **m** 11.99 **n** 899.9959 **o** 0.0 **p** 0.01 **q** 0.0 **r** 78.393 **s** 200.00 **t** 5.1

Exercise 1G

1 **a** 50 000 **b** 60 000 **c** 30 000 **d** 90 000 **e** 90 000 **f** 50 **g** 90 **h** 30 **i** 100 **j** 200 **k** 0.5 **l** 0.3 **m** 0.006 **n** 0.05 **o** 0.0009 **p** 10 **q** 90 **r** 90 **s** 200 **t** 1000 **2** **a** 65, 74 **b** 95, 149 **c** 950, 1499 **3** Elsecar 750, 849; Hoyland 1150, 1249; Barnsley 164 500, 165 499 **4** Huddersfield 10 500, 11 499; Leeds 27 450, 27 549; Middlesborough 15 000, 24 999 **5** **a** 56 000 **b** 27 000 **c** 80 000 **d** 31 000 **e** 14 000 **f** 5900 **g** 1100 **h** 850 **i** 110 **j** 640 **k** 1.7 **l** 4.1 **m** 2.7 **n** 8.0 **o** 42 **p** 0.80 **q** 0.46 **r** 0.066 **s** 1.0 **t** 0.0098 **6** **a** 60 000 **b** 5300 **c** 89.7 **d** 110 **e** 9 **f** 1.1 **g** 810 **h** 5000 **i** 67 **j** 1 **k** 9 **l** 9.75 **m** 13 **n** 20 **o** 870 **p** 30 **q** 0.074 **r** 0.0099 **s** 0.09 **t** 0.0709

Exercise 1H

1 a 35000 **b** 15000 **c** 960 **d** 12000 **e** 1050 **f** 4000 **g** 4 **h** 18 **i** 1200 **j** 50 **k** 20 **l** 6 **m** 5 **n** 4 **o** 20 **p** 30 **2 a** 14 **b** 10 **c** 1.1 **d** 1 **e** 5 **f** $\frac{2}{3}$ **g** 4 **h** 0.4 **i** $\frac{1}{2}$ **j** 20 **k** 1.2 **l** 2 **m** $1\frac{1}{2}$ **n** 5 **o** 1 **p** $\frac{4}{5}$ **3 a** £3000 **b** £2000 **c** £1500 **d** £700 **4 a** £15000 **b** £18000 **c** £17500 **5** 8 **6** £21000 **7** 8p **8** 25 **9** 27 kg **10 a** 40 **b** 10 **c** £30 **11 a** 10000 **b** 30000 kg (30 t) **12** 1200 **13 a** 30 **b** 120 **c** 1440 **14** 400 **15 a** 3 kg **b** 200 **16** 24 min

Exercise 1I

1 a 1.7 m **b** 6 min **c** 240 g **d** 80°C **e** 35000 **f** 600 **g** 16 miles **h** 284519 **i** 14 m^2 **2** 82°F, 5.3 km, 110 min, 43000 people, 6.289 s, 67th, 1788, 15, 4.67 s **3** 40 **4** 40 min **5 a** £2500 **b** £600 **c** £90 **6** 60 **7** 70 mph **8** 70 **9** 300 **10** 80000 kg (80 t)

Examination questions (Chapter 1)

1 £6348 **2** 15% **3 a** 34650 **b** 34749 **4 a** £450000 **b** 20% decrease **5 a** 0.70223554 **b i** $\frac{6 \times 100}{600 + 200}$ **ii** 0.75 **6 a** £12.42 **b** £14.60 **7 a** 150000, 511000 **b** 3.4 **8** £53.14 **9 a** 3407 **b** 1999 **10 a** £43.18 **b** £598.03 **11 a** 29.6 min **b** 9375 litres **12** 12 **13 a** £44781120 **b** 10.6 **14** 5

Exercise 2A

1 a 15.7 cm **b** 25.8 cm **c** 25.1 cm **d** 36.4 cm **e** 37.7 m **f** 56.5 m **g** 4.1 cm **h** 23.2 m **i** 11.9 cm **j** 14.5 **k** 18.2 m **l** 5.0 cm **2 a** 188.5 cm **b** 26526 **3** 8.8 m **4 a i** 1.5 mm **ii** 8.8 cm **iii** 211 cm **b i** 4.7 mm **ii** 79.2 cm **iii** 0.08 mm **5 a** 201 m, 207 m, 214 m, 220 m, 226 m **b** 88.9% **6 a** 440 cm **b** 5 **7 a** 9.42 cm **b** 15.4 cm **8** 38.6 cm **9** 36.0 cm **10** 181436 **11 a** Sue 62.8 cm, Julie 69.1 cm, Dave 75.4 cm, Brian 81.7 cm **b** The difference between the distances round each waist of two people is 2π times the difference between their radii **c** 6.28 m **12 a** 3770 cm **b** 2653

Exercise 2B

1 a 5 cm, 10 cm, 31.4 cm, 78.5 cm^2 **b** 4.5 cm, 9 cm, 28.3 cm, 63.6 cm^2 **c** 4 cm, 8 cm, 25.1 cm, 50.3 cm^2 **d** 3.50 cm, 7.00 cm, 22 cm, 38.5 cm^2 **e** 2.9 m, 5.8 m, 18.2 m, 26.4 m^2 **f** 17.5 m, 35.0 m, 110 m, 963 m^2 **g** 3.8 m, 7.6 m, 23.9 m, 45.4 m^2 **h** 19.3 m, 38.5 m, 121 m, 1170 m^2 **i** 0.08 mm, 0.16 mm, 0.503 mm, 0.0201 mm^2 **2 a** 78.5 cm^2 **b** 63.6 m^2 **c** 530.9 cm^2 **d** 0.8 m^2 **e** 380.1 m^2 **f** 3525.7 cm^2 **3** 1p : 3.1 cm^2, 2p : 5.3 cm^2, 5p : 2.3 cm^2, 10p : 4.5 cm^2 **4 a** 56.5 cm^2 **b** 19.6 cm^2 **c** 115.5 cm^2 **5 a** 49.1 m^2 **b** 54.9 cm^2 **c** 16.8 cm^2 **6** 201 m^2 **7 a** 50.3 m^2 **b** 44.0 cm^2 **c** 28.3 cm^2 **8 a** 15 **b** 33.7% **9** 158 **10** 31.4 cm, 58.9 cm^2

Exercise 2C

1 a i 5.59 cm **ii** 22.3 cm^2 **b i** 8.29 cm **ii** 20.7 cm^2 **c i** 16.3 cm **ii** 98.0 cm^2 **d i** 15.9 cm **ii** 55.6 cm^2 **2** 16.1 cm, 48.4 cm^2 **3 a** 37.7 cm **b** 38.6 cm **c** 73.8 cm **d** 20.3 cm **4 a** 47.0 cm^2 **b** 173 cm^2 **c** 18.8 cm^2 **d** 34.9 cm^2 **5 i** 1676 km **ii** 28 km **iii** 0.5 km **6** 36.5 cm^2 **7 i** 13.9 cm **ii** 7.07 cm^2 **8** 41.1 cm^2 **9** 23.3 cm **10** 53.7° **11** 9.4 cm

Exercise 2D

1 a 30 cm^2 **b** 77 cm^2 **c** 24 cm^2 **d** 42 cm^2 **e** 40 m^2 **f** 6 cm **g** 3 cm **h** 10 cm **i** 3 cm **j** 2.5 cm **k** 12 cm **2 a** 27.5 cm, 36.25 cm^2 **b** 33.4 cm, 61.2 cm^2 **c** 39.1 m, 90 m^2 **3 a** 57 m^2 **b** 702.5 cm^2 **c** 84 m^2 **4 a** 47 m^2 **b** 51 m^2 **c** 86 m^2 **5** Shape *c*, 25.5 cm^2 **6** Any pair of lengths that add up to 10 cm. For example: 1 cm, 9 cm; 2 cm, 8 cm; 3 cm, 7 cm; 4 cm, 6 cm; 4.5 cm, 5.5 cm **7** Shape *a*, 28 cm^2 **8** 80.2% **9** 1100000 km^2 **10 a** 30 m, 48 m^2 **b** 52 cm, 150 cm^2

Exercise 2E

1 0.75 g/cm^3 **2** $8\frac{1}{3}$ g/cm^3 **3** 32 g **4** 120 cm^3 **5** 156.8 g **6** 3200 cm^3 **7** 2.72 g/cm^3 **8** 36800 kg (36.8 t) **9** 1.79 g/cm^3 **10** 1.6 g/cm^3

Exercise 2F

1 a i 226.2 cm^2 **ii** 207.3 cm^2 **b i** 445.3 cm^3 **ii** 325.2 cm^2 **c i** 2147.1 cm^3 **ii** 922.5 cm^2 **d i** 24.9 m^3 **ii** 50.5 m^2 **2 a i** 226 cm^3 **ii** 207 cm^2 **b i** 14.9 cm^3 **ii** 61.3 cm^2 **c i** 346 cm^3 **ii** 275 cm^2 **d i** 1060 cm^3 **ii** 636 cm^2 **3** £80.16 **4** 1.23 tonnes **5** 2.8 cm **6** 3.0 cm **7** 6.2 cm **8** 696 cm^3 **9** 297 cm^2 **10** 332 litres **11** 1.71 g/cm^3 **12 a** 3691 cm^3 **b** 29.2 kg **13** 0.461 mm **14** 7.78 g/cm^3 **15** 270 km **16** 340 km

Exercise 2G

1 i a

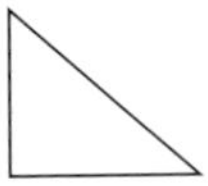

b

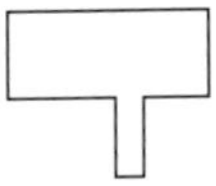

c

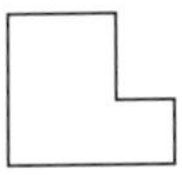

ii a 21 cm^2 **b** 48 cm^2 **c** 36 m^2 **iii a** 63 cm^2 **b** 432 cm^3 **c** 324 m^3 **2 a** 432 m^3 **b** 225 m^3 **c** 1332 m^3 **3** 525 m^3 **4** 146 cm^3 **5 a** 21 cm^3, 210 cm^3 **b** 54 cm^2, 270 cm^2 **6** 7.65 m^3 **7** 19 600 m^3 **8** 327 litres **9** 1.024 t **10** Solid *b* heaviest (2880 g), solid *a* lightest (2851 g) **11** 905 g

Exercise 2H

1 a 56 cm^3 **b** 168 cm^3 **c** 1040 cm^3 **d** 84 cm^3 **e** 133.3 cm^3 **2** 270 cm^3 **3 a** 73.3 m^3 **b** 45 m^3 **c** 3250 cm^3 **4** 208 g **5** 1.5 g/cm^3 **6 a** 201.6 g **b** 441 g **c** 47.25 g **7 a** 9 cm **b** 6 cm **8** 260 cm^3

Exercise 2I

1 a i 3560 cm^3 **ii** 1430 cm^2 **b i** 314 cm^2 **ii** 283 cm^2 **c i** 1020 cm^3 **ii** 679 cm^2 **2** 935 g **3** 75.4 cm^2 **4** 283 cm^2 **5 a** 2560 cm^3 **b** 2260 mm^3 **6 a** 30.2 cm **b** 4.8 cm **c** 6 cm **d** 90.5 cm^2 **e** 3.6 cm **f** 86.9cm^3 **7** 2.8 cm **8 a** 178 cm^3 **b** 50.2 cm^3 **c** 8.39 cm^3 **9 a** 140 g **b** £670 **10** 0.3 cm

Exercise 2J

1 i 3590 cm^3 **ii** 14 140 cm^3 **iii** 8180 cm^3 **2 i** 866 cm^2 **ii** 1720 cm^2 **iii** 3850 cm^2 **3** 65 400 cm^3, 7850 cm^2 **4 i** 1960 cm^2 **ii** 8180 cm^3 **5** 125 cm **6** 6232 **7 a** 3.5 cm **b** 3.3 cm **8** 3.63 cm **9** 489 cm^3 **10** 165 cm^2 **11** 21.1 cm^3 **12 a** 1.4 mm **b** 521 or 522 **c** 0.001 15 mm

Examination questions (Chapter 2)

1 a 48 **b** 1200 cm^2 **c** 19.6 cm^2 **d** 21.5% **2 a** 157 cm **b** 31 830 **3 a** 400 m **b** 10 150 m^2 **4 a** 9.8 m^3 **b** 6860 kg **5 a** 5 litres **b** 26.1 litres **6 a** 38.5 cm^2 **b** 323 cm^3 **8 a** 500 cm^2 **b i** 400 cm^3 **ii** 80% **c i** 42 cm^2 **ii** 9.52 cm **9 a** 462 cm^3 **b** 3 cm **10** 1575 cm^3 **11** 216 m^2 **12 a** 497 cm^3 **b** 319 cm^2 **13 a** 11.9 cm^3 **b** 1 cm **14** 161 cm^3 **15 a** 88.5 cm^3 **b** 106 cm^2

Exercise 3A

1 a $2f + 6$ **b** $3k - 12$ **c** $4t + 4$ **d** $6d + 9$ **e** $12t - 8$ **f** $10m + 6$ **g** $20 + 8w$ **h** $6 - 8x$ **i** $12 + 15p$ **j** $10t + 15w$ **k** $12m - 8d$ **l** $6x + 15y$ **m** $8f + 6$ **n** $40 - 10t$ **o** $12g + 6t$ **2 a** $9x + 14y$ **b** $16t + 23p$ **c** $10x + 23y$ **d** $21p + 13t$ **e** $14x + 2y$ **f** $22x - 21t$ **g** $14p + 10m$ **h** $15t - 23q$ **i** $4x + 2y$ **j** $4t - 10n$ **k** $3p + 16t$ **l** $4x - 11y$ **3 a** 75 pence **b** $15x$ pence **c** $4A$ pence **d** Ay pence **4** £$(A - B)$ **5** £$\frac{A}{5}$ **6** $72 + x$, $T + x$ **7 a** $\frac{T}{2}$ **b** $\frac{T}{2} + 4$ **c** $T - x$ **8 a** £t **b** £$(4t + 3)$ **9 a** $8x$ **b** $12m$ **c** $18t$ **10 a** 51.5 km **b** 15.4 km **c** $(11 + x)$ km **d** $(s + b + r)$ km **e** 112 miles **f** $(T - 20)$ km **11 a** £5000 **b** £$(8M + 5N)$ **c** £$(GM + NT)$

Exercise 3B

1 i 8 **ii** 17 **iii** 32 **2 i** 3 **ii** 11 **iii** 43 **3 i** 9 **ii** 15 **iii** 29 **4 i** 9 **ii** 5 **iii** –1 **5 i** 13 **ii** 33 **iii** 78 **6 i** 10 **ii** 13 **iii** 58 **7 i** 4 **ii** 7.2 **iii** 26.4 **8 i** 6.5 **ii** 0.5 **iii** –2.5 **9 i** 1 **ii** –3 **iii** 6 **10 i** –7 **ii** –10 **iii** 6.5 **11 i** 0 **ii** –12 **iii** 18 **12 i** 12 **ii** 14 **iii** 4.4 **13 i** 13 **ii** –3 **iii** 5 **14 i** 15.4 **ii** –20 **iii** –0.5 **15 i** 13.5 **ii** –16 **iii** $2\frac{2}{3}$ **16 i** 5 **ii** 12.6 **iii** $6\frac{1}{2}$ **17 i** 2 **ii** 8 **iii** –10 **18 i** 3 **ii** 2.5 **iii** –5 **19 i** 6 **ii** 3 **iii** –2 **20 i** –4.8 **ii** 48 **iii** 32

Exercise 3C

1 a 2.2 **b** 2.125 **c** 1.3 **2 a** 1.4 **b** 1.4 **c** –0.4 **3 a** 1.8 **b** 3 **c** $1\frac{7}{9}$ (Accept 1.78) **4 a** 9 **b** 25 **c** 1.44 **5 a** 2.375 **b** –19.5 **c** 6.02 **6 a** 13 **b** 74 **c** 17 **7 a** 27 **b** 5 **c** 0 **8 a** 4 **b** –3 **c** 1.5 **9 a** 75 **b** 8 **c** –4 **10 a** 75 **b** 22.5 **c** –30 **11 a** 9.08 **b** 63.6 **c** 191 **12 a** 6.84 **b** 5 **c** 7.17 **13 a** 0.889 **b** 1.4 **c** 0.2 **14 a** ±3.32 **b** ±2.24 **c** ±4.06 **15 a** ±7.21 **b** ±8.75 **c** ±7.62

Exercise 3D

1 2 **2** 13 **3** 13 **4** 6 **5** 1 **6** 3 **7** 12 **8** 1 **9** 9 **10** 56 **11** 2 **12** 5 **13** 3 **14** 4 **15** 2.5 **16** 3.5 **17** 2.5 **18** 4 **19** 4 **20** 4.5 **21** 1.5 **22** 3.5 **23** 1.2 **24** 1.8

Exercise 3E

1 15 **2** 6 **3** 28 **4** 16 **5** 40 **6** 24 **7** 8 **8** 16 **9** 30 **10** 21 **11** 72 **12** 56 **13** 10 **14** 6 **15** 12 **16** 6 **17** 10.5 **18** 12.5 **19** –0.4 **20** –1.4

Exercise 3F

1 –1 **2** –3 **3** –2 **4** –3 **5** –1 **6** –2 **7** –3 **8** –6 **9** –10 **10** 7 **11** 17 **12** –4 **13** 7 **14** 2.8 **15** 1.75 **16** 7 **17** 6 **18** 1 **19** 11.5 **20** 0.2

Exercise 3G

1 3 **2** 7 **3** 5 **4** 3 **5** 4 **6** 6 **7** 8 **8** 1 **9** 1.5 **10** 2.5 **11** 0.5 **12** 1.2 **13** 2.4 **14** 4.5 **15** 3.5 **16** 2 **17** –2 **18** –1 **19** –2 **20** –2 **21** –1 **22** –4 **23** –2 **24** –1.5

Exercise 3H

1 a 4, 5 **b** 7, 8 **c** 23, 24 **2 a** 5.3 **b** 6.7 **c** 8.4 **3 a** 2.7 **b** 5.8 **c** 1.7 **4 a** 8.3 **b** 4.3 **c** 7.2

Exercise 3I

1 7.8 cm × 12.8 cm **2** 19.0 m × 29.0 m **3** 5.68 m × 6.68 cm **4** 10.3 cm × 9.3 cm **5** 7.8 cm × 7.8 cm × 7.8 cm **6** 7.1 cm **7** 3.5 cm **8** 1.80 cm **9 a** 5.2 **b** 3.2 **c** 1.4 **10** 2.6

Exercise 3J

1 $x = 4, y = 1$ **2** $x = 1, y = 4$ **3** $x = 3, y = 1$ **4** $x = 5, y = 2$ **5** $x = 7, y = 1$ **6** $x = 5, y = \frac{1}{2}$ **7** $x = 4, y = 2$ **8** $x = 2, y = 4$ **9** $x = 3, y = 5$ **10** $x = 2.25, y = 6.5$ **11** $x = 4, y = 3$ **12** $x = 5, y = 3$

Exercise 3K

1 $x = 2, y = 3$ **2** $x = 7, y = 3$ **3** $x = 4, y = 1$ **4** $x = 2, y = 5$ **5** $x = 4, y = 3$ **6** $x = 1, y = 7$ **7** $x = 2, y = 1$ **8** $x = 3, y = 5$ **9** $x = 6, y = 3$ **10** $x = 8, y = 2$ **11** $x = 1, y = 5$ **12** $x = 4, y = 3$

Exercise 3L

1 $x = 2, y = 5$ **2** $x = 3, y = 4$ **3** $x = 1, y = 4$ **4** $x = 6, y = 2$ **5** $x = 7, y = 3$ **6** $x = 4, y = 3$ **7** $x = 5, y = 1$ **8** $x = 3, y = 8$ **9** $x = 9, y = 1$ **10** $x = 7, y = 3$ **11** $x = 4, y = 2$ **12** $x = 6, y = 5$

Exercise 3M

1 $x = 3, y = -2$ **2** $x = 2, y = \frac{1}{2}$ **3** $x = -\frac{3}{7}, y = 3\frac{2}{7}$ **4** $x = 1.5, y = 4$ **5** $x = 3.5, y = 1.5$ **6** $x = -2, y = -3$ **7** $x = -1, y = 2.5$ **8** $x = -3, y = -2$ **9** $x = 2.5, y = -0.5$ **10** $x = -1.5, y = 4.5$ **11** $x = -2.5, y = -3.5$ **12** $x = -0.5, y = -6.5$

Exercise 3N

1 Amul £7.20, Kim £3.50 **2** £1.49 **3** £2.25 **4** 84p **5** 10.3 kg **6** £4.40 **7** £62.00 **8** £195 **9** 2 h 10 min

Exercise 3P

1 i $n = \frac{W-t}{3}$ **ii** $t = W - 3n$ **2 i** $y = \frac{x+w}{5}$ **ii** $w = 5y - x$ **3 i** $m = \frac{p-t}{7}$ **ii** $t = p - 7m$ **4 i** $k = \frac{t+f}{2}$ **ii** $f = 2k - t$ **5 i** $m = \frac{g-v}{6}$ **ii** $v = g - 6m$ **6** $m = \sqrt{t}$ **7** $p = \sqrt{k}$ **8** $b = \sqrt{(a-3)}$ **9** $h = \sqrt{(w+5)}$ **10** $p = \sqrt{(m-2)}$ **11 i** $t = u^2 - v$ **ii** $u = \sqrt{(v+t)}$ **12 i** $m = k - n^2$ **ii** $n = \sqrt{(k-m)}$ **13** $r = \sqrt{\left(\frac{T}{5}\right)}$ **14** $t = \sqrt{\left(\frac{P}{3}\right)}$ **15 i** $w = K - 5n^2$ **ii** $n = \sqrt{\left(\frac{K-w}{5}\right)}$

Examination questions (Chapter 3)

1 a $2\frac{3}{8}$ (Accept 2.375) **b** $\frac{5}{8}$ (Accept 0.625) **2 a** £$6x$ **b** £$4y$ **c** £$(6x + 4y)$ **d** £$(20x - 40)$ **3 a i** $8y$ **ii** $6y + 6$ **b** 3 **c** 6 cm^2 **4 a** $x + 3$ **b** $2(2x + 3)$ **c** $4x + 6 = 32$, 6.5 cm and 9.5 cm **5 a** $y = 2x + 1$ **b** 4 **6** 2.5 **7 i** 2, 3 **ii** 2.7 **8 a** 51 **b** $t = \frac{v-u}{g}$ **c** 7.5 **9 i** $x + y = 40$, $2x + 3.5y = 92$ **ii** $x = 32$, $y = 8$ **10** $x = 3$, $y = -2$ **11** $a = 3.5$, $c = 1.5$ **12 a** £129 **b i** $t = \frac{c-500}{80}$ **ii** 5

Exercise 4A

1 10.30 cm **2** 5.92 cm **3** 8.49 cm **4** 20.62 cm **5** 18.60 cm **6** 17.49 cm **7** 32.2 cm **8** 2.42 m **9** 500 m **10** 707.11 m **11** 6.73 cm **12** 1.06 cm

Exercise 4B

1 a 15 cm **b** 14.66 cm **c** 6.33 cm **d** 18.33 cm **e** 5.40 cm **f** 217.94 m **g** 0.44 cm **h** 8 m **2 a** 19.85 m **b** 15.49 cm **c** 15.49 m **d** 12.38 cm **e** 22.91 m **f** 19.85 m **g** 7.14 m **h** 0.64 m **i** 16.61 m **j** 10.20 m **k** 4.53 m **l** 10.04 cm

Exercise 4C

1 6.63 m **2** 2.06 m **3** 10.82 m **4** 11.31 m **5** 9.22 m **6** 19.21 km **7** 147.05 km **8** 2.37 km **9 a** 127 m **b** 99.62 m **c** 27.38 m **10** 12 ft **11 a** 3.87 m **b** 1.74 m **12** 3.16 m **13** 5.10 **14 a** 4.74 **b** 4.54 m **15** 16.47 cm^2 **16** 58.59 km **17** 192.35 **18** 120.01 m **19** $25^2 = 24^2 + 7^2$: therefore, right-angled **20** 7.21

Exercise 4D

1 32.25 cm^2, 2.83 cm^2, 49.99 cm^2 **2** 22.25cm^2 **3** 15.59 cm^2 **4** 27.71 **5 a**

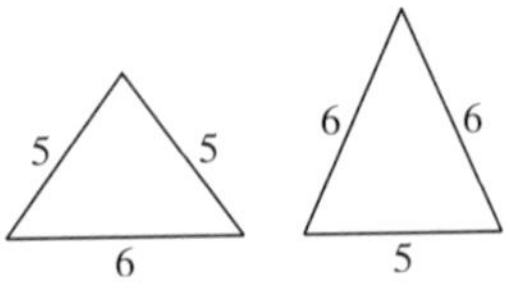

b 166.26 cm^2

b Triangle with 6 cm, 6 cm, 5 cm **6 a**

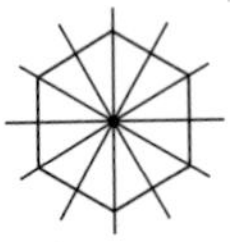

7 259.81 cm^2 **8** 8.25 cm, 11.66 cm, 5.72 cm

Exercise 4E

1 a i 14.4 cm **ii** 13 cm **iii** 9.4 cm **b** 15.3 cm **2** No **3 a** 24 cm and 20.6 cm **b** 15.0 cm **4** 21.3 cm **5** 4.24 m, 5.19 m **6 a** 8.94 cm **b** 5 cm **c** 8.54 cm **d** 9.43 cm **7 a** 11.3 cm **b** 7 cm **c** 8.06 cm **8 a** 13 cm **b** 15 cm **c** 15.8 cm **9 a** 50 cm **b** 54.8 cm **c** 48.3 cm **d** 27.0 cm

Exercise 4F

1 a 0.682 **b** 0.829 **c** 0.922 **d** 1.00 **e** 0.707 **f** 0.342 **g** 0.375 **h** 0.00 **i** 0.574 **j** 0.966 **k** 1.0 **l** 0.946 **2 a** 0.731 **b** 0.559 **c** 0.388 **d** 0.00 **e** 0.707 **f** 0.940 **g** 0.927 **h** 1.00 **i** 0.819 **j** 0.259 **k** 0.017 **l** 0.326 **3** 45° **4 a i** 0.574 **ii** 0.574 **b i** 0.208 **ii** 0.208 **c i** 0.391 **ii** 0.391 **d** Same

e **i** sin 15° is the same as cos 75° **ii** cos 82° is the same as sin 8° **iii** sin x is the same as cos $(90° - x)$ **5** **a** 0.933 **b** 1.483 **c** 2.379 **d** Infinite **e** 1.000 **f** 0.364 **g** 0.404 **h** 0.000 **i** 0.700 **j** 3.732 **k** 57.290 **l** 5.145 **6** **a** 0.956 **b** 0.899 **c** 2.164 **d** 0.999 **e** 0.819 **f** 0.577 **g** 0.469 **h** 0.996 **i** 0.754 **j** 0.956 **k** 0.191 **l** 5.145 **7** Has values > 1 **8** **a** 4.532 **b** 4.459 **c** 3.500 **d** 0.624 **e** 6.000 **f** 0.000 **g** 3.508 **h** 1.871 **9** **a** 10.723 **b** 5.402 **c** 3.669 **d** 14.114 **e** Infinite **f** 0.000 **g** 39.250 **h** 1.913 **10** **a** 3.564 **b** 8.960 **c** 14.375 **d** 9.900 **e** 28.356 **f** 8.912 **g** 66.261 **h** 2.622 **11** **a** 5.612 **b** 7.075 **c** 19.940 **d** 4.483 **e** 6.000 **f** 10.000 **g** 12.548 **h** 43.288 **12** **a** 1.463 **b** 7.774 **c** 17.893 **d** 14.372 **e** 0.401 **f** 7.151 **g** 8.152 **h** 19.801 **13** **a** 7.727 **b** 48.627 **c** 2.279 **d** 15.187 **e** 28.430 **f** 6.725 **g** 21.459 **h** 16.935 **14** **a** 29.856 **b** 44.761 **c** 20.329 **d** 2.376 **e** 16.710 **f** 7.032 **g** 17.791 **h** 194.311 **15** **a** 6.568 **b** 12.803 **c** 57.870 **d** 9.697 **e** 1.555 **f** 7.779 **g** 7.927 **h** 16.984 **16** **a** 6.973 **b** 19.940 **c** 14.432 **d** 12.051 **e** 15.681 **f** 28.954 **g** 21.139 **h** 4.659

Exercise 4G

1 **a** 30° **b** 51.7° **c** 39.8° **d** 61.3° **e** 87.4° **f** 45.0° **g** 5.9° **h** 46.2° **i** 62.6° **j** 11.5° **k** 44.4° **l** 48.6° **2** **a** 60° **b** 38.3° **c** 50.2° **d** 28.7° **e** 2.6° **f** 45.0° **g** 84.1° **h** 43.8° **i** 27.4° **j** 78.5° **k** 45.6° **l** 41.4° **3** **a** 31.0° **b** 20.8° **c** 44.2° **d** 13.9° **e** 17.0° **f** 41.8° **g** 46.4° **h** 52.2° **i** 60.7° **j** 63.1° **k** 69.5° **l** 77.1° **4** **a** 53.1° **b** 41.8° **c** 44.4° **d** 56.4° **e** 2.4° **f** 22.6° **g** 73.7° **h** 14.5° **5** **a** 36.9° **b** 48.2° **c** 45.6° **d** 33.6° **e** 87.6° **f** 67.4° **g** 16.3° **h** 75.5° **6** **a** 31.0° **b** 37.9° **c** 15.9° **d** 60.9° **e** 57.5° **f** 50.2° **g** 36.9° **h** 5.2° **7** Error message, largest value 1, smallest value –1 **8** **a** **i** 17.5° **ii** 72.5° **iii** 90° **b** Yes

Exercise 4H

1 **a** 17.5° **b** 22.0° **c** 32.2° **2** **a** 5.288 cm **b** 5.755 cm **c** 13.248 cm **3** **a** 4.573 cm **b** 6.860 cm **c** 100.4 cm **4** **a** 5.119 cm **b** 9.766 cm **c** 6.292 cm **d** 15.53 cm **e** 9.506 cm **f** 10.199 cm **g** 17.058 cm **h** 22.17 cm **5** **a** 47.2° **b** 5.416 cm **c** 13.681 cm **d** 38.0° **e** 14.153 cm **f** 51.1° **g** 6.698 cm **h** 44.0°

Exercise 4I

1 51.3°, 75.5°, 51.3° **2** 6.474 cm, 32.640 cm, 136.941 cm **3** **a** 5.353 cm **b** 14.833 cm **c** 12.041 cm **d** 8.619 cm **e** 12.306 cm **f** 5.871 cm **g** 4.767 cm **h** 43.415 cm **4** 7.325 cm, 39.066 cm, 134.817 cm **5** **a** 5.592 cm **b** 46.6° **c** 4.264 cm **d** 40.1° **e** 13.268 cm **f** 40.4° **g** 11.873 cm **h** 56.918 cm

Exercise 4J

1 33.7°, 36.9°, 52.1° **2** 5.094 cm, 30.353 cm, 1119.6 cm **3** 8.242 cm, 61.971 cm, 72.794 cm **4** **a** 9.020 cm **b** 7.507 cm **c** 7.143 cm **d** 8.895 cm **e** 13.083 cm **f** 8.104 cm **g** 11.301 cm **h** 50.780 cm **5** **a** 13.738 cm **b** 48.4° **c** 7.032 cm **d** 41.2° **e** 8.360 cm **f** 19.845 cm **g** 58.2° **h** 5.236 cm

Exercise 4K

1 **a** 12.586 **b** 59.588 cm **c** 74.724 **d** 15.973 **e** 67.881 **f** 20.054 **g** 20.128 **h** 9.139 **i** 1.545 **2** **a** 44.4° **b** 39.8° **c** 44.4° **d** 49.5° **e** 58.7° **f** 38.7° **g** 48.2° **h** 38.9° **i** 66.4° **3** **a** 67.4° **b** 11.326 **c** 133.512 **d** 28.1° **e** 39.725 **f** 263.459 **g** 50.2° **h** 51.3° **i** 138.198 **j** 22.776

Exercise 4L

1 65.4° **2** 2.05–3.00 m **3** 44.4° **4** 6.82 m **5** 7.03 m **6** 31° **7** 5.657 cm **8** 25.3° **9** 19.6°, 4.776 m **10** 0.498 m **11** 42.45 m **12** 21.138 m

Exercise 4M

1 10.101 km **2** 21.8° **3** 428.9 m **4** 156.26 m **5** 222.4 m, 42° **6** **a** 21.46 m **b** 17.79 m **7** 13.4 m **8** 19.5°

Exercise 4N

1 **a** 73.36 km **b** 15.59 km **2** **a** 14.72 km **b** 8.5 km **3** 120.3° **4** **a** 59.4 km **b** 8.4 km **5** **a** 15.89 km **b** 24.11 km **c** 31.185 km **d** 37.7° **6** 2.28 km **7** **a** 66.22 km **b** 11.74 km **c** 13.14 km **d** 260.4° **8** 43.29 km, 101.5°

Exercise 4P

1 5.786 cm **2** 48.2° **3** 7.416 cm **4** 81.63 cm **5** 9.865 m **6** **a** 36.40 cm^2 **b** 115.44 cm^2 **c** 90.6 cm^2 **d** 159.93 cm^2

Examination questions (Chapter 4)

1 8.20 m **2** **a** 1:25000 **b** 24.41 km **3** **a** 38.11 m **b** 697.5 m^3 **4** Kevin, because $14^2 \neq 11^2 + 9^2$ **5** 40.17 cm^2 **6** **a** 17000 ft **b** 39.8 miles **7** **a** **i** 60 mm^2 **ii** 2.4 **iii** 67.4° **b** 23.42 cm **8** **a** 7.616 m **b** ≈ 31° **9** **a** **i** 19.08 m **ii** 72.5° **b** 27.19 m **10** **a** 75.5° **b** 7.75 m **11** **a** 1.9° **b** 450 m **c** ≈ 0.9 km/h **12** **a** 4.49 m **b** 35.95 m^2 **13** **a** **ii** 226° **b** 170 km **c** **i** 28.1° **ii** 344°

Exercise 5A

1 **a** 1440° **b** 2340° **c** 17640° **d** 7740° **2** **a** 150° **b** 162° **c** 140° **d** 174° **3** **a** 9 **b** 15 **c** 102 **d** 50 **4** **a** 15 **b** 36 **c** 24 **d** 72 **5** **a** 12 **b** 9 **c** 20 **d** 40 **6** **a** 130 **b** 95 **c** 130 **7** **a** 50° **b** 37° **c** 64.375° **8** Hexagon **9** **a** Octagon **b** 89° **10** $a = b = 70°, c = 50°, d = 80°, e = 55°, f = 70°, g = h = 57\frac{1}{2}°$ **11** **a** 75° **b** 50° **c** 62° **d** 40° **12**

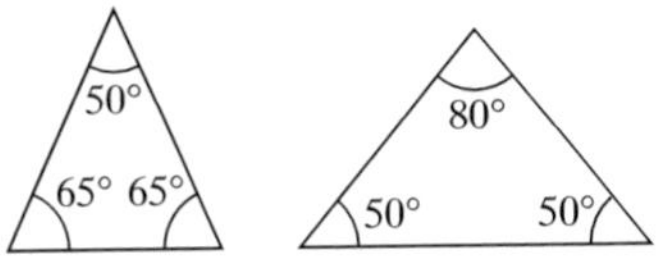

13 40°, 40°, 100° **14** $a = b = 65°, c = d = 115°, e = f = 65°, g = 80°, h = 60°, i = 60°, j = 60°, k = 20°$ **15** **a** 108° **b** 36° **c** 72° **16** **a** 120° **b** 90° **c** 60° **17** **a** 135° **b** 67.5° **c** 22.5°

Exercise 5B

1 $a = 110°, b = 55°, c = 75°, d = 115°, e = 87°, f = 48°$ **2** $a = c = 105°, b = 75°, d = f = 70°, c = 110°, g = i = 63°, h = 117°$ **3** $a = 135°, b = 25°, c = d = 145°, e = f = 94°$ **4** $a = c = 105°, b = 75°, d = f = 93°, e = 87°, g = i = 49°, h = 131°$ **5** $a = 58°, b = 47°, c = 141°, d = 37°, e = g = 65°, f = 115°$ **6** **a** $x = 25°, y = 15°$ **b** $x = 8°, y = 17°$ **c** $x = 7°, y = 31°$ **7** $a = 40°, b = 75°, c = 15°, d = 75°, e = 75°, f = 105°, g = 105°, h = 10°, i = 95°, j = 35°$ **8** **a** $x = 60°, y = 30°$ **b** $x = 7°, y = 40°$ **9** **a** $x = 65°$ **b** $x = 73°$ **c** $x = 55°$ **10** **a** $w = 25°, x = 15°, y = 65°$ **b** $x = 23°, y = 88°$ **c** $a = 65°, b = 45°, c = 135°, d = 25°, e = 45°, f = 70°, g = 135°, x = 20°$ **11** **a** $x = 50°$: 60°, 70°, 120°, 110° – trapezium **b** $x = 60°$: 50°, 130°, 50°, 130° – parallelogram **c** $x = 30°$: 20°, 60°, 140°, 140° – kite **d** $x = 20°$: 90°, 90°, 90°, 90° – square

Exercise 5C

1 **a** 56° **b** 62° **c** 105° **d** 115° **e** 55° **f** 45° **g** 30° **h** 60° **i** 32° **j** 145° **k** 133° **l** 24° **2** **a** 55° **b** 52° **c** 50° **d** 24° **e** 39° **f** 80° **g** 34° **h** 30° **3** **a** 41° **b** 49° **c** 41° **4** 109° **5** **a** 72° **b** 37° **c** 72° **6** 68° **7** **a** $x = y = 40°$ **b** $x = 131°, y = 111°$ **c** $x = 134°, y = 23°$ **d** $x = 32°, y = 19°$ **e** $x = 59°, y = 121°$ **f** $x = 155°, y = 12\frac{1}{2}°$

Exercise 5D

1 **a** $a = 50°, b = 95°$ **b** $c = 92°, x = 90°$ **c** $d = 110°, e = 110°, f = 70°$ **d** $d = 99°, e = 105°$ **e** $j = 89°, k = 89°, l = 91°$ **f** $m = 120°, n = 40°$ **g** $p = 44°, q = 68°$ **h** $x = 40°, y = 34°$ **2** **a** $x = 64°, y = 128°$ **b** $x = 48°, y = 78°$ **c** $x = 137°, y = 47°$ **d** $x = 36°, y = 72°$ **e** $x = 55°, y = 125°$ **f** $x = 35°$ **g** $x = 48°, y = 45°$ **h** $x = 66°, y = 38°$ **3** **a** $x = 49°, y = 49°$ **b** $x = 70°, y = 20°$ **c** $x = 80°, y = 100°$ **d** $x = 100°, y = 75°$ **4** **a** $x = 50°, y = 62°$ **b** $x = 92°$ **c** $x = 93°, y = 42°$ **d** $x = 55°, y = 75°$ **5** **a** $x = 95°, y = 138°$ **b** $x = 14°, y = 62°$ **c** $x = 32°, y = 48°$ **d** 52° **6** **a** 71° **b** $125\frac{1}{2}°$

Exercise 5E

1 **a** 38° **b** 110° **c** 15° **d** 45° **2** **a** 6 cm **b** 10.8 cm **c** 0.47 cm **d** 8 cm **3** **a** $x = 12°, y = 156°$ **b** $x = 100°, y = 50°$ **c** $x = 62°, y = 28°$ **d** $x = 30°, y = 60°$ **4** **a** 62° **b** 66° **c** 19° **d** 20° **5** 191.6 cm^2 (Radii are 6, 4, 3 cm) **6** 64.1 cm^2 **7** 19.5 cm

Exercise 5F

1 **a** $a = 65°, b = 75°, c = 40°$ **b** $d = 79°, e = 58°, f = 43°$ **c** $g = 41°, h = 76°, i = 76°$ **d** $k = 80°, m = 52°, n = 80°$ **2** **a** $a = 75°, b = 75°, c = 75°, d = 30°$ **b** $a = 47°, b = 86°, c = 86°, d = 47°$ **c** $a = 52\frac{1}{2}°, b = 52\frac{1}{2}°$ **d** $a = 55°$ **3** **a** 36° **b** 70° **4** **a** $x = 25°$ **b** $x = 46°, y = 69°, z = 65°$ **c** $x = 38°, y = 70°, z = 20°$ **d** $x = 48°, y = 42°$

Examination questions (Chapter 5)

1 a i 50° **ii** Equal angles in isosceles triangle and angle sum is 180° **b** 110° **c** 213.6 cm **2 a** 50°: EAC is isosceles triangle **b** 80°: sum of angles in triangle = 180° **3 a** 45° **b** 135° **4 a** 90° **b i** 72° **ii** 108° **5 a** 80° **b i** Rhombus **ii** All sides equal, opposite angles equal **6 a** 60° **b** 120° **c** On a straight line (120° + 60° = 180°) **d** 60° **e** Parallel (alternate angles equal) **7 i** 20° **ii** Alternate angle to 32° **iii** 48° **8** $x = 126°$, $y = 121\frac{1}{2}°$ **9 a** 80° **b** 74° **10 a** $p = 192°$, $q = 84°$ **b** 72° **11 a** $m = 35°$, $n = 126°$ **b i** $3x$ **ii** x **iii** $180° - 6x$ **c** Because both CD and DE are altitudes of triangle ACE. Area of triangle ACE = $\frac{1}{2}$ CD × AE = $\frac{1}{2}$ BE × AC **12 a** 65° **b** 130° **c** 50°

Exercise 6A

1 a Yes : SAS **b** Yes : SSS **c** No **d** No **e** Yes : ASA **f** Yes : RHS **g** Yes : SSS **h** Yes : ASA

2

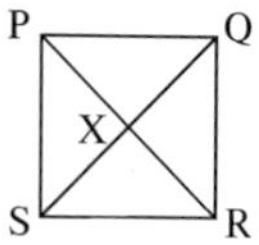

PQR to PSR to SPQ to SRQ, PXS to PXQ to QXR to RXS

3

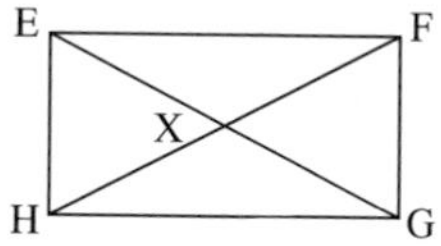

EGF to FHE to GEH to HFG, EXH to FXG, EXF to HXG

4

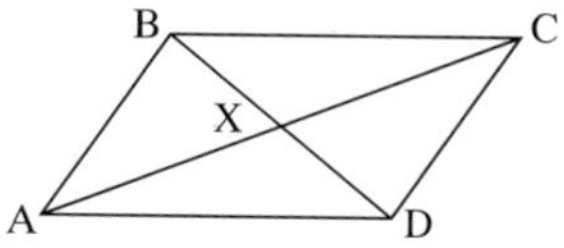

ABC to ADC, BDC to DBA, BXA to DXC, BXC to DXA

5

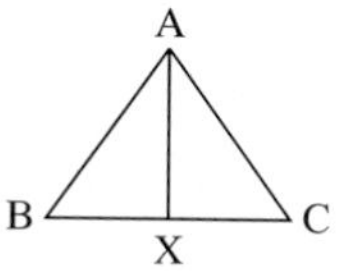

AXB to AXC

6 a Yes: SSS. A to R, B to P, C to Q **b** No **c** Yes : SAS. A to R, B to Q, C to P **d** No **7 i** 60° **ii** 80° **iii** 40° **iv** 5 cm **8 i** 110° **ii** 55° **iii** 85° **iv** 110° **v** 4 cm

Exercise 6B

1 a i $\begin{pmatrix}1\\3\end{pmatrix}$ **ii** $\begin{pmatrix}4\\2\end{pmatrix}$ **iii** $\begin{pmatrix}2\\-1\end{pmatrix}$ **iv** $\begin{pmatrix}5\\1\end{pmatrix}$ **v** $\begin{pmatrix}-1\\6\end{pmatrix}$ **vi** $\begin{pmatrix}4\\6\end{pmatrix}$

b i $\begin{pmatrix}-1\\-3\end{pmatrix}$ **ii** $\begin{pmatrix}3\\-1\end{pmatrix}$ **iii** $\begin{pmatrix}1\\-4\end{pmatrix}$ **iv** $\begin{pmatrix}4\\-2\end{pmatrix}$ **v** $\begin{pmatrix}-2\\3\end{pmatrix}$ **vi** $\begin{pmatrix}3\\3\end{pmatrix}$

c i $\begin{pmatrix}-4\\-2\end{pmatrix}$ **ii** $\begin{pmatrix}-3\\1\end{pmatrix}$ **iii** $\begin{pmatrix}-2\\-3\end{pmatrix}$ **iv** $\begin{pmatrix}1\\-1\end{pmatrix}$ **v** $\begin{pmatrix}-5\\4\end{pmatrix}$ **vi** $\begin{pmatrix}0\\4\end{pmatrix}$

d i $\begin{pmatrix}3\\2\end{pmatrix}$ **ii** $\begin{pmatrix}-4\\2\end{pmatrix}$ **iii** $\begin{pmatrix}5\\-4\end{pmatrix}$ **iv** $\begin{pmatrix}-2\\-7\end{pmatrix}$ **v** $\begin{pmatrix}5\\0\end{pmatrix}$ **vi** $\begin{pmatrix}1\\-5\end{pmatrix}$

2

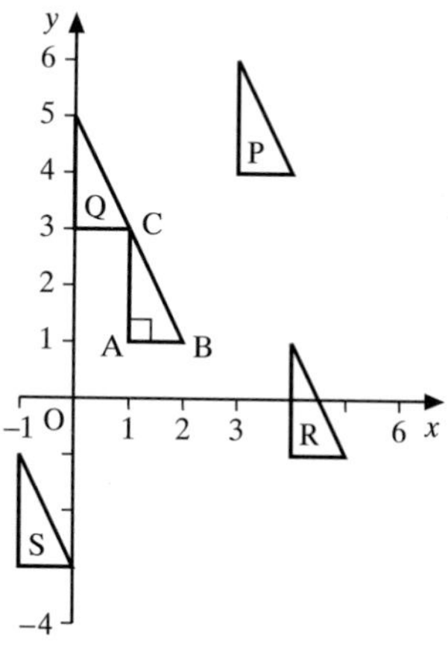

3 a $\begin{pmatrix}-3\\-1\end{pmatrix}$ **b** $\begin{pmatrix}4\\-4\end{pmatrix}$ **c** $\begin{pmatrix}-5\\-2\end{pmatrix}$ **d** $\begin{pmatrix}4\\7\end{pmatrix}$ **e** $\begin{pmatrix}-1\\5\end{pmatrix}$ **f** $\begin{pmatrix}1\\6\end{pmatrix}$

g $\begin{pmatrix}-4\\4\end{pmatrix}$ **h** $\begin{pmatrix}-4\\-7\end{pmatrix}$

4 19 × 19 = 361 (including $\begin{pmatrix}0\\0\end{pmatrix}$)

Exercise 6C

1

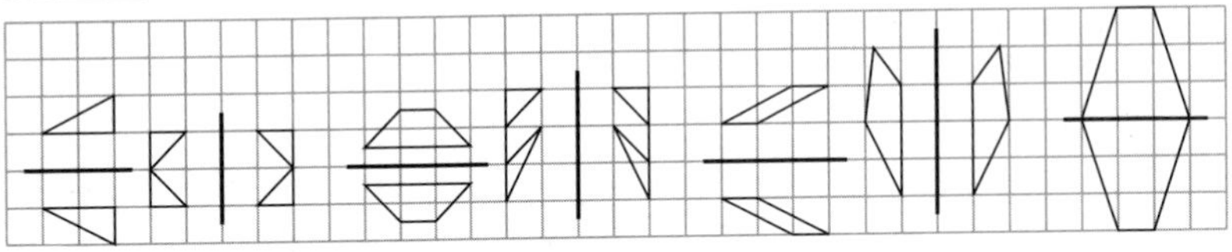

2

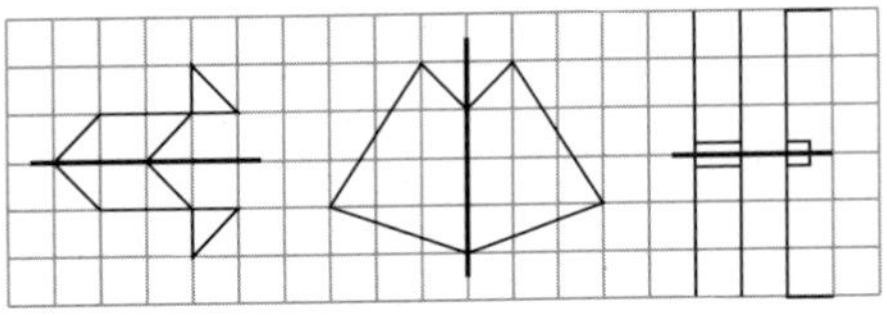

3 a–e

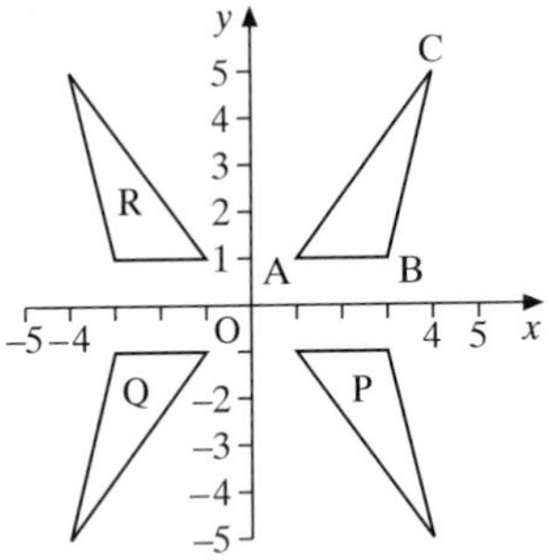

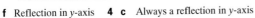

f Reflection in *y*-axis **4 c** Always a reflection in *y*-axis

5

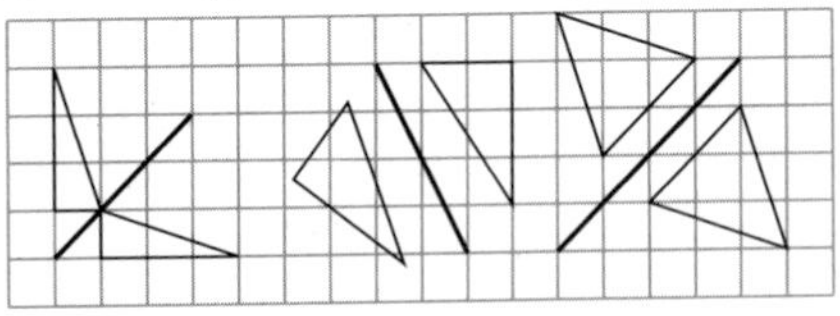

6

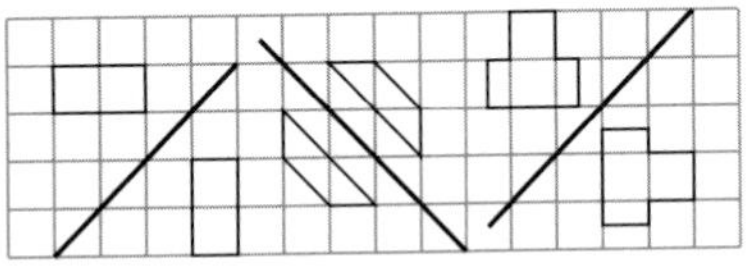

7 a–i

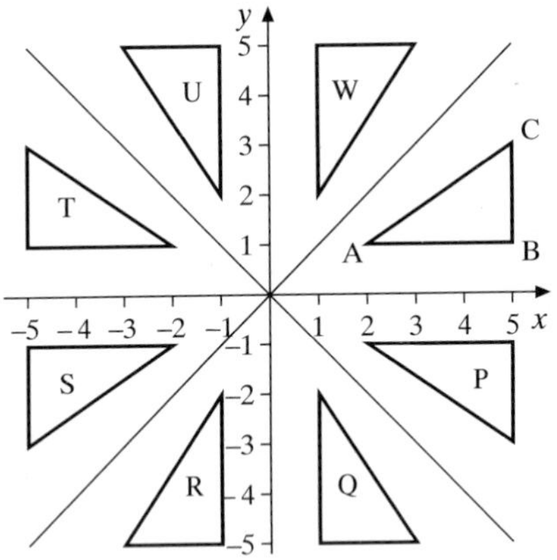

j Reflection in $y = x$ **8 c** Always a reflection in $y = x$
9 c iii *x*-co-ordinates stay the same, *y*-co-ordinates change sign (+ to –, – to +) **iv** Yes **10 c iii** *y*-co-ordinates stay the same, *x*-co-ordinates change sign (+ to –, – to +) **iv** Yes **11 c iii** *x* and *y*-co-ordinates change over **iv** Yes **12 c iii** *x* and *y*-co-ordinates change over and change sign **iv** Yes

Exercise 6D

1 a

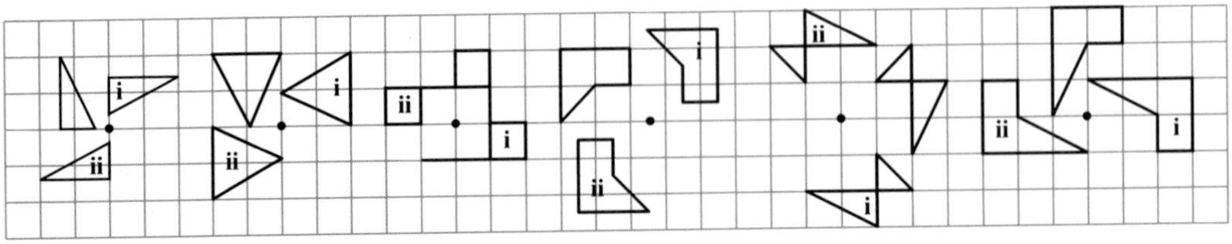

b Rotation 90° anticlockwise *or* rotation 270° clockwise

2 a

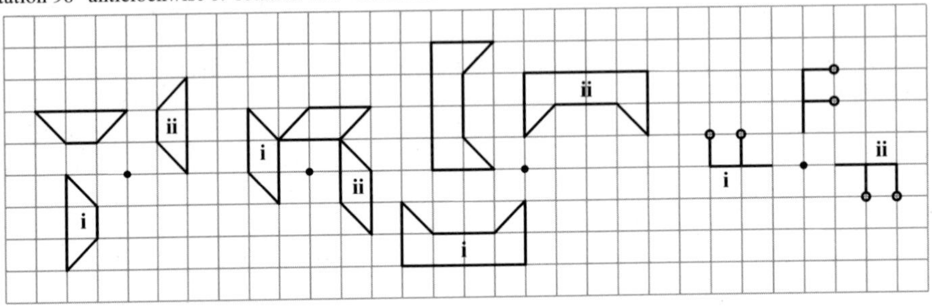

b Rotation 90° clockwise **c** Rotation 270° anticlockwise **4 a** 90° anticlockwise **b** 270° anticlockwise **c** 300° clockwise **d** 260° clockwise **5 c iii** Original co-ordinates (x, y) become $(y, -x)$ **iv** Yes **6 iii** Original co-ordinates (x, y) become $(-x, -y)$ **iv** Yes **7 iii** Original co-ordinates (x, y) become $(-y, x)$ **iv** Yes

8 a–c

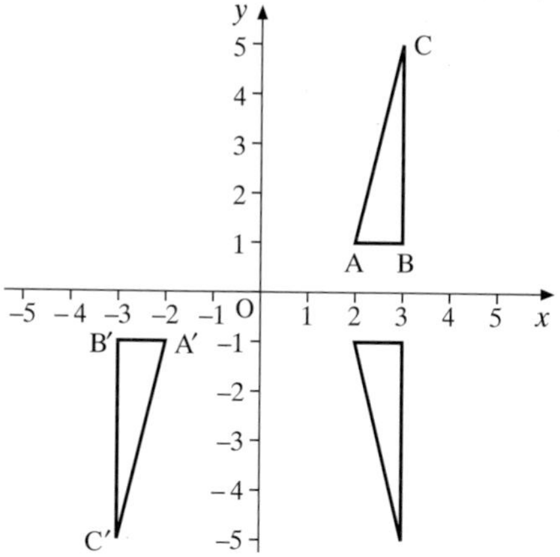

d Rotation 180° **e** Yes **f** Yes

9 a

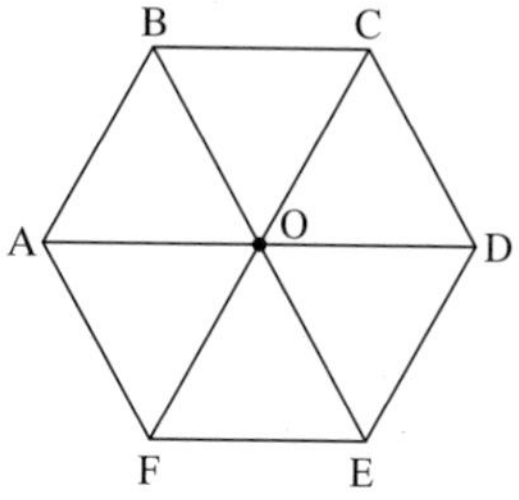

b i Rotation 60° clockwise about O **ii** Rotation 120° clockwise about O **iii** Rotation 180° about O **iv** Rotation 240° clockwise about O. **c i** Rotation 60° clockwise about O **ii** Rotation 180° about O **10 a i** Rotation 72° clockwise about O **ii** Rotation 72° clockwise about O **b i** BOC, COD, DOE, EOA **iii** BDE, CAE, DAB, EBC

Exercise 6E

1

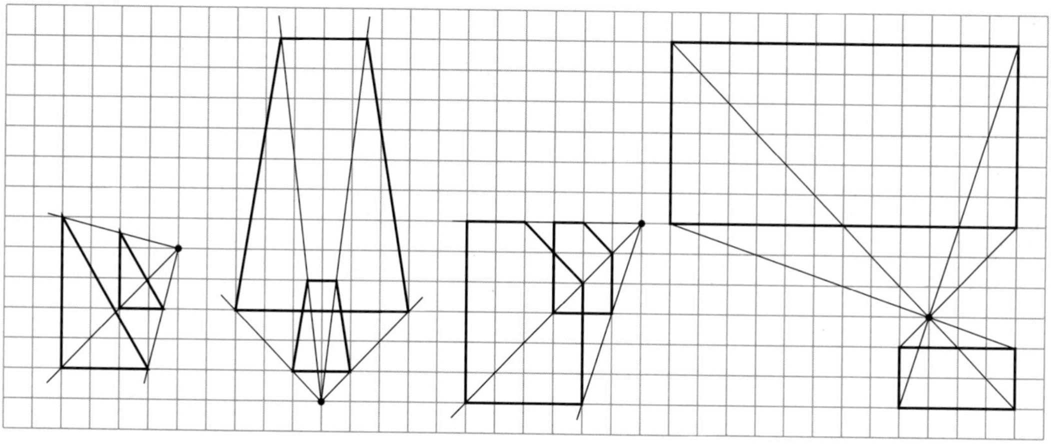

2

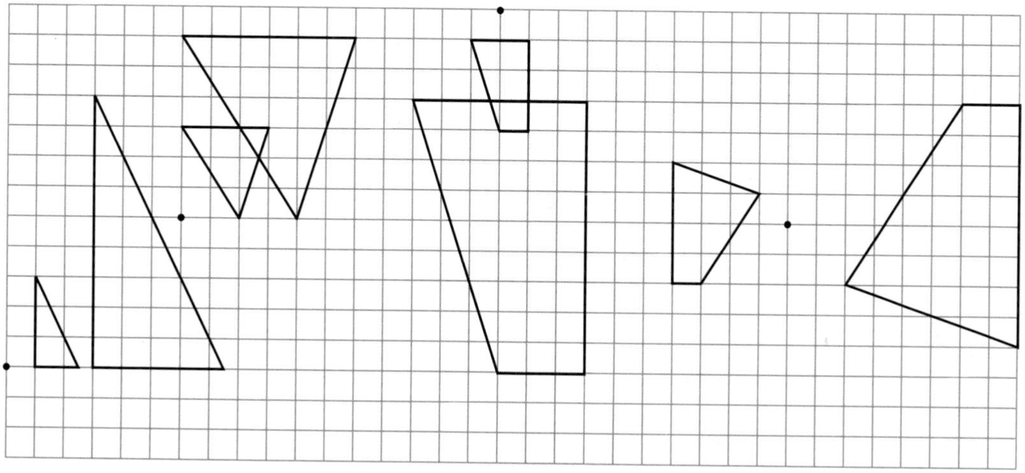

3 d All shapes the same

4

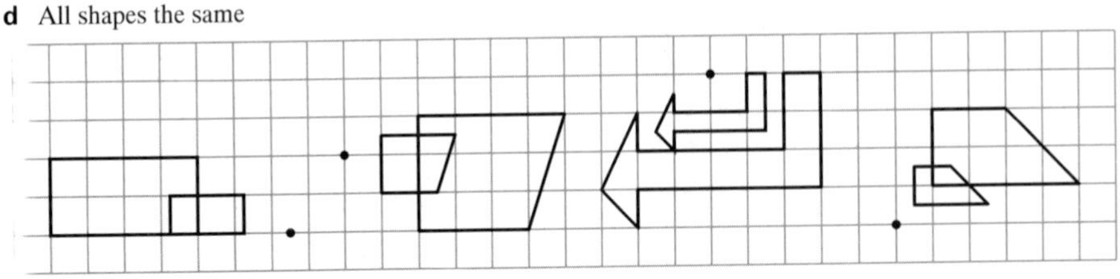

5

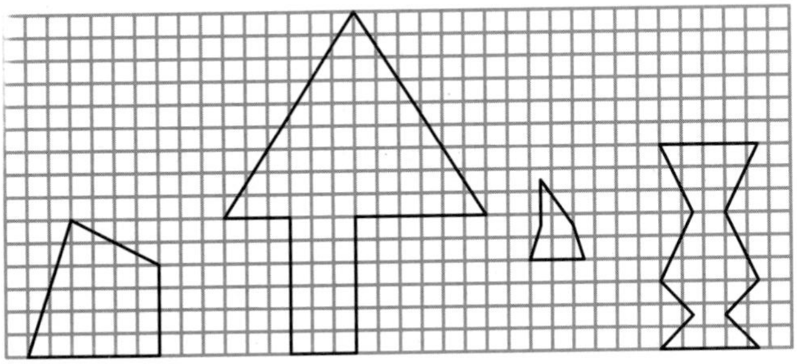

6 a Shape moves ('opposite' to centre of enlargement) **b** Shape and size of enlargement.

Exercise 6F

1 A translation $\begin{pmatrix}1\\-2\end{pmatrix}$, B reflection in y-axis, C rotation 90° clockwise about (0, 0), D reflection in $x = 3$, E reflection in $y = 4$, F enlargement by scale factor 2, centre (0, 1) **2 a** T_1 to T_2: rotation 90° clockwise about (0, 0) **b** T_1 to T_6: rotation 90° anticlockwise about (0, 0) **c** T_2 to T_3: translation $\begin{pmatrix}2\\2\end{pmatrix}$ **d** T_6 to T_2: rotation 180° about (0, 0) **e** T_6 to T_5: reflection in y-axis **f** T_5 to T_4: translation $\begin{pmatrix}4\\0\end{pmatrix}$ **3 a–c**

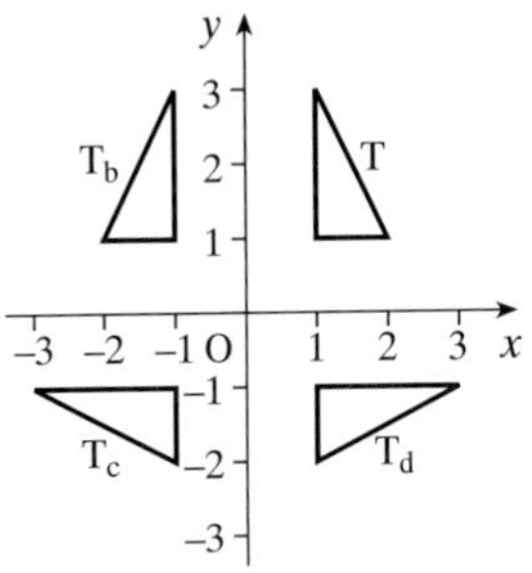

d T_d to T: rotation 90° anticlockwise about (0,0)

4 (–4, 3) **5 a** (–5, 2) **b** Reflection in y-axis **6** (3, 1) **7** Reflection in x-axis, translation $\begin{pmatrix}0\\-1\end{pmatrix}$, rotation 90° clockwise about (0, 0) **8** Translation $\begin{pmatrix}0\\-8\end{pmatrix}$, reflection in x-axis, rotation 90° clockwise about (0, 0) **9** Rotation 180° clockwise or anticlockwise about (0, 0)

Examination questions (Chapter 6)

1 ADC: SAS **2 a** x one of 3 equal angles around a point, totalling 360° **b**

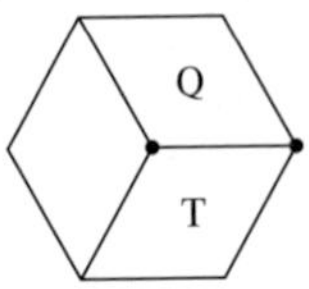

There are two possible centres of rotation, as shown. Examples of angles of rotation are:

120° clockwise about LH dot

60° anticlockwise about RH dot

3 a Reflection in $y = -x$

b–c

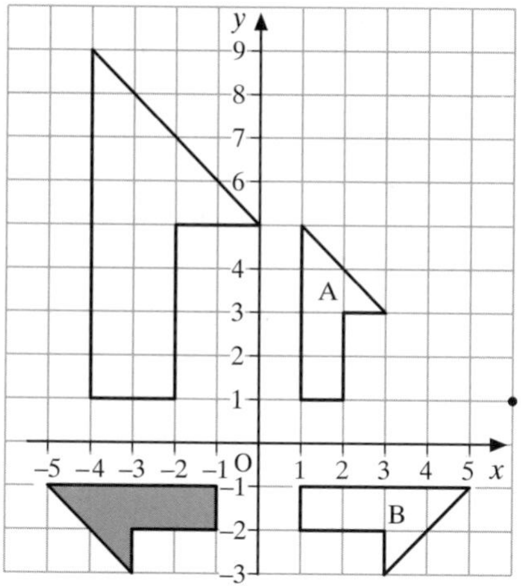

4 a

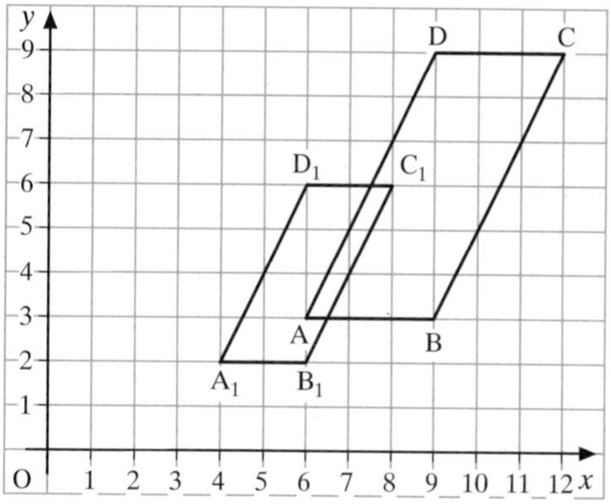

b Enlargement sf $\frac{3}{2}$, centre (0,0)

5 a (10, 11) **b** (–3, 4) **c** (8, 6) **6** BDE, CEA, DAB, EBC **7** Rotation 90° anticlockwise about (0,0)

8 a AB = $\begin{pmatrix} -5 \\ 0 \end{pmatrix}$ **b** EF = $\begin{pmatrix} 4 \\ -2 \end{pmatrix}$ **c** $\begin{pmatrix} 4 \\ 3 \end{pmatrix}$ **9** Rotation 180° clockwise or anticlockwise about (0,0)

Exercise 7B

5 a i Construct 60° angle and bisect it **ii** Bisect 30° angle **iii** Construct 90° angle and bisect it to get 45°. Bisect 45° angle **iv** Construct 45° angle on upper arm of 30° angle **8 b** AC = 5.2 cm, BC = 6.3 cm **9 b** PR = 5.9 cm, RQ = 4 cm

Exercise 7C

1 Circle with radius **a** 2 cm **b** 4 cm **c** 5 cm **3** Circle with radius 4 m **4**

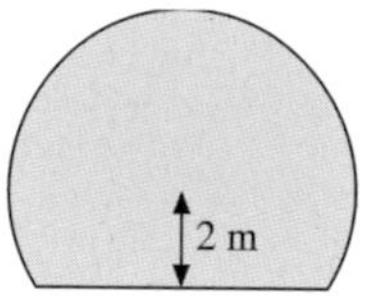

5 a

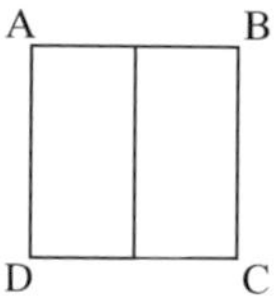

b

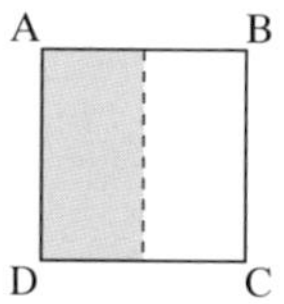

c

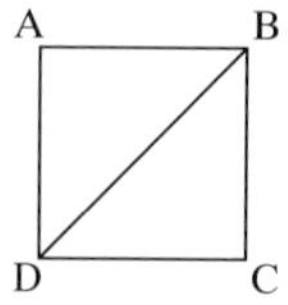

d

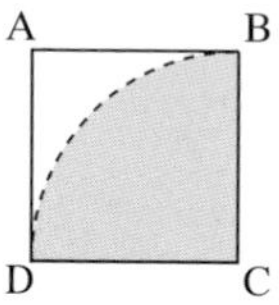

e

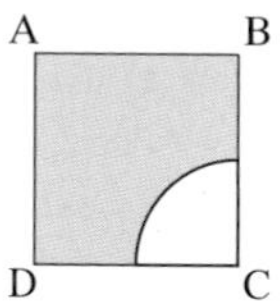

f

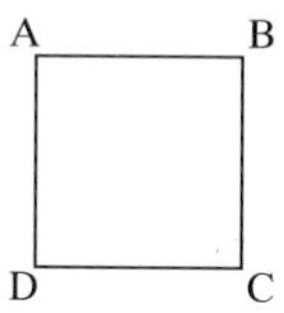

6 Diagram *c* **7**

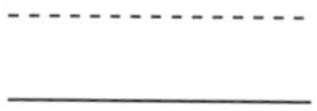

Exercise 7D

1

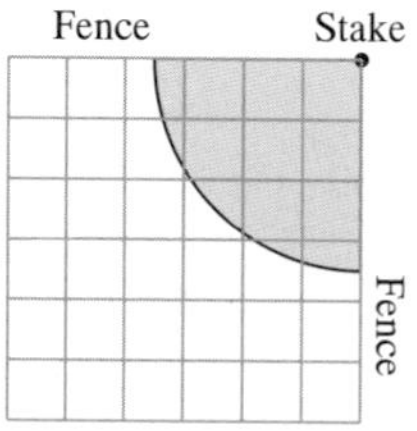

2

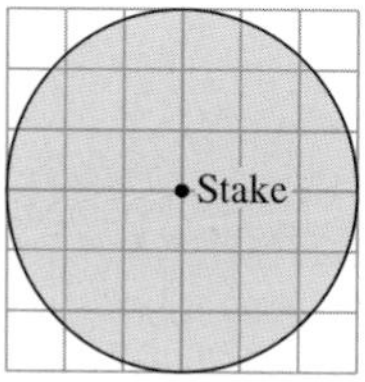

3

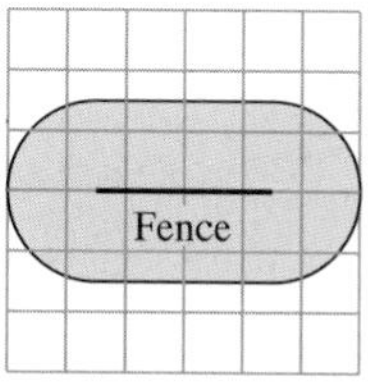

4

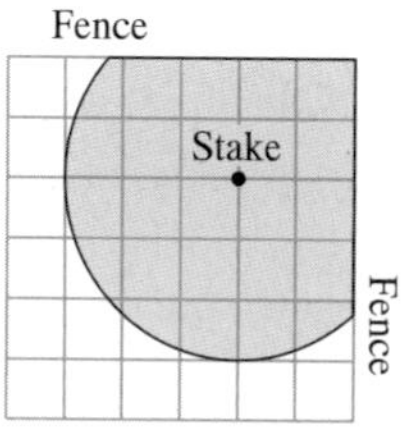

5

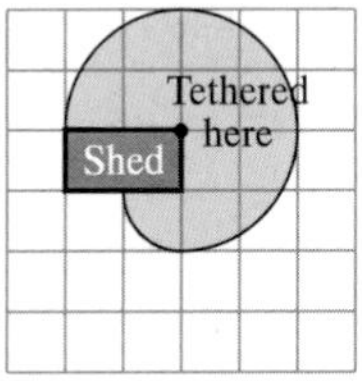

6

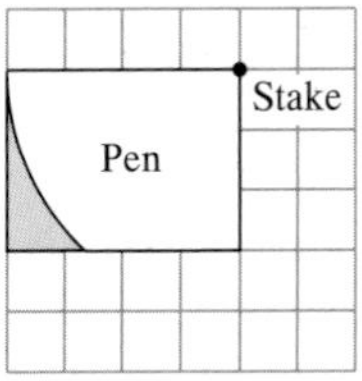

7

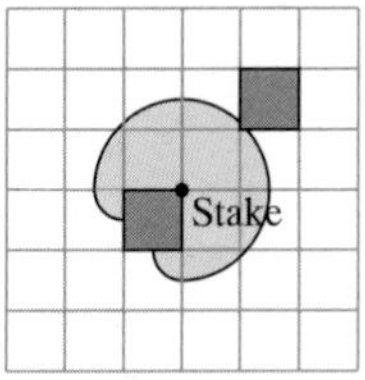

8 **a**

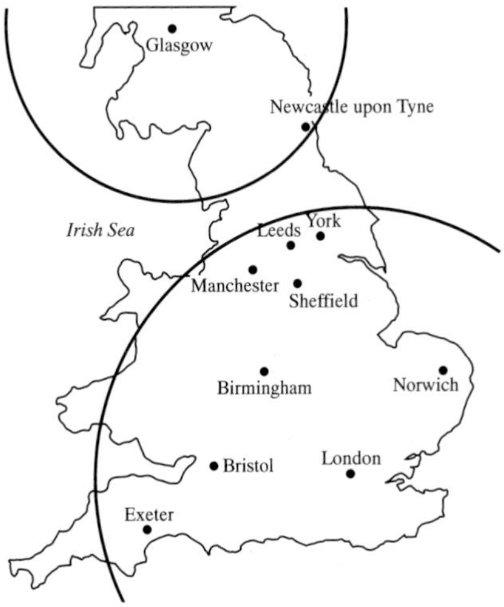

b No **c** Yes

9 **a** Yes

b Shaded region

10

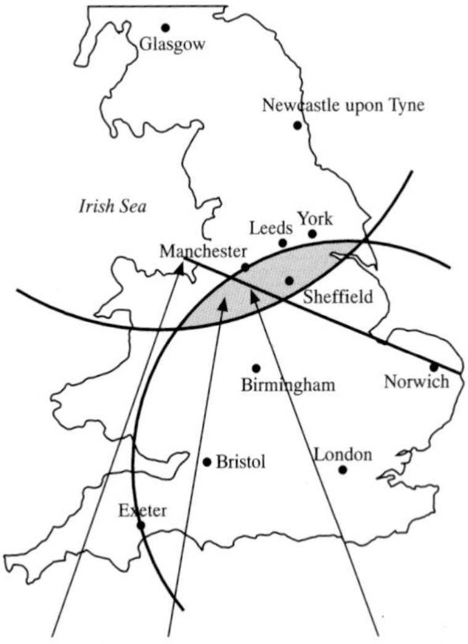

a The line **b** The region **c** This part of line

11

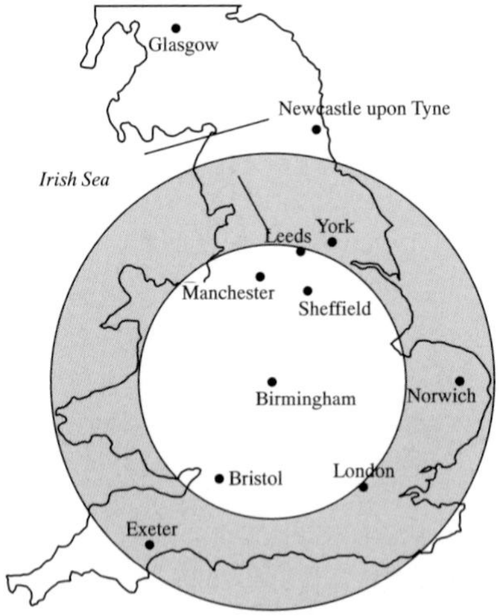

12

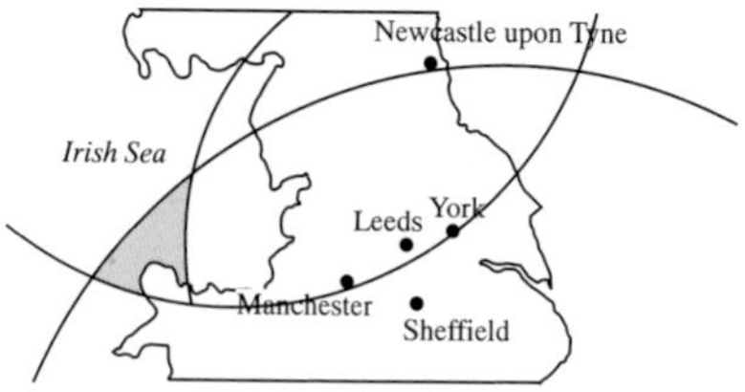

13

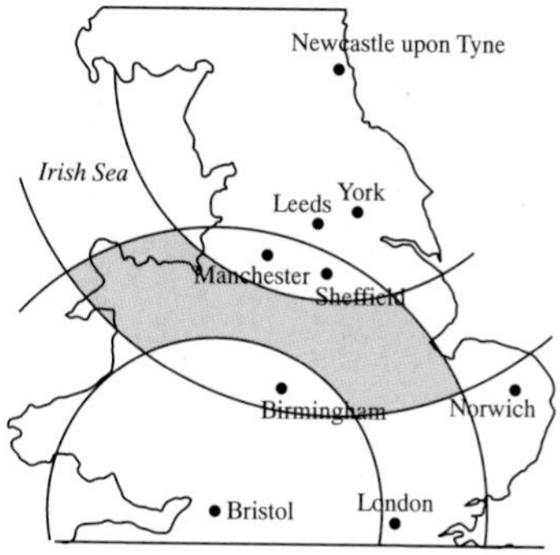

14

15

16

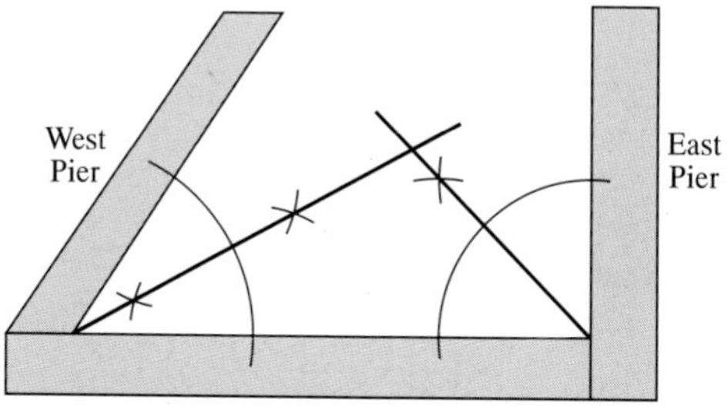

Examination questions (Chapter 7)

1 a

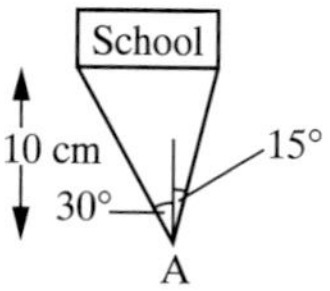

b 83 m **2**

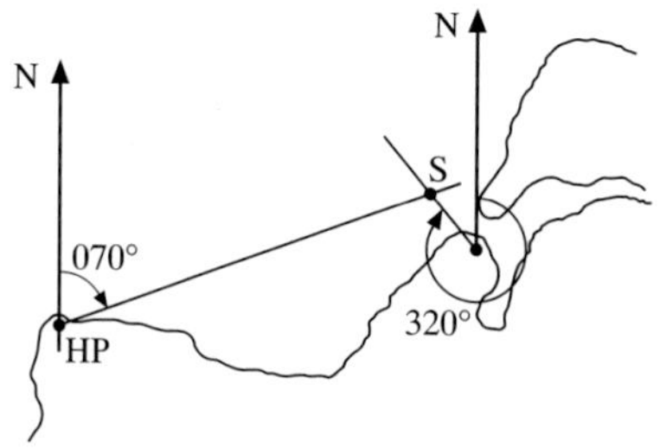

3

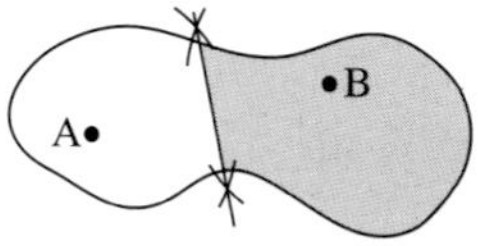

4

5

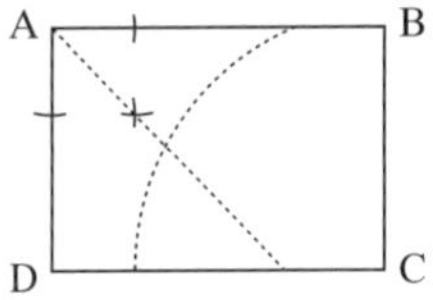

6

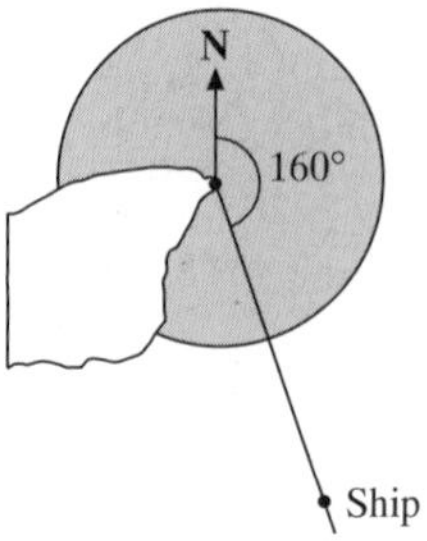

7

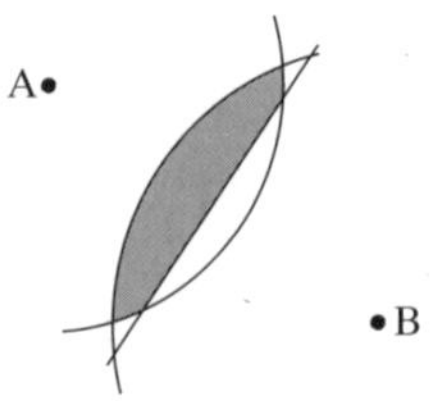

8 a

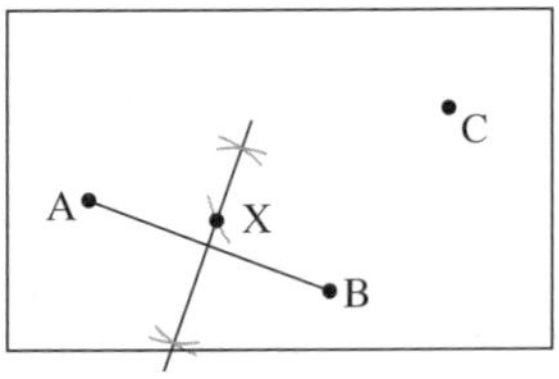

b Distance 71.5 km, time 17 min

9

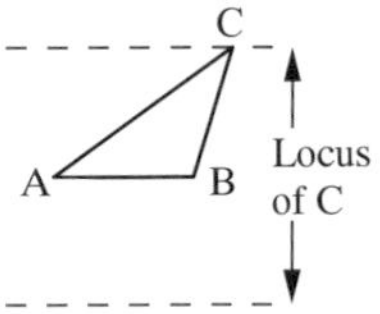

10 a 20 m
b

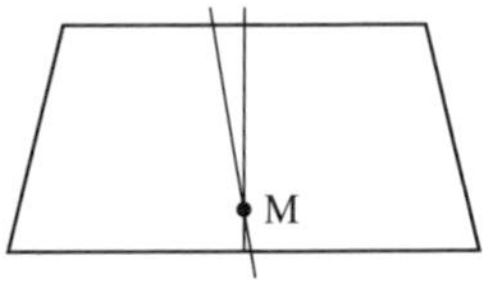

c 69 m^2

Exercise 8A

1 a 2^4 **b** 3^5 **c** 7^2 **d** 5^3 **e** 10^7 **f** 6^4 **g** 4^1 **h** 1^7 **i** 0.5^4 **j** 100^3 **2 a** $3 \times 3 \times 3 \times 3$ **b** $9 \times 9 \times 9$ **c** 6×6 **d** $10 \times 10 \times 10 \times 10 \times 10$ **e** $2 \times 2 \times 2 \times 2 \times 2 \times 2 \times 2 \times 2 \times 2 \times 2$ **f** 8 **g** $0.1 \times 0.1 \times 0.1$ **h** 2.5×2.5 **i** $0.7 \times 0.7 \times 0.7$ **j** 1000×1000 **3 a** 16 **b** 243 **c** 49 **d** 125 **e** 1000000 **f** 1296 **g** 4 **h** 1 **i** 0.0625 **j** 1000000 **4 a** 81 **b** 729 **c** 36 **d** 100000 **e** 1024 **f** 8 **g** 0.001 **h** 6.25 **i** 0.343 **j** 1000000 **5 a** 1 **b** 4 **c** 1 **d** 1 **e** 1 **6** Always 1 **7** 10^6 **8** 10^6 **9 a** 1 **b** –1 **c** 1 **d** 1 **e** –1 **10 a** 1 **b** –1 **c** –1 **d** 1 **e** 1 (even powers give 1, odd powers give –1)

Exercise 8B

1 a $\frac{1}{5^3}$ **b** $\frac{1}{6}$ **c** $\frac{1}{10^5}$ **d** $\frac{1}{3^2}$ **e** $\frac{1}{8^4}$ **f** $\frac{1}{9}$ **g** $\frac{1}{w^2}$ **h** $\frac{1}{t}$ **i** $\frac{1}{x^m}$ **j** $\frac{4}{m^3}$ **2 a** 3^{-2} **b** 5^{-1} **c** 10^{-3} **d** m^{-1} **e** t^{-n}

3 a i 2^4 **ii** 2^{-1} **iii** 2^{-4} **iv** $(-2)^3$ **b i** 10^3 **ii** 10^{-1} **iii** 10^{-2} **iv** 10^6 **c i** 5^3 **ii** 5^{-1} **iii** 5^{-2} **iv** 5^{-5}

d i 3^2 **ii** 3^{-3} **iii** 3^{-4} **iv** $-(3^8)$ **4 a** $\frac{5}{x^3}$ **b** $\frac{6}{t}$ **c** $\frac{7}{m^2}$ **d** $\frac{4}{q^4}$ **e** $\frac{10}{y^5}$ **f** $\frac{1}{2x^3}$ **g** $\frac{1}{4m}$ **h** $\frac{3}{4t^4}$ **i** $\frac{4}{5y^3}$ **j** $\frac{7}{8x^5}$

5 a $7x^{-3}$ **b** $10p^{-1}$ **c** $5t^{-2}$ **d** $8m^{-5}$ **e** $3y^{-1}$ **6 a i** 25 **ii** $\frac{1}{125}$ **iii** $\frac{4}{5}$ **b i** 64 **ii** $\frac{1}{16}$ **iii** $\frac{5}{256}$ **c i** 8 **ii** $\frac{1}{32}$ **iii** $\frac{9}{2}$ or $4\frac{1}{2}$ **d i** 1000000 **ii** $\frac{1}{1000}$ **iii** $\frac{1}{4}$

Exercise 8C

1 a 5^4 **b** 5^{10} **c** 5^5 **d** 5^3 **e** 5^{15} **f** 5^9 **g** 5^2 **h** 5^3 **i** 5^{-5} **2 a** 6^3 **b** 6^5 **c** 6^1 **d** 6^0 **e** 6^1 **f** 6^{-2} **g** 6^6 **h** 6^{-7} **i** 6^2 **3 a** 4^6 **b** 4^{15} **c** 4^6 **d** 4^{-6} **e** 4^6 **f** 4^0 **4 a** a^3 **b** a^5 **c** a^7 **d** a^4 **e** a^2 **f** a^1 **5 a** $6a^5$ **b** $20a^4$ **c** $8a^3$ **d** $9a^2$ **e** 15 **f** $8a^6$ **g** $-6a^4$ **h** $8a^8$ **i** $-10a^{-3}$ **6 a** $3a$ **b** $4a^3$ **c** $3a^4$ **d** $6a^{-1}$ **e** $4a^7$ **f** $5a^{-4}$ **7 a** $8a^5b^4$ **b** $10a^3b$ **c** $30a^{-2}b^{-2}$ **d** $2ab^3$ **e** $8a^{-5}b^7$ **8 a** $3a^3b^2$ **b** $3a^2c^4$ **c** $8a^2b^2c^3$

Exercise 8D

1 5 **2** 10 **3** 8 **4** 9 **5** 25 **6** 3 **7** 4 **8** 10 **9** 5 **10** 8 **11** 12 **12** 20 **13** 5 **14** 3 **15** 10 **16** 3 **17** 2 **18** 2 **19** 6 **20** 6 **21** $\frac{1}{4}$ **22** $\frac{1}{2}$ **23** $\frac{1}{3}$ **24** $\frac{1}{5}$ **25** $\frac{1}{10}$ **26** $\frac{5}{6}$ **27** $\frac{5}{3}$ **28** $\frac{8}{9}$ **29** $\frac{9}{5}$ **30** $\frac{5}{8}$ **31** $\frac{3}{5}$ **32** $\frac{1}{4}$ **33** $\frac{5}{2}$ **34** $\frac{4}{5}$ **35** $\frac{8}{7}$ **36** $\frac{2}{3}$ **37** $\frac{3}{4}$ **38** $\frac{2}{3}$ **39** $\frac{5}{7}$ **40** $\frac{7}{8}$

Exercise 8E

1 a 16 **b** 25 **c** 216 **d** 81 **2 a** $t^{\frac{2}{3}}$ **b** $m^{\frac{3}{4}}$ **c** $k^{\frac{2}{5}}$ **d** $x^{\frac{3}{2}}$ **3 a** 4 **b** 2187 **c** 64 **d** 3125 **e** 125 **f** 279936 **g** $\frac{1}{32}$ **h** 177147 **4 b** 1.4 **5 b** 1.4 **6 a** 2.43 **b** 2.23 **c** 3.14

Exercise 8F

1 a 31 **b** 310 **c** 3100 **d** 31 000 **2 a** 65 **b** 650 **c** 6500 **d** 65 000 **3 a** 0.31 **b** 0.031 **c** 0.0031 **d** 0.000 31 **4 a** 0.65 **b** 0.065 **c** 0.0065 **d** 0.000 65 **5 a** 250 **b** 34.5 **c** 4670 **d** 346 **e** 207.89 **f** 56 780 **g** 246 **h** 0.76 **i** 76 **j** 89 700 **k** 865 **l** 10 050 **m** 999 000 **n** 23 456 **o** 98 765.4 **p** 43 230 000 **q** 7867.9 **r** 2036.7 **s** 764.3 **t** 3 457 800 **u** 345.78 **v** 6000 **w** 56.7 **x** 560 045 **y** 9090.7 **z** 70 086 **6 a** 0.025 **b** 0.345 **c** 0.004 67 **d** 3.46 **e** 0.207 89 **f** 0.056 78 **g** 0.0246 **h** 0.0076 **i** 0.000 076 **j** 0.000 008 79 **k** 0.000 865 **l** 1.005 **m** 0.000 000 999 **n** 2.3456 **o** 0.098 765 4 **p** 0.000 4323 **q** 0.786 79 **r** 20.367 **s** 7.643 **t** 0.000 345 78 **u** 0.000 000 034 578 **v** 0.000 000 000 06 **w** 0.000 000 567 **x** 0.005 600 45 **y** 0.000 090 907 **z** 0.070 086 **7 a** 60 000 **b** 120 000 **c** 10 000 **d** 42 000 **e** 21 000 **f** 300 **g** 150 **h** 1400 **i** 100 000 **j** 200 000 **k** 28 000 **l** 900 **m** 400 **n** 8000 **o** 160 000 **p** 4500 **q** 8000 **r** 250 000 **s** 10 000 **t** 600 **u** 3000 **v** 60 000 **w** 4 000 000 **x** 360 000 **y** 48 000 000 000 **z** 1 200 000 000 **8 a** 5 **b** 50 **c** 25 **d** 30 **e** 7 **f** 300 **g** 6 **h** 30 **i** 4 **j** 5 **k** 2 **l** 100 **m** 40 **n** 200 **o** 20 **p** 20 **q** 2 **r** 1 **s** 16 **t** 150 **u** 12 **v** 15 **w** 40 **x** 5 **y** 40 **z** 320 **9 a** 230 **b** 57 8 900 **c** 4790 **d** 57 000 000 **e** 216 **f** 10 500 **g** 0.000 32 **h** 9870

Exercise 8G

1 a 0.31 **b** 0.031 **c** 0.0031 **d** 0.000 31 **2 a** 0.65 **b** 0.065 **c** 0.0065 **d** 0.000 65 **3 a** 9999999×10^{99} **b** 0.000001×10^{-99} (Depends on number of digits displayed) **4 a** 31 **b** 310 **c** 3100 **d** 31 000 **5 a** 65 **b** 650 **c** 6500 **d** 65 000 **6 a** 250 **b** 34.5 **c** 0.004 67 **d** 34.6 **e** 0.020 789 **f** 5678 **g** 246 **h** 76 **i** 7600 **j** 897 000 **k** 0.008 65 **l** 100.5 **m** 0.000 009 99 **n** 234.56 **o** 9876.54 **p** 4 323 000 **q** 0.078 679 **r** 0.203 67 **s** 76.43 **t** 0.000 034 578 **u** 345 780 **v** 60 000 000 **w** 0.000 567 **x** 56 004.5 **y** 90 907 **z** 0.007 0086 **7 a** 2.5×10^2 **b** 3.45×10^{-1} **c** 4.67×10^4 **d** 3.4×10^9 **e** 2.078×10^{10} **f** 5.678×10^{-4} **g** 2.46×10^3 **h** 7.6×10^{-2} **i** 7.6×10^{-4} **j** 8.97×10^{-1} **k** 8.65×10^3 **l** 1.005×10^2 **m** 9.99×10^{-1} **n** 2.3456×10^2 **o** 9.87654×10 **p** 4.323×10 **q** 7.8679×10^3 **r** 2.0367×10^2 **s** 7.643×10 **t** 3.4578×10 **u** 3.4578×10^{-3} **v** 6×10^{-4} **w** 5.67×10^{-3} **x** 5.60045×10 **y** 9.0907×10^{-1} **z** 7.0086×10 **8** 7.2×10, 1.5×10^3, 5.7×10^4 **9** 2.7797×10^4 **10** 2.81581×10^5, 3×10, 1.382101×10^6 **11** 1.298×10^7, 2.997×10^9, 9.3×10^4 **12 a** 5.67×10^3 **b** 2.346×10^5 **c** 6×10^2 **d** 3.46×10^{-1} **e** 7×10^{-4} **f** 5.6×10^2 **g** 6×10^5 **h** 7×10^3 **i** 3.5×10^{-6} **j** 1.6 **k** 1 **l** 1×10^3 **m** 2.3×10^7 **n** 3×10^{-6} **o** 2.56×10^6 **p** 1.08×10^8 **q** 4.8×10^2 **r** 1.12×10^2 **s** 2.7×10^2 **t** 6×10^{-1} **u** 2.8×10^6

Exercise 8H

1 *a, b, e, g, h, i, j* **2 a** $\sqrt{7}$ **b** $\sqrt{70}$ etc. **c** $\sqrt{443}$ etc. **d** $\sqrt{3079}$ etc. **3 a** $-\sqrt{3}$ **b** $-\pi$ **c** -5π **d** $\sqrt{3} - \sqrt{2}$ **e** $-\pi$ **4 a** $\frac{1}{\pi}$ **b** $\frac{1}{\sqrt{7}}$ **c** $\sqrt{\frac{3}{2}}$ **d** π **e** $\frac{1}{\pi^2}$ **5 a** False **b** False **c** True

Exercise 8I

1 a 0.5 **b** $0.\dot{3}$ **c** 0.25 **d** 0.2 **e** $0.1\dot{6}$ **f** $0.\dot{1}4285\dot{7}$ **g** 0.125 **h** $0.\dot{1}$ **i** 0.1 **j** $0.\dot{0}7692\dot{3}$ **2 b** Same digits recur in cyclic order **3** $\frac{9}{22}$ $\frac{3}{7}$ $\frac{16}{37}$ $\frac{4}{9}$ $\frac{5}{11}$ $\frac{6}{13}$ **4** $\frac{7}{24}$ $\frac{3}{10}$ $\frac{19}{60}$ $\frac{2}{5}$ $\frac{5}{12}$ **5 a** $\frac{1}{8}$ **b** $\frac{17}{50}$ **c** $\frac{29}{40}$ **d** $\frac{5}{16}$ **e** $\frac{89}{100}$ **f** $\frac{1}{20}$ **g** $2\frac{7}{20}$ **h** $\frac{7}{32}$ **6 a** 24.242 242 … **b** 24 **c** $\frac{8}{33}$ **7 a** $\frac{8}{9}$ **b** $\frac{34}{99}$ **c** $\frac{5}{11}$ **d** $\frac{21}{37}$ **e** $\frac{4}{9}$ **f** $\frac{2}{45}$ **g** $\frac{13}{90}$ **h** $\frac{5}{110}$ **i** $2\frac{7}{9}$ **j** $7\frac{7}{11}$ **k** $3\frac{1}{3}$ **l** $2\frac{2}{33}$ **8 a** True **b** True **c** Recurring

Exercise 8J

1 a $\sqrt{6}$ **b** $\sqrt{15}$ **c** 2 **d** 4 **e** $2\sqrt{10}$ **f** 3 **g** $2\sqrt{3}$ **h** $\sqrt{21}$ **i** $\sqrt{14}$ **j** 6 **k** 6 **l** $\sqrt{30}$ **2 a** 2 **b** $\sqrt{5}$ **c** $\sqrt{6}$ **d** $\sqrt{3}$ **e** $\sqrt{5}$ **f** 1 **g** $\sqrt{3}$ **h** $\sqrt{7}$ **i** 2 **j** $\sqrt{6}$ **k** 1 **l** 3 **3 a** $2\sqrt{3}$ **b** 15 **c** $4\sqrt{2}$ **d** $4\sqrt{3}$ **e** $8\sqrt{5}$ **f** $3\sqrt{3}$ **g** 24 **h** $3\sqrt{7}$ **i** $2\sqrt{7}$ **j** $6\sqrt{5}$ **k** $6\sqrt{3}$ **l** 30 **4 a** $\sqrt{3}$ **b** 1 **c** $2\sqrt{2}$ **d** $\sqrt{2}$ **e** $\sqrt{5}$ **f** $\sqrt{3}$ **g** $\sqrt{2}$ **h** $\sqrt{7}$ **i** $\sqrt{7}$ **j** $2\sqrt{3}$ **k** $2\sqrt{3}$ **l** 1 **5 a** a **b** 1 **c** $\sqrt{a}$ **6 a** $3\sqrt{2}$ **b** $2\sqrt{6}$ **c** $2\sqrt{3}$ **d** $5\sqrt{2}$ **e** $2\sqrt{2}$ **f** $3\sqrt{3}$ **g** $4\sqrt{3}$ **h** $5\sqrt{3}$ **i** $3\sqrt{5}$ **j** $3\sqrt{7}$ **k** $4\sqrt{2}$ **l** $10\sqrt{2}$ **m** $10\sqrt{10}$ **n** $5\sqrt{10}$ **o** $7\sqrt{2}$ **p** $7\sqrt{7}$ **7 a** 36 **b** $16\sqrt{30}$ **c** 54 **d** 32 **e** $48\sqrt{6}$ **f** $48\sqrt{6}$ **g** $18\sqrt{15}$ **h** 84 **i** 64 **j** 100 **k** 50 **l** 56 **8 a** $20\sqrt{6}$ **b** $6\sqrt{15}$ **c** 24 **d** 16 **e** $12\sqrt{10}$ **f** 18 **g** $20\sqrt{3}$ **h** $10\sqrt{21}$ **i** $6\sqrt{14}$ **j** 36 **k** 24 **l** $12\sqrt{30}$ **9 a** 6 **b** $3\sqrt{5}$ **c** $6\sqrt{6}$ **d** $2\sqrt{3}$ **e** $4\sqrt{5}$ **f** 5 **g** $7\sqrt{3}$ **h** $2\sqrt{7}$ **i** 6 **j** $2\sqrt{7}$ **k** 5 **l** 24 **10 a** $2\sqrt{3}$ **b** 4 **c** $6\sqrt{2}$ **d** $4\sqrt{2}$ **e** $6\sqrt{5}$ **f** $24\sqrt{3}$ **g** $3\sqrt{2}$ **h** $\sqrt{7}$ **i** $10\sqrt{7}$ **j** $8\sqrt{3}$ **k** $10\sqrt{3}$ **l** 6 **11 a** abc **b** $\frac{a}{c}$ **c** $c\sqrt{b}$ **12 a** 20 **b** 24 **c** 10 **d** 24 **e** 3 **f** 6 **14 a** $\frac{3}{4}$ **b** $\frac{25}{3}$ **c** $\frac{5}{16}$ **d** 12 **e** 2

Examination questions (Chapter 8)

1 i 6561 **ii** $\frac{1}{25}$ or 0.04 **2 a** 7.75×10^8 **b** 1833 **3 a** 2.493×10^{-23} g **b i** 2.994×10^{-23} g **ii** 3.34×10^{22} **4 a** 5×10^{101} **b** 5×10^{-8} **5** 4.23 light years **6 a** 52 000 000 **b** 1.2×10^{-1} **7 a** 2 **b** 2^{-5} **c** $\frac{1}{5}$ **8 a** i and ii **b** $\sqrt{2}$ and $\sqrt{8}$ etc. **c** $\frac{2}{55}$ **9 a i** –24 **ii** $\sqrt{5}$ **iii** $-\frac{1}{343}$ **b** $21 - 8\sqrt{5}$ **10 a** $\frac{161}{100}$ **b i** 17.777… **ii** 16 **iii** $\frac{16}{9}$

c $\sqrt{\frac{21}{2}}$ etc.

Exercise 9A

1 a i 7 **ii** 6 **iii** 6.4 **b i** 4 **ii** 4 **iii** 3.7 **c i** 8 **ii** 8.5 **iii** 8.2 **d i** 0 **ii** 0 **iii** 0.3 **2 a** 668 **b** 1.9 **c** 0 **d** 328 **3 a** 2.2, 1.7, 1.3 **b** Better dental care **4 a** 42 **b** 7 **c** 3 **d** 2 **e** 2.4 **f** Mode **g** 2.6 **5 a** 46 **b** 2 **c** 2.8 **6 a** 0 **b** 1.0 **7 a** 7 **b** 6.5 **c** 6.5 **8 a** 1 **b** 1 **c** 1.0 **9 a** Roger 5, Brian 4 **b** 3, 8 **c** 5, 4 **d** 5.4, 4.5 **e** Roger, smaller range **f** Brian, better mean **10 a** 34 **c** $x = 10, y = 24$ **d** 2.5

Exercise 9B

1 a i 31–40 **ii** 29.9 **b i** 0–100 **ii** 158.6 **c i** £5.01–£10 **ii** £9.44 **d i** 7–9 **ii** 8.4 **2 a** 81–90 g **b** 8617.5 g **c** 86.2 g **3 a** 207 **b** 19–22 cm **c** 20.3 cm **4 a** 41–50 **b** 49.8 **c** 13.4% **5 a** 160 **b** 52.6 min **c** Modal group **d** 65% **6 a** 5.25 min **b** Modal group **c** Yes, 50% were over 5 min late **7 a** 176–200 h **b** 31% **c** 193.6 h **d** No **8 a** 132 **b** 134.4 g **9** 24 **10** Average price increases: Soundbuy 17.7p, Springfields 18.7p, Setco 18.2p

Exercise 9C

1 iii 140.9 cm **2 ii** Boys 12.9, girls 13.1 **3 ii** 1.9 **4 ii** 6.2 goals **5 ii** Mon 28.9, Wed 21.4, Fri 21.8 min **6 i** Boys **ii** 111 **v** Boys 4.8 kg, girls 4.5 kg **7 i** 1.8 **8 i** Age 16–17: £13.31, age 18–20: £16.21 **9 ii** 45.8 words/min **iii** $33\frac{1}{3}$% **10 i** 63 **ii** 2.9

Exercise 9D

1 a Frequency density: 5, 6.5, 6, 4, 3, 2 **b** 16, 18, 12.4, 5 **c** 17, 18, 12, 5 **d** 0.4, 1.2, 2.8, 1 **e** 9, 21, 18, 7

2 a i

Age	9	10–11	12–13	14–16	17–18	19
Frequency	5	12	8	9	5	2

ii 10–11 **iii** $12\frac{1}{2}$ **iv** $13\frac{1}{2}$

b i

Temperature, t (°C)	$9.5 < t \le 10.5$	$10.5 < t \le 11.5$	$11.5 < t \le 13.5$	$13.5 < t \le 15.5$	$15.5 < t \le 18.5$	$18.5 < t \le 20.5$
Frequency	10	15	50	40	45	10

ii 11.5–13.5 °C **iii** 14 °C **iv** 14.3 °C

c i

Weight w, (kg)	$45 < w \le 65$	$65 < w \le 95$	$95 < w \le 135$	$135 < w \le 145$	$145 < w \le 155$
Frequency	200	360	240	80	40

ii 65–95 kg **iii** 87 kg **iv** 92kg

3 a 9 h **b** 9.2 h **4 a** 775 **b** 11.1 min **c** 410

5 a

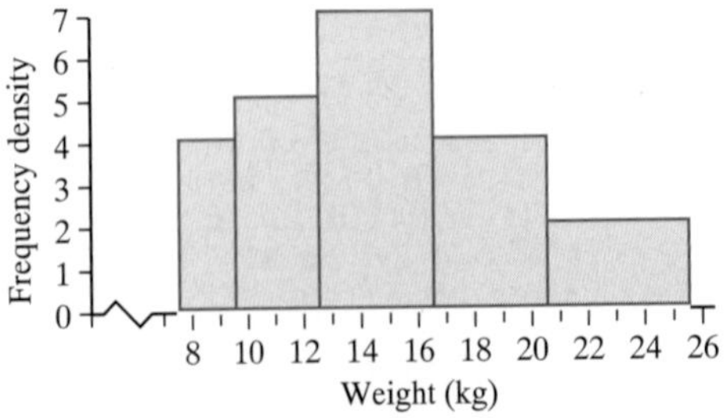

b 14.7 kg **c** 15.1 kg **d** 37

6 a

Frequency	80	10	40	110	60	60

b 360 **c** 64.5 mph **d** 59.2 mph

7 a

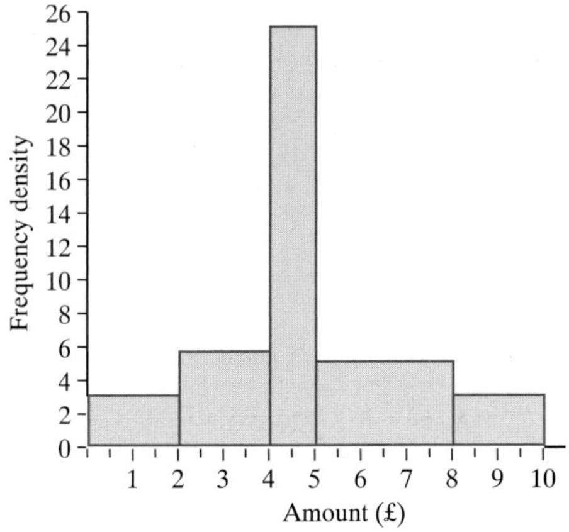

b

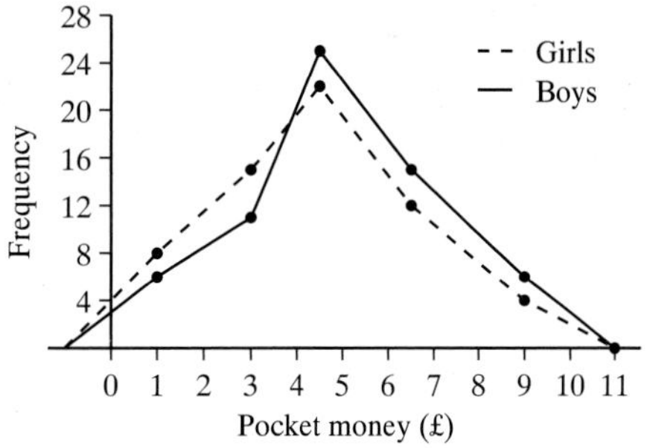

c Girls £4.36, boys £4.81. On average, boys tend to get more

8

a

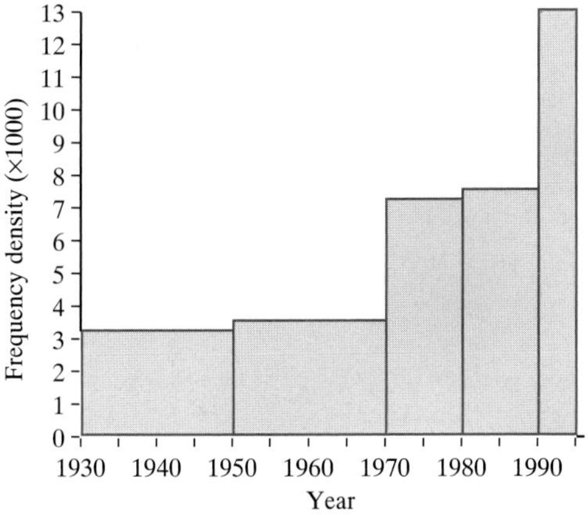

b

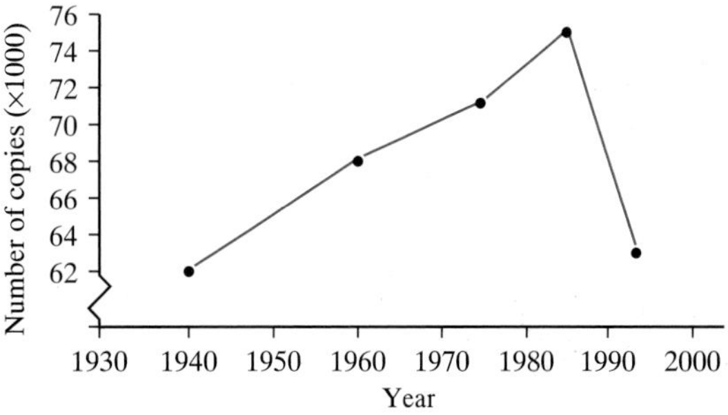

c Histogram

Examination questions (Chapter 9)

1 a £18.90 **b** 6.4 miles **2 a** 150–155 litres **b** 155.8 litres **c** Mean: all values used **3 a** 0–£1 **b** £1.43
4 a 12.55 m **6 a** £2.01–£3.00 **b** £2.14 **9 a** Not. **b** 9 boys and 6 girls
10 a

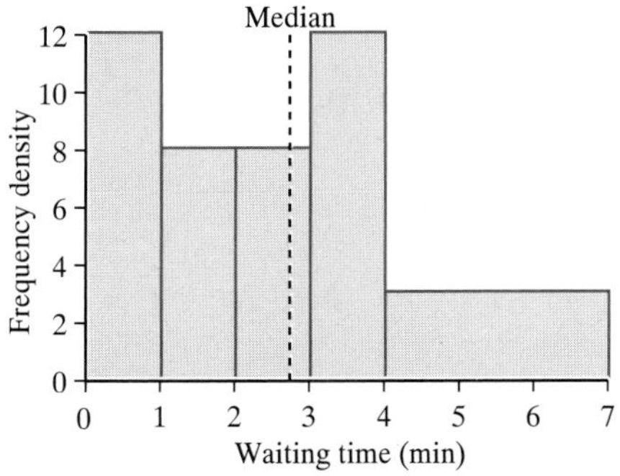

b Median 2.75 min

Exercise 10A

1 $6t$ **2** $12y$ **3** $15y$ **4** $8w$ **5** $3t^2$ **6** $5b^2$ **7** $2w^2$ **8** $15y^2$ **9** $8p^2$ **10** $6t^2$ **11** $12m^2$ **12** $15t^2$ **13** $2mt$
14 $3wy$ **15** $5qt$ **16** $6mn$ **17** $6qt$ **18** $12fg$ **19** $10hk$ **20** $21pr$ **21** y^3 **22** t^3 **23** $3m^3$ **24** $4t^3$ **25** $6n^3$
26 $20r^3$ **27** t^4 **28** h^5 **29** $12n^5$ **30** $10t^7$ **31** $6a^7$ **32** $4k^7$ **33** t^3 **34** $6y^2$ **35** $12d^3$ **36** $15p^6$
37 $3mp^2$ **38** $6t^2y$ **39** $6m^2n$ **40** $8m^2p^2$

Exercise 10B

1 $6+2m$ **2** $10+5l$ **3** $12-3y$ **4** $20+8k$ **5** $6-12f$ **6** $10-6w$ **7** $3g+3h$ **8** $10k+15m$ **9** $12d-8n$
10 t^2+3t **11** m^2+5m **12** k^2-3k **13** $3g^2+2g$ **14** $5y^2-y$ **15** $5p-3p^2$ **16** $3m^2+12m$ **17** $4t^2-4t$
18 $8k-2k^2$ **19** $8g^2+20g$ **20** $15h^2-10h$ **21** $15t-12t^2$ **22** $6d^2+12de$ **23** $6y^2+8ky$ **24** $15m^2-10mp$
25 y^3+5y **26** h^4+7h **27** k^3-5k **28** $3t^3+12t$ **29** $4h^4-4h$ **30** $5g^4-10g$ **31** $12m^3+4m^2$ **32** $10k^4+5k^3$
33 $15d^3-3d^4$ **34** $6w^3+3tw$ **35** $15a^3-10ab$ **36** $12p^4-15mp$ **37** $5m^2+4m^3$ **38** t^4+2t^4 **39** $5g^2t-4g^4$
40 $15t^3+3mt^2$ **41** $12h^3+8gh^2$ **42** $8m^3+2m^4$

Exercise 10C

1 a $7t$ **b** $9m$ **c** $3y$ **d** $9d$ **e** $3e$ **f** $2g$ **g** $3p$ **h** $2t$ **i** $5t^2$ **j** $4y^2$ **k** $5ab$ **l** $3a^2d$ **2 a** $22+5t$
b $21+19k$ **c** $10+16m$ **d** $16+17y$ **e** $22+2f$ **f** $14+3g$ **g** $10+11t$ **h** $22+4w$ **3 a** $2+2h$ **b** $9g+5$
c $6y+11$ **d** $7t-4$ **e** $17k+16$ **f** $6e+20$ **g** $7m+4$ **h** $3t+10$ **4 a** $4m+3p+2mp$ **b** $3k+4h+5hk$
c $3n+2t+7nt$ **d** $6pq+3p+7q$ **e** $6h+6j+13hj$ **f** $21ty+6t+8y$ **g** $24p+12r+13pr$ **h** $20k-6m+19km$
5 a $13t+9t^2$ **b** $5y+13y^2$ **c** $18w+5w^2$ **d** $14p+23p^2$ **e** $7m+4m^2$ **f** $22d-9d^2$ **g** $10e^2-6e$ **h** $14k^2-3kp$
6 a $17ab+12ac+6bc$ **b** $18wy+6ty-8tw$ **c** $16gh-2gk-10hk$ **d** $10ht-3hp-12pt$ **e** $ab-2ac+6bc$
f $12pq+2qw-10pw$ **g** $14mn-15mp-6np$ **h** $8r^3-6r^2$

Exercise 10D

1 $6(m+2t)$ **2** $3(3t+p)$ **3** $4(2m+3k)$ **4** $4(r+2t)$ **5** $m(n+3)$ **6** $g(5g+3)$ **7** $2(2w-3t)$ **8** $2(4p-3k)$
9 $2(8h-5k)$ **10** $2m(p+k)$ **11** $2b(2c+k)$ **12** $2a(3b+2c)$ **13** $y(3y+2)$ **14** $t(4t-3)$ **15** $2d(2d-1)$ **16** $3m(m-p)$
17 $3p(2p+3t)$ **18** $2p(4t+3m)$ **19** $4b(2a-c)$ **20** $4a(3a-2b)$ **21** $3t(3m-2p)$ **22** $4at(4t+3)$ **23** $5bc(b-2)$
24 $2b(4ac+3ed)$ **25** $2(2a^2+3a+4)$ **26** $3b(2a+3c+d)$ **27** $t(5t+4+a)$ **28** $3mt(2t-1+3m)$ **29** $2ab(4b+1-2a)$
30 $5pt(2t+3+p)$ **31** Not possible **32** $m(5+2p)$ **33** $t(t-7)$ **34** Not possible **35** $2m(2m-3p)$ **36** Not possible
37 $a(4a-5b)$ **38** Not possible **39** $b(5a-3bc)$

Exercise 10E

1 x^2+5x+6 **2** $t^2+7t+12$ **3** w^2+4w+3 **4** m^2+6m+5 **5** $k^2+8k+15$ **6** a^2+5a+4 **7** x^2+2x-8
8 $t^2+2t-15$ **9** w^2-2w-3 **10** f^2-f-6 **11** g^2-3g-4 **12** y^2+y-12 **13** x^2+x-12 **14** p^2-p-2
15 k^2-2k-8 **16** $y^2+3y-10$ **17** a^2+2a-3 **18** t^2+t-12 **19** x^2-5x+4 **20** r^2-5r+6 **21** m^2-4m+3
22 g^2-6g+8 **23** $h^2-8h+15$ **24** n^2-5n+4 **25** $x^2+9x+20$ **26** $18-3t-t^2$ **27** $15-2b-b^2$ **28** y^2-6y+5
29 p^2-p-6 **30** $7k-k^2-10$ **31** x^2-9 **32** t^2-25 **33** m^2-16 **34** t^2-4 **35** y^2-64 **36** p^2-1 **37** $25-x^2$
38 $49-g^2$ **39** x^2-36

Exercise 10F

1 $6x^2+11x+3$ **2** $12y^2+17y+6$ **3** $6t^2+17t+5$ **4** $8t^2+2t-3$ **5** $10m^2-11m-6$ **6** $12k^2-11k-15$
7 $6p^2+11p-10$ **8** $10w^2+19w+6$ **9** $6a^2-7a-3$ **10** $8r^2-10r+3$ **11** $15g^2-16g+4$ **12** $12d^2+5d-2$
13 $8p^2+26p+15$ **14** $6t^2+7t+2$ **15** $6p^2+11p+4$ **16** $6-7t-10t^2$ **17** $12+n-6n^2$ **18** $6f^2-5f-6$
19 $12+7q-10q^2$ **20** $3-7p-6p^2$ **21** $4+10t-6t^2$ **22** $8r^2-10r+3$ **23** $8x^2-22x+5$ **24** $17m-12m^2-6$
25 $2x^2+5xy+3y^2$ **26** $6y^2-10ty-4t^2$ **27** $8x^2-6xy-5y^2$ **28** $2x^2-7xy+6y^2$ **29** $5m^2+13mp-6p^2$
30 $4t^2-13kt+3k^2$

Exercise 10G

1 $4x^2-1$ **2** $9t^2-4$ **3** $25y^2-9$ **4** $16m^2-9$ **5** $4k^2-9$ **6** $16h^2-1$ **7** $4-9x^2$ **8** $25-4t^2$ **9** $36-25y^2$
10 a^2-b^2 **11** $9t^2-k^2$ **12** $4m^2-9p^2$ **13** $25k^2-g^2$ **14** $a^2b^2-c^2d^2$ **15** a^4-b^4

Exercise 10H

1 $x^2+10x+25$ **2** $m^2+8m+16$ **3** $t^2+12t+36$ **4** p^2+6p+9 **5** m^2-6m+9 **6** $t^2-10t+25$ **7** $m^2-8m+16$
8 $k^2-14k+49$ **9** $9x^2+6x+1$ **10** $16t^2+24t+9$ **11** $25y^2+20y+4$ **12** $4m^2+12m+9$ **13** $16t^2-24t+9$
14 $9x^2-12x+4$ **15** $25t^2-20t+4$ **16** $25r^2-60r+36$ **17** $x^2+2xy+y^2$ **18** $m^2-2mn+n^2$ **19** $4t^2+4ty+y^2$
20 $m^2-6mn+9n^2$

Exercise 10I

1 $(x+2)(x+3)$ **2** $(t+1)(t+4)$ **3** $(m+2)(m+5)$ **4** $(k+4)(k+6)$ **5** $(p+2)(p+12)$ **6** $(r+3)(r+6)$
7 $(w+2)(w+9)$ **8** $(x+3)(x+4)$ **9** $(a+2)(a+6)$ **10** $(k+3)(k+7)$ **11** $(f+1)(f+21)$ **12** $(b+8)(b+12)$
13 $(t-2)(y-3)$ **14** $(d-1)(d-4)$ **15** $(g-2)(g-5)$ **16** $(x-3)(x-12)$ **17** $(c-2)(c-16)$ **18** $(t-4)(t-9)$
19 $(y-4)(y-12)$ **20** $(j-6)(j-8)$ **21** $(p-3)(p-5)$ **22** $(y+6)(y-1)$ **23** $(t+4)(t-2)$ **24** $(x+5)(x-2)$
25 $(m+2)(m-6)$ **26** $(r+1)(r-7)$ **27** $(n+3)(n-6)$ **28** $(m+4)(m-11)$ **29** $(w+4)(w-6)$ **30** $(t+9)(t-10)$
31 $(h+8)(h-9)$ **32** $(t+7)(t-9)$ **33** $(d+1)^2$ **34** $(y+10)^2$ **35** $(t-4)^2$ **36** $(m-9)^2$ **37** $(x-12)^2$
38 $(d+3)(d-4)$ **39** $(t+4)(t-5)$ **40** $(q+7)(q-8)$ **41** $(p+2)(p-1)$ **42** $(v+7)(v-5)$ **43** $(t+1)(t+3)$
44 $(m+1)(m-4)$ **45** $(x+2)(x-3)$

Exercise 10J

1 $(x+3)(x-3)$ **2** $(t+5)(t-5)$ **3** $(m+4)(m-4)$ **4** $(3+x)(3-x)$ **5** $(7+t)(7-t)$ **6** $(k+10)(k-10)$ **7** $(2+y)(2-y)$
8 $(x+8)(x-8)$ **9** $(t+9)(t-9)$ **10** $(x+y)(x-y)$ **11** $(x+2y)(x-2y)$ **12** $(x+3y)(x-3y)$ **13** $(3x+1)(3x-1)$
14 $(4x+3)(4x-3)$ **15** $(5x+8)(5x-8)$ **16** $(2x+3y)(2x-3y)$ **17** $(3t+2w)(3t-2w)$ **18** $(4y+5x)(4y-5x)$

Exercise 10K

1 −2, −5 **2** −3, −1 **3** −6, −4 **4** −3, 2 **5** −1, 3 **6** −4, 5 **7** 1, −2 **8** 2, −5 **9** 7, −4 **10** 3, 2 **11** 1, 5
12 4, 3 **13** −4, −1 **14** −9, −2 **15** 2, 4 **16** 3, 5 **17** −2, 5 **18** −3, 5 **19** −6, 2 **20** −6, 3 **21** −1, 2 **22** −2
23 −5 **24** 4 **25** −2, −6 **26** 5, −3 **27** 7 **28** −6, −4 **29** 2, 16 **30** −6, 4 **31** −9, 6 **32** −10, 3 **33** −4, 11
34 −8, 9 **35** 8, 9 **36** 1

Exercise 10L

1 $(2x+1)(x+2)$ **2** $(7x+1)(x+1)$ **3** $(4x+7)(x-1)$ **4** $(3t+2)(8t+1)$ **5** $(3t+1)(5t-1)$ **6** $(4x-1)^2$
7 $3(y+7)(2y-3)$ **8** $4(y+6)(y-4)$ **9** $(2x+3)(4x-1)$ **10** $(2t+1)(3t+5)$ **11** $(x-6)(3x+2)$ **12** $(x-5)(7x-2)$

Exercise 10M

1 a $\frac{1}{3}, -3$ **b** $1\frac{1}{3}, -\frac{1}{2}$ **c** $-\frac{1}{5}, 2$ **d** $-2\frac{1}{2}, 3\frac{1}{2}$ **e** $-\frac{1}{6}, -\frac{1}{3}$ **f** $\frac{2}{3}, 4$ **g** $\frac{1}{2}, -3$ **h** $2\frac{1}{2}, -1\frac{1}{6}$ **i** $-1\frac{2}{3}, 1\frac{2}{5}$ **j** $1\frac{3}{4}, 1\frac{2}{7}$ **k** $\frac{2}{3}, \frac{1}{8}$ **l** $-\frac{1}{4}$
m $-1\frac{1}{2}$ **n** $\frac{2}{5}$ **p** $1\frac{1}{3}$ **2 a** 7, −6 **b** $-2\frac{1}{2}, 1\frac{1}{2}$ **c** 7, −6 **d** $-1, \frac{11}{13}$ **e** 3, −2 **f** $-\frac{2}{5}, \frac{1}{2}$ **g** $-3\frac{2}{3}, \frac{4}{13}$ **h** $\frac{3}{8}, \frac{5}{12}$ **i** 4 **j** $3, -\frac{1}{2}$
k $-1, -2\frac{1}{2}$ **l** $-3, 4\frac{1}{2}$ **m** $1\frac{2}{3}$ **n** $3\frac{1}{2}$ **p** $3, -2\frac{1}{2}$

Exercise 10N

1 1.77, −2.27 **2** −0.23, −1.43 **3** 3.70, −2.70 **4** 0.29, −0.69 **5** −0.19, −1.53 **6** −1.23, −2.43 **7** −0.41, −1.84 **8** −1.39, −2.27 **9** 1.37, −4.37 **10** 2.18, 0.15 **11** −0.39, −5.11 **12** 0.44, −1.69 **13** 1.64, 0.61 **14** 0.36, −0.79 **15** 1.89, 0.11

Exercise 10P

1 0.87, −1.54 **2** 3.77, −0.27 **3** 1.29, 0.31 **4** 1.37, −1.70 **5** 1.10, 0.34 **6** 5.12, −3.12 **7** No solution **8** No solution
9 0.74, −0.54 **10** 0.16, −6.16 **11** No solution **12** 0.54, −5.54

Exercise 10Q

1 6, 8, 10 **2** 15 m, 20 m **3** 29 **4** 6.54, 0.46 **5** 3.22, 0.78 **6** 16 m by 14 m **7** 48 km/h **8** 45, 47 **9** 2.54 m, 3.54 m
10 6 cm **11** 30 km/h **12** 10p **13** 1.25, 0.8 **14** 10 **15** 5 h **16** 0.75 m

Examination questions (Chapter 10)

1 $3t(1+2t)$ **2 a** $3pq(4p-5q)$ **b** $2x^2+7x-15$ **c** $n=\frac{C-120}{40}$ **3 a** $a(2b-1)$ **b i** 6 **ii** 2, 3 **4 a i** $2\pi r(r+h)$
ii $2x^2+11x+12$ **b i** 75 **ii** $M=\sqrt{\frac{P}{a}+b}$ **5 a** $2x^2-11x+15$ **b** $b=\frac{c-fc}{f}$ **6 a** $4\frac{1}{2}$ **b ii** 7 **7 a i** $4x^2+12x$
ii $4x^2+12x+9$ **b** 9 **8 a** $\frac{x+3}{3}$ **b** $1\frac{1}{3}, \frac{3}{4}$ **9** 6.14, −1.14 **10 b** 2.62, 0.38 **11 a** $\frac{15}{x}+\frac{11}{x-2}$ **b** $\frac{15}{x}+\frac{11}{x-2}=4$
c ii $7\frac{1}{2}$ mph **12 b** 8.7 cm, 1.3 cm

Exercise 11A

1 a i 9 am **ii** 10 am **iii** 12 noon **b i** 40 km/h **ii** 120 km/h **iii** 40 km/h **2 a i** 125 km **ii** 125 km/h **b i** Between 2 and 3 pm **ii** 25 km/h **3 a i** 250 m/min **ii** 15 km **b** 500 m/min **c** Paul, 1 min **4 a** He fell **c i** 400 m/min **ii** 20 km/h **5 a** Ravinder – car, Sue – bus, Michael – cycle **b** 4.00 pm, 4.20 pm, 4.35 pm **c** 0.4 km/min **d** 14.4 km/h **6 b** 1.67 m/s **ii** 6 km/h

Exercise 11B

1 a 1.5 **b** 0.5 **c** −0.5 **d** −1 **c** 0.6 **f** 3 **g** $\frac{4}{3}$ **h** 0.2 **i** −1 **2 a** $\frac{15}{2}$ **b** 3 **c** $\frac{5}{4}$ **d** $\frac{2}{25}$ **e** $\frac{6}{35}$ **f** $\frac{1}{2}$ **g** $-\frac{4}{5}$ **h** 25 **i** $-\frac{25}{9}$ **j** $\frac{25}{6}$ **k** $\frac{25}{18}$ **l** $\frac{2}{3}$ **m** $\frac{4}{5}$ **n** 4 **p** −4 **3 a** $2\frac{1}{2}$ km/h **b** 3.8 m/s **c** $2\frac{1}{2}$ km/h **4 a** 30 km/h, 6 km/h, 0, 36 km/h **b** 4 m/s, 16 m/s, 2 m/s, 16 m/s

Exercise 11C

1 b i 3 m/s **ii** 2.75 m/s **c i** 2 m/s **ii** 3 m/s **2 b i** 3 m/s **ii** 15 m/s **c i** 10 m/s **ii** 10 m/s **3 b** 40 km/h **c i** 20 km/h **ii** 30 km/h **4 b i** 10 km/h **ii** 35 km/h **5 b i** 12 km/h **ii** 10 km/h **c i** 10 km/h **ii** 12 km/h **6 b** 56 km/h **c i** 70 km **ii** 80 km/h

Exercise 11D

1 a i 20 m/s^2 **ii** 13 m/s^2 **b** 154 m **2 a** 875 m **b** 1050 m **3 a** 2–4 h and 8–10 h **b** 400 km **c** 22 km/h

4 a

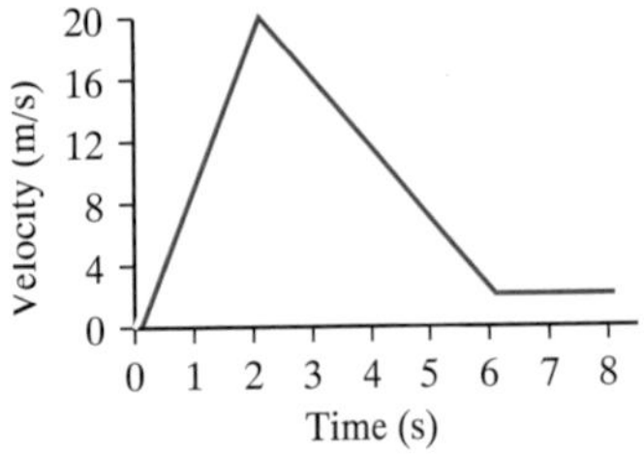

b 54 m **c** 129 s

5 a

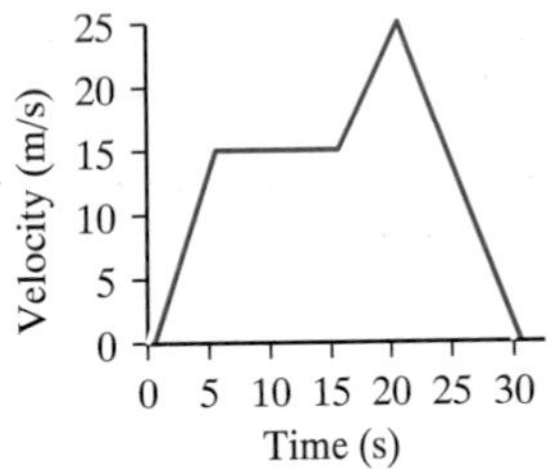

b 3 m/s^2 **c** 412.5 m **d** 13.75 m/s

6 a 90 m/s

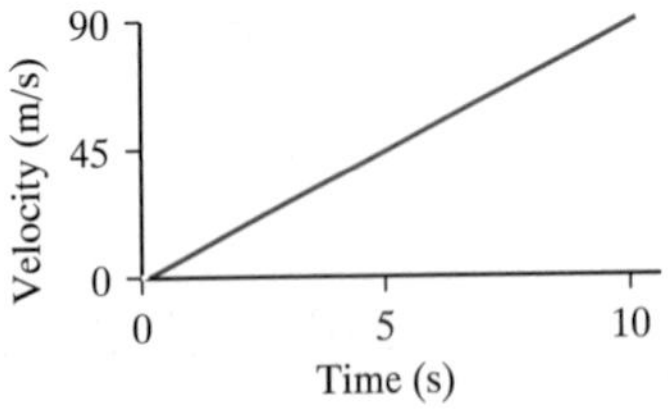

b i 45 m/s **ii** 9 m/s^2

Exercise 11E

1 a 15.5 **b** 134 **c** 30 **d** 94 **2 a** 116 **b** 230 **c** 136 **d** 21.2

Exercise 11F

1 b Decelerating **c i** –0.5 m/s^2 **ii** –1.4 m/s^2 **d** 74.24 m **2 a i** 64 m/min^2 **ii** –32 m/min^2 **b** 20.6 km **c** 515 m/min **3 b i** 1.3 m/s^2 **ii** 1 m/s^2 **c** 1480 m **4 b** 4.23 km **5 b** 27 km/min^2 **c** 13.38 km **d** 16.35 km **6 a** $7\frac{1}{2}$ m/s^2 **b i** 70 m **ii** $33\frac{1}{2}$ m **iii** 325 m **c** 27.1 m/s **7** $\frac{1}{2}$ km **8** ≈ 250 m

Examination questions (Chapter 11)

1 a 58 miles **b** 45 mph **c** 10.40–11.50 **2 a** 9.30 **b** 7 miles **c** 90 **d** 4 mph **3 b** 55 mph **c** 24 min **d** Gradient of line **f** 9 miles **4 a** 0.5 m/s^2 **b** 2.18 km **5 a ii** $\frac{3}{2}$ **b** 91 m **6 a** 1.5 m/s^2 **b i** 163 **ii** Distance travelled **7 a** 20 m/s **b** 12.3 m/s **c** 684 m **8 a i** 12 **ii** 0.05 **b** 3.3 km **9 a** 1/A, 2/B, 3/D, 4/E
C
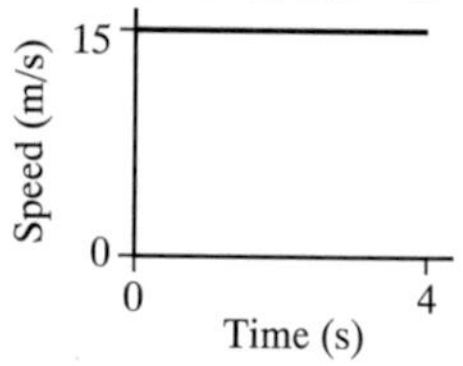

Exercise 12A

1 2, 3 **2** Sf = 4, not similar **3 a** Enlargement **b** 1 : 3 **c** Angle R **d** AB **4 a** Sides in same ratio **b** 2 : 1 **c** Angle Q **5 a** Sides in same ratio **b** Angle P **c** PR **6 a** Sides in same ratio **b** Angle Q **c** AR **7 a** 8 cm **b** 7.5 cm **c** 3.5 cm **d** 12 cm, 10 cm **e** $6\frac{2}{3}$ cm, $13\frac{1}{3}$ cm **f** 24 cm, 13 cm **g** 10 cm, 6 cm **h** 4.2 cm **8 a** Sides in same ratio **b** 1 : 3 **c** 13 cm **d** 39 cm **9** 4.8 m

Exercise 12B

1 a 9 cm **b** 6 cm **2 a** 9 cm **b** 5 cm **c** 14 cm **d** 5 cm **e** 60 cm, 75 cm **f** 56 cm, 24 cm **g** 45 cm, 60 cm **h** 10 cm, 8 cm **3** 82 m **4** 220 ft **5** 15 m **6** 8 cm, 10 cm, 16 cm **7** 3.09 m **8** 6 m

Exercise 12C

1 5 cm **2** 6 cm **3** 10 cm **4** 16 cm **5** 6 cm, 7.5 cm **6** 8 cm, 11.2 cm **7** 15 cm, 21 cm **8** 3 cm, 2.4 cm

Exercise 12D

1 a 4:25 **b** 8:125 **2 a** 16:49 **b** 64:343 **3** Linear scale factor: 2, 3, $\frac{1}{4}$, 5, $\frac{1}{10}$, 7, $\frac{1}{5}$, $\frac{1}{2}$; Linear ratio: 1:2, 1:3, 4:1, 1:5, 10:1, 1:7, 5:1, 2:1; Line: $\frac{2}{1}$, $\frac{3}{1}$, $\frac{1}{4}$, $\frac{5}{1}$, $\frac{1}{10}$, $\frac{7}{1}$, $\frac{1}{5}$, $\frac{1}{2}$; Area scale factor: 4, 9, $\frac{1}{16}$, 25, $\frac{1}{100}$, 49, $\frac{1}{25}$, $\frac{1}{4}$; Volume scale factor: 8, 27, $\frac{1}{64}$, 125, $\frac{1}{1000}$, 343, $\frac{1}{125}$, $\frac{1}{8}$ **4 a** 1:2 **b** 1:8 **c** 8 pints **d** No **5** 135 cm^2 **6 a** 56 cm^2 **b** 126 cm^2 **7 a** 48 ft^2 **b** 3 ft^2 **8 a** 2400 cm^3 **b** 8100 cm^3 **9 a** 3750 cm^3 **b** 3.75 cm^3 **10** 4 litres **11** 91.125 litres **12 a** 5.0625 litres **b** Height **13 a** 5.4 m^2 **b** 1.35 m^2 **14** 1.38 m^3 **15** £6 **16** 6, 8, 10 cm **17** $3r$ **18 a** 9, 36 **b** 16, 80 **c** 9, 45 **d** 36, 270 **e** *b* and *d*

Exercise 12E

1 6.2 cm, 10.1 cm **2** 4.3 cm, 6.7 cm **3** 9.6 cm **4** 3.38 m **5** 35 min **6** 8.4 cm **7** 26.5 cm **8** 17 cm **9 a** 4.3 cm, 7.8 cm **b** 143 g, 839 g **10** 2480 millilitres **11** 53.76 kg **12** 1.73 kg **13 a** $\sqrt{5}$:$\sqrt{8}$ **b** 0.99 litres **14** 92.8 cm **15** 1.30 m^2, 4.42 m^2

Examination questions (Chapter 12)

1 $4\frac{1}{2}$ cm **2** 63 cm **3** 280 m **4** 27 cm **5 a i** BCD **ii** 3 cm **b** Stays the same **6 a** All corresponding angles equal **b** 3.75 m **7** 2.8 m **8 a** Triangles ABC and ADE **b i** 6 cm **ii** 20 cm **9** 250.7 cm^3 **10** 1.6 cm^3

Exercise 13A

1 13.1 cm **2** 73.7° **3** 9.81 cm **4** 33.5 m **5 a** 10.0 cm **b** 4.69 cm **6** 63.0°

Exercise 13B

1 a 58.6° **b** 20.5 cm **c** 2049 cm^3 **d** 64.0° **2 a** 3.46 **b** 75.5° **c** 73.2° **d** 60.3 cm^2 **3 a** 24.0 **b** 48.0 **c** 13.5 cm **d** 16.6° **4 a** 32.0° **b** 35.9° **5 a** 3.46 m **b** 51.9°

Exercise 13C

1 36.9°, 143.1° **2** 53.1°, 126.9° **3** 48.6°, 131.4° **4** 21.7, 158.3° **5** 40.8°, 139.2° **6** 224.4°, 315.6° **7** 194.5°, 345.5° **8** 198.7°, 341.3° **9** 190.1°, 349.9° **10** 234.5°, 305.5° **11** 28.1°, 151.9° **12** 71.3°, 108.7° **13** 200°, 340° **14** 185.6°, 354.4° **15** 33.6°, 146.4° **16** 210°, 330° **17** 8.3°, 171.7° **18** 198.5°, 341.5° **19** 48.2°, 131.8° **20** 243.3°, 296.7°

Exercise 13D

1 53.1°, 306.9° **2** 54.5°, 305.5° **3** 62.7°, 297.3° **4** 54.9°, 305.1° **5** 79.3°, 280.7° **6** 216.9°, 143.1° **7** 104.5°, 255.5° **8** 100.1°, 259.9° **9** 111.2°, 248.8° **10** 166.9°, 193.1° **11** 78.7°, 281.3° **12** 44.4°, 315.6° **13** 114.7°, 245.3° **14** 107.9°, 252.1° **15** 56.1°, 303.9° **16** 93.2°, 266.8° **17** 131.6°, 228.4° **18** 59.7°, 300.3° **19** 37.3°, 322.7° **20** 109.5°, 250.5°

Exercise 13E

1 a 0.707 **b** –0.9998 (–1.0) **c** –0.819 **d** 0.731 **2 a** –0.629 **b** –0.875 **c** –0.087 **d** 0.999 **3 a** 21.2°, 158.8° **b** 209.1°, 330.9 **c** 50.1°, 309.9° **d** 150°, 210° **e** 60.9°, 119.1° **f** 29.1°, 330.9° **4** 30°, 150° **5** –0.755 **6 a** 1.41 **b** –1.37 **c** –0.0367 **d** –0.138 **e** 1.41 **f** –0.492 **7** True **8 a** sin 25° = cos 65° **b** sin 130° = sin 50° = cos 40° **9 a** $x = 10°, 130°$ **b** $x = 12.7°, 59.3°$ **10** $x = 38.1°, 141.9°$

Exercise 13F

1 14.5°, 194.5° **2** 38.1°, 218.1° **3** 50.0°, 230.0° **4** 61.9°, 241.9° **5** 68.6°, 248.6° **6** 160.3°, 340.3° **7** 147.6°, 327.6° **8** 135.4°, 315.4° **9** 120.9°, 300.9° **10** 105.2°, 285.2° **11** 54.4°, 234.4° **12** 42.2°, 222.2° **13** 160.5°, 340.5° **14** 130.9°, 310.9° **15** 76.5°, 256.5° **16** 116.0°, 296.0° **17** 174.4°, 354.4° **18** 44.9°, 224.9° **19** 50.4°, 230.4° **20** 111.8°, 291.8°

Exercise 13G

1 a 3.64 m **b** 8.05 cm **c** 19.45 cm **2 a** 46.6° **b** 112° **c** 36.2° **3** 50.3°, 129.7° **4** 2.88 cm, 20.91 cm **5 a** 30° **b** 40° **c** 19.45 m **6** 36.55 **7 a** 36.82 m **b** 22.16 m **8** 3.47 m **9** 767 m **10** 15.3 km/h

Exercise 13H

1 a 7.71 cm **b** 29.1 cm **c** 27.4 cm **2 a** 76.2° **b** 125.1° **c** 90° **3** 5.16 cm **4** 72.3°

5

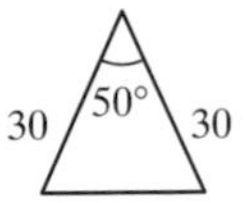

25.4 cm,

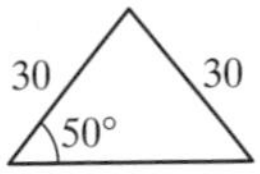

38.6 cm **6** 65.5 cm **7** 64 km at 088.6° **8** 21.8° **9 a** 10.7 cm **b** 41.7° **c** 383° **d** 6.69 cm **e** 54.4 cm^2 **10** 82.8° **11** 8.89 cm

Exercise 13I

1 a 8.60 m **b** 90° **c** 27.2 cm **d** 26.9° **e** 41.1° **f** 62.4 cm **g** 88.4° **h** 866.1 cm **i** 86.6 cm **2** 7 cm **3** 11.1 km **4** 19.9 knots **5 a** 27.8 km **b** 262.2°

Exercise 13J

1 $\frac{3}{5}$ **2** $\sqrt{\frac{2}{5}}$ **3** $\sin x = \frac{\sqrt{6}}{\sqrt{19}}, \cos x = \frac{\sqrt{13}}{\sqrt{19}}, \tan x = \frac{\sqrt{6}}{\sqrt{13}}$ **4 a** $\sqrt{157}$ **b** $\sin A = \frac{6}{\sqrt{157}}, \cos A = \frac{11}{\sqrt{157}}$ **5** $144\sqrt{3}$ cm^2

6 400 cm^2

Exercise 13K

1 a 24 cm^2 **b** 26.7 cm^2 **c** 242.5 cm^2 **d** 21 096.6 cm^2 **e** 1123.8 cm^2 **2** 4.26 cm **3** 102.6 cm^2 **4 a** 42.3° **b** 49.6° **5** 2033 cm^2 **6** 20.98 cm^2 **7 a** 33.2° **b** 25.3 cm^2

Examination questions (Chapter 13)

1 48.7° **2** **b** 6.81 km **3** **a** 16.2 km **b** 35° **4** **a** **i** 80° **ii** 6.99 cm **b** **i** 79° **ii** Max 7.09 cm, min 6.899 cm (≈ 6.90 cm) **5** **a** 11.43 m **b** 15.4° **6** **a** **i** 7.79 m **ii** 20 m **b** 75.3° **c** 47.8 m **7** **a** 3.11 m^2 **b** 5.16 m **8** **a** 24.6° **b** 8.37 yd **9** 65.8 m **10** 26.8 m

Exercise 14A

1 **a** $y = \frac{3}{2}x - 2$ **b** $y = x + 1$ **c** $y = 2x - 3$ **d** $y = \frac{1}{2}x + 3$ **e** $y = x$ **f** $y = x - 4$ **g** $y = 2x$ **h** $y = \frac{1}{5}x + 3$ **i** $y = \frac{3}{2}x + 1$ **2** **a** **i** $y = 2x + 1, y = -2x + 1$ **ii** Reflection in *y*-axis **iii** Different sign **b** **i** $y = \frac{2}{5}x - 1, y = -\frac{2}{5}x - 1$ **ii** Reflection in *y*-axis **iii** Different sign **c** **i** $y = x + 1, y = -x + 1$ **ii** Reflection in *y*-axis **iii** Different sign **3** **a** $y = -2x$ **b** $y = -\frac{1}{2}x$ **c** $y = -x + 1$ **d** $y = -\frac{2}{5}x - 1$ **e** $y = -\frac{3}{2}x - 3$ **4** **a** **i** $y = 1 - 2x, y = \frac{1}{2} - \frac{1}{2}x$ **ii** Lines reflected in $y = x$ (also applies to **b** and **c**) **iii** One gradient reciprocal of the other (also applies to **b** and **c**) **b** **i** $y = 2.5x + 2.5, y = 0.4x - 1$ **c** **i** $y = 2, x = 2$

Exercise 14B

2 **b** (2, 0) **3** **b** (2, 2) **4** **b** (4, 2)

Exercise 14C

1 **a** 32°F **b** $\frac{9}{5}$ (Accept 1.8) **c** $F = 1.8C + 32$ **2** **a** 0.07 **b** £10 **c** Charge = £10 + 7p/unit **3** **a** $\frac{5}{2}$ **b** £2 **c** Charge = £20 + £2.50/day **4** **a** $\frac{1}{2}$ **b** £50 **c** Charge = £50 + 50p/person **5** **a** $\frac{1}{10}$ **b** 25.4 cm **c** 1 mm **d** Length = 25.4 cm + 1 mm/kg

Exercise 14D

1 4, 1 **2** 2, 3 **3** 3, 10 **4** 5, 5 **5** 1, 5 **6** 3, 16 **7** –2, 6 **8** –6, –9 **9** 1, –1 **10** 2, 6 **11** 2, 8 **12** $7\frac{1}{2}, 3\frac{1}{2}$

Exercise 14E

1 **a** Values of *y*: 27, 12, 3, 0, 3, 12, 27 **b** 6.8 **c** 1.8 or –1.8 **2** **a** Values of *y*: 27, 18, 11, 6, 3, 2, 3, 6, 11, 18, 27 **b** 8.3 **c** 3.5 or –3.5 **3** **a** Values of *y*: 40, 28, 18, 10, 4, 0, –2, –2, 0, 4, 10 **b** 1.75 **c** 4.2 or –1.2 **4** **a** Values of *y*: 27, 16, 7, 0, –5, –8, –10, –8, –5, 0, 7 **b** –8.8 **c** 3.4 or –1.4 **5** **a** Values of *y*: 18, 10, 4, 0, –3, –2, 0, 4 **b** 6.8 **c** 0.2 or 4.8 **6** **a** Values of *y*: 2, –1, –2, –1, 2, 7, 14 **b** 0.25 **c** 0.7 or –2. **e** (1.1, 2.6) and (–2.6, 0.7) **7** **a** Values of *y*: 18, 11, 6, 3, 2, 3, 6 **b** 2.25 **c** 2.4 or –0.4 **e** (–1, 6) **8** **a** Values of *y*:18, 12, 8, 6, 6, 8, 12 **b** 9.75 **c** 2 or –1 **d** Values of *y*: 14, 9, 6, 5, 6, 9, 14 **e** (1, 6) **9** **a** Values of *y*: 4, 1, 0, 1, 9, 16 **b** 7.3 **c** 0.4 or –2.4 **e** (1, 4) and (–1, 0) **10** **a** Values of *y*: 15, 9, 4, 0, –3, –5, –5, –3, 0, 4, 9 **b** –0.5 and 3

Exercise 14F

1 **a** Values of *y*: 12, 5, 0, –3, –4, –3, 0, 5, 12, **b** 2 and –2 **2** **a** Values of *y*: 7, 0, –5, –8, –9, –8, –5, 0, 7 **b** 3 and –3 **3** **c** Values of *y*: 15, 8, 3, 0, –1, 0, 3, 8, 15 **d** Values of *y*: 11, 4, –1, –4, –5, –4, –1, 4, 11 **e** 1 and –1, 2.2 and –2.2 **4** **a** Values of *y*: 5, 0, –3, –4, –3, 0, 5, 12 **b** –4 and 0 **5** **a** Values of *y*: 16, 7, 0, –5, –8, –9, –8, –5, 0 **b** 0 and 6 **6** **a** Values of *y*: 10, 4, 0, –2, –2, 0, 4, 10, 18 **b** –3 and 0 **7** **c** Values of *y*: 10, 4, 0, –2, –2, 0, 4, 10 **d** Values of *y*: 6, 0, –4, –6, –6, –4, 0, 6, 14 **e** 0 and 3, –5 and 0 **8** **a** Values of *y*: 4, 1, 0, 1, 4, 9, 16 **b** –2 **c** Only 1 root **9** **a** Values of *y*: 10, 3, –2, –5, –6, –5, –2, 3, 10 **b** 0.6 and 5.4 **10** **a** Values of *y*: 19, 6, –3, –8, –9, –6, 1, 12 **b** 0.9 and –3.4

Exercise 14G

1 **a** Values of *y*: 10, 5, 4, 2.5, 2, 1.33, 1, 0.67, 0.5 **b** **i** 0.8 **ii** –1.6 **2** **a** Values of *y*: 10, 8, 5, 4, 2, 1, 0.8, 0.5, 0.4 **b** **i** 0.7 **ii** –0.7 **3** **a** Values of *y*: 10, 5, 3.33, 2, 1.25, 1, 0.33, 0.2, 0.1, 0.07 **b** **i** 0.13 **ii** –0.25 **4** **a** Values of $5\sqrt{x}$: 0, 5 and –5, 7.1 and –7.1, 8.7 and –8.7, 10 and –10, 11.2 and –11.2 **b** **i** 9.4 and –9.4 **ii** 2.6 **5** **a** Values of $\frac{1}{2}\sqrt{x}$: 0, $\frac{1}{2}$ and $-\frac{1}{2}$, 0.71 and –0.71, 0.87 and –0.87, 1 and –1, 1.1 and –1.1 **b** **i** 0.8 and –0.8 **ii** 2.25 **6** **a** Values of $\sqrt{x-3}$: 0, 1 and –1, 1.41 and –1.41, 1.73 and –1.73, 2 and –2, 2.23 and –2.23 **b** **i** 1.9 and –1.9 **ii** 5.25 **7** **a** Values of *y*: 10, 5, 2.5, 2, 1.25, 1, 0.5, 0.33, 0.25 **b** **i** –0.67 **ii** 25 **8** **a** Values of *y*: 10, 5, 2.5, 2, 1, 0.5, 0.4, 0.25, 0.2 **c** 4.8 and 0.2 **9** **a** Values of *y*: 25, 12.5, 10, 5, 2.5, 1, 0.5, 0.33, 0.25 **c** 0.48 **10** **a** Values of *y*: 0.5, 0, –0.33, –1, –1.5, –3, –4, –9, 11, 6, 5, 3.5, 3, 2.33, 2, 1.5 **b** Values of *y*: –3.5, –4, –4.33, –5, –5.5, –7, –8, –13, 7, 2, 1, –0.5, –1, –1.67, –2, –2.5 **c** These two graphs are translations of $y = \frac{2}{x}$

Exercise 14H

1 a Values of *y*: –24, –12.63, –5, –0.38, 2, 2.9, 3, 3.13, 4, 6.38, 11, 15.63, 30 **b** 4.7 **2 a** Values of *y*: –54, –31.25, –16, –6.75, –2, –0.25, 0, 0.25, 2, 6.75, 16, 31.25, 54 **b** 39.4 **3 a** Values of *y*: 27, 15.63, 8, 3.38, 1, 0.13, 0, –0.13, –1, –3.38, –8, –15.63, –27 **b** 0.2 **4 a** Values of *y*: –36, –23.13, –14, –7.88, –4, –1.63, 0, 1.63, 4, 7.88, 14, 23.13, 36 **b** 0.6 **5 a** Values of *y*: –45, –26.88, –14, –5.63, –1, 0.63, 0, –0.63, –5, –7.88, –10, –10.63, –9 **b** –9.3 **6 a** Values of *y*: –17, –7.13, –1, 2.13, 3, 2.38, 1, –0.38, –1, –0.13, 3, 9.13, 19 **b** –1.9, 0.3, 1.5 **7 a** Values of *y*: –19, –9.13, –3, 0.13, 1, 0.375, –1, –2.38, –3, –2.13, 1, 7.13, 17 **b** 3.2 **8 a** Values of *y*: –7, 1.38, 6, 7.63, 7, 4.88, 2, –0.88, –3, –3.63, –2, 2.63, 11 **b** –2.7, 0.5, 2.1 **9 a** Values of *y*: –16, –5.63, 1, 4.63, 6, 5.88, 5, 4.13, 4, 5.38, 9, 15.63, 26 **c** –1.6, –0.4, 1.9 **10 a** Values of *y*: –20, –9.63, –3, 0.63, 2, 1.88, 1, 0.13, 0, 1.38, 5, 11.63, 22 **c** –1.9, 0.4, 1.5 **11 a** Quadratic **b** Linear **c** Reciprocal **d** Reciprocal **e** None **f** Cubic **g** Linear **h** None **i** Quadratic

Exercise 14I

1 a –1.4, 4.4 **b** –2, 5 **c** –0.6, 3.6 **d** 0.3, 2.7 **2 a** –5, 1 **b** –5.3, 1.3 **c** –4.8, 0.8 **d** –3.4, –0.6 **3 a** 0.7, 4.3 **b** 0.2, 4.8 **c** –0.4, 5.4 **d** 0, 6 **4 a** –1.4, 1.4 **b** –2.3, 2.3 **c** –2, 2 **d** –1.6, 2.6 **5 a** 0, 2 **b** 2.4 **c** –0.6, 1, 1.6 **d** 2.8 **e** –0.8, 0.6, 2.2

6

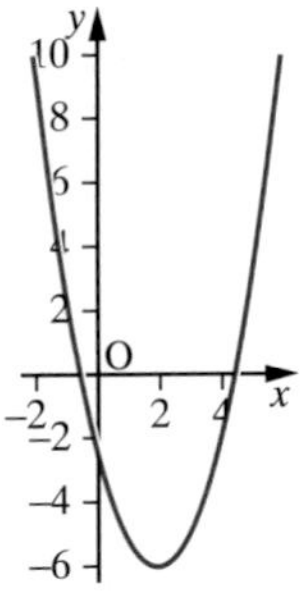

a 4.5, –0.5 **b** 5, –1

7

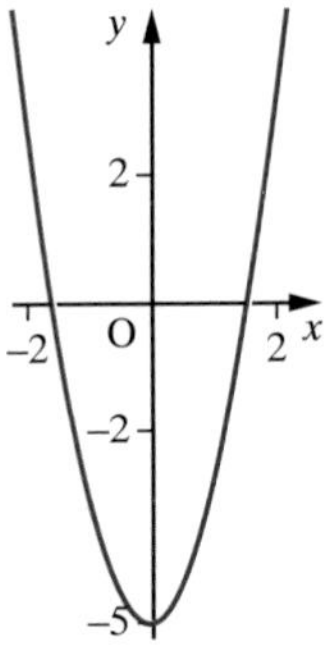

a 1.6, –1.6 **b** –1.2, 1.2

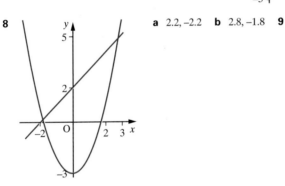

8

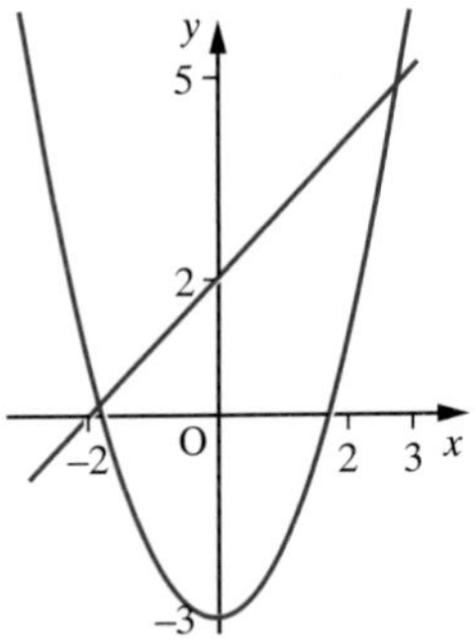

a 2.2, –2.2 **b** 2.8, –1.8

9

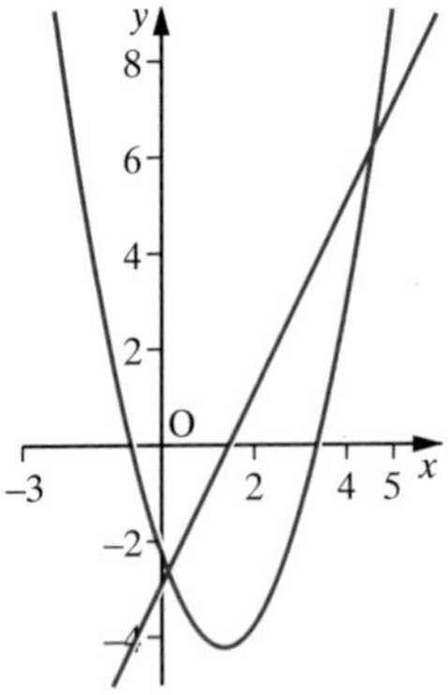

a 3.3, –0.3 **b** 4.8, 0.2

10

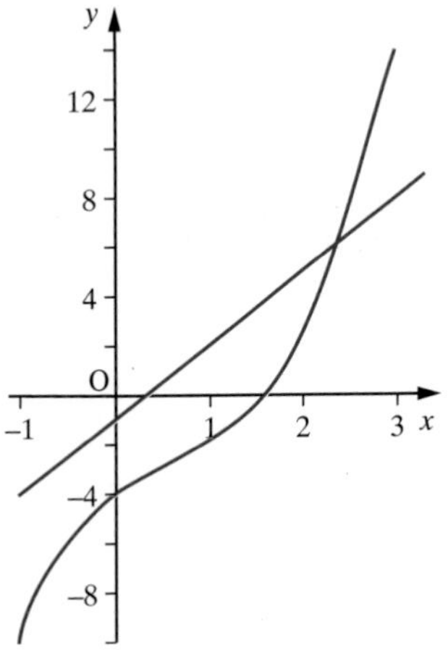

a 2, **b** 2.5

Exercise 14J

1

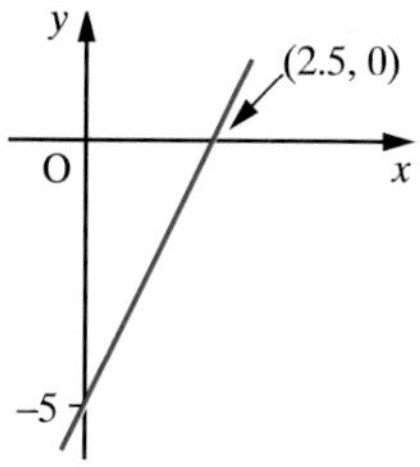

2

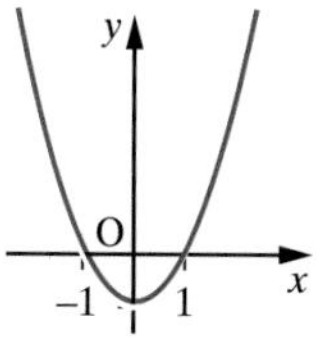

3

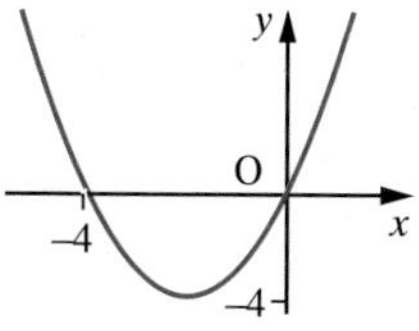

4

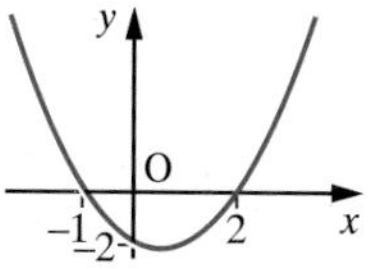

5

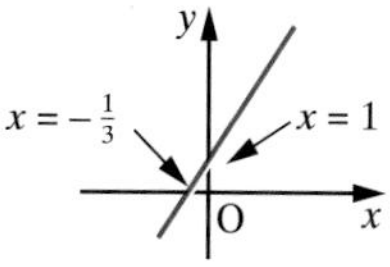

6

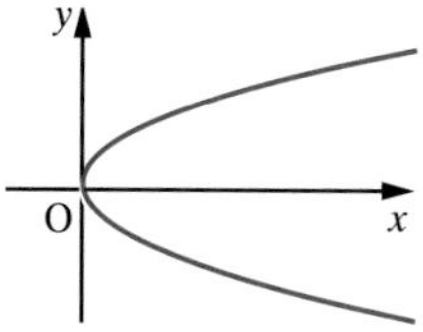

7

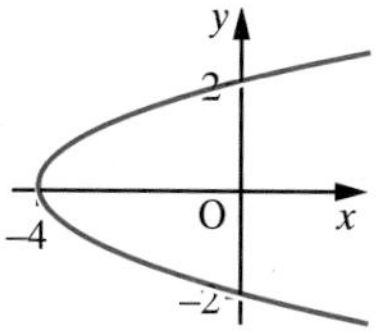

8

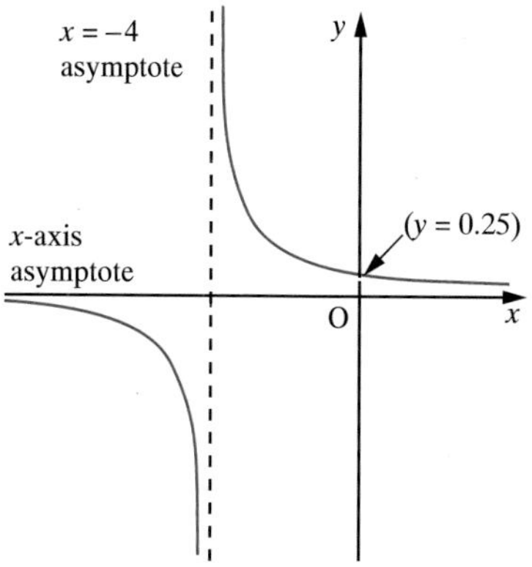

9

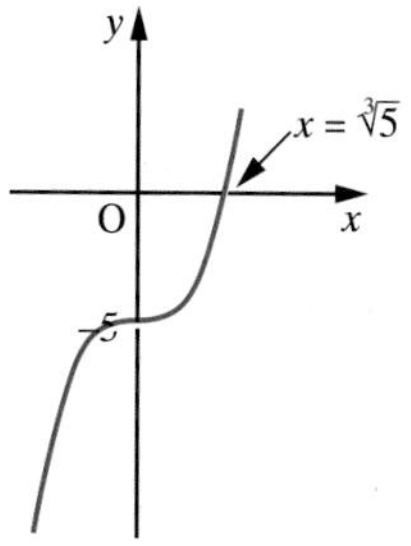

10

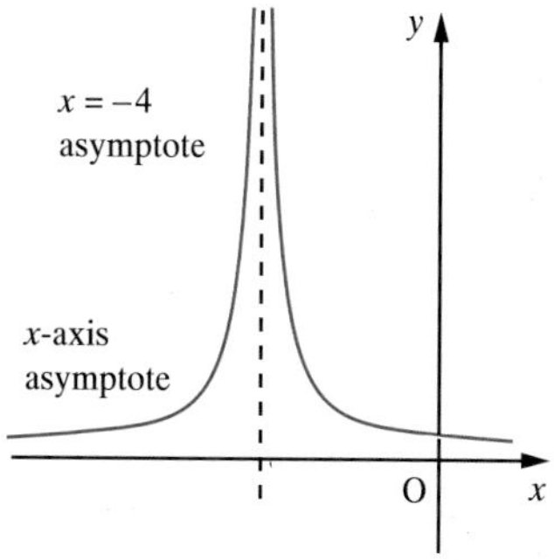

11

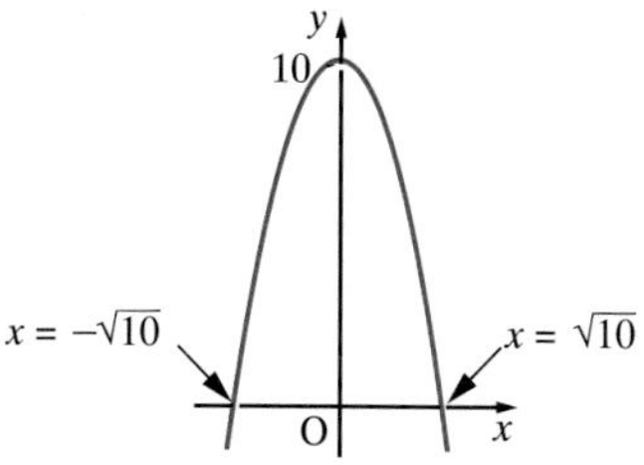

12

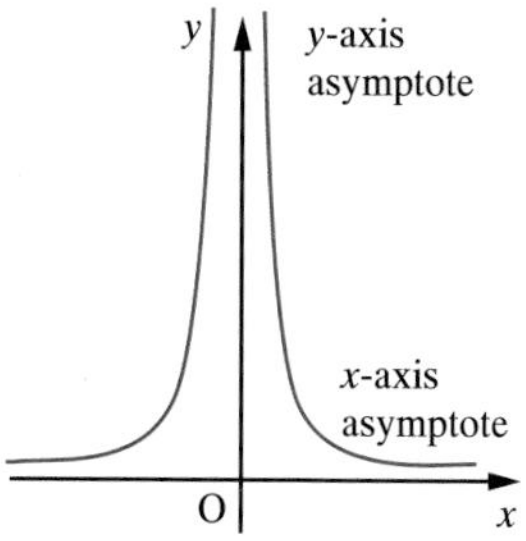

Examination questions (Chapter 14)

1 b i $\frac{1}{2}$ **ii** $\frac{1}{2}$ **iii** $y = \frac{1}{2}x + \frac{1}{2}$ **2 b** $x = 1\frac{1}{2}, y = 3$ **3 b ii** 32.5 °C **iii** 68 g **c i** $a = 0.4, b = 50$ **iii** 88 g **4 b** 60p **5 a** Graph C **b** $v = kr^2$ **6 a** 0.54, 2.15 **c i** –2, –0.4, 2.42 **ii** $x^3 - 5x + x - 2 = 0$ **7 a** Values of d: 0, 2.5, 10, 22.5, 40, 62.5, 90, 122.5, 160 **c** 106 m **d** 4.5 s **8 a** Values of y: 10, 4, 0, –2, –2, 0, 4, 10 **c** 2.6, 0.4

9 a

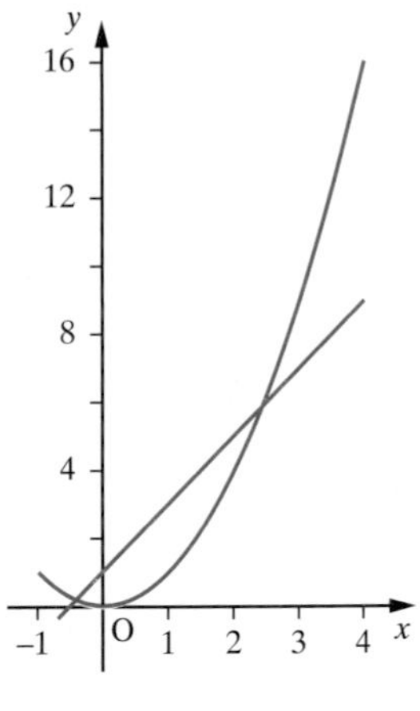

b Draw $y = 2x + 1$: −0.4, 2.4 **10 a** $y = 2x + 3$ **b i** 2 **ii** 0 **c** 2.7, −0.7

Exercise 15A

1 a Positive correlation **b** Negative correlation **c** No correlation **d** Positive correlation **2** A person's reaction time increases as more alcohol is consumed **3** As people get older, they consume less alcohol **4** No relationship between temperature and speed of cars on M1 **5** As people get older, they bank more money **6 c** ≈ 20 cm/s **d** ≈ 35 cm **7 b** Greta **c** ≈ 70 **d** ≈ 72 **8 c** Yes, usually (good correlation) **9 c** ≈ £75 000 **d** Locality, improvements **e** Yes, positive correlation **10 b** No correlation **c** No

Exercise 15B

1 c 53 s, 16 s **2 c** 56 s, 17 s **d** Children: lower median **3 c** 605, 277 **d** 37/38 **4 c** 67°F, 17°F **5 c** 48, 43 **d** 18% **6 c** £2.25, £1.08 **7 a** Cumulative frequency 8, 22, 47, 82, 96, 100 **c** Median £810, IQR £80 **d** 28%

Exercise 15C

1 a Mean 6, SD 2.45 **b** 11.6, 3.77 **c** 108, 4.43 **d** 203, 1.41 **e** 73.65, 3.57 **f** 1, 2.51 **g** 77.2, 5.19 **h** 35, 3.98 **2 a** Mean 7.6, SD 2.24 **b** 21.6, 3.77 **c** 87.2, 3.43 **d** 203, 1.41 **e** 72, 4.53 **f** 1, 3.63 **g** 97.2, 5.19 **h** 36.2, 5.01 **3 a** 6 **b** 1.41 **4 a** Mean 8, SD 2.61 **b** 18, 2.61 **c** 28, 2.61 **5** 10 **6** 11 **7** 5 **8 a** Mean 8, SD 1.94 **b** 8, 4.73 **c** Paula, because she is more consistent. Rose occasionally gets high scores. **9** 12, 16 **10 a** Salford Harriers: Mean 19 min 45.2 s, SD 9.48 s; Bingley Harriers: 19 min 53.8s, 20.63 s; Sunderland: 20 min 15s, 30.25 s **b** Salford Harriers, because they are fastest and most consistent

Exercise 15D

1

Time	2	3	4	5	6	7	8	9	10	12
Frequency	5	1	1	5	1	3	1	1	1	1

Mean 5.4, SD 2.82

2 a Mean 2.15, SD 1.19 **b** 24.3, 1.51 **c** 102.15, 1.19 **d** 7.79, 0.47 **e** 3.55, 0.88 **f** 0.166, 0.066 **3 a i** Mean 3.49, SD 1.73 **ii** 3.00 **b i** 6.96, 2.42 **ii** 5.85 **c** Mean is about double, square of SD is also about double **d** Mean about 10.5, SD about 3 **4 a** Mean 135.2, SD 7.44 **b** Mean 2.84, SD 1.49 **i** 135.2 **ii** 7.44 **c** Same **d** Smaller numbers **5 a** Class 1: Mean 5, SD 2.24; Class 2: Mean 5, SD 1.51 **b** Class 2, because it had a lower SD, so was more consistent **6 a** Mean 90.16 min (≈ 90 min 10 s), SD 7.24 min **b** She will be late on more than 15 days, so not a good idea

Examination questions (Chapter 15)

1 b 65 **2 a** 25 **d** ≈ 22 **c** Positive correlation **3 c** 16 **4 a** The older the runners were, the longer they took **c** The 'peak' is at a higher time, and the variation is less **d i** 4–5 h **ii** 5–6 h **5 b i** 100 **ii** 13 **c i** Joy: smaller interquartile range **ii** Laura: smaller median **6 a** 57 **c i** 57 **ii** 78 **7 b i** 44 mph **ii** 11 mph **iii** 76% **8 b i** 235 **ii** 44 **iii** 51 **9 b** 53, 45, 60, 15 **c** 51 **10 a** 2.4 min **c i** 2.2 min **ii** 2.9 min **d** 5 **11 a** Mean 493.5, SD 10.6 **b** 483.5, 10.6. To compensate for the fault, Cathy reduced each reading by 10, thereby reducing the mean by 10. But the SD would be the same for both calculations. **12 a** 60 **b** Mean increases to £261.50, SD unaltered **c** Mean and SD increase by 10% **d** Manager's scheme better for 6 lowest paid workers, foreman's for 4 highest paid. Manager's scheme benefits more

Exercise 16A

1 a $\frac{1}{5}, \frac{1}{25}, \frac{1}{10}, \frac{21}{200}, \frac{37}{250}, \frac{163}{1000}, \frac{329}{2000}$ **b** 6 **c** 1 **d** $\frac{1}{6}$ **e** 1000 **2 a** $\frac{19}{200}, \frac{27}{200}, \frac{4}{25}, \frac{53}{200}, \frac{69}{200}$ **b** 40 **c** No **3 a** 32, **b** Yes **4 a** $\frac{1}{5}, \frac{1}{4}, \frac{39}{100}, \frac{21}{50}, \frac{77}{200}, \frac{1987}{5000}$ **b** 8 **5 a** 0.429, 0.326, 0.294, 0.289, 0.303, 0.306 **b** 0.286, 0.168, 0.190, 0.152, 0.202, 0.201 **c** 0.5, 0.3, 0.2 **d** 1 **e** Red 10, white 6, blue 4 **6 b** 20 **7 a** 6 **8 a** B **b** B **c** C **d** A **e** B **f** A **g** B **h** A **9 a** Caryl **b** $\frac{107}{275}, \frac{169}{550}, \frac{91}{550}, \frac{38}{275}$ **c** Yes **10 a** Not likely **b** Impossible **c** Not likely **d** Certain **e** Impossible **f** 50–50 chance **g** 50–50 chance **h** Certain **i** Quite likely

Exercise 16B

1 a $\frac{1}{6}$ **b** $\frac{1}{6}$ **c** $\frac{1}{2}$ **d** $\frac{1}{13}$ **e** $\frac{1}{4}$ **f** $\frac{1}{2}$ **g** $\frac{1}{3}$ **h** $\frac{1}{26}$ **i** $\frac{1}{13}$ **j** 0 **2 a** $\frac{1}{2}$ **b** $\frac{1}{2}$ **c** $\frac{1}{2}$ **d** $\frac{1}{52}$ **e** $\frac{4}{13}$ **f** $\frac{1}{52}$ **3 a** 0 **b** 1 **4 a** $\frac{1}{10}$ **b** $\frac{1}{2}$ **c** $\frac{2}{5}$ **d** $\frac{1}{5}$ **e** $\frac{2}{5}$ **5 a** $\frac{1}{3}$ **b** $\frac{1}{3}$ **c** $\frac{2}{3}$ **6 a** $\frac{6}{11}$ **b** $\frac{5}{11}$ **c** $\frac{6}{11}$ **7 a** $\frac{1}{5}$ **b** $\frac{1}{2}$ **c** $\frac{1}{2}$ **d** $\frac{7}{10}$ **8 a** $\frac{7}{15}$ **b** $\frac{2}{15}$ **c** $\frac{8}{15}$ **d** 0 **e** $\frac{8}{15}$ **9** $\frac{1}{50}$ **10 a** AB, AC, AD, AE, BC, BD, BE, CD, CE, DE **b** 1 **c** $\frac{1}{10}$ **d** 6 **e** $\frac{6}{10}$ **f** $\frac{3}{10}$ **11 a** $\frac{2}{5}$ **b i** 3 **ii** 9 **c i** $\frac{1}{3}$ **ii** $\frac{2}{3}$ **12 a** $\frac{1}{3}$ **b** $\frac{1}{2}$ **c** $\frac{5}{6}$ **d** 0 **e** 1 **13 a** $\frac{1}{4}$ **b** $\frac{3}{8}$ **c** $\frac{1}{4}$ **d** $\frac{3}{8}$ **e** $\frac{1}{2}$ **f** $\frac{3}{4}$

14

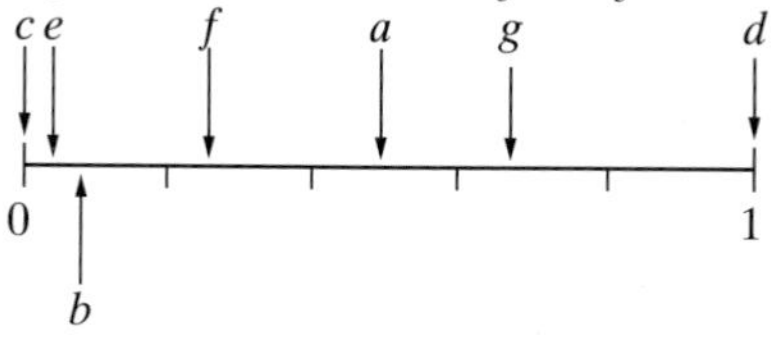

15 a $\frac{5}{20}$ cancels to $\frac{1}{4}$ **b** Either $\frac{4}{19}$ or $\frac{5}{19}$

Exercise 16C

1 a Yes **b** Yes **c** No **d** No **e** Yes **f** Yes **2** Events **a** and **f** **3** $\frac{3}{5}$ **4 a i** $\frac{3}{10}$ **ii** $\frac{3}{10}$ **iii** $\frac{3}{10}$ **b** Events *i*, *ii* and *iv* **c** *iv* **5 b i** $\frac{1}{10}$ **ii** $\frac{3}{10}$ **iii** $\frac{3}{10}$ **iv** $\frac{7}{10}$ **c** Events *i* and *ii* **d** Event *ii* **6 a** $\frac{3}{8}$ **b** $\frac{1}{8}$ **c** Events *i* and *iv* **d** Outcomes overlap **7** $\frac{3}{20}$ **8** Not mutually exclusive events **9 i** *a* and *b* **ii** *c*, 9 **iii** *c*, 6 **iv** *c*, 36 **v** *c*, 12 **vi** *c*, 1 **vii** *c*, 10 **viii** *c*, 15 **ix** *a* **x** *c*, 12 **10 a i** 0.25 **ii** 0.4 **iii** 0.7 **b** Events are not mutually exclusive **c** Man/woman, American man/American woman **d** Man/woman

Exercise 16D

1 25 **2** 1000 **3 a** 260 **b** 40 **c** 130 **d** 10 **4** 5 **5** 400 **6 a** 150 **b** 100 **c** 250 **d** 0 **7 a** 167 **b** 833 **8** 1050 **9 a** 10, 10, 10, 10, 10, 10 **b** 3,5 **c** Find the average of the scores ($\frac{21}{6}$)

Exercise 16E

1 a $\frac{1}{6}$ **b** $\frac{1}{6}$ **c** $\frac{1}{3}$ **2 a** $\frac{1}{4}$ **b** $\frac{1}{4}$ **c** $\frac{1}{2}$ **3 a** $\frac{1}{13}$ **b** $\frac{1}{13}$ **c** $\frac{2}{13}$ **4 a** $\frac{2}{11}$ **b** $\frac{4}{11}$ **c** $\frac{6}{11}$ **5 a** $\frac{1}{3}$ **b** $\frac{6}{15}$ **c** $\frac{11}{15}$ **d** $\frac{11}{15}$ **e** $\frac{1}{3}$ **6 a** 0.6 **b** 120 **7 a** 0.8 **b** 0.2 **8 a** 0.75 **b** 0.6 **c** 0.5 **d** 0.6 **e ii** Not mutually exclusive **iii** 0.4 **9 a** $\frac{17}{20}$, **b** $\frac{2}{5}$ **c** $\frac{3}{4}$ **10** Probability cannot exceed 1

Exercise 16F

1 a 7 **b** 2 and 12 **c** $P(2) = \frac{1}{36}$, $P(3) = \frac{1}{18}$, $P(4) = \frac{1}{12}$, $P(5) = \frac{1}{9}$, $P(6) = \frac{5}{36}$, $P(7) = \frac{1}{6}$, $P(8) = \frac{5}{36}$, $P(9) = \frac{1}{9}$, $P(10) = \frac{1}{12}$, $P(11) = \frac{1}{18}$ $P(12) = \frac{1}{36}$ **d i** $\frac{1}{12}$ **iii** $\frac{1}{3}$ **iii** $\frac{1}{2}$ **iv** $\frac{7}{36}$ **v** $\frac{15}{36}$ **vi** $\frac{5}{18}$ **2 a** $\frac{1}{12}$ **b** $\frac{11}{36}$ **c** $\frac{1}{6}$ **d** $\frac{5}{9}$ **3 a** $\frac{1}{36}$ **b** $\frac{11}{36}$ **c** $\frac{5}{18}$ **4 a** $\frac{5}{18}$ **b** $\frac{1}{6}$ **c** $\frac{1}{9}$ **d** 0 **e** $\frac{1}{2}$ **5 a** $\frac{1}{4}$ **b** $\frac{1}{2}$ **c** $\frac{3}{4}$ **d** $\frac{1}{4}$ **6 a** $\frac{1}{8}$ **b** $\frac{3}{8}$ **c** $\frac{7}{8}$ **d** $\frac{1}{8}$ **7 a** 16 **b** 32 **c** 1024 **d** 2^n **8 a** $\frac{1}{12}$ **b** $\frac{1}{4}$ **c** $\frac{1}{6}$ **9 a** 6 **b i** $\frac{4}{25}$ **ii** $\frac{13}{25}$ **iii** $\frac{1}{5}$ **iv** $\frac{3}{5}$

Exercise 16G

1 a $\frac{1}{4}$ **b** $\frac{1}{2}$ **c** $\frac{3}{4}$ **2 a** $\frac{2}{3}$ **b** $\frac{1}{2}$ **d i** $\frac{1}{6}$ **ii** $\frac{1}{2}$ **iii** $\frac{5}{6}$ **e** 15 **3 a** $\frac{2}{5}$ **b i** $\frac{4}{25}$ **ii** $\frac{12}{25}$ **4 a** $\frac{1}{13}$ **b** $\frac{12}{13}$ **c i** $\frac{1}{169}$ **ii** $\frac{25}{169}$ **5 a i** $\frac{2}{5}$ **ii** $\frac{3}{5}$ **b i** 4 **ii** 1 **c i** 4 **ii** 2 **e i** $\frac{2}{5}$ **ii** $\frac{7}{10}$ **6 a** $\frac{1}{8}$ **b** $\frac{3}{8}$ **c** $\frac{7}{8}$ **7 a** 0.14 **b** 0.41 **c** 0.09 **8 a** $\frac{3}{5}$ **c i** $\frac{1}{3}$ **ii** $\frac{7}{15}$ **iii** $\frac{8}{15}$ **9 a** $\frac{1}{4}$ **b** 0 **d i** $\frac{1}{2}$ **ii** $\frac{1}{2}$ **iii** 0 **10 a** 1 **b** 1 **c**

	$\frac{1}{4}$	$\frac{1}{4}$	$\frac{1}{10}$
$\frac{3}{5}$	$\frac{1}{3}$	$\frac{3}{5} \times \frac{1}{3}$	
	$\frac{2}{3}$	$\frac{3}{5} \times \frac{2}{3}$	$\frac{2}{5}$

Exercise 16H

1 a $\frac{4}{9}$ **b** $\frac{4}{9}$ **2 a** $\frac{1}{169}$ **b** $\frac{2}{169}$ **3 a** $\frac{1}{221}$ **b** $\frac{8}{663}$ **4 a** $\frac{1}{4}$ **b** $\frac{1}{2}$ **5** $\frac{1}{216}$ **6 a** $\frac{4}{25}$ **b** $\frac{12}{25}$ **7 a** $\frac{3}{20}$ **b** $\frac{1}{2}$ **8 a** 0.08 **b** 0.32 **c** 0.48 **9 a** 0.336 **b** 0.452 **c** 0.024 **10 a** $\frac{1}{6}$ **b** 0 **c i** $\frac{2}{3}$ **ii** $\frac{1}{3}$ **iii** 0

Exercise 16I

1 a $\frac{125}{216}$ (0.579) **b** $\frac{191}{216}$ (0.421) **2 a** $\frac{11}{16}$ **b** $\frac{15}{16}$ **3 a** 0.378 **b** 0.162 **c** 0.012 **d** 0.988 **4 a** $\frac{4}{25}$ **b** $\frac{9}{25}$ **c** $\frac{16}{25}$ **5 a** $\frac{2}{15}$ **b** $\frac{1}{3}$ **c** $\frac{2}{3}$ **6 a i** $\frac{1}{216}$ (0.005) **ii** $\frac{25}{216}$ (0.579) **iii** $\frac{91}{216}$ (0.421) **b i** $\frac{1}{1296}$ (0.00077) **ii** $\frac{625}{1296}$ (0.482) **iii** $\frac{1671}{1296}$ (0.518) **c i** $\frac{1}{7776}$ **ii** $\frac{3125}{7776}$ (0.402) **iii** $\frac{4651}{7776}$ (0.588) **d i** $(6)^{-n}$ **ii** $(\frac{5}{6})^n$ **iii** $1-(\frac{5}{6})^n$ **7 a** $\frac{32}{243}$ (0.132) **b** $\frac{1}{243}$ (0.0041) **c** $\frac{242}{243}$ (0.9959) **8 a** $\frac{3}{8}$ **b** $\frac{1}{120}$ **c** $\frac{119}{120}$ **9 a** $\frac{33}{150}$ (0.22) **b** $\frac{117}{150}$ (0.78) **10 a** $\frac{1}{30}$ **b** $\frac{29}{30}$

Exercise 16J

1 a $\frac{27}{1000}$ **b** $\frac{189}{1000}$ **c** $\frac{441}{1000}$ **d** $\frac{343}{1000}$ **2 a** $\frac{8}{125}$ **b** $\frac{36}{125}$ **c** $\frac{54}{125}$ **d** $\frac{27}{125}$ **3 a** $\frac{1}{1296}$ (0.00077) **b** $\frac{625}{1296}$ (0.482) **c** $\frac{125}{324}$ (0.386) **4 a** $\frac{1}{9}$ **b** $\frac{7}{18}$ **c** $\frac{7}{18}$ **d** $\frac{1}{9}$ **5 a** 0.154 **b** 0.456 **6 a** 0.3024 **b** 0.4404 **c** 0.7428 **7 a** 0.9 **b** 0.6 **c** 0.54 **d** 0.216 **8 a** 0.6 **b** 0.6 **c** 0.432 **d** Independent events **9 a** $\frac{1}{9}$ **b** $\frac{1}{9}$ **c** $\frac{4}{27}$ **d** $\frac{4}{27}$ **10 a** 0.126 **b** 0.4 **c** 0.42 **d** 0.054

Exercise 16K

1 a i $\frac{3}{8}$ **ii** $\frac{5}{8}$ **b ii** $\frac{5}{12}$ **iii** $\frac{7}{12}$ **2 a i** $\frac{5}{13}$ **iii** $\frac{8}{13}$ **b ii** $\frac{15}{91}$ **iii** $\frac{4}{13}$ **3 a i** $\frac{1}{3}$ **ii** $\frac{2}{15}$ **b** $\frac{4}{15}$ **c** $\frac{1}{6}$ **d** 1 **4 a** $\frac{1}{60}$ **b** 50 **5** Both events are independent **6 a** $\frac{1}{120}$ **b** $\frac{7}{40}$ **c** $\frac{21}{40}$ **d** $\frac{7}{24}$ **7 a** $\frac{1}{9}$ **b** $\frac{2}{9}$ **c** $\frac{2}{3}$ **d** $\frac{7}{9}$ **8 a** 0.000495 **b** 0.00198 **c** 0.000018 **d** 0.00024 **9 a** 0.54 **b** 0.38 **c** 0.08 **d** 1 **10 a** RFC, FRC, CRC, CFC **b** $\frac{1}{3}$ **c** $\frac{1}{3}$ **d** $\frac{1}{3}$ **e** Whichever day he chooses to run by the canal, the probability is the same

Exercise 16L

1 a $\frac{1}{4}$ **b** $\frac{3}{4}$ **2 a** $\frac{1}{16}$ **b** $\frac{1}{16}$ **c** $\frac{15}{16}$ **3 a i** $\frac{16}{343}$ **iii** $\frac{316}{343}$ **b i** $\frac{4}{35}$ **iii** $\frac{34}{35}$ **4** 0.4375 **5** 0.441 **6 a** 0.3 **b** 0.7 **7** 0.419 **8 a** $\frac{11}{36}$ **b** 0.421 **c** 0.518 **d** $1-(\frac{5}{6})^n$ **9 a** $\frac{1}{8}$ **b** $\frac{5}{12}$ **10 a** $\frac{1}{10}$ **b** $\frac{1}{2}$ **c** $\frac{5}{12}$ **d** $\frac{1}{30}$ **e** $\frac{29}{30}$ **11 a** $\frac{1}{2}$ **b** $\frac{47}{120}$ **c** $\frac{1}{2}$ **d** 1000 **12 a** $\frac{1}{5}$ **b i** 0.4096 **ii** $\frac{1}{5}$ **iii** 0.32768 **iv** 0.67232 **13 a** 1 **b** $\frac{2}{5}$ **14 a** $\frac{3}{10}$ **b** $\frac{1}{10}$ **c** $\frac{2}{5}$ **d** $\frac{3}{5}$ **15 a** $\frac{1}{210}$ (0.00476) **b** 0 **c** $\frac{209}{210}$ (0.99524) **16 a** $\frac{2}{9}$ **b** $\frac{2}{9}$ **c** $\frac{7}{9}$ **d** $\frac{2}{15}$ **17 a** 0.56 **b** 0.06 **c** 0.94 **18 a** 1×10^{-10} **b** 0.349 **c** 0.651 **19 a** $\frac{1}{8}$ **b** $\frac{3}{8}$ **c** 10 or 11

Examination questions (Chapter 16)

1 a 0.09 **b** P(same) = 0.46, P(different) = 0.54: Sarah wins **2 a i** 3, 4, 4, 5, 5, 6 **ii** $\frac{1}{3}$ **iii** $\frac{2}{3}$ **b i** 9 **ii** New totals 6, 7, 8 **iii** $\frac{2}{9}$ **3** No. She was assuming one of her tickets had to win **4 a i** AC, AD, BC, BD, CD **ii** $\frac{1}{6}$ **b** 0.67 **5 a i** $\frac{1}{6}$ **ii** $\frac{1}{36}$ **b** $\frac{13}{36}$ **6 a i** 0.2 **ii** 0.5 **iii** 0.7 **b** 20 **7 i** $\frac{3}{20}$ **ii** $\frac{8}{20}$

8 a

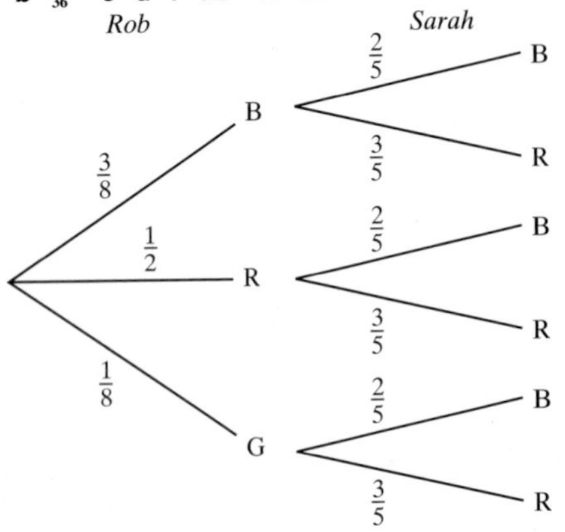

b $\frac{3}{20}$ **c** $\frac{11}{20}$ **9 a** 0.08 **b** 0.23 **10 a** $\frac{7}{12}$ **c i** $\frac{1}{4}$ **ii** $\frac{31}{60}$

Exercise 17A

1 a 3, 5, 7, 9, 11 **b** 1, 4, 7, 10, 13 **c** 7, 12, 17, 22, 27 **d** 1, 4, 9, 16, 25 **e** 4, 7, 12, 19, 28 **2 a** 4, 5, 6, 7, 8 **b** 2, 5, 8, 11, 14 **c** 3, 8, 13, 18, 23 **d** 0, 3, 8, 15, 24 **e** 9, 13, 17, 21, 25 **3** $0, \frac{1}{3}, \frac{2}{4}, \frac{3}{5}, \frac{4}{6}, \frac{5}{7}$ **4 a** 1, 3, 6, 10, 15, 21 **b** Triangle numbers **5 a** 24, 120, 720 **b** 69

Exercise 17B

1 a $2n + 1$ **b** $4n + 1$ **c** $5n + 3$ **d** $6n - 4$ **e** $3n + 2$ **f** $7n - 5$ **g** $4n - 3$ **h** $4n - 1$ **i** $3n - 1$ **j** $10n - 8$ **k** $4n + 4$ **l** $5n - 1$ **2 a** 151 **b** 105 **c** 248 **d** 197 **e** 394 **f** 54 **g** 256 **h** 395 **i** 148 **j** 168 **k** 355 **l** 393 **3 a** 33rd **b** 30th **c** 100th = 499 **4 a i** $4n + 1$ **ii** 401 **iii** 101 **b i** $2n + 1$ **ii** 201 **iii** 99 or 101 **c i** $3n + 1$ **ii** 301 **iii** 100 **d i** $2n + 6$ **ii** 206 **iii** 100 **e i** $4n + 5$ **ii** 405 **iii** 101 **f i** $5n + 1$ **ii** 501 **iii** 101 **g i** $3n - 3$ **ii** 297 **iii** 99 **h i** $6n - 4$ **ii** 596 **iii** 98 **i i** $8n - 1$ **ii** 799 **iii** 103 **j i** $2n + 23$ **ii** 223 **iii** 99 or 101 **5 a** $\dfrac{2n + 1}{3n + 1}$ **b** Terms decrease **c i** 0.667 774 **ii** 0.666 777 74 **d** 0.666 677 7774 and 0.666 666 777 777 74 **6 a** $\dfrac{4n - 1}{5n - 1}$ **b** Terms increase **c i** 0.7964… **ii** 0.799 64… **d** 0.799 964… and 0.799 999 64…

Exercise 17C

1 b $4n - 3$ **c** 97 **d** 50th diagram **2 b** $2n + 1$ **c** 121 **d** 49th set **3 a** 18 **b** $4n + 2$ **c** 12 **4 b** $2n + 1$ **c** 101 **d** 149th diagram **5 a i** 24 **ii** $5n - 1$ **iii** 224 **b** 25 **6 a i** 20 **ii** 162 **b** 79.8 km **7 a i** 20 cm **ii** $(3n + 2)$ cm **iii** 152 cm **b** 332 **8 a i** 14 **ii** $3n + 2$ **iii** 41 **b** 66 **9 a i** 10 **ii** $2n + 2$ **iii** 20 **b** 14 **10 a i** 5 **ii** n **iii** 18 **b** 20

Exercise 17D

1 a i 35, 48 **ii** $n^2 - 1$ **b i** 38, 51 **ii** $n^2 + 2$ **c i** 39, 52 **ii** $n^2 + 3$ **d i** 34, 47 **ii** $n^2 - 2$ **e i** 35, 46 **ii** $n^2 + 10$ **2 a i** 37, 50 **ii** $(n + 1)^2 + 1$ **b i** 35, 48 **ii** $(n + 1)^2 - 1$ **c i** 41, 54 **ii** $(n + 1)^2 + 5$ **d i** 50, 65 **ii** $(n + 2)^2 + 1$ **e i** 48, 63 **ii** $(n + 2)^2 - 1$ **3 a i** 30, 42 **ii** $n(n - 1)$ **b i** 60, 84 **ii** $2n(n - 1)$ **c i** 56, 72 **ii** $(n + 1)(n + 2)$ **d i** 15, 21 **ii** $\frac{1}{2}n(n - 1)$ **e i** 54, 70 **ii** $n(n + 3)$

Examination questions (Chapter 17)

1 a i 13 **ii** Add previous 2 terms: 21 **b** $3n - 2$ **2 a i** $\frac{11}{12}$ **ii** $\dfrac{n}{n + 1}$ **b** $\frac{2}{1}, \frac{3}{2}, \frac{4}{3}, \frac{5}{4}$ **3 a** 23, 27 **b** Add 4 **c** $4n - 1$ **4 b** 15, 18, 21, 24, 27 **c** 63 **d** $3n + 3$ **5 a** n^2 **b** $n^2 + n$ **6 a i** 26 **ii** 37 **b i** 22 **ii** 48 **c i** $2n + 2$ **iii** $k = 2$ **7 a** 40 **b i** 57 **ii** Differences increase by 3 each time **c ii** $a = 1.5, b = 0.5$

Exercise 18A

1 $P = a + b$ **2** $P = a + b + c + d$ **3** $P = 4x$ **4** $P = p + 2q$ **5** $P = 2\pi r$ **6** $P = 2h + (2 + \pi)r$

Exercise 18B

1 a $A = xy$ **b** $A = \pi r^2$ **c** $A = 2ad - a^2$ **d** $A = 2rh + \pi r^2$ **2 a** $A = \frac{1}{2}bh$ **b** $A = bh$ **c** $A = \frac{1}{2}bh + \frac{1}{2}bw$ **d** $A = \frac{1}{2}h(a + b)$ **e** $A = \frac{1}{8}\pi d^2 + \frac{1}{2}dh$ **f** $A = \frac{1}{8}\pi D^2 + \frac{1}{2}w(b + D)$

Exercise 18C

1 $V = pqr$ **2** $V = \pi r^2 h$ **3** $V = aqt + bpt - apt$ **4** $V = abl + adl + 2cdl$ **5** $V = \frac{1}{2}bhw$ **6** $V = \frac{1}{2}bhl$

Exercise 18D

1 a L **b** V **c** L **d** A **e** L **f** L **g** V **h** V **i** N **j** L **k** N **l** A **m** V **n** A **o** V **p** V **q** N **r** L **s** A **t** V **u** L **v** N **w** N **x** N **y** L **z** N **2 a** A **b** L **c** L **d** A **e** V **f** V **g** V **h** A **i** L **j** V **k** A **l** L **m** V **n** A **o** V **p** A **q** V **r** A **s** A **t** A **u** L **v** A **w** A **x** A **y** V **z** V

Exercise 18E

1 a C **b** I **c** C **d** I **e** C **f** I **g** C **h** I **i** C **j** I **k** C **l** C **m** C **n** C **o** C **p** I **q** C **r** C **s** I **t** C **u** C **v** C **w** C **x** C **y** C **2 a** C, L **b** I **c** C, V **d** C, L **e** I **f** I **g** C, V **h** C, V **i** C, V **j** C, V **k** C, L **l** I **m** C, V **3 a** 2 **b** 2, 3 **c** 2 **d** 2, 2 **4** Inconsistent

Examination questions (Chapter 18)

1 Length: 4, area: 2, 3, volume: 1, 5 **2** Formula *iii*: $[L^2]$ units **3** $\pi r^2 h$, lbh **4 a i** A **ii** V **iii** L **iv** A **v** N **b** Inconsistent **5** abc: volume, $2(a + b)$: perimeter, bd: area **6 a** [L] units **b** Formula *iii*: $[L^2]$ units **7** πab, $\pi(a + b)l$

Exercise 19A

1 a 15 **b** 2 **2 a** 75 **b** 6 **3 a** 225 **b** 6 **4 a** 24 **b** 6 **5 a** 150 **b** 6 **6 a** 22.5 **b** 12 **7 a** 19.8 **b** 14 **8 a** 175 **b** 8 **9 a** £66.50 **b** 175 kg **10 a** 44 **b** 84 m^2

Exercise 19B

1 a 100 **b** 10 **2 a** 27 **b** 5 **3 a** 75 **b** 2 **4 a** 20 **b** 5 **5 a** 24 **b** 6 **6 a** 56 **b** 1.69 **7 a** 192 **b** 2.25 **8 a** 11.44 **b** 81 **9 a** 25.6 **b** 5 **10 a** 25.6 **b** 5 **11 a** £50 **b** 225 **12 a** 3.2°C **b** 10 atm **13 a** 259.2 g **b** 2.5 mm **14 a** 2 J **b** 40 m/s **15 a** £78.26 **b** 400 miles

Exercise 19C

1 $Tm = 12$ **a** 3 **b** 2.5 **2** $Wx = 60$ **a** 20 **b** 6 **3** $H(p + 2) = 28$ **a** 2.8 **b** 0.8 **4** $Q(5 - t) = 16$ **a** −3.2 **b** 4 **5** $Mt^2 = 36$ **a** 4 **b** 5 **6** $cf^2 = 144$ **a** 5.76 **b** 4 **7** $W\sqrt{T} = 24$ **a** 4.8 **b** 100 **8** $H\sqrt{g} = 36$ **a** 4.5 **b** 1.44 **9** $gp = 1800$ **a** £15 **b** 36 **10** $td = 24$ **a** 3°C **b** 12 km **11** $pw = 60$ **a** £10 **b** 25 **12** $ds^2 = 432$ **a** 1.92 km **b** 8 m/s **13** $p\sqrt{h} = 7.2$ **c** 2.4 atm **b** 100 m **14** $W\sqrt{F} = 0.5$ **a** 5 t **b** 0.58 t

Examination questions (Chapter 19)

1 8 **2 i** $Y = \frac{18}{X^2}$ **ii** 0.72 **3 i** $y = \frac{20}{x + 3}$ **ii** 2 **4 a** $h = 0.05\,s^2$ **b** 20 m/s **5 a** $y = \frac{80}{x^2}$ **b** 3.2 **6** 4.72 kg **7** 1 candle power **8** 31.6 km **9 a** $T = 8\sqrt{M}$ **b** 60 **c** 2.56 **10 a** $y = \frac{108}{x^2}$ **b i** 3 **ii** 2

Exercise 20A

1 a $5.5 \le 6 < 6.5$ **b** $16.5 \le 17 < 17.5$ **c** $31.5 \le 32 < 32.5$ **d** $237.5 \le 238 < 238.5$ **e** $7.25 \le 7.3 < 7.35$ **f** $25.75 \le 25.8 < 25.85$ **g** $3.35 \le 3.4 < 3.45$ **h** $86.5 \le 87 < 87.5$ **i** $4.225 \le 4.23 < 4.235$ **j** $2.185 \le 2.19 < 2.195$ **k** $12.665 \le 12.67 < 12.675$ **l** $24.5 \le 25 < 25.5$ **m** $35 \le 40 < 45$ **n** $595 \le 600 < 605$ **o** $25 \le 30 < 35$ **p** $995 \le 1000 < 1005$ **q** $3.95 \le 4.0 < 4.05$ **r** $7.035 \le 7.04 < 7.045$ **s** $11.95 \le 12.0 < 12.05$ **t** $6.995 \le 7.00 < 7.005$

Exercise 20B

1 a 6.67% **b** 1.96% **c** 2.04% **d** 0.59% **e** 0.21% **f** 33.3% **g** 9.09% **h** 20% **i** 7.69% **j** 0.13% **k** 3.03% **l** 2.44% **2 a** 2620 g **b** 2580 g **c** 0.78% **d** 0 **3 a i** 100% **ii** 20% **iii** 11.1% **iv** 7.7% **v** 5.9% **b** Decreasing **4 a i** 4.35% **ii** 3.7% **iii** 3.22% **iv** 2.86% **v** 2.7% **b** Decreasing **5 a i** 5.26% **ii** 5.26% **iii** 5.26% **iv** 5.26% **v** 5.26% **b** All the same

Exercise 20C

1 a i $38.25 \le \text{Area} < 52.25$ cm^2 **ii** 18.95% **b i** $37.1575 \le \text{Area} < 38.4475$ cm^2 **ii** 1.74% **c i** $135.625 \le \text{Area} < 145.225$ cm^2 **ii** 3.56% **2 a** $5.5 \le 6 < 6.5$ m, $3.5 \le 4 < 4.5$ m **b** 29.25 m^2 **c** 18 m **d** 27.27% **3** $79.75 \le \text{Area} < 100.75$ m^2 **4 a** $216.125 \le \text{Volume} < 354.375$ m^3 **b** 34.4% **5** $20.9 \le \text{Length} \le 22.9$ m **6 a** $16.43 \le \text{Area} < 21.69$ cm^2 **b** 5.18 cm **7 a i** $64.08 \le \text{Volume} < 69.58$ cm^3 **ii** £22570 ≤ Cost < £24500 **b** £23642.87 ≤ Price ≤ £23661.12 **c** Three errors possible in **a** but only one in **b** **8 a** $14.65 \le \text{Time} < 14.75$ s **b** $99.5 \le \text{Length} < 100.5$ m **c** 6.86 m/s **9 a** 1.27% **b** 1.92% **10** $3.4 \le \text{Length} < 3.43$ cm **11 a** $5.8 \le \text{Length} < 5.9$ cm **b** 1.81%

Examination questions (Chapter 20)

1 a $27.5 \le \text{Length} < 28.5$ cm **b** $15.5 \le \text{Width} < 16.5$ cm **c** $110 \le \text{Length} < 114$ cm **d** $11 \le \text{Gap} < 13$ cm
2 a i $59.5 \le \text{Orange lace} < 60.5$ cm **ii** $44.75 \le \text{Purple lace} < 45.25$ cm **b** 119 cm **c** 15.75 cm **3** 48.74° **4** 451.5 kg
5 a 22.8125 cm^2 **b** 15 rectangles **6** 6.7% **7 a** 4328.6 litres **b** 5177 cartons **8 a** $41.75 \le \text{Time} < 41.85$
b 19.00 m/s **c** 70.98 mph, which lies between 71.007 and 70.953 mph **9 a** 30 ohms **b** $28 \le R \le 32.21$ ohms
10 a $10.35 \le \text{Time} < 10.45$ s **b** $99.95 \text{ cm} \le \text{Length} < 100.05$ m **c** 9.667 m/s (≈ 9.7 m/s)

Exercise 21A

1

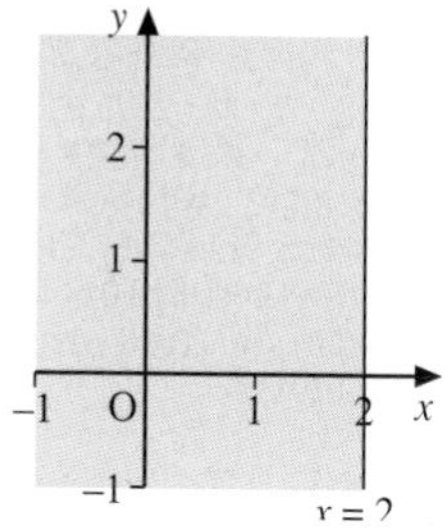

2

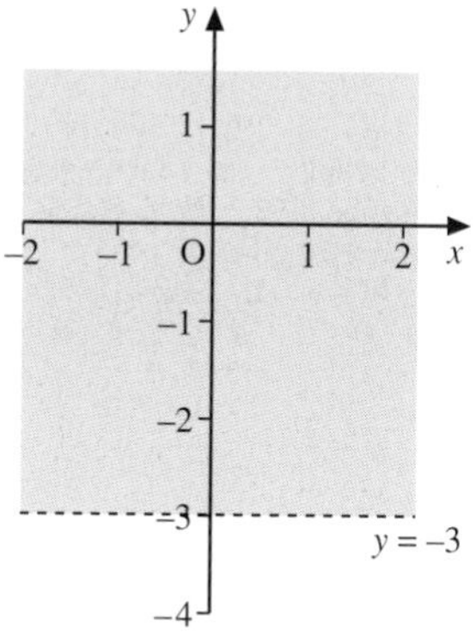

3

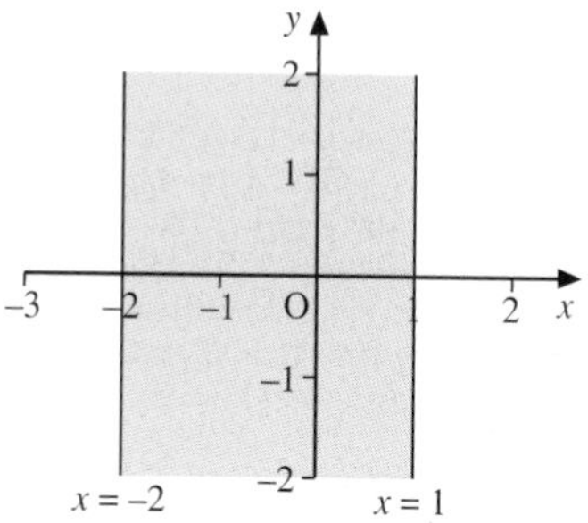

4

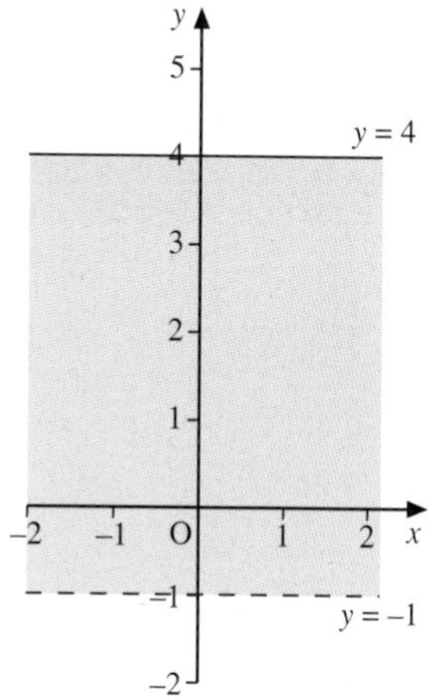

5 a

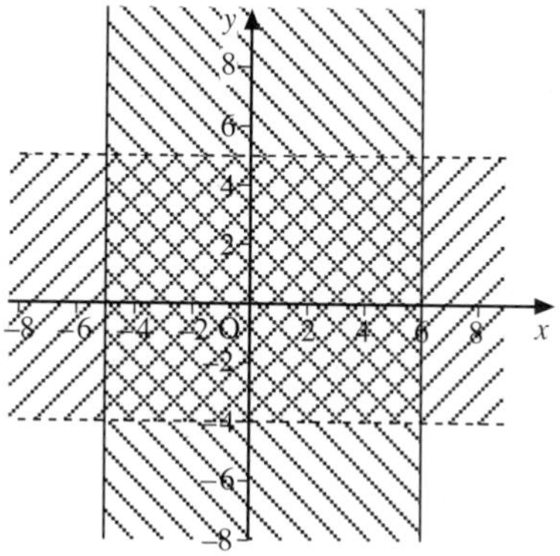

b i Yes **ii** Yes **iii** No

6

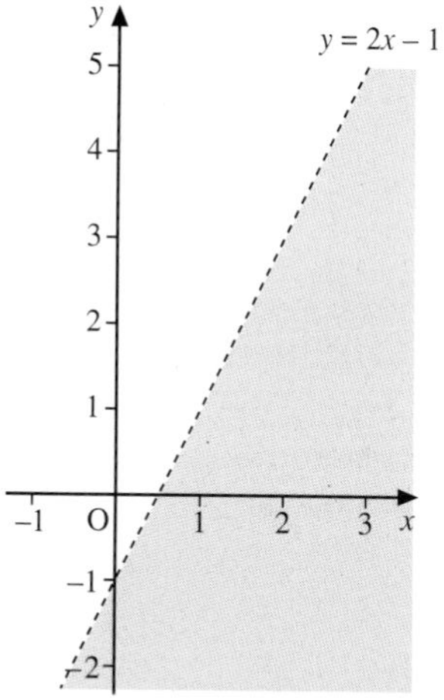

7

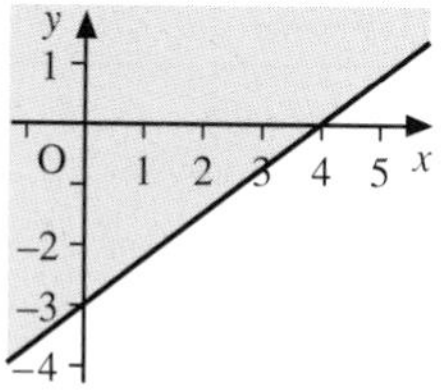

8

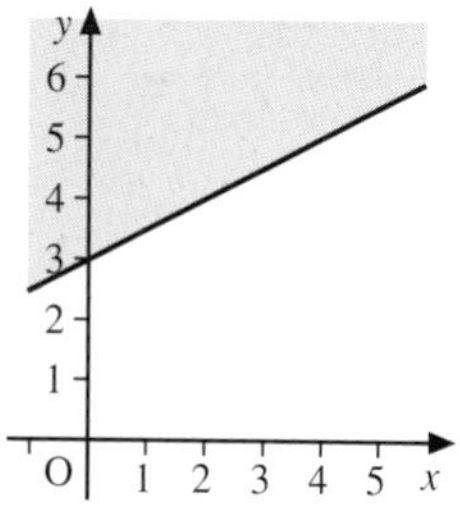

9

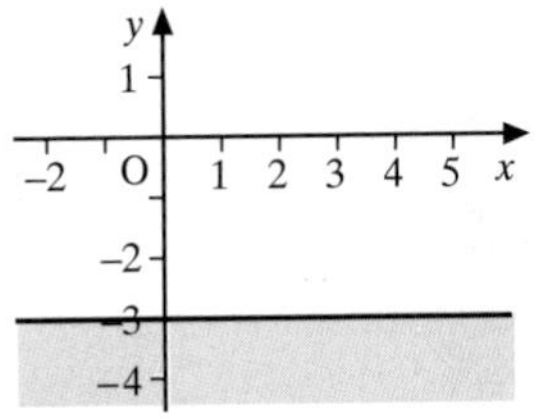

10 e i No **ii** Yes **iii** Yes **11 g i** No **ii** No **iii** No
12 b i No **ii** Yes **iii** Yes **iv** No

Exercise 21B

1 a £148x **b** £125y **c** £(148x + 125y) **2 a** 53p **b** $19x + 15y$ **c** $19x + 15y + 3z$ **d** $19d + 15f + 21$ **3 a** £($Ax + By$) **b** £($Ax + 2Bx$) **c** £(9A + (9 + y)B) **4 a** May be true **b** Must be false **c** May be true, e.g. $x = 30$, $y = 20$ **d** May be true, e.g. $x = 3$, $y = 40$ **5 a** May be true **b** May be true **c** Must be false **6** E Excels hold 40E; S Storms hold 50S. There must be more than 1500 seats, so $40E + 50S \geq 1500$. Cancelling through by 10 gives $4E + 5S \geq 150$ **7 a** W rides cost £1.50W. This cannot exceed £6.00, so $1.50W \leq 6.00$. Cancelling through by 1.5 gives $W \leq 4$ **b** Likewise $2D \leq 6$, giving $D \leq 3$ **c** Total cost is $1.50W + 2D \leq 6.00$. Multiplying through by 2 gives $3W + 4D \leq 12$ **d** $D \leq 2$ **e i** Yes **ii** No **iii** No **iv** Yes
8 a $45x + 25y \leq 200 \Rightarrow 9x + 5y \leq 40$ **b** $y \geq x + 2$

Exercise 21C

1 a i Cost $30x + 40y \leq 300 \Rightarrow 3x + 4y \leq 30$ **ii** At least 2 apples, so $x \geq 2$ **iii** At least 3 pears, so $y \geq 3$ **iv** At least 7 fruits, so $x + y \geq 7$ **b i** No **ii** No **iii** No **iv** Yes **2 a i** Space $4x + 3y \leq 48$ **ii** Cost $300x + 500y \leq 6000 \Rightarrow 3x + 5y \leq 60$ **b i** Yes **ii** No **iii** Yes **iv** Yes **3 a i** Number of seats required is $40x + 50y \geq 300 \Rightarrow 4x + 5y \geq 30$ **ii** Number of 40-seaters $x \leq 6$ **iii** Number of 50-seaters $y \leq 5$ **b i** Yes **ii** Yes **iii** Yes **iv** Yes **c** Combination *iii*, which costs £760 **d** Five 40-seaters and two 50-seaters cost £740 **4 a i** Time $30x + 45y \geq 180 \Rightarrow 2x + 3y \geq 12$ **ii** Cost $75x + 100y \leq 600 \Rightarrow 3x + 4y \leq 24$ **b** $x \geq 2, y \geq 2$ **c i** Yes **ii** No **iii** No **iv** Yes **d** Combination *iv*, which costs £4.25
5 a i Volume of water $x + 2y \leq 30$ **ii** Cost $2.50x + 1.50y \leq 37.50 \Rightarrow 5x + 3y \leq 75$ **iii** More rainbow, so $x < y$ **b** $x \geq 1, y \geq 1$ **c i** No **ii** Yes **iii** No **iv** No **v** Yes **d** Combination *ii*, which costs £29.50 **6** $2x + 3y \leq 48$, $1.25x + 2.5y \leq 37.5 \Rightarrow x + 2y \leq 30$ **7** $2x + 1.5y \leq 300 \Rightarrow 4x + 3y \leq 600$; $50x + 40y \geq 6000 \Rightarrow 5x + 4y \geq 600$; $x \leq 2y$ **8** $2x + 4y \geq 40 \Rightarrow x + 2y \geq 20$; $100x + 150y \leq 1800 \Rightarrow 2x + 3y \leq 36$; $x \leq 10$; $y \leq 7$ **9** $x \geq y$; $15x + 30y \leq 180 \Rightarrow x + 2y \leq 12$; $8x + 20y \geq 100 \Rightarrow 2x + 5y \geq 25$
10 $4x + 6y < 24 \Rightarrow 2x + 3y < 12$; $300x + 500y > 1500 \Rightarrow 3x + 5y > 15$; $x \leq 4$; $y \leq 3$

Exercise 21D

1 a

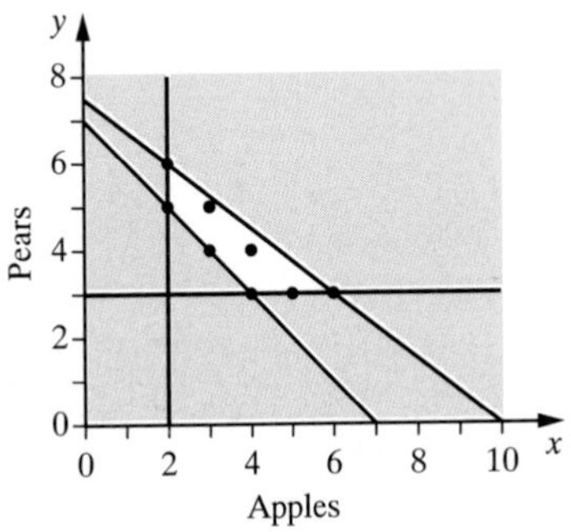

b 6 apples and 3 pears = 9 fruits
c 4 apples and 3 pears, costing £2.40

2 a

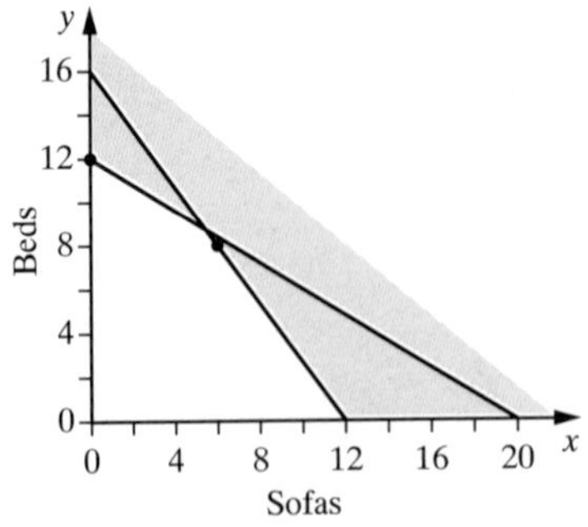

b 6 sofas and 8 beds = 14 items
c 12 beds worth £6000

3 a $4x + 5y \geq 30, x \leq 6, y \leq 5$

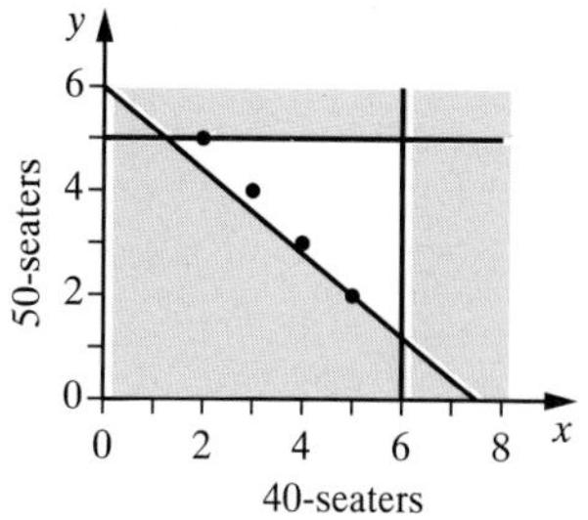

b 7 coaches: (2, 5), (3, 4), (4, 3) or (5, 2)
c Five 40-seaters and two 50-seaters

4 a

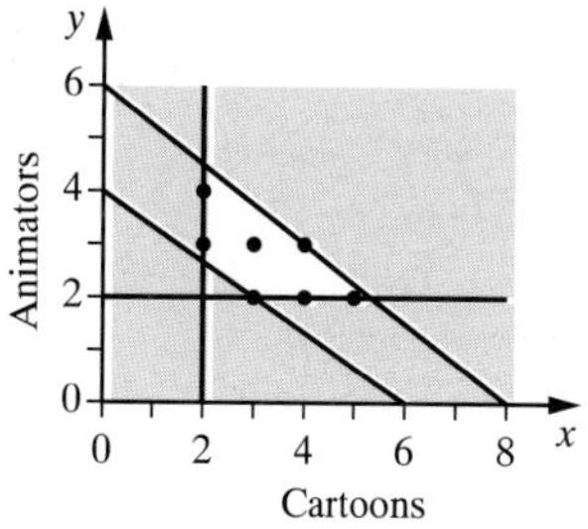

b Longest time: 4 cartoons and 3 animations
c Least cost: 3 cartoons and 2 animations

5 a $x + 2y \leq 30, 5x + 3y \leq 75, x < y, x \geq 1, y \geq 1$
b 19 fish = 8 fantails and 11 rainbows
c 3 fish = 1 fantail and 2 rainbows

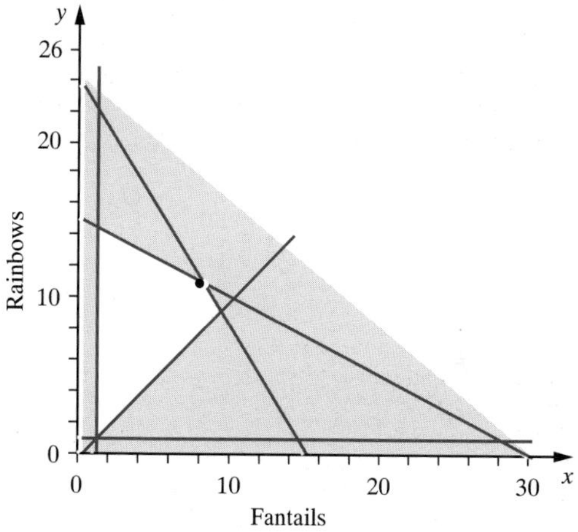

6 a $2x + 3y \leq 48, 5x + 10y \leq 150$

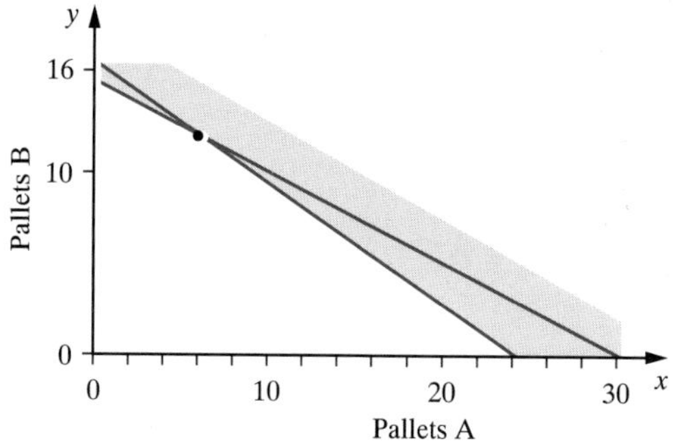

b 6 pallets A and 12 pallets B give £393 profit

7 a $4x + 3y \leq 600, 5x + 4y \leq 550, x \leq 2y$

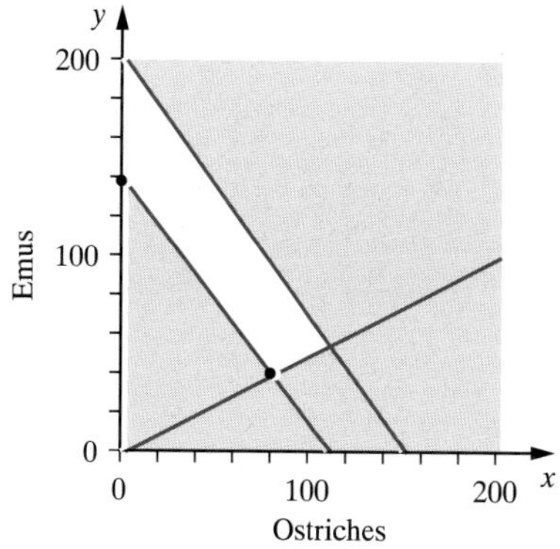

b 120 birds = 80 ostriches and 40 emus **c** Cheapest: 138 emus at £414/week

8 a

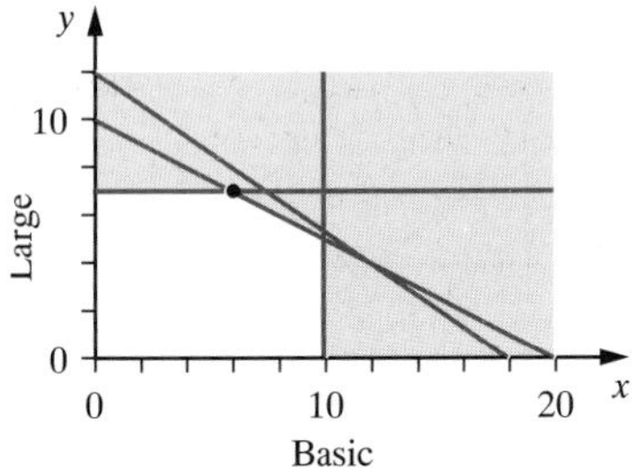

b Cheapest: 6 basic and 7 large **c** Forgotten that boys must not share rooms with girls

9 a $x \geq y, x + 2y < 12, 2x + 5y \geq 25$

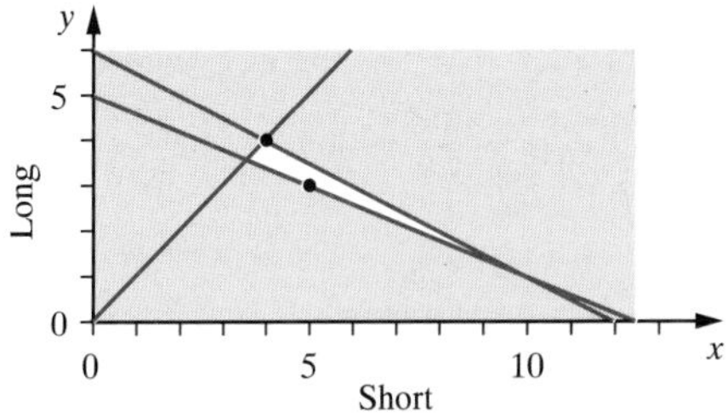

b 8 questions: (4, 4) or (5, 3) **c** (4, 4) gives 112 marks, (5, 3) gives 100 marks **d** (4, 4) takes 3 h, (5, 3) takes 2 h 45 min

10 a

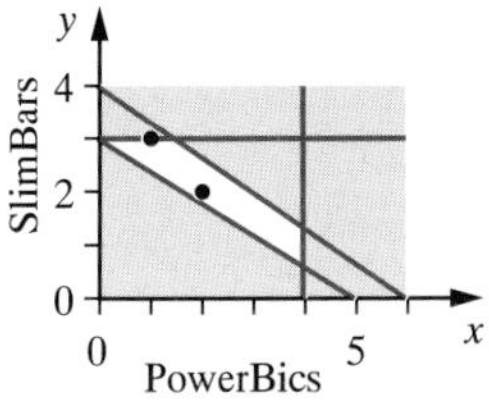

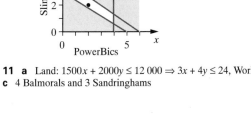

b 4 comprising (2, 2) or (1, 3) **c** 1 PowerBic + 3 SlimBars at £13

11 a Land: $1500x + 2000y \leq 12\,000 \Rightarrow 3x + 4y \leq 24$, Workers: $5x + 3y \leq 30$ **b**

c 4 Balmorals and 3 Sandringhams

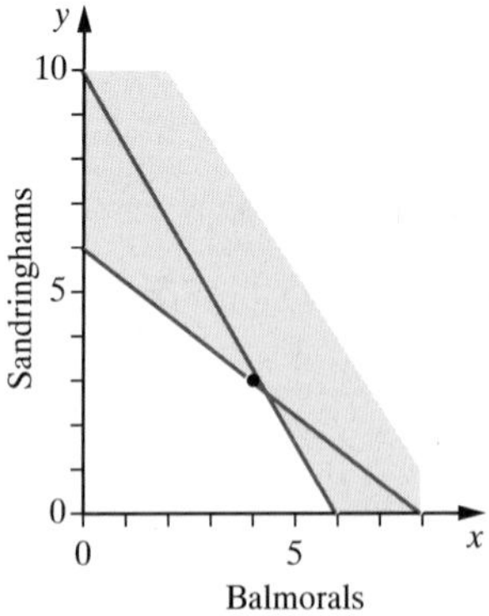

12 a $4x + 5y \geq 20, 5x + 6y \leq 30, x \leq 4, y \leq 3$ **b**

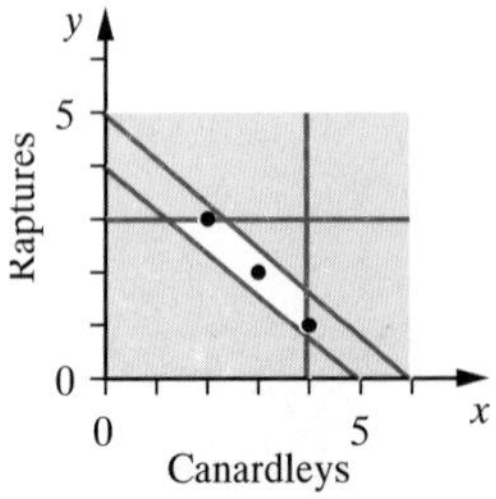

c 4 Canardleys and 1 Rapture

Examination questions (Chapter 21)

1 a i Total number of people is $x + y \leq 200$ **ii** Money from sale of tickets is $2x + 3y \geq 450$ **iii** Number of £3 tickets < Twice number of £2 tickets, $y \leq 2x$ **b**

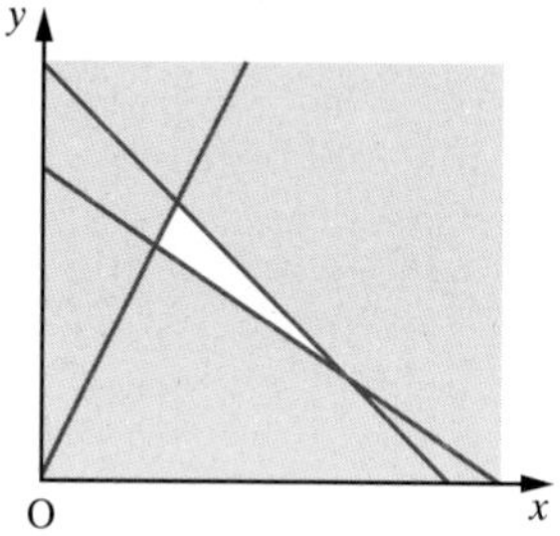

c 132 £2 tickets and 66 £3 tickets. Profit £462

2 a

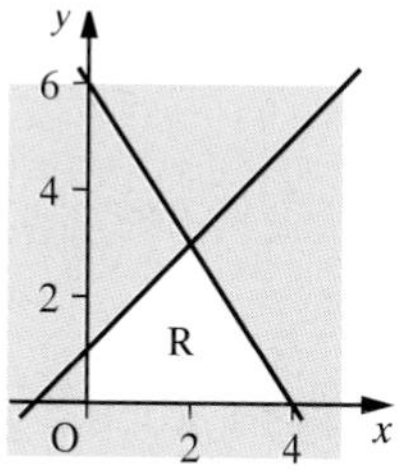

$x = 2, y = 3$ **b** At (2, 1), $s = 0, t = 8$; at (4, 6), $s = 5, t = 24$
c R is required region

3 $x \leq 3, x + y \geq 4, y < 2x + 1$

4 a

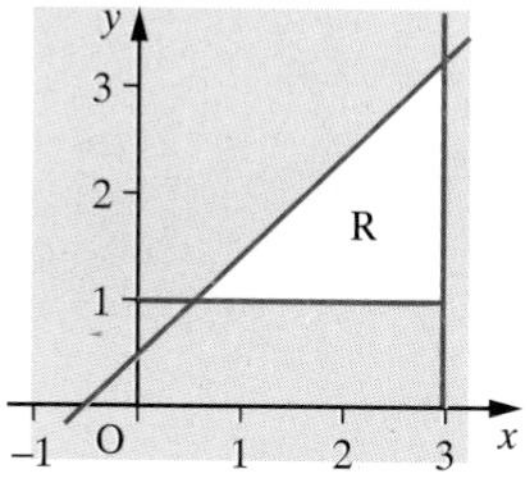

R is required region **b** (3, 2), (3, 3), (2, 2)

5 a i $x = 1.5$ **ii** $y = \frac{1}{2}x$ **iii** $x + y = 6$ **b** $x \geq 1.5, y \geq \frac{1}{2}x, x + y \leq 6$ **c** $p = 1.5, q = 4.5$

6 a Area of plots is $100c + 50t \leq 1000 \Rightarrow 2c + t \leq 20$; council rule $t \leq 2c$; profit $3c + 7t \geq 42$

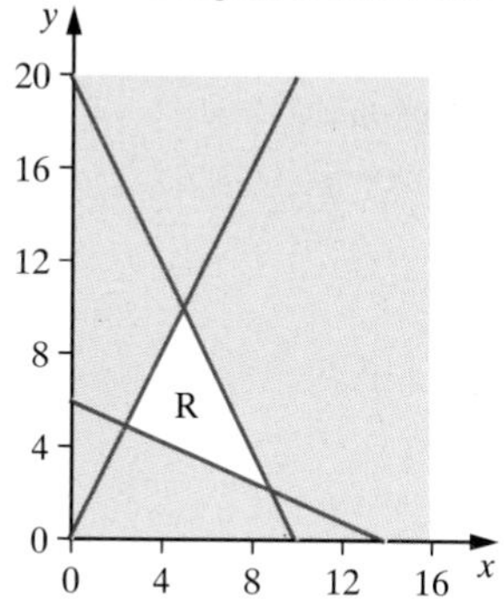

R is required region **b** 5 caravans and 9 tents

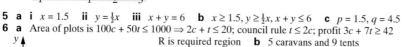

7 a Seating of x double deckers is $60x$ and of y single deckers is $40y$. So $60x + 40y \geq 560 \Rightarrow 3x + 2y \geq 28$
b

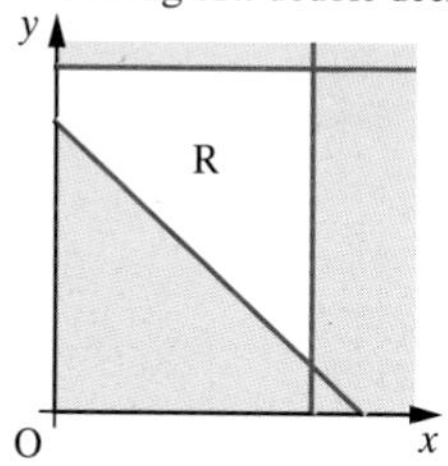

R is feasible region **c** $x = 6, y = 5, C = £500$

8 a $4 \le c \le 8$ ($c \ge 4$, $c \le 8$: two inequalities), $d \ge 3$, $c + d \le 14$

b

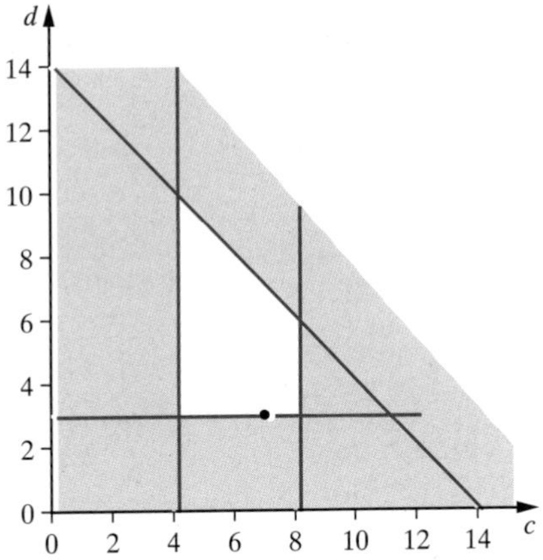

c 12 boats costing £940 (7 canoes and 3 dinghies)

Exercise 22A

1 a Any 3 of $\overrightarrow{AC}$, $\overrightarrow{CF}$, $\overrightarrow{BD}$, $\overrightarrow{DG}$, $\overrightarrow{GI}$, $\overrightarrow{EH}$, $\overrightarrow{HJ}$, $\overrightarrow{JK}$ **b** Any 3 of $\overrightarrow{BE}$, $\overrightarrow{AD}$, $\overrightarrow{DH}$, $\overrightarrow{CG}$, $\overrightarrow{GI}$, $\overrightarrow{FI}$, $\overrightarrow{IK}$ **c** Any 3 of $\overrightarrow{AO}$, $\overrightarrow{CA}$, $\overrightarrow{FC}$, $\overrightarrow{IG}$, $\overrightarrow{GD}$, $\overrightarrow{BD}$, $\overrightarrow{KJ}$, $\overrightarrow{JH}$, $\overrightarrow{HE}$ **d** Any 3 of $\overrightarrow{BO}$, $\overrightarrow{EB}$, $\overrightarrow{HD}$, $\overrightarrow{DA}$, $\overrightarrow{JG}$, $\overrightarrow{GC}$, $\overrightarrow{KI}$, $\overrightarrow{IF}$ **2 a** 2**a** **b** 2**b** **c** **a** + **b** **d** 2**a** + **b** **e** 2**a** + 2**b** **f** **a** + 2**b** **g** **a** + **b** **h** 2**a** + 2**b** **i** 3**a** + **b** **j** 2**a** **k** **b** **l** 2**a** + **b** **3 a** Equal **b** $\overrightarrow{AI}$, $\overrightarrow{BJ}$, $\overrightarrow{DK}$ **4 a** $\overrightarrow{OJ} = 2\,\overrightarrow{OD}$ and parallel **b** $\overrightarrow{AK}$ **c** $\overrightarrow{OF}$, $\overrightarrow{BI}$, $\overrightarrow{EK}$ **5**

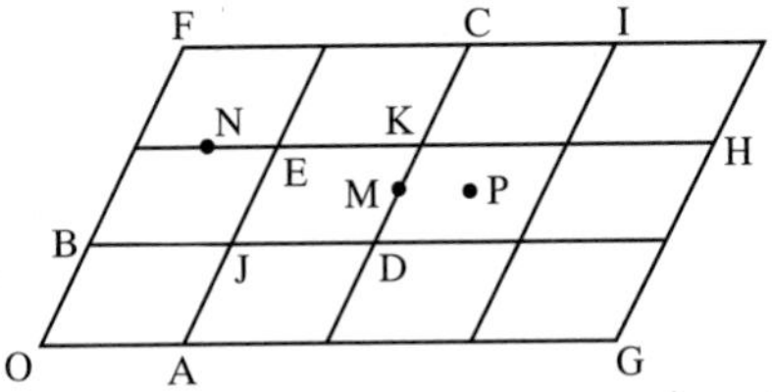

6 a Lie on same straight line **b** All multiples of **a** + **b** and start at O **c** H **d i** $\overrightarrow{OQ} = \mathbf{a} + \frac{1}{2}\mathbf{b}$ **ii** $\overrightarrow{OR} = 3\mathbf{a} + \frac{3}{2}\mathbf{b}$ **e** $n\mathbf{a} + \frac{n}{2}\mathbf{b}$

7 a –**b** **b** 3**a** – **b** **c** 2**a** – **b** **d** **a** – **b** **e** **a** + **b** **f** –**a** – **b** **g** 2**a** – **b** **h** –**a** – 2**b** **i** **a** + 2**b** **j** –**a** + **b** **k** 2**a** – 2**b** **l** **a** – 2**b** **8 a** Equal but in opposite directions **b** Any 3 of $\overrightarrow{DA}$, $\overrightarrow{EF}$, $\overrightarrow{GJ}$, $\overrightarrow{FI}$, $\overrightarrow{AH}$ **9 a** Opposite direction and $\overrightarrow{AB} = \frac{1}{2}\,\overrightarrow{CK}$ **b** $\overrightarrow{BJ}$, $\overrightarrow{CK}$ **c** $\overrightarrow{EB}$, $\overrightarrow{GO}$, $\overrightarrow{KH}$ **10 a**

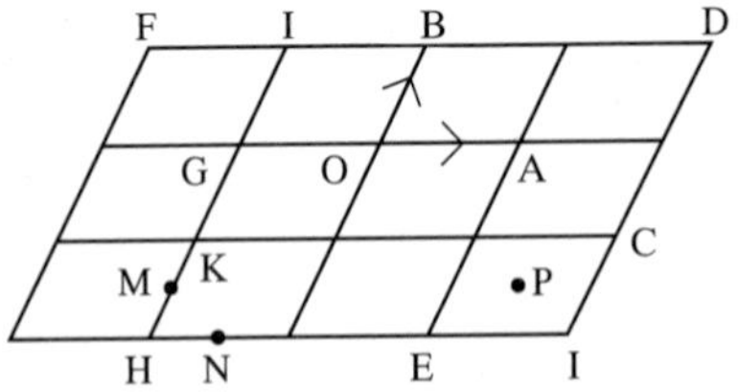

11 a Any 3 of $\overrightarrow{MJ}$, $\overrightarrow{AG}$, $\overrightarrow{HC}$, $\overrightarrow{BD}$, $\overrightarrow{OH}$, $\overrightarrow{NA}$, $\overrightarrow{PO}$, $\overrightarrow{KB}$, $\overrightarrow{IE}$ **b** Any 3 of $\overrightarrow{DG}$, $\overrightarrow{HJ}$, $\overrightarrow{AL}$, $\overrightarrow{EH}$, $\overrightarrow{BA}$, $\overrightarrow{OM}$, $\overrightarrow{FB}$, $\overrightarrow{IO}$, $\overrightarrow{KN}$ **c** Any 3 of $\overrightarrow{GD}$, $\overrightarrow{HE}$, $\overrightarrow{BF}$, $\overrightarrow{JH}$, $\overrightarrow{AB}$, $\overrightarrow{OI}$, $\overrightarrow{LA}$, $\overrightarrow{MO}$, $\overrightarrow{NK}$ **d** Any 3 of $\overrightarrow{CH}$, $\overrightarrow{DB}$, $\overrightarrow{EI}$, $\overrightarrow{GA}$, $\overrightarrow{HO}$, $\overrightarrow{BK}$, $\overrightarrow{JM}$, $\overrightarrow{AN}$, $\overrightarrow{OP}$ **e** Any 3 of $\overrightarrow{FH}$, $\overrightarrow{EG}$, $\overrightarrow{IA}$, $\overrightarrow{BJ}$, $\overrightarrow{KM}$, $\overrightarrow{OL}$ **f** Any 3 of $\overrightarrow{JD}$, $\overrightarrow{AE}$, $\overrightarrow{OF}$, $\overrightarrow{LH}$, $\overrightarrow{MB}$, $\overrightarrow{NI}$ **g i** $\overrightarrow{FG}$, $\overrightarrow{IJ}$ or $\overrightarrow{KL}$ **ii** $\overrightarrow{OC}$, $\overrightarrow{KE}$, $\overrightarrow{NG}$, $\overrightarrow{PH}$ **iii** $\overrightarrow{FJ}$ or $\overrightarrow{IL}$ **iv** $\overrightarrow{FL}$ **v** $\overrightarrow{LF}$ **vi** $\overrightarrow{PC}$ **vii** $\overrightarrow{CP}$ **viii** Same as part *d* **ix** Same as part *a*

12 Parts *b* and *d* could be, parts *a* and *c* could not be **13 a** Any multiple (positive or negative) of 3**a**–**b** **b** Will be a multiple of 3**a**–**b**

Exercise 22B

1 a i $-\mathbf{a}+\mathbf{b}$ **ii** $\frac{1}{2}(-\mathbf{a}+\mathbf{b})$ **iii**

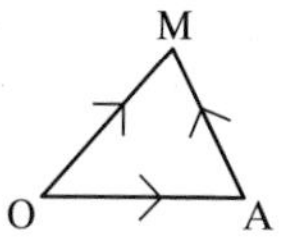

iv $\frac{1}{2}\mathbf{a}+\frac{1}{2}\mathbf{b}$ **b i** $\mathbf{a}-\mathbf{b}$ **ii** $\frac{1}{2}\mathbf{a}+\frac{1}{2}\mathbf{b}$ **iii**

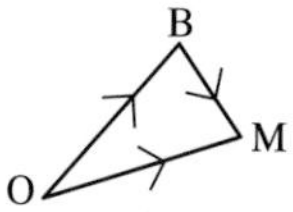

iv $\frac{1}{2}\mathbf{a}+\frac{1}{2}\mathbf{b}$

c

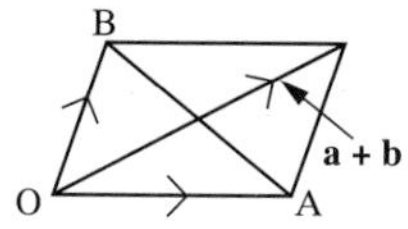

d M is mid-point of parallelogram of which OA and OB are two sides

2 a i $-\mathbf{a}-\mathbf{b}$ **ii** $-\frac{1}{2}\mathbf{a}-\frac{1}{2}\mathbf{b}$ **iii**

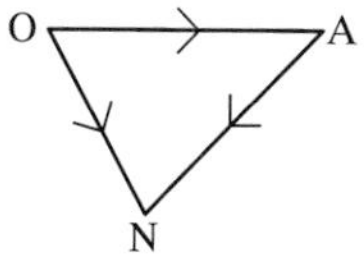

iv $\frac{1}{2}\mathbf{a}-\frac{1}{2}\mathbf{b}$ **b i** $\mathbf{b}+\mathbf{a}$ **ii** $\frac{1}{2}\mathbf{b}+\frac{1}{2}\mathbf{a}$ **iii**

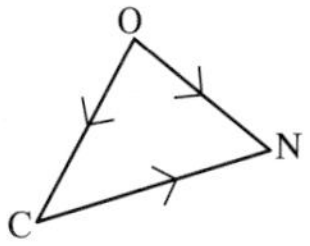

iv $\frac{1}{2}\mathbf{a}+\frac{1}{2}\mathbf{b}$ **c**

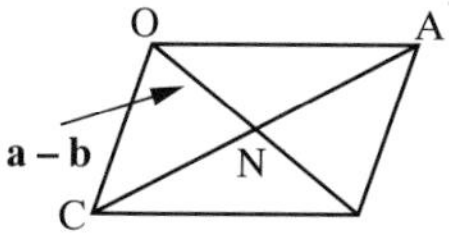

d N is mid-point of parallelogram of which OA and OC are two sides

3 a

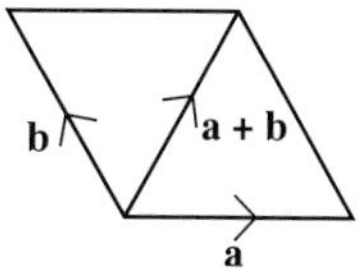

b

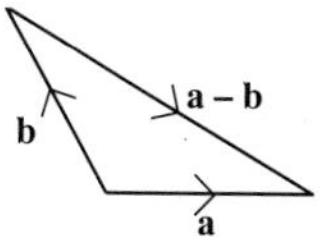

4 a i $-\mathbf{a}+\mathbf{b}$ **ii** $\frac{1}{3}(-\mathbf{a}+\mathbf{b})$ **iii** $\frac{2}{3}\mathbf{a}+\frac{1}{3}\mathbf{b}$ **b** $\frac{3}{4}\mathbf{a}+\frac{1}{4}\mathbf{b}$ **5 a i** $\frac{2}{3}\mathbf{b}$ **ii** $\frac{1}{2}\mathbf{a}+\frac{1}{2}\mathbf{b}$ **iii** $-\frac{2}{3}\mathbf{b}$ **b** $\frac{1}{2}\mathbf{a}-\frac{1}{6}\mathbf{b}$
c DE = DO + OE = $\frac{3}{2}\mathbf{a}-\frac{1}{2}\mathbf{b}$ **d** DE parallel to CD (multiple of CD) and D is a common point

6 a

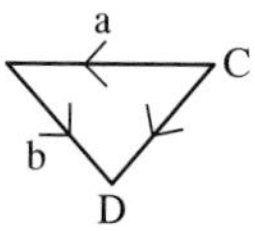

$\overrightarrow{CD} = -\mathbf{a}+\mathbf{b} = \mathbf{b}-\mathbf{a}$ **b i** $-\mathbf{a}$ **ii** $-\mathbf{b}$ **iii** $\mathbf{a}-\mathbf{b}$ **c** 0, vectors return to starting point
d i $2\mathbf{b}$ **ii** $2\mathbf{b}-2\mathbf{a}$ **iii** $-2\mathbf{a}$ **iv** $2\mathbf{b}-\mathbf{a}$ **v** $-\mathbf{a}-\mathbf{b}$

7 a

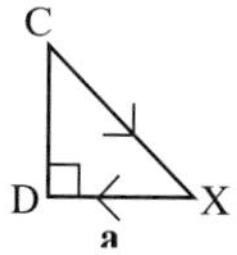

$CX = \sqrt{1^2+1^2} = \sqrt{2}\mathbf{b}$
$\overrightarrow{CD} = \overrightarrow{CX}+\overrightarrow{XD} = \sqrt{2}\mathbf{b}-\mathbf{a}$

b

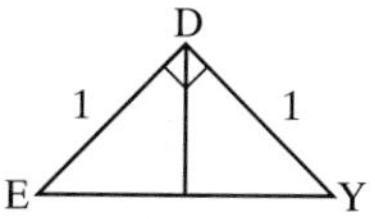

$YE = \sqrt{1^2+1^2} = \sqrt{2}\mathbf{a}$.
$\overrightarrow{DE} = \overrightarrow{DY}+\overrightarrow{YE} = \mathbf{b}-\sqrt{2}\mathbf{a}$

c i $-\mathbf{a}$ **ii** $-\mathbf{b}$ **iii** $\mathbf{a}-\sqrt{2}\mathbf{b}$ **iv** $\sqrt{2}\mathbf{a}-\mathbf{b}$ **v** $\sqrt{2}\mathbf{a}+\mathbf{a}$ **vi** $\sqrt{2}\mathbf{b}+\mathbf{b}$ **vii** $-2\mathbf{b}+\sqrt{2}\mathbf{b}-\mathbf{a}-\sqrt{2}\mathbf{a}$ **viii** $-2\mathbf{b}+\sqrt{2}\mathbf{b}-2\mathbf{a}-\sqrt{2}\mathbf{a}$
8 a i $-\mathbf{a}+\mathbf{b}$ **ii** $\frac{1}{2}(-\mathbf{a}+\mathbf{b}) = -\frac{1}{2}\mathbf{a}+\frac{1}{2}\mathbf{b}$ **iii** $\frac{1}{2}\mathbf{a}+\frac{1}{2}\mathbf{b}$ **b i** $\frac{1}{2}\mathbf{b}+\frac{1}{2}\mathbf{c}$ **ii** $-\frac{1}{2}\mathbf{a}+\frac{1}{2}\mathbf{c}$ **c i** $-\frac{1}{2}\mathbf{a}+\frac{1}{2}\mathbf{c}$ **ii** Equal
iii Parallelogram **9 i** $\mathbf{b}-\mathbf{a}$ **ii** $\frac{1}{2}\mathbf{b}-\frac{1}{2}\mathbf{a}$ **iii** $\frac{1}{2}\mathbf{a}+\frac{1}{2}\mathbf{b}$ **iv** $\frac{1}{3}\mathbf{a}+\frac{1}{3}\mathbf{b}$ **v** $\frac{1}{3}\mathbf{b}-\frac{2}{3}\mathbf{a}$ **vi** $-\mathbf{a}+\frac{1}{2}\mathbf{b}$ **b** $k=\frac{3}{2}$ **10 a i** $\frac{1}{2}\mathbf{a}$
ii $\mathbf{c}-\mathbf{a}$ **iii** $\frac{1}{2}\mathbf{a}+\frac{1}{2}\mathbf{c}$ **iv** $\frac{1}{2}\mathbf{c}$ **b i** $-\frac{1}{2}\mathbf{a}+\frac{1}{2}\mathbf{b}$ **ii** $-\frac{1}{2}\mathbf{a}+\frac{1}{2}\mathbf{b}$ **c** Opposite sides are equal and parallel **d** NMRQ and PNLR
11 a $\overrightarrow{AB} = \mathbf{a}-\mathbf{b}$, $\overrightarrow{AC} = 3\mathbf{a}-3\mathbf{b}$, $\overrightarrow{BC} = 2\mathbf{a}-2\mathbf{b}$ **b** These vectors lie on the same straight line, because they are parallel and have a common point B **c** Only two parallel vectors with a common point are needed to prove that three points are colinear
12 a i $-\frac{1}{6}\mathbf{y}+\frac{1}{3}\mathbf{x}$ **ii** $\mathbf{y}-\mathbf{x}$ **iii** $-\mathbf{x}-\frac{3}{4}\mathbf{y}$ **c** ZR : RP = 3 : 1

Exercise 22C

1 a

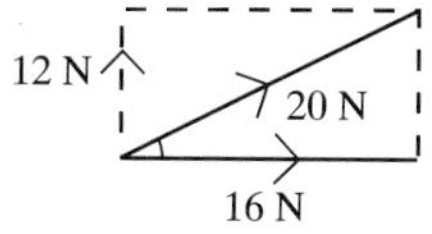

20 N at 36.9° to **A**

b

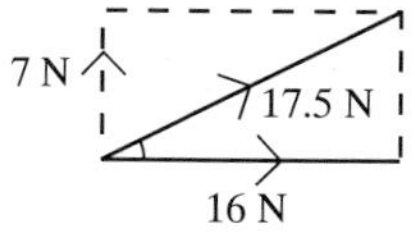

17.5 N at 23.6° to **A**

c

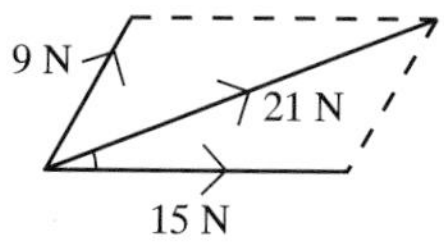

2 N at 21.8° to **A**

d

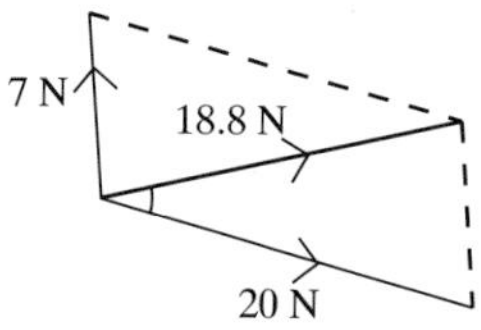

18.8 N at 19.2° to **A**

2 009° **3** Upstream at 60° to bank **4** Resultant upward force 138 kN, so locomotive not lifted **5** Beryl, because her pull (15.7 N) greater than Ann's (13.7 N) **6** 437 km/h at 328.3° **7** 83 km/h at 320.5° **8** 12 km/h at 107° **9 a** Upstream at 67.7° to bank **b** 23.4 s **10** 5.79 km/h at 88.3°

Examination questions (Chapter 22)

1 i $\mathbf{p} + \frac{1}{2}\mathbf{q}$ **ii** $\mathbf{q} - \mathbf{p}$ **iii** $\mathbf{q} + \frac{1}{2}\mathbf{p}$ **2 a** $\overrightarrow{AC} = \overrightarrow{AB} + \overrightarrow{BC}$ **c** $2\mathbf{p} + 4\mathbf{q}$ **d** On same straight line **3 i** $\mathbf{b} - \mathbf{a}$ **ii** $\frac{3}{4}\mathbf{b} - \frac{3}{4}\mathbf{a}$ **iii** $\frac{1}{4}\mathbf{a} + \frac{3}{4}\mathbf{b}$ **4 a i** 0.85 m/s **ii** Downstream at 61.9° to bank **b i** 8 m **ii** 20 s **5** PS : SR = 2:1. P, S and R on same straight line **6 i** $\mathbf{b} + \mathbf{c}$ **ii** $-\mathbf{c} + \mathbf{b}$ **iii** $\frac{1}{2}\mathbf{a} + \frac{1}{2}\mathbf{b} + \frac{1}{2}\mathbf{c}$ **iv** $-\frac{1}{2}\mathbf{b} + \frac{1}{2}\mathbf{c}$ **7** 17.6 km/h at 90° **8** Upstream at 70.5° to bank

Exercise 23A

1 a–d

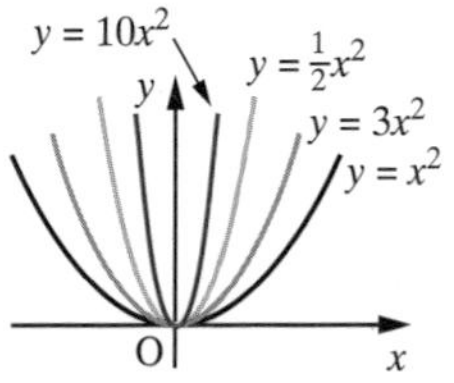

e Stretch sf in y-direction: 3, $\frac{1}{2}$, 10

2 a–d

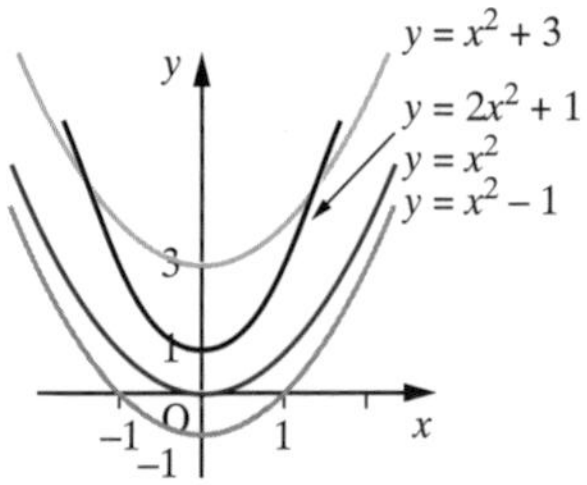

e b Translation $\begin{pmatrix} 0 \\ 3 \end{pmatrix}$ c Translation $\begin{pmatrix} 0 \\ -1 \end{pmatrix}$

d Stretch sf 2 in y-direction, followed by translation $\begin{pmatrix} 0 \\ 1 \end{pmatrix}$

3 a–d

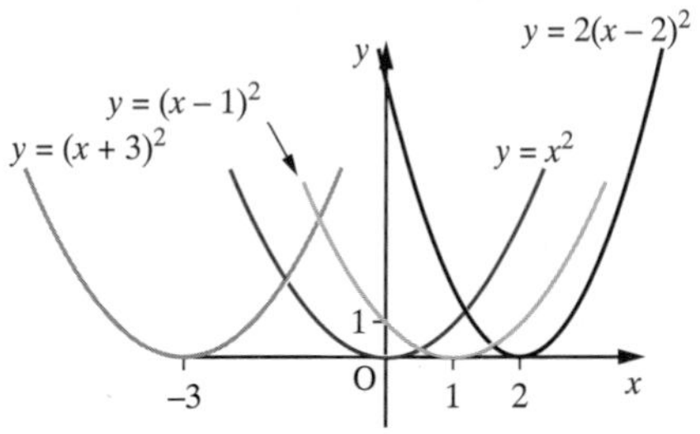

e b Translation $\begin{pmatrix} -3 \\ 0 \end{pmatrix}$ c Translation $\begin{pmatrix} 1 \\ 0 \end{pmatrix}$

d Stretch sf 2 in y-direction, followed by translation $\begin{pmatrix} 2 \\ 0 \end{pmatrix}$

4 a–c

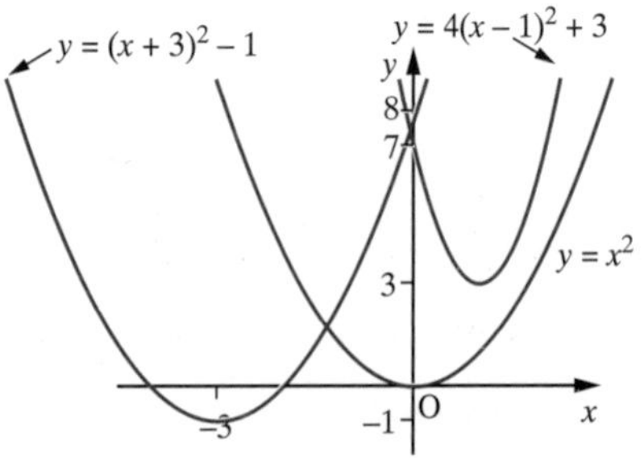

d b Translation $\begin{pmatrix} -3 \\ -1 \end{pmatrix}$

c Translation $\begin{pmatrix} 1 \\ 3 \end{pmatrix}$ followed by stretch sf 4 in y-direction

5 a–d

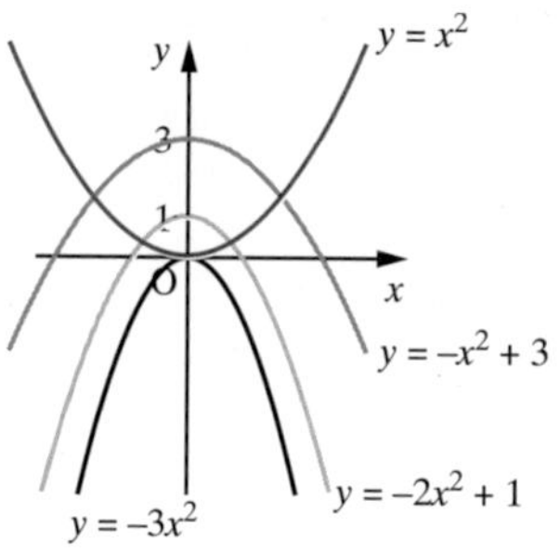

e *b* Reflection in x-axis, followed by translation $\begin{pmatrix} 0 \\ 3 \end{pmatrix}$

c Reflection in the x-axis, followed by stretch sf 3 in y-direction

d Reflection in x-axis, followed by stretch sf 2 in y-direction and translation $\begin{pmatrix} 0 \\ 1 \end{pmatrix}$

6 a–d

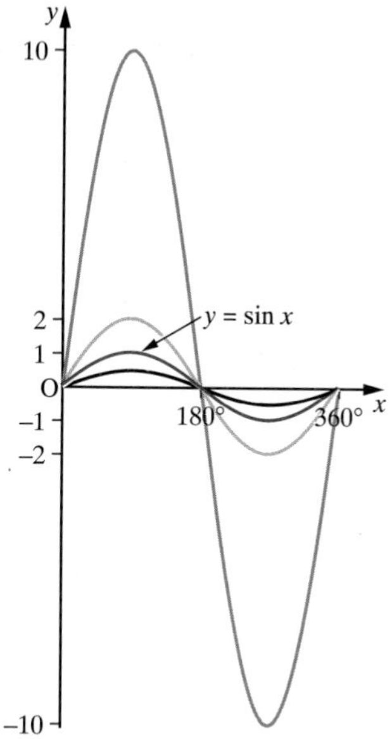

e Stretch sf in y-direction: 2, $\frac{1}{2}$, 10

7 a–d

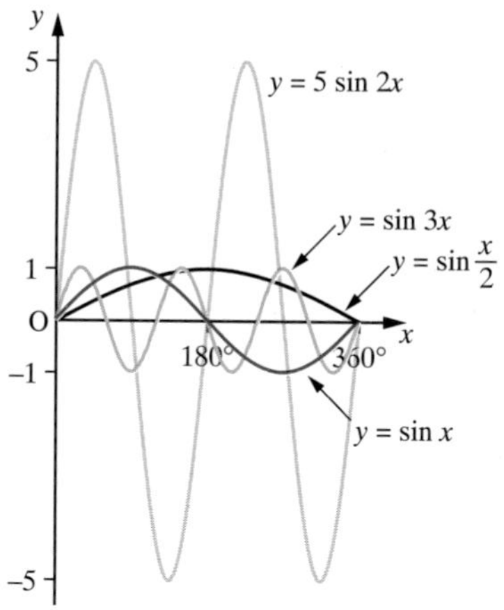

e *b* Stretch sf $\frac{1}{3}$ in x-direction *c* Stretch sf 2 in x-direction

d Stretch sf 5 in y-direction, followed by stretch sf 2 in x-direction

8 a–d

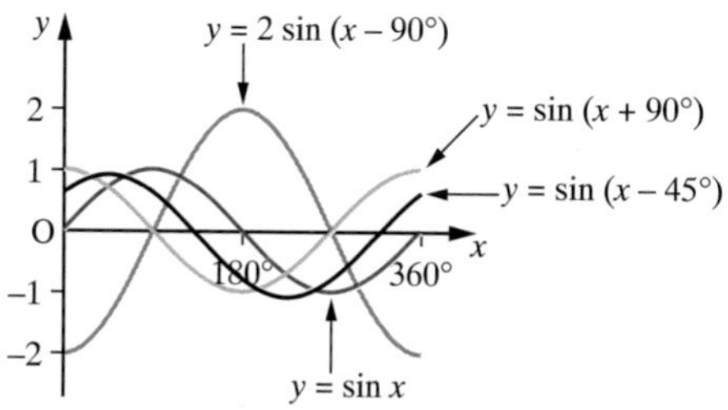

e *b* Translation $\begin{pmatrix} -90 \\ 0 \end{pmatrix}$ *c* Translation $\begin{pmatrix} 45 \\ 0 \end{pmatrix}$

d Stretch sf 2 in y-direction followed by translation $\begin{pmatrix} 90 \\ 0 \end{pmatrix}$

9 a–d

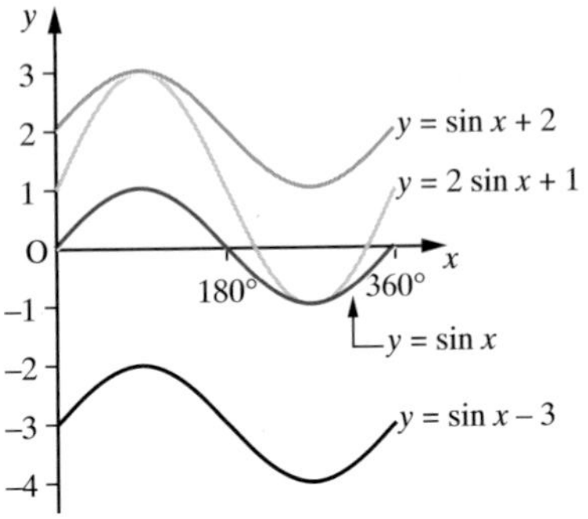

e *b* Translation $\begin{pmatrix} 0 \\ 2 \end{pmatrix}$ *c* Translation $\begin{pmatrix} 0 \\ -3 \end{pmatrix}$

d Stretch sf 2 in *y*-direction followed by translation $\begin{pmatrix} 0 \\ 1 \end{pmatrix}$

10 a–d

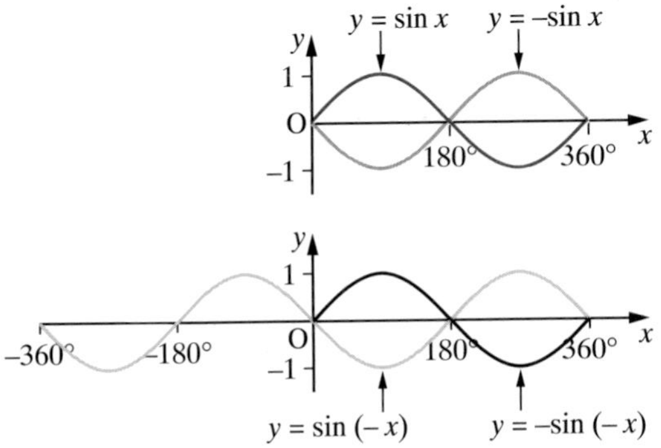

e *b* Reflection in *x*-axis *c* Reflection in *y*-axis *d* This leaves the graph in the same place and is the identity transform

11 a–d

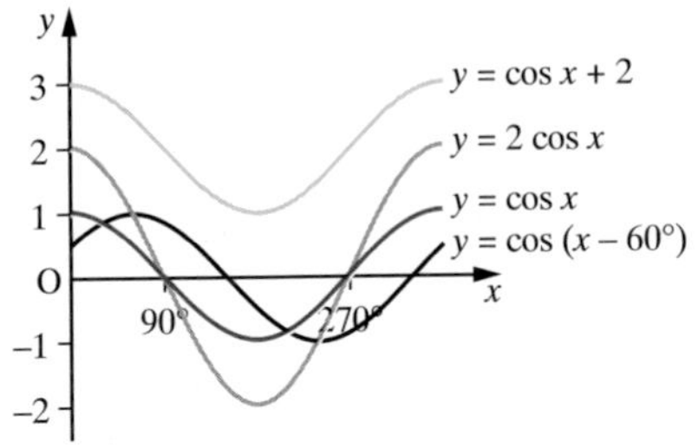

e *b* Stretch sf 2 in *y*-direction *c* Translation $\begin{pmatrix} 60 \\ 0 \end{pmatrix}$

d Translation $\begin{pmatrix} 0 \\ 2 \end{pmatrix}$

12 Because tan *x* repeats itself every 180°, so tan (*x* – 180°) is the translation $\begin{pmatrix} 180 \\ 0 \end{pmatrix}$

13 a i Stretch sf 4 in *y*-direction **ii** Stretch sf 9 in *y*-direction **iii** Stretch sf 16 in *y*-direction **b i** Stretch sf $\frac{1}{2}$ in *x*-direction **ii** Stretch sf $\frac{1}{3}$ in *x*-direction **iii** Stretch sf $\frac{1}{4}$ in *x*-direction **c** Stetch sf a^2 in *y*-direction, or stretch sf $\frac{1}{a}$ in *x*-direction

14 a

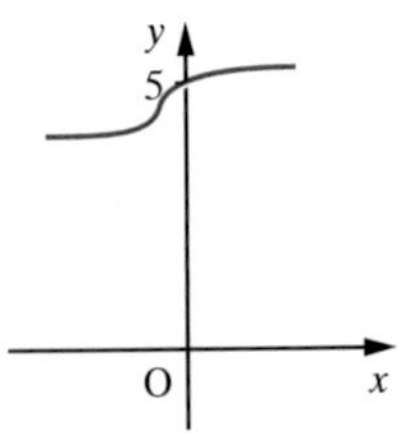

b

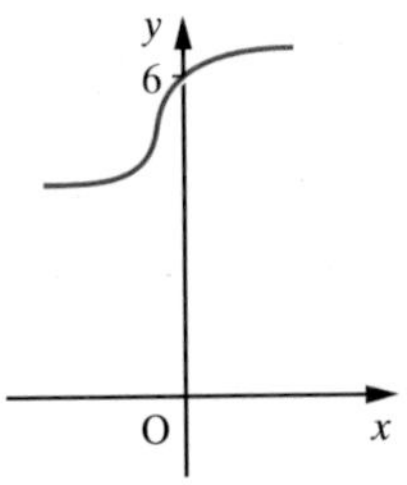

c

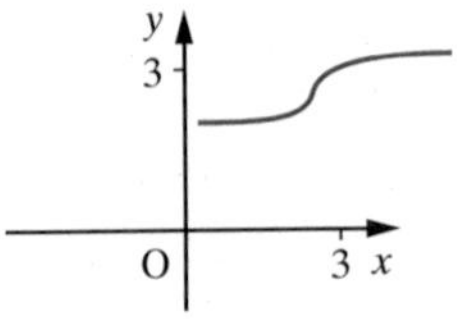

d

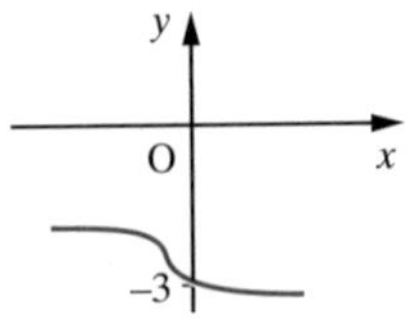

e

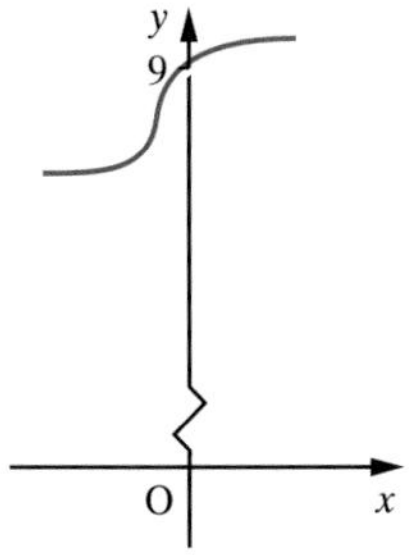

f

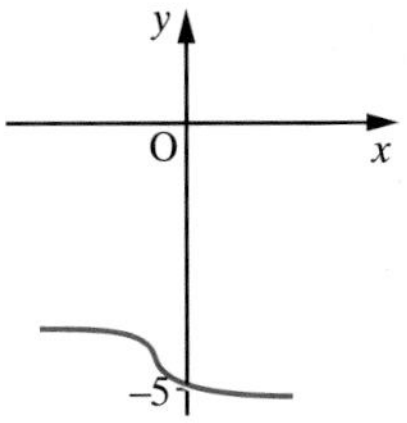

15 **a** $y = 5x^2$ **b** $y = x^2 + 7$ **c** $y = (x + 3)^2$ **d** $y = 3x^2 + 4$ **e** $y = (x + 2)^2 - 3$ **f** $y = -3x^2$ **16** **a** $y = 6 \cos x$ **b** $y = \cos x + 3$ **c** $y = \cos (x + 30°)$ **d** $y = 3 \cos x - 2$ **e** $y = \cos (x - 45°) - 2$

17 **a**

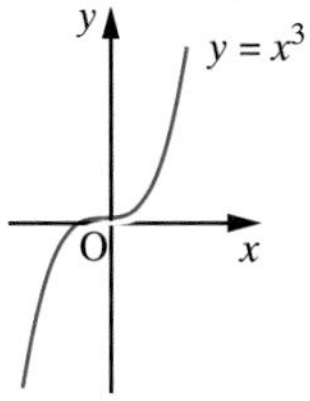

b **i**

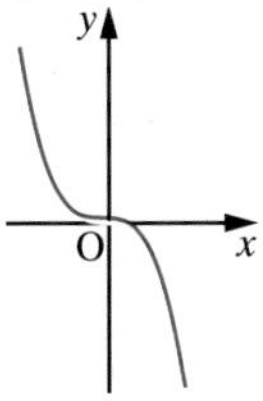

ii

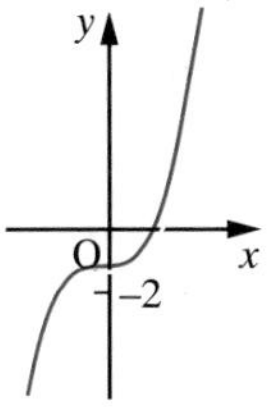

iii

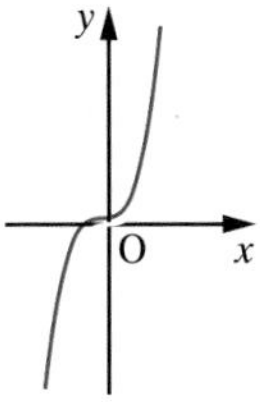

iv

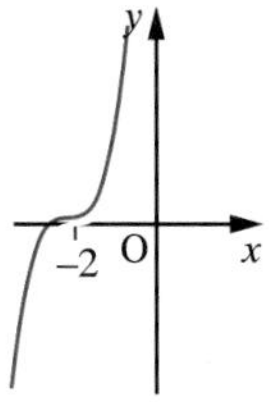

c **i** $y = -x^3$ **ii** $y = x^3 - 2$ **iii** $y = 3x^3$ **iv** $y = (x + 2)^3$

18 **a**

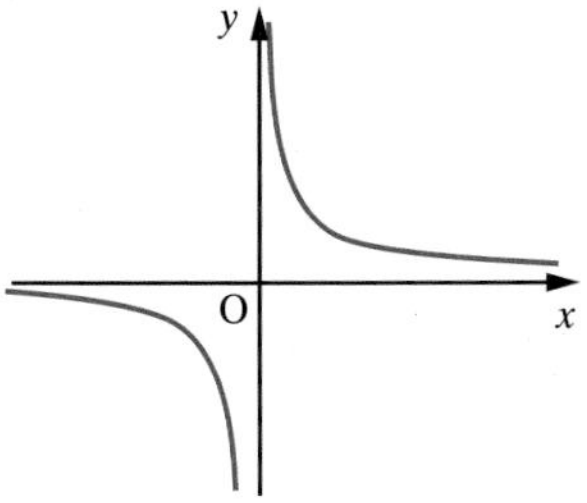

b **i**

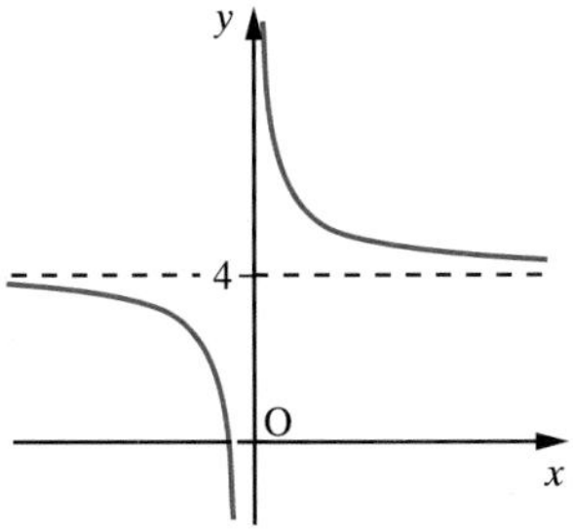

ii

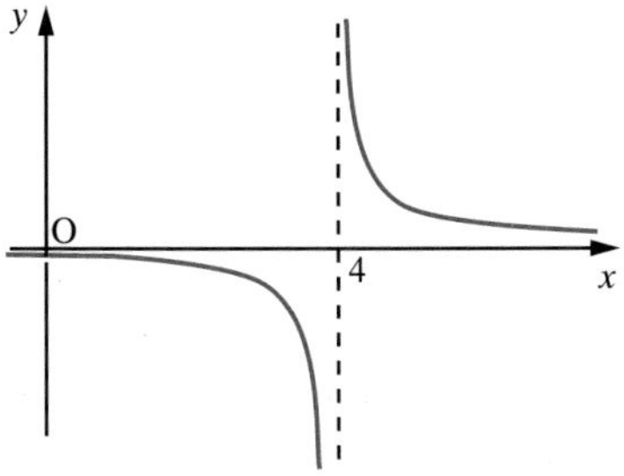

iii

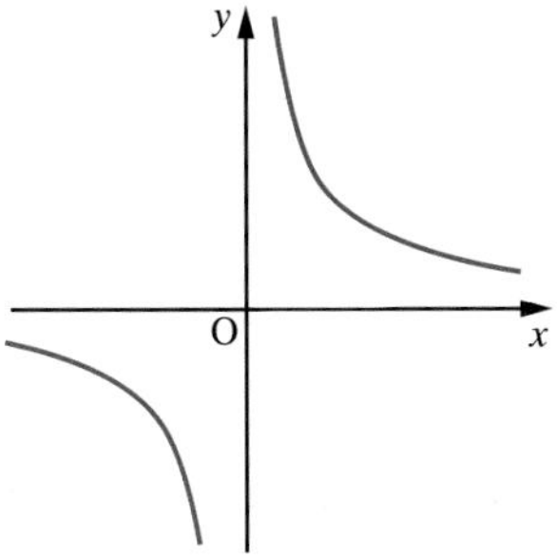

iv

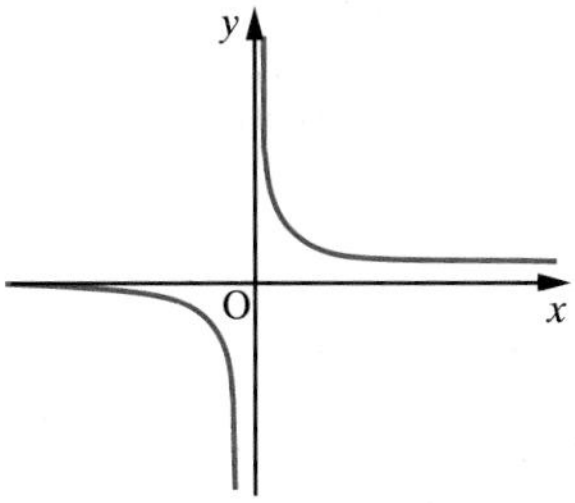

c **i** $y = \frac{1}{x} + 4$ **ii** $y = \frac{1}{x - 4}$ **iii** $y = \frac{3}{x}$ **iv** $y = \frac{1}{2x}$ **19** **a** $y = x^2 + 2$ **b** $y + (x - 2)^2$ **c** $y = 2x^2$ **d** $y = -x^2 + 4$

20 **a** $y = 2 \sin x$ **b** $y = \sin(x - 30°)$ **c** $y = 2 \sin(x - 60°)$ **d** $y = \sin 2x$ **21** **a** Translation $\begin{pmatrix} 0 \\ -90 \end{pmatrix}$ **b** **i** Equivalent **ii** Equivalent **iii** Not equivalent **22** **i** A **ii** D **iii** E **iv** C **v** B

Examination questions (Chapter 23)

1 a 24 **b**

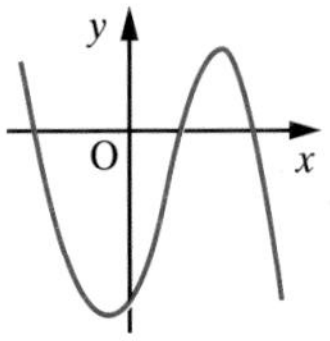

c Reflection in x-axis **d** 3

2 a

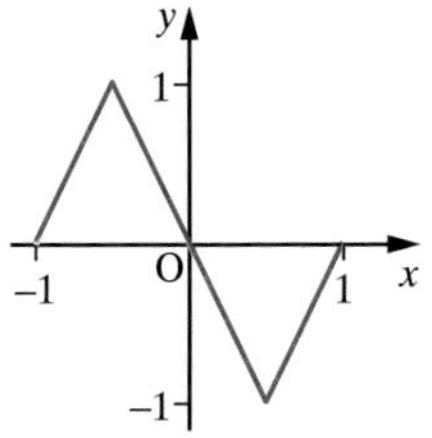

b

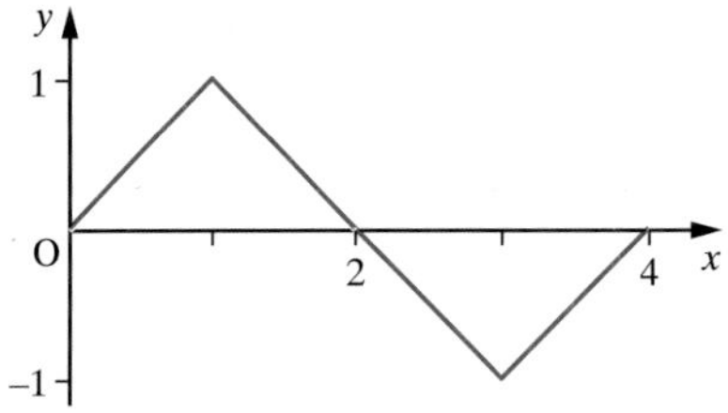

c Translation $\begin{pmatrix} 2 \\ 4 \end{pmatrix}$

3 a–b

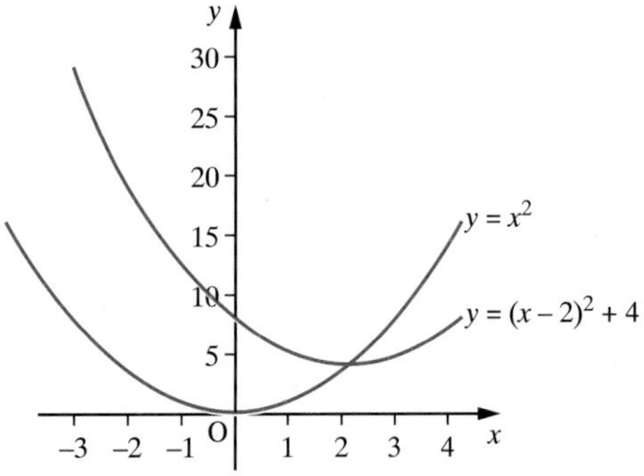

4 i

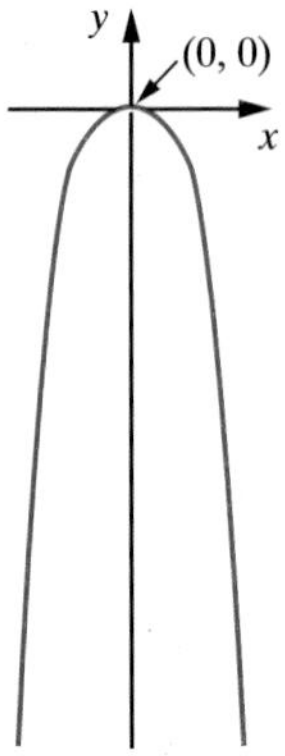

ii

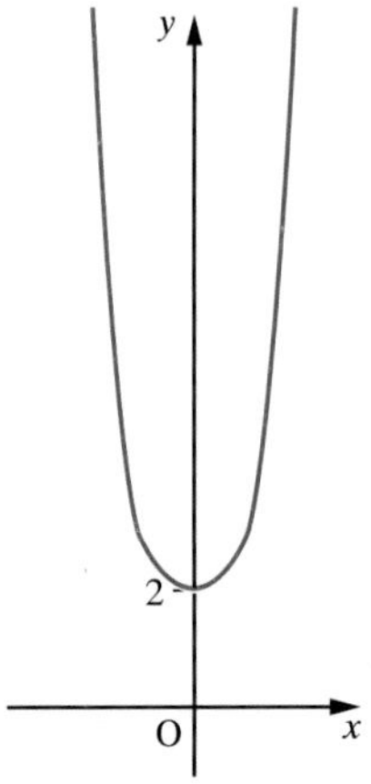

iii

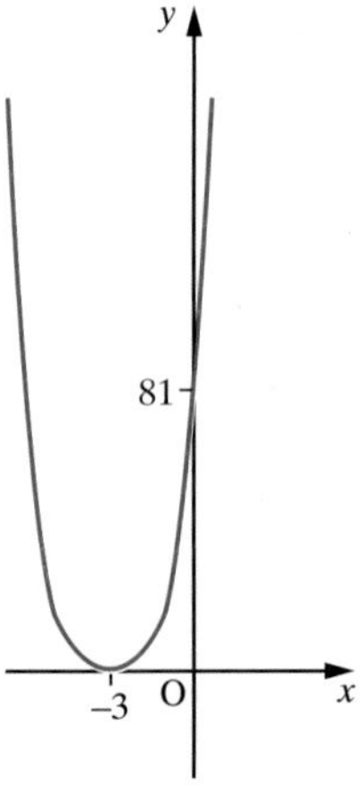

5

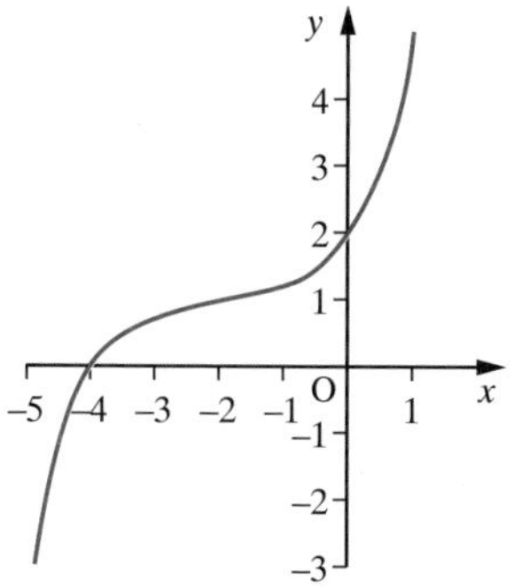

6 i

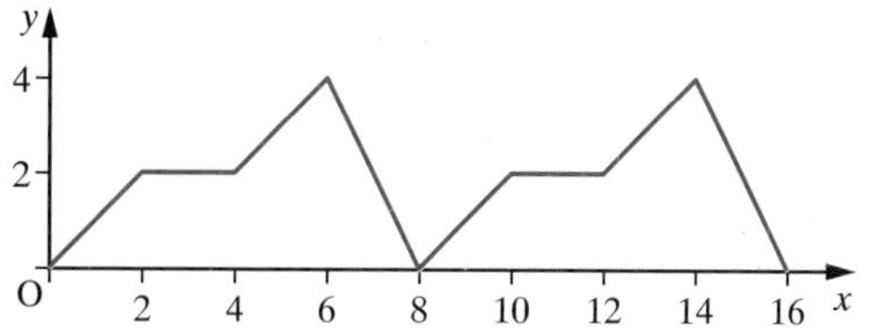

ii $y = \mathrm{f}(x - 1) + 2$

7

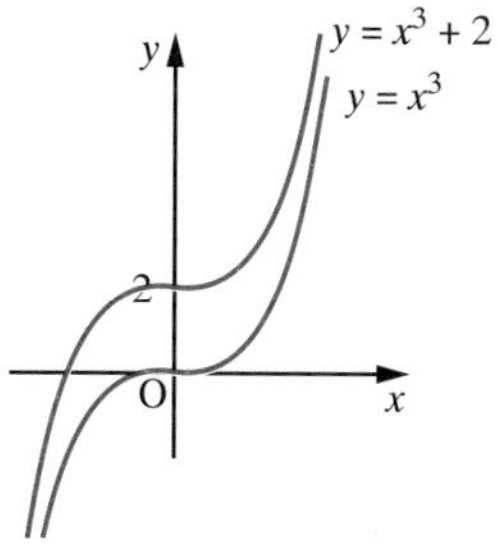

8 i

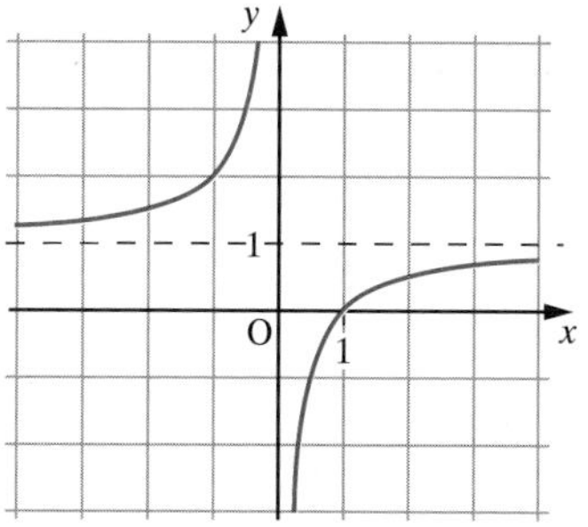

ii

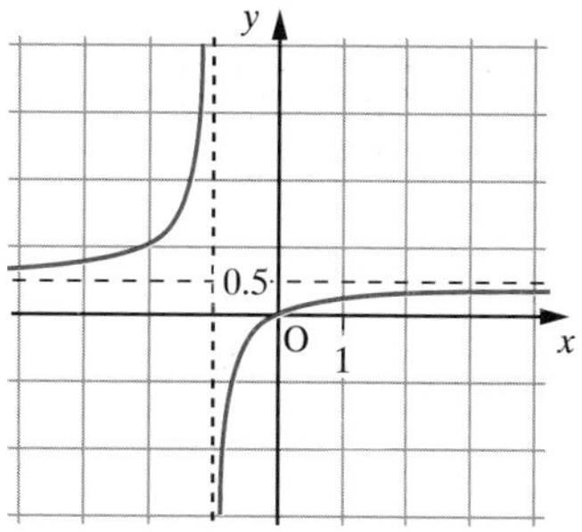

9 i

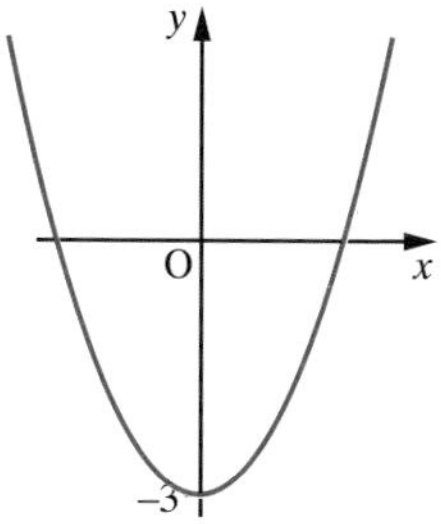

ii

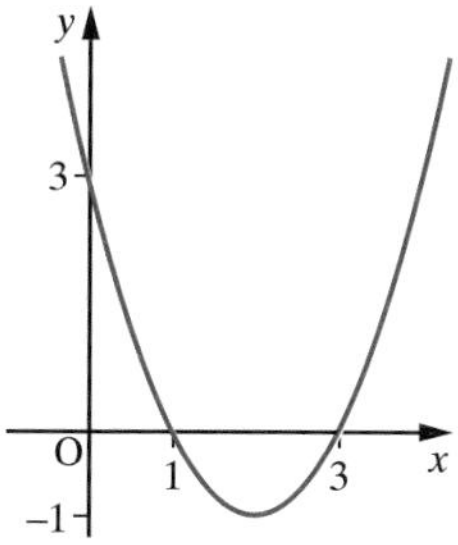

10 i

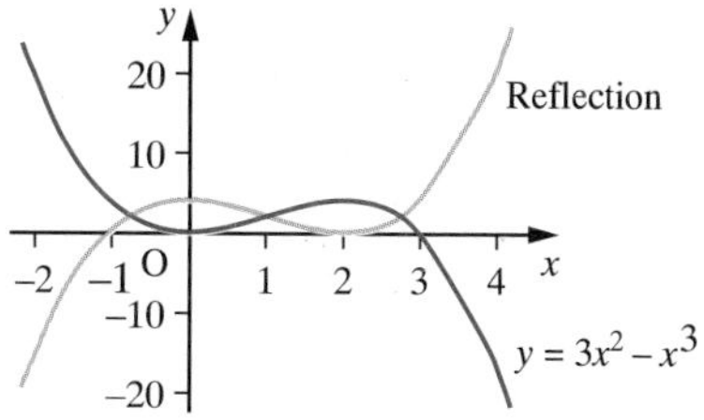

ii $y = x^3 - 3x^2$